# Innovative
# Energy &
# Environmental
# Applications

# INNOVATIVE ENERGY & ENVIRONMENTAL APPLICATIONS

Published by
**THE FAIRMONT PRESS, INC.**
700 Indian Trail
Lilburn, GA 30247

# INNOVATIVE ENERGY & ENVIRONMENTAL APPLICATIONS

OCLC 29318935

Library of Congress Catalog Card No. 92-85510

Published by
THE FAIRMONT PRESS, INC.
700 Indian Trail
Lilburn, GA  30247

Printed in the United States of America

10  9  8  7  6  5  4  3  2  1

ISBN 0-88173-159-5   FP

ISBN 0-13-466194-X   PH

While every effort is made to provide dependable information, the publisher, authors, and editors cannot be held responsible for any errors or omissions.

Distributed by PTR Prentice-Hall, Inc.
A Simon & Schuster Company
Englewood Cliffs, NJ  07632

Prentice-Hall International (UK) Limited, London
Prentice-Hall of Australia Pty. Limited, Sydney
Prentice-Hall Canada Inc., Toronto
Prentice-Hall Hispanoamericana, S.A., Mexico
Prentice-Hall of India Private Limited, New Delhi
Prentice-Hall of Japan, Inc., Tokyo
Simon & Schuster Asia Pte. Ltd., Singapore
Editora Prentice-Hall do Brasil, Ltda., Rio de Janeiro

# CONTENTS

# SECTION 4: ENERGY MANAGEMENT APPLICATIONS

# SECTION 5: ADVANCES IN LIGHTING EFFICIENCY AND APPLICATIONS ..... 407

# SECTION 6: ELECTRICAL SYSTEM OPTIMIZATION ..... 447

# SECTION 7: FEDERAL ENERGY MANAGEMENT ... 471

# SECTION 8: HVAC SYSTEM OPTIMIZATION ... 517

# INTRODUCTION

The year 1992 marks the 15th anniversary of the World Energy Engineering Congress (WEEC). It also marks the rebirth of the energy management industry. Society now recognizes the importance of energy management as a primary way to prevent further deterioration of this planet's environment. The United Nations' Conference on Environment & Development (UNCED), or Earth Summit, in Rio de Janeiro has mandated the efficient production and consumption of all forms of energy as primary vehicles in preventing global warming.

For example, if energy efficient lighting was used everywhere profitable, the electricity required for lighting would be cut by 50%, and national electricity demand would be reduced by 10%. In addition, carbon dioxide emissions would be reduced by 232 million tons, or 4% of the national total emissions—the equivalent of the carbon dioxide emissions of 42 million cars, or one-third of all cars on U.S. roads.

Demand-side management has become the buzz word of the '90s. Utilities, in order to postpone building power generation facilities, are encouraging their customers to reduce demand. Over the next decade utilities will spend $100 billion dollars on incentive and rebate programs aimed at energy conservation. Reducing the need for power plants significantly helps the environment.

This extensive reference is based on papers presented at the World Energy Engineering Congress, October 28-30, 1992, Georgia World Congress Center, Atlanta, Georgia. The WEEC is the nation's premier event and puts into perspective the myriad of changes impacting our industry. The growing awareness of the interrelated nature of energy and the environment is thoroughly presented in the companion World Environmental Engineering Congress.

The WEEC is more important than ever before because energy management is a driving force of most companies' plans. Spurred by new legislation, federal energy conservation requirements, utility rebate and incentive programs, and the EPA's Green Lights Program, organizations are now requiring efficient use of energy. This year's WEEC includes extensive presentations on demand-side management and power generation options for securing a reliable electric supply.

We congratulate our sponsors—The Alliance To Save Energy, AT&T, Electric Power Research Institute, *Environmental Protection* Magazine, Georgia Office of Energy Resources, National Registry of Environmental Professionals, Rocky Mountain Institute, U.S. Department of Energy/Office of Institutional Conservation Programs, U.S. Department of Energy/State Energy Programs Division, and U.S. Environmental Protection Agency/Green Lights Program—for supporting this program and playing a major role in fostering technology transfer.

We also congratulate the Association of Energy Engineers and its 8,000 members for providing the leadership for the industry to develop.

For 15 years the World Energy Engineering Congress has provided the essential forum for industry. The sharing of information is important to the continued growth of the energy engineering profession. AEE is proud to play a major role in sponsoring this vital conference.

Albert Thumann, P.E., CEM
Executive Director
Association of Energy Engineers

# CONTRIBUTORS

Abdulally, Iqbal F., *Foster Wheeler Energy Corporation*
Achinger, Sara K., *Dahlen, Berg & Co.*
Allen, Paul, P.E., *Walt Disney World*
Altibi, Naser, *University of Florida*
Andresen, Mark, *Basic Measuring Instruments*
Armstrong, James H., P.E., CEM, CERS, *Tejas Engineering & Mgmt. Services, Inc.*
Audin, Lindsay, CEM, *Columbia University*
Bachschmidt, Rebecca A., *University of Tennessee*
Bagstad, Stephen S., *Aluminum Company of America*
Baker, Timothy J., *Combined Refrigeration Resources, Inc.*
Barrett, Larry B., *Barrett Consulting Associates*
Bartkus, Vincent E., P.E., *Pennsylvania Power & Light Company*
Bass, Keith, *Montana Power Company*
Bates, Andrew J., *Amber Consolidated, Inc.*
Baumer, Ronald R., P.E., *Environmental Control Engineering, Inc.*
Beers, Allen R., *Anheuser-Busch, Inc.*
Bentley, Richard, *Consultant*
Bladykas, Michael P., P.E., *Lizardos Engineering Associates, P.C.*
Blanton, Jeffrey S., *SBM, Inc.*
Block, David L., Ph.D., P.E., *Florida Solar Energy Center*
Boresow, Steve, *AT&T*
Bortone, Vincente, MSMS, *The University of Kansas*
Bowen, Paul T., P.E., *Rhode Island Dept. Mental Health, Retardation & Hosp.*
Braithwait, Cara Lee Mahany, *Independent Consultant*
Bramble, P.R., *Pennsylvania Power & Light Company*
Brown, Sherman, *Trane, Montana*
Burger, Robert, *Burger and Associates, Inc.*
Burroughs, H.E., *IAQ Building Wellness Consultancy*
Campbell, Walter R., *Foster Wheeler Energy Corporation*
Capehart, Barney L., Ph.D., *University of Florida*
Chastain, Brice, MSPH, CIH, *Life Cycle Engineering, Inc.*
Catlin, Joel O., *AWWA Research Foundation*
Chen, Chu-Chen (C.C.), P.E., *Southern University*
Cilia, John P., *IBM, Inc.*
Clark, Terry, *Finelite, Inc.*
Clark, Steven J., P.E., CEM, *Energy Engineering*
Coccaro, Charles J., *Public Service Electric & Gas Company*
Cress, Kevin, CEM, *New England Power Service Company*
Crowley, Joseph C., *Kraft General Foods*
Dahle, Douglas E., *Naval Facilities Engineering Command, Alexandria, VA*
Dahlen, Derick O., *Dahlen, Berg & Co.*
Dalton, John, *Reed Consulting Group*
Davey, Don, *Bonneville Power Administration*
Davis, Sonya D., *State of Louisiana*
Deb, Arun K., Ph.D., P.E., *Roy F. Weston, Inc.*
Dingle, R., John, *Reed Consulting Group*
Dinh, Khanh, *Walt Disney World*
Dixon, William T., *Citizen's Conservation Corp.*
Dong, Mitchell, *FulCircle Ballast Recyclers*
Donoghue, John P., *Boston Edison Company*
Duchane, David V., *Los Alamos National Laboratory*
Dutta-Choudhury, K., M.S., CEM, *Louisiana Army Ammunition Plant*
Elgendy, Youssef, A.M., Ph.D., *Georgia Institute of Technology*
Feldman, Shel, *Wisconsin Center for Demand-Side Research*
Fetters, John L., CEM, CLEP, *AT&T Columbus Works*
Finleon, Jane, *Public Service of Colorado*
Flood, Newell, *Directorate of Engineering & Housing*, Ft. Lewis, WA
Fournier, Donald F., Jr., *U.S. Army Construction Engineering Research Labs*
Galamaga, Donald P., CCP, *Rhode Island Dept. Mental Health, Retardation & Hosp.*
Gillespie, Adrian, *Army Forces Command, Atlanta, GA*
Gilyard, Y.O., *Enact, Inc.*
Ginsberg, Mark, *U.S. Dept. of Energy*
Goldner, Fredric S., CEM, *Energy Management & Research Associates*
Good, Larry, *National Capital Chapter-AEE*
Gordon, Harry, *Burt Hill Kosar Rittlemann Associates*
Gould, M. Scott, CEM, *Standford University*
Gras, Seaton, *Global Ozone Solutions, Inc.*
Hackner, Richard J., P.E., *Wisconsin Center for Demand-Side Research*
Haijie, Chen, *Shanghai China Energy Research Society*
Harris, Louis, *U.S. Department of Energy*
Hassler Curt C., *West Virginia University*
Heis, Mel, P.E., CEM, *Fountain Square Management Company*
Hills, Alan L., *Cogeneration Finance, Inc.*
Hoff, Tom
Hutchins, Paul F., P.E., Ph.D., *Reynolds, Smith & Hills, Inc.*
Hyre, Regi Ann, *Oklahoma State University*
Jendrucko, Richard J., Ph.D., *University of Tennessee*
Johnson, Brian K., P.E., *Energy, Minerals & Natural Resources Dept./NM*

Johnson, Robert P., P.E., *Pennsylvania Power & Light Company*
Kane, Christopher, P.E., Esq., *Lyon and McManus*
Keith, Larry W., *Anheuser-Busch, Inc.*
Kinser, Donald E., P.E., *Environmental Design*
Krane, Robert, Ph.D., *University of Tennessee*
Kun, Gao Shu, *The Central Coal Mining Research Institute*
Lain, Chen Wen, *The Central Coal Mining Research Institute*
Levy, David J., *Iowa Gas and Electric Co.*
Liechty, Randall L., P.E., CEM, *R.J. Miller Associates, Inc.*
Lowthian, Walter E., P.E., *Dean Oliver & Associates*
Mac Nish, Stephen M., *International Business Machines Corporation*
MacCracken, Calvin D., Pte, *Calmac Manufacturing Corporation*
Marietta, Karl E., P.E., *Dahlen, Berg & Co.*
Martin, Gene, P.E., *Colorado Interstate Gas*
Martin, Mark G., *Detroit Edison Company*
McCagg, Brin, *FulCircle Ballast Recyclers*
McKay, Hayden, *Hayden McKay Lighting Design*
McKenna, Joshua, *Certified Engineering & Testing Company, Inc.*
McKinzie, Lance, *Purdue University*
Milam, Joseph A., P.E., *Environmental Design*
Morse, O., *Lawrence Berkeley Laboratory*
Mozingo, Carl, *Tower Inspection, Inc.*
Mozzo, Martin A., Jr., P.E., CEM, *Kennetech Energy Management, Inc.*
Mull, Thomas D., P.E., CEM, CLEP, *Carolina Consulting Group*
Neal, Charles E., P.E., *Department of the Air Force*
Ness, Robert O., Jr., *University of North Dakota*
Nezhad, Hameed G., Ph.D., *Moorhead State University*
Oliver, Wayne J., *Reed Consulting Group*
O'Neill, Patrick J., *Honeywell, Inc.*
Packard, Cristina Padlan, *Baltimore Gas & Electric Company*
Parker, Graham, *Pacific Northwest Laboratory*
Paton, James B., *Fort Devens, Massachusetts*
Perez, Richard, *AWS Scientific*
Perrault, George A., *Perrault Consulting*
Phillips, W. Curtis, CEM, *North Carolina Energy Division*
Pierce, A.R., *Detroit Edison Company*
Pino, Joseph F., *Boston Edison Company*
Poole, James N., *CRS Sirrine Engineers, Inc.*
Porter, Gregory J., *PSI Energy, Inc.*
Purcell, Charles W., *Pacific Northwest Laboratory*
Ray, Sumit, *University of Florida*
Rhodes, Wallace W., *Enact, Inc.*
Rideau, Harold M., *Exxon Chemical Company*
Rubinstein, F., *Lawrence Berkeley Laboratory*
Schiess, Klaus, P.E., CEM, *KS Engineers*
Secrest, Tom, *Pacific Northwest Laboratory*
Sharp, Laura L., *University of North Dakota*
Sherif, R.A., Ph.D., *IBM*
Sherif, S.A., Ph.D., *University of Florida*
Shrivastava, S. Ram, P.E., *Larsen International, Inc.*
Siebens, Christopher W., *Jersey Central Power & Light Company*
Silveria, Kent B., *CUH2A, Inc.*
Singh, Jitendra B., P.E., *Pennsylvania Power & Light-Company*
Sorensen, Thomas C., *Thermal Gas Systems, Inc.*
Sparrow, F.T., *Purdue University*
Stebbins, Wayne L., *Hoechst Celanese Corporation*
Stewart, Alan, *Honeywell, Inc.*
Sullivan, Cindy, *SouthCoast Air Quality Management District*
Szlenski, Theodore P., P.E., *Pennsylvania Power & Light Company*
Szydlowski, Richard F., *Pacific Northwest Laboratory*
Tang, John T., *Foster Wheeler Energy Corporation*
Teets, Steven J., *AT&T Network Systems*
Tillson, David K., P.E., *Tillson Engineering Laboratory*
Triplett, Kelly, *Public Service of Colorado*
Tsatsaronis, George, Ph.D., *Tennessee Technological University*
Tucker, R. Arnold, P.E., CEM, *GTE Electrical Products*
Vaillencourt, Richard R., P.E., *Energy Investment, Inc.*
Vasenda, Sandra K., *West Virginia University*
Wagner, Van E., *Detroit Edison Company*
Walker, Thomas H., *General Services Administration*
Warren, Carlos S., Ph.D., P.E., *Reynolds, Smith & Hills, Inc.*
Wenger, Howard, *Pacific Gas & Electric Company*
Wert, Douglas A., *Ahlstrom Development Corporation*
Williams, Dan R., *National Capital Chapter-AEE*
Williams, Larry, J., Ph.D., *Electric Power Research Institute*
Wilson, Paul, P.E., *Dean Oliver & Associates*
Wolpert, Jack S., Ph.D., CEM, *E-Cube, Inc.*
Wolpert, Susan, B., *Nederaland Refrigeration*
Woods, James, CEM, *General Services Administration*
Wrench, Laura E., *Pacific Northwest Laboratory*
Yun, Z., *The Central Coal Mining Research Institute*
Zhong, Wei Ping, *The Central Coal Mining Research Institute*

# ACKNOWLEDGEMENTS

Appreciation is expressed to all those who have contributed their expertise to this volume, to the conference chairmen for their contribution to the 15th World Energy Engineering Congress, and to the officers of the Association of Energy Engineers for their help in bringing about this important conference.

---

The outstanding technical program of the 15th WEEC can be attributed to the efforts of the 1992 Advisory Board, a distinguished group of energy managers, engineers, consultants, producers and manufacturers:

Richard Aspenson
Director of Governmental Affairs - AEE

Karlin J. Canfield
Naval Civil Engineering Lab

Keith Davidson
Director Industrial Utilization & Power Generation

Jon R. Haviland, P.E., CEM
Consultant

Konstantin K. Lobodovsky
Pacific Gas & Electric Company

Dilip Limaye
Synergic Research Corporation

William H. Mashburn, P.E.
Virginia Polytechnic Institute

Malcom Maze
Abbott Laboratories

Harvey Morris
Independent Power Producers

Martin A. Mozzo, Jr., P.E.
Kenetech Energy Management Inc.

Patricia Rose
U.S. Department of Energy

Frank Santangelo, P.E., CEM
Consultant

Walter P. Smith
BASF Fibers

Albert Thumann, P.E., CEM
Association of Energy Engineers

Wayne C. Turner, Ph.D., P.E., CEM
Oklahoma State University

Gerald Decker
Decker Energy

Ron Smith
GM

Shirley Hansen, Ph.D.
Hansen Associates, Inc.

MaryAnne Lauderdale, P.E.
Energy Investment, Inc.

The following organizations have given outstanding support in promoting principles and practices to help achieve energy savings, greater productivity, and lower operating costs.

## CORPORATE SUSTAINING MEMBERS
*Association of Energy Engineers*

ABB Standard Drives Division
Abbott Laboratories
Alliance to Save Energy
American Institute of Plant Engineers
Association of Physical Plant Administrators of
   Universities and Colleges
Bailey Controls Company
Baskin-Robbins, USA, Co.
Bath Iron Works Corporation
Battelle Pacific Northwest Laboratories
Byucksan Engineering & Construction Co., Ltd.
California Energy Commission
City of Houston
CP National/Trident Energy Group
Datastream Systems Incorporated
Department of Corrections/Office of Capital
   Management /Boston
Destec Energy
Diesel & Gas Turbine Publications
DMC Services
Energy Initiatives, Inc.
Energy Investment Inc.
Energy Management Associates, Inc.
Energy Management Specialists Inc.
Engineering Management Corporation
Engineer's Digest
Enron Gas Marketing, Inc.
Ferreira Service Inc.
Florida Power & Light Company
HaVAC Control Systems, Inc.
Hydra-Co Operations, Inc.
IBM Corporation
International Energy Society
H.F. Lenz Company
Los Angeles Dept. of Water & Power
Luis Malheiro da Silva, Lda
Mission Energy Company
NALMCO (intN'l. Assoc. of Lighting Mgmt.
   Companies)
National Electrical Contractors Association
National Wood Energy Association
NEOS Corporation

New York State Electric & Gas
Niagara Mohawk Power Corporation
Northern Illinois Gas Company
Northern States Power Company
Northstar Energy Corporation
Norwalk Hospital Engineering Department
Old Dominion Electric Cooperative
Philadelphia Thermal Energy Corporation
Process Systems Inc.
PSI Energy
Rocky Mountain Institute
Shanghai Society of Energy Research
Southwire Company
SSI Services Inc.
State Industries, Inc.
Stone & Webster Engineering Company
Sverdrup Corporation
Synergic Resources Corporation
Tennessee Valley Authority
Texas A&M University/Physical Plant Dept.
3 M Company
Trend Control Systems
Turlock Irrigation District
United Assoc. of Journeymen Apprentices
   of the Plumbing & Pipefitting Industry in
   the US & Canada
United States Air Force/Tyndall
University of Mass/Amherst/Physical Plant Dept.
University of Missouri/Campus Facilities
US Army Construction Engineering
   Research Laboratory
US Army Logistics Evaluation Agency
US Dept of Energy/Chicago
US Dept of Energy/New Mexico
US Dept of Energy/New York
Utah Association Municipal Power Systems
V.E.I. Inc
Verle A. Williams & Associates Inc.
Wentworth Institute of Technology
Western Area Power Administration/California
Western Area Power Administration/Colorado
Zurich-American Insurance Group

# SECTION 1
# ENVIRONMENTAL MANAGEMENT

Chapter 1

# A Holistic Approach to Improving Indoor Environmental Quality: A Case Study

J. A. Milam, D.E Kinser

## INTRODUCTION

One of the "big six" accounting firms recently consolidated several offices into a regional headquarters located in a southern metropolitan city. This regional headquarters involved seven floors totalling 187,000 square feet of tenant space in a new high rise building.

The accounting firm realized that improving their employees' work environment would provide significant savings from increased worker productivity and reduced absenteeism. Therefore, the firm retained Environmental Design International (EDI) to provide consulting services to create and maintain an environmentally healthy office space.

The creation of a healthy, productive and safe indoor environment involves a total, holistic approach to the various elements that affect indoor environmental quality (IEQ) in a building. A holistic approach requires detailed evaluation of all areas that impact indoor environmental quality and not just the more common review of HVAC systems.

This case study shows that the optimization of a healthy indoor environment is an endless, all inclusive process: beginning with the initial construction material selections and environmental systems design; continuing through the construction and commissioning phases; and progressing to pro-active monitoring of IEQ parameters to protect the tenant's investment in a healthy, productive and safe indoor environment.

## CONSTRUCTION MATERIALS AND FURNISHINGS

Because the materials and furnishings used in a building can adversely affect Indoor Environmental Quality, you must view these building elements from an IEQ perspective.

### Construction Materials

Construction materials are a major source of pollutants. Construction materials can contain many harmful chemicals that are out-gassed into the indoor environment. In addition, some construction materials are more susceptible to microbial infestation than others. This is of particular importance in areas containing plants or susceptible to water damage. Finally, many construction materials produce tremendous amounts of

fibers, dust, and airborne particulates that are known indoor air contaminants.

Construction materials conducive to a healthy indoor environment do not necessarily cost more than others. We made positive changes to improve the tenant's indoor environmental quality during construction by selecting "environmentally friendlier" materials. Some of the construction materials examined and specified were:

- Insulation
- Cabinets
- Particle boards
- Sealing and spackling compounds
- Adhesives
- Glues
- Wall coverings
- Tile grout
- Paints, stains and varnishes
- Plasters and cements

### Furnishings

Furnishings are another major source of pollutants in the indoor environment. For example: furnishings contain many harmful chemicals that are out-gassed into the indoor environment; some furnishings are more susceptible to microbial infestation than others; and some furnishings shed many fibers which become airborne particulate contaminants.

Through proper furnishing selection, an indoor environment can be comfortable, aesthetically pleasing and healthy. Some particular furnishings addressed were:

- Furniture
- Carpeting
- Draperies
- Systems furniture and work stations
- Ornamental fabrics.

Results from early environmental testing indicate that this attention to furnishings and construction material selection has a great impact on improving the space's indoor environmental quality. For instance, EDI sampled for formaldehyde in the tenant's space and another tenant constructed at the same time in the same building. Chart One shows that the formaldehyde concentrations recorded in the other tenant space were fifty to seventy-five percent higher than those recorded in the space with IEQ conscious materials and furnishings selection.

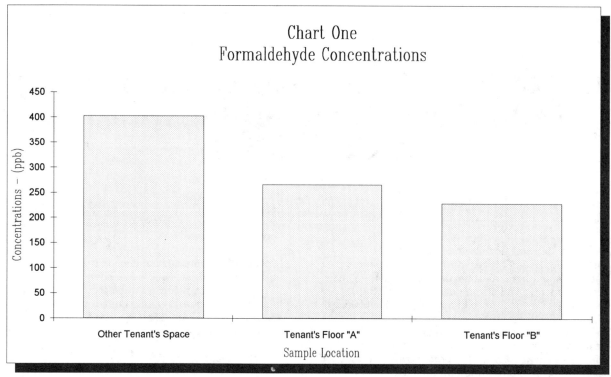

**Chart One
Formaldehyde Concentrations**

Concentrations – (ppb)

450
400
350
300
250
200
150
100
50
0

Other Tenant's Space    Tenant's Floor "A"    Tenant's Floor "B"

Sample Location

## PEST CONTROL

Control of pests did not wait for infestation to occur - it began during the construction phase. One aspect of this process included application of low toxicity pesticides to the interior surfaces of wall cavities. This will minimize future insect infestation within walls.

EDI reviewed and modified the pest control chemicals and procedures to promote better indoor air quality. EDI provides ongoing training of tenant personnel and pest control subcontractors on issues pertaining to pesticides and Indoor Environmental Quality.

## HVAC SYSTEM DESIGN AND AIR DYNAMICS

The HVAC systems and associated air dynamics with it are among the most important components contributing to a buildings indoor environmental quality. IEQ problems attributed to poor HVAC design have been numerous and well documented. Therefore, EDI approached the tenant HVAC system design and air dynamics from an improved Indoor Environmental Quality perspective. Our design included:

- System compliance with ASHRAE Standard 62-89. The base building outside air system was limited in capacity. Therefore, we used the "Indoor Air Quality Procedure" of ASHRAE Standard 62 to reduce occupant and building generated contaminants within the space.

- Modifications to the base building air handling units to accept gaseous phase and high efficiency filters. Special filter racks were constructed to adapt to the existing air handling units. These racks contained 4" deep, 30% efficient pre-filters; activated charcoal gas phase filters; and 95% DOP high efficiency particulate filters. All filters and

racks were installed with gaskets and edge seals to minimize bypass leakage.

These high efficiency filters have significantly reduced the amount of respirable particulates in the tenant space. Airborne particulate samples taken in the supply air of tenant's space were compared to samples taken on other floors in the same building with conventional filtration. Chart Two shows the level of respirable particulates and the percent reduction over the conventionally filtered system.

- A localized exhaust system in the print shop photographic developing room connected to the base building toilet exhaust riser.

- Equipment locations designed to insure accessibility and maintainability.

- Fan filtration units containing gaseous and high efficiency particulate filtration in several high contaminant areas such as:

  - Print Shops
  - Copy Rooms
  - Break Rooms
  - Cafeteria

- Careful examination of pressure relationship between various areas of the building to prevent migration of contaminants to other areas of the building.

## LIGHTING SELECTION

Poor lighting is often a concurrent stressor in indoor environmental quality complaints. The complaints usually result from insufficient light levels, poor light "quality", glare on CRT screens and flickering lights.

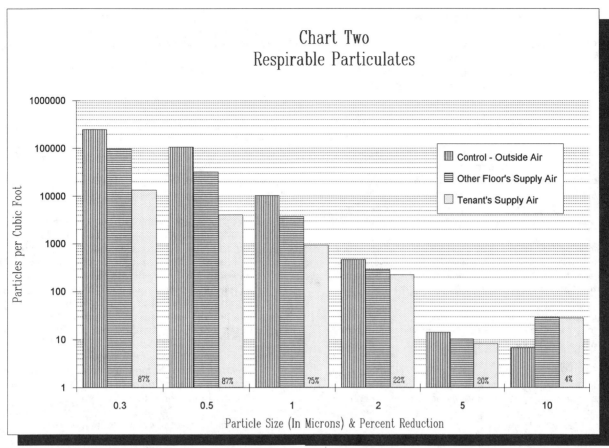

## Chart Two
## Respirable Particulates

Particles per Cubic Foot

Legend:
- Control - Outside Air
- Other Floor's Supply Air
- Tenant's Supply Air

Particle sizes (In Microns) & Percent Reduction: 0.3 (87%), 0.5 (87%), 1 (75%), 2 (22%), 5 (20%), 10 (4%)

EDI paid special attention to the lighting of workstations and offices. The lights installed in these areas were fluorescent fixtures with low glare lenses. The lamps in these fixtures were specified with a high color rendition index for improved lighting quality. Lights were installed to maintain a minimum of fifty footcandles in all workstations.

Light fixtures were also specified with energy efficient ballasts, return air and heat removal capabilities. This provided energy savings to the tenant. The lights' return air capabilities had an aesthetic impact by decreasing the number of return air grilles installed in the ceiling.

### WATER PURIFICATION

Water purification systems were installed in all tenant breakrooms and cafeterias. These systems are restaurant quality purification units designed with replaceable cartridges. The water purification units:

- Remove common off-tastes and odors, such as chlorine.

- Filter suspended particles as small as 0.5 micron.

- Reduce mineral and scale deposits in ice machines, coffee makers and soda dispensers. This reduces maintenance and increases machine life.

### ENVIRONMENTAL SYSTEMS COMMISSIONING

One of the most crucial steps in creating and maintaining a healthy indoor environment is Commissioning of the building's Environmental Systems. This Environmental

Systems Commissioning does not replace traditional Test and Balance (T&B) work. System commissioning is an ongoing process. It begins with the design phase and continues through the construction, acceptance and building occupancy phases. EDI functioned as the Commissioning Authority for the project to develop and implement the overall commissioning process. This process:

- Developed environmental benchmarks with which to evaluate the final building performance and acceptance criteria.

- Incorporated tenant revisions and review comments on construction materials, HVAC systems, lighting, etc. into the design and construction process.

- Verified occupant requirements versus design parameters for indoor environmental impact on various systems such as the HVAC, electrical, data, voice, plumbing, fire protection, life safety and security systems. Specific areas examined were:
  - Basic system type
  - Major components
  - Capacity and sizing criteria
  - Type of control
  - Operating sequences

- Verified occupant requirements versus operation and performance parameters for indoor environmental impact under various conditions such as:

- Operation under all seasonal loads
- Changeover procedures
- Part-load operation periods
- Occupied versus unoccupied modes
- Control system setpoint adjustments
- Operation of system components in life-safety modes
- Operation of system components in energy conservation modes

■ Monitored the construction and test and balance procedures to determine compliance with commissioning plan. This included a detailed inspection of equipment and material installation, observation of major equipment start-up, testing, balancing, adjusting and calibration activities.

■ Included direct training of environmental operations and maintenance personnel. We provide ongoing training of tenant and landlord personnel pertaining to indoor environmental issues.

■ Determined minimum standards for operation and maintenance manuals, as-built drawings and other documentation.

■ Observed and verified performance acceptance testing for environmental systems, provided acceptance checklist and documentation specific to each system.

■ Provided direction to implement corrective measures when acceptable system performance was not achieved with some systems.

## CONTAMINANT FLUSH OUT

The air handling units, toilet exhaust and outside air systems were run continuously to "flush out" potentially harmful fumes and vapors from construction materials. This "flush out" period took place during the last month of construction and the first sixty days of occupancy.

Air sampling indicated a marked reduction in total volatile organic compounds (TVOC's) during the first few weeks of occupancy. For example, samples taken in the tenant's space before the flush out period began and three weeks after flush out started indicated reductions in TVOC concentrations ranging from sixty-four to eighty-nine percent.

## CONSTRUCTION FILTRATION

EDI requested that the central air handling units not be operated during construction to prevent dust contamination in the units and ductwork. However, the building owner and contractor elected to operate the HVAC system during construction.

In order to protect the tenant's IEQ investment, EDI required the contractor to install 4" deep, 30% efficient filters and roll media prefilters on all air handling units during construction. 1" thick, 30% efficient filters were also installed on all fan powered induction units (PIU's) during construction. EDI regularly monitored the filters

for bypass leakage and overloading. At the end of the construction process, the supply and return duct systems were then vacuumed by a qualified duct cleaning firm.

## IEQ RISK ASSESSMENT

A crucial step to maintaining a healthy indoor environment is the IEQ Risk Assessment of the building, just before initial occupancy. The IEQ Risk Assessment included a review of many items that affect the tenant's IEQ and provides the foundation for future IEQ efforts.

EDI conducted on-site review and observation of the many factors which effect building IEQ, such as:

■ Re-introduction of construction materials as a source of pollutants in the indoor environment. Touch-up on moving related damaged furniture and painted surfaces occurred for several weeks after move in. EDI worked with the tenant's furniture repair contractor on products and procedures to minimize release of potential chemical irritants. In addition, all touch-up painting was performed after hours and during the flush out period.

Such items will never be completely avoidable. However proper communications and training can decrease the possibility of spoiling an otherwise healthy indoor environment.

■ Examined mechanical systems environmental parameters including:

- Actual outside air quantities
- Ventilation efficiency
- Filtration efficiency
- Equipment condition
- System balance

■ Occupancy and space use to determine any differences or deficiencies in the design and actual usage.

■ General housekeeping practices. Specific recommendations are made on an on-going basis.

■ Quantitative Sampling for $CO_2$, temperature, relative humidity, airborne microbials, volatile organic compounds (VOC's) and airborne particulates to establish equipment performance and baseline concentrations.

## MAINTENANCE, JANITORIAL AND OPERATING PROCEDURES

You must also address the important operational aspects of the building from an IEQ perspective. This includes maintenance, janitorial and operating protocols. Often subtle and inexpensive changes to these procedures can greatly increase a building's indoor environmental quality.

This phase included review and preparation of the following:

## Maintenance and Janitorial Procedures

Evaluation of regular and preventive maintenance procedures including janitorial cleaning methods. EDI recommended changes and wrote protocols for all environmental systems to help optimize indoor environmental quality.

Important Maintenance concerns included:

- Filtration efficiency and change out frequency

- Condensate system cleaning

- Insecticides and other purposeful chemicals used in the building.

- General maintenance (i.e., responsiveness to leaks and other problems).

We also evaluated janitorial procedures and their impact on IEQ. Areas evaluated were:

- Cleaning chemicals

- Vacuum cleaner types

- Furniture oils/polish, floor waxes and polishes, etc.

- Overall housekeeping effectiveness

## Operating Procedures

EDI evaluated base building and tenant building operating procedures. We recommended changes and protocols to help optimize indoor environmental quality.

This phase included:

- Review and modifications to the operation of major base building and tenant HVAC systems.

- Review of HVAC test and balance reports to determine current supply air settings and outside air quantities.

- Review of control system procedures to determine current operation of the HVAC system.

- Training of building and tenant operating staff.

- Appointing an Indoor Environmental Quality Manager and two Assistant IEQ Managers within the tenant's organization. These employees received intensive hands-on training regarding environmental systems and procedures within their space.

   The IEQ Managers will address everyday environmental issues such as

   - Logging initial occupant complaints
   - Reporting water leaks or spills
   - Reporting odors, etc.

   More complicated environmental issues will be handled by EDI personnel.

## PRO-ACTIVE MONITORING PROGRAM

The final step in maintaining a healthy indoor environment and protecting the tenant's IEQ investment involves routine monitoring. Proper monitoring can detect potential IEQ concerns and prevent them from becoming problems. We call this approach a Pro-active Monitoring Program.

A Pro-active Monitoring Program combines the attributes of an IEQ Risk Assessment with review of maintenance, janitorial and operating procedures on a continuing, routine basis.

EDI conducts an "IEQ Check-Up" twice a year in the tenant space - at the beginning of the cooling season and at the beginning of the heating season. This Pro-active Monitoring Program includes:

- On site review and monitoring of:

   - Mechanical systems condition
   - Occupancy levels and space usage
   - Housekeeping effectiveness

- Routine update of maintenance, janitorial and operating protocols developed by EDI and tailored specifically to the tenant's needs.

- Written summary report indicating the general health of the space and any changes that have occurred since the last observation. This is an important part of any risk management program and demonstrates "due diligence."

- Providing the tenant access to the latest information and knowledge of IEQ issues.

- Evaluation of the strategic impact of IEQ issues on the tenant's business.

## POST-ACCEPTANCE ENVIRONMENTAL COMMISSIONING

A crucial step in maintaining a healthy indoor environment is commissioning of the *environmental systems after acceptance of the building*. This Post-Acceptance Environmental Commissioning will ensure the effective, ongoing performance of the building's environmental systems. As use and function of the facility change, environmental systems need to be adapted to the changing occupant and utilization requirements. EDI provides Post-Acceptance Commissioning for the tenant which includes the following:

- Maintain a history of the facility and record changes and effect on the previously commissioned systems.

- Update as-built documents as required to reflect modifications of the facility or environmental systems.

- Evaluate impact of planned alterations to the environmental systems.

- Periodically re-test portions of the environmental systems to measure actual versus design performance.

- Develop and maintain system complaint reports and procedures.

- Develop plans for re-commissioning of systems should discrepancies occur between predicted and actual performance.

## CONCLUSION

Presently, we are evaluating fulfillment of our ultimate goal - improving employee productivity and reducing absenteeism. The short period in which the offices have been occupied prevents us from drawing a definitive statistical conclusion at this time. However, we have several reports of improvement in employee health since moving from the previous office space. For example:

■ A partner in the firm reported that "his allergies have reduced markedly since moving into the new office."

■ Another account from a worker in the print shop is most compelling, "I've had respiratory problems since the time I started work in the print shop until we moved into the new offices. Those units in the ceiling really help."

While these testimonials are no substitute for statistical data on productivity and absenteeism, they are extremely promising. Because employees perceive improvement in their indoor work environment, they are happier with their jobs and more likely to perform higher quality work, in less time. In essence, the first step towards increased employee productivity and reduced absenteeism has already occurred.

Chapter 2

# The Usage of Filtration as Fulfillment of Acceptable Indoor and Optimal Energy Management

H. E. Burroughs

ABSTRACT

The role of filtration is a significant
factor in the prevention and mitigation of
indoor air quality problems. ASHRAE Standard
62-89, "Ventilation for Acceptable Indoor Air
Quality", makes broad and non-specific
references to filtration. This paper
provides guidelines for the usage of
filtration as a means of fulfillment of the
Standard's requirements. The paper also
references the specific authorities as
iterated in the Standard. The discussion
will include the usage of filtration in
treating contaminated outside air, protection
of equipment and systems, protection of
occupants, reduction of ventilation air, and
source control. The reduction of ventilation
air through filtration has significant and
positive energy management benefits. Other
energy benefits accrue from clean heat
exchange surfaces.

DISCUSSION

The usage of high efficiency particulate and
gas phase filtration has been widely applied
and well established in the space,
electronics, pharmaceutical, computer, and
health care industries. However, this well
developed technology has been generally
under-utilized and largely ignored in the
area of commercial buildings. The wide
array of filter types, configurations,
efficiencies, capabilities, and costs provide
the designer with many versatile approaches
to employ air filtration to comply with the
emerging requirements for improved air
cleanliness and quality in public buildings.

The widespread concern for the health,
wellbeing, and productivity of building
occupants is driving the construction design
industry to improve the performance of
commercial buildings in this regard.
ASHRAE's Standard 62-1989 (1) provides the
design professional with guidance in
attaining acceptable air quality in
conditioned space. There are a number of
areas referenced in this standard where
filtration can aid in attaining quality, cost
effectiveness, and energy effectiveness:
treating outside air when it has unacceptable
quality; protecting mechanical equipment and
systems; protecting occupants from microbial
and respirable contaminants; treating return
air to supplement ventilation air; and
providing localized control of specific
sources of identified contaminants.

DEFINITIONS

The following definitions, which are quoted
from Standard 62, provide basic rationale for
the use filtration. They are referenced with
appended comments as background for the
detailed discussion on application that
follows.

Acceptable Indoor Air Quality: air in which
there are no known contaminants at harmful
concentrations as determined by cognizant
authorities and with which a substantial
majority (80% or more) of the people exposed
do not express dissatisfaction. (the key
phrases are "known harmful concentration" and
"dissatisfaction").

Air-Cleaning System: a device or combination
of devices applied to reduce the
concentration of airborne contaminants such
as microorganisms, dusts, fumes, respirable
particles, other particulate matter, gases,
and/or vapors in air. (The critical factor
is that the system provide the ability to
control all of the referenced contaminants to
attain acceptable air quality).

Air Conditioning: the process of treating air
to meet the requirements of a conditioned
space by controlling its temperature,
humidity, cleanliness, and distribution.
(The operative word is "cleanliness" which is
usually forgotten in the design of air
conditioning systems).

Air-Ventilation: that portion of supply air
that is outdoor air plus any recirculated air
that has been treated for the purpose of
maintaining acceptable indoor air quality.
(The key reference is that ventilation air
can be defined as treated return air as a
component of required ventilation rates).

Treatment of Outside Air for Ventilation

The pretreatment of air introduced to
occupied space is an important application
area for both gas phase and particulate
filtration. Standard 62 prescribes in Table
1 the acceptable concentration levels for
several gases and total particulates and also
references by note other listed contaminants
in Appendix C.

"4.1 Acceptable air quality is achieved by providing ventilation air of the specified quality and quantity to the space..."Step 1: Contaminants in outdoor air do not exceed the concentrations listed in Table 1..."Step 2: If the outdoor air is thought to contain any contaminants not listed in Table 1, guidance on acceptable concentration levels may be obtained by reference to Appendix C. "6.1.2 If the outdoor air contaminant levels exceed the values given in Table 1, the air should be treated to control the offending contaminants. Air cleaning systems suitable for the particle size encountered should be used. For removal of gases and vapors, appropriate air-cleaning systems should be used." (Underlining added by author for emphasis).

Studies of EPA and State Air Quality Board data indicate that a number of urban areas exceed the Table 1 maximum levels as a routine occurrence. In addition, building site locations near expressways, airports, industry, high traffic areas, and nearby neighboring exhaust or other pollution sources can cause excessive contaminant loads in the make-up air. For example, soot dropout in U. S. urban areas has been reported to range from 20 to 200 tons per square mile per month.(2) Work by Whitby, Et al, (3) demonstrates that 99% of this airborne particulate burden is less than 12 microns in size. These conditions mandate higher efficiency particulate filters, (85% to 95% ASHRAE rated) as well as some form of high capacity gas phase cleaners selected on the basis of the gases being experienced.

## Protecting Mechanical Equipment and Systems

Traditionally, low efficiency throw-a-way filters, panel filters, roll media, and metal washable filters have been used in an effort to keep lint and gross particulates from coils and heat exchange equipment. Anecdotal experience has proven that such low efficiency filters do not adequately protect the equipment, the system, or the occupants. Coils foul, causing energy loss that cannot be completely regained with coil cleaning; dirt accumulates in the air handler and the distribution system providing nutrients for microbial growth; and visible dirt is introduced to the occupied zone increasing housekeeping costs.

As additional rationale for the protection of the system, refer to the definition of air conditioning which includes notation of "cleanliness", and this reference from the body of Standard 62, "5.6 Ventilating ducts and plenums shall be constructed and maintained to minimize the opportunity for growth and dissemination of microorganisms through the ventilation system." Visible particles are defined as 10 micron and larger in size and dominate this category of housekeeping contaminant load. Particulate filters in the medium efficiency range, such as 30% to 55% ASHRAE rating, provide removal efficiencies in the range of 99% + against 10 micron sized particles.

Therefore, they provide excellent equipment and system protection while saving in energy efficiency, coil and system cleaning costs, and housekeeping costs. Energy savings alone will demonstrate virtual immediate payback in energy savings over the cost and additional horsepower penalty of the higher efficiency filter.

For example, in a 100,000 sq. ft. building located in New York State, 95% ASHRAE rated filters were installed. The increased filtration saved $.49 per sq. ft. in annualized energy premium and cleaning cost of fouled coils. In turn, the filtration cost $.11 per sq. ft. per year, including labor and energy operating costs. The net savings of $.38 represented a 336% return on investment in filtration.(4)

## Protection of Occupants

The recent focus on air quality problems in public buildings has provoked growing concern about health effects of occupants. This can potentially be the result of poor air quality in the space. The presence of high concentrations of microbial matter, such as fungal spores; bacteria; virus-carrying particles; and respirable particles can affect the wellbeing and productivity of occupants. Standard 62-89 defines the size of bacteria as "(99% exceed 1 micron in size) and are attached to larger particles such as human skin flakes. Lung-damaging particles that may be retained in the lungs are 0.2-5 micron in size.

When it is necessary to remove particulate contaminants, air filters---should be used." The previous reference to avoiding the dissemination of microorganisms through the ventilation system again applies. Filtration equipment for the control of respirable particles should have at least an ASHRAE rated efficiency of 95% and an actual efficiency of approximately 95%+ against 1 micron particles. Should control of the lowest limit of 0.2 microns for microbial matter be required, filters having a rating of 95% DOP should be applied.

These filtration levels will provide excellent protection for the occupants of the building from airborne respirable and microbial particulates. Though more expensive in cost and energy demand, they still demonstrate reasonable paybacks compared to the costs of fouled coils and equipment failures. The cost savings of health insurance, productivity, absenteeism, and employee morale are less tangible but equally compelling.

For the employer or tenant occupying the space, the most dramatic return on investment comes from the productivity of their most valuable asset, their human capital. Cost of human capital--their salaries and wages, their fringes, and their health cost--can be the most important asset or expense on the company financial report. These costs can range from as much as $200 to $400 per square foot of occupied space per year. The enlightened employer should therefore compare the productivity potential provided by clean, healthful air with their cost of human capital to analyze the real return on investment for their operation.

The American Management Association has stated that productivity loss due to IAQ problems could reach 18% and the Journal of the American Medical Association cites that the health cost related to IAQ is 15 billion dollars and involves 150 million mandays per year in absenteeism. In a recent study, it was demonstrated that potential increases of productivity in office workers due to improved environmental quality would average $697 per employee per year.(5)

Reduction of Ventilation Air by Return Air Filtration

Standard 62-89 references the usage of treated return air in the definition of ventilation air. It specifically provides the protocol in section 6.2 which enables the designer to apply control technologies for contaminant abatement as an alternative to the prescribed ventilation rates as provided in Table 2. under the Ventilation Rate Procedure. The alternate Indoor Air Quality Procedure provides a performance method for achieving acceptable air quality which allows the control of specific contaminants rather than reliance on a specified ventilation rate. This method is particularly effective when a known contaminant being generated within the space mandates even higher levels of ventilation than prescribed in Table 2.

Pertinent language authorizing the usage of filtration is found in section 6.1.3.2 of the Standard, "Properly cleaned air may be recirculated....The recirculation rate for the system is determined by the air-cleaning system efficiency...The air-cleaner used to clean recirculated air should be designed to reduce particulate and, where necessary and feasible, gaseous contaminants. The system shall be capable of providing indoor air quality equivalent to that obtained using outdoor air at a rate specified in Table 2. Appendix E may be referenced for assistance in calculating the air flow requirements for commonly used air distribution systems."

The reference to Appendix E is noteworthy for it provides the engineering protocol and authority for ventilation substitution. These application of these formulas are well developed and cross interpreted into filter efficiencies in a paper presented at the World Energy and Environmental Congress '91.(6) The author developed the engineering selection process using the Indoor Air Quality Procedure using the filter efficiency formulas as detailed in the Standard Appendix.

Using this methodology, the return air should be treated with high efficiency particulate filters and high capacity chemical control devices such as adsorbers (activated charcoal), absorbers (permanganated alumina), or electron modification (bipolar ionization). These approaches can be used as alternates or in combination to attain the desired control over the specific contaminant loads in the return air so that ventilation air introduced from the outside can be reduced. This, in turn, will lower the latent heat loads introduced during high humidity periods and lowers the amount of internally accumulated contamination. Based upon current rate structures in Atlanta, Georgia for example, the energy cost savings for reduced ventilation could average $1.50/cfm/year.

The Standard creates a baseline for reducing ventilation air, however; "6.2.3...contaminants that are not appreciably reduced by the air-cleaning system may be the controlling factor in design and prohibit the reduction of air below that set by the Ventilation Rate Procedure." This latter reference applies to the control of carbon dioxide ($CO_2$) which is specifically limited to a maximum of 1000 ppm by the Standard. This is critical because the commonly applied filtration technologies for gaseous control do not control this chemical compound. The rationale for this limit and the appropriate dilution rate of 15 cfm per person is elaborated in Appendix D. Although the assumption is that reduction potential through the usage of filtration is only to 15 cfm, the usage of $CO_2$ monitoring controls could enable further reductions during light building occupancy periods. Control protocols should then be engineered into the buildings systems controls to call for additional outside ventilation to specifically control the $CO_2$ by dilution when and if it accumulates. Overall capacity of the HVAC system would therefore have to reflect the peak condition of 15 cfm per person total ventilation air load.

Treatment of Sources

An effective method for controlling contaminant accumulation in the conditioned space is to eliminate sources through selection of low outgassing building components and by controlling at the point of generation. This keeps the contaminants from reaching the occupied zone and avoids recycling them to the central air treatment system. This allows down sizing of equipment and employs control tactics at specific stress points lowering capital and operating costs. "5.7 Contaminants from stationary local sources within the space shall be controlled by collection and removal as close to the source as practicable."

Localized exhaust can be an effective control protocol for

excessive heats and ultra high contaminant levels that would excessively burden central air conditioning and air filtering systems. Such areas as high capacity copier/printer space, smoking/breakrooms, and internal transmission/vacuum-tubes are probably most practically controlled by exhaust. Air from areas such as restrooms, lunchrooms, conference rooms, and specialized activity areas which produce recognizable but lighter odor levels could be treated and recycled using localized self contained filtration systems.

These should be selected on the basis of the anticipated contaminant nature and generation rate. Control can be localized and manual as required. This would reduce proportionately that amount of outside ventilation make-up air that would have to be introduced to compensate for the additional exhaust or contaminant load on the system. Generally, the cost of localized filtration equipment is more expensive per cfm than centralized systems because of auxiliary power and controls. However, it is still very cost effective when compared to the ventilation burden it replaces.

CONCLUSION

As this discussion has indicated, there is substantial authority and reference to the utilization of filtration in the fulfillment of the ASHRAE Standard 62-89. This also fulfills the objective of designing for acceptable indoor air quality. Furthermore, the proper usage of filtration can protect systems and occupants while saving energy and operating costs. These are compelling motives to fully utilize the benefits and advantages available through modern filtration technology. Furthermore, these technologies are well-proven and currently available from a number of competent well-established equipment manufacturers.

REFERENCES

(1) Standard 62-1989. Copies are available from the American Society of Heating, Refrigerating, and Air-Conditioning Engineers, Inc., 1791 Tullie Circle, NE, Atlanta, GA. 30329. (Cost $40 non-members).

(2) Handbook of Fundamentals, 1989. American Society of Heating, Refrigerating, and Air Conditioning Engineers.

(3) "Atmospheric Aerosols: Size Distribution Interpretation," Klaus Willeke & Kenneth Whitby, University of Minnesota, APCA Journal, Vol 25 #5, May 1975.

(4) "A Discussion of Filtration: Its Cost and Benefits", 1991. H. E. Burroughs

(5) "Using Office Design to Increase Productivity," Michael Brill, Stephen T. Margulis, Ellen Konar, and Buffalo Organization for Social & Technological Innovation, Inc. (BOSTI) 1989.

(6) "Filter Selection on an Engineering Basis", Forrest Fencl. World Environmental and Energy Congress, 1991.

## Chapter 3

# Microbial Contaminants, Human Allergies, Building Deterioration: Remedial Requirements

W. Rhodes, Y.O. Gilyard

### ABSTRACT

A long term program was instituted at a large southeastern coastal highrise hotel to assess the problems relating to human hypersensitivity and severe interior building deterioration associated with microbiological contamination to endeavor to provide effective remedies. Air and surface microbial samples were collected before and after each major incremental mechanical modification (primarily the heating, ventilating and air conditioning system). These data results, carefully evaluated, showed very high levels of microbiological infestation of a variety of taxa.

During the course of this project numerous other commercial and institutional facilities were evaluated for IAQ problems related to human microbial exposure and building deterioration. Recommended remedial actions in all cases were successful in enhancing IAQ for occupants and rectifying the destructive issues.

This highly contaminated large hotel located in a high humidity region shall be used as a case study because of the extreme methods necessary to remedy the multiplicity of problems and to prevent a recurrence. All air handling systems and building interiors were examined, evaluated and diagnosed to assure that proper solutions could be instituted. After three years, practically no microbial regrowth on surfaces is evident from laboratory cultures. The results observed suggests significant new concepts and methodologies for indoor air enhancement, reduction in human symptomatic responses to microbial antigens and prevention of building interior deterioration.

### INTRODUCTION

Buildings are designed and constructed primarily for human or animal occupancy or for storage of various materials and substances. They also contain, as an integral part, numerous active functional systems specifically employed to serve a definite purpose to enhance building usage for a designated objective. For example, a large multistory office complex occupied by humans will normally require an actively operating heating, ventilating, and air conditioning (HVAC) system, a plumbing system, elevators, an electrical system, etc., which could be classified as dynamic constituents. In addition, it will require a fire protection system, stairwells, structural integrity, aesthetical properties, etc., which could be classified as static constituents. Metaphorically then, a "building is a living entity" requiring proper diagnosis of any poorly operating dynamic mechanisms or static conditions, proper treatment and correction of any impairments, and a reasonable prognosis of its overall life cycle.

Considering a facility in this light suggests that with diversified maintenance personnel and other building "physicians" employing conscientious attention and care can extend the useful purpose of the structure so that its active complement of "human cells" working within its internal environment can maintain their normal and healthy posture to achieve the functional goals for which the building was created. The building, its systems, and its occupants, are fluid and continuously changing. Recognition of this phenomenon unequivocally demands that the viewpoint of its status must be progressively flexible to all changes required by the building as well as the change of the times. Buildings are constructed solely for the value they can contribute, either directly or indirectly, to the human occupants (the structure's life blood) and therefore should be designed, constructed, operated, and maintained to assure the optimum comfort, health and well being of those integral human occupants, their objectives and activities in its interior environment.

### PHYSICAL DESCRIPTION OF THE BUILDING

The building has twin nine story guest room towers connected by a beach level and main level lobby. Two restaurants, meeting and banquet rooms, office areas, a gift shop and a bar are the other main areas that are part of the facility. The building is on the beach and for much of the time is subjected to high relative humidities. The exterior of the building has a stucco finish which in many areas was quite porous until a sealant was applied. The public spaces are quite spacious and functional as well as aesthetically pleasing. The ratio of fenestration area to solid wall area is rather high. The guest rooms are very well designed and each has sliding glass doors to an exterior balcony.

## HVAC DESCRIPTION

The central HVAC system consists of two large electrically driven chilled water centrifugal units located in a basement equipment room with dual chilled water pumps (piped in parallel to the chillers), dual condenser water pumps, an automatic water treatment system for the condenser water and a large cooling tower on the roof. The public areas are cooled, dehumidified, heated and ventilated by numerous horizontal chilled water fan coil units (FCU's) with electric heat suspended above the ceilings. Some minimum outside air is furnished to most of these units.

The guest room units and corridor units are vertical chilled water fan coil units also with electric heat located in furred out areas in each guest room and the FCU's in the corridors are recessed in the wall. No outside air is furnished to any of these units. The bathroom for each guest room is mechanically ventilated by exhaust fans on the roof which exhaust the air from common shafts.

## INITIAL MAJOR BUILDING AND HVAC PROBLEM

* The exterior of the building was not adequately sealed permitting excessive moisture penetration when the outdoor vapor pressure exceeded the interior pressure [1]. This vapor pressure differential exacerbated condensation problems in numerous locations in the building interiors.
* There was no outside air furnished to the fan coil units in the guest rooms and to compound the condition insufficient outside air to the public fan coil units permitted a negative pressure in the building with respect to the outside, consequently, large quantities of untreated outside air were being infiltrated into the building.
* The refrigeration capacity of the fan coil units were excessive for the heat gain design requirements in all of the guest rooms relative to sensible heat removal; therefore, the thermostat would become quickly

satisfied prior to adequate latent heat removal and the interior relative humidity would rise to over 75%.

* The fan coil units in the guest rooms did not operate continuously which intensified the latent heat in the space. The thermostat was set too low in many instances subcooling the room. When the sliding glass doors were opened the humid outdoor air condensed on some of the walls and ceiling areas in addition to the furnishings.

* The stairwells were not tightly sealed adding to the problem of "stack effect" within the building and entraining additional humid outdoor air into the building.

* The chilled water piping risers to the numerous guest rooms were improperly insulated and vapor sealed permitting extreme moisture problems within each furred cavity housing the vertical fan coil unit. This added to the problem of damp sheet rock in many areas in the rooms.

* Fungal growth was quite visible on much of the walls and ceiling. Portions of the walls were covered by wall paper and microbiological growth was occurring on not only the wall paper but on the sheet rock surfaces under the wall paper [6].

* Human reactions and their perception of the intense fungal odors were very obvious from the number of complaints received.

* Fungal growth on the interiors of all of the fan coil units in all spaces was quite dense, especially on the fiberglass liners in the units and in the duct systems.

* The condensate drain pans in most of the fan coil units were improperly draining and contained high levels of microbial sludge and contamination.

* The carpets in the guest rooms were vacuumed with standard vacuums and a strong volatile odor-emitting-chemical was used for cleaning. Additionally, a strong deodorizer was sprayed in the rooms and furnishings primarily for masking tobacco smoke odors. Attempts were also made to mask the mildew (fungal) odor.

\* The elevator shafts had smoke dampers improperly controlled causing not only a strong "stack effect" in the shaft, but the action of the elevator created a piston effect causing further moisture problems within the building and also microbiological transfer [2].

SOLUTIONS: APPLYING THEORETICAL AND PRACTICAL ENGINEERING CONCEPTS

Problems requiring remedies of an obvious nature, e.g., installing proper insulation and adequately vapor sealing the chilled water piping risers will not be covered in this paper. The more complex engineering solutions however, will be explained in brief detail to show alternative methods that can be equally effective in rectifying problems.
Explanations for rectifying several of the major engineering problems associated with indoor air quality are as follows:

1. The refrigeration capacity of the fan coil units (as previously indicated) was excessive with respect to the actual room load at design conditions. The cooling coil in the large FCU's had the capability of rapidly removing the sensible heat at an approximate rate of 4 to 1 in relation to the latent heat. This rapid sensible heat removal afforded little time for the FCU to adequately remove the proper latent heat to maintain the design relative humidity.
The thermostat controlled a two-position, two-way chilled water valve and as soon as the thermostat indicated a need for cooling, the valve opened and the room sensible load was removed almost immediately, satisfying the thermostat and closing the valve. Very little latent heat was removed. The room temperature would begin to rise and the entire control procedure would be duplicated. In other words the thermostat would cause the chilled water valve to "short-cycle", and the results of this repeated action caused excessively high relative humidities in the room. It had been suggested by others that all of the room FCU's be removed (approximately three hundred and fifty) and replaced with properly sized units. As an alternate plan, the fan speed was "locked" to its lowest speed in addition to installing a baffle plate over the FCU fan discharge so that the air quantity theoretically matched the room design load. The cooling cycle of the FCU then operated for a longer period of time to remove the room sensible heat because of the FCU's reduced refrigeration capacity. This minor modification allowed considerably more latent heat removal or dehumidification. The lowered air quantity reduced the FCU total capacity and the ratio of sensible-latent heat removal was more appropriate with the actual room conditions as there was an internal change in the cooling coil dew point and the psychrometric slope of the theoretical (and actual) sensible heat factor between the coil apparatus dew point and the room design condition.

Consequently, a relative simple psychrometric engineering principle pragmatically applied averted a massive monetary expenditure and contributed in resolving one of the problems.

2. The externally damp condition in the furred cavities of the FCU's was rectified by sealing the building exterior and eliminating the moisture built-up on the improperly insulated and sealed chilled water risers. This was necessary for several reasons: a) the small openings in the fan suction side of the FCU would draw additional moisture from the cavity further intensifying the problem of high relative humidity in the room. b) The dry wall was deteriorating and required replacement. c) The moisture problem in the wall cavity between the sheet rock layers supported extensive microbiological growth and required complete replacement. The replacement in most instances was accomplished after the major moisture sources were corrected.

3. The microbiological growth-primarily fungal-was extremely intense, destructive to the building, and most importantly potentially hazardous to the health and well being of human occupants over an extended time period. This fungal formation was corrected by a) removing heavily contaminated building materials and replacing them with new materials b) reducing or eliminating excessive moisture sources c) identifying the amplification sites of the fungal agents and taking positive steps in eliminating these sites, e.g., improper condensate pan drainage, moisture carry-over from the chilled water coil to the lined discharge supply plenum due to excessive supply air quantities, etc. d) thoroughly cleaning the interiors of all the rooms, including walls, ceilings, carpets (with HEPA vacuums), and room

furnishing (soft and hard materials) e) thoroughly
cleaning all of the interior components of the FCU's
and their surfaces to reduce microbial aerosolization
as a function of temperature, humidity, air velocity [3],
and extensive reproduction and "bloom".

4.  Prevention of the recurrence of fungal growth would
have been impossible if further corrective measures had
not been implemented.  Therefore, a paint containing an
antimicrobial agent was applied [7] to all room surfaces,
i.e., the walls and ceilings and to some of the hard
surfaces of the room furnishings.  Additionally, the
interior components of the FCU's, the fan blades,
condensate pans, fan housings, supply air plenums (all
lined with fiberglass) and grilles, return air plenums
and FCU interior plenum walls also all lined with
fiberglass, etc. (Prior to applying this paint product
an independent private laboratory had tested the
product for off-gassing at the request of a large
Southwestern University where the authors conducted a
prior three year research study because of similar
fungal problems).  After three years no visible fungal
growth has occurred within any of the rooms and very
little has occurred in the interiors of the FCU's.
Also periodic microbiological samples are periodically
collected and evaluated to determine which specific
small surface areas may require a reapplication of the
paint due to an uncontrollable event.

5.  All of the carpets are now vacuumed with a HEPA
vacuum to contain all microscopic particulates, spores,
vegetative microorganisms, etc., of a minimum size of
0.3 micrometer.  The older "dust-scattering" vacuums
are no longer used.  When necessary the carpets are
steam cleaned.  Particularly difficult stains are
"spot" cleaned with a mild detergent type cleaner.
Very little chemical spray is utilized and must be
preapproved by the head of housekeeping.

6.  Booster fans were installed in some of the ducts
furnishing outside air to the fan coil units in the
public areas to assist in pressurizing and diluting
contaminants [4] in the building interior.  Also 100% 
outside air FCU's were installed on each floor in the
corridors to the guest rooms to provide additional
positive pressure in the building interior.

## CONCLUSIONS

The incidence of human hypersensitivity reactions to
the interior environment is highly suggestive to their
exposure to ubiquitous microbial contaminants [5].  An
additional problem of exposure of some sensitive humans
to chemical vapors and gasses from cleaning and
deodorizing agents in the rooms also appears to have
created an irritant response in some individuals but
not necessarily the same persons.

The majority of allergic responses decreased
dramatically when the air and surface microbial
contaminants were significantly reduced suggesting
hypersensitivities were primarily occurring from
exposure to microbial agents.  A valid indication of
this is that these microbiological agents were reduced
by one to two orders of magnitude in the air and four
to five orders on the surfaces over a year before the
chemical agents were changed.  Alteration of chemical
usage further enhanced the indoor air quality for human
occupants and their reactions.
The authors suggest that various ubiquitous microbial
taxa are significant contributors to human
hypersensitivity reactions and that chemical gasses and
vapors significantly contribute to irritant effects.
There is also the decided possibility of the additive
or synergistic effect.
It has been established by studies in this complex as
well as approximately thirty other buildings that the
application of a paint containing and antimicrobial
applied in proper locations is far superior to cleaning
alone.  The paint application increases the
effectiveness of microbial reduction for several years
(the longevity of the effect of the paint cannot be
established at present as its efficiency in the oldest
project is seven years); whereas, cleaning will provide
an immediate improvement for a few weeks to perhaps a
year depending on the facility.  Cleaning alone offers
no lasting biocidal or biostatic results.

It is necessary to conduct a very through professional
study based on extensive experience and the application
of appropriate engineering and scientific principles to
resolve indoor air quality problems in any facility.
Microbial agents can cause mild to serious
hypersensitivity reactions in susceptible humans [8].
Chemical gasses even at low levels can cause overt
irritant responses in some individuals.  Extensive
building deterioration and destruction can occur from
microbiological contamination.

Microbiological contamination does not have to be
visually apparent on surfaces in a building and its
systems to cause hypersensitivity reactions or to cause
intensive short and long term building deterioration.

<u>REFERENCES</u>

1. Wong,S.P.W. and Wang,S.K., <u>Fundamentals of Simultaneous Heat and Moisture Transfer Between the Building Envelope and the Conditioned Space Air</u>, ASHRAE Transactions 1990, Vol. 96, Pt. 2.

2. Cohen, D.and Wanner, R.G., <u>The Case of the Intoxicated Cells - An Epidemiologic Note</u>, American Journal of Epidemiology, Vol. 113, No. 3, 1981.

3. Pasanen,A.L., Pasanen,P., Jantunen,M.P., and Kalligkoksi, P., <u>Significance of Air Humidity and Air Velocity for Fungal Spore Release into the Air</u>, Atmospheric Environmental, Vol. 25A, No. 2, pp 459-462, 1991.

4. Kethley, T.W., <u>Air: Its Importance and Control</u>, National Conference on Institutionally Acquired Infections, pp 35-46, September, 1963.

5. Hodgson, M.J., Morey, P.R., Attfield, M., Sorenson,W., Fink, J.N., Rhodes, W.W., Visvesvara, G.S., <u>Pulmonary Disease Associated with Cafeteria Flooding</u>, Archives of Environmental Health, Vol. 40, No. 2, 1985.

6. Rytkonen,A.L., Pasanen,P., Kalliokoski,P., Nevalainen,A. and Jantunen,M. (1988) <u>The Effect of Air Temperature and Humidity on the Growth of Some Fungi</u>. Proceedings of Healthy Buildings '88, Vol. 2, pp. 345-350. Swedish Council for Building Research, Goransgaian 66, S-11233 Stockholm, Sweden.

7. Rhodes,W.W., <u>Efficacy and Longevity of Application of a Research Chemical in Interior Air Handling Systems for Reduction Trends of Viable Fungal Dissemination in Occupied Public Buildings</u>, 8th World Clean Air Congress, The Hague, The Netherlands, Vol. 1, 1989.

8. Solomon,W.R., and Burge,H.A., Allergens and Pathogens, Indoor Air Quality, P. Walsh, (Ed.), Chap. 10, Boca Raton, FL., 1984.

# Chapter 4
# HVAC Design Guidelines for Effective Indoor Air Quality

M.P. Bladykas

Due to combined effects of decreased ventilation rates and tighter building construction to produce "energy-efficient" buildings, as well as increasing volumes and types of office-generated air pollutants, many buildings are experiencing problems with indoor air quality.

Indoor air quality awareness is increasing rapidly as more information is made available on contaminant detection, resulting health hazards, and the cost of poor productivity and/or litigation due to sick or uncomfortable workers.

In the past, energy-efficiency was the primary design driver. However, today HVAC system designers must respond with system solutions that offer both high indoor air quality as well as energy-efficiency.

Systems that are both energy-efficient and promote healthy environments are realized through careful consideration of design parameters which directly affect indoor air quality. These include the proper use of economizers, variable air volume systems, airflow measurement, air filters, humidification, drain pan design and sound attenuation. Also included are many design options that when considered collectively during pre-planning stages can significantly improve indoor air quality throughout the life of a building.

## INDOOR AIR QUALITY

In the past, HVAC systems adapted well to the energy crunch by implementing designs for greater energy-efficient operation. Considering that almost 10% of the total U.S. energy consumption is attributed to heating, cooling, distributing and otherwise processing ventilation air for buildings, it is no surprise that most designs meant a reduction in ventilation [1].

Evolving with such reduced ventilation systems were new building materials and furnishings which incorporated contaminants, such as formaldehyde. In addition, new buildings were being designed for very low air leakage, with permanently closed windows.

Published information on the health hazards, combined with improved instrumentation to detect contaminants has resulted in workers who are more aware of their indoor air quality (IAQ).

Because a business' cost of conditioning building air is about $2 per square foot, while the cost of an adequately productive work force is about $150 per square foot, the economies of indoor air quality are gaining importance.

Many indoor air contaminants stem from a building's every day use such as copy equipment exhaust, cleaning solvents, floor waxes, aerosols, radon gas, cosmetics, smoking, and human body odor. Also a problem in maintaining IAQ are volatile organic compounds (VOCs) which are produced from synthetic furnishings, carpets and some building materials.

In addition, the HVAC system itself adds to the IAQ problem with dust and microbe accumulation in filters, duct linings, cooling coils, drain pans and humidifiers. Other causes of IAQ contaminants may be the location of outdoor air intakes resulting in the introduction of automotive exhaust; or an inadequate outdoor air supply volume which results in $CO_2$ and other contaminant build-up (see Figure 1).

| COMMON CAUSES OF INDOOR AIR QUALITY COMPLAINTS | |
|---|---|
| Ventilation Systems | 48.3% |
| Inside Contamination (other than smoking) | 17.7% |
| Contamination from Outside Sources | 10.3% |
| Poor Humidity Control | 4.4% |
| Contamination from Building Materials | 3.4% |
| Hypersensivity (Pneumonitis) | 3.0% |
| Cigarette Smoking | 2.0% |
| Other or Unknown | 10.9% |

*Source: National Institute for Occupational Safety and Health (NIOSH)*

FIGURE 1.

Because occupant- and building-generated contaminant sources are difficult to eliminate, remedies are directed at contaminant dilution and removal. In contrast, HVAC system-generated contaminants are more easily controlled through proper system design which actually removes the pollutant source.

Conventional energy-efficient HVAC systems with minimal ventilation keep indoor air contaminants recirculating in building air. This results in higher concentrations of internally-generated pollutants.

The fact that "Sick Building Syndrome" (defined when more than 20% of a building's occupants have illnesses such as respiratory infections, headaches and eye irritations perceived to be caused by indoor air contaminants) is now a well known term means that companies and their employees are aware of the standards they want in IAQ.

Achieving adequate IAQ consistently over the long term requires thoughtful analysis of the many IAQ contaminant countermeasures.

Some straightforward countermeasures include adequate outdoor air ventilation, clean air filters and properly pitched and trapped cooling coil drain pans. Other countermeasures require more pre-planning such as installing means to isolate building ventilation zones where building renovations may take place; planning for office equipment and its direct exhaust; measurement of outdoor air intake to assure a minimum standard while maintaining heating/cooling economy.

The best HVAC design for achieving adequate IAQ is one that considers all possible countermeasures and their contribution to both a healthful and energy-efficient environment.

## OUTDOOR AIR INTAKES

A first step in achieving high quality indoor air is to start with high quality outdoor air for building ventilation.
Substantial progress has been made in the improvement of outdoor ambient air quality through research and regulatory activity aimed at the environment and industry [1]. The Environmental Protection Agency, the National Institute for Occupational Safety and Health, as well as state and local authorities monitor air quality and conformance to air quality standards. These standards include limits for sulfur dioxide, carbon monoxide, ozone, nitrogen dioxide, lead and total particulate counts in outdoor air (see Table 1) [2].

National Primary Ambient-Air Quality Standards
for Outdoor Air as Set by the
U.S. Environmental Protection Agency

| Contaminant | Long Term | | | Short Term | | |
| | Concentration ug/m$^3$ | Averaging ppm | | Concentration ug/m$^3$ | Averaging ppm | |
| --- | --- | --- | --- | --- | --- | --- |
| Sulfur dioxide | 80 | 0.03 | 1 year | 365 | 0.14 | 24 hours |
| Total Particulate | 75[a] | ---- | 1 year | 260 | --- | 24 hours |
| Carbon monoxide | | | | 40,000 | 35 | 1 hour |
| Carbon monoxide | | | | 10,000 | 9 | 8 hours |
| Oxidants (ozone) | | | | 235[b] | 0.12[b] | 1 hour |
| Nitrogen dioxide | 100 | 0.055 | 1 year | | | |
| Lead | 1.5 | ---- | 3 months[c] | | | |

[a]  Arithmetic mean

[b]  Standard is attained when expected number of days per calendar year with maximal hourly average concentrations above 0.12ppm (235 ug/m$^3$) is equal to or less than 1, as determined by Appendix H to subchapter C, 40 CFR 50

[c]  Three-month period is a calendar quarter.

TABLE 1

However, conforming to standards alone is not enough. To some building occupants, odors from a nearby fast-food restaurant may be quite noticeable and bothersome, and complaints may quickly mount. One means to minimize several possible outdoor air contaminants is to properly locate outdoor air intakes. Thoughtful design of outdoor air intakes can reduce the need for costly outdoor air treatment and cleaning systems in the future (see Figure 2).

Some items to consider are: odors from restaurants, beauty salons, laundries; roadway, gas station, parking garage and "drive-up" carbon monoxide exhausts; and sulfur exhausts from landfills and garbage dumps.

Nearby undeveloped lots should be considered with respect to lot zoning and the type of business that may appear there in the future. Other more subtle intake contaminants to consider include bird nests with associated fecal material, the close proximity of cooling towers, and standing water such as a pond which may result in odors and airborne microbes [3]. In addition, the location of outdoor air intakes should insure that no cross contamination from the same building's exhaust will be possible.

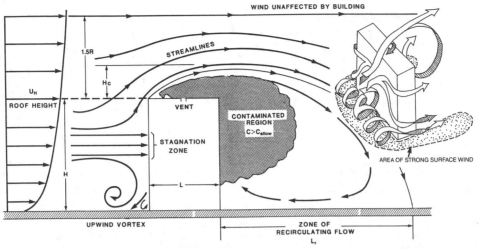

Flow Patterns Around a Rectangular Building

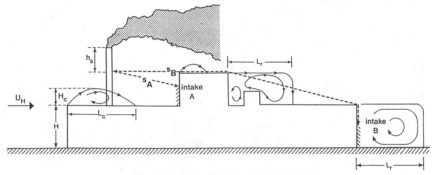

Flow Recirculation Regions and Exhaust to Intake
Stretched String Distances (Wilson 1982)

(SOURCE: 1989 ASHRAE HANDBOOK-FUNDAMENTALS)          FIGURE 2

### ECONOMIZER SYSTEMS

Although effective in reducing operating costs with respect to cooling building air, some economizer designs do not include provisions for maintaining required minimum outdoor air ventilation or outdoor air purge capabilities.

Before 1989, the ASHRAE standard for minimum outdoor air ventilation for office occupancies was five cubic feet per minute (cfm) per person. However, the standard is now at 20 cfm per person for office occupancies [2,4]. This four-fold increase in the minimum standard has left many existing economizer designs operating below adequate ventilation levels (see Figure 3).

For example, during ambient outdoor temperatures in the 50°F to 60°F range, the economizer opens outdoor air dampers achieving ventilation levels far above the minimum requirements for outdoor air intake per person. However, during higher or lower outdoor temperatures where cooling or heating energy is required, the economizer unit restricts outdoor air dampers electing to re-cool the building's return air.

| OUTDOOR AIR REQUIREMENTS FOR VENTILATION* | |
|---|---|
| Room Type | Outside Air |
| Hotel Guestroom | 30 CFM |
| Office Space | 20 CFM |
| Reception Area | 15 CFM |
| Theater | 15 CFM |
| Classroom | 15 CFM |
| Library | 15 CFM |
| Hospital | |
| Patient Room | 25 CFM |
| Operating Room | 30 CFM |

*According to American Society of Heating, Refrigerating and Air ConditioningEngineers (ASHRAE )ventilation standards.
(CFM = Cubic Feet of Outdoor AirPer Minute)

FIGURE 3.

21

Figure 4. depicts a standard commercial rooftop economizer design containing return, exhaust and outdoor air dampers and a supply fan. A fault in this design is the lack of an exhaust or return fan and the resultant inability to assure minimum ventilation and effectively purge building air with outdoor air.

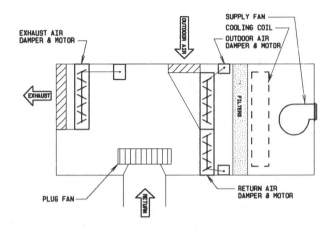

ALTERNATE COMMERCIAL ROOFTOP
ECONOMIZER/RETURN-EXHAUST FAN ARRANGEMENT
FIGURE 5

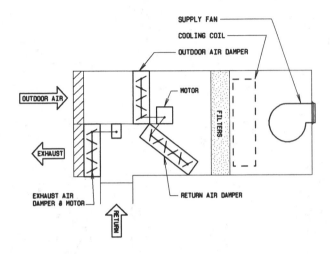

STANDARD COMMERCIAL ROOFTOP
ECONOMIZER ARRANGEMENT    FIGURE 4

Purge capability is desired for emergencies such as smoke exhaust; but in other less urgent situations purge capability can economically support IAQ by flushing out space contaminants. For example: a weekend or evening purge with no heating or cooling required in an unoccupied building, or purging after a building renovation has been completed to rapidly remove construction material contaminants.

In addition, an exhaust or return fan allows more control in maintaining proper building pressurization and assures proper economizer operation. Without a return or exhaust fan the economizer system relies on space pressurization to "push" the exhaust through the air return system and economizer exhaust damper. More often than not, this is not possible and the economizer never operates as intended.

An exhaust fan offers purge capability, proper building pressurization, and proper economizer operation. One design option is a special fan arranged to accomplish both exhaust and/or return for purge and pressure control capability. Figure 5. is an alternative using a conventional plug fan. This design provides the most efficient, precise economizer operation. In economizer installations where minimal outdoor air is employed, the double fan action assures that enough return air is exhausted for the amount of outdoor air intake desired.

AIRFLOW TRACKING

The use of variable air volume (VAV) systems results in fluctuations of outside air intake, similar to that of economizers. When demand for cooling is lower, VAV controllers reduce the flow of supply air so that the desired space temperature is maintained and less energy is expended in transporting the air.

However, the reduction of supply airflow results in a proportionate reduction in outdoor air intake. Because of the many factors involved, including the use of air-side and water-side economizers, as well as building leakage, the actual amount of outdoor air supplied to a space may not be precisely calculable.

At lower supply airflows, the minimum outdoor air intake of 20 cfm per person may be inadvertently compromised.

For example, on a design day, a VAV system takes in 20% outdoor air. Building cooling requires a supply flow of 10,000 cfm. With decreasing outside temperature, building cooling load is lower, therefore the VAV system reduces the supply flow to 5,000 cfm. Outdoor air intake is now reduced to 10% or less which may not be sufficient to assure the minimum ventilation rate of 20 cfm per person.

One way of tracking outdoor air intake is to measure the $CO_2$ levels in occupied spaces. High $CO_2$ levels indicate inadequate ventilation. However, using $CO_2$ levels to control ventilation rate is difficult at best. A much more effective method is to employ a VAV system design which incorporates airflow measurement devices (see Figure 6).

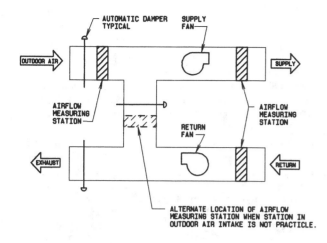

TYPICAL LOCATION OF AIRFLOW MEASURING
STATIONS IN A CONVENTIONAL AIR HANDLING SYSTEM
FIGURE 6

A measuring station in the outside air intake
is first and foremost to measure actual flow
against the required flow and to present an
alarm condition to an operator when below that
limit.

Additionally, measuring stations in the supply
and return systems, in combination with an
intake measuring station, provide complete
data on building pressurization as well as
minimum ventilation airflow. When an outdoor
airflow measuring station cannot be physically
located within the outside air intake, an
option is to place a station in the return to
the mixing box, in addition to the supply and
return air stations, so that outside air flow
can be calculated.

### FILTERING SYSTEMS

Since one hundred percent outdoor air
ventilation is not cost effective, almost
every HVAC system recirculates a portion of
the supply air. Proper air filtering removes
many contaminants, making the return air fit
for reuse.

In most areas today, outdoor air also contains
a number of contaminants and also requires a
level of filtering depending on the
surrounding building environment.

In most cases, air filters should be located
after the outdoor air/return air mixing box
and before HVAC equipment. In this location,
filters remove contaminants in the air, and
also prevent contaminants from accumulating in
the equipment.

While filters act to reduce air contaminants,
they can also be contaminant producers. When
exposed to cool, damp air, filters can become
a source of microbial growth.

Microbes feed on dirt which accumulates within
the filter over time. The accumulation of
dirt restricts the air path within the filter
and actually increases filter efficiency.
However, the increasing air restriction causes
an increased pressure drop across the filter,
resulting in more energy expended to push air
past the filter. Filter replacement
schedules are commonly based on the economic
consideration of when the operating costs
associated with an increased pressure drop
approach the cost of a new filter. For
effective indoor air quality control, more
frequent filter replacement should occur,
based on reducing the level of dirt and
microbe accumulation in a filter, and not
solely on the system operating costs.

Filtration downstream of equipment may be
required to accommodate ultra-low particulate
demands in hospitals, laboratories, and
manufacturing clean rooms. However, filters
downstream of coiling coils and fans are
exposed to cool, moist air. Even the most
anti-fungal fiber glass filters are at risk of
growing biological contaminants. In this
configuration, highly consistent filter
maintenance including cleaning and replacement
is vital to maintaining air quality (see
Figure 7).

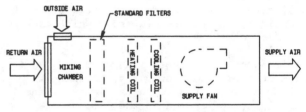

STANDARD AIR HANDLING UNIT

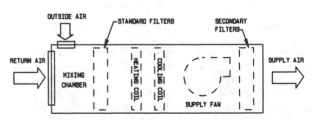

AIR HANDLING UNIT WITH SECONDARY
FILTERS DOWNSTREAM OF EQUIPMENT
(SECONDARY FILTERS EXPOSED TO COLD DAMP AIR)

FIGURE 7

High Efficiency Particulate Air (HEPA) filters, with particulate removal efficiencies of 99.97% to 99.99%, are useful in removal of air particulates such as smoke, atmospheric dust and microbes. However gaseous contaminants such as volatile organic compounds and odors require adsorption filtration by activated carbon filters or other means. While advantageous for this purpose, the use of carbon filters is not permitted in many municipalities due to their lack of adequate fire resistance. An emerging technology is the use of ozone in removing VOCs and other indoor air pollutants.

### DUCT SILENCERS

The use of internal acoustic duct lining to reduce equipment noise can be a major contributor to indoor air quality problems. Duct lining is typically installed in the ductwork near air conditioning units, variable air volume units, return fans, and in transfer ducts to help prevent the transmission of noise.

The duct lining material, although chemically treated and coated, can break down over time due to general degradation and turbulent air flow, as well as damage during initial installation. Lining damage can introduce particulates into the air. In addition, the lining surface area, exposed to damp, cool air, can become a source of microbial growth, especially in the damaged areas which create breeding cavities.

Cleaning of lined ducts is highly unsuccessful. In most cases, cleaning with vacuum hoses serves to further disrupt the lining surface. Because the linings are usually installed by permanent fixation to the duct surface, replacement of damaged lining requires replacement of the entire duct section.

An excellent alternative to duct lining is the use of duct sound traps or duct silencers. There are two basic types of duct silencers, "packed" and "packless."
In packed silencers, perforated metal baffles are filled with acoustic material which performs sound absorption, in addition to sound attenuation performed by the tuning effect of the perforated baffle structures.

Packless silencers do not contain fill material. The non-perforated baffles work on the tuning principle only to attenuate sound. Packless duct silencers maintain the highest indoor air quality. Because they do not contain any fiber fill material, there is no chance for particulate generation or microbial growth in the vulnerable duct sections downstream of cooling coils and fans.

### HUMIDIFICATION SYSTEMS

Adequate indoor air quality requires that indoor air humidity be held between about 30% and 70% relative humidity. Lower or higher levels promote microbial growth, occupant discomfort, etc. Standard air conditioning inherently results in relative humidities below 70%. However, in cold climates, where building heating results in very low humidity levels, indoor air humidification is required to maintain relative humidity above 30%.

Several types of humidification systems are available and all have varying affects on the quality of indoor air (see Figure 8).

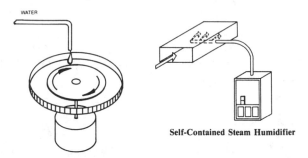

Self-Contained Steam Humidifier

Atomizing Humidifier

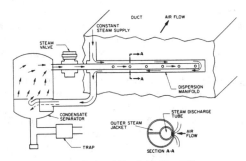

Jacketed Dry-Steam Humidifier

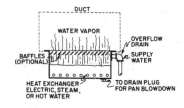

Heated Pan Humidifier

(SOURCE: 1988 ASHRAE HANDBOOK-EQUIPMENT)

FIGURE 8

While atomizing systems may be energy-efficient, their use can significantly contribute to indoor air quality problems. An atomizing system injects a fine spray of water into the air stream. The spray generates tiny water droplets which sometimes do not fully evaporate and can fall on duct surfaces, promoting microbial growth.

In an evaporative pan-type humidification system, there is no water spray introduced into the air stream. However, this type of unit includes an internal water pan over which ventilation air passes. Stagnant water in the pan results in mineral and dirt deposits and can promote microbial growth. These contaminants are then introduced into the ventilation air passing through the evaporative humidifier.

More preferred are steam humidification systems which inject moisture into the air stream in a vapor form. The water vapor does not support microbial growth.

One type, a central steam humidification system, makes use of a building's boiler steam. Although energy-efficient, boiler steam may contain oil, gas and other residue contaminants. In addition, boiler steam may contain chemical treatments that can introduce harmful contaminants into the humidifying steam.

An electric steam generating humidifier best supports high quality indoor air. The electric unit boils tap water to create steam. The steam is then injected into the air stream. The resulting steam contains minimal contaminants, and the vapor supports no microbial growth.

Although energy intensive, the electric system provides the most sanitary operation.

### ROOM AIR DISTRIBUTION

Room air distribution provides both fresh air renewal and contaminant removal in a space. The most effective means of room air distribution is displacement distribution or once-through flow of ventilation air through a space (see Figure 9). For example, ventilation air enters a room at the floor and room air exits at the ceiling.

Displacement offers the highest removal rate of room air contaminants. Thus it is often the method of choice for hospitals and clean rooms.

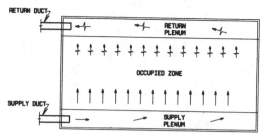

ROOM AIR DISTRIBUTION SYSTEM - DISPLACEMENT
(CONTAMINANTS REMOVED DIRECTLY VIA DISPLACEMENT PROCESS)

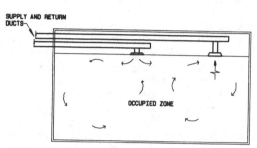

ROOM AIR DISTRIBUTION SYSTEM - OVERHEAD MIXING
(CONTAMINANTS REMOVED VIA DILUTION PROCESS, NOTE POSSIBLE SHORT CIRCUITING OF SUPPLY AIR)

FIGURE 9

Floor plenums can be used to distribute air to floor outlets for room supply. In addition, special carpeting is available which permits airflow through carpeted floor grates.

While displacement distribution offers the highest air quality, it is also the most costly system to operate. The high air-exchange rate demands more energy to condition and transport the air, and zoning is more difficult.

The most common room air distribution system is overhead mixing. In this system, ventilation air enters at the ceiling and room air also exits at the ceiling.

Overhead mixing blends ventilation air with room air, continuously exhausting a portion of the mixed air. In this way, room air contaminants are diluted and eventually removed.

The air-exchange rate is less for overhead mixing systems than for displacement systems. Overhead mixing systems commonly use only about one-third the volume of air as displacement systems. This results in less energy for air transport and conditioning. In addition, overhead mix supply air is usually maintained at about 10°F less than the temperature of displacement system supply air.

Room air distribution systems that often fall short in maintaining adequate indoor air quality include induction and fan coil units. Both designs consist of cooling/heating coils, air filters and associated coil drain pans. The drain pans and air filters can promote significant microbial growth if not frequently maintained.

DRAIN PAN DESIGN

The design of drain pans for coiling coils must provide for total water removal because stagnant water remaining in a drain pan quickly promotes microbial growth.

Drain pan and condensate trap design parameters include air system static pressure, trap height, pipe sizing, proper pitching of drain pans, and capacity of the equipment. Some considerations include, for example, that drain "U"-trap heights be greater than fan static pressures. Blow-through fan units create positive air pressure at the drain pan outlet and pan drainage is usually not a problem (see Figure 10). Draw-through equipment traps must be designed with enough height between the equipment drain pan and floor drain to accommodate the minimum trap dimensions required to assure proper pan drainage. This may require installing the equipment at elevated heights (see Figure 11). In addition, the diameter of a drain pipe should not be less than the diameter of the drain pan connection.

A condensate trap should provide an adequate water seal to prevent air at atmospheric pressure from entering the trap and impeding drainage at a lower pressure. Properly designed drain pans and condensate traps eliminate stagnant water, thus eliminating microbial growth and its contamination of indoor air. In addition, proper designs will avoid significant maintenance and equipment downtime costs.

PLANNING AHEAD

To achieve expected air quality performance levels throughout the life of a building, an HVAC design must be adaptable to a building's air quality needs. For example, planning ahead for future building renovations, painting, furnishing and office equipment.

Renovations taking place in occupied buildings pose a significant threat to indoor air quality, introducing dust from plaster, fiberglass, etc., and many types of VOCs into the air.

However, a properly zoned duct distribution design can effectively cut off the zone under renovation and protect the rest of the building from ventilation contaminants (see Figure 12). In addition, duct zoning combined with purge capability can quickly eliminate contaminants, such as after construction work, interior painting or a fire.

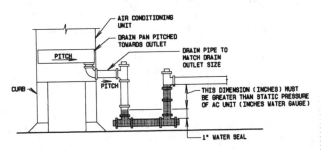

BLOW THROUGH UNIT CONDENSATE TRAP

FIGURE 10

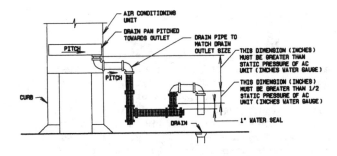

DRAW THROUGH UNIT CONDENSATE TRAP

FIGURE 11

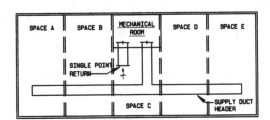

TYPICAL PLENUM RETURN SYSTEM WITH SINGLE POINT RETURN - REQUIRES RETURN AIR TO TRANSFER ACROSS SPACES VIA CEILING PLENUM

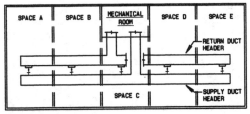

TYPICAL PLENUM RETURN SYSTEM WITH DISTRIBUTED RETURN - ELIMINATES TRANSFER ACROSS SPACES AND ALLOWS FOR ISOLATION OF SPACES UNDER CONSTRUCTION

FIGURE 12

When selecting furnishings and carpeting, as well as building materials, duct sealants and insulation adhesives, it is important to consider the level of VOC contamination the products will contribute to indoor air. Many manufacturers now test and label products with VOC off-gassing rates. VOC contamination can be subtle. For example, while a carpet product may claim very low VOC contamination rates, the adhesive with which the carpet is applied may pose a great VOC problem.

Steps can be taken to lessen the VOC contamination from furnishings. These include allowing several weeks of furniture storage for VOC off-gassing before the products are installed. For the first few weeks of building occupation, daily purges with 100% outdoor air can significantly improve the indoor air quality.

Office equipment can be a major contributor of VOCs and particulate contaminants. For example, carbon particulates from copy machines; ammonia odors from blue print machines; and VOCs from film developers. In addition, the equipment produces heat which affects the space cooling load.

A ventilation design should consider the equipment to be installed within the space and, where possible, include special dedicated exhausts that will directly remove the contaminants.

Possibly the most important HVAC design element is the control system that will regulate building temperature and humidity. The ability to maintain acceptable limits of temperature and humidity is what is most noticeable to building occupants, and what may generate the largest number of complaints.

While many air quality contaminants go unnoticed--even at harmful levels--workers quickly notice an uncomfortable room temperature or humidity level. Additionally, humidity levels outside the comfort range can cause dryness and irritation in the eyes, nose and throat, increased microbial growth, as well as static electricity discharge.

## CONCLUSION

Building owners, designers and occupants need to consider all the design measures that contribute to high indoor air quality.

Building occupants, furnishings, equipment, and ambient air pollution all contribute to surmounting indoor air quality concerns. However, these can be minimized by following HVAC design guidelines which promote high indoor air quality while maintaining reasonable energy-efficiency.

The possible liabilities and loss of business productivity due to air quality problems are too great to ignore.

## REFERENCES

[1] ASHRAE. 1987. Indoor Air Quality Position Paper. Atlanta: American Society of Heating, Refrigeration, and Air-Conditioning Engineers, Inc.

[2] ASHRAE. 1989. ASHRAE Standard 62-1989, Ventilation for Acceptable Indoor Air Quality. Atlanta: American Society of Heating, Refrigeration, and Air-Conditioning Engineers, Inc.

[3] Meckler, M., P.E. 1991. Indoor Air Quality From Commissioning Through Building Operations. ASHRAE Journal, Nov. 1991, pp. 42-48.

[4] Roberts, J.W., P.E. 1991. "Outdoor Air and VAV Systems." ASHRAE Journal. Sept. 1991, pp. 26-30.

Chapter 5

# Leak Monitoring for CFC's, HCFC's, HFC's and Oxygen Depletion: Recent Developments

T.C. Sorenson

## INTRODUCTION

The implementation of the Montreal Protocol and Title VI of the Clean Air Act of 1990 are having significant effects on the supply and cost of halocarbon refrigerants. In the US, there will be no new CFC's produced after 1995. Conservation measures which include recovery and recycling are enhanced by continuous monitoring for leaks in refrigeration systems.

Some of the non-ozone depleting substitutes for CFC's have toxicity and flammability properties which require continuous monitoring for health and safety. Both economic and safety considerations have led to an increased use of monitoring instruments for halocarbon refrigerant emissions.

Halocarbon refrigerants are colorless, odorless and, in general, boil at or below room temperature. In addition, they are high molecular weight compounds with vapor densities three to five times that of air. When refrigerants escape from closed systems, they can be expected to settle into low lying areas (in the absence of air movement).

These physical and chemical properties combined make CFC's, HCFC's and HFC's likely candidates for continuous electronic monitoring because:

1) They cannot be detected by human senses (color, odor)

2) They will be in the vapor phase under normal conditions

3) They will concentrate differentially

4) They diffuse slowly.

In the past, notification of refrigerant loss has been by pressure, temperature, or liquid level sensor alarms caused either by inability of the system to maintain temperature or by mechanical malfunction of the equipment. Perhaps 20 to 40% of the total refrigerant in a system can be lost before temperature, pressure, or liquid level sensors alarm. This can amount to hundreds and sometimes thousands of pounds of refrigerant being lost.

Detection through leak monitoring has the ability to detect the presence of minute concentrations (parts-per-million) in the air of enclosed spaces thereby providing early and rapid notification that a leak exists. In most circumstances, refrigerant loss can be reduced significantly by monitoring. For example, in a 10,000 cu.ft. 90°F machine room, the loss of less than one pound of R12 would trip a 300 ppm alarm. If the leak rate was 1/2 lb/min., an alarm would be given in less than 2 minutes.

### Cost Considerations

The Alliance for Responsible CFC Policy has estimated that only 39% of CFC demand can be made up by HFC's and HCFC's by the year 2000. Conservation (including recovery, recycling & reuse) of CFC's will have to make up almost 30% of the shortfall. Since many refrigeration systems lose 20-30% annually through leaks, any leaks which develop will have to be quickly identified and repaired.

The decreased availability of CFC's will have three effects:

1) Price will continue to increase dramatically due to supply-demand market forces and taxation.

2) Shortages will develop and allocation will replace market based distribution systems.

3) Eventually, equipment and systems will be replaced or converted to function on non-ozone depleting varieties.

In addition to normal supply-demand economics, which will increase the price of refrigerants, the U.S. government has implemented a tax on CFC and HCFC inventories which will further amplify the cost escalation as refrigerants move through the chain of distribution.

The Omnibus Budget Reconciliation Act of 1989 imposes taxes based on the ODP (ozone depletion potential) of refrigerants. The tax began in 1990 with a $1.37/lb (1.0ODP) and increases to $2.65/lb. in 1994. Beginning in 1995, taxes are increased $0.45/lb/yr. to eventually reach $4.90/lb in 1999.

The taxation of refrigerants based on ODP has been so successful for the government that there will likely be additional taxes based on the GWP (global warming potential, i.e., "green house" effect) of these same gases. If implemented, GWP taxes could dwarf both ODP taxes and supply-demand price increases in magnitude particularly for the low ODP R22 and zero ODP R134a.

As the available stocks of CFC's dwindles in the years ahead, supply disruptions are virtually certain. Thus, it may not be possible to obtain replacement refrigerants at any price in the timely and orderly manner that you are accustomed to from traditional suppliers.

The replacement HCFC's and HFC's are more costly to manufacture. In addition, because of their initial limited supply, some are presently much more expensive. For example, a recent price on R134A, which is the replacement for R12, was $15 per pound; and for R123, the R11 replacement, $8.00 per pound.

The chemical and equipment manufacturer have concluded that there will be no "drop-in" CFC replacements. Converting from R11 to R123 or R12 to R134a is not a simple or inexpensive matter. In addition to the cost of the new refrigerant, in many circumstances significant equipment modifications must be made to accept the new refrigerants even though the efficiencies and thermodynamic properties are similar.

For example, to convert a typical commercial building with two existing 450 ton chillers presently running on R11 to R123 would cost about $30,000 to $150,000, depending on the chiller design. To convert an existing R502 low temperature refrigeration system in a supermarket to R22 (two stage) would cost about $100,000 - $150,000 and to change an R12 medium temperature system to R134a would cost about $40,000 for the refrigerant alone.

## Health & Safety Considerations

ASHRAE has promulgated the Safety Code for Mechanical Refrigeration (BSR/ASHRAE 15-1989R) and the Number Designation and Safety Classification of Refrigerants (BSR/ASHRAE 34-1989R). Taken together, these two standards reclassify refrigerants into six new categories and establish monitoring levels for machine room refrigerant leaks and oxygen depletion.

The proposed new ASHRAE standards classify refrigerants on the basis of toxicity (A or B) and flammability (1, 2 or 3). Class A refrigerants have TLV-TWA's greater than 400 ppm; Class B refrigerants have TLV-TWA's less than 400 ppm. A Class A1 refrigerant would be non-flammable and have no toxicity, whereas a Class B3 refrigerant would be highly flammable and have high toxicity.

Category A-1 (which includes all present CFC's) would require refrigerant leak detection through oxygen depletion

monitoring. Categories A2, A3, B2, B3 would require monitoring at the 20% LFL level and category B1 would require TLV-TWA PPM monitoring.

For those of you unfamiliar with this terminology, LFL stands for Lower Flammability Limit, which is in the range of 3 to 14% for most category A2 and B2 refrigerants and 1 to 3% for category A3 and B3 refrigerants. Thus, 20% of the LFL would be in the area of 0.4 to 1.0% (4,000 to 10,000 PPM).

TLV-TWA stands for Threshold Limit Value-Time Weighted Average which is the maximum average exposure level that a person should be exposed to in an 8 hour day 40 hour week. Sometimes there will be an additional exposure limit called the STEL, which is a 15 minute short-term TWA maximum exposure level. The ACGIH (American Conference of Governmental Industrial Hygienists) establishes TLV's, TWA's, and STEL's.

| CFC | Group | TWA/TLV ppm | LFL% | $O_2$% |
|---|---|---|---|---|
| 11 | A1 | 1000 | - | 19.5 |
| 12 | A1 | 1000 | - | 19.5 |
| 113 | A1 | 1000 | - | 19.5 |
| 114 | A1 | 1000 | - | 19.5 |
| 115 | A1 | 1000 | - | 19.5 |
| Azeotrope | | | | |
| 500 | A1 | 1000 | - | 19.5 |
| 502 | A1 | 1000 | - | 19.5 |
| HCFC | | | | |
| 22 | A1 | 1000 | - | 19.5 |
| 123 | B1 | 10* | - | - |
| 142b | A2 | - | 20 | - |
| 152a | A2 | - | 20 | - |
| HFC | | | | |
| 134a | A1 | 1000* | - | - |
| Other | | | | |
| 717 | B2 | 25 | - | - |

*Recommended, not yet established

TABLE 1 - ASHRAE AND ACGIH MIN/MAX RECOMMENDED EXPOSURE LEVELS

The ASHRAE standards and ACGIH are primarily concerned with health and safety, rather than economics. The basic control strategy for safety purposes is to dilute the refrigerant in the air of the machine room by introduction of clean air through mechanical ventilation.

The normal indoor machine room ventilation requirement is equal to the large of:

a) 0.5 cfm/sq.ft. or

b) the amount required to maintain a maximum 18°F above the ambient with all heat producing machinery running.

The minimum mechanical ventilation required to exhaust a potential refrigerant leak for an indoor machine room is calculated by:

$Q = 100 \times G^{0.5}$ where
$Q$ = air flow in CFM;
$G$ = the mass of refrigerant lbs. (in the largest system, any part of which is located in the machine room).

In a typical example, there might be two 400 ton chillers each with 800 pounds of R123 centrally located in a mechanically ventilated machine room of approximately 1500 sq. ft. floor area and 15 foot ceiling height (22,500 cu. ft. room volume). Normal ventilation would be about 800 cfm and emergency ventilation about 3000 cfm. The exhaust would be to the outside.

A typical alarm sequence for R123 might be a visual indication at the 5 PPM level, mechanical ventilation started at a 10 PPM level, followed by local and remote audible and visual alarms at a 200-300 PPM level.

For Class A1 refrigerants, ASHRAE 15 requires a 19.5% oxygen alarm. A normal atmosphere contains about 21% Oxygen. The minimum safe atmosphere is considered to be 19.5%, at 16% most will be disoriented and at 12% most are unconscious.

A typical alarm sequence for Oxygen might be to alarm and start ventilation at the 19.5% level and initiate a second remote alarm at 16% to caution persons entering the area to be equipped with SCBA.

## Leak Detection Considerations

The basic control strategy for leak monitoring, on the other hand, is to provide notification so that remedial actions (repairs) can be undertaken. Concentration levels are usually significantly below that which would cause concern for safety.

In leak detection monitoring, the primary concern is the amount of refrigerant lost and the time before an alarm condition is reached. The amount lost and time to alarm depends on the leak rate, room net volume and the amount of fresh or recirculated air.

Refrigerant leak rates are usually expressed in dynamic terms (pounds per minute or ounces per year). Leak monitors measure PPMv (parts per million vapor volume/room volume). The general formula to calculate PPMv is:

$$PPMv = \frac{LRv \times T \times 10^6}{Vo}$$

Where $LRv$ = vapor leak rate, cfm
$T$ = time, minutes
$Vo$ = Room Net volume, cu. ft.
and $LRv = LRm \times Vg$
Where $LRm$ = Leak rate, lbs/min. and
$Vg$ = gas volume, cu. ft./lb.

Multiple sensors should be used for monitoring in very large rooms where diffusion must be relied on to move the gas to the sensor. For example, 4-450 ton chillers are located side by side in a plant room with dimensions 60'x200'x20' high. The release of 10 lb. of R134a vapor would raise the overall room contamination level to 150 PPM; however, the area in the immediate vicinity of the leak could temporarily exceed 500 PPM.

In the absence of air movement, it could take 20 to 30 minutes for the refrigerant to perfectly mix in the entire room volume. Multiple sensors should be located in low lying areas near the potential leak sources. In some cases, the number of sensors will be equal to the number of chillers in these large plant rooms.

A good rule of thumb is that there should be one sensor for each 20-40,000 cu. ft. room volume or one sensor fewer than the total number of chillers, whichever is less. If there is a continuous draft in the room, then a sensor should be located downstream from the last potential leak source.

Monitoring both oxygen depletion and Class A1 refrigerants at the ppm level can have significant cost benefits by increasing the sensitivity almost 1000 times. For example, the 1.5% difference between a normal and depleted atmosphere equals 15,000 ppm. Reliable leak monitoring for Class A1 refrigerants can be done at 100-300 ppm.

Many buildings are now installing R123 compatible chillers but presently running on R11. By installing a multi-gas monitor, oxygen deprivation can be monitored now and the conversion to R123 will require only the addition of a halocarbon sensor at conversion time (a simple 10 minute plug-in procedure). The installation and field wiring would stay the same; alarm levels and protocols are preprogrammed or field adjustable.

## Technology and Equipment

The two technologies most commonly applied for leak monitoring of halocarbon refrigerants are infrared (IR) and ceramic metal-oxide sensors (CMOS). Infrared technology is based on the absorption of a certain specific wave length of IR light by the halocarbon molecule. CMOS technology is based on the change in conductivity of certain sensitized metaloxides upon exposure to halocarbon gases.

From a performance standpoint, the major difference between the two technologies is that IR can be quite selective to the gas of interest whereas CMOS technology is less specific. IR technology is preferred in those circumstances where the air of a machine room might be contaminated by a variety of halocarbons or flammables.

On the other hand, CMOS technology is lower cost, requires less maintenance, and does not require frequent recalibrations. CMOS is much more adaptable to multiple sensor installations.

Electrochemical sensor technology is typically used for Oxygen depletion monitoring. Essentially this is a battery which runs on atmospheric oxygen. This technology is very specific to oxygen and has a wide dynamic range.

The latest multi-sensor, multi-gas microprocessor controlled instruments offer both IR and CMOS halocarbon monitoring, and also oxygen depletion sensing. Once installed, alarm protocols can be changed without disturbing connected equipment like fans and remote devices.

The basic requirements of a leak monitor are that it:

1) be designed for continuous unattended operation during the three, six, or twelve month periodic maintenance cycle of the associated equipment

2) provide a display and signal proportional to the concentration of refrigerant in the atmosphere since 100 ppm might be case for investigation while 1000 ppm might be cause for evacuation or the use of SCBA;

3) have the ability to "stand-alone" or interface with other systems; such as BAS/EMS since machine rooms are seldom occupied;

4) have the ability to quickly initiate some action when an alarm condition is reached such as turning a fan ON or providing remote visual or audible alarm;

5) have the sensing element remote from the controller to take advantage of differential concentration of vapors settling in low lying areas.

6) have a failure/fault alarm; and

7) responsed to an alarm condition within three or four minutes.

If the instrument is to be used for safety purposes:

1) multiple alarm levels

2) local and remote audible and visual alarm capability

3) battery back-up or access to UPS

Depending on the particular application, additional features may be indicated or required, such as:

1) multiple sensor capability;

2) field adjustable alarm levels;

3) high selectivity to a specific halocarbon;

4) limited access;

5) automatic recalibration; and

6) the ability to display an alarm on both a TWA and instantaneous basis.

## Summary

The Montreal Protocol and Clear Air Act of1990 are facts of life. In the US, no newCFC's will be made after 1995. For the next decade, rapid price increases and supply uncertainties can be expected for all halocarbon based refrigerants.

Some non-ozone depleting substitutes pose a health and safety risk at fairly low concentrations. ASHRAE has proposed two new standards which re-classify refrigerants and establish monitoring limits. As ASHRAE standards are promulgated into local codes and regulations, continuous monitoring in machine rooms will become a way of life.

Leak detection by continuous monitoring has been demonstrated to provide not only a increased margin of safety, but also provides the economic benefit of conserving of increasingly precious refrigerants.

Thermal Gas Systems is working to provide the HVAC&R industry with low cost, highly reliable leak detection instruments for CFC's, HCFC's HFC's and oxygen depletion.

## References

1. BSR/ASHRAE, 34-1989R; Number Designation and Safety Classification of Refrigerants; American Society of Heating, Refrigerating and Air Conditioning Engineers, March 1991.

2. BSR/ASHRAE 15-1989R; Safety Code for Mechanical Refrigeration; American Society of Heating, Refrigeration, and Air-Conditioning Engineers, March 1991.

HALOGUARD SINGLE SENSOR REFRIGERANT LEAK MONITOR

OXYGUARD SINGLE SENSOR OXYGEN DEPLETION MONITOR

HALOGUARD II MULTI-SENSOR MULTI-GAS MONITOR

# Chapter 6

# Handling of CFC's— On-Site Recycling Versus Off-Site Reclamation

S. Gras

Implementation of the Clean Air Act has resulted in an enormous amount of discussion and confusion on the management of CFCs. The delay of implementing rules and overall lack of federal leadership has contributed to this confusion and undoubtedly caused many to continue releasing CFCs until we know what the game rules are going to be. CFC dependent industries must now focus on new concepts, such as CFC management, while at the same time keeping their focus on their principle business activity. For example, if the principle business activity is to repair air conditioning or refrigeration equipment, then it may not make sense to make a large capital investment of equipment and labor to recycle CFCs on-site. The question, "What is my business", has never been more important. It is my hope that this paper will help you to better evaluate your options and reduce some of the confusion.

## BACKGROUND

### Terms

The three terms most often used to describe the processes of CFCs are:

> Recover - to retrieve gas from a
>            system.
> Recycle - to perform some level of
>            cleaning the gas with filters,
>            dryers, separators, etc.
> Reclaim - to bring the gas to (and
>            certify) virgin quality.

These terms are frequently substituted for one another, which adds to the confusion.

### Old Ways

In the normal course of servicing refrigeration and air conditioning equipment technicians vent CFCs and HCFCs into the atmosphere. This was the standard practice deal with used refrigerants since one did not know if they were clean enough for reuse and they were cheap. After nearly two decades of research, we have a better understanding of CFC based chemicals and their impact on the Earth's ozone layer.

### Ozone layer

Scientists believe that the stratospheric ozone layer is being destroyed by the gases that we all thought were benign. As the ozone layer is depleted more UV radiation reaches the Earth and this poses a very serious risk to every web of life. While some still dispute this cause/effect relationship, most believe that the risks are so great that we should not risk breaking something we cannot fix. The logical result is to adopt a practice of not venting. Besides being an environmentally sound practice, intentional venting is prohibited by the Clean Air Act and carries penalties as high as $25,000 per day.

## OPTIONS

Okay, so you have just stopped venting. Congratulations! It is the right thing to do. Now, what are you going to do with the collected gas? There are two basic solutions to this problem.
1) Recycle them on site;
2) Get them to a reclamation center.
A simple decision, right? Perhaps not.

### Recycling

Recycling machines process CFCs through a series of components designed to remove the various contaminants from the refrigerants at the service site. Water and particulates are removed with the replaceable desiccant filter, oil is removed with an oil separator, and non-condensible gas is removed by purging.

### Reclamation

Reclamation is accomplished off-site by processing the gas through a number of steps akin to the manufacturing process. The oil, water, particulates and noncondensible gases are removed by distillation. The gas is then analysed to verify that the gas has been reclaimed to virgin specifications.

## COMPARISONS

|                  | ON-SITE | OFF-SITE |
|------------------|---------|----------|
| Equipment Cost   | HIGH    | LOW      |
| CFC Quality      | LOW     | HIGH     |
| Recycle Time     | LONG    | N/A      |
| Documentation    | LOW     | HIGH     |
| Waste Products   | PROBLEM | EASY     |
| Support          | LOW     | HIGH     |

### Pro Recycling

You do not have to transport the gas. Minimum tanks required.

### Con Recycling

Technician's time to run recycler is

33

expensive. CFCs cannot change ownership unless quality is certified.
No proof that the gas meets quality standards
Machines are more involved to use/maintain.
Higher cost for equipment.
Purging may vent some CFCs.
Recirculation takes time.
Waste materials to handle.

<u>Pro Reclamation</u>

Equipment is less expensive.
Virgin quality gas.
Paper trail to show compliance with law/rules.
No waste materials to handle.

<u>Con Reclamation</u>

Transportation of tanks.

## POINTS TO CONSIDER

In order to prove compliance with the Clean Air Act one should take measures to document proper CFC management.

In order to ensure your customers satisfaction you want to make certain that the CFCs are not contaminated prior to reuse. Also, most compressor manufacturers' warranties require ARI 700-88 quality refrigerant.

If you are recycling you must change filters as often as needed.

Waste materials must be disposed of properly.

DO NOT use throw away tanks for recovery. They are very dangerous.

If you remove CFCs from a customers site you must have them <u>reclaimed</u> before using the gas.

Non-condensable gases reduce the efficiency and life expectancy of refrigeration and air conditioning equipment.

## CONCLUSION

Most contractors will be doing **both** programs to one degree or another. There will be times when the refrigerant is brand new, when a very minor problem requires servicing and the CFCs will be put right back in with no concerns about quality. There will be other times that it makes more sense to have the gas reclaimed because of burn-out.

Where equipment reliability is a prerequisite and the quality of the gas is imperative, the CFC management process should be through a reclamation center. Contractors can do this themselves or deal with a low cost/no cost CFC service that will do it for them.

Both options have their merits and on every recovery occasion the contractor will have to make a judgement call. They are, after all, the ones that will carry all the associated risks and responsibilities. Let's hope they make the right decisions,

and within the context of good CFC management.

Chapter 7
# Clean Air Act Amendments of 1990

C. Mozingo, R.A. Hyre

### I. INTRODUCTION

In November of 1990, in one of its last acts in the session, Congress passed the Clean Air Act Amendments of 1990. The Clean Air Act (CAA) had remained virtually unchanged since the last CAA amendments in 1977. Based on the ineffectiveness and complete lack of coverage in some areas, the CAA has been modified and expanded. The 1990 amendments expand the act to cover additional problem areas and take different approaches to solving old problems. This paper highlights the major provisions of the 1990 amendments and discusses the possible impact on industry.

Before going into the highlights of the amendments an explanation of the structure of the amendments and how they fit into the amended act is needed. The 1990 amendments consist of eleven titles, see Table One.

**Table One - Titles of the CAA 1990 Amendments**

> *Title I - Nonattainment Provisions*
> *Title II - Provisions Relating to Mobile Sources*
> *Title III - Hazardous Air Pollutants*
> *Title IV - Acid Deposition Control*
> *Title V - Permit Provisions*
> *Title VI - Stratospheric Ozone Protection*
> *Title VII - Federal Enforcement Provisions*
> *Title VIII - Miscellaneous Provisions*
> *Title IX - Clean Air Research*
> *Title X - Disadvantaged Business Concerns*
> *Title XI - Clean Air Employment Transition Assistance*

The eleven titles of the 1990 amendments fit into the six titles of the Clean Air Act, see Figure One. The CAA previously consisted of three titles. The 1990 amendments have added three new titles dealing with acid deposition, permits, and stratospheric ozone protection, as shown in Figure One. Following is a discussion on the highlights of the CAA amendment titles, and the probable impact on industry.

### II. THE CLEAN AIR ACT AMENDMENTS OF 1990

#### Title I - Provisions for Attaining and Maintenance of NAAQS

Title one can be looked at as the "nonattainment" provisions, since it addresses the problem of areas in excess of the NAAQSs. As before, the act will rely on the states to implement the necessary programs needed to improve air quality in their airspace through the implementation of the SIP. The entire nation is divided into air quality regions. Regions that meet or exceed NAAQs are classified as "attainment" areas, areas that do not meet NAAQs are classified as "nonattainment". The pollutants being monitored for NAAQS purposes are, ozone (smog), carbon monoxide (CO), particulates, nitrogen oxides ($NO_x$), sulfur dioxide ($SO_2$), and lead. Some nonattainment areas are further categorized based on the severity, and type of pollution. CO and particulate nonattainment areas are broken into two categories, *moderate* (reach attainment by 1995) or *serious* (reach attainment by 2000). Ozone areas are classified as:

> *Marginal* - attainment by 1993
> *Moderate* - attainment by 1996
> *Serious* - attainment by 1999
> *Severe* - attainment by 2005, 2007 in Chicago, Houston, and New York
> *Extreme* - attainment by 2010 (Los Angeles)

Ozone Nonattainment: The amended act seeks a continuous improvement in ozone nonattainment areas. This is accomplished by requiring all nonattainment areas (except marginal areas) to have a 15% reduction in Volatile Organic Compounds (VOCs) by 1996, and a 3% annual reduction thereafter until attainment is reached.

Reaching ozone attainment through VOC emission reductions is a major part of Title One. This is because VOCs are precursors to ozone. VOCs concentrate in the atmosphere where influenced by sunlight they combine with $NO_x$s to form photochemical oxidants. Photochemical oxidants, or smog, is a mixture of pollutants including ozone. Ozone is an unstable, toxic form of oxygen. One of the more visible changes to the public is the requirement that service stations use vapor recovery devices of pumps to reduce VOC emissions. These recovery devices will be required at stations that dispense 10,000 or more gallons per month.

The definition of a "major' source has changed. Previously it was any source that emitted 100 TPY of VOC or $NO_x$. The new definition of a "major" source is based on the type of nonattainment area where the source is located. Major sources are:

> *Extreme* - 10 TPY of VOC or $NO_x$
> *Severe* - 25 TPY of VOC or $NO_x$
> *Serious* - 50 TPY of VOC or $NO_x$
> *Moderate* - 100 TPY of VOC or $NO_x$
> *Marginal* - 100 TPY of VOC or $NO_x$

There are several measures EPA will use to improve ozone in nonattainment areas. As shown above, the overall goal appears to be reduction in VOC emissions. Until these amendments, ozone attainment was sought mainly through VOC emission reduction. Under the revised act, reduction of $NO_x$ emissions is also desired in the more highly polluted areas. The use of Reasonably Available Control Technology (RACT) on $NO_x$ sources is now required in certain areas and will be applied to "major" sources. EPA is charged with developing a set of generic RACTs for specific industrial source categories. RACTs are to be issued in the form of Control Technology Guidelines (CTGs). CTGs, in essence, have the same authority of a federally mandated rule. To date there are about thirty CTGs. Under the new amendments, EPA is charged with developing CTGs for eleven new specific industrial sources. Table Two shows when RACT and BACT is required.

**Table Two - Attainment and Nonattainment Requirements**

```
┌─────────────────────────────────────────────┐
│             Nonattainment                    │
│                                              │
│     Old Sources - RACT                       │
│     New Sources - LAER                       │
│     Emission Offsets                         │
│                                              │
│             Attainment                       │
│                                              │
│       PSD   │   NAAQS                        │
│       BACT  │   Based                        │
│                                              │
│ New Sources must meet NSPS - Emission Based  │
└─────────────────────────────────────────────┘
```

The effectiveness of $NO_x$ emission reductions is to be determined by November of 1991. Depending on EPAs findings the $NO_x$ control measures could change. Furthermore, if it can shown that no net air quality improvement results from using these controls then sources can petition EPA for exemption. Another measure that affects both ozone and CO nonattainment areas is vehicle Inspection & Maintenance (I&M) programs. I&M programs that already exist must be upgraded, and in most ozone nonattainment areas where I&M programs do not exist they must be implemented.

Other Criteria Pollutant Nonattainment: Areas can also be in nonattainment for particulate matter less than 10 microns in size ($PM_{10}$) or for not meeting $SO_2$, and CO standards. At present there are 41 CO nonattainment areas and 70 $PM_{10}$ Nonattainment areas.

SIPs and Federal Involvement: State Implementation Plans (SIPs) must provide for attainment and maintenance of NAAQSs in areas within the state. If EPA finds that the SIP is not effective or inadequate, then it can develop a Federal Implementation Plan (FIP) for use in the state. FIPs can be whole plans or partial plans designed to meet specific needs. If for some reason a state makes an inadequate effort towards implementing this title or meeting NAAQSs, the act has provided certain sanctions that can be applied. Cutoff or restriction of federal highway funds, or a requirement that new industry offset emissions by a 2 to 1 ratio, are sanctions EPA has available.

Title I Impact on Industry: The classification of the Air Quality Control Region (AQCR) in which a facility is located is the major factor for determining the impact of Title I. Since Title I mainly deals with nonattainment problems, facilities in attain-

ment areas are not affected. The full impact of Title I will be felt in nonattainment areas. Therefore, facilities in nonattainment areas will have to comply with the above provisions. Obviously, this is a more complicated structure to operate under. Facilities in attainment areas need to be aware of any problems that arise in their AQCR. If an attainment area is reclassified as non-attainment, a company could have to drastically alter its operating procedures. Basically the idea is to strive for attainment, and once achieved, work to keep it.

**Title II - Provisions Relating to Mobile Sources**

The amendments takes two approaches to reducing mobile source emissions, reducing tailpipe emissions and using "clean" fuels. Additionally, there are provisions for fleet vehicles. An annual, centralized Inspection and Maintenance (I&M) program is required in nonattainment areas classified as "serious" and above.

Tailpipe Emission Reduction: The traditional approach to mobile source emissions has been to reduce, as much as possible, tailpipe emissions. By 1994 all automobile manufacturers are required to reduce tailpipe emissions on 40% of the cars produced. These emissions consist of Non-methane-hydrocarbons (NMHCs), Carbon Monoxide (CO), and oxides of Nitrogen ($NO_x$s). Currently, light duty vehicles are allowed to emit 0.41 grams NMHC per mile. The 1990 amendments lower the emission standard to 0.25 NMHC. The new emission standards for CO and $NO_x$ are 3.4 gpm and 0.4 gpm respectively. The tighter CO emission limits must be achieved for all new cars by 1998, 1995 for $NO_x$. If EPA finds that it is both necessary and technologically feasible, it will reduce these emissions further in 2003. Important requirements affecting consumers are the recall provisions. The period for which cars are subject to recall due to emission system failures was doubled to 10 years or 100,000 miles, whichever comes first. Also, car manufacturers must install warning systems to alert drivers when emission controls fail. States have the option of using the federal emission standards or the more stringent California standards. States cannot adopt their own standards, as this would put too much burden on the auto industry.

Reformulated and Oxygenated Fuels: The "clean" fuels approach to emission reductions consists of reformulated gasolines and oxygenated fuels. Reformulated gasolines are initially for use in nine ozone nonattainment areas (Los Angeles, San Diego, New York, Houston, Chicago, Milwaukee, Baltimore, Philadelphia, and Hartford) starting in 1995. Other nonattainment areas can opt into this program. Reformulated gasolines after January 1, 1995 must meet the following fuel content specifications:
1. 2% average oxygen.
2. 1% average benzene.
3. Use detergents.
4. Contain no heavy metals.
5. Cannot increase $NO_x$ emissions.

Oxygenated fuels will be required in CO nonattainment areas during the four winter months (the time of year prone to high CO levels). EPA can allow a shorter oxygenated fuel period if it will not cause any exceedances of the CO standard. Starting in 1992, a minimum oxygen content of 2.7% will be required in fuels sold in nonattainment areas.

Additional Vehicle Provisions: In addition to emission controls, the revised act calls for evaporative controls. Beginning in 1995 auto makers must install onboard canisters to capture a minimum of 95% of the hydrocarbon vapors that normally escape during refueling. Also, beginning in 1994 new mass transit buses must use cleaner fuels (natural gas or methanol) to cut particulate emissions by 50%. Cleaner diesel engines are encouraged along with new procedures for testing diesel equipped vehicles.

Fleet Vehicle Provisions: Under the new CAA fleet vehicles in ozone nonattainment areas classified as, serious, severe, or extreme, and one CO nonattainment area (Denver), will face new requirements. A fleet vehicle is defined as belonging to a group of 10 or more vehicles capable of being centrally fueled, with the exception of vehicles normally garaged at personal residences at night. Generally the standards require emissions to be about 60%-70% less than non fleet vehicles.

There are two tailpipe emission standards to choose between, the California low emission vehicle (LEV) standard, or the federal "wrap around" standard. The LEV standard will be in effect in California in 1998, 2001 for everywhere else, for vehicles less than 6000 lbs. The California (LEV) tailpipe standard is 0.075 gpm non-methane hydrocarbon compared to 0.25 gpm for non fleet vehicles. EPA is directed under the amendments to develop "wrap around" standards. These standards are to be based on LEVs using reformulated gases. Automakers will be able to choose between the two standards.

EPA is required to study off-road vehicles (except locomotives) to determine if they are significant emitters of ozone and CO, and if necessary regulate them. Within five years EPA is to regulate emissions from new locomotives.

California Pilot Program: Starting in model year 1996, 150,000 vehicles meeting LEV standards must be produced for sale in California, this number will rise to 300,000 cars by 1999. Initially these vehicles must meet transitional LEV standards, these standards are:

> 0.125 gpm non-methane
> hydrocarbons.
> 0.4 gpm $NO_x$.
> 3.4 gpm CO.
> 0.015 gpm formaldehyde.

By the year 2000 these vehicles must meet the following lower LEV standards:

> 0.075 gpm non-methane
> hydrocarbons.
> 0.2 gpm $NO_x$.
> 3.4 gpm CO.
> 0.015 gpm formaldehyde.

Other states with serious, severe, or extreme, ozone nonattainment areas can adopt this program.

Title II Impact on Industry: The auto and oil industries will be greatly affected by Title II. It is the auto manufacturers who will design and produce cars to meet the new emission standards. Automakers will have to build LEVs for sale in affected areas and for use by companies that have fleet vehicles. The oil industry will be responsible for developing and produce reformulated and oxygenated fuels. Overall, Title II will force automakers and oil refiners to redesign their products so that they will comply with the amendments.

## Title III - Hazardous Air Pollutants (NESHAPS)

The basic approach the amendments have taken to control toxic emissions is to first apply the maximum available control technology (MACT) to a source, then determine if there is any "residual risk" above what the MACT can control. Congress has mandated that 189 additional air pollutants are to have NESHAPs developed for them.

Types of Hazards: Three classes of hazardous air pollutant sources have been targeted for regulation, these are:

1. Routine everyday stack & fugitive emissions from **major sources** (oil refineries, manufacturing plants, etc.).
2. Routine everyday stack & fugitive emissions from **small (area) sources** (gas stations, dry cleaners etc.).
3. **Accidental**, catastrophic releases that are life threatening.

Emission Control Standards for Major Sources: A major source is defined as any source emitting 10 tons per year of a single listed pollutant, or a total of 25 tons per year of a combination of any listed pollutant. A list of major source categories is to be developed by EPA.

Emission reduction standards for major sources will be based on the Maximum Available Control Technology (MACT) for each major source category. For new major sources, MACT will be the most restrictive available controls. For existing sources MACT will be the control technologies used in the cleanest 12% of a source category.

After MACT rules have been set for major source categories EPA is to determine if adequate protection is provided, or if there is any residual risk posed. EPA and other federal agencies will determine acceptable residual risk levels. More to the point, if the MACT provides sufficient protection against listed hazardous air pollutants then all is well. Its when there is still not enough protection against unwanted emissions, after installation of MACT, that the area of risk between what is desired and what is possible needs to be evaluated. If this area is determined to be acceptable by EPA then no further controls are needed, if the risk is not acceptable then further steps will have to be taken. Each major source that is subject to the new NESHAPs standards is required to apply for an operating permit under Title V of the 1990 amendments.

Emission Controls for Area Sources: Area sources are subject to the same NESHAPS list as major sources. EPA is to develop a list of categories and subcategories for area sources. Enough categories are to be identified to assure reduction of 90% of the 30 most serious toxic air pollutants emitted from area sources. MACT rules will be established for area sources in the same manner as for major sources.

Accidental Releases: The above provisions are concerned with the normal operations of a source. The following provisions deal with unplanned or accidental release of extremely hazardous substances. EPA is to develop a list of at least 100 extremely hazardous substances (EHSs). EHSs are pollutants that would likely cause death, injury, or require evacuation of the immediate area if an accidental release were to occur.

If the threshold amount of a listed EHS is exceeded at a source, then the facility has to meet certain requirements. An engineering analysis of the facility will be done to determine any public health hazards, also, risk management plans must be developed. These studies and plans are to be made available to the public. EPA is directed to develop plans to deal with facilities handling EHSs. In addition reporting requirements will increase beyond the current SARA Title III requirements.

A new board designed to investigate non-transportation chemical accidents, called the Chemical Safety Board, is established. This board will consist of five members. The board is to determine the cause of accidents and to recommend ways to avoid similar accidents in the future.

Title III Impact on Industry: Facilities will have to determine what type of hazardous air pollutant source they would be classified as. Based on this classification, they will have to take steps to comply with the regulations. Any source has the potential of an accidental release occurring, these provisions and the resulting regulations could have a significant impact to industry as a whole. Sources will need to pay attention to the Congressional mandated list of materials for which NESHAPS are to be developed. This list will be greatly expanded and will have a significant effect on industry.

## Title IV - Acid Deposition Control

Title IV deals with reducing emissions from electric utility powerplants. $SO_2$ reductions will occur in two phases, basically emissions are to be reduced by 10,000,000 tons a year until 2000.

Marketable Allowances: Utilities will be able to emit set levels (allowances) of $SO_2$ equal to a permitted emission level. Basically, an allowance is a marketable permit to emit one ton of $SO_2$. If a utility reduces it emission of $SO_2$ below its permitted emission level, then it will accumulate whatever allowances it does not use. These allowances can be saved for future use, or given to another plant owned by the same company, or sold outright to another utility. If allowances are sold to another facility it would allow the purchasing facility to emit above its own permitted emission level, yet remain in compliance with the regulations. The idea is reduce emissions overall in the most cost effective manner.

Sources emitting amounts of $SO_2$ and $NO_x$ over what their allowances are valued at (both permitted and bought allowances) will be required to pay an excess emission fee of $2,000 per ton. Sources that over emit and become subject to fees must submit a plan showing how it will correct the problem. Also, continuous emission monitoring equipment will be required at affected facilities. Record-keeping and reporting requirements have been changed to better keep track of emissions.

Phase I - Sulfur Dioxide Reduction: Beginning in 1995, Phase I is designed to reduce $SO_2$ emissions at over 100 powerplants current-ly emitting over 2.5 pounds per million BTU (lbs./mmBTU). The 1985-87 average fuel consumption is used as a base for compliance. EPA is also authorized to provide certain incentives to powerplants using scrubbers and reducing emissions, some of these incentives are:

1. Plants that use scrubbers can postpone compliance until 1997.
2. Plants that use scrubbers can receive an early reduction bonus allowance for actual reductions achieved between 1995 and 1997.
3. Plants using certain control technologies will receive a 2 - 1 credit for every ton of reduction below 1.2 lbs./mmBTU.

For powerplants in Illinois, Indiana, and Ohio, a special allocation of 200,000 allowances was set aside to aid in the transition to Phase I.

For new plants, allowances can be obtained to offset their emissions or they might be exempt from the program altogether. If a new plant needs allowances, it must obtain them from a sister plant or from EPA. EPA will withhold a certain number of allowances to be sold to those plants that cannot obtain them on the open market. In Phase I, these allowances will be sold through an auction.

Phase II - Sulfur Dioxide Reduction: Phase II begins January 1, 2000. As of this date, allowable utility emission rates will be lowered from 2.5 lbs./mmBTU to 1.2 lbs./mmBTU. Plants currently emitting less than 1.2 lbs./mmBTU can increase by roughly 20% between now and the year 2000, but after that emissions are capped. As a whole, emissions are all to be capped as of 2000. Any allowances withheld by EPA during Phase II will be made available through direct sales and auctions.

$NO_x$ Emissions: Overall the act aims to reduce $NO_x$ by 2,000,000 tons. Utilities that come under Phase I must also reduce their $NO_x$ emissions to some performance standard to be determined by EPA no later than 1993. These standards are to be based on the type of boiler being used. Because of retrofit problems, cyclone boilers or wet-bottom boilers are excluded. All remaining types of utility boilers must meet performance standards to be set no later than 1997, and implementation is to be completed by the Phase II deadline. All of the standards are to be based on low $NO_x$ burner technology.

Title IV Impact On Industry: Title IV directly targets emissions from coal fired electric utilities. The regulations that will come out of this provision will require many utilities to refit to come into compliance. As a result, industry can look for higher energy costs.

## Title V - Permit Provisions

A significant addition to the CAA is the provisions for a federal permit program to be overseen by EPA. These provisions have been added to the CAA by the 1990 amendments. Title V of both the act and the amendments contains the new permit provisions. Previously, only new or modified sources were required by federal regulations to obtain a permit. In order to ensure that all regulatory provisions of the CAA were met, the title V permit provisions were added. The new permit program is similar to the National

Pollution Discharge Elimination System (NPDES) permit required by the clean water act (CWA).

The responsibility for implementing and maintaining permit programs is delegated to the state, to be integrated into the existing SIP. The state will design its own program to meet requirements set by EPA. These permit requirements are to be promulgated by EPA by November of 1991. The program must be in place nationwide by November 1994. This gives the states three years to install a permit program. If a state does not develop or adequately enforce a permit program then EPA can move in and develop its own. States are allowed to develop and add more measures as long as they are more stringent than EPAs.

Title V permit provisions are directed at significant contributors to air emissions. Sources that emit more than 100 tons per year (major source) and smaller sources in more polluted areas (according to nonattainment classification, extreme, serious, etc.) are required to have a permit. Sources that emit title III air toxics of 10 tons or more of any single listed hazardous air pollutant or 25 tons or more of any combination of listed hazardous air pollutants, are require to obtain a permit. New sources subject to NSPSs are still required to obtain permits.

Sources have a year after the programs start up to apply for a permit. If a permit is applied for in a reasonable amount of time, the source can continue operations during the review and issuance process. After the first year of the program, permit applications must be acted on by the state within 18 months. The state is to send draft permit applications to EPA for approval. EPA has the authority to reject permits. If EPA objects to a permit application, the state has 90 days to revise it. If the state does not revise the permit, then EPA can revise it or deny it.

If, after a source receives its permit, it decides to modify its operations, no formal permit revision will be required if the following requirements are met:

1. The changes are not defined as modifications according to existing statutes.
2. An increase in emissions will not occur because of the changes.
3. Seven days written notice to state and EPA, prior to the changes.

To fund this program states are allowed to collect a permit application fee of not less than $25 per ton of emitted regulated air pollutants, except CO. This amount cannot exceed $100,000 because no fees will be assessed for emissions above 4,000 tons a year. If a source exceeds its permitted emissions, then a fee of not less than $10,000 a day can be imposed.

Citizen Review: While processing permit applications prior to issuance, the state is required to allow for public comment and hearing. Any person can petition EPA to issue an objection to a permit application. EPA has 60 days to act on the petition. The objections in these petitions need to have been raised during the public comment period in order for EPA to act on them. Once a permit is issued, a citizen petition cannot delay its use.

Title V Impact On Industry: Initially the responsibility for this program lies with the states. After a permit system has been implemented then industry can apply for a permit. A system like that of the National Pollutant Discharge Elimination (NPDES) under the Clean Water Act (CWA) can be expected. Industry will have to build on existing record keeping and reporting structures used for other environmental permits.

## Title VI - Stratospheric Ozone Protection

Title VI provisions are intended to prevent deterioration in the stratospheric ozone. This title contains many do or die provisions. Its sets firm deadlines for the phase out of production of certain substances. These substances are chlorofluorocarbons (CFCs), halon, carbon tetrachloride, and methyl chloroform. The intent is to phase out the use and production of these substances and force industry to develop new and more environmentally safe substitutes.

There are two classes of substances to be phased out and regulated. Class I includes CFCs, halons, methyl chloroform, and carbon tetrachloride. Class I substances are to be phased out by the year 2000, except for methyl chloroform which has until 2002. Class IIs principle substance is hydrochlorofluorocarbons (HCFCs). In 2015 production of HCFCs, except for certain uses, is to be banned. HCFCs can continue to be used as a refrigerant until 2020. HCFC production will be completely banned in 2030.

The most noticeable changes as far as the public is concerned is the provisions concerned with the recovery, recycling, and disposal of Class I and II substances. These new regulations will be in effect after January 1, 1992. The servicing of air conditioners and refrigerators will become tightly regulated. After July 1, 1992 no direct venting of refrigerants during service (including car air conditioners) will be allowed. Cars produced in model year 1994 and thereafter will be required to use refrigerants that will not deplete the ozone.

Title VI Impact on Industry: Replacements for CFCs used in industry will have to be found. These provisions force new development by gradually banning all use of CFCs. Manufacturers of CFCs will have to respond, this will probably translate into higher costs for these products.

## Title VII - Federal Enforcement Provisions

This title basically increases federal control and punishment for violations of SIP, permits, or any other provisions of the new act. EPA can use title VII to go after states that allow SIP or permit violations.

Criminal penalties can be up to $250,000 and five years in prison for individuals or $500,000 for corporations. Basically, criminal penalties can result from any knowing violation of the revised act or SIPs, or knowingly endangering others.

The amendments do deal with individuals involved in violations. Employees that knowingly release air toxics that have the potential of doing severe bodily harm to others can be fined $250,000 a day and 15 years in prison, for corporations the fine can be $1,000,000. When dealing with unknowing violations the new act places responsibility on employers or senior personnel rather than actual operators.

Field Citations: Government officials now have the ability to write on-site citations for minor violations. These "tickets" can be up to $5,000 a day for each violation. Facilities that have been given a citation have the right to a hearing.

Other Provisions: Citizen suits regarding violations or noncompliance can be brought against facilities to force them to obtain a permit and comply with the SIP. In cases where the violation has been repeated, the suit can also cover past violations. Another innovative provision is the Award Program for individuals providing information on violations, in effect a "bounty" program.

Title VII Impact On Industry: Title VII gives the federal government broad powers to enforce these amendments. Individual and corporate liability seems to be clearly defined. One provision that has the potential to cause trouble is the "bounty" provision. If industry complies with these amendments and conducts business in an environmentally responsible manner, these provisions probably will not be used against them. One way for industry to respond to environmental concerns as a whole is to make use of environmental audits to provide a "picture" of their environmental operations.

## Titles VIII thru XI

Title VIII contains miscellaneous provisions, ranging from studying Class I PSD areas, to analysis of costs and benefits. Title IX deals with clean air research into problems such as acid rain and the health effects of both long and short term air pollution. Title X contains provisions for disadvantaged business concerns. Title X requires EPA to make sure that no less than 10% of total federal funding for clean air research goes to disadvantaged business concerns. Disadvantaged business concerns are those which women or minorities own a majority interest. Title XI contains provisions for clean air employment transition assistance. These provisions set up a program dealing with employees displaced because of compliance with the Clean Air Act.

### III. Summary

The Clean Air Act Amendments of 1990 set ambitious goals and deadlines for the various provisions. How some of these provisions will be transferred into actual regulations, and how effective these regulations will be, remains to be seen. Only after several years and after the regulations are tested in both the courts and the work environment, will the true impact of the 1990 amendments be known. These amendments have the potential for a far reaching economical impact, not just now, but for years in the future. Most of these provisions and their resulting regulations will translate into expenses for industry. Ultimately, it will be up to those in industry to implement the CAA 1990 in an environmentally responsible manner.

### References

1.  Graves, Michael D.; Jones, Randolph L.; Livingood, Mathew G.; Bentley, Royce H.; The Historical Perspective on the Clean Air Act; Hall, Estill, Gable, Golden, & Nelson, P.C., Tulsa, Ok.; Oklahoma State University, Engineering Extension, Stillwater, Ok.; 1991.

2.  Graves, Michael D.; Jones, Randolph L.; Livingood, Mathew G.; Bentley, Royce H.; The (New) Clean Air Amendments; Hall, Estill, Gable, Golden, & Nelson, P.C., Tulsa, Ok.; Oklahoma State University, Engineering Extension, Stillwater, Ok.; 1991.

3.  Doughty, Dennis G.; The New Clean Air Act from the States Perspective; Oklahoma State Dept. of Health, Air Quality Service, Oklahoma City, Ok.; Oklahoma State University, Engineering Extension, Stillwater, Ok.; 1991.

4.  Quarles, John; Lewis, William H.; The NEW Clean Air Act, A Guide to the Clean Air Program as Amended in 1990; Morgan, Lewis & Bockius, Washington, D.C.; 1990.

5.  Findley, Roger W.; Farber, Daniel A.; Environmental Law in a Nutshell; West Publishing Co., St. Paul Minn., 1988.

# Chapter 8
# Balancing the Need for Electricity with Clean Air

C. Kane

## INTRODUCTION

Electricity is a clean, efficient, relatively safe and highly transportable form of energy. Increased use of electricity may well be the answer to some of our environmental problems, particularly in the area of transportation. However, since electricity does not occur naturally as a fuel source, other forms of energy need to be converted to produce electricity. The different fuels used in the conversion process have varying impacts on the environment, the economy and society.

The majority of our electricity is produced by burning fossil fuels (coal, oil and natural gas). More than half of the electricity used by American consumers today is produced from coal burning power plants. Although our coal reserves are plentiful, unabated coal burning produces ash particulates and emissions associated with acid rain, namely sulfur dioxide ($SO_2$) and nitrogen oxides (NOx). Fossil fuels such as coal also contribute to global warming by the release of carbon dioxide ($CO_2$).

In the next 20 years, our country will have many new opportunities to decide what type of power plants should be built. The Department of Energy's (DOE) Energy Information Administration (EIA) anticipates growth in demand during that time could be 245,000 megawatts[1] or almost 50% more than 1990 levels (See Figure 1). Regardless of the accuracy of these projections in demand growth, a significant amount of the coal-fired power plants are aging and will need to be replaced or retrofited. Furthermore, the nuclear power industry will need to justify plant license renewal with the Nuclear Regulatory Commission (NRC) or shut down units when current licenses expire, starting with the first unit in the year 2000.

Last year, President Bush produced a National Energy Strategy (NES)[2] to help guide the Nation's energy future. One response to the National Energy Strategy (NES) has been published by a number of environmental groups led by the Union of Concerned Scientists entitled America's Energy Choices (AEC)[3]. These two reports outline the somewhat counter positions on electrical energy for the future; increasing production and reliance on nuclear and fossil fuels versus reducing demand and more reliance on renewables.

As with most debates in a democracy, the outcome will probably fall somewhere in the middle of these two positions. Improved methods for evaluating alternatives and resolving the conflicts must be developed to maximize the overall energy, environmental and economic benefits to society of our electricity use. Before discussing some of the competing alternatives and improved methods of evaluating them, it is worthwhile to review the current state of environmental regulation with respect to clean air.

## CLEAN AIR REQUIREMENTS FOR ELECTRICITY PRODUCTION

Up until the past few years, our approach to environmental protection was one of "command and control", where levels of clean up are dictated for all newly constructed and, to a much lesser extent, existing facilities. With the recent enactment of the Clean Air Act Amendments, a shift has begun toward a market-based approach to environmental clean up. Theoretically, under a market-based system, the same results can be achieved but with the clean up occurring at the least cost opportunities. This shift to a market-based approach is likely to spread beyond the Clean Air Act. A brief outline of the federal law will introduce the principal requirements.

### The Clean Air Act

The Clean Air Act has had a dramatic effect on power plant construction since its enactment 20 years ago. In 1970, the Clean Air Act was first passed to "protect and enhance" the nation's air quality. As a result of the Act, the Environmental Protection Agency (EPA) set "New Source Performance Standards" for emissions of $SO_2$, NOx and several other pollutants. These standards put a limit on new coal-fired power plants for emission of no more than 1.2 pounds of $SO_2$ per million Btu of coal burned.

Amendments to the Act were passed in 1977 that further required all plants built or altered after September 18, 1978, to reduce $SO_2$ emissions by 70% to 90% from the levels that would be emitted if no sulfur controls were installed. Requirements for using the Best Available Control Technology (BACT) and Prevention of Significant Deterioration (PSD) in attainment areas were requirements instituted in the Amendments of 1977.

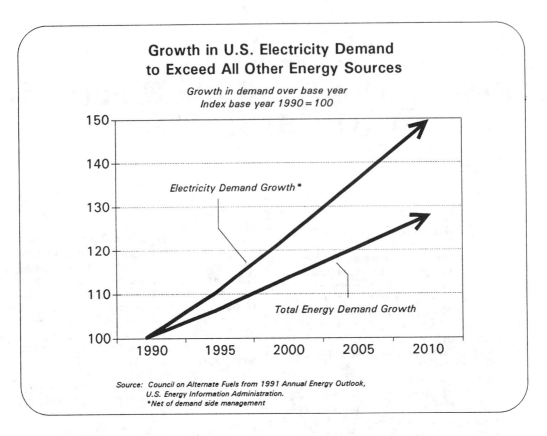

**Growth in U.S. Electricity Demand
to Exceed All Other Energy Sources**

*Growth in demand over base year
Index base year 1990 = 100*

*Electricity Demand Growth\**

*Total Energy Demand Growth*

Source: Council on Alternate Fuels from 1991 Annual Energy Outlook,
U.S. Energy Information Administration.
\*Net of demand side management

**FIGURE 1**

The BACT analysis is done on a case-by-case basis. The reviewing authority evaluates the energy, environmental, economic and other costs associated with each alternative technology, and the benefit of reduced emissions that the technology would bring. The reviewing authority then specifies an emissions limitation for the source that reflects the maximum degree of reduction achievable for each subject pollutant regulated under the Act which must be below any applicable standard of performance.

On December 1, 1987, the EPA Assistant Administrator for Air and Radiation issued a memorandum that implemented the "top-down" method for determining BACT. In brief, the top-down process provides that all available control technologies be ranked in descending order of control effectiveness. The PSD applicant first examines the most stringent -- or "top" -- alternative. That alternative is established as BACT unless the applicant demonstrates, and the permitting authority in its informed judgment agrees that technical considerations, or energy, environmental, or economic impacts justify a conclusion that the most stringent technology is not "achievable" in that case. The failure of this analysis seems to be that economic impacts are given little consideration.

## Operating Permits

Since 1970, the Clean Air Act has had the State Implementation Plan (SIP) as its focal point. The EPA set nationwide standards for the principal air pollutants of concern and specified concentrations that would be allowed over a given period of time. The states then modeled their significant sources. Based on the modeling results, states developed SIP's by rulemaking, setting out enforceable measures to achieve the necessary reductions. The EPA then by notice-and-comment rulemaking approved each state's rules or if disapproved, issued a federal plan.

SIP's are not typically a single document, but rather may fill a file cabinet full of rules, amendments, technical, analytical and modeling information. These SIP's are extremely complex, difficult to revise and frequently ambiguous. To address these problems, the Clean Air Act Amendments of 1990 contain a permit program fashioned after the highly successful National Pollution Discharge Elimination System (NPDES) permit program under the Clean Water Act, while preserving the Clean Air Act's focus on environmental results.

Operating permits are required for all major sources. A source is major if it has the potential to emit any pollutant regulated under the Act in amounts exceeding thresholds of typically 100 or 250 tons per year. Permits will have to be renewed every 5 years and will set forth all those requirements of the Clean Air Act that apply, as well as monitoring and reporting requirements.

States must develop their own permit program but EPA will maintain back-up authority as well as a veto power on permits that don't comply with federal law. The permit program will facilitate enforcement of the Act and facilitate emissions trading. The rules on operating permits have not been issued and still are the subject of much debate.

## Allowances Trading Program

Title IV of the 1990 Clean Air Act Amendments addresses acid rain deposition control and the goal of reducing annual emissions of sulfur dioxide and nitrogen oxides. The ultimate goal of Title IV is to reduce by the year 2000, overall emissions of $SO_2$ nationally by 10 million tons per year from a 1980 level of 18.9 million tons. The 8.9 million tons permitted by 2000 would then become a cap for the future. The law does not displace the normal permitting process but rather superimposes a new market-based approach on the existing regulatory process. All utilities will receive a limited number of "allowances" in order to emit $SO_2$. An allowance is basically a permit to emit one ton of $SO_2$ in a single calendar year.

In order to "throw on the switch" at any fossil-fueled power plant, a utility owner/operator must first control, or purchase in the market, enough allowances to cover the amount of pollutants that the unit will emit. Temporary increases and decreases in emissions within utility systems or power pools do not require allowance transfers or recordation so long as the total tonnage emitted by the utility system in any year matches its allowances for that year. Thus, utilities must "true up" at year's end to ensure that allowances match emissions for each unit. The allowance program applies to both existing and new utility units to ensure that the cumulative annual emission of $SO_2$ from utility units does not exceed the established ceiling.

Title IV divides the allowances program into two phases. Phase One will go into effect on January 1, 1995 and run to the end of 1999. This phase will cover the largest and highest emitting units in the nation. Phase Two goes into effect in the year 2000 and will cover all units, including those previously addressed by Phase One. The goal is also to reduce NOx emissions by two million tons, below 1980 levels. New emission limits for NOx will become effective for coal-fired units in 1995.

Recently, the first two transactions of national allowance trading were announced. Allowance prices in these transactions ranged from $250 to $400 per allowance according to reports. Wisconsin Power and Light sold the allowances to Duquesne Light and the Tennessee Valley Authority. The sales were relatively small of 10,000 to 25,000 allowances but they heartened utility officials around the country as a beginning. Now, there is a market.

## Global Warming

Although there is no current legislation in the U.S. covering production of carbon dioxide, it appears to be inevitable. The NES states that "despite the large uncertainties regarding potential global climate change, there is sufficient scientific concern to have persuaded the world community to start acting to curb the build-up of the so-called Greenhouse Gases[4]". Combustion of fossil fuels in power plants is a contributor of carbon dioxide, which is a greenhouse gas.

Last year, the National Academy of Sciences in conjunction with other groups produced a report on Policy Implications Of Greenhouse Warming[5]. The recommendations of the panel are summarized as follows:

(1) Study in detail the **"full social cost pricing"** of energy with a goal of gradually introducing such a system.

(2) Reduce the emission of greenhouse gases during energy use and consumption by **enhancing conservation and efficiency**.

(3) Make greenhouse warming a key factor in planning for our future energy supply mix. The United States should adopt a **systems approach** that considers the interactions among supply, conversion, end use and external effects in improving the economics and performance of the overall energy system. (emphasis added)

The concepts expressed in these recommendations contain the building blocks for our future approach in choosing among the alternatives discussed further below.

There are still key questions about the extent to which human activities contribute to the Greenhouse Effect - fossil fuel combustion vs. deforestation for example. U.S. coal combustion is estimated to contribute less than 8% of the total worldwide release of $CO_2$ and $CO_2$ constitutes only half of the "Greenhouse Gases"[6]. Based on the world attention that is focused on this issue and the growing evidence of some impact, the alternatives we select for the future must give some consideration to the $CO_2$ effect.

## ALTERNATIVES FOR PRODUCING ELECTRICITY MORE EFFICIENTLY, CLEANER AND SAFER

Technology advances are emerging rapidly in the electrical power industry that will improve environmental performance and plant efficiency. When applied to our plentiful coal resources, these technological advances can also improve performance of our existing plant inventory and enhance our future energy security. Other technological advances in combined cycles, energy conservation, improved efficiency and use of renewables provide additional alternatives for the future.

## Energy Conservation and Increased Efficiency

Energy conservation is a concept that became popular in the 1970's as a direct result of the oil price shock and the Carter Administration's declaration of the "moral equivalent of war" on U.S. dependence on foreign oil. Unfortunately, momentum was lost in the 1980's when oil prices began falling. But the war in the Persian Gulf and the recent passage of the Clean Air Act Amendments have given America new motivation to conserve energy both to reduce our dependence and to prevent pollution. According to a recent report by the National Association of Regulatory Utility Commissioners, the U.S. could save between $27 billion and $120 billion a year on its energy bill through conservation measures[7].

Technology for the efficient use of energy continues to improve. Examples of technology advances shown with the relative percent increase in efficiency over the existing baseline, include the following:

| | |
|---|---|
| Residential Compact Fluorescents (IBW) | 50-70% |
| New T-8 lamps | 10-15% |
| Electronic Dimmable Ballast | 20% |
| Automatic Lighting Control Systems | 15% |
| Outside Lighting with Halogens | 60% |
| Variable Speed Motor Drives | 10-40% |
| Proper Sizing of Motors | 5-15% |
| Evaporative Air Coolers | 10-20% |

Florida has recently taken a statewide initiative to look at the potential of energy conservation. The Florida Energy Office contracted for a study of the "achievable potential" for demand-side management which is to be completed this year. The study will identify the kinds of energy efficiency programs that are "technically possible and achievable".

Increased use of cogeneration also increases the overall efficiency of our fuel consumption. Cogeneration is the production of electricity with the combined utilization of waste heat. Where applications provide for utilization of the waste heat for district heating or for other industrial uses, overall efficiencies can reach 60% or greater. Levels of efficiency must be given more weight in evaluating the total societal costs of alternatives if such higher efficiency technologies are to be given full credit for the multiple benefits they produce.

The disparity between opinions on the potential for energy conservation and increased efficiency is demonstrated by the AEC's Market-Based Scenario for growth in electric power needs. According to this study, electric power generation needs will be slightly _less_ in the year 2010 than what we needed in 1988. The current projections of DOE on the otherhand, forecast an increase in electrical demand of approximately 50% by the year 2010.

## Clean Coal Technologies[8]

Over the last two decades, the most common means of reducing emissions of coal combustion has been by the use of the flue gas scrubber developed during the 1960's. Until recently, the flue gas scrubber was the only commercial technology capable of achieving the 70% to 90% SO2 reduction required under the 1977 Clean Air Act Amendments. According to DOE, a little over 20% of currently operating U.S. coal-fired power plants have installed scrubbers. Due to the time frame in meeting Phase One requirements, scrubber installation could double by 1995.

However, the future of clean coal burning for power generation will have to go beyond the scrubber technology available today. Today's scrubbers are expensive to build and consume 5% to 8% of a power plant's thermal energy in order to operate. Additionally, the current scrubber technology does not reduce the emissions of NOx. A brief discussion of some new clean coal technologies can be addressed by reviewing how coal can be cleaned at several points in the fuel chain.

Precombustion Cleaning: An estimated 40% of the coal bound for U.S. utility boilers receives some cleaning before it is burned. The Electric Power Research Institute has estimated that wider use of coal cleaning processes could reduce total SO2 emissions by 10% nationwide. To achieve greater reductions, improved coal cleaning techniques need to be developed including chemical and biological cleaning. According to DOE, chemical or biological coal cleaning appears to be capable of removing as much as 90% of the total sulfur in coal. Some chemical techniques also may remove 99% of the ash.

Cleaning During Combustion: In fluidized bed combustors, crushed coal is mixed with limestone and the mix is suspended on jets of air. As the coal burns, the limestone acts like a chemical "sponge" to capture the sulfur before it enters the exhaust system. More than 90% of the sulfur released from coal can be captured this way and turned into solid dry waste. Also, since combustion temperatures can be kept to around 1400 to 1600 degrees F, or almost half the temperature of a conventional boiler, much less nitrogen pollutants form. Thus, fluidized bed combustors can meet both SO2 and NOx standards without any additional pollution control equipment (See Figure 2).

Post-Combustion Cleaning: Advanced post-combustion SO2 controls include in-duct sorbent injection systems inside the ductwork leading from the boiler to the smokestack. Sulfur absorbers (such as lime) are sprayed into the center of the duct. 50% to 70% of the SO2 can be removed as the reaction produces dry particles that can be collected downstream. This technique will be particularly attractive for retrofitting smaller, older, plants where space is limited.

Advanced scrubber technology is being developed to make these devices more economical and to remove both SO2 and NOx. The addition of adipic acid in the process can achieve as much as 97% SO2 removal. "Jet bubbling reactors" are also being developed where the flue gas is bubbled through a sulfur absorbing slurry which greatly improves the process efficiency compared to today's wet scrubbers.

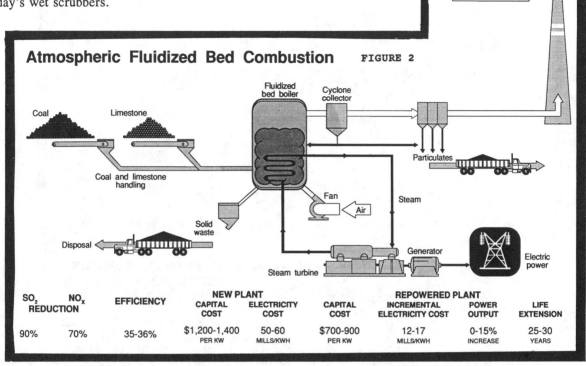

## Atmospheric Fluidized Bed Combustion   FIGURE 2

| SO₂ NOₓ REDUCTION | | EFFICIENCY | NEW PLANT | | REPOWERED PLANT | | | LIFE EXTENSION |
|---|---|---|---|---|---|---|---|---|
| | | | CAPITAL COST | ELECTRICITY COST | CAPITAL COST | INCREMENTAL ELECTRICITY COST | POWER OUTPUT | |
| 90% | 70% | 35-36% | $1,200-1,400 PER KW | 50-60 MILLS/KWH | $700-900 PER KW | 12-17 MILLS/KWH | 0-15% INCREASE | 25-30 YEARS |

Post combustion nitrogen oxide controls are also being utilized in some new commercial plants using the concept of selective catalytic reduction (SCR). Although this technology is considerably more expensive than low NOx burners which are today's standard for NOx reduction, EPA is in some instances requiring this level of control. Ammonia is mixed with fuel gas which then passes through a reaction chamber separated from the scrubber vessel. By use of a catalyst, ammonia converts the NOx to molecular nitrogen and water. This process is projected to reduce nitrogen emissions by 50% to 80%.

### Gas Turbines and Combined Cycle

The combination of gas and steam turbines account for the name combined cycle. Clean gases are burned and the very hot exhaust is routed through a gas turbine to generate electricity. The resid/ual heat in the exhaust is used to boil water for a conventional steam turbine-generator to produce more electricity.

Natural gas today appears plentiful and cheap. Although coal is cheaper and even more plentiful, natural gas is cleaner. Environmental considerations are driving utility demand because natural gas is a way to reduce nitrogen oxide and sulfur dioxide emissions. The big problem of natural gas is getting the gas to go where it needs to be due to regulatory procedures governing pipeline routing and construction.

Coal gasification, used in the gas turbine/combined cycle method for generating electricity, has progressed from the research laboratory to the threshold of commercial application (See Figure 3). Coal gasification combined cycle systems are among the cleanest of the emerging clean coal technologies. Sulfur, nitrogen compounds and particulates are removed before the fuel is burned in the gas turbine. This results in SO2 reductions of 95-99% and nitrogen oxide reduction of greater than 90%. This technology appears to be one of the much more promising means to utilize our plentiful coal reserves cleanly in the next century.

Combined cycles have the additional benefit of a higher conversion efficiency of 40-42% as compared to 33% for conventional pulverized coal-fired steam turbine systems. The increased efficiency produces a proportionate decrease in CO2 emissions and other emissions for a given electrical output[9]. Increased efficiencies also use the "non-renewable" resources at a slower rate and reduce other fuel cycle costs proportionately.

### Renewables

The AEC analysis of renewable energy considered 13 technologies from hydroelectric-plant upgrades to advanced geothermal technologies (geopressured and hot dry rock). The direct costs were considered along with

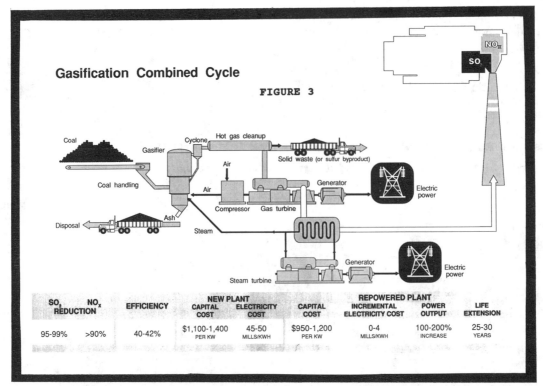

## Gasification Combined Cycle

### FIGURE 3

| SO₂ NOₓ REDUCTION | | EFFICIENCY | NEW PLANT CAPITAL COST | ELECTRICITY COST | REPOWERED PLANT CAPITAL COST | INCREMENTAL ELECTRICITY COST | POWER OUTPUT | LIFE EXTENSION |
|---|---|---|---|---|---|---|---|---|
| 95-99% | >90% | 40-42% | $1,100-1,400 PER KW | 45-50 MILLS/KWH | $950-1,200 PER KW | 0-4 MILLS/KWH | 100-200% INCREASE | 25-30 YEARS |

physical limitations on the resource and the incremental cost of storage needed to compensate for variations of solar and wind output[10].

Wind, solar, advanced geothermal and biomass account for the largest shares of new renewable supply. Under AEC's various scenarios, renewable energy resources will play an increasingly important role over the next 40 years[11], accounting for between 40% and 60% of our electrical generating capacity by the year 2030. Policies are outlined that will promote greater use of renewables. NES's projections on the use of renewables are far less optimistic increasing to approximately 22% by the year 2010.

A good example of the potential of renewables occurred recently in wind energy as a result of a relatively simple technology breakthrough[12]. The new technology is a variable-speed turbine developed by U.S. Windpower Company. The prior technology had to operate a near constant speed in order to provide a constant level of power. Addition of a new converter between the generator and utility line now allows the rotor and generator to speed up in gusts of wind and convert more energy into electricity.

The Electric Power Research Institute (EPRI) participated in the development, and estimates the new model can generate electricity at a cost of 5 cents per kilowatt hour. This cost is already competitive with other sources of energy, without even considering other societal costs. Due to wind availability and geographic requirements, wind generation mainly is available in certain areas of midwestern states and therefore, the power must be transmitted to other regions. Still EPRI claims wind energy has the potential of delivering 50,000 MW by 2010 with the new technology which is over 25 times the wind power produced today.

## PROCESSES FOR COMPARING ALTERNATIVES AND MAKING DECISIONS

Utilities and regulators need to be able to determine which investments are most likely to provide the greatest overall social benefits to consumers at the least cost. Historically, the utility was rewarded a rate of return only for its costs of power generation and, therefore, had no incentive to reduce customer demand. This rate structure guaranteed growth in new power plant construction without adequately considering system inefficiencies or least cost solutions.

Furthermore, better forums need to be developed for timely and efficient decision-making on when, where and how to add new generating capacity. While improvements have been made in some states over the last decade, nationally, there is a great need for improvement. In particular, there must be greater emphasis on negotiated solutions to our environmental and energy problems in lieu of the adversarial relationship that has developed between industry and environmental regulators.

### Least Cost Planning (Integrated Resource Planning)

Planning instruments are in place in many states that now compare the costs and benefits of electricity supply and demand options. These instruments are variously known as Least Cost Planning or Integrated Resource Planning (IRP). Many of these programs are new and are only beginning to address the regulatory changes necessary to implement IRP procedures. Both the NES and the AEC support the premise that investments in electricity conservation and efficiency should be allowed to compete on an equal playing field with supply options. AEC goes further to ensure least-cost investments are the most profitable investments for the utility.

The best IRP approach for any given locale will vary because of regional differences in utility costs, supply options, pricing policies and other characteristics. States and utilities are in the best position to determine which approach is most responsive to local needs. The federal government can take a lead in experimenting with research in publicly owned systems.

Under the "command and control" philosophy of environmental protection, environmental policy has been many times more expensive then is necessary to achieve given improvements in environmental quality. Regulators have traditionally taken as a given whatever costs were necessary to meet environmental regulations. Under the new market-based philosophy of the Clean Air Act Amendments, regulators should create a regulatory atmosphere that encourages utilities to prevent environmental degradation at the lowest possible cost. It is anticipated that the market-based approach will create opportunities to meet significantly tighter emission constraints at a cost roughly half what it would be under the "command and control" approach. However, to achieve this cost reduction, regulators must fully get on board.

A recent example of the current command and control philosophy involved a utility that sought permitting to build a second coal-fired power plant at a two unit site, the first unit having operated for only 5 years. The issue was the required level of NOx reductions. The designer proposed upgrading the 1st unit with improved low NOx burners and using the same improved low NOx burners for unit 2 for a total cost of $11 million. Using the "top down" BACT "command and control" approach, the regulator rejected that proposal and instead required expensive SCR NOx control to be used on the new unit at a cost of $26 million with no upgrades to unit 1. The same amount of overall NOx reduction will be achieved but at more than twice the cost.

## Power Plant Siting and Land Use

Siting of power plants creates a particular difficulty in balancing between local quality-of-life concerns with regional or national needs for new energy facilities. The impacts are felt locally while the benefits cover broader regions. In addition, there has been a perception that the state and federal planning bodies have not given adequate considerations to local concerns of public health. The result is frequent and vehement opposition from local communities to new energy-facilities.

The NES promotes expansion of model state siting programs such as Florida's consolidated process for facility siting and environmental permitting. The siting and certification of electrical power plants are governed by the Florida Electric Power Plant Siting Act. An equally important land use and siting issue involves the location of transmission lines which in Florida are governed by the Transmission Line Siting Act. The two acts in Florida involve a coordinated review process under the supervision of the Department of Environmental Regulation (DER)[13]. The process is subject to an administrative hearing and the ultimate

certification by the Governor and cabinet. The state review process preempts local government decision making in this area and provides one-stop, coordinated permitting. The DER receives applications with a substantial mandatory fee and forwards copies to other state agencies who prepare evaluation reports on the impacts of the proposal which are submitted back to DER. The process then goes through three principal hearings.

Land Use Hearing: A land use hearing takes place in the county of the proposed site to determine if the proposed project complies with existing zoning plans. A hearing officer then issues recommendations to the Governor and cabinet sitting as the siting board. If zoning variances are not granted by the local government, the applicant can appeal to the siting board for a zoning vacancy.

Need Determination Hearing: This hearing is conducted before the Public Service Commission (PSC) considering energy demand, cost, reliability, and any other factors including mitigation to energy demand. The PSC's determination of need is binding on the hearing officer and the siting board. An affirmative determination of need is required to proceed with a certification hearing by the siting board.

Certification Hearing: A hearing officer of the Division of Administrative Hearings then conducts a certification hearing which results in findings of facts and conclusions of law. The hearing officer then submits a recommended order to the siting board. The siting board must then issue a written order approving, denying or approving with modifications the certification. This order by the board is the final administrative action required for the application.

Such a streamlined consolidation of this process can provide an efficient and comprehensive hearing on the issues without the expense and delay experienced in fragmented processes that still exist in many states. In Florida, the law requires that the process be completed within 14 months. This streamlining is essential in order to provide timely and responsible decision making on new power plants with consideration of energy conservation and improved efficiency.

Public utility commissions and state government agencies need to give more attention to local site specific impacts of new power plants that are not dealt with easily by the broader environmental laws. People do not generally want power plants or transmission lines anywhere near their homes and frequently will use any means available to prevent it. State agencies and public utilities need to get local communities involved up front and insure that they have accurate information about the details of the project. Local interests need to have a voice in the negotiation of the parameters of new and existing power plants.

## Total Fuel-Cycle Cost Analysis

A lot of discussion is taking place today on how our environmental analyses fail to identify and quantify all impacts to health, the environment and society. The total fuel cycle cost must be addressed. For a new coal combustion technology, this would include the environmental impacts of the added coal mining, cleaning, transportation, and the transportation of ash and sulphur pollution control waste.

Such analyses should also include the full costs of complying with regulations and permit conditions; operating costs or environmental impacts associated with the construction of a facility and the manufacture of its capital equipment. Still other factors could be included to broaden the analysis even further to reflect the costs or benefits to the Nation of building and operating generating facilities or the indirect costs associated with electricity use. This analysis would provide a distorted view if the benefits are not also considered, such as tax base enhancement, job creation, energy independence and indirect benefits in electricity use.

Another concept considered by some regulatory agencies for comparing different alternatives involves the use of "environmental externalities". Environmental externalities represent damages that occur to the environment from an operating plant. Estimating a monetary value for environmental externalities provides

an approximation of the societal value of reducing impacts on human health and the environment from electrical energy. Dr. Paul Joskow, Professor of Economics and Management at MIT provides an interesting discussion of environmental externalities and how they may be properly utilized[14].

According to Dr. Joskow, emissions of wastes into the environment are an "externality problem" because the associated costs for clean air beyond what is regulated are "external" to the emitting firms' production and pricing decisions. The critical issue is how to price the incremental emissions so that the decisionmaker takes the cost of environmental impacts into account when it makes decisions about how much to pollute and how much to control emissions. The answer to these decisions will be reflected in the price charged for its products. The whole idea for Government regulation of power plant emissions is to force owners of the plant to take account of the external effects of the emissions on air, water and resources by internalizing a cost for abatement[15].

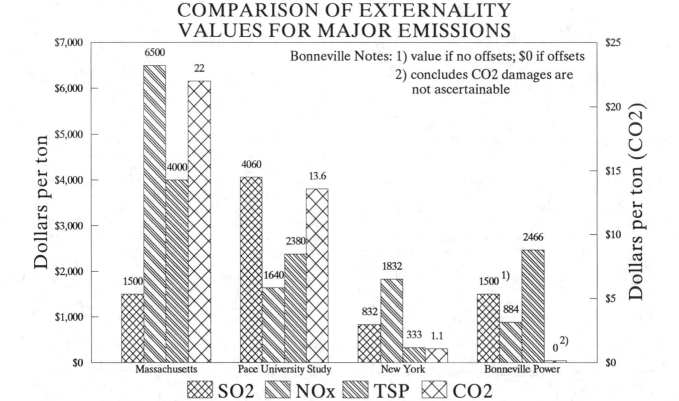

FIGURE 4

One solution to environmental externality problems is the establishment of tradable emissions permits market which is essentially what is being done in Title IV of the Clean Air Act. By creating this market, we are internalizing this external "cost". The cost of emissions are then reflected in the prices of emission rights. Once the externality is fully "internalized", there will still be residual emissions but they will no longer be of policy concern once they are priced properly[16].

For greenhouse gases, some states may believe costs of control to be a valid way of estimating the value of reducing emissions but most economists feel a damage based approach is better. There is discussion of adopting a federal carbon tax and several states are trying to reduce $CO_2$ emissions by a target percentage. The stabilization effort will come either from reducing $CO_2$ emissions or increasing $CO_2$ sinks. We can stabilize the global climate by improving energy efficiency, halting the destruction of forests, and increasing carbon sinks, including tree-planting and $CO_2$ scrubbing.

A few states and the Bonneville Power Administration (BPA) are attempting to implement consideration of environmental externalities in the decision making process. However, the results to date in valuation of externalities are quite varied and demonstrate the difficulty in understanding the economics involved (See Figure 4). This apparent confusion may do little more than increase the costs to consumer without having any notable effect on the environment. Regional, national, and international environmental problems require coordination and considerations beyond state boundaries.

## Environmental Mediation And Facilitation

Litigation is very rarely the best or most efficient method for solving a problem since lawsuits are strictly a win-lose proposition. Lawsuits are time consuming and expensive. Money and time that could be spent on solving the problem is spent on lawyers. Frequently, litigation or other forms of adversarial dispute resolution are instigated with more emotion than a clear understanding of the facts or the real interests involved.

As a practitioner, experienced in disputes resolution, I have seen the toll on individuals and businesses that result from litigation and other adversarial administrative processes. Not surprisingly, the accomplishments of which I am proudest in my 20 years of experience, have involved participating in several structured negotiations of complex, multimillion dollar disputes where settlements were reached without resorting to litigation.

Mediation is the facilitation of negotiations by a person, not a party to the dispute, who has no power to decide the issues but whose sole function is to assist the parties in reaching a settlement. The mediator serves to schedule and structure negotiations, acts as a catalyst between the parties, focuses the discussion, facilitates exchange between the parties, and serves as an assessor - not a judge - of the positions taken by the parties during the course of negotiations[17].

One of the most infamous environmental court cases of the 1960's and 1970's, Scenic Hudson[18], was ultimately resolved by mediation. The Federal Power Commission was petitioned by Consolidated Edison (Con Ed) for a hydroelectric permit on the Hudson River in New York. EPA had the duty of evaluating the power plant's effect on fish. EPA required cooling towers be built which the utility thought was unnecessary. A battle of the wills ensued which resulted in 14 years of fighting and litigation.

Con Ed took the initiative in finally seeking mediation of the dispute. The parties in the mediation included state and federal agencies as well as public interest groups and sportsmen. The mediation lasted 16 months and was ultimately successful in producing an agreement among all the parties[19]. Mediation accomplished in 16 months what the courts were unable to do in 14 years. When mediation has been utilized in environmental disputes, the results have been very positive. Yet, there is still a certain amount of distrust in the process on the part of regulators.

## CONCLUSION

The prior framework of environmental laws dictated standards of environmental performance but have failed to adequately account for the economics involved. With the new Clean Air Act, we are beginning a system of market-based incentives to improve environmental quality at the least cost opportunities. Various promising alternatives exist or can be commercially developed for reducing demand or for producing electricity in a safer, more efficient and healthier manner than what the old system would dictate. Evaluation and dispute resolution methods must go beyond the present processes to make better choices for our long term energy and environmental future. Least-cost planning, total fuel-cycle analysis, coordinated power plant siting and greater use of mediation and facilitation are ways to improve the process.

## REFERENCES

1.  Annual Outlook For U.S. Electric Power 1991, Energy Information Administration, July 1991.

2.  National Energy Strategy; Powerful Ideas For America (NES), Washington, D.C., February 1991.

3.  America's Energy Choices; Executive Summary (AEC), Published by the Union of Concerned Scientists, 1991.

4.  NES, Pg. 172, Supra, Note 1.

5.  Policy Implications of Greenhouse Warming, National Academy of Sciences, et al., 1991.

6.  Clean Coal Technology: The New Coal Era, U.S. Department of Energy, Office of Fossil Energy, June 1990.

7.    "Profile" & "Conservation Techniques & Tips", <u>Washington Business Journal</u>, Pg. 6, November 26, 1990.

8.    Supra, Note 6.

9.    Id., Pg. 34.

10.   Supra, Note 2.

11.   Supra, Pg. 18, Note 2.

12.   "Future of Wind Power Gets A Lift", <u>The Washington Post</u>, November 17, 1991, Pg. H1, by Thomas W. Lippman.

13.   <u>Florida Environmental and Land Use Law</u>, Section 15, Pg. 23-24, The Florida Bar, 1991 Edition.

14.   <u>Dealing With Environmental Externalities: Let's Do It Write!</u> by Dr. Paul L. Joskow, Professor of Economics and Management, MIT., prepared for Harvard Northeast Electric Utility Executive Conference, Killington, Vermont, October 17 and 18, 1991.

15.   Id. Pg. 36 - 42.

16.   Id.

17.   <u>Guidance On The Use of Alternative Dispute Resolution Techniques In Enforcement Actions</u>, EPA, August 6, 1987, 18 ELR 35123 (1-88).

18.   Scenic Hudson Preservation Conference v. Federal Power Commission, 354 F.2d 608 (2d Cir. 1965).

19.   <u>Kindling The Environmental ADR Flame: Use Of Mediation And Arbitration In Federal, Planning, Permitting And Enforcement</u>, by Sandra M. Rennie, 19 ELR 10479 (11-89).

# Chapter 9
# California's Experience with Alternative Fuel Vehicles

C. Sullivan

## INTRODUCTION

California is often referred to as a nation-state, and in many aspects fits that description. The state represents the seventh largest economy in the world. Most of California does not have to worry about fuel to heat homes in the winter. What we do worry about is fuel for our motor vehicles, approximately 24 million of them. In fact, California accounts for ten percent of new vehicle sales in the United States each year. Petroleum consumption in California is 15 billion gallons a year, much of it used in the transportation sector. The state is the third largest consumer of gasoline in the world, only exceeded by the United States as a whole and the former Soviet Union.

California is also a "leader" in air pollution. Of the nine worst ozone areas in the country cited in the 1990 Clean Air Act Amendments, two areas -- the Los Angeles Basin and San Diego -- are located in California. Five of California's cities made the "top 20" smoggiest cities in the United States. In reality, all of California's major metropolitan areas have air quality problems.

This paper will discuss the beginnings of California's investigations of alternative fuels use in vehicles; the results of the state's demonstration programs; and future plans to improve California's air quality and energy security in the mobile sector.

## BACKGROUND

California began to look seriously at alternative fuels in the late 1970s, in response to the oil crises. Although California experienced only a three to five percent shortfall in petroleum supplies during that period, the impact on the state was severe. Long lines formed at service stations, and a rationing plan for the agricultural sector was put in place. As the Governor's agency for energy conservation, supply and demand, the California Energy Commission (Commission) was given responsibility for seeking alternatives to petroleum fuels for our transportation sector.

The potential significant air quality benefits from the use of alternative fuels was not immediately recognized. However, both an extensive emissions test program on the vehicles and air quality modeling studies were conducted which validated the potential air quality benefits. This air quality component has become increasingly important as California seeks avenues to meet federal air quality standards.

In 1990, the Board passed landmark regulations requiring manufacturers of light-duty vehicles to produce increasingly lower emission vehicles between 1994 and 2003. Low emission vehicle regulations have also been passed for medium-duty vehicles. California currently has the most stringent standards for heavy-duty engines for transit applications. In fact, the only engine currently certified for use in California in a transit coach is a Detroit Diesel methanol engine. Moreover, the Board is planning to implement low emission standards for this sector in 1996.

All these Low Emission Vehicle regulations have provided an additional impetus to engine and vehicle manufacturers to develop of clean, alternative fuel technologies.

## LIGHT-DUTY VEHICLE ACTIVITIES

### Alcohol Fuels

In the late 1970s, alcohol fuels were considered to be the most viable alternative to petroleum fuels. Germany was the world's leader at that time in investigating alcohol fuels, and dedicated methanol and ethanol Volkswagens, as well as transit buses, were being demonstrated throughout West Germany. The Commission purchased 40 Volkswagen Rabbits, 20 methanol, 19 ethanol, and one gasoline "control" vehicle, and placed these vehicles with state agencies in Sacramento. In addition, 20 dedicated methanol Ford Escorts were placed with Los Angeles County for demonstration in a variety of government applications.

At the same time, the Commission began an investigation to determine the feasibility of producing ethanol in California for use as a transportation fuel. The results of this study, including construction and operation of one production facility, indicated that ethanol produced in California was not cost-effective as a motor vehicle fuel.

In 1983, based on the technical success of the Volkswagen and Ford demonstrations, 500 dedicated methanol Ford Escorts were placed with local and state government agencies throughout California. The Commission attempted to establish a fueling network for the vehicles using small independent gasoline stations, and a meager network of about 15 stations was established from Chico to San Diego. These stations were often not conveniently located to major freeways, and drivers sometimes found them difficult to locate. Still, with careful planning, a driver could travel from Northern to Southern Califonia, a distance of over 500 miles, in a dedicated methanol vehicle.

The state placed 150 of the Escorts at Thrify Rent-A-Car at Los Angeles International Airport (LAX). Thrifty had a contract with the state to provide rental vehicles to state employees in Los Angeles on business. Previous research had indicated that state employees typically went to Los Angeles on one-day trips; they drove to downtown LA and back to the airport, and did not fuel their vehicles. So, the fact that there were only three places in the LA Basin to obtain methanol fuel was not considered a problem.

That assumption could not have been more incorrect. When state employees went to the counter at Thrifty and identified themselves as state employees, they were handed the keys to a methanol Escort and maps to the fuel stations. People paniced. They often abandoned the vehicles two or three miles from the airport, with a quarter tank of fuel remaining. After several months, the cars were removed from this service and placed with government fleets in the Los Angeles area. Those vehicles performed successfully, with many achieving 100,000 miles or more before being removed from service.

Some of these Escorts remain in service today. But because of the LAX-Thrifty experience, this demonstration is referred to as, "a technical success, but an emotional failure".

Fortunately, automotive engineers recognized the problem and made another technological breakthrough -- the fuel flexible vehicle (FFV). FFVs will operate on methanol or gasoline or an infinite combination of the two fuels, in a single fuel tank. (With a change in the computer chip, the vehicles will also operate on ethanol and/or gasoline.) No more were the drivers of methanol vehicles tied to a limited fuel network. If methanol fuel was not available, the driver could simply fill the car's fuel tank with gasoline. The Energy Commission, South Coast Air Quality District and the Air Resources Board collectively took delivery of seven prototype fuel flexible Ford Crown Victorias in 1987.

General Motors conceived their own version of the fuel flexible technology, calling their cars Variable Fuel Vehicles. The Commission entered into formal agreements with Ford and General Motors to support engineering costs to produce up to 5,000 fuel flexible cars for California. The vehicles were to be introduced over time in increasing numbers, with the goal of 5,000 vehicles in 1993. The differential costs were spread over the entire 5,000 vehicles at $2,000 per vehicle.

The District entered into a separate demonstration program with Chrysler to develop and demonstrate "gasoline tolerant" technology, a fuel flexible vehicle optimized to operate on methanol fuel. In addition, the District and Volvo are cooperating on the demonstration of fuel flexible Volvos utilizing electrically-heated catalysts for optimum emission control.

The Japanese automobile manufacturers entered the demonstration program in 1989. Currently, prototype fuel flexible vehicles produced by Nissan, Mitsubishi, Mazda, and Toyota are being operated by the Commission, District, and Board.

Initially, fuel flexible vehicles were placed exclusively with government fleets. But the models that General Motors and Ford chose to build -- the Chevrolet Corsica and Lumina and Ford Crown Victoria and Taurus -- are not typical government fleet cars. Even though the Commission paid $1,500 of the $2,000 differential cost for government fleets, these vehicles still cost several thousand dollars more than conventional "fleet" vehicles. For many fleets with defined vehicle purchase budgets, the decision to purchase FFVs meant that they could not buy as many vehicles. Moreover, vehicles like the Crown Victoria project an image of prosperity or opulence, an image not appreciated by taxpayers.

In 1991, the Commission began to approach private organizations to purchase FFVs. In 1992, a variety of incentives were offered to purchasers of FFVs. For instance, on orders or 20 or more vehicles, the Commission agreed to pay the full $2,000 differential cost, and the Sacramento Metropolitan Air Quality Management District offered an incentive of $1,000 to purchasers of FFVs. The District marketed the vehicles to organizations required to comply with Regulation XV, a commute trip reduction program. Under this regulation, organizations can receive enhanced credits for meeting average vehicle ridership by using alternative fuel vehicles in a rideshare program.

In 1993, Ford, General Motors and Chrysler will offer FFVs to the general public. Chrysler has made a public announcement that their fuel flexible vehicles, the Dodge Spirit and Plymouth Acclaim, will cost no more than their gasoline counterparts. In the spirit of competiveness, the other manufacturers are likely to follow suit. This will be an incentive both to the private purchaser and public and private organizations. The Chrysler models are more typical government fleet vehicles and will fill a need that the Luminas and Taurus could not meet.

A continuing obstacle to convincing fleets to purchase FFVs has been the lack of an adequate refueling network. After the initial efforts with independent stations proved less than satisfactory, the Commission sought the cooperation of major oil companies. In 1989, the Commission and ARCO entered into an agreement to place methanol refueling pumps at commercial stations. Other oil companies soon joined the effort. The Commission now has agreements with all the major oil companies in California, and commitments to place methanol refueling facilities at 68 stations by the end of 1993. The current network numbers 43 throughout the state. The fuel is accessed through the use of a credit card system, similar to a bank ATM card. The credit card company, GasCard, administers the distribution of fuel cards and monthly billing for methanol fuel accessed. The credit card system was initiated for two reasons. First, to control fuel access so that consumers would not be able to put methanol in their gasoline vehicles. And second, to provide a convenient way for fleets to track methanol useage and to pay for fuel. As more vehicles are sold, particularly to the public, this system becomes increasingly cumbersome. One solution being considered is a change in the shape of the nozzle, similar to the differences between nozzles for unleaded and leaded gasoline.

The Board's Low Emission Vehicle regulations includes a mechanism to require the oil companies to provide alternative fuels at public refueling stations. If the number of low emission, alternative fuel vehicles in California reaches 20,000 in 1993 and 1994, a requirement for the establishment of a minimum of 90 stations in the Los Angeles Air Basin in 1994 becomes effective. The number of stations then increases to a minimum of 200 in 1995. Other air quality management districts can "opt in" to this requirement through their Air Quality Management Plans. Thus far, seven districts, representing 90 percent of California's population, have exercised this option. The number of stations in each region is based on population. This requirement applies to any low emission vehicles. It appears at this time that FFVs, of all the alternative fuel vehicles, have the best likelihood of reaching 20,000 in the mid-1990s.

Compressed Natural Gas

In the 1970s, the gas utilities in California looked seriously at compressed natural gas (CNG) as a vehicle fuel. Hundreds of cars were converted to operate on CNG, and were placed in utility fleets for employee use. Unfortunately, these early conversions exhibited poor performance compared to their gasoline counterparts, and employees did not like the fact that the trunk was completely filled with the CNG cylinder. The vehicles were reconverted to gasoline in the early 1980s and the programs abandoned.

However, there continued to be a niche market for CNG use in vehicles, and the vehicle conversion industry was very active. Again, some enthusiasm for this alternative was lost because of poor vehicle performance. And with virtually no public refueling sites, CNG was really only an option for fleets.

These and later conversions were done for energy security reasons, not as an emissions reduction strategy. ARB regulations required only that the converted vehicle's emissions not exceed those of its gasoline counterpart at the time of conversion. Many of these early conversions were not performed properly and the vehicles not maintained very well. Three years ago, when the ARB was studying the emissions from both alternative and conventional fuel vehicles, they found that in-use emissions on CNG and propane (LPG) conversions were often very high. In fact, one LPG vehicle conversion owned by the District had emissions 300 times higher than its gasoline counterpart!

Because of renewed interest in natural gas as a motor vehicle fuel, and the active participation of the gas utilities, the gas industry, and the automotive manufacturers, compressed natural gas vehicle technology has made important strides in recent years. In 1992, GMC offered a limited number of CNG Sierra pickup trucks, and Chrysler offered the Dodge Ram van. In 1993, it is likely that Ford, GM and Chrysler will all have CNG vehicles available. Currently, the target market for natural gas vehicles is fleets. This is a logical avenue because of the fueling limitations for natural gas vehicles. In 1992-93 the federal General Services Agency plans to place up to 600 CNG vehicles with federal fleets in the LA Basin.

Between 1990-91, California privately-owned gas utilities received approval from the California Public Utilities Commission to ratebase demonstration and commercialization activities for natural gas vehicles. P G & E, SoCal Gas and San Diego Gas and Electric Company have all begun major vehicle marketing campaigns. Refueling stations are being sited, but the majority of these stations will be sited at specific users' sites and not available to the public. Fleets continue to be the logical near-term market for CNG vehicles.

## Electric Vehicles

The District is actively sponsoring the development of electric vehicle technologies through a variety of demonstration programs. These programs are conducted in concert with the Board and the electric utilities. The District has purchased one electric retrofit vehicle, which is displayed at various events in the Basin. The vehicle is made available to the Board for emissions and performance evaluations. The District is also sponsoring the development and testing of battery technologies such as the sealed bi-polar lead acid battery.

The District is part of an extensive demonstration program with Federal Express to demonstrate methanol, CNG, propane, reformulated and electric technology in delivery vans. Partners in this program include the federal Department of Energy, automotive manufacturers, fuel producers, the Commission, the Board and several Federal Express sites in the LA Basin.

## MEDIUM-DUTY VEHICLES

An area that seems ripe for alternative fuel development is the medium-duty vehicle area. Airport shuttles, delivery vans and similar vehicles are usually centrally located and fueled, and have assigned routes in a limited geographic area. Some fleets, such as the Los Angeles Times have used alternative fuels for years. Many of these fleets use liquified petroleum gas (LPG). These vehicles have been retrofitted to use LPG mostly for economic reasons. For years, there was no optimization work performed on these systems, and often these vehicles had very high emissions. This situation has now changed, and there is development work for propane-fueled engines in progress on a number of fronts by engine manufacturers, engine retrofitters, and research organizations.

## Methanol

Detroit Diesel's 4-71 engine is currently under development for use in shuttle bus applications. Demonstrations include airport shuttle buses at Sacramento Airport and employee shuttles with TRW in Los Angeles. Aside from this work, there is very little development occurring with methanol, medium-duty engines.

## Compressed Natural Gas

Hercules Engine Company, Tecogen, Ford, and others are pursuing development of compressed natural gas engines to meet medium-duty vehicle needs. The District is a cosponsor to a demonstration of Hercules engines in airport equipment, including trucks and ground support equipment. The District is also sponsoring the demonstration of CNG Hercules engines in shuttle buses at an airport and a university, and the Ford engine in a local government utility truck.

## Methanol

In 1982, California began investigating the use of alternative fuels in heavy-duty vehicles with the Commission-sponsored demonstration of methanol in transit buses at the Golden Gate Transit District, near San Francisco, California. Two methanol buses were utilized -- one M.A.N. from West Germany and one Detroit Diesel 6V92 -- plus a diesel control vehicle from each manufacturer. The DDC 6V92 represented the first time methanol had been used in a heavy-duty, compression-ignition engine. With the assistance of the Urban Mass Transportation Administration (UMTA), the project continued until 1990. Methanol One (the DDC bus) is now in service with the South Coast Area transit in Ventura, California, and Methanol Two and its diesel counterpart (M.A.N.) are in service with the Southern California Rapid Transit District (SCRTD) in Los Angeles.

The Golden Gate demonstration gave Detroit Diesel the confidence to improve the technology and bring it to commercialization. The DDC 6V92 methanol engine is currently the only heavy-duty engine certified in California for use in transit buses. SCRTD currently operates 30 methanol engines in its fleet, and expects delivery soon of 303 additional methanol buses. Other districts in California operating methanol transit buses include Riverside Transit Agency, Orange County Transit District, and South Coast Area Transit.

One concept that appears to make the retrofit of existing transit bus engines viable is the use of Avocet, a cetane improver, with methanol. The Avocet is used in small percentages (less than 5 percent) as an additive to M100. This enables the fuel to ignite without making substantial changes to the engine itself. This strategy has been demonstrated at SCRTD with excellent results. DDC 6V92 engines, with mechanical injectors, utilized in 1981 transit buses, were retrofitted with electronic injectors, and fueled with a 3 percent concentration of Avocet in methanol. When these retrofitted buses are compared to similar, older diesel buses, NOx emissions are reduced more than 50% and particulate emissions are reduced by more than 75%. SCRTD continues to perfect this retrofit strategy and plans to reduce the amount of Avocet to less than two percent.

Based on the success of the bus demonstrations, the Commission initiated a demonstration of methanol in heavy-duty engines used in trucking applications. The District is a cofunder of this demonstration, which included nine methanol engines at eight sites. All major engine manufacturers in the United States were represented in this demonstration, the purpose of which was to determine the feasibility of using methanol in the trucking industry. This demonstration is coming to a close at this time. The performance of the engines in service was assessed, and the most promising technologies are now being demonstrated in an effort to gain long-term durability information.

In 1989, the Commission began a demonstration of methanol in school buses. The program is targeted at replacing pre-1977 school buses with alternative fuel or advanced diesel technologies. Phase I includes 50 methanol buses, powered by DDC 6V92 engines. Phase II, which is currently underway, will include 100 methanol buses (also utilizing the 6V92).

Most of the heavy-duty vehicles utilize M100, or pure methanol. The school buses, however, use M85. Although emissions benefits are lower with M85, there is a concern about safety, specifically flame luminosity, with the use of M100 in school buses. The Board recently passed regulations, effective in 1996, requiring the use of an additive to provide flame luminosity, effective in 1996. Although the Board and the District cosponsored an effort by Southwest Research Institute to find such an additive, a low cost, readily available additive has yet to be found.

Although emissions reductions using methanol as a diesel substitute are dramatic, it is difficult for methanol to be cost-competitive with diesel. Because of its low volumetric energy content, 2.3 gallons of methanol are required to equal 1 gallon of diesel fuel. And, on some duty cycles, this ratio is increased to 2.5 or more. The "rack" price of methanol is currently $.42/gallon. Simply translating this raw price into its diesel equivalent would be over $.96/gallon; adding transportation, taxes and markup increases the price even more. When Avocet is added to methanol, the cost of the fuel rises dramatically. Two actions may help equalize this cost differential. In 1993, refiners in California will be required to produce a "reformulated" diesel, estimated to add up to $.20/gallon to the current diesel price. The Board is also considering a "low emission vehicle" standard for heavy-duty engines/vehicles. They expect to lower the NOx standard to 2.5 g/bhph and particulates to .05. Meeting this proposed standard with diesel will be difficult, if not impossible.

## Compressed Natural Gas

Cummins produced the first original equipment manufacturer compressed natural gas engine, an L10, and has targeted the transit bus market. They are in the process of engine certification to meet California transit bus standards. California demonstration sites for this engine include Southern California Rapid Transit District and Orange County Transportation Authority. Sacramento Regional Transit Authority recently placed an order for up to 75 CNG-powered transit buses.

Santa Barbara Air Pollution Control District has several CNG projects. One of these is a CNG pilot-ignition intercity bus. The pilot-ignition technology, by Stewart & Stevenson, uses diesel fuel for starting and under idle conditions; the remainder of the time, the engine uses CNG. These buses operate in intercity commuter service from outlying towns to Santa Barbara Monday through Friday.

In 1990, as part of the Phase I School Bus Demonstration, the Commission purchased ten Bluebird school buses, equipped with Tecogen CNG engines. Phase II of that program will place 100 buses equipped with turbo-charged Tecogen CNG engines with California school districts. The Tecogen CNG engine is certified in California; however, the turbo-charged version is not yet certified.

Finally, the District, in a costshared program with the Commission, The Gas Company and the federal Department of Energy, is demonstrating the use of CNG in heavy-duty trucks. Currently under demonstration is a Caterpillar 3406 CNG engine being used in a tractor-trailer grocery delivery truck. This truck originates in the LA Basin and goes over the Tehaichipi Mountains to Bakersfield on a daily basis. This is an extremely hard duty cycle with grades of up to 6 percent. We hope to have enough fuel capacity for the truck to make the round trip daily -- about 250 miles -- but there will be CNG available in Bakersfield at a utility fueling station. We anticipate adding two CNG engines and trucks to this demonstration in 1992-93.

## Electric and Fuel Cell Technologies

The District participates in a number of investigations into the feasibility of using electric and fuel cell technologies in the heavy-duty sector, primarily buses. These projects include funding support for the demonstration of an electric shuttle bus in the community of Palm Dessert, participation in DOE's fuel cell bus program, and a fuel cell bus demonstration in cooperation with BC Research.

Santa Barbara APCD sponsors the operation of an electric shuttle bus in downtown Santa Barbara. They are also considering a demonstration of a hybrid electric-CNG bus.

## FUTURE ACTIVITIES

As an air quality strategy, the future of alternative fuels is uncertain. The first Transitional Low Emission Vehicle (TLEV) certified under the Board's Low Emission Vehicle regulations was a gasoline Ford Escort. The consensus of the automotive manufacturers is that they can meet TLEV and LEV standards with gasoline. ULEV standards are less certain, but those standards are not effective until 1998. A manufacturer could simply skip production of ULEVs, and produce electric vehicles early.

The future is no more certain for the heavy-duty sector. The use of reformulated diesel fuel and particulate traps or other controls will most likely meet future EPA standards.

Energy security is also not a compelling reason for a fleet or the public to start using alternative fuels. The public has forgotten past oil crises. And no wonder; gasoline is actually cheaper than it was in the late 1970s. In a recent editorial in Road & Track magazine, Patrick Bedard stated the current perception of the need for energy security very succinctly, "Apparently state planners haven't heard the news that the Arab oil embargo has been over for ten years and the market is so awash in cheap petroleum, most of it non-Arabian, that we enjoy the luxury of refusing to buy from three Arab OPECers (Iran, Iraq, and Libya) because we don't like their politics."

In the absence of government pressure to use alternative fuels, we would not have seen the development of reformulated gasoline and diesel fuels, nor the advances made in engine and emissions control technologies.

It may be that methanol, compressed natural gas and propane are interim strategies to electric vehicles and fuel cells. California will continue to pursue a variety of strategies to reach our goals of clean air and energy security.

# Chapter 10
# CNG/Diesel Buses for Texas School Districts

J. H. Armstrong

At the present time, the preponderance of trucks, buses and other heavy duty vehicles are powered by diesel engines. The reasons for the change from gasoline to diesel engines are all basically economic, due to the longer life and lower operating costs of diesel engines, as compared to gasoline engines. This provides a compelling reason to continue to use these engines, even if powered by fuel other than diesel. A major strategy within the industry has been the various attempts to adapt diesel engines to alternative fuels. These conversions have been largely to either methanol or natural gas, with propane joining the race just recently. This strategy takes advantage of the remaining life of existing vehicles by converting engines rather than purchasing a new engine (and/or vehicle) designed for and dedicated to an alternate fuel. Although diesel engines have been converted to run on natural gas, there are substantial challenges that must be met. The following describes some of the technical approaches being used for diesel engine conversions.

One of the primary advantages of diesel fuel is its high cetane rating which allows the fuel to autoignite when sufficiently compressed (cetane rating discussed below). The term dieseling comes from this autoignition phenomenon. Compression ignition or autoignition simplifies the diesel engine, as compared with spark ignition engines, by eliminating spark plugs, distributors, and other electrical components. Ordinarily natural gas, propane or methanol do not autoignite due to their low cetane rating. Therefore, some means of igniting the alternate fuel must be provided. Some of the proven ignition methods are to add spark plugs or glow plugs, or use a fumigation system. The cetane rating is a number indicating a fuel's ability to self ignite - the higher the number, the easier it self-ignites. Diesel's cetane rating averages 47, while natural gas and alcohol fuels have ratings no higher than 10-typically closer to zero. A cetane number of at least 40 is required for diesel fuel.

It should be noted that new natural gas engines are being designed which are dedicated to the use of a single fuel. These engines are designed from the ground up to run on Compressed Natural Gas (CNG) and their operating characteristics should approach those of a diesel engine. The design of these engines is substantially different from what is described below, since these new engines can take advantage of the unique characteristics of natural gas.

The traditional thought to have a diesel engine burn natural gas would mean adding spark plugs and associated electronics. Rather than make these extensive engine modifications, an approach that works for natural gas conversions has been to use diesel in tandem with natural gas, particularly in four-cycle diesel engines. For this type of conversion, diesel is used as a "pilot fuel' for starting and for low engine RPM (revolutions per minute) operation. The amount of natural gas is increased as engine speed increases (higher RPM) as shown in the chart below. The operating percentage of natural gas averages 80 to 90 percent. Rather than the engine being dedicated to operate on a single fuel or having the capability to run on either diesel or an alternate fuel, both fuels are used with varying mixtures, depending upon engine load. Since diesel engines generally rely on the diesel fuel for additional lubrication and cooling, the diesel fuel used in conjunction with natural gas provides these functions. Without this additional lubricant, engine life would be substantially reduced.

| ENGINE SPEED RPM | PERCENT CNG % |
|---|---|
| 0 | 0 |
| 400 | 0 |
| 800 | 0 |
| 1200 | 20 |
| 1600 | 80 |
| 2000 | 82 |
| 2400 | 83 |
| 2800 | 84 |

Another advantage of converting a diesel engine to run on natural gas is the effect on emissions. Emission testing has shown that running a diesel engine on an combination of diesel and natural gas (dual fuel operation) significantly reduces the particulates released to the atmosphere. Although the Total Hydrocarbon emissions do increase under dual fuel operation, the Carbon Monoxide, Carbon Dioxide and Nitrous Oxide emissions decrease. A result of the conversions has also been that the power of the converted diesel engine is noticeably increased, but not to a point higher than rated output, and the amount of black smoke typically emitted by diesel engines is significantly reduced. An alternate and more complex retrofit for use of natural gas is accomplished with the addition of gas injection valves and electronic control systems, including a high-speed solenoid valve. Such a system must address problems of metering the fuel mixture in rapidly changing fuel conditions, proper timing of fuel injection, and the need to deliver fuel directly to each cylinder. The electronics for this more sophisticated system can achieve better emissions results, but must be designed to fit each particular engine type. This system is very expensive.

With the natural gas dual fuel fumigation conversion, equipment can be added to the engine without major physical modifications - retrofit equipment is added on rather than built into the engine. Electronic controls are added without major engine modifications. The natural gas retrofits discussed above apply primarily to four-cycle diesel engines found in school buses and in many heavy trucks.

Many school districts utilize diesel because of the long life of engines, high miles per gallon and low maintenance costs. The fuel conversion technique described herein should be of interest to those school districts.

In August 1990, the San Benito Independent School District approved funds to convert 28 diesel school buses and 5 gasoline mini vans to use CNG. San Benito ISD was the first school district to accomplish this particular conversion. They opted to convert all but a few older buses that are scheduled for replacement in the next few years.

San Benito ISD, located in the Lower Rio Grande Valley, has an enrollment of approximately 8,000 students and provides transportation to an area of 101 square miles. A total of 43 vehicles operated by the district travel 1,150 miles each day on their routes with total fleet mileage of about 500,000 miles per year.

It is not uncommon to hear that diesel engines will not run on any alternative fuel. Diesel engines have not been modified to run on an alternative fuel alone by simply adding conversion equipment. However, it is possible to use natural gas in combination with diesel. The San Benito ISD buses are powered by both natural gas and diesel. In the year they have been operating, the San Benito buses are running on an overall average mixture of 60 percent natural gas and 40 percent diesel.

San Benito ISD began studying conversion to an alternative fuel more than a year before making a decision. They began their program with two test buses which were converted to a mixture of diesel and natural gas. The buses use a KG5000D conversion kit developed and patented by Carburetion Labs, Inc. in Miami, Florida. The test buses demonstrated sufficient cost savings for the school district to initiate larger scale conversion.

The district believes that natural gas fueled vehicles will produce savings in fuel costs and maintenance, and will reduce pollution.

Retrofitting a diesel engine for natural gas use is similar in many respects to gasoline conversion (as described in Alternative Fuels Transportation Brief Number 2-1, January 1991 published by the Center for Global Studies in Houston, Texas). As in a gasoline engine conversion, the conversion kit adds a patented air-fuel mixer. The major difference is the need for an RPM monitoring device to control the mixture of diesel and natural gas. The mixture of fuels is controlled by either mechanical or solenoid switches. Diesel is then used to start the engine and is decreased as engine speed increases (higher RPM). When RPM drops during gear shifts, diesel again becomes the primary fuel. The average percent of natural gas in day-to-day full load operations is about 80 percent. Actual in-use percentages in 15 diesel vehicles at San Benito in recent experience ranged from 32 to 73 percent (See attached report for the 91-92 school year). This analysis does not include the 5 gasoline buses or the six diesel buses with the 7.31 International engines that San Benito ISD also converted and is running on CNG. CNG was not used on some days during the reporting period due to compressor problems.

Cost savings is the primary reason given for the San Benito ISD's converting to CNG from diesel. Tejas Engineering & Management Services, Inc. in Helotes, Texas conducted a preliminary analysis, published in April, 1991, which included projections of costs savings. Their estimates included 21 diesel conversions and 5 gasoline conversions. Estimated costs for conversions and an electrical powered natural gas compression station were $144,195. Estimated annual savings attributable to reduced fuel cost from CNG use was $20,065. An additional $14,500 was added for anticipated maintenance savings, yielding an estimated total annual savings of $34,565, or more than $1,300 per vehicle. The compression station was analyzed separately with part of the payoff being provided in fuel costs. This analysis indicated that fuel cost savings would pay for vehicle conversion costs in 3.7 years. Compression stations costs would be covered by these cost savings in 7.5 years.

Recent fuel cost and milage figures were compiled for 22 diesel converted buses and 5 gasoline converted buses, not all of which were brought on line at the same time. These buses were driven a total of 261,041 miles (235,071 for diesel and 25,970 for gasoline) from March 26, 1991 to March 31, 1992. During this time an estimated $29,823 in fuel was consumed: $27,573 for diesel buses and $2,250 for gasoline buses. The fuel estimate includes the cost of compression and a portion of the compressor cost built into the cost of natural gas. Diesel for this mileage with unconverted engines could cost $37,274, a conversion fuel cost savings of 35 percent. The estimated savings from both fuel and maintenance costs is 5.53 cents per mile.

This is about 19 percent higher than the 4.654 cents per mile indicated in the April 1991 feasibility analysis mentioned above.

To date the school district indicates relatively few problems with the transition to natural gas fueled vehicles. San Benito's transportation director, Alfredo Salinas, notes that the only problems have been electrical rather than mechanical, including disconnected wires or broken switches.

In September 1991, La Joya Independent School District approved funds to convert 38 diesel and 11 gasoline school buses to use CNG and became the second Texas school district to convert their diesel vehicles. La Joya ISD, also located in the Rio Grande Valley, has an enrollment of approximately 9000 students. A total of 134 vehicles operated by the district travel 7500 miles each day over their 105 routes with total fleet mileage of about 1,320,000 miles per year.

One major question regarding the use of any conversion kit on vehicles is the effect on a new vehicle's warranty. In this particular project, letters had been requested by Carburetion Labs clarifying this question. The letters suggest that conversions, in and of themselves, will not void a OEM company's warranty. However, this statement does not imply that failures resulting from the use of conversions will be covered under the OEM company warranty. The certified contractor installing conversion kits should warrant that the installation does not alter or modify in any way the vehicle's pre-existing emission control equipment.

Advantages of Compressed Natural Gas.

1. Burns well in conventional spark ignition engines and in dual fuel operation. Natural gas can be adapted for use in existing gasoline and some diesel engines with a variety of conversion kits available for light and heavy duty vehicles. Because it is a gas, there is no problem with cold weather starting.

2. Demonstrated experience in U.S. and other countries. CNG has been used fairly widely in the United States and other countries as compared with liquid alternative fuels.

3. Established distribution system. There is familiarity with natural gas as a fuel (although not for transportation) and an established gas distribution system. With minimal modifications, the existing distribution system can be used safely to provide fuel at many locations.

4. U.S. produced fuel. Natural gas is considered to be an abundant fuel in the United States, with Texas being one of the major producing states. This supply provides an energy security incentive for using natural gas rather than imported petroleum products.

5. Low emissions levels. Natural gas is a relatively clean transportation fuel as compared with gasoline, diesel, or methanol. The possible exception is Nitrous Oxide emissions which are believed to be manageable with known emission control technology.

6. Possible reduced maintenance costs. Although not yet well established, most reports indicate lower maintenance costs with CNG. This is attributed to the cleaner and more complete burning that occurs with natural gas due to its chemical nature and relatively simple composition compared with gasoline or diesel.

7. Contrary to the beliefs of those who do not understand CNG vehicles, they are actually safer than diesel or gasoline vehicles. CNG is lighter than air so it dissipates into the atmosphere if a leak occurs. Since CNG can only ignite in a range of 5 to 15 percent gas to air, a match held in a CNG stream will not ignite this stream because of insufficient oxygen. In addition, the DOT requirements for CNG fuel tanks makes them much safer than gasoline or diesel tanks.

Disadvantages of Compressed Natural Gas.

1. Heavy and bulky fuel tanks. The steel or aluminum high pressure tanks are heavy and bulky. The tank weight and bulk increases fuel consumption and reduces vehicle storage capacity. Research is underway to develop higher volume and lighter weight storage tanks.

2. Longer time to refuel--slow fill method. Slow fill fueling requires several hours. With fleet operations where vehicles are centrally stored overnight, this is not a major problem.

3. Limited range of travel. A single CNG fuel tank normally holds a gasoline equivalent of four to five gallons. At 20 miles per gallon, this is a range of only 80 to 100 miles, significantly below the 300 miles normally experienced with gasoline fueled vehicles.

4. Relatively high cost of converting existing vehicles. Cost estimates for converting passenger cars and light duty trucks range from $1,000 to $2,000 (EPA/GAO), substantially more than methanol or ethanol conversions.

5. Cost and limited availability of refueling stations. Very few public fueling stations are currently available in Texas, and CNG fueling stations typically cost from $125,000 to $400,000 to construct.

Chapter 11

# Technical Overview on FW-CFB Boiler Technology Burning Refuse Derived Fuel

J.T. Tang, I.F. Abdulally, W.R. Campbell

## INTRODUCTION

Municipalities in towns and cities across U.S. and in other developed countries are urgently seeking solutions for the disposal of municipal solid waste (MSW). This is because landfill sites are rapidly becoming inundated. Many of these municipalities are considering various methods to incinerate the wastes efficiently and cleanly while recovering energy.

Municipal wastes vary greatly in size and composition, depending on the town, city or country where it is generated. Incinerating MSW directly requires complex combustion systems which include a moving or travelling grate furnace, stoker boiler or rotary kiln incinerator. These combustion systems have many moving parts and burn at an elevated furnace temperature that often result in a high furnace corrosion rate, frequent equipment failures and low plant availability. Additionally, they produce flue gas with high emissions of pollutants requiring expensive back end emission control systems. An alternate to incineration is to transform MSW to refuse derived fuel (RDF) and burn it in a fluidized bed boiler.

A typical non-reheat, Foster Wheeler circulating fluidized bed boiler (FW-CFB) is depicted in Figure 1 The Foster wheeler CFB process which evolved from the conventional bubbling fluidized bed combustion technology, has proven commercial operation demonstrating fuel

flexibility, process simplicity, boiler reliability and excellent boiler performance with high combustion efficiency and low pollutant emissions. Its high performance is attributed to intensive mixing of gas and solids in the lower furnace region, high solid recycle to the furnace via steam-cooled cyclones and relatively low operating furnace temperature that results in low emissions of pollutants. However, to minimize risks associated with the burning of RDF in the CFB, the following additional considerations need to be considered for the design and selection of the plant:

1)  Investigate a waste-preparation system that can produce refuse derived fuel (RDF) acceptable to a circulating fluidized bed boiler. Ideally, the RDF is prepared to have sizes less than 4 inches (102 mm) and uniformly consistent. In addition, it should not contain materials that can cause bed particles to agglomerate and plug solid flow systems;

2)  Modify the CFB to minimize risks associated with RDF burning.

This paper will discuss RDF quality and its impact on the fluid-bed boiler performance, risk associated with RDF burning, and boiler modifications which will minimize the potential risks involved when burning of RDF.

## RDF QUALITY

Controlling RDF quality is one of the most important criteria for the successful burning of RDF in a circulating fluidized bed combustion system. Aspects of RDF quality that are important to boiler performance are as follows:

•  Top RDF size fed to the furnace;

•  The moisture, ash, metal content, and heating value

Functional problems can arise when RDF having a size greater than 4 inches (102 mm) and consisting of a large quantity of long wire, and aluminum and ferrous objects are fed into a CFB at a high input rates. Typical problems are bed material agglomeration and defluidization; pluggage of bed drain, air nozzles, and recycle loop; and damage of furnace refractory and waterwall tubes and grid floor nozzles. Boiler performance and emissions in the flue gas leaving the boiler are also affected.

The type of RDF preparation process and equipment used is crucial to the quality of RDF produced. The quality of RDF will in turn affect the overall performance of the CFB boiler. There are five different types of RDF processing systems currently available that produce several grades of RDF. Figure 2 depicts the different types of RDF processing systems. The selection of any one of these preparation systems will depend on the type of RDF incinerator chosen and the quality of the garbage during collection as a result of recycling programs adopted by the municipality. Table 1 illustrates the affect on the quality of RDF by choosing various combinations and quantities of metal separation, screening and shredding equipments. In general, the greater the number of stages of metal separation, size screening and shredding the better the quality and size distribution of the RDF. By this it is implied that the removal of aluminum and ferrous material is maximized and top size is reduced to a minimum (see Table 2). The diversified RDF i.e., RDF-5, is the best grade of RDF that is currently, commercially

**Figure 1**
**Typical CFB Steam Generator Arrangement**

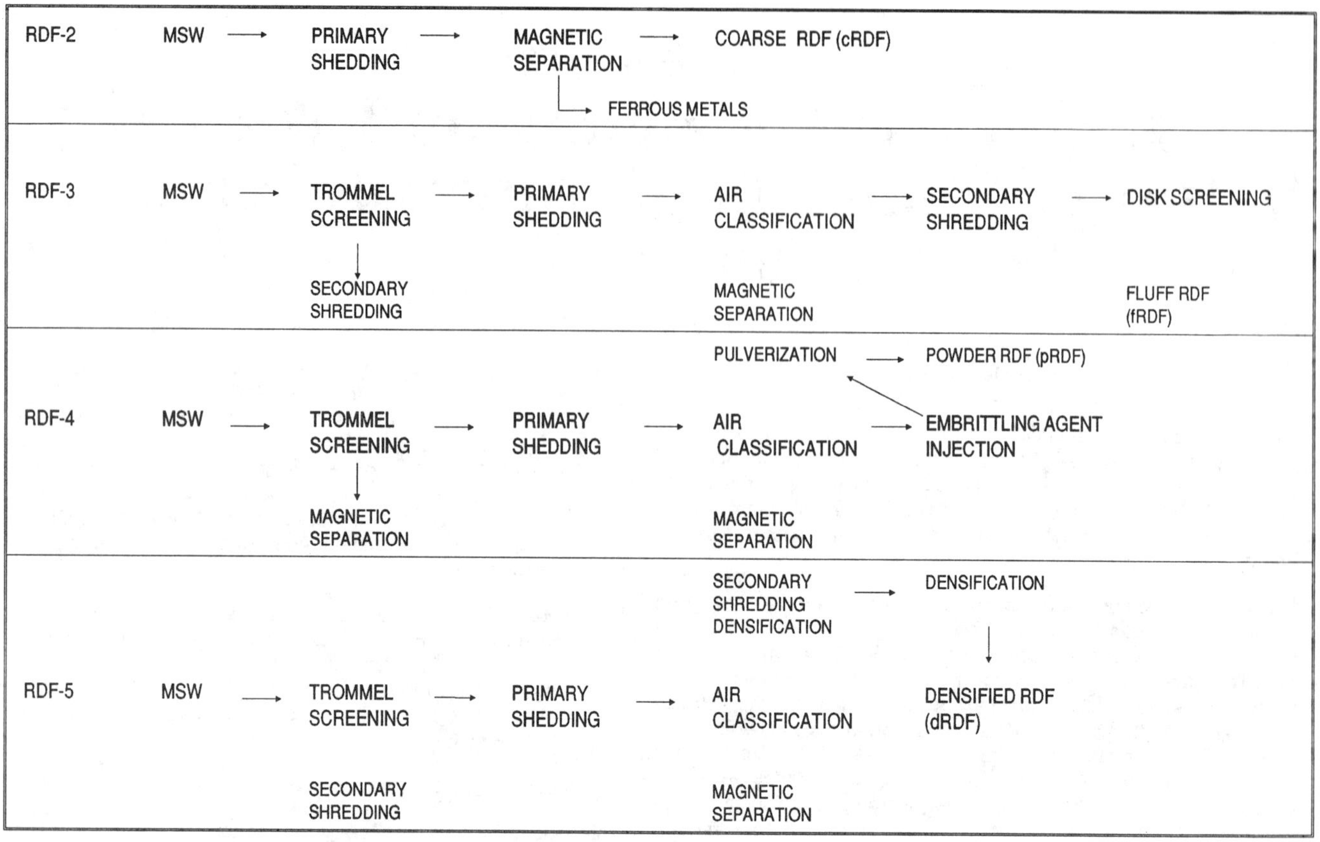

RDF-2   MSW → PRIMARY SHEDDING → MAGNETIC SEPARATION → COARSE RDF (cRDF)
     → FERROUS METALS

RDF-3   MSW → TROMMEL SCREENING → PRIMARY SHEDDING → AIR CLASSIFICATION → SECONDARY SHREDDING → DISK SCREENING
     SECONDARY SHREDDING      MAGNETIC SEPARATION      FLUFF RDF (fRDF)

PULVERIZATION → POWDER RDF (pRDF)

RDF-4   MSW → TROMMEL SCREENING → PRIMARY SHEDDING → AIR CLASSIFICATION → EMBRITTLING AGENT INJECTION
     MAGNETIC SEPARATION      MAGNETIC SEPARATION

SECONDARY SHREDDING DENSIFICATION → DENSIFICATION

RDF-5   MSW → TROMMEL SCREENING → PRIMARY SHEDDING → AIR CLASSIFICATION → DENSIFIED RDF (dRDF)
     SECONDARY SHREDDING      MAGNETIC SEPARATION

**FIGURE 2**
**RDF PROCESSING SYSTEMS**

**TABLE 1**

**CLASSIFICATION OF REFUSE FUELS**

| Class | Form | Description |
|-------|------|-------------|
| **RDF-1** | Raw (MSW) | Municipal solid waste as a fuel as discarded form without oversized bulky waste |
| **RDF-2** | Coarse (CRDF) | MSW processed to coarse particle size with or without ferrous-metal separation, such that 95% by weight passes through a 6 inch square mesh screen |
| **RDF-3** | Fluff (fRDF) | Shredded fuel derived form MSW processed for the removal of metal, glass and other entrained inorganics; particle size of this material is such that it has at least 85% passing through 2 inches and 98% passing through 3 1/4 inches. |
| **RDF-4** | Powder (pRDF) | Combustible waste fraction processed into powdered form, 95% by weight passing through a 2000 micron screen size |
| **RDF-5** | Densified (dRDF) | Combustible waste fraction densified (compressed) into pellets, slugs, cubettes, briquettes, or similar forms |

produced. Almost all of the commercially available combustion systems can burn RDF-5 requiring little or no major modification. However, the cost associated with producing densified RDF is several times higher than that of RDF-1,2 and 3. Consequently, use of RDF-5 is more or less limited to a few specialized applications. The fluff RDF i.e., RDF-3, however, is less costly and can be burnt in a circulating fluidized bed boiler adapted for this application.

**MAIN CONCERNS BURNING RDF IN A CIRCULATING FLUIDIZED BED BOILER**

The following are the main concerns when burning RDF in a circulating fluid-bed boiler:

(a) RDF quality

RDF quality is of utmost importance when considering the main items affecting the performance of the CFB. The potential impact of RDF quality on the design and operation of the CFB is discussed below:

(i) Oversized RDF feed

The performance of the boiler is adversely affected, if the sizing of the RDF is greater than four inches (102mm). The following problems can be expected if RDF sizing is greater than 4 inches.

· A higher variation in RDF density will result which can lead to a non-uniform RDF feed rate into the boiler.

· Higher burning of RDF in the freeboard, cyclone and boiler backpass. This is because of the RDF consisting of mostly very light combustible materials

TABLE 2

## COMPARISON OF REFUSE DERIVED FUEL PROPERTIES

| Fuel Type: | MSW | Coarse RDF | Wet RDF | Fluff RDF | Dust RDF |
|---|---|---|---|---|---|
| **Fuel Preparation:** | None | Shredding Magnetic Separation | Hydrapulping Cyclone Separation | Screening, Two-stage Shredding, Air Classification, Magnetic Separation | Trommel Screening, Magnetic Separation, Air Classification, Ball Mill Drying |
| **Composition:** | | | | | |
| % Moisture | 25.2 | 26.4 | 50.0 | 25.2 | 2.0 |
| % Ash | 24.9 | 21.1 | 7.0 | 7.9 | 10.9 |
| Gross Btu/lb | 4450 | 4677 | 3835 | 5841 | 7656 |
| **Major Components:** | | | | | |
| % Paper | 43.0 | 45.5 | 29.9 | 74.1 | 71.7 |
| % Plastic | 3.0 | 3.2 | 2.3 | 3.8 | 4.5 |
| % Glass, Ceramics | 9.0 | 9.6 | 0 | 0.04 | 0.5 |
| % Iron and Steel | 6.0 | 0.3 | 0 | 0.2 | 0 |
| Particle Size: | | 95%<6 in. | — | 98%<3 1/4" | 45%<200 mesh |
| **% Yield In RDF Product:** | | | | | |
| Weight | 100.0 | 94.0 | 111.2 | 75% | 42.0 |
| Btu | 100.0 | 98.8 | 95.9 | 85 | 72.3 |

such as paper. The burning of excessive oversized combustible materials in the furnace freeboard will result in higher gas temperature in the cyclone and boiler backpass and higher CO emission. The higher gas temperature will also increase the potential of boiler tube corrosion from hydrogen chloride species, cause ash to soften and lead to ash agglomeration.

(ii) Shredded plastic bottles and automobile tires

Typically there is less than 5% of these items in the RDF feed stream. However, the combustion of these constituents will release chloride compounds, form wire nest and add trace heavy metals to the flue gases. Presence of significant chloride gaseous compounds can result in severe boiler tube deterioration and assist in the formation of toxic dioxin and furan. The burning of radial tires will increase the steel wire input into the boiler which will cause wire nest to form. Also, zinc oxide is released which will cause certain bed material to swell causing poor bed fluidization.

(iii) Sodium-based glasses and aluminum

These materials soften and melt at a relatively low bed temperature (below 1500 F). Softening and melting of these materials can result in the formation of bed agglomerates; the sticking of the molten material to the furnace refractory

and pressure parts affecting their integrity; and the plugging of the air nozzles and the bed drain with sintered material.

(iv) bricks, wires and metals

When these materials are present in significant quantities and in large pieces, damage of the air nozzles and furnace refractory, plugging of the bottom ash drain and ash handling systems and the erosion of boiler pressure parts can occur.

In order to improve boiler performance, it is, therefore, imperative to control the RDF quality by carefully selecting the RDF preparation system to minimize the presence of these materials. Having a high quality RDF feed increase boiler reliability, minimize pollutant emissions and give satisfactory boiler performance.

(b) Feeding of RDF to furnace

Unlike other types of fuel, RDF consist mostly of combustible paper and ash. The ash in the RDF which is about 5 to 10% by weight consist mainly of wire, glass, metal, brick and ceramic materials. The heating value and bulk density of the RDF vary greatly on an hourly, daily and seasonal basis. To overcome the problems caused by this variation a satisfactory feed system and good operating practice is imperative to insure the best boiler performance and minimize boiler outages. Common problems that can be expected with RDF feeding are:

- non-uniform RDF feed rate,

- pluggage of feed system,

- frequent equipment failure,

- under capacity of feed system and insufficient redundancy.

- insufficient penetration of RDF to the furnace which can results in the maldistribution of heat release in the furnace

(c) Moving and draining of RDF bottom ash

RDF contains metal, steel wire and brick. These materials can restrict air nozzles and bed drain ports, which in turn can cause bed to defluidize. Defluidization can also occur if these materials are allowed to accumulate sufficiently on the grid floor. A further concern is that if these materials are not continuously and quickly removed, then plugging of the bed drain pipe and ash conveying system can develop.

(d) Fouling, eroding and corroding of boiler pressure parts and refractory.

Since majority of the RDF ash is either too fine or too coarse which is not suitable for bed material, addition of sand, or another inert material is, therefore, required to satisfy the furnace solids inventory requirements for ensuring proper bed turbulent and, hence, good combustion performance when firing RDF. Both sand and RDF ash have abrasive qualities. This along with the corrosive nature of the combustion gases can lead to the corrosion and erosion of the boiler pressure parts and the refractory. Additionally, the alkaline constituents in the entrained RDF ash can foul the heat transfer tubes and reduce the thermal performance of the boiler to the point that the guarantee conditions cannot be met.

(e) Meeting stringent emission guidelines

Meeting the current stringent emission requirements is a major challenge when attempting to burn RDF or other waste materials. In recent years, because of increasing public awareness of environmental issues, more stringent emission permit requirements were implemented as time progressed. The following is a list of current emission permitting limits for units burning RDF, in the U.S.

- total hydrocarbon emission: 10 ppm

- carbon monoxide: 100 ppm

- sulfur dioxide: 30 ppm

- nitrogen oxide: 130 ppm

- hydrogen chloride: 25 ppm

- opacity: 10%

- dioxin:   30 Ng per normal cubic meter for total dioxin and furance, or
           2 Ng per normal cubic meter for toxic equivalent factor.

The above emission values are based on a 24 hour average and corrected to 7% $O_2$ and a moisture free basis. Meeting these guidelines is a challenge which requires careful selection of the design guidelines for the combustion system.

(4) Boiler design approaches to burning RDF

During the early 1970's, bubbling fluidized bed combustion technology was applied worldwide burning a wide range of fuels.

This experience extended into the circulating fluidized bed combustion technology in the 1980's.

Circulating fluidized bed boilers (CFB) were discussed in great details in the referenced papers (1) to (3) and their successful operating experiences are discussed in papers (4) and (5). The success of Foster Wheeler's CFB boiler is attributed to its unique design features which include:

- steam-cooled cyclone (Figure 3),

- directional air distributor (Figure 4),

- fluidized bed stripper and cooler,

- refractory anchoring methods (Figure 5).

For a recent project, the challenges and potential problems associated with the burning of 100% RDF in a CFB have been studied and appropriate modifications to the CFB design have been made to minimize the aforementioned risks.

Figure 6 shows a typical CFB system for burning 100% RDF. The system consists of the following special or unique features:

¤ **FUEL FEEDER**

A special feed system developed by Detroit Stoker Co. for handling waste fuels that uses a combination of hydraulic ram and variable speed inclined apron feeder is used (see Figure 7). Feeding of RDF to the CFB is accomplished by steep feed angle and air swept distributor. The system is designed to achieve the objectives of a) minimal storage capacity b) maintain a seal against back pressure from the furnace and c) give uniform RDF distribution and penetration into the furnace.

¤ **PROVISIONS FOR FURNACE PRESSURE PART PROTECTION**

The furnace pressure parts are protected from corrosion and erosion by the following methods:

- A layer of corrosion-resistant, high alumina, low iron refractory with stainless steel reinforcing fibers is mounted on a high density stud pattern in the lower furnace region where solid mixing is intense and reducing conditions are prevalent.

- A layer of corrosion-resistant alloy cladding is applied to the water-wall immediately above the refractory. The covered area extends up to furnace freeboard.

¤ **MAIN FURNACE AND STRIPPER/COOLER GRID**

A sloped grid with situated directional air nozzles is provided both in the main furnace and the stripper/cooler (see Figure 8). The grid system is capable of forcibly directing coarse material from immediately below the fuel feeder discharge to the drain, through the drain line and the stripper/cooler and finally into the ash disposal system. Draining large and heavy material from the furnace grid floor, quickly and effectively, is essential to avoid the potential plugging of air nozzles and bed drain ports.

¤ **SOLIDS STRIPPER/COOLER**

A unique stripper cooler depicted in Figure 9, is used for the RDF application. The drains to the stripper/coolers are located at the opposite end wall of the furnace from the feeders. The stripper/coolers performs many useful functions. They are as follows:

- Separation, by air classification, of relatively fine but usable particles from the coarse and large particles. These fine particles are returned to the furnace since they are beneficial to the process.

- Cooling of the remaining larger particles sufficiently for discharge into the ash screening, bed ash recycling and removal system.

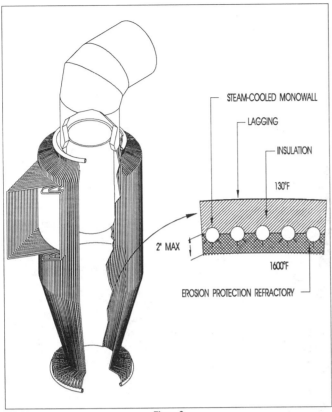

**Figure 3**
**Steam-Cooled Cyclone**

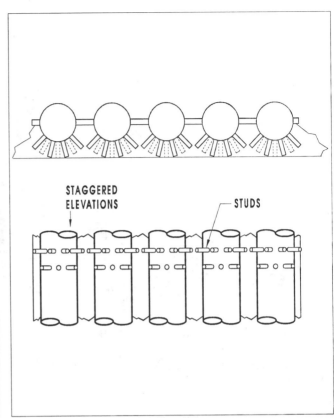

**Figure 5**
**Refractory Anchoring Method**

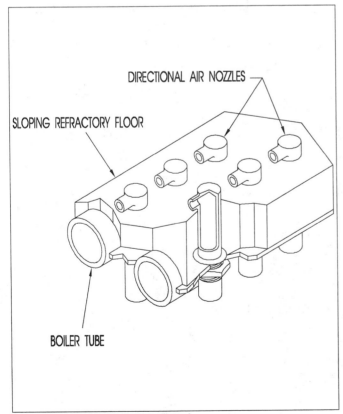

**Figure 4**
**Directional Air Distributor on Water Cooled Grid**

- To perform the preceding functions, independent control is provided for the air flows to the stripper and cooler zones.

▫ **STEAM COOLED CYCLONE**

Past experience has shown that the reliable and trouble free operation of a CFB depends on having a reliable refractory system, especially for the cyclone. The Foster Wheeler patented and developed steam-cooled cyclone is illustrated in Figure 3. The entire cyclone enclosure is steam cooled. The internal surface of the cyclone is protected by a thin layer of high erosion-resistance, high conductivity, alumina phosphate-bonded refractory. The refractory is generally anchored by a high density stud pattern similar to that used in the bottom of the furnace. This arrangement, which has been proven for over an accrued 80,000 hours of commercial operation, has the following advantages:

- Enables rapid unit furnace heat-up and cool down during startup and shutdown of the unit.

- minimizes thermal stress and spalling of refractory,

- reducing cyclone and therefore, structural steel weight,

- minimizes heat loss through cyclone skin.

When burning RDF, or any waste fuel, temperature swings and high temperature gradient are expected in the furnace and the cyclone. Also, attack by corrosive gas and abrasive particle is expected. For these reasons it is important to select a cyclone design that can withstand these adverse conditions. The steam-cooled cyclone is able to satisfy these requirements resulting in trouble free operation proven in commercial operation.

3) Heat Recovery Area (HRA)

The HRA design for RDF fired CFB unit is similar to that proven reliable on MSW boilers. The design is arranged to minimize tube corrosion and erosion and facilitate tube cleaning. A unique horizontal gas pass HRA is provided immediately down stream of

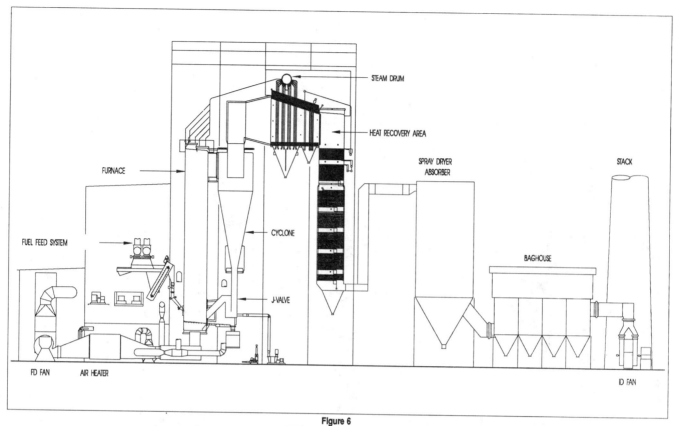

**Figure 6**
**FW-CFB Boiler Burning RDF**

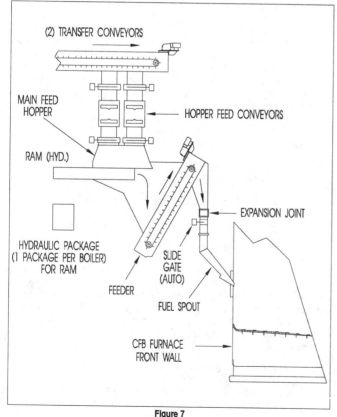

**Figure 7**
**Feed System for CFB Boiler Burner 100% RDF**

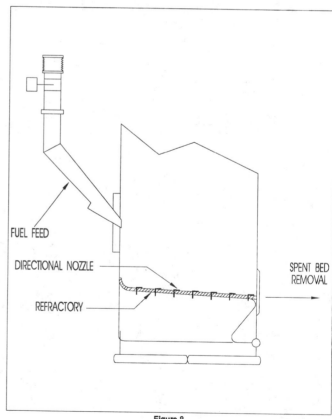

**Figure 8**
**Sloping Grid with Directional Nozzles**

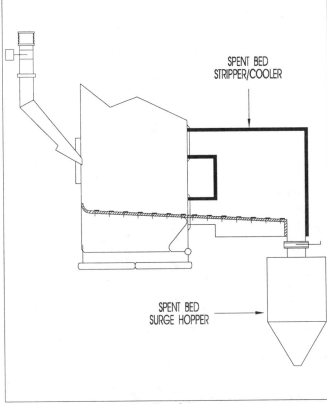

**Figure 9**
**CFB Unit for RDF — Spent Bed Stripper/Cooler**

the cyclone (see Figure 12). In this pass an evaporator section is provided before the final superheater bank. This is done in order to reduce the gas temperature in the evaporator section to an acceptable temperature before entering the relatively high temperature superheater tubes. The evaporator tube spacings and tube material are suitably selected to minimize erosion and corrosion when burning RDF. A arrangement, provided at the bottom headers of the evaporator sections and special headers at the bottom of each superheater loop, enables effective cleaning of these surfaces from potential ash fouling.

5)  Dry Scrubber

Because of the low sulfur content in the RDF and the unusual temperature profile anticipated in the furnace i.e., (relatively low bed temperature and a relatively high upper furnace temperature), sulfur capture in the furnace is expected to be poor. This has been confirmed by pilot plant testing. Any attempt to reduce sulfur and hydrogen chloride emissions in the furnace will require a very high calcium-to-sulfur ratio, which will increase the $NO_x$ emissions. Therefore, dry scrubber should be included for the final control of sulfur dioxide and hydrogen chloride emissions in preference to

providing emission control in the furnace. The use of dry scrubber with lime solution can achieve sulfur capture in excess of 90%. Moreover, when the dry scrubber system is used in conjunction with the baghouse, it can greatly reduce emissions of ammonia chloride, hydrogen chloride and dioxin.

### CONCLUSION

The successful burning of RDF in a circulating fluidized bed boiler largely depends on having satisfactory RDF quality and an intentionally well designed fluidized bed boiler and plant which addresses all the challenges brought upon in trying to burn RDF. Some of these challenges are to provide **a)** suitable and reliable RDF preparation and feed systems, **b)** an efficient bottom ash removal system, **c)** a suitable boiler design that is not susceptible to corrosion and erosion attack and **d)** adequate emission controls to meet the stringent permitting requirements. By accomplishing these objectives in the design, CFB boilers can sucessfully burn 100% RDF and achieve the following advantages over existing refuse fired units:

- Lower overall risks

- Greater reliability

- Lower maintenance

- Higher thermal efficiency

- Lower emissions

### REFERENCES

1)  I. F. Abdulally, *"Basic Consideration For The Selection And Design Of A Foster Wheeler Circulating Fluidized Bed Steam Generating Unit"*, 9th FWEC International Engineering Conference, May 14-17, 1990.

2)  S. J. Goidich, M Seshamani, *"The Foster Wheeler Approach To Circulating Fluidized Bed Technology"*, December 4-6,1990. The tHird International Power Generation Industries Conference & Exhibition, Orlando, Florida.

3)  A. V. Harrington, J.A. Brown *"Design Considerations for a 40 MWe cogeneration anthracite culm fired CFB"*.

4)  B. Studley, D. Parham *"Foster Wheeler - Mt. Carmel Anthracite Culm Fired Circulating Fluidized Bed Steam Generator Experience"* 1990 CIBO AFBC Conference, December 11, 1990.

6)  I. F. Abdulally, Randy W. Voyles, Arlyn Libal, *"Multiple Fuel Firing Experience in a Circulating Fluidized Bed Boiler"*, Annual Meeting of the American Power Conference, Chicago, Illinois, April 13-15, 1992.

Chapter 12

# AT&T Network Systems Methane Gas Supply Project

S.J. Teets, J.S. Blanton

## INTRODUCTION

SBM, Inc. recently commissioned an alternate fuel supply for AT&T Network Systems in Columbus, Ohio. The project involves recovering methane gas (MG) generated from the Bedford I Landfill located 1.5 miles northwest of AT&T's facility. The gas is gathered and compressed at the landfill and piped to AT&T's power house where it is used to fuel the primary plant boiler.

## BACKGROUND

SBM, Inc. is a specialized energy company dedicated to the recovery and utilization of methane gas as an alternate fuel source. Their current operations are based at the Bedford I Landfill on the east side of Columbus, Ohio.

SBM principals have developed two other successful methane gas recovery projects. The first is located in Martinsburg, WV where MG is transported via a 3 mile pipeline and used by a VA medical center as boiler fuel. The second project is in Pittsburgh, PA where the gas is used to drive generator sets producing 1.8 megawatts of electricity which is sold to the local utility.

AT&T's Columbus Works is a major manufacturer of telecommunications equipment and employs over 5,000 people. More than 100,000 different items are made at the Columbus Works, including AUTOPLEX® System 1000 cell site equipment; 4 ESS™ electronic switching systems; and DATAKIT® Virtual Circuit Switches. In addition to manufacturing, new technology researched and developed at Columbus is a key contributor to the success and growth of AT&T's global business.

The methane gas being delivered to AT&T is used to fuel a plant boiler generating 125 PSIG steam at 65,000 pounds per hour (peak load). The steam is used mainly for process applications, space heating, and domestic hot water purposes at the 2.2 million square foot facility.

## SUPPLY SOURCE

Methane gas is a naturally occurring byproduct of modern landfills. The gas is produced from the biological decomposition of refuse. MG production at the Bedford I Landfill is expected to last between 20 to 30 years.

The gas being produced at this landfill is a medium BTU fuel, consisting of roughly 57% methane and 43% carbon dioxide. It has a heating value in the 500 BTU/SCF range.

SBM has exclusive rights to methane gas reserves at the landfill. They began commercial recovery of the methane gas in 1987 with construction of a system to supply the gas to a continuous brick kiln operation adjacent to the landfill.

The landfill recently reached capacity and the total reserves of methane gas approached a point that supply of the MG to AT&T became economically feasible.

## DESIGN DEVELOPMENT

SBM first approached AT&T with the concept of the project during the summer of 1989. A unique joint effort evolved and all facets of the supply system design and boiler operation were evaluated. During a ten-month period, all major design and engineering issues were reviewed and finalized between the two companies.

Areas of key concern were supply capability and reliability of the methane gas. In addition, the design needed to conveniently allow for switching to and from natural gas in the event SBM experienced a short-term interruption such as the loss of electrical power at the compression station.

An important design objective of SBM was to allow for the minor variations in recoverable quantities of methane gas. In essence, the burner system would always use the maximum quantities SBM would have available to support AT&T's demand for steam.

Primary concerns of AT&T were that the installation provide for a safe, reliable, and economical operation of the MG in their plant boiler.

Once the basic system had been agreed to by both parties, key contractors and suppliers were evaluated and selected for the boiler upgrade. These companies were made part of the project team and detailed planning for system integration began.

Refinement of the methods and logic to be used to join all aspects of the project continued until all parties agreed that a premier installation would result from their efforts.

The design stage was essentially complete at this point, allowing for unforeseen details which could emerge as the project matured. Therefore, discussion began regarding the supply agreement.

## SUPPLY AGREEMENT

The concept initially presented to AT&T provided for SBM advancing all capital required for the project and providing AT&T with a savings over their natural gas costs. Presented in this manner, the risk associated with the project on AT&T's part was greatly reduced. Also, the incentive of discounted fuel rates was very attractive.

AT&T reserved the right of approval for all phases and specifications concerning the project. In this regard, they were assured that material and methods of construction met their quality standards as well as those of their primary insurance carriers.

SBM presented a well-crafted draft of the supply agreement to AT&T's engineers for review. The document helped to speed discussions concerning the supply agreement and negotiations were completed in a short four months. This was also in large part due to the efforts of both SBM and AT&T's management teams that supported the project along with a superb effort by the purchasing and legal departments within AT&T.

### Main Points of Agreement

Seller's Obligation: SBM was responsible for obtaining the necessary authorizations, easements, and rights-of-way; Providing the MG recovery system; Constructing the pipeline to AT&T's facility; Modifying the boiler and gas trains to permit burning of methane gas and/or natural gas in the new burner; and providing start-up assistance as required by AT&T.

Buyer's Obligation: AT&T agreed to purchase a stated percentage of its boiler fuel requirements (or up to the quantities SBM was able to supply) for the term of the contract. Also, due to environmental regulations, AT&T was required to obtain a Permit to Operate (PTO) the modified boiler.

Price: The purchase price for each MMBTU of MG delivered will be calculated according to formulas developed using AT&T's natural gas price as an index. In this manner, AT&T was assured a discount to prevailing natural gas costs.

Product Specification: SBM is to deliver MG to AT&T at a concentration and pressure sufficient to properly burn in the boiler without detrimental effects.

Burner Specifications: The COEN Company's proposal for the new burner application was made part of the contract. Therefore, AT&T was insured that burner performance specifications were met.

## PRIORITY OF SUPPLY

SBM is supplying the methane gas on a first-priority basis to AT&T. During the summer months, any excess fuel will be supplied to the brick kiln operation.

At the brick kiln operation, an automated system is being installed that will take natural gas and blend it with air so that it has the same combustion characteristics as MG. This blended gas will then be fed to the kiln in place of the methane gas, on an as needed basis. This will allow for unattended switch over of fuels because the blended gas will require no fuel/air ratio adjustment.

## CONSTRUCTION PHASES

### Project Management

AT&T was designated as having the overall project management. SBM was responsible for the construction management and oversaw all contracts for the project. In this way, AT&T was assured of the highest quality project but relieved of the day-to-day supervisory details.

SBM's previous experience in successful application of this technology proved to be a valuable resource which AT&T relied on heavily during both the design and construction phases.

### Well Field and Collection Systems

The Bedford I Landfill closed in 1991 after receiving municipal waste for 20 years. The 70-acre landfill is approximately 80 feet deep and has 2.5 million tons of refuse in place. This makes the landfill of moderate size when compared to other landfills in the United States.

The well field is comprised of 70 wells spaced at 150 feet intervals. This spacing is somewhat tighter than typically found. However, it was SBM's goal to have the highest recovery efficiency possible. Also, since SBM owns and operates its own drilling equipment, the cost of the wells was easily justified.

A vacuum is placed on the wells and the MG is gathered through a horizontal collection system. The compression facility tempers the gas for either transporting or flaring any excess quantities for environmental considerations.

The adjustments to the wells (well-tending) are currently being conducted manually on a weekly basis. Methane concentrations and vacuums are monitored at each well and adjustments are made to achieve maximum production.

Additionally, data is gathered on a quarterly basis to provide a baseline evaluation of MG production. This includes flow measurements at preset vacuums, and the temperature and depth of leachate in the wells. This baseline data will be used to evaluate quantities of methane gas being produced and project the life of MG production at the landfill.

## Expansion of Compression Facility

SBM expanded its compression facility originally constructed for the nearby brick kiln operations. The design objective was to provide for continuous operations without on-site personnel.

The expansion involved installation of eight reconditioned Lamson Gas Turbo-blowers purchased from a defunct steel mill. Also, a custom air-to-gas heat exchanger was installed for inter-blower cooling of the gas and to protect against transporting MG above 160° F in the proposed polyethylene pipeline.

One key feature of the compression facility is the electronic controls which include a state-of-the-art programmable controller to monitor all functions.

A 32-channel data logger with alarm capability provides for continuous monitoring of all operating parameters. This unit also allows for remote reporting to a personal computer equipped with a modem.

## Pipeline

The pipeline design criteria was to provide for a low pressure system in the 6 to 10 PSIG operating range. As such, SBM installed a 12 inch diameter polyethylene (PE) material. This provided for minimal pressure drop when transporting high volumes of MG during the winter heating season.

The PE pipe represents the optimum installed cost of any approved material for installations of this nature. SBM installed the pipeline using its own seasoned staff. Subcontracts were let for excavation equipment and other specialty items as needed. In this way, SBM was able to take the risk out of the equation and accomplish the work at a very competitive cost.

The pipeline route of 8000 feet presented a wide variety of challenges and adventures. Routing of 3000 feet of pipe through a local industrial park and boring operations under a railroad demanded that strict installation techniques be followed.

Coupled with these assignments were the obstacles presented by winter weather. Despite these conditions, the pipeline was completed within the projected 12-week schedule and just slightly over budget.

## Boiler Upgrade

The design criteria for the boiler upgrade dictated convenience and reliability while maintaining boiler efficiencies and safety standards similar to AT&T's previous operations. Also, the MG piping train, safety devices, and control arrangements were to approximate those of the existing natural gas facilities to ease transition for power house operators.

The primary operational objective is to utilize methane gas up to its availability and then supplement with natural gas on an as-needed basis.

These benchmarks were met by a combined effort of both the burner manufacturer, COEN Company, Inc. of Woodland, CA, and the primary labor contractor, Combustion Systems, Inc. (CSI) of Camby, IN.

The boiler control logic also allows for unattended switch-over to natural gas in the event the MG supply is interrupted. The system also accounts for the slight variations of methane concentrations in the MG by automatically adjusting combustion fuel/air ratios in the burner.

The integration of the COEN burner management system and CSI's control system, a series of programmable controllers, allowed all design objectives to be fully met.

Proper burner and ancillary equipment application has allowed MG to be introduced to the boiler as effectively and conveniently as natural gas.

Training

Power house operators were included in burner and control design activities. In this manner, a "buy in" of the project was achieved and strengthened the chances of success.

Each operator was included in different phases of prove-in activities to allow hands-on training while completing the project.

Prior to final acceptance of the new system, all operators were briefed on added or modified equipment and thoroughly directed in each aspect of the operation. What-if scenarios and practical exercises were conducted by CSI, the system's installer and SBM.

In addition, documentation and operational procedures were registered and reviewed with all power house operators.

KEY PROJECT ADVANTAGES

Methane Gas Supply Agreement

- Provides substantial savings in AT&T's fuel costs.
- Required no capital investment by AT&T.
- Provided state-of-the-art burner and controls with dual fuel capability and flexibility.
- Reduces boiler maintenance costs.
- Utilizes a long-term renewable energy source.

Environmental

- Reduces methane gas emissions from landfill.
- Mitigates "Greenhouse Effect."
- Provides an EPA and DOE recommended utilization of methane gas.
- Reduces AT&T's overall air emissions, particularly nitrous oxides (through low NOx burner).

Energy

- Dedicates long-term renewable fuel supply to AT&T.
- Decreases dependence on foreign oil.
- Optimizes combustion efficiency with state-of-the-art controls and boiler upgrade.

FUTURE UPGRADES

The planned primary upgrade is the automation of SBM's well-tending function. Two distinct advantages would be gained by SBM in automating this function.

First, labor savings to SBM of up to $30,000 per year may be realized. Second, and even more compelling, is the opportunity to maximize MG production.

The current design calls for individual stations located on the landfill that can handle up to 20 wells. Each station will have its own methane gas analyzer that will be automatically calibrated.

The MG will be drawn from a particular well by a high capacity vacuum pump which will supply a sample to the methane analyzer. Depending on the methane concentration, a programmable controller will then adjust the valve at the wells to maintain a preset methane level.

Individual stations will be interconnected by means of a two wire loop to a single personal computer that will recount information for all wells for management purposes. Once completed, it will then be possible to maximize BTU production on a sustaining basis.

This system is scheduled to be on-line by the fall of 1992 when peak gas production is slated.

CONCLUSION

This project has provided a "win" situation for all parties involved. SBM acquired a long-term supply agreement for an otherwise wasted resource; AT&T was furnished discounted boiler fuel rates; and the overall environment was improved.

Chapter 13

# Pyrolysis of Automotive Shredder Residue for the Production of Fuel-Grade Gas

L.L. Sharp, R.O. Ness, Jr.

## INTRODUCTION

Every year eight to ten million cars and trucks are disposed of by shredding at one of the 200 auto shredders located in the United States. Automotive shredder residue (ASR) is a by-product created in the dismantling of automobiles. Figure 1 illustrates the process by which ASR is generated. An automobile is stripped of useful and/or hazardous items, such as the gas tank, battery, tires, and radiator. Although it is beneficial to have these items removed for safety and environmental concerns, this is not always accomplished. After removal of some or all of these items, the automobile is shredded to provide a material less than 4 inches in size and composed of approximately 50% organic and 50% inorganic fractions. Ferrous scrap is then separated out magnetically. This ferrous scrap supplies the steel industry with 12 to 14 million tons per year for electric arc furnace feedstock. Air cyclone separators isolate a low density "fluff" from the nonferrous fraction (aluminum, copper, etc.). This fluff (shredder residue) is composed of a variety of plastics, fabrics, foams, glass, rubber, and an assortment of contaminants.[1] Fluff bulk density is approximately 20 lb/ft[3].[2]

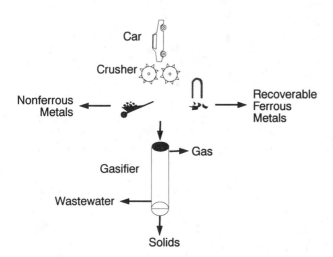

Figure 1. Automotive Shredder Residue Generation.

In 1990, the average car processed in a shredder facility produced 300 pounds of fluff.[3] Between 2.5 to 3 million tons of shredder residue are generated in this process per year.[1] This figure is expected to rise, since cars are increasingly being manufactured with more and more plastics. One study estimates that the fraction of ASR will double between 1987 and 1997, based on the relative amounts of plastics in 1977 and 1987 model cars and the fact that the average age of a car being shredded is 10 years. The cost of

landfilling all of this material is now between $12 to $100 per ton, depending on location (shipping not included).[2]

Along with autos, "white goods," or old appliances such as refrigerators and washing machines, are disposed of in combination with the automobiles in the shredders. White goods are the main contributor of polychlorinated biphenyls (PCBs) in ASR. Shredder residue also contains a wide variety of heavy metals and halogens, making ASR a good candidate feed material for a variety of waste-processing schemes as it will present many of the common problems to be considered when using waste as a gasification feedstock. A typical composition of fluff is shown in Table 1.

TABLE 1

Typical Auto Fluff Composition[2]

|  | % Dirt, Stone, and Glass Fines Removed | % after Screening and Trommeling |
|---|---|---|
| Fiber | 42.0 | 47.8 |
| Fabric | 3.1 | 3.6 |
| Paper | 6.4 | 7.3 |
| Glass | 3.5 | 0.5 |
| Wood | 2.2 | 2.5 |
| Metals | 8.1 | 0.5 |
| Foam | 2.2 | 2.5 |
| Plastics | 19.3 | 22.0 |
| Tar | 5.8 | 6.6 |
| Wiring | 2.1 | 0.5 |
| Elastomers | 5.3 | 6.2 |
|  | HHV = 5400 Btu/lb | HV = 6163 Btu/lb |

Bulk Density: Approx. 20 lb/ft[2]

If ASR is to be processed, whether for energy generation or just disposal, there are several difficulties that need to be addressed. The most troublesome are the heavy metals (especially cadmium) content and the aforementioned PCBs. Other heavy metals that need to be addressed include lead, arsenic, barium, chromium, selenium, and mercury. Table 2 is a typical analysis from one shredder facility. Lead in ASR can come from car batteries, wheel weights, exhaust systems, body repair filler, and highway contaminants, to name a few. Lead in ash resulting from processing automotive shredder residue has been known to occur in the form of lead chloride, which would indicate a high leachability.[2] Shredder residue is not yet considered a hazardous waste by the United States Environmental Protection Agency, but could conceivably be classified as such in the future. Any process selected to treat shredder residue will either have to eliminate heavy metals before processing, for instance with leaching, or will have to be able to deal with these substances in the ash.

### TABLE 2

#### Automotive Shredder Residue

| | |
|---|---|
| pH | 6.4 |
| PCBs | 19 ppm |
| Odor | Oil |
| Color | Black & Brown |
| Phenolic | 8.25 ppm |
| Cyanides | <0.031 |
| Sulfides | 2.7 ppm |
| Flash Point | >140°F |
| Physical State | Solid |
| % Free Liquids | None |
| Specific Gravity | 0.0432 |
| | |
| **EP TOXICITY METALS** | |
| Arsenic | <0.02 |
| Barium | <0.1 |
| Cadmium | 0.92 ppm |
| Chromium | <0.05 ppm |
| Lead | 0.81 ppm |
| Mercury | <0.0002 ppm |
| Selenium | <0.002 ppm |
| Silver | <0.01 ppm |

Reproduced with permission

There is an urgency associated with the problem of shredder fluff disposal. Shredder operators indicate that in three to four years the rising cost of land-filling will make shredder operations unprofitable. The volume of fluff needs to be reduced, and that volume reduction will necessarily produce ash. Since fluff has a reasonable heating value, 5400 Btu/lb, any process for volume reduction which takes advantage of this energy-producing potential seems a logical course of action. Energy production will generate revenue that will help to offset the cost of ash stabilization and disposal. Shredder operators make a profit by selling scrap metal to the steel industry for use in electric arc furnaces. It is highly desirable to recycle scrap metal from a steel manufacturer's point of view, since 74% less energy is required to produce steel when an arc furnace is charged with scrap instead of iron ore.[2] Shredders, then, not only dispose of a tremendous number of unwanted cars and trucks, but provide the steel industry with a valuable feedstock. Shredder residue is a problem that must be dealt with soon if the shredder industry is to continue to be a viable member of the recycling community.

#### Process Options

Several processes have been proposed as ways to reduce the volume of ASR, including combustion and incineration. Pyrolysis or gasification followed by combustion (IGCC) might prove to be a workable process (Figure 2). Proximate analyses of ASR show a low fixed carbon content, indicating that pyrolysis would be preferable over gasification. Screening tests in the thermogravimetric analyzer were done to find steam reactivities. The thermogravimetric analysis (TGA) tests indicate that a medium-high Btu gas can be produced from gasification of ASR. Pyrolysis has an advantage over combustion technologies in that the gas stream can be used for a variety of purposes. Additionally, gas cleanup is somewhat easier in a reducing atmosphere. One scenario would place the ASR gasifier near a utility IGCC unit. Product gas would be mixed with the IGCC gas in a gas-fired turbine. The ASR produced gas could be used for electrical peaking purposes or to offset a fractional amount of coal that is fed to the electrical utility. Another option would be to place the ASR gasifier near a shredder facility. Shredders are high energy consumers, using somewhere between 15 and 25 kWh per ton of material processed.[1]

Deriving energy from fluff would reduce the need for purchasing electricity by the shredder facility.

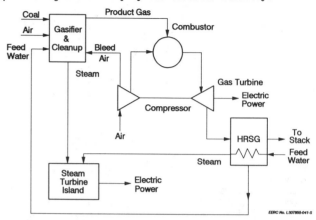

Figure 2. IGCC Process.

#### Automotive Shredder Residue TGA Results

Screening tests with ASR were conducted in the TGA instrument to determine test matrix conditions for larger scale tests. Five tests were conducted to determine reactivity with steam and one catalyst at temperatures of 600°, 650°, 700°, 800°, and 850°C.

In all tests, the reactant mixtures were heated to the desired reaction temperature and held at temperature until approximately half of the fixed carbon in the sample had been converted to gas, at which point the reaction was terminated by cutting off the steam and heat supply. All tests were performed under flowing argon gas. To determine the point at which half of the fixed carbon had been converted, TGA proximate analyses were carried out on each sample prior to the reactivity tests. These analyses (Table 3) showed that volatiles are removed from the reactant mixtures, and the remaining material consists of about 8.2% fixed carbon and 27.3% ash for ASR with catalyst and about 9.2% fixed carbon and 17.3% ash for ASR without catalyst. Size of the ASR was -⅛ in all tests.

### TABLE 3

#### Automotive Shredder Residue Proximate Analysis

| | Without Catalyst | | With Catalyst | |
|---|---|---|---|---|
| | as received | mf | as received | mf |
| Moisture, wt% | 2.9 | --- | 6.1 | --- |
| Volatiles, wt% | 70.6 | 72.7 | 58.4 | 62.2 |
| Fixed Carbon, wt% | 9.2 | 9.5 | 8.2 | 8.7 |
| Ash, wt% | 17.3 | 17.8 | 27.3 | 29.1 |

The TGA graphs start at time = 0. This point marks the beginning of the heatup period. Weight loss during the heatup period (as measured by a decreasing weight percent value) is due to moisture loss and devolatilization. When devolatilization is complete, temperature is held at a constant value, and steam is added. When 50% of the fixed carbon is converted, heat is turned off and the steam flow terminated. The point at which 50% of the fixed carbon is converted is determined by examination of proximate analysis data.

As stated, each reactivity test was terminated when about half of each devolatilized sample had been converted to gas: about 31.4 weight percent of the sample in the case with catalyst, and about 21.9 wt% of the sample in the case with no catalyst. After the termination of heat and steam, the conversion line still continued until the instrument was turned off, since some residual steam was still present, but it was not linear.

Table 3, the proximate analysis of the ASR, indicated a high volatile content, about 58.4% in the case of ASR with catalyst and about 70.6% in the case of ASR without catalyst. During continuous fluid-bed tests, devolatilized material will most likely be cracked and further reacted since its residence time in the reactor will be much longer than the time required for devolatilization, and the temperature at which devolatilization occurs, 260°-520°C, is much lower than the temperature which will be present in the reactor. Time for devolatilization in the case of ASR without or without catalyst is about 5 minutes.

In the case of ASR without catalyst, at 800°C, time for complete conversion is about 19 minutes (Figure 3). At 850°C, conversion time is only 5 minutes (Figure 4). Addition of a $K_2CO_3$ catalyst decreases conversion time considerably. Times for 100% conversion and their corresponding temperatures are shown in Table 4. Gas analyses from the 700°C test and the 850°C test are shown in Table 5.

### Table 4

Steam Reactivities of ASR with $K_2CO_3$ Catalyst

| Temperature | Time |
|---|---|
| 600°C | 18 minutes (Figure 5) |
| 650°C | 12 minutes (Figure 6) |
| 700°C | 7 minutes (Figure 7) |

### Table 5

ASR TGA Gas Analyses

| Inert Free Basis | 700°C ($K_2CO_3$ Catalyst) | 850°C (No Catalyst) |
|---|---|---|
| $H_2$ | 92.3 | 69.7 |
| $CO_2$ | 7.7 | 19.7 |
| CO | --- | 10.5 |
| Btu/scf, dry 300 | --- | 260.0 |

| With Inert Gas | 700°C ($K_2CO_3$ Catalyst) | 850°C (No Catalyst) |
|---|---|---|
| $H_2$ | 0.60 | 0.53 |
| $CO_2$ | 0.05 | 0.15 |
| CO | --- | 0.08 |
| $N_2$ | 3.95 | --- |
| Ar | 95.40 | 99.24 |
| Btu/scf | 2.00 | 2.00 |

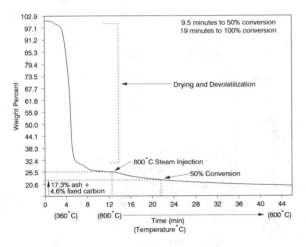

Figure 3. Steam Reactivity of ASR at 800°C.

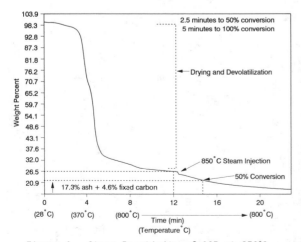

Figure 4. Steam Reactivity of ASR at 850°C.

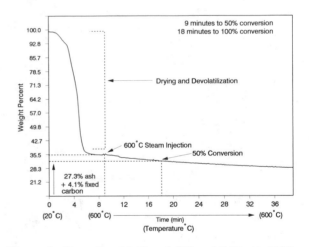

Figure 5. Steam Reactivity of ASR and $K_2CO_3$ at 600°C.

### Continuous Fluid-Bed Reactor (CFBR) System

Figure 8 is a schematic of a 1-to-4 lb/hr continuous fluid-bed reactor (CFBR) bench-scale test unit which will be used to pyrolyze ASR. The reactor consists of a 33-inch-high bed, having a nominal 3-inch inner diameter (ID). The freeboard section is 17 inches high, with a nominal 4-inch ID. Any liquid used in the fluidization gas mix is first preheated and then mixed with heated fluidization gas. The mix is heated to reaction temperature in a superheater. Because ASR has a very low density, an inert bed material is used to facilitate adequate fluidization. Solids are fed into the reactor via a dual auger arrangement. The first auger, horizontally situated, meters out the feed material.

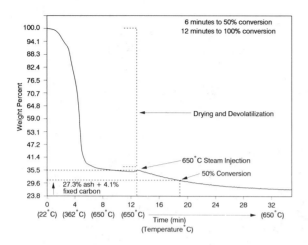

Figure 6.  Steam Reactivity of ASR and $K_2CO_3$ at 650°C.

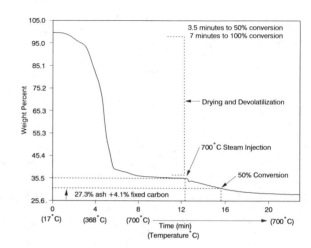

Figure 7.  Steam Reactivity of ASR and $K_2CO_3$ at 700°C.

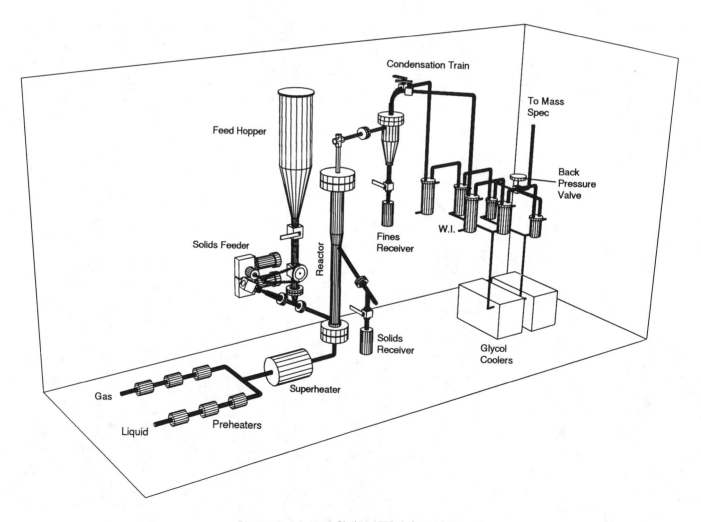

Figure 8.  1-to-4 lb/hr CFBR Schematic.

The metered feed gravity drops to the second auger. This second auger, at a 30° angle from horizontal, delivers the feed material quickly into the hot reactor. Because plastics in the ASR soften and get sticky at a fairly low temperature, it is important to keep the feed at a low temperature until it enters the reactor. Spent solids are collected from the reactor through a top bed drain leg. Material is collected in a lock hopper-type pot. Gas, volatiles, and fines leave the top of the reactor and enter a 3-inch ID cyclone where fines are removed. The gas stream enters one of two condensation trains. One train is used for start-up and shutdown, while the other is used for material balance purposes. The two condensation trains are identical, each consisting of a water-cooled indirect heat exchanger, followed by two glycol-cooled indirect heat exchangers. The stream is then depressurized, and the gas sampled and metered. Data collection and process control are achieved with a Genesis software package.

Future Tests

Further tests are planned to determine:

- The yield structure for automotive shredder residue
- Optimal fluidization velocity
- Carbon conversion with reduced fluidization velocity
- The effect of increased pressure on gas yields
- The fate of vaporized heavy metals
- Methods of ash stabilization
- The feasibility of hot-gas cleanup
- Leachability properties of unreacted material

The heavy metals that are vaporized will either condense in the condensate train, which will cause scaling over a long period of time, or possibly recondense as particulates in the gas stream. More information will be needed on where these metals condense in order to determine the best way to deal with them.

## SUMMARY

The future of waste disposal appears to be moving away from landfilling and incineration and toward recycling and using waste materials as a source of energy. New technology in pollution control and in energy generation techniques make energy production from waste materials an environmentally acceptable alternative. Tests on ASR, a waste product of automotive shredders, indicate that a medium-high Btu gas can be produced in a reasonable residence time. Some work remains to be done to optimize operating conditions and to determine how to deal best with heavy metals and chlorine and sulfur compounds.

## REFERENCES

1. Schmitt, R.J. "Automobile Shredder Residue--The Problem and Potential Solutions," CMP Report No. 90-1; Center for Materials Production: Pittsburgh, PA, 1990; pp iii, 1-1.

2. Hubble, W.S.; Most, I.G.; Wolman, M.R. "Investigation of the Energy Value of Automotive Shredder Residue," USDOE Contract No. DE-AC07-84ID12551; Energroup, Inc.: Portland, ME, 1987; pp VI-8-8, VI-8-23.

3. Eller, R. "Solid Waste Management in Japan," *Waste Age*, May 1992.

# Chapter 14
# Contribution of Waterborne Radon to Indoor Air

A.K. Deb, J.O. Catlin

## INTRODUCTION

Radon-222 is a member of the uranium decay chain and is formed from the decay of radium-226 (Figure 1). Once radon is formed in the soil, it can move through the soil to reach the atmosphere. Radon and its decay products emit alpha particles during the decay process. Alpha particles emitted from inhaled radon and its daughters increase the risk of lung cancer. Radon enters a house from soil gas through the basement floor and walls and from water. It has been estimated that about 10% of all homes in the United States have radon levels exceeding the U.S. Environmental Protection Agency (EPA) corrective action level of 4 pCi/L of radon in indoor air. Above this level, radon in indoor air may be a serious health risk.

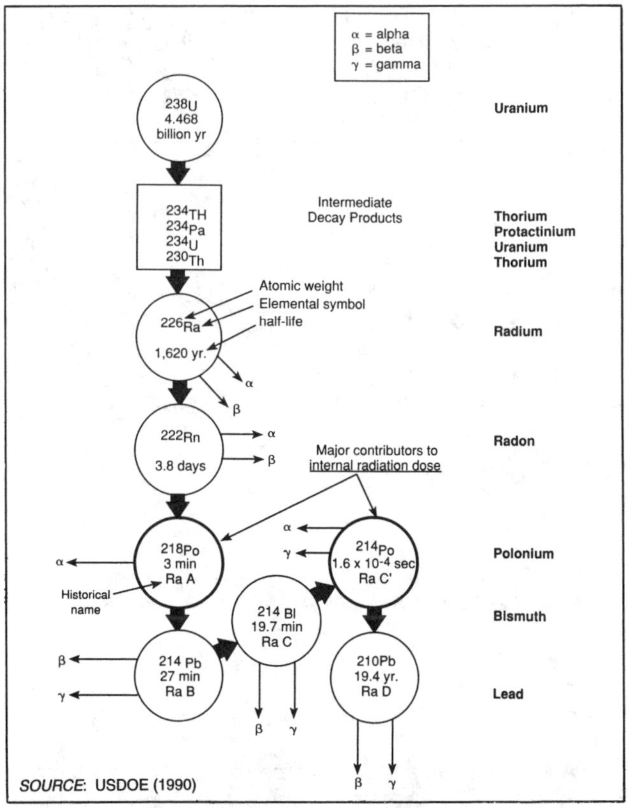

Radon is soluble in water; thus when radon comes in contact with groundwater it dissolves. The radon concentration in groundwater may range from 100 pCi/L to 1,000,000 pCi/L. When water with a high radon level is used in the home, radon is released from the water to the air and thus can increase indoor air radon concentration. Considering the estimated health risk from radon in public water supply systems, EPA has proposed a maximum contaminant level (MCL) of 300 pCi/L for radon in public drinking water supplies serving more than 25 residences.

In order to address the health risks of radon in water and the proposed regulations, the American Water Works Association Research Foundation (AWWARF) initiated a study to determine the contribution of waterborne radon to radon levels in indoor household air.

## OBJECTIVE

The main objective was to perform a controlled experiment to explore the contribution of waterborne radon to home air quality and the effect of radon removal from a centralized water system on indoor radon levels in three communities with widely variant waterborne radon contamination levels.

## STUDY SETUP

### Community Description

Three small communities in New Hampshire served by groundwater systems have been selected for this study. Data from participating homes in three communities are shown in Table 1.

Table 1

DATA FROM PARTICIPATING COMMUNITIES

FIGURE 1  RADIOACTIVE DECAY OF URANIUM-238 SHOWING THE PRODUCT RADIONUCLIDES, MASS NUMBERS, HALF-LIVES, HISTORICAL NAMES, AND TYPES OF RADIATIONS

| Community | Number of Hours | Number of Participating Homes | Number of Sampling Sites |
|---|---|---|---|
| A | 25 | 19 | 60 |
| B | 182 | 85 | 256 |
| C | 27 | 15 | 45 |

Homeowner participation from these three communities was solicited: 19 homes from Community A, 85 homes from Community B, and 15 homes from Community C participated in this study. The indoor air radon testing program was carefully developed so that airborne radon contributions from waterborne radon could be estimated. In participating homes, indoor air radon concentrations in at least three locations and water radon concentrations were measured. Packed tower aeration (PTA) systems were installed in all three community water treatment systems to remove radon from water. Measurements of airborne radon and waterborne radon in each of the participating homes were repeated to determine posttreatment air and water radon concentrations.

## Airborne Radon Measurements

Airborne radon measurements were made using electret-passive environmental radon monitors (E-PERMs). An E-PERM is a device that uses an electrostatically charged Teflon disc, called an electret, to measure the radon concentration in air. Once activated, the electret surface, which has a positive charge, attracts negative ions produced by the alpha particles generated from decaying radon. The radon enters a filtered ionization chamber housing the electret, and negatively charged ions are drawn to the surface of the electret, thereby reducing its surface voltage. The electret surface voltage is read using a portable digital meter (surface potential electret reader, or SPER) before and after exposure to radon. The resulting differential voltage is then used to calculate the average radon concentration present during the exposure period. For a 7-day exposure period, the lower level of detection (LLD) of airborne radon measurements using E-PERM is about 0.3 pCi/L (EPA 1989).

## Radon Monitor Placement

Release of waterborne radon to indoor air depends on waterborne radon concentrations, water temperature, and the degree of agitation of water. Thus, the largest releases of waterborne radon in the home are due to activities such as taking showers and washing dishes or clothes.

Radon monitor locations were selected to best differentiate between airborne radon contributions from the soil and those from household water. The air radon contribution from domestic water should be the highest in areas or rooms where household activities cause radon/water separation. Radon monitors were placed within each house in areas with varying potentials for radon/water separation. These areas included the following:

Area 1: Areas of high potential for release of radon from water and high potential for airborne contribution from soil gas (e.g., basement laundries)

Area 2: Areas of low potential for release of radon from water but with high potential for airborne contribution from soil gas (e.g., basement family rooms)

Area 3: Areas of high potential for release of radon from water and low potential for airborne contribution from soil gas (e.g., first-floor kitchens or bathrooms and second-floor laundries)

For each selected house, E-PERMs were placed in each of the three areas for a continuous 7-day period before and after the installation and operation of the community-wide radon removal water treatment systems. A 7-day period for indoor air radon measurements was selected to cover the weekly cycle of household water-related activities in a house. The voltage of the electret was measured at the beginning and at the end of the 7-day period, and the difference in voltage between the two measurements was used to calculate the 7-day average radon concentration.

## Water Sample Collection and Analysis

Samples of household water were collected for radon analysis concurrently with the placement of the airborne radon monitors for both the pretreatment and posttreatment testing phases. Water samples were collected only at the time monitors were placed. Samples were collected following EPA (1983) protocols. The analysis of radon in water was completed using the scintillation method.

## Waterborne Radon Removal System

In this study a Packed Tower Aeration (PTA) system was used to remove radon from water in the three communities. PTA systems were installed at the well-head supply for each of the communities. A general schematic of the PTA radon removal system used in Communities A, B, and C is shown in Figure 2.

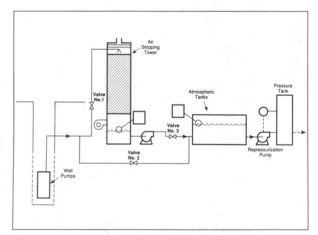

**FIGURE 2   SCHEMATIC OF PTA RADON REMOVAL SYSTEMS**

## DATA ANALYSIS

Airborne radon and waterborne radon were measured in selected houses in the three communities during pre- and post-treatment periods. In order to facilitate the analysis of data, both airborne and waterborne data were entered into a relational computer database system.

Average waterborne radon concentrations in household water in Communities A, B and C during pre- and posttreatment conditions were 1,292 and 126 pCi/L; 2,411 and 241 pCi/L; and 21,295 and 520 pCi/L, respectively. It should be pointed out that the concentration of radon in water in Community C will not meet the proposed MCL of radon of 300 pCi/L even after installation of a treatment system. Matched pair statistical regression analysis of pre- and posttreatment indoor air data was conducted for each community (Figures 3 to 5) and also separately for locations in each community.

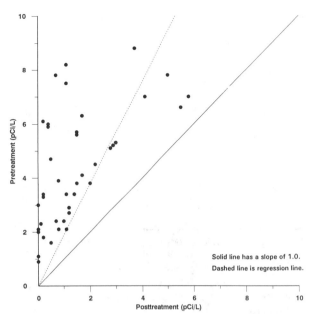

FIGURE 5  MATCHED PAIR ANALYSIS, COMMUNITY C

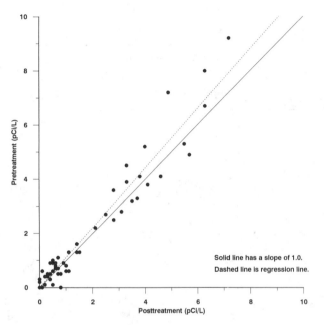

FIGURE 3  MATCHED PAIR ANALYSIS, COMMUNITY A

The slopes of the regression lines of the matched pair data for Communities A, B, and C were 1.11, 1.03, and 1.87, respectively, indicating small indoor air radon reductions in Communities A and B compared with Community C. Background indoor air radon concentrations for the three communities were estimated from posttreatment indoor air radon concentrations in basement family room (BF) and basement laundry room (BL) locations. Background radon concentrations for Communities A, B, and C were estimated at 3.7 pCi/L, 1.0 pCi/L, and 1.6 pCi/L, respectively, indicating lower-than-national-average background indoor air radon concentrations in Communities B and C and a higher-than-national-average background radon concentration in Community A. Community A had a high background radon concentration (3.7 pCi/L) and a relatively low waterborne radon concentration (1,292 pCi/L), Community B had a low background indoor radon concentration (1.0 pCi/L) and a moderate waterborne radon concentration (2,411 pCi/L), and Community C had a low background indoor radon concentration (1.6 pCi/L) and a very high waterborne radon concentration (21,295 pCi/L). Analysis of the reduction of indoor air radon concentration between pre- and posttreatment periods indicated that very little average reduction of indoor air radon occurred in Community A (0.1 pCi/L) and Community B (0.2 pCi/L) and a large average reduction of indoor air radon occurred in Community C (2.9 pCi/L).

Analysis of Radon Reduction Data

A regression analysis of the reduction of all household waterborne radon concentrations ($\Delta Rn_{water}$) and the corresponding reduction of household airborne radon concentrations ($\Delta Rn_{air}$) for all three communities together was conducted. A plot of all data, the regression line, and the 95% confidence lines appear in Figure 6. The fitted regression equation with a correlation coefficient ($R^2$) of 0.71 is:

$$\Delta Rn_{air} = (0.00013)\Delta Rn_{water}$$

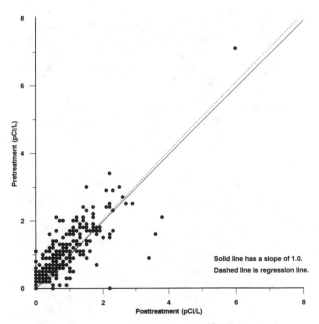

FIGURE 4  MATCHED PAIR ANALYSIS, COMMUNITY B

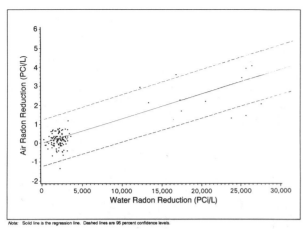

Note: Solid line is the regression line. Dashed lines are 95 percent confidence levels.

**FIGURE 6   AIR RADON REDUCTION VERSUS WATER RADON REDUCTION**

This equation gives an average ratio of radon concentration in air to radon concentration in water of $1.3 \times 10^{-4}$.

## Analysis of Distribution of Data

In order to obtain an overall, community-wide distribution of airborne radon concentration reduction due to reduction of waterborne radon for each community, a cumulative distribution analysis of pre- and posttreatment airborne radon concentrations was conducted. A cumulative distribution of measured airborne radon concentration values (both before and after treatment) provides a picture of the overall reduction of radon in each community. Figures 7, 8, and 9 show the cumulative distribution of pre- and posttreatment measured radon concentrations in Communities A, B, and C, respectively.

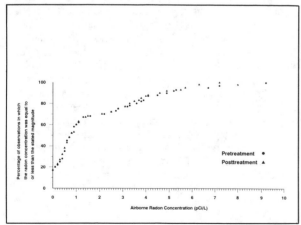

**FIGURE 7   AIRBORNE RADON CUMULATIVE DISTRIBUTION, COMMUNITY A**

Community A essentially shows very little difference in the cumulative distribution of measured airborne radon values before and after treatment of water for removal of radon. The difference of mean of pre- and posttreatment airborne radon data in Community A is 0.1 pCi/L.

In Community B, there is a small but discernible difference in the cumulative distributions. Approxi-

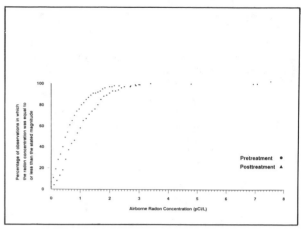

**FIGURE 8   AIRBORNE CUMULATIVE DISTRIBUTION, COMMUNITY B**

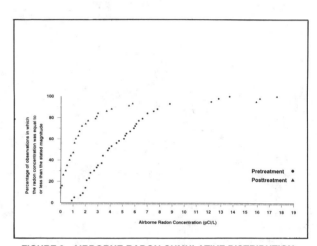

**FIGURE 9   AIRBORNE RADON CUMULATIVE DISTRIBUTION, COMMUNITY C**

mately 95% of the airborne radon observations in Community B were less than 2 pCi/L, and the concentration difference in the mean of pre- and posttreatment radon concentration in air is approximately 0.2 pCi/L.

Community C shows a greater difference in the cumulative distributions. The difference in the mean concentration of pre- and posttreatment airborne radon for Community C is 2.9 pCi/L.

## CONCLUSIONS

The following conclusions were made from this study:

1. In Community A, the contribution of waterborne radon to indoor air radon is small relative to the contribution from soil gas and other sources. Thus, the water treatment system for radon removal had little effect on indoor air radon in Community A. This situation could create a false sense of safety for Community A. Residents could be led to believe that the radon problem is solved by the installation of a water treatment system.

2. In Community B, average pretreatment indoor air radon concentrations in all locations are low. The small difference in pre- and posttreatment indoor air radon concentrations indicates a small contribution of waterborne radon to indoor air radon.

3. In Community C, a relatively large reduction of indoor air radon between pre- and posttreatment measurements at all locations indicates a large contribution of waterborne radon to indoor air radon and the effectiveness of a water treatment system in indoor air radon reduction. Community C, with a pretreatment waterborne radon concentration of 21,295 pCi/L, will not be able to meet the proposed MCL of 300 pCi/L, even after installation of the PTA treatment system.

4. The effect of reducing waterborne radon on indoor air radon concentrations has been found to be a reduction of $1.3 \times 10^{-4}$ pCi/L of indoor air radon for every reduction of 1 pCi/L of waterborne radon.

5. Installation of water treatment systems for radon removal in water for Communities A and B containing radon concentrations of up to 2,400 pCi/L did not produce any significant improvement in indoor air quality.

## REFERENCES

1. USDOE. 1990. Radon, Washington D.C.: Office of Health and Environmental Research, Radon Research Program, DOE/ER-0448P.

2. USEPA. 1989. Indoor Radon and Radon Decay Product Measurement Protocols, Las Vegas; Office of Radiation Programs, Eastern Environmental Radiation Facility.

## ACKNOWLEDGMENT

The sponsorship of the American Water Works Association Research Foundation (AWWARF) of this project is acknowledged.

# Chapter 15

# Reducing Energy Consumption while Improving IAQ Using Sensors and Improved Filtration

M. Heis

## Introduction

ASHRAE Standard 62-1989 requires a minimum ventilation rate of 15 CFM/person. Office spaces have a minimum requirement of 20 CFM/person of outdoor air for ventilation. Table 2 of the Standard lists different types of building usages (offices, bars, conference rooms, schools, etc.), estimated maximum occupancy per 1000 square feet, and the recommended amount of outdoor air in CFM/person. Although this paper will discuss mostly commercial office space usage, the same principles apply to other uses. When ASHRAE TABLE 2 is used for design purposes, the process is called The Ventilation Rate Procedure. Most of the outdoor air flow rates are given as a volumetric flow rate per occupant. The minimum rate of 15 CFM/person is based on a carbon dioxide ($CO_2$) level of 1000 ppm. For 20 CFM/person the $CO_2$ level in the space should be no higher than 825 ppm. Therefore, $CO_2$ sensing can be used as a method of controlling the ventilation system.

Because people naturally exhale carbon dioxide, it is considered a good indicator of the amount of outdoor air delivered to a space based on the number of people in the space. Outside levels of carbon dioxide range from 300-400 ppm. Indoor levels of carbon dioxide typically range from 500 ppm to 1000 ppm, or more depending on the number of people and the rate of ventilation. Exposure to carbon dioxide levels exceeding 10,000 ppm is considered a health risk. An inside carbon dioxide concentration of 1000 ppm is considered equal to a ventilation rate of 15 CFM/person using outside air with a $CO_2$ level of 300 ppm. If the outside air contains 400 ppm of $CO_2$, then the acceptable inside level will be higher than 1000 ppm for a ventilation rate of 15 CFM. By ventilating based on occupancy, $CO_2$ control provides a method of reducing energy consumption in spaces with variable occupancy. Conference rooms, classrooms, theaters and other variable occupancy spaces are good applications for $CO_2$ sensors. Spaces with contaminant sources not related to human occupancy should not be controlled this way. There would be a problem created when occupant density was low and the contaminant levels were allowed to increase because of decreased ventilation levels. Filtration systems designed for those contaminants could be used to allow lower levels of ventilation. The ASHRAE AIR Quality Procedure should be followed to assure good IAQ when contaminant sources are present.

## Intermittent and Variable Occupancy

ASHRAE Standard 63-2989 states "When the contaminants are associated only with occupants or their activities, and do not present a short-term health hazard, and are dissipated during unoccupied periods to provide air equivalent to acceptable outdoor air, the supply of outdoor air may lag occupancy. When contaminants are generated in the spaces or the conditioning system independent of occupants or their activities, supply of outdoor air should lead occupancy so that acceptable conditions will exist at the start of occupancy.

The first statement allows the supply of outdoor air to lag occupancy when the air in the space is restored to the equivaltent contamination level of outdoor air. This provision allows the outside air dampers to remain closed while the HVAC system is conditioning the space prior to occupancy and contaminant build up. Energy can be saved because the space can be heated or cooled without the need for conditioning outside ventilation air at the same time. This control sequence is often referred to as the "warm up/cool down" control sequence. The building is being brought into the temperature comfort zone without the benefit of outdoor air for ventilation purposes. $CO_2$ sensors can be used to determine the optimum time to open the outside air dampers for ventilation. The HVAC system can condition the building better and faster while saving money using this provision. If the economizer system could be used for cooling during this time, the "cool down" sequence should not be used.

The second statement requires the outdoor air for ventilation to lead occupancy because contamination occured during unoccupied hours. The necessary lead time must be provided to lower the contaminant level to acceptable levels. The ASHRAE Standard provided two figures for determining the lag or lead time.

Where peak occupancies are less than three hours in duration, the Standard allows the outdoor airflow rates to be determined on the basis of average occupancy, provided that the average occupancy used is not less than half the maximum. This provision can be used for restaurants, training rooms and conference rooms where the length of peak occupancy is less than three hours.

A procedure is included in ASHRAE 62-1989 to permit averaging of loads. Credit can be taken for the excess outdoor air that is recirculated from the overventilated spaces. This procedure is used where one common air-handling system serves high occupany density areas, open spaces, conference rooms and private offices. Carbon dioxide sensors can be used to determine the amount of overventilation taking place and the amount of outdoor air possible.

## Filtration

Good filtration is essential for good indoor air quality. The air must be kept clean to prevent dirt build-up inside the equipment, on coils and inside the ductwork. The IAQ requirement for proper maintenance, clean equipment and clean air can actually reduce energy costs and increase equipment efficiency. Dirt and moisture work together to cause microbiological growth. Good filtration will prevent the excessive buildup of airborne contaminants that can cause symtoms associated with "sick building syndrome". High efficiency filtration can pay for itself in higher equipment efficiencies, lower equipment maintenance costs and reduced risks of IAQ problems.

Good filtration starts with a good pleated prefilter rated 25 - 30% efficient. This prefilter should be followed by a high efficiency final filter rated 90 - 95%. This combination will provide effective filtration for particles of .5 micron size. These filters will protect equipment from contaminant buildup on surfaces. Occupants will also be protected from respirable particulates.

For control of volatile organic compounds (VOCs) such as formaldehyde, filters made of either activated carbon or permanganated aluminum are normally used. Activated carbon has the ability to remove a wide range of fumes and odors. It is readily available and relatively inexpensive. Activated aluminum coupled with potassium permangarate makes an excellent oxidizing agent. This filter material is effective for filtering many hydrocarbons including formaldehyde.

The removal of VOCs and other gases is not as easily accomplished as particulate removal. Some trial and error will probably be necessary. Air flow rates are critical and may need to be reduced through the filters for effective odor removal and lower pressure drops across the filters.

The use of contaminated outdoor air for ventilation should be avoided whenever possible. However, the outside air in some cities may have to be cleaned before using for ventilation. The same rules apply as for filtering recirculated air.

## Increased Outdoor Air

Using 100% outside air to control contaminants may not be anymore effective than using one-third outside air and two-thirds recirculated air. A study done by the City of Columbus, Ohio found that when outside air was increased to 100%, no significant improvement in IAQ occurred; no noticeable improvement in the measured IAQ from the ASHRAE Standard 62-1989 recommendations. Furthermore, questionnaires to employees found no perceived difference between lower levels of outside air and higher levels of outside air. The study was sponsored by the Urban Consortium Energy Task Force with funding from the U. S. Department of Energy.

## Summary

Good filtration and carbon dioxide monitoring can assure excellent IAQ in office buildings. Using $CO_2$ sensors can help fine tune a building to the minimum outdoor air levels needed for proper ventilation. Less outdoor air during very hot or very cold weather can result in large energy savings and better indoor comfort conditions. $CO_2$ sensors can also provide early warning of ventilation problems. High levels of $CO_2$ in the space would indicate an outside damper problem or an air flow problem. Good filtration is needed to control dirt buildup on surfaces and protect occupants from respirable particulates. In addition, activated carbon or permanganated aluminum may be needed to control volatile organic compounds, fumes and odors.

## References

ASHRAE, 1989. ASHRAE Standard 62-1989: Ventilation for Acceptable Indoor Air Quality, ASHRAE, Atlanta, GA.

Ventresca, J. A. and Shrack, J., 1991. "Measured Indoor Air Quality and Energy Demand with Increased Fresh Air Ventilation", Power Generation, Energy Management and Environmental Sourcebook, pages 549-558, Association of Energy Engineers, Atlanta, GA.

# Chapter 16

# Worker Exposure to Toxic Combustion Gases from Forced Draft Boilers

J. McKenna

## INTRODUCTION

A major concern for steam-electric generating utilities in the 1990's is how to comply with recent amendments to the Clean Air Act (CAA). The CAA amendments mandate controls for air toxics (hazardous air pollutants) in emissions from sources such as utilities. Utilities with Forced Draft Boilers (FDBs) have the additional concern of worker exposure to air toxics in combustion gases before the gases exit through the stack. Recently, a fossil-fired utility with FDBs decided to address concerns posed by air toxics to protect the health of station workers as well as the environment.

## WORKER EXPOSURE TO TOXIC COMBUSTION GASES FROM FDBs

FDBs operate with forced draft fans to supply air to the furnace for combustion. Unfortunately, the high pressure of FDBs, coupled with environmental control systems downstream from the furnace, causes increased discharge pressures. Increased discharge pressures, in turn, result in combustion gas leaks from furnace access seals, casing holes and penetrations. These leaks may lead to worker exposure. For example, a worker may enter an area around the boiler to record a temperature or pressure reading from a system and only be exposed to the gases (including particulates) for a few minutes. On the other hand, however, a worker may endure an eight hour day of exposure to the gases while repairing or maintaining equipment. The degree of worker exposure to toxic combustion gases varies with the length of exposure and concentration of toxins in the gases. In addition, the type and concentration of toxins potentially present in the gases depends on the type and source of the fuel used (see Exhibit 1). The Occupational Safety and Health Administration (OSHA) regulates most of the toxins associated with combustion gases and particulates.

## UTILITY DECIDES TO ADDRESS TOXIC GASES ISSUE:

Recently, a utility with FDBs decided to protect workers from gases leaking from the furnace. Worker protection from toxic gases at this utility was non-existent until sample analysis from stack emissions and furnace leaks inside the plant recorded consistently high levels of sulfur dioxide. Gas leaks from the universal pressure once-through unit were located on the gas recirculating ducts, windbox, burner fronts, boiler walls, gas exhaust ducts and air preheaters. To immediately reduce sulfur dioxide levels, the utility permanently switched to low sulfur fuel oil and will burn natural gas instead of oil for the majority of the year. Realizing that other hazards may be present and compounding the problem, the utility implemented a toxic gas respiratory protection and training program for all station workers. The OSHA compliance respiratory protection program at this utility is crucial as the FDBs are 150 feet tall and are partially enclosed by a building structure and roof. As a result, the roof prevents the escape of gases and the floors below the roof contain high concentrations of sulfur dioxide and toxic gases. Ultimately the utility will install induced draft fans to eliminate exposure to toxic gases inside the plant. Induced draft fans are located downstream of the furnace, before the stack. The existing boiler unit required some design modifications to accommodate the induced draft fans. Induced draft fans are larger than forced draft fans and reduce the furnace pressure by handling combustion gases from the furnace. Although the new design of combining forced draft fans with induced draft fans is referred to as balanced draft (0 psia), the furnace will be slightly below atmospheric pressure (called draft). The new balanced draft will eliminate combustion gas leaks from the furnace. In addition, to reduce the potential sulfur dioxide and toxic gas emissions and deposits outside the plant, the utility has increased the height of the existing stacks. The higher stacks will carry the emissions further up into the atmosphere and disperse the emissions away from the immediate vicinity of the utility site.

| Source Category | Potential HAPs[a] | | | | Potential Emission Sources | | |
| | Organic | | Inorganic | | Process Point | Process Fugitive | Area Fugitive |
| | Vapor | Particulate | Vapor | Particulate | | | |
|---|---|---|---|---|---|---|---|
| Coal combustion | 3,14,19, 21,25,28 | 19 | 1,2,8,9,13, 17,27,31 | 1,2,5,6,8,9, 10,11,15,16, 18,20,22,24 | A,B | I | H |
| Oil combustion | 14 | 19 | 13,17,27 | 1,2,5,6,8,9, 10,11,15,16,29 | A,B,E | | |
| Natural gas combustion | 14 | 19 | | | A,B,E,F | | |
| Gasoline combustion | 12,14 | 12,19 | 17 | 15 | G | | |
| Diesel combustion | 12 | 12,19 | | 6,18 | G | | |
| Wood combustion | 3,4,12,14,25 | 12,19 | 27 | 16,20 | A,B,C | | |
| Waste oil combustion | 7,12,21,23,26 | 12,19 | | 6,8,9,15,18 | A,B,D | | |

**Pollutant Key**

| | | | |
|---|---|---|---|
| 1 | - arsenic | 16 | - manganese |
| 2 | - antimony | 17 | - mercury |
| 3 | - acetaldehyde | 18 | - nickel |
| 4 | - acetic acid | 19 | - polycyclic organic matter (POM) |
| 5 | - barium | 20 | - phosphorus |
| 6 | - beryllium | 21 | - polychlorinated biphenyls (PCB) |
| 7 | - benzene | 22 | - radionuclides |
| 8 | - cadmium | 23 | - trichloroethylene |
| 9 | - chromium | 24 | - zinc |
| 10 | - cobalt | 25 | - phenols |
| 11 | - copper | 26 | - ethyl benzene |
| 12 | - dioxin | 27 | - chlorine |
| 13 | - fluorides | 28 | - pyridine |
| 14 | - formaldehyde | 29 | - vanadium |
| 15 | - lead | 30 | - dibenzofuran |

**Source Key**

A - furnace
B - boiler
C - woodstove/fireplace
D - incinerator
E - gas turbine
F - reciprocating engine
G - industrial engine and/or equipment
H - coal storage pile
I - ash handling system

EXHIBIT 1

**SUMMARY:**

Air toxics emissions that exit the stack are a hazard to humans and the environment. However, utilities with FDBs should address the issue of worker exposure to toxic gas emissions that leak from the furnace. Questions to ask include: what air toxics are present in my plant? what are the present levels? what are the OSHA regulations and how do I reduce the air toxics levels to protect all workers in my plant? Obviously, not all utilities are as ambitious as the utility described here or they may not have the necessary funds to implement long term solutions such as balanced draft modifications or increasing the height of the stacks. However, utilities with FDBs should acknowledge that worker exposure to toxic gases can exist. Then, in the short term, fuel changes, personal and ambient air monitoring, respiratory programs and employee training can be developed to help ensure a safe working environment for station personnel.

Reference: EPA Handbook:
Control Technologies for Hazardous Air
Pollutants, EPA/6-91/014 June 1991

# Chapter 17
# Recognition, Evaluation, and Control of Indoor Air Pollution

B. Chastain

Indoor air pollution is typically associated with terms "sick building syndrome," "tight building syndrome," "building related illness," and "problem building". Indoor air pollution is a relatively new public health concern (approximately 15 years old) although this issue is an age-old problem dating back to prehistoric times when humans came to live indoors. Through this presentation I hope to summarize indoor air quailty issues in order to provide you with usable information concerning the recognition and evaluation of indoor air quality (IAQ) problems and the subsequent control measures which can be used for maintaining or improving the indoor air environment for better occupant health and comfort control.

Why has the subject become so vocalized in the last fifteen years? Why the sudden interest and awareness concerning indoor air quality issues?

During the last half of the 1970's and all of the 1980's, buildings were built or remodeled to minimize air handling, heating, and cooling costs, often limiting the amount of outside air brought into the buildings to near minimums. Paralleling these developments, complaints related to modern buildings increased. The new terms "tight building syndrome," "sick building syndrome," and "indoor air quality" became widely used by health and safety professionals and subsequently by newspaper columnist and the general public.

Concurrent with the increase of complaints that have arisen concerning IAQ, our expectations for comfort have arisen. No longer do we tolerate hot, humid summers by opening a window or fanning ourselves. When it gets cold, we don't always go for our sweaters, we head for the thermostat. This has increased the cost of both summer cooling and winter heating, a cost issue for building owners.

Many reports also point out the single most important area of liability litigation facing building designers is the environmental performance of buildings. For example, recent areas of litigation have included asbestos materials, formaldehyde products, and microbial growth in mechanical and plumbing systems. According to estimates, 90 percent of office buildings have the potential for similar problems. Fortunately, such problems can be identified and controlled.

Thus, to summarize, the reasons for the increased interest and awareness in indoor air quality include:

- Tighter building construction for energy conservation.
- Reduced levels of outdoor air provided to building interiors.
- New buildings and construction materials: insulations, foams, glues, fabrics, particle boards, fibrous glass.

- Large percentage of the time spend indoors (e.g., 90%).
- Increased public awareness, education, and expectations.

Historically, indoor air quality referred to comfort issues - temperature, humidity, drafts, stuffiness, and odor control. In past years, more attention has been paid to health. Low concentrations of indoor contaminants have resulted in many physical and psychological symptoms and complaints, particularly among hypersensitive persons. Typical complaints and symptoms include:

- Upper respiratory irritation: itching eyes, coughing, sneezing
- Congestion
- Headache, dizziness, nausea
- Fatigue, listlessness, inability to concentrate
- Shortness of breath
- Discomfort of a non-specific nature
- Skin irritation

In some instances occupant complaints and symptoms have lead to actual illnesses. Typical IAQ-related illnesses include:

- Humidifier fever (high incidence, mild flu-like symptoms, no deaths)
- Pontiac fever (similar to humidifier fever, non-pneumonia, no deaths)
- Legionnaires disease (incidence thought to be low, pneumonia, high fever, 10-20% mortality)
- Sinusitis
- Asthma
- Hypersensitivity Pneumonitis

Although many occupant complaints and symptoms typically do not result in clinical illness we must recognize the IAQ problem is real, particularly to the person involved. IAQ problems, real or imagined, always affect morale, efficiency, productivity, and attendance of the person affected, thus, producing "hidden" costs not easily measured.

What are the sources of the complaints and symptoms? At one end of the spectrum is "mass psychogenic disease" caused by the suggestion that people should be feeling sick. At the other end are contagious diseases (colds, flu) that simply pass around the plant or office. In either case, time and education often cure these problems.

Between the two extremes are a number of factors, conditions, and agents which can genuinely create complaints, symptoms, and illnesses:

(1) Bioaerosols. The presence of pollen, microbial agents, or organic toxins in the air may result in hypersensitivity pneumonitis and other

respiratory complaints. Often originating in the ventilation system, these problems have in the past been called "humidifier chills." Now it is known that more significant illnesses (e.g., Legionnaires' disease) are also associated with air handling equipment.

(2) Chemicals. The presence of reactive and organic chemicals (e.g., formaldehyde) may cause complaints and health problems. The source of chemicals can be almost anything - process emissions, process materials, building materials, carpet, cleaning materials, etc.

(3) Tobacco smoke. Tobacco smoke may cause similar complaints to those described above. Reductions in air exchange rates and tighter buildings can increase this problem.

These agents often originate within the building, but outdoor sources can also be involved, e.g., motor vehicle exhaust, pollen, reentrained exhaust air, smoke, dust, etc.

The National Institute of Occupational Safety and Health (NIOSH), in studies of over 1,000 IAQ episodes, categorized the major sources or factors associated with IAQ problems as follows: (estimates are rounded to nearest 10%)

· 50% related to deficiencies in the ventilation of the building (e.g., lack of outside air, poor air distribution, uncomfortable temperatures and humidities, and sources of contaminants in the system.
· 30% related to some indoor air contaminant (e.g., formaldehyde, solvent vapors, dust, microbiological agents).
· 10% could be attributed to an outside source (motor vehicle exhaust, pollen, fungi, smoke, construction dusts).
· 10% had no observable cause.

Of the indoor sources, about 5% were related to suspected microbial contamination, and about 5% were attributed to furnishings and fabrics.

NIOSH compiled a list of the frequency of the buildings it investigated.

| Complaint | Percent of buildings where occupants registered complaint |
|---|---|
| Eye Irritation | 81 |
| Dry Throat | 71 |
| Headache | 67 |
| Fatigue | 53 |
| Sinus Congestion | 51 |
| Shortness of Breath | 33 |
| Cough | 24 |
| Dizziness | 22 |
| Nausea | 15 |

The information presented in the NIOSH studies suggests some important conclusions. The ventilation system and the space itself are often significant sources of indoor pollution. People, through human respiration, metabolism, and cigarette smoking, are also significant sources, but not the only source, nor the major source in many cases, as has been assumed in the past.

"Tight building syndrome," often seen in buildings constructed during the past two decades, can create or exacerbate all of the problems previously described. Remedial measures include:

· adding more outside air,

· rearranging building occupancy
· restructuring air handling equipment, and
· increasing the mixing of ambient air with free-standing fans.

"Sick building syndrome," refers to a class of complaints and symptoms expressed by building occupants during an IAQ episode. Typical "sick building syndrome" complaints include nonspecific discomfort, headache, upper respiratory irritation, cough, dry, itchy skin, difficulty concentrating, and sensitivity to odors. In this syndrome, the cause or source of the complaints is difficult to find. Symptoms often disappear after occupants leave the building.

Common patterns emerge when looking at "sick building syndrome":

· Symptoms are mostly nonspecific
· Forced ventilation is common
· Buildings are energy efficient
· People complaining also perceive they have little control over their environment
· More complaints come where population densities are higher
· Symptoms are more likely in afternoon than morning.

"Building related illness," like "sick building syndrome," refers to a class of illnesses related to IAQ problems (e.g., sinusitis, asthma, legionnaires disease, Pontiac fever, flu, colds).

Adequate prevention and control of indoor air quality problems require (1) defining the nature of the problem, (2) determining causes and sources, and (3) implementing cost-effective controls. Typically in gathering information, evaluating the problem, and applying controls you might:

· Investigate the nature and extent of the complaints, e.g., by conducting walkthroughs, interviews, and literature searches.
· Identify and evaluate potential causes, e.g., by conducting air sampling, utilizing IAQ questionnaires, and conducting interviews.
· Assess ventilation conditions, e.g., temperature, humidity, outside air, air distribution, settled water, air flow parameters, etc.
· Suggest ways of controlling or eliminating contributing sources or causes, e.g., improve ventilation, remove sources, provide preventive maintenance, schedule custodial activities after work, isolate, substitute, control smoking, etc.
· Assist in education and training of persons affected, and
· Provide follow-up.

The indoor environment and its associated air quality can be improved through the use of traditional controls: engineered solutions, work practice changes, and administrative measures. Engineered solutions usually include isolation, removal of sources, process changes to reduce sources, and ventilation. Ventilation is improved by directly exhausting contaminant sources, provided additional outside air for dilution, and improving the efficiency of mixing. Air mixing efficiencies can be improved by:

· Limit or modify office partitions to allow more mixing,
· Provide fans for those complaining of "stagnant air,"

- Balance the air handling system to maintain consistent pressures between different zones,
- Place supply diffusers and return grills where they will provide the greatest mixing, and
- Open air supply diffusers and vents to proper setting.

The heating, ventilation, and air conditioning (HVAC) system should receive periodic preventive maintenance, be configured to filter objectionable aerosols, provide comfortable temperatures (e.g., 68-76 degrees F), and maintain humidities between 30-70% (40-60% better).

Preventative HVAC system maintenance is the keystone of an administrative solution to indoor air problems. Good preventative maintenance include:

- Periodic checks of damper settings, controls, drive belts, ductwork integrity and system balance,
- Periodic measurements of air flows and pressures,
- Checking temperatures and humidities routinely,
- Replacement of filters on schedule,
- Cleaning of system components on a regular schedule,
- Control of all wet or settled water problems, to include removal of damp materials, disinfection of contaminated waters, blowing out drain pipes routinely,
- Maintaining pressures in the building which will not cause furnace and water heater exhaust air to flow backward into the building.

Other administrative controls include:

- Training and education of occupants on IAQ.
- Perform cleaning, remodeling, and building construction during non-working hours.
- Provide additional dilution ventilation during remodeling and cleaning activities.
- Prohibit flow of air from high contamination areas (e.g., industrial process areas) to areas of less contamination (e.g., office spaces).
- Provide medical attention to those affected, as necessary. For example, persons with allergies or hypersensitivity should be evaluated. In occupational settings, employees should be screened for suitability to work in environment.
- Establish smoking policies.

Evaluating indoor air quality problems often require professionals such as industrial hygienists or air quality specialists and the use of testing and sampling equipment. Typical equipment includes: velometers, manometers, portable infrared analyzers, particle counters, carbon dioxide meters, detector tubes, radon samplers, and microbiological samplers. Because these equipment require some knowledge and experience to use, you may want to bring in sampling experts such as the industrial hygienist if you have no experience. The quality of your results will depend, in large part, on correct sampling procedures and correct sample analysis.

There are four basic types of sampling for qualifying and quantifying indoor air contaminants: (1) spot sampling - usually performed with real-time indicator tube-type indicator samplers; is quick and usually not very quantitatively accurate test. It is often performed during the preliminary stages of study (e.g., during the walk-through) to check for the presence or absence of a particular chemical compound. (2) Personal Monitoring - a sampling device (filter, charcoal tube, passive dosimeter, impinger, indicator tube) is placed near the breathing zone of the person being sampled. Some samplers are worn on the lapel or collar, others are held in place by a stand, and still others may be held by someone standing alongside the person sampled. Sample times may vary from 1 minute to 8 hours or more. Sampling results are immediate with real-time monitors. Others will be sent to a lab for analysis. Results are usually in "parts per million (ppm) by volume" (for gases and vapors), "milligrams per cubic meter ($mg/m^3$) air (for aerosols or particulate)," colony forming units per cubic meter ($CFU/m^3$) air (for microbes), and can provide an estimate of the persons actual exposure. Personal monitoring is often used when there is a question about personal health effects, or a concern about compliance with exposure standards as set forth by the Occupational Safety and Health Administration (OSHA). (3) Area Monitoring - (also, fixed sampling, area sampling, environmental monitoring, station sampling) uses a sampling device similar to those mentioned in personal monitoring. The sampler is usually placed in a fixed location, or moved about in the space to be tested, sample results suggest background concentrations of the chemical contaminant at the location of the sampler, and may not represent actual exposures at the breathing zone of people. (4) System Monitoring - like stack sampling, air samples can be obtained from the ductwork itself, or at supply and return registers, or at air intakes. This type of sampling allows the investigator to identify pathways of chemical contaminants, and whether or not the HVAC system is contributing to the problem.

Potential building and air contaminants typically sampled for and their sources are provided below:

- Formaldehyde - tobacco smoke, insulation, paneling, furnishings, carpet, stay-pressed cloth, deodorizers, paper products
- Ozone - photocopiers, laser printers, electrical equipment, electrostatic air cleaners
- Nitrogen Dioxide ($NO_2$) - vehicles, gas heating and cooking, industrial processes
- Carbon Dioxide ($CO_2$) - people density, flame operations, vehicles
- Organic Chemicals - photocopiers, industrial processes, labs, new furniture, furnishings, building materials, cleaning materials, paint
- Allergens - pollen, fungi, bacteria, mold, mites, dust, tobacco smoke
- Fibers - insulation, fire proofing, equipment
- Sulfur Dioxide ($SO_2$) - industrial processes
- ETS - environmental tobacco smoke
- Radon - soil containing uranium - enters through cracks, holes in basement wall/flooring, drains, or sump pump openings.

There are a number of standards and codes which affect or influence indoor air quality but the standard, against which all indoor air quality performance will be measured in the 1990s was published by the American Society of Heating, Refrigeration, and Air Conditioning Engineers (ASHRAE) in October 1989. This consensus standard is titled ASHRAE 62-1989 Ventilation for Acceptable Indoor Air Quality. This standard's purpose is to establish acceptable indoor air quality by describing procedures, equipment, and systems required to achieve acceptable indoor air quality. ASHRAE 62-1989 is an excellent reference document in combating indoor quality problems.

In review, there are many issues, causes, and affects
associated with the recognition, evaluation, and
control of indoor air quality problems in buildings.
By using the information provided and furthering your
study of this issue you will better be able to
understand and address IAQ problems in your buildings
and facilities with the goal of maximizing occupant
comfort and health concurrently with controlling IAQ
problems and the "hidden" costs associated with this
issue.

# Chapter 18

# Managing the Environmental Impacts of Utility Lighting Retrofits Programs

K. Cress

## INTRODUCTION

One of the most popular demand-side management (DSM) programs currently being sponsored by electric utilities is the removal of old fluorescent light ballasts and replacing them with more efficient models. This type of program, however, can produce a substantial waste stream of the old ballasts, many of which contain Polychlorinated Biphenyl(s) (PCBs), a regulated hazardous substance. The proper disposal of spent light ballasts should be an integral component of DSM programs.

This paper will discuss the experience that New England Electric System (NEES)[1] has had with disposing of spent light ballasts resulting from the implementation of our Small Commercial & Industrial Program (a direct install lighting program which provides for the installation of energy efficient lighting measures which include fluorescent fixtures, ballasts and lamps, specular reflectors, compact fluorescent systems, high intensity discharge fixtures, and occupancy sensors. This innovative program is one of the largest in the country and has achieved over 6,000 installations). In this paper, we will review why PCBs are classified as hazardous substances and what effect State and Federal regulations have on the transportation and disposal of ballasts that contain PCBs. Second, we will explain our ballast disposal process which includes collecting, processing, storing, shipping and ultimate disposal. Third, we will discuss our experiences with two different methods of disposal - incineration and recycling. And last we will report on program results.

## PCB REGULATIONS

Polychlorinated Biphenyl or "PCB" is an organic chemical that was widely used in electrical equipment i.e. transformers, capacitors, switchgear and voltage regulators. Synthetically manufactured, PCBs have very desirable cooling properties, and, thus, were used extensively in capacitors of fluorescent light ballasts through 1979.

Today, the EPA classifies PCBs as a hazardous substance. This is because PCBs are not easily biodegradable when released into the environment and are suspected carcinogens. Thus, the EPA has determined that PCBs are harmful to human health and the environment.[2]

### Regulations

When Congress passed the Toxic Substance Control Act (TSCA) of 1976, it enabled the EPA to regulate the manufacture, storage, use, records and disposal of PCBs. The EPA banned the manufacturing of PCBs in 1978.

The regulations for disposal of fluorescent light ballasts containing PCBs depends on the condition of the ballast when it is removed. If the ballast is not leaking, then it is not regulated under TSCA. A leaking ballast, however, is regulated under this law and is required to be disposed of at a chemical waste landfill or incinerator permitted under TSCA. The disposal of ballasts without PCBs is not regulated.

The disposal of PCB ballasts may also be regulated by individual state laws. According to the EPA, there are 21 states that presently have some form of Regulation for PCB disposal.[3]

The Commonwealth of Massachusetts is the only state in our three-state service territory that has a policy for PCB ballast disposal. In agreement with the EPA, the Massachusetts Department of Environmental Protection (DEP) requires all leaking ballasts to be managed as a hazardous waste, requiring use of a licensed hazardous waste transporter, manifest, and disposal by incineration or burial at a chemical waste landfill. For non-leaking ballasts, the Massachusetts policy differs from the EPA's. Massachusetts identifies the capacitors in ballasts as a hazardous waste when PCB concentration is greater than 50 parts per million. Therefore, the DEP requires all capacitors with PCBs to be disposed of at a licensed hazardous waste treatment facility if located in Massachusetts. Out-of-state disposal of capacitors is to be done in compliance with state laws where ultimate disposal occurs.[4]

The Massachusetts policy has an interesting caveat that helps make a ballast disposal program practical. Quoting from the policy:

"Under this policy, the Department will consider a contractor's central receiving location the site of hazardous waste generation. Accordingly, the Department will not require the use of a licensed hazardous waste transporter and manifest for transport of intact non-leaking lighting ballasts to the contractor's central location for subsequent processing (removal of capacitors) or accumulation provided that all such ballasts and/or components are subsequently properly transported off-site in accordance with 310 CMR 30.000, either as a hazardous waste for disposal, or as a regulated recyclable material for recycling. If any of the ballasts and/or capacitors are leaking, they must be managed as a hazardous waste. A hazardous waste manifest shall not be used for transport of non-leaking lighting ballasts to the contractor's central location unless such location is a treatment, storage or disposal facility. A licensed hazardous waste transporter and manifest MUST be used and the waste disposed of as a hazardous waste if the ballasts and/or capacitors are leaking. If the capacitors are being disposed of in another state, the generator must comply with that state's requirements for disposal of PCB capacitors."[4]

In effect, the Commonwealth of Massachusetts requires spent ballasts that contain PCBs to be managed and disposed of as a hazardous waste. Not only does our program fully comply with this policy, it did so before this policy was established.

BALLAST DISPOSAL PROCESS

This section describes in detail the process of our Ballast Disposal Program, starting with the collection of removed ballasts from a customer's facility to the recycling or incineration of the ballasts and their components.

Notification

The process begins when a lighting installation is completed and the spent ballasts are placed in 9 mil plastic bags and stored at the site. These completed installations are tracked in a computer data base. A list of these sites is generated and given to a dispatcher on a periodic basis. Each list contains the customer name, address, contact person, telephone number, and the quantity of ballasts to be picked up. The dispatcher uses the list to develop the daily schedule for the pick-up crews.

"Milk-Runs"

We refer to the task of traveling to each customer site,

collecting the removed ballasts and transferring them to a central collection warehouse as "milk-runs". To fully appreciate the unique challenge this task poses, we need to briefly describe our service territory.

As the map (Figure #1) shows, NEES' service territory is large and extends into three states. To efficiently perform the milk-runs, operations are based out of our corporate headquarters located in Westborough, Massachusetts. Figure #1 also illustrates the maximum roundtrip distances our drivers travel to cover our service territory. On average, our trucks travel 146 miles and collect at 5 sites per day.

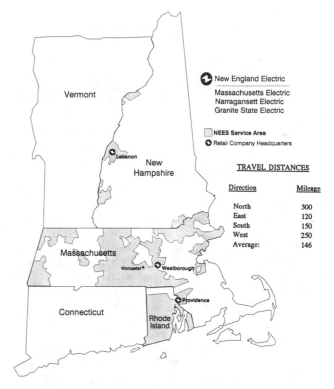

**FIGURE 1: NEES SERVICE TERRITORY**

The type of truck used is an 18 foot van body with a hydraulic tailgate. They have a gross weight rating of 30,000 lbs. and a cargo weight capacity of 15,000 lbs.

One driver and one helper perform the pickups which involves traveling to the customer site, finding the removed ballasts, carrying the bags to the truck, and emptying the bags into 55-gallon D.O.T. 17C drums. The drums, which typically hold between 100-150 ballasts and weigh around 650 lbs., are covered and lifted into the trucks using the hydraulic tailgate. The plastic bags are either reused or discarded.

The drivers are Hazardous Waste Certified in addition to having their Commercial Drivers License (CDL). This certification is technically not required to locally transport PCB ballasts, but NEES has instituted it as policy. The certification is secured by the successful completion of

Transportation of Hazardous Waste Training in compliance with USEPA, USDOT and State requirements (see Figure #2). This is an annual training and certification process.

**FIGURE 2: TRANSPORTATION OF HAZARDOUS WASTE CERTIFICATE**

Also, the trucks used to collect and transfer the ballasts are licensed by the State as hazardous waste transport vehicles. Vehicles must pass a State inspection to receive this license.

Collection and Processing

When the milk-run trucks reach their maximum weight capacity, they are off-loaded at a division warehouse located in Worcester, Massachusetts. This facility is one of NEES' three large distribution warehouses, chosen for its central location. The trucks are unloaded using forklifts equipped with a special gripping device for drums. Each drum is placed on a pallet, four drums per pallet, making up what is called a "four-pack".

The following four steps are followed in the processing of each drum. Each drum is:

1. Numbered using a company sequence number.
2. Labeled, using labels that identify the contents as PCBs and Hazardous Waste (see Figure #3).
3. Weighed as a four-pack, and
4. Stored in a hazardous waste area located inside the warehouse.

According to state regulations, the ballasts can be stored at this location for a maximum of 30 days; however, we typically transfer them to a long-term storage facility within 5 days of receipt.

Storage and Shipping

After the drums containing ballasts have been processed, they are transferred to the long-term storage facility where they are kept until they are shipped to the ultimate disposal site. This storage facility is capable of storing PCB waste for up to 9 months.

All drums are stored in lots in preparation for shipping. An average of 60 drums makes up one lot or truckload. Semi-tractors with 45' trailers are used by commercial hazardous waste transporters to ship the ballasts to the ultimate disposal site. Hazardous waste transporters are designated by the disposal company receiving the waste ballasts.

All ballast shipments are manifested according to State and Federal regulations. This involves the use of 3 additional labels for each drum containing ballasts. A "Material Profile Label", a "PCB Shipping Label", and a sequence number label is supplied by the particular disposal firm that will receive the shipment (Figure #4). Strict compliance to the manifest and documentation procedure is enforced by our Division Storeskeeper who oversees all processing and shipping related to the ballast disposal program.

ULTIMATE DISPOSAL

This section addresses the "What" and "Where" of the ballast disposal program. What happens to the ballasts and where do the ballasts (or their separated components) go to final destruction? NEES uses two different methods of ultimate disposal -- incineration or recycling.

**FIGURE 3: PCB AND HAZARDOUS WASTE LABELS**

93

**FIGURE 4: SHIPPING LABELS**

## Incineration

This method involves the burning of the complete ballast at a TSCA licensed PCB incinerator. NEES has used this method since the beginning of the program. Initially, the waste management firm of Clean Harbors, Inc., was utilized to broker for incineration of the entire ballast at the ChemWaste Management facility in Illinois. The unexpected shutdown of this facility in late 1991 led NEES to secure another disposal contract with Rollins Environmental Inc. of Deer Park, Texas.

The process of incinerating ballasts at Rollins is simple. Ballasts are first shredded and then placed inside the incinerator. The PCBs in the ballasts are completely destroyed as well as the asphalt and metal. The only by-product of the incineration process is ash which is approximately 5% of the original weight.

The advantage of the incineration method of disposal is that the PCB waste is completely destroyed and the long-term liability for the customer and utility is greatly reduced. The disadvantages of incinerating ballasts include the increase of atmospheric emissions, the consumption of extra fuel to completely burn the non-combustible metals in the ballasts, and the waste of valuable metals.

It is interesting to note that there are only three TSCA PCB incinerators currently operating in the United States. The demand for these PCB incinerators is subsequently very high. Securing reliable disposal slots from these incinerators has been increasingly difficult over the past year. The impact this situation can have on utility DSM programs is potentially great. More and more utility companies are hopping on the DSM bandwagon and will most likely promote programs that will result in light ballast retrofits. This will further increase the demand for PCB incineration.

At this time, it is uncertain whether other PCB incinerators will become available to meet the growing demand for incineration of PCB ballasts. Companies that are planning ballast retrofit programs are advised to secure reliable sources of ultimate disposal before they begin such programs. This will help prevent potential interruptions due to unavailable incinerator slots.

## Recycling

The high demand for disposal of lights ballasts has not only kept the PCB incinerator business strong but it has also sparked the entrepreneurial spirit. Several new companies specializing in recycling fluorescent light ballasts have recently come into existence. Most of the firms are only in start-up phase; however their potential impact on the ballast disposal business is substantial.

NEES has recently added recycling as an option for the ultimate disposal of ballasts. We view this decision to be prudent because it reduces our dependence on a single hazardous waste disposal firm. It also reduces some adverse environmental impacts associated with the whole ballast incineration method.

## Recycling Process

Roughly 48,000 ballasts from our program have been recycled by Salesco Systems, U.S.A. at their recycling facility in Phoenix, Arizona. The process involves a series of steps that separate each ballast into the component materials of steel, copper or aluminum wire, asphalt, and the capacitor. The capacitor and asphalt are placed in drums and shipped to a licensed PCB incinerator for destruction. The reclaimed metals are sold as scrap.

The waste reduction of the recycling process has been impressive. The volume of waste sent for incineration was reduced by 60% and the weight was reduced by 80%. The latter is more important because incinerators charge by the pound and therefore, substantial cost savings can be realized.

The major concern about recycling is the production capabilities of recycling companies. According to our investigation, the recycling process can be very labor-intensive, and therefore potentially limiting to production. Perhaps a process refinement will improve production as the recycling industry matures.

## RESULTS

Since NEES started the Small C&I ballast retrofit program in June 1990, over 350,000 ballasts have been disposed of. The table below shows the specific quantities disposed of according to each program year. This table also shows that roughly 87% of the ballasts have been incinerated and 13% recycled. We expect the recycled percentage to continue to increase in the future.

The costs for ballast disposal depends on which method is used (incineration, recycling or chemical waste landfill). Clearly, incineration of the complete ballast is the most expensive method, recycling less expensive. Approximately 80% of the cost is attributed to shipping and incineration or recycling and 20% for the initial collection.

### Ballast Disposal

| Program Year | Incinerated | Recycled | Total Qty. |
|---|---|---|---|
| 1990 | 142,958 | N/A | 142,958 |
| 1991 | 137,438 | N/A | 137,438 |
| 1992* | 29,764 | 48,000 | 77,764 |
| Total | 310,160 | 48,000 | 358,160 |

* through 6/1/92

## CLOSING

Demand side management is a pro-active approach to efficiency and conservation which is considered to be good for the environment. A reliable measurement of the net environmental impact of DSM programs has yet to be established.

We believe at NEES that the positive effects of DSM programs outweigh the negative, but we also believe in reducing known averse impacts where feasible and prudent. The NEES ballast disposal program has proven to be one example of effectively and responsibly managing the environmental impacts of a DSM program. Hopefully, the information contained in these pages will allow others to do likewise.

## ACKNOWLEDGEMENTS

The success of the Ballast Disposal Program is due to the assistance of many people. Likewise, the completion of this paper is due to the help of several people the author wishes to acknowledge. I want to thank Charlie Foster, Joe Kwasnik, Ken McMillan and Jim Tyler for their input of information; my supervisor, Michael Horton, for the freedom to undertake the project, and Eileen Gumma and Jeanne Hackathorn for word processing and layout assistance.

## SOURCES

1. New England Electric System is a public utility holding company headquartered in Westborough, Massachusetts. Its retail subsidiaries are Massachusetts Electric Company ("Mass. Electric"), The Narragansett Electric Company ("Narragansett"), and Granite State Electric Company ("Granite State"). These subsidiaries provide electricity to 1.2 million homes and businesses of approximately 3 million people in Massachusetts, Rhode Island and New Hampshire. Its wholesale generation and transmission subsidiary, New England Power Company ("NEP"), owns and operates 21 electric generating stations in New England. As used in this paper, the terms "NEES" and the "System" refer to one or more of the subsidiaries of New England Electric System.

2. EPA Fact Sheet "PCBs in Fluorescent Light Fixtures" January, 1985.

3. EPA Greenlights Program "Light Brief" January, 1992, and U.S. Environmental Protection Agency Greenlights Program "Lighting Upgrade Waste Disposal Report" February, 1992.

4. Bureau of Waste Prevention, Division of Hazardous Waste, Policy for Disposal of Lighting Ballasts From Fluorescent Lights Containing PCB-Impregnated Capacitors, Commonwealth of Massachusetts Department of Environmental Protection, January 1992.

# Chapter 19
# Methods for Quantifying Environmental Externalities

J. Dalton

## INTRODUCTION

The quantification of environmental externalities is a complex and often subjective task. This subjectivity and the difficulty of reliably expressing complex and uncertain relationships between environmental pollutants and the resulting damages and then expressing these damages in dollar costs, results in a wide divergence of opinions regarding the appropriate environmental externality values. Outlined below is a review of the generally accepted methods for incorporating environmental externalities into the resource evaluation process and for quantifying environmental externalities in terms of monetary values.

Environmental externalities are "the cost of environmental damages caused by a project or activity for which compensation to affected parties does not occur." (Massachusetts Department of Public Utilities, 86-36-G, p. 77) An example of an environmental externality for the electric utility industry are the costs imposed on society of electric generating units' uncontrolled (residual) emissions, e.g., the damage costs of acid rain caused by the sulfur dioxide emissions from Midwestern power plants. These acid rain damage costs are external costs since they are borne by society in general and are not considered by the electric utilities as part of their planning process. Public awareness of the externality costs of acid rain has resulted in legislation requiring utilities to reduce their sulfur dioxide emissions and will cause electric utilities to internalize these acid deposition costs, i.e., reflect them in their planning processes and overall costs of electricity.

There are a number of ways in which environmental externalities can be incorporated into utilities' resource planning processes. The two methods that have received the most attention are a weighting and ranking approach and the monetization of externalities, i.e., the expression of externality values in dollars. The monetization approach is more complex and has received wider acceptance from regulators. Consequently, this discussion focuses primarily on methods for monetizing externalities.

## METHODS FOR INCORPORATING EXTERNALITIES INTO THE IRP PROCESS

While the monetization of externalities has been more widely applied, the weighting and ranking approach offers one compelling advantage; it is relatively simple and easy to incorporate into the existing resource evaluation process. As an example, for self-scoring requests for power supply proposals conducted by electric utilities, the environmental externality value can be a separate score which is added to the scores of other evaluation criteria. However, the administrative simplicity of the weighting and ranking approach masks the more fundamental issue of how the weights and rankings should be developed. One confronts many of the same issues that are present when attempting to monetize externalities. In both approaches it is necessary to estimate environmental impacts and the value of

these impacts.[1] Alternatively, one could assume that a conservation measure has a lower environmental impact than a natural gas-fired combined cycle which has a lower environmental impact than an oil-fired steam unit. However, this does not resolve the issue of how to measure the degree of difference in environmental impacts among competing projects. Thus, whether the weighting and ranking approach or the monetization of damages is used, the environmental impacts and the value of these impacts must be determined.

Monetizing externalities offers several advantages relative to the weighting and ranking approach: (1) externality costs can be added to direct resource costs enabling a comparison of the resources' total societal costs, i.e., market prices and externality costs; and (2) innovation to improve projects' overall thermal efficiency, pollution control efficiency, externality costs is encouraged. The major disadvantage of monetizing externalities is the uncertainty associated with many of the values produced in the various steps of the monetization process and the risks of giving uncertain externality values the same weight as direct market prices.

## METHODS FOR MONETIZING EXTERNALITIES

There are four methods for monetizing externalities: (1) polling of experts; (2) estimating the relative potency of various pollutants; (3) estimating and valuing the damages; and (4) calculating costs of control.

The first method is not frequently used and is subject to significant bias since it is difficult and often impossible to the independently evaluate the underlying assumptions of the participants' externality value estimates. The second method, basing the externality value on the pollutants potency relative to a pollutant with a known externality value, is attractive since it is straightforward and appears to have a high degree of theoretical support. However, the results of this method are subject to question since any bias in the original externality value estimate can be compounded. Finally, the relative potency method is based on the dose-response relationship which is often subject to a significant amount of uncertainty. Nonetheless, this method can be useful in providing an independent check of the reasonableness of an externality value or a "ballpark estimate".

The last two valuation methods have received the most attention and the widest application. Estimating and then valuing the damage (damage cost estimates) is the most attractive valuation method from a theoretical perspective, but the most troubling from a methodological perspective. The major drawback of this approach is the difficulty of developing the damage cost estimates and the significant uncertainties and subjectivity associated with the values developed in the valuation process.

---

1. This is necessary in weighting and ranking approaches if the variations in environmental impacts among various resources are to be accounted for properly.

For example, to determine the externality value for sulfur dioxide emissions the analyst must: (1) determine the dispersion of the pollutant; (2) evaluate chemical transformations of the pollutant; (3) determine the actual resources to be affected; (3) estimate the amount of the pollutant that these resources will be affected by; (4) estimate the resulting damages to the resource; and (5) estimate the economic value of the effect on the resource. Typically each of these steps is subject to a significant amount of uncertainty and judgement. For example, dispersion modeling can only provide estimates of the levels of ambient concentrations and the results provided are extremely site specific, reflecting local topography and meteorological conditions. The impacts on receptors are calculated based on the actual densities of the resources and their existing condition (resources in a weakened condition might be more susceptible to damages). Dose-response relationships are subject to uncertainty regarding the nature of the dose-response relationship (linear vs. curvilinear) and whether there are effects below a certain threshold. Finally, the economic valuation of the actual damages typically requires that values be placed on the increased mortality and morbidity risks. These economic valuation methods can be classified in two ways: (1) revealed preference or actual valuation methods; and (2) direct or contingent valuation methods. Both methods are discussed in greater detail below.

Revealed preference methods "infer values for changes in natural resources as 'revealed' by actual behavioral data" (Violette, p. 13). One commonly used revealed preference method that is used to value recreational activities is to estimate travel costs, including out-of-pocket costs for gas and food and the opportunity cost of the travel time. A second revealed preference method is the hedonic price method. For example, the hedonic price method is used to estimate the value of differences in air pollution levels by evaluating the differences in property values and their relation to air pollution levels.[2] By relying on actual expenditures and behavior, revealed preference-based valuation estimates are often assumed to be more reliable than the contingent valuation method. (This discussion of revealed preferences does not pertain to the application of control costs as a revealed preference. The use of control costs as an indication of externality values is discussed below.) However, in some instances revealed preferences can understate externality values since the value to consumers of a day of fishing is likely to be greater than the total costs of the fishing outing, otherwise the consumer would not have gone fishing. Another drawback of this valuation method is that there are a limited number of areas where revealed preferences can be used given the availability and quality of data (Violette, p. 13).

Contingent valuation methods use survey techniques and contingent or hypothetical markets to reveal what expenditures and behavior would be if those markets existed (Violette, p. 13). For example, contingent valuation methods are often used to value changes in visibility. Contingent valuation methods are attractive because they can be used to value damages in a wide range of circumstances; however they also are subject to criticism because they rely on consumers' representations regarding their willingness to pay to avoid a certain result, but do not require any financial confirmation. Thus, contingent valuation studies can potentially overestimate willingness to pay. In sum, all of these economic valuation methods rely on a significant degree of judgement, and as such, all are subject to criticism and uncertainty.

The fourth method for monetizing externalities is to use the cost of pollution control expenditures.[3] For example, the Massachusetts Department of Public Utilities' oxides of nitrogen ($NO_x$) externality value is based on the marginal cost of selective catalytic reduction on a 10 MW gas turbine. (This $NO_x$ control technique was determined to be the highest cost control technique required by Massachusetts environmental regulators.) The implied valuation method assumes that "through the political process that government mandated levels of pollution control provides, a reasonable, rough proxy for of [sic] what society is willing to pay to avoid environmental externalities" (Massachusetts Department of Public Utilities, 89-239, p. 67) This rationale appears to assume that consumers in their role as voters are able to communicate to elected officials and to environmental regulators through the public comment process about their willingness to pay for environmental control programs. According to this line of reasoning, if consumers believed that an environmental control program were too costly, they would protest to the environmental regulators and elected officials and if the public outcry was great enough the control program would be rescinded. However, this rationale argues for the use of average not marginal control costs, since consumers actually pay average not marginal control costs, i.e., the consumer sees a total cost of x which produces a benefit of y. Thus, if acceptance of pollution control program costs is assumed to represent society's willingness to pay, then average not marginal control costs should be used as the basis for the implied valuation methodology.

Alternatively, one might argue that it is not consumers who determine society's willingness to pay, but regulators, who base their decisions on the cost-effectiveness of control techniques on marginal costs, with the highest marginal control costs equal to the marginal benefits of control. However, environmental regulators have the same difficulty quantifying the marginal benefits of emission control programs as other analysts. Furthermore, in many instances decisions regarding the appropriateness of control techniques are not based on how the technique's marginal costs compare to its marginal control benefits. In sum, decisions regarding society's willingness to pay made by both regulators and consumers are based on average, not marginal, control costs.

The reasonableness of using marginal control costs as an indication of the appropriate externality value is further called into question by the environmental regulatory process. Under federal legislation and EPA rules, in many instances there is no direct relationship between the costs of environmental control programs and the benefits of the control program. This is particularly true with respect to programs to maintain and achieve the National Ambient Air Quality Standards (NAAQS). As required by federal legislation, the primary NAAQS are established by the EPA to protect the most sensitive populations (e.g., the elderly) with an adequate margin of safety. All states are required to achieve and maintain these standards without regard to the cost of attaining the standards.[4] Thus, control programs that are developed to achieve and maintain these standards are not based on a careful balancing of the costs of control with the benefits of control. Furthermore, if a state already satisfies the primary and secondary NAAQS then by definition the externalities value for that pollutant must be zero.

---

2.   The hedonic price method is often plagued with statistical problems. For example, multicolinearity can make it difficult to distinguish between the relative significance and contribution of conditions that often occur together, e.g., in urban areas air pollution and congestion. Thus, one would be unable to definitively determine the degree to which air pollution and congestion individually affect property values.

3.   This method is also commonly referred to as the "implied valuation method".

4.   In addition to primary standards, the Clean Air Act provides for secondary standards which are also based on general welfare considerations and reflect a balancing of the costs and benefits of controls.

## CONCLUSIONS: THE IMPACTS OF EXTERNALITIES ON ELECTRIC RESOURCE'S RELATIVE COSTS

The preceding discussion has indicated that attempting to express externality values in terms of dollars of damage costs is a difficult and subjective task. Nonetheless, many state public utility commissions have undertaken this task and have ordered utilities in their jurisdictions to include commission-approved externality values in their resource evaluation processes. Table 1 presents a comparison of externality value estimates for sulfur dioxide, oxides of nitrogen, and carbon dioxide for various jurisdictions. All of the externality value estimates shown except for the California Energy Commission and the Bonneville Power Administration are based on the implied valuation method. The California Energy Commission and the Bonneville Power Administration estimates are based on damage cost estimates. A comparison of the implied valuation and the damage-based estimates indicates that the two methods by no means give consistent results.[5] This is further evidence of the difficulty and subjectivity of developing reliable externality value estimates.

In spite of the uncertainty and the subjectivity associated with these externality value estimates, they can have a significant impact on utilities' resource decisions. Table 2 shows the cost impact of the externality values adopted by the Massachusetts Department of Public Utilities on two different electric generating technologies: (1) fluidized bed coal units; and (2) natural gas-fired combined cycle units. Clearly, under these externality value estimates a fluidized bed coal unit is under a significant competitive disadvantage relative to a natural gas-fired combined cycle unit.

5.   One must be careful when attempting to compare these results since they are for different jurisdictions with different air quality levels. For example, the externality value estimates for sulfur dioxide and nitrogen oxides in California are significantly higher than for other areas, reflecting the state's air quality problems.

TABLE 1
### COMPARISON OF SO₂, NOₓ AND CO₂ EXTERNALITY COSTS
### (1990 NOMINAL LEVELIZED DOLLARS PER TON)

| Institution | Notes | $SO_2$ | $NO_x$ | $CO_2$ |
|---|---|---|---|---|
| | | ----------------- ($/ton)----------------- | | |
| NYS Energy Plan 1991 Update: General Revenue Tax | | $ 1,274 | $ 6,081 | $107 |
| Trust Fund Tax | | $   280 | $ 1,406 | $   7.9 |
| New York State 1989 Energy Plan: Preliminary Draft Report | a | $ 830 | $ 1,968 | $ 18 |
| Final Draft Report | b | $ 630 | $ 2,569 | $ 1 |
| NYS Public Service Commission: | c | $ 830 | $ 1,967 | $ 1 |
| Massachusetts Department of Public Utilities: | d | $ 2,304 | $ 9,981 | $ 35 |
| Nevada Public Utilities Commission: | e | $ 2,278 | $ 9,928 | $ 32 |
| California Public Utilities Commission (SCAQMD): | f | $18,300 | $24,500 | $ 7 |
| California Energy Commission: In State: | g | $27,436 | $27,676 | $ 12 |
| Out of State: | | $ 2,386 | $ 6,442 | $ 12 |
| Bonneville Power Administration: East of the Cascades: | h | $ 3,073 | $   101 | $ 9 |
| West of the Cascades: | | $ 5,259 | $ 1,291 | $ 9 |

Source:        New York State Energy Plan

## Notes to Table 1

a. Source: <u>Draft New York State Energy Plan</u>, "Environmental Externalities Issue Report", Preliminary Draft, February 1989.

b. Source: <u>Draft New York State Energy Plan</u>, Vol. VI, "Environmental Externalities Issue Report:, may 1989. Revised estimates. Estimates are used for consideration of externality costs in all aspects of least cost planning.

c. Source: <u>Draft New York State Energy Plan</u>. "Environmental Externalities Issue Report", Preliminary Draft, February 1989 for $SO_2$ and $NO_x$. The $CO_2$ estimate is a value judgement by NYS DPS Staff. Estimates are used for consideration of externality costs in utility resource selection (competitive bidding programs) and in special studies.

d. Estimates prepared for Massachusetts DPU by Tellus Institute. Based on marginal control costs under the implied valuation approach. Used for consideration of externality costs in resource planning and selection, conservation programs and contract evaluation.

e. Estimates prepared for Nevada PSC by Tellus Institute. Based on marginal control costs under the implied valuation approach. Pertain to EPA attainment areas in-state. Used for consideration of externality costs in all aspects of least cost planning.

f. Based on marginal control cost estimates for California's South Coast Air Quality Management District's (SCAQMD) proposed Tier I control measures for compliance with the California Clean Air Act. Used by the California PUC, Division of Ratepayer Advocates for estimating residual emissions adders for Pacific Gas & Electric, Southern California Edison and San Diego Gas & Electric service territories.

g. Based on average control cost estimates for California's South Coast Air Quality Management District's (SCAQMD) proposed Tier I control measures for compliance with the California Clean Air Act. Used in Southern California Edison service territory.

h. Based on damage function analysis. These estimates apply to all aspects of least cost planning.

Source:    New York State Energy Plan

TABLE 2

COMPARISON OF EXTERNALITY VALUES FOR FLUIDIZED BED COAL VS. NATURAL GAS—FIRED COMBINED CYCLE UNITS
MASSACHUSETTS DEPARTMENT OF PUBLIC UTILITIES ADOPTED EXTERNALITY VALUES

| Pollutant | DPU Adopted Externality Value ($ 1990/ton) | Fluidizied Bed Coal | | Natural Gas—fired Combined Cycle | | Externality Value Difference (¢/kWh) |
|---|---|---|---|---|---|---|
| | | Emission Factor (lbs/MMbtu) | Externality Impact (¢/kWh) | Emission Factor (lbs/MMbtu) | Externality Impact (¢/kWh) | |
| Sulfur Dioxide | $1,578 | 0.3 | 0.24 | 0.01 | 0.01 | 0.23 |
| Nitrogen Oxides | $6,896 | 0.29 | 0.99 | 0.036 | 0.10 | 0.89 |
| Carbon Dioxide | $24 | 207.3 | 2.49 | 109.1 | 1.11 | 1.37 |
| Volatile Organic Compounds | $5,574 | 0.01 | 0.03 | 0.009 | 0.02 | 0.01 |
| Particulate Matter | $4,207 | 0.03 | 0.06 | 0.006 | 0.01 | 0.05 |
| Carbon Monoxide | $915 | 0.13 | 0.06 | 0.022 | 0.01 | 0.05 |
| Methane | $231 | 0.16 | <u>0.02</u> | 0 | <u>0.00</u> | <u>0.02</u> |
| | | Total | 3.88 | Total | 1.27 | 2.62 |

Note: These estimates are assumed emission levels for new generating units permitted in New England. The externality values for existing units would be much higher.

Source: Reed Consulting Group

## REFERENCES

1. D.P.U. 86-36, 12/6/89, Massachusetts Department of Public Utilities

2. D.P.U. 89-239, 8/31/90, Massachusetts Department of Public Utilities

3. New York State Energy Office, Department of Public Service, Department of Environmental Conservation, New York State Energy Plan, 7/91.

4. Violette, Dr. Daniel, Carolyn Lang and Dr. Philip Hanser. 10/1/91. "A Framework for Evaluating Environmental Externalities in Resource Planning: A State Regulatory Perspective." In: <u>Proceedings of the National Conference on Environmental Externalities</u>, Jackson Hole, WY. Washington: National Association of Regulatory Utility Commissioners.

# Chapter 20
# Converting Wastes into Energy

S. R. Shrivastava

## INTRODUCTION

Many industrializing nations faces a formidable agenda of environmental cleanup tasks as well' as rising energy costs. Therefore, it is essential that pollution control be achieved without additional increase in energy demand. Ironically, waste materials, both solid and liquid, contain biomass which can be converted into a renewable source of energy, namely methane. Many industrial wastewaters contain high concentrations of organics, which is ideal for the anaerobic treatment process.

In the USA, recovering energy from solid waste is a goal established by the Environmental Protection Agency. The anaerobic treatment process can integrate the treatment of solid waste, waste treatment plant sludge, and high strength leachates generated in sanitary landfills. This paper discusses some high rate anaerobic process applications which are currently treating wastes while generating biogas.

## TREATMENT PROCESS

The two basic biological treatment processes available for treating waste are the aerobic and anaerobic treatment processes. Aerobic treatment is accomplished in the presence of dissolved oxygen, whereas anaerobic treatment occurs in the absence of dissolved oxygen. Both the anaerobic and aerobic processes can be further classified into suspended growth and attached growth processes. The suspended growth process is a biological process in which the microorganisms responsible for the conversion of the organic matter or other constituents to gases and cell tissues are maintained in suspension within the liquid. In the attached growth process the microorganisms are attached to some inert medium such as rock, slag or specially designed ceramic or plastic materials. Attached growth treatment processes are also known as fixed film processes. The characteristics of the waste being treated dictate the choice of treatment process.

## ANAEROBIC TREATMENT

Anaerobic treatment processes for high organic strength wastes have been studied for over 100 years. The anaerobic degradation of waste (biological process) takes place in two or three steps. In a three step sequence the first step involves the enzyme-mediated reconstruction of higher weight molecular compounds suitable for use as a source of energy and cell carbon. The second step involves bacterial conversion of the compounds resulting from the first step into identifiable lower-molecular-weight intermediate compounds. The third step involves the bacterial conversion of the intermediate compounds into simpler end products, namely $CH_4$ and $CO_2$. In the two step sequence, the first two steps described above are considered to occur simultaneously and are defined as a single step. The two step process is more commonly referred to as acid formation followed by methane formation.

The treatment of leachate by the anaerobic process has the following advantages:

* Reduced operation and maintenance costs:

* Less sludge production and improved sludge dewaterability;

* More stable system-seasonal and intermittent operation is possible; and

* 70% +/- conversion of biodegradable DOC to methane.

## ANAEROBIC DIGESTION OF MSW

Typical municipal solid waste (MSW) contains paper, food waste, yard, and garden debris which are amenable to the biological conversion to methane ($CH_4$) and carbon dioxide ($CO_2$). When MSW is placed into landfills the biological decomposition takes place at a slow, uncontrolled rate with questionable methane recoveries. The energy content of MSW is about 4,500 BTU per pound on a wet basis. The energy potential from MSW generated in the USA is estimated to be $2 \times 10^{15}$ BTU/year of which 85% can be recovered. Currently, only about ten percent of this energy potential is being recovered.

A typical anaerobic digestion treatment system includes three processing streams including front end processing units, a digestion unit, and a final processing unit. The front end process contains size reduction and sorting units where the organic portion of the waste is separated from the waste stream. In the digestion unit the organic portion of the waste stream is mixed with water, sludge, or leachate to obtain an optimum moisture content and is conveyed to the reactor. The biogas produced in the digestor is compressed and injected throughout the reactor to mix the contents. The typical post processing unit includes dewatering and curing equipment. The digested material, upon its further curing, may serve as a soil conditioner, thus reducing the landfill space required. The water contained in the digestate is re-circulated back into the system. The typical retention time for the process is about 20-40 days. In general, most of the pre-processing and post processing is similar to that of a typical materials recovery facility for solid waste. A typical system is conceptually illustrated in Figure 1.

In the United States a few small pilot projects have been developed. The most highly publicized include the Disney World System in Orlando, Florida sponsored by the Gas Research Institute, the University of California Davis project, developed in conjunction with the California Prison Authority, the U.S. Department of Energy Pompano Beach Project, and the University of Florida Seback Project.

None of the US pilot projects focused on the entire municipal waste stream. However, two systems for the anaerobic digestion of MSW currently exist in Europe. They are 1) DRANCO (DRy ANaerobic COposting), a Belgian system, and 2) VALORGA, a French System. The varied capacities of these systems indicate that, unlike the incineration process, the anaerobic process does not need require large volumes of MSW in order to be economically feasible.

## LEACHATE TREATMENT

Larsen Engineers designed "a centralized, anaerobic leachate pretreatment facility" to treat the leachate generated from four landfills owned by Steuben County, New York. The leachate pretreatment facility was constructed and put in operation in February, 1989. The expected leachate quantities and organic strengths from these landfills are given in Table 1.

### LEACHATE PRETREATMENT FACILITY (LTF)

The Stueben County Leachate Treatment Facility is located in Mt. Washington near Bath, New York. The facility essentially consists of two treatment streams to be operated in parallel the majority of the time. However, when needed the facility can be operated in series to achieve greater organic removal rates.

The facility has the following provisions for each waste stream (see Figure 2):

- Influent storage tank

- Influent pumps and heat exchanger to convey the leachate to the top of the reactor;

- Above ground, insulated reactor and plastic media;

- Recycling pump and heat exchanger to maintain the process temperature;

- Effluent storage tank; and

- Chemical/nutrient feed pumps.

In addition, the LTF has a boiler room to provide the necessary heat to raise the temperature of the process liquid, a control room where the entire process is controlled and maintained through a computer system, and a small analytical laboratory to analyze the various parameters important to the process. Each treatment stream was designed to handle 10,000 gallons of leachate per day at a strength of 13,000 mg/L. As this treatment facility was designed based on the mass loading per unit volume, the organic strength of the influent is monitored and the volumetric loading of the leachate can be adjusted accordingly. Table 2 presents representative operating results of the pretreatment facility.

When there is a need for a full treatment of leachate, or any other liquid waste stream, a floating biological contactor, such as the unit described below, can be used for polishing or secondary treatment.

## "MONITOR" - A BRIDGE BETWEEN TWO BIOLOGICAL PROCESSES

Biological treatment of waste is becoming increasingly popular in the environmental cleanup industry. The following is a brief description of two principal methods of biological treatment processes and how they are being utilized in the latest bioremediation technology.

The success of any cleanup project can be maximized by retaining the highest possible concentration of "active biomass" (microorganisms) within a treatment system. The growth and activity of microorganisms depends on availability of food (contaminants), nutrients, maintenance of optimal operating parameters (pH, temperature, etc.), absence of inhibitory conditions, and minimization of loss/washout of microorganisms.

The typical concentration of microorganisms present in suspended growth processes varies from 1000 to 4000 mg/L as opposed to a range of 2,000 to 70,000 mg/L in attached growth processes. The suspended growth processes are, in general, more reliable when compared to attached growth processes.

In an attempt to increase the active biomass while incorporating the reliability of the suspended growth process, Larsen Engineers in conjunction with KLV Technologies is offering a treatment system known as a "Floating Biological Contactor," also known as "MONITOR" (see Figure 3). MONITOR is constructed on pontoons and is capable of floating in any water body. Contained within the superstructure beneath the water surface are hundreds of plastic webs which act as media to immobilize the biomass. MONITOR has the provision to supply the necessary air to sustain the microbiological activity.

MONITOR is ideally suited for the removal of nutrients (nitrogen) from polishing lagoons which are characteristic of many waste treatment plants. Additionally, MONITOR has the potential to be used in the bioremediation of hazardous waste sites. In this case the contaminants can be leached out of a contaminated soil matrix and the leachate conveyed to a dual containment structure. The MONITOR(S) can be floated in these containment structures and be inoculated with the appropriate bacterial strain to treat the leachate. The treated leachate can be sprayed back on the contaminated soil where it can be collected and further treated by MONITOR(S) in a closed loop system until the site is remediated. The ease of portability offers the flexibility for utilizing MONITOR(S) in a wide variety of applications.

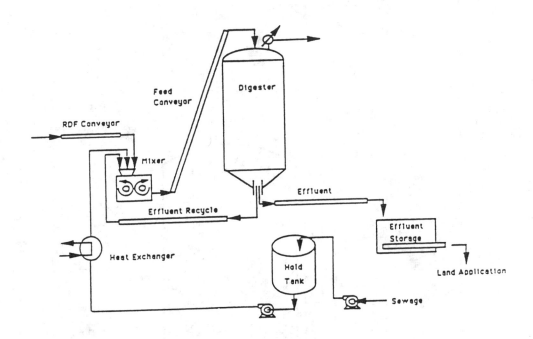

**FIGURE 1**

Anaerobic composting removes energy before a final aerobic curing step. Final product is sold to the public as natural organic fertilizer. In this system our garbage becomes the source for alternative energy production, helping our environment and solving our energy problems at the same time.

FIGURE 2

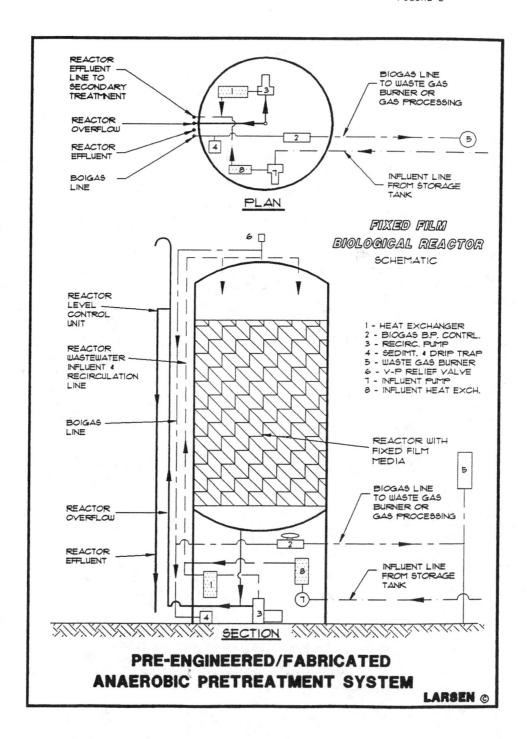

**PRE-ENGINEERED/FABRICATED
ANAEROBIC PRETREATMENT SYSTEM**

LARSEN ©

# M✷NITOR

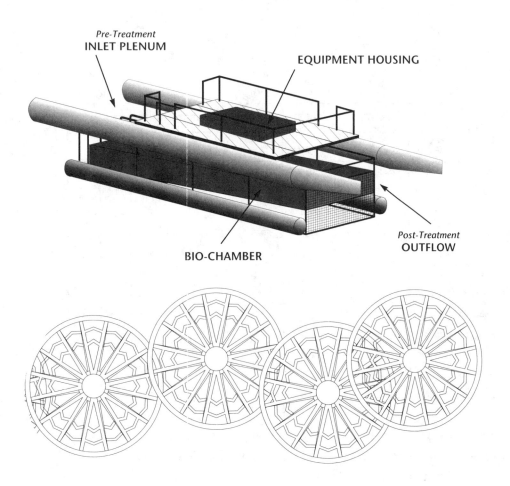

Pre-Treatment
**INLET PLENUM**

**EQUIPMENT HOUSING**

**BIO-CHAMBER**

Post-Treatment
**OUTFLOW**

## TABLE 1.  EXPECTED LEACHATE GENERATION FROM STEUBEN COUNTY LANDFILLS

| ORIGIN | ANNUAL LEACHATE GENERATION (M.GALS) | EXPECTED BOD (mg/L) |
|---|---|---|
| LINDLEY (NORTH) | 1.2 | 2000-15,000 |
| LINDELY (SOUTH) | 2.1 | 2,000 - 20,0000 |
| BATH (NEW) | 2.0 | 10-100 |
| BATH (OLD) | 0.8 | 2,000 - 25,000 |
| TOTAL | 6.0 TO 8.0 | |

## TABLE 2.  LEACHATE PRE-TREATMENT FACILITY OPERATING RESULTS

| MONTH | FLOW (GAL.) | COD (in) | COD (out) | % REMOVAL | ALKA. | VOLA. Acids | pH (in) | pH (out) | TSS (in) | TSS (out) |
|---|---|---|---|---|---|---|---|---|---|---|
| March 89 | 37,900 | 7369 | 1300 | 82.4 | 2172 | 148 | 6.87 | 7.1 | 612 | 652 |
| April 89 | 117,000 | 3036 | 522 | 82.8 | 2184 | 428 | 6.23 | 7.27 | 275 | 282 |
| May 89 | 241,000 | 5944 | 599 | 89.9 | 1814 | 149 | 6.22 | 7.75 | 375 | -- |
| June 89 | 222,500 | 10013 | 1014 | 89.8 | 2098 | 188 | 6.4 | 7.07 | -- | -- |
| July 89 | 255,500 | 10483 | 3699 | 64.7 | 1748 | 290 | 5.94 | 6.98 | -- | -- |
| August 89 | 172,000 | 17162 | 1772 | 89.6 | 2179 | 409 | 5.91 | 6.87 | -- | -- |
| September 89 | 117,000 | 13979 | 1683 | 87.9 | 2004 | 396 | 5.85 | 6.65 | -- | -- |
| October 89 | 180,000 | 13,600 | 3,450 | 74.6 | 1,804 | 1,076 | 6.16 | 6.99 | 312 | 276 |
| November 89 | 315,000 | 10,580 | 2,750 | 74.0 | 4,325 | 1,729 | 6.34 | 6.84 | -- | -- |
| December 89 | 170,000 | 12,419 | 2,707 | 78.2 | 2,238 | 1,044 | 6.29 | 6.99 | -- | -- |
| January 90 | 181,000 | 10,370 | 2,179 | 78.9 | 2,337 | 379 | 6.56 | 7.19 | 75 | 124 |
| February 90 | 294,000 | 7,504 | 1,229 | 83.6 | 2,200 | 138 | 6.5 | 7.09 | 290 | 318 |
| March 90 | 304,000 | 9,196 | 1,663 | 81.9 | 2,100 | 234 | 6.53 | 7.21 | -- | 289 |
| April 90 | 383,000 | 9,980 | 1,358 | 86.4 | 1,947 | 196 | 6.47 | 7.10 | -- | 432 |
| May 90 | 406,000 | 10,705 | 2,175 | 79.7 | 1,988 | 277 | 6.41 | 7.32 | -- | 181 |
| June 90 | 286,000 | 12,800 | 1,950 | 84.8 | 2,333 | 302 | 6.38 | 7.29 | -- | 432 |
| July 90 | 281,000 | 10,925 | 2,275 | 79.2 | -- | -- | 6.51 | 7.3 | -- | 139 |
| August 90 | 290,000 | 12,010 | 3,850 | 67.9 | 2.252 | 348 | 6.68 | 7.24 | -- | -- |

# Chapter 21

# Metrologic Analysis of Energy and Economic Growth Rate and Study of the Countermeasures in China

W.P. Zhong, Z. Yun, C.W. Lain, G.S. Kun

## Abstract

Coal output in China increased from 872mt in 1985 to 1080mt in 1990, representing an annual growthrate of 4.37%. As the biggest coal burning country, it gives out a large amount of $CO_2$ and other pollutants into air, resulting in serious air pollution and sharing a great part in creating the global greenhouse effect. On the other hand, China faces severe energy shortage. Coal will remain to be the most important energy resource for a long time. Using the method of econometrics, this paper analyses the relations between China's energy production, comsumption increase and national economic growth in the last forty years, makes comparisons with other countries, and points out problems of China's energy consumption increase and economic development. On this basis the strategy for developing China's energy industry is put forward. In the end, the authors advance that the leading posititon of energy industry in the national economy must be established and economic developing speed in China must be determined according to that of the energy industry, and China's national economy can then develop continuously, steadily and coordinately, Environment problems will become restrictive condition of china's energy developing strategy and technology choice.

## 一. Primary Energy Consumption and Envionment Protection Policy In China

A national energy Consumption structure depends on its resource, economy, society, and technical conditions. China is one of the few Countries in the world that depends mostly on coal for the energy consumption. In 1990, Coal accounted for 76.2% of the primary energy Comsumption. The Characteristics of energy Consumption in China are quite different from those of other countries in the world ( see Table 1)

According to the facts in China, the proved reserves of Coal acounted for 90% of the total proved energy reserves. In recent years, it is impossible for China to increase the specific gravity of oil and natural gas in primary energy consumption, Using coal as the main energy consumption will not be Changed in the following years. According to the forcasting method for energy demamds of Research Institute of Energy offiliated to the State Planning Commission, namely **MEDEE-S** Primary energy demamds forcasting modeling in China, and its demands Show in Table 2.

1. Although the specific gravity of Coal in primary energy consumption will decrease gradually, it will be the principal energy in China in the following 30 years. Coal will account for about 60% to the year 2015.

2. High-qualiy energy demands will be increased quickly. Starting from 1985 to 2015, oil, natural gas, and hydroelectricity will averagely increase by 5.24%, 7.393% and 5.70% a year respectively, and nuclear electricity also will increase by 12.69% from the period of 2000 to 2015.

3. High development of Hydroelectricity and nuclear electicity.

Table 2: Primary Energy Demands And Structure In China In 1985~2015

| | 1985 | | 2000 | | 2015 | |
|---|---|---|---|---|---|---|
| | Mtoe | % | Mtoe | % | Mtoe | % |
| Coal | 407.73 (816.83) | 77.98 | 724.70 (1450.57) | 71.03 | 1024.11 (2049.65) | 62.61 |
| Oil | 95.17 | 18.20 | 244.05 | 24.00 | 440.25 | 26.91 |
| Natural gas | 12.03 (129.30) | 2.38 | 27.92 | 2.74 | 115.51 (1241) | 7.06 |
| Hydroelectricity | 7.95 (92.4) | 1.52 | 28.64 (240.0) | 2.82 | 43.00 (500.0) | 2.63 |
| Nuclear electricity | | | 2.15 (25.0) | 0.21 | 12.90 (150.0) | 0.79 |
| Total | 522.88 | 100 | 1020.34 | 100 | 1635.77 | 100 |

Notes: The data in brackets are real number: Coal Mt, Natural gas Hurdred Million $M^3$ Hydroelectriciy TWH

In a word, energy structure in China will not be Changed thoroughly in recent 30 years. China is the greatest Coal consuming country in the world. Coal output in China increased from 872 Mt in 1985 to 1080Mt in 1990, averaging the annual increase rate of 4.37%. With the increasing of Coal consumption by large margin and rural population, effective measures must be adopted to protect against the urban atmospheric pollution due to a large amount of Coal burning and serious ecological damages, caused by excessive consumption of biomass energy in rural areas, otherwise the situation will be worse. in 1989

Coal burning emitted 14.4 Mt of $SO_2$ and 10.2Mt of particulates in China, accounting for 92% and 73% of total amount of emissions respectively. Economic losses due to air polluted by Coal burning was great

Perhaps the supreme potential risk is $CO_2$ emission

from Coal burning Which will cause the 'greenhusse effect' problem of global warm. If once signing an international Conventions, China will face the pressure of utilized Coal reduction caused by limitation of $CO_2$ emission. Therefore, the environmental will be the principal restrained conditions of prospective energy development Strategy and technological selections in China. As a developing country, China must take the responsibility for protecting environment and developing its economy. The Chinese Government attaches great importance to environmental protection and effect of energy on weather and environment. China carries out the basic policy such as laying equal emphasis on both exploitation and Conservation of energy, encouraging energy saving and improving the efficiency of energy utilization, developing clean energy. population Control, and plantation.

Table 1. Comparison of Primary energy Consumption in China betweem other conuntries 1990

| | China | USA | Soviet Union | Japan | Germany | Great Britain | France | World |
|---|---|---|---|---|---|---|---|---|
| Consumption Mtce Mix % | 987.8 | 2935.5 | 1902.8 | 667.7 | 494.8 | 382.6 | 381.2 | 11476.1 |
| Oil | 16.6 | 41.3 | 31.8 | 58.5 | 36.7 | 39.4 | 48.9 | 36.8 |
| Natural gas | 2.1 | 23.8 | 41.8 | 10.5 | 15.6 | 22.5 | 12.8 | 21.7 |
| Coal | 76.2 | 23.4 | 20.8 | 17.8 | 35.8 | 29.6 | 9.5 | 27.3 |
| Hydroelectricity | 5.1 | 3.6 | 6.8 | 4.3 | 0 | 0.7 | 8.3 | 6.7 |
| Nuclear electricity | | 7.6 | | 9.7 | 10.8 | 7.8 | 37.2 | 5.7 |
| Other | | 0.3 | 2.8 | | 1.9 | | 0.1 | |
| Total | 100.0 | 100.0 | 100.0 | 100.0 | 100.0 | 100.0 | 100.0 | 100.0 |

All of thess have made great progress, being in keeping with the international policy for weather and environmental protection.

二. Metrologic Analysis of Short Energy supply in China

Table 3: Companison of energy production and Consumption growth between national income

| | growth rate of energy produc-tion % | growth rate of electric power % | gorwth rate of energy con-sumption % | growth rate of electric power consumption % | growth rate of national income % | elasticity of energy production % | elasticity of elec-tric power production % | elastic-ity of ener-gy cons-umption % | elasticity of electric power consumpti-on % |
|---|---|---|---|---|---|---|---|---|---|
| 1953~1957 | 15.5 | 21.46 | 15.54 | 20.35 | 8.90 | 1.78 | 2.41 | 1.75 | 2.29 |
| 1958~1962 | 11.75 | 10.07 | 11.39 | 10.07 | -3.10 | | | | |
| 1963~1965 | 3.80 | 13.06 | 4.55 | 13.06 | 14.78 | 0.21 | 0.94 | 0.31 | 0.91 |
| 1966~1970 | 10.48 | 11.39 | 9.16 | 11.39 | 8.30 | 1026 | 1.37 | 1.10 | 1.37 |
| 1971~1975 | 9.49 | 11.06 | 9.17 | 11.06 | 5.50 | 1.73 | 2.01 | 1.67 | 2.01 |
| 1976~1980 | 5.51 | 8.95 | 5.82 | 8.95 | 6.10 | 0.90 | 1.47 | 0.95 | 1.47 |
| 1981~1985 | 6.86 | 6.44 | 4.93 | 6.68 | 10.8 | 0.61 | 0.64 | 0.49 | 0.65 |
| 1986~1988 | 3.85 | 9.90 | 6.64 | 9.91 | 9.70 | 0.40 | 1.02 | 0.68 | 1.02 |

Although energy industries in China had been developed rapidly at the average growth yate of more than 10 percent every year during the past 40 years, total primary energy production in 1988 increased 40.4 times that of in 1949, it has failed to keep up with the economic develpment. The metrologic analysis is as follows:

1. A low growth rate of energy production

In recent years, economy in China has developed rapidly, energy industries lagged behind processing industries due to their sharp development According to Calcuation of fixed price in 1988, growth rate of GNP was 11.2%, gross value of industrial output was increased by 20.7%, of which processing industries accounted for 23%, rural industry accounted for 35%, but primary energy production was increased by 4.4%. comparison between energy production and consumption growth and national economic growth, we can find that the growth rate of national income was higher than energy production. (see Table 3)

2. Low Elasticity Of Primary Energy In China

In order to develop national economy coordinately, the energy production elasticity of developing countries should be more than 1 and electric energy elasticity should be approached to 1.5 according to most specialists opinions and experiences in development of internationl economy. Starting from 1977 to 1987, the elasticity of the electric energy production of HONGKONG and TAIWAN were 1.36 and 1.23 respectively so as to ensure to develop economy. The elasticity of electric energy production of the United States was more than 2.0 during the period from 1920 to 1980. The forcast from International Energy Conference shows that the elasticities of principal energy and electric energy for developing countries will be 1.0 to 1.04 and 1.30~1.37 respectively during the period from 2001 to 2020 (see Table 4).

Table 4 Growth prediction of energy production for developing countries (except middle East)

| years | growth rate of total output value △GNP% | growth rate of principal energy △E% | growth rate of electric energy △ELEC% | $\frac{\triangle E}{\triangle GNP}$ | $\frac{\triangle ELEC}{\triangle GNP}$ |
|---|---|---|---|---|---|
| 1972~2000 | 3.8~5.8 | 3.0~4.0 | 5.5~6.0 | 0.8 | 1.46~1.36 |
| 2001~2020 | 3.5~4.6 | 3.5~4.8 | 4.8~6.0 | 1.0~1.04 | 1.37~1.30 |

in the Sixth Five-year Plan (1980 to 1985), the elastictity of primary energy and electric energy in China were 0.54 and 0.58 respectively (see Table5).

Table 5 Growth rate and elasticity of energy production in China

| years | annual growth of gross output value of industry and agriculture % | annual growth rate of primary energy % | annual growth rate of electricity % | elasticity of primary energy | elasticity of electricity |
|---|---|---|---|---|---|
| 1981~1985 | 11.0 | 6.0 | 6.44 | 0.54 | 0.58 |
| 1986~1988 | 13.0 | 3.9 | 9.91 | 0.30 | 0.76 |

These showed that the growth rate of energy production in China lagged behind in its economic development, particularly electrie power was wery short. Since the Seventh Five—year Plan, the growth rate of primary energy decreased obviously, an annual growth rate of primary energy in 1986 to 1988 was 3.9%, and the elasticity of primary energy production has been dropped to 0.30, Although the percentage of electric power has rised to some extent, averaging out to 9.91% than 1. As a result, energy supply fell short of demand in China.

3. Electric power Shortage Caused By Uncoordinated Proportion Of Electricity Consuming Equipment

The statistics of electric power sector shows as fallows:

In 1980 elecricity consumption fell Short of 40 TWH due to 10 GW of installed capacity Shortage of power generating equipment in China.

In 1986 elecricity Consumption also fell short of 70 TWH caused by 15 GW of installed capacity Shortage of power generating equipment in China.

Owing to the blind development of processing industries, the proportion between power generating and electricity consuming equipment was very uncoordinated, Power generating and electricity Consuming equipment has been in proportion as 1:2.4 for long time (see Table 6)

Table 6 The proportion of power generating and electricity consuming equipment

| year | capacity of generating equipment 10⁴KW | capacity of electricity consuming equipment 10⁴KW | proportion of capacity of power and electricity consuming |
|---|---|---|---|
| 1980 | 6587 | 15248 | 1:2.31 |
| 1981 | 6900 | 16041 | 1:2.32 |
| 1982 | 7236 | 17240 | 1:2.38 |
| 1983 | 7644 | 18635 | 1:2.44 |
| 1984 | 8012 | 19846 | 1:2.48 |
| 1985 | 8705 | 21258 | 1:2.44 |
| 1986 | 9382 | 23411 | 1:2.50 |
| 1987 | 10290 | 26095 | 1:2.54 |
| 1988 | 11550 | 28596 | 1:2.48 |

Power generating and electricity consuming equipment in China should be in proportion as 1:2 from its experience. According to this proportion newly installed electricity consuming equipment was about 25.69 GW during the period from 1986 to 1988, in other words, one third of these equipment has no power generaation Capacity to supply power. In recent years, installed capacties of power generating

units in China have been increasing year after year but electricity consuming equipment has also been increasing sharply. These newly installed power generating Capacities could not alleviate shortfall in power supply and would not meet the demands for newly installed electricity consuming equipment, thus causing in rather short power supply. The Ministry of Energy estimated that 20—30 percent of industrial production capacities could not bring into play to operation, in other words. 20—30 percent of gross value of industrial output have been suffered a loss, thus gross national product lost about 1700—2500 handred million yuan a year by it.

4. The Growth Of Coal Consumption Exceeds That Of Coal Producion In China And The Reasion Of Electricity Shortage Will Mainly Be Shortfall In Coal Supply In The Future.

Coal shortage is the source of shortfall in energy supply because Coal accounted for more than 70% of the primary energy consumption. The main pressure of Coal demands Comes from thermal power Stations, at the present time more than 70% of power stations fuel Coal, accounting for about 25% of annual coal production.

The total Capital construction investment of energy industires can be found that investment for electric industry was higher than coal industry. That is to say that the demands of Coal burning power generation will increase steeply (see Table 7).

Table 7 The growth of coal for power generation unit: MT

| year | coal output | increase over las year | power station coal | increase over last year | newly installed power-station coal accounting for the in crease incoal output |
|---|---|---|---|---|---|
| 1981 | 621.63 | | 123.81 | | |
| 1982 | 666.32 | 44.69 | 134.27 | 18.46 | 23.3 |
| 1983 | 714.53 | 48.21 | 143.11 | 8.84 | 18.8 |
| 1984 | 789.24 | 74.87 | 162.87 | 18.96 | 25.6 |
| 1985 | 872.28 | 83.05 | 174.96 | 12.09 | 15.5 |
| 1986 | 894.04 | 21.76 | 195.92 | 20.96 | 96.3 |
| 1987 | 928.89 | 34.85 | 221.96 | 26.04 | 76.5 |

159 medium and large—sized thermal power station constructed in 1988 and 2.07 hundred million tons of coal will be increased for power generation. 11.5 hundred million tons of raw coal output will be planned in 1995, and 1.8 hundred million tons of coal output will be increased over 9.7 hundred million tons of coal in 1988, in other words, Coal burning for power generation will account for 87% of the increase in coal output. Evidently it is difficut to meet coal burning for power generation.

5. Inadequate Investment Of Energy, Large Population And Lower Percapita Energy In China.

Overseas countries attach great importance to investment of principal energy sector which is the concentrated funds.

According to relevant data, investment of principal energy sector in other developing countries generally accounted for 20% of the total investment, and investment of power generation sector in the USA was 10% in 1989 and 1990, investment of prinicpal energy sector in China respectively accounted for 14.9% and 15.4% of the total national investment, Energy industries failed to be suited to development of national economy by reason of insufficient investment of energy, with a large population and lower percapita energy consumption. In 1989, percapita energy consumption was 0.9 tce(0.9toa of coal equwalent) and percapita installed capacity of electric generator was 0.1 **KW**, the former was inferior to 1/15 the latter approached 1/28 of the two in the USA. One can find in Table 8 that percapita energy consumming level in China is low, While the potentialities of the demands will be great.

Table 8: Percapita principal energy consumption and installed capacity of electric generator in 1989

| comparison | China | USA | Japan | HongKong | Taiwan |
|---|---|---|---|---|---|
| percapita principal energy consumption tce | 0.9 | 13.8 | 5.7 | 2.4 | |
| percapita installed capacity of electric generator KW | 0.1 | 2.87 | 1.53 | 1.32 | 0.28 |

6. Low Efficiency Of Energy Utilization And High Energy Squander in China

The total energy consumption of the unit gross national product in China is among the highest in the world. Comparing with other countries and regions in the world, 3 tce(3 tons of coal equivalent) and 1780 KW of electricity are consumed for produce of 1000 USD worth gross national product, or 3.95 times and 2.97 times respectively that with advanced world levels, energy consumption of maijor industrial products is very high, e.g. 32% higher for thermal power generation, 40%for rolled steel, 66% for cement, 45% for plate glass, 83% for synlhetic ammonia, and 38% for paper. The high energy consumption is a major cause for short energy supply in China and also a huge potential for energy conservation.

Table 9: Efficiencises of principal energy utilization of countries 1989

| | t. c. e $1000GNP | KWh $1000GNP |
|---|---|---|
| China | 3.00 | 1780 |
| Japan | 0.35 | 420 |
| United states | 0.76 | 600 |
| Hongkong | 0.38 | 600 |

三. The Problems Concerned Growth Of Energy Consumption And Economy

1. In accordance with specific conditions principal energy in China is shorter, and raw oil reserves is conparative limit. coal hydroelectricity and power supply are very far from the major induslrial bases and transportation price is much high.

2. Energy Prices Are Low. The Low Energy Prices Leads Energy Industries To Have Poor Capacity Of Self—Acumulation and Self—development And Are Unfavourable For Develping Energy Conservation And Improving Efficiency Of Energy Utilization.

3. Principal Energy Needs To Support Social Daily and Burden Of energy Supply Is Very Heavy due To Low Efficiency Of Energy Utilization And Serious Squander With Large Population. In Rural Area There Are Still Short Electricity Supply; And The Consequences Are Very Serious.

4. By the Year 2000, The Total Coal Consumption In Proportion To Energy Mix Will Be High. The Effect Of Coal Burning On Atmospheric Pollution, Acid Rain and Damages Of Ecology, Lakes, Forests, And Social Environment Is Very Great And Economic Paid Are Very High.

5. Owing to low long — term investment energy industries, they are uncoordinated to develop national economy. This will restrict Inevitably the development of the national economy in China.

四. Strategical Suggestion

1. To establish an important place of enerngy in the national economy. The rate of energy development should be taken into consideration when the medium and long — term development programmes of the national economy will be worked out, so as to determine the rate of the national economy. Economic development pla will be arranged on the basis of accurately evaluated quantity of energy avaible for supply particularly overall balance for coal, electricity and transportation.

2. To put into effect the Preferential policy for energy, getting raise in proportion of investments for energy, and increasing input for energy industries, The proportion of government invesment for energy increasing should be higher than societywide fied investmants so as to ensure energy industries to be suitable for the development of the national economy. Internal capital arrangement in energy industries must be overall planning, thus development of coal and electric industries will be well coordinated, Every effort is made to quicken to increase workable reserves by adding investment of exploration of petroleum and natural gas, so as to provide the development of oil and gas industry.

3. Great efforts are made to improving energy structure and rational distribution, to develop hydropower generation, and to exploit petroloum and natural gas resources. Nuclear power station will be constructed safely. And various kinds of new energy districts.

4. Energy prices should be rationalized. Reform of

energy prices will take as the basis of the whole price reforms. Energy prices should be readjusted step by step. The price readjustment will make up for consumption gradually, paying bank loans, and reaching a fairly high level for profit. As a result, enterprises in energy sectors are ability for own profit and loss responsibility and self—development

This is determined upon the cradical place of energy in the national economy and its present unfair prices in the whole price system.

5. In Process of the growth of economic development of developing countries, the elasticity of electric energy will approach1.5 appropirately. China is now under the initial stage of industriatization electric energy must develop in advance. The rate of electric power development will be high than that of economic development, so as to effectively promote economic development. Elasticity of electricity should be more than 1. So this will be an important target of the long—term programme, five — year plan and macro cntrol. While restricting the rate of electricity consuming equipment, proportion of installed capacity of power generation unit will be fair.

6. To pay qeual ettention to both exploition and conservation of energy. The stable medium and long — term strategies and programmes suited to the actual conditions for energy development will be planned out. Energy development will be on the basis of coal with electricity as center. Energy prodution and utilization efficiency should be improving by relying on technologic progress. Energy Conservation will be encouraged and chosen as the state policy. In order to promote energy saving technical innovation, its investment will be increased by large margin.

7. To Develop Commerial Coal The Chinese Grovernment will energetically develop coal washing, processing and utilization of coal and low BTU fuels. New technologies for processing and utilizaton of coal particularly gasification, being easy of centralized desulfurization and denitrification. In order to put an end to the urban atmospheric pollution due to a large amount of coal burning and malignant eclogical cycle caused by excessive consumption of biomas energy in rural areas, a policy of restricted coal direct combustion should be adopted progressively.

8. To increase specific gravity of coal Converted to electricity. In the domestic total coal consumption, the present specific gravity of coal converted to secondary energy ( electricity, gas and coking coal) is about 35%, of which electricity accounts for 23%, Corresponding figur for the United States accounts for 86%. Efficiency of coal utilization will be improved, and pollutant emissions will be easy of centralired control and treatment, and $CO_2$ emissions will be reduced by increasing specific gravity of coal converted to electricity.

The author: Wei Ping Zong,
Address:     Research Institute of Economy
             The Central Coal Mining Research
             Institute Hepingli,  Beijing
             The People's Republic of China
Tel:         (01)4214931Ext.; 808
Fax          (01)4219234
Cable:       4282 Beijing
Telex:       22504 CCMRI CN
The authors: Zhang Yun  Chen Wenlain   Gao Shu Kun
Address:     Pingdingshan Coal mining Administration
Tel:         (0375)222212
Fax:         (0375)23462

# SECTION 2
# DEMAND-SIDE MANAGEMENT

# Chapter 22
# The Common Denominator between DSM and Power Quality

G. Porter

A key focus of every demand side management (DSM) program in the U.S. today is efficiency improvement. This is a radically different approach from the push made in the late 1970's when conservation meant cutting back on use or sacrificing performance and function. Today, conservation simply means doing the same thing, or even more, with less energy. DSM does not mean shivering with the lights off, it means using ultra-high efficiency lighting, heating, and cooling equipment that not only keeps our environments comfortable but our electric bills low.

The reason all this is now possible is due to the advances in technology that have occurred since the 1970's. And the key to these advances is a family of devices called power electronics. However, these new technologies, and the power electronics inside, use power differently, resulting in a sensitivity to power abnormalities.

Does this mean our global push for efficiency improvement is also exacerbating the power quality problem? Possibly. But only if we don't understand why it's happening and fail to do something to prevent it.

Something for Nothing?

Demand side management techniques, or efficiency improvements, fall into three categories: low technologies, controls and new technologies. Low technology includes using water heater wraps, installing low flow shower heads, repairing malfunctioning equipment, and eliminating wasteful techniques.

The second technique, controls, can greatly improve the operation of air compressors, assist in load control strategies, perform energy management functions and perform complex optimizing functions.

The final technique, new technologies, holds the greatest promise for DSM because the benefits are not subject to personal whim and generally persist, even if the property changes hands. New technologies are employed in thousands of new end-uses from light dimmers to permanent magnet motors. Although most DSM programs rely on the long term contributions of devices like high frequency ballasts, some end-uses can illuminate the issues surrounding power quality.

The enabling technology that has made all these advances possible is power electronics. Our bulk 60 Hz power, which was designed for powering lights and motors, has limited versatility, in and of itself. In the last couple of decades we have been looking for ways to alter it to make it more closely match end-use needs by turning in into d.c, raising the frequency, and varying the frequency.

A family of devices called power electronics (electronic devices that can switch power on and off at high speeds), along with new circuit topologies, have made all this possible. They are in large part responsible for today's motor drives, compact power supplies, grid interfaces for solar cells and wind power, UPS systems, induction heating systems, microwave ovens, and high frequency lighting. They will also be the necessary ingredient for future efficiency advances such as the electric vehicle and fuel cells.

As the number of ways to improve efficiency using power electronics increases, so do the number of ways they impact the electric supply system. The old adage, "you don't get something for nothing" truly applies in the case of improving efficiency. The "something" you get is sensitivity to power abnormalities, as well as the possible corruption of the power line. Cases abound where companies install adjustable speed drives to save energy and then experience wide scale shutdowns every morning at 6:05 am when the utility company automatically corrects for power factor. And just as common are the cases where large drives, installed for efficiency reasons, interfere with the operation of neighboring businesses.

Today's DSM Needs Technology

The flagship DSM program of virtually every utility company is lighting. In the Commercial sector alone, lighting accounts for as much as 25% of the total energy consumed. But technologies exist to easily cut that figure by half or even three-quarters. There are several reasons why such large improvements are possible: advances in fluorescent bulbs, improvements in fixtures, and application of power electronics in the ballasts. Of the total possible improvement, bulbs may account for 15%. High frequency electronic ballasts can cut power by half compared to magnetic ballasts. And new reflectors and fixtures, if applied properly, can reduce the total number of bulbs needed.

115

Bulbs and fixtures do not affect power quality but ballasts may. Some of the first types of electronic ballasts that showed up in the market at the beginning of the "DSM Era" had great performance but distorted the sign-wave so much they created harmonics with THD in the 60-80+ range. Many of the recent products have resolved the harmonics issue but others haven't and it's important to check.

The second element of most utilities' programs is generally "motors and drives." Although there are some important advances in motors on the horizon (Variable Reluctance, Brushless Doubly Fed, Permanent Magnet), the primary efficiency improvement in today's motor market is created by high efficiency motors. They can result in improvements in the 2-6 % range, depending on horsepower and speed. It is important to note, however, that these improvements are considered "low tech" since they require only bulk 60 Hz power.

Drives, on the other hand, offer a high tech approach to ensuring that the motor uses only enough power to meet the needs of the application. Traditional speed controls use mechanical equipment to alter speeds and flows. ASDs actual alter nature of the energy going to the motor to accomplish the necessary tasks. ASDs can be excellent retrofit candidates in pumping, HVAC, and process systems. Not every motor in use, however, is a candidate for speed control, but many of the large process motors in use today are unnecessarily running at full power.

Switching Power is the Key

The 60 Hz power flowing on the power lines of the U.S. can be used directly for turning motors and lighting incandescent lamps but must be converted to other forms for use by computers, welders and microwave ovens. Comparing bulk 60Hz power to the high frequency power found inside switched-mode power supplies is like comparing rough-sawn logs to the versatility of 2x4's. If the job at hand is to build a house, both the log and the 2x4 can do the task, it's just so much easier and less wasteful to use 2x4's. The parallels in this illustration point out why the designers of today's end-uses have chosen power electronics -- the electric industry's 2x4's -- as an essential part of the system. They're smaller, less expensive, more functional, and much more efficient than the alternative of mechanically altering bulk power.

Devices such as the Power MOSFET and IGBT can switch a dc power source on and off with enough efficiency that they can create high-frequency power in a very small package. The benefit of this feat is the size of power supplies can be greatly reduced because transformers can be much smaller at high frequencies than at 60 cycle. Being able to switch off and on at any frequency also makes it possible to supply a motor with a smooth sine-wave and any frequency, including 60 Hz.

Even though power electronics devices, with their high-frequency switching capabilities, are needed to produce a.c. from d.c. (invertor section), it's still traditional semiconductor devices like Thyristers and SCR's that convert 60 Hz power into a d.c. voltage (rectifier section). Figure 1 shows a block diagram for a typical variable frequency drive. Figure 2 shows the block diagram for a switched-mode d.c. power supply. Both of these devices use rectifier bridges that 1) lie exposed to all of the transients on the power delivery system and 2) draw a very non-linear current from the source. This means they're not only sensitive to activity on the power delivery system but also require some type of mitigation device. Luckily, most of today's power supplies are equipped with some sort of varister (MOV) to help mitigate transients.

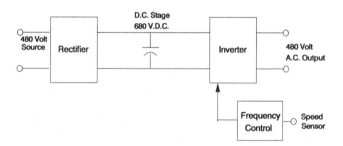

FIGURE 1. BLOCK DIAGRAM OF VARIABLE FREQUENCY DRIVE

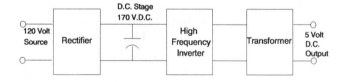

FIGURE 2. BLOCK DIAGRAM OF SWITCHED-MODE POWER SUPPLY

Why are DSM Devices so Sensitive?

As DSM programs around the world put more and more emphasis on using efficient technologies -- and nations put more emphasis on alternative energy sources (i.e. wind ,solar, fuel cells) -- we all need to ensure new products are designed with a couple of ideas in mind. First, knowing the importance of power electronics, designers must account for the reality that these devices are just semi-conductors, subject to all sorts of hazards like static electricity, lightning and switching transients. Secondly, when our end-use products become dependent upon "intelligent" power, failure of even a small internal device becomes critical. Serviceability and backup will become extremely important power quality issues.

In addition to changing power into a variety of forms, most drives and power supplies are also intelligent and have the capability to protect themselves from the myriad of power quality abnormalities by quickly shutting themselves down. This "watchdog" function is one important method of protecting critical components. The trick here is to set the threshold for the shutdown at the proper level -- one that protects the equipment from damage but doesn't interrupt productive use every time minor events occur.

Devices are also sensitive to the non-linear voltages created by the non-linear currents from large, neighboring devices. This phenomenon generally occurs with large drives that use a substantial portion of the facility's power; however, smaller drives located in close proximity to many others can cause interference too. Also, harmonic generating devices may resonate with on-site capacitors, resulting in nuisance trips on breakers and overheating of distribution equipment such as transformers.

## Sensitive to What?

Table 1 is a matrix showing some of the typical power abnormalities and how various DSM products react to them. Some of the abnormalities are common to every one of the products - high-energy transients, grounding and overvoltage. This reflects the fact that all of these devices have semiconductors inside them and require that the wiring, and especially the grounding, be installed correctly and in good repair.

| DSM Products | POWER ABNORMALITIES | | | | | | |
|---|---|---|---|---|---|---|---|
| | High-Frequency, High-Energy Transients | Low Frequency Capacitor Switching Overvoltage | Momentary Sags (3-30 cycle) | Outages (>30 seconds) | Harmonics | Grounding & Wiring | Momentary Overvoltage >140 volts |
| Lighting Ballasts | D | | | | S | N,D | D |
| Adj. Speed Drives | D | N | R | B | | N,D | D |
| High Efficiency Motors | D | | | | S | | |
| Variable Speed Heat Pumps | D | N | R | B | S | N,D | D |
| Load Controllers | D | N | R | B | | N,D | D |
| Dispatch Systems | D | N | R | B | | N,D | D |

N - nuisance    S - a source of the problem    R - ride through needed
D - damage possible    B - backup may be needed

TABLE 1. POWER ABNORMALITIES AND THEIR EFFECTS ON DSM PRODUCTS

Other abnormalities, such as momentary dropouts and transient overvoltages from capacitor switching, are generally problems only for drives that utilize watchdog circuits to help protect internal components from the external world. The degree of sensitivity of the watchdog is a function of the designer's perception of what abnormalities the product might experience in the real world. Some devices shut down for voltage sags of 10% that may last for only 5 cycles. Others recognize that momentary dips occur frequently, even on the best of electrical distribution systems, and provide ride-through in the range of 60% for 30 cycles. The criteria for evaluating which set specifications are needed for a given application must be looked at carefully to ensure that critical processes are protected and also nuisance tripping is minimized.

## Solutions to Potential Problems

Luckily, for every power quality problem there is a proven solution. On the other side of the equation, however, is the fact that these solutions are generally not free, and some are extremely expensive. Although it's doubtful the cost of mitigation devices and techniques will ruin the cost-effectiveness of a utility's DSM efforts, they are costs, nonetheless, that must be included. And including the costs is a step that must be taken to ensure that the DSM programs are received successfully.

The solutions include:
1. Correcting the wiring and grounding mistakes
2. Transient voltage surge suppressor (TVSS)
3. In-line reactors (chokes) for ASD's
4. Energy Storage devices on critical applications
5. Harmonic filters for large variable speed drive applications
6. Tuned filters to eliminate resonance
7. EMI/RFI shielding
8. Low impedance isolating transformers

## Conclusion

As utilities implement programs to push for energy efficiency, one of the results may be an increased population of end-uses that have a propensity to be sensitive to power delivery abnormalities. Some may view this as the price we have to pay for increasing the functionality of bulk 60 Hz power. Others may view this as a good reason to stay away from DSM. The utility industry **must** view this situation as an important element of their DSM planning and reflect the costs of mitigating potential power quality problems in the overall program.

Power quality mitigation costs will not drastically add much to the total DSM bill, but the costs of poor power quality could definitely negate the positive benefits of new technologies. Failure to properly plan for the sensitivities of energy efficient equipment will be a major mistake considering the solutions are fairly well known. Proper understanding, education, design, and protection, using a systems approach to problem solving, will ensure that power quality problems won't force us to abandon beneficial efficiency improvement programs.

# Chapter 23
# The Likely Market Potential for Electricity Saving ASD Devices

F.T. Sparow, L. McKenzie

Many utility demand-side management (DSM) programs encourage the adoption of adjustable speed drives (ASD) in the industrial and commercial sectors, since such devices save KW and KWh.

The term "adjustable speed drives" is used to refer to any device which allows the speed of the motor to be adjusted to better match process requirements. Thus, motor input control devices, such as electronic adjustable speed drives for AC motors (i.e., adjustable frequency drives (AFD)), voltage controlled DC motors, and the use of floating pressure setpoint controls, or other devices which better control on/off compressor operation, would be considered ASD devices. Also included would be motor technologies, such as multi-speed windings, etc., which allow the synchronous speed of the motor to be altered. Not included in this definition would be mechanical systems such as gear boxes, friction disks, etc., which maintain motor speed, but alter the drive r.p.m. to the equipment. The importance of the distinction is that ASDs, as defined above, have the potential to substantially reduce KW and KWh consumption if the equipment duty cycle is varying, while mechanical drive r.p.m. varying devices don't.

Utilities are offering as an inducement substantial rebates on the cost of electricity saving ASD devices, finding it cheaper to subsidize the resultant reductions in electricity use than to construct new, more expensive generating capacity.

Table 1 shows the subsidy offered for electricity saving ASD devices by a representative capacity constrained utility. Such incentives are bound to accelerate the pace of ASD introduction into electricity user power systems.

What fraction of electricity demand in the industrial sector can be expected to be met by motors equipped with adjustable speed drives of any type, and what electricity savings can be expected from such installations?

Table 2 summarizes the results of recent studies which relate to the problem. Those interested in estimates of likely ASD market shares of total industrial demand will be interested in column (6); those with interests in the estimates of the KWh likely to be saved by ASDs will be interested in column (8).

The market share estimates in column (6) are of two types:

(i) The maximum technical potential for ASDs expressed as a percent of sales -- i.e., the share of the electricity use market that would be served by ASDs if they were installed in every application where they were feasible, regardless of economics. This estimate is of little value to anyone except "true believers" in energy conservation. Such estimates in the table will have "100%" entries in column (5).

(ii) The maximum economic potential -- e.g., the percent of total electricity use where ASD can be expected to economically serve industrial demand. Such estimates will have market penetration estimates less than 100 percent in column (5). Market penetration estimates range from less than 1 percent in the early years up to 40 percent by early next century, with electricity savings ranging from a fraction of a percent in the early years up to above 2 percent early in the next century.

Table 1. ASD Rebates [1], [2].

| Motor Size | Rebate Amount | | Typical Installed Cost/HP for AFD |
|---|---|---|---|
| Up to 30 HP | $160/HP | motors in use | 900–1400 |
| 31–60 HP | $140/HP | more than | 650–900 |
| 61 HP and above | $125/HP | 5,000 hours/year | 170–650 (up to 2500 HP) |
| All motors | $100/HP | less than 5,000 hours/year | |

Table 2.  Summary of ASD Market Share and Conservation Impact Studies.

| Study (date) and scope | (1) Year of Forecast | (2) Total KWh x $10^9$ | (3) Motor % | (4) % ASD Possible | (5) % Market Penetration | (6) % Market (3)x(4)x(5) | (7) Avg. % Savings | (8) Savings KWh x $10^9$ (% of (2)) |
|---|---|---|---|---|---|---|---|---|
| EM 4527 (1988) (National) | 1980 | 717 | 67 | 100 | 3-6 | 2-4 | 25 | 5.1 (.7%) |
|  | 1985 | 728 | 67 | 100 | 8-14 | 5-9 | 25 | 14.7 (2.02%) |
| Comment:  This study was to estimate existing penetration. | | | | | | | | |
| NYS ERDA (1988) (New York State) | 1986 | 20.364 | 77.7 | 100 | 100 | 77 | 22.5 | 3.56 (17.48%) |
| Lovins (1989) (National) | 1987 | 890 | 68-78 | 50 | 100 | 34-39 | 20-45 | 61-157 (6.8-17.6%) |
| Comment:  Both of the above studies are technical potential estimates. | | | | | | | | |
| Mich. Options (1988) (Michigan) | 1995 | 30.212 | 72 | 33-94 | 23-27 | 5-18 | 24-27 | .218-.247 (.72-.82%) |
|  | 2005 | 33.549 | 72 | 33-94 | 39-63 | 9-43 | 24-27 | .289-.469 (1.2-1.95%) |
| Comment:  Uses SIC specific end use, motor size, and variable load %. | | | | | | | | |
| PEAC (1988) | 1987 |  |  | 50-60 |  |  | 25 | 150,000 units sold |
| Comment:  Makes important point that "vast majority of ASD products 50 HP and below are coming from off-shore manufacturers." | | | | | | | | |
| CU-6746 (1990) | 1987 | 845 | 67 | 100 | 100 | 67 | 25-35 implied | 141-198 implied (17-23%) |
| (National) | 2000 | 1167 | 67 | 100 | 100 | 67 | 25-35 implied | 195-274 implied (17-23%) |
| Comment: Study lumps high efficiency motors and ASD; above are implied amounts for ASD; technical potential only. | | | | | | | | |
| CU-6953 (1990) (National) | 1990 | 987 | 67 | 100 | 1 | .7 | 25 implied | 2.31 (.23%) |
|  | 2000 | 1241 | 67 | 100 | 9.8 | 6.6 | 25 implied | 28.46 (2.29%) |
| PNL-5665 (1986) | 1995 | 1110 | ? | motors>50HP | 20 | ? | 57-156 (a) | 34 (3.06%) |
|  | 2000 | 1213 | ? | motors>50 HP | 20 | ? | 57-156 (a) | 51 (4.2%) |
| Comment:  Projects % new motors installed that are ASD; database not motor population, but US DOC estimates of new motor sales! | | | | | | | | |
| Baldwin (1989) | 1986 | 200,000 ASDs sold in 1986 | | | | | | |
| Comments:  Not a forecast; makes important point that 10-15% torque derate when retrofit with ASD, 2% increase in motor kwh because of harmonics. | | | | | | | | |

(a)     x $10^3$ KWh/motor.

[EM 4527]    Resource Dynamics Corp., "Electrotechnology Reference Guide," EPRI EM-4527, Revision 1, Vienna, VA, August 1988.

[NYS ERDA]    New York State Energy Research and Development Authority, "The Potential for Electricity Conservation in New York State," Energy Authority Report 89-12, Albany, NY, September 1989.

[Mich. Options]    Battelle Memorial Institute, "Industrial Sector Energy Analyses and Audits.  Volume 1: Project Summary and Recommendations to Michigan Electricity Options Study," Columbus, OH, January 21, 1988.

[PEAC]    Giesecke, A.B., and See, C.S., "The U.S. Market Opportunity for Adjustable Speed Drives: A Scoping Study," EPRI Power Electronics Applications Center (PEAC), Research Report No. PEAC.0014R, Knoxville, TN, September 1988.

[CU-6746]    Barakat & Chamberlin, Inc., "Efficient Electricity Use:  Estimates of Maximum Energy Savings," EPRI CU-6746, Oakland, CA, March 1990.

[CU-6953]    Barakat & Chamberlin, Inc., "Impact of Demand-Side Management on Future Customer Electricity Demand:  An Update," EPRI CU-6953, Oakland, CA, August 1990.

[PNL 5665]    Pacific Northwest Laboratory, "The Electric Energy Savings from New Technologies," PNL-5665, Rev. 1, UC-95, Richland, WA, September 1986.

[Baldwin]    Baldwin, Samuel F., "Energy-Efficient Electric Motor Drive Systems," in  Electricity, Efficient End-Use and New Generation Technologies, and Their Planning Implications, Thomas B. Johansson, Birgit Bodlund, and Robert H. Williams, Editors, Lund University Press, Lund, Sweden, 1989.

[Lovins]    Lovins, Amory B., "The State of the Art: Drivepower," Rocky Mountain Institute, Snowmass, CO, April 1989.

How are these estimates created? Most follow the following sequence. Estimate, by Standard Industrial Classification (SIC):

(a) the fraction of KWh use consumed by motors;

(b) the fraction of motor use where it is likely to be technically feasible to use ASDs;

(c) the likely maximum market penetration into this technical market potential, given the installed cost of ASD devices, and the likely yearly energy and other savings which would be associated with their introduction. The product of the percentage estimates in steps (a), (b), and (c) yield the likely market potential for ASDs; and

(d) the likely electricity savings that would result if this market share were captured by ASD devices is obtained by multiplying the total KWh sales by the market potential, and then multiplying that by the likely percent KWh savings associated with introducing ASD devices.

Each step in the sequence will be discussed, and options presented for likely values.

### Percent of KWh Use in Motors

Several estimates, by two-digit SIC, are available:

(a) The estimates contained in Table 4-6 of EPRI report EM-4527, revision 1, prepared by the Resource Dynamics Corporation, shown in column (1) of Table 3.

(b) Estimates contained in Table 1-18 of the Industrial Sector Analysis report in the Michigan Electricity Options Study prepared by Battelle Memorial Institute, shown in column (2) of Table 3.

(c) Four-digit SIC estimates contained in the IMIS database prepared by Battelle for use by EPRI members, which were used with some additional assumptions as to the fractions of end use provided by motors to estimate motor use for a major utility.

(d) The mother of all these estimates, contained in the 1980 ADL study [3].

The problem with this and all other data presented at the two-digit level is that (a) they are not independent estimates, and (b) the two-digit level of aggregation is simply not detailed enough to be anything but "best guesses." KWh weighted sums of four-digit SIC electricity end-use data have some chance of reflecting the actual distribution, but even here problems arise, since most four-digit electricity end-use estimates are based on plant manager estimates, and not on metered electricity end-use.

If a way could be found to organize and summarize the wealth of establishment energy end-use data collected during the energy audits conducted by utilities and the federal and state governments over the past 15 years, these estimates could certainly be improved. Lacking such data, the estimates given in Table 3 must suffice to define the range of possible values for motor use share by two-digit SIC.

Table 3. Motor Use as a Percent of Total Use.

| SIC | STUDY | | | |
|---|---|---|---|---|
| | EM-4527 | Michigan Options | Battelle | ADL |
| 20 | 87 | 80 | 87 | 81 |
| 21 | 75 | - | - | 73 |
| 22 | 81 | 88 | 71 | 79 |
| 23 | 72 | 90 | 86 | 73 |
| 24 | 89 | 91 | 74 | 74 |
| 25 | 76 | 80 | 76 | 74 |
| 26 | 89 | 89 | 94 | 81 |
| 27 | 68 | 85 | 68 | 73 |
| 28 | 65 | 84 | 39 | 83 |
| 29 | 92 | 88 | 88 | 83 |
| 30 | 90 | 52 | 71 | 87 |
| 31 | 50 | - | 49 | 73 |
| 32 | 83 | 81 | 87 | 92 |
| 33 | 53 | 53 | 45 | 77 |
| 34 | 51 | 59 | 69 | 86 |
| 35 | 57 | 60 | 57 | 81 |
| 36 | 87 | 72 | 62 | 83 |
| 37 | 64 | 74 | 58 | 76 |
| 38 | 93 | 66 | 69 | 70 |
| 39 | 92 | - | 79 | 70 |
| Overall | 70 | - | 62 | 74 |

### Percent of Motor Use Which Could Reasonably Use ASD

Problems exist here at both the conceptual and data level. Several methods can be used to estimate the technical limits on the fraction of motor use possible for ASDs.

#### Method #1

There are two markets for new adjustable speed drives:

(a) a replacement for motors which are already speed controlled, usually in cases where exact control of speed is a process requirement (e.g., steel rolling mill motors, paper making machine motors, etc.);

(b) penetration into markets where the motor duty cycle varies over time, but currently motor speed is roughly maintained under partial load conditions (e.g., throttling liquid flow by valves, air flow by discharge dampers, etc.). These applications now offer enough economic benefit from the electricity savings and utility rebates to make ASD a viable option.

The former market is fairly limited both in terms of volume and additional conservation potential, and thus should not receive much attention from utilities in designing their DSM programs. The second, typically associated with motors driving pumps, fans, and compressors, dwarfs the first market in conservation potential, since considerable energy savings result when the energy lost in throttling constant speed motors is eliminated, and hence substantial utility subsidies can be expected.

While most would agree that motors which drive compressors are good opportunities for ASD devices (these are estimated to consume 13 percent of industrial electricity), there is some disagreement about the type of ASD device most likely to dominate the market. Early on, electronically controlled adjustable frequency drives (AFD) for AC motors were thought to be the best opportunity. For instance, the studies summarized in Table 2 implicitly assumed that all ASD demand would be met by AFD devices, since KWh savings were based on case studies involving installation of AFD devices on AC motors.

It now appears that compressor performance and expected life may be adversely affected by continuous variation in motor speed. A more viable option appears to be to use compressor capacity modulation techniques which control the on/off cycling of the motor to change compressor suction and discharge pressures to better match process needs [6]. Not only do such control approaches save electricity -- savings in the range of 10-30 percent are reported -- but the cost of the devices is low relative to AFC devices. Payback periods from 4 to 12 months have been reported in a range of applications, much shorter than the payback times usually associated with electronic AFD devices.

Two sources for the fraction of motor demand associated with pumps, fans, and compressors are available, and are shown in columns (1) and (2) of Table 4.

Method #2

A second approach would limit ASD market shares to those motor sizes which are likely to be candidates for possible ASD devices. The argument goes that most small motors either operate at full load, or are off, with little partial load operation, and hence will never be good candidates for ASD installations. The disagreement is over how small is small. Some [6] argue that only motors under 5 HP should be eliminated. If this is the case, the limitation is minor, since less than 1 percent of total industrial electricity use is consumed in such motors [3].

Table 4. Percent Motor Use Likely Suitable for ASD

| SIC | STUDY | | |
| --- | --- | --- | --- |
| | EM-4527 (1) | Michigan Options (2) | ADL (3) |
| 20 | 44 | 62.5 | 66 |
| 21 | 17 | - | 40 |
| 22 | 20 | 30 | 75 |
| 23 | 18 | 33 | 40 |
| 24 | 21 | 35 | 60 |
| 25 | 18 | 23 | 60 |
| 26 | 37 | 55 | 86 |
| 27 | 26 | 22 | 40 |
| 28 | 75 | 84 | 65 |
| 29 | 75 | 94 | 69 |
| 30 | 31 | 52 | 79 |
| 31 | 20 | - | 40 |
| 32 | 20 | 31 | 72 |
| 33 | 20 | 51 | 86 |
| 34 | 22 | 64 | 77 |
| 35 | 18 | 45 | 68 |
| 36 | 31 | 42 | 70 |
| 37 | 35 | 53 | 66 |
| 38 | 16 | 44 | 47 |
| 39 | 16 | - | 47 |
| Total | | | 75 |

(1) Pumps, fans, and compressors only.
(2) Air conditioners, refrigerators, air compressors, other variable applications (Michigan estimate of percent of motor drive powering variable loads).
(3) Percent of motor KWh provided by motors greater than 50 HP [5].

Another major (1986) study [7] described in the backup for Table 2 concluded that no major market existed for ASD equipment below 50 HP because of payback periods in excess of 20 years [8]. This presumption is contradicted by actual data collected by CRS Sirrine and reported in the various editions of the *ASD Directory* [2], which indicate that substantial numbers (> 200,000) of units have been sold in the 7.5-50 HP range. If this > 50 HP restriction were true, the market for ASDs would be reduced to 75 percent of the KWh used for motors. Estimates of the percent of motor KWh consumed by motors over 50 HP by SIC are given in column (3) of Table 4.

This data could be used to adjust downward the likely potential estimates in columns (1) and (2) by assuming that pump, fan, and compressor motor sizes were distributed the same way all motor use sizes were distributed. In this case, it would be appropriate to multiply the entries in columns (1) and (2) by the percentages in column (3) to obtain an estimate of the motor KWh consumed in each SIC by pumps, fans, and compressors greater than 50 HP. (Note this screen is really an economic, not a technical, screen.)

## Likely Penetration Into Maximum Market Potential

Finally, estimates of the likely penetration into the maximum market potential need to be considered. Economic adoption decisions are a function of the payback period associated with ASD adoption -- i.e., how many years it takes for the cumulative annual savings in the form of electricity bill reductions, etc., to exceed the purchase and installation cost of the ASD device. Table 5 is a compendium of values of electricity saved in recent ASD installations found in the literature. This compendium cannot be considered "average" but only "best results expected" for obvious reasons.

The examples found in Table 5 also illustrate the wide range of electricity savings which can be expected. The savings are calculated, using a three step process:

(a) Forecast the duty cycle of the equipment over the planning horizon. The duty cycle would show the percent of time during the unit time interval the fan, pump, or compressor would be at a given partial load condition, expressed as a percent of the full load of the equipment. Thus, motor "A" would operate x percent of the time at y percent of the full load during year "z" of the planning horizon.

### Table 5. ASD KWh Savings Found in the Literature

- **Municipal Utilities**
  - ASD installed on air blowers in water aeration system: 24% savings

- **Commercial Buildings**
  - ASD installed on water pumps: 33% savings
  - ASD on HVAC fan reduces consumption: 22% (lecture hall)
  - ASD replaces fan dampers in HVAC: 17 to 30% savings depending on building type, geographic location
  - ASD for chiller compressors: 10% savings

- **Glass Industry - Automotive Glass**
  - ASD replaces vane control in glass tempering: 30% savings

- **Chemical/Petroleum Industry**
  - ASD replaces valve on 10,000 HP compressor: 11% savings
  - ASD replaces valve on 100 HP centrifugal pump: 43% savings
  - ASD replaces valve on 2000 HP pump: 25% savings,
  - ASD replaces valve on 100 HP pump: 30% savings
  - ASD replaces valve on 2500 HP pump: 6% savings
  - ASD replaces valve on compressor: 12% savings,
  - ASD replaces fan damper on 400 HP fan: 45% savings
  - ASD replaces inlet guide vane on 300 HP boiler fan: 75% savings

    (Why? Average fan load 50% due to oversizing 2 boilers so each could handle entire steam load.)

- **Pipelines**
  - Gas
  - Oil - 3500 HP ASD drive

- **Pulp & Paper Industry**
  - ASD for I.D. fan on recovery boiler now directly driven
  - ASD for turbine lineshaft drive: increased electricity use
  - ASD for constant speed pump: 70% savings
  - ASD for sludge pump

- **Textile Industry**
  - ASD replaces fixed speed 100 HP fan: 61% savings
  - ASD replaces DC motor drive in mill: 0 savings

- **Wood Industry**
  - ASD on kiln fans decrease air flow as moisture drops: 40% savings

- **Iron & Steel Industry**
  - ASD for roller, motors on continuous caster

123

(b) Calculate the KWh consumption the present motor would utilize serving this load, given the motor's part load performance function which relates KW use to the various loads.

(c) Calculate the reduced KWh consumption, if the motor were retrofitted with an adjustable speed device, using the ASD part load performance function.

All this is summarized for fans in Figure 1, taken from Eto & De Almeida [9]. Table 6 shows representative calculations of annual energy savings for a representative 100 HP motor.

Figure 1. Part-Load Performance for Several Variable Air Flow Techniques

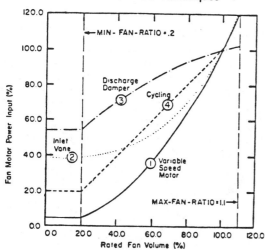

The value of the steam of annual KWh and KW savings in the form of likely bill reductions are then annualized, and divided into the installed cost of the device to obtain an estimate of the payback period.

Since the cost of ASD devices is falling, subsidies provided by utilities vary in time and place, and the value of KWh saved may be rising, these calculations are also dependent on when the calculation is done.

Conceivably, ASD costs could fall and electricity prices and utility subsidies could rise until 100 percent of the maximum market potential could be realized. But this is unlikely. The Michigan Electricity Options Study assumes the maximum achievable market share is 50 percent; the PNL report [10] assumes at most 20 percent of the target market will be penetrated "with the current (1986) market situation for this equipment."

New developments in technology could result in increases or decreases in the maximum potential. Two examples will suffice:

• The trade talk concerning Japanese adjustable frequency drives falling below $25/HP when mass produced in high quantities for small motors could drive the penetration toward 100 percent.

• Continued market penetration of high efficiency motors into the constant speed drive market would reduce the savings associated with ASD device installation. However, high efficiency motor savings are small relative to ASD savings except for the very smallest motors.

For our purposes, a range of 20 to 50 percent of the total market will be adopted.

Table 6. ASD Savings Depends on Time at Percentage of Full Load

| Example 100 HP, 92% Efficiency (KW = HP/Eff * .746 = 81) | | | | | | | | |
|---|---|---|---|---|---|---|---|---|
| | % Full Load Input Power | | Full Load Input Power | Existing Motor Input (KW) | ASD (KW) | Savings (KW) | Hours | Annual Energy Savings (KWh) |
| % Full Load | Existing Motor | Proposed ASD | | | | | | |
| 0 | 0 | 0 | 81 | 0 | 0 | 0 | 2780 | 0 |
| 30 | .60 | .08 | 81 | 49 | 6 | 43 | 880 | 37,840 |
| 40 | .63 | .14 | 81 | 51 | 11 | 40 | 1030 | 41,200 |
| 50 | .65 | .21 | 81 | 53 | 17 | 36 | 1120 | 40,320 |
| 70 | .75 | .44 | 81 | 61 | 36 | 25 | 1040 | 26,000 |
| 90 | .93 | .73 | 81 | 75 | 59 | 16 | 980 | 15,680 |
| 100 | 1.09 | 1.05 | 81 | 88 | 85 | 3 | 930 | 2,790 |
| | | | | | | | | 163,830 (44%) |

## Resultant KWh Savings, if Penetration Achieved

If the markets are penetrated as expected, the likely annual savings as a percent of total industrial KWh use can be calculated by:

(1) Obtaining the percent economic potential by multiplying the assumed percent of motor use where it is reasonable to expect ASD to be applicable times the percent penetration likely to be achieved under current and projected ASD equipment and electricity KW and KWh costs.

(2) Multiplying the economic potential percent by the expected KWh savings if ASD devices are installed to obtain the likely percent KWh savings associated with achievement of the economic potential. As Table 5 shows, these percents are extremely variable. Until better "average" data are collected, the 25 to 35 percent range of savings reported in column (7) of Table 2 are reasonable to use.

## Estimates of U.S. Economic Potential for ASD Devices

Table 7 shows in columns (H) and (I) the range of ASD potential and KWh savings obtained by multiplying the high estimates from each range, shown in columns (D) through (G), and then multiplying the low estimates from each range shown in the columns.

Column C is obtained by adding purchased KWh and KWh generated less KWh sold for each SIC from "The Annual Survey of Manufactures" [11].

Column D is obtained from the high and low values for each SIC shown in Table 3.

Column E is obtained from the high and low values for each SIC shown in Table 4.

Column F is obtained by assuming the 20 to 50 percent range of maximum market penetration mentioned in a previous section holds.

Table 7. Likely Market Potential for Electricity Saving ASD Devices

| A   B SIC Industry | C 1989 Total Elec Energy Use (million KWh) | D Motor % Low | High | E Suitable % Low | High | F % Penetration Low | High | G % Savings Low | High | H % of Use Saved Low | High | I KWh Saved (million KWh) Low | High |
|---|---|---|---|---|---|---|---|---|---|---|---|---|---|
| **PROCESS INDUSTRIES** | | | | | | | | | | | | | |
| 28  Chemicals | 163179.0 | 65 | 84 | 65 | 84 | 20 | 50 | 25 | 35 | 2.11% | 12.35% | 3447.16 | 20149.34 |
| 26  Pulp & paper | 102410.7 | 81 | 94 | 37 | 86 | 20 | 50 | 25 | 35 | 1.50% | 14.15% | 1534.62 | 14488.04 |
| 20  Food | 55054.5 | 81 | 87 | 44 | 66 | 20 | 50 | 25 | 35 | 1.78% | 10.05% | 981.07 | 5532.15 |
| 29  Petroleum & Coal | 43785.2 | 83 | 92 | 69 | 94 | 20 | 50 | 25 | 35 | 2.86% | 15.13% | 1253.79 | 6626.45 |
| 22  Textile Mills | 30623.9 | 71 | 88 | 20 | 75 | 20 | 50 | 25 | 35 | 0.71% | 11.55% | 217.43 | 3537.06 |
| 21  Tobacco Products | 1788.9 | 73 | 75 | 17 | 40 | 20 | 50 | 25 | 35 | 0.62% | 5.25% | 11.10 | 93.92 |
| | | | | | | | | | | | | | |
| **METALS PRODUCTION** | | | | | | | | | | | | | |
| 33  Primary Metals | 155263.1 | 45 | 77 | 20 | 86 | 20 | 50 | 25 | 35 | 0.45% | 11.59% | 698.68 | 17992.66 |
| | | | | | | | | | | | | | |
| **MATERIALS FABRICATION** | | | | | | | | | | | | | |
| **METALS FABRICATION** | | | | | | | | | | | | | |
| 35  Non-Elec Machinery | 36325.2 | 57 | 81 | 18 | 68 | 20 | 50 | 25 | 35 | 0.51% | 9.64% | 186.35 | 3501.39 |
| 37  Transportation | 39322.3 | 58 | 76 | 35 | 66 | 20 | 50 | 25 | 35 | 1.02% | 8.78% | 399.12 | 3451.71 |
| 36  Electrical Equipment | 33133.7 | 62 | 87 | 31 | 70 | 20 | 50 | 25 | 35 | 0.96% | 10.66% | 318.41 | 3531.22 |
| 34  Fab Metal Products | 33371.6 | 51 | 86 | 22 | 77 | 20 | 50 | 25 | 35 | 0.56% | 11.59% | 187.21 | 3867.27 |
| 38  Instruments | 13943.7 | 66 | 43 | 16 | 47 | 20 | 50 | 25 | 35 | 0.53% | 3.54% | 73.62 | 493.15 |
| 39  Misc Mfg Industries | 4966.3 | 79 | 92 | 16 | 47 | 20 | 50 | 25 | 35 | 0.63% | 7.57% | 31.39 | 375.80 |
| | | | | | | | | | | | | | |
| **NON-METALS FABRICATION** | | | | | | | | | | | | | |
| 32  Stone, Clay, Glass | 33855.5 | 81 | 92 | 20 | 72 | 20 | 50 | 25 | 35 | 0.81% | 11.59% | 274.23 | 3924.53 |
| 30  Rubber & Plastics | 35345 | 52 | 90 | 31 | 79 | 20 | 50 | 25 | 35 | 0.81% | 12.44% | 284.88 | 4397.80 |
| 24  Lumber & Wood | 21886.2 | 74 | 91 | 21 | 60 | 20 | 50 | 25 | 35 | 0.78% | 9.56% | 170.06 | 2091.23 |
| 27  Printing & Publishing | 16663.6 | 68 | 85 | 26 | 40 | 20 | 50 | 25 | 35 | 0.88% | 5.95% | 147.31 | 991.48 |
| 23  Apparel | 5875.2 | 72 | 90 | 18 | 40 | 20 | 50 | 25 | 35 | 0.65% | 6.30% | 38.07 | 370.14 |
| 25  Furniture | 6295.3 | 74 | 80 | 18 | 60 | 20 | 50 | 25 | 35 | 0.67% | 8.40% | 41.93 | 528.81 |
| 31  Leather | 986.3 | 49 | 73 | 20 | 40 | 20 | 50 | 25 | 35 | 0.49% | 5.11% | 4.83 | 50.40 |
| TOTALS | 834075.2 | | | | | | | | | 1.24% | 11.51% | 10301.27 | 95994.56 |

Note: Column C obtained by adding purchased KWh and KWh generated less sold from Table 4 of *ASM Industry Statistics* (1989) [11].

Column G is obtained by assuming the 25 to 35 percent range of market penetration in column (7) of Table 2 holds.

Column H is the range of likely percent of total manufacturing KWh sales that could be economically served by ASD. It is obtained by multiplying the high values of columns D, E, and F together, and then the low values together.

Column I, the range of likely KWh savings associated with column G, is obtained by multiplying the ranges of column G by the savings ranges in column F.

Finally, the totals for all SICs are shown in the last row of the table.

## Conclusions

We can conclude from this exercise that:

- The range of estimates for the likely market penetration of electricity saving ASD devices into the market for manufacturing use and the resultant KWh savings is almost an order of magnitude.

- Still, the range of impact of such ASD devices is small, relative to other uncertainties (such as the rate of growth of GNP) which directly influence electricity demand growth.

- The range of estimates could be improved if:

  (a) the analyses were carried out at the four-digit SIC level to take advantage of existent audit information on electricity end use;

  (b) data were collected systematically by four-digit SICs on the motor drive end uses which have been successfully fitted with electricity saving ASDs; and

  (c) data so collected would include actual KWh and KW savings together with information on payback experience.

## References

[1]   *The DSM Letter,* 19(7) (April 1, 1991).

[2]   *ASD Directory,* Second Edition, EPRI/ PEAC (1987).

[3]   A.D. Little, "Classification and Evaluation of Electric Motors and Pumps," DOE/TIC-11339 (September 1980).

[4]   Applied Energy Systems, Inc., "Applications of Compressor Capacity Modulation in the Industrial and Commercial Sectors," EPRI TR-100035 (October 1991).

[5]   Argonne National Laboratory, "Classification and Evaluation of Electric Motors and Pumps," DOE/TIC-11339 (September 1980), p. 3-35, 3-36.

[6]   Michigan Electricity Options Study, Industrial Sector Analysis, Vol. 1, p. 2-32.

[7]   Pacific Northwest Laboratory, "The Electric Energy Savings from New Technologies," PNL-5665, Rev. 1, UC-95, Richland, WA (September 1986).

[8]   Ibid., p. 13-9.

[9]   Eto, Joseph H., and De Almeida, Anibal, "Saving Electricity in Commercial Buildings with Adjustable-Speed Drives," *Transactions on Industry Applications,* Vol. 24, No. 3 (May/June 1988): 439-443.

[10]  Pacific Northwest Laboratory, "The Electric Energy Savings from New Technologies," PNL-5665, Rev. 1, UC-95, Richland, WA (September 1986). p. 13-11.

[11]  Bureau of the Census, *Annual Survey of Manufactures, Industry Statistics* (1989), Table 4, p. 1-37.

# Chapter 24
# Adjustable Speed Drives - Industrial and Commercial Applications

J.N. Poole

## ABSTRACT

Electric motors are significant users of electricity within the United States. Approximately 70 percent of the total electricity produced by the utilities and independent power producers is consumed by electric motors. The use of variable speed to control industrial and commercial processes rather than the traditional constant speed method can save energy, lower maintenance cost and improve process control. By providing a variable frequency voltage to AC motors through the use of electronic adjustable speed drives (ASDs), the speed of AC motors can be controlled and thus the speed of the driven equipment can be matched to process requirements.

This paper describes the benefits that can be derived from variable speed control, the methodology for ASD candidate evaluation and some specific case studies of ASD applications.

## INTRODUCTION

Electronic adjustable speed drives (ASDs) are more efficient and cost-effective than ever before due to recent advancements in solid state technologies. As a result, they are significantly changing the way induction AC motors are used and operated, and are providing commercial, industrial and utility plant operators immediate opportunities to save energy, reduce operating and maintenance cost, and improve product quality.

Induction AC motors are limited, primarily by the AC frequency of their power supply, to operation at constant speed. At constant speed, the flow requirements of AC motor driven equipment must be controlled by the use of mechanical or hydraulic devices such as couplings, clutches, gears, vanes and valves. By the use of electronic ASDs, AC motor speed can be varied and controlled to match the flow from the driven equipment to the process requirements.

ASDs save energy by sensing the power requirements of the driven process equipment and then varying the motor speed to provide the actual power required to satisfy the process demand.

ASDs improve equipment reliability by permitting soft starts, controlled acceleration and deceleration.

ASDs provide improved process control by providing a finer degree of automatic control of equipment speed to match the changes in process demand.

ASDs reduce maintenance cost and improve equipment life by reducing the stress in shafts, bearings, couplings, rotors, and starters.

There are a wide range of applications of ASDs for utility commercial and industrial customers. Some of the applications are:

- Office building heating, cooling and ventilation systems
- Municipal water pumping stations
- Municipal waste water treatment plants
- Industrial process pumps and fans
- Industrial process conveyors and mixing equipment
- Industrial variable rate manufacturing equipment
- Industrial drying equipment

### Process Control

Seventy percent of the electrical power generated in the United States is used by electric motors. Only a small proportion of the industrial and commercial motor driven equipment is operated at or near full load on either a continuous or intermittent basis. The majority of industrial and

commercial processes operate
continuously at varying load
requirements.

There are three basic methods used for
controlling process flow rate in fluid
systems, they are:

   o  Throttling, such as fan dampers
      or control valves.
   o  Fluid recirculation, by-pass
      lines.
   o  Equipment speed control,
      adjustable speed drives (ASDs).

Under throttling control, as
indicated in Figure 1, each piece
of equipment runs near full load at
constant speed. Energy input in
excess of the process requirement
is wasted by dissipating it across
a control valve or damper. The
pressure drop across a fan damper
or pump control valve consumes
energy, in addition to fluid
friction. Throttling control is
the conventional design practice,
dating back to the earliest days of
continuous process design. Fluid
recirculation, as indicated in
Figure 2, wastes energy by
maintaining a constant rate of
power consumption on the motor,
regardless of process requirements. This method is used with
some specialized fluid processes.

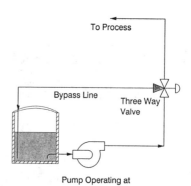

Pump Operating at
Constant Speed

FIGURE 2
CONSTANT SPEED PUMPING
WITH BYPASS CONTROL

Speed control as indicated in
Figure 3 is more energy efficient
because it matches the speed of the
driven equipment to the actual
requirements of the process. There
are several types of equipment that
are designed to provide variable
speed operation of pumps. These
are:

   o    eddy current clutches
   o    fluid drives
   o    adjustable frequency drives

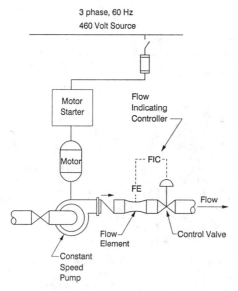

FIGURE 1
CONSTANT SPEED PUMPING WITH
THROTTLE VALVE CONTROL

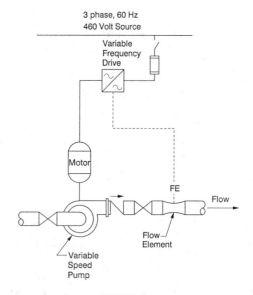

FIGURE 3
PUMPING WITH ADJUSTABLE
SPEED CONTROL

The relative consumption for a
centrifugal fan operating with
different capacity controlling
devices is indicated in Figure 4.
The electronic adjustable frequency
drive (AFD) is the most efficient
of the devices used to control air
flow as indicated in Figure 4.

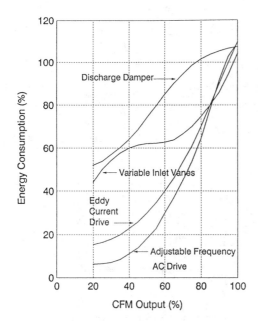

FIGURE 4

TYPICAL ENERGY CONSUMPTION OF A
CENTRIFUGAL FAN SYSTEM USING
SELECTED SPEED CONTROL TECHNIQUES

When specifying adjustable
frequency drives, understanding the
process requirements is more
important than understanding the
details of drive technology. A
drive should be selected on the
basis of what it can do, not on how
it accomplishes the task.

AC adjustable frequency drives are
the most popular choice of the ASD
alternatives. They use standard
squirrel cage induction or
synchronous motors, offer a speed
regulation accuracy of 0.1% or
better, and are available from
fractional to 20,000 HP.

## AC Induction Motors

Alternating current (AC) induction
squirrel cage motors are the work
horse of commercial and industrial
processes. These motors are
typically connected to a constant
frequency power supply (60HZ) and
consequently are limited to
operation at a fixed speed.

Induction motor synchronous speed
is established by the number of
motor poles and the frequency of
the applied AC voltage. The
adjustable frequency output from an
ASD provides drive speed control.

$$n = \frac{120 * f}{p}$$

n = motor speed in RPM
f = frequency in Hertz
p = number of motor poles

For a 2 pole motor operating at 60 Hz,
the synchronous speed is 3600 RPM as
indicated below. If the frequency is
changed to 30 Hz, then the synchronous
speed is reduced to 1800 RPM. Speed is
a linear relationship based on the
frequency.

$$n = \frac{120 * 60 \text{ Hz}}{2 \text{ poles}} = 3600 \text{ RPM}$$

The actual operating speed will be
slightly less than the synchronous
speed due to the slip which is a
function of the motor NEMA design
classification and the load.

The NEMA design letter on the nameplate
of a squirrel cage induction motor
defines the torque, slip, and starting
current characteristics of the motor.
Polyphase squirrel cage induction
motors are offered in a choice of four
NEMA designs.

Design A  These motors are quite
comparable to Design B motors, having
normal torque and slip and normal
starting current. The most significant
difference is that starting currents
are limited by NEMA for Design B and
not for Design A.

Design B  This motor is overwhelmingly
the general purpose motor of industry.
Its combination of low starting current
and normal torque and slip makes it an
excellent choice for driving many types
of industrial loads.

Design C  Design C motors have high
starting torque, low starting current,
and low slip. The high breakaway
torque makes the Design C a good choice
for hard-to-start loads.

Design D  These motors have very high
starting torque, high slip, and
relatively low starting current.
Design D permits high breakaway torque
and high running horsepower to be
concentrated in a relatively small
frame size.  Design D motors are
offered as NEMA standard in slips of 5
to 8 percent and 8 to 13 percent; some
manufacturers offer motors with even
higher slips by special order.

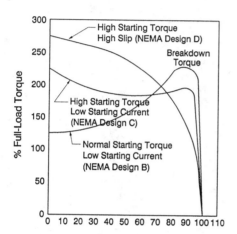

FIGURE 5
AC INDUCTION MOTOR TORQUE
SPEED CHARACTERISTIC AT
CONSTANT VOLTAGE AND FREQUENCY

NEMA Design Letters A through D
prescribe the torque, slip, and
starting current of polyphase squirrel
cage induction motors.  Of these three
characteristics, torque is the most
important because any attempt to
compensate for poor torque
characteristics with power transmission
equipment adds substantially to the
cost of the installation.  The motor
should be selected with a torque that
will turn the crank under all
anticipated loads.  Figure 5 depicts
the torque speed characteristics of AC
induction motors.

ASD Basics

The basic elements of an ASD are shown
in Figure 6.  Although there are
numerous designs and devices used by
the various manufacturers, all ASDs
employ electronic switching devices
such as thyristors and transistors to
first convert the 60 Hz input to direct
current (DC) power in the rectifier
stage and then reconstruct the DC to a
variable frequency AC power output in
the inverter stage.  Through the use of

the switching devices and control
circuitry, output frequency and voltage
are controlled.  Filter stages are used
to shape and smooth the DC wave forms
produced by electronic switching.

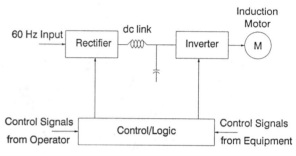

FIGURE 6
TYPICAL VFD COMPONENTS

Output voltage and frequency from
the inverter section is controlled
by input signals from operator
controls and feedback signals from
process equipment.

APPLICATIONS SCREENING

When properly applied, variable
frequency AC drives are economical
to operate, and have an energy
savings potential from 20 to 50
percent when compared to throttling
control.  Every load is not
necessarily a good application.  A
good application will have a large
number of annual operating hours
and a high degree of valve or
damper throttling for a large
number of the total operating
hours.  Energy cost savings can be
readily determined based on
calculations, using established
principles.

From an energy economics viewpoint,
applications with the following
characteristics are the most
attractive for ASD installations:

o    High annual operating hours
o    Variable load characteristic
o    Moderate to high horsepower
     rating    (50 HP and larger)

is very steep, near full rated speed.

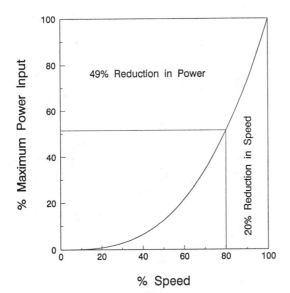

FIGURE 7
VARIABLE SPEED POWER CURVE

TABLE 1

| Speed | Flow | Required HP |
|-------|------|-------------|
| 100% | 100% | 100.0% |
| 90% | 90% | 72.9% |
| 80% | 80% | 51.2% |
| 70% | 70% | 34.3% |
| 60% | 60% | 21.6% |
| 50% | 50% | 12.5% |
| 40% | 40% | 6.4% |
| 30% | 30% | 2.7% |
| 20% | 20% | 0.8% |

VARIABLE POWER
LOAD CHARACTERISTICS

In this operating region, modest decreases in speed yield significant reductions in power consumption as shown in Table 1.

In most cases, an ASD will not lower the demand. Motors are sized based on the highest load requirement they will have to satisfy for some percentage of the operating cycle. This peak load, for most drives, will occur one or more times during the billing period. Demand cost is typically based on the highest demand established during a 15 minute interval during the billing period.

An exception would be for a fan on a cooling tower or similar load where the load peak would occur on a seasonal basis.

The demand may also be lowered through the use of ASDs if several ASDs are in operation. The more ASDs in service, the more likely that the demand will be lower when compared to the demand established using constant speed drives. It is very unlikely that the peak load for all drives would occur within the same 15 minute interval.

The screening methodology described in this section is the first step to be taken in the evaluation of a potential ASD candidate. The information needed to screen a candidate is:

o The horsepower rating of the motor
o The annual number of hours the equipment operates (duty cycle).
o The percent of time the equipment operates at less than rated full load (load cycle).
o The amount of flow variation typically used in the operation of the equipment.

In order to determine if an application is a good candidate for an ASD, the load duty cycle must be estimated. A rough estimate of the load duty cycle may be constructed from operating records or from discussion with the operating personnel.

Examination of the load duty cycle can reveal features of system operation that favor the use of ASD technology. The load duty cycle indicated in Figure 8 is an excellent candidate for an ASD retrofit. There is a high degree of throttling for a large part of the total operating hours. This is depicted in the figure by the number and height of the operating points that are below 100% flow.

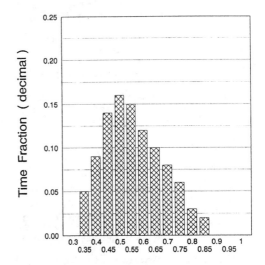

Flow / Rated Flow

FIGURE 8

The load duty cycle indicated in Figure 9 is a moderate candidate for an ASD retrofit. The figure indicates that there is some throttling of the equipment but most of the operating points are near the rated capacity of the equipment. The total operating hours, horsepower, and cost of electric power, would determine if there is a reasonable financial payback for the installation of an ASD.

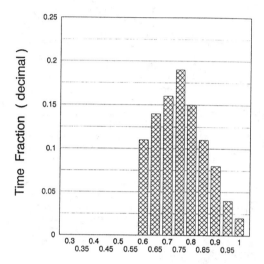

Flow / Rated Flow

FIGURE 9

The load duty cycle indicated in Figure 10 is a poor candidate for an ASD retrofit. If the drive operates near full load (no throttling) for the majority of the operating year, there is no potential for energy savings where this type of load duty cycle applied.

Factors that influence the success of an ASD application are as follows.

o  High degree of throttling
o  High annual operating hours
o  Large horsepower, 50 HP or larger
o  Cost of electrical power

The drive applications that have the greatest potential for energy savings are:

o  Pumps
o  Fans
o  Blowers

The screening process should also identify if there are other potential benefits in addition to energy savings. Some of the other benefits could be one or more of the following:

  o  Reduced stress due to soft start
  o  Lower maintenance cost
  o  Improved process control
  o  Improved product quality
  o  Increased equipment life

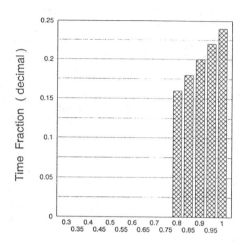

Flow / Rated Flow

FIGURE 10

APPLICATION CASE STUDIES

When considering an ASD application, it is important to realize that a generalization of a particular type of application is not always practical because the energy savings potential is a function of:

  o  the number of hours a year that the equipment is operated
  o  the horsepower rating of the equipment
  o  equipment operating practices
  o  the design rated conditions relative to normal operating conditions
  o  cost of energy

Each one of these aspects affect the feasibility of an ASD application. With a proper understanding of the technology involved, many potential candidates can be identified. The following case studies are discussed to illustrate the thought processes needed to identify the potential for the use of ASD technology for a particular system with reasonable accuracy.

Case 1:  HVAC Condenser Cooling Water Pump

A research center of a large computer firm located in the northeast has many facility support systems. The HVAC condenser cooling water system was identified as a system which could benefit from an ASD retrofit. The system consists of three 3500 GPM vertical pumps, two 3750 GPM horizontal pumps and three cooling towers that are used in various combinations, depending on the load of the HVAC system. The system is in some mode of operation at all times. Normal summer peak load condenser cooling water demand is 11,500 GPM. This demand will require some combination of 4 of the 5 pumps supplying all 5 of the chillers and a glycol system. The normal winter load is reduced to 1875 GPM to supply one of the 1000 ton chillers as shown in Figure 11. This mode of operation requires one of the pumps to be throttled or the use of a cooling tower bypass arrangement in order to meet this flow requirement.

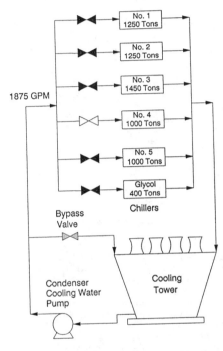

FIGURE 11
HVAC CONDENSER COOLING WATER
SYSTEM DIAGRAM

Retrofitting one of the vertical pumps with a 400 HP ASD will allow the low flows during the winter months to be achieved with a reduction in energy consumption. This mode of operation was projected to be valid for six months out of the year.

The ASD analysis performed in the evaluation of this application is summarized below:

Estimated Equipment Cost  $50,000
Estimated Installation Cost 70,000
Total Cost of Retrofit    $120,000

Energy Saving      757,576 kWh/yr
Cost of Energy        $0.066/kWh
Energy Cost Savings   $50,000/yr

$$\text{Simple payback} = \frac{\$120,000}{\$50,000} = 2.4 \text{ years}$$

Key features in considering this system as a potential ASD candidate were.

   o High number of operating hours
   o Large HP rating of pumps
   o Large reduction in required flow for a substantial number of operating hours during the year
   o The use of a throttling valve or bypass arrangement to achieve flow control

Case 2:  HVAC Supply Fan

This case study describes the application of an ASD to a 75 HP HVAC supply fan for a variable air volume (VAV) system. A VAV system is designed to control room temperature by varying the amount of cool air delivered to the conditioned space. This is achieved by modulating variable air boxes located in each conditioned space with a thermostat. The design of a VAV system inherently requires the variable volume operation of the supply fan air flow to accommodate the temperature swings encountered in the conditioned space. The supply fan flow is modulated by variable inlet guide vanes (VIGV). An ASD provides the same function with improved energy efficiency. Figure 12 is a representation of this system shown for one of the wings of the building.

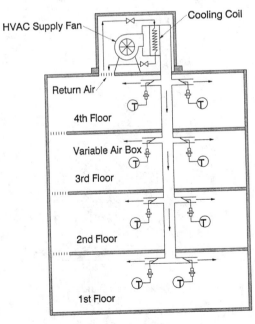

FIGURE 12
FLOW DIAGRAM OF A VAV HVAC
OFFICE BUILDING AIR CIRCUIT

133

## Operating Data and Equipment Performance

Daily operating data was not available for this fan. However, cooling loads were estimated based on the size of the building and design data obtained from the management of the property. Given the size of the conditioned space as 76,000 square feet, the lighting loads could be estimated at 3 watts/sq. ft. and the occupancy load may be estimated at 10 occupants per 1000 square feet with each occupant contributing 150 watts. these estimates compared favorably with the design capacity of the cooling coils that were used in the HVAC system. The fan curve was obtained from the manufacturer using the nameplate data recorded from the fan housing.

## Load Duty Cycle

The output of an HVAC system is tied to the weather conditions of the area. Due to the lack of actual operating data, one year of local weather data was obtained so that a load duty cycle could be estimated. The load duty cycle was constructed based on the high temperature for each day. Figure 13 shows the fraction of the total days in the year that the daily high temperature occurred in a particular temperature range. An estimate for the air required to satisfy the heating or cooling load for a given daily high temperature was derived from the HVAC system design data. Figure 14 depicts the fraction of the total operating hours that the fan operates at each flow rate. This is the load cycle.

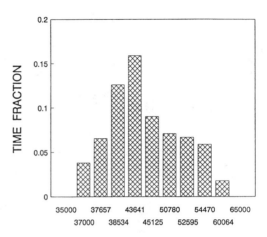

FIGURE 14
THE LOAD CYCLE

Conversation with the operating personnel indicated that the fans were run from 6:00 a.m. to 5:00 p.m., five days of the week. This gives a duty cycle of

$$\frac{11 \text{ hrs/day} * 5 \text{ days/wk} * 52 \text{ wks/yr}}{8760 \text{ hrs/year}}$$

which is equal to 0.326.

## System Resistance Curve

The design data for this fan indicates an operating point of 64,000 CFM, 738 RPM, 5.5 in. wg. To determine the behavior of the system, it was assured that a 1.5 in. wg. duct pressure is used as a control point. This pressure indication is used to position the inlet vanes to the fan and will be used as an input to the ASD to control the fan motor speed. A system resistance curve was drawn on the fan performance curve beginning at 1.5 in. wg. and intersecting the design point of 5.5 in. wg., 64,000 CFM. Figure 15

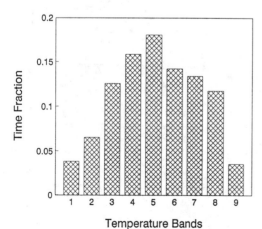

FIGURE 13

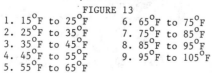

1. 15°F to 25°F    6. 65°F to 75°F
2. 25°F to 35°F    7. 75°F to 85°F
3. 35°F to 45°F    8. 85°F to 95°F
4. 45°F to 55°F    9. 95°F to 105°F
5. 55°F to 65°F

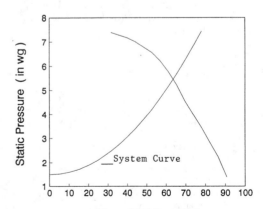

FIGURE 15
SYSTEM CURVE SUPERIMPOSED ON THE VANES WIDE OPEN PRESSURE RISE PERFORMANCE CURVE

shows the estimated system
resistance curve superimposed on
the vanes wide open fan performance
curve.

## Energy Savings

Using the procedure outlined
earlier to customize VIGV
performance curves, a specific set
of performance curves were
developed. These curves were used
to determine the BHP required for
each air flow rate in the load duty
cycle. From this, an estimate for
the total annual energy requirement
for the operation of the fan at
constant speed was determined to be
344,000 kWh.

An estimate of the total annual
energy requirements for the fan
operating in adjustable speed was
determined using the system
resistance curve, the fan
performance curve, and the load
duty cycle. The total annual
energy required with adjustable
speed operation was estimated to be
234,000 kWh. Both of these
estimates were determined with
consideration for the varying motor
and ASD efficiencies that are
encountered at loads and speeds
different from rated conditions.
The energy calculations indicate
that an annual energy savings of
110,000 kWh is possible with the
use of ASD technology. This
represents a 32% reduction in
annual energy consumption for this
piece of equipment.

The ASD analysis performed in the
evaluation of this application is
summarized below.

Estimated Equipment Cost  $10,400

Estimated Installation Cost 16,000

Total Cost of Retrofit    $26,000

Energy Saving        10,000 kWh/yr

Cost of Energy         $ 0.13 /kWh

Energy Cost Saving $14,300 /yr

$$\text{Simple Payback} = \frac{\$26,000}{\$14,300} = 1.8 \text{ yrs}$$

The features of this system that
support an ASD retrofit are,

- The use of a cooling tower
  bypass arrangement to
  maintain proper condenser
  cooling water temperature
- A large number of operating
  hours
- An intermediate size HP
  rating

This case describes a small
military base in the vicinity of
New York City. Among the many
utilities required to operate such
an installation, it is of course
necessary to provide potable water
on a continuous basis. The supply
of potable water to the base
requires the full time operation of
a distribution system. The potable
water distribution pumps were
identified as potential ASD
candidates because of their heavy
use under variable loads.

A potable water system exhibits a
daily cycle that reflects the water
consumption habits of the community
it serves. Typically, such a
system will exhibit peaks in the
early morning and early evening.
These peaks can be as much as twice
the normal baseload demand of the
system. Presently, system pressure
and flow control is maintained by
the use of pressure reducing check
valves located at the discharge of
each of the water distribution
pumps. Figure 16 is a flow diagram
of this system showing the
equipment configuration. This ASD
application involves the adjustable
speed operation of the 75 HP water
distribution pumps to match the
system demand and maintain a
constant distribution header
pressure, thus eliminating the need
for the energy inefficient pressure
reducing check valves.

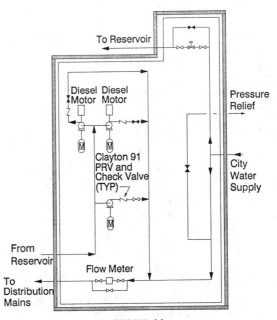

FIGURE 16
FLOW DIAGRAM OF THE POTABLE
WATER DISTRIBUTION SYSTEM

## Operating Data and Equipment Performance

Through discussions with the operations personnel at this facility it was discovered that only one of the three pumps is in operation at any time. Also 29 chart disks were obtained. The data on the disks was placed by a chart recorder which continuously monitored the flow of potable water into the distribution header. The pump performance curve for the pumps was obtained from the operations records. Also, the model and manufacturer of the pressure reducing check valve was recorded.

## Load Duty Cycle

One of the pumps operates at all times, so the duty cycle is unity. The chart disks obtained from the facility records were used to develop a load cycle for the distribution system. Each chart was intended to hold one week of operating data. However, some of these charts had more data on them. The approximately 35 weeks of data were used to estimate the operating profile for the year. This is a lot more data than is usually available for an energy savings evaluation. Figure 17 represents the load duty cycle that was estimated from the charts.

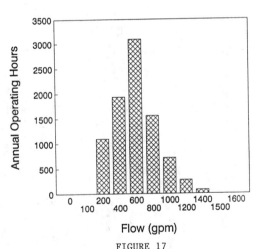

FIGURE 17
LOAD DUTY CYCLE

## System Resistance Curve

From the pump performance curve, a system resistance curve was estimated. The operating data indicated that the maximum flows

encountered in the system rarely exceed 1400 gpm. This point on the pump performance curve indicates a discharge pressure of 150 feet. This was taken as the end point of the system resistance curve that gradually decreases to 40 feet at zero flow. The static head of 40 feet provides service to the remotest single story user in the distribution network. This pressure is always present on the system. The multiple story users have booster pumps. After estimating the system resistance curve, system pressures were obtained for each of the operating flows to be used in the analysis of the adjustable speed operation of the pumps. Figure 18 depicts the estimated system resistance curve for the water distribution system superimposed of the head/flow performance curve.

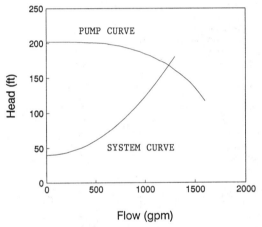

Flow (gpm)

FIGURE 18
SYSTEM CURVE SUPERIMPOSED
ON THE PUMP PERFORMANCE CURVE

## Energy Savings

Energy calculations were based on the estimated system resistance curve and the load duty cycle constructed from the operating data obtained from the customer. The annual energy consumption of the pump operated at constant speed was calculated to be 249,000 kWh, while the adjustable speed operation of the pump was estimated to consume only 153,000 kWh annually. This represents a potential energy saving of 96,000 kWh per year or a 39% reduction in energy requirements.

The results of the ASD analysis are summarized below.

Estimated Equipment Cost   $10,400

Estimated Installation Cost <u>16,000</u>

Total Cost of Retrofit   $26,400

Energy Saving      96,000 kWh/yr

Cost of Energy     $ 0.17 /kWh

Energy Cost Saving   $16,320 /yr

$$\text{Simple Payback} = \frac{\$26,400}{\$20,910} = 1.6 \text{ yrs}$$

The features of the system that favor an ASD retrofit are.

- The high number of operating hours

- An intermediate HP rating

- The large fluctuations in the required system flow

- The present use of pressure reducing check valves   as a means of flow control

## Case 5:  Steam Turbine Replacement

Historically, recovery boilers in the pulp and paper industry have used a variable speed drive to power the boiler induced draft fan. The majority of the drives have been either a mechanical steam turbine or a synchronous or induction motor driving the fan through a fluid drive variable speed coupling.  Either drive will satisfactorily vary the speed of the fan to meet the boiler demand. The motor drive is much more efficient than the steam turbine and reliability of the two types of drives has proven to be equal.  The usual practice has been to select the type of drive based on the mill's heat and energy balance. This was the method used in selecting the original drive for the I.D. fan.

The turbine drive was specified and purchased in 1974.  During the 12-year period between 1974 and 1986, the mill energy conditions changed to the point that it became desirable to re-evaluate the drive economics.  The economic analysis favored an AC motor drive and indicated a retrofit would provide a potential savings of $338,000 per year.  This would represent a simple return of capital in less than 1 1/2 years.

## Application

The application consisted of replacing the steam turbine drive with an AC motor variable frequency drive system.  The existing I.D. fan steam turbine drive cycle, as indicated in Figure 19, takes 43,000 lb/hr of 600 psig, 703° F steam from the 600 psig steam header, with an enthalpy of 1352 BTU/lb.  The output of the desuperheater sends 47,304 lb/hr of 60 psig, 342°F steam to the paper mill process.  Desuperheating was necessary in order for the steam temperature to be compatible with the steam users in the pulp producing and paper drying process. Installing a motor and a variable frequency drive system and shutting down the drive turbine provided a much more efficient energy cycle for the I.D. fan drive.  As indicated in Figure 20, an additional 47,304 lb/hr of 600 psig, 702°F steam from the 600 psig steam system will be passed through the more efficiency No. 8 turbine generator, thereby producing an additional 2,037 kW of electrical power.  728 kW of the additional power generated will be consumed by the I.D. fan motor drive.  The difference of 1309 kW will be used to reduce the amount of power purchased from the utility.

INCREMENTAL STEAM PROCESS

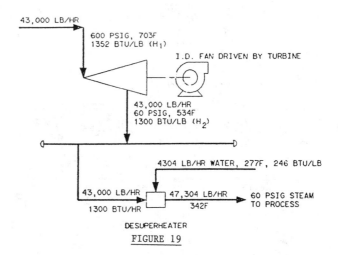

DESUPERHEATER

FIGURE 19

The recovery boiler I.D. Fan is
equipped with a double extended
shaft.  The equipment arrangement
with the steam turbine drive is
indicated in Figure 22.

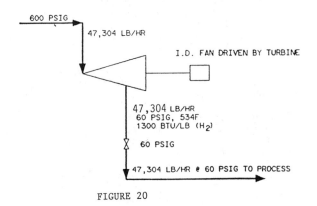

600 PSIG

47,304 LB/HR

I.D. FAN DRIVEN BY TURBINE

47,304 LB/HR
60 PSIG, 534F
1300 BTU/LB ($H_2$)

60 PSIG

47,304 LB/HR @ 60 PSIG TO PROCESS

FIGURE 20

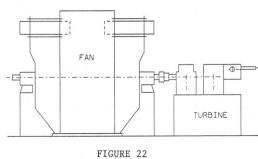

FAN

TURBINE

FIGURE 22

The mill generators and the utility
ties are synchronized and operate
in parallel, as indicated in Figure
21.  Based on a utility power cost
of $.04126/kWH and 8400 operating
hours per year, the potential gross
savings is $453,700/yr.  The net
savings is $338,000/yr.  The delta
between gross and net savings is
due to the additional steam that
must be generated in the boiler to
make up the difference between
43,000 lb/hr and 47,304 lb/hr that
is required to satisfy the process
demand of 60 psi steam.

The equipment arrangement with the
synchronous motor drive is
indicated in Figure 23.  The steam
turbine drive was decoupled and is
being maintained for immediate use
as an installed spare in the event
of an electric drive malfunction.
The installed drive is a 1250 hp,
900 RPM, 0.9PF, synchronous motor
with a brushless exciter.

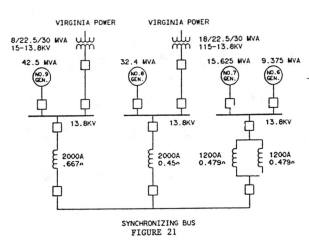

VIRGINIA POWER       VIRGINIA POWER

8/22.5/30 MVA                    18/22.5/30 MVA
15-13.8KV                        115-13.8KV

42.5 MVA      32.4 MVA      15.625 MVA   9.375 MVA
NO.9          NO.8          NO.7         NO.6
GEN.          GEN.          GEN.         GEN.

13.8KV        13.8KV        13.8KV

2000A         2000A         1200A        1200A
.667Ω         0.45Ω         0.479Ω       0.479Ω

SYNCHRONIZING BUS
FIGURE 21

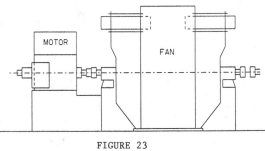

MOTOR        FAN

FIGURE 23

The motor is powered by a 12 pulse
load commutated inverter (LCI).
The total installed capital cost
was $480,000.  The net energy
saving was $338,000.  This
represents a simple return of
capital in 1.4 years.

### Case 6: Steel Mill BOF Fan

A steel mill located in the mid west operates two large ID fans serving Basic Oxygen Furnaces (BOF). These fans draw combustion gases from the furnace and pass them up a nearby stack during a cyclic lancing process as shown in Figure 24. During the actual lancing or firing process, which lasts about 20 minutes, the fans produce maximum air flow. After lancing, the air flow is reduced substantially by throttling the inlet dampers for a period of 30 minutes until the next cycle begins. Due to the frequent and significant throttling, significant savings can be achieved by the application of an adjustable speed drive. Based on operating data received from mill personnel, an accurate history of the load duty cycle for the BOF fan was determined. The "20 minute firing – 30 minute idle" cycle mentioned earlier is maintained continuously except for an 8-hour shutdown period every Wednesday and 5-day shutdown each quarter. An operating record was obtained indicating the pressure in the oxygen tank used to store the oxygen used in firing the furnace. The duration and frequency of the firings could be identified by a drop in the oxygen tank pressure. From the operating record we determined that the average number of firings per day was 26.

The ASD will be controlled by a signal from the existing process computer. Only two speeds will be required for the BOF fan, 1180 rpm and 300 rpm. The high speed will be used during the 20 minute firing periods, while the low speed will be used during the 30 minute non-firing periods. Since motor speed is directly proportional to the AC frequency applied, the drive will operate at two frequencies – 60 Hz for 1180 rpm operation and 15 Hz for 300 rpm operation.

The fan was a size 7111 Sturtevant fan, SWSI Class 1200, Arrangement 3 with inlet boxes. A fan curve was obtained for the 300 RPM and 1180 RPM speeds. The fan performance curve and the system resistance curve is indicated in Figure 25. The system curve is a quadratic relationship that describes the pressure losses in the system as a function of flow through the system and intersects the 1180 rpm fan curve (the current mill operating speed) at the mill's current operating air flow of 125,000 cfm. Although no required minimum flow rate exists, the air flow reduction capability was determined to be about 90% based on the throttling operation with the inlet dampers. Therefore, with a non-firing air flow of 15,000 cfm together with a naturally induced draft, an adequate amount of air flow will be maintained and the build-up of particulate matter on the fan blades will be minimized. Using the affinity laws, 15,000 cfm air flow corresponds to a speed of 300 rpm and 33 brake horsepower (bhp). Also, the frequency setting for the 300 rpm operation is 15 Hz which is well within the adjustable frequency range of the ASD.

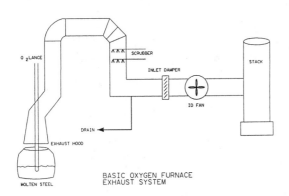

FIGURE 24
BOF EXHAUST SYSTEM

The ASD retrofit would consist of a 2000 hp adjustable frequency drive installed in parallel with the motor's existing starter. This would allow the mill to have a drive "bypass" mode so that the motor could be operated at either constant or adjustable speed.

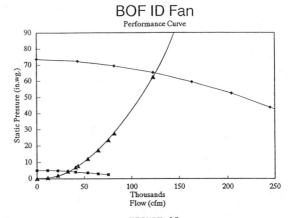

FIGURE 25
BOF FAN PERFORMANCE CURVE
AND THE SYSTEM CURVE AT BOTH
OPERATING MODES

The annual energy savings is calculated as the annual energy cost for the present operation during times when minimum air flow is used minus the operating cost at 300 RPM (minimum air flow) with an ASD.

The fan operating load cycle is as follows:

Operating hours at maximum air flow     2,841 hours

Operating hours at minimum air flow     5,023 hours

Total annual operating 7,864 hours time

Based on measured electrical data, the horsepower used with the inlet damper throttled is 1200 HP for 5,023 hours per year. The electrical energy consumed is 4,657,726 kilowatt hours at a cost of $186,309 based on a cost of electrical energy of $.041 kWh.

The calculated horsepower used based on the affinity laws is:

$$\frac{(300 \text{ RPM})^3}{(1180 \text{ RPM})^3} * 2000 \text{ HP} = 33 \text{ HP}$$

The motor and ASD efficiency at 300 RPM operating at 15 hertz is .45 and .7 respectively. The annual energy consumed at 300 RPM is 392,599 kilowatt hours. The annual cost of electrical energy at 300 RPM $15,703 based on energy cost of $.04 kWh.

The annual savings is     $186,309
                           -$15,702
                           $170,607

The cost estimate for the ASD and associated equipment installed is as follows:

Equipment Cost    $295,000
Installation Cost    75,000
                    -------
                  $370,000

The simple return of the capital cost is:

$$\frac{\text{Cost}}{\text{Net Savings}} = \frac{\$370,000}{\$170,607} = 2.17 \text{ yrs}$$

## Conclusions

The results of the case studies indicate energy reduction potential from 23% to 75% depending on the application and the load duty cycle. ASD applications are difficult to generalize because the energy savings potential hinges on the amount of time a piece of equipment is in operation as well as the variability of its operating range. There is no specific characteristics that inherently favor a particular type of ASD application. e.g., HVAC Supply Fan. such that all applications in that particular category can be said to produce a given energy savings. Each case must be reviewed in light of the best available operating data and equipment performance information.

While a certain amount of detailed analysis is desirable, most economically viable ASD applications can be judged to be feasible using the prescreening methods previously discussed. Applications that the prescreening procedure identify as acceptable will typically produce a 15% to 40% reduction in energy consumption. Larger horsepower ASD applications exhibit a favorable cost benefit at lower overall energy reductions because of the magnitude of the kWh savings and the cost of installation decreases on a horsepower basis. Smaller horsepower ASD applications (i.e., below 75 HP) must have higher overall energy savings to be economically attractive because the magnitude of the kWh savings is less and the cost per horsepower for the installation is greater.

# Chapter 25
# Customer Value - The Missing Link

A. R. Pierce, M.G. Martin, V.E. Wagner

For many years electric utilities found it easy to provide value to their shareholders. With a monopoly service and decreasing costs it was easy to sell 7% more electricity each year and earn attractive returns. In the last 20 years electric utilities have learned that it is not possible to provide value to their shareholders without providing value to their customers.

At Detroit Edison we are learning that customer value is not always what the utility thinks it is. There is no better way to find out what customers value than to ask them. We have done a lot of direct asking in the last couple of years, through market research and individual interviews. And we have learned indirectly from our customers when a particular program does not succeed as we thought it should. Two areas where we are learning more about customer value are Demand Side Management (DSM) and Power Quality.

## DEMAND SIDE MANAGEMENT

Detroit·Edison's experience with DSM programs is limited. We recently completed a three year "Demand and Energy Management Plan" in December of 1991. The programs were only pilots and are still being evaluated, but we were able to make some generalizations about successful and unsuccessful programs.

### Limited Experience

One of the most successful pilot programs was the dispersed generation pilot. It offered non-manufacturing and manufacturing customers an incentive to operate new or existing generators during system peak days. Customers installing new generators were given an annual incentive of $100/kW, while customers with existing generators were given $50/kW per year. The customer response to this pilot was very positive, and the pilot incentive money was fully committed by the second quarter of 1991. Ten customers received incentives, resulting in a potential peak savings of 3 to 5 MW.

One of the least successful programs was a residential water heater financing program. Making highly efficient electric water heaters easier to acquire simply did not add enough value for our customers to cause them to participate in the program.

Our Performance Contracting pilot was of questionable value. The pilot offered manufacturing and non-manufacturing customers a feasibility study performed at their facility by an approved energy service company (ESCO), in most cases at no charge to the customer. Upon completion of the study, the ESCO would propose to finance the installation of the viable energy savings measures

in exchange for a share of the energy savings. The customer response to this pilot was poor. Although many customers received the study, very few customers followed through by signing a performance contract with the ESCO. We cannot be sure of the reason(s) for the poor performance of the pilot until our evaluation is complete.

### Overall DSM Strategy

Following our mixed results and reviewing some mixed results from other utilities, we concluded that we needed an overall strategy for choosing and implementing effective and efficient DSM programs. Targeting value-creating DSM programs to meet customer needs/values is the most cost effective way to elicit customer participation in DSM programs. But DSM programs cost money. If the increased cost of the DSM programs is borne by customers, how can we be sure that the positive value of the program is greater than the decreased value which results from the higher rates which pay for the programs. Providing cost effective customer value through DSM programs requires a delicate balance between the funding level of value-creating DSM programs and the associated rate impacts/net benefits.

The first step in developing a DSM strategy was to determine customer needs/values. The customers were segmented by market. Once segmented, we used "brainstorming" sessions with customer account executives to identify the key elements of customer value for each customer market. We later incorporated customer value research results that were important from a DSM perspective. We also used program results from other utilities as a proxy for customer value in Michigan. Although we plan to test our programs with Michigan customers before full implementation, a reasonable proxy was necessary for the preliminary evaluations which followed.

The next step in developing a DSM strategy was to evaluate approximately 60 potential DSM programs, based on identified customer value elements, from three different perspectives (as shown in Figure 1). The three points of view come from: the utility (or shareholders), customers (both participants and non-participants), and society (considering externalities). Each party has its own perspective as to the value created by potential DSM programs. The corresponding perspectives are: utility value, total value (customer value plus utility value), and societal value. We focus on "total value", which includes programs with a net aggregate benefit to the customer and the utility. We do not use a societal value test because of difficulty of measurement.

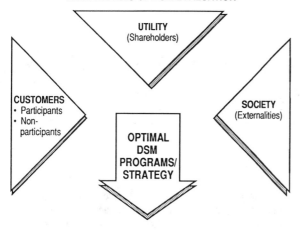

THREE LEVELS OF DSM EVALUATION

UTILITY
(Shareholders)

CUSTOMERS
• Participants
• Non-participants

SOCIETY
(Externalities)

OPTIMAL
DSM
PROGRAMS/
STRATEGY

EVALUATION PERSPECTIVE

SOCIETAL "VALUE"
• Programs net beneficial to all of society
(incorporating environmental impact value)

"TOTAL" VALUE
• Programs net beneficial to customers
and the utility

UTILITY VALUE
• Programs net
beneficial to the utility
(pre rate increase)

FIGURE 1. DSM PROGRAM EVALUATION
PERSPECTIVES

DSM programs create "total value" when the sum of the utility's avoided capacity, avoided energy, and customer non-electric savings, exceed the utility's incremental DSM costs (i.e., administration) and the customer investment costs. The DSM costs and benefits can vary widely among programs that create total value. Figure 2 is an example showing the benefits and costs making up total value for three DSM programs: Efficient Motors, Dispersed Generation, and Exit Sign Lighting.

DSM programs passing the total value test provide a net aggregate benefit for the utility and the customer, but the economics to the utility alone are often negative. This occurs if the utility loses revenues and is required to pay participant incentives (costs which are considered transfer payments from the total value perspective) and those costs are not fully offset by the avoided cost savings. Figure 3 is an example showing the benefits and costs making up "utility" value for the same three DSM programs: Efficient Motors, Dispersed Generation, Exit Sign Lighting. Note that of the three total value-creating programs previously discussed, only Dispersed Generation leaves the utility whole before lost revenue and participant incentive recovery.

We next matched the value-creating DSM programs to the customer value elements associated with specific markets/customers. DSM programs targeted to specific customers/markets in this way have a higher probability of reaching a receptive customer. Proper targeting is also important in cost effectively administering a DSM program.

Making DSM Program Recommendations

The utility decision on the optimal amount of DSM funding often requires making a trade-off between increased rates and customer value creation. Figure 4 depicts a graph of the rate impact/net benefits versus the funding levels for DSM programs. We believe a reasonable amount of DSM spending is somewhere between funding only DSM programs which decrease rates

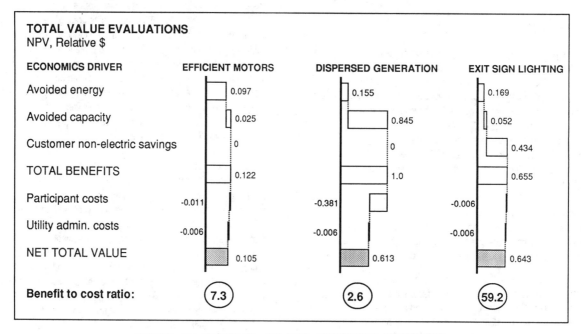

FIGURE 2. EXAMPLES OF DSM PROGRAMS EVALUATED
BY "TOTAL VALUE"

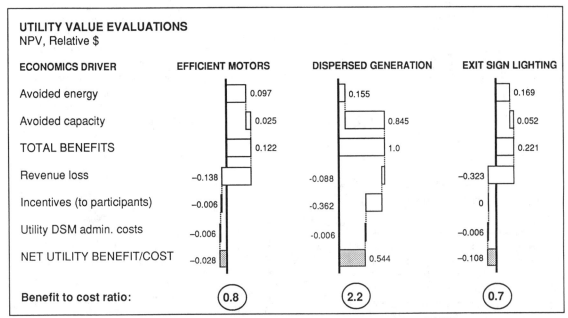

FIGURE 3.    EXAMPLES  OF  DSM  PROGRAMS  EVALUATED
BY  "UTILITY  VALUE"

(minimal spending) and funding all DSM programs which increase the net benefit to the utility and its customers (maximum spending). Typically, very few DSM programs are net beneficial to customers and the utility while reducing rates, and those programs should be implemented first. As DSM programs are added with marginal total value, rates increase, until additional DSM programs actually decrease the net benefit to the utility and its customers. Detroit Edison management had to decide on a recommended DSM funding level based on both economic and regulatory considerations, but the overall strategy project clearly outlined the economic considerations for both the utility and the customers.

The decision as to the appropriate DSM program mix and the level of funding will depend, in part on a utility's customers. The utility must know its customers well in order to determine the proper balance between the number of value-creating DSM programs required to meet their needs/values versus their customers' sensitivity to the associated rate impacts.

### POWER QUALITY

Our customer value research has shown that power quality is an issue in virtually all markets. Moreover, it is expected to increase in significance in the next 5 years in many of our markets.

The definition of power quality has evolved substantially since the introduction of the microprocessor. Previously the responsibility of power engineers, it encompassed reliability, voltage control, and flicker. Today, the proliferation of microcomputer, telecommunication, and control equipment has forced a new definition of power quality for utilities, manufacturers, and users in order to accommodate the needs of electronic equipment.

The new definition of power quality involves the fitness for use of electric power. A power quality problem is any power

### RATE IMPACT/NET BENEFITS VERSUS DSM PROGRAM SPENDING

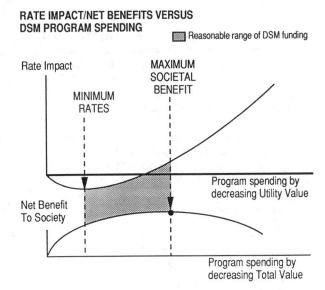

FIGURE 4.    RANGE  OF  DSM  SPENDING

variation that results in equipment downtime. In some cases it may only be a nuisance such as resetting a digital alarm clock. The opposite extreme is the loss of $300,000 by a steel company due to a switching transient tripping a continuous steel caster. Grounding, although not perhaps considered a power variation, has a similar effect and is considered part of power quality. Computer network lock-up and damaged circuit boards are frequently caused by grounding problems.

The types of disturbances commonly causing power quality problems are shown in Figure 5. The surge is a unidirectional pulse less than 4 ms in duration and is generated by switching off an inductive load or lightning. The capacitor switching transient is shown next. Utilities and their customers switch capacitors to control power factor. When the capacitor is switched on, it generates a characteristic transient that affects some types of equipment.

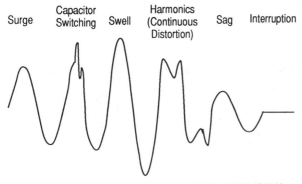

Surge | Capacitor Switching | Swell | Harmonics (Continuous Distortion) | Sag | Interruption

FIGURE 5. TYPES OF DISTURBANCES COMMONLY CAUSING POWER QUALITY PROBLEMS

Harmonics is a repetitive distortion of the voltage or current and is caused by nonlinear loads. There are several mechanisms by which harmonics affect equipment. A voltage sag is a momentary reduction in voltage due to a fault on the utility network. It has the same effect on equipment as a short interruption. The swell is the inverse of the sag. It is the momentary increase in voltage, most commonly due to a neutral shift as a result of a fault. Swells rarely affect equipment. Finally, an interruption is the complete absence of voltage due to the disconnection from the power source.

There have been several large power quality surveys that showed the occurrence of disturbances. Unfortunately most are quite dated. The most recent is coordinated by the National Power Laboratory and is the result of 450 site-months of data from 74 residential, commercial, and industrial locations nationwide. Figure 6 shows the percent occurrence of the disturbances.

Sags are by far the most common type of disturbance at 60%. This is in contrast to popular articles on power quality that portray surges as the most common problem. Sags cause significant economic loss. Swells are the next most common but do not adversely affect most equipment. These are followed by surges at 8 % and interruptions at 3.4%.

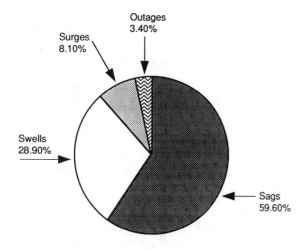

FIGURE 6. PERCENT OF OCCURRENCE OF DISTURBANCES

There are no standards on power quality either for utilities or equipment. Existing utility voltage standards and manufacturers' specifications apply to steady state voltage variation. One criteria that has been widely applied as a guideline was originally published by the Computer Business Equipment Manufacturers Association as a recommendation for mainframe computers (see Figure 7). It was reproduced in IEEE Standard 446 as a guide for facilities. While no manufacturer meets the guide, it is used as a reasonable limit for power variation.

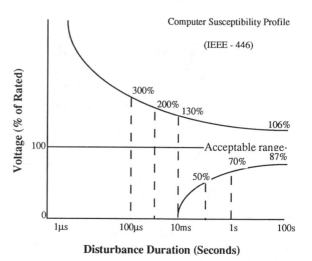

FIGURE 7. IEEE STANDARD 446 GUIDE FOR FACILITIES

Downtime is the result of more than just power variation. Figure 8 shows the relationship between the three factors that cause power related downtime. Power variation is the most obvious cause resulting from utility faults, switching, etc. However, the user's facility also contributes to power variation with harmonics, grounding, surges, and wiring problems. Surges cannot travel far on building wiring and, therefore, those present are largely generated within the user's facility. As will be shown, utilities are working to reduce their variation and helping users to reduce building variation.

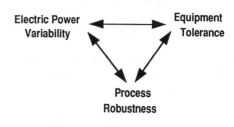

FIGURE 8. THREE FACTORS CAUSE POWER RELATED DOWNTIME

Equipment tolerance is the next factor in the triangle. Thirty years ago there was hardly any electronic control equipment in business. Computers were large centralized pieces of hardware and most control functions were performed by relays. If the voltage dropped below 60% the relay would drop-out. They were unaffected by surges, grounding, or transients. Today electronic controls may reset if the voltage drops below 85% of rated. Voltage distortion (transients, harmonics) or grounding may cause disruption. Of the three elements of the triangle, equipment tolerance has changed the most over the last two decades, in the wrong direction.

Process robustness is the third element in the power quality triangle. This is how the equipment is applied in the power environment. If the equipment is applied blindly, a power variation that exceeds the tolerance of the equipment will result in downtime. Power conditioning equipment increases the robustness of the application so that wide power variation can be tolerated by very sensitive equipment. A fiber optic computer network makes the network immune to grounding problems. The shielding of low voltage signal cables from magnetic or electronic interference is another example of increasing the robustness of an application. The latter is the least frequently applied.

Utility Role

Utilities have assumed the leadership role for power quality in many cases. Although 60% to 80% of power quality problems originate within the user's facility (improper wiring, grounding problems, interfering equipment, etc.), our research has shown that users expect utilities to provide power quality expertise and to work to minimize the problem. Such activities increase customer trust and confidence, positioning the utility as the preferred energy supplier in an increasingly competitive energy market. In the future, utility customers may be able to select their energy provider, much as telephone customers can select their long distance provider. But even before that is possible, some utility customers can turn to self-generation in cases of extreme power quality problems.

Equipment is more sensitive, and user's expectations of product quality in everything from automobiles to electricity have increased. As a result, utilities are shifting to a more customer defined quality criteria. Traditionally, electric utilities have been primarily concerned with reliability or the prevention of long-term outages. Their design, planning, and operating criteria as well as performance measures focused on reliability. Depending on the utility, long-term outages were defined as 3-5 minutes. Today, a 30 second outage can have the same consequence as a 30 minute outage. Many have or are in the process of redefining their outage criteria to include an outage of any duration.

Harmonics are another problem where utilities may establish limits. IEEE Standard 519 sets limits on utility voltage distortion that a few utilities have adopted. A revision of the standard due late in 1992 also limits the current distortion that utility customers return to the utility. Most harmonic problems are caused by users and the utility becomes involved to provide consultation or to mediate neighboring users' interference with each other.

Users expect utilities to reduce the variability of their product. The first step in that process is to measure actual performance.

Unfortunately, the traditional utility measurement methods are aimed at reliability and not the types of deviations users may be complaining about. Some utilities have installed permanent monitors to track power quality performance and it is expected more will follow. The data from the monitors show that power quality is very location specific, varies by time-of-day, and improves with higher voltage service levels. From the data utilities will develop specific action plans to address excessive variability.

Many utilities have power quality specialists who work with their customers to resolve problems. This is an opportunity for them to transform a negative experience for their customers to a positive one. These specialists can positively affect a much larger group of users through education and prevention. By working cooperatively with electrical contractors, architectural and engineering firms, power quality problems can be minimized in design and construction. Utilities are also educating their customers on how power quality should be a consideration in purchase and application decisions. If users can anticipate power quality problems rather than be surprised by them, less frustration will be generated. For long term effectiveness, education is the most powerful tool available to the utility.

Manufacturer's role

The greatest change over the last couple of decades in the compatibility triangle is the decrease in equipment tolerance to power quality disturbances. Manufacturers are under enormous pressure to reduce costs to remain competitive in the world market. Apparently power quality sensitivity is not a characteristic they feel their customers demand. If they felt their customers were demanding improved power quality, they would eventually have to provide this value to their customers.

In many cases, equipment designers are not aware of the actual disturbances their equipment will experience in service. Without this information, they assume that steady state voltage variation, extended interruptions, and surges are the major power considerations. The equipment will experience those disturbances as well as momentary interruptions, sags, capacitor switching transients, and harmonics. The hardware changes to accommodate those disturbances are often minor. Yet, without the knowledge of their existence, improvements are not possible. Utilities and some users are trying to communicate power quality issues to the manufacturers' decision makers. However, it may be years before this effort succeeds.

Power quality requirements may also be added to equipment standards documents. Yet, there is no one organization whose standards necessarily will cause the change. Most manufacturers compete in the world market and design to perceived international requirements. Furthermore, many standards groups consists of manufacturers who may not yet appreciate the magnitude of the problem. The standards that will first reflect power quality requirements will be those that include outsiders, such as users and utilities, in their membership. With time, standards will incorporate more realistic power quality requirements.

The Electric Power Research Institute (EPRI), the research vehicle of the electric utility industry, is attempting to bring utilities' and manufacturers' needs together with a proposed Utility Compatibility Rating. EPRI is developing an acceptance test that would certify that manufacturers' equipment meets minimum power quality performance requirements. The manufacturer could then use the rating for promotional purposes. It may well be that a nonstandard approach such as this will the be most successful.

## User's Role

The users responsibility is to plan for power quality in the application of their equipment. Electricity is part of the environment within which their equipment must operate within. As with ambient temperature and humidity, there will be voltage variation; and the equipment selected must operate within the band that is expected to occur. This means the user should know what power variation to expect and that information should be available from the utility. The utility should provide either site specific data from monitoring the location or generic information on reasonable expectations of disturbance activity.

Users should also try to obtain power quality tolerance data from manufacturers before they purchase. Some manufacturers such as mainframe and minicomputer manufacturers may already have the necessary information. Nevertheless, most manufacturers will not. The most the user can do is to pressure the manufacturer for the performance data. If enough customers ask for the data, manufacturers will eventually provide it. They will then begin to accept power quality tolerance as a customer requirement.

Power quality as a specification requirement has not been successful. It appears that specification requirements work best when they address mutually understood performance. Adding a new requirement that is not considered a standard item will not necessarily change the manufacturer's response.

Armed with general knowledge of power quality, the user should apply it in their application. For instance, critical computer information that could be lost after a momentary interruption requires a battery back-up for the computer. A more subtle problem is an electrically operated magnetic lathe chuck. A brief interruption could cause the part to be thrown from the rotating chuck creating a considerable hazard.

Although not all users need be power quality experts, they should apply some common sense to prevent possible future equipment problems. And although all power quality problems are not of a utility's making, the utility is in an ideal position to help customers with power quality issues.

# Chapter 26
# DSM - The Iowa Experience
D.J. Levy

The Iowa Legislature passed a landmark bill in the 1990 session which became effective July 1, 1990. This legislation had several components, the most significant being a requirement for rate-regulated utilities in Iowa to begin implementing energy efficiency programs.

The legislation sets spending targets of 2% of gross electric revenues and 1½% of gross gas revenues. It also requires five specific program areas to be considered.

Administrative rulemaking to comply with the legislation was completed in early 1991 and all utility plans were filed by July 1, 1991. The plans were reviewed in individual contested proceedings and most were approved by February 1, 1992. The final orders in all of the proceedings required the utilities to begin the programs in 1992.

Iowa-Illinois Gas and Electric Company proposed and received approval on eight programs spanning all customer classes. Most of the programs include both gas and electric measures. The four residential programs were implemented on March 1, 1992 and the four commercial/industrial programs were implemented on April 1, 1992.

Costs of the programs are deferred in special accounts until a contested cost recovery proceeding is convened. The legislation requires cost recovery from customers to lag the program implementation by at least two years. Therefore, those proceedings will commence in 1994 with amortization to be spread over four years following an order in that proceeding.

The presentation will follow the sequence of the following charts as well as detail experience in the programs to date.

---

# Senate File 2403

■ Became Law July 1, 1990

■ Set Spending Targets

■ Established Schedule

■ Targeted Five Programs

---

# Spending Targets

- 2% of Gross Electric Revenues

- 1 1/2% of Gross Gas Revenues

- Paid for by customers

# Schedule

- Rulemaking in 1990

- Submit plans early 1991

- Plan approval late 1991

- Programs start in 1992

- Cost recovery start 1994

# Targeted Programs

■ Residential Water Heater Blankets

■ Commercial Lighting

■ Energy Efficiency Goods

■ Low Income

■ Tree Planting

# Programs in the Plan

■ Residential Weatherization

■ Residential Equipment Rebate

■ Residential Low-Income

■ Residential New Construction

■ Non-Res Buildings - Shopping List

■ Non-Res Buildings - Custom

■ Industrial Process

■ Non-Res New Buildings

# 1992-1994 Budget

- Electric - $7,317,544 (1.4%)

- Gas - $9,991,538 (2.6%)

## Program Administration Costs

|                 | 1991     | 1992      | 1993      | 1994      |
|-----------------|----------|-----------|-----------|-----------|
| RESIDENTIAL     | $22,501  | $212,504  | $212,504  | $212,504  |
| NON-RESIDENTIAL | $85,957  | $368,480  | $368,480  | $368,480  |
|                 |          |           |           |           |
| TOTAL           | $108,458 | $580,984  | $580,984  | $580,984  |

# Program Penetration Rates

## Year

|  | 1 | 2 | 3 | 4 | 5 | 6 | 7 | 8 | 9 |
|---|---|---|---|---|---|---|---|---|---|
| **RESIDENTIAL:** | | | | | | | | | |
| WEATHERIZATION | 3% | 8% | 15% | 22% | 29% | 36% | 42% | 47% | 50% |
| HIGH-EFF. REBATES | 10% | 25% | 33% | 33% | 33% | 33% | 33% | 33% | 33% |
| LOW INCOME | 3% | 8% | 15% | 22% | 29% | 36% | 42% | 47% | 50% |
| NEW CONSTRUCTION | 10% | 25% | 40% | 40% | 40% | 40% | 40% | 40% | 40% |
| **NON-RESIDENTIAL:** | | | | | | | | | |
| COOLING | 2% | 4% | 8% | 10% | 10% | 10% | 10% | 10% | 10% |
| LIGHTING | 20% | 25% | 30% | 30% | 30% | 30% | 30% | 30% | 30% |
| HEATING | 10% | 15% | 20% | 20% | 20% | 20% | 20% | 20% | 20% |
| CUSTOMIZED | 2% | 5% | 10% | 10% | 10% | 10% | 10% | 10% | 10% |
| MOTORS | 1% | 3% | 5% | 7% | 10% | 10% | 10% | 10% | 10% |
| PROCESS | 1% | 1% | 2% | 3% | 3% | 3% | 3% | 3% | 3% |
| NEW CONSTRUCTION | 0% | 5% | 10% | 15% | 20% | 20% | 20% | 20% | 20% |

# Labor Requirements

|  | PROGRAM MANAGER | PROGRAM ANALYST | ENGINEER | CLERICAL |
|---|---|---|---|---|
| **RESIDENTIAL:** | | | | |
| WEATHERIZATION | 3/4 TIME | 1/2 TIME | | |
| HIGH-EFF. REBATES | 1/2 TIME | FULL TIME | | |
| LOW INCOME | 1/4 TIME | | | |
| NEW CONSTRUCTION | 1/2 TIME | | FULL TIME | |
| **NON-RESIDENTIAL:** | | | | |
| COOLING | | | | |
| LIGHTING | 1/2 TIME | | FULL TIME | FULL TIME |
| HEATING | | | | |
| CUSTOMIZED | 1/2 TIME | | FULL TIME | 3/4 TIME |
| MOTORS | 1/2 TIME | | 2 - FULL TIME | 3/4 TIME |
| PROCESS | | | | |
| NEW CONSTRUCTION | 1/4 TIME | | 1/2 TIME | 1/4 TIME |

# Pre-determined Rebates
### Residential
### Furnaces and boilers

| AFUE | Rebate |
|---|---|
| 84.0%-84.9% | $210 |
| 85.0%-85.9% | $245 |
| 86.0%-86.9% | $280 |
| 87.0%-87.9% | $315 |
| 88.0%-88.9% | $350 |
| 89.0%-89.9% | $385 |
| 90% and over | $420 |

# Pre-determined Rebates
### Residential
### Central Air & Heat Pumps

| SEER | Rebate |
|---|---|
| 11.0-11.4 | $150 |
| 11.5-11.9 | $225 |
| 12.0-12.4 | $300 |
| 12.5-12.9 | $375 |
| 13.0-13.4 | $450 |
| 13.5-13.9 | $525 |
| 14.0 and over | $600 |

# Pre-determined Rebates
## Residential
## Water Heaters

| Type | EF | Rebate |
|---|---|---|
| Gas | .60 and over | $50 |
| Electric | .95 and over | $50 |

# Pre-determined Rebates
## Residential
## Room Air Conditioners

| EER | Rebate |
|---|---|
| 9.5-9.9 | $35 |
| 10.0 and over | $50 |

# Pre-determined Rebates
### Commercial/Industrial
### Motors (sample)

| Size (HP) | Efficiency (TEFC) | Efficiency (ODP) | Rebate |
|---|---|---|---|
| 1 | 84.0 | 82.5 | $ 6 |
| 5 | 88.5 | 87.5 | $ 12 |
| 20 | 93.0 | 92.4 | $ 21 |
| 50 | 94.1 | 94.1 | $ 68 |
| 200 | 95.4 | 95.0 | $293 |

# Pre-determined Rebates
### Commercial/Industrial
### Lighting (sample)

| Measure | Description | Rebate |
|---|---|---|
| Lamps | 32-34 watt T-12 | $ .50 |
| Lamps | 60 watt T-12 | $ 1.00 |
| Ballasts | 2-4 4ft T-12 | $ 6.00 |
| Ballasts | 2-4 8ft T-12 | $ 7.00 |
| T-8 Systems | 2-32 watt | $ 8.00 |
| T-8 Systems | 4-32 watt | $12.00 |
| Delamping | 2X4 fixture | $ 6/lamp |
| Delamping | 1X8 fixture | $12/lamp |

# Pre-determined Rebates
## Commercial/Industrial
## HVAC

| Description | Rebate |
|---|---|
| Air conditioners | Same as residential |
| Heat pumps | Same as residential |
| Prgrm thermostat | $30 |

# Risks & Opportunities

■ **Risks**

– Lost Revenue and Margin from DSM Reduction in Sales

– Regulatory Response to Resulting Rate Cases

– FASB Treatment of Program Cost Capitalization

– Recovery of Costs and Capitalized Return

■ **Opportunities**

– Unique Opportunity to Improve Customer Productivity & Relationships

– Program Performance Rewards

– More Economic Development without Capacity Addition

# Chapter 27
# Demand-Side Management Bidding - Lessons Learned

J.L. Finleon, K. Triplett

## SYNOPSIS

This paper describes lessons learned by Public Service Company of Colorado, participating in Demand Side Management Bidding as a soliciting utility.

## ABSTRACT

This paper examines Public Service Company of Colorado's, (PSC's) successful implementation of a 50 Megawatt (50 MW) Demand Side Management bidding program. PSC experienced DSM bidding through implementing a small pilot program and later, through a 50 MW DSM bidding program which was successful in achieving a response of 63 proposals, totaling 130 MW, at an average price of $329/kW.

This paper will discuss key issues associated with DSM bidding such as scoring techniques, security deposits, timing of payments, eligibility, etc., and how PSC decided to resolve the issues based on its previous experience. In addition, the paper will review changes PSC would make in future DSM bidding programs.

Based on the issues described in this paper it is concluded that a balance must be struck between a utility's need for reliable, low cost, long lived, demand and energy savings and the amount of burden a utility can place upon potential bidders.

## INTRODUCTION

Demand Side Bidding is a process whereby a utility initiates a Request for Proposals (RFP) to its customers and/or energy service companies (ESCOs) or other third parties for implementing Demand Side Management (DSM) technologies. The RFP typically specifies the types of DSM technologies desired by the utility and the criteria used to evaluate the proposals. The premise behind DSM bidding is that the competitive natute of bidding will drive down the costs of implementing DSM measures.

PSC's bidding experience began in mid-1989 with a pilot program consisting of the release, by PSC, of a Request for Proposals for Demand Side Management prop jects for a total of 2 MW. With little advertising this solicitation received a response of 9 proposals totaling 6 MW at a cost of approximately $240/kW. Based on the initial success of the pilot project, PSC initiated a second solicitation for 50 MW in December 1990. With a little more advertising the 50 MW bidding program was successful in attracting 63 proposals totaling 131 MW at an average price of $329/kW.

A further breakdown of the results of the 50 MW bidding program included proposals from 45 customers and 18 third parties. The following is a summary of the technologies represented by the 131 MW submitted:

| | |
|---|---|
| Electric heat conversions | 38.70 MW |
| Lighting | 32.00 MW |
| Energy Cooperative | 15.00 MW |
| Indst. Process Efficiency | 12.50 MW |
| Snowmaking | 9.90 MW |
| Energy Management Systems | 7.50 MW |
| Motor Efficiency | 5.40 MW |
| Gas/Steam Cooling | 3.90 MW |
| A/C Efficiency | 2.70 MW |
| Other | 3.00 MW |
| Total | 130.60 MW |

The remainder of this paper describes issues that should be addressed by utilities when conducting their DSM bidding programs. These issues are broken down into three general categories: RFP Objectives, RFP Design and RFP Process. A description of each issue, some options and recommendations will be discussed.

## RFP OBJECTIVES

The utility should clearly identify objectives for pursuing demand side management bidding, and should develop the Request for Proposal around those objectives. Some of the issues around setting objectives include the following:

* How should the program integrate with existing direct utility incentive programs?

* Should DSM savings be maxmized per site, or should overall cost per unit of savings be minimized?

* Does the utility want participation from both customers and ESCOs?

* What loas shape does the utility want to achieve?

The objectives of the program may be determined and driven by regulatory incentives, the existence of other DSM programs offered by the utility, the amount of experience a utility has in implementing DSM, and by the system resource needs.

### Program Integration with Existing Utility Programs

The utility must decide if and how the bidding program should be integrated with its existing programs. Some utilities allow their DSM bidding programs to compete directly with rebates they offer for the same measures.

In this case, it is unlikely that the cost of the bidding program will be less than the utility's rebate program, because the financial incentive to the customer must, at a minimum, be equal to the rebate allowed through the utility program. Changing the amount of the rebates in a utility program during the bidding process can wreak havoc on an ESCO's ability to market the bidding program under a fixed price. Competing programs can also result in the alienation of the utility's customer representatives who would, in essence, be competing with ESCOs to persuade customers to install DSM measures.

Utility customer representatives may have individual quotas for encouraging their customers to take advantage of utility rebates, a third party or ESCO could impede their progress. The reverse is also true, in that ESCOs have a harder time selling their proposals when a utility has a direct rebate for the same measure. One recommendation is to target bidding either to a specific market segment or to DSM measures not already eligible for utility rebates. An option that would reduce competition between a utility's representatives and ESCOs would be to solicit bids from ESCOs to assist with the marketing and follow-up work associated with existing DSM rebate programs.

## Maximize Savings Per Site vs. Minimize Cost Per Unit Savings

Utilities need to decide if their goal is to maximize the cost effective savings per site or to minimize the cost of the overall program per unit of savings. The answer to this issue may be dependent upon the regulatory incentives to minimize the cost per unit of demand savings. In this case, it is recommended that within a proposal each DSM measure be broken out and evaluated individually. It is likely more cost effective to implement the cheapest measure at several sites than to implement all possible measures at one site. Individual evaluation of each DSM measure by the utility creates some incertainty for bidders, who risk having only part of their proposal accepted, in knowing how to price individual measures in order to recover their overhead costs. If the utility's objective is to maximize savings per site, then a means for allocating additional possible points for additional DSM measures installed at one site should be included when designing the scoring mechanism.

## Participation by Customers and/or Energy Service Companies

Allowing direct participation by customers, in addition to ESCOs, can lower the overall cost of the bidding program to the utility. ESCOs need to retain close to 50% of the bid award payment to cover their costs of managing the project. If customers participate directly, care should be taken to make the bidding process as simple as possible. PSC learned that providing constant communication to customers, and educating utility customer representatives about the bidding process generated customer enthusiasm for the program and encouraged customer participation.

Pre-bid conferences allowed bidders to meet face to face with the utility DSM bidding program staff. Establishing a personal rapport between utility staff and bidders is paramount to customer participation. Without this essential communication, customers and the utility's representatives may become disenchanted with the process, and overall customer satisfaction will suffer. PSC's DSM solicitation was extended to customers, ESCOs and other third parties. Approximately two thirds of the proposals received were from customers and one third from ESCOs and other third parties. The final award group was comprised of roughly the same mix of customers to ESCOs and third parties.

## Load Shape Objectives

Setting load shape objectives can help the utility obtain DSM measures that will benefit its system. One objective might be to "see what the marketplace desires" by leaving the type of DSM technology open. At the other end of the spectrum a utility can specify the DSM measure down to the level of the allowed equipment.

Bids were received for a wide variety of technologies providing valuable data on costs and savings for a number of DSM technologies. PSC's system requirements were for DSM savings to occur in winter, summer, and year round due to the company's existing high load factor.

### RFP DESIGN

When designing an RFP utilities should, at a minimum, consider the following factors: a) verification, b) pricing, c) scoring, d) security deposits, e) bidder qualifications and experience, f) measure lifetime, g) minimum size requirements, and h) timing of payments.

## Verification

Determining the amount of DSM savings achieved is of paramount importance to the utility. In PSC's MW pilot program, verification and site inspection were interchangeable terms, until the utility found an application whereby the project was installed and savings were not what was predicted.

For the 50 MW program, PSC better defined verification into three specific categories of evaluating the savings resulting from the installation: engineering calculations, metering, and statistical analyses of energy bills.

Bidders were allowed to choose specific methods and were responsible for conducting the verification with final review and approval of the verification to be the utility's responsibility. As a result, the costs of verification, and justification of the technique, become the responsibility of the bidder. Problems in the 50 MW program arose because bidders had little experience in designing verification techniques appropriate for their particular measure, and PSC had to review and approve the technique and results. Recommendations for future programs will include the utility designing and performing the verification to appropriately fit the particular measure and to assure consistency for similar proposals. Taking on more of the verification responsibility will likely result in a slight increase of overall administration costs for the utility, but should lower the bid price because bidders will not bear the burden.

## Pricing

Rather than using "avoided costs" as the ceiling for proposals, PSC utilized a reference price of $240/KW for the 50 MW program based on the results from the first 2 MW solicitation. Bids were scored, in part, based on the difference between the reference price and the bidder's proposed price. The reference price seemed to have a psychological effect of forcing bid prices near the reference price mark rather than near the avoided cost price. The average price of the final award group from the 50 MW program was $220/KW.

## Scoring

The scoring methodology should be designed to meet the utility's objectives. PSC used an objective scoring system in which bidders scored themselves. Bidders benefited by knowing exactly how they would be scored, leaving less potential for PSC to be accused of preferential treatment. The disadvantage to a self scoring RFP is the potential for "gaming" the system by the bidders.

For example, PSC awarded points in the 50 MW solicitation for providing combinations of verification techniques that utilized billing analysis, engineering calculations, and metering.. Once the bidders were chosen they attempted to negotiate out of some of the methods. Many times the methods were not appropriate to the individual technologies, making the negotiation process more difficult. It is recommended that the items being self-scored be limited to price and possibly measure lifetime, and that the utility be allowed to subjectively score certain items such as bidder qualifications.

It is important that the scoring criteria be described up front in the RFP itself. Submitting proposals is costly to bidders, therefore, in developing their proposals, they should understand clearly the utility's objectives.

## Security Deposits

Security deposits are needed to ensure the utility receive sincere proposals. Utilities invest time in evaluation of each proposal they receive. There are three specific points in the bidding process that require some kind of security be provided to the utility. The first is in the proposal submission state. Some type of application fee will help ensure that once a proposal is chosen, the bidder will negotiate in good faith to secure a contract. Once the contract is negotiated, the utility needs security that the bidder will install the DMS measure and achieve the savings. Once the DSM measure is installed, the utility needs assurance that the savings will be maintained over the life of the proposal.

PSC required a $100 non-refundable application fee and, upon contract execution, a $20/kw security to be held, through installation, over the measure lifetime. In future programs, the application fee may be variable, tied to the kw proposed, and then refunded should a contract be executed or the proposal eliminated.

## Bidder Qualification and Experience

Evaluating the experience and qualifications of the bidder can provide information to the utility regarding the riskiness of the proposal. However, experience may not always be necessary to ensure a good proposal. PSC utilized a self-scoring mechanism that gave bidders more points for having completed similar projects in the past. This kind of system may be disadvantageous for customers who are bidding on their own facilities.

The use of some type of sujective scoring by the utility that weighs a bidder's qualifications, based on references and the quality of the proposal submitted, is recommended.

## Measure Lifetime

Lifetime of the measure is important in determining the length of time the utility can rely on the demand and energy reduction occurring. One option for assessing the measure lifetime is to utilize ASHREA type standards for individual pieces of equipment. Another option is to allow bidders to propose a lifetime whereby they agree to replace and maintain equipment if the proposed lifetime is longer than the industry-accepted standard lifetime. The second option increases the value of the savings but is riskier in terms of the length of a contract.

There are many unknowns about technological advancement 10 to 15 years in the future, although it is assumed that at a minimum, the energy efficiency of technologies will increase. PSC allowed bidders to propose a lifetime from 10 to 20 years. Almost all of the proposals were for DSM measures with 20 year lifetimes. It is questionable whether some businesses will be in place in 20 years, therefore longer contracts are riskier to the utility.

## Minimum Size Requirements

PSC required a minimum bid size of 300 kw per proposal for an ESCO or third party bidder and 100 kw for a customer. Proposals could consist of any number of seperate measures with no minimum kw size per measure. Because measures were treated separately within a proposal, contracts for part or all of a proposal were negotiated. The minimum kw size requirement was to ensure proper economies of scale for the investment in evaluating proposals and negotiating contracts. The minimum size requirement should be balanced with the utility's desire to allow customers to submit their own proposals, as single customers must be large enough users to achieve a demand reduction of 100 kw or more. PSC is currently considering a 50 kw minimum size pre measure to prevent hours of staff time being spent preparing contracts for very small kw amounts.

## Timing of Payments

Timing of payments is important to bidders in terms of cash flow. Bidders want to offset their investment in the energy efficiency measure upfront while the utility wants to ensure payment for the savings as they are achieved.

PSC paid the bidders after the measure was installed and verification of savings achieved was performed. In some cases, where the verification included metering or billing analysis, payment did not occur until 6 months to a year following installation. PSC agreed to pay part of the bid award based on engineering calculations until the final verification was achieved. Other utilities have declined to pay more than the savings were worth for each year, making the award payment annually over the term of the contract. Understandably, making payments over time will increase the overall cost. It is simpler and less expensive for the utility to make the payments up front, however there is a risk that the savings will not be maintained over time. This risk can be mitigated somewhat with contract language and with the security deposit.

### RFP PROCESS

After the objectives are set and the RFP designed, the utility must determine how the bidding program will be conducted. Some of the issues associated with the process of a bidding program are a) degree of flexibility in contract negotiation, b) utility assistance offered to bidders, c) communications, and d) data management.

## Degree of Flexibility in Contract Negotiation

Bidding programs can take 1 to 2 years to complete, from the time of release of an RFP to having signed contracts. During measures a bidder wishes to market, the business conditions of potential customers and the availability and prices of technologies.

The utility needs to balance flexibility with the need to obtain verifiable and reliable measures. If everything were negotiable the utility would have no idea what it was actuallygetting until all the contracts were signed. The utility may find that its contracts are of little value. PSC allowed bidders to negotiate a decrease in bid size and measures, however increases were not permitted. This created some problems when it came close to signing contracts as some large proposals were reduced in size necessitating PSC to offer contracts to lower ranked proposals to get a total of 50 MW. Not allowing bidders to reduce their size would have resulted in more proposals being withdrawn. Allowing bidders to increase their bid size could result in a utility signing contracts for more DSM than is needed. Having a non-refundable application fee tied to the proposal size ($2/kW) may help to reduce this problem in the future.

## Assistance Offered to Bidders

In the first programs offered by PSC, the utility tried to stay at "arm's length" from all bidders, customers and ESCOs. Customers felt they were treated unfairly compared to past experiences with the utility when they were given greater flexibility. Some ESCOs used PSC's program to market to customers and later blamed the utility when problems occurred. Customer representatives became frustrated when program requirements got in the way of their objective of maintaining relationships with their customers. It is recommended that the utility provide assistance to all bidders through workshops to help bidders with proposal preparation. More upfront time from the utility may be required, but should result in fewer problems down the road.

Finding ways to leverage the utility's marketing advantage can help ESCOs lower their costs. The utility should be prepared to provide energy service companies with customer data to help them target customers. The utility should also provide assistance to the successful ESCOs' targeted customers, in educating them about the program. A utility representative, calling on a customer along with the ESCO, adds credibility to the process and should improve the ESCO's selling power. Utility involvement with the ESCO also provides the utility with some control over how information is presented to customers. This involvement may increase the administrative costs to the utility because they are more involved in the ESCO marketing process.

Alternatively, allowing ESCOs to come between the utility and its customers could hurt the relationship the utility has with its customer.

## Communications

Communication is very important during the bidding process. The department within the utility, responsible for managing the bidding process, must be in constant communication with other departments within the utility regarding the status of the program.

Customer representatives need to fully understand the rules and procedures of the program and know the status of proposals submitted by their customers. Informed representatives will refrain from providing contradictory information and can assist in communicating progress to the bidders. Regular newsletters outlining the status and reviewing the procedures are other ideas. PSC learned that not everyone will read and understand the rules if they are written only in the RFP.

## Data Management

Bidding programs are complex. Keeping track of the information supplied by bidders is crucial. Having a computerized data management system can save time when extracting information from proposals. Information

regarding construction schedules, types of DSM measures, bid size, price, verification, etc., are often needed to summarize the status and results of the program. It also would be helpful to include documentation of every phone and meeting conversation held with bidders in the event disagreements occur.

## CONCLUSIONS

It is important that a utility consider the costs and risks to itself and to potential bidders when designing and implementing a bidding program. Finding ways to share the risks with the bidders will result in programs with lower costs and more reliable savings.

This paper described issues associated with setting objectives for a bidding program, designing an RFP to meet the objectives and then managing the process of the bidding program.

Clear objectives must be established by the utility when designing an RFP for a competitive bid program. Procedures and policies must be developed for communicating those goals internally and presenting a unified company perspective to potential bidders. The RFP should concisely and clearly state the utility's expectations of potential bidders.

The more information a bidder has about what the utility wants and how it is to be presented, the higher the quality of information will be submitted. Leveraging the market power a utility has to work with customers and ESCOs can improve the overall effectiveness of the program. Organizing the data into a computerized database can improve the efficiency of evaluating the proposals and developing contracts.

Chapter 28

# Demand-Side Management Process Evaluations - The Management Perspective

G.A. Perrault, L.B. Barrett

## INTRODUCTION

A demand-side management (DSM) process evaluation is a qualitative, expert assessment of how a utility marketing program is being conducted. It reviews the efficiency and effectiveness in which a utility plans, manages, executes, and monitors the delivery of DSM programs to its marketplace. Process evaluations, also known as operational reviews, are becoming an increasingly significant component of the entire evaluation process which includes load impact, customer satisfaction and cost-effectiveness analysis.

The focus of the process evaluation is on the program planning and delivery *process* as opposed to the energy *impacts* resulting from the specific measures or products of the program. Because of this process-oriented focus, such evaluations can identify important opportunities for improving the cost-effectiveness of a program without significantly changing product lines.

The evaluation may identify administrative or delivery process improvements which may improve cost-effectiveness by lowering costs or increasing participation. In addition, the evaluation may identify ways of improving the degree to which the customer is satisfied with the program or the utility.

Since process evaluations are usually conducted as part of a utility's mandated DSM measurement and evaluation plan, they tend to focus mainly on the stated needs of the regulator as opposed to company management. This can be a problem. Although the regulatory perspective is important, in an increasingly competitive business environment, utilities must not overlook management's business and operational needs for specific information regarding DSM program planning, control, execution, and evaluation.

This paper discusses some of the conflicts that exist between the regulator's and management's needs for DSM program evaluation results and presents some approaches for assuring that both needs are met. It is organized to first discuss the scope of a process evaluation, then the evaluation issues, the management concerns, and finally reporting of results.

## SCOPE OF A PROCESS EVALUATION

A process evaluation is a qualitative, expert assessment of the effectiveness in which a utility *plans, manages, executes* and *monitors* the delivery of DSM programs to its marketplace. As such, the focus of the process evaluation is on the

marketing *process* rather than the program *product*. The specific scope of the evaluation may be narrow or broad. It may focus on one specific program element or, as illustrated in Figure 1, it may examine all four elements of the DSM activity.

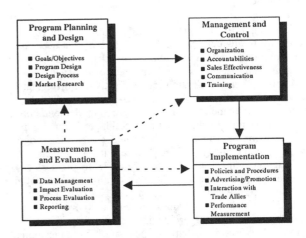

FIGURE 1: THE FOUR INTER-RELATED DSM PLANNING AND DELIVERY FUNCTIONS

The *Program Planning and Design* element includes the goals and objective setting process, program design, market research, market needs assessment, measurement and evaluation plan development, and any shareholder incentive mechanism. The *Management and Control* element examines the marketing and sales organization, work unit and personal accountabilities and responsibilities, employee training, communication, goal setting at the work unit level, resource allocation, and organizational flexibility. The *Program Implementation* element examines written policies and procedures, reporting systems, quality of field representatives, problem detection and reporting, and program implementation process. The *Measurement and Evaluation* element examines the M & E resources for adequacy, data collection process, progress reports, and budget and variance reporting process.

In examining each of these elements, the process evaluation focuses on the process which was followed, as opposed to the specific actions. For example, it examines the program planning and design process to determine whether goals and objectives were stated at the outset. It doesn't concern itself with whether the specific goals of the program were appropriate, but rather were goals established, and were they consistent, or in conflict with other stated corporate goals (financial, regulatory, public relations, customer satisfaction, marketing, etc.). If conflicts were identified, what actions were taken to resolve them?

The process evaluation examines the program design process to determine, for instance, whether all the appropriate parties, both within and outside the company, were involved in program design. Was an effort made to identify who should be involved and to include them? In short, the process evaluation examines some of the non-quantifiable management and organizational aspects of demand-side management program performance. As such, recommendations coming out of a process evaluation can impact significantly the overall cost-effectiveness of a DSM program. This is especially the case when administrative costs represent a large portion of overall program costs (such as with customer energy audit and information programs). The process evaluation may identify options for using resources more effectively or for streamlining procedures thereby resulting in improved efficiencies.

In planning a process evaluation, care must be made to recognize the two distinct audiences which have a need for specific process evaluation results — regulators and company management. Each has their own need for information which the process evaluation can help satisfy. For regulators, process evaluations can provide information regarding the efficient development of energy resources, implementation of state energy policies, customer satisfaction, etc. For company management, information can be provided regarding program planning and delivery, staffing consideration, customer satisfaction, and corporate image. Since many process evaluations are conducted as a result of a requirement by the regulator, results must be made public. However, it is conceivable that the state does not need to know all the detailed information regarding the process. Some information, especially that regarding specific organizational, personnel or strategic business issues, are more appropriate for internal use only. It is important that these differences be recognized and discussed thoroughly at the beginning of the process evaluation.

As illustrated in Figure 2, process evaluations may have two components: an internal evaluation and an external evaluation. The internal evaluation may be further divided into two reviews: a process evaluation of the utility staff and a process evaluation of the field or line organization. Similarly the external evaluation may be divided into two reviews: a process evaluation involving trade allies and an evaluation of customer participation.

Most process evaluations may be expected to include an internal review. After programs have been underway, external evaluations grow in value. Part of the value of process evaluations involving external components comes from identifying barriers to implementation and participation by free riders.

Process evaluations draw their information from many sources (see Figure 3). First, is the documentation of programs through marketing strategy and planning documents, regulatory filings, policy statements, program procedures, organization descriptions, budget/variance reports, as well as advertising and promotional materials.

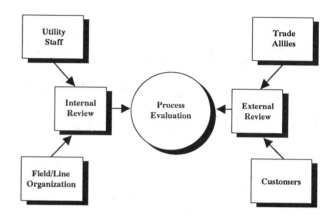

FIGURE 2:    INTERNAL AND EXTERNAL COMPONENTS OF A PROCESS EVALUATION

Second, process evaluations draw their information from interviews of utility personnel, trade allies, and customers. Interviews with utility personnel may include staff from market research, planning, program management, field operations, advertising, and information systems. Field interviews with utility personnel may include energy analysis and engineering, sales, installation, and service. Other utility interviews could include rates, credit and billing, customer service and district operations. Where multiple interviews are considered in the same job category, focus groups may be appropriate, such as for field or customer service representatives.

FIGURE 3:    SOURCES OF INFORMATION IN A PROCESS EVALUATION

Trade ally interviews may include manufacturers, distributors and installation contractors. Where programs are directed at new construction, other trade allies would include developers, builders, architects and engineers.

Customer interviews may also be conducted individually or through focus groups. These methods are particularly appropriate where the objective is to uncover problems with program implementation and explore solutions.

The third approach is through mail or telephone surveys. Surveys could be used for utility personnel where many are involved over a larger service area. Surveys are probably more useful for trade allies and most useful for customers. Surveys are appropriate where the purpose is to document behavior or customer satisfaction. Surveys are not as effective to discuss problems and explore solutions. This can be done better through interviews and focus groups.

In the early stages of a program or one with few participants, focus groups and interviews are likely to be more productive. In the early stages the objective may be to determine what is inhibiting participation and affecting results rather than to determine general measures of satisfaction.

It may be better to look for problems with trade allies and customers first in order to get them corrected before many more participate or greater expenditures are undertaken. Utility customers and trade allies are generally willing to cooperate and share their views on utility programs and procedures. Recommendations from trade allies and customers can be particularly valuable in improving delivery effectiveness and efficiency.

## ISSUES ADDRESSED

Depending on whether the process evaluation was mandated by the state regulator or initiated by management, the specific issues addressed and the method of presenting the results may differ. For the public arena, the evaluation may focus on documenting program evolution and procedures. For management, the evaluation may focus on identifying internal inconsistencies with other corporate activities or on organizational issues. Some of the specific issues the process evaluation may examine include:

### Program Planning and Design

— How were program goals and objectives developed? Are program goals consistent with corporate goals?

— Who was involved in program design? Was market research/load data used? What was its quality? How was it used? How were successes/failures of past programs incorporated into the program design? Were trade allies consulted and do any program elements pose problems?

— Do the programs meet the demand for services? Are all market segments adequately addressed by the programs?

— Is there a measurement and evaluation plan? Is there a strategy for implementing the measurement and evaluation plan?

— Are regulatory reporting requirements identified? If a potential shareholder incentive exists, is the calculation procedure clear to staff and management?

### Management and Control

— How are the various functional areas linked that are involved in DSM? What mechanisms are used to coordinate and communicate between organizational units?

— Does everyone understand their role/responsibility? How closely are accountabilities, responsibilities and authority linked? How is the organizational structure designed to develop and deliver service that meets customer needs? Are spans of control appropriate?

— Does the employee training program meet the needs of the DSM activity?

— How are management expectations communicated to staff and field? Is there a mechanism in place to accurately communicate to program managers field conditions, activities, and program problems and successes?

— How are program objectives translated into goals by work unit?

— Have program policies and procedures been written? Are job descriptions complete and current?

— Are resources being budgeted adequately to meet goals? How is recruiting of staff and field being conducted?

— How does the organization remain flexible to implement program changes? How are program changes made?

### Program Implementation

— Do formal written program policies and procedures exist and are they understood? Are procedures followed in a timely manner? How are policies and procedures periodically updated or revised? Are policies and procedures consistent with goals and objectives?

— Is there a reporting system to indicate program progress and comparison to goal? How is field performance monitored and managed? Are budgeted resources being used as planned?

— Are high standards of quality control and quality assurance maintained? Are field representatives adequately trained and motivated for their roles?

— Are the delivery mechanisms appropriately matched to the individual market segments? Are the local infrastructures capable of supporting the programs?

— How are problems detected and reported to management?

— Was the information that promoted and explained the program useful to the customer? Was the process of installation burdensome to the customer? To the utility? To the installer? Was the utility field representative responsive to questions and able to solve customer problems? Did the DSM activity function as expected?

### Measurement and Evaluation

— Are the measurement and evaluation resources adequate to perform the task? Is appropriate data

163

being collected? Did the measurement and evaluation plan indicate when the process and impact evaluations were to be performed?

— What progress reports are being produced and at what frequency? Are budget and variance reports produced and distributed? Are the reports timely? Are the reports distributed to the appropriate individuals? Are the reports actionable?

## ADDRESSING MANAGEMENT CONCERNS

Prior to the current "collaborative" approach to utility resource planning and marketing, process evaluations were conducted at the exclusive direction of management. Results were not necessarily included in a report to the regulatory body and therefore much less public. Management could minimize posturing, recognize problems areas and take corrective actions without the accompaniment of public scrutiny.

Today's process evaluations are usually part of a broader measurement and regulatory reporting requirement involving complete public disclosure of all findings and conclusions. Such openness can lead to a more limited and superficial scope for the process evaluation. To minimize potential adverse publicity, management may concentrate on program operational characteristics and avoid the broader strategic issues related to financial, regulatory, public relations, customer satisfaction and overall marketing objectives. Addressing these management issues, especially in today's more competitive environment, may result in findings and recommendations inappropriate for a public document.

One way these issues can be addressed is to first clearly identify the objectives of the process evaluation and the audience for the final report. To the extent possible, utilities must also identify the specific questions that senior and functional area management want addressed by the study. In the event that the evaluation is to meet both the needs of the regulator and utility management, conflicts must be identified and resolved. One solution could be a supplemental report to management discussing in more detail specific organizational, personnel and strategic business issues.

For the process evaluation to provide optimal value to both utility management and regulators, evaluations must have the latitude to be candid with utility management, and utilities must feel that they will have ample opportunity to improve upon their DSM programs, consistent with other corporate objectives.

## KEY CONSIDERATIONS IN REPORTING RESULTS

Process evaluations can provide valuable information to DSM program operators and staff, utility management, and regulators. A thorough understanding of the issues surrounding the evaluation and an identification of the audience for which the evaluation is intended is important. In order for management to gain maximum value from this measurement and evaluation investment, it is important that the evaluation:

■ Satisfies the need for a business review of the marketing process — not just the regulatory reporting requirement

■ Recognizes the realities of the politics which may surround the DSM planning and delivery process

■ Includes interim reports and briefings to
  — verify key findings (statements of fact)
  — identify gaps in the process evaluation
  — preview conclusions and recommendations

■ Recognizes what is being done well and recommends ways to improve overall program results

■ Recognizes areas where improvements can be made and offers reasonable, realistic, and actionable recommendations for improvements

## SUMMARY

A process evaluation is particularly useful for utilities to improve the efficiency and effectiveness of their DSM programs. The evaluation can identify administrative and delivery process improvements which may improve cost-effectiveness by lowering implementation costs or increasing participation. In addition, the evaluation may identify ways of improving customer satisfaction with the program and the utility.

While driven largely by regulatory needs, a process evaluation should also address management's specific needs for information. Some of this information — especially that regarding organization, personnel, or competitive implications — may not be appropriate for public disclosure. Care must be taken to assure that both the regulator's and management's needs for DSM program evaluation results are met.

In addition, the process evaluation must recognize a utility's broader corporate goals and objectives and recommend realistic and actionable ways to improve results consistent with these broader objectives.

## BIBLIOGRAPHY

Barrett, Larry, "Process Evaluations Improve DSM Programs," *Barrett Consulting Associates Report*, January, 1991.

Freeman, Luisa, "Process Evaluation: Current Status and Future Outlook," *Evaluation Exchange*, December, 1991.

McRae, Marjorie R., "Don't Shoot the Messenger: Conducting DSM Process Evaluations in (Inevitably) Political Environments," *Proceedings — ACEEE 1990 Summer Study on Energy Efficiency in Buildings*, Volume 6, Pages 99–107.

National Association of Regulatory Utility Commissioners, *Management Audit Manual, Volume I — Fundamentals of Management Audits*, November, 1988.

Perrault, George A., "DSM Process Evaluations: What, Why and How," 1991 International Energy Program Evaluation Conference, Chicago, Illinois, August 22, 1991.

# Chapter 29
# Demand-Side Management: The Perspective of a Combination Utility

C.P. Packard

## ABSTRACT

During the 1980's, Baltimore Gas & Electric (BG&E) met part of the rapid growth in demand for electricity in its service territory by implementing cost-effective demand-side management (DSM) programs--specifically, peak shaving and load shifting strategies. BG&E's focus in the 1990's has been expanded to include all DSM options with an increasing emphasis on those which promote overall energy efficiency or strategic conservation. This change in focus is being driven by Federal legislation, state regulatory requirements and the perceived potential benefits for both the customer and the Company. Current activities related to DSM include involvement in a Collaborative Process to design cost-effective electric and gas conservation programs for all customer classes--low-income, residential, commercial and industrial. Program design consists of four steps: 1) data gathering and technology assessment; 2) development of program concepts; 3) detailed program design and 4) monitoring and evaluation. Significant reductions in the projected peaks as well as in sales in future years are the anticipated results of our efforts. As a combination utility, unique opportunities and challenges face BG&E: fuel switching, eligibility of non-full requirements customers, and energy options for customers.

## I. INTRODUCTION

Baltimore Gas and Electric provides natural gas service and electricity to Baltimore City and all or part of nine Central Maryland counties. The area served with electricity is approximately 2,300 square miles with 2,528,000 residents, while the area served with gas includes 616 square miles with a population of 1,910,000. As the first gas utility and one of the first electric utilities in the United States, BG&E celebrated its 175 year anniversary in 1991.

In the 1980's, BG&E experienced a rapid growth in demand and consumption of electricity. From 1980 to 1990 the peak demand for electricity grew 38% from 3,969 MW to 5,477 MW, respectively and annual sales of electricity grew 43% from 17,228 GWh to 24,620 GWh, respectively. For the 1990's, BG&E expects continued growth in sales, peaks and customers but at growth rates noticeably lower than those experienced in the 1980's.

The rapid growth in demand for electricity in the 1980's was met in part by demand-side management (DSM), specifically, load management--peak shaving and load shifting strategies. BG&E's DSM focus in the 1990's has been expanded and includes an emphasis on the promotion of overall energy efficiency or strategic conservation. This paper will discuss BG&E's experiences and perspectives in three major sections:

. Benefits of DSM
. DSM Program Design
. Issues and Unique Opportunities with DSM

## II. BENEFITS OF DEMAND-SIDE MANAGEMENT

Demand-Side Management (DSM) involves utility activities designed to influence customer energy use in ways that can be beneficial to both the customer and the utility. Utility programs falling under the umbrella of DSM can be characterized as load management or conservation.

BG&E defines load management as the concept of altering a pattern of electricity use in order to: 1) improve the system load factor, 2) reduce the loads during daily, weekly, monthly or yearly on-peak periods, and, ultimately, 3) reduce operating costs and generating capacity requirements. BG&E is able to reduce risk by managing future power demands rather than passively responding to them. As a result, load management can provide opportunities to optimize the use of existing generating facilities, delay the need for future investments in new generating capacity and operate its more efficient plants, which, in turn helps conserve our natural resources. All these effects enable BG&E to minimize the cost of service to its customers.

Currently, BG&E is offering its customers the following load management programs:

Residential Options
    Air Conditioner Radio Control
    Water Heater Radio Control
    Optional Time-of-Use Rates
    Standard Time-of-Use Rates for New
      Construction

Commercial/Industrial Options
    Curtailable Service
    Emergency Generation
    Air Conditioner Radio Control
    Time-of-Use Rates for customers with
      demands greater than 60 kW

Optional Time-of-Use Rates for customers
with demands less than 60 kW
Cool Storage

In the 1990's, BG&E expanded its DSM focus to include conservation. There are three reasons for this change: Federal legislation, State regulatory requirements and the perceived potential benefits to BG&E and its customers.

In 1990, the Clean Air Act was amended to, among other things, encourage the pursuit of conservation for environmental reasons, stating: "The Administrator shall allocate allowances to an electric utility under this subsection only if ... such electric utility has adopted and is implementing a least cost energy conservation and electric power plan ...".

In the 1991 Maryland State Legislative Session, House Bill 520 was passed, which states that "each gas and electric company shall develop and implement programs and services to encourage and promote the efficient use and conservation of energy...". This Bill also directs the Commission to adopt rate-making policies that provide cost recovery and financial incentives.

In April of 1991, BG&E signed a Memorandum of Understanding (MOU) which established a Collaborative Process for BG&E to work with its regulators, several consumer groups, state agencies, and the Sierra Club. Under the terms of the MOU, BG&E will aggressively encourage cost-effective conservation programs and the use of energy-efficient technologies. One of the goals of the Collaborative Process is to create the opportunity for an exchange of information and perspectives on the development of a comprehensive plan for the implementation of cost-effective conservation. Another goal is to resolve issues of program design and regulatory practice with respect to BG&E's activities, including: lost revenues, cost recovery, cost allocation, utility incentives, and avoided cost.

As one would expect, BG&E, like other utilities, was reluctant to encourage customers to purchase less of its product because of the loss in revenues. Lost revenues are the base rate revenues that are not collected due to the implementation of DSM programs above the level of impacts reflected in the test year from BG&E's most recent base rate proceeding. It has been agreed to by the Collaborative Process participants that BG&E can recover lost revenues between rate cases. The base rates stated in BG&E's Electric and Gas Service Tariffs and collaboratively determined demand and energy savings estimates (per unit) will be used to estimate lost revenues.

The Collaborative parties have also agreed to provide BG&E with an incentive for successfully meeting DSM program goals. BG&E will have the opportunity to earn an incentive equal to 7.5% of the difference between the avoided cost and the program cost, if 75% of the total annual goal for energy savings is met.

With the traditional utility disincentives negotiated away, conservation is appealing not only to customers but also BG&E. Conservation is recognized as a way to enhance the partnership between BG&E and its customers by further improving quality of service and controlling the cost of gas and electric utilities. BG&E's conservation efforts will provide incentives to customers to purchase new technologies that save money today and in the future. By enabling customers to save money, they can become more competitive. Healthy businesses and a strong local economy keep the citizens of Central Maryland employed and prosperous.

All costs associated with the design and implementation of DSM programs as well as lost revenues will be recovered through a surcharge, which will take the form of an adder to base rates. The surcharge will be estimated prospectively on an annual basis and calculated separately for each Tariff Schedule. The electric surcharge will be established as a rate per kWh purchased from BG&E. The gas surcharge will be established as a rate per therm based on gas purchased from BG&E. Actual receipts from the surcharges will be trued-up to authorized amounts annually. An interest rate equal to the most recent authorized rate of return will be applied to any differences resulting from the true-up process. All Collaborative parties agreed that the mechanism may be reviewed after the first two years of use.

Costs to be collected in the surcharge will be assigned directly to participating customer classes whenever possible. Program costs common to more than one customer class will be allocated to the customer classes on the basis of the proportion of directly assignable costs. The customer classes have been defined as follows:

Electric Customer Classes

Tariff Schedules R, RL -- Residential
    Customers
Tariff Schedule G -- General Service
    Customers
Tariff Schedule GL -- Large General
    Service Customers
Tariff Schedule P -- Primary Voltage
    Service Customers

Gas Customer Classes

Tariff Schedule D -- Residential
Tariff Schedule C -- General Service

Unfortunately, the current classifications do not result in costs that can be allocated to residential, commercial and industrial customers. Commercial and industrial customers can be billed under Schedule G, GL or P. As a result, some industrial customers may perceive themselves to be subsidizing lighting improvements or the implementation of other conservation measures in a commercial customer's facility; alternatively, in the future, when more industrial programs are developed, commercial customers could subsidize industrials. While the allocation of costs can solve interclass cross-subsidization concerns, the issue of interclass cross-subsidization remains; however, by proving a broad range of options to all our customers, BG&E's ratepayers should all benefit from the energy and environmental benefits of cost-effective DSM programs.

The current conservation programs provide incentives for customers who buy high efficiency residential heating and air conditioning equipment, provide financial and design assistance to make new commercial buildings much more efficient, provide incentives and assistance to insure that industrial customers use the most efficient equipment feasible. The current conservation programs are:

Residential High-Efficiency Replacement Heating/Cooling Program Comprehensive Commercial Construction Program
Industrial Plant Expansion and Major Equipment Replacement Program
Commercial Efficient Lighting Program
Gas Air Conditioning Program

## III. PROGRAM DESIGN

As mentioned previously, BG&E signed a MOU last Spring, which stated that BG&E would Collaboratively develop programs to aggressively encourage conservation. The Collaborative Process agreed upon an organizational structure which established a Policy and Oversight Committee for addressing key policy issues; three working groups for developing detailed designs for programs to be marketed to BG&E's residential, commercial and industrial customers; and a final working group charged with developing a monitoring and evaluation plan for the assessment of program performance, customer satisfaction, program costs and the energy and demand savings. The working groups design cost-effective DSM programs in four steps: 1) data gathering and technology assessment; 2) development of program concepts; 3) detailed program design; and 4) monitoring and evaluation. Program design within a Collaborative Process provides unique challenges which will be highlighted below.

### Data Gathering and Technology Assessment

In this first step of program design, intensive market research is conducted. The main objective is to assess the existing market situation and attempt to understand the customers, their current uses of electricity, their potential for DSM, and their requirements for program participation. The research also investigates the advantages and disadvantages of elements of other existing utility programs and studies existing and future technologies and their applications. Finally, internal and external resources for implementing and tracking program results must be identified and evaluated.

The involvement of the various Collaborative participants can be beneficial in terms of their prior experience in program design and expertise with technologies. In addition, customer involvement in program design can provide immediate market research that would otherwise be discovered later in surveys or focus groups. Finally, trade ally contacts and consulting engineering expertise can quickly be identified by some of the participants.

### Development of Program Concepts

In the second step of program design, the program goals and target market are identified; preliminary discussions on incentive strategy, marketing approach and program administration takes place; and measures identified are screened against BG&E's avoided cost.

In this stage of design, discussions among the participants can become interesting due to the different opinions and objectives of the parties. BG&E is challenged with balancing the many differing goals of the Collaborative participants. For example, one participant of the Collaborative Process lobbied for BG&E to develop programs to avoid lost opportunities, while BG&E was committed to minimize lost opportunities. As a result, this participant encouraged BG&E to adopt an aggressive rebate strategy which would result in a relatively quick payback period. In contrast, BG&E was committed to a payback strategy that seems to be getting significant penetration and participation as compared to other utility programs. Another view on the matter was that of the customers who would ultimately pay the surcharges. These customers were trying to minimize expenses and costs and supported the less aggressive rebate strategy. In another case, BG&E proposed vendor incentives, but the customer groups, looking to minimize costs and keep benefits limited to BG&E's ratepayers, refused to agree.

### Detailed Program Design

In the third step of program design, program parameters such as broad marketing strategy, penetration estimates, demand and energy savings, incentive levels, and program costs are finalized.

During this detailed program design stage, several of the Collaborative participants were interested in reviewing BG&E's broad marketing strategy and implementation plans for its conservation programs. While BG&E was open to providing a broad/conceptual overview of the marketing strategy, there was hesitation to formally file a plan which could limit flexibility and the ability to respond quickly to changing market needs.

For determining penetration estimates, demand and energy savings, one of BG&E's Collaborative participants decided, several days prior to the filing deadline, that they could not agree to the proposed demand and energy savings. Ultimately, BG&E filed its first set of conservation programs without Collaborative agreement on impacts. This was discouraging, since the Collaborative Process was intended to have all parties agree on program design and impacts, minimize litigation; and provide an open forum for input from regulators and other interested parties.

In this step of design, the final assumptions are also analyzed for cost-effectiveness: do the benefits out-weigh the costs? Agreement on avoided costs is critical to be able to calculate benefit cost ratios. For BG&E first filing, since avoided costs issues were unresolved, it was agreed that BG&E's numbers, which were lower, would be used.

## Monitoring and Evaluation

The final step of program design involves developing provisions for the monitoring and evaluation of the program in terms of three broad categories: process, market and impacts. The purpose of monitoring and evaluating programs is to estimate and validate program impacts, recommend refinements to programs and improve overall program performance.

BG&E has placed much emphasis on monitoring and evaluation activities since results can help with decision making and marketing. Results can help determine how to improve a program or if a program is not worth continuing. In addition, verified impacts can help market measures to skeptical customers who need "proof" that savings will be realized.

For process evaluation, BG&E will determine if the program was implemented as planned, if implementation was effective and if any improvements can be made. For market evaluation, BG&E will determine the penetration rate, customer satisfaction, and reasons for nonparticipation. Demand and impact verification is also performed and used to determine the cost-effectiveness of a program.

## IV. ISSUES AND UNIQUE OPPORTUNITIES WITH DSM

As a combination utility BG&E must address many difficult issues and can capitalize on unique opportunities when appropriate. Currently, BG&E is working to resolve the issues of fuel switching and eligibility of non-full requirements customers.

For a combination utility fuel switching presents less of a problem as compared with fuel switching between competing electric and gas utilities. In fact, fuel switching as a DSM option for a combination utility can be viewed as an opportunity which can benefit all ratepayers. For example, BG&E's Gas Air Conditioning Program provides incentives for customers to implement a gas air conditioning technology, which reduces summer electric peak and increases gas purchases in the summer period when there is surplus capacity. Fuel switching offers customers a choice in energy service, which is often very important to the individual customer. Another example is a customer with an electric heat pump needing replacement can receive a rebate for either installing a high efficiency electric high pump or a high efficiency gas furnace. The ability to provide our customers with energy choices enables us to meet BG&E Corporate goals related to customer satisfaction and service.

BG&E is considering fuel switching as technologies that switch fuels used 1) from electricity to BG&E purchased gas or 2) from BG&E purchased gas to electricity. Opportunities of fuel switching from or to steam, oil or transported gas are generally not considered. In evaluating measures, the fuel switching opportunity must be more energy efficient than the next best alternative on a total Btu basis; must pass the initial screening for cost-effectiveness; and must

be an applicable technology with a market within the BG&E service territory. Currently, BG&E is evaluating, through pilot projects, packaged cogeneration and gas engine driven heat pumps. Next year, BG&E plans to test two gas engine driven air compressors.

Another equally complicated issue that the Collaborative Process participants are trying to resolve is the eligibility of non-full requirements customers. For BG&E, a non-full requirements customer can take many forms: a customer that generates, via cogeneration, part of its electricity requirements; a customer that has standby generation equipment; a customer with interruptible gas service and standby, back-up fuel capabilities; or a customer that transports and purchases its own gas. At this point, a cogeneration customer is lobbying to either be ineligible for the DSM program incentives and exempt from the surcharge or be eligible for all rebates and surcharges. The latter proposal would effectively enable a customer with a relatively large number of conservation opportunities to participate in the programs while paying a relatively small portion of the total surcharge. It is possible for a non-full requirements customer to participate in a program, receive a rebate, then provide its own energy needs, which, ultimately, results in the captive customers subsidizing the DSM investment.

The resolution of these issues and the completed detailed design of additional programs could provide BG&E with significant impacts from DSM activities. The 1992 current forecast of existing DSM programs projects the following impacts:

|  | Impacts by (MW) | | |
| --- | --- | --- | --- |
|  | 1995 | 2000 | 2006 |
| Existing Programs: | | | |
|  |  |  |  |
| Residential | 275 | 417 | 570 |
| C/I | 240 | 353 | 473 |
|  |  |  |  |
| Total Impacts | 515 | 770 | 1043 |

TABLE 1 - PROJECTED IMPACTS OF EXISTING PROGRAMS

The actual range of impacts is quite wide, which is a result of uncertainty associated with penetrations and impacts and how programs are marketed and promoted to eligible customers. Meeting customers' growing demands through DSM is certainly more uncertain than meeting customers' demand through the construction of new generation capacity. As a result, deferred kW from DSM activities contains a degree of risk. Nevertheless, BG&E is committed to DSM as a viable option for meeting demand requirements. Since 1986, BG&E has relied more and more on DSM. Previous projections for DSM impacts by 2000, shown below, demonstrate BG&E's growing involvement and utilization of DSM over the years.

| DSM Plan Filing | BG&E Corporate Forecast Without DSM (MW) | DSM Impact (MW) |
|---|---|---|
| 1986* | 5,847 | 97 |
| 1988 | 6,140 | 256 |
| 1989 | 6,480 | 417 |
| 1990 | 6,909 | 514 |
| 1991 | 7,075 | 752 |
| 1992 | 7,100 | 770 |

*Filed December, 1986

TABLE 2 - DSM IMPACT ON CORPORATE FORECAST - YEAR 2000

## V. CONCLUDING REMARKS

Since the 1980's, when BG&E met the growing demand for electricity by load management strategies, many changes have occurred in terms of BG&E's involvement with DSM. Originally, DSM activities emphasized load shifting and peak clipping. Currently, BG&E is also promoting gas and electric energy conservation and capitalizing on fuel switching as a DSM option through a Collaborative Process.

Many issues are still being resolved, but the framework has been established for design and monitoring and evaluation of successful DSM programs. BG&E is prepared to aggressively pursue conservation in order to satisfy three major corporate objectives: (1) improve the quality of service to customers; (2) improve the living environment in Central Maryland; and, (3) earn a fair return on our conservation investments. The time is right for conservation--technology is available to provide significant load relief without inconveniencing the customer.

BG&E, like other utilities, is facing transitional times. Two challenges that face BG&E include meeting customers' expectation and maintaining Corporate profitability. Investments in DSM can help deal with both challenges. DSM investments, if done efficiently, can result in not only recovery of all costs but also additional earnings for stockholders. Meeting customers' needs will result in business retention as well as economic growth and development. Through DSM BG&E can position itself as an energy company of choice.

# Chapter 30

# The Energy Efficiency Partnership - Kraft General Foods and Boston Edison Company

J.C. Crowley, J.P. Donoghue

During the past twenty years, inordinate shifts in the supply and demand of energy have forced both electric utility companies and their customers to investigate new and innovative ways to satisfy the ever increasing demand for electricity. The ENERGY EFFICIENCY PARTNERSHIP, developed between Kraft General Foods and Boston Edison Company, presents an exemplary study of how two corporate giants creatively solved the problem of uncontrolled energy costs and its positive effect on the overall operations of Kraft General Foods, Framingham.

But the ENERGY EFFICIENCY PARTNERSHIP did more than reduce energy costs, it provided benefits to all parties on the playing field. To understand its significance, a review of the partnership's history is paramount.

The first official announcement of the ENERGY EFFICIENCY PARTNERSHIP was made on April 9, 1990.

"Framingham, MA. . .The Commonwealth of Massachusetts, Kraft General Foods Framingham, and Boston Edison Company have joined forces in a $3.6 million dollar energy partnership that will help keep 250 industrial jobs in Massachusetts and could lead to the future expansion of the international food company's Framingham facility.

That announcement heralded the beginning of what has become a world recognized effort on the part of two corporate giants to reduce energy costs, conserve the environment, retain industrial viability in a state that has been experiencing the devastating effects of the recession and last but no means least, put to rest what had been at times an adversarial relationship between Boston Edison Company and Kraft General Foods, the largest ice cream and frozen dessert manufacturer in the United States.

An additional benefit has also been realized from the PARTNERSHIP, one that never could have been forecasted, and that is the ownership that all participants have taken toward making the ENERGY EFFICIENCY PARTNERSHIP a working success.

## WHY THE PARTNERSHIP AND HOW IT WORKS

The decade of the '80's proved to be a time of transformation for both Kraft General Foods and Boston Edison Company. It was a ten year period that brought many changes to both companies which made it possible for them to initiate and achieve the ENERGY EFFICIENCY PARTNERSHIP in the '90's.

By the late 1970's, Joe Crowley, Operations Manager of Kraft General Foods Framingham realized that increased energy costs, especially electricity, was having a negative effect on the overall budget for the manufacturing facilty. They had been successful in implementing energy conservation measures which produced savings on natural gas, fuel oil, and water, but not electricity.

An analysis of consumption showed that most of the electricity use went into maintaining the storage facility and running the hardening system 24 hours a day, 365 days a year, except during defrost. This was due to the type of system which was installed in the mid-60's. Twelve years ago, a total replacement would have been necessary to improve the system's efficiency. Kraft General Foods wasn't interested in making that kind of investment in a "dated" plant.

Over time, alternative conservation measures were reviewed and analyzed in a continued effort to reduce the electric bill. Co-generation was seriously explored as it could supply both the Framingham manufacturing facility and neighboring office buildings with ample self-generated power.

Although natural gas was desirable, it wasn't a readily available alternative. And, the development of an industrial electric rate, which is common practice in come industrial states, was proposed to the Boston Edison executives. It was flatly refused.

By 1988 the situation was critical. Kraft General Foods Framingham production costs were not competitive with other manufacturing facilities in the Dairy Division and they were faced with the real possibility of closure.

The concept of co-generation was re-explored and it's benefits could not be ignored. It would reduce electrical cost, which was the major factor in keeping the plant from getting its operating costs in line with other dairy division facilities, as well as produce additional revenues from the excess steam that could be sold to neighboring buildings.

Kraft General Foods proceeded with its plans and notified Boston Edison of its decision. This raised a red flag at Boston Edison that did not go unnoticed.

Just as Kraft General Foods had been forced to make changes in the 1980's so had Boston Edison. It was a decade that changed how the electric utility did business with it's customers. This situation was propelled by a variety of issues. First, increased energy demands from new and existing customers during the "Massachusetts Miracle" boom years had the company searching for cost effective ways to generate power. Second, cost overruns of plant construction in the '70's all but made new generating facilities in the 1980's an impossible dream. And third, a renewed commitment for the environment presented a multitude of issues to be addressed.

To take Boston Edison forward, a new management team was put in place. From them emerged a new corpoate mission directing the development of programs that would make Bosotn Edison a company easy to do business with and harvest additional capacity (electricity) by making existing and new cusotmers more efficient.

In 1987, conservation and load management programs offering seven of a total package of forty end use specific programs was introduced. In 1988, the effort was referred to as Demand Side Management. It was intended to offer a comprehensive program for all end users, but as John Donoghue, Manager Load Containment Division, of Boston Edison explains, "By 1989 the customers were telling us that the program was too complicated and confusing."

As the Company worked towards rectifying those problems, The DSM programs were experiencing some success in the commercial sector but not in the industrial sector due to the complexity of the industrial facilities. To address this, it was proposed that audits be provided to five industrial customers and then use that audit as the first step of the DSM effort.

Concurrently, the Massachusetts Executive Office of Energy was offering the Energy Advisory Service to the industries of Massachusetts. The service was funded from an Exxon oil overcharge settlement. Specifically, industrial customers were being offered energy audits for $100 a day. Kraft General Foods Framingham presented an optimal industrial site to receive one of the first five audits.

THE AUDIT

The facility evaluation began with a sixteen day on-site analysis. The goal was to provide a fuel blind audit of energy consumption. Kraft General Foods systems, used for cooling, storage, manufacturing, packaging end use products, and sanitation were all examined. The extensive three month audit was conducted by Pequod Associates, an engineerng firm specializing in energy conservation and Stahlman Engineering, experts in industrial refrigeration. Their findings recommended replacing the current refrigeration system, replacing the air handling units, retrofitting the lighting system and replacing 40% of the motors and installing a heat recovery system.

The retrofit would include, replacing a 1700 ton freon refrigeration system with a 2000 ton ammonia system, complete with an automated system for centralized refrigeration control. In addition to saving energy, it addressed the CFC issue that would have to be managed in the mid to late 1990's.

Second, replace the air handling equipment in the ice cream hardener and freezer. With the new system, air handlers are defrosted with hot ammonia gas from compression rather than electricity as with the old system.

Third, install high-efficiency motors for homogenizing and pasteurizing equipment.

Fourth, install a new lighting system that would include T-8 lamps, relectors and electronic ballasts and fifth, install a heat recovery system.

The retrofit is designed to save more than 6 million kilowatt-hours of electricity a year. That equals the amount of energy it takes to power 1000 homes in the Greater Boston area. For Kraft General Foods Framingham, it would reduce their energy costs by 33 percent on an annual $1.4 million electric bill.

In February 1990, the results of the audit were presented to Kraft General Foods. It was then that Kraft General Foods chose to be involved with the ENERGY EFFICIENCY PARTNERSHIP, a new comprehensive program developed by Boston Edison that offered a one year pay back of the initial retrofit investment over a two year period.

Calculations for payback are determined by monitoring the equipment for two years. Boston Edison's incentive payment is based on a cents-per-kWh formula. That is determined by the cost divided by the total 2-year projected energy savings in kWh's. For example, the air handling system would be figured accordingly.

---

### Incentive Payment Based on Cents-per-kWh Formula

### Air Handling

| | | |
|---|---|---|
| Cost | $1,000,000 | |
| Estimated Annual Savings | $100,000 | 2,000,000 kWh |
| Maximum Incentive | $900,000 | |
| Actual Incentive | $\dfrac{\$900,000}{(2)\,2,000,000} = \$0.225/\text{kWh}$ | |

FIGURE 1

---

MANAGING THE PARTNERSHIP

Both Joe Crowley of Kraft General Foods and John Donoghue of Boston Edison recognized that if a strict time frame wasn't adhered to, the goal of achieving complete installation by the end of March 1991 would be missed. That first quarter of 1991 presented the best time for a change-over as it coincided with the plant's slowest production period and was the least disruptive to the continued operation of the facility.

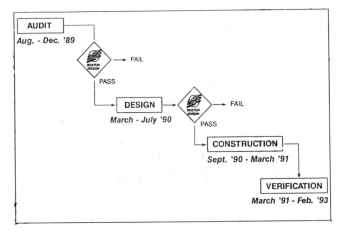

FIGURE 2

By March 1990 when all the audit recommendations were presented and the necessary approvals ascertained, the design team was organized. It was comprised of a coalition of Kraft General Foods management, operating personnel, refrigeration and electrical engineers and Boston Edison's demand-side management representatives. The ENERGY EFFICIENCY PARTNERSHIP presented a mutual challenge for the dozen people working towards mutual solutions. When they came to the meetings, they parked their ego's at the door. Together, they developed an installation and project management schedule which was reviewed in weekly meetings. Through this team approach, the group created and implemented better solutions than were originally proposed. The audit recommendations and the final result are radically different.

Because the audit had been developed with very little input from the plant operating personnel, it stepped on some sacred cows . . . especially the hardening system and refrigeration compressors. The roller bed hardening system was a simple design, very flexible and extremely reliable. Operations wanted to improve it rather than replace it.

Refrigeration, an old ammonia freon cascade system, had to be removed because of its limited turn down capability. Screw compressors are 20 year old technology and the past two decades have shown that it isn't the answer to all applications. Operations wanted to create a partnership between the two, the reciprocating technology and the screw technology.

The goal to issue bid documents by early July was achieved and the bids were returned by early August. A month of bureaucratic indecision ensued. This caused us a loss of four weeks from the planned schedule. Four weeks was critical to successfully completing the retrofit on time. Construction began in September and the twelve member design team gained a dozen new members to become the project team of twenty-four.

The strength of the relationship developed and the design team solidified the project team which now inlcuded the three contractors; refrigeration, electrical and general. Unfortunately for the contractors, they blindly accepted the schedule and agreed to work within the parameters of the bid. When the first change-order was presented it became very obvious that the margin for project cost-effectiveness was minimal and that any change-orders would drive the project over budget. Joe Crowley made it very

clear that when Kraft General Foods secured bids they stuck to them. In the first meeting the contractors were told in no uncertain terms that change orders would not equal add-on's to the bill. They agreed.

It also became obvious during the project meetings that because the operating personnel were present, solutions were arrived at that could accomodate the proposed change-orders without going over the budget. Rather than utilize outside contractors, Kraft General Foods used their own operating people and charged their time to the project.

The project was in construction for seven months. During those thirty weeks, the team was involved in project meetings for four hours a week, or 120 hours for the duration of the retrofit. It proved to be 120 hours of constant finessing and juggling the completedness of the documents, the contractors perception of scope of work as compared to the customers scope of work, scheduling, and cost control issues.

The final retrofit included eliminating the freon from the refrigeration system which created an ammonia based system with three different temperature stages that are utilized in the processing and storage of frozen desserts; -50 degrees for hardening, -35 degrees for processing and storage, and +17 degrees for ingredient storage.

To obtain the most efficient operation, new air handling units were installed which utilize hot ammonia gas off the compressors for defrosting. This eliminated the need for electric defrost. The new system runs automatically about four times weekly for 15 minute intervals. With each unit capable of functioning separately, the need for a total system shut-down has been eliminated. The old electric defrost units used to run four times a day for two hour periods, pluse a twelve hour total system shut down on Saturday.

The new air handling units are equipped with vane axle fans instead of the centrifugal fan. They use 50% less horse power to move twice as much air.

The heat recovery system removes excess heat from the compressors to heat hot water, which is used primarily for cleaning. The new system eliminates the need for 2500 gallons of No. 2 oil per week which had been used to fuel steam boilers.

Although construction was completed in mid-March, 1991, that did not automatically mean that the verification of savings period could begin as had been originally scheduled. There were two learning curves associated with the computerized control system that interfaced to the new refrigeration system and air handling units. One, the systems operators were accustomed to manual controls and required training and experience to become computer proficient. Second, the original control settings were determined empirically. The systems had to be cycled down over their entire operating range for identification and setting at the most efficient control settings.

After a six week trial period, everyone felt about 95% ready to begin the verification stage.

VErification of savings actually began in June of 1991 with the first year ending on May 31, 1992. Results are presented in Figure 3.

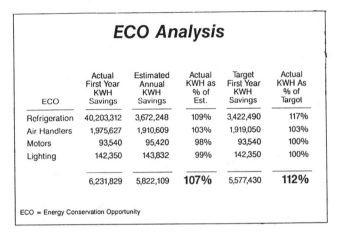

## ECO Analysis

| ECO | Actual First Year KWH Savings | Estimated Annual KWH Savings | Actual KWH as % of Est. | Target First Year KWH Savings | Actual KWH As % of Target |
|---|---|---|---|---|---|
| Refrigeration | 40,203,312 | 3,672,248 | 109% | 3,422,490 | 117% |
| Air Handlers | 1,975,627 | 1,910,609 | 103% | 1,919,050 | 103% |
| Motors | 93,540 | 95,420 | 98% | 93,540 | 100% |
| Lighting | 142,350 | 143,832 | 99% | 142,350 | 100% |
| | 6,231,829 | 5,822,109 | **107%** | 5,577,430 | **112%** |

ECO = Energy Conservation Opportunity

FIGURE 3

The original estimaged energy savings were formulated on a normal production level of 20 million gallons of ice cream a year. Actual first year verification was for 22.4 million gallons, an increase of 2.4 million gallons.

The refrigeration system savings was 3.4 million kWh versus the estimated 3.6 million kWh. This is attributed to the fact that most of the energy savings were estimated to occur during the non-produciton hours which were less than speculated. Therefore, the actual refrigeration system energy savings of 4 million kWh is 109% of the estimated savings of 117% of the target savings.

The air handling system savings are less affected by production activity. Verification of energy savings are right on target at 103%.

Motors and lighting are not affected by the production activity.

Specific savings in air handling and refrigeration electric consumption are illustrated by the next two graphs.

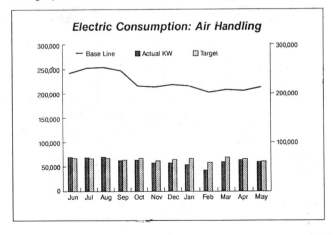

### Electric Consumption: Air Handling

FIGURE 4

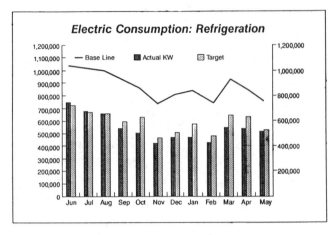

### Electric Consumption: Refrigeration

FIGURE 5

The success of this project can be traced directly to the input of operating personnel. From the very beginning they took ownership of this project which is now exceeding projections in all phases at all times.

Joe Crowley loves to quote a statement that he has heard often since the retrofit began. "I can't believe you actually functioned in that plant while at that work was going on." To which he replies, "Not only did we continue to operate, but we realized some very positive benefits.

During the forced down-time, Kraft General Foods employees received training on new computer programs, overhauled existing equipment, installed a new inventory control system, retrofited the lighting systems in the office area, warehouse storage and the building exterior which reduced lighting consumption 30% overall and upgraded forty motors, ranging in size from 5 to 40 hp, which increased their efficiency by approximately 10%. Kraft General Foods Framingham likes to say that everything was being retrofited.

The financial commitment from Kraft General Foods really motivated the worker's "buy-into" the program. It immediately became their program and they have since continued to demonstrate ownerhsip of their jobs and the company. "We have successfully taken the Total Quality Management theory from concept to reality. We have just experienced our best quarter ever, in all measures" sites Joe Crowley. An example of this is shown in the increase of line efficiencies as shown in figure 6.

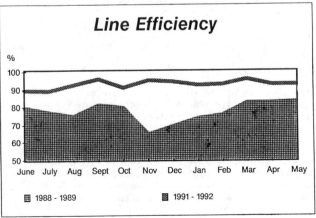

## Line Efficiency

FIGURE 6

Joe says that one word can describe the success of
the program. "Commitment."

"Without the commitment of all parties, from
corporate president to in-plant personnel, the
project didn't have a chance of getting to first
base. We were fortunate in having that commitment
across the board, both at Boston Edison Company and
Kraft General Foods."

Yes, the ENERGY EFFICIENCY PARTNERSHIP has been
successful, probably far more sussessful than any
of the involved parties could imagine.

# Chapter 31
# DSM/Federal Energy Efficiency Partnership Program at Fort Lewis, Washington

G. Parker, T. Secrest, N. Flood, A. Gillespie

## ABSTRACT

The Energy Systems Modernization Office (ESMO) at Pacific Northwest Laboratory (PNL)[a] is developing and applying the Federal Energy Decision Screening (FEDS) system for federal installations in cooperation with the servicing utility(s). In the process, we conduct an installation-wide, fuel-blind energy-efficiency resource assessment, identify the most life-cycle cost-effective technologies, work with the servicing utility to develop a program to implement energy conservation projects and technologies, evaluate rates and rate structures, and contribute to the design and implementation of an energy savings verification procedure to evaluate the impact of installed technologies.

Working with the U.S. Army Forces Command (FORSCOM) and the U.S. Department of Energy Federal Energy Management Program (DOE-FEMP), Fort Lewis was identified as a site for a pilot program which would result in a model approach for FEMP and FORSCOM to apply to other federal installations. Fort Lewis, a large (population 35,000) military installation in Tacoma, Washington, purchases electricity through Tacoma Public Utilities (TPU). TPU in turn purchases electricity through the Bonneville Power Administration (Bonneville), a regional federal power marketing agency. Fort Lewis has an annual electric load of about 195,000 megawatt-hours (MWh)(~40 MW).

An energy conservation supply curve for the Fort was developed showing the amount of electric energy savings that can be achieved at different prices for energy saved. From these data, a proposal was prepared for acquiring approximately 43,000 kilowatt-hours (kWh) (~4 MW) of annual cost-effective electric energy savings, which TPU presented to Bonneville. This proposal identified investment requirements at the Fort and the likely energy and dollar savings which will result from the investment. Approximately $10 million of investment in electrical energy efficient end-use technology was estimated to be cost-effective at Fort Lewis under this arrangement.

In the agreement with Fort Lewis, TPU will finance 100% of this investment and will procure the energy services contractor who will conduct the detailed audits and install the technologies. The Fort will repay TPU 15% of the total installed cost of the technology over the time period of the installation of the technologies. The result is that Fort Lewis will see a reduction in its electric bill of approximately $500,000/year, depending on the final program design.

---

[a] Pacific Northwest Laboratory is operated for the U.S. Department of Energy by Battelle Memorial Institute under Contract DE-AC06-76RLO 1830.

## INTRODUCTION

The mission of DOE-FEMP is to lead the improvement of energy efficiency and fuel flexibility within the federal sector. Through ESMO at PNL, FEMP is developing and applying the FEDS system for identifying and acquiring all cost-effective energy projects at large federal facilities such as military installations.[1]

The FEDS process includes conducting an installation-wide, fuel-neutral energy-efficiency resource assessment, identifying the most life-cycle cost-effective retrofit technologies, working with the servicing utility to develop a program to implement energy conservation projects and technologies, evaluating rates and rate structures, and designing and implementing an energy-savings verification procedure to evaluate the impact of installed technologies.

The FEDS process is currently being applied at over 15 federal installations with a combined annual energy cost exceeding $100 million. FEMP has concluded that each federal installation can typically invest 1 to 2 times its annual energy bill in cost-effective energy system modernization projects. The result will be annual energy cost savings of 20 to 35%, lower operations and maintenance expenditures, and increased reliability, comfort and user productivity. For electric energy savings, the biggest target is typically lighting retrofits with a substantial potential in heating, ventilating, air conditioning, pumps, and motors retrofits, and electrical transmission and distribution system upgrades.

This paper describes the initial FEDS application projects at Fort Lewis. The paper focuses on the electric energy resource potential and acquisition in cooperation with the servicing electric utility, TPU. Fort Lewis has an annual fuel consumption of about 2.5 trillion Btu, of which 26% is in the form of electricity. The annual electric bill is $4.5 million.

## BACKGROUND

In developing a pilot FEDS program, FEMP believed that Bonneville, as part of the federal sector and DOE, could actively support the identification, characterization, and procurement of electric energy-efficiency resources from federal customers within the Bonneville service territory. Bonneville is required by the Northwest Electric Power Planning and Conservation Act (PL 96-501) to implement the integrated resource plan developed by the Pacific Northwest Power Planning Council (NPPC). The NPPC plan identifies energy efficiency (conservation) as the least-cost resource to meet load growth. Thus, Bonneville is designing several approaches to purchasing energy efficiency from retailers (utilities), third parties, and end-users of electricity.

For these reasons, FEMP approached Bonneville with the proposal to develop a pilot FEDS program with a large federal customer in Bonneville's service territory. FEMP emphasized that, to the extent possible, the pilot program should not require the federal customer to either procure an energy services contractor (ESCO) or provide up-front capital funds for the electric technologies. FEMP has identified these two requirements as major obstacles in the path of federal agencies/installations attempting to aggressively pursue energy-efficiency programs. FEMP and Bonneville agreed to fund PNL, to identify and recruit a federal customer, and to conduct a FEDS assessment at the federal facility.

It was agreed that the pilot program should be designed to be transferable to other federal customers within the Bonneville service territory. To have maximum impact, the program should also be transferable to federal customers outside of Bonneville's service territory. This condition meant that the program would likely have greater transferability if the federal customer were not served directly by Bonneville but by a utility that purchased power from Bonneville. This would give the program maximum credibility when FEMP/PNL transfer the "lessons learned" to other utility service territories and other states.

A necessary condition for the program to be successful was that the federal customer be thoroughly committed to working through the process. We also knew that the federal customer needed to be served by a utility committed to innovative approaches in demand-side management (DSM) programs--ideally, a utility that had demonstrated commitment to the fundamental principles of least-cost planning.

Fortunately, all conditions were quickly met. FEMP has a cooperative program with FORSCOM for providing technical assistance to FORSCOM installations. FEMP and FORSCOM have agreed to cost-share activities in developing innovative approaches to energy efficiency at the latter's installations. Fort Lewis is a FORSCOM installation within the Bonneville service territory, with whose key staff PNL had already developed a working relationship. In addition, Fort Lewis is served by a utility (TPU) that has demonstrated a commitment to energy-efficiency programs over the years with staff who enthusiastically embraced the concept. All these parties became involved in the pilot program.

The overall goals of the pilot program are:

- to demonstrate the FEDS approach such that it can be transferred to other federal installations;

- to acquire all cost-effective energy efficiency identified and characterized at Fort Lewis; and

- to acquire all cost-effective electric energy efficiency at Fort Lewis through a TPU/Bonneville agreement that would not require the Fort to either procure an ESCO or provide any up-front capital.

The latter goal could best be accomplished through the Targeted Resources Acquisition Program offered by Bonneville. This program enables utilities that purchase power from Bonneville to identify and buy electric energy-efficiency resources from the utilities' customers, then sell those resources back to Bonneville for use elsewhere in its service area. However, to take full advantage of this program, utilities such as

TPU must prepare a proposal to Bonneville that tells the agency where and what the potential resources are and how the utility plans to evaluate those estimated resources to determine their actual extent. The federal installation whose potential resources are being estimated also needs this information so that it can decide whether or not to commit its share of the installed cost of the recommended retrofits.

In this paper, we focus on PNL's assessment of the electric energy-efficiency resource potential at Fort Lewis and provide a summary of the contracting process for DSM services from TPU. A comprehensive report describing the analyses process and data used in the assessment was prepared and presented to TPU.[2]

Consistent with the FEDS process, an assessment has also been undertaken by PNL for the fossil fuel efficiency resource and fuel-switching potential. Unlike the electric efficiency projects funded through the utility DSM program, these projects will require government and/or third-party financing strategies. A comprehensive report for the fossil-fuel assessment is under preparation.

For the electric assessment, we develop an estimate of the electricity use baseline and efficiency improvement potential for major sectors and end uses at the site. Developing the baseline is essential to segment the end uses that are targets for broad-based efficiency improvement measures and to provide TPU with the basis for its proposal to Bonneville to acquire the resource. The efficiency resource estimate is a conservative (minimum) estimate of savings potential. We did not identify all possible efficiency opportunities, but instead identified the majority of the resource. Additional opportunities will likely be uncovered through the detailed building-by-building audit to be conducted by the ESCO.

## BASELINE ELECTRICITY USE

The first step in the process was to quantify the baseline energy use by facility type and end use. To develop the baseline electricity use we undertook a two-step process. We first segmented the Fort into sectors, subsectors, and end uses to reflect major areas of consumption and efficiency potential. The four sectors identified were: 1) buildings; 2) pumps/motors; 3) distribution system; and 4) exterior lights. The four sectors were further segmented into subsectors and, in the case of buildings, end uses (i.e., interior lighting, domestic hot water [DHW], refrigeration, and Other).

The second step entailed estimating baseline consumption through the development of subsector consumption and end-use intensities (EUIs) measured in kilowatt-hours per square foot (kWh/ft²) for subsectors in which end uses are identified. The process to develop the baseline electricity use is described in more detail below.

### Sector Segmentation

The real property data base for the site was used to divide the site facilities into sensible building types. The site contains approximately 4450 buildings with floorspace of 24 million ft². We segmented the buildings sector into 16 subsectors (building types) based upon function and uniqueness of operation. End uses identified in the buildings sector include five lighting type categories, domestic hot water supplied by residential-type water heaters, refrigeration (Refrig.) supplied by residential-type refrigerators, and all other uses. The Other category contains heating, ventilating, and air-conditioning (HVAC) energy end uses that are specific to each building type. HVAC energy use was not separated because almost all heating energy is supplied by fossil fuel and few buildings are cooled; electricity use for HVAC is primarily for fans and pumps.

The pumps/motors sector reflects electricity use for large pumps and motors (10 to 250 horsepower) used for the water supply and sewage treatment subsectors. The distribution sector accounts for the losses incurred for electricity distribution through the transformer and feeder subsectors. We segmented the exterior lights sector into three subsectors: residential, non-residential (building exterior and parking lot lighting), and street lighting.

## End-Use Intensities

The estimated baseline electricity consumption was developed through a combination of EUIs developed for the buildings sector end uses and estimated subsector consumption for the other three sectors. Estimates were developed using primary data for energy use at Fort Lewis, input from Fort Lewis staff, and secondary information from other studies conducted for the Pacific Northwest region.[3,4,5]

The baseline electricity use is displayed in Table 1. The data were developed for the buildings sector end uses and estimated subsector consumption or losses for the other three sectors.

## Metered Data

Typical with large federal installations, the limited availability of submetered data created a challenge in developing the baseline electricity use. The Fort is served by three substations. Each is metered separately by TPU for both demand and power usage. Aside from the commercial (nonappropriated) buildings on the Fort, these are the only sites where electricity usage for the installation is metered. Seventeen feeder lines from these three substations provide all electrical power to the Fort.

We metered each of the substations and feeders separately and collected time-series data for four consecutive months. The primary purpose of the metering was to measure the electric demand profile of the Fort and determine the relative contributions to that demand of each of the three substations and 17 feeders. The secondary purpose was to provide the only metered data for an accurate assessment and reconciliation of the electrical energy use intensity estimates.

### ELECTRIC EFFICIENCY RESOURCE SUPPLY ASSESSMENT

The supply of the electric efficiency resource was estimated for all subsectors and end uses except the Other category in the building subsectors. The quantity of energy resource available through the installation of energy-efficient measures and technologies was

TABLE 1. ESTIMATED BASELINE ANNUAL ELECTRICITY USE BY SECTOR, SUBSECTOR, AND END-USE

| Sector | Estimated Annual Baseline Electricity Use (MWh) | | | | |
|---|---|---|---|---|---|
| | Lighting | DHW | Refrig. | Other | Total |
| **Building** | | | | | |
| Single-Family | 4,210 | 9,287 | 2,477 | 9,339 | 25,313 |
| Multifamily | 3,713 | 7,650 | 2,040 | 7,707 | 21,110 |
| Concrete Barracks | 10,431 | | | 12,064 | 22,495 |
| Wood Barracks | 1,088 | | | 982 | 2,071 |
| Office/Admin. | 10,368 | 1,817 | | 10,478 | 22,663 |
| Warehouse | 6,025 | 26 | | 4,990 | 11,041 |
| Motor Pool | 5,122 | 1,140 | | 3,682 | 9,944 |
| Hangar | 1,084 | 92 | | 912 | 2,088 |
| Dining Halls | 1,252 | | | 5,955 | 7,207 |
| Clubs | 1,154 | | | 2,410 | 3,565 |
| Old Madigan | 4,502 | | | 8,807 | 13,309 |
| New Madigan | 5,959 | | | 2,023 | 7,982 |
| Commissary | 735 | | | 4,515 | 5,250 |
| Computer Center | 118 | | | 376 | 494 |
| Simulators | 230 | 3 | | 4,564 | 4,797 |
| Other | 4,873 | 637 | | 4,249 | 9,759 |
| Subtotal | 60,867 | 20,653 | 4,517 | 83,053 | 169,088 |
| | | | | | |
| **Pumps/Motors** | | | | | |
| Water Supply | | | | 3,600 | 3,600 |
| Sewage Treatment | | | | 1,160 | 1,160 |
| Subtotal | | | | 4,760 | 4,760 |
| | | | | | |
| **Distribution Losses** | | | | | |
| Transformers | | | | 13,000 | 13,000 |
| Lines | | | | 2,000 | 2,000 |
| Subtotal | | | | 15,000 | 15,000 |
| | | | | | |
| **Exterior Lights** | | | | | |
| Residential | 1,290 | | | | 1,290 |
| Other Building | 2,453 | | | | 2,453 |
| Street | 4,000 | | | | 4,000 |
| Subtotal | 7,744 | | | | 7,744 |
| | | | | | |
| Total | 68,611 | 20,653 | 4,517 | 102,813 | 196,591 |
| | | | | | |
| % of Total | 34.9 | 10.5 | 2.3 | 52.3 | 100.00 |

estimated for three electricity price ranges: $0 through $0.023/kWh, $0.024 through $0.045/kWh, and $0.046 through $0.075/kWh. The endpoint of the first price range is the approximate price that Fort Lewis currently pays for electricity (blended rate); the endpoint of the second price range is the approximate long-run avoided cost for new electricity generation in the Pacific Northwest (Bonneville) region;[6] and the endpoint of the last cost range is an arbitrary price beyond which there is likely no cost-effective technology options.

The potential menu of energy resource opportunities (EROs) was discussed and agreed upon in consultation with the utility. The EROs selected were those that were current technology, technically applicable, and acceptable to the installation. They are identified below by sector and end use.

## Buildings

### Interior Lighting

- Replace 15% of the incandescent lamps in indoor residential fixtures, 75% of the indoor fixtures in other buildings, and 100% of the exterior fixtures with compact fluorescent fixtures.

- Replace standard magnetic ballasts with energy-efficient magnetic ballasts in two-tube fluorescent fixtures using 34-, 40-, and 75-W tubes.

- Replace standard magnetic ballasts with electronic ballasts in two-tube fluorescent fixtures using 34-, 40-, and 75-W tubes.

- Replace standard magnetic ballasts with tuneable electronic ballasts in two-tube fluorescent fixtures using 34-, 40-, and 75-W tubes.

- Add parabolic reflectors (refl.) to two-tube fluorescent fixtures using 34-, 40-, and 75-W tubes.

- Replace two-tube fluorescent fixtures using 34-, 40-, and 75-W tubes with new fixtures with reflectors and electronic ballasts.

- Replace two-tube fluorescent fixtures using 75-W tubes with 150-W high-pressure sodium lamps.

- Replace two-tube fluorescent fixtures using 75-W tubes with single-tube 75-W very-high-output (VHO) fixtures.

- Replace two-tube fluorescent fixtures using 34- and 40-W tubes with F-30 T-8 fixtures.

Lighting system retrofits were made on a constant level of service basis. That is, if a retrofit put out twice the level of light (measured in lumens), a one-for-two replacement was used.

## Domestic Hot Water

- Increase the insulation level of the tanks by wrapping all of the water heaters with insulation.

- Wrap only new water heaters (less than 2 years old) with insulation.

- Replace 100% of existing water heaters with high-efficiency water heaters with nonmetallic or lined tanks. (Information from Fort Lewis staff indicates that life expectancy for water heaters is less

than 5 years due to tank corrosion caused by carbonic acid. In addition, TPU staff encouraged consideration of a water heater replacement program with high-efficiency models, as the utility has experienced greater success with a replacement program than with wrap programs.)

- Replace water heaters upon failure (ROF) with high-efficiency water heaters with nonmetallic or lined tanks.

## Refrigeration

- Replace 100% of existing residential-type refrigerators.

Replacing refrigerators with high-efficiency models as they wear out rather than implementing a straight replacement program as above was not considered because it is understood that all models now available are of the "efficient" variety. Consequently, there is little differential among replacement option.

## Pumps/Motors

### Water Supply (WS)

- Totally replace well pump motors with high-efficiency motors.

- Replace well pump motors with high-efficiency motors upon failure.

### Sewage Treatment (ST)

- Totally replace sewage treatment pump motors with high-efficiency motors.

- Replace sewage treatment pump motors with high-efficiency motors upon failure.

For both the water supply and sewage treatment subsectors, existing motors were assessed individually for replacement because the number of operating hours varied significantly, which has a large effect on the economic analysis. The cost and efficiency improvement also varies with motor size.

## Distribution

### Transformer (TRANS)

- Replace existing transformers with high-efficiency units. Existing transformers were assessed by size category for replacement.

### Line Loss

- Regulate the voltage of the distribution system so that the most distant point on individual feeders meets minimum voltage requirements under all load conditions.

Although insufficient information was available to quantify the resource it was estimated to provide a reduction of 1% to 3.5% in total base load at a very low cost.

## Exterior Lighting

### Residential

- Replace 100% of incandescent bulbs with compact fluorescent fixtures.

## ECONOMIC ANALYSES OF THE RESOURCE

Two economic figures of merit were used for depicting the financial attractiveness of the EROs. The first was the levelized energy cost (LEC), which is the metric commonly used by utilities to express the cost of supply- and demand-side resources on a dollars per kilowatt-hour (or kilowatt) basis. The LEC of an ERO is calculated as the annualized total cost divided by the annual energy savings. The LEC is used to develop a supply curve relating the quantity of resource available at a schedule of prices. Typically, utilities with aggressive DSM programs are only interested in, and will only pay for, energy-efficiency measures that cost no more than their long-run avoided cost to acquire new generating resources calculated in the same manner as the LEC.

The second economic figure of merit is the life-cycle-cost (LCC), net present value (NPV) metric that federal agencies are required to use to evaluate cost-effectiveness.[7] Each ERO has an associated initial capital cost, as well as a stream of costs (e.g., operations and maintenance), over the term of analysis (typically 25 years). In addition, each ERO saves some amount of energy, which translates into savings on the Fort's utility bill. The NPV employs the concept of the present value of a stream of savings or costs that will be enjoyed or incurred in the future. Built into the LCC algorithm is a fixed discount rate and real energy price escalation rate. For federal facilities, any project or action with a positive NPV is considered cost-effective. And the project with the lowest LCC and maximum positive NPV among a choice of projects should be considered first.

For each ERO considered, PNL determined the capital cost, operations and maintenance costs, and energy savings used in the LEC and LCC/NPV analyses. The initial capital cost in the LCC analysis is the cost to the government. Because of the size of the resource, the single "owner" of the resource and the aggressive DSM program offerings, TPU agreed to pay for 85% of the installed cost of the EROs, leaving the government's (Fort's) share at 15%.

The LEC, NPV, and annual energy-efficiency resource availability (kWh) of each measure considered were determined. The results of the analyses are shown in Table 2. The data in Table 2 allow the utility and the Fort to choose the electric energy-efficiency measures to install in the site-wide retrofit.

Using the LEC values, efficiency measures up to the cost of the marginal supply resource for Bonneville (~$0.045/kWh), or other negotiated cost near this value (agreed upon between Bonneville and TPU since Bonneville will "pay" TPU a cost to deliver the efficiency resource to Bonneville), may be considered cost-effective.

All options that are not part of mutually exclusive sets that have an LEC less than the avoided (or Bonneville/TPU negotiated) cost should be selected. Options that are part of mutually exclusive sets should be chosen if they have the LEC closest to the avoided (or negotiated) cost of energy, but not exceeding it. For example, based on the NPV, the best choice for retrofitting fluorescent lighting fixtures having 40-W tubes was determined to be a total new fixture having a standard electronic ballast and parabolic reflector. This choice also shows an LEC of $0.0166/kWh, which will also be acceptable to the utility.

Examination of the results of the analyses with the cost-sharing split shows that the choice of criteria (LEC or NPV) will not significantly affect the ultimate choice of the EROs to be installed at the Fort. The most desirable measures, in terms of both overall energy savings and NPV, could be selected and implemented using either criteria.

The LEC and resource availability are displayed in Figure 1 in the form of a supply curve. This supply curve shows availability of about 43,000 average annual MWh of electric efficiency at a cost of less than $0.037/kWh. Above $0.037/kWh, less than an additional 1,500 MWh are available.

Figure 2 shows the resource availability by end-use for LEC ranges of $0 to $0.023/kWh, $0.024 to $0.045/kWh, and $0.046 to $0.075/kWh. In the lowest cost range, over 37,000 MWh annually (equivalent to over 4 average MW of capacity) are provided by efficiency improvements to water heaters, water supply pumps, interior lighting, exterior lighting, water treatment pumps, and transformer upgrades/voltage regulation.

Other transformer and water supply pump replacements, in addition to a different set of lighting and water heating improvements, contribute another 5,907 MWh to the resource potential for the mid-range cost. The upper cost range contains another 412 MWh provided by additional water supply pump and transformer replacements. Note that lighting measures account for over 90% of the efficiency resource available at less than $0.024/kWh.

The estimated capital cost for all cost-effective electric EROs is approximately $10 million. Based on the Fort's payment of 15% of the installed cost, the NPV of the EROs exceeds $15 million and the cost to Fort Lewis for the installed technologies is $1.5 million. The Fort's estimated annual electrical energy savings is between $500,000 and $1 million depending on the final selection of the technologies to be installed.

## FOSSIL FUEL RESOURCE ASSESSMENT

A similar assessment was undertaken for fossil fuel efficiency measures, including fuel-switching (e.g., oil to natural gas) opportunities. The analyses showed a resource potential (savings) of nearly 300,000 MMBtu/year with EROs and fuel-switching costing approximately $6.6 million. The NPV of all cost-effective measures was ~$44 million based on the government (Fort) paying for 100% of the installed cost of the technologies.

## CONTRACTING AND IMPLEMENTATION

The Fort Lewis-TPU contract for installing energy-efficient technologies has been under development since the inception of the baselining activity in March 1990. Early in the negotiations, TPU agreed to up-front finance the entire cost of the installation of the technologies. TPU understood that this was the best way to effectively and quickly acquire the resource potential of this size. This was also one of the necessary conditions for the project to be a success. TPU, as a public (non-regulated) utility, received endorsement from the Tacoma City Council and Utility Board to pursue the project and acquire the necessary capital for the project (installed technologies) through bond sales. The magnitude of the investment requested by TPU was based on the PNL resource assessment.

The Fort issued a public notice of intent to enter into a contract with the utility to accept the DSM program and technologies. The result was a sole-source contract with TPU since only TPU can offer the utility DSM programs to its customers (e.g., Fort Lewis). The utility DSM offerings, combined with recent federal

TABLE 2. LEVELIZED ENERGY COST, NET PRESENT VALUE, AND RESOURCE AVAILABILITY BY EFFICIENCY MEASURE

| Efficiency Measure | Levelized Energy Cost ($/kWh) | Marginal Levelized Energy Cost ($/kWh) | Net Present Value (1991 $ thousands) | Marginal Annual Resource Availability (kWh) | Marginal Initial Capital Cost (1991 $ thousands) |
|---|---|---|---|---|---|
| DHW: ROF[a] | 0.0056 | 0.0056 | 1,935 | 2,427,754 | 1,439 |
| WS: ROF - Well #18 | 0.0066 | 0.0066 | 4 | 13,810 | 1 |
| DHW: Complete replacement[a] | 0.0057 | 0.0081 | 2,126 | 2,595,185 | 1,572 |
| Fl-75-W: New fix. w/refl., ballast | 0.0098 | 0.0098 | 410 | 1,318,273 | 220 |
| Fl-40-W: New fix. w/refl., ballast[b] | 0.0166 | 0.0166 | 7,453 | 25,915,995 | 6,662 |
| Fl-34-W: New fix. w/refl., ballast[c] | 0.0167 | 0.0167 | 278 | 957,498 | 250 |
| ST: ROF - Effluent pumps | 0.0181 | 0.0181 | 9 | 30,747 | 8 |
| Inc.: Replace w/compact fl | 0.0203 | 0.0203 | 981 | 6,199,405 | 754 |
| TRANS: 50 kVA Transformers | 0.0210 | 0.0210 | 518 | 1,500,308 | 619 |
| TRANS: 37.5 kVA Transformers | 0.0228 | 0.0228 | 238 | 699,314 | 313 |
| WS: ROF - Well #19 | 0.0251 | 0.0251 | 1 | 5,522 | 2 |
| WS: ROF - Well #15 | 0.0263 | 0.0263 | 2 | 6,955 | 3 |
| TRANS: 25 kVA Transformers | 0.0275 | 0.0275 | 198 | 606,455 | 327 |
| TRANS: 75 kVA Transformers | 0.0335 | 0.0335 | 267 | 865,947 | 569 |
| WS: ROF - Well #10 | 0.0357 | 0.0357 | (d) | 32 | (d) |
| TRANS: 100 kVA Transformers | 0.0373 | 0.0373 | 36 | 120,387 | 88 |
| WS: ROF - Sequal spring | 0.0562 | 0.0562 | 5 | 24,573 | 21 |
| WS: ROF - Well #13 | 0.0567 | 0.0567 | (d) | 2,869 | 2 |
| TRANS: 200 kVA Transformers | 0.0605 | 0.0605 | 86 | 374,132 | 443 |
| WS: ROF - Well #14 | 0.0613 | 0.0613 | (d) | 3,528 | 3 |
| WS: ROF - Well #12 | 0.0613 | 0.0613 | 1 | 7,498 | 7 |
| TRANS: 15 kVA Transformers | 0.0771 | 0.0771 | 37 | 205,211 | 310 |
| TRANS: 300 kVA Transformers | 0.0800 | 0.0800 | 35 | 206,202 | 324 |
| Fl-40-W: Install F30 T-8 fixtures[b] | 0.0245 | 0.1061 | 7,059 | 28,399,233 | 9,690 |
| Refrigerators: Replace | 0.1113 | 0.1113 | 80 | 1,387,167 | 1,843 |
| WS: ROF - Well #9 | 0.1165 | 0.1165 | (d) | 494 | (d) |
| TRANS: 500 kVA Transformers | 0.1180 | 0.1180 | 13 | 208,314 | 482 |
| TRANS: 750 kVA Transformers | 0.1333 | 0.1333 | 3 | 176,512 | 461 |
| TRANS: 1000 kVA Transformers | 0.1410 | 0.1410 | (d) | 53,305 | 147 |
| TRANS: 1500 kVA Transformers | 0.1419 | 0.1419 | (d) | 92,446 | 257 |
| TRANS: 5 kVA Transformers | 0.1564 | 0.1564 | (d) | 6,398 | 20 |
| TRANS: 2500 kVA Transformers | 0.1582 | 0.1582 | (d) | 15,074 | 47 |
| WS: ROF - Well #17 | 0.2615 | 0.2615 | (d) | 878 | 3 |
| Fl-34-W: Install F30 T-8 fixtures[c] | 0.0245 | 3.7801 | 246 | 959,483 | 340 |

(a) These measures are mutually exclusive and only one will be selected.
(b) These measures are mutually exclusive and only one will be selected.
(c) These measures are mutually exclusive and only one will be selected.
(d) NPV is negative and therefore not considered as a viable measure.

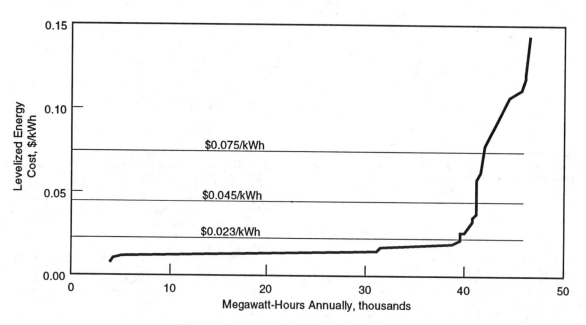

FIGURE 1. ELECTRIC EFFICIENCY SUPPLY CURVE

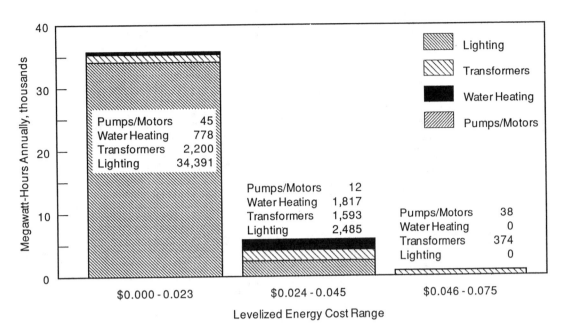

FIGURE 2. ELECTRIC EFFICIENCY RESOURCE BY END-USE AND COST RANGE

legislation and policy to encourage federal agencies to participate in utility DSM programs, gave the necessary incentive and authority for the Fort to pursue this project.[8,9]

The contract developed between TPU and the Fort is a "blanket ordering agreement" (BOA), separate from the existing utility service contract. Under this BOA, the utility will contract with a single competitively-selected ESCO to audit and recommend the installation of electrical retrofit technologies at the Fort.

The recommendations and installation schedule will be reviewed by TPU and Fort staff and agreed-upon by the Fort prior to any work at the site. The Fort will then accept the technologies once installed and commissioned by the ESCO. TPU will then reimburse the ESCO for the installed technologies according to the terms of the ESCO-TPU contract. The Fort will pay back 15% of the installed cost to the utility, likely through a direct payment. TPU will be reimbursed by Bonneville, under the terms of the TPU-Bonneville contract, for the delivered efficiency resource.

Perseverance and commitment on the part of the Fort Lewis technical and contractual staff, FORSCOM program office and contracting staff, and TPU has resulted in a precedent-setting contract vehicle for this project that was finalized during a formal proclamation ceremony on May 13, 1992. The award of the ESCO contract is expected by September 1992. The installation of technologies is expected to begin the first quarter of fiscal year 1993 and continue for 5 to 7 years.

The verification of the energy savings is an issue currently under discussion between TPU and Bonneville.

REFERENCES

1. J. W. Currie, R. W. Reilly, R. W. Brancato, and J. A. Dirks. "Modernizing Federal Energy Systems: The FEDS Development Approach." *Energy Engineering*, Vol. 88, No. 4, 1991.

2. T. J. Secrest, J. W. Currie, J. G. De Steese, J. A. Dirks, T. J. Marseille, G. B. Parker, E. E. Richman, and S. A. Shankle. *Fort Lewis Electric Energy Baseline and Efficiency Resource Assessment*. PNL-7763, Pacific Northwest Laboratory, Richland, Washington, October 1991.

3. *Description of Electric Energy Use in Single Family Residences in the Pacific Northwest*, DOE/BP-13795-21, July 1989.

4. *Description of Electric Energy Use in Commercial Buildings in the Pacific Northwest*, DOE/BP-13795-22, December 1989.

5. *Fort Lewis Energy Savings Opportunity Survey*. Fort Lewis, Washington, 1987.

6. *1991 Northwest Conservation and Electric Power Plan*. Volume I, 91-04. Northwest Power Planning Council, April 1991.

7. 10 CFR Part 436 *Federal Energy Management and Planning Programs*.

8. Executive Order on Federal Energy Management, E.O. 12759. *Federal Register*, Vol. 58, No. 76, April 19, 1991.

9. *Defense Energy Program Policy Memorandum (DEPPM) 91-2*. Office of the Assistant Secretary of Defense, March 19, 1991.

# Chapter 32
# The Trials and Tribulations of Designing a DSM Data Base at Boston Edison

A.J. Bates, J.F. Pino

## OVERVIEW

This paper highlights the iterative steps necessary in developing a real-world mission-critical application at Boston Edison. The DSM System is the result of over two years of effort to develop a workable Demand Side Management (DSM) tracking system. Today, the system continues to evolve and change but Boston Edison no longer is *"fitting square pegs into round holes."*

## HISTORY

### DSM at Boston Edison
Boston Edison pursued various conservation programs in the mid 1980's. The initial programs were developed in response to regulatory requirements where some direct costs were paid for through a conservation charge by the customer while others were capitalized in the rate base. In effect there was no monetary incentive for the utility to encourage conservation programs.

The first generation of programs was called "Impact 2000" which included:

- Water heater wrapping
- Refrigerator coil cleaning
- Direct load control pilot programs.

The second generation of DSM programs included:

- Lighting Rebates
- Energy Audits
- ENCORE
- Design Plus
- Load Management.

### Tracking Early Programs
Tracking the results of these conservation programs was the responsibility of the program managers. The managers had the discretion to use whatever method they deemed necessary to track their program's progress. A variety of tools were used, such as Lotus 1-2-3 Alpha 4, dBase, etc. The data collection for the Residential programs and the Commercial/Industrial programs was handled in two different ways. The Residential programs were maintained by outside energy contractors who did the installation and audit work. Summary statistics were provided by the contractor for both invoicing and reporting purposes. The Commercial/Industrial programs were tracked at Boston Edison using a variety of methods, the method depending on the type of program and who was in charge.

In all cases, the information recorded was geared toward the day-to-day management needs of the program managers. Specific DSM data requirements had not been formulated; no systematic evaluation was undertaken.

### DSM is Linked to Rates
In 1989, the Massachusetts Department of Public Utilities (DPU) and other public interest agencies approved a negotiated rate settlement agreement which initiated a significant effort in conservation through DSM programs in exchange for future rate case considerations (referred to as the Settlement).

As part of the Settlement, Boston Edison had agreed to spend $75 million over a three year period on conservation programs. The spending of this money would be monitored by a Settlement Board composed of members of the Attorney General's Office, the Executive Office of Energy Resources, the Conservation Law Foundation, and the Company. For any expenditure in excess of $75 million, Boston Edison would be permitted to recover all program costs and earn a conservation incentive, provided that the Company could document the savings for each program. This "cost recovery" provision now created a revenue opportunity, making reliable program monitoring a priority.

### New Programs

The original programs rapidly evolved into over twenty initiatives:

- Efficient Lighting
- New Construction - Residential
- Boston Public Housing
- Public Housing Authority
- Energy Fitness
- A/C and Heat Pump Tune Up
- HVAC Rebate
- High Use Electric Heat Retrofit
- Multi-family energy audits
- ENCORE
- New Construction - Government
- Equipment Replacement
- Small C/I Retrofit
- Level II Retrofits
- Large C/I Retrofit
- New Construction - C/I
- Remodeling
- Load Management (BEEC, GAP, TOULC, A/C Cycling)
- Energy Audits 1-4
- Appliance Labeling
  (For complete program information contact Boston Edison)

As a result of the expanded initiatives, the program management staff grew from twenty to nearly seventy people.

### Managing Many Programs
With the new DSM programs, the added scrutiny of the Settlement Board, and the financial incentives of "cost recovery", DSM data integrity became a priority while data collection became a nightmare.

Program managers and contractors attempted to maintain their existing methods of data collection. They continued to use the dBase, 1-2-3, and Alpha 4 applications. Problems with this strategy became apparent during program evaluations. Each manager's data base could be defined differently. For example, a data element might be defined as a character code ("A" for "Attic") in one data base, as a numeric code (4 for "Roof/Attic") in a second data base, and as a text field ("Attic") in yet another. When there were few programs these inconsistencies were a nuisance. However, on a large number of programs with thousands of participants, analyzing and reconciling these differences became unmanageable.

The simple self-contained applications were no longer suitable or able to support the increased reporting requirements and the need for accurate information. The staff became overwhelmed. The old way of data management with the new requirements was like *"fitting square pegs into round holes."*

## MANAGING CHANGE - DESIGNING A DATA BASE

### Identifying the Problem
In order to relieve program managers of some DSM reporting and reconciling processes, a new area called Monitoring and Evaluation (M&E) was formed. This new group immediately recognized the need for a centralized data base to insure more accurate reporting. Individual data bases could no longer produce the reports in a timely manner and the information they ultimately contained was prone to errors.

Senior management concurred with M&E and decided to investigate the development of a centralized data base application. M&E lacked expertise in the computer field so Boston Edison's Management Information Services (MIS) area was consulted on developing a data base. As is the case with most large corporations today, MIS did not have the resources available to develop a new application. Rather than postponing the development process, a steering committee was formed to select a data base vendor or consultant who could build the new system.

### Data Base Committee
This committee, composed of 3-4 managers and 10-15 staff members, developed the initial data base requirements and the specifications for a Request For Proposal (RFP). The RFP was submitted to the bidding process and a consulting firm was engaged to devise a prototype database system. The consulting staff was incorporated into the data base committee.

Over the course of several months this group attempted to establish data definitions and data entry screens. The DSM Program managers' and users' perspective was: "We know what to implement but not what to save.." That is, they could design and develop a program to save energy, but they did not know what information was needed to prove cost effectiveness and energy savings to the Settlement Board. The managers' responsibilities involved marketing their programs, not necessarily collecting specific data. They collected the information they thought might be needed. The intent of the central data base project was to determine what information should be collected, then impose this structure on the programs.

The consulting firm determined that:

"Current operational activities appear unique between divisions because of a lack of uniform procedures and different priorities on activities. For example, recording and tracking of leads is handled differently in each division and is accorded differing levels of importance in each. Despite these differences, operations are uniform enough that

a single system model can be demonstrated to address all divisions."

By developing universal standards, data collection should be easier. Unfortunately, the members of the committee could not agree on a standard; each area had different interests in the data collected and collection process. Program Management, Marketing Communications, Demand Planning and M&E all had distinctly different needs and agendas. In order to begin to move the process, a decision was made to devise a simple prototype application which could "grow" and change as the newly formed groups developed and implemented new programs.

Up to this point the customary phases of systems development were followed closely: users were interviewed, needs identified, specifications planned, RFPs issued. However, a final plan was not agreed upon, so there was no ownership of the program. Since no group wanted to take charge of the project, M&E was put in charge. Management reasoned that M&E acting as an auditor would insure that the information necessary for demonstrating savings and costs to the Settlement parties and the DPU would be collected.

### The Prototype System
The prototype application was originally simple and recorded basic information such as participants' names and addresses. The organization of the data base followed a simple hierarchy.

> Lead information file
> > Business information file
> > > Customer information file
> > > > Program information file
> > > > > Measure information file

The files were linked together with a system generated identification number.

Efficient Lighting was the first program implemented. As the new DSM programs began to evolve, the data base also evolved. More and more fields, files, and features were added. The simple data base became unwieldy and still didn't fulfill the needs of the users.

The flat data base design could accommodate simple programs like Efficient Lighting but ultimately forced management to make compromises and perform various contortions to accommodate reasonable data in more complicated programs. Depending on what segment a program was in and what type of customer was participating, the data base field "Actual kWh" could mean "Proposed number of fixtures." Generic fields were created where free text and comments could be entered . Many fields had no validation or integrity checks and when analyzed could provide no useful consistent information. There was limited documentation which further hindered the analysis process. The new system had imposed a structure which did not meet the users' needs; they were trying to *"fit square pegs into round holes."*

## RECOGNIZING PROBLEMS
Computer systems typically develop through a process called the "System Development Lifecycle". This process includes: Requirements Analysis, Design, Programming, Implementation, Use, and Revisions. The intent of this process is to develop a system which attempts to match the business environment where it is in use. At Boston Edison, the requirements analysis phase was never really completed. As a result:

- Control of the system was lost
- Development costs doubled
- System became un-maintainable (features hard coded, no documentation)

# Prototype System Model

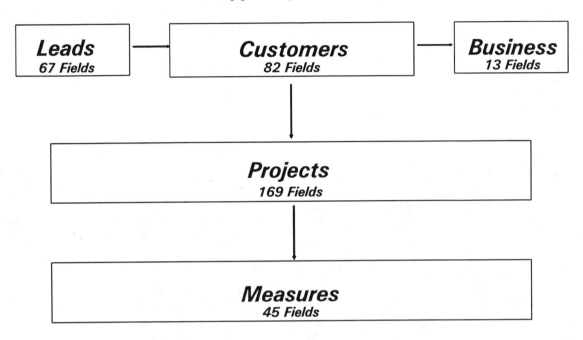

*All Combinations Must Be Accommodated*

- Network, multi-user, hardware/software problems difficult to track
- Prototype became a "run-away".

## Prototype Failure

After approximately six months of development, it be came clear to M&E that there were significant deficiencies in the prototype, both in the system software and the actual data base. Management recognized these problems and decided to review the prototype to determine what corrective action should be taken.

The analysis covered many aspects of the system, including data storage requirements, system maintenance, hardware requirements, and the user interface:

- The user interface was not intuitive, required duplicate data to be entered in multiple places, and over-all retrieval time was excessive (10-20 seconds per customer).

- Data storage statistics showed that, despite the effort by the consultants and the data base committee, the data base was not being used effectively.

  - Only 4 of 20 major programs implemented into the system
  - 80% of fields completely blank
  - 10% of fields more than 50% blank
  - Only 10% of fields less than 50% blank

- The design of the prototype software made it impossible for the consulting company's programmers to keep up with the data base changes.

- The projected hardware needs for the production system showed requirements for over 500 megabytes of disk space and additional network hardware by mid 1992, even though only 20% of the data base actually contained data.

Based on these findings, Boston Edison management posed the questions:

- Will the environment always be changing, if not monthly at least seasonally?

- Would the system hardware ever handle the requirements?

- Was the DSM area headed in the right direction? Hardware, software etc?

- Had the prototype failed? Could it be salvaged?

- Could, would it meet the long term needs of a production system?

- Was good money going after bad?

To answer these questions and to find solutions, Boston Edison engaged a new data base consulting firm to perform an independent analysis.

## INDEPENDENT SYSTEM REVIEW

The new consulting firm identified several fundamental issues to be considered:

- The environment - corporate culture
- Type of users - managers, clerks
- Data requirements - program managers, contractors, DPU
- Growth needs - data base size 1992, 1993

The following system areas were reviewed:

- Software
  - user interface
  - data storage model
  - ease of access/retrieval
  - application code
  - security

- Users/Management:
  - management goals
  - User group needs
  - key areas of commonality across groups

## Critical Findings.

The data base strategy of "making everything look the same" was not workable when expanded to all DSM programs. At Boston Edison, DSM is divided into major areas: Residential Programs, Government Programs, Commercial/Industrial Programs, Load Management, and Monitoring & Evaluation. The original consultant's reasoning for the flat data base design was based on the premise that all programs, activities and initiatives would conform to a single set of requirements. However, the data needed to support a Residential lighting "mail-in rebate" program is radically different than that needed for a Commercial/Industrial "HVAC retrofit" program, even though there are some similarities. A secondary problem with the flat data base design was that it used dozens of "generic" fields which consume space even if they are not used and require substantial backup documentation to be properly analyzed.

The application software could not be easily changed. It had been developed using programming techniques which require an application to be fully defined before the system is completed. Features and functions needed to be individually coded into the application which caused the programming backlog to become unacceptably long.

## Recommendations.

The central system should not impose an umbrella data base design. It should provide a uniform method to access data. These two objectives could be achieved by utilizing the few aspects all programs shared, such as a facility address which is recorded in all Boston Edison programs.

In the DSM environment, change would be continuous, so any application would need to be:

- Flexible to accommodate change

- Able to be maintainable by non-technical users

- Modular in design.

After presenting these and other findings, combined with the analysis already performed in-house, Boston Edison determined that the system could not be saved.

## BUILDING A FLEXIBLE DATABASE

Boston Edison needed a system which could allow very different types of information to be collected and accessed through a uniform interface.

In order to create this new system a new implementation plan was developed:

- Redesign the data model and software strategy to:

  - Accommodate change
  - Provide for a logical flow of information from the facility to program participation and from program participation to the specific activities called measure installation

- Management approval of design

- Acquire necessary management commitments

- Create new software interface.

## Results

In order to accommodate many data tracking requirements, a unique software strategy was required. Rather than building a generic data base that could store any type of information and customizing the software for special requirements, the new data base consultant developed a generic data base interface which could access any data base. Using this paradigm, every user group could have data files specially designed for their needs. Users would not have to "fit square pegs into round holes" anymore.

The benefits of this new model are significant:

- Unused data fields could be eliminated, reducing clutter and cutting network storage requirements by 50%

- "Custom" programming could be greatly reduced or eliminated

- Data entry screens could be customized to reduce training times

- Program documentation was virtually eliminated as the data base now could have meaningful intuitive names rather than generic ones

- The system could accommodate an unlimited number of programs and measures.

The new DSM System (DSMS) was developed as a "table driven" application which utilizes tightly integrated program modules that allow custom features to be easily attached.

New DSM initiatives and programs are implemented by creating data base files and screens according to the user's specifications. Entries are then made in three files which control the software. Once these steps are complete, the new program is active in the DSMS application and the process can be accomplished without shutting down the system.

The three system control files allow custom program software to be individually attached to any DSM data base. When a program needs a customized feature, such as an energy savings calculation, the formula is programmed and compiled into a special file. This custom code is accessed by making an entry in one of the system control files which is checked while the program is running. If an entry exists, the normal processing stops and the custom code is executed, after which normal processing resumes. Using this technique the DSMS application can have validations on any and all fields, complex computations, and more.

This technique eliminates many of the problems associated with the old system, particularly the programming backlog. Now users can design a data base to track a new program and can have it integrated in a few hours. The only programming required is for special formulas. If no special formulas are required, non-technical users can setup their own programs (if they have proper access rights). The core application code is never changed.

# New System Model

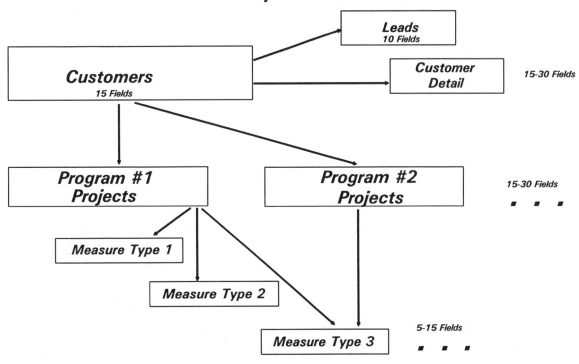

*Unlimited Number Of Programs and Measures*

The new data base is designed to support an unlimited number of independent programs and measures. This feature eliminates the need for program managers to agree on all data base changes, allowing them to concentrate on managing their programs instead of overall data base design. Programs can be phased in, rather than attempting to solve all of the design problems at once.

Development Time

The basic system software was developed in approximately three months using pre-existing software libraries provided by the new consultant. These software libraries contained many of the features required by Boston Edison which reduced both development time and cost.

Once the basic application was created, a year's worth of existing data was loaded into the system in approximately six weeks. This data came arrived in various file formats which needed to be converted for the new system to accept.

Today, 15 programs are on-line, only four months after the core software was completed. The combined data bases contain over 130 megabytes of data for 75,000 customers.

LOOKING AHEAD

Boston Edison management does not expect that there will be significant new growth in DSM initiatives, but it does expect that existing programs will change. This will be due to changes in reporting requirements, program management needs, and regulatory changes. In any event, the Boston Edison DSM System should be able to accommodate these changes as they happen without *"fitting square pegs into round holes."*

# Chapter 33
# Acquiring Energy Savings in Manufactured Housing

D. Davey

## MANUFACTURED HOUSING ACQUISITION PROGRAM

FIGURE 1. THE NORTHWEST'S "MAP" PROGRAM ACQUIRED ENERGY SAVINGS FROM HOME MANUFACTURERS

In 1991, the Northwest utilities faced a complex situation. They needed new sources of electrical power to avoid future deficits. A significant block of energy savings was available in the manufactured housing sector in the form of energy savings from increased insulation to new manufactured homes. The manufacturers were interested in saving the electricity in the homes, but would only deal with the utility sector as a whole.

Half of the homes targeted were sited in investor-owned utility (IOU) service territories, and half in the public sector made up of utilities that purchased some or all of their electricity from the Bonneville Power Administration.

Utilities agreed to acquire energy from manufacturers n the form of thermal efficiency measures specified by the Bonneville Power Administration. The program that resulted from over one year of negotiations was called the Manufactured Housing Acquisition Program, or MAP.

Manufacturers, the utilities, State Energy Offices, the Northwest Power Planning Council and Bonneville all worked closely and with tenacity to build the program that went into effect on April 1, 1992, and should save the region between 7 and 9 megawatts, enough energy to supply 11,000 homes in the Northwest.

### LOCKING IN WITH THE MANUFACTURERS

Amazingly, given the diversity of participants, a "Manufacturers Acquisition Committee" was formed that included representatives of IOU and public utilities, and manufacturers. The manufacturers agreed to build to high standards of thermal efficiency in exchange for an energy acquisition payment of $2,500 over a four-year contract cycle.

## MAP PARTICIPANTS
### (MANUFACTURED HOUSING ACQUISITION PROGRAM)

- MANUFACTURERS
- UTILITIES
- STATES
- SUPPLIERS
- REGIONAL COUNCIL
- BPA

FIGURE 2. PARTICIPANTS FROM BOTH THE PUBLIC AND PRIVATE SECTORS COOPERATED TO ENSURE SUCCESS OF THE PROGRAM

Since these payments were to be made by Bonneville within 15 days of shipment from the plants, a tracking system was required to determine where the homes were to be sited. Bonneville would be reimbursed by the IOU and cost share utilities for homes sited in their service territories.

Inspection at the plant was also of concern to assure a quality product. The State Energy Offices offered to provide both the tracking and inspection of the homes for a flat rate of $150 per home . This amount was to be reimbursed by IOUs and cost shares to Bonneville.

Finally, to help the manufacturers over the conversion to a new administrative process, a one-time administrative payment was agreed to. Manufacturers estimated a wide array of administrative costs, ranging from $10,000 to $60,000. The problem was that by reimbursing on an individual basis, Bonneville would be penalizing those manufacturers that had already borne the costs of certain technical changes to their manufacturing methods. The solution came in the form of an agreement on a flat $10,000 amount for each manufacturer.

## MANUFACTURERS IN THE NORTHWEST WITH SUPER GOOD CENTS MODELS

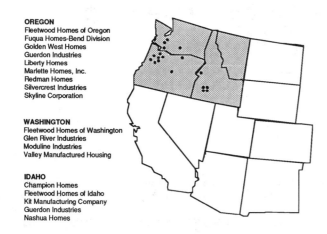

**OREGON**
Fleetwood Homes of Oregon
Fuqua Homes-Bend Division
Golden West Homes
Guerdon Industries
Liberty Homes
Marlette Homes, Inc.
Redman Homes
Silvercrest Industries
Skyline Corporation

**WASHINGTON**
Fleetwood Homes of Washington
Glen River Industries
Moduline Industries
Valley Manufactured Housing

**IDAHO**
Champion Homes
Fleetwood Homes of Idaho
Kit Manufacturing Company
Guerdon Industries
Nashua Homes

FIGURE 3. ALL 18 NORTHWEST MANUFACTURERS PARTICIPATED

### AGREEMENT WITH THE UTILITIES

Negotiations proceeded simultaneously both through the acquisition committee, and individually with manufacturers and utilities. Once the agreement with the manufacturers was shaped, Bonneville was able to show utilities how much energy they would be acquiring through the program. The next step was to arrange for reimbursement from the investor-owned and cost-share utilities for acquisition payments advanced to manufacturers by Bonneville (see figure 4). Each utility would reimburse Bonneville for homes sited in its service area, plus a $150 administrative charge per unit. Bonneville covered the payments of the 100 percent utilities because the agency was, in effect, acquiring that energy for its own use.

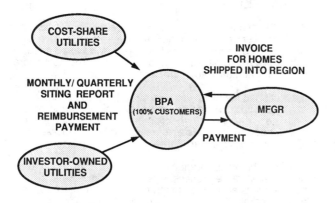

## PAYMENT PROCESS

FIGURE 4. MAP ACQUISITION PAYMENTS WERE BROKERED THROUGH BPA

### RISK AND MANAGEMENT REINFORCEMENT

Each sector took risks in putting this deal together. The manufacturers modified the design of already successful products and added efficiency measures that could increase the price beyond the offset of the acquisition payment (see figure 5). About 30 percent of the new homes built each year in the Northwest are manufactured. At 10,000 to 13,000 homes per year, the manufacturers have a great deal at stake.

### MAP REFERENCE PATH FOR ELECTRICALLY HEATED MANUFACTURED HOMES

| COMPONENT | | CLIMATE ZONE (ALL CLIMATE ZONES) |
|---|---|---|
| CEILINGS | FLAT | U-0.025 |
| | SLOPED | U-0.030 |
| WALLS | ABOVE GRADE | U-0.052 |
| FLOORS | (STEADY STATE) | U-0.033 |
| GLAZING | U-FACTOR | U-0.35 |
| | AREA (% OF FLOOR) (3) | 15.0% |
| EXTERIOR DOORS | | U-0.19 |
| ASSUMED INFILTRATION RATE (4) | | 0.35 ACH |
| CROSSOVER DUCT INSULATION | | R-8 |
| MAIN TRUNK DUCT INSULATION | | R-4 |

FIGURE 5. STRINGENT U-FACTORS AND R-VALUES WERE SPECIFIED FOR MAP HOMES

Utilities were purchasing energy savings that looked good on paper and were based on solid research and demonstration projects, but had yet to be proven in the open market. The risks were worthwhile, though, because energy acquired through the acquisition program should cost only about 2.5 cents per kilowatt hour, compared to 11 cents per kilowatt hour for power from new generating plants.

Bonneville also extended itself. Bonneville management had directed its program managers to take risks in the pursuit of conservation resources. The MAP was an excellent opportunity to put that directive into action. Bonneville took the risk of guaranteeing manufacturers start-up materials costs for one month prior to the activation date of the acquisition program. That amounted to some $2 million.

Manufacturers indicated they needed a guarantee from utilities to proceed in ordering materials so that they could begin on time. Faced with this dilemma, Bonneville distributed a memorandum of understanding to IOU and cost-share utilities asking for them to indicate their intent to participate as a sign of good faith.

Utilities representing 70 percent of the homes in the region indicated that they would participate. Bonneville management, realizing that attracting 100 percent was unlikely, set 80 percent as a decision plateau for proceeding with a guarantee to the manufacturers.

With the guarantees, manufacturers began to sign the agreement and proceed in stocking up on their necessary materials to build the homes to MAP.

## THE DEFINITION OF COMPROMISE

Negotiations went down to the wire, with one of the largest utilities being among the last to sign. Bonneville's management worked closely with the utility to resolve policy conflicts, and approximately one week before the April 1 deadline an agreement was reached that brought an additional 20 percent of the region's production into a program that had already reached the threshold of viability. Neither party was totally pleased with the arrangement, which probably is the best definition of a compromise.

## NINETY PERCENT COVERAGE

The agreement between Bonneville and Puget Power raised the percentage of homes covered by utility participation in MAP from 70 to 90 percent. Bonneville will continue to work with the remaining utilities, encouraging them to join the program during the next year.

The MAP went into effect on April 1 and has been enjoying the participation of all 18 manufacturers. The tracking, administrative and invoicing systems have all been functioning smoothly. Bonneville uses a computerized tracking system developed and installed by the State Energy Offices to track and verify the production, inspection and installation of each MAP home.

## THE NEXT STEP

The next step will be a six month review in October. Utilities and manufacturers will have the opportunity to make adjustments to the contract that can help the process flow more smoothly. Bonneville may also update its technical specifications at that time. While anything could happen at that, and subsequent annual reviews, However, it is reassuring to note that everyone involved in the MAP has made every effort to see that the program succeeds.

# Chapter 34

# Lighting Improvements - A Demand-Side Strategy that Works

T.D. Mull

In the early eighties Demand Side Management (DSM) became a recognized planning strategy for most electric utilities. You might say that it finally gained acceptance as a valid approach to meeting future customer needs. Prior to that time the supply side strategy, of simply building more power plants to meet ever increasing customer requirements for power, was the predominant utility mindset. Plant construction costs, growing customer interest in conservation and the environment, and regulatory concerns for the future availability of power focused utility management on the potential benefits of a DSM planning approach.

One of the first areas that utilities looked to for DSM opportunities was in commercial and industrial interior lighting. The conservation efforts of the seventies had made customers aware of the potential benefits of turning off fixtures when they left a room. However, many utilities in general viewed this, and other lighting measures, only as revenue erosion. In fact, that is exactly what it was. Initial conservation efforts focused on reducing "energy" consumption, not peak demand. But as utilities began to more closely examine the potential for demand control, some realized that controlling certain lighting applications could reduce peak demand in acceptable proportions.

Initial lighting DSM program efforts generally centered around encouraging the use energy efficient fluorescent lamps and ballasts and the application of high pressure sodium (HPS) fixtures, for replacement of mercury vapor (MV). Today, the opportunities for DSM applications in lighting have been significantly enhanced by recent improvements in source technology, luminaire design and system control. Even so, it is still quite common to find large facilities, including utilities, with minimal lighting control capability and utilizing inefficient sources.

Studies done by electric utilities indicate that as much as thirty to forty percent (30%-40%) of the energy consumed in the commercial sector may be used for interior lighting. For the industrial sector this value is typically ten to twenty percent (10%-20%). Over the past three years we have had the opportunity to survey over fifty industrial, commercial, and governmental facilities, ranging in size from 25,000 to 2.8 million square feet. The surveys have confirmed these estimates. The results have also indicated that the DSM potential is significant.

The are several factors that make lighting an attractive DSM area for utilities to focus their efforts. These include:

- Lighting is an end use that is readily understood by most customers.
- Potential savings are easily quantified.
- Once a measure has been installed, there is a reasonable degree of assurance that it will be retained.
- Demand and energy savings can be readily tracked.

Recent utility lighting DSM program activity has been mixed. In some portions of the country, such as the Northeast, utilities are taking a proactive approach and aggressively promoting such items as electronic ballasts, T-8 fluorescent lamps, and occupancy sensors. ~n other areas utilities are letting market forces dictate customer actions. The advent of the EPA Green Lights Program may provide sufficient inducement for some of the less active utilities and customers to become more involved.

Today, there are a number of proven off-the-shelf DSM options available to commercial and industrial customers that offer opportunity to minimize lighting costs and control peak demand. The lighting surveys we have conducted have indicated that a typical potential saving of 10%-20% in lighting expenditures is possible. Depending upon the measures implemented and annual operating hours, the associated lighting demand reduction can be even larger.

The following is a brief summary of the most commonly chosen lighting DSM customer options.

## LAMP SOURCES:

- Compact fluorescent lamps (PL) have had a dramatic impact on the lighting industry. They offer energy and demand saving options to what has been considered a strictly incandescent market segment. PL lamps are used to replace R or even ER lamps in recessed can fixtures. Fixture designs now offer two 13 watt PL lamps as an option to the standard 100/150 watt incandescent lamp. Now available in sizes from 5 watts to 40 watts, PL lamps are a viable option for many applications.

- T-8 fluorescent lamps are growing in popularity as replacements for F40T12 34 watt energy saving lamps. Mated with electronic ballasts these lamps have a higher lumen output and lower wattage input to optimize most four foot fluorescent systems. A four-lamp four foot fluorescent fixture with T-8 lamps can save approximately 32 watts over a similar fixture with 34 watt lamps and an energy efficient electromagnetic ballast.

- Improvements in high pressure sodium lamp technology have produced more acceptable color and even "energy emcient" lamps. Now receiving a greater level of acceptance, especially in the industrial sector,

HPS lamps offer high efficacy and provide a cost effective option to other HID and fluorescent systems.

## EQUIPMENT/FIXTURES:

- Quality electronic ballasts, for fluorescent lighting systems, have resulted in dramatic improvements in system operating efficiencies. In standard two lamp eight foot HO fixtures, the use of energy saving lamps and an electronic ballast can drop the overall input watt by approximately 93 watts per fixture. Efficiencies obtained with energy saving lamps and electronic ballasts can approach that of certain high pressure sodium configurations (100t lumens per watt).

- Specular reflectors for fluorescent systems offer meaningful demand savings potential, when properly applied. In applications when the lighting levels are excessive, quality reflectors offer a potential for reducing the total number of lamps required. Available in three basic types (silver film laminate, dielectric-coated aluminum, and polished aluminum), specular reflectors come in configurations for most popular sizes of fluorescent fixtures.

- Three-lamp fluorescent fixtures offer another option in retrofitting office areas. Replacement of four-lamp four foot fixtures with three-lamp fixtures has gained popularity over the past several years. With many existing office having elevated lighting levels, three-lamp fixtures offer significant demand and energy savings potential.

## CONTROLS

- Occupancy sensors provide individualized lighting control for spaces such as conference rooms, storage areas, and offices. These sensors remove the human element from switching control and ensure that lighting is off when a space is unoccupied. Since occupancy sensors are installed in infrequently occupied spaces, in which the lighting is normally left on, they provide a demand control component of savings as well as the generally accepted energy savings.

- With the adaption of electronic ballasts and controls the dimming of fluorescent lighting systems have become an affordable DSM option. Dimming, in controlled increments or to maintain an ambient lighting level can now be done effectively and for minimal additional cost.

The utilization of these basic lighting technologies has shown that DSM lighting programs can be effective and beneficial, for both utilities and customers. The customer benefits from lower operating costs, now and in the future. The utilities benefit from the better utilization of their existing facilities. This enhanced utilization allows them to defer, or potentially eliminate, the addition of costly generating capacity and the need for additional capital. Therefore, lighting DSM programs truly provide a win-win opportunity.

Chapter 35
# DSM Research and Tailored Technology Transfer

R.J. Hackner, S. Feldman, C.L.M. Braithwait

## ABSTRACT

The increasing utility and regulatory need for specialized and consistent Demand-Side Management (DSM) information has spawned the growth of several statewide, non-partisan research organizations, including the Wisconsin Center For Demand-Side Research (the Center). Their primary purpose is to gather and disseminate DSM information relevant to statewide conditions to program planners, implementers and load forecasters, as well as regulators and a variety of other private and public interest groups.

Such organizations have difficulties in meeting the specific needs of their constituents. The idea of "being all things to all people" leaves research organizations grappling with the problem of how to tailor and transfer results to match these needs.

The focus of this paper is to detail the process used to identify technology transfer needs and their impact on the development of DSM research project objectives and strategies. We define steps in the process and illustrate salient points using the development of a commercial cooling program agenda.

## BACKGROUND

Traditionally, research organizations have taken a producer-centered approach to disseminating research results where it is incumbent on the user to identify useful information. That is, research is performed and the results are positioned from the researcher's perspective, with sometimes minimal regard to presenting or packaging the information for specific audiences. It is left to the discretion of the audience to attach meaning to the information, based on their particular interests or information needs. The producer-centered approach is warranted for organizations whose main emphasis is on fundamental, or basic, research, where the audience is well-defined and fairly homogeneous.

In contrast, a client-centered approach, one in which the research is designed to meet a client-driven information need, is necessary for applications research. In this case, the client (or audience), although well-defined, may be more heterogeneous in nature. It is, therefore, incumbent on the information provider to synthesize and package the pertinent information on behalf of the audience. Thus, the

fundamental differences between the producer- and client-centered research approaches require distinct strategies to effectively communicate results.

The client-centered research approach is well suited to providing DSM information to utilities and their customers alike. The need to effectively communicate information internally and externally is extremely critical in the case of utilities as they move forward with evaluating and promoting increasingly sophisticated DSM technology options and techniques. Internally, utility program planners, implementers and load forecasters need sound technical, market and economic information on which to base program decisions. Also, the ability to meet external information needs, covering such topics as DSM technology applicability, versatility, customer acceptance and persistence is important if utilities are to act in an advisory capacity to their DSM program participants.

Clearly, utilities need to do their homework before committing oftentimes enormous resources to the implementation and continuing support of a major DSM program. As the energy awareness of utility customers rises and program costs for more sophisticated DSM options increase, so too will the need for utilities and regulatory agencies to have access to quality information. Tailored technology transfer should provide added value to the quality information needed to address the myriad of questions and concerns facing DSM professionals and program participants.

DSM research organizations, such as the Center, have obligations to their sponsoring organizations to not only provide quality, primary information, but to further ensure realization of the information's value via tailored technology transfer. This can not be not a matter of happenstance. Careful planning is needed to envision, develop and execute individual projects and research programs that meet information needs in a comprehensive and cost-effective manner. The focal point for this planning is the concept of tailored technology transfer.

### TAILORED TECHNOLOGY TRANSFER - THE PLAN

In a nutshell, tailored technology transfer is using the right tool for the right job. A hammer would no sooner be used to screw in a compact fluorescent light bulb than a technical journal article would be used to promote a DSM technology to the general public. Appropriate format and level of information are needed for technology transfer materials to be effective.

In a sense, the process of incorporating tailored technology transfer principles into a research agenda can be likened to the development of an advertising program. Table 1 provides a comparison between the steps for implementing these two concepts.

TABLE 1
COMPARISON OF STEPS FOR TAILORED TECHNOLOGY
TRANSFER AND ADVERTISING PROGRAM

| Advertising Program | Tailored Technology Transfer |
| --- | --- |
| Analyze the market | Define target audiences and information needs |
| Set concrete goals and objectives | Same |
| Set a budget | Establish priorities |
| Develop a creative strategy | Design and perform the research |
| Choose the medium or media | Select the specific transfer mechanism(s) |
| Evaluate the results | Same |

The format for the remainder of the paper will be to walk through the steps of tailored technology transfer. Salient points are illustrated using the development of a commercial cooling program agenda.

Define target audiences and information needs

Defining target audiences and information needs answers the questions "who" and "what."

Resource limitations and just plain common sense dictate that except for unique instances, information and information exchange are most effective when they are designed for and directed toward a specific audience. Marketing and advertising persons use the term "target marketing" to define the concept of zeroing in on a specific segment of the population who are most likely to purchase a product or service.

Likewise, it is important to define information needs at the very start. Opportunities to cost-effectively obtain information are frequently lost when planning is done on an ad hoc basis, rather than being systematized.

As an example, let us consider a current Center project.

Commercial cooling has received considerable attention by many utilities and DSM research organizations. Wisconsin utilities and the Center are no exception. Faced by the state's growth of summer electric demand, several Wisconsin utilities have recently proposed the construction of up to seventeen combustion turbine peaking plants. While accepting the need for near-term supply-side relief, the staff of the Public Service Commission has called for improved estimates of summer demands, as well as development and implementation of load control measures and other demand-side programs designed to mitigate the growth of summer peak.

Figure 1 depicts Wisconsin's statewide peak electric demand by end-use for the commercial sector. Space cooling represents the single most peak intensive end-use for the commercial sector, particularly in the summer months.

FIGURE 1. COINCIDENT PEAK DEMAND BY END-USE (%)

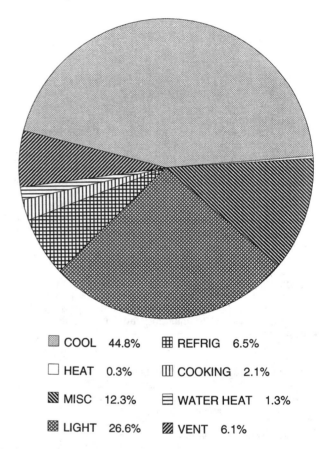

| | | | |
| --- | --- | --- | --- |
| ▨ COOL | 44.8% | ⊞ REFRIG | 6.5% |
| ☐ HEAT | 0.3% | Ⅲ COOKING | 2.1% |
| ▧ MISC | 12.3% | ▤ WATER HEAT | 1.3% |
| ▨ LIGHT | 26.6% | ▨ VENT | 6.1% |

SOURCE: THE ELECTRIC DEMAND-SIDE OPTIONS DATABASE, WISCONSIN CENTER FOR DEMAND-SIDE RESEARCH, 1990

For this reason, the Center participants (Wisconsin gas and electric utilities, the Public Service Commission of Wisconsin, University representatives and Center staff) concluded that understanding commercial cooling loads and their associated electric demand represents a key link in forecasting peak electric load profiles. The belief was that utility load forecasting can be improved if better estimates of commercial cooling loads were available. Furthermore, the impact of new cooling technologies on the present and future load profiles can be established if accurate cooling load data are available. Finally, the level of customer benefits that can be derived from applying state-of-the-art cooling technologies can be established by demonstrating the technologies in real applications and then provided as input to customer decisions.

Four target audiences and their information needs were identified. The four main audiences were utilities, their customers, contractors/installers and design architects/engineers. The utility audience was further subdivided into customer service representatives, program

198

planners, load forecasters and rate designers. Each audience has a distinct set of technology and market information needs. The needs run the gamut from technology performance characteristics to market demographics. Table 2 summarizes the target audiences and their specific information needs.

## Set concrete goals and objectives

Once the target audience(s) and information needs have been defined, the next step is to establish project goals and objectives. It is important to set precise goals and objectives to focus the use of resources and so that the ultimate success of the efforts can be measured during the evaluation step.

For the commercial cooling program, the primary goals are to:

- Aid utilities in forecasting and customer support

- Enable utility customers to compare the benefits and costs of different systems on the basis of metered data and/or simulations

- Analyze market barriers (e.g., customer perceptions, capital constraints, etc.) to increased adoption of new technologies

## Establish priorities

Access to unlimited resources may obviate the need to establish priorities; however, the real world dictates that resources (time, budget and human) are finite. Thus, establishing priorities is a critical step in ensuring that goals and objectives can be and are met in a cost-effective manner.

Using the principle of divide and conquer, the first order of business was to split the overall program development along the most logical line, that between technical and market information needs. In the interests of brevity, the focus of this paper will be on the technical side.

To aid in establishing priorities, a scoping study was commissioned to systematize the available research on cooling technologies, identify gaps and assess the benefits and costs in filling those gaps. More specifically, this scoping study focused on identification of the cooling technologies that require additional testing in Wisconsin,

and the types of commercial buildings in which such tests should be conducted.

Once the available data were compiled, an evaluation was made of the quantity and quality of information. Quality issues covered the reliability, maintenance and compatibility of each technology, the energy and demand requirements under standard conditions and any information available regarding head-to-head comparisons with other technologies.

Based on this review, areas were identified where additional research was required. The scoping study concluded that:

- The general lack of (thermal) cooling load data offers an opportunity for near-term, relatively low-cost, data-gathering efforts.

- The technology and methodology of end-use and technology field test metering is well established. End-use electric load data for commercial buildings is becoming widely available from many sources, and additional metering programs by many utilities continue to add to the database. However, much of the data relate to conventional cooling technologies.

- Abundant end-use cooling electrical energy consumption data from a previous project provide an excellent base for understanding demand impacts of conventional technologies, but in the absence of (thermal) cooling load data, they provide little help in understanding the impacts of newer, "unconventional" commercial cooling technologies.

- The availability of data on the newer technologies, which often does include thermal load, approximately follows the penetration of the technology in the market. This is not surprising given the high cost of metering, as well as the cost of subsidizing the purchase and installation of an alternative cooling technology.

- Data developed through computer simulations of commercial buildings paired with conventional and unconventional technologies are abundant. While the scoping study only examined studies by Synergic Resources Corporation and the Gas Research Institute directly, conversations with

TABLE 2.  COMMERCIAL COOLING USER/INFORMATION MATRIX

| USER | TECHNOLOGY INFORMATION | | | | MARKET INFORMATION | | |
| --- | --- | --- | --- | --- | --- | --- | --- |
| | PERFORMANCE | O&M | DESIGN | ECONOMICS | DEMOGRAPHICS | ECONOMIC TREND | OTHER |
| UTILITY CUSTOMERS | X | X | X | X | | | |
| CONTRACTORS/INSTALLERS | X | X | X | | | | |
| DESIGN ARCHITECTS/ENGINEERS | X | | X | | | | |
| UTILITY - CUSTOMER SERVICE | X | X | X | X | | | |
| LOAD FORECASTERS | | | | X | X | X | X |
| RATE DESIGNERS | | | | | X | X | X |
| PROGRAM PLANNERS | | | | X | X | X | |

X    INDICATES INFORMATION IS NEEDED

individuals at the Electric Power Research Institute, Energy Edge, the Center for Electric End-use Data and private research firms conducting energy studies indicate a very large database across building types, technologies, and climates. An opportunity which this presents is the potential for developing a library of input decks for various building types (and variations within building types) which would allow the Wisconsin Center to consider a representative sample of buildings through simulation, while minimizing costs for data development.

Based on these conclusions, the initial task list consisted of

- Establishing a Cooling Load Library for Wisconsin-specific commercial buildings using available end-use data.

- Developing/enhancing computer models of commercial cooling technologies.

- Conducting metered field tests of selected emerging cooling technologies.

## Design and perform research

Once priorities have been established, the design and performance of research requires that the myriad of details, decisions and tasks must be considered, made and performed to successfully complete a research effort.

Design parameters were established by consensus among the Center participants. The four main requirements placed on the research included: 1) All currently feasible commercial cooling systems will be considered, regardless of energy source; 2) In documenting the applicability of different cooling systems to commercial buildings, note will be taken of particularly successful technology/building type pairings, as well as particularly unsuccessful pairings; 3) The results will be applicable to buildings in Wisconsin and 4) Results of both experimental and simulation approaches will be included in the database.

These conditions formed the basis for a detailed Request For Proposal (RFP). Following RFP development, proposals were solicited from appropriate contractors, bids were received, evaluated and a contractor selected.

Key to the successful performance of the research is the establishment of open communications among the contractor, the Center staff and Center participants, beginning with an extensive project kick-off meeting and continuing throughout the project.

## Select the specific transfer mechanism

Each technology transfer mechanism has its own unique set of advantages and disadvantages. Research papers, reports, technical briefs and promotional materials comprise several of the printed media that can be used. In addition, electronic (applications software, database, etc.) and audio-visual media have been used effectively as transfer media. Likewise, seminars, workshops and presentations have their place as transfer mechanisms. All in all, decisions must be made to determine the appropriate media given the target audience and their information needs.

The cornerstone for the commercial cooling program is the availability of detailed information contained in the commercial cooling database. From this database, two sets of technology transfer tools are being developed:

- Customer-specific tools designed to establish the impact of new technologies on:

  Electric Demand
  Electric Use
  Occupant comfort
  Operation and maintenance
  procedures and cost

- Utility-specific tools that will enable load forecasters, program planners and rate designers to establish the actual and predicted impact that the new technologies have (or will have) on:

  System electric demand
  System electric use

Other technology transfer methods that will be employed as appropriate include:

- Brochures/pamphlets to promote "proven" technologies

- "Open Houses" to showcase installations

- Technical research papers

- Promotional videos

- Customer forums which bring together project participants (customers, manufacturers representatives and utility representatives) and other potential technology "consumers"

- Contractor forums which bring together manufacturers representatives, utility representatives and installation contractors to establish the infrastructure necessary to install and maintain the new technologies.

Figure 2 is a sample of a technology transfer needs assessment, along with a sample promotional brochure outline.

## Evaluate the results

Evaluation of the results represents the final step in the tailored technology transfer process. The evaluation step not only seeks to answer the question, "Did the results justify the resources expended?" but also the question, "What lessons can be applied to the next technology transfer effort?"

Successful technology transfer is measured by the ability to influence decision-makers based on the presentation of information. Unsuccessful technology transfer occurs when the decision-maker(s) is (are) left with too little, or inaccurate, information on which to base their decision.

Results can be classified into two broad categories: tangible and intangible benefits. Tangible benefits, such as increased adoption of efficient technologies and increased participation in utility DSM programs, albeit somewhat difficult to quantify, can have a real dollar value associated with them. Although they certainly do have real value, intangible benefits, such as an increased understanding of technologies or an increased awareness of utility DSM efforts, are generally even more difficult to value.

Audience evaluations are done at appropriate junctures during the course of individual projects. Evaluation of overall Center efforts, including the commercial cooling program area, is conducted biannually by all Center participants. For each project area, a value is assigned by each participant on the basis of, "What would our organization have paid in order to have these research results?" Although somewhat subjective, the exercise is essential to evaluating current programs, as well as setting future research direction.

Information from the audience and internal evaluations, combined with budget, resource and other information is then incorporated into the overall planning process.

## CONCLUSIONS

A comprehensive plan to identify technology transfer needs and their impact on the development of DSM research project objectives and strategies has been described.

FIGURE 2. TECHNOLOGY TRANSFER NEEDS ASSESSMENT AND PROMOTIONAL BULLETIN OUTLINE SAMPLE

| AUDIENCE | | | KEY INFORMATION NEEDS | TECHNOLOGY TRANSFER MEDIUM/MEDIA | FORMAT |
|---|---|---|---|---|---|
| PRIMARY | SECTOR | TITLE | | | |
| UTILITY CUSTOMERS | COMMERCIAL | BUILDING MANAGER | INTRODUCTION/ PERFORMANCE | PROMOTIONAL BULLETIN | CASE STUDY |
| • | COMMERCIAL | BUILDING OPERATOR | OPERATION AND MAINTENANCE | PAMPHLET & DETAILED HANDBOOK | TROUBLESHOOTING GUIDE |
| • | | • | • | • | • |
| • | | • | • | • | • |
| | | • | • | • | • |
| | | | • | • | • |
| | | | | • | |

Promotional Bulletin Outline

| Technology | : | Gas Cooling |
| Primary Audience | : | Utility Customers |
| Sector | : | Commercial Buildings |
| Audience Subcategory | : | Building Managers |
| Additional Information | : | Buildings > 50,000 square feet |
| Format | : | Case Study |

Key Topics
- Why gas cooling
  - Energy savings
  - Environment
- Basic Concept of gas cooling
- Typical installation
  - Description of facility and equipment
  - Photograph
- Testimonial from Building Manager
- Energy savings comparisons
- Operation and maintenance comparison
- Checklist to see if gas cooling is for you
- For more information . . .

# ACKNOWLEDGMENTS

This work was sponsored in part through a grant from the Oil Overcharge Fund administered by the Wisconsin Energy Bureau. The authors are extremely grateful to the Center's staff and Commercial Cooling Steering Committee for their assistance in project design, review and support.

# Chapter 36
# PSE&G Standard Pricing Offer: The Price is Right... So Come on Down

C.J. Coccaro

Public Service Electric and Gas Company (PSE&G) is the major energy provider of electricity and natural gas in the State of New Jersey, serving 71% of its population. Of the corporation's more than 13,250 employees, the Electric Business Unit has 9,525 who provide for the energy needs of:

1,639,899 Residential Customers (representing 25% revenue)
221,362 Commercial Customers (representing 50% revenue)
7,620 Industrial Customers (representing 25% revenue)

Electric revenue exceeds $3.5 Billion, representing sales of almost 38 Billion Megawatthours. In 1991, PSE&G had 10,116 megawatts Net Installed Generating Capacity. The Maximum Net Peak Load of 9,085 megawatts was delivered on July 23, 1991. Natural gas revenue exceeds $1.3 Billion, representing sales of more than 2,611,000 kilotherms.

PSE&G first became involved in DSM fifteen years ago and up until 1989 the focus of activities has been primarily on utility designed and implemented information programs, direct installation of weatherization measures, and gas and electric equipment rebate programs. With new incentive regulations, PSE&G has begun to take an even more proactive approach towards implementing DSM programs and services. Energy conservation will be primarily discussed from the electric perspective because, to date, this has been the bulk of PSE&G's experience. The incentive regulations will offer utilities the opportunity to gain experience in natural gas Demand Side Management (DSM).

This paper will briefly describe the evolution of Demand Side Management in New Jersey. It will describe the treatment of DSM as a firm resource option under an integrated competitive bid as well as the evolution to the Standard Offer concept under New Jersey's recently adopted incentive conservation regulations. Finally, it will describe certain of the key contractual provisions in the Standard Energy Savings Agreement.

LARGE SCALE CONSERVATION INVESTMENT:

In recent years, the State of New Jersey has embraced the concept of Integrated

Resource Planning (IRP), which includes DSM. As a general matter, IRP requires that utilities pursue a mix of supply and demand-side measures that will provide safe, reliable utility service at the lowest overall cost. In this regard, our state public utility commission, the New Jersey Board of Regulatory Commissioners (BRC) has expressed the view that "DSM measures offer an alternative resource which can be tapped to offset the need for new electric generating and transmission plant or natural gas supply sources and transmission facilities, and the concomitant environmental impacts."

In 1989, PSE&G, in compliance with a state commission approved Stipulation of Settlement (Stipulation), issued a Request for Proposals (RFP) to solicit Large Scale Conservation Investments (Bidding) as part of an integrated bid block for 200 Megawatts of electric capacity. As a threshold requirement, DSM proposals were required to contribute at least 400 kW of Summer Prime (hours from 12:00 noon to 6:00 p.m., Monday through Friday, except holidays, between June 1 and September 30, inclusive) electric capacity, and to do so below PSE&G's published kWh avoided cost. One of two bid price options were available: The Energy Service Company (ESCO) could bid separate On-peak and Off-peak prices, or a levelized kWh price for all hours.

Announcements of the bid were advertised in the Wall Street Journal, The New York Times, local newspapers and trade journals.

This promotion prompted 290 requests for both supply-side and demand-side RFPs. Eight supply side proposals were bid for 654 MW. Seven (ESCOs) and one major industrial customer bid a total of 53 Megawatts of Summer Prime electric capacity, and energy savings of almost 280 million kWhs.

The following conservation measures were bid:

1. High-efficiency lighting.
2. High-efficiency motors;
3. Variable speed drives;
4. High-efficiency chillers; and
5. Energy Management Systems.

Not all ESCOs bid all the above measures. The largest portion of the bid was lighting (70%), followed by cool storage (14%). ESCOs were required by the RFP to install only those measures cited in their project proposal.

ESCOs were also requested to propose Measurement and Verification Plans (MVPs) that addressed the following measurement concerns:

1. Demand reduction of affected end-uses;

2. Maintenance of existing lighting levels;

3. Selection of representative circuits, areas, or end-uses which will be monitored by run-hour meters, data loggers, or similar device to document hours of operation for affected measures.

All eight DSM proposals and four supply side proposals were accepted based upon a scoring system which included the following categories:

1. Economic/price factors;

2. Project and viability factors;

3. Measurement and verification factors. The final award group was announced on March 22, 1990.

All but one of the DSM contracts have been executed and approved, by the BRC. PSE&G will pay the ESCOs, monthly, for estimated energy savings (in kWhs). True-ups of these monthly estimates will occur quarterly, after reading meters which will monitor the hours of operation during the Summer Prime, On-peak, and Off-peak periods. The payment formula follows:

kW demand reduction X metered hours of operation X ESCO's bid price per kWh = PSE&G payment to the ESCO.

PSE&G will begin to pay ESCOs for energy savings delivered in 1992. By 1995, when the full obligations of the ESCOs are delivered, PSE&G's payments will exceed $14 million per year until the end of the 10-year contract (in most cases first contract year is 1992). The bids from the ESCOs ranged from 73.5% of avoided cost to 98.2% of avoided cost. **The bids are 86.7% of avoided cost on a weighted average basis.** Utility payments to the ESCOs are to be recovered in rates. There is no mechanism under the Stipulation for recovery of almost $16.5 million per year of lost revenue (1991 dollars).

CONSERVATION INCENTIVE REGULATIONS:

The DSM incentive regulations entitled "Demand Side Management Resource Plan" (N.J.A.C 14:12 et seq.), which were adopted by the BRC -- (the successor agency to the New Jersey Board of Public Utilities (BPU)) - on October 9, 1991, are the result of a rulemaking proceeding that

spanned over a 2.5 year period. The current regulations find their genesis in a June 4, 1990 Prepeoposal entitled "Limiting Barriers to Effective Conservation Programs and Implementing Conservation Ratemaking Incentives." This Prepeoposal identified the existence of certain barriers to more extensive investment in energy conservation by consumers and utilities in the State. It also outlined possible utility ratemaking incentive mechanisms to remove some of the existing barriers and to encourage energy conservation investments.

The BPU cited the following as barriers to implementation of cost-effective energy efficient measures:

1. Lack of information;

2. Lack of available capital;

3. Insufficient payback periods for many customers.

Following a public hearing and the submittal of written comments by interested parties, the BRC found that:

It was the view of the majority of commenters to the Prepeoposal that the provision of some form of financial incentive to the utilities would foster an increased penetration of installed conservation, load management and energy efficiency measures in the homes and businesses of New Jersey.

The BPU noted that the majority of commenters felt that utilities couldplay a vital role in the expansion of conservation and DSM and observed that in those states (New York, California, Wisconsin, Massachusetts, among others) where utility incentives have been approved, that "DSM activity has increased dramatically."

In December 1990, the BRC proposed new rules which provided utilities with the opportunity to recover program costs, lost revenues, and to earn returns on investments in energy efficiency measures based upon a sharing of program savings between utilities and ratepayers. In response to certain concerns, the rules were re-proposed on May 6 and, among other changes, included an additional utility incentive mechanism the Standard Offer approach. Under the Standard Offer, the utility itself can offer DSM services and receive payment on the same basis as other competing DSM service suppliers in the marketplace. The utility is also fully at risk for the unsuccessful DSM ventures.

The final rules as adopted by the BRC on October 9, 1991, state that their purpose and scope is to:

Foster the increased penetration and use of energy efficiency technologies applicable to the use and supply of electric and gas energy in the State. One mechanism to encourage cost-effective investment in such demand side management initiative is the provision of financial

incentives to electric and gas utilities with respect to investment aimed at fostering the increased use of energy efficiency technologies... These rules are designed to put in place mechanisms which permit utilities to earn financial returns equivalent to or, in recognition of the potential positive impact our society greater than, the returns provided on utility owned supply side projects. The rules are also designed to create an environment for utilities to utilize their resources and unique position as major energy providers in the State to foster increased energy efficiency. Finally, the rules are intended to provide significant increased opportunities for the delivery of energy efficiency services and measures by independent non-utility energy services companies, contractors and suppliers. N.J.A.C 14:12-1.1.
The incentive regulations have engendered an active debate among regulators, utilities, independent contractor groups, distributors, and ESCOs. Independent contractors have opposed the proposal because they believe the rules will encourage the direct sale and installation, by utilities, of 'high-efficiency appliances and technologies in direct competition with their services. ESCOs, while endorsing the Standard Offer incentive approach are, nonetheless, concerned with the manner in which the utility will compete in the DSM marketplace.

Utilities have filed DSM Resource Plans with the BRC as required by regulation. Under PSE&G's Plan, DSM activities are divided into two principal areas: Core Programs and Performance Based Programs.

The BRC's regulations define Core programs as those programs that are not cost-effective or profitable, and are thus not eligible for incentives. PSE&G's Core Programs under the Plan include:
1.    Home Energy Savings Program (HESP);

2.    Low Income Grant and/or Seal-Up Programs;

3.    Commercial and Apartment Conservation Service (CACS) energy audit program;

4.    Energy Thrift Home program -- PSE&G's equivalent to the Good Cents Program offered by many utilities; and

5.    Programs offered by PSE&G to residences utilizing energy sources other than natural gas for space heating purposes.

Nonetheless, if a utility can design and implement any of these programs so that it passes the TRC test (which remains the primary test in New Jersey), that program may be included in a utility's DSM incentive plan.

Utilities have a choice of participating in either a Standard Offer program or a Shared Savings program. Both programs allow utilities the opportunity to earn a return on investment, up to a price cap based upon avoided costs, for each

Performance Based Program (as opposed to a "Core" program). The difference in the two programs lies in the funding of the measures to be installed, opportunities to earn a return on a DSM investment, and the scope of utility control.

The Shared Savings program allows utilities to earn a return, based upon energy savings resulting from the installation of high-efficiency measures through rebate programs, etc. The incentive amount (capped at the same Standard Offer price cap) is to be calculated as a retention by the utility of a percentage of the net benefits achieved by virtue of each program. An example of the formula for utility incentive payment under the Shared Savings program follows:

Standard Offer Price Cap = $.04

Program Costs = $.03

Savings to be shared by Utility and Ratepayers = $.01

The Shared Savings incentive approach allows for recovery of program costs through rates. The utility and the ratepayers would share in the net benefits of any program. The sharing formula will be established through negotiations between the utility and the BRC. The target is about 25% of the net benefit to utility shareholders and the balance of 75% to be passed along to ratepayers as their share of the net benefits. Shared Savings offers greater utility control because the utility decides which measures are to be rebated or directly installed through a utility program.

Standard Offer

By contrast, the Standard Offer requires shareholder funding of measures installed by the utility if the utility elects to compete with ESCOs for market share. Under the Standard Offer Incentive Mechanism, in return for its investment in energy efficiency, the utility will have the opportunity to earn a return that is set by the marketplace. (i.e. price not profit is subject to regulation) Likewise, the utility, not its ratepayers, will be exposed to the costs of unsuccessful DSM ventures. In concept, the Standard Offer is relatively straightforward and, as a contracting vehicle, is one with which there has been considerable experience in New Jersey and elsewhere. The Standard Offer is applicable to all performance-based DSM measures. The utility, its customers, energy service companies, and independent contractors, are all eligible project sponsors under the Standard Offer. The Standard Offer itself consists of the price to be paid for electric and gas energy savings delivered and the terms and conditions that will govern performance. Once approved by the Commission, these terms of trade will be applicable to all participants.

The formulas which establish the maximum Standard Offer Price and the level of the Total Resource Cost Test are as follows:

Note 1:

Under the Standard Offer approach, PSE&G, for example, would issue standard contract terms and a standard price per conserved kilowatthour for a fixed amount of DSM capacity. An ESCO, utility or contractor functioning as an ESCO would earn a return based on the its ability to competitively install DSM measures in host customers' facilities and receive the Standard Offer payment for energy savings delivered to the utility. There would also be an opportunity to share in some level of the host customers' bill savings. The difference between the cost to install and maintain the measures and the total revenue stream would be profit (or loss) to the ESCO or the utility.

The formula used to determine the appropriate level of payments from all ratepayers considers the rate impact caused by fixed cost revenue erosion. Fixed cost revenue erosion is calculated as the non-fuel related revenue (average retail rate of the utility in its last test year less fuel costs and gross receipts and franchise taxes) multiplied by a factor of 0.5.

For example, the proposed PSE&G levelized Standard Offer payment per conserved kilowatthour for the ten year period 1992-2001 is:

Standard Offer= TRC - (Non Fuel Related Revenue X .5)

Standard Offer = 6.51¢ - (5.88¢ X .5)

Standard Offer = 3.57¢/kWh

This example is based on the all hour average price per conserved kWh. The actual Standard Offer price would be time and seasonally differentiated.

Note 2

This results in payments from PSE&G electric ratepayers being capped at 3.57¢/kWh with the balance of up to 6.51¢/kWh coming from a share of reduced utility bills from host customers where the DSM measures have been installed. **Non participating ratepayers are now purchasing DSM at 54.8% of avoided cost under the Standard Offer approach vs. 86.7% of avoided cost under the bid.**

Maximum host payment=6.51¢ - 3.57¢ = 2.94¢

These additional contributions from participating customers, in the form of direct payments of a share of the bill savings (or customer contributions that offset first cost) will be permitted up to the point where the total of payments from the utility plus participant costs equals the benefits as defined in the TRC.

Note 3
Total Resource Cost Test

The rule establishes the Total Resource Cost (TRC) as a test of the cost-effectiveness of a program to society. The current definition of the Total Resource Cost Test in New Jersey has been amended to include environmental externalities.

In order to receive BRC approval for incentives, Performance-based programs must be demonstrated to result in a ratio of at least 1.0 as defined by the Total Resource Cost Test. For electric utility DSM programs, an average environmental externality value shall average $.02 per kWh starting in 1991.

The TRC test establishes a cap on payments from all parties for any DSM measure. This cap is defined as the avoided cost of a supply-side kilowatthour plus the environmental adder. The avoided costs of supply include both avoided energy and capacity at the generation level adjusted for losses, and avoided transmission and distribution costs. PSE&G's avoided cost do not currently include avoided transmission and distribution costs. The level of these avoided costs, if any, are currently being evaluated.

For example, the current TRC limit on average for all hours for the period 1992-2001 for PSE&G is:

TRC = Avoided Supply + Loss Factor + Environmental Adder

TRC =   3.64¢ + 0.4¢ + 2.47¢

TRC =   6.51¢ per conserved kWh

This allows an ESCO to collect payments of up to 6.51¢ as a combination of payments from all ratepayers and payments of a portion of bill savings from the participating host customer. A program must be demonstrated to cost less than or be equal to the avoided TRC to pass the TRC test and gain initial approval by the NJBRC.

### *REVENUE FLOW TO ESCO UNDER STANDARD OFFER*

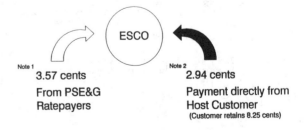

Note 1
3.57 cents
From PSE&G
Ratepayers

Note 2
2.94 cents
Payment directly from
Host Customer
(Customer retains 8.25 cents)

**10 year levelized, 1992-2001**
Estimated Retail Rate = 11.19 cents
Note 3
TRC = 6.51 cents

## STANDARD ENERGY SAVINGS AGREEMENT

Current utility planning in New Jersey reflects the inclusion of DSM as a "firm" resource and as such, DSM is an essential element in a mix of supply-side and demand-side resources which will be used to meet future customer demands for reliable supplies of electric and gas service. The operative adjective word is "firm" when PSE&G is evaluating the inclusion of various types of DSM in its long term capacity plan. It is probably this aspect of PSE&G's DSM program that distinguishes it from many existing utility DSM programs. Indeed, the cornerstone of the incentive DSM in New Jersey is the performance aspects of DSM that will be installed under the utility programs. It is imperative that not only cost-effective DSM measure be installed but that these measures continue to perform at specified levels for a known period.

The controlling mechanism is the "Standard Energy Savings Agreement" which is part of the Standard Offer. This agreement establishes the "take and pay" obligation of the utility for actual energy savings delivered to PSE&G during the contract term. It also defines the responsibility of the third party contracting with PSE&G to compensate PSE&G for any damages caused either by a delay in the date of commercial operation of the DSM measures or their failure to produce the required level of energy and capacity savings.

The following is a brief description of a few of the key performance based provisions of the agreement:

1.  ARTICLE IV - Purchase Price and Payment Obligation

This Article establishes PSE&G's obligation to pay the Seller for the delivery of energy savings that have passed the Cost-Effectiveness Test and have been demonstrated to be capable of the delivery of energy savings at the specified level.

> Section 4.03 - Regulatory Risk limits the risk to PSE&G shareholders of the recovery of payments to ESCOs either being impaired or disallowed. If an agency having jurisdiction, disallows or impairs the recovery by PSE&G of payments to ESCOs then the ESCO has the ability to enter into an amendment to adjust the price to a level found to be acceptable by the BRC or the ESCO may terminate the agreement after 30 days notice to PSE&G.

> Section 4.04 - Replacement Capacity Costs is intended to insure the continued "persistence" of the energy savings from a group of DSM measures installed at host facilities. A Seller will pay a penalty if the installed measures fail to produce 80% of the level of committed savings during PSE&G's Summer Prime Period. The penalty is equal to the

difference between the 80% level and the actual level of committed energy savings multiplied times the capacity deficiency charge established by the Pennsylvania, New Jersey, Maryland (PJM) power pool of which PSE&G is a member.

> Section 4.05 - Liquidated Damages for Failure to Meet In-Service Deadline Date is a fund that has been created to protect PSE&G from any cost required to mitigate damages caused by a Seller's failure to deliver committed energy savings by a date certain. The current Standard Offer as proposed requires that a Seller deposits $164 per kW of Summer Prime Period Average Demand Reduction. These funds will be released when the Seller achieves his date of commercial operation.

2.  ARTICLE VI - Monitoring

This article outlines the requirements for measurement and verification of the energy savings produced by the DSM measures installed at the various host facilities.

> Section 6.01 (a) - Pre-Implementation Audit establishes PSE&G's right to audit the existing end use equipment located at proposed host facilities so that the "before" types of installed equipment and consumption can be verified. All audits are performed by PSE&G at the Seller's expense.
> Section 6.01 (b) - Implementation Audit establishes PSE&G's right to audit the process of end use equipment retrofit at proposed host facilities.

> Section 6.01 (c) - Post-Implementation Audit establishes PSE&G's right to audit a host facility to verify that the end use equipment specified in the agreement was actually installed at proposed host facilities.

3.  ARTICLE IX - Force Majeure

As with any agreement, there will be events which will occur that are beyond the control of and which occur without the fault of the party claiming force majeure. The Standard Energy Savings Agreement provides for the typical events of strikes, natural disturbances and restraints of government and regulatory agencies. It also provides for relief from damages resulting from the total cessation of operation of a host facility.

## CONCLUSION

The Standard Offer is a mechanism that is superior to a bidding process both in administrative efficiency and in the resulting cost for " performance based" DSM:

> The timing is improved. DSM measures must be installed during the period

of the Standard Offering (about 2 years).

- There is surety of a contract if an ESCO can negotiate a    commitment from a host.

- In the PSE&G process, the contract provisions are being developed through a collaborative process chaired by the BRC with participation from all the major groups that will either participate in, or pay for the Standard Offer.

- The ultimate price to non partici-pating ratepayers has been predeter-mined to be a significant discount from avoided cost.

- The timing of the Standard Offer provides for new capacity blocks to be determined every two years with redefined avoided cost associated with each new offering.

Chapter 37

# DSM—A Perspective for the 90's

M.A. Mozzo, Jr.

## ABSTRACT

Demand Side Management (DSM) Programs are becoming important facets in the resource planning activities of many utilities. These programs have made substantial impacts to some utilities during the late 1980's, especially those in the Northeast. They will continue to play major roles in utility activities through the 90's. There are major issues which will be addressed and answered in the 90's in order for DSM to continue to play a role in the 1990's.

## INTRODUCTION

During the past decade the electrical consumers of the United States have substantially reduced the growth of electrical demand and consumption on utilities. While these efforts have reduced the growth on demand, they have not resulted in negative growth. Electrical demand today is still increasing at a rate of approximately 1-3% per year. This growth will have to be met by an increase in the supply side of the electrical utilities or through Demand Side Management (DSM) projects. This paper will discuss some perspectives regarding DSM and its impacts on utilities and customers.

## SUPPLY STRATEGIES

Utilities who are experiencing growth can meet their increasing demand in a number of ways: (1) build more power plants, (2) buy power from other utilities, (3) buy from cogenerators, (4) use selective brown outs, or experience black outs, and (5) support energy efficiency.

Today, very few utilities are building new power plants outside of construction of peaking gas turbines. The lead time to construct new coal or oil power plants, let alone the unheard of nuclear plants, is many years. Permits for environmental issues have to be met, certificates of need are required, and of course, the NIMBY (Not In My Back Yard) syndrome is an extremely sensitive social issue. Most utilities would rather avoid the issue of building new powerplants and develop alternative means of generating power requirements.

Another common method of obtaining power is to buy it from other utilities. In New Jersey, the major electrical utility is connected to what is known as th ePJM Grid. This interconnection allows a sharing of power resources among the participating utilities during periods of shortages. This really is an acceptable method of meeting electrical demands as long as there is power readily available for sharing, **AND** it makes economical sense to purchase additional power requirements from the grid.

A third option is to buy from cogenerators and independent power producers. This is an acceptable means of obtining power as long as the project is technically feasible, makes economic sense, and will be a stable, long-time source of power. Most utilities, when they build power plants, assume that this plant will be in service for many years, twenty five or longer. In fact, if one was to look at the age of our power plants today, one would see this expectation is being met. Most utilities have entered into life extension programs which rejuvenate their older pwoer plants to extend their useful life. I believe it is safe to assume that utilities do engage in long range planning which insures that their own generating supplies will be predictable. If a utility is to accept the position that power generated from cogenerators or independent power producers is an acceptable means of supply, then the utility must be assured that this supply is of a long-term in nature. There is obviously risk involved in entering into such ventures.

A fourth option, and one that I'm sure the utilities would not want to use is to nothing about meeting increasing demand except through selective brown-outs and/or blackouts. I think this option can be readily dismissed as not acceptable.

The fifth and last option is for the utilities to support improving energy efficiencies of the end use of their product, better known as Demand Side Management programs. Obviously, if the end use of the product is more efficient, then growth will be reduced and the need for more supply side projects will be reduced. A word of caution here however. Just like in option 3, the use of cogenerators or supply side projects, DSM projects **MUST** likewise prove to be reliable and long term options. DSM projects cannot be installed today just to disappear tomorrow. The utilities, in order to make DSM an effective supply tool, must be able to plan on having both supply side and demand side projects installed for long time frames, or their ultimate customers could be significantly hurt.

I believe that DSM projects can become an integral part of a utility's resource planning if proper planning and control is assured. All parties must recognize that in order to successfully implement a DSM project, they must work in unison as a team to effect these programs. If any one of the parties perceives a threat to their well being, and refuses to cooperate fully, the effectiveness of a DSM program will be reduced. DSM programs should be viewed as one leg of the resource planning table, the other options mentioned previously with the exception of selective brownouts, being the other three legs. Each leg plays a major role in supporting the resource planning requirements of a utility.

## FORMS OF DEMAND SIDE MANAGEMENT

Demand Side Projects take many forms and vary from utility to utility. Obviously, any customer should determine what programs exist in his utility region, evaluate the pros and cons of each program, and select the one that best meets his needs.

One of the more popular programs is a direct rebate program. This type of program occurs between the end user or customer dealing directly with the utility. It usually takes the form of a cash rebate to the customer upon proven installation of an energy conservation measure. Some types of rebates may be for high efficiency air conditioning units installed in residential and/or commercial sites, installation of more efficient lamps and/or ballasts in cimmercial sites, installation of more efficient lamps and/or ballasts in commercial and/or industrial facilities, and replacement of electric motors with more energy efficient units. Utilities may also make available the purchase of such energy efficient products such as compact fluorescent lights to residential customers which are convient and at reasonable costs. Typically, rebate programs do not require any verification of continued use, only verification of the installation of the ECM in the first place. I would suspect that the assumption is made that once higher efficiency measures are undertaken, they will continue to remain in place. Further verification to insure continued use becomes costly and probably not very productive.

Another form of a DSM program is through a bid program utilizing Energy Service Companies (ESCO's). In this form, an ESCO submits a bid to provide to provide a stated KW and/or KWH reduction to a utility through the installation of Energy Conservation Measures, ECM's, at one or more sites. During the term of the contract, the ESCO identifies specific sites and ECM's eligible for the program, purchases and installs materials used on the ECM, and monitors and verifies the energy savings throughout the life of the bid. In return for this effort, the utility will pay the ESCO for documented electrical savings throughout the life of the bid. This type of program is limited to those companies who successfully submit a bid to the utility.

Our world is constantly undergoing change, and the DSM program is no exception. As issues and problems develop in the administration of DSM programs, resolutions are made and appropriate changes are made. New forms of DSM programs are constantly evolving all the time. The cunning electrical consumer will be aware of all programs as they evolve, and he will continually analyze what is in his best interest and act accordingly. One word of caution, however, do not wait until a better offer comes along. The customer who waits will never see any savings, he'll always be waiting for a better offer.

## ENERGY SERVICE COMPANIES(ESCO'S)

Use of an ESCO provides many advantages for commercial and industrial facilities in taking advantage of DSM Programs. First, ESCO's may be the only way to participage in a DSM program in order to obtain utility rebates. Even if another program exists, such as a rebate program, this may not be the most economically attractive and feasible method that a customer should employ. Some utility rebate programs pay very little, especially for an industrial customer. Additionally, a reputable ESCO will use his payment from the utility to help pay down the cost of the project. In this manner, the customer will receive a project which has a higher value than his expenditure outlay, and everyone benefits.

A second reason to utilize an ESCO, is the ESCO's access to funding. ESCO's have found that one way to grow their business is to have a ready access to funding for energy projects. Use of this funding is not required by the customer, but access to this funding allows the customer to use his resources, which are probably scarce, for other purposes such as improvements to manufacturing processes. The ESCO can then recover his investment form the utility payments, as well as a payment from the customer either in the form of shared savings or a lump sum payment. Obviously, this requires a financial analysis of a customers cost of money versus the ESCO, and the potential use the customer may have for the monies on other projects. Another fact to consider is that some ESCO's base their payment of shared savings on performance, that is, savings must meet expected levels in order for the ESCO to receive adequate payments.

A third reason to use an ESCO is that energy conservation is their business. Customers are typically in the business of manufacturing widgets or running hospitals, not researching and building energy conservation projects. During the 1970's, many corporations had energy managers whose sole job was to develop energy projects. Unfortunately, most of these departments no longer exist. Energy projects become local plant responsibilities and typically, they just don't get done. ESCO's on the other hand, have engineering staffs who are knowledgeable about the latest technologies in energy efficiency improvements. They also have project management staffs who have experience in installing energy projects. The ESCO has the capabilities and are in the business of assisting different sites in reducing energy consumption and costs. The ESCO can become an extension of a customers capabilities, without distracting everyday activities.

## ISSUES AND PERCEPTIONS OF ESCO's AND DSM

There have been issues and perceptions regarding ESCO's and DSM programs which have created negative feelings about the acceptance of such programs. As with any new program or product, there always is good and bad. The customer should be well aware of significant issues regarding DSM programs and to thoroughly study all potential projects for any adverse impacts. A reputable ESCO will work with the customer to achieve a satisfactory relationship.

One issue that has developed frequently is "cream skimming." As should be expected in developing potential ECM's at a site, the list will contain projects with various savings payback. Some ESCOs have proposed projects which accomplish just portions of the projects. While no one should advocate doing ECMs with long paybacks, one also should not advocate doing projects in a half way manner. For example, assume a facility has a variety of lighting fixtures which are inefficient. A good lighting retrofit project will consider all fixtures for retrofit under a DSM project except those that economically do not make sense, such as patient rooms in a hospital, which have very few burn hours. Some ESCOs however, have made it a practice of replacing only a portion of a total lighting system, or have used an inappropriate technology in order to maximize electrical savings and their utility payouts. This action typically will leave a customer with a mixed system, difficult to maintain. In evaluating an ESCO, the customer should insure that the firm is evaluating any and all potential ECMs and is willing to provide them to the customer if it makes financial sense.

Another issue revolves around Customer Relationships. The customer should assure himself that the ESCO he selects is one tha will work for him in the accomplishment of the DSM Energy project, that the ESCO is committed to developing a relationship which will achieve all parties objectives.

A third issue is quality assurance. Too often when work is done by third parties, substandard materials and workmanship are utilized. This arises because a DSM company is cutting corners to meet certain financial objectives which may not be the same as the customer. The customer should insist in complete review and approval of all materials and labor that go into a project. The relationship between ESCO and a customer should be a long relationship if the DSM program is to succeed.

A fourth issue is measurement and verification of projected energy savings. In most DSM programs, this topic is adequately covered by uitilities. All ECMs must be accurately measured and savings verified for utility payments. These measurents in most cases, are not done with engineering calculations, but rather with point measurements of the ECMs on at least a statistical sample of the ECM. In fact, it is a fair statement to say that measurement of energy savings achieved under DSM programs is a growing business.

## FUTURE OF DSM PROGRAMS

Unless the people of the United States and the electrical utilities are willing to commit to a program of extensive construction of new nuclear powerplants, DSM programs will continue to play a key role in reducing electrical growth patterns. These programs will continually change in form in attempts to improve their implementation. Efforts must continue to develop satisfactory relationships and teamwork between utilities, customers, ESCOs, and other DSM companies in order to make this a viable business.

Chapter 38

# DSM Bidding - What Field Are We Leveling, Anyway? Or How Do You Level the Field without Killing the Crop

C.W. Siebens

## Introduction

Since the first regulated monopoly was established, there has been regulatory concern over the "level playing field" issue. This concern can be valid, but its character is relatively nebulous, and situational. Most recently, regulators have expressed their concern over the level playing field issue relative to demand side bidding, and demand side management (DSM) incentives regulation which provides utility shareholder returns for DSM initiatives.

The playing field issues relative to DSM <u>can</u> be extensive. Utility ESCO subsidiaries are being formed, utility service contracts for HVAC equipment exist, and utilities have special access to customers and customer energy information. At the same time, all source bidding processes are required in some states allowing DSM projects to effectively displace supply side projects, customers must choose between utility DSM programs and ESCO offerings, and the list goes on.

The following discusses the broad concept of the "level playing field" as it relates to DSM programs, and explores the potential merits of leveraging the status society has invested in utilities, as well as the validity of attempts to artificially level the field for markets in which the utility is a player.

The views presented are based primarily within the context and upon experience from regulation in New Jersey, where the first round of All Source Bidding was started in 1989, and DSM incentives regulation is nearing implementation. While some aspects of the New Jersey experience are unique, the framework of perceived "playing field" issues will be common with other jurisdictions.

The general conclusion presented is that if DSM incentives regulation which are initiated to "recruit" committed utility resources to maximize efficiency improvements in the marketplace, and these efficiency improvements are implemented through energy service providers selected through a competitive process by the utility or customers, the level playing field issue becomes fundamentally bogus.

An apt metaphor can be drawn between the DSM incentives environment and farming. Both have

concerns about maintaining a level field, planting seed, and reaping a harvest that benefits consumers and the farmers. In keeping with this image, certain attempts to artificially level the field can effectively "kill the crop", by reducing or eliminating utility motivation to enthusiastically support an aggressive DSM agenda.

## New Jersey Background for DSM Incentives

A number of recent regulatory initiatives have been attempting to stimulate utility support and investment in Demand Side Management (DSM). New Jersey incentives regulation specifically sought to address a general recognition of a) barriers inhibiting the full development and public adoption of energy efficient technologies, b) significant practical/and economic disincentives for utilities to invest in energy savings and c) the absence of other viable mechanisms (such as State or Federally funded initiatives) to accomplish the task.[1]

DSM Incentives regulation were adopted in September 1991 following roughly three years of debate and consideration of alternative provisions of the rules. The regulations, as they are being implemented, include the highest standard of accountability for DSM results in the country, providing incentives based almost entirely on measured results. They provide utility shareholders, as an incentive for cost effective DSM programs, some accepted percentage of the net benefits of the program, where net benefits are defined as the difference between the value of accepted (generally measured) savings over the life of the measure, and the program cost. The "Purpose and Scope" of the final New Jersey regulations state:

"The rules in this chapter are designed to encourage & promote cost effective investment in demand side management initiatives. ... These rules are designed to put in place mechanisms which permit utilities to earn financial returns equivalent to or, in recognition of the potential positive impact on society, greater than the returns provided on utility owned supply side projects. The rules are also designed to create an environment for utilities to utilize their resources and unique position as major energy providers in the State to foster increased energy efficiency. Finally the rules are intended to provide significant increased opportunities for the delivery of energy efficiency services and measures by independent non-utility energy service companies, contractors and suppliers."[2]

The manner in which the regulations are implemented, as well as the details of the regulations themselves will determine how well New Jersey will meet the stated purpose.

A brief summary of the regulations is required to understand the basis for any "playing field" issues. A grossly simplified summary follows:

A group of "core programs" are required in the regulations, including residential and commercial energy audits, information and education programs, a weatherization program for income qualifying residential customers, and a program supporting increasing the efficiency of new construction.

Detailed mechanisms for the recovery of program costs, as well as of incentives and lost revenues for all programs would be proposed by the utility for regulatory review and approval. Jersey Central Power and Light has proposed that costs associated with core programs would be expensed and recovered on a current year basis through a new DSM cost recovery mechanism paralleling the mechanism for fuel cost recovery.[3] Costs and incentives for performance based programs are proposed to be amortized over a period associated with the "payback period" for non-participants.

The details of all programs, as well as measurement procedures and incentive structure, would be proposed by the utility for regulatory review and approval.

The value of savings is based on a unique formula, which includes avoided energy and capacity costs, a stipulated value of environmental externalities, and a portion of "fixed cost revenue erosion." Utilities are allowed to incorporate values for avoided transmission and distribution costs. Measurement plans are required for all incentive programs, and include adjustments for line losses.

The approval process has evolved to a settlement roundtable format with ten "chairs at the table" for parties representing different interest groups. The roundtables (one for each gas or electric utility) are not required to develop consensus if consensus is not forthcoming, but rather they identify consensus where it exists, as well as

outstanding issues where it does not for the Commission to resolve.

The regulations offer utilities two options for designing incentives structures for performance based utility DSM programs: shared savings or standard offer. The standard offer involves the utility defining a block of energy and capacity to be satisfied, publishing a set of fixed terms, conditions, measurement plans and pricing (for measured power savings), and competing with the marketplace for DSM projects, generally through a company subsidiary. Utility incentives, like independent ESCO incentives, are based on the difference between the standard price offer and the cost of the projects (net of any customer contribution). Since the standard offer is comparable to a DSM bidding program, utilities electing this option are exempted from a state requirement that an All Source Bidding process will be used to meet new generation capacity requirements.

The shared savings option provides a share of the net savings (the difference between the value of power savings resulting from a program over the life of the measures and the costs of the program on a net present value basis) to utility shareholders. Utilities must present a portfolio of programs addressing essentially all cost effective DSM technologies, with measurement plans, and assessment of competitive impacts for review and approval. Utilities electing this option are also required to implement an All Source Bid capacity procurement process, using the avoided cost values and standards for measurement proposed for their own programs, ensuring that if the utility programs are less than aggressive, an independent initiative can develop.

An important feature of the shared savings option is that the utility is allowed to request incentives and lost revenues associated only with the utility's programs. The utility receives neither for the success of projects awarded through the All Source Bidding process, which creates a climate of competition between the utility programs and independent projects.

The perspectives addressed in the following are based on the election of the **shared savings option**, which relies on implementation of DSM projects through energy services providers selected through a competitive process by customers or the utility.

How do You Level the Field Without Killing the Crop?

During the hearings leading to these regulations, and during the settlement roundtables currently in progress, the issue of a "level playing field" between utilities and the competitive "free market" of energy service providers has persistently and aggressively raised its head. Quoting from "Public Comments" on the proposed regulations:

"The most cost effective level of energy conservation investment is best achieved through a competitive market. The proposed rules leave too much discretion to the utilities and Board Staff will not be able to ensure that all utility costs are property accounted for".[4]

Several cures for this "problem" have been discussed & considered, including: a) requiring the release of customer lists and information traditionally held as confidential, b) for the purposes of computing incentives, developing a formula for adding overhead costs to the costs of utility programs to simulate private sector costs, and c) allocating costs of certain programs required by the regulations over performance based programs.

Each of these attempts to artificially handicap the utility's inherent strengths also diminishes utility motivation in the DSM market contradicting the original basis for the regulations. The regulations are founded on an intent to "create an environment for utilities to utilize their unique position ... to foster increased energy efficiency."[5]

What incentive is provided to plow the field and plant the seed for energy savings through objective information and education programs, energy audits, or other programs, if the costs associated with those programs directly reduce any incentive and essentially com directly from the pockets of utility shareholders. Certainly this kind of provision would eliminate any reason for utilities to present information that does not directly support enrollment in a utility program.

While each of these ideas may soothe a potential sore spot of interested parties at the table, they also undermine the intent of the process.

## Any DSM Incentives are artificial in nature

What naturally occurring market provides its suppliers additional earnings for selling less product. While "negawatts" are gaining standing in the regulatory environment, they are not generally recognized in the marketplace.

To restate the obvious, creating incentives for utility shareholders for delivering power savings effectively and efficiently involves creation of an instrument of reward for utilities accomplishing specified objectives in the marketplace. They generally provide some dividend to shareholders for producing improved end use energy performance (whatever the state defines that to be) through rebate programs, direct installation services, performance contracting, DSM bidding or other approved means of influencing the market place.

In the case of Jersey Central Power and Light, and the vast majority of utility DSM initiatives in the country, DSM services and technologies are provided by or through contractors and vendors in the market place, with payments, marketing, partnership or other means of support from the utility. Unlike supply projects where utilities receive reasonable returns for approved utility managed and installed power supply investment and performance, DSM Incentive Programs reward utilities for their influence in the market place.

The formulas for shared savings incentives attempt to simulate what is available to unregulated DSM service suppliers, but the "product" being delivered is market support from information, rebates, consultation, and other activities and services. These generally support development of a market for efficiency improvements, and do not directly compete with the marketplace.

## Utility Program Services are Inherently Supportive of the DSM Market - Not Competitive with the Market

Utility programs which provide rebates, information, training, project coordination or advice to customers are not necessarily services that exist in the marketplace outside the utility context. These are initiatives or services that regulators are striving to encourage through DSM incentives, and which generally support the development of a DSM market. The direct beneficiaries of the stimulated market are the participants and contractors, manufacturers and ESCOs making increased sales.

Some features, such as the addition of "market based overheads" to utility program costs in this context, such as for a rebate program, make no sense. The product offered is not the installation of a high efficiency appliance, but the processing of a rebate application. The overhead associated with that function is dramatically different from that associated with selling and installing appliances. Undue artificial allocation of costs to the program simply reduces the resource available to support customer DSM projects.

The structure of incentives regulation needs to be designed around basic objectives and principles, and avoid real or perceived disincentives of the players to maximize market adoption of efficient technologies.

## Ten Ingredients Which Will Make the Market Work

The following goals of DSM incentives regulations and implementation will develop a healthy DSM marketplace.

1.  Create a win-win-win-win environment for customers, utilities, energy service providers, and regulators (who are too frequently in a no win position). If any of the players lose, the process will not work well, and can get tied up in litigation. There needs to be a motivation for

215

each player to bring their strengths cooperatively and enthusiastically to the table.

2. Understand the strengths of the players, such as their relative willingness to take risks, business flexibility, financial flexibility and stability, business longevity, stake in the process, trustworthiness, commitment to DSM, etc.

3. Understand the needs of the players. Core values and perceptions (or misperceptions) of corporate mission and business risk associated with DSM (or DSM incentives regulation) implementation can cause tremendous upheaval in the negotiation or communication process. There exist "deal killer issues" (herbicides) which can include fuel switching, statewide fuel selection standards, earnings surveillance, earnings caps, release of confidential customer information and other utility specific value based issues. During implementation, certain players will attempt to superimpose a new agenda on the plan. These need to be assessed objectively and carefully, and balanced against the costs of time, delays, possible litigation, and the relative importance of the stated intent of the regulations.

4. Create a motivation for alliances and cooperation. The way the New Jersey regulations impose competition between utility and ESCO projects (previously noted) will create future difficulties for all parties. A means of avoiding this is desirable.

5. Create healthy competition between energy service providers, by encouraging a diversity of options and technologies, creating avenues for market participation for all players, and providing special rewards for programs which maximize savings, and cost non-participants less.

6. Require accountability for DSM results. Trust is an essential element for DSM in particular. One gains long term trust through accountability for results.

7. Avoid new inefficiencies. Are existing energy codes and standards strong enough and are they being enforced by the appropriate state agency? If not, someone will be paid for efficiency improvements later.

8. Upgrade the public stake and consciousness of DSM through education, requiring investment of the participants, rate designs which provide appropriate market signals, trade ally incentives, etc.

9. Separate demand from supply side bidding. Allow or encourage a DSM bidding process which will provide the most savings for specified targeted markets and technologies at the least cost.

10. Use a results oriented regulatory process supporting the intent of the regulation. Avoid micro-management, and allow sufficient flexibility for utilities to manage a profitable por

## Utility Programs are generally Implemented through the Marketplace

Where utilities are competing head to head delivering DSM measure installations in competition with the marketplace, the playing field issue can be germane. However, several key questions need to be answered to assess the nature of the competition and the "field". Is the utility using its personnel to market and install the measures? If not, devices like assessing artificial overheads comparable to that in the competitive market are already captured through the utility payments to its contractors. Further attempts to capture overheads constitute double counting.

If utility personnel are used to market and install the measures, the most effective means of "leveling the field" is to require that such services are performed by an unregulated subsidiary, and require an "arms length relationship" between the parent and subsidiary.

## Leveling the Field for Power Supply

Starting in the 1980's, considerable attention focussed on the perceived need for the development of a more competitive, less regulated supply of non-utility generation to balance perceived inefficiencies of the regulated suppliers. During that period, and continuing today, significant legal and regulatory efforts attempted to inject competition into the regulatory formula for power supply, and presumably "get a better deal" for customers.

In New Jersey, the State, in implementing the requirements of PURPA, established an avoided energy cost for cogeneration projects with a ten percent adder to the short term avoided cost of the utilities of purchasing power from the Pennsylvania New Jersey Maryland (PJM) Power Pool. Non-utility generators (NUGs) and cogeneration facilities were exempted from several significant tax provisions required of other energy suppliers. Finally, and more importantly, the NUGS, unlike the public utilities, did not have to go through an extensive and time consuming Certificate of Need process.

As a result of these, and other initiatives including standard offers, and competitive bidding, over 15% of utility capacity in New

Jersey will be procured from non-utility generators by the mid-1990's.

In a recent speech, Commissioner Carmen Armenti of the New Jersey Board of Regulatory Commissioners stated,

> "However, it seems to me that we have tilted too far away from pursuing a fair and balanced regulatory policy... have we thought that perhaps the utilities are not building new facilities because it has become impossible to do so in view of the current regulatory climate?"

> "I am concerned about the direction we are going in - particularly the replacement of the compact system, under the guise of competition, with a power generating supply system that would drive public utilities out of the electricity business and leave no one to take responsibility for safety, adequacy, economy or reliability of supply."[6]

## Conclusion

The regulatory environment is at a dynamic and historic turning point which has potential to redirect or redefine the character of utility motivations and introduce new features to the "regulatory compact." This represents a significant opportunity that should be approached with care and enthusiasm, and with a goal of developing a win-win-win outcome for customers, utilities, and the energy service delivery industry. Successful implementation in this will count as a win for regulators.

Regulation related to the DSM market needs to benefit from lessons from other contexts. The objectives of DSM incentives are stated well in the Purpose and Scope of the New Jersey regulations. Cautious consideration should be given to ideas that conflict with or undermine those intentions.

The importance of bringing utility cooperation and enthusiasm to the DSM market is too frequently ignored by regulators and those players that advocate using a stick rather than a reward to produce a desired behavior. While the stick is effective in some contexts, the regulatory community has recognized the significance of the fundamental disincentives for utilities to fully embrace aggressive DSM. Enthusiastic farmers will produce better harvests.

217

## REFERENCES

1  <u>New Jersey Register</u>, Monday November 4, 1991, Cite 23 NJR 3368.

2  <u>New Jersey Register</u>, Monday November 4, 1991, Cite 23 NJR 3380.

3  Jersey Central Power and Light. "Demand Side Management Plan" Section.

4  <u>New Jersey Register</u>, Monday November 4, 1991, Cite 23 NJR 3371.

5  <u>New Jersey Register</u>, Monday November 4, 1991, Cite 23 NJR 3380.

6  Armenti, C.   "Remarks of Carmen J. Armenti, Commissioner New Jersey Board of Regulatory Commissioners Before THe Public Utility Law Section New Jersey State Bar Association", May 14, 1992.

DSMbid.cws

# SECTION 3
# POWER GENERATION, COGENERATION AND INDEPENDENT POWER

# Chapter 39

# Meeting Changing Conditions at the Rhode Island Medical Center Cogeneration Plant

D.P. Galamaga, P.T. Bowen

## OVERVIEW – THE DEPARTMENT AND THE CENTRAL POWER PLANT – A SPECIAL PARTNERSHIP

The Rhode Island Department of Mental Health, Retardation and Hospitals is one state department in Rhode Island whose basic function is to provide services to seriously disabled individuals throughout the state. Operating under a Director who reports to the Governor of Rhode Island, the Department has three major divisions, approximately 2500 employees, and a budget of 200 million dollars. Its operations extend throughout the state and the major focus for hospital or institutional levels of care reside in three major locations, the Dr. U.E. Zambarano Memorial Hospital in northern Rhode Island, the Dr. Joseph Ladd Center in southern Rhode Island, and the Rhode Island Medical Center in the middle of the state. Besides these institution-based operations, the Department sponsors a wide range of rehabilitative programming in the community either through direct operations of facilities such as group homes or through contracts with private non-profit providers of service.

Interestingly, the three major divisions of the Rhode Island Department of Mental Health, Retardation and Hospitals each have national reputations for providing services to disabled citizens. The Division of Hospitals and Community Rehabilitative Services provides long term care hospital-based services to frail, elderly populations with debilitating illnesses ranging from severe stroke to amyotropic lateral sclerosis (Lou Gehrig's disease). This division also sponsors several innovative programs including an out-patient geriatric assessment unit which allows persons in the state to bring elderly friends or relatives in for a complete multi-disciplinary work-up so that the individual concerned can continue to live productively in the least restrictive environment possible consistent with their stage of illness. Offering programs principally at the Rhode Island Medical Center, the Rhode Island General Hospital and at the aforementioned Zambarano Memorial Hospital, this division's programs have been widely acclaimed as being at the cutting edge of offering long term hospital-based care services and alternatives to hospital services to individuals in the state. Programs are offered in conjunction with Brown University School of Medicine, the University of Rhode Island School of Pharmacy, the Community College of Rhode Island, Harvard University School of Public Health, and other institutions of higher education. The second major division, that of Retardation and Developmental Disabilities, similarly has a national and international reputation for providing extraordinary care and services to these special individuals. This division was able to proceed in a deliberate way to provide resources from its own budget and with the support of the Governor and General Assembly to lead to a publicly announced policy of closing state institutions for the mentally retarded while providing a wide range of community options. This action will be completed sometime in fiscal year 1993, given appropriate resource availability. The third major division, that of Mental Health and Management Services, provides institutional and community care to the severely mentally disabled in the state and has been recognized by the Nader organization and by Dr. E. Fuller Torrey as having the Number One mental health system in the country. The state Institute of Mental Health, a psychiatric hospital, similar to the General Hospital and Zambarano Hospital, operates programs at the cutting edge of mental health research in conjunction with the previously mentioned institutions of higher education and schools of medicine and pharmacy. Similar to the Ladd Center, resources have been able to be moved from the hospital to the community with a view towards a very small state specialty psychiatric hospital as part of a unified system of mental health care throughout the state offering a wide range of residential options with temporary community hospitalization available where necessary.

These three key divisions, all having programs of widely recognized excellence, also have a unique relationship with the efforts of the Division of Facilities and Maintenance within this same department, which is part, uniquely, of the Division of Mental Health and Management Services. This relationship specifically is focused on the fact that major benefits accruing from savings realized by improvements in the Rhode Island Medical Center Central Power Plant have been able to accrue to the benefit of operating funds for the programs of the three divisions. In like manner, when the state has offered bond referenda to the citizens of the state of Rhode Island who have been similarly impressed by the nature of the three major programs of this Department, the voters have consistently approved bond issues, not only to develop community residences for severely disabled individuals and to provide funds for capital maintenance and repair of institutions, but also to provide some funds for the maintenance of the Rhode Island Central Power Plant and its steam and electrical distribution system. In a very true sense, this relationship can be said to be "symbiotic." For example, the Central Power Plant has saved a cumulative total of 10 million dollars in operating expenditures over the past 10 years from 1982 to 1992. These 10 million dollars in avoided costs have been able to be put directly into programs for the mentally ill, the mentally retarded, and those persons requiring long term hospitalization for other illnesses. This is truly a major benefit.

The future of the Rhode Island Department of Mental Health, Retardation and Hospitals is focused on providing care to disabled individuals in the least restrictive environment consistent with the individual's capacity to deal with that environment. What has been able to happen based upon this policy is that the Department, under the leadership of its Director, Mr. Thomas D. Romeo, has been able to systematically decrease hospital and institution-based patients and residents to programs in the community with appropriate financial supports in the community so that the environment provided is truly the "least restrictive." This has not been the experience in other states where state hospitals have, in effect, dumped patients into the communities to have them wander the streets without any resources to provide for their needs. In Rhode Island, the experience has been that state bond funds approved by the voters over the past 15 years have built group homes, apartments and other forms of residential facilities, buildings to house programs of rehabilitation for various clients, and funds to develop community facilities in partnership with other agencies so that the disabled can benefit from living in mainstream, modern and very habitable living arrangements. The characteristics, thus, of the Department of MHRH's institutional population during this period of time has decreased substantially from well over 3,000 patients at the Rhode Island Medical Center to about 400 at the General Hospital and about 150 at the Institute of Mental Health today in 1992. These populations have been replaced, by and large, with prison populations who have taken over old hospital buildings and with programs housing activities for other populations including juvenile detention facilities. In 1992, at the time of writing of this paper, the Department of MHRH, which has the expertise to manage the Central Power Plant at the Rhode Island Medical Center along with the distribution systems, finds itself in an interesting situation whereby the division charged with the responsibility to run the utilities system has also capital oversight responsibility for a wide range of community facilties throughout the State of Rhode Island. For the time being, though, the policy of the state will be for the Department of MHRH to continue to run the Central Power Plant and this Department does not mind us keeping responsibility for that facility, since there have been continued benefits to the Department from savings that have accrued systematically over the past 10 years in a major way. In recent years, starting with the oil shocks of the 1970's, many vendors attempted to sell state government on the possibility of having the private sector take over the Central Power Plant and sell utilities to the state while modernizing the plant. Up until this time, the state has chosen to go it alone, financing improvements to the plant directly from either operating budget revenues or from capital bond referenda. There was one attempt at a shared savings arrangement competitively bid with Scallop Thermal Corporation, a sub-division of Royal Dutch Shell, successfully bidding on major overhaul of the system. Significant drops in the price of oil, though, made it not economically feasible and the parent company pulled out of the final arrangement. As of this writing, the Department is again considering a shared savings arrangement for improvements to the Central Power Plant and the distribution system along with some demand side management activities with a vendor who went through a competitive selection process back in 1986. After a long hiatus, the state and the vendor have agreed to go forward with the shared savings arrangement. Significant increases in the prison population have also stimulated the Department of MHRH to update an RFP for enhancing its current cogeneration capacity and this RFP will probably be let sometime in the Fall of 1992, again looking for some form of shared savings arrangement with the state. The lack of capital finances in the state and a heavy overall state debt burden are the major reasons forcing the Department to move towards shared savings arrangement at this time. With these general comments in mind, we will now proceed to review the Central Power Plant specifically as part of the Rhode Island Medical Center; however, it should be kept in mind that one of the major motivations for the kind of attention that the power plant has received has been its special partnership with operating programs for disabled citizens in the state.

## HISTORICAL BACKGROUND

In 1902 the Central Power Plant (CPP) was established at the Rhode Island Medical Center (RIMC) to provide heat and electricity for the facility and to make the Center self-sufficient. The plant consisted of coal fired boilers and steam engine driven generators.

In 1936 a new cogeneration plant was built and consisted of two General Electric Company steam turbine generators rated at 750 KW - 0.80 PF. Throttle conditions were 400 PSIG and 600 degrees F with steam extraction at 100 PSIG and exhaust (back pressure) at 15 PSIG. This plant has been in continuous operation since 1936.

A 1956 expansion added two Elliott Company steam turbine generators rated at 2,000 KW - 0.80 PF and a 120,000 #/Hr. Riley Corporation steam boiler.

The Central Power Plant operated as an isolated plant until 1974, at which time it was interconnected with the Narragansett Electric Company (NECO) system. The interconnection was required due to increased imbalance of the steam and electrical loads.

The facility served by the CPP is a 200 acre site off Route 95, three miles south of Providence. There are 160 buildings and structures of various types on the site. The buildings house programs of the Departments of Administration (DOA), Corrections (DOC), Children, Youth & Families (DCYF), Mental Health, Retardation & Hospitals (MHRH), and the Rhode Island Lottery. Presently there are 3,000 inmates, patients, and over 6,000 staff and workers at the site. Total building floor area is approximately 2,800,000 square feet. See Figure I.

## FUEL PURCHASING

The fuel usage at the RIMC is expressed in equivalent barrels of #6 oil; Figure 2 shows the usage in recent years. The high usage in the late 1960's and early 1970's is due to a combination of deteriorated distribution systems (leaks), the steam dumped to the atmosphere to meet electrical loads prior to the 1974 connection to NEC and the inefficiency of older 1933 boilers.

Oil consumption estimates prepared in February 1992 project the fuel usage will increase to 190,000 equivalent barrels for the 1993 - 1994 season, see Figure 2.

The boilers at the CPP are equipped with combination gas/oil burners, except for Boiler #6, which is equipped only for oil. Oil used is #6, 1 percent sulphur. Natural gas is generally supplied by the Providence Gas Company on an interruptable basis.

Past practice was to bid #6 oil on an annual basis. Pricing is based on the lower (day of delivery) of the Boston or Providence posted Tank Car Schedule as published in the New York Journal of Commerce, plus or minus a fixed amount determined by the bidders. There is no fixed quantity of purchase, though bid data shows historical usage. Starting in 1990, an additional bid was taken for a fixed quantity of oil to be delivered between the months of November through April. In 1990 the fixed quantity was 75,000 barrels, in 1991 - 80,000 barrels, and in 1992 - 88,000 barrels. These quantities represent slightly less than the projected usage for the winter months. The bid usually is taken in July and August and requires a financial commitment the day of the bid. In 1992 the fixed quantity bids were taken in June with option of 44,000 or 88,000 bbls. A commit-

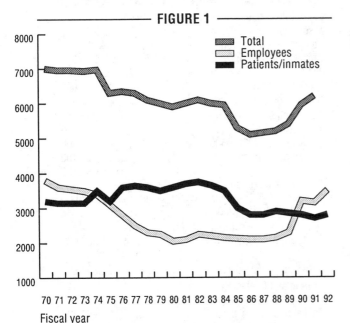

**Population at RIMC 1970-1992**

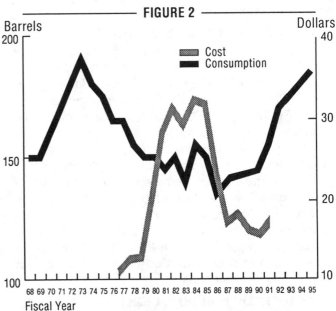

RIMC Central Power Plant
Fossil Fuel Consumption (Thousands of Barrels)
and Fuel Cost (Dollars Per Barrel 77-91)

ment was made for 44,000 bbls. of oil at $18.14 per barrel. A second bid for the second 44,000 bbls. will be taken in August. Needless to say, this type of bidding is essentially dealing in the commodities market.

The first serious attempt to purchase natural gas competitively occurred in the summer of 1987 as a result of discussions with gas suppliers. The first contract was initiated on a monthly basis with the Providence Gas Company in September, 1987. There exists a problem with the rates approved by the Public Utilities Commission (PUC), which permits a variable charge for local transport from $.10 to $.85 per thousand cubic feet of gas. Since September, 1987 MHRH has purchased gas from various suppliers with payment to the LDC for local transport by the supplier or the State. While MHRH is certainly not completely satisfied, due to variable transport rates charged by the LCD, it has forced the price down so that generally gas is the fuel used from April through October. MHRH has burned natural gas as late as December 15 in some years.

People who have worked for or with governmental agencies will appreciate the effort required by the people in the Departments of MHRH, Purchasing and Administration to overcome historical practices and required public bidding procedures.

Increased gas pipeline capacity and new distribution systems within Rhode Island should improve competition and result in lower gas prices.

The availability of pipeline natural gas has resulted in increased competition between oil and gas, as well as competition between the local gas company and gas supply companies. All of this has been beneficial to our fuel budgets. Figure 2 shows the annual cost of fuels per equivalent barrel of #6.

## STEAM ABSORPTION CHILLER

Because of the invested capital in the steam distribution system and our lower summer steam loads, the incremental cost for use of steam absorption chillers for air conditioning is minimal and improves the cogeneration. Figure 3 is a typical analysis of the comparative economics for a 200 ton electric and steam absorption chiller. It will be noted the added capital investment for the steam absorption chiller has a simple payback of 5.8 years. The electrical demand reduction is an important element in the analysis due to impact on the building electric system design, secondary transformer size, distribution system capacity and the CPP switchgear capacity. There are a total of 2600 tons of steam absorption units installed at the RIMC, ranging in size from 100 to 448 tons.

## RETROFIT OF BUILDING LIGHTING SYSTEMS

The Department of MHRH initiated an energy conservation program in 1982. The program started with the typical "energy audits." The measures included such

items as boiler blowdown heat recovery, feedwater heater addition to the CPP steam cycle, and lighting systems retrofit. On its own, MHRH replaced incandescent lights, removed florescent fixture tubes, and replaced ballast.

In 1988 NECO started its rebate program. Lighting system improvements under the rebate program are tabulated below:

Energy Reduction Measures
Narrangansett Electric Company
Rebate Program

| YEAR | KWH RED. | KW RED. |
|---|---|---|
| 1990 | 987,000 | 318 |
| 1991 | — | — |
| 1992 | 422,000 | 130 |
| TOTAL | 1,409,000 | 448 |
| 1993 | 1,800,000 | 600 (Proposed) |

Energy reduction measures have consisted primarily of ballast and tube replacement, new reflectors (tube reduction) and use of high pressure sodium lamps. Proposed 1993 program will include use of high efficiency motor replacement as well as lighting measures.

This program has been satisfactory; MHRH is as eager to reduce electrical usage and the electrical demand as is our public utility. Demand loadings on our generating and distribution systems are critical concerns. The next phase of energy conservation may well be with an Energy Service Company agreement to

## FIGURE 3
## COMPARATIVE COSTS
## 200 TON ELECTRIC AND ABSORPTION CHILLER

**1. Capital Investment**

| | |
|---|---|
| Absorption Chiller, 200 ton installed | $102,000 |
| Electric Chiller, 200 ton installed | 160,000 |
| Capital Cost Difference | $ 58,000 |
| Reduction Transf. Size, 150 KVA | $4,000 |
| Net Difference | $ 54,000 |
| Added Debt Services (Absorption Unit) | $6,156 |

**2. Operating Cost**      Cost/Yr.

A. Electric Chiller

Electricity - (200)(1500 FLH)(0.10) = ... $ 30,000

Electricity Demand - (200)(2)(11) = ... $4,400

$ 34,400

B. Steam Absorption

Steam - $\frac{(200)(18)(1500)}{1000}$ x 5.00 = ... $ 27,000

Cogenerated Electricity (Credit)

$\frac{(200)(18)(1500)}{30}$ x .045 = ... $8,000

Net Operating Cost ... $ 19,000

**3. Owning and Operating**

| | |
|---|---|
| Operating Cost Difference | $ 15,400 |
| Capital Cost | −$6,200 |
| Net Cost Difference | $ 9,200 |
| Simple Payback = 58,000 = | 5.8 years |
| | $9,200 |

reduce the State's expenditure of dollars. A tentative program for FY 1993 is shown in the table above. The program will be expanded to include motor replacement with energy efficient motors as well as lighting retrofits. Since many of our buildings operate on a 24-hour basis, potential savings are higher than average. Since many of our motors are now showing age, the replacement has an added advantage of cost saving in both maintenance and normal replacement costs.

## CPP STEAM CYCLE & STEAM DISTRIBUTION SYSTEM

The steam distribution system for the RIMC consists of over 20 miles of steam and return piping. Steam is distributed at two pressure levels, namely 100 PSIG and 20 PSIG nominal. The higher pressure steam was originally dictated for sterilization, cooking and laundry requirements for the hospital. In recent years changes in operation have resulted in less need for high pressure steam.

The CPP Flow Diagram is shown in Figure 4; steam is extracted from the turbines at 100 PSIG and exhausted at 20 PSIG into the distribution systems. An analysis of the Elliott steam turbine generator performance data indicates as a simple rule that 60 pounds of steam is required per KWH when extracted at 100 PSIG, and 30 pounds are required per KWH when exhausted at 20 PSIG. These figures are higher than the original performance data on the Elliott turbines and allows for lower performance due to age. Stating the operation in another way, twice as much power can be cogenerated with 20 PSIG steam as with 100 PSIG extracted steam.

Two areas where changes have been made to improve cogenerated power follow. First, the laundry, constructed in 1958, had a criteria for 150 PSIG steam, which could only be obtained by reducing of 400 PSIG steam and without any cogeneration. Review and tests revealed the laundry could operate satisfactorily with 100 PSIG steam system. The piping system was modified to utilize 100 PSIG steam, which provides cogeneration power of 640,000 KWH per year, a saving of $50,000 with a simple payback of 0.5 years. Secondly, the General Hospital Regan Building has a 250 ton steam absorption chiller, which had been run on the 100 PSIG steam system since start-up in 1981. In 1989 an investigation was made to determine reasons for inability to operate on low pressure steam. It appears the problem was due to lack of trapping on the unit and the arrangement and trapping on the steam piping. Modifications to piping and trapping resulted in satisfactory operation on low pressure steam, providing an addi-

## FIGURE 4

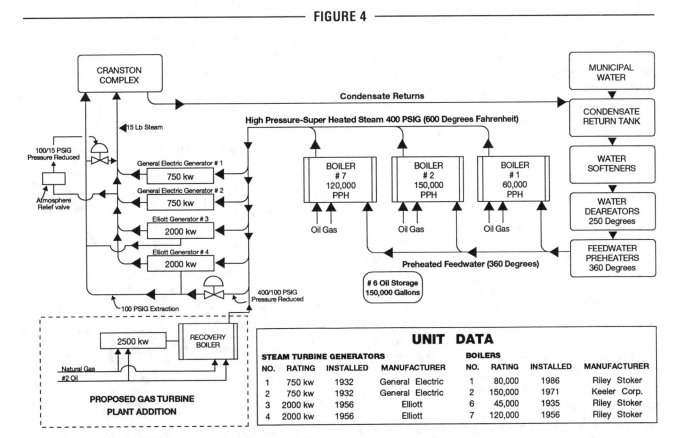

**UNIT DATA**

| STEAM TURBINE GENERATORS | | | | BOILERS | | | |
|---|---|---|---|---|---|---|---|
| NO. | RATING | INSTALLED | MANUFACTURER | NO. | RATING | INSTALLED | MANUFACTURER |
| 1 | 750 kw | 1932 | General Electric | 1 | 80,000 | 1986 | Riley Stoker |
| 2 | 750 kw | 1932 | General Electric | 2 | 150,000 | 1971 | Keeler Corp. |
| 3 | 2000 kw | 1956 | Elliott | 6 | 45,000 | 1935 | Riley Stoker |
| 4 | 2000 kw | 1956 | Elliott | 7 | 120,000 | 1956 | Riley Stoker |

**Rhode Island Department of Mental Health, Retardation and Hospitals**

**Central Power Plant, Cranston, RI**

tional cogenerated power of 107,000 KWH per year, a savings of $4,800, and a simple payback of one-half year. Other areas are being investigated.

## UTILITY COMPANY COOPERATIVE AGREEMENT

In 1990 the Department of MHRH entered into a Cooperative Interruptable Agreement with the Narragansett Electric Company. Under the terms of this agreement, MHRH would, "on call" from the utility, reduce its purchased power demand by 500 KWH in the summer and 300 KWH in the winter. This agreement resulted in a reduction of $100,000 in electrical charges for the year or about $.00625/KWH of purchased electricity.

To meet load reduction requirements, MHRH had three alternatives - reduce load by use of building emergency generators, load shedding or increase steam turbine generation by exhausting low pressure steam to the atmosphere. The latter alternative is four times more expensive and least desirable.

## 1936 STEAM TURBINE GENERATOR UPGRADE

The General Electric Company steam turbine generators generally have been little used in recent years until about 1988 when problems with the Elliott Turbines resulted in loss of power during the winter months. The turbines have been operated at reduced loads, 300 KW. In 1990, as a result of a major short circuit, the bus bars, switches, instrument transformers and associated items were damaged. In connection with repair work, bids were taken, and General Electric was awarded a contract to test and repair the generators, exciters and switchgear and to provide new controls and instrumentation for synchronizing the generators. The work was completed in 1992. Tests indicate the generators are capable of 800 KW, 0.90 PF. The cost of reconditioning for both units was $130,000. Upgrade of the turbine generators has enhanced their reliability and increased the total generating capacity by 900 KW, a cost of $144 per KW.

## PLANT EXPANSION ALTERNATIVES

A study of the RIMC steam loads and total electric load requirements indicates the electric load is increasing faster than the steam load. This results in less opportunity for steam cogenerated power and increased quantities of the more expensive purchased electricity. See Figure 5. Plant expansion alternatives could include diesel engine generators or gas turbine, both with heat recovery. A gas turbine with heat recovery at steam conditions to permit use in the existing steam turbines (a combined cycle) would appear most attractive; this cycle is indicated in Figure 4.

A simplified feasibility analysis prepared in 1988 (Figure 6) indicates a simple payback of 3.7 years based on a single 2500 KW gas turbine generator. Electric usage

has increased more than anticipated in 1988, which should improve the economics for gas turbine generation.

In-depth studies must be made for final selection of new cogenerating unit(s), which would address the many issues involved.

## PRIVATIZATION STUDIES

While the evaluation of plant expansion alternatives has been proceeding, the state has also engaged the Army Corps of Engineers on a project which is seen to be both mutually beneficial to the engineers and to the Department of MHRH. The engineers are looking to develop further expertise in the area of utilities analysis and cogeneration and the state is looking for some confirmation or other options regarding who should run the Central Power Plant in the future. To this end, a study has been commissioned where the state and the Army Corps of Engineers share fifty-fifty in the costs of an overall project aimed at determining or validating the future requirements for the Central Power Plant at the Rhode Island Medical Center and to supplement this study with a cost benefit analysis to indicate whether the operation should be taken over by the private sector or whether there are more savings accruing to the state if it continues to run the project itself. It is anticipated the outcome of this study will occur late sometime in the Fall of 1992.

## CONCLUSION

In conclusion, it is quite evident that the Rhode Island Medical Center Central Power Plant and its utilities distribution system are a major resource to the State of Rhode Island and a major benefit to the taxpayers of the

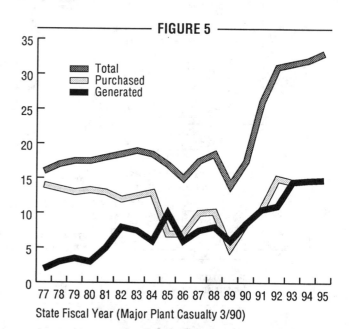

**FIGURE 5**

State Fiscal Year (Major Plant Casualty 3/90)

**RIMC Central Power Plant
Electricty Generated & Purchased**

state. The direct beneficiaries of the savings realized by the Central Power Plant have been Rhode Island's most disabled citizens. Resources saved by the Rhode Island Central Power Plant have been allowed to be applied to programs for the chronically ill, the severely mentally ill, and the mentally retarded in the state with the result that leadership in the overall Department and specific leadership within divisions has been able to focus on program development and program services for these patients and clients. The result has been a set of nationally recognized programs with an unusual cogenerating partner.

### FIGURE 6
### RHODE ISLAND MEDICAL CENTER CENTRAL POWER PLANT
### GAS TURBINE COGENERATION ANALYSIS

#### COGENERATION PARAMETERS

1. ASSUMED ELECTRIC & THERMAL LOADS
   Electric Usage (1993) = ...............................28,000,000 KWH
   Steam Usage (1993) =...................................850 MM Lbs.

2. STEAM/ELECTRIC RATIO # Steam/KWH
   Lbs. Steam/KWH = 850 x 10 MM = ...............30.35
   28 x 10 MM

3. STEAM GENERATION PARAMETERS
   Steam Turbine Generation ...........................55 lbs./KWH
   (Assumes Extr. Operation)
   Gas Turbine Generation ................................5 lbs./KWH

4. ELECTRIC/STEAM BALANCE
   The combination of steam and gas turbine electric generation must result in 30.4 lbs. of steam\KWH to satisfy the thermal load.
   If "X" equals the KWH of Steam Turbine Generation and an adjustment factor (5/55 = .09) is made for steam turbine power from the HRSG (Gas Turbine), then:

   $$(X)(55)+(1-X)(5)(1.09) = ...........30.4$$
   $$x = ...........504$$

   i.e., 51% of the electric generation should be from the steam turbines and 49% from the gas turbine.

   Turbine Electric Generation = ...........................14.3x10MM KWH
   Turbine Steam Required = 14.3x10MMx55 = ......786.5 MM Lbs.
   Gas Turbine Electric Generation = ....................13.7x10MM KWH
   Gas Turbine Steam (HRSG) = 3.7x10MMx5 = ....68.5 MM Lbs.

5. COST OF STEAM & POWER
   **Case I - Present System**
   Steam & Electric Cost
   Base Fuel Cost: Oil #6 1% = ..........................$18.00 Bbl.
   Cost/M Lbs. = (1,000) (1,028) (18.00) = ..........$3.58
   (150,000)(42)(.82)

   Purchased Electricity = ...................................7.5 Cents/KWH
   Fuel Oil #2 1,000,000 x .54 =..........................$4.10/MMBTU(LHV)
   138,500    .95

   Boiler Fuel = (850)(1,000)(3.58) = ................$3,043,000
   Elec. Gen. = (850)(1,000,000) = ....................5.455 MM KWH
   55
   Elec. Purchased = 28.0 - 15.455 =..................12.545 MM KWH
   Elec. Cost = (12,545)(1000000)(.075) =..........$940,875
   Total Energy Cost = ......................................$3,983,875

#### Case 2 - Gas Turbine (95% Availability)
1. Gas Turbine Fuel
   Elec. Gen. = ........................................13,600,000 KWH
   Avg. Load - 13,700,000 = .....................1627 KW
   8,420 Hrs.
   Gas Turbine Fuel Rate = .......................21.7 MM BTU/HR.
   Fuel Usage = 8,420 Hrs. x 21.4 =..........182,714 MM BTU
   Fuel Cost = (182,714)(4.10) = ................$749,128

2. Steam Turbine Fuel Cost
   Gen = (14.3)(100,000)(55) = .................786.5
   Fuel Cost = 786.5 x 1000 x 3.58 = ........$2,816,000

3. Total Energy Cost
   Steam Generation .............................$2,816,000
   Gas Turbine ........................................522,800
   Total .....................................................$3,338,800
   Credit Electric Cost Saving .................$ -878,150
   Total .....................................................$2,460,650
   O & M Expense (Exc. Fuel) .................  -137,000
   Net Cost .............................................$2,597,650

4. Savings - Case 2 vs Case 1
   I. Case I................................................$3,983,875/Yr.
   Case 2 ...............................................  2,597,650
   Savings ..........................................$1,323,500/Yr.

   2. Simple Payback
   Gas Turbine Capital Cost
   (2500 KW)(1800) = .........................$4,500,000
   Annual Savings................................$1,250,022
   Simple Payback
   4,500,000 = 3.7 Yrs.
   1,214,000

# Chapter 40
# Feasibility Study of Wood-Fired Cogeneration at a Wood Products Industrial Park, Belington, WV

S.K. Vasenda, C.C. Hassler

## ACKNOWLEDGEMENTS

The preparation of this report was financially assisted through a grant administered by the U.S. Department of Energy, Southeastern Regional Biomass Energy Program (SERBEP). The development of an Energy Conservation Program was prepared as a cooperative effort with the West Virginia Fuel and Energy Office, Governor's Office of Community and Industrial Development.

## INTRODUCTION

Wood residue is gaining favor as an alternative renewable energy; however, in West Virginia wood as an energy source is substantially underutilized (1). This project is an attempt to employ wood residue as fuel for a cogeneration facility in one location in West Virginia.

The Belington Industrial Park was selected for this study because it exhibits three key criteria which make cogeneration an attractive option: 1) some companies generate wood residue which may be used as fuel; 2) the dry kilns consume process steam on a 24-hour basis; and 3) the companies may be better able to combine equity to attract potential investors of a cogeneration system than would a single company. Figure 1 (below) shows the 74-acre Belington Industrial Park, along with its location in West Virginia. All companies in the park are either primary or secondary wood products firms.

Companies in this study were divided into three groups: group 1 consisted of all companies presently inside the industrial park, group 2 comprised two companies locating soon inside the park, and group 3 consisted of a radiofrequency kiln presently out of business.

Several alternatives were developed based upon feedback received from engineers, manufacturers and developers with experience in cogeneration systems. For each alternative, only wood residue from industrial processes is considered as fuel. These alternatives were:
1. A plant sized to service all companies in the park;
2. A plant sized to take in additional residue produced within a 25- and 50-mile radius surrounding Belington;
3. A small system sized to meet the steam demands of a steam user(s) and supply electricity to only one company.

In addition, as part of the study, a Request for Proposals was sent to 90 developers of biomass energy projects to determine what would be most suitable for the site.

### Considerations for this Study and Assumptions Made

Considerations: Data was collected from all companies inside the park on amount of residue produced and energy consumed. Based upon this data, equipment size and type, cost of equipment, cost of annual operation/maintenance, savings and/or revenue was determined. After the data was obtained, economic feasibility, specifically net present value of each alternative, was calculated. Additionally, social and regulatory aspects were also considered. The following general and specific tasks were performed:
1. Characteristic and amount of wood residue available for fuel from wood products companies were examined;
2. An energy profile for each company inside the park of maximum, average, and annual use based upon energy bills was defined;
3. Size of systems for each alternative were estimated;
4. Configurations of appropriate systems were determined;

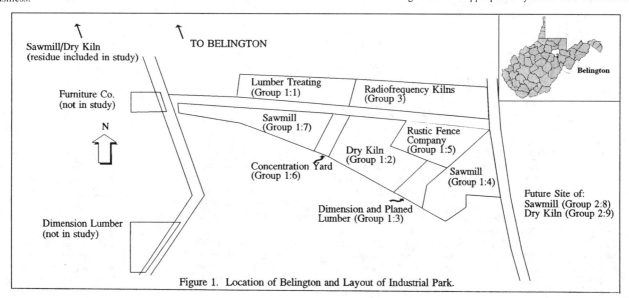

Figure 1. Location of Belington and Layout of Industrial Park.

5. Approximate capital and operating costs, along with savings and revenue were determined;
6. Cash flow analyses based upon approximate costs and revenues (if applicable) were calculated;
7. Sentiments of park tenants, the community, and surrounding wood products industry were examined; and
8. Applicable Federal and State rules, regulations, and laws pertaining to cogeneration at this location were researched.

Assumptions: It was necessary to make some assumptions regarding residue production, energy consumption, and equipment selected (assumptions regarding energy consumption are mentioned in that section of the report):
1. All wood residue used is considered 50% moisture content (wet basis);
2. Approximately 2.5 lbs. of steam are produced per lb. of residue;
3. One van (trailer) holds 20 tons of wet residue;
4. Of all residue available from outside the park, only 80% of available sawdust is considered as fuel for this study;
5. The plant would operate 8,400 hrs./yr.;
6. Used turbine/generator obtained for 10% cost of new (17);
7. Maintenance of new equipment is calculated at 5% for the first 5 years, and 7.5% thereafter (33);
8. Maintenance of used equipment is calculated at 7.5% (of the cost of new equipment) for the first 5 years and 10% thereafter.

Pertaining to the cash flow analysis:
1. No inflation rate is considered;
2. Feasibility would be achieved with a discounted payback period of four years (the same criteria used by most companies to evaluate a cogeneration investment);
3. Plant life is 20 years;
4. State tax rate is 9.6%, Federal tax rate is 34%;
5. Minimum acceptable rate of return (MARR) is 8%, 10%, and 12%;
6. The cogeneration plant would be funded entirely by state tax-free industrial revenue bonds (IRBs) and one annual payment of IRBs at an interest rate of 8%;
7. Project losses cannot be applied to another business component of the company owning the cogeneration plant.

## DATA COLLECTED

Data was collected on residue production from wood products companies within a 50-mile radius of Belington. First, residue production will be discussed, then energy consumption.

### Residue Production

Wood residue from sawmill operations is the only type of fuel considered for this study. Residue is generated as bark, sawdust, shavings, chips, and slabs. The amount of residue available was obtained from estimates provided by sawmills and secondary wood products companies generating residue in tons/day, or vans/day.

Belington Site: At the present time, all residue produced at Belington is either disposed off-site or stored on-site, none is used to create energy. Sawdust is mostly hauled to a local charcoal manufacturer, or other small manufacturer, or burned in wood-fired boilers; sawdust has the lowest economic value of all wood residue. Bark is hauled to several mulch plants, and chips are hauled to several paper companies located outside of West Virginia. Slabs which are not hogged are often given away for firewood. The distance to haul residue is often quite far in this mostly-rural area, and little, if any money is made on the sale of residue. One hundred and twenty tons of residue per day can be used for a facility is produced by all the companies in and surrounding the park.

Within 50-Mile Radius of Belington: Data on wood residue production was collected from sawmills and secondary wood products companies within a 50-mile radius of Belington, as illustrated in Figure 2. Often, the distance is much greater than what is measured because the roads are quite twisting.

Table 1 is a summary of residue availability in this area, categorized by Belington area, 25-mile radius, and 50-mile radius (excluding amounts used in wood-fired boilers). Individual amounts and company names are confidential. Only sawdust, bark and chips are considered because it was thought that shavings and slabs would be minimal. Data from only sawmills was obtained from a 25-to 50-mile radius because it is likely that smaller secondary industries outside 25-miles would not have enough residue to economically haul such an extended distance.

Residue availability was obtained by calling each company and asking the following questions: 1) How much (sawdust, bark, chips) are generated in tons/day?; and 2) What becomes of these residues?

Table 1. Residue availability within 50-mile radius of Belington.

| Type of Residue | Tons/Day | | | |
|---|---|---|---|---|
| | Belington area | Within 25-miles | Between 25-and 50-miles | Total |
| Sawdust | 50 | 190 | 287 | 527 |
| Bark | 40 | 183 | 288 | 511 |
| Chips | 30 | 193 | 497 | 720 |
| Total | 120 | 566 | 1,072 | 1,758 |

### Energy Usage

Electric and natural gas bills were analyzed to determine approximate peak, average and annual energy usage for each company. Two years of bills were requested from companies in Group 1 that covered 1989-1990. Energy data for companies in Group 2 was estimated from conversations with owners regarding anticipated energy requirements. Group 3 data was obtained from the previous owner of the radiofrequency kilns and covers only 1989.

An approximation of energy usage for each company is shown in Table 2. This table was produced without consideration of seasonal changes in energy usage because energy usage is limited by the market for wood products, which is somewhat unpredictable.

Table 2. Energy profiles of all companies in study.

| Company (1) | ----------Electrical---------- | | | | -----------Thermal----------- | | |
|---|---|---|---|---|---|---|---|
| | peak kW[1] (2) | peak kW[2] (3) | avg kWh/h (4) | annual kWh (5) | peak mmBtu/h (6) | avg mmBtu/h (7) | annual mmBtu (8) |
| Group 1: Presently In Park: | | | | | | | |
| 1. Lumber Treating | 69.3 | 44.7 | 34.5 | 70,275 | 1.0 | 0.2 | 400 |
| 2. Steam Dry Kiln | 376.0 | 104.0 | 78.8 | 662,235 | 7.2 | 5.8 | 50,750 |
| 3. Dimension/Planing | 70.0 | 70.0 | 50.0 | 102,500 | na | na | na |
| 4. Sawmill | 214.0 | 122.0 | 72.2 | 150,625 | 0.7 | 0.2 | 400 |
| 5. Rustic Fencing Mfg. | 516.5 | 197.8 | 166.2 | 336,350 | na | na | na |
| 6. Concentration Yard | 19.4 | 19.4 | 17.0 | 34,300 | 0.1 | 0.05 | 100 |
| 7. Sawmill | 314.0 | 136.0 | 100.3 | 205,063 | na | na | na |
| TOTAL GROUP 1: | 1579.2 | 693.9 | 519.0 | 1,561,34 | 9.0 | 6.25 | 51,650 |
| Group 2: Future In Park: | | | | | | | |
| 8. Sawmill | 128.4 | 73.2 | 43.3 | 90,338 | 0.4 | 0.1 | 100 |
| 9. Steam Dry Kiln | 236.9 | 39.4 | 46.9 | 394,149 | 4.0 | 3.0 | 26,250 |
| TOTAL GROUP 2: | 365.3 | 112.6 | 90.2 | 484,486 | 4.4 | 3.1 | 26,450 |
| Group 3: R/F Kiln: | 569.5 | 389.5 | 234.8 | 1,974,25 | 0.1 | 0.05 | 100 |
| TOTAL GROUPS 1+2: | 1944.5 | 806.5 | 609.2 | 2,045,83 | 13.4 | 9.35 | 78,100 |
| TOTAL GROUPS 1+2+3: | 2514.0 | 1218.6 | 844.0 | 4,020,08 | 13.5 | 9.4 | 78,200 |

[1] Determined by highest demand on bill;
[2] Determined by adding all equipment horsepower.

Electricity Consumption at the Belington Site: Electricity consumption is shown in columns 2-5. Columns 2 and 3 show two different values for peak electrical demand. The peak demand in Column 2 represents the total of all equipment horsepower, while the peak demand in column 3 represents the highest demand shown on any electric bill; column 3 is considered a more accurate representation of demand.

Monthly bills (or estimations of monthly usage if bills were not available) were totalled to obtain a rough estimation of annual kWh used. This rough determination of annual consumption was used to obtain an accurate representation of average (col. 4) and annual (col. 5) kWh used. The calculation for col. 4 took into account the type of business; hours operated per month was either:
168 (plants/offices open 8 hours/day x 21 days/mo. = 168), or
128 (plants/offices during holiday weeks in July & Nov. when open 8 hrs./day x 16 days/mo.).

Based upon the value obtained in column 4, column 5 was calculated using two different methods based upon company usage of electricity:

1. Companies expected to use electricity 2000 hrs/yr:
   a. *Assume* that peak kW occurs for 2, 15-min. periods/day (1/16 of an 8-hour day or 125 hours/year);
   b. *Assume* that average kWh/h occurs 7.5 hours/day (15/16 of an 8-hour day or 1,875 hours/year);
   c. *Therefore* annual kWh = (peak kW x 125 hrs./yr)+(avg. kWh/h x 1,875 hrs./yr.);
2. Companies expected to use electricity 8400 hrs/yr:
   a. *Assume* that peak kW occurs for 1, 15-minute period/week (12.5 hrs./yr.);
   b. *Assume* that average kWh/h occurs 8,387.5 hrs./yr.;
   c. *Therefore* annual kWh = (peak kW x 12.5)+(avg.kWh/h x 8,387 hrs./yr.).

Thermal Consumption at the Belington Site: Although it could not be determined what portion of gas was used for heating/cooling just by examining gas bills, it is assumed that gas usage for dry kilns is used primarily as process steam.

It was more difficult to calculate thermal consumption than electricity consumption, as bills to be used as a basis were difficult to obtain. Thermal data is shown in columns 6-8. Peak mmBtu/hour (col. 6) was obtained by determining the month which had the highest gas consumption, then dividing the total amount for that month by the number of days the company operated that month.

Average mmBtu/hour (col. 7) was calculated the same way as average kWh/hour by determining how many hours/month each type of company operated:
732 (for the steam kilns operating 24 hours/day x 30.5 days/mo.),
168 (for offices open 8 hours/day x 21 days/mo.), or
128 (for offices during holiday weeks in July & Nov. when open 8 hours/day x 16 days/mo.).

Annual mmBtu (col. 8) was obtained by totalling all Btu consumed during one year and multiplying by either 2,000 or 8,750 hours/year.

## TECHNICAL/ECONOMIC FEASIBILITY

It is difficult to determine exact equipment and equipment sizes required at this point. Costs are also site-specific. Use of general cost information is limited; the more costly equipment required is normally customized and the price for this equipment will be unique (33).

Capital cost estimates for equipment were provided by developers and by equipment manufacturers based upon preliminary descriptions of this project; no on-site visits were conducted. Percentages of capital cost to be allocated to insurance, operation/maintenance, and engineering were, in some cases provided by developers of similar projects and, in other cases are general

industry rules-of-thumb. The four major alternatives will be discussed in the order listed in the introduction. First, technical feasibility will be discussed for the first case in each alternative, then economic feasibility.

Technical Feasibility

Alternative 1. Plant sized to service companies only inside park: We examined four possibilities within this alternative: 1A) excluding RF kilns, new equipment; 1B) include RF kilns, new equipment; 1C) exclude RF kilns, used equipment; and 1D) include RF kilns, used equipment.

Alternative, 1A, which excludes the RF kilns and considers all new equipment is the one featured for discussion; changes made to consider alternatives B-D are discussed in the sections entitled "Alternative 1B", "Alternative 1C", and "Alternative 1D", which follow.

From Table 2, column 2, maximum electric demand for Groups 1 and 2 is 806.5 kW. A condensing turbine was selected for this alternative to maximize production of electricity; a non-condensing turbine would produce electricity based upon steam usage, which is low. The amount of steam required by the kilns can be diverted to them. The single stage condensing turbine/generator that should effectively meet this demand is approximately 800 kW. The amount of steam necessary to meet this generator capacity is:

800 kW x 17.43 lbs. of steam per hour/kW = 19,944 lbs. of steam./hr.

From Table 2, column 7, average use for process steam is 9.95 mmBtu/hr. The steaming capacity required for dry kilns:

9.95 mmBtu/hour / 970 Btu/lb. of steam = 10,257 lbs. of steam/hr.

The maximum total boiler capacity required for both steam and electricity is:

13,944 lbs. + 10,257 lbs. = 24,201 lbs. of steam.
24,201 lbs. of steam x 970 Btu/lb. of steam = 23,474,970 Btu
23,474,970 Btu / 33,475 Btu/BHP = 701 BHP

Since steam is bled off before reaching the turbine, the amount of wood waste required per week to meet this boiler capacity can be divided between: 1) peak periods of 40 hours/week (8 hrs./day x 5 days/week) when the demand for electricity and process steam are at maximum, and 2) non-peak periods of 128 hours/week ((16 hrs./day x 5 days/week) + 48 hrs. during weekends) when the demand for electricity is low and process steam is still required. The calculations to determine waste required for these two instances are:
1. peak periods:
   24,201 lbs. of steam x 970 Btu/lb. of steam = 23,474,970 Btu/hr.
   23,474,970 Btu/hr./0.662 combustion efficiency = 35,460,680 Btu/hr.
   35,460,680 Btu/hr./3,000 Btu/lb. = 11,820 lbs. of residue/hr.
   11,820 lbs. of residue x 40 hrs./week = 472,800 lbs. of residue/week
   472,800 lbs. of residue/week/2,000 lbs./ton = 236 tons/week

2. non-peak periods:
   10,257 lbs. of steam x 970 Btu/lb. of steam = 9,949,290 Btu/hr.
   9,949,290 Btu/hr./0.662 combustion efficiency = 15,029,139 Btu/hr.
   15,029,139 Btu/hr./3,000 Btu/lb. = 5,010 lbs. of residue/hr.
   5,010 lbs. of residue x 128 hrs./week = 641,280 lbs. of residue/week
   641,280 lbs. of residue/week/2,000 lbs./ton = 321 tons/week

Total amount of residue needed = 557 tons/week (236+321).

Major decisions regarding alternative 1A are mentioned; Table 3 shows a list of capital and start-up costs for alternative 1A.

It is estimated that a plant will use approximately 557 tons/week of green sawdust (density 20 lbs./ft$^3$ (32). Therefore, a slab 5,000 ft$^2$ will store 600 tons at an average height of 12 ft., more than 5 days of fuel.

Table 3. Capital cost estimates for alternative 1A.

| Equipment | Item Cost | Total Cost |
|---|---|---|
| Site prep & concrete | 60,000 | |
| Belt conveyer | 40,000 | |
| Truck dumper, conveyers | 135,000 | |
| Hogger | 50,000 | |
| Installation | 110,000 | |
| Total Fuel Storage and Handling | | 395,000 |
| Boiler | 250,000 | |
| Metering bin, controls, valves, pumps | 10,000 | |
| Installation | 230,000 | |
| Total Boiler System | | 490,000 |
| Condensing Turbine/Generator | 170,000 | |
| Controls, relays, switchgear, piping, valves, | 60,000 | |
| Installation | 95,000 | |
| Total Turbine/Generator | | 325,000 |
| Cooling Tower | 75,000 | |
| Pumps, piping, valves | 40,000 | |
| Installation | 65,000 | |
| Total Cooling Tower | | 180,000 |
| Piping | 271,900 | |
| Installation | 200,900 | |
| Total Piping to Steam Dry Kilns | | 472,800 |
| Equipment | 150,000 | |
| Installation | 75,000 | |
| Total Cyclone Collector | | 225,000 |
| Foundation | 22,500 | |
| Interior mechanics (plumbing,gas) | 15,000 | |
| Excavation and site prep. | 22,500 | |
| Fees | 7,500 | |
| Construction of Building | 75,000 | |
| Permits | 7,500 | |
| Total Plant | | 150,000 |
| Engineering | 125,268 | |
| Project Management | 62,634 | |
| Contingency | 208,780 | |
| Construction Insurance | 20,878 | |
| Construction Financing | 125,268 | |
| Total Construction Cost | | 542,828 |
| Legal Fees | 75,000 | |
| Interconnection | 60,000 | |
| Permits | 50,000 | |
| TOTAL CAPITAL COST | | 2,965,628 |

This amount of residue is produced by the companies within and surrounding the park. Since all the companies that have residue also own their own vans, they can continue to blow the residue into their vans, then drive to the site where they will be unloaded. A truck dump and scale will be needed to unload vans; about 5 vans/day will unload at the site. A hogger will be used to size bark and slabs which will need to be separated at the mills prior to arriving at the site.

One 700 BHP spreader stoker, with combination watertube furnace and multi-pass firetube boiler is able to handle wet fuel and can quickly change firing rates. The system includes metering system and controls.

An 800 kW single-stage condensing turbine/generator with inlet pressure of 125 psig and outlet pressure of 15 psig is considered for this system. This system includes turbine controls, synchronous generator, pressure lubrication system and water condenser.

A cooling tower is installed in all condensing systems to dissipate the heat produced by the condenser. This system will include cooling water pump, piping and valves.

Steam lines will carry the extraction steam from the cogeneration plant to both dry kiln companies. This piping will be above ground and insulated. Throttle pressure is 250 psig (saturated) and exhaust is 15 psig.

Bel-Bar Dry Kiln is approximately 0.5 miles and Abenaki Timber will be approximately 0.125 miles from a possible location of the cogeneration plant. Total length of piping required is 0.625 miles (0.500 + 0.125), or 3,300 feet. Cost is estimated at $143/ft. (23).

Since the park is located in a rural county and not a PSD Class I area, it is anticipated that a mechanical collector, such as a multitube cyclone will be adequate to meet air quality requirements. Because this emissions control device has a relatively low efficiency, several cyclones might need to be operated in series to remove finer particles. This type of pollution control system will reduce particulates to levels of 0.1-0.5 lb./MMBtu, acceptable for most areas.

It is estimated that a building approximately 75' x 40', with an eave of 30' will be adequate. From contact with construction companies, it is estimated that the cost will be approximately $150,000. This includes the possibility of excess excavation, since the potential site for the plant is on hilly terrain.

Additional project costs that a developer would encounter need to be considered. These can be calculated as a percentage of total plant and equipment as shown in Table 4.

Table 4. Estimation of construction cost based upon percentages.

| | | | |
|---|---|---|---|
| Engineering | $2,087,800 | x 0.06 = | $125,268 |
| Project Management | | x 0.03 = | 62,634 |
| Contingency | | x 0.10 = | 208,780 |
| Construction Insurance | | x 0.01 = | 20,878 |
| Construction Financing | | x 0.06 = | 125,268 |
| TOTAL | | | $542,828 |

It is estimated that approximately ten acres will be required. It is assumed that land will be made available for the project by the Barbour County Development Authority free-of-charge.

The two primary benefits from a cogeneration plant are savings of electricity and process steam that would otherwise need to be purchased from the utility, and revenue from the sale of excess electricity to the utility. Since revenue is not being considered in this alternative, only savings will be calculated.

Savings of thermal energy is based upon the assumption that all energy can be obtained from the cogeneration facility. The cost of natural gas for industrial use in West Virginia is approximately $2.00/MCF (9). Estimated annual Btu consumption for both dry kiln companies is 77,000 mmBtu (50,750 mmBtu Bel-Bar + 26,250 mmBtu Abenaki). Annual savings in natural gas is $148,077 (77,000 mmBtu x (1,000,000 MCF/1,040,000 Btu) x $2.00/MCF).

To determine savings of electricity, annual kWh was multiplied by $0.05/kWh. Therefore, savings for all companies excluding the RF kilns is calculated to be 2,045,834 kWh x $0.05/kWh = $102,292. Savings including the RF kilns is calculated to be $201,004 (4,020,088 kWh x $0.05/kWh). Total savings is then $148,077 + $102,292 = $250,369 ($349,081 for the R/F kilns).

Wood fuel systems generally experience higher operating costs than non-biomass systems because of reduced levels of automation and increased personnel requirements (32). Since the cogeneration plant will operate 24-hours/day, one operator will need to be on-site during all three shifts. Two additional operators, possibly people already working nearby, will be needed to operate the plant during the weekends. The weekday operators might also work weekends, so that weekend operators would not have to work two shifts in a row. If no person is hired to specifically do maintenance (this study assumes no extra maintenance personnel), operators will need to be trained in maintenance. A plant manager will oversee the operators and wood handlers and a part-time secretary will handle the paperwork. Table 5 shows the breakdown of labor; only the values for *direct* and *indirect* cost are shown on the cash flow projections in the Economic Feasibility section.

Table 5. Breakdown of labor cost for 6 employees.

| Labor | Hourly Wage | Hours/ Yr. | Annual Wage |
|---|---|---|---|
| Operators (3) | $ 9.00 | 2,000 | $54,000 |
| Wood Handler (1) | 7.50 | 2,000 | 15,000 |
| Plant Manager (1) | 11.50 | 2,080 | 23,920 |
| Secretary (1) | 5.00 | 1,000 | 5,000 |
| TOTAL Annual Wages | | | $97,920 |
| Fringe Benefits @ 10% | | | 9,792 |
| *Direct* TOTAL Wages + Benefits | | | $107,712 |
| Worker's Compensation | $97,920 x 0.0333 | | 3,260 |
| Unemployment Insurance | $40,000 x 0.027 | | 1,080 |
| Liability Insurance | $25 x $98 | | 2,450 |
| Social Security Matching | $97,920 x 0.060 | | 5,875 |
| *Indirect* TOTAL Compensation, Insurance, Matching | | $12,665 | |
| TOTAL, Wages, Compensation, Matching | | | $120,377 |

The plant will require regular maintenance on all items of equipment in addition to building maintenance. It is reasonable to expect that maintenance will cost about 5% of original equipment (less installation) cost during the first 3 to 5 years, then increase to 7.5% thereafter (33). Cost of equipment less installation is $1,311,900. Therefore, during the first five years @ 5%, maintenance cost is approximately $65,595 ($1,311,900 x 0.05) while after the fifth year it will be $98,393 ($1,311,900 x 0.075).

Although insurance on building and equipment may vary, equipment insurance can be estimated to be approximately $1.50 per $100 of equipment cost (11). Since cost of equipment less installation is $1,311,900, annual insurance cost is estimated to be $19,679 annually. Insurance on buildings can range from $2.50 - $3.00 per $100 of building cost. The average of $2.75 will be used for this study; therefore, insurance for the $150,000 building is estimated to be $4,125 annually. Total insurance is $19,679 + $4,125 = $23,804.

In addition, money must be set aside for items that will be needed during the year, such as parts, computer equipment, contingency, office supplies, etc. This study assumes $10,000 for parts, $6,000 for supplies, and $15,000 for contingency.

Water is used to cool the condenser; most of the water is recirculated and what is not is dissipated by the cooling tower. A water-cooled, direct combustion facility uses an average of 490 to 550 GPM (gallons/minute); however, most of it is recirculated (6). From conversations with developers of similar projects, it is estimated that a likely amount of consumption is approximately 164,000 gallons/month. Based upon water rates obtained for the city of Belington, it is anticipated that cost of water will be approximately $168.05/month, or $2,017 annually.

A standby charge will need to be paid to the electric utility to remain connected with them; this charge is estimated to be $28,000 annually.

For wood combustion plants, chemicals are required to treat water that is used to transport boiler ash. Dry wood ash is not toxic, but the solution of ash when combined with water is corrosive (2). Although this wastewater may be discharged directly into the sewer system, the water is sometimes pretreated prior to discharge. The cost, which is estimated from a similar project, is approximately $14,600.

Ash left over after combustion could be given away or hauled to a landfill (ash is considered valuable, especially by gardeners). It is estimated that for a plant this size, about 3 tons of ash will be produced/week. With a tipping fee of approximately $20/ton, about $3,120 will be spent on ash disposal annually (3 tons/week x $20/ton x 52 weeks/year).

Capital and operating cost differences between alternatives 1a-1d are shown in Table 6. For alternative 1B which include the radiofrequency kilns, turbine size increased to 1,200 kW ($425,000) and boiler size increased to 900 BHP ($630,000). The increase in equipment costs consequently increased construction cost to $605,228, as this cost is calculated as a percentage of equipment cost. Therefore, total capital cost increased to $3,268,028.

Annual operating costs that are tied in to capital costs, such as maintenance and insurance, increased. Maintenance for the first five years was $72,810 and $109,215 thereafter. Insurance increased to $25,968. Savings increased from $102,292 to $201,004 as the radiofrequency kilns consume a great deal of electricity (nearly double of the rest of the park). There was still ample fuel available from the companies within and surrounding the park for a plant of this size.

Table 6. Comparison of key costs for alternatives 1A-1D.

| | T/G | Construction | Total | ---Maintenance----- | | | |
| | | | | First 5 yrs | After 5 yrs | Total First 5 yrs | Total > 5 yrs |
|---|---|---|---|---|---|---|---|
| 1A | $325,000 | $542,828 | $2,965,628 | $65,595 | $ 98,393 | $288,513 | $321,311 |
| 1B | 425,000 | 605,228 | 3,268,028 | 72,810 | 109,215 | 297,893 | 334,298 |
| 1C | 32,500 | 466,778 | 2,597,028 | 76,370 | 112,930 | 296,183 | 332,743 |
| 1D | 42,500 | 505,778 | 2,786,078 | 86,900 | 128,225 | 307,923 | 349,248 |

Alternative 1C takes into account a used turbine/generator. A used turbine may be purchased for 10% of original cost; other equipment is often custom-made and rarely purchased used (17). Cost of the turbine/generator was $32,500.

This decrease in capital cost decreased construction cost to $466,778; this is a consequence of using percentages to calculate construction cost. Total capital cost was then $2,597,028.

Annual maintenance cost for used equipment is difficult to predict (17), but was calculated to be 7.5% for the first five years (of the cost of new equipment), and 10% thereafter ($76,370 and $112,930). Insurance costs decreased to $20,669.

For alternative 1D, Cost of used turbine/generator was estimated at $42,500. This subsequently decreased construction cost to $505,778, and total capital cost was estimated at $2,786,078. Maintenance for the first five years was $86,900, and $128,225 thereafter. Insurance was estimated to be $21,908.

Alternative 2. Plant Sized to Take Residue Within 25-and 50-Mile Radius. The radiofrequency kilns are excluded for all options. The options explored within this alternative are: 1) Servicing companies within park, new equipment, savings and revenue; 2) Servicing companies within park, used equipment, savings and revenue; 3) Selling all power, new equipment; and 4) Selling all power, used equipment. For these four alternatives, analysis was performed for both 25-mile versus 50-mile radius. Alternative 2A(25-mi), which includes servicing companies within the park, selling excess to the utility, new equipment, and within a 25-mile radius is the alternative featured for discussion; changes made to alternatives B-D are discussed in the section Alternatives 2B-2D, which follows.

While alternative 1 based system size upon energy demand, alternative 2 based system size on amount of waste wood available. Only sawdust was considered from companies outside Belington, as this waste has the least value and could be made available at a cost less than what might be paid for bark or chips. The amount of waste available for fuel was determined by adding the amount of waste that might be hauled to Belington (from within a 25- and 50-mile radius) to the 120 tons/day already produced there.

The amount of waste available was calculated from Table 3. Approximately 190 tons/day of sawdust is generated from within a 25-mile radius of Belington. An additional 287 tons/day is generated from between 25- and 50-miles. Assuming that only 80% of this sawdust could be made available to the plant, an additional 152 tons/day (190 x 0.80) and 230 tons/day (287 x 0.80) are considered. Therefore, adding in the 120 tons/day from the Belington area, 272 tons/day (120 + 152) is available from within 25-miles, and 502 tons (120 + 152 + 230) is available from within 50-miles.

Boiler size based upon 272 tons/day was determined to be:
272 tons/day x 5 days/week = 1,360 tons/week
1,360 tons/week / 7 days/week = 194.3 tons/day
194.3 tons/day x 2,000 lbs./ton = 388,600 lbs./day
388,600 lbs./day / 24 hrs./day = 16,192 lbs./hr.
16,192 lbs./hr. x 2.5 lbs. of steam/lb. of wood = 40,480 lbs. of steam
40,480 lbs. of steam / 34.5 = 1173 BHP

The single-stage condensing turbine/generator to fit this is 2.322 MW

The plant for alternative 2 was configured identically to alternative 1, except for the addition of fuel cost. Fuel storage and handling, boiler, steam turbine/generator, cooling tower, and cyclone collector increased in size, therefore cost increased. Piping to both dry kilns remained the same distance.

It is estimated that a larger building will be needed, including the possibility of excess excavation, since the potential site for the plant is on hilly terrain.

Even though there is ample residue so that the users might possibly become self-sufficient from the electric utility, it is wise to remain connected to the utility, which would provide power during times of maintenance and outages at the cogeneration plant.

Interconnection costs include relays and circuit breakers for the connection, transformers to match incoming lines, and extension, if necessary, to connect the plant with the utility lines (6). To accurately determine the cost of connection, a site visit by the utility will be required since the cost depends on the proximity of the plant to the kV line that would support the expected amount of power from the plant. From conversations with the electric utility, it was estimated that a system of this size would require either a 138 kV line, or only a 23 kV line (if the 23 kV line has the ability to handle the excess power) (5,2).

It is estimated that savings would incorporate both dry kiln companies, for a total of $148,077. Savings in electricity is $102,292. Revenue from the sale of electricity is calculated by determining annual production of electricity then subtracting from it the number of kWh used on-site. The total annual electric production of a 2.3 MW plant is 2,300 kW/h x 8,400 hrs./yr. = 19,320,000 kW/yr.

Two laborers (one operator and one wood handler) were added for alternative 2, bringing the total to 8. Cost of equipment less installation is $1,386,900. Therefore, during the first five years, maintenance cost will be approximately $69,345 and after the fifth year $104,018. Equipment and building insurance totalled to $25,891.

Cost of fuel that the plant will have to purchase within a 25-mile radius is designated as $7.00/ton. Therefore, annual cost of fuel is ($7.00 x 152 tons x 250 days) = $266,000.

Comparisons between alternative 2A(25-mi) and the rest of the alternatives associated with #2 are shown in Table 7. A larger plant (estimated 6 MW) could be constructed with the additional residue obtained from a radius of 50-miles. There were differences of capital and operating costs, and revenue between 2A(25-mi) and 2A(50-mi). The increase in plant size increased both capital and operating costs, but not proportionally. Increase in boiler and turbine/generator costs had the greatest effect on capital cost.

Operating cost items affected by the increase in capital cost were operation and maintenance ($153,595, $230,393) and insurance

($51,785). Cost of fuel increased to $668,500 ((152 tons + 230 tons) x $7.00/ton x 250 days/yr.).

Revenue increased to $725,312 from $259,112, as annual production of a 6 MW plant is 50,400,000 kWh/yr ((50,400,000 kWh - 2,045,834 kWh (RF kilns)) x $0.015). However, fuel requirements are not proportional to the size of the cogeneration plant and tend to decrease for larger-scale plants. A plant that uses 108,800 tons/yr. of wood residue can support a generator of 5 MW (2); at 125,500 tons/yr., this plant will be sized at approximately 6 MW.

For Alternatives 2B(25-mi and 50-mi), servicing companies inside park, used equipment, used equipment again reduced the cost of a turbine/generator from $1,700,000 to $170,000. This decreased project cost to $600,028 (25-mi) and $831,428 (50-mi). Total capital cost decreased to $3,367,828 and $4,511,728 for 25-mile and 50-mile, respectively. Total operating cost was $648,480 (25-mi) and $1,146,824 (50-mi); the increase from the 50-mile radius was due to the increase in cost of fuel.

Alternatives 2C(25-mi and 50-mi), selling power to the utility, new equipment, capital and operating costs correspond to 2A. Since there is no savings, all 50,400,000 kWh are sold to the utility, generating $756,000.

Alternatives 2D(25-mi and 50-mi), selling power to the utility, used equipment correspond to 2B except that all power is sold, generating $756,000.

Table 7. Comparison of key costs for alternatives 2A-2D.

| | T/G | Construction | Total | Maintenance First 5 yrs | After 5 yrs | Total First 5 yrs | Total > 5 yrs |
|---|---|---|---|---|---|---|---|
| 2A(25-mi) 2C(25-mi) | $ 750,000 | $ 775,528 | $4,218,328 | $ 94,095 | $141,143 | $ 631,905 | $ 678,952 |
| 2A(50-mi) 2C(50-mi) | 1,700,000 | 1,229,228 | 6,439,528 | 153,595 | 230,393 | 1,112,374 | 1,141,434 |
| 2B(25-mi) 2D(25-mi) | 75,000 | 600,028 | 3,367,828 | 118,095 | 173,393 | 648,480 | 703,377 |
| 2B(50-mi) 2D(50-mi) | 170,000 | 831,428 | 4,511,728 | 205,595 | 299,893 | 1,146,824 | 1,241,952 |

Alternative 3: Plant sized for one company: An alternative to a large-scale system servicing the companies in the park is a small-sized system to service either one company for both steam and electricity, or one company for electricity and run steam lines to a dry kiln. A plant that is downsized to meet the energy requirements of one user would lower the capital and operating costs (i.e., using labor already available), and avoid the problem of selling electricity back to the utility.

Based upon electricity and steam usage of the companies within the park, three likely alternatives were developed. Two are designed solely for the two dry kiln companies. However, since the system for Bel-Bar dry kiln company will generate more electricity than they require, a third alternative was developed. The variations are: 1) Bel-Bar using steam and electricity; 2) Abenaki using steam and electricity; and 3) RF kilns using electricity and selling steam to Bel-Bar.

Only alternative (a) will be discussed; the others will be discussed in terms of variations to alternative 3A.

A backpressure turbine/generator was considered for this alternative. Therefore, size of the system would depend upon the amount of steam Bel-Bar uses. From Table 2, it was estimated from monthly gas bills that Bel-Bar uses 5.8 mmBtu/hr. on the average. Therefore, 9,131 tons/yr. is required to supply this amount of steam to Bel-Bar, and 109 kW could be generated from a system this size.

5.8 mmBtu/hour / 970 Btu/lb. of steam = 5,979 lbs. of steam/hr.
5,979 lbs. / 2.75 lbs. steam / lb. of waste = 2,174 lbs. of waste/hr.

2,174 lbs/hr. x 8,400 hrs/yr. = 9,131 tons of waste required/yr.
5.8 mmBtu/hour / 33,475 Btu/BHP = 173 BHP
5,979 lbs. of steam/hr. / 55 turbine steaming rate = 109 kW/hr.

Capital costs for alternative 3a are shown in Table 8. Since Bel-Bar presently uses natural gas to heat their kilns and has no boiler on-site, a wood-fired boiler must be purchased ($170,000 includes installation). The cost of a fuel storage and handling system is estimated to be $40,000. The cost of a 110 kW turbine/generator is about $145,000 (includes installation). Additional amounts for piping are estimated to be $10,000.

Table 8. Capital cost estimates for alternative 3A.

| Equipment | Item | Total |
|---|---|---|
| Site prep & concrete | 7,500 | |
| Belt conveyer | 11,000 | |
| Hogger | 5,000 | |
| Installation | 16,500 | |
| Total Fuel Storage and Handling | | 40,000 |
| Boiler | 85,000 | |
| Metering bin, controls, valves, pumps | 5,000 | |
| Installation | 80,000 | |
| Total Boiler System | | 170,00 |
| Condensing Turbine/Generator | 50,000 | |
| Controls, relays, switchgear, piping, valves, pumps | 10,000 | |
| Installation | 85,000 | |
| Total Turbine/Generator | | 145,00 |
| Piping | | 10,000 |
| Building | | 23,750 |
| Permits | | 5,000 |
| TOTAL CAPITAL COST | | 393,75 |

An additional building might be constructed to house the boiler and turbine/generator. This study will assume an extra building constructed at a cost of $23,750. It is estimated that permitting and paperwork will total approximately $5,000. Therefore, total capital cost is estimated at $393,750.

Bel-Bar is able to save money on all their process steam, the savings will amount to $105,560 (52,780 MCF x $2.00/MCF). It is possible for Bel-Bar to save all of their electricity, as this system is able to produce 915,600 kW/yr (109 kW x 8,400 hrs/yr.). Since they only need 662,235 kWh/yr, they can save (662,235 kWh/yr.x $0.05/kW) $33,112 annually.

Operating costs were estimated using the same percentages as were used for the previous alternatives. Operation and maintenance cost is estimated at $19,438 for the first five years and $29,156 thereafter. Using the same percentages as before, insurance cost is calculated as $5,831. Parts are calculated at 0.01 of equipment cost or $3,888.

For this alternative, we are assuming that fuel is free (there is ample fuel from the industrial park area), and that no extra personnel for maintenance need to be hired.

Alternative 3B is similar to 3A; data for Abenaki was substituted and the system was downsized, accordingly. Total equipment cost decreased to $175,000, while the cost of building and permits remained the same. Therefore, total capital cost became $203,750. Savings of process steam was $54,600 and electricity $19,707, based upon a 65 kW turbine. Operation/maintenance was $8,750, insurance $2,625, and parts $1,750.

Alternative 3C included a boiler and turbine/generator in an existing building, and running steam lines to Bel-Bar Dry Kiln. The cost of the boiler and turbine/generator would be the same as that of 3A, $365,000. The cost of piping, while only $10,000 for 3A, is increased to $144,400 for this option (800 ft. x $143/ft.). Total capital cost was $484,400. Operation/maintenance is $23,470, insurance is $7,041 and parts/contingency is $4,694.

Send Request For Proposals to Potential Developers: The request for proposals (RFP) is a summary of this project along with information on all the data collected. This RFP was reviewed by Bill Willis and John F. Herholdt of the West Virginia Fuel and Energy Office; David Warner, West Virginia Economic Development Authority; Lynette Woda, WV Governor's Office of Community and Industrial Development; Dave Stephenson, SERBEP; and the tenants of the Belington Industrial Park. All comments received were incorporated into the document; the RFP was sent to 90 developers and owners/operators of biomass energy projects on April 6, 1992. The list of recipients was obtained from an industry directory (15) and from a list provided by SERBEP.

It was requested that responses must be postmarked by June 30, 1992. At that time, a task force will have been formed consisting of representatives from the Fuel and Energy Office, Appalachian Hardwood Center, Barbour County Development Authority, and the Belington Industrial Park who will review any responses received.

Economic Feasibility

Economic analysis incorporates the data collected on capital costs, operating costs, and savings and/or revenue, to produce a discounted cash flow for the 20-year estimated life of the project which is used to determine project feasibility.

Depreciation Methods: Biomass property which is also a qualifying small power production facility within the meaning of section 3(17)(c) of the Federal Power Act, is classified for depreciation purposes in Section 48(1)(15) of the Internal Revenue Code (12). Depreciation was taken on two classes of items: 1) equipment, and 2) business start-up costs. Depreciation was taken on the building as nonresidential real property.

Biomass equipment was depreciated using 5-year MACRS (modified accelerated cost recovery system) 200% declining balance with a half-year convention. The building is considered nonresidential real property and is depreciated over 31.5 years using a straight-line method.

Permitting and legal fees, along with project cost are considered business start-up expenses and can be amortized for not less than 60 months; an amortization period of 60 months was chosen for this project.

Cash flow was calculated by the following procedure:
1. Savings and/or Revenue - Operating Cost - Depreciation (Equipment + Building + Start-Up) - Loan Payment (Interest) = Earnings Before Income Taxes;
2. If there is a net operating loss (NOL), the loss may be carried back 3 years, or carried forward 15 years. NOL is subtracted from income before Federal taxes to determine taxable income for that year);
3. Earnings After NOL - State Income Tax = Earnings After State Tax;
4. Earnings After State Tax - Federal Income Tax = Earnings After Taxes;
5. Earnings After Taxes + Depreciation (Equipment + Building + Start-Up) + - Loan Payment (Principal) = Net Cash Flow;
6. Net Cash Flow x MARR = Present Value of Cash Flow;
7. Net present value calculated (next section).

A discounted cash flow technique is used to account for the annual inflows and outflows and takes into consideration the time value of money. The technique used for this analysis is the net present value method (discounted payback period). The formula for calculating net present value (NPV) of cash flow is:

Table 9. Cash flow projection for alternative 1A.

ALTERNATIVE 1A:
Exclude RF Kilns; New Equipment
MARR = 10%
20-Year Loan Interest Rate = 8%

| | Year: Initial | 1 | 2 | 3 | 4 | 5 | 6 | 7 | 8 | 9 | 10 |
|---|---|---|---|---|---|---|---|---|---|---|---|
| Project Cost: | | | | | | | | | | | |
| TOTAL Equipment | 2,087,800 | | | | | | | | | | |
| TOTAL Plant | 150,000 | | | | | | | | | | |
| TOTAL Start-up | 727,828 | | | | | | | | | | |
| TOTAL Capital Cost | 2,965,628 | | | | | | | | | | |
| | | | | | | | | | | | |
| Savings: | | | | | | | | | | | |
| Natural Gas for Process Steam | | 148,077 | 148,077 | 148,077 | 148,077 | 148,077 | 148,077 | 148,077 | 148,077 | 148,077 | 148,077 |
| Electricity | | 102,292 | 102,292 | 102,292 | 102,292 | 102,292 | 102,292 | 102,292 | 102,292 | 102,292 | 102,292 |
| TOTAL Savings | | 250,369 | 250,369 | 250,369 | 250,369 | 250,369 | 250,369 | 250,369 | 250,369 | 250,369 | 250,369 |
| Operating Cost: | | | | | | | | | | | |
| Fixed Costs: | | | | | | | | | | | |
| Labor | | | | | | | | | | | |
| Direct | | 107,712 | 107,712 | 107,712 | 107,712 | 107,712 | 107,712 | 107,712 | 107,712 | 107,712 | 107,712 |
| Indirect | | 12,666 | 12,666 | 12,666 | 12,666 | 12,666 | 12,666 | 12,666 | 12,666 | 12,666 | 12,666 |
| Operation & Maintenance | | 65,595 | 65,595 | 65,595 | 65,595 | 65,595 | 98,393 | 98,393 | 98,393 | 98,393 | 98,393 |
| Insurance | | 23,804 | 23,804 | 23,804 | 23,804 | 23,804 | 23,804 | 23,804 | 23,804 | 23,804 | 23,804 |
| Property Tax | | 0 | 0 | 0 | 0 | 0 | 0 | 0 | 0 | 0 | 0 |
| Parts | | 10,000 | 10,000 | 10,000 | 10,000 | 10,000 | 10,000 | 10,000 | 10,000 | 10,000 | 10,000 |
| Supplies | | 6,000 | 6,000 | 6,000 | 6,000 | 6,000 | 6,000 | 6,000 | 6,000 | 6,000 | 6,000 |
| Contingency | | 15,000 | 15,000 | 15,000 | 15,000 | 15,000 | 15,000 | 15,000 | 15,000 | 15,000 | 15,000 |
| TOTAL Fixed Costs | | 240,776 | 240,776 | 240,776 | 240,776 | 240,776 | 273,574 | 273,574 | 273,574 | 273,574 | 273,574 |
| Variable Costs: | | | | | | | | | | | |
| Water | | 2,017 | 2,017 | 2,017 | 2,017 | 2,017 | 2,017 | 2,017 | 2,017 | 2,017 | 2,017 |
| Electricity | | 28,000 | 28,000 | 28,000 | 28,000 | 28,000 | 28,000 | 28,000 | 28,000 | 28,000 | 28,000 |
| Chemicals for Water Treatment | | 14,600 | 14,600 | 14,600 | 14,600 | 14,600 | 14,600 | 14,600 | 14,600 | 14,600 | 14,600 |
| Ash Disposal | | 3,120 | 3,120 | 3,120 | 3,120 | 3,120 | 3,120 | 3,120 | 3,120 | 3,120 | 3,120 |
| TOTAL Variable Costs | | 47,737 | 47,737 | 47,737 | 47,737 | 47,737 | 47,737 | 47,737 | 47,737 | 47,737 | 47,737 |
| TOTAL Operating Costs (Fixed & Variable) | | 288,513 | 288,513 | 288,513 | 288,513 | 288,513 | 321,311 | 321,311 | 321,311 | 321,311 | 321,311 |
| (Net Savings + Revenue)-Operating Cost | | (38,145) | (38,145) | (38,145) | (38,145) | (38,145) | (70,942) | (70,942) | (70,942) | (70,942) | (70,942) |
| (Depreciation Equipment) | | (417,560) | (668,096) | (400,858) | (240,515) | (240,515) | (120,257) | | | | |
| (Depreciation Building) | | (4,762) | (4,762) | (4,762) | (4,762) | (4,762) | (4,762) | (4,762) | (4,762) | (4,762) | (4,762) |
| (Depreciation Start-up) | | (145,566) | (145,566) | (145,566) | (145,566) | (145,566) | | | | | |
| (Loan Payment - Interest) | | (236,753) | (232,066) | (226,468) | (220,419) | (213,889) | (206,835) | (199,218) | (190,991) | (182,105) | (172,510) |
| Earnings before Income Taxes | | (842,785) | (1,088,635) | (815,797) | (649,406) | (642,876) | (402,797) | (274,922) | (266,695) | (257,810) | (248,214) |
| If (Net Operating Loss) | | | | | | | | | | | |
| Earnings after NOL | | 0 | 0 | 0 | 0 | 0 | 0 | 0 | 0 | 0 | 0 |
| (Less State Income Taxes) | | 0 | 0 | 0 | 0 | 0 | 0 | 0 | 0 | 0 | 0 |
| Earnings before Federal Taxes | | 0 | 0 | 0 | 0 | 0 | 0 | 0 | 0 | 0 | 0 |
| (Less Federal Income Taxes) | | 0 | 0 | 0 | 0 | 0 | 0 | 0 | 0 | 0 | 0 |
| Earnings after Taxes | | (842,785) | (1,088,635) | (815,797) | (649,406) | (642,876) | (402,797) | (274,922) | (266,695) | (257,810) | (248,214) |
| (Depreciation Equipment) | | 417,560 | 668,096 | 400,858 | 240,515 | 240,515 | 120,257 | | | | |
| (Depreciation Building) | | 4,762 | 4,762 | 4,762 | 4,762 | 4,762 | 4,762 | 4,762 | 4,762 | 4,762 | 4,762 |
| (Depreciation Start-up) | | 145,566 | 145,566 | 145,566 | 145,566 | 145,566 | | | | | |
| Loan Payment - Principal | | (64,805) | (69,990) | (75,589) | (81,636) | (88,167) | (95,220) | (102,838) | (111,065) | (119,950) | (129,547) |
| Net Cash Flow | | (339,703) | (340,201) | (340,202) | (340,201) | (340,202) | (372,998) | (372,998) | (372,998) | (372,998) | (372,999) |
| PVIF @ 10% | | 0.909 | 0.826 | 0.751 | 0.683 | 0.621 | 0.564 | 0.513 | 0.467 | 0.424 | 0.386 |
| Present Value of Cash Flow | | (308,821) | (281,158) | (255,598) | (232,362) | (211,238) | (210,548) | (191,407) | (174,006) | (158,188) | (143,807) |
| Net Present Value | (3,050,773) | | | | | | | | | | |

$$NPV = \sum_{t=1}^{N} \frac{Y_t}{(1+i)^t} - CI$$

where:

t = the year under consideration (1,2,...10);
$Y_t$ = the net cash flow for year t (outflow - inflow);
i = the minimum acceptable rate of return (MARR);
N = the life of the project;
CI = total capital investment.

This method finds the present value of the expected net cash flows of an investment, discounted at the cost of capital, and subtracts from it the initial cost outlay of the project. If the net present value is positive, the project is acceptable, if negative, the project should be rejected (34). The cost of capital is the minimum acceptable rate of return (MARR) the investor will accept.

Comparison of Alternatives: Table 9 shows 10 years of the 20-year cash flow projection for Alternative 1A at MARR of 10%; this table also contains breakdowns of operating costs; other tables are not shown. Projections were performed for each alternative for 8%, 10%, and 12% MARR.

Cash flow was used as a basis to determine NPV. The NPV derived is used exclusively in this report as the basis for discussion and as an indicator of feasibility.

Alternative 1: Table 10 shows the NPV of alternatives 1A-1D; numbers in () indicate a negative NPV. It can be seen that all NPVs are negative, evidence that this alternative is not a viable one. Alternative 1D which incorporates savings of RF kilns and has an NPV of ($1,939,658) @ 12% MARR, is the best of the group.

Using this analysis as a starting point, an effort was made to achieve feasibility, using alternative 1D as a basis. Feasibility could be obtained by either increasing savings or decreasing cost. Since savings could not be increased, capital and maintenance costs were decreased. Capital costs and maintenance costs were decreased to $1.5 Million and $150,000, respectively. Feasibility using our criteria still could not be obtained as the NPV was ($37,790).

Table 10. NPV for variations of alternative 1.

| | MARR | | |
|---|---|---|---|
| Alternative: | 8% | 10% | 12% |
| 1A: Excluding RF kilns, new equipment | ($3,530,752) | ($3,050,773) | ($2,667,425) |
| 1B: Including RF kilns, new equipment | ($2,965,214) | ($2,561,139) | ($2,238,245) |
| 1C: Excluding RF kilns, used equipment | ($3,259,481) | ($2,814,317) | ($2,458,925) |
| 1D: Including RF kilns, used equipment | ($2,562,436) | ($2,216,738) | ($1,939,658) |

The conclusion reached for this alternative is that, it is not only unlikely that a cogeneration system could service all the companies within this park, but, even if they could be serviced, it would not be feasible to do so; it is impossible to rely only on savings for such a large-scale project.

Alternative 2 considered a larger-scale system. The same type of economic analysis that was performed for alternative 1 was also performed for this alternative, but in addition, avoided cost rate was increased to determine what rate would be needed to achieve feasibility. Costs were not decreased in this analysis. Tables 19-20 show the NPV at avoided cost rate of $0.015/kWh and the avoided cost rate required to achieve feasibility.

All initial NPV values are negative, again indicating an unfeasible alternative. From Table 11, it can be seen that the increase in avoided cost rates required for feasibility range from $0.1115 to $0.1524, clearly unobtainable. However, as can be seen from Table 20, avoided cost rates required for feasibility decreased, as economies of scale at this size (approximately 6 MW) are approached. Avoided cost rates range from $0.0637 to $0.0888 at this size, possibly obtained through wheeling power.

Table 11. Alternative 2 (25-mile radius): NPV at avoided cost rate $0.015/kWh, avoided cost rate required for feasibility.

| ALTERNATIVES | Minimum Acceptable Rate of Return | | |
| --- | --- | --- | --- |
| | 8% | 10% | 12% |
| 2A: Companies in park, new equip., savings & revenue. | ($5,693,739) $0.1415 | ($4,921,648) $0.1470 | ($4,304,857) $0.1524 |
| 2B: Companies in park, used equip., savings & revenue. | ($5,054,163) $0.1185 | ($4,364,360) $0.1227 | ($3,813,629) $0.1276 |
| 2C: Sell all power to utility, new equipment. | ($6,396,759) $0.1319 | ($5,531,255) $0.1367 | ($4,839,701) $0.1417 |
| 2D: Sell all power to utility, used equipment. | ($5,757,183) $0.1115 | ($4,973,966) $0.1153 | ($4,348,472) $0.1190 |

Table 12. Alternative 2 (50-mile radius): NPV at avoided cost rate $0.015/kWh, avoided cost rate required for feasibility.

| ALTERNATIVES | Minimum Acceptable Rate of Return | | |
| --- | --- | --- | --- |
| | 8% | 10% | 12% |
| 2A: Companies in park, new equip., savings & revenue. | ($8,228,003) $0.0828 | ($7,109,356) $0.0857 | ($6,215,927) $0.0888 |
| 2B: Companies in park, used equip., savings & revenue. | ($5,771,499) $0.0643 | ($4,973,543) $0.0662 | ($4,337,205) $0.0683 |
| 2C: Sell all power to utility, new equipment. | ($8,931,024) $0.0815 | ($7,718,963) $0.0843 | ($6,750,771) $0.0872 |
| 2D: Sell all power to utility, used equipment. | ($7,443,695) $0.0637 | ($6,423,547) $0.0656 | ($5,609,378) $0.0677 |

Economies of scale at wood-fired plants are best maximized at 15 MW, 150,000 lbs./hr. steaming capacity. A 10 MW plant would require 184,000 tons/yr. of fuel (14). A 15.5 MW plant in Bridgewater, NH consumes 258,420 tons of waste/yr.(11). For this alternative, it may be possible to utilize additional waste or decrease cost in order to better approach scale; it is predicted that scale might be achieved by taking in between 184,000 and 258,420 tons/yr. (this alternative considered 125,000 tons/yr.).

The conclusion reached for alternative 2 is that a larger-scale system is certainly more viable than a small-scale system designed to meet the energy requirements of the park. However, while economies of scale are best met at larger systems, avoided cost is also a major consideration. The alternative that incorporates residue obtainable from a 50-mile radius and incorporates used equipment is, again, the best of the group. However, even for this case, the avoided cost rate required for feasibility is greater than $0.06/kWh, clearly unobtainable. Therefore, this alternative, although promising, is not sufficient to achieve feasibility.

Alternative 3: Alternative 3, a smaller-scale system servicing one or two companies, is the most viable option. Table 21 shows NPV's and discounted payback periods for all alternatives.

Although NPV for each alternative is positive (indicative of a good investment) none of the alternatives achieved payback in four years. The best scenario, alternative 3, at 8% MARR, discounted payback period is estimated to be 14.16 years.

Table 13. Alternative 3: NPV and discounted payback periods (in years), MARR 8%, 10%, and 12%.

| Alternatives | MARR | | |
| --- | --- | --- | --- |
| | 8% | 10% | 12% |
| 1A: Bel-Bar Dry Kiln | $381,989 > 20 | $342,132 >> 20 | $309,104 >> 20 |
| 1B: Abenaki Dry Kiln | $223,077 14.16 | $199,342 > 20 | $181,825 > 20 |
| 1C: RF Kilns/Bel-Bar Dry Kiln | $336,554 >> 20 | $304,819 >> 20 | $279,242 >> 20 |

Although a positive NPV is important, it is also fundamental to have a reasonable payback period. Therefore this alternative could be considered most viable.

## SOCIAL/REGULATORY FEASIBILITY

### Social Feasibility

Social feasibility is becoming increasingly important in cogeneration projects. Social feasibility takes into consideration acceptance by various sectors of the community. A cogeneration plant burning wood waste would assuredly be welcome by the tenants of this park and the primary and secondary wood products companies in the surrounding area, because of the existing problems in disposing of wood residue and the possibility of savings of energy bills that the plant would provide.

However, the industrial park is located very close to a residential area and they are the ones who would have to live with emissions resulting from the plant. It is likely that a cogeneration plant that burns solely wood waste would be acceptable to not only the residents surrounding the park, but also those living in the nearby community. The additional truck traffic into the industrial park area might pose a problem, but it would not represent any new traffic patterns as many of the trucks that would dispose of their waste at the park already use Route 92 to the present disposal site in Parsons. However, one potential problem lies with the 6 MW plant; approximately 25 trucks/day are anticipated to enter the park. Some will go through Belington, others will come from the south. Some coordination must be involved that takes into account new patterns of truck traffic.

It is recommended to any developer of this project that the citizens of Belington and the surrounding area be kept informed of stages of the project through public meetings and in making available documents open and available to interested parties.

### Regulatory Feasibility

Environmental Regulations: A new cogeneration plant at this location would be governed by several types of environmental regulations, including air quality, water discharge, and emergency planning and community right-to-know. Some regulations are regulated at the federal level, while others are regulated at both the federal and state levels.

Air quality permits are issued by a state to enforce limitations of both Federal and state air quality emissions. The West Virginia Air Pollution Control Commission (WVAPCC) handles permits and monitoring.

Various agencies regulate the withdraw, allocation, and use of water. The requirements are determined by whether the water will be pumped from groundwater, withdrawn from a natural body of water, or supplied by a municipal wastewater system (8).

West Virginia requires a National Pollution Discharge Elimination System (NPDES) permit. This is handled by the Water

Resources Section, Division of Natural Resources. A plant burning solely wood waste should have little problem obtaining an NPDES permit.

PURPA Regulations: From preliminary discussions with Monongahela Power Co., the local utility which is a subsidiary of Allegheny Power Systems (APS) of Greensburg, PA, it is expected that they are not interested in purchasing any power produced by a cogenerator. However, in preliminary talks with Virginia Electric Power Company (VEPCO) and Philippi Municipal Utility, located approximately 12 miles away from this location, they are both interested in purchasing power. An agreement to wheel power is a potential that needs to be examined more closely.

## LITERATURE CITED

1. Aton, Carol L., Lawrence P. Fisher, J. Craig Wyvill, and Jerry L. Birchfield. November 1979. Wood Energy Potential in West Virginia. Technology Applications Laboratory, Engineering Experiment Station, Georgia Institute of Technology, Project A-2297.

2. Binder, Regis, Monongahela Power Company., Greensburg, PA, personal conversation, Mar., 1990.

3. Davidson, J. Peale, Manager, Customer Service. Monongahela Power Co., Fairmont, WV, personal conversations, June, 1991 and Jan., 1992.

4. De Zeeuw, R.E., R.L. Gay, L.S. Craig. T.R. Miles, and J.N. Cole. August 1986. Permits/Regulations for Biomass Energy Facilities in the Southeast. Prepared for Southeastern Regional Biomass Energy Program under TVA Contract No. TV-67243A, 124 pp.

5. Energy User News. November 1991. Ranking of Gas Utility Prices by State: Industrial, Vol. 16, No. 11, p. 27.

6. Hassler, C.C., Sims, H.C., Bean, T.L., and Ponzurick, T.G.. November 1988. Evaluating a Wood Densification System for Producing Fuelwood Logs. Final Report, 54 pp.

7. Hassler, C.C. and Jones, K.D. 1986. Biomass Energy Systems: A Preliminary Investment Decision-Making Guide for the Small Business. Prepared for Southeastern Regional Biomass Energy Program under contract TV-72848A, 97 pp.

8. Hourigan, P.D. "Cogeneration and Independent Power Plants: The Role of Environmental Regulations" in World Cogeneration, Vol. 3, No. 2, pp. 6-7.

9. Independent Energy. December 1991. The 1992 Industry Directory, Section 2, Biomass Energy.

10. Kern, A.L., President. International Power Machinery Company, Cleveland, OH, personal conversation, November 1991.

11. McKinney, Mark, Director of Development, Harbert Cogen, personal correspondence, June 1990.

12. Oliker, I and Major, W. 1988. Developing Energy-Integrated Industrial Parks. Prepared by Burnes and Roe Company for Electric Power Research Institute, EM-5853, Research Project 1276-5, p. A-1.

13. Technology Applications Laboratory of the Georgia Institute of Technology. 1984. The Industrial Wood Energy Handbook. Van Nostrand Reinhold Company, 240 pp.

14. Vranizan, J.M., P. Neild, L.S. Craig, L.F. Brown, R.L. Gay, and R. DeZeeuw. 1987. Biomass Energy Project Development Guidebook. Prepared for the Pacific Northwest and Alaska Regional Biomass Energy Program. 289 pp.

15. Weston, J.F., and Brigham, E.F. 1977. Essentials of Managerial Finance, Fourth Edition. The Dryden Press, Hinsdale, IL, 617 pp.

# Chapter 41

# The Evolution of the Competitive Bidding Proces

W.J. Oliver, R.J. Dingle

## I. BACKGROUND TO COMPETITIVE BIDDING

### A. The Public Utility Regulatory Policy Act

From the 1920s to the early 1970s, the structure of the electric utility industry remained fairly constant. Up until this time, the generation, transportation and distribution of electricity was provided by local electric utility companies. The dominant pricing method was cost-of-service based rates, which relies on the premise that generation of electricity is not a competitive market, but a natural monopoly. This environment included close scrutiny by state and federal regulatory bodies to ensure that electric utility companies were making prudent management decisions.

This stable environment changed with the passage of the Public Utility Regulatory Policies Act (PURPA) in 1978. The primary intent of PURPA was to encourage the use of renewable energy sources, energy efficiency measures, and cogeneration and small power production. The act guaranteed firms and developers interconnection with the host utility company and administrated avoided costs for the basis of payment for sales of power by qualifying facilities to the host utility.

By the early 1980s, the primary change that PURPA brought to the structure of the electric utility industry was the introduction of the small power producer (SPP). Since then, however, the emergence of new suppliers has challenged the basic infrastructure of the electric generation industry. Along the way, the concept that electric generation is a natural monopoly has been called into question.

As the independent power market expanded, numerous problems arose primarily because of ambiguities in some parts of PURPA. The first problem to arise concerned the methodology which should be used by a utility company in calculating avoided costs. Since PURPA simply required utility companies to purchase power from cogenerators or small power producers at not more than their avoided costs, but offered no assistance in the development of these avoided costs, individual state regulators were left to deal with this issue. As a result, interpretation of this requirement differed from state to state.

The second problem that arose from the expansion of the independent power industry was that utility companies soon began to receive capacity bids for more capacity than they needed. This meant that any type of random awarding of contracts would allow the best option to be chosen only by chance; thus keeping the utility industry from realizing the full potential benefits of competitive forces resulting from the development of the independent power industry.

### B. Invitation for Competitive Bidding

As a result of the increased number of proposed projects relative to need, utilities and state commissions had to develop a method for selecting projects. The result has been the emergence of a competitive bidding process for the selection of projects.

The competitive bidding or competitive selection process had its roots in the standard offer contract process in California, but the first formal bidding systems originated in the Northeast, notably with the development of the competitive bidding process in Massachusetts in 1986.

Competitive bidding has provided numerous benefits to the electric utility industry. The first benefit is that it has provided utility companies, and ultimately electricity consumers, with alternative competitive sources of power generation. By allowing competitive bidding for resources, utility companies are provided with more options from a variety of suppliers, including utility companies and non-utility generation developers.

The second benefit of competitive bidding is the role this process has played in bringing market forces together to affect price. Whenever numerous suppliers are brought in from a single market, competition will allow the solicitor to choose from the best the market has to offer. This concept holds true for both price and non-price factors such as quality and dependability of service, technology type of generators, fuel types, location, etc. Under competitive bidding most contracts signed by utilities have been at prices below the utility's long run avoided cost.

Third, the bidding experiments have spawned the development of more mature, viable projects by shifting some of the risk from the consumer to the developer.

### C. Initial Bidding Experiments

During the mid-1980s, several states and utility companies began to consider and implement competitive bidding experiments to address the numerous problems which were being encountered throughout the industry. The first utility to implement a competitive bidding solicitation was Central Maine Power Company (CMP) in 1984. CMP's solicitation was issued as a response to avoided cost rates developed by the Maine Public Service Commission which were based on construction of a nuclear power plant.

By taking the initiative and issuing a power solicitation, CMP established a competitive framework for the evaluation of all producers, while developing a logical method for choosing an award group which would best serve the capacity needs of the company. This approach allowed CMP to pay market-based prices for its additional capacity instead of the inflated avoided cost rates developed by the Maine PSC.

On December 31, 1986, the Massachusetts Department of Public Utilities issued regulations which established rules for determining rates, terms, and conditions concerning the sale of electricity by qualifying facilities to electric utility companies. These rules were intended to implement the provisions of PURPA, Title II, Sections 201 and 210, and regulations issued by the FERC. The Massachusetts regulations resulted in one of the more detailed competitive bidding systems developed at that time.

The rules adopted in Massachusetts outlined the guidelines for developing and implementing a competitive bidding system and identified the evaluation methods and criteria to be included in an RFP. Boston Edison Company developed the initial RFP, a self-scoring system that awarded points to each project for price and non-price factors.

In the development of the regulations, Massachusetts Electric Company (MECO), an affiliate of New England Power Company (NEP), requested and received an exemption from the competitive bidding system so that the company could continue to contract with QFs through negotiation methods. MECO also proposed to conduct an experiment which would compare the bidding and negotiation processes. MECO submitted annual reports to the DPU outlining the state of the competitive power market in Massachusetts.

This request was granted by the Massachusetts Department of Public Utilities, and as a result the wholesale power company of Massachusetts Electric Company, New England Power Company, issued its own request for proposals (RFP) outside of the Massachusetts Department of Public Utilities jurisdiction in 1988.

New England Power sought to capture the advantages of the negotiation process by inserting enough judgement into the process so that the most flexible of options were chosen  The concept employed was based on the premise that the company had certain system needs that not every project could fulfill.  By using judgement in the scoring process, extraneous non-price attributes of each proposal were given careful consideration and weighting.  This represented a deviation from the rigid self-scoring system intended by regulations, and actually gave the utility a measure of judgement in the evaluation process.  This process, which has been referred to as competitive negotiations, has established a framework around which the IRM process is based.

## II. COMPARISON OF BIDDING PROCESSES

The sophistication of the bidding process has expanded rapidly from the early administered bids of Maine and Connecticut. These systems have ranged from self-scoring processes to integrated resource planning.

### A.  Self-Scoring Mechanisms

Self-scoring based RFPs represent the second stage of the RFP process after administered bids and have become relatively common in the electric utility industry.  In this type of process, the issuing utility company generally assigns weightings and point values to the crucial factors in project development, including price and non-price factors.  Once these values are determined, a scoring mechanism is developed and directions are supplied with each RFP.

The concept behind this process is for each sponsor to fill out the submission material, self-scoring their project in the process. This was initially developed to streamline the bidding process. But as the industry became more competitive with a greater number of large developers, more utility companies found themselves re-scoring inaccurate project bids, which actually increased the work of company personnel while delaying the selection process.

The Self-Scoring process is unique, not only in each state but usually within each RFP, due to the individual needs and objectives of each utility company.  Because of this, the scoring factors are not the same in each RFP.  There are, however, general aspects of project development which are covered in most processes such as price factors (overall bid price relative to avoided cost and degree of front-loading), project development factors, operational longevity indicators, and system operational attributes.

### B.  System Evaluation

Recently, utility companies have been integrating their resource planning activities much more closely with the RFPs they issue. This is evident through the types of evaluation methods employed by these companies on each proposal.  Since most utility companies use some type of detailed production costing method or software in their resource planning function to develop budgets, regulatory filings, etc., it is clearly appropriate to use these capabilities when evaluating potential new resource additions.

Subsequently, one of the most recent trends seen in the competitive bidding process is that of system evaluations.  This approach enables the utility company to evaluate exactly how the various operating and pricing characteristics of a generating facility will react within its specific power supply system.  While removing the assumptions concerning operating levels of each plant, this approach indicates to the company approximately what operating level can be expected from the facility within its power system.

An example of this type of analysis can be found in the recent Delmarva Power and Light Company (DPL) RFP.  The evaluation process used in the Delmarva RFP entails four stages; non-responsiveness test, price screen, non-price screen, and detailed evaluation.  The company screened all of the proposals to eliminate offers that had an evaluated cost greater than the evaluated cost of the proxy unit (gas-fired combined cycle project).  This process included the use of production cost models to evaluate each project's production cost impact to Delmarva.  Each successful project (priced lower than the proxy) was then scored on the basis of non-price factors.  DPL then subjected each remaining proposal to sensitivity analysis, evaluating each under differing fuel price assumptions, discount rates, etc.

### C.  Integrated Resource Management

The latest approach in the evolution process for competitive bidding is the concept of integrated resource management (IRM), which can include an all-source bidding process.  This approach has been embraced by several state regulatory agencies.  The concept behind this approach is to manage the entire resource planning function in a succinct and efficient manner, while ensuring that enough judgement is included in the process so that obvious positive and negative project attributes are considered.  These processes have also included environmental externalities as part of the evaluation process.

The general resource planning incorporated in the IRM process includes the following steps:  (1) determining the amount and time of need for additional resources; (2) the issuance of an RFP soliciting proposals to fulfill the estimated power needs; (3) design of the evaluation process to be applied to these proposals; (4) the development of an updated resource plan with the selected project(s); (5) the negotiation and signing of contracts with the winners of the RFP.  As with other processes, specifics may be slightly different but the issues addressed and the concept are the same from state to state.

For the supply-side resources, this process is intended to have all types of options compete against each other to determine the best mix of options for the utility system.  These options include Qualifying Facilities (QFs) as outlined by PURPA, utility-built resources, and non-utility owned generation such as Independent Power Producers (IPPs).  Also to be considered are all types of Demand-Side Management (DSM) and conservation programs.

The objective of this concept is to provide utility companies with all possible options, supply and demand, to meet their capacity and energy needs at the lowest possible cost and in a reliable manner.  Since this is the latest evolutionary stage in the competitive bidding process, it is seen as the ultimate in resource planning strategies.  This process moves the utility industry closer to a competitive marketplace at the generation level.

## III. TRENDS IN BIDDING

A number of trends in bidding have been emerging since the advent of competitive bidding in the mid-1980s. Several of these trends are likely to continue into the future and have important implications on the structure of bidding systems. They include the following:

### A. Balance Between Price and Non-Price Factors

The early bidding systems placed a disproportionate emphasis on the price bid with little emphasis on non-price factors. As a result, many of the projects which received power contracts were immature projects that proposed a certain price but were not certain if the price bid could be justified. Under this scheme, project developers secured the power contract early in the development process, then had to combine all the pieces for a successful project to fit into the power contract. Many of these ultimately failed, with the causes of failure ranging from siting and permitting problems to fuel supply and financing.

As an example, in the first Boston Edison RFP (issued in January 1987) approximately 90% of the points awarded were on the basis of price (price relative to avoided cost, break-even factor and price risk factor). In the second Boston Edison RFP (April 1989), approximately 50% of the points were awarded on the basis of price and 50% on the basis on non-price factors.

Currently, bidding systems have evolved to a more equitable balance between price and non-price factors. In recent solicitations, a breakdown of points on the basis of 60% price and 40% non-price appears to represent the current balance. Utilities now recognize that low prices do not guarantee successful projects. Utilities, counting on projects they have contracted with to provide capacity and energy during the time frame proposed, recognize that project failures could place them in a precarious position from a capacity standpoint. Because of this, utilities are placing a greater premium on such non-price factors as project maturity, project viability, site issues, technology, environmental permitting status, fuel supply status and financial viability.

### B. The Decreasing Reliance on Avoided Cost as the Basis of Project Pricing

One of the major implications of the competitive bidding process has been the decreasing reliance on avoided costs in establishing market prices. In most of the bidding processes which have occurred, avoided costs only serve as a cap on price and as a guide to determining the level of front-end loading. Instead, successful projects in these RFPs have generally bid prices substantially below avoided costs resulting in a market price based more on market forces, rather than on established avoided cost rates.

The role of avoided costs in utility solicitations is being eroded further as avoided costs are now replaced by a proxy unit, or are not even published or considered in the evaluation. For example, in the recent Delmarva RFP, the costs of building a proxy unit served as the basis for price comparisons. If a project had a lower price (defined by its impact on Delmarva's system costs) than the proxy unit, that project would pass to the next stage of evaluation. If no project bid a price lower than the proxy unit, Delmarva would move forward with its plans to build the proxy unit.

In the recent New England Power (NEP) RFP released in April 1992, there are no targets established for comparison. Instead, NEP will evaluate projects on a relative basis based on the impacts of each project on total system costs.

### C. More Comprehensive Threshold Requirements

The initial threshold criteria that a project must meet to be considered in the RFP process are becoming stricter. Projects generally must own or have leased a site, and must identify all necessary permits, have a letter of intent for fuel supply, have developed a critical path for the project, identified the equipment of choice and have negotiated a letter of intent with a steam host, if a QF. Again, the intent of requiring stricter threshold requirements is designed to identify "real" projects and ensure that project developers have at least initiated the development process.

### D. More Sophisticated and Comprehensive Scoring Systems

The evolution of competitive bidding scoring systems from self-scoring to an integrated system approach reflects a considerable improvement in the project evaluation process and overcomes many of the problems associated with the rigid self-scoring systems.

One of the obvious benefits of the integrated system approach is that the utility can evaluate the impact of each project bid on its total system costs. Since decisions to purchase capacity and energy from outside sources represent billion dollar decisions over a 20-30 year period, it is in the best interest of the utility to ensure that the project selected will provide the greatest benefits to utility ratepayers. The recent Delmarva Power and Light RFP offers an example of such a system. Delmarva received 27 bids for power supplies and conducted a detailed production cost analysis of each project to determine the impact on system costs resulting from the integration of each project into the utility's generation plan. Delmarva's approach not only allowed for a detailed system analysis but also provided the ability to compare projects of different contract lengths (20 or 30 years) and type (baseload, intermediate and peaking) of project. Since the project developer cannot determine with accuracy its price score because the ultimate ranking of the project will depend on its impact on system cost and its ranking relative to other projects, gamesmanship of the pricing system is not possible.

Self-scoring and less sophisticated bidding systems, on the other hand, contain a number of flaws which inhibit effective project evaluation:

1. The ranking of projects under these systems is generally based on a busbar cost analysis, with no consideration of the impact on utility system cost. This could result in the selection of projects which do not produce the lowest system cost.

2. The ability of a project developer to game the process is enhanced under a self-scoring system since a sophisticated developer can estimate the score of competitors and propose options to maximize its score.

3. The self-scoring system can lead to disputes between project developers and utilities over the awarding of price and non-price points since it is incumbent on the utility to disprove the contentions of the developer.

4. Self-scoring systems are not well conditioned to compare projects of different lengths or type of capacity, or capacity factor. Generally, project evaluation horizons under a self-scoring system have been 20 years, which favors combined cycle units at the expense of coal or other higher capital cost options which are best evaluated over 30 years. Additionally, these systems specify a capacity factor at which projects will be evaluated.

### E. Preference For Dispatchability

The issue of dispatchability has become very popular in recent competitive bidding processes. In order to serve the load shape of a utility company most effectively and minimize cost, the resources within its system must be able to ramp up and down, or dispatch, on a real-time basis. When the cost of energy generated by the project is greater than the utility system marginal cost, the utility would prefer to dispatch the project off-line and purchase lower cost power to minimize total production costs. This allows the utility to reduce the cost to its customers. Because a large number of QF projects that were contracted under PURPA are must-run plants, and these plants produced high-cost power whether the utility needed the power or not, dispatchability has become one of the most important non-price features currently sought by utility companies.

The recent BECO RFP #3 assigned 20 points, or 5.5% of the scoring to dispatchability. This made up one-half of the total System Optimization Score. Another example of the increased importance placed on this facility attribute can be seen in the Virginia Power Company (VEPCO) RFP. VEPCO placed such a high importance on dispatchability that it reserved the right to reject any proposal that was not at least partially dispatchable.

F. Inclusion of Environmental Costs

One of the recent trends in the RFP process has been the inclusion of environmental costs (environmental externalities) in the scoring process. While several RFPs have included the implications of project environmental impacts in the non-price evaluation, recent solicitations have attempted to include externalities in the price component. Interestingly, the process of calculating environmental costs or externalities for different emission sources has produced drastically different values between states as well as heated debate among utilities, project developers, environmental and conservation groups, and state agencies within the same state. Internalizing the value of environmental externalities for inclusion in the RFP system is a process which is continuing to expand and will continue to be included in evaluation systems.

## IV. INDUSTRY TRENDS AFFECTED BY BIDDING

The advent of competitive bidding has spawned a number of new market participants, including large and well-financed independent development firms, utility subsidiaries, subsidiaries of equipment manufacturers, and large construction companies. In essence, these developers which have supplemented or replaced utilities as the builders of power generation projects resemble utilities themselves. Five trends have emerged from the competitive bidding process:

1. Increased level of competition

   The first and most important trend which has emerged from the competitive bidding process is an enhanced level of competition. A general rule of thumb is that at least a 10:1 ratio exists in each solicitation. That is, for every 1MW of power required, at least 10MW is proposed. In keeping with the large number of project sponsors who actively compete to supply power there has been an attendant reduction in price. In recent years, the electric power industry can again be characterized as a declining cost industry. This has been due to lower fuel costs and lower equity returns accepted by project sponsors who have realized that to be competitive requires lower prices.

2. Larger projects are being proposed

   The competition which has been created in the electric generation industry has led developers to propose larger scale projects to take advantage of economies of scale and be more competitive in RFPs. While these are not the same 400 - 1000MW projects built in the 1970s, 240MW combined cycle units are not unusual. Although projects of this size can generate power at lower per unit costs, a problem that remains is the fact that capacity and energy will generally have to be sold to more than one utility. Project sponsors are continually assessing the tradeoffs between project size and the related economies of scale

benefits and the size of the market into which the capacity is to be sold.

3. Projects have become more mature prior to securing a power contract

   Under the competitive bidding process, the critical path of a project has been revamped. Prior to competitive bidding, project sponsors secured the power contract first and then proceeded to develop the project within the power contract. Under competitive bidding and the premium placed on non-price criteria such as project viability and environmental permitting status, more and more developers recognize that to maximize the project score requires that the project be fairly far along the critical path. As a result, projects are now securing permits and negotiating firm fuel supply arrangements prior to securing the power contracts. This trend can be expected to lead to the selection of more mature projects and a greater probability of project success.

4. Larger development budgets are being required

   Consistent with the third trend noted above is the requirement to maintain a large development budget prior to securing the power contract. It is not unusual for projects today to spend $4-5 million on project development before they even secure a power contract, if at all. This has resulted in three other important factors:

   • Only large-scale, well-financed developers are in a position to propose larger scale projects;

   • Since development costs are not linearly related to the size of the project, larger scale projects are being proposed to spread the development costs over more capacity; and

   • These larger scale project developers are spending a considerable amount of money on developing the project bid and have become sophisticated in understanding the utility systems into which they are bidding.

5. Electric generating technology is improving rapidly

   One of the major implications of the competitive bidding process is the dramatic improvement in electric generating technologies driven by competitive forces. Equipment manufacturers have greatly improved unit heat rates while actually lowering project capital costs. These companies recognize that a breakthrough in technology that allows a developer to gain a competitive advantage in the RFP process will place that vendor in a favorable situation. It can be expected that new generations of equipment will be superior to previous generations and that technology improvements will continue in such a competitive environment.

## V. THE FUTURE OF COMPETITIVE BIDDING

There appears to be little doubt that competitive bidding as a means of procuring power supplies will expand into more states and utilities in the future and will become more sophisticated. While bidding is likely to expand, questions remain as to the form in which bidding systems will take, the issues to be addressed in developing bidding systems, and the components of individual systems. The following represents the thoughts of the authors regarding these issues:

1. The integrated system approach to project evaluation, similar to the approach undertaken by Delmarva Power, will likely be the standard for bidding systems, replacing self-scoring systems. These systems allow for a comprehensive evaluation of each project or a

combination of projects on a consistent basis to minimize total system costs. With billion dollar decisions on the line, cursory evaluations cannot guarantee the best results.

2. Bidding systems have to come to grips with the evaluation of all sources of capacity, including both demand and supply side resources. The current issues surrounding the integration of demand- and supply-side resources will need to be resolved to completely capture the benefits of the integrated resource planning concept.

   The initial problem with this process is the question of how to completely equate the demand- and supply-side options. Since they are fundamentally different types of resource options, the same evaluation process which has been used for supply-side alternatives needs to be changed so that demand-side options are evaluated on an equal basis. There have been several concepts developed, but none to date has completely eliminated any bias in the evaluation process.

3. The evaluation of environmental costs and consequences will continue to be incorporated in bidding systems. While recent solicitations have incorporated environmental externality values in project pricing, several other issues need to be addressed. With the passage of the Clean Air Act and speculation over the value of emission allowances, bidding systems will need to incorporate these factors. One option, consistent with the integrated system evaluation approach in which the system is optimized to produce the lowest costs, is to calculate the environmental emission levels consistent with the system optimization. Utilities can then value the environmental costs/benefits associated with their evaluation of each project in a manner consistent with their production cost analysis.

4. Credit rating agencies have begun to raise concerns about the impacts of increased purchased power costs on the debt rating of the utility. These agencies are, in effect, treating purchased power obligations as long-term debt for rating purposes. Bidding systems in the future will have to address this concern particularly if the utility has the opportunity to build its own unit. At the same time, utilities will continue to be concerned about eroding rate base.

5. Public Utility Commissions should re-examine the traditional approach to rate base regulations in light of eroding rate base and concern over increased purchased power obligations. This could include allowing utilities to bid their own projects, participating as an equity participant in a project, or treating a portion of purchased power as rate base. In each of these cases, issues of self-dealing and fair and efficient evaluation of projects bid to a utility will become important components of the bidding system.

# Chapter 42
# Financing Power Facilities in the Competitive Bidding Environment

A.L. Hills

## INTRODUCTION

In 1988 the Federal Energy Regulatory Commission ("FERC") issued proposed rules as guidelines for the use of competitive bidding by state utility commissions to chose new power supplies. Since then, more than 20 states have implemented bidding programs to determine the price and sources of incremental generating capacity.

This presentation discusses the impact of the use of competitive bidding on how lenders and equity investors perceive the risks of project-supported financing arrangements and describes the actions that project developers have taken to adapt the project financing process to win bidding contests and as importantly, successfully obtain project financing in spite of the "credit crunch" market environment.

## FINANCIAL IMPACTS OF BIDDING

### 1. Increased "Up-Front" Financial Risks

The most immediate impact of formalized bidding programs has been to significantly increase the development risk capital that developers must expend on engineering and other costs related to analysis of bidding requests and preparation of bidding proposals. This greatly increased financial exposure has accelerated the consolidation of participants in the Independent Power Industry, forcing smaller, entrepreneurial developers to either affiliate with or sellout to "deep pocket" corporate developers and/or bring financial institutions and venture investment firms into co-development arrangements at the outset of specific bidding requests.

This trend has also been enhanced by the closing of the public debt and equity markets to development companies, unless they already have a significant portfolio of operating power facilities.

### 2. Earlier Involvement of Financing Sources

In the non-bidding environment of the 1980's, project developers attempted to negotiate power sales agreements with the goal of obtaining the highest possible power prices consistent with the ability to sell project output on a continuous or nearly continuous basis. In this environment, only a general outline of the probable financing terms and sources was necessary to determine the basic economic feasibilty of a proposed project.

However, in the highly competitive bidding environment, the ability to offer the lowest possible power rates has become the dominant criteria for selection of winning bidders. As a consequence, it is now extremely important for developers to work closely with their legal and financial advisors while preparing bid packages, to develop detailed ownership and financing plans for their projects. Only with such specific financial terms is it possible for a developer to bid the lowest possible power prices, with the minimum necessary "economic margin" for unforeseen costs, that are consistent with successfully financing the project if selected by the bidding utility.

In addition, certain competitive bidding programs have included various non-price "qualitative" factors to narrow the field of responsible bidders, including the extent to which the actual financing terms and sources for a project have been committed prior to the bid. Such non-price requirements have made it necessary for developers and their financial advisors to negotiate formal commitment letters with lenders and/or equity investors, conditioned upon the successful selection of the proposed project and completion of power sales and other project-related contracts with risk allocation provisions, as proposed in the bid submission.

## 3. Necessary Changes in Power Price Bids

In addition to having a more precise understanding of the financing terms and costs when preparing bids, it has also become necessary for project developers, utility purchasers, state commissions and financing sources to better understand the interrelationship between the operating mode desired by a competitively bid project and required changes in the traditional "avoided cost" pricing mechanisms.

The easily comparable "cents per kilowatt hour delivered" method of pricing can be incompatible with the requirements of "non-recourse" project financing, if the bid includes the possibility of significant dispatchability by the purchasing utility. In simple terms, as purchasing utilities show increased preference for bid power sources that mimic the operation of the utility's own resources, the resulting power pricing terms for bid contracts have had to more closely mirror traditional utility costing methods.

For example, a highly dispatachable private power project will not satisfy the credit criteria of project lenders or equity investors unless it can be clearly shown that all project-related fixed costs (including financing charges) will be recovered through "capacity charges", the payment of which are subject only to reasonable, agreed upon levels of operational availability. Likewise, the variable costs of project operations must be recoverable through an "energy charge" based upon actual power deliveries.

However, when individual projects bid greatly different pricing schemes based upon differing proposed operating modes, the objective comparison of these bids in both the near term and on a "life cycle" basis has become much more difficult. As a consequence, the possibility that protests or legal challenges to the results of bidding by unsuccessful developers is greatly increased.

## 4. Increased Financial Risk Perceptions

The single most important effect of the trend towards competitive bidding for power supplies has been to increase the perceived riskiness of lending to or investing in bid projects. In particular, the tendency of "all-out" bidding to reduce the economic and cash flow margins of projects have resulted in lower debt service coverage ratios and/or reduced percentages of debt leverage (75-85% versus 90% or more).

Similarly, equity investors may require increased levels of return to compensate for the increased amounts of risk capital during development of projects and also a higher level of equity investment in the construction phase of projects.

This potential conflict between the increased return desires of financing sources and the narrowed profit margins due to competitive bidding is the single greatest impediment to the long-run viability of bidding as the method of obtaining future power resources.

The potential damage to the Independent Power Industry of this financial conflict has been exacerbated by the "credit crunch shakeout" in the commercial banking and insurance lending industries over the past two years. During most of the 1980's, the financing of private power projects had benefited from an increasing number of financial institutions interested in this market.

However, increased concerns by these institutions over highly leveraged loans (so-called HLTs), increased bank capital requirements, bad loans to real estate and takeover transactions, losses in the Toyko Stock Market and the general effects of a worldwide recession have reduced the number of active players in the project finance arena from 50 to 60 in 1989 to approximately 15 to 20 today.

Along with this reduction in the number of active financing sources, the credit terms and costs of project financings have also increased to reflect the increased risk aversion of lenders and the reduced number of competitors for any particular financing.

## CONCLUSIONS

As a consequence of the factors described above, the long-term impact of competitive bidding for new power supplies may result in unrealistically predatory energy prices resulting in either: (1) increasing financial costs to actually develop and build economically viable power supplies; or (2) the failure of many winning bidders to actually carry through and deliver bid power sources at the expected costs and within the needed timeframes.

Additionally, the use of competitive bidding as the exclusive means for obtaining power contracts in many states, has accelerated the consolidation trend in the Independent Power Industry, thereby reducing the number of entrepreneurial, non-utility affiliated power project development companies.

At worst, if competitive bidding programs do not properly address the financing concerns discussed above, the ultimate result of bidding could be failure to actually obtain sufficient quantities of reliable power supplies. Such a result would likely hasten a return to the traditional, monopolistic regulated utility power generation and pricing methodologies.

# Chapter 43
# The Time Has Come for Retail Wheeling

D.O. Dahlen, S.K. Achinger

## I. INTRODUCTION

Retail wheeling, the transmission and distribution of electric power for end users, fosters competition and promotes the efficient use of resources. Access to electric-utility transmission and distribution systems would establish competitive electric markets by permitting retail customers to obtain the lowest cost for energy which would meet their specific needs. Among electric utilities and their customers, the idea of allowing market forces to attract supply and set prices is a current controversy. To counter the anticompetitive effects of recent mergers in the wholesale market, the Federal Energy Regulatory Commission (FERC) has mandated open transmission access for wholesale customers. However, the FERC denied access to retail customers and qualifying facilities (QF) in both its Northeast Utilities (FERC case No. EC-90-190) and PacifiCorp (U.S. Circuit Court of Appeals for D.C., 89-1333) decisions.

Retail wheeling will benefit both consumers and producers. The ability of large customers to purchase power from the lowest cost sources and have it transmitted to their facilities, will save American industrial and commercial customers at least $15 billion annually. The increased efficiency resulting from competition would also reduce residential electric bills.

Through retail wheeling, independent power producers can market their capacity to a greater customer base, and traditional utilities will benefit from access to other utilities' markets with the more efficient utilities prospering. Retail wheeling will, therefore, reward efficient utilities and encourage inefficient utilities to improve.

These benefits substantially outweigh the objections utility companies have raised. This paper demonstrates and quantifies the benefits of retail wheeling to both energy consumers and producers in the United States. This paper explores the history of electric utility regulation, describes the benefits of retail wheeling, and refutes the arguments against retail wheeling most frequently raised by utility companies. The discussion of regulation and the electric utility industry includes a model for the life cycle of a regulated industry, the origins of electric utility regulation, and a summary of current regulatory trends. The discussion then focuses on the benefits of retail wheeling, and addresses the technical, policy, and legal arguments most frequently made by those who oppose retail wheeling. The conclusion presents some alternatives to retail wheeling, such as public ownership of the transmission system.

## II. REGULATION AND THE ELECTRIC UTILITY INDUSTRY

William G. Shepard developed a model for the four-stage life cycle of a regulated industry in his 1985 work entitled, "Public Policies Toward Business." While these stages are not definitive, his approach provides insight into the electric utility industry.

Brief but fierce competition characterizes the first stage of development of a regulated industry in Shepard's model. As the industry grows and innovates, a few firms begin to dominate the market in stage two. After achieving some market domination, these companies may seek regulation to stabilize their companies and secure market control in return for a guaranteed rate of return on invested capital. Stage three is, therefore, characterized by market stability, product saturation, and increased regulation. Regulation is a comfortable and profitable environment. While natural monopoly conditions may have disappeared by stage four (if they ever existed), the regulated business is unlikely to seek a competitive environment and leave the regulated environment. Regulated businesses will face competition because market forces and the economic interests of customers and society will overcome the resistance of unwilling utilities.

While the existence of economies of scale is debatable in the early phases of industry development, according to Shepard any such savings disappear in stage three. This event permits the unbundling of services and the full-scale competition characteristic of stage four. For electric utility companies, this would mean separating generation, transmission, and distribution services. However, the benefits of competition will not be not realized under the current regulatory system unless legislators and regulators adopt policies which encourage competition.

Rate-regulated companies do not have the incentives to maintain efficient operations. Because government has granted the protection of a monopoly to the regulated business, they know that competition could reduce their profits, reduce their market shares, or drive them out of business. Therefore, some industry leaders wish to maintain the protection of regulation and no competition. This creates the potential for inefficient monopolists to obstruct competition by capturing the attention of legislators and regulators. Although most firms in the electric utility industry have not sought competition, a few companies have already allowed limited retail wheeling. The utility industry has reached the point in its development where it needs to accept the competition that unbundling and retail wheeling will create because society needs the benefits of competition.

"Not all natural monopolies have been regulated (e.g., computers, autos, and aluminum), and not all regulated industries have been natural monopolies (e.g., natural gas production)." (Bonbright, p. 557) Thus, utilities may not have been regulated simply because they were natural monopolies. In fact, the idea for industry regulation can be traced back to a speech given in 1898 by the president of the National Electric Light Associations (NELA), Samuel Insull. Insull reasoned that it would be easier for utility companies to find investors willing to accept risk if the companies had no competition. Initially, the NELA did not subscribe to Insull's idea, but as the number of municipal systems grew, the idea of regulation became more appealing. In the ten-year period between 1896 and 1906, the number of municipal utilities tripled, and as a result, the NELA adopted a position favoring state regulation of electric utilities. In 1907, three states created such regulatory bodies, and within nine years 33 states had utility commissions. The historical development of electric utility regulation supports the life cycle

analysis of Shepard because the industry sought regulation in exchange for monopoly power.

As the electric utility industry faces inevitable competition, retail wheeling has been the subject of litigation in several recent utility merger cases before the Federal Energy Regulatory Commission (FERC). The merger of Utah Power and PacifiCorp, as well as the merger of Northeast Utilities and the Public Service Company of New Hampshire, represent significant advances in the development of transmission access. In both cases, the FERC refused to require retail wheeling, but it mandated wholesale wheeling.

Prior to the proposed PacifiCorp merger case, both companies controlled extensive transmission networks throughout their service territories. Therefore, when the FERC considered these applications, "the Commission's primary concern was with the possible anticompetitive effect of the merger in the bulk energy sales and transmission markets." To alleviate this concern, the Commission conditioned PacifiCorp's merger on the company's provision of firm wholesale transmission services to any utility that requests such service. The order required PacifiCorp to establish cost-based rates for such services. However, the FERC specifically excluded QF's and end users from the mandated list of transmission customers. Since the initial decision, the U.S. Court of Appeals has required the FERC to justify its exclusion of QF's and end users. As a result, the Commission has ordered a hearing on retail wheeling to determine if it is necessary to alleviate the anticompetitive effects of the merger.

The second important case involved the merger of Northeast Utilities and the Public Service Company of New Hampshire. In an August 9, 1991 Order, the Commission approved this merger, but once again based its approval on assured transmission access for other utilities. Just as in the PacifiCorp case, the FERC refused to force these northeastern utilities to wheel power for retail consumers.

## III. BENEFITS OF RETAIL WHEELING

American industrial companies have realized that the long-term savings possible from retail wheeling and competitively-priced power are necessary for their long-term success in world markets. As their involvement in the recent FERC cases demonstrates, these companies are acutely aware of the benefits of retail wheeling which include: lower electricity rates, availability of more services, increased utility innovation, increased utility efficiency, conservation of capital, and conservation of natural resources.

Retail wheeling would create competition. To compete with other electricity providers, utilities would need to be more efficient. This increased efficiency would result in reduced energy rates-- the most direct benefit of retail wheeling.

## Lower Electricity Rates

Competitive power supply procurements have been conducted by Dahlen, Berg & Co. in wholesale markets in which rate-regulated utilities were the suppliers. Savings in these procurement efforts have ranged from 15% to more than 20%. With 1991 U.S. commercial and industrial electricity sales of approximately $104 billion, 15% savings would be approximately $15.6 billion while 20% savings would be $20.8 billion.

## Availability of More Services

Retail wheeling and the attendant unbundling of services would also permit customers to select the combinations of services which best fit their individual needs. Many in the utility industry falsely assume that all customers want the same quality of service. Some customers desire a lower quality of service at a reduced price. These customers do not currently have this option. The separation of generation, transmission, and distribution would be similar to the unbundlings that have taken place in the computer industry, the telecommunications industry, and the natural gas industry. Like customers for those services, electric utility customers would have more products and services from which to choose.

## Increased Utility Innovation

Without an increase in competition in the utility industry, utility innovation suffers. Unlike a competitive environment which encourages innovation to permit the survival of a company, the current system of rate regulation of bundled products discourages innovation because the regulated business is not permitted to fail or to earn a higher return based on its innovation. A competitive market would reward innovation with survival and higher profits.

Innovation is not, however, the implementation of demand-side management or least-cost planning which are initiatives of regulators across the U.S. These initiatives would be better-characterized as "copying" by the utility rather than "innovation." Utilities should not be allowed higher returns for copying.

The external threat of losing sales makes companies in other industries innovative. The threat of losing sales to other utilities or to independent power producers would similarly make the U.S. electric utility industry innovative. Our society and economy need the innovation and cost reduction that is possible by the development of competition in the electric utility industry.

Under the current regulatory system, utilities are rewarded for their abilities to influence regulatory agencies which causes them to expend resources filing rate cases and persuading legislators and regulators. In a competitive environment, electric utilities would be rewarded for innovation rather than for well-developed political skills. If the average rate case costs $1 million and 75 are filed annually, another $75 million would be saved in a competitive market.

## Increased Utility Efficiency

Utility efficiency is discouraged by utilities' vertical integration and the current regulatory scheme.

Currently, most utility companies are vertically integrated with all the key functions of the industry (i.e. production, transmission, and distribution) performed within each firm. This does not permit them to take advantage of their areas of expertise, or to tailor services to fit the needs of industrial customers. According to the FERC Transmission Task Force, 75% of the energy generated in the United States is produced by vertically-integrated utility companies. Because no firm can excel at everything, vertical integration dilutes the comparative advantage of a firm by bundling services in the company's area of expertise with services the company provides less efficiently.

Investor-owned utilities are judged by their ability to deliver profits to the stockholders. In the current regulatory framework, utilities appear to have two alternatives to increase profitability. They can either apply for an increase in their rates, or they can attempt to become more efficient. Efficiency improvement will not increase profits because regulators will order lower rates if the utility's profits are too high. This dilemma produces a disincentive for utilities to innovate because they are guaranteed profitability under the current system whether they innovate or not.

Promoting competition between utilities will increase efficiency, and these savings will benefit American industry and the general public. In an era of international competition, industry cannot afford to pay rates higher than a competitive market would provide.

Competition in the Japanese automobile industry shows us the benefits of many suppliers in a market. Japanese automobile manufacturers recently have been more successful than their U.S. competitors. There are eight Japanese manufacturers competing in a smaller domestic market. Despite lower sales volumes than U.S. manufacturers, Japanese automobile company costs are lower, quality is higher, and Japanese innovation has captured an increasing market share. This performance is not achieved by restricting competition. These companies are successful in competing in world markets because competition is so keen at home. The U.S. electric utility industry can benefit from competition just as the Japanese automobile industry has benefited. If the U.S. is to remain the world's industrial leader, American industry needs the benefit of electricity sold in a competitive market.

Utility companies have successfully reduced costs when forced to do so, either during periods of high inflation or at the behest of a regulatory agency. Detroit Edison trimmed $100 million from its annual budget after the state public service commission froze its rates. This example is, however, unusual because regulators are seldom able to force utilities to control costs. Therefore, society, industry and utilities need the discipline of the market to compel them to control costs.

## Conserve Capital

The U.S. electric utility industry is capital-intensive with more than $500 billion invested. Annual capital expenditures exceed $30 billion annually. A competitive market would reward those utilities which make more-efficient use of assets, thereby releasing capital for other uses.

## Conserve Natural Resources

Through the increased competition retail wheeling will produce, only the most efficient generating units will be run. Other units will be retired over time. These more efficient units will use less fuel. Retail wheeling would also encourage cogeneration with its more efficient use of fuel. In each of these cases, less fossil fuels will be burned and the environmental impacts of electrical generation, such as acid rain and global warming, will be mitigated.

Transmission access will also improve generation siting as a larger number of potential sites can be considered. This should also produce environmental benefits. Generation at the customer's location would also reduce transmission and distribution losses.

## IV. UTILITIES' TECHNICAL ARGUMENTS AGAINST RETAIL WHEELING

Utilities make three arguments against retail wheeling which are based on the physics of electricity. Those arguments are that electricity cannot be stored, the need for frequency control, and that electricity follows the path of least resistance.

## Electricity Cannot be Stored

Utilities claim that electricity is a unique commodity because it cannot be stored. This argument is irrelevant. The issue in retail wheeling is access to a transmission and distribution system. Viewed as a system, the electric utility transmission and distribution system is essentially the same as the natural gas transmission system, the publicly-switched telephone system, the airline system, or a hotel. That is, no two users can use the same unit of capacity at the same time. Further, this problem has already been solved in utilities' transactions with their wholesale wheeling customers. There is no reason to believe that they can not apply this expertise to retail wheeling.

## Frequency Control

Utilities argue that retail wheeling will disrupt frequency control, resulting in equipment damage. Frequency control is a function of interconnections under the National Electric Reliability Council guidelines and not a responsibility of any one utility. Because they all operate at 60hz, frequency control should remain unchanged. There is no reason to expect that frequency control will be imperilled. If any generator fails to maintain 60hz, it could be disconnected from the system.

## Path of Least Resistance

Electricity is difficult to direct because it follows the path of least resistance, but this is not a valid argument against retail wheeling. Similar to the need for instantaneous delivery, utility companies must deal with this reality whenever electricity is transmitted. Because utility companies handle this issue in wholesale wheeling and in transactions between themselves, there is no reason to believe that it will be problematic in retail wheeling.

## V. UTILITIES' POLICY ARGUMENTS AGAINST RETAIL WHEELING

### Reliability Concerns

The argument that retail wheeling will harm system reliability is often proposed by utilities. Reliability concerns expressed by utilities would appear to fall into two categories--generation and transmission. If generation is unreliable, the wheeling utility should charge fair backup power supply rates to satisfy the customer's reliability desires. Transmission system reliability for an existing system should remain unchanged unless the generation source to be wheeled causes an increased flow on limited capacity lines. In that case, supply from that delivery point may not be wheelable or may require additional investment. Distribution reliability should remain the same for nearly every situation in which a customer is currently receiving service. Utilities should not, therefore, be permitted to deny retail wheeling for reasons of limited distribution capacity.

Utilities should be required to construct facilities to provide retail wheeling because transmission and distribution are the only parts of a utility's system that are natural monopolies. Because these are natural monopolies, the rates for transmission and distribution services must remain regulated.

In addition, no utility makes a credible argument that reliability of transmission systems has been affected by wholesale wheeling transactions. Large industrial customers have the same general use characteristics as municipal utility distributors of electricity. Therefore, utilities could provide retail wheeling with the same system reliability as is presently maintained.

### Facility Duplication

Many utility advocates argue that it is not socially beneficial to have competition in the electric utility market because facilities would be duplicated. This argument is an attempt to mask the inefficiencies intrinsic in any monopoly. There is duplication of facilities in every industry whether competitive or not. In agriculture, cows produce more milk than can be consumed. In the automobile industry, foreign manufacturers are establishing U.S. plants at the same time as domestic manufacturers are closing plants. In the steel industry, special purpose plants are constructed while older, less-efficient plants are abandoned. There is apparent waste in each duplication. However, a competitive market works because the benefits of competition outweigh the cost of duplication of facilities and even their abandonment. There is no reason to expect that the electric utility industry is different from any other industry in this respect.

Many electric utilities are haunted by the excess capacity that their protected status permits them to purchase and continue to hold. The cost of that excess capacity is, typically, passed on to ratepayers. This could never happen in a competitive market. Further, the discipline of the marketplace (a major benefit of competition and retail wheeling) would provide a substantial disincentive to overexpansion.

### Increased Risk

Without risk, an industry stagnates and becomes less efficient. As demonstrated by the collapse of planned economies where enterprise has no risk, risk is essential to economic health because it compels efficiency and innovation which are the engines of economic growth. Risk to the utility is not adequate justification for industrial customers being prohibited from purchasing from a more efficient supplier.

### Planning Problems

Retail wheeling will require utilities to contend with more uncertainty than in the past. Careful planning will allow them to adjust to changing system needs. As long as regulators are vigilant, alterations in system flows should occur with no change in reliability. Similar arguments were made by AT&T and the gas industry before those industries were deregulated, and they have successfully adjusted without compromising quality. The inconvenience to utilities of having to improve planning is small compared to the economic benefits of retail wheeling described earlier in this paper.

### Residential Customers

Another concern expressed by utility advocates is that residential electricity bills will increase. There is an implication in this argument that utilities will sell below cost to large customers and recover their losses from residential customers. A competitive market would not permit this. Any company that would sell below cost will lose money, attract more customers, and reach the day when it goes out of business. Instead, companies that become more efficient as the result of competition will have rates which are lower for residential customers, as well as, for commercial and industrial customers. The natural gas industry raised this same argument when it faced deregulation; however, as a result of competition, well-head gas prices dropped and reliability was maintained.

## VI. UTILITIES' LEGAL ARGUMENT AGAINST RETAIL WHEELING

All fifty states have either territorial statutes, or the requirement for a certificate of public convenience and necessity which define utility service in each state. Twenty-three states have territorial statutes that specify the utility company and its obligations for each of the territories established by these statutes. The remaining states operate under certificates of public convenience which do not explicitly define service territories. Some would argue that these statutes, especially the territorial ones, would not permit retail wheeling because they apparently grant monopolies.

However, the advent of retail wheeling should give an entirely different meaning to the word service. There are retail power customers that desire to purchase retail wheeling instead of bundled generation, transmission, and distribution. Service to these customers is currently inadequate. These customers desire to purchase a product which is not offered by the franchised utility. This inadequacy can be remedied by unbundling generation, transmission, and distribution. To continue to narrowly define service as power sold at the customer's door step, permits entrenched monopolists to prevent customers from purchasing a product they need.

## VII. CONCLUSIONS AND ALTERNATIVES

Retail wheeling is an idea whose time has come. The utility industry cannot permanently block competition. At some point, this industry will have to leave regulatory protections behind and face full-scale competition. There are examples of retail wheeling. Northern States Power Company wheels power from the Western Area Power Administration (WAPA) to the University of North Dakota and to the South Dakota State Penitentiary. Consolidated Edison wheels power for the Power Authority of New York to retail loads within Consolidated Edison's service territory. Iowa Electric Light & Power Company wheels power which permits its customers to interrupt their power take from Iowa Electric and substitute remote generation. This is especially interesting because this wheeling takes place at the time of system peaks. These examples suggest that utilities' technical, policy, and legal arguments against retail wheeling are without merit.

Access to retail wheeling must be implemented to secure the economic benefits described in this paper to both ratepayers and utilities. If utilities will not provide retail wheeling, the transmission system in the U.S. should be owned by the government to provide the substantial economic benefits of retail wheeling and competition to the general public. Retail wheeling is necessary for U.S. companies to remain competitive in world markets.

## REFERENCES

Bonbright, James C; Danielsen, Albert L; and Kamerschen, David R., Principles of Public Utility Rates, Public Utilities Reports, Inc., Arlington, Virginia, (1988).

Hyman, Leonard S., America's Electric Utilities: Past, Present, and Future, Public Utilities Reports, Inc., Arlington, Virginia, (1983).

Porter, Samuel H., and Burton, John R., "Legal and Regulatory Constraints on Competition in Electric Power Supply," Public Utilities Fortnightly, Vol 123, No. 11, (1989).

Porter, Samuel H., and Maliszewski, Raymond M., "Technical and Economic Constraints on Competition in Electric Power Supply," Public Utilities Fortnightly, Vol 122, No. 10, (1988).

# Chapter 44

# Northern States Power Company's Open Transmission Tariff from a Customer's Perspective

K.E. Marietta, S.K. Achinger

## I. INTRODUCTION

In October of 1990, Northern States Power Company (NSP or Company), filed a unique open transmission tariff for both captive customers and through-system transactions. This is an important step towards expanding transmission services in the United States. Many individuals in the utility industry, who may be considering imposing generation costs on transmission services, have been closely monitoring NSP's case which is currently before the Federal Energy Regulatory Commission (FERC). NSP's innovative generation costs include charges for reactive power production, frequency control, load dispatching, and load following. The results of this case may also have an important impact on the future of open transmission tariffs. Rates for these services depend on the customer's classification as either a captive or through-system consumer. The proposed tariff raises critical issues related to the costing of these transmission services. NSP's methodology has caused serious concern because the proposed tariff would increase transmission costs by an average of 53%. This paper will discuss the benefits of transmission, proposed rates, contract terms, and costing methodologies of NSP's plan.

### Northern States Power:

NSP, an investor-owned utility serving Minnesota, Wisconsin, North Dakota, South Dakota and the Upper Peninsula of Michigan, generates, transmits, and distributes electricity to approximately 1.3 million customers and employs 7,100 individuals. Minnesota consumers accounted for 63% of the company's 1991 revenues which totaled approximately 2.2 billion dollars. NSP's peak electric demand for 1990 was 6,733 megawatts. The Company purchased 18% of its capacity from other utilities and generated 47% of its capacity from coal, 31% from nuclear power, and the remaining 4% from other sources.

## II. TARIFF OVERVIEW

### Case History:

The Federal Energy Regulatory Commission, in an order issued December 28, 1990, consolidated three NSP transmission cases before the Commission under Docket No. ER91-21-000. The initial case, Docket No. ER90-349-000 filed on June 25, 1990, involved a transmission service agreement ("Eastern Agreement") between NSP and the eastern Wisconsin municipal members of Wisconsin Public Power System, Inc. (WPPI). NSP filed the second docket, Docket No. ER90-406-000, on August 8, 1990, which contained a transmission service agreement between NSP and the municipal members of WPPI located in western Wisconsin ("Western Agreement"). At the direction of the Wisconsin Public Service Commission (WPSC), NSP filed the generic transmission tariff, Docket No. ER91-21-000, on October 29, 1990. This tariff provided for the supply of firm and non-firm transmission services by NSP to its existing and new transmission customers.

Dahlen, Berg & Company represented Minnesota Cities, a group consisting of the NSP's Wheeling Association and NSP's wholesale customers (the River Electric Association). As a result of the expert testimony given by Dahlen, Berg & Company and the other intervenors in this consolidated proceeding, NSP made a settlement offer and revised its filing. On July 12, 1991, the Wisconsin Public Service, Wisconsin Electric Power Company, Citizen's Power & Light Corporation, and the Wisconsin Intervenor Group accepted NSP's settlement offer. The Commission approved the settlement agreement on October 23, 1991.

NSP filed the revised case on September 20, 1991, through its rebuttal to the Minnesota Cities, the FERC staff, and the other non-consenting parties. This second filing basically parodied the company's July settlement offer. In its rebuttal filing, NSP changed several terms in both the Eastern and Western Agreements and amended many of the tariff provisions. In the revised case, NSP restructured its reactive power costing and reduced the tariff charges overall. Only the base rate increased from $16.70 to $17.67 in the revised filing. At the suggestion of the FERC trial staff, NSP included step-up transformers in the base rate calculation, resulting in the $1.07 increase. NSP reduced the load following charge from $2.00 to $1.35 per kilowatt-year, and the frequency control charge from $0.94 to $0.93 per kilowatt-year, The Company also reduced the maximum reactive power charge from $23.99 to $2.69 per kilowatt. NSP's Wheeling Association members currently pay $14.77 per kilowatt-year for transmission services; therefore, contracting for services under the revised tariff would increase the members' costs by 53% to $22.65 per kilowatt-year. While the rates in the rebuttal case are lower, the real issue is the inclusion of generation costs which could become the industry standard.

After extensive discovery, the hearing began on October 7, 1991, cross examination ended October 11, 1991, and the record closed on October 31, 1991. The parties involved filed their initial briefs on December 17, 1991, and their reply briefs on January 17, 1992. The Commission Trial Staff issued its Brief on Exceptions on May 15, 1992, in response to the presiding administrative law judge's April 15, 1992, Initial Decision. In its Brief on Exceptions issued May 15, 1992, the Commission Staff requested that the FERC reverse the Initial Decision regarding NSP's proposed reactive power charge, its frequency control charge, and its nonfirm transmission service rate. The Minnesota Cities requested reversal of the same issues as those addressed by the Commission Staff.

## NSP's Transmission Policy:

Since the 1950s, NSP has voluntarily provided transmission services to municipalities located on its transmission system who had an allocation of power generated and sold by the Western Area Power Administration (WAPA). Under the Mid-Continent Area Power Pool (MAPP) Agreement of March 31, 1972, and through the company's interconnections, NSP has transmitted power generated by other utilities and provided transmission services to other electric providers. The Company furnishes transmission services when such transactions will not endanger reliability and service to NSP's native load customers. Over the past several years, the number of requests for transmission services from municipalities, municipal agencies, and non-MAPP utilities has increased dramatically. NSP

proposed the open transmission tariff, in response to the increasing demand for transmission services and pressure from the Wisconsin Public Service Commission, to provide greater access to the company's transmission system.

NSP's current policy provides transmission service, subject to availability and system reliability, between the point of receipt and the point of delivery, based on the fully allocated cost of the specific service requested. NSP will only provide these services by contract, and after it has met its prior contractual commitments and native load needs. Under these agreements, the customer is responsible for losses and costs of both NSP and any third parties involved in the transaction.

## NSP's Proposed Tariff:

NSP's rates under the proposed tariff differ depending on the customer's location and classification as a captive or through-system user. The proposed transmission tariff would charge customers for generation support services such as: reactive power, frequency control, and load following. These new costs would have a major impact on transmission user rates. NSP claims that if generation support services are not allocated to the transmission function, then the transmission customers benefit from a generation subsidy. However, in its rate calculations, NSP failed to recognize the benefits its system receives from transmission.

## Intervening Parties:

The parties intervening in this case sought increased accessibility to NSP's transmission system, but not under the conditions set forth in NSP's open transmission tariff. Services under NSP's proposed tariff would make transmission available to municipal electric utilities, generating and non-generating electric utilities, non-utility generators, and qualified facilities. The intervenors in this case include: the Northern States Power Wheeling Association, a group of municipal electric utilities consisting of existing transmission service customers, the River Electric Association, and companies and associations desiring to purchase services under the proposed tariff. Other Minnesota and Wisconsin investor-owned utilities, Wisconsin Public Power Inc., Central Minnesota Municipal Power Agency, and the state Public Service Commissions for Minnesota and Wisconsin also chose to intervene in this case.

## Historical Approach:

Historically, NSP employed the FERC-accepted "bright line" approach which completely separates the power supply function from the transmission function. This method bases rates on the cost of service. The proposed generation support charge which is a dramatic departure from this methodology, includes charges which have traditionally only been part of the power supply function. For customers purchasing transmission services under the company's existing policy, NSP implemented a cost based methodology. Under this approach, NSP computed the rate for transmission services by dividing its calculated revenue requirements by its wheeling load. NSP's calculated revenue requirement for transmission service was $1,303,000, based on 1991 budget data, which yields a calculated rate of $12.15 per kilowatt-year. In contrast, NSP's settlement rate offer was $22.65, or 86% higher than traditionally calculated costs.

## III. BENEFITS OF TRANSMISSION

The most significant error in NSP's tariff is that the Company failed to recognize the benefits of transmission when structuring the tariff rates. While generation may benefit transmission by the production of reactive power and by following load, the benefits of transmission should not be overlooked. These transmission benefits include: the delivery of power and energy from other utilities; the sale of power and energy to other utilities; the reduced reserve margins required for the same level of reliability; the construction of lower cost and larger scale generation units; and the sharing of diversity and geographically dispersed loads.

Interconnections permit the delivery of power and energy from other utilities to NSP's service area. The Company estimated that it saved $139.9 million dollars from such purchases in the 1991 test year. NSP admitted that it would have to reduce its energy sales to native load customers by 559 gigawatts to avoid the $45 million dollar MAPP penalty for failure to meet reserve requirements if the Company did not purchase from other utilities. For the 1991 test year, NSP earned $20.3 million dollars from sales to other utilities. These transactions are only possible through interconnections, transmission lines, transmission substations, and associated facilities. MAPP membership, made possible through the company's interconnections, allows NSP to maintain a 15% reserve margin instead of a 25% reserve margin. The 10% savings equals 545,949 kilowatts of generation, or approximately $77 million dollars based on the average system generation cost of $141.20 per kilowatt for the 1991 test year.

The construction of lower cost and larger scale generation units and the sharing of diversity and geographically dispersed loads are difficult to quantify. However, the benefits from the delivery of power and energy from other utilities, the sale of power and energy to other utilities, and the maintenance of lower reserve margins yields a total cost savings of $282.2 million dollars. These savings ($282.2 million dollars) divided by NSP's total transmission system load (5,811,358 kilowatts) results in a net benefit of $48.56 dollars per kilowatt-year. The benefits of transmission, therefore, exceed the highest rate proposed by NSP.

Costing Approaches:

As the numbers demonstrate, charging the transmission function with the benefits provided by generation and then crediting the function with the benefits provided by transmission is unworkable. NSP's traditional approach represents the other costing option, which involves drawing a "bright line" between the power supply function and the transmission function. Application of the "bright line" to NSP's costs would create a rate of $16.70 per kilowatt-year before the Company revised its filing and $17.67 per kilowatt-year after the step-up transformers were added.

## IV. PROPOSED RATES

However, NSP asserts that transmission service customers should be allocated costs of generation, so that alleged burden would not fall upon electric power customers. NSP based the rates for its open transmission tariff on the type of customer receiving the service and the alleged generation support needed for the transaction. Generation costs claimed by NSP include reactive power, frequency control, load dispatching, and load following.

## A. CUSTOMER CLASSIFICATIONS

The tariff originally discriminated between captive and through-system customers and among captive customers based upon their location within NSP's service area. NSP divided its transmission customers into two service categories, "Reserved Service Inside" and "Reserved Service Outside". "Reserved Service Inside" refers to the transmission services that NSP would provide to its captive customers. Transmission service would cost these customers between $19.64 and $43.63 per kilowatt-year in contrast to the current FERC-filed rate of $14.77/kilowatt-year. "Reserved Outside Service," rates for through system customers, would cost between $17.64 and $30.79 per kilowatt-year under NSP's proposal. Distance, direction and destination of power flow determine the amount of transmission required to support a transaction. Longer transactions directly impact more transmission facilities and should, therefore, cost more than transactions across shorter distances. It is nearly impossible to construct a through transaction which would be shorter than the average "inside" transaction of forty miles. Based on this line of reasoning, outside customers should pay more instead of less for transmission services because of the generally greater distances involved in these transactions.

At the Minnesota Cities' suggestion, NSP bifurcated the tariff into an "Inside Tariff" and an "Outside Tariff" in the settlement offer and rebuttal case. The Company also adopted uniform rates for all captive customers, but retained the geographic distinction for Outside customers. Under the revised tariff, outside customers would pay between $18.60 and $21.29 per kilowatt-year, and all inside customers would pay $22.65 per kilowatt-year.

## B. FREQUENCY CONTROL AND LOAD DISPATCH CHARGES

Production Energy Management System (EMS) fixed charges and the FERC Account 556 serve as the basis for NSP's frequency control and load dispatch charge. Fixed charges for NSP's net EMS investment include return, income taxes, book depreciation, deferred taxes, and property taxes, totaling $1.6 million dollars for NSP's Minnesota and Wisconsin operations. Under the FERC's Uniform System of Accounts, a utility may apportion labor and expenses incurred for system control and load dispatch services to Account 556 (System Control and Load Dispatching - Production) Account 561 (Load Dispatching - Transmission) and Account 581 (Load Dispatching - Distribution). NSP allocated its frequency control and load dispatch costs to all three of these accounts. According to NSP's 1990 FERC Form 1, the Company had $10.3 million dollars in system control and load dispatching expenses and apportioned $3.4 million dollars to Account 556, $3.2 million dollars to Account 561, and $3.7 million dollars to Account 581.

NSP added the $3.5 million dollars from Account 556 to the $1.6 million dollars in EMS expenses for a combined total of $5.1 million dollars per year. NSP established the total delivery demand by combining its native load less transmission losses with its transmission load. By dividing the total costs by the total demand, NSP arrived at a frequency control and dispatch charge of $0.94 per kilowatt-year. However, NSP did not identify any additional expenses not already covered in its FERC Form 1 filing to justify charging the transmission customers a portion of the production Account 556. Under this scheme,

NSP could potentially recover an extra $245,000 dollars from existing captive transmission customers who are already paying for frequency control and dispatch services under the FERC Account 561. If the Commission approves this method for calculating frequency control and dispatch services, it should then require NSP to credit Account 561 with the revenues received from the Account 556 charge.

According to NSP, the EMS operates the entire integrated generation and transmission system, and thus the EMS and Account 556 expenses relate to transmission. Delivery related costs in Account 556 include: monitoring, controlling and matching generation to load, as well as operation and maintenance expenses. Therefore, NSP did not significantly alter the frequency control and dispatch charges in the company's September 1991 filing. However, NSP eliminated seven percent from Account 556 expenses and five percent of the EMS expenses from its original filing, resulting in a rate decrease from $0.94 to $0.93 per kilowatt-year. The seven percent NSP deducted from Account 556 included production expenses associated with billing, sale for resale, and accounting for interchange transactions and economic dispatch.

## C. LOAD FOLLOWING

Under the proposed tariff, NSP would reserve 75 megawatts for following the loads of the company's inside customers. Originally, NSP proposed a cost of $2.00 per kilowatt-year based on the assumption that all generating units follow load. However, the response time for some units is too slow and for others the marginal cost of following load is too high. Base load units cannot respond quickly enough to meet the megawatt per minute response standard for error correction within its control area. Therefore, these units, along with any others that do not satisfy the National Electric Reliability Council's (NERC) response rate, should be removed from the load following calculation. Reserving capacity from all NSP generating units for load following purposes would be uneconomical. The units with the lowest marginal costs should be operated at the highest possible capacity factors. The marginal costs of nuclear units essentially prohibits NSP from reserving capacity for transmission services from these. Therefore, NSP should remove from its average generation cost calculation for load following any units which do not meet the minimum response rates, and any units with marginal costs which preclude them from load following.

At the intervenor's suggestion, NSP removed its nuclear units from the load following calculations and based the new load following rate on the three Sherburne County units. According to

NSP's data for the previous twelve months, the Company used these units for generation control between 99.38% and 82.37% of the time. The average of the other suitable units comprised the remaining generation control. The revised calculations based on the Sherburne units produced the lower rate of $1.35 per kilowatt-year.

## D. REACTIVE POWER

The reactive power component of the tariff has four flaws: the model assumptions are inconsistent with the facts; the assumptions for critical calculations are borrowed from an incomplete case regarding Southern Company, an unrelated utility; the turbo-generator investment allocation is not realistic; and the sole source of reactive power is generation.

Reactive Power Model:

Four problems arise from the reactive power model NSP used to support its tariff filing. First, NSP did not compare the results from their computer simulation to actual transactions. Second, the power factor for NSP's load cannot be characterized as 98%. Third, NSP cannot treat all its transmission customers as incremental to its system. Lastly, NSP's model does not work for smaller loads.

NSP attempted to measure all transmission transactions by simulating the MAPP transmission and generation system with a computer load flow model, but the Company did not compare these results with actual operation of its system. The computer model cannot determine the reactive power necessary for individual transmission transactions and this presents an accounting problem, because NSP does not have the capability to collect this data. To solve this accounting problem, NSP's generic transmission computer model simulated the relationship between real and reactive energy relative to the delivery rate. From this simulated relationship, NSP developed a reactive power average of $38.60 per kilovar-year, to be applied to all individual transmissions based on the portion of the supporting unit's annual cost, as defined in NSP's Var tables. This methodology assumes that the relationship between Vars and Watts is linear across all levels of load transactions from the same source to the same destination. The Company admitted, however, that the "[t]total NSP generator megavar output is not strictly a function of NSP load." Therefore, the Var to Watt relationship is nonlinear and dependant on other variables not present in NSP's rate computations.

In the revised filing, NSP continued to rely on its computer model, based on the fact that this particular program has been universally accepted within the MAPP region. Further, NSP asserts that the computer generated results do not have to be compared with actual transactions because the software developers made this comparison when they created the program. NSP also claims that such a comparison would be impossible to make at this time. The Company concluded that the parameters it chose and the combinations thereof should produce results within the range expected by actual conditions.

NSP incorrectly assumed that all transmission customers would be incremental to its system. However, NSP's cannot treat all of its transmission customers as incremental, because the Company has been planning for these customer loads and treating them as part of its system for years. By entering these existing customer loads in the computer analysis as incremental, NSP accounted for these loads twice.

In the settlement offer, NSP stated that, for long-term inside transactions, it would not specifically base the reactive power requirements on the incremental load flow studies. Under the revised tariff, NSP plans to use the average Var per Watt, as determined by the incremental studies for short inside transactions. The average produced by this method was 34.75%, but for administrative purposes NSP decided to reduce the figure to 34%, the highest outside reactive power factor. NSP also continued to treat all outside transactions as incremental, because of the different reactive power requirements needed for individual transactions.

Further, NSP's model assumed that all metro area substations had a 98% percent power factor at time of system peak, but NSP does not possess any studies confirming this finding, and the actual figures available for NSP's substations at the time of the filing varied widely. NSP based the 98% power factor on the average power factor for the metro area which was approximately 99% on the high side of the transformer. While urban or heavily loaded substations typically achieve unity power factors, smaller or rural substations do not maintain such a high power factor. NSP cannot characterize its load based on the urban power factors, because the Company serves many rural areas in Northern Minnesota and parts of the Dakotas. In the revised filing, NSP maintained the 98% percent power factor, and this false characterization of the company's load created yet another error in NSP's model.

The cumulative effect of all these errors inherent in NSP's model made the model unusable for loads of approximately ten megawatts or less, and a substantial portion of NSP's wheeling customers have loads of ten megawatts or less. To alleviate the problems in calculating the company's costs for smaller loads, NSP offered to negotiate separately with these customers as part of the settlement agreement. However, individual negotiations for the bulk of NSP's transmission customers defeats the purpose of having the generic tariff.

Southern Company:

Initially, NSP based its reactive power charge on the assumption that all of its production costs, including piles of coal and land rights, were being used to generate reactive power. NSP later adopted Southern Company's figures as the standard for its reactive power charge, after an individual from Minnesota Power and Light, an intervenor in the case, mentioned Southern Company in his testimony to refute the turbo-generator allocation studies of NSP. Southern Company, a completely unrelated utility, also had a filing before the FERC, Docket No. ER91-150-000, which included a reactive power charge. Once mentioned, the Southern Company filing played a key role in NSP's presentation of its case, and NSP relied on Southern Company's filing for many of the critical assumptions in the calculation of NSP's transmission tariff rates.

However, NSP did not enter any evidence into the record to support the comparability of its system to Southern Company's system, or any other evidence which demonstrated that Southern Company's costs represented the industry standard. In fact, the Commission had not yet ruled on the validity of Southern Company's cost allocators and reactive power charge when the Administrative Law Judge issued his Initial Decision. As a result, Southern Company's cost allocators could become the industry standard by precedent from this case, without any evidenciary support. As a matter of public policy, while opening transmission systems would encourage more customers to use them, any potential gains may be defeated by unsupported costs. Utility rates must be based on utility-specific costs. NSP has violated this fundamental tenet of ratemaking in this case.

Turbo-Generator Costs:

The turbine of a turbo-generator does not produce turbo generator reactive power, so NSP had to separate the cost of the turbines from the fourteen turbo-generation units involved. To accomplish this task, the Company made three cost allocations: between the generators and the turbines, between the excitor and non-excitor components of the generators, and between the portions of the non-excitor component involved with real and reactive power production.

While utilities make various estimates and allocations throughout the ratemaking process, they have always done so based on their utility-specific costs. However, instead of contacting the manufacturers of its equipment, NSP based turbo-generator investment information on numbers it borrowed from Southern Company after abandoning a study conducted by an NSP employee. According to the NSP study, generator-excitor cost equaled 50% of the turbo-generator's total cost, and only 5% of the generator-excitor cost was attributable to the excitor. Data obtained from the equipment manufacturers would have been a more credible and logical source for the cost information, even if these manufacturers could only supply an approximation. Furthermore, no evidence was entered into the record to demonstrate that NSP turbo-generators are comparable to Southern Company's units or whether Southern Company's assumptions were valid, representing another violation of the fundamental tenet of ratemaking.

NSP blames this lack of information on the FERC accounting regulations because the FERC does not require cost separations for turbines, generators, and excitors. However, Southern Company is governed by the same regulations and had this information. Further, the federal regulations represent the bare minimum required by law and do not prevent NSP from keeping more specific records. Under the Federal Power Act (FPA), if a utility wishes to depart from standard industry practice, then that Company has the burden of proof to justify such a departure. See, e.g., Village of Chatham and Riverton Illinois v. FERC, 662 F.2d 699, 708 (7the Cir. 1982) ; Nantahala Power and Light Co. v. FERC, 727 F.2d 1342, 1345 (4the Cir. 1984) ; 16 USC sec. 824d. NSP's reactive power component of its transmission service charge is a departure and, therefore, NSP must carry the burden of proof as to the justness and reasonableness of this novel charge.

NSP cannot base radical departures from accepted transmission ratemaking on the fact that the FERC accounting system did not require the information. NSP has provided transmission services separately since the 1950s, and has performed many cost allocations to support its past filings. There should be no need to rely on speculation or borrowed data to support this tariff filing. Ratepayers are entitled to rates based on the costs of the utility actually supplying the service, not rates based on the costs of an unrelated utility in a distant market. Furthermore, NSP relied on costs from only four units of Southern Company's many generating units rather than Southern Company's entire system.

## Reactive Power Sources:

NSP's current proposal does not acknowledge reactive power supplied from either line charging, capacitors, or the amount of loss compensation that it already collects from its transmission customers. All the company's calculations assume that only generators produce reactive power. However, in response to a data request from the Commission Staff, NSP stated that it receives 2473 megavars of reactive power from sources other than its generators, but the Company did not account for any of this production capability in the tariff filing. This omission resulted in higher reactive power rates since the lower costs associated with other types of reactive power production would reduce the rate NSP proposed. Also, in NSP's last rate case, the Commission approved the cost of capacitors as a transmission related expense, so through the fully allocated cost of service the company's existing customers already pay for reactive power support from these capacitors. Therefore, NSP would receive double recovery for reactive power support under the proposed tariff. In the rebuttal case, NSP maintained its position that the reactive power necessary to support wheeling transactions under the tariff would originate solely from generators, because the Company did not plan to add capacitors or other reactive devises to support these transactions.

## V. COST METHODOLOGIES

The facts of this case do not support the costing methodology NSP used. The company's methodology contains four flaws. First, the Company used obsolete costs and load data in calculating the tariff rates which inflated the cost to consumers. Second, the transmission tariff discriminates against captive customers who have no transmission alternatives to NSP. Third, the tariff would charge inside service customers different rates depending on their location within NSP's service area. Finally, reserve requirements and other expenses increase the cost to inside customers, notwithstanding the shorter distances involved in their transactions.

## NSP's Data:

NSP calculated both its costs and loads with obsolete data. While NSP did not file with the FERC until mid-October 1990, the Company based its costs on a forecast of its 1991 budget prepared during the first quarter of 1990. On August 2, 1990, six weeks before the open transmission tariff filing, NSP filed a wholesale rate case which contained cost data based on its 1990 second quarter forecasts for 1991. In response to unfavorable decisions in recent retail rate cases, NSP had reduced its projected

expenses and capital expenditures in both 1990 and 1991. As a result of these omissions, NSP inflated its costs by performing the cost calculations based on the obsolete data, which yielded a much higher figure than the Company would have obtained if it had used the information available at the time of the tariff filing.

NSP also understated its wheeling load by approximately 14,600 kilowatts, or 10.5%, but supported its filing with wheeling information derived from projections for 1991 made in the fall of 1989. As a result, NSP spread its costs over fewer units resulting in higher overall unit costs. NSP's projections made in November of 1989 showed a long term wheeling load of 123,981 kilowatts, but by January 1991, the company's wheeling forecasts revealed loads of 138,613 kilowatts. According to NSP's projections, the City of Blue Earth has a wheeling load of 9,267 kilowatts; however, NSP did not include Blue Earth as a transmission service customer in its tariff filing, even though the contract between NSP and Blue Earth became effective on December 20, 1990. For its native load projections, NSP again used obsolete data from November 1989, which disclosed a 5,454,942 kilowatt load. NSP supplemented its wholesale filing of January 1991, by updating its total native load to figure 5,523,499 kilowatts, but the Company did not update this figure in its tariff filing until the intervenors brought this omission to the attention of the Commission. Therefore, NSP understated its native load by 68,000 kilowatts in its initial filing. However, in the revised filing, NSP included its most recent load and budget data, correcting the earlier omissions.

## Inside Transmission Customers and Zone Rates:

As NSP initially structured its tariff, inside service transmission customers to the north and east of the Twin Cities would pay more than those to the south and west, even though NSP's transmission system was theoretically designed to produce the lowest overall cost and to benefit all NSP customers. NSP's proposed zone rates transfer the benefits of an integrated system to those customers located in the zone which happens have the lower cost at the time the study was performed. Zone rates are unfair to a captive wheeling customer because location is a factor beyond the customer's control; public utility ratemaking has long recognized the fairness of "postage stamp" rates for captive customers. "postage stamp" rates mean that all customers pay the same rate regardless of their location. This scheme is similar to the twenty-nine cent stamp required to send a letter across town or across the country. Unlike outside transmission customers, the inside customer has no alternatives to NSP's transmission system;

261

therefore, "postage stamp" rates are essential for these customers.

NSP's zone rates present a further problem in that at least three suppliers are located in more than one zone. The Missouri Municipal Power Agency is located in both the Nebraska/Wyoming zone, where annual service ranges from $19.64 to $24.67 per kilowatt-year, and the Dakotas zone, where the same service ranges from $24.67 to $28.15 per kilowatt-year. For the Ottertail Power Company, located in two zones (Northern Minnesota and the Dakotas), and for United Power Association, located in three zones (the Twin Cities, Northern Minnesota, and the Dakotas), the maximum price for service differs by $4.64 per kilowatt-year, or 15%.

As a result of the intervenors efforts, NSP substantiality revised its rate structure for inside customers. In the September filing, NSP partially corrected the problems of multiple rate zones by adopting "postage stamp" rates for its inside customers; however, the Company retained the zone rates for outside transactions.

### Reserve Requirements:

Captive customers must meet the reserve requirements of the MAPP Agreement to which NSP is a member, regardless of the customer's MAPP status. However, Section 6(b) of the Transmission Services Tariff does not impose these same reserve requirements on the outside customers. MAPP requires that its members maintain a 15% reserve margin to insure reliability, meaning NSP's proposed contract would bind parties to agreements which they never signed. Thus, this provision imposes added costs on captive customers who do not receive the benefits of power pool membership for their added expense. As part of the September filing, NSP retained the reserve requirements for inside customers, stating that through-system customers would have to meet the requirements their outside host utility placed on them; and therefore, this obligation for inside customers was fair.

### VI. CONTRACT TERMS

Not only are the terms in NSP's open transmission tariff one-sided, many of the company's transmission customers have been receiving services for years under contracts which are substantially different. NSP's contract permits the Company to make changes to the agreement and absolves the Company of liability for events beyond its control. However, the contract does not afford its customers similar protection. Also, captive customers do not receive priority or flexible rescheduling terms,

making the tariff unworkable. Finally, the transmission customers must reimburse NSP for any third party charges incurred as a result of the customer's transaction.

### Existing Contracts:

First, NSP's availability provision in its proposed contract is unreasonable because it requires existing captive transmission customers to execute new transmission service agreements, and the existing contracts differ substantially from the proposed transmission service agreements in five respects. One, the existing agreements do not state a generation source, rather they specify interconnection points between NSP and an adjacent control area. Generator specification precludes purchases of power from other utility systems making the tariff unworkable. Two, numerous contracts which have been in place for many years had initial terms that exceed the six year limitation under the new contract. Three, the existing contracts contain no third party liability language, but the language of Section 4.01 of the proposed contract states that NSP shall not be liable to the transmission customers for events beyond NSP's control. However, there is no provision for customer liability protection for events beyond the customer's control. According to Section 4.02 of the contract, the customer would be liable to NSP if the customer fails to comply with service curtailment procedures when requested to do so by NSP. However, Section 4.02 does not provide any exceptions for the customer, even if the customer is unable to comply with the request for the same reasons NSP is unable to perform the service. Four, customers under existing contracts have been paying rates based on embedded fully allocated costs of service, the approach historically employed by NSP. Embedded fully allocated costs means that each customer pays an equal share of the expenses which are embedded in the cost of service. Existing customers who have no economic transmission alternatives to NSP should not be required to conform to NSP's proposed incremental costing approach. Five, Section 2.03 of the proposed contract, also grants NSP another unilateral power, that is the ability to make changes to signed customer agreements pending FERC approval. This provision should either allow the customer to make similar filings with the FERC or be removed entirely from the contract. In addition to these specific problems, the proposed contract differs from existing agreements in several other terms and conditions.

In the revised filing, NSP required existing transmission customers to either sign the tariff agreement, or renegotiate their existing agreements. Realistically, these customers will receive essentially the same terms whether they sign the agreements or negotiate because they have no power to negotiate since they have no other transmission options. The six year contract limit did not change under the revised scheme because NSP's planning horizon is only six years, and the Company plans to treat these transactions as incremental and not to install any capacitors or other equipment for the benefit of its transmission customers. However, the liability issues raised by the intervenors were addressed, and the contractual obligations of the parties balanced. To accomplish this objective, Sections 4.01 and 4.02 were modified to include equal liability protection for the customers. These sections now excuse the customers from their obligations when uncontrollable forces are present which prevent the customer from complying with the provisions of the contract. NSP also changed Section 2, which originally granted the Company the unilateral power to change the terms under the tariff, to include customer complaint rights and a provision which states that no changes to the contract shall be effective until both parties have agreed to such changes in writing.

Priority:

Captive inside customers do not have priority in either their transmission service requests or in their curtailment orders, according to Sections 3(c)(1) and (2). The language of these sections suggests that NSP could deny service if the Company had a pre-existing commitment to outside transactions or a commitment for a longer duration. NSP has the right to reduce or interrupt any transmission, if the Company feels it is necessary in its sole technical judgement, without prior notice to the customer. This provision highlights the need for captive customer priority, because these customers have no economic alternatives to the purchase of transmission services and the possible reduction or interruption of these services. For these reasons, the tariff language should include a provision which commits NSP to adding facilities to provide transmission service to captive customers. Under the September filing and settlement agreement, NSP provided that the MAPP Line Loading Relief Procedure would dictate curtailment procedures and transaction priority when problems arise. NSP made other changes to the priority provisions in the tariff contracts, however, these modifications do not assure captive customer service.

Rescheduling of Power and Energy:

Originally, NSP's contract required transmission notice periods which were longer than necessary to maintain reliable service, and had no provision for hourly rescheduling. Under this agreement, daily service is the shortest duration that NSP

will provide. According to Sections 3(b) and 3(c) of the Transmission Services Tariff, the transmission customer must notify NSP at least two business days in advance of the delivery, and NSP does not have to respond to that request until noon on the business day preceding the date of the transaction. Also, rescheduling of power and energy lost during transmission would not be possible under the proposed tariff; therefore, potential customers could not make long-term purchases of power and energy unless other wheeling sources were available to them. For inside-service customers this would be an impossibility because they have no other options. In September, the Company reduced the notice required for rescheduling requests to the same business day for its daily service, but imposed a rescheduling fee when a customer changes the destination of a transmission request to a secondary source. Overall, the Company made the rescheduling provisions more reasonable in the revised filing.

Third Party Charges:

The basic agreement between the customer and NSP should be that the customer pays for the service provided, and NSP takes any measures necessary to provide such service. However, Section 6(b) of the Transmission Service Tariff requires that the customer reimburse NSP for any third party charges incurred as a result of services provided by NSP in addition to the amount NSP already collects from the customer under the rate schedule. NSP retained the third party language with only minor modifications, stating that such language was standard in the industry contracts.

## VII. CONCLUSION

Ironically entitled, "open transmission tariff," which has been available to customers for approximately a year, has had minimal use. The unworkable scheme for inside-service customers created by NSP defeats the goal of the tariff because open access is meaningless if no one uses the system. NSP's initial filing was badly flawed, but the efforts of the intervenors brought about significant improvements in the proposed rates, contract terms, and costing of the company's revised September filing. However, the revised tariff still contains flaws which will limit its use. The potential precedent, the inclusion of generation costs in transmission costing, is the most significant outcome of NSP's open transmission tariff filing thus far. If the Commission allows this precedent when it issues its final decision this fall, it will substantially increase transmission rates and discourage usage of transmission systems.

# Chapter 45
# Hot Dry Rock: A New Energy Source for Clean Power

D.V. Duchane

## INTRODUCTION

Almost everyone knows that the interior of the earth becomes progressively hotter with depth. Volcanic eruptions provide a vivid illustration of the vast amount of thermal energy stored within the earth, while geysers, hot springs, and related geothermal features demonstrate that this energy can be brought to the surface in a more benign manner over extended time periods. These latter phenomena have, in fact, been utilized as sources of heat since ancient times.

During the second half of this century, the use of natural geothermal fluids to generate electricity has rapidly expanded. Today, in excess of 5,000 megawatts of electric power are produced from geothermal energy sources around the world.[1] Geothermal electric power development in the United States began in 1960. With an installed capacity of more than 2,000 megawatts, it is concentrated in the far western part of the country.[2]

The vast majority of geothermal energy is found, however, not in the form of hot fluids, but rather as hot dry rock (HDR) which exists almost everywhere beneath the surface of the earth. The object of this paper is to review and summarize the current state of development of HDR technology in the United States and around the world, including preliminary results of a long-term test now underway at the HDR heat mine in Fenton Hill, NM.

## HDR HEAT MINING

### The HDR Resource

The total amount of energy available in the form of HDR is, of course, directly related to the depth that one is willing to drill to in order to recover it. Within about 6 miles of the surface, a depth that is reachable with today's drilling technology, the worldwide HDR resource base has been estimated at about 10 million quads.[3] As a point of comparison, the world's consumption of all forms of energy is in the range of 300 quads per year.[4] Thus, if only a small fraction of the energy present in HDR could be mined, the energy needs of the world could be met for thousands of years.

Although the HDR resource exists almost everywhere, access to it is much easier in some places than in others. Figure 1, a geothermal gradient map of the United States, shows that the increase in temperature of the earth with depth varies greatly from place to place. In the eastern U. S. rock temperatures increase only slowly with depth, while in many parts of the west the geothermal gradient is relatively high. Obviously, drilling and related costs to reach

rock of equivalent temperatures will be much lower in the west than in the east. In general, parts of the world with active volcanism or growing mountains tend to have high thermal gradients. Japan, for example, has an abundance of high grade HDR resources. Northern Europe, however, like the eastern United States, is almost uniformly a region of low thermal gradients.

### The Heat Mining Concept

In the early 1970's, several scientists at the Los Alamos National Laboratory conceived the idea of mining heat from HDR using drilling and hydraulic fracturing techniques that had been developed in the petroleum and geothermal industries. A patent covering the basic technique was issued in 1974 and has since expired.[5]

An idealized picture of such an HDR heat mine is shown in Figure 2. A well is first drilled deep enough to reach usefully hot rock. Water is then pumped down this well at pressures high enough to open up natural joints in the rock, thus creating a reservoir consisting of a relatively small amount of water dispersed in a very large volume of hot rock. The characteristics of the reservoir are determined primarily by the nature of the rock, the amount of water injected, and the pressure under which the hydraulic fracturing operation is carried out. Seismic technology is employed to detect and locate the microearthquakes which occur as the reservoir is being formed. These provide a three-dimensional picture of the reservoir's size, orientation, and location, and this information is in turn used to guide the drilling of a second well which is designed to penetrate the reservoir at some distance from the first.

The system is operated by pumping water down one well (the injection well) at a pressure sufficiently high to hold the rock joints open but not so high as to cause further growth of the reservoir. The water is heated as it flows across the reservoir rock to the low pressure outlet provided by the second well (the production well), and is returned to the surface. After extraction of its useful thermal energy, the same water is recirculated to mine more heat.

### Environmental Considerations

Because of the closed-loop nature of the process, HDR is an inherently clean energy source. Only heat is removed from the earth and released to the atmosphere as a result of normal operations. Water, air, and terrestrial pollutants resulting from operation of an HDR facility are practically zero. HDR plants occupy only a small space since the fuel is stored naturally

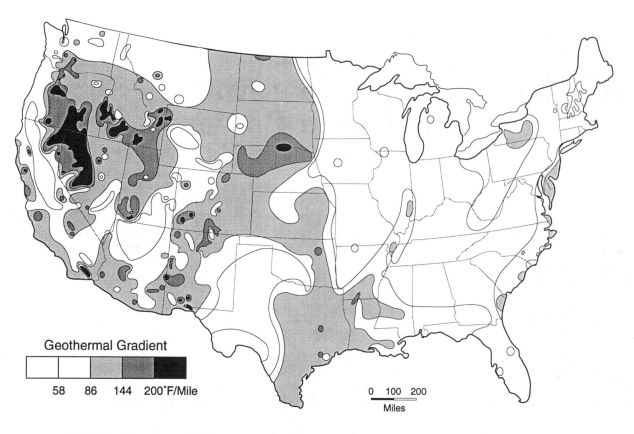

FIGURE 1. A Geothermal gradient map of the United States. High grade HDR resources are located primarily in the west.

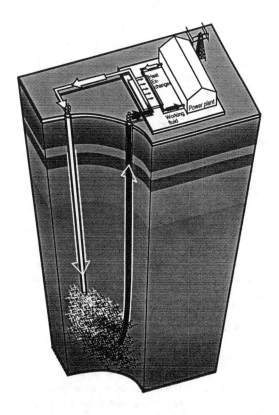

FIGURE 2. An idealized conception of an HDR heat mine.

underground. Furthermore, no toxic waste products accumulate as a result of normal operations to present disposal problems for future generations. For all these reasons, HDR is among the most environmentally promising energy alternatives.

Economic Factors

Economic electricity production from geothermal resources generally requires fluid at a temperature on the order of 300°F or more but direct thermal applications have been shown to be practical with fluids of 150°F or even less. A number of economic evaluations of HDR energy have been carried out. Table 1 shows data from one of these studies which estimates the cost of production of electricity and thermal energy from HDR resources of various grades using presently available technology and optimized engineering.[6]

| Geothermal Gradient °F/Mile | Breakeven Electricity Price, ¢/kWh | Cost of Thermal Energy, $/10^6 BTU |
|---|---|---|
| 230 | 5-6 | 2-4 |
| 144 | 8-9 | 4-7 |
| 86 | 16-18 | 10-17 |

TABLE 1. Estimated costs of energy from HDR resources using current technolgy and optimized engineering.

Clearly, electric power production from HDR is at present cost competitive only in regions with high geothermal gradients and in the United States, that means in the west. Electricity generation to produce saleable power is expected to be the first commercial use of HDR energy, but as confidence in HDR as a reliable energy source is developed, it is expected that site-specific direct thermal uses for this ubiquitous energy source, perhaps utilizing relatively low grade resources, will begin to grow rapidly.

## DEVELOPMENT OF HDR TECHNOLOGY AT LOS ALAMOS

### Early Work

Work on the extraction of energy from HDR began in 1974 with the establishment of an experimental facility at Fenton Hill, NM about 35 miles by road west of Los Alamos. The site is located just a few miles outside the crater of the largest volcanic caldera in the United States. The area had been recently burned over so experimental work could be carried out with little additional deleterious environmental impact. Other factors important in the selection of the site were its location near a paved road, and its relative proximity to Los Alamos. Granitic basement rock lies about 2,000 ft below the surface at Fenton Hill, and the geothermal gradient is about 190°F/mile. While this gradient is considerably higher than the average, it is by no means the highest in the country.

Between 1974 and 1978, the worlds first heat mine was developed at a depth of about 10,000 ft. Flow tests of this Phase I reservoir were conducted over a two-year period between 1978-1980 in a series of runs during which water was brought to the surface at temperatures of 275-285°F.[7] Thermal power was produced at rates as high as 5 megawatts. Operation of this small system, with the reservoir volume estimated to be on the order of about 120,000 cubic yards, demonstrated conclusively that the HDR technology conceived at Los Alamos could be applied to mine thermal energy from the depths of the earth.

### The Phase II HDR System

In 1980, work was begun at Fenton Hill on the creation of a larger, deeper, and hotter HDR reservoir. In developing this Phase II system, two wells were drilled to depths in excess of 14,000 ft. The last 3,000 ft of each well was angled at about 30° to the vertical with one wellbore located directly above the other. On the basis of analytical work in the Phase I reservoir, it was expected that hydraulic stimulation in the lower wellbore would create vertical fractures which would connect to the upper well.

In spite of repeated injections of large amounts of water at pressures as high as 7,000 psi, no connection between the two wells was achieved. Microseismic monitors were used during these hydraulic stimulations to detect and locate the numerous microearthquakes occurring as the joints were opened. From the locations of these microearthquakes, it was possible to obtain a picture of the location and dimensions of the growing reservoir, and it eventually became apparent that the two wellbores would never become connected. A decision was therefore made to redrill the bottom of the upper wellbore into the zone where the microseismic data showed the reservoir was being formed. Once this was done, a connection between the two wells was rapidly established.

Figure 3 shows one view of the phase II system as it exists today. The reservoir is centered at approximately 12,000 ft, is elongated in shape, and is tilted roughly along the axis of the lower wellbore. It has been determined by a variety of measurement techniques that the fluid-connected volume of the reservoir is in the range of 25 million cubic yards. As currently configured, the original upper well is the injector while the lower well serves as the producer.

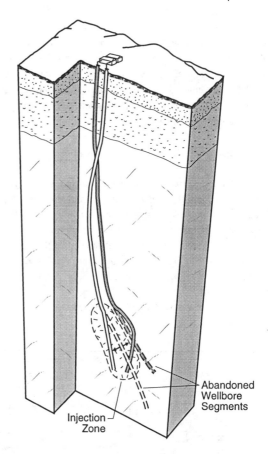

FIGURE 3. The Phase II HDR heat mine at Fenton Hill, New Mexico.

### Initial Flow Testing of the Phase II Reservoir

The drilling, fracturing, and well completion work associated with development of the Phase II reservoir took nearly six years to accomplish so that it was not until May 1986 that the system was ready for flow testing. At that time, a 30-day flow test was conducted using rented pumping equipment and temporary surface piping.[8] The results of this test are summarized in Table 2.

| Injection Conditions: | Pressure, psi | 4570 |
|---|---|---|
| | Flow Rate, gpm | 290 |
| | Temperature, °F | 60 |
| Production Conditions: | Backpressure, psi | 500 |
| | Flow Rate, gpm | 214 |
| | Temperature, °F | 375 |
| | Thermal Power, MW | 9.8 |
| Water Loss, gpm (%) | | 76 (26) |

TABLE 2. Operating results of the 30-day flow test, May-June, 1986.

267

In order to achieve the impressive fluid production rate shown in Table 2, it was necessary to run the test at pressures high enough to cause growth of the reservoir. Although a large amount of fluid could be pumped through the system under these conditions, a significant fraction of the water was consumed in extending the reservoir. Water losses, as measured by the difference between injected and produced volumes, declined over the length of the test but were still about 26% of the injected volume at its termination.

There were many interruptions in flow during this short test, but the overall results were highly positive in showing that considerable amounts of water hot enough to be useful for electrical power production could be produced from the Phase II reservoir. On the basis of these results, repairs were made to the lower wellbore, which had been damaged by the extensive fracturing operations carried out during the creation of the reservoir, and construction of a permanent surface facility was begun.

### The Phase II Surface Plant

Construction of the surface plant was completed in late 1991.[9] Figure 4 is a diagram showing the main components of the plant. Two injection pumps, each capable of delivering 200 gallons of water at up to 5,000 psi form the primary motive force in the loop. Typically only one pump is operated at a time while the other is on standby status. A high-pressure stainless steel pipeline carries the water from the pump to the injection well. After circulating through the underground system and extracting thermal energy from the rock, the water returns to the surface through the production well.

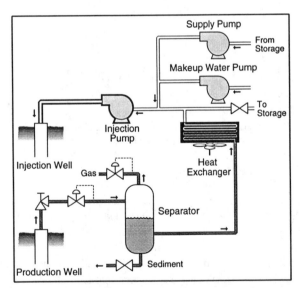

FIGURE 4. Schematic drawing of the Fenton Hill Phase II HDR surface plant.

Valves on the production wellhead permit a backpressure of several thousand pounds to be maintained on the underground system. The hot water from the production wellhead passes through a series of control valves which reduce its pressure to 700 psi or less, a separator which removes gases and particulates that may have been entrained in the fluid, and a heat exchanger where the thermal energy is measured and dissipated.

The cooled water is then recirculated back to the injection pump. A pumphouse just upstream from the injection pump contains two types of makeup water pumps: High volume/low pressure pumps can be used to fill the system rapidly or add large amounts of water quickly if operating at production pressures of less than 200 psi. Low volume/high pressure pumps deliver water against heads of up to 700 psi and permit more efficient operations when relatively small amounts of makeup water are needed.

The surface plant has been constructed to conform to power plant pressure codes and strict materials standards. It is highly automated with control set-points and automatic shutdown features which allow it to be run in an unmanned mode of operation for up to eight hours or more. Continuous collection of flow, pressure, and temperature data is carried out automatically at a number of points in the circulation loop. Recent experience has shown that this plant will operate as designed with an extremely high degree of reliability. During the entire month of May 1992, the plant ran on a 24-hour-a-day schedule with no unplanned shutdowns.

### The Long-Term Testing Program

A long-term testing program of the Phase II HDR system began in December 1991 with a 3-day flow test to evaluate the new plant under actual operating conditions and assess the state of the reservoir which had been pressurized but not flowed for several years. After minor plant modifications, two more short flow tests were conducted in February 1992. In early March, a ten-day test was conducted. Finally, on April 8, 1992, continuous flow testing began. As this paper is being written, the test has been underway for about 2 months. Table 3 summarizes some important operating data as of early June, 1992.

| Injection Conditions: | Pressure, psi | 3926 |
| | Flow Rate, gpm | 117 |
| | Temperature, °F | 65 |
| Production Conditions: | Backpressure, psi | 1401 |
| | Flow Rate, gpm | 100 |
| | Temperature, °F | 364 |
| | Thermal Power, MW | 4.4 |
| Water Loss, gpm (%) | | 12.8 (10.8) |

TABLE 3. Operating parameters of the Fenton Hill Phase II HDR Plant, June 5, 1992.

### HDR DEVELOPMENT OUTSIDE THE UNITED STATES

#### Western Europe

Since development of HDR heat mining began in the United States in 1974, worldwide interest in the technology has developed. The British began work in 1978 at a site in Cornwall, England.[10] There they drilled wells to depths in excess of 6,600 feet, carried out hydraulic fracturing operations, and conducted extensive flow testing over a number of years. Unfortunately, due to a relatively low thermal gradient, their reservoir was created in rock at temperatures of less than 200°F, and so could not produce water hot enough to be useful in generating electricity. Work in the United Kingdom has thus been concentrated on scientific aspects of HDR technology such as studies of rock mechanics and of fluid flow in fractures. Recently, they have de-emphasized their Cornwall HDR project and have begun to participate more actively in a broader European HDR effort.

Several years ago, the European Community (EC) began a program of HDR development involving intensive participation by Germany, France, and more recently, as mentioned above, Great Britain.[11] At present the principle experimental site of the EC work is at Soultz in northeastern France but some work is also underway at Urach in Germany. A consortium of private industrial firms has formed a group known as European Hot Dry Rock Industries. It is anticipated that in 1994 a site will be selected to begin a $300 million, 10 year HDR effort aimed specifically at developing the low-gradient resources of northern Europe. Financing for the project is expected to come primarily from the EC.

## Japan

The Japanese have had an extensive HDR development program for a number of years. They currently have three active sites, with reservoirs in rock at temperatures of about 360-390°F being developed at two of the locations. Water loss problems plagued the early Japanese effort, but in late 1991 they conducted a 3-month flow test in which 80% of the injected water was recovered.[12] After deepening their present wells and creating an improved reservoir, the Japanese expect to begin long-term testing similar to the current Los Alamos experiment sometime during 1994-1995.

## Russia

The Russians have had a longstanding interest in HDR but began experimental work only recently. They have carried out drilling and fracturing operations at a site near Mt. Elbrus in the Caucusus Mountains, modeling their efforts on the work which was done in developing the system at Fenton Hill. The goal of the Russian program is to supply thermal and electric energy for a local tungsten mine.

## THE FUTURE OF HDR

The tests now being conducted at Fenton Hill should set the stage for the development of a second HDR site in the United States. Ideally this new HDR system will be constructed and run by private industry although, as with many new technologies, government support may be required to make it happen. This second HDR facility should be designed to make and sell power in order to provide a clear demonstration of the economics of HDR energy production.

Work should also continue to explore advanced techniques for the design of HDR systems. Modeling studies have indicated that as much as a sevenfold increase in energy production could be achieved by simply drilling a second production well into the Fenton Hill reservoir. Experimental work must be conducted to verify that multiple production wells per injector can indeed markedly improve the productivity of HDR reservoirs. Cyclic operational schedules, in which the production well is flowed only on a periodic basis, perhaps to provide electric power during periods of peak demand for example, also appear to warrant experimental evaluation.

Finally, an investigation of the application of HDR technology for other purposes such as desalination, gray-water purification, and the treatment of certain industrial wastes would appear to be worthwhile as the technology matures. In fact, the wide variety of options for utilizing HDR bode well for its successful transition from an experimental technology to commercial reality within the next decade.

## SUMMARY

Geothermal energy in the form of HDR is an abundant, widely distributed resource which has significant environmental advantages and holds the promise of favorable economics. The technology to gain access to HDR and successfully bring its energy to the surface has been under development over the past two decades at the Los Alamos National Laboratory in the United States and, more recently, in a number of other countries. A test to evaluate the feasibility of extracting energy from HDR over an extended time period is now underway at a pilot facility in Fenton Hill, NM. Initial results are promising.

The current test will form the basis for the construction of future HDR facilities which will generate and sell electric power. Innovative design and operational techniques may significantly improve the performance of HDR systems and should make HDR even more competitive with conventional energy sources. In the future, HDR technology may be useful, not only to produce energy on a wide scale, but also to solve a variety of other serious world problems involving water purification and pollution control.

## REFERENCES

1. Huttrer, G. W., 1990. Geothermal Electric Power-A 1990 World Status Update, Geothermal Resources Council Bulletin, July-August, pp 175-187.

2. Rannels, J. W. and D. V. Duchane, 1990. Geothermal Development in the USA: A Vast Potential Resource, Power Generation Technology, London: Sterling Pub., pp 177-180.

3. Armstead, H. C. H. and J. W. Tester, 1987, Heat Mining, London: E. F. Spon.

4. Tester, J. W., D. O. Wood, and N. A. Ferrari, Ed., 1991. Energy and the Environment in the 21st Century, The MIT Press, Cambridge, MA.

5. Potter, R. M., E. S. Robinson, and M. C. Smith, 1974. Method of Extracting Heat From Geothermal Reservoirs, U. S. Patent 3,786,858.

6. Tester, J. W. and H. J. Herzog, 1990. Economic Predictions for Heat Mining: A Review and Analysis of Hot Dry Rock (HDR) Geothermal Energy Technology, Massachusetts Institute of Technology Energy Laboratory Report, MIT-EL 90-001.

7. Dash, Z. V., H. D. Murphy, and G. M. Cremer, eds., 1981. Hot Dry Rock Geothermal Reservoir Testing: 1978-1980, Los Alamos National Laboratory Report, LA-9080-SR.

8. Dash, Z. V., ed., 1989. ICFT: An Initial Closed-Loop Flow Test of the Fenton Hill Phase II HDR Reservoir, Los Alamos National Laboratory Report, LA-11498-HDR.

9. Ponden, R. F., 1991. The Design and Construction of a Hot Dry Rock Pilot Plant, Proceedings of U. S. Department of Energy Geothermal Program Review IX, pp 149-151.

10. Parker, R., 1989. Hot Dry Rock Geothermal Energy Research at the Camborne School of Mines, Geothermal Resources Council Bulletin, vol 18, no. 9 (Oct.) p. 3-7.

11. Kapplemeyer, O., A. Gerard, W. Schloemer, R. Ferrandes, F. Rummel, and Y. Benderitter, 1991. European HDR Project at Soultz-sous-Forets General Presentation, Geothermal Sciences and Technology, vol 2, no. 4 (Apr.) p. 263-289.

12. Matsunaga, I., 1991. Japan New Energy Development Organization, personal communication.

# Chapter 46

# Application of Fluidized Bed Combustion for Use of Low Grade and Waste Fuels in Power Plants

D.A. Wert

## EXECUTIVE SUMMARY

In a span of less that 15 years, CFB combustion technology has progressed from a concept to a demonstrated capability of providing clean, reliable energy from low-cost, low-grade fuels. In fact, one of the major advantages of CFB technology is its ability to burn fuels with high moisture, high ash and high sulfur levels, allowing the users the option of using inexpensive "opportunity" fuels.

CFB technology has demonstrated reliable operation while burning low-grade, easily available fuels which other combustion technologies preclude or cannot easily accommodate (such as peat, waste coals, sludges, municipal wastes and lignite). The CFB units can be designed to burn a wide range of different fuels, alone or in combination. This capability allows the user to take advantage of various fuel supplies to lower operating costs while still complying with ever increasing environmental regulations. This paper will review the evolution and experience of CFB technology and discuss the operating history of the first culm-fired (anthracite mine tailings) power plant.

The development of opportunity-fueled power plants has been associated with the establishment of the Independent Power Industry in the United States. Traditional utilities have relied on premium fuels (oil, natural gas, coal and nuclear) due to availability and the ability to pass fuel costs through to consumers. With the development of privatized power plants, more emphasis has been placed on fixing fuel costs over the life of the plant to minimize investor risk. An analogy can be drawn between the growth of the Independent Power Industry in the United States over the last ten years with the need for capacity in many Developing Countries today.

The interest in privatized or Project Financed power plants is quickly spreading to Developing Countries because the host countries and multilateral agencies can only finance a small portion of the projected capacity needs. For example, for the next decade, it has been estimated that the annual investment for electric power supply in all Developing Countries alone lies between US$ 60 to 125 billion per year.[1] At present the combination of bilateral and multilateral funds allocated for electric power investment is approximately US$ 10 billion per year and the prospects for any significant increase in the amount of aid funds available is slight.

Given their urgent need for more electricity and given their precarious financial situation and often negative balance of trade payments, Developing Countries will have to rely on indigenous fuels and foreign investment to provide for their rapidly expanding energy needs. Far too often in the past, these countries have relied on oil imports for their primary energy needs, and in the process have exported their limited investment capital to meet fuel and energy needs. This trend must change if these countries are going to build enough electrical generating capacity to satisfy their growing demand. Most Developing Countries are not using their available resources to solve this problem: low-grade, indigenous solid fuels (i.e. opportunity fuels).

CFB combustion technology has proven to be an effective means of using indigenous resources to produce reliable, cost-effective, environmentally clean electricity. Simply put, Developing Countries can burn indigenous solid fuels in CFBs to produce low-cost energy. Thus, the most viable solution for many of these nations is to encourage privatized power plant development and Project Financing to fund solid-fueled projects using indigenous fuels to provide the power these countries desperately need. The experiences of private developers in the U.S. using Project Financed, CFB power projects burning low-grade fuels can be used as examples for how independent Project Financing and CFB technology can be used to assist Developing Countries in meeting their rising electrical needs.

## SUMMARY OF CFB EXPERIENCE

With several generations of proven design and many unit-years of successful operation, CFBs are a mature technology. Some of the CFB's greatest advantages are fuel combustion efficiency, proven environmental performance, and the ability to burn a wide range of premium and low quality fuels. The high intensity of solids mixing in a CFB facilitates the burning of a wide range of fuels and eliminates a number of shortcomings experienced in a pulverized coal combustion system or bubbling fluidized bed combustion system. Examples of these advantages are:

- higher combustion efficiencies
- better sulfur capture
- higher heat transfer coefficient
- better load reduction with faster turndown rate
- fewer feed points
- lower $NO_x$ emissions
- multi-fuel capability

CFB technology, with its strong operating and performance characteristics, continues to gain worldwide acceptance. Currently, CFB units are operating in approximately 20 countries, with additional countries focusing on this technology to solve environmental, waste and fuel problems. The worldwide CFB sales by country are illustrated in Figure 1.

## COMMON FUELS FOR A CFB:

agriculture waste/biomass
bark
bitumens and asphaltines
coals (all grades):
    anthracite
    bituminous
    subbituminous
    lignite
    bituminous gob
    anthracite culm
diatomite
gases:
    natural
    "off" gases
gasifier fines
oil
oil shale
peat
petroleum coke:
    delayed
    fluid
refuse-derived fuel (RDF)
residual and waste oils
sludge:
    de-inking
    municipal
    paper mill
tires
washery waste and rejects
wood and woodwaste

TABLE 1.  CFB FUEL CAPABILITY

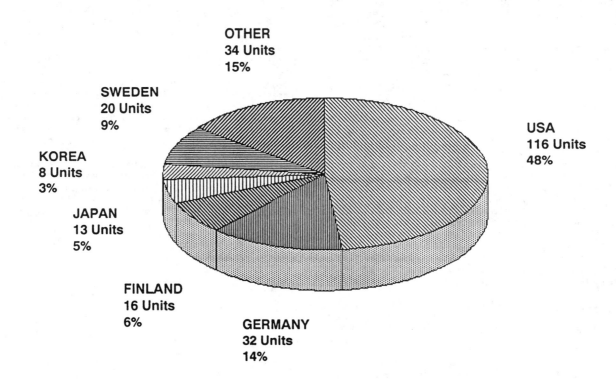

FIGURE 1.  CFB SALES WORLDWIDE BY COUNTRY (1992)

The circulating, fluidized nature of this combustion system permits the burning of many fuels in a clean and efficient manner. The many varieties of fuels that can be burned effectively and efficiently in a CFB are listed in Table 1. As an example, there are over 25 CFB boilers operating on brown coal and 9 units operating on waste coal while meeting the rigid U.S. and EC emissions standards.

In addition to the variety of fuels that can be burned alone or in conjunction with other fuel(s), the size and scope of CFB technology has steadily increased from small industrial applications to large utility-scale boiler systems. The technology has been scaled up in size from the first commercial units in 1979 (7 MWth) to the 409 MWth plants being constructed for Nova Scotia Power Corporation. Utility plants (> 100 MWe) are designed with reheat steam to improve plant efficiency. The reheat steam design operates with approximately 10% better thermal efficiency than does a traditional non-reheat design. Currently, units are being designed up to 600 MWth.

The experience summary has shown that CFBs are a proven, reliable technology that can burn difficult, low-grade fuels with availability factors in excess of 90%. CFBs have evolved into utility-size boilers, with manufacturers offering CFBs in the 250-300 MWe size.

GILBERTON/PANTHER CREEK EXPERIENCE

Located in Frackville, Pennsylvania, the Gilberton Power Facility began Commercial Operation in October, 1988, and has shown continuous improvement in its operating performance. A photograph of Gilberton is shown in Figure 2. The 2 AHLSTROM PYROFLOW® CFBs at Gilberton are a first generation design (first application for anthracite culm), and these Pyroflow boilers operated with annual capacity factors as shown below:

| Year | Capacity Factor (%) |
|---|---|
| 1989[1] | 75.0 |
| 1990 | 85.7 |
| 1991 | 92.5 |

[1] First full year of operation

TABLE 2. CAPACITY FACTORS AT GILBERTON POWER COMPANY

As the first processed anthracite culm-fired CFB power plant, Gilberton faced many problems associated with the specific characteristics of this fuel for the first time. Since 1988, 9 CFB units have begun commercial operation on culm (waste anthracite) and gob (waste bituminous) and 9 more are in construction. These projects have developed a reputation for high reliability. As an example, the members of the Anthracite Region of Independent Power Producers Association (ARIPPA), who burn waste coal (culm and gob) to generate electricity, had an average capacity factor of 87.5% in 1991. It is clearly evident from these results and from Gilberton's results that producing electricity from waste coals has the potential to be reliable, environmentally clean and economically rewarding.

FIGURE 2. GILBERTON POWER COMPANY

In addition to the economic benefits of these projects, each 80 MWe plant is removing 1-2 million tons of environmentally polluting mine waste each year. Over the life of these projects, each will consume 30-60 million tons of waste and leave behind ash which neutralizes the mining areas and promises to reclaim areas devastated by up to 150 years of mining activity.

The Panther Creek Energy Project, located in Nesquehoning, Pennsylvania, is a duplicate of the Gilberton Power Company plant with modifications based on Gilberton's operating experience. Gilberton was the first processed anthracite culm plant to go into operation, and several problems arose in its first year of operation. The second generation Pyroflow CFBs, such as those at Panther Creek, have incorporated the lessons learned at Gilberton. Several examples of the problems that arose at Gilberton and the resulting design improvements at Panther Creek are discussed below:

a) Bottom Ash System Capacity: Gilberton was designed for a 70% bottom ash/30% fly ash split based on performance fuel with normal margins using both ash coolers. Initially, during operation with the worst case fuel, the total ash content increased from an average 37% to the mid 40's and the bottom ash/fly ash split increased to a 90%/10% split. This higher split overloaded the ash removal system, decreasing plant capacity, increasing system erosion, and causing plant outages.

For Panther Creek, the ash removal system was designed for 80% bottom ash removal for the worst case fuel, with only three of four ash coolers operating. The fourth bottom ash removal drain will allow full operation under all operating conditions.

273

b) Fuel Feed System: The Gilberton fuel feed system was designed with drag chain conveyors. The highly corrosive and erosive nature of the fuel caused this system to suffer higher than anticipated forced outage rates. To eliminate this problem, Panther Creek's design has been upgraded to include belt feeders.

c) Fuel Processing: Gilberton uses a heavy media separation fuel processing facility to process the raw anthracite culm to 7,762 Btu/lb fuel. This process captures the maximum amount of carbon but allows some variation in fuel sizing and quality. Panther Creek has selected a jig processing facility which provides a higher quality fuel, allowing for higher boiler efficiencies and improved boiler bed maintenance.

d) Fuel Silos: The Gilberton fuel silos were constructed of carbon steel. In just over one year of operation, the anthracite culm wore through the silos. The problem was corrected by installing stainless steel liners. The Panther Creek silos are designed with stainless steel in the critical areas.

e) Moisture Content in Fuel: Gilberton's fuel can contain up to 18% moisture content. The high fuel moisture content causes front wall fuel feed pluggage and pluggage in other fuel feed system components.

The fuel preparation plant at Panther Creek has improved drainage control to lower the fuel moisture content, which will result in fewer fuel plugs and in reduced fuel loading. The maximum moisture content of the fuel fed to the boilers at Panther Creek will not exceed 12%.

f) Refractory: Early during the operating phase at Gilberton, it was discovered that the cyclone wall refractory had eroded away and that the cyclone vortex finders, also made of gunnite refractory, needed to be replaced. The gunnite refractory in the barrel and scroll areas of the cyclones were replaced with brick. The cyclone roofs/cones and vortex finders were also rebuilt.

Panther Creek's design reflects maximum brick refractory and improved anchors to hold the brick in place.

g) Fuel Feed Points: Gilberton experienced material handling problems in transferring the fuel from the in-plant storage bunkers into the boilers. Each boiler was equipped with two volumetric feeder systems: one to the rear wall area feeding into the loop seal chutes and the other feeding into the front wall of the boiler. The front wall feeder system consisted of a series of bi-directional ribbon feeders and was inoperable with most normal fuel. It plugged in minutes and required several hours of hard, hot, dirty work to clear.

After trying to rectify this situation, it was learned that the boilers would operate efficiently with the loop seal feeders only. Thus, Panther Creek incorporated a redundant fuel delivery system to the loop seal feed area only and did not bother with a front wall feed system. In addition to simplifying the design, the loop seal feed system will ease the day-to-day operating requirements as well as the overall maintenance of the materials handling system.

The plant modifications identified above are just a few examples of the design enhancements and changes resulting from the detailed plant review of Gilberton's operating experience. Even in spite of these first generation problems, Gilberton's operating performance has been very good. The second generation design at Panther Creek has benefitted from this review process, and it is anticipated that the capacity factors at Panther Creek, which will begin commercial operation this fall, will be significantly higher in the first years of operation than were the capacity factors at Gilberton.

In addition to the design enhancements at Panther Creek, the guaranteed emissions at Panther Creek are also significantly lower than at Gilberton, and well within the limits established by the 1990 Amendments to the Clean Air Act. The guaranteed emissions limits for Gilberton and Panther Creek, as well as the limits specified by the Clean Air Act are listed below in Table 3.

Guaranteed/Required Emissions

All emissions levels are measured in lb/MMBtu.

| Pollutant | Gilberton | Panther Creek | Clean Air Act 1995 | 2000 |
|---|---|---|---|---|
| SO2 | 0.370 | 0.156 | 2.500 | 1.200 |
| NOx | 0.600 | 0.150 | | |
| CO | | 0.180 | | |
| TSP | | 0.017 | | |
| VOC | | 0.005 | | |

Notes: 1. The Environmental Protection Agency will establish target levels for NOx compliance after the year 2000.

2. There are no guaranteed emissions levels for CO, TSP and VOC pollutants at Gilberton.

TABLE 3. GUARANTEED EMISSIONS LEVEL

## INTERNATIONAL DEMAND

The world-wide demand for clean, reliable electric generating capacity has never been greater. In Developing Countries the trend toward increased use of electricity as the preferred energy source continues while more stringent environmental legislation makes aging technology (polluting) obsolete. In the Developing Countries the need for a reliable supply of electricity is essential for social and economic development. Current shortages in the Developing Countries are delaying economic growth with a resulting loss of US\$ 1-3 per kwh not supplied.

Demand for new capacity in developed countries (with approximately 75% of current installed capacity) is 1-2% per year while demand in Developing Countries is increasing at over 7% per year based on modest economic growth projections. Some countries, such as Indonesia, India, Pakistan and Brazil project capacity needs of 10-15% per year. According to a recent report, titled "Power Shortages in Developing Countries,"[2] the U.S. Agency for International Development projected that Developing Countries will need an additional power generation capacity of over 1,500,000 MWs by the year 2008 (See Figure 3).

Estimates of the capital investment needed to meet this demand vary from US\$ 60 - 125 billion per year in the Developing Countries alone. Currently, bilateral and multilateral funds for investment in electrical capacity represent approximately US \$10 billion per year with limited prospects for any increased funding. This fact, coupled with the historically poor performance of state owned and operated utilities (on reliability, environmental and financial factors) has initiated the trend toward privatization (or Project Financing) in power generation.

Many Developing Countries are actively implementing programs to encourage the development of privatized power plants. The programs, patterned after the success of the U.S. Independent Power industry, are hoping to expand sources of investment capital by "Project Financing" future capacity needs. A privatized power plant is financed through traditional (bilateral and multi-lateral) and non-traditional (commercial, equity) sources, but does not depend (directly) on the borrowing capacity of the host country. This approach can "free" capital for other investment options which could enhance infrastructure development and accelerate industrial growth.

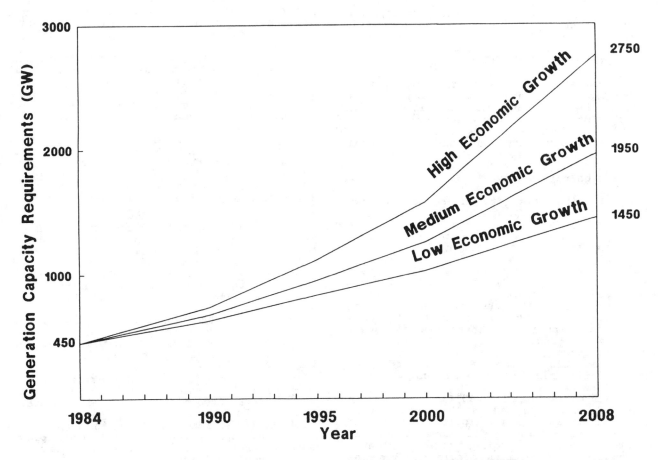

FIGURE 3. ELECTRICITY GENERATION CAPACITY REQUIREMENTS
FOR DEVELOPING COUNTRIES (1988 - 2088)

## CFB APPLICABILITY

WHAT DOES A SPECIFIC COMBUSTION TECHNOLOGY HAVE TO DO WITH THE TREND TOWARD PRIVATIZATION OF POWER PLANTS IN DEVELOPING COUNTRIES?

**A GREAT DEAL.**

One of the largest investor risks in Project Financed power projects is the ability to manage the operating costs of the project, mainly fuel costs. Any project based on imported fuel has two problems: uncertainty over future fuel costs (on the international market) and the resulting transfer of capital overseas to pay for the fuel. The cost of fuel can vary due to both international market forces and currency fluctuations. If a Developing Country would use its indigenous fuel reserves, the cost of fuel (and electricity) could be stabilized (in local terms) and the capital otherwise sent off-shore to pay for imported fuel could be used for in-country investment, such as infrastructure and industrial development.

The use of indigenous fuels solves both problems, by avoiding the unfavorable balance of trade payments due to gas and oil imports and by freeing up capital to develop other in-country industries, such as mining and transportation. From a Project Finance standpoint, the use of indigenous fuels can reduce or eliminate the fuel cost risk and reduce currency risk exposure. While these options have existed for many years, few Developing Countries have undeveloped premium fuel reserves and the technology to utilize low quality or waste fuels did not exist prior to the development of CFBs.

As demonstrated in Table 1, CFB power plants are capable of burning a wide range of low quality fuels in an environmentally clean, reliable manner. The technology offers:

- fuel diversity independent of global energy prices,

- high reliability,

- pricing tied to in-country labor indices, and

- the ability to reduce unfavorable balance of trade payments.

Since the price of fuel can be fixed or tied to local indices, the fuel cost risk is minimized for Project Financing and local infrastructure and jobs are created (on average, at least one job is created for each MW of new capacity). These new employees create an additional demand for new infrastructure (housing, services, etc.) and pay taxes. The net societal benefit from the use of indigenous fuels is enormous.

Typically these fuels have little or no market value and can be mined (or harvested) at a cost less than imported fuels. Since the capital cost of solid-fueled power plants is greater than gas/oil fixed plants, international developers should develop and build the privatized solid fuel power plants and state utilities should build the oil/gas plants which have lower capital costs (higher fuel costs) and shorter construction schedules. Developing Countries can, therefore, reduce capital investment in power plants and use scarce capital for other infrastructure and industrial development.

## SUMMARY

CFB combustion experience has demonstrated that low quality, waste fuels can be burned in an environmentally clean manner, that CFB power plants can be built in utility sizes and that CFB power plants operate at high capacity factors (even using waste fuels).

Based on the operating experiences at Gilberton and other waste fuel power plants, developers and owners have clearly shown us that the early startup problems with waste fuel plants have been solved and that second generation plants have incorporated the lessons learned from the first generation design.

The experience of the Independent Power Industry in the United States has taught us that Project Financing is a viable method of power plant development, and that independent developers can provide economically competitive, reliable electrical and thermal generating capacity.

The experiences from the developed countries with industrialization has clearly shown that we need to protect the environment and implement a program of sustainable growth using environmentally friendly technologies.

A careful review of the economies in the Developing Countries has demonstrated and continues to demonstrate that the lack of electrical generating capacity is constraining industrial growth and further limits the rate of industrial expansion and world trade.

Due to the lack of availability of capital in international markets, Developing Countries can not obtain the investment capital from traditional sources to build needed power plants, expand industrial capacity and raise the standard of living at desired rates.

The combination of the factors outlined above point to a viable, although partial, solution for most Developing Countries. This solution involves developing privatized (Project Financed) solid-fueled power plants using low quality indigenous fuels. The benefits to the Developing Countries are substantial:

- The construction and operation of new generating capacity without the need for the Developing Country's government to invest its limited capital.

- Environmentally clean, price stable, reliable electricity produced by experienced international developers.

- Added societal value and infrastructure development associated with power plant operations and associated industries such as mining.

The benefits to the developed countries are equally large:

- Increased trade in environmentally clean technology - an investment in the future of the planet.

- Opportunities for investment in power plants using proven technology and price stable fuels.

- Expanded worldwide trade resulting from the growth in Developing Countries' economies.

The time is right for Developing Countries, power plant developers, equipment suppliers and investors to work together to create an opportunity for mutual success. While visible failures in some countries have eroded developer and investor interest, the potential exists for creative and innovative solutions to the international need for additional capacity. Only time will tell whether the parties succeed together or fail alone.

## REFERENCES

[1] Vincento Vadacca, CEO, Ansaldo Energia, Washington, D.C. Paper entitled "International Power and Co-Generation Projects" and presented at the Forbes-sponsored Project Financing & Construction in the 1990's Conference, New York City, January 9-11, 1992.

[2] U.S. Agency for International Development, A Report to Congress, "Power Shortages in Developing Countries: Magnitude, Impacts, Solutions, and the Role of the Private Sector," Washington, D.C., March, 1988.

# Chapter 47

# Analysis of Technologies and Economics for Geothermal Energy Utilization of Electric Power Plant

C. Haijie

## INTRODUCTION

Geothermal energy -- it is a kind of heat energy which pertains to the internal heat of the earth. It carries the heat of the earth outward by the underground water of the rock section of the earth. Normally, the temperature of the thermal water is 50°-140°c. During the 20th century, the rapid development of industry and agriculture quickly increased the need for large amounts of electric power. Now, although there are coal power plants, oil and nature gas power plants, hydroelectric power and nuclear power plants, all countries of the world attach importance to the prospect of geothermal power plants. It is the most economic (no consumption fuel) and safe (no pollution) power plant. (present author considered that the chlorofluorocarbon refrigerants such as R11, R12, and etc. are not used)
In 1904, Italy established the first geothermal power plant in the world. Soon afterwards, the U.S.A., Iceland, Japan, Russia, and New Zealand also established geothermal power plants. In 1970, China, North China, Jiang province and Guangdong province also established geothermal power plants. In 1975, the U.S.A. geothermal power plant capacity of 522mw was the first in the world.
In general, the principle of the geothermal power plant process uses the Rankine cycle. In this power plant process, the generator is driven by the turbine. Because the temperature of the cooling water is limited by the weather (average temperature of the cooling water is about 28°c, except in the winter cooling water is 4°-5°c) the thrust out pressure of the turbine through the condenser is unable to condense at very low levels. Therefore, its enthalpy drop (isentropic expansion process) is very small and the output power and thermal efficiency are very small and low. Due to above mentioned, the technologies of the geothermal power plant process are imperfect. The present author considered that it must need further improvement (above mentioned: output power 2.0-8.0Kw/hrT, $\eta=2\%$--$10\%$.)

## GEOTHERMAL ENERGY UTILIZATION OF ELECTRIC POWER PLANT SYSTEM SET AND WORKING PRINCIPLE

Geothermal energy utilization of electric plant system sets are illustrated by Fig-(1).

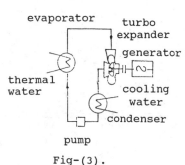

Fig-(1).

It consists of the turbine, generator, evaporator, condenser, pump and pipe. The principle of the geothermal power plant process uses the Rankine cycle, such as the a-line diagram shown in Fig-(1) and Fig-(2).

In Fig-(1) the working substance is adding the heat by the thermal water in the evaporator and it is gaseous through the turbine to drive the generator. The expansion gas (working substance) is out of the turbine and through the condenser and then the pump carries the working substance (liquid) to the evaporator. Such as mentioned above the working substance is finished a Rankine cycle.
Fig-(2) is the T-S diagram. In Fig-(2) T-S diagram: the addition of heat process 4-1, and the isentropic expansion, process 1-2, the rejection of heat, process 2-3, the work input to the pump carried the working substance to the evaporator, process 3-4. The Rankine cycle output work from the thermodynamics First Law:
$W=(h_1-h_2) -T(s_1-s_2)$.
the thermal efficiency of the Rankine cycle: (isentropic)
$$\eta= \frac{h_1-h_2}{h_1-h_4}$$

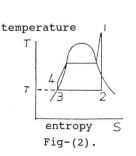

Fig-(2).

The T-S diagram is not to scale in particular, the actual temperature rise in the pump is very small. So the $h_4$ is very close to the $h_3$. In Fig-(1), the output work is very small (2.0--8.0Kw/hrT thermal working substance steam $T=10^3$Kg.) and the thermal efficiency (isentropic) of the Rankine cycle is very low ($2\%$--$10\%$).
Above mentioned: as shown in the Table-(1). the present author considered: that excepting the Rankine cycle process raised the temperature of the geothermal water (working substance) can be increased the output work and thermal efficiency because the cooling water temperature is limited by the weather throughout the year. (Average cooling water temperature is about 28°c, except in the winter cooling water temperature is 4°--5°c, may gain good profit.) The geothermal power plant process, only the most efficient way, that the turbine must be replaced by the turboexpander as shown in Fig-(3) and Fig-(4).
Fig-(4) T-S diagram shows the geothermal power plant process use of the turboexpander. It can drop the thrust pressure of the turboexpander ie the outlet temperature of the turboexpander is very low so that $T'<T$, ($h_2'<h_2$) it can obtain the maximum outlet enthalpy

Fig-(3).

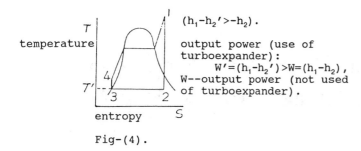

$(h_1-h_2' > -h_2)$.

output power (use of turboexpander):
$$W'=(h_1-h_2') > W=(h_1-h_2),$$
W--output power (not used of turboexpander).

Fig-(4).

At the same time the present author calculated that: the different temperature of the evaporated working substance (geothermal water) through the single stage turboexpander (expansion ratio $\epsilon=4$), it can increase the output power and thermal efficiency. As shown in Table-(2). The output power increased (15-60% above). The thermal efficiency of the Rankine cyclerised (4%--20%). It may save 50%--60% investment of the working substance. Above mentioned, it may be used to recover the low temperature waste heat. (50°--140°c.)

Table-(1). Output power and thermal efficiency of the geothermal power plant driven the generator by the turbine (average cooling water temperature 28°c).

| working substance | outlet temperature (with working substance) of the evaporator °c | evaporated pressure bar | enthalpy Kcal/Kg $h_1$ | enthalpy Kcal/Kg $h_2$ | output power $h_1 - h_2$ | isentropic expansion work $h_1 - h_4$ | thermal efficiency $\eta$ |
|---|---|---|---|---|---|---|---|
| ammonia $NH_3$ | 50 | 20.727 | 352.5 | 351.72 | 0.78= 0.906Kw | 352.5-83.68= 264.82 | 0.27% |
| | 70 | 33.6 | 333.89 | 328.4 | 5.49= 6.38Kw | 333.89-65.42= 268.47 | 204% |
| n-butane $CH_3CH_2CH_2CH_3$ | 50 | 5.0 | 110.0 | 104.92 | 5.08= 5.906Kw | 110.0-21.30= 88.7 | 5.7% |
| | 100 | 15.5 | 145.24 | 125.42 | 19.32= 22.46Kw | 145.24-42.25= 103 | 18.75% |
| isobutane $CH_3(CH_3)_3$ | 50 | 6.9 | 102.14 | 97.33 | 4.81= 5.59Kw | 102.14-21.35= 80.79 | 5.9% |
| | 100 | 21.2 | 136.3 | 118.6 | 17.7= 20.58Kw | 136.3-47.78= 88.52 | 19.9% |
| propane $CH_3CH_2CH_3$ | 50 | 17.58 | 224.5 | 222.1 | 2.4=2.79Kw | 224.5-146.3= 78.2 | 3.06% |
| | 65 | 24.73 | 226.8 | 222.1 | 4.7=5.46Kw | 226.8-146.3= 80.5 | 5.83% |

Table-(2). Output power and thermal efficiency of the geothermal power plant for driven the generator by the turboexpander (expansion ratio $\epsilon=4$).

| working substance | °c | bar | $h_1$ | $h_2$ | output power | isentropic work | $\eta$ |
|---|---|---|---|---|---|---|---|
| ammonia $NH_3$ | 50 | 20.727* | 332.9* | (5.18bar) 326.9* | 6.0= 7.44Kw | 332.9-23.92*= 208.92 | 3.06% |
| | 70 | 33.6* | 334.38* | 330.4* | 3.98= 4.63Kw | 334.38-37.03*= 297.35 | 1.34% |
| n-butane $CH_3CH_2CH_2CH_3$ | 50 | 5.0 | 110.0 | (1.25bar) 94.45 | 15.55= 18.08Kw | 110.0-4.0= 106 | 14.66% |
| | 100 | 15.5 | 145.24 | (3.875bar) 125.42 | 19.82= 23.03Kw | 145.24-42.25= 103 | 19.24% |
| isobutane $CH_3(CH_3)_3$ | 50 | 6.96 | 102.14 | (1.725bar) 87.36 | 14.78= 17.17Kw | 102.14-3.87= 98.27 | 15% |
| | 100 | 21.2 | 136.3 | (5.3bar) 117.1 | 19.2= 22.3Kw | 136.3-43.95= 92.38 | 20.78% |
| propane $CH_3CH_2CH_3$ | 65 | 24.73 | 119.44 | (6.18bar) 110.12 | 9.325= 10.83Kw | 119.44-27.28= 92.16 | 10.1% |

Data*; present author found and calculated from 6. (References).

## WORKING SUBSTANCE

As is known to all, choosing the working substance for the geothermal power plant is a very important problem because it directly effects the profit and loss of the output power and thermal efficiency and the investment of the geothermal power plant. On the other hand, in general, the geothermal power plants used chlorofluorocarbons (CFC'S). In recent years, due to the chlorofluorocarbon refrigerants (R11, R12, R500 and etc.) causing depletion of the stratospheric ozone ($O_3$) layer, and the global warming, the production of the CFC'S was limited. In the year 2000, a complete cessation of CFC'S production is expected.

The present author considered that the working substance must satisfy the following requirements:

1. the working substance must have a low normal boiling (temperature) point, moderate evaporated pressure, high chemical stability and in the thermodynamics process, no chemical reaction.
2. the working substance must not cause depletion of the stratospheric ozone ($O_3$) layer and not be toxic to humans and animals.
3. the working substance should not be corrosive towards the equipment and pipes.
4. the working substance costs and sources are cheap and easy.

Above mentioned: Table-(1) and Table-(2) illustrated the thermodynamics data of ammonia, n-butane, isobutane and propane. It may be adapted for the geothermal power plant. The n-butane and isobutane are the best working substances of them, and have a large output power, high thermal efficiency, and moderate evaporated pressure. In same diameter of the equipments, due to the moderate pressure, it can save investment of the equipments (because the thickness $s_1/s_2 = p_1/p_2$ here p is evaporated pressure.) About 40--60% total (equipment). At 50°c outlet temperature (with working substance) of the evaporator, n-butane: $h_1-h_2$=5.906Kw/hr·T (working substance steam) T=1000Kg. Propane: $h_1-h_2$=2.79Kw/hr·T, it can save 50% about weight of the working substance. The present author considered: that above mentioned four kinds of the working substance all completely replaced the CFC'S. All also completely satisfied above mentioned requirements.

## TURBOEXPANDER AND EXPANSION RATIO

Turboexpander has a long history of use in air separation, but more recent has come to the fore in liquid gas industry. The turboexpander is the radial reaction turbine. There is a high efficiency ($\eta$=0.8 above) and very small fraction loss. It does so by the mechanism of constant entropy expansion, together with the production of power (by-product). The power comes from the decrease in enthalpy of the working substance itself. So that the radial reaction turbine is the most efficient of the three (among the pulse turbine, the reaction turbine, and the radial reaction turbine).

On the other hand, the turboexpander is suited to the high speed turbine rotors and nozzles capable of reliable operation under extreme condition of low temperature and a wide range of the pressure. The structure is shown in Fig-(5). 1--nozzles, 2--blade and impeller,

3--diffuser, 4--inlet pipe, 5--inlet pipe, 6--outlet pipe.

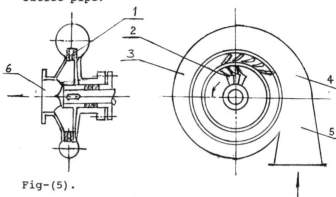

Fig-(5).

When the first turboexpander was designed, how to accurately calculate the expansion ratio $\epsilon$ of the turboexpander of the geothermal power plant was of great concern to the designer. N. Watson calculated the isentropic thermal efficiency $\eta$ and expansion ratio $\epsilon$ of the turbocharger of the internal combustion engine (single stage) as follows:

isentropic thermal efficiency

$$\eta = \frac{actual\ work}{isentropic\ expansion\ work}$$

i.e. 
$$\eta = \frac{h_1 - h_2}{h_1 - h_{2s}} \qquad ----(1)$$

here: $h_{1,2,2s}$--enthalpy Kcal/Kg.

towards the ideal gas ($C_p$= constant).thermal efficiency also may be written as following:

$$\eta = \frac{T_1 - T_2}{T_1 - T_{2s}} \qquad ---(2)$$

here:$T_{1,2,2s}$--absolute temperature °K. due to the isentropic expansion, may be obtained:

$$\frac{P_1}{P_2} = \left(\frac{T_1}{T_2}\right)^{\frac{r}{r-1}} \qquad ----(3)$$

here: 
$$r = C_p / C_v$$

$C_p$---specific heat at constant pressure.
$C_v$---specific heat at constant volume.

from (2) and (3),obtained:

$$\eta = \frac{T_1 - T_2}{T_1 - T_{2s}} = \frac{1 - T_2/T_1}{1 - (P_2/P_1)^{\frac{r-1}{r}}}$$

expansion ratio:

$$\varepsilon = \frac{P_1}{P_2} = \left(\frac{T_1}{T_1 - (T_1 - T_2)/\eta}\right)^{\frac{\gamma}{\gamma-1}} ---(4)$$

here: $P_1$--- inlet pressure of turboexpander.
$P_2$--- outlet pressure of turboexpander.

Above mentioned formula, the expansion ratio is suited for the single stage turboexpander. The present author considered that: the working principle and structure of the turbocharger are the same as the turboexpander, so the formula (4) may be calculated for the expansion ratio of the turboexpander of the geothermal power plant process.

Table-(3) expansion ratio ε with the different type of turbine

| type | application field | ε | source |
|------|-------------------|---|--------|
| (1) turboexpander, | deep low temperature refrigeration industry (air separation) | ε =2.83--3.18, | ( present author measured at industry pratice). |
| (2) Helical rotary screw expander | the geothermal power plant test | ε =3.0, | References: 1. |
| (3) turbocharger, | internal combustion engine | ε =4.0, | References: 5. |

In general, expansion ration ε of the single stage turboexpander is given 2.5--4.0. The present author found and proved that the expansion ration ε is used of two or multi stages as follows:

hence, the single stage expansion ration ε:

$$\varepsilon_1 = \frac{P_1}{P_2} = \left(\frac{T_1}{T_1 - (T_1 - T_2)/\eta}\right)^{\frac{r}{r-1}} \quad ---(5)$$

due to: $r>1$, $r'>1$, $r/(r-1)>1$, $r'/(r'-1)>1$.

At same condition, two single stage connected in series as Fig-(6) may be obtained the second stage expansion ratio:

$$\varepsilon_2 = \frac{P_2}{P_3} = \left(\frac{T_2}{T_2 - (T_2 - T_3)/\eta}\right)^{\frac{r'}{r'-1}} > 1 \quad ---(6)$$

(5)×(6), obtained:   (in which $T_2 > T_3$).

$$\varepsilon = \frac{P_1}{P_2} \cdot \frac{P_2}{P_3} = \frac{P_1}{P_3}$$
$$= \left(\frac{T_1}{T_1 - (T_1 - T_2)/\eta}\right)^{\frac{r}{r-1}} \left(\frac{T_2}{T_2 - (T_2 - T_3)/\eta}\right)^{\frac{r'}{r'-1}} > 4$$

Above mentioned, the present author considered that r and r' must be needed further to test and industry experiment.

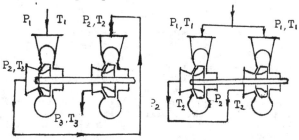

Fig-(6)       Fig-(7).

Fig-(7). is use of the large volumetric flow condition (single stage connected in parallel).

About designed the turboexpander's formula, it may be found from textbook and handbook, here will not mention (above mentioned, if we know ε and thermal water t°c, i.e. determined W and η of the turboexpander so very easy designed it.)

PAYBACK PERIOD

The geothermal power plant system project its payback period may be calculated by the following formula:

$$\text{payback period} = \frac{\text{investment}}{\text{gross profit}}$$

Let us site an example:
The geothermal power plant system project, its technological data as follows:
electric power capacity  2 x 375 Kw·hr
geothermal water temperature  90°--110°c.
average temperature of the cooling water about 28°c.

Investment:
(not included the prospecting and well drilling expense).
1.  turboexpander cost        $8x10^4$
2.  evaporator cost           $8x10^4$
3.  condenser cost            $12x10^4$
4.  pump cost                 $1x10^4$
5.  pipe and valve cost       $2x10^4$
6.  instrument cost           $3x10^4$
7.  working substance cost    $10x10^4$
8.  design expense            $3x10^4$
9.  installation cost         $4x10^4$
10. building cost             $10x10^4$
11. contingency cost          $6x10^4$
                 total =      $67x10^4$

Gross profit:
1. geothermal power cost      $27x10^4$/yr
   (China at present condition)

In addition:
Maintenance & repair expense  $1x10^4$/yr

$$\text{payback period} = \frac{67\times10^4}{27\times10^4-1\times10^4}$$
$$= 2.57 \text{ years} \leqslant 3.5 \text{years}.$$
(is possible).

In this system, if not uses the turboexpander, it uses the turbine, that the payback period would be prolonged due to increased equipment, working substance, and repair expense.

$$\text{payback period} = \frac{98\times10^4}{27\times10^4-2\times10^4}$$
$$= 3.92 \text{ years} > 3.5 \text{years}.$$
(not economic).

CONCLUSIONS

1.  The ammonia, n-butane, isobutane and propane working substance all completely replaced the chlorofluorocarbon refrigerants and also completely satisfied the requirement of Rankine cycle.
2.  Geothermal power plant process, the turbine is replaced by the turboexpander, it may be obtained:
    (1) the thermal efficiency of the

Rankine cycle raised: (4% -- 20%).
(2) the output power increased: (15% -- 60%) and can have a good economic effect.
3. The expansion ratio $\epsilon$ of the turboexpander:
   (1) single stage $\epsilon$ = 2.5--4.0.
   (2) two or multi stage $\epsilon$ must be needed further to test and industry experiment.
   Towards large volumetric flow, it may be connected in parallel and towards the high evaporated pressure, it may be connected the single in series as shown in Fig-(6) and Fig-(7) (single stage turboexpander)
4. The system payback period = 2.57 years <3.5 years is possible. The use of the turboexpander would effectively shorten the payback period and can increase with great effect.

References:

1.  McKay R. A. and R.S. Sprankel "Helical Rotary Screw Expander Power System" Proceeding on Research for the Development of Geothermal Energy Resources, Pasadena Calif., Sep23-25, 1974.

2.  Jesse S. Doolittle and Francis J. Hale "Thermodynamics for Engineers" John Wiley & Sons, New York, 1983.

3.  Robert Goldstick and Albert Thumann CEM, PE. "Principles of Waste Heat Recovery" The Fairmont Press, Inc., Atlanta, Georgia, 1986.

4.  Loyal Clarke and Robert L. Davidson "Manual for Engineering Calculations" McGraw Hill book company., 1962.

5.  N. Watson and M.S. Janota "Turbocharging the Internal Combustion Engine", MacMillan Press Ltd., 1982.

6.  F. A. Holland and F. A. Watson "Thermodynamic Design Data for Heat Pump Systems" Pergamon Press, 1982.

# SECTION 4
# ENERGY MANAGEMENT
# APPLICATIONS

# Chapter 48

# A Simple In-Plant Technique for Quantifying Leaks in Compressed Air Systems

R.J. Jendrucko, R.A. Bachschmidt

Other than electricity, compressed air is the most widely-used energy form in manufacturing plants. As a form of potential energy compressed air has distinct advantages including the fact that it is non-toxic and convenient in use for effecting mechanical action. However, it is normally the most expensive energy form employed due to the inherent inefficiencies in producing compressed air, usually with the use of electrically-powered motors. For this reason, compressed air system leaks often represent a significant fraction of total energy losses associated with plant operations.

The frequency of the occurrence of significant leaks in industrial compressed air systems remains relatively high; among 227 industrial energy audits performed by the University of Tennessee Energy Analysis and Diagnostic Center over a several year period, 122 recommendations to repair compressed air system leaks were made (1).

Plant compressed air leaks are commonly overlooked as being of minor concern. In part, this may be due to the relative difficulty of locating, and repairing all existing leaks. While leaks can usually be located sequentially by the sound of leak air jets, repair may be difficult and time-consuming due to system complexity and the need for process interruption and system dissembly to replace defective parts and reseal joints. In the face of such disincentives, it is distinctly desirable to be able to quantify the energy value of leaks to establish a priority for leak repair.

For a typically complex compressed air distribution system, efforts at leak quantification usually focus on single leaks or total system loss rate. Normally, attention is directed to the former in order to demonstrate that significant energy may be associated with single leaks (2, 3). Historically, individual leaks are typically modeled as ideal gas choked flow through simple circular orifices. Although such models may provide useful order-of-magnitude estimates of typical leak rates, accurate experimental measurement or mathematical model prediction of air loss through actual leaks of irregular geometry have not yet been documented. For this reason it is usually more useful to address leaks on a total system basis. Such estimates also focus attention on the total gross cost of all leaks and thus provide a stronger incentive for improved plant maintenance leading to the repair of existing leaks.

A recent publication (4) outlines a simple method for quantifying total leak air loss as a function of pressure decay during system bleed-down. However, use of this method requires the measurement or reliable estimation of total distribution system confining air volume. Since in a typically complex system this volume is difficult to quantify, the bleed-down method may be subject to large errors in predicted air loss rates. In view of this limitation a modification of this method is shown to circumvent the problem and to allow a direct calculation of system volume and total leakage rate.

The approach is as follows: For a system of assumed constant temperature and volume (V), the total leakage rate is assumed proportional to the system-atmospheric pressure difference (first-order model). A simple mass balance and integration over time yields the expression:

$$\ln (P_{system} - P_{atmosphere}) = K_1 \text{ (unknown constant) } t \text{ (elapsed time)}/V$$

Now, if an additional intentional leak is added to the system by tapping into the system with a valve-controlled branch, the mass balance becomes

$$\ln (P_s - P_a) = [(K_1 + K_2) t]/V$$

If two semi-logarithmic plots are now made of $P_s - P_a$ versus elapsed time, t, two constant slopes can be determined:

$$\text{slope } 1 = K_1/V$$
$$\text{slope } 2 = (K_1 + K_2)/V$$

These expressions constitute two independent, algebraic equations with three unknowns. However, $K_2$ can be evaluated if the artificial leak can be directly quantified, for example by orifice flow metering. The leak air mass flow is

$$m_{measured \; leak} = K_2(P_s - P_a)$$

From this additional relationship, $K_1$ (and V) can be determined and

$$m_{system \; leaks} = K_1(P_s - P_a)$$

defines total leakage rate for the unknown system leaks at any system pressure. Thus, with a simple system modification and flow metering of an added intentional "test" leak, total unidentified system leaks can be easily quantified.

This modified approach, while improved, is still based on the assumed first-order model. This modeling basis is valid as long as the leak parameters $K_1$ and $K_2$ are constant and the system pressure is instantaneously uniform throughout the system volume. For systems having significant in-line flow restrictions (such as those resulting from partially-closed valves, system pressure will not be uniform and a higher-order model may be needed to accurately describe system behavior.

## REFERENCES

(1) Jendrucko, R. J. and K. L. Binkley, "Factors Affecting the Implementation of Energy Conservation Measures Identified During Audits of Manufacturing Facilities," Proc. 14th World Energy Engineering Cong., pp. 433-434, 1991.

(2) Ingersoll-Rand Catalog A, Compressors Accessories, p. 163, 1978.

(3) Cunningham, E. R., "Air Compressors," Plant Engineering, p. 58, May 1980.

(4) Dutta-Choudhury, K., "Characterization and Evaluation of Leaks from Compressed Air Lines," Proc. 14th World Energy Engr. Cong., pp. 435-438, 1991.

# Chapter 49
# Systems Approach in Energy Management

K. Dutta-Choudhury

## INTRODUCTION:

Several years ago when I was working in the chemicals division of a paper company in Instrumentation and Controls, I had an experience which had a lasting impact on my work approach which is systems approach. I was going out of town on company business when I was called by the maintenance manager. He told me that a very important piece of boiler instrument of the power plant had broken down and I needed to expedite the delivery of the replacement instrument when I arrived at a certain city. The instrument was ordered over the phone.

When I landed in the city, I went straight to the supplier's office, delivered the purchase order for the instrument, and made sure that the instrument was put on the next flight. Having done so, I took care of my other businesses in the city and returned to my work place in about a week. To my dismay I found out from the maintenance manager that the particular instrument still had not arrived in the plant and he could not run the power plant. Thus the company incurred substantial losses. On further inquires, I found out that the instrument did indeed arrive at the plant stores on time. But, in the absence of any instructions thereon, the instrument was not delivered to the power plant. The sense of urgency was lost in the existing delivery process. In other words, the process or system failed. The whole process from requisitioning to delivery of ordered items was analyzed and corrective procedures were incorporated to prevent future repetitions. This brings up the subject of systems approach in engineering management in general and energy management in particular. This involves defining an objective and designing a system for an effective way of getting there.

## SYSTEM DEFINITION:

What is a system? Simply stated, any system has a set of inputs and a set of outputs and a well-defined rectangular box in-between which describes the system. The inputs and outputs are materials, utilities and informations (Figure 1 Single Stage System; Figure 2 Single Stage System with Feedback). A well-conceived and well-designed system transforms system inputs to desired outputs. A system may also have information only as inputs and information only as outputs. For example, the chief executive officer of an organization acts on a set of informations brought to him in the form of decision options. He then gives directives to his subordinates through his system to carry through his decisions to attain desired objectives. These actions and outcomes are all information-oriented.

## SYSTEM CHARACTERISTICS:

A boiler plant has a set of inputs (water, chemicals, fuel, knowledge and experience of boiler operators) and a set of outputs (steam, delivery system and quality of steam). With inappropriate combinations of inputs you will certainly obtain inappropriate outputs and the right combination of inputs will deliver the right combination of outputs in a properly maintained system. The objective is to optimize the performance of the system, the boiler system, i.e. increase the efficiency, safety and longevity of the boiler and prevent steam losses. What applies to the boiler system applies to any system, small or big, simple or complex. Y-Line at Louisiana Army Ammunition Plant is a fine example of how rectangular bars of iron are converted to projectile by a set of successive operations which constitute the sub-systems of the

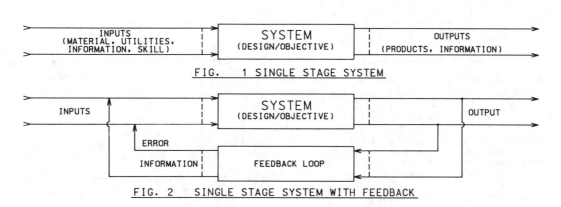

FIG. 1 SINGLE STAGE SYSTEM

FIG. 2 SINGLE STAGE SYSTEM WITH FEEDBACK

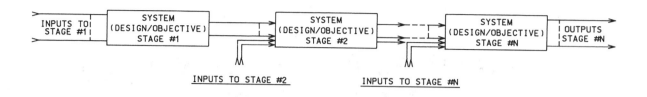

FIG. 3   MULTI-STAGE SEQUENTIAL SYSTEM

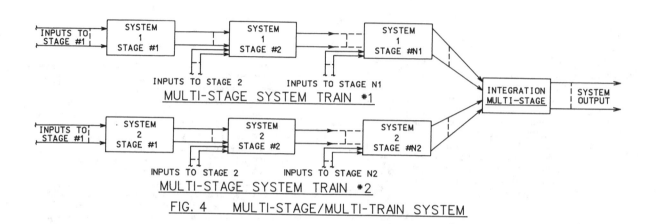

MULTI-STAGE SYSTEM TRAIN #1

MULTI-STAGE SYSTEM TRAIN #2

FIG. 4   MULTI-STAGE/MULTI-TRAIN SYSTEM

large aggregate system (Figure 3 Multi-Stage Sequential System, Figure 4 Multi-Stage/Multi-Train System). Inputs of each sub-system operation consists of materials, utilities and expertize of the system operators. The outputs at each stage consist of value-added products and information on the quality of the products. Optimizing the performance of the sub-systems does improve the overall system performance of Y-Line. The same is true of any other production operations in the plant.

### DEVIATION OF SYSTEM CHARACTERISTICS:

Any system has certain characteristics and it operates within certain upper and lower limits of desired objectives. When measured parameters in performance evaluation show degradation of performance from desired values, it is time to take corrective measures. Any system that performs poorly, deviates from desired objectives outside designed limits is an expensive and, consequently, an undesirable system. It must be rectified or the system must be replaced. It may also involve imparting training to the operators of the system i.e. provide better knowledge input.

### SYSTEM PERFORMANCE MEASUREMENT:

How do you analyze the performance of a system? That depends on your system perspective. For boiler operation, it is the amount of steam generated against the fuel consumed as well as a comprehensive analysis of the flue-gas. If you are a quality control specialist, you measure the quality and tolerances of the manufactured product and feed the information back to production; if you are in finance, you measure the cost of making the product and determine what factors are causing price deviations and control them, if necessary; if you are in maintenance you maintain the equipment within

manufacturer's tolerance limits at all times. If you are in energy, you measure the cost of utility components and bring them down by enhancing the performance of energy sub-systems. None of these perspectives of a system work at cross-purposes and are truly additive that cause improved results i.e. lower cost and higher performance of products.

### SYSTEM NOISE:

It must also be recognized that there is also a lot of misinformation, intentional or unintentional, between measured performance parameters and their interpretation for corrective actions. That creates a noisy environment and is not conducive for an objective evaluation of the performance of a system. The aim is to filter out the noise factors by emphasizing/deemphasizing output informations collected from different measurements or sources. This will ensure significant elimination of biases for an objective evaluation of system performance.

### ROLE OF SYSTEMS APPROACH:

Systems Approach is a simple and effective tool in defining objectives and then defining and designing systems within the constraints of input resources. It has to be well defined. Once the system has been put into operation, then by measuring the deviation from objectives and taking corrective actions, you can create a very satisfying and productive environment. Systems approach provides a clearer perspective of what the system is designed to do or the system is not designed to do. System evaluation and corrective actions are necessarily an ongoing and continuous processes. The truism is a system designed for making nuts and bolts don't make good commemorative gold coins and vice-versa.

# Chapter 50

# Domestic Hot Water Use Study, Multi-Family Building Energy Monitoring and Analysis for DHW System Sizing Criteria Development

F.S. Goldner

## ABSTRACT

Thirty New York City multifamily building combined steam heating and domestic hot water (DHW) plants were instrumented for monitoring (mostly hourly) apartment, outdoor, boiler and DHW temperatures and burner on-off times. In nine of these buildings, which had been upgraded, additional data collected were: stack temperature, DHW flow in 15-minute increments, oil & boiler make- up water flows, and DHW temperature before and after the mixing (tempering) valve and on the circulating return line. The data set collected between July 1990 and September 1991 amounts to a database of over 100 megabytes.

The project's objectives are to develop comprehensive operating data on combined DHW and heating systems to be used in system design and specifications and for improving operating procedures. DHW requirements in multi-family buildings are currently calculated on the basis of questionable standards. These new, more precise DHW flow data (broken down by occupied apartment, per capita and other demographic data) result in a better basis for sizing than existed heretofore.

There is a critical need for improved specifications and performance in newly constructed and renovated buildings. The practice has been to oversize by applying safety factors because of unknown consumption levels and patterns. This often causes excessive burner cycling, a clear indication of inefficient fuel use. Better system choices among various instantaneous generation and storage scenarios will result in savings derived from smaller initial equipment investments as well as more energy efficient operations.

Furthermore, energy audit calculations to determine savings on conservation measures rely too often upon gas or oil bills that have to be divided between space heating and inaccurate DHW figures, at best, or worse, some "best guess" method. The data being generated define figures for DHW energy use so that more reliable and accurate predictions of savings can be calculated.

This paper presents DHW demand patterns, seasonal variations, weekday *vs.* weekend consumption, consumption *vs.* occupancy levels, coincidence of 15- and 60-minute demand periods, and average *vs.* peak demand levels.

This project is sponsored by New York State Energy Research and Development Authority (NYSERDA). The results of this research are being reviewed for inclusion in a revision of DHW guidelines for the next edition of the ASHRAE Handbook.

## INTRODUCTION

Energy engineers have long been frustrated by the lack of reliable data upon which to size domestic hot water (DHW) generating equipment. Design engineers and contractors know that strict adherence to ASHRAE data often results in undersized equipment. To be on the safe side, many of these oversize equipment and the resultant systems can be very inefficient.

The ongoing research reported here reflects the particular concern for the energy efficiency and economic viability of multi family buildings. New construction of these buildings (particularly in New York City) is rare now, but thousands of units of dilapidated buildings are being renovated and fitted with new boilers that do double duty, as is the custom, as steam heating and DHW generators. Public money for housing as well as building self improvement funds are very scarce; hence it is imperative that none is wasted on oversized boilers and inefficient operation.

What are presented here reflects analyses of fourteen months of real-time monitored data toward developing reliable data on DHW consumption and demand patterns for system sizing criteria. The research has been performed by Energy Management & Research Associates (EMRA) under a contract with New York State Energy Research and Development Authority (Energy Authority).

With the proliferation of personal computers and modems, multifamily building managers/owners have begun to install on- line systems for remotely monitoring heating plants and building equipment. They are currently installed by a number of management firms. Characteristically, on-line systems monitor such variables as indoor temperatures (in one-to-ten room sampling), burner on/off times and heating timer control device settings. Such systems are usually managed by a supervisor in a central management office who, on a daily or some other basis "calls up" each building and observes current and past data summaries.

These systems, installed in multifamily buildings, provided the research project with a significant and economical opportunity to track more data points and to analyze and summarize operational data to form what is potentially the largest multi-family building operations/energy use database in existence. EMRA was fortunate to be able to use the systems in buildings managed by Ralph Langsam Associates. The systems were upgraded with additional monitoring points to collect more detailed information on DHW use.

DHW requirements in NYC buildings have been calculated on the basis of national ASHRAE and other standards of many years standing, which have proved to be inaccurate.[1] This project measured DHW flows precisely in the observed buildings, producing a better base of experience for sizing and operation. This is a critical need in the process of renovating buildings. (There is additional applicability in New York City because all multifamily buildings are to be metered for water consumption by 1996. Initial indications are of much higher than expected water use and costs.)

Energy audit calculations used to determine fuel savings on energy conservation measures rely upon fuel bills, in the case of systems where DHW is generated within the space heating boiler, that have to be divided between consumption for space heating and DHW consumption based on the inaccurate data discussed above, or some other "best guess" method. The exception are those very few cases where separate DHW systems and related fuel delivery data exist. Investment decisions are then made on payback figures presented in the audit reports. We will now have definitive data for DHW energy use so that more reliable predictions of savings can be made.

In principle, a boiler and its burner should be sized so that on the coldest design day it will just satisfy the steam requirements of the installed radiation (plus pickup factors) and the DHW load by running continuously. In practice, oversizing often causes cycling on the coldest days, indicating inefficient operation. The data developed in this project will contribute to better sizing of the boiler plants, virtually all of which currently are done on a rule-of-thumb basis.

This research project is: (a) developing and analyzing a comprehensive set of multifamily building operational energy performance data and (b) developing, based on the observed data, analyses of DHW consumption demand and energy requirements, boiler sizing versus installed radiation and versus heating requirements, all to be used in specification preparation and revision.

### RESEARCH APPROACH

Building Selection

Critical to the success of the project has been the reliability of the data and the cooperation of Langsam Associates, which has a reputation as a well run building management firm. The firm's cooperation and reliable management of its buildings has paid enormous dividends in monitoring equipment upkeep, availability of historical building records and access to both building facilities and operating personnel. The building selection was made from a set of about seventy Langsam sites that had had OAS Heat Computers (heating system controllers) installed. An effort was made to include a diversity of

building sizes, income levels, ethnic backgrounds and locales.

The demonstration buildings are characteristic of the older and predominant stock of the over 120,000 New York City multi-family buildings. The buildings selected range in size from 17 to 103 apartments in either five or six above-ground stories. As noted in Table 1, these buildings were built before 1902 (in the parlance of NYC code, "old law" buildings) or between 1902 and 1928 ("new law"). All have combination steam and DHW generating, steel tube boilers with (primarily) Nos. 4 or 6 oil, air-atomizing burners. DHW is generated in a "tankless" coil just under the surface of the boiler water. A summary of general building characteristics is given in Table 1.

Data Collection

The data were collected, from July 1990 through September 1991, by the computerized heating controllers, which monitor these data points in all thirty buildings: Temperatures - in apartments, of outdoor air, boiler water (aquastat) and DHW; and burner on-off times. The nine upgraded buildings (Bldg. Nos. 1-3 & 5-10) had additional data monitoring equipment installed to record stack temperature, boiler make-up water flow, DHW flow in 15-minute increments, oil flow, DHW temperature before and after the mixing valve and on the return line. These devices were polled every 15 minutes, hourly or daily, depending on the particular device by the computer which stored the data in memory. Via modem, the management company staff called each building every third day to download the data onto disks that were delivered to Energy Management & Research Associates.

EMRA then put the data through a FORTRAN data translation program, rearranging it to an Rbase (database) readable format while performing a number of preliminary calculations. The data were then loaded into a specially designed database where macros performed a second level of calculations. The Rbase environment was then used to perform specific analyses, outputting smaller data sets to Quattro Pro for graphical analyses and presentations.

Note that project monitoring examined _operational_ conditions, which should be distinguished from monitoring

## BUILDING CHARACTERISTICS

| BLDG ID # | TOTAL APTS | Persons per apt. | Sq. ft/ apt | % Children | public laundry | In-apartment | | % low flow shower-heads | fuel type | # of stories | bldg type |
|---|---|---|---|---|---|---|---|---|---|---|---|
| | | | | | | % dish-washers | % cloths-washers | | | | |
| 1 | 23 | 1.455 | 900 | 3% | - | - | 65% | - | 4 | 5 | new law |
| 2 | 30 | 3.393 | 745 | 41% | - | - | 67% | - | 6 | 5 | new law |
| 3 | 34 | 2.688 | 757 | 31% | - | - | 44% | 50% | 4 | 5 | new law |
| 5 | 90 | 2.571 | 558 | 36% | 2 | - | 67% | - | 6 | 5 | new law |
| 6 | 49 | 2.174 | 1265 | 10% | - | 6% | 31% | 75% | 6 | 6 | new law |
| 7 | 60 | 1.842 | 946 | 9% | 3 | 40% | 70% | 50% | 6 | 6 | old law |
| 9 | 80 | 1.683 | 768 | 7% | 3 | 8% | 25% | 20% | 6 | 6 | old law |
| 10 | 102 | 2.000 | 720 | 38% | - | - | 26% | 25% | 4 | 6 | new law |
| Average - | | 2.226 | 832 | 22% | 1.0 | 7% | 49% | 28% | | | |
| Maximums - | | 3.393 | 1265 | 41% | 3.0 | 40% | 70% | 75% | | | |
| Minimums - | | 1.455 | 558 | 3% | 0.0 | 0% | 25% | 0% | | | |

Table 1

# TENANT DEMOGRAPHICS

|  | "At Home Patterns" | | | | "Family Types" | | | | | "Income Levels" | | | |
|---|---|---|---|---|---|---|---|---|---|---|---|---|---|
| BLDG ID # | all work | 1 works & 1 @ home | seniors | No work | single | couples | family | 1 parent | seniors | Public Assist. | Low Income | Middle Income | Other |
| 1 | 48% | 9% | 43% | 0% | 48% | 4% | 4% | 9% | 35% | 4% | 0% | 52% | 43% |
| 2 | 20% | 30% | 7% | 43% | 10% | 7% | 67% | 17% | 0% | 43% | 57% | 0% | 0% |
| 3 | 0% | 52% | 12% | 39% | 6% | 12% | 85% | 36% | 12% | 39% | 79% | 0% | 0% |
| 5 | 6% | 17% | 6% | 76% | 0% | 27% | 93% | 72% | 6% | 23% | 77% | 0% | 0% |
| 6 | 31% | 21% | 21% | 21% | 10% | 31% | 31% | 2% | 21% | 15% | 42% | 42% | 4% |
| 7 | 52% | 3% | 43% | 5% | 2% | 66% | 10% | 0% | 26% | 0% | 9% | 95% | 0% |
| 9 | 41% | 41% | 14% | 14% | 14% | 68% | 14% | 7% | 7% | 3% | 20% | 81% | 4% |
| 10 | 25% | 0% | 10% | 65% | 0% | 50% | 50% | 0% | 0% | 50% | 25% | 25% | 0% |

Table 2

building thermal characteristics, *e.g.*, heat loss.

## Data Set

The data set covers all of the data collected by the building monitoring devices, building operational and tenant information requested from superintendents and property managers via questionnaires and interviews, and equipment and building condition data obtained through energy audits (performed by the author and colleagues).

As of this writing, data only from July 1990 through February 1991 has been loaded into the database and analyzed, amounting to approximately 60 of an anticipated 100 megabytes when all data are fully loaded. Various tables in the database contain about 5 million data points. It is anticipated that the additional data will serve to further substantiate the findings presented here, and be used for further research into related areas.

This paper, then, will focus on the a subset of eight of the nine buildings that had the additional monitoring equipment installed. Building #8 (of the nine-building subset) has been excluded due to anomalies in the (unusual nocturnal) patterns of DHW use. In addition, Summer 1990 data for building #5 has been excluded because of a changeover in operation from the boiler serving one 45-unit building to serving two sister buildings (with a total of 90 apartments).

### DATA ANALYSIS

Throughout the data, several relationships have been examined: daily and seasonal variations in DHW demand patterns; consumption *vs.* occupancy levels; frequency and coincidence of 15- and 60-min DHW demand periods; average consumption *vs.* peak demand levels; and boiler on-and-off cycle lengths.

*A focal point for this research has been the examination of DHW consumption on a per capita basis.* Historically, published data for DHW consumption was presented on a per apartment basis. While this may have been the most convenient way to review and present the data in the past, the current figures suggest that per capita analyses may be an important parameter. The per capita denominator has been chosen on the basis that it is people that consume water, not apartments or square footage. Per capita data can be converted to per apartment figures by using actual or estimated occupant populations.

The first step to providing an accurate accounting of DHW use is to determine occupancy levels. Monthly vacancies compiled from management's rent roll records were used

to calculate the number of occupied apartments for all buildings. Data collection included fractions, which were used to represent occasions where leases ran into 1/2 or 1/3 of a month.

Review of these data revealed that there was a variance in the occupancy of the different buildings over the time period investigated. Monthly occupancy rates in the buildings ranged from 85 to 100 percent, the average for all of the buildings being 95 percent. Vacancy figures have been used to eliminate (both inter- and intra-building) DHW use variances due to differing occupancy levels, and to calculate the consumption of DHW per occupied apartment.

The next step was to take a snapshot of how many occupants were in each apartment and determine the number of persons per apartment for each building. This was done with the assistance of the building superintendents. These figures were then used as the denominator in all subsequent computations.

In order to analyze the data more thoroughly, monthly summaries were produced and then used to create consumption levels and patterns for the summer (July and August), fall (October and November) and winter (December, January, and February) periods.

### FINDINGS

**Consumption per Capita:** The number of persons per apartment (Table 1) in the building set ranged from 1.5 to 3.4, with an average of 2.2. Using a per occupied apartment analysis, the consumption levels differed 3.8 fold, from a low of 52.57 to a high of 198.87 gallons per occupied apartment, the average being 115.46. When population density is considered, usage ranges from 31.23 to 76.44 gal per capita, with an average of 51.04, a difference of 2.4 fold.

**Seasonal Variations:** One of the most distinct findings is seasonal variation in DHW consumption. Figure 1 clearly illustrates that consumption levels rise from summer to fall to winter. This was true in all but one building. The average per capita DHW consumption of 44.14 gallons in summer rose by 14 percent to 50.38 in fall and then by 13 percent, to 57.01 during the winter period.

**Weekday vs. Weekend:** A weekday vs. weekend comparison for each building (Figure 2) reveals that there is generally a slightly higher level of consumption on weekends (Saturday and Sunday) than on weekdays. A more detailed analysis, (figures not shown here), reveals that this is true in all but a few individual building cases

## SEASONAL COMPARISON OF DHW CONSUMPTION
### AVERAGE GALLONS PER CAPITA PER DAY

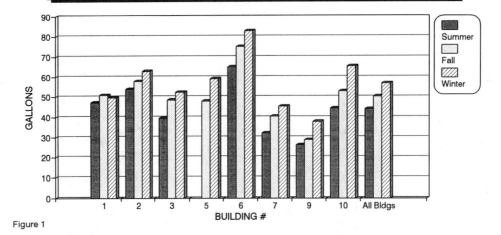

Figure 1

## WEEKDAY vs. WEEKEND CONSUMPTION
### GALLONS PER CAPITA : 7/90 - 2/91

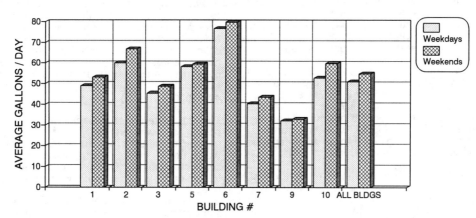

Figure 2

## WEEKDAY vs. WEEKEND CONSUMPTION
### GALLONS PER CAPITA, COMPOSITE 7/90-2/91

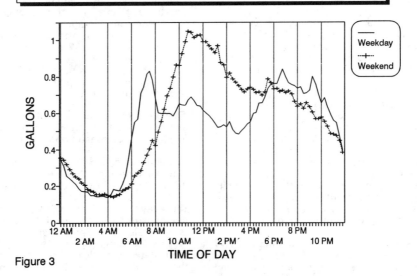

Figure 3

during the summer period. For the eight-month period of data, the average weekend day per capita consumption of 54.71 gallons is 7.5 percent greater than the average weekday day level of 50.89 gallons.

Much work has gone into the 15-minute DHW flow meter data analysis to produce demand-flow curves (see Figs. 3, 4 & 5). There is a distinct difference between weekday and weekend DHW consumption patterns. Weekday data exhibit minimal overnight usage followed by a morning peak, then by lower afternoon demand and finally, an evening or night-time peak. On the other hand, weekends have just one major peak; it begins later in the morning and continues on until around 1:00 to 2:00 p.m. Usage then tapers off fairly evenly through the rest of the day. Examination of the composite weekday and weekend graph (Figure 3) illustrates that the weekend peak is greater, at 1.05 gal per capita, than any of the weekday peaks, at 0.84.

**Affects of Workers and Children:** In examining the composite weekday curve (Figure 3), two morning peaks can be observed; the first is between 6:00 and 8:00 a.m.;

the second, between 9:30 a.m. and noon. When examining individual building data, one observes that particular sites fall into one of these two peaking patterns. Some general knowledge of the tenant populations (Tables 1 and 2) may serve to explain this difference. The buildings with occurrence of large numbers of either working tenants or middle-income populations experience the early morning peak. Buildings with a large percentage of children seem to fall into the later morning peak category (especially so during the summer).

Building #1 (Figure 6) is an example of a working class building with a large 6:00-8:00 a.m. spike, low mid-day use, and an "after dinner - wash the dishes" peak at around 7:00 p.m. Building #3 (Figure 7) is an example of the later morning, 10:00- noon peak. There are, of course, buildings with a mix of these two patterns. This area requires more research before any concrete conclusions can be drawn.

Figures 8 and 9 clearly illustrate the seasonal variation in both consumption levels and usage patterns between summer, fall and winter. Note that the highest peaking level occurs during winter weekends.

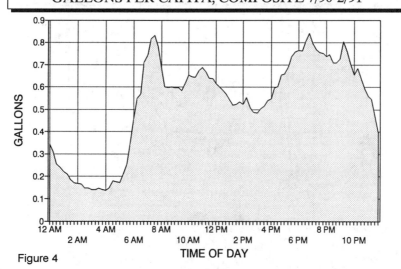

**WEEKDAY CONSUMPTION OF DHW**
GALLONS PER CAPITA, COMPOSITE 7/90-2/91

Figure 4

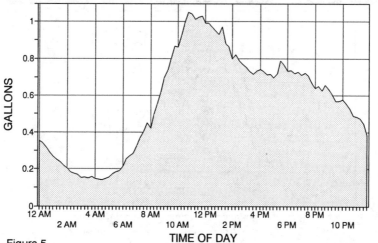

**WEEKEND CONSUMPTION OF DHW**
GALLONS PER CAPITA, COMPOSITE 7/90-2/91

Figure 5

## WEEKDAY vs. WEEKEND CONSUMPTION
### GALLONS PER CAPITA - BLDG #1 (Summer)

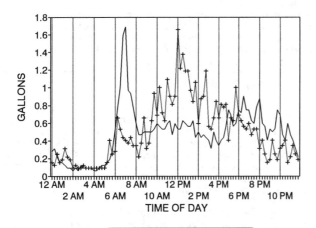

Figure 6

## WEEKDAY vs. WEEKEND CONSUMPTION
### GALLONS PER CAPITA - BLDG #3 (Summer)

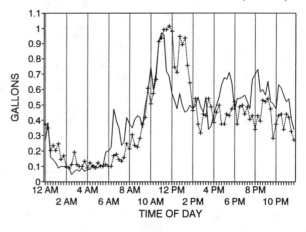

Figure 7

## SEASONAL VARIATIONS, WEEKDAY CONSUMPTION
### GAL per CAPITA, COMPOSITE

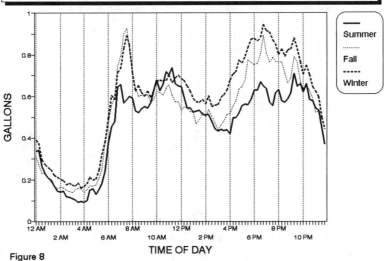

Figure 8

## SEASONAL VARIATIONS, WEEKEND CONSUMPTION
### GAL per CAPITA, COMPOSITE

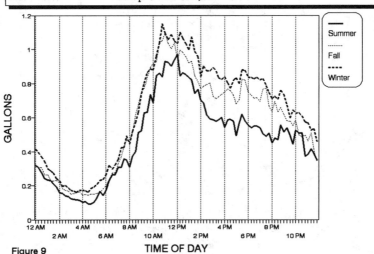

Figure 9

**Identifying Demands on Equipment:** While flow curves show us general usage patterns of a building, peaking times and flows can be used to more closely identify demands on the boiler. Maximum 15-min demand times (Figures 10 and 11) occur most often at 7:45 a.m. and 7:00, 7:15, 8:45 and 9:15 p.m. on weekdays; and 10:45 and 11:15 a.m. and 6:15 p.m. on weekends. This can then be compared to the maximum 60-min demand periods (Figures 12 and 13). *(Note: The times listed on the frequency graphs represent the 15- or 60-min periods ending at XX:XX.)*

There is an exact coincidence of 60- and 15-min maximum demand times on the weekends. During weekdays, the mornings have a close match of 60- and 15-min demands, and there is an exact match during the evening periods. The most frequent minimum 60- min consumption periods occurred at 4:00 a.m. on both weekends and weekdays. This demand period data will be used when evaluating DHW system sizing and storage options. It will also be used when comparing the coincidence of DHW and heating demands on the boiler.

**Generating Storage Capacity:** Fifteen and 60-min maximum demand and hourly average consumption data were compiled to examine peak needs, in contrast to total volume. This type of analysis will be useful in setting out new system design and sizing parameters and evaluating a mix of instantaneous generation and storage options. An examination of Table 3 reveals that, in comparison to the use in a maximum 60-min period the average hourly consumption is only 41 percent of that peak. This suggests that there is a possibility of generating storage capacity to meet that peak during many other average or below-average demand hours of the day.

Comparisons of 15- and 60-min peak periods shows that the highest (15-min) peak is equal to about one third (34%) of DHW consumed in the peak hour.

Lastly, there is slightly (25%) more DHW consumed in the average hour than in the highest 15-min period of the day. This again makes a case for some type of off-peak generation and storage strategy. These peaking and hourly consumption figures must be considered in conjunction with coincidence of peaks and overall consumption patterns to further evaluate this issue.

## Maximum 15 Minute Times Frequency
### Weekday - All Bldgs (Winter)

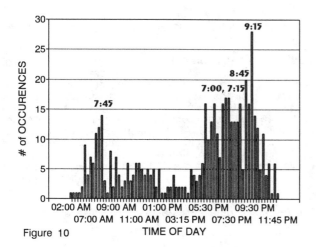

Figure 10

## Maximum 15 Minute Times Frequency
### Weekend All Bldgs (Winter)

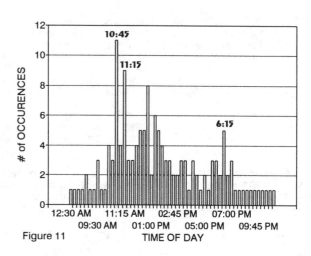

Figure 11

## Maximum 60 Minute Times Frequency
### Weekday All Buildings (Winter)

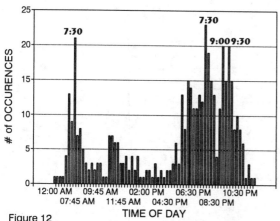

Figure 12

## Maximum 60 Minute Times Frequency
### Weekend All Bldgs (Winter)

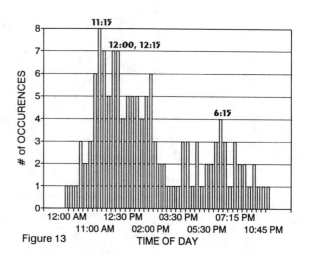

Figure 13

# GALLONS OF DHW USAGE (PER CAPITA) - WINTER

| TOTAL APTS | BLDG ID # | AVERAGE HOUR | difference avg / 15 max | 15 MIN. MAX. | difference 60 / 15 max | 60 MINUTE MAXIMUM | difference avg / 60 max |
|---|---|---|---|---|---|---|---|
| 23 | 1 | 2.072 | 77% | 2.681 | 37% | 7.210 | 29% |
| 30 | 2 | 2.626 | 123% | 2.130 | 32% | 6.732 | 39% |
| 34 | 3 | 2.183 | 90% | 2.436 | 38% | 6.405 | 34% |
| 90 | 5 | 2.469 | 161% | 1.532 | 30% | 5.140 | 48% |
| 49 | 6 | 3.452 | 148% | 2.337 | 32% | 7.319 | 47% |
| 60 | 7 | 1.895 | 114% | 1.668 | 36% | 4.698 | 40% |
| 80 | 9 | 1.579 | 118% | 1.343 | 34% | 3.950 | 40% |
| 102 | 10 | 2.728 | 171% | 1.597 | 30% | 5.338 | 51% |
| Average - | | 2.265 | 125% | 1.835 | 34% | 5.500 | 41% |
| Maximum - | | 3.452 | 171% | 2.681 | 38% | 7.319 | 51% |
| Minimum - | | 1.380 | 77% | 0.791 | 30% | 2.704 | 29% |
| Fold difference - | | 2.50 | | 3.39 | | 2.71 | |

Table 3

Figure 14 illustrates the actual consumption curve in a sample building (#7 - Fall, 1990 data). The bottom line (0.75) represents average consumption (for a 15-min period, the period for which all data are taken). This is equivalent to levelizing the building's DHW consumption equally across the entire day. Under one possible scenario, the building's DHW needs would be met by generating storage during low consumption periods, represented by the white areas under the line, to be used during peak times. The other two lines illustrate, respectively, levels of 10 and 25 percent excess storage capacity.

It is apparent from the data that both the highest consumption levels and peak volumes occur on winter weekend days. It is therefore logical, as suggested by Olivares[2] of Ontario Hydro that we choose this level of

consumption with which to base any potential sizing parameters.

**ASHRAE vs. Monitored Data:** As previously discussed, currently available DHW consumption data have not been considered suitable for system sizing decisions. Table 4 illustrates that the ASHRAE (industry standard) data, at 39.25 gal, is 66 percent below the monitored consumption of 115.46 gal for the daily average gallons of DHW per apartment. The ASHRAE per apartment figure is, in fact, 23 percent lower than the per capita consumption of 51.04 gal/day. Examining maximum hourly consumption (Table 5) we see that the ASHRAE data, 9.38 gallons, is 25 percent below the monitored consumption of 12.38 gal, on a per apartment basis.[3]

The results to date indicate that one's use of ASHRAE

## STORAGE POTENTIAL
### BLDG # 7 - Weekday (Fall)

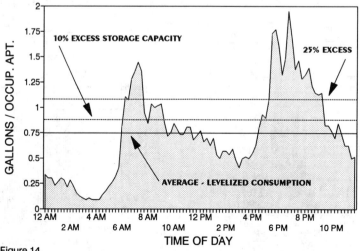

Figure 14

estimates will result in undersizing. When this research is concluded, specific sizing criteria will be put forth. Such guidelines will be based on per capita consumption and estimated maximum occupancy levels based on apartment size.

## AVERAGE GALLONS OF DHW PER DAY

| | Monitored data | | | ASHRAE[4] | |
|---|---|---|---|---|---|
| TOTAL APTS | Per Capita | Per Occup. Apt. | | # of Apts | Per Apt. |
| 23 | 49.70 | 72.29 | | 20 or less | 42.0 |
| 30 | 58.61 | 198.87 | | | |
| 34 | 45.98 | 123.57 | | | |
| 49 | 76.44 | 166.18 | | 50 | 40.0 |
| 60 | 40.42 | 74.45 | | | |
| 80 | 31.23 | 52.57 | | 75 | 38.0 |
| 90 | 53.61 | 137.85 | | | |
| 102 | 54.92 | 109.85 | | 100 | 37.0 |
| Average | 51.04 | 115.46 | | | 39.25 |

Table 4

## MAXIMUM GALLONS OF DHW PER HOUR

| | Monitored data | | | ASHRAE[4] | |
|---|---|---|---|---|---|
| TOTAL APTS | Per Capita | Per Occup. Apt. | | # of Apts | Per Apt. |
| 23 | 6.86 | 9.98 | | 20 or less | 12.0 |
| 30 | 6.76 | 22.92 | | | |
| 34 | 5.87 | 15.78 | | | |
| 49 | 6.80 | 14.79 | | 50 | 10.0 |
| 60 | 4.32 | 7.95 | | | |
| 80 | 3.28 | 5.53 | | 75 | 8.5 |
| 90 | 4.68 | 12.03 | | | |
| 102 | 5.03 | 10.06 | | 100 | 7.0 |
| Average | 5.45 | 12.38 | | | 9.38 |

Table 5

**Energy to Generate DHW:** An evaluation of the energy used to produce DHW was conducted for the summer period, when the systems are used only for DHW generation. This analysis revealed (Figure 15) that an average of 146.3 gallons of DHW (used at the tap) was produced for each gallon of #6 oil (or equivalent) consumed by the burner. The volume of DHW produced by one gallon of #6 oil equivalent ranged from 102 to 206 gallons, a factor of 2. Included in these figures are various levels of combustion efficiency, pipe insulation, standby loses and other real time factors that effect the operation of systems in occupied buildings. These numbers can be used as a check against results of energy savings predictions from audit calculations, for DHW conservation related measures, *e.g.,* low-flow showerheads.

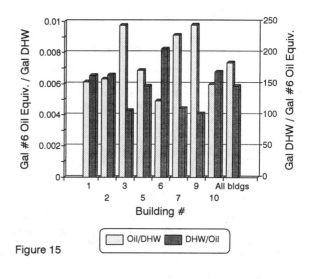

## ENERGY USED TO PRODUCE DHW
### JULY - SEPT. 1990 DATA

Figure 15

### DISCUSSION: OVERSIZING

A principal impetus behind this research was the lack of reliable data on DHW consumption in multifamily buildings. A consequence is that DHW generating systems and, particularly, combined heating/DHW boilers, which represent 90-95 percent of the systems in New York City, are frequently oversized by between 30-200 percent.[5]

When installing a boiler, either as a replacement during rehabilitation or for new construction, it is necessary to provide for both heating and hot water loads.[6] Generally, the individual responsible will use a "what was there before", "looks like ...", or some rough rule-of-thumb sizing method. In new construction, the correct method would be to design the radiation to meet the heat loss of the envelope and then to add the DHW load. The starting point in an inhabited building is to size the boiler to supply the existing radiation; *i.e.,* to the total EDR (Equivalent Direct Radiation), then add the DHW load.

Given that DHW demand is not known, excessive safety factors are employed. In fact, the author has seen a *doubling* of the space heating load. These factors contribute to considerable oversizing, even when the heating portion is done properly.

Guidelines developed from this research will enable proper sizing which will save buildings money (1) in lower initial equipment investments, for the smaller, more correctly sized equipment, and (2) in lower annual operating costs due to higher operating (seasonal) efficiencies as cycling is reduced because equipment is operating closer to full load. Additional savings may be achieved by using DHW consumption patterns to evaluate different scenarios for optimizing storage *vs.* instantaneous generation configurations.

### FUTURE WORK

In near-term, goals are to complete the analysis of the 14-month data set by evaluating 1991 spring and summer data against the parameters discussed in this report. This will be used to create a year-round summary. Figures for maximum 2- and 3-hour demands, and maximum daily consumption loads will be developed to better analyze supply and storage models. The seasonal efficiency of the boiler/burner units employed to make DHW (during the non-heating periods) will be calculated. Through additional work on both DHW consumption data and energy requirements, boiler sizing needed to produce DHW may be determined.

## Recommendations

Further analysis of the 14-month data set that should be pursued includes complete modeling of a DHW system (boiler operations, storage tank temperature fluctuations and water flows); calculation of the percentage of energy used for DHW *vs.* heating; coincidence of DHW demand *vs.* heating calls; and calculations of oversizing of existing boilers (in study buildings) based on actual DHW and EDR loads.

In the process of creating the database for this project, much boiler operation and apartment temperature data were collected. Analysis of these data will reveal insights pertaining to heating production and distribution.

## ACKNOWLEDGEMENTS

This paper was prepared in conjunction with a research project funded by the New York State Energy Research and Development Authority (Energy Authority). The opinions, findings, conclusions and recommendations expressed herein are solely those of the author and do not necessarily reflect the view of the Energy Authority.

The author would like to gratefully acknowledge the cooperation and assistance of Norine Karins of the Energy Authority; Dick Koral of the Apartment House Institute; Mark Engel, Larry Conner and the staff of Ralph Langsam Associates; David Suthergreen of Optimum Applied Systems Inc.; Peter Judd former Assistant Commissioner of HPD-ECD; Perry Tripi of EMRA; Howard Silverman; and others who have helped review this work. The genesis of this work was derived from analysis and field work of the Energy Conservation Division of New York City's Department of Housing Preservation and Development between 1984 and 1991.

## ENDNOTES

[1] Derived by the work of the N.Y.C. Dept. of Housing Preservation and Development's - Energy Conservation Division (ECD) in the analysis of buildings for energy audits, boiler replacement and other programs. Substantiated in phone conversations by various members of ASHRAE Technical Committee 6.6 (Service Hot Water).

[2] Olivares, T.C.. 1987. HOT WATER SYSTEM DESIGN FOR MULTI-RESIDENTIAL BUILDINGS. Report No. 87-239-K, Ontario Hydro Research Division, Ontario.

[3] The figures for monitored data are per occupied apartment. The difference between the research and ASHRAE gallonages would be greater if full occupancy had existed at all times. Percent differences were calculated using the "average" gallon figures.

[4] *1987 ASHRAE Handbook, HVAC Systems and Applications.* (Chapter 54 - Service Hot Water), ASHRAE, Atlanta.

[5] Experience of ECD. Oversizing percentages were computed against the building's radiation load plus an estimated DHW load.

[6] It would be most efficient to install separate space heating and DHW systems, but it is unlikely that a large percentage of the New York market will take this route any time soon, in the light of the resistance to having an additional mechanical system to care for.

# Chapter 51
# The Museum of New Mexico and Energy Management

B.K. Johnson

## PREFACE

There are unique indoor conditioning and energy management challenges in museums. In Santa Fe, the Museum of New Mexico (MNM) is located in a unique climate and must stay within utility expenditure limits allocated through the State government budget process, while handling valuable collections with specific environmental requirements. Adequate humidity for indoor exhibitions is the top priority for heating, ventilating, and air-conditioning (HVAC) systems. Energy management systems (EMS) implemented by the Energy, Minerals and Natural Resources Department (EMNRD) in two MNM exhibition facilities avoid energy costs, but must be maintained regularly. Energy savings goals must yield priority in favor of maintaining proper indoor conditions.

MNM is one of six Divisions within the State of New Mexico's Office of Cultural Affairs (OCA). The mission of OCA is

> to foster, preserve, and protect current and past expressions of culture and the arts, which are determined to be in the best interests of New Mexico.

As a part of their mission, OCA is well-known for excellence in cultural collections, through MNM. MNM is comprised of the

- Museum of Fine Arts
- Museum of Southwest History
- Museum of International Folk Art
- Laboratory of Anthropology
- Museum of Indian Arts and Culture.

There are eight separate physical facilities that house these operations, including administration. Behind the scenes, there are operational costs that must be managed carefully; the costs of heating, cooling, and lighting the buildings that MNM uses are a part of this. EMNRD has assisted OCA in meeting its mission through the expertise of the Energy Conservation and Management Division (ECMD). ECMD is designated by the Governor as the State Energy Manager agency.

There have been a variety of obstacles that ECMD and MNM have been challenged with as they pursue preservation of collections and control of operational costs. As new situations present themselves, solutions have come forward from the ECMD/MNM collaborative efforts. These experiences, described herein, may assist and encourage other organizations as they take on energy management jointly with a strong mission to accomplish.

The significant issues encountered, in the joint pursuit of energy management and culture, have involved

- HVAC systems in museums
- EMS in museums
- energy implications of operating museums
- communication.

Two MNM buildings, both in Santa Fe, where ECMD has had extensive involvement, are the Museum of Fine Arts and the Museum of Indian Arts and Culture. The buildings are shown in Figures 1 and 2. With EMNRD funds and ECMD technical assistance, EMS was implemented in each of the buildings, followed by EMS maintenance.

FIGURE 1. MUSEUM OF FINE ARTS: SANTA FE, NEW MEXICO

FIGURE 2.  MUSEUM OF INDIAN ARTS AND CULTURE: SANTA FE, NEW MEXICO

Currently, there are new opportunities for energy management that ECMD is pursuing and that can be utilized by MNM.  The main avenues through which they will occur are:

- 1991 State Energy Policy
- Green Lights program for State government.

MNM is developing plans for improving its ability to preserve collections as it embarks on expanding into additional facilities.  An environmental preservation consultant is now retained by MNM.  The consultant is recommending improved indoor conditions by making humidity the highest priority in museum operations.  Humidity control is a significant issue for MNM, given the dry ambient conditions of the southwest U.S. region, as a whole, and the unique weather patterns of Santa Fe.

## STATE AGENCIES' BACKGROUNDS

### Museum of New Mexico

New Mexico is often referred to as a tri-cultural state, because of the Native American, Hispanic, and Caucasian peoples that live side-by-side.  Unique expressions in art and culture are produced; the mixture of culture and the natural world are frequently cited for the beautiful and diverse works created.  MNM is an important part of this natural collaboration of people and land, with ties to a variety of significant endeavors, such as

- current art of the three cultures
- ancient art of indigenous peoples
- musical performance
- anthropology
- archaeology.

The essence of the above is coordinated within the museum buildings and the environment that they provide.  Shows, research, education, performances, and exhibitions are constantly being juggled, with the facilities used to the fullest.  This is a tremendous administrative challenge.  The buildings, themselves, are also a part of the essence, having been produced through the art of architecture, with several of them being of historical value.

A survey of the current status of MNM facilities would lead one to conclude that they should upgrade maintenance and administration of the buildings and their systems.  MNM's rule-of-thumb for the proper indoor environment, given New Mexico's dry climate, is 70 degrees F, while 35% relative humidity (RH) should be maintained.  MNM has documented that they are not maintaining these conditions, causing an untold amount of damage to cultural collections.

MNM is also increasing their square footage with expansion of existing buildings and construction of new buildings.  This includes administrative space as well as museum program space.  With expansion seeming to be at an apex now, MNM knows that it is wise to investigate indoor conditioning and energy management.

### Energy, Minerals and Natural Resources Department

EMNRD provides consultation services to State agencies in the areas of energy efficiency and renewable resources.  This effort is led by ECMD.  Among its many capabilities, ECMD has expertise in building systems engineering.  Through ECMD, State agencies have access to experience with building systems, which are usually thought of as the three areas of

- envelope
- HVAC systems
- lighting.

Maintaining proper temperature and humidity conditions to ensure that collections are protected, while controlling energy consumption, is possible through a fourth component: EMS. These four components interact, along with human intervention, to provide building spaces with a level of comfort. Systems powered by renewable resources (e.g., passive solar, active solar thermal, photovoltaics) are also integrated into building systems. Passive solar systems for space heating, which are integrated into envelope design, exist, to a certain degree, in the two MNM buildings discussed here.

EMNRD has supported the Office of Cultural Affairs (OCA) with several projects in the past ten years, assisting them to avoid excessive energy costs and to investigate building systems' problems. The simple payback criterion that ECMD uses is ten years or less (i.e., the time in which a project's first cost is paid for in energy cost avoidance accrued through implementation of the project). Examples of ECMD projects for MNM are

- installation of energy management systems
- maintenance of energy management systems
- test and balance of HVAC systems
- energy modeling.

The above listed projects follow in step with the focus of the ECMD vision, which is

to be the catalyst for implementing energy efficiency measures in State agencies which control costs.

This vision does not exclude comfort or other space function criteria which are important to the mission of the agency being assisted; energy-efficient operation and comfort are values which can be achieved simultaneously. It is not the function of EMNRD to alter the quality of services of another State agency by restricting or changing usage of building systems. Ideally, energy efficiency measures should be implemented and costs avoided through projects that customers (i.e., museum visitors) do not even notice.

Temperature and humidity conditions which preserve museum collections (e.g., pottery, weavings, paintings) are top priority. Museum collections, which MNM has built a reputation on, require humidity-based environment control for satisfactory preservation. This means that relative humidity conditions for collections are actually of higher priority than conditions for people, which are temperature-based in typical institutional building design.

## GOALS AND CHALLENGES

Ideally, proper indoor conditions would be maintained for a wide variety of exhibition types and storage areas in MNM facilities, continuously. The HVAC systems are designed to distribute conditioned air to all spaces in the Museum of Fine Arts and Museum of Indian Arts and Culture buildings. There is no differentiation between the collection-occupying areas of galleries and storage rooms and the people-occupying areas of administrative offices, theaters, lobbies, and gift shops. This means that the HVAC systems should maintain the top-priority temperature and humidity requirements needed for galleries and storage rooms in all building spaces. This is a practical solution and can be programmed into the EMS to coordinate the necessary HVAC control functions. However, in practice at these two museums, the conditioning goal has been a difficult challenge.

The conditioning goals of MNM are made of a combination of local needs and international requirements for maintaining collections[1]. First, temperature control is relatively easy to manage, because designers and building occupants are used to relating to the temperature-based requirements of conventional buildings. The 65 to 80 F range is fine for people using the building spaces as well as museum collections. However, a constant temperature within the range, 72 F, for example, must be established. Night setback of HVAC systems or any other type of temperature fluctuation, on a daily or weekly basis, is not acceptable. It may be possible to have a seasonal adjustment of the setpoint (e.g., 72 F for winter, 78 F for summer). A gradual swing from one setpoint to the other should be planned to occur over a long period; one degree F change per two days may be adequate to museum conservators. Temperature control is not a difficult issue for museums in Santa Fe.

Second, but of top priority, is how to manage humidity control for collections. The typical international requirement widely recommended is 55% RH, plus or minus 5% RH[2]. By maintaining this humidity in museums, one meets an important requirement for accessing the international market of touring collections. MNM has a requirement of 35% RH, plus or minus 5% RH. Their practical reasons for having lower humidity levels are:

- 55% RH has been established by museum conservators from high-humidity climates in the eastern U.S.
- New Mexico has a dry climate
- 75% of MNM's total collection is locally created
- humidity equipment breakdowns would expose collections to damaging humidity changes[1]
- maintaining 55% RH in a dry, cold climate incurs high energy costs and possible condensation damage to building envelopes[2].

With a high percentage of the total collection being created in New Mexico, dry conditions in the collection materials are already established. For international collections, micro-climate containment methods are frequently used when exhibiting and transporting collections to maintain adequate humidity.

To continue striving for the goal of proper conditions for a wide variety of exhibition types, while maintaining collections in storage, MNM has a number of challenges. The challenges are being addressed in a number of ways. New flexible standards for the museum environment will be released soon that are more accomodating to the unique New Mexico situation. As a part of its expansion plans, MNM is considering converting one museum to specifically meet the higher 55% RH requirement. MNM is also consulting with an art preservation specialist to evaluate the current status of their museums and propose specific options for cost-effective solutions[1]. ECMD is working with MNM by contributing to the consultant's evaluation, continuing its technical assistance (especially concerning EMS issues), and briefing OCA administration on responding to the State Energy Policy and the State's potential Green Lights program.

## ENERGY MANAGEMENT

The two buildings being addressed herein are different in design and purpose. It is a challenge for MNM to administer and maintain different types of buildings, while continuing a unified mission of preserving delicate cultural collections within those buildings.

### Two Museums

The Museum of Fine Arts is housed in a brick two-story building, with 52,000 square feet. Constructed in 1917, it is one of Santa Fe's many historic buildings. Collections predominantly displayed in the galleries are paintings. A basement is used to store paintings and other collections. A conventional chiller and boiler are located in the basement; ductwork distributes conditioned air throughout the building. Humidity is increased through a hot water coil that creates steam in the ductwork. An EMS was installed in 1985 for $45,000, which resulted in significant reduction of the building's utility bills during the 1985-86 fiscal year period. An ice thermal storage system provides cooling for the St. Francis Auditorium, a musical performance space in the museum. The annual energy bill is approximately $1.10 per square foot.

Pottery, weavings, paintings, silverwork, and other anthropological materials are displayed and stored in the recently-constructed Museum of Indian Arts and Culture. The building has two levels, one being a basement, is 32,000 square feet in area, and incorporates passive solar and daylighting features in the envelope. A conventional boiler and chiller serve administration, a store, a theater, and classrooms; rooftop units provide heating, cooling, and humidity control for three gallery spaces. An EMS was installed with the original HVAC controls for $85,000 in 1986. Humidity is provided by replaceable, water-filled cannister units which run on electricity. The annual energy bill is approximately $1.50 per square foot.

### Energy Management Systems, Maintenance, and Results

The two MNM buildings described both have the same type of EMS: Barber-Colman Network 2100. EMS provides computerized coordination of conventional HVAC control systems. Instead of directing each of the myriad of system valves and dampers to open, close, or modulate through a series of local discrete electric and pneumatic switches, controllers, transmitters, or thermostats, there is sophisticated computer-based logic (i.e., IF-THEN-ELSE) which has been programmed to control these systems. The logic resides in software subroutines and effects the same changes, while coordinating operation of all building systems. Computerized coordination of control offers the opportunity for MNM to control spaces under close tolerances for relative humidity and temperature. Closer control of space conditions means avoided energy costs.

In 1988 it was apparent that there were HVAC systems' control problems, as well as increasing energy costs, that needed to be investigated. EMS maintenance was conducted in 1989 and 1990, as part of a $0.5 million HVAC maintenance program funded by EMNRD. The $23,264 EMS maintenance project for the Museum of Indian Arts and Culture realized $3,925 in avoided energy costs during the July 1989 through June 1990 fiscal year period, which is a simple payback of 5.9 years. Similar cost avoidance was achieved in the following fiscal year (1990-91), compared to the July 1988 through June 1989 pre-maintenance period.

A before-and-after monthly comparison of energy costs for the building is shown in Figure 3. Note that avoidance first shows up in September 1989, which coincides with substantial completion of the work. Utility billing histories for electricity and natural gas were normalized for weather and billing period variables to present an accurate picture of the avoided costs.

The Museum of Fine Arts did not fair as well; the $17,918 spent for its EMS maintenance did not achieve a positive payback through the same type of normalized utility billing analysis. This is due to the variation in activities held at the building, additional electricity load from office equipment, and varying operating policies for HVAC systems. In addition, analysis of utility billing data of the more recent 1991-92 fiscal year shows that the Museum of Indian Arts and Culture is no longer achieving a positive payback. The mixed results show that EMS maintenance projects may be hard to justify on avoided costs, depending on the project. However, ECMD's experience with EMS indicates that maintenance is needed on a regular basis (e.g., annually) to keep systems, computer hardware, and energy costs in line.

In both buildings, the funding was used for

- HVAC control programming
- replacement and repair of EMS components, as necessary
- limited replacement and repair of HVAC components
- training.

Previous HVAC programming was revised or totally replaced. Museum administrators and maintenance staff, who had worked with the buildings' operations for several years, were consulted. Consensus was reached

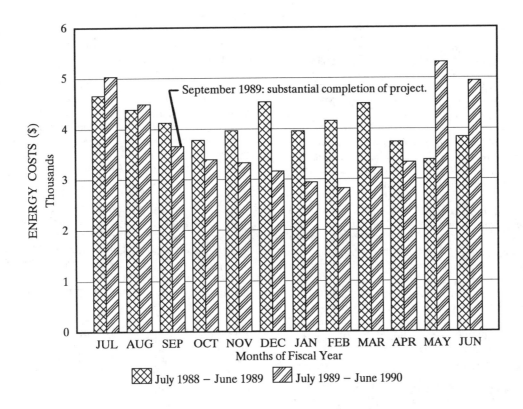

FIGURE 3. ENERGY COSTS, MUSEUM OF INDIAN ARTS AND CULTURE

on how to go about the programming. Main points followed were

- programming should be simplified
- maintain constant indoor conditions, 24 hours a day, in all spaces
- give low EMS user levels to MNM staff and high levels to EMNRD staff and their contractor.

Concerning the last point, higher user levels were eventually given to MNM staff.

It was found that many EMS components had failed or degraded severely since the EMS was installed. Sensors, relays, and computer hardware were replaced. HVAC components closely related to EMS operation, such as control valves, were also repaired or replaced.

Training was conducted for MNM maintenance and administrative staff, to get them more familiar with EMS and to achieve energy savings through more extensive use of EMS capability. With hindsight, it appears that the training did not payback as anticipated, because

- the entire maintenance staff was provided training, instead of reserving it for specific personnel
- maintenance staff are not familiar with the computer interface, typically

- incentives are lacking for maintenance staff to pursue new skills
- training quality by the contractor was fair, but not excellent.

EMS training should be reserved for selected individuals of the maintenance staff that have already shown knowledge and leadership in operation of HVAC systems. During the training, it was apparent that many of the maintenance staff were not truly interested. Much of this might be attributed to, simply, the inability to type on the computer keyboard. In addition, the wages for State government maintenance personnel are low, compared to the private sector, so this labor force is difficult to retain.

The contractors appeared to treat training as an afterthought, having to be pushed and reminded to satisfy the training requirements listed in their agreement with EMNRD. Hypothetical situations were most often used to lead maintenance staff through the training, while there was minimal attention paid to the current HVAC problems at the site; the latter would have provided excellent training opportunities. Extensive one-on-one training during the real life of the building's HVAC would have been beneficial to the maintenance staff, perhaps more than anything else.

## HVAC Test and Balance

During the EMS maintenance at the Museum of Indian Arts and Culture, a HVAC test and balance procedure was recommended. There appeared to be severe HVAC equipment problems in the newer of the two buildings, because computer programming revisions and EMS hardware maintenance by the contractor were not effecting the expected improvements in indoor environment conditions. An amendment to the existing contract was approved and $5,300 worth of diagnostic testing was performed. The in-place performance of the heating and cooling systems was documented[3].

It was also found that several terminal units had terminal piping that was smaller than specified on the construction drawings. This meant that fluid flow to the units, in cooling mode or heating mode, was not sufficient. From performance data, it was determined that about five terminal piping runs should be replaced, due to actual poor performance on the cooling side. Amazingly, negotiations begun in late 1990 to have the original mechanical contractor replace the piping continues, with litigation in the offing.

## Energy Modeling

At about the same time as the test and balance procedure, a $5,000 project was initiated to quantify the energy performance of the Museum of Indian Arts and Culture. With EMS and HVAC systems issues on our minds, we thought that documenting energy consumption with the DOE-2.1d simulation would be an excellent tool for current and future reference. This was combined with the need for ECMD to upgrade its building energy simulation capabilities, so the necessary software was purchased and installed. Some of the more challenging modeling tasks turned out to be

- HVAC equipment
- self-shading effects on the building envelope
- scheduling.

The model came to within 30 percent of annual energy consumption of actual utility billings for the building[4]. MNM has shown interest in using the model to explore energy implications of expansion options for the building.

### CONTINUING ON

## Future Strategies

The future will see MNM conservators advocating better exhibition conditions, MNM and OCA administration planning for facilities' expansion, ECMD pushing for responsiveness to the State Energy Policy, an increasing number of visitors to the museums, and increased variety of museum activities. Energy consumption and costs will increase, as a result. However, there are innovative strategies available that may help avoid costs and maintain the necessary indoor conditions.

Temperature can be allowed to float off of setpoint to accomodate humidity requirements: Indoor conditioning for people is temperature-based; for collections, they should be humidity-based. When humidity is high and HVAC systems reach their dehumidification limit on a hot, but wet, summer day, allow the HVAC system to float and the temperature to move up[5]. These conditions do occur during the monsoon season in July and August. A look at the psychrometric chart for 5,000 feet elevation[6] (Santa Fe is at 7,000 feet) shows that an unacceptable 44% RH at 72 F would become an acceptable 36% RH at 78 F, based on MNM's acceptable range of 30 to 40% RH.

The collections can accept the temperature variation more than humidity variation. By programming the necessary subroutines into the existing EMS, HVAC systems can be controlled to produce this result. For storage areas that are usually not occupied with people, this strategy has great utility. This strategy can reduce energy costs and can be an interim solution before systems are upgraded.

Hire a HVAC technician: This person would

- manage building automation systems
- consult with MNM administrative and maintenance personnel on HVAC equipment, systems, control, and indoor conditioning issues
- review specifications, design, cost estimates, scheduling, and procurement of equipment and services for automated building control systems.

A minimum of a high school Diploma, with several years experience in maintenance of HVAC systems and EMS, would be required for employment.

Green Lights for MNM: A significant portion of MNM energy costs is for lighting. Many of MNM's lighting systems must be specialized to enhance presentation of exhibitions, while protecting them from heat and radiation damage. This often intensive use of lighting should be reviewed by ECMD and proposals developed, with MNM input, on how to reduce the energy use, but maintain or upgrade the quality of the light. There are conventional lighting systems throughout the museums, in administrative, public, and storage areas, where energy efficiency can be improved.

ECMD is actively investigating how the State of New Mexico can be a Green Lights Partner with the U.S. Environmental Protection Agency. On becoming a Partner, ECMD will work with MNM and OCA to achieve Green Lights goals of improved energy efficiency in existing and new lighting systems.

Energy Management Plan for MNM: The Governor's Executive Order on energy, based on the 1991 State Energy Policy, directs each State agency to develop and carry out an energy management plan. An energy management goal has been established that, between

1992 and 1995, State government should reduce energy consumption in State facilities and transportation fleets by 10% over the projected State utility and fuel expenditures for 1995. ECMD will assist MNM and OCA to prepare a plan and meet the energy management goal.

## Communication and Collaboration

Two key occurrences in late 1991 that will spur MNM and ECMD on to further joint efforts are

- release of the 1991 State Energy Policy
- serious investigation of indoor environment conditions by MNM conservators.

These two activities were developed independently, but MNM conservators inquired about ECMD technical assistance, which then brought the two groups together for serious negotiations. MNM is working with an art preservation consultant to present recommendations to OCA management. ECMD is offering technical assistance through the Policy. Roles are being defined so that MNM and ECMD can proceed with a reasonable program.

Communication is now much improved. Previously, in the administration of preserving the arts and culture for New Mexico, certain responsibilities were not defined. This led to

- communication gaps
- short-term solutions
- damaged art.

Among MNM administration, OCA administration, MNM maintenance, EMNRD, and EMNRD's contractors, there were many communication gaps. There are different ways in which people see maintenance needs, technical needs, budget allocation, budget planning, and new MNM programs. One perspective of EMNRD is: if maintenance and repair budgets are funded adequately, indoor environment conditions can then be offered for exhibition of prestigious collections, while continuing to display and store MNM's own wonderful collections. Energy efficiency improvements on MNM facilities can help fund the maintenance and repair budgets.

In the preservation of cultural collections at MNM it is now defined as the first priority that

> indoor environment conditions should be based on humidity requirements of the collections and not on the temperature-based requirements of people.

The challenge will be for MNM to achieve optimum humidity and temperature in all of its facilities. ECMD is looking forward to providing technical assistance to do this at the lowest operational expense feasible.

## ACKNOWLEDGEMENTS

Numerous consultations have been held with Ron Vigil, Deputy Director, OCA, on energy efficiency of MNM facilities. Claire Munzenrider, Chief Conservator, MNM, has communicated the needs of art conservation to EMNRD. John J. McGowan, CEM, former Director, ECMD, contributed significantly to development of the relationship between OCA and EMNRD. Through his work as a consultant to OCA, Steven Weintraub, Art Preservation Services, has raised issues concerning preservation of collections, the building environment, and control of humidity. Key ideas of the above mentioned people, developed during the normal course of State activities, are contained in this work.

## REFERENCES

1. Munzenrider, C., personal communication, Chief Conservator, Museum of New Mexico, Office of Cultural Affairs, Santa Fe NM, May 1992.

2. Thomson, G., The Museum Environment, Second Edition, Butterworths, London, 1986.

3. Sedillo, P. M., "Mechanical System Study for the Museum of Indian Arts," report prepared for Energy, Minerals and Natural Resources Department, Contract No. 77-521.33-134A, Miller Metal Co., Albuquerque NM, July 1990.

4. Jones, R. W., "Installation and Verification of Building Energy Simulation Software: DOE2 Model of Museum of Indian Arts and Culture," report prepared for Energy, Minerals and Natural Resources Department, Contract No. 78-521.03-272, Balcomb Solar Associates, Santa Fe NM, February 1991.

5. Weintraub, S., personal communication, Conservation Consultant, Art Preservation Services, New York NY, November 1991.

6. ASHRAE Psychrometric Chart No. 4, American Society of Heating, Refrigeration, and Air-Conditioning Engineers, Atlanta GA, 1965.

# Chapter 52

# Metering Revisited - Innovative Concepts for Electrical Monitoring and Reporting Systems

W.L. Stebbins

## ABSTRACT

For the first three-quarters of this century, the monitoring of electrical power and energy has been dominated by conventional electromechanical voltmeters, ammeters, and watthour meters. Only in the last decade have solid state microprocessor-based digital devices become available for application in the commercial and industrial marketplace.

These new devices perform the tasks of up to 24 conventional indicating meters for about the price of three. Communication via a RS-485 data link to a PC allows monitoring of up to 70 values including times and dates, min/max history, temperature indications, and energy management alarms.

Complex waveform analysis can also be carried out for harmonic problems typically associated with adjustable speed drives that have been installed on fans and pumps for energy management savings. Since metering systems are absolutely essential to a successful Energy Management Process, consideration should be given to applying the latest in metering technology.

It should be noted that meters by themselves do not save money, they only cost money to install and maintain. Proper monitoring, recording, and analysis lead to corrective actions which produce the desired result of reducing energy per unit of production or per service performed.

Experience has shown that a 1 to 2% reduction can be achieved after meters are installed just by letting the users know that they are being monitored. Up to a 5% reduction can occur when the users then become proactive toward better managing of their energy. Ultimately up to 10% reduction can be achieved when metering is tied directly to the process through a PLC or DCS, in a closed loop automated process control arrangement.

## INTRODUCTION

Details presented include basic electrical measurements, a layman's guide to available metering equipment, techniques to employ and pitfalls to avoid, and evaluation of claims made by vendors. All dollar values presented are approximate, and are based on 1993 energy and equipment costs in the Southeast. Brand names are included to present a cross-section of equipment available and the listing is not intended to be all inclusive.

There are a variety of firms with the capabilities to supply satisfactory equipment, hardware, and software. Application of this equipment, hardware, and software for these specific requirements should not be construed as a general endorsement by either Hoechst Celanese or by the Author. It is important to note that a variety of brands and suppliers should be evaluated by anyone considering a similar application.

Values given for flows, temperatures, pressures, and unit energy costs approximate actual numerical quantities and are used to illustrate the methodology employed.

## BACKGROUND

Since 1973, the Celanese plants of Hoechst Celanese Textile Fibers have had an extensive energy management process in place. Results of this process have yielded, within the Celanese plants, a reduction of over 30% in BTU/NGP.

Energy cannot be well managed unless there is a way to identify the major users and then easily trend the consumption patterns to identify potential reductions in energy per unit of production or per service performed. In the words of one old sage, "If you can't meter it, you can't manage it."

For example, if someone were willing to pay your home utility bills for the next six months, how would that change your life style? Would lights be left on, doors left open, and the air conditioning turned cold enough to hang meat on the walls? All of the good energy management approaches learned over the years would be almost immediately forgotten.

Then what happens when you start back again paying your own bills? You resume employing good energy management techniques. The same principle applies to energy consumption per unit of production or per service performed in the commercial, institutional, and industrial sectors.

## ESTABLISHING AND JUSTIFYING METERING SYSTEMS

Any energy management process must follow certain economic guidelines before it can be justified. Meters, by themselves, can save no money. They only indicate and record what is happening. It takes action and reaction by people to save money.

Experience shows that substantial savings can result from metering and trending. The percentage saved depends on how much was being wasted and how conscientious employees are in taking corrective actions. However, once a metering system is installed and operating, a minimum of 1 percent energy savings annually can be expected as a result of the detection of utility system losses.

For example, if a plant spends $3,000,000 annually for electricity and fuel, $30,000 gross annual savings using a metering and trending system could be expected. If taxes were 50 percent, the net annual savings would be $15,000. With a maximum pay-back period of 3 years, the plant could spend up to $45,000 for the metering and trending system.[1]

## SIX REASONS TO METER:

### 1. CHARGE OUT ENERGY TO INDIVIDUAL DEPARTMENTS

This is the most basic reason to meter. Each month the total energy bill is proportioned to the various departments. This data is used to compare costs against the department's budget and thus develop a variance-dollar value. Also included is the use of meters for revenue billing when energy is sold to a third party such as in a cogeneration arrangement.

### 2. ACCOUNTABILITY FOR ENERGY USED

Trending of energy consumption per unit of production or per service performed is the basis for initial analysis and resulting corrective actions.

### 3. EFFICIENCY OF UTILITY EQUIPMENT AND SYSTEMS

The experience HCC has gained from their Utility Test Process [2] provides the following guidelines values:

1) Centrifugal air compressors at 125 psig:
   3.2-4.0 kWh/1,000 standard cubic feet (scf)

2) Centrifugal chiller drives producing 45 degree F. water:
   0.6-1.0 kW/ton refrigeration or
   0.6-1.0 kWh/ton-hour refrigeration

3) Refrigeration delivered to the conditioned space:
   1.0-2.0 kW/ton refrigeration or
   1.0-2.0 kWh/ton-hour refrigeration

4) Steam boilers at 250 psig:
   Number 6 fuel oil = 7.1-9.0 gal/1,000 lb steam
   Natural gas = 1,000-1,300 scf/1,000 lb steam
   Pulverized coal = 100-120 lb/1,000 lb steam
   (Fuel Consumption values will be 25 percent higher at 600 psig.)

### 4. PROVIDE INFORMATION FOR AUDITS OF ENERGY PROJECTS

With funding becoming increasingly difficult to obtain, audits of cost reduction energy management projects have been required more frequently over the past five years.

### 5. MAINTENANCE WORK, IDENTIFY PERFORMANCE PROBLEMS, FEEDBACK TO MANAGERS

The collection of energy-consumption data in support of maintenance work is seen as a viable tool, greatly aiding in the identification of equipment performance problems. As a side issue, performance problems associated with the people operating the equipment are also identified, allowing managers to take any necessary corrective action.

### 6. IDENTIFY POTENTIAL FUTURE ADDITIONAL ENERGY SAVINGS

With the long-term goal of management being one of continual improvement, metering and trending systems provide data on which to base resource allocation decisions.

## FUNDAMENTALS OF ELECTRICAL METERING

Before taking steps to reduce your electric bill, it pays to become familiar with the instruments utilities use to meter your electric power consumption. The basic unit is the watthour meter, and the standard industrial meters are very similar to those used in residential service in your home.[3]

Watthour meters measure electrical energy through the interaction of magnetic fluxes generated by the voltage and current coils acting to produce eddy currents in the rotating aluminum disk. Eddy current flow generates magnetic lines of force which interact with the flux in the airgap to produce turning torque on the disk. The meter is thus a carefully calibrated induction motor, the speed of which depends on the energy being measured. Each revolution of the meter disk represents a fixed value of watthours. The register counts these revolutions through a gear train and displays this count as watthours. Jewel or magnetic bearings are used to support the disk and the gear assembly is designed to impose minimum load on the disk.

The upper part of Figure 1 details in simplified fashion how the kW demand value is obtained from the utility kWh meter. Each time the meter disk makes one complete revolution under the influence of the voltage and current coils, the photocell energizes the relay and transfers contacts A and B, providing kWh output pulse. At the end of the demand interval, usually 15, 30 or 60 minutes, a clock pulse is given for two to six seconds, signifying that a new interval has begun.

The A, B, and clock contacts are used by the demand monitoring or control equipment to develop the curve shown in the left part of Figure 2. The kWh pulses are merely added to each other over the demand interval. A line connecting the tops of the columns of pulses describes the accumulation of kWh pulses during the interval. The actual kWh per pulse and the number of total pulses recorded during the interval will depend on the plant load and the Potential Transformer (PT) and Current Transformer (CT) ratios for the specific kWh meter. The fictitious mouse fanning the lower bearing in Figure 1 illustrates that the disk speed increases proportionally to an increasing demand for power, hopefully not to the level that causes bearings to overheat!

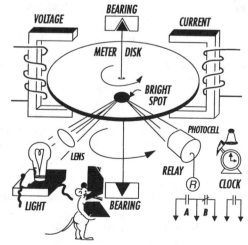

Figure 1:   Simplified Watthour Meter.

It is important to note at this point that the slope of the line in Figure 2, mathematically speaking, is defined as rise over run, which is kWh divided by time, (one half hour in this case), which is equal to kW demand. That is to say, the total kWh of energy consumed, divided by the time over which it was consumed, yields the *average* kW demand (kWd) for power over that time interval. This means that by detecting the slope of the line early in the interval, corrective action can be taken to reduce the slope by shutting off loads, lowering the *average* kWd to a more acceptable value. It follows that a flat line of zero slope would indicate no further energy consumption, a zero demand for power. Taken to the extreme, a line with a negative slope would indicate negative energy consumption, with a reversal of power flow; i.e., on-site generation of power back into the utility company's transmission system. This could occur if large capacity generation equipment was a part of the plant utility system.

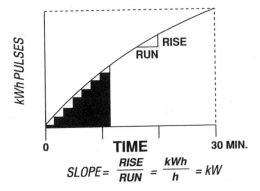

Figure 2: Demand Curve.

$$SLOPE = \frac{RISE}{RUN} = \frac{kWh}{h} = kW$$

The exact length of the demand interval will vary by power company, one of the most common being 30 minutes. This interval length is most frequently associated with the time for power company generators, transformers, and transmission lines to build up sufficient heat due to overload conditions to do permanent damage to the equipment.

However, as kWd peaks increase, and as a few power company customers attempt "peak-splitting," the demand intervals are being reduced to 15 or even five minutes. In a few cases, a "sliding interval" is used, where there is no identified beginning and end to the interval. The kWd peak is then the highest average kWd for *any* successive 30 minutes during the power company billing period. There are some extreme situations where the power company will refuse to supply the customer with kWh pulse information. In that case, the customer has to install his own PTs and CTs and appropriate kWh meter or other transducer, if he wishes to obtain kWd information.

## ELECTROMECHANICAL METERS

The face of a conventional electromechanical kWh meter is shown in Figure 3. The diagram illustrates a Potential Transformer (PT) and a Current Transformer (CT) connected to one of the three input phases to the meter. The CTR on the meter face stands for "CT ratio" and the 800 to 5 indicates that when 800 amps flow through the phase conductor, 5 amps flow through the CT secondary into the meter. The PTR on the meter face stands for "PT ratio" and the 60/1 indicates that with 120 volts on the secondary serving the meter potential coils, the primary is connected to a 7,200 volt supply (120 volts X 60 = 7,200 volts).

Reading the dial to obtain the kWh value is sometimes a great source of confusion, because the dials turn in opposite directions. The right most dial turns one complete revolution which advances the left adjacent dial one number. In this example, the right most dial is read as 5 (and remains a five until the hand actually touches the mark for the 6). The second dial from the right is read as an 8, and will become a 9 when the right most dial hand points straight up to 0. The third dial from the right is read as a 9 (not a 0 as you might expect), and will not become a 0 until the hand on the second dial from the right points straight up to 0.

Using the same reasoning, the second dial from the left is read as a 5, and the left most dial is read as a 1. It becomes apparent that the meter dials must be read from right to left to determine the correct values from the dial hand position. The meter reading would thus be recorded as 15985. That value would be used as the current reading, from which a previous reading would be subtracted. That difference is then multiplied by 10,000 to obtain the kWh that passed through the primary feeders during the specified time interval, such as a week or month.

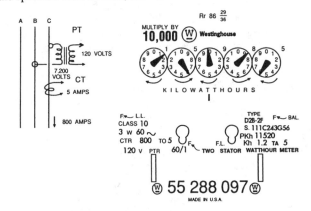

Figure 3: Electromechanical kWh Meter.

Six sample meter faces are presented in Figure 4 with their meter readings to allow you to practice your dial reading technique.

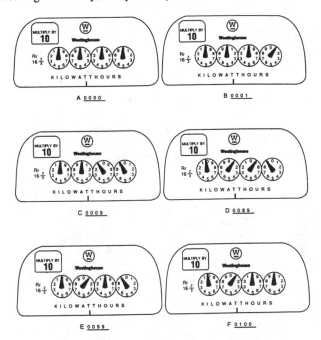

Figure 4: Typical kWh Meter Readings.

311

# MULTI-TASKING SOLID STATE METERS

For many decades, the only type of meter was an electro-mechanical device that measured power consumption. These meters perform their task satisfactorily, operate reliably, and have remained virtually unchanged for many years. Even today, electromechanical meters are the dominant measurement device on power system, and utilities continue to use and purchase them. However, there is a growing niche of applications where a more advanced device has advantages. This niche has fostered the development of the solid-state meter.

The oil embargoes and rising fuel costs of the 1970's forced utilities to increase their electric rates substantially and bill customers in a more equitable way, one that better reflected the actual cost to supply power to a particular user. This require-ment gave rise to advanced purchase contracts. A utility, for example, might charge a customer more if it consumed reactive power in excess of a prescribed limit. Alternatively, a contract might provide a discount if a customer used a higher percentage of off-peak power. Another variable, which is considered when implementing demand-side management programs, is flexibility: A customer might get a lower rate in exchange for interruptible supply. Although there are exceptions, these types of contracts are widespread only with large industrial customers.

The first compatibility concern dealt with the physical nature of the meter rather than its electronic characteristics. Millions of electromechanical meters use a standard socket. In general, electronic meters do not require a socket for installation. Early suppliers of solid-state meters did not package their meters with the standard sockets, which met with utility resistance. Vendors soon realized that they had to package their meters to fit these sockets.

While adapting to the standard socket was important, it pales in comparison to the protocol problem. Protocol refers to the communications structure that software uses to transfer data between computers and metering equipment. Examples of protocol are the commands a system uses to instruct meters to transfer data, keep track of where data were last read from, and reset itself. Each device has unique commands to accomplish these tasks. Of course, if a utility intends to use manual methods to read their meters, protocol is irrelevant.

While most manufacturers agree that the industry would benefit from a standard protocol, it remains very difficult to actually establish one. A prime reason is that, over the years, each vendor has developed its own protocol. With all the money invested in the equipment to match this standard, a vendor is hesitant to give it up. In some cases, certain equipment would not even be able to adapt to another standard, forcing a vendor to abandon a product line.

Efforts toward establishing a standard continue, and industry meetings are still held regularly to discuss the issue. Various group – notably the Edison Electric Institute – have devoted much attention to the problem. It still is conceivable that a standard can be developed that proves satisfactory – or at least tolerable – to all parties. Some feel that efforts will lead to two or three standards, which still is an improvement over the 30 or so around today.

A typical solid state meter is based on:

– A 16-bit microprocessor for speed and processing power.

– A multi-tasking operating system that controls the sharing of processor time among various tasks, such as communica-tions, engineering unit calibration, and totalization.
– An application program, written in a high-level language, composed of specific tasks for specific metering functions.
– User control of the tasks through tables of operating parameters.
– A bus architecture that, in the QUAD4 meter, allows optional boards to be added for such functions as monitoring quality-of-service and loss-of-metering potential.
– Additional memory for storage of data, the application program, and operating parameters.

*Features include:*

– 2- or 4-quadrant metering
– Directly measure watts and vars (kWh and kvarh)
– Calculate kVAh, kVA, power factor, associated demands, and kQh (if needed)
– Local communication and control through internal serial port and internal switches
– Factory-set parameters; also user-programmable with a DOS-based device
– Easy field maintenance via board swapping without scrambling memory
– Demand functions with demand reset switch (turn-to-reset type)
– Two programmable display sequences, user-selectable
– Ability to change/restore dial readings while in test mode.

## APPLICATION OF SOLID STATE METERS

Electric utility applications have ranged from Supervisory Control And Data Acquisition (SCADA) systems primarily concerned with remote operations to distribution automation, which focuses on operating efficiency. Today, systems designed specifically for industrial customers of electric utilities provide similar functions but are tailored to meet the specific requirements of an industrial power system.[4]

New power equipment assemblies such as low- and medium-voltage switchgear, switchboards, and motor control centers can be supplied with monitoring equipment to provide remote access of power system information. In addition, this equipment can be augmented to perform various automatic control functions and provide elaborate local display of system conditions in the power equipment. See figures 5 and 6.

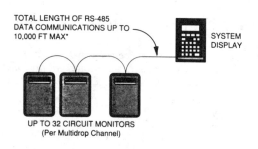

Figure 5:  Local Monitoring.  (Courtesy of Square D Company).

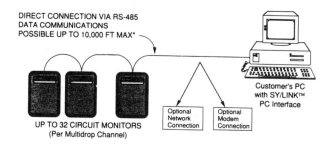

DIRECT CONNECTION VIA RS-485
DATA COMMUNICATIONS
POSSIBLE UP TO 10,000 FT MAX*

UP TO 32 CIRCUIT MONITORS
(Per Multidrop Channel)

Optional Network Connection

Optional Modem Connection

Customer's PC with SY/LINK™ PC Interface

Figure 6:    Remote Monitoring. (Courtesy of Square D Company).

The retrofit of existing power systems is becoming an increasingly important aspect of power monitoring and control. The vast majority of today's installed equipment was furnished with little or no remote communications capability. New devices employing high sampling rates and efficient data communications are now available, which can provide data far in excess of previous methods, even in those cases where some telemetry exists.[5] [6] [7] [8] [9]

## SYSTEM ARCHITECTURE

To ensure that both present and future monitoring and control needs can be supported,the system architecture must allow for efficient transfer of information and be sufficiently flexible to provide for future expansion.

A high-performance local area network (LAN) provides a communications backbone to support multiple equipment locations. Operating at speeds of up to 500 kilobaud, the ability of this network to support transfer of large quantities of information ensures that acceptable data throughput times are achieved.

One or more in-plant personal computer workstations can be directly connected to the network, taking full advantage of network performance. In addition, off-site workstations can gain access to power system information via telephone modem.

## WAVEFORM CAPTURE FOR HARMONIC ANALYSIS

The problem of harmonics in industrial plants has received increasing attention over the past few years. Adjustable speed drives, static converters, and other industrial equipment are sources of potentially hazardous harmonic distortion. Even plants free of such equipment may experience problems due to the influence of other customers on the same utility circuit.

To detect and diagnose harmonic problems adequately, a monitoring system must be capable of capturing data from all three voltage and current waveforms at monitored points throughout the system. Sampling rates in excess of 4 kHz are needed to measure current and voltage accurately through the 35th harmonic.

Identifying which harmonics are present as well as their relative magnitudes allows the plant engineer to take necessary corrective action. In today's dynamic industrial environment, the monitoring system serves a continual need to identify and diagnose harmonic problems when they arise.

## FUTURE OUTLOOK

Awareness of monitoring and control of industrial power systems has increased in recent years, and interest is growing rapidly. Electronic monitoring and control functions are likely to become as commonplace for both new power equipment and existing power installations as conventional metering is today. The expected payback times typically range from 1 to 3 years.

The ability to network power equipment efficiently throughout the distribution system will be of paramount importance to industrial plants. Network performance requirements will include speed, reliability, and the capacity to transfer large amounts of data. In addition, connectivity with other plantwide systems will become an important consideration.

Automatic control of equipment is anticipated to represent the next logical step in the progression from passive monitoring toward plantwide automation. Automatic transfer functions, loadshedding, and loadsequencing are expected to find increasing application.

Finally, the application of computers – especially personal computers – to solve industrial power system problems will have significant impact in years to come. The availability of extensive power system data, coupled with the software to manipulate, analyze, and present this information, is certain to become a powerful source of value for commercial, institutional, and industrial power users.

### SUMMARY

The ultimate goal of a metering system is to assist the plant or facility in managing the energy required to produce a specific product or service. Monitoring and trending energy consumption allows for close control while minimizing expenses.

Unless energy consumption is measured, it is next to impossible to know where to direct time and energy. Metering and trending systems provide that vital ingredient to a successful energy-management process.

Space does not permit a detailed review of all data, concepts, and approaches. Additional practical metering examples have been published previously.[10] It is hoped that information presented will encourage those involved in the measurement and use of energy to do further investigation into this challenging field.

### REFERENCES

[1]  W.L. Stebbins, "Highly Efficient Energy Metering and Trend Analysis Techniques for Maximum Control." In *Proceedings Of The 14th World Energy Engineering Congress*, The Association of Energy Engineers, Atlanta, GA. October 1991.

[2]  W.L. Stebbins, "Implementing An Effective Utility Testing Process: A Keystone For Successful Energy Management." In *Proceedings Of The 13th World Energy Engineering Congress*, The Association of Energy Engineering, Atlanta, GA. October, 1990.

[ 3] W.L. Stebbins, *The Dranetz Handbook For Electrical Energy Management.* Dranetz Technologies, Inc. P.O. Box 4019, Edison, NJ. 00818-4019. March, 1992.

[ 4] Adapted from, "Monitoring and Control of Industrial Power Systems." Robert A. Kennedy and Donald N. Rickey. *IEEE Computer Applications In Power,* Vol. 2, No. 4, October 1989.

[ 5] EMON Corporation, One Oxford Valley, Suite 418, Langhorne, PA 19047.

[ 6] Process Systems Incorporated, P.O. Box 240451, Charlotte, NC 28224.

[ 7] Westinghouse Electric Corporation, 170 Industry Drive, RIDC Park West, Pittsburgh, PA 15275.

[ 8] Square D Company, Engineered Products Division, 200B Weakley Road, Smyrna, TN 37167.

[ 9] Allen-Bradley, 1201 South Second Street, Milwaukee, WI 53204

[10] W.L. Stebbins, "Utility Monitoring Systems: Key To Successful Energy Management," in *Proceedings Of The 6th World Energy Engineering Congress,* The Association of Energy Engineers, Atlanta, GA, November, 1983.

# Chapter 53
# A Methodology for Evaluating Annual Energy Use for Large Multifacility Complexes

P.F. Hutchins

## INTRODUCTION

Evaluating the energy use performance of large multibuilding complexes (called "installations" here) can be difficult, especially when the only energy use values available are single-point monthly utility invoices. Many factors complicate the situation - weather, plus changes in the number, size and use of buildings. What can the Energy Manager conclude when faced with old buildings being demolished, new computer facilities coming on-line, ever-changing weather conditions and a single meter for each fuel type? An analytical method is presented here that will help the Energy Manager evaluate his/her installation's energy performance. This method can be used to adjust actual energy usage to account for the effects of these factors. This allows meaningful comparisons on a year-to-year basis and between similar installations.

## METHODOLOGY DEVELOPMENT

Two factors are proposed that are used to adjust annual energy use for comparison purposes. They are called Building energy Intensity Factor, BIF, and Weather Intensity Factor, WIF. The BIF is used to account for variations in building types/uses that vary from year-to-year and from installation-to-installation. To account for these variations, the expected annual energy use amounts for all building types are normalized to a baseline. The baseline used here is the annual energy use for the most common installation floor space, office areas. Therefore, office buildings will have a BIF equal to 1.0. A building that utilizes 50 percent more energy than the typical office building will have a BIF of 1.50 and so on.

In a similar manner, the WIF is used to account for variations in weather that in turn cause variations in energy use. The "average" weather year will generate a WIF equal to 1.0. A weather year that would cause an increase in energy use by 10 percent will result in a WIF equal to 1.10.

### BIF, Building Energy Intensity Factor

The BIF is the ratio of the annual energy use in a specific building type to the annual energy use for typical office space utilized 10 hours/day, 5 days/week for a particular locale. BIFs can be developed from various sources [1, 2, 3 and 4] concerning building energy performance standards and related topics.

A composite BIF for the entire installation, can be calculated as an average of the individual building BIFs weighted by the amount of floor area for each building type. This is shown mathematically in Equation (1).

$$BIF_M = \frac{\sum_{i=1}^{n} BIF_i * f_i}{\sum_{i=1}^{n} f_i} \qquad (1)$$

where,

$BIF_M$ = installation Building energy Intensity Factor in fiscal year M

$BIF_i$ = Building energy Intensity Factor for building type i

$f_i$ = floor area for building type i

$n$ = number of building types

Note that $\sum_{i=1}^{n} f_i$ is the total installation floor area.

### WIF, Weather Intensity Factor

Using regression analysis techniques, a linear equation can be developed relating installation energy use, heating degree-days (HDD) and cooling degree-days (CDD) with a high degree of correlation. The U.S. Army Construction Engineering Research Laboratory has developed many such equations [5]. The equation has the form as shown below.

$$E_M = a_0 + a_1 * H_M + a_2 * C_M \qquad (2)$$

where,

$E_M$ = installation energy use (MBtu) in fiscal year M

$H_M$ = annual heating degree days in fiscal year M

$C_M$ = annual cooling degree-days in fiscal year M

$a_0$ = regression equation constant (MBtu)

$a_1$ = regression equation coefficient (MBtu/HDD)

$a_2$ = regression equation coefficient (MBtu/CDD)

The WIF is the ratio of the energy use, $E_M$, using actual HDD and CDD data and the energy use, $\overline{E_M}$, using average HDD and CDD data. Both are calculated using Equation (2).

$$WIF_M = \frac{E_M}{\overline{E_M}} \qquad (3)$$

where,

$WIF_M$ = Weather Intensity Factor for fiscal year M

$\overline{E_M}$ = $a_0 + a_1 * \overline{H} + a_2 * \overline{C}$

$\overline{H}$ = Average heating degree-days

$\overline{C}$ = Average cooling degree-days

## Installation Comparisons

Actual annual energy use values can now be normalized with respect to building use/type, weather and floor area. The result is called the adjusted energy index.

$$EUI_M^* = \frac{E'}{BIF_M * WIF_M * F_M} \qquad (4)$$

where,

$EUI_M^*$ = adjusted energy use index (Btu/sf), fiscal year M

$E_M'$ = installation measured annual energy use (MBtu), fiscal year M

$F_M$ = installation total floor area (square feet), fiscal year M

It is $EUI^*$ that can be used to compare installation energy use on a year-to-year basis. The $EUI^*$ can also be used to compare similar installations in similar climatic regions.

## Detailed Installation-To-Installation Comparisons

Comparisons between installations in different climatic regions are much more difficult. The $EUI^*$s cannot be used for this purpose since the weather influence is normalized with respect to one particular installation's average weather conditions. One must look at the individual regression equation coefficients. These are developed using Equation (2). Also, care must be taken to compare installations with similar activities. Any substantial atypical energy use, such as production-related energy should be removed from the annual energy data and evaluated independently.

For a meaningful comparison, the Equation (2) coefficients must be normalized with respect to building type and floor area.

$$
\begin{aligned}
E_M &= \frac{a_0 + a_1 * H_M + a_2 * C_M}{BIF_M * F_M} \\
&= \frac{a_0}{BIF_M * F_M} + \frac{a_1}{BIF_M * F_M} * H_M + \frac{a_2}{BIF_M * F_M} * C_M \\
&= A_{0,M} + A_{1,M} * H_M + A_{2,M} * C_M \qquad (5)
\end{aligned}
$$

where,

$A_{0,M}$ = $\dfrac{a_0}{BIF_M * F_M}$, normalized regression equation constant

$A_{1,M}$ = $\dfrac{a_1}{BIF_M * F_M}$, normalized regression coefficient for HDD

$A_{2,M}$ = $\dfrac{a_2}{BIF_M * F_M}$, normalized regression coefficient for CDD

These coefficients $A_{0,M}$, $A_{1,M}$ and $A_{2,M}$ can be used for installation-to-installation comparisons.

### EXAMPLE - INSTALLATION - YEAR-TO-YEAR COMPARISON

The following example is based on actual data collected at a U.S. Army installation located in the continental United States. For this example, the installation will be called Fort X.

## FY 90 Analysis

BIF Development: As stated earlier, BIFs can be developed using data gathered from a number of sources. The following uses Reference 1, the U.S. Air Force's ETL 87-4. Table I was constructed using data from this ETL for Region 7.

TABLE I. BIF DEVELOPMENT

| # | Building Category | Energy Budget Figure[1] (kBtu/sf/yr) | BIF |
|---|---|---|---|
| 1 | Office | 35 | 1.0 |
| 2 | Hospital | 100 | 2.9 |
| 3 | Clinics | 50 | 1.4 |
| 4 | School | 35 | 1.0 |
| 5 | Community Fac. | 35 | 1.0 |
| 6 | Storage (Heated) | 35 | 1.0 |
| 7 | Commissary/Clubs | 60 | 1.7 |
| 8 | Maintenance | 55 | 1.6 |
| 9 | Military Housing | 40 | 1.1 |
| 10 | Utilities | 20 | 0.6 |
| 11 | Family Housing | 40 | 1.1 |
| 12 | Other | 35 | 1.0 |

[1]ETL 87-4

Fort X FY 90 property records were reviewed. Building data were sorted by construction type code and placed into the categories shown in Table I. The results are contained in Table II.

TABLE II. FORT X FLOOR AREA BY BUILDING TYPE FY 90

| # | Building Category | Floor Area (sf) | BIF |
|---|---|---|---|
| 1 | Office | 1,000,997 | 1.00 |
| 2 | Hospital | 137,200 | 2.75 |
| 3 | Clinics | 31,411 | 1.50 |
| 4 | School | 919,360 | 1.25 |
| 5 | Community Fac. | 504,112 | 1.00 |
| 6 | Storage (Heated) | 555,067 | 1.13 |
| 7 | Commissary/Clubs | 143,583 | 1.63 |
| 8 | Maintenance | 167,494 | 1.63 |
| 9 | Military Housing | 1,326,000 | 1.38 |
| 10 | Utilities | 14,497 | 0.50 |
| 11 | Family Housing | 2,100,000 | 1.38 |
| 12 | Other | 118,708 | 1.25 |
| | Totals | 7,018,429 | 1.29[1] |

[1]Average, weighted by floor area.

The BIF for Fort X for FY 90 is calculated by applying Equation (1)

$$BIF_{90} = \frac{\sum\limits_{i=1}^{12} BIF_i * f_i}{\sum\limits_{i=1}^{12} f_i}$$

$$= \frac{9,075,060}{7,018,429}$$

$$= 1.29$$

WIF Calculation: Weather and energy data were evaluated for FY 89. Below is the regression equation that was developed which characterizes the annual energy use at Fort X in MBtu.

$$E_M = 395,280 + 68.6 * H_M + 32.4 * C_M \quad (6)$$

where,

$H_M$ = annual heating degree-days
$C_M$ = annual cooling degree-days

The following data were collected for FY 90.

TABLE III. FORT X FY 90 DATA

| | |
|---|---|
| Energy Use (MBtu) | 742,800 |
| Floor Area (sf) | 7,018,429 |
| HDD | 3511 |
| CDD | 1537 |

The average HDD and CDD for Fort X are 3960 and 1336, respectively. The WIF for FY 90 can be calculated using Equations (3) and (6).

$$WIF_{90} = \frac{E(3511,1537)}{E(3960,1336)}$$

$$= \frac{395,780 + 68.6 * 3511 + 32.4 * 1537}{395,280 + 68.6 * 3960 + 32.4 * 1336}$$

$$= \frac{685,933}{710,222}$$

$$= 0.97$$

EUI*, Adjusted Energy Use Index Calculation: The measured energy use at Fort X during FY 90 was 742,800 MBtu. The EUI* can be calculated by applying Equation (4).

$$EUI^*_{90} = \frac{742,800}{1.29 * 0.97 * 7.02}$$

$$= 84,590 \text{ Btu/sf}$$

The results of the analysis thus far are summarized in Table IV below.

TABLE IV. FORT X - FY 90 ANALYSIS RESULTS

| | |
|---|---|
| Energy Use (MBtu) | 742,800 |
| Floor Area (sf) | 7,018,429 |
| EUI (Btu/sf) | 105,840 |
| BIF | 1.29 |
| WIF | 0.97 |
| EUI* (Btu/sf) | 84,590 |

The adjustment process decreased the EUI from 105,840 to 84,590 Btu/sf due to:

(1) The presence of building types which use 29 percent more energy than typical office types, and

(2) Weather conditions that should result in a three-percent decrease in annual energy use.

This means that if Fort X was composed of only administrative type buildings and had an "average" weather year, the energy use would have been 84,590 Btu/sf. This value can now be used to compare installation energy use on a year-to-year basis. Similar installations in similar climatic regions can also be compared.

FY 91 Analysis

In FY 91 Fort X added barracks, containing 316,200 square feet of floor space. The winter was warmer than in FY 90, and the summer was warmer than normal. The HDD and CDD were 3117 and 1880, respectively. How does this change the adjustment factors, BIF and WIF? Table V contains the pertinent data for FY 91. Table VI contains the FY 91 building classification data.

TABLE V. FORT X FY 91 DATA

| | |
|---|---|
| Energy Use (MBtu) | 707,100 |
| Floor Area (sf) | 7,334,597 |
| HDD | 3117 |
| CDD | 1880 |

TABLE VI. FORT X FLOOR AREA BY BUILDING TYPE - FY 91

| No. | Building Category | Floor Area (sf) | BIF |
|---|---|---|---|
| 1 | Office | 1,000,997 | 1.00 |
| 2 | Hospital | 137,200 | 2.75 |
| 3 | Clinic | 31,411 | 1.50 |
| 4 | School | 919,360 | 1.25 |
| 5 | Community Fac. | 504,112 | 1.00 |
| 6 | Storage | 555,067 | 1.13 |
| 7 | Commissary/Clubs | 143,583 | 1.63 |
| 8 | Maintenance | 167,494 | 1.63 |
| 9 | Military Housing | 1,326,000 | 1.38 |
| 10 | Utilities | 14,497 | 0.50 |
| 11 | Family Housing | 2,100,000 | 1.38 |
| 12 | Other | 118,708 | 1.25 |
| | Totals | 7,334,597 | 1.30[1] |

[1]$BIF_{91}$ = 1.30, average of BIFs, weighted by building area.

Using Equation (1) $BIF_{91}$ is calculated

$$BIF_{91} = \frac{9,509,791}{7,334,597}$$

$$= 1.30$$

Using the HDD and CDD data, $WIF_{91}$ is calculated using Equation (3).

$$WIF_{91} = \frac{670,018}{710,222}$$

$$= 0.94$$

317

$EUI_{91}^{*}$ is calculated using equation (4) as before.

$$EUI_{91}^{*} = \frac{707,100}{1.30 * 0.94 * 7.33}$$

$$= 78,940 \text{ Btu/sf}$$

The results for FY 91 are summarized below in Table VII.

TABLE VII.  FORT X - FY 91 ANALYSIS RESULTS

| | |
|---|---|
| Energy Use (MBtu) | 707,100 |
| Floor Area (sf) | 7,334,597 |
| EUI (Btu/sf) | 96,400 |
| BIF | 1.30 |
| WIF | 0.94 |
| EUI* (Btu/sf) | 78,940 |

FY 90 - FY 91 Comparison:  Actual energy use for Fort X in FY 91 was 707,100 MBtu.  This is a five-percent decrease from FY 90.  However, the weather was milder, building area increased and some energy intensive buildings were added in FY 91.  What is the installation energy performance? Was the gross energy use decrease due to increased energy efficiency or other factors?  Using the BIF and WIF, the following Table VIII compares the two years.

TABLE VIII.  FORT X - COMPARISON FY 90 AND FY 91

| | FY 90 | FY 91 | Difference (%) |
|---|---|---|---|
| Energy Use (MBtu) | 742,800 | 707,100 | -4.8 |
| Floor Area (sf) | 7,018,000 | 7,334,600 | +4.5 |
| EUI (Btu/sf) | 105,840 | 96,400 | -8.9 |
| BIF | 1.29 | 1.30 | +0.8 |
| WIF | 0.97 | 0.94 | -3.1 |
| EUI* (Btu/sf) | 84,590 | 78,950 | -6.7 |

The EUI, which is the most often used energy performance indicator, decreased 8.9 percent between FY 90 and FY 91.  However, after adjusting for weather and floor area data, the EUI* decreased only 6.7 percent.  Since the floor area utilization changed little between FY 90 and FY 91, the analysis shows that about 25 percent of the 8.9-percent decrease in the EUI was due to changes in weather.

## CONCLUSIONS AND RECOMMENDATIONS

A method is developed that will aid in the understanding of changes in annual energy use for large multifacility complexes.  Where similar installations exist, this method can be used to compare one installation to another.

The methodology is straightforward and can be easily accomplished using any of the well-known computer spreadsheet programs.  It should also lend more credibility to energy performance evaluations and goal-oriented energy programs.

REFERENCES

1.  "Engineering Technical Letter (ETL) 87-4: Energy Budget Figures (EBFs) for Facilities in the Military Construction Program," U.S. Department of the Air Force.

2.  "Base Data for Building Energy Performance Standards for New Buildings," U.S. HUD and U.S. DOE.

3.  "Performance Standards for New Construction and Multi-Family High Rise Residential Buildings," U.S. DOE, DOE/CE-0304T, January 30, 1989.

4.  "Standard 90.1-1989, Energy Efficient Design of New Buildings Except Low-Rise Residential Buildings," ASHRAE.

5.  "A Model of U.S. Army Material Command (AMC) Energy Consumption, Volume II: Installation Equations and Related Statistics," U.S. Army Construction Engineering Research Laboratory, Technical Report E-86/02, March 1986.

# Chapter 54
# Quantification of Variables That Affect Energy Consumption

C.S. Warren

## INTRODUCTION

Facility energy consumption is the summation of a number of contributory factors, caused by equipment that uses energy in response to demands placed by the user and according to its particular design. While energy efficiency improvements usually concentrate on individual parts or systems, overall energy consumption is analyzed by examining the use of specific fuels. Because independent variables effect the consumption of these fuels, accurate comparisons of a facility's energy consumption for time-measured periods must include these effects.

In many cases, it is possible to determine and quantify the effects of one or more of the independent variables through a statistically valid regression analysis of the data. The regression model can be linear, or be dependent on other functions such as powers, time lead or lag, or exponential. The most common model is linear, but other dependencies are often encountered.

Regression analyses are not difficult to accomplish, and are included as one of the tools in most spreadsheet software. The analyses provide the energy manager with a means to better understand the energy consumption of his/her facility.

## METHODOLOGY

Multiple regression analyses of fuel consumption and various independent variables were conducted using the computer spreadsheet Lotus 123 and a regression software package called SpreadSheet Regression Version 2, developed by Background Development Company. Three procedures were used in the modeling process: correlation, multiple regression, and stepwise regression.

The Correlation procedure calculates a correlation matrix for up to 16 input variables. In addition, the procedure also returns descriptive statistics for each variable including the mean, the population and sample standard deviations, and the coefficient of variation.

The Multiple Regression procedure estimates a multiple regression equation with one dependent and up to 15 independent variables. A full array of diagnostic statistics are provided, as well as options to automatically calculate the regression estimates and residuals.

The Stepwise Regression procedure also estimates a multiple regression equation with one dependent and up to 15 independent variables. The stepping algorithm is based upon the t-statistics of the regression coefficients and includes an option for forced entry of selected variables.

The model equations for fuel consumption were obtained using the following procedures:

1.  Historical values of fuel consumption were tabulated and graphed along with major independent variables that were judged to have some correlation with the dependent variable. The graphic comparison gave a pictorial clue as to the variables most likely to show strong correlations.

2.  A correlation matrix was calculated for each fuel using major variables which appeared to affect energy consumption. The independent variables which had high correlation coefficients with respect to the dependent variable were selected to be included in the regression equation. Of those independent variables that were highly correlated with each other, the one that was most strongly correlated with the dependent variable was chosen.

3.  A stepwise regression was run using the variables selected from the correlation procedure. Those variables which improved the adjusted R-square were then included in the multiple regression analysis. Generally, no more than one independent variable was included for each four observations.

4.  Various combinations of the selected independent variables were used on a trial-and-error basis in the multiple regression analysis. The following criteria were used in the order shown for the final determination of each model equation:

    a.  The value of the adjusted R-square ($R^2_{adj}$) for the equation was maximized. The adjusted R-square is a measure of the goodness of fit of a regression equation. The adjusted R-square measures the percentage of the variation of the dependent variable that is explained by the regression equation. For example, an adjusted R-square of 0.90 indicates that the regression equation explains 90 percent of the variation of the dependent variable.

        Unlike the R-square statistic, the adjusted R-square statistic is adjusted for the number of variables and observations used to estimate the regression equation. This provides an unbiased estimate of the variation of the dependent variable that is explained by the regression equation.

The following equation is used by the program to calculate the adjusted R-square:

$$R^2_{adj} = R^2 - [(1 - R^2)\ \frac{(V-1)}{(OB-V)}]$$

where:

V  = the number of variables
OB = the number of observations

b.  The t-statistic (t-stat) for the regression coefficients was maximized. The t-statistic measures how many standard errors the regression coefficient is away from zero. This statistic is useful for testing the hypothesis that a particular coefficient is significantly different from zero.

c.  The determinant (Det.) of the normalized matrix adjusted for the number of independent variables and observations should equal a number close to one. This determinant provides a measure of the degree of the multicollinearity existing among the independent variables. The determinant will have a value of one when there is no multicollinearity, and a value of zero when there is perfect multicollinearity. Multicollinearity arises whenever values of the independent variables stands in an exact or almost-exact linear relation to each other.

## RESULTS

### Example 1

The first example involves both heating and cooling energy use at a large Army troop installation. At the time the data were taken (1987), approximately 66,462 persons worked on the post including both military and civilians. The majority of the military population was housed on site. The primary fuels used by the installation are natural gas and electricity.

Data from October 1982 through September 1986 were analyzed; the methodology described in the previous section revealed that the predominant independent variables were heating-degree-days for natural gas use, and cooling-degree-days for electricity use, showing that the variations in energy use throughout the year are almost entirely due to weather.

Analyses were done for each year of FY 82 through FY 86, plus the composite for the five years. The results are shown below along with the respective adjusted $R^2$ values:

|  | Adjusted-$R^2$ | |
| Fiscal Year | NAG | Elec |
|---|---|---|
| 82 | .981 | .954 |
| 83 | .766 | .891 |
| 84 | .967 | .957 |
| 85 | .898 | .960 |
| 86 | .954 | .957 |
| Composite 82-86 | .907 | .915 |

Figures 1 and 2 show the actual and calculated values for the five-year composite for electricity and natural gas, respectively.

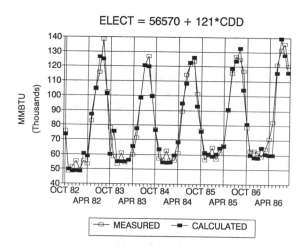

FIGURE 1.  FIVE-YEAR ELECTRICITY CONSUMPTION

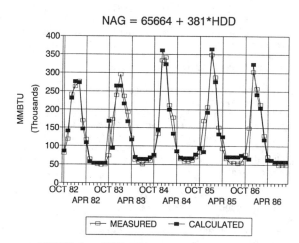

FIGURE 2.  FIVE-YEAR NATURAL GAS CONSUMPTION

The regression equations may be expressed by:

E  =  X * CDD + KC
N  =  Y * HDD + KH

where

| E | = | monthly electric use (MMBtus) |
| X | = | cooling-degree-day coefficient (MMBtu/CDD) |
| CDD | = | monthly cooling-degree-days |
| KC | = | cooling constant (MMBtus) |
| N | = | monthly natural gas use (MMBtus) |
| Y | = | heating-degree-day coefficient (MMBTU/HDD) |
| HDD | = | monthly heating-degree-days |
| KH | = | heating constant (MMBtus) |

Values for each of the variables are:

| FY | X | KC | Y | KH |
|---|---|---|---|---|
| 82 | 130 | 48,167 | 423 | 53,105 |
| 83 | 118 | 55,087 | 357 | 64,424 |
| 84 | 126 | 54,556 | 362 | 67,057 |
| 85 | 117 | 59,010 | 393 | 70,215 |
| 86 | 132 | 57,890 | 432 | 57,013 |
| Composite | 121 | 56,570 | 381 | 65,664 |

The coefficients, X and Y, may be viewed as the weather-related consumption of energy with the units of MMBtu/HDD or MMBtu/CDD. The constants represent the monthly base-load of electricity and natural gas in MMBtus.

The table below shows the annual consumption percentages attributed to weather and base-load.

| FY | NAG | | Electricity | |
|---|---|---|---|---|
| | % Weath. | % Base | % Weath. | % Base |
| 82 | 58.3 | 41.7 | 38.1 | 61.9 |
| 83 | 52.3 | 47.7 | 29.6 | 70.4 |
| 84 | 51.8 | 48.2 | 33.5 | 66.5 |
| 85 | 48.0 | 52.0 | 30.4 | 69.6 |
| 86 | 53.2 | 46.8 | 33.9 | 66.1 |

This installation has a high constant base load of electricity that accounts for approximately 2/3 of the annual electricity consumption; approximately 1/2 of the natural gas consumption is due to weather.

Example 2

The second example shows the dependency of heating-fuel use for an Army installation located in the northeastern section of the United States. Unlike the first example, this installation is a depot activity that was constructed in 1942. The original facility was built for ordnance storage and tank maintenance. The installation's components have evolved and improved over the years, but the basic mission is still supply, ammunition, and maintenance.

Regression analyses of monthly fuel use from October 1987 through September 1990 was attempted for both electricity and boiler fuels to determine the quantitative dependence of energy consumption on weather, production, and/or manpower. The variables that were examined were heating-degree-days, cooling-degree-days, labor force, supply manhours, and labor hours.

Boiler Fuels: As expected, the variation in boiler fuel use is explained by demands on heating during the year. The monthly consumption over the three-year period is best approximated by the equation

$$FUEL = 5462 + 44.8 * HDD$$

Figure 3 shows a comparison of measured fuel use and calculated fuel use. The statistical fit of the calculated data to the observed data is good, with an adjusted $R^2$ of 93 percent. Integration of the energy-dependence equation reveals that approximately 80 percent of boiler fuel use is directly related to weather (Figure 4).

When examined individually, all three years showed a significant correlation with heating-degree-days with respective $R^2$s of 0.928, 0.919, and 0.958.

Figure 5 shows the calculated boiler fuel use as a function of heating-degree-days for the three separate years. FY's 88 and 90 show essentially the same dependence on HDD. FY 89 shows less dependence on HDD, suggesting that some major heating component was off-line that year, or that the equipment operated at a higher efficiency than in the other years.

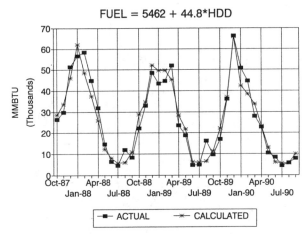

FIGURE 3.   FOUR-YEAR BOILER FUEL USE

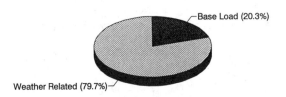

FIGURE 4.   BOILER FUEL USE PERCENTAGES

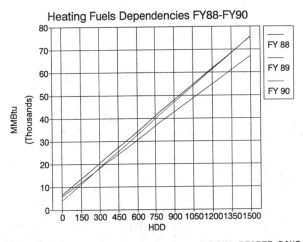

FIGURE 5.   FUEL USE DEPENDENCY ON HEATING-DEGREE-DAYS

Electricity: No significant correlation between electricity and any independent variable could be found, suggesting that the base electrical load of the installation is predominant.

## Example 3

The third example involves an Army installation that shows fuel dependencies on variables in addition to weather. This particular installation is located in the southeastern United States and was first opened in 1941. The initial mission was the production of gunpowder, and has since expanded into manufacturing of all types of military propellants. the facility has produced over two billion pounds of propellants and gunpowder since 1941.

The two primary use fuels, coal and electricity, were analyzed for the period October 1984 through September 1989. Since there are a number of components that make up the final product, each of the components was considered in addition to weather.

Coal: Monthly consumption of energy produced from coal was best approximated by the equation

$$Coal\ MMBtu = 95,000 + 200 * HDD + 0.061 * NC$$

The term NC in the equation represents the monthly production of pounds of nitrocellulose. The coal consumption model has an adjusted $R^2$ value of 0.802. The actual and the calculated values of coal consumption are shown in Figure 6.

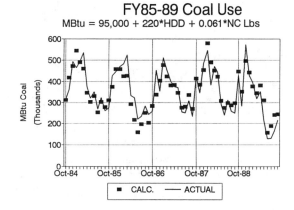

### FY85-89 Coal Use
MBtu = 95,000 + 220*HDD + 0.061*NC Lbs

FIGURE 6. FIVE-YEAR COAL CONSUMPTION

Integration of the equation components show that approximately 26 percent was related to weather, 47 percent to nitrocellulose production, and the remaining 27 percent related to neither quantity.

Electricity: Variations in electricity use at manufacturing facilities are difficult to analyze, because of the pervasive use in the processes. Nevertheless, a reasonable correlation was obtained with the production of the sum of two components, pounds of ammonia oxides (AOP) and concentrated acid (NAC/SAC). The model equation for monthly electricity use is expressed by

$$ELECT\ MMBtu = 26,880 + 0.00171 * (AOP + NAC/SAC)$$

which has an $R^2$ value of 0.603.

As expected, there is no correlation with weather for electricity use, and about 60 percent is not subject to variations of production. The actual and the calculated values of electricity consumption are shown in Figure 7.

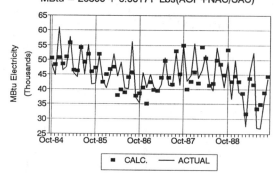

### FY85-89 Electricity Use
MBtu = 26800 + 0.00171*Lbs(AOP+NAC/SAC)

FIGURE 7. FIVE-YEAR ELECTRICITY CONSUMPTION

## Example 4

Thus far, we have shown applications of the regression model at individual installations. The fourth example deals with analysis of electricity and natural gas use on a statewide basis for various industries.

Historical energy consumption by industries included in Standard Industrial Codes (SIC) 20 through 39 were for a southeastern state. Variables were taken from historical economic, demographic and climatological data. The results of the analyses produced energy consumption models for each industry category in each utility service area dependent on one or two independent variables. In all, 40 independent variables were examined for correlation, including fuel prices, gross state product by industry, employment by industry, and producer price indices.

Illustrations of the results for a few industries are shown below.

Electricity: Figure 8 shows the model for SIC 20, Food and Kindred Products. It was found that the variables employment for SIC 20 and constant gross state product (EMPLOY and CONGSP) produced the best correlation with an adjusted $R^2$ of 0.944. The model equation is expressed by

$$ELSALES = -220 + 8.41 * EMPLOY + 371 * CONGSP$$

where electric sales (ELSALES) are in giga-watt-hours, employment is in thousands of persons, and gross state product is in billion dollars. The rise in sales reflects the increasing sales and employment in the industry.

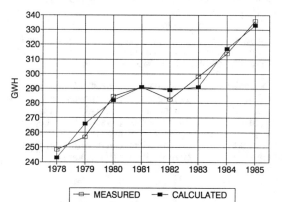

ELSALES = -220+8.41*EMPLOY+371*CONGSP

FIGURE 8. ELECTRICITY SALES FOR SIC 20

<u>Natural Gas</u>: The chemicals industry (SIC 28) shows the effect of fuel pricing on sales (Figure 9).

NGSALES = 208 - 40.4*CURPRI

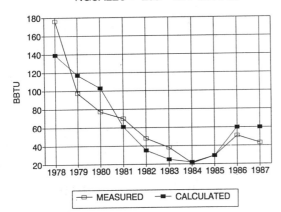

FIGURE 9.  NATURAL GAS SALES FOR SIC 28

The model equation is

$$NGSALES = 208 - 40.4 * CURPRI$$

where gas sales (NGSALES) is expressed in billion Btu's and current fuel price (CURPRI) is in $/MMBtu. The negative coefficient reflects the decrease in sales with the increase in price.

### SUMMARY

While statistical analysis of energy consumption data is not a new idea, it is a tool that many energy managers do not use.  Although it is not always possible to produce a model equation of energy use due to data limitations and/or complexities of the variables, regression models can help energy managers gain insight into what is really happening to their energy use.

# Chapter 55
# Performance Ratio - A Better Design Tool

R. Bentley

A successful job requires a good plan. And, a good plan is built on sound decisions. Most of these decisions are a tug-of-war between first cost and future performance.

Suppose you are designing a house. You are considering two different wall structures where the main difference will show up in the heat bill. You know how they differ in cost (NET COST). And, you can figure yearly fuel cost (PERFORMANCE COST) for each. How do you choose the better design?

When future performance may be measured in dollars, the decision becomes a matter of cost comparison. Unfortunately, you cannot directly compare first costs with future costs. A few attempts to deal with this have been around for a long time. Some folks like YEARS-TO-PAYBACK (YP). Others use COST-PERFORMANCE-INDEX (CPI). Many work from the seat of their pants.

## THE FOLLY OF SIMPLE PAYBACK

YEARS-TO-PAYBACK should take the cost of money, and inflation into account. Most disregard this, and use SIMPLE-PAYBACK, dividing NET COST by the yearly PERFORMANCE COST difference between two options. Regardless of how you get YP, you take the shortest payback as the better design. Think about it. A design change that has zero NET COST, and a tiny PERFORMANCE COST advantage, will deliver a top score of zero. It will beat out another design with a small NET COST, but very large PERFORMANCE COST advantage.

YEARS-TO-PAYBACK may tell you how quickly you should recover an investment. It is **not** a **valid** measure of the better alternative!

The words COST-PERFORMANCE-INDEX might make you think CPI is the tool you need. If you have used it, you know a higher CPI means a better CPI. However, the CPI curve delivers its maximum value at zero. Check out a range of designs. As NET COST and NET PERFORMANCE go to zero, CPI goes max. If you use CPI, you have a built-in argument for believing your design cannot be improved.

Actually, CPI and YP are inverse relationships. If one fails, they both fail. You can not depend on YP or CPI to steer you straight. *(See the description of YP and CPI in APPENDIX A).*

## DOING IT THE RIGHT WAY

I have worked for the past 20 years at the cutting edge of innovative building design. Low cost, low energy buildings have been the goal. Life would have been easier with a good performance test. Well, they say if you want something done right, do it yourself.

PERFORMANCE RATIO is a fairly simple idea. It compares the COSTS of two alternatives to provide a specific BENEFIT. A benefit might be work done, or the maintenance of a building's inside environment. Costs are the total of FIRST COST, and the PRESENT VALUE of all future costs.

PRESENT VALUE has a very specific meaning. It represents the current value of a future expectation. Future expectation is an estimate based on future interest and inflation rates. Suppose you make an investment today, placing $1000 in a savings account. You expect the value of that account to become considerably greater in the future. However, the PRESENT VALUE of that account is $1000.

FIRST COSTS and PRESENT VALUE are equivalent. They may be summed, and compared. Lets look at two alternatives. Providing the benefit for the first alternative represents a PRESENT VALUE of $1000. This means an investment of $1000 would produce income that precisely covers the expense of all future benefits. The second alternative costs $200 more than the first alternative. This greater FIRST COST is directly responsible for a reduction in the PRESENT VALUE cost of providing the benefit. The PRESENT VALUE of providing the benefit for the second alternative happens to be only $600. Adding this to the $200 first cost, we get $800. This is less than the $1000 required by our first alternative. Clearly, the second alternative would be our wisest investment.

PERFORMANCE RATIO makes this comparison by dividing first alternative costs by second alternative costs ($1000/$800=1.25). Division removes the effects of scale, making the result more useful for universal comparison.

When PERFORMANCE RATIO will be used to compare several alternatives, you will find it convenient to establish one of the alternatives as a BASE LINE. All PR values calculated using this BASE LINE may then be directly compared and ordered. Alternatives to standard practice are most easily compared using the STANDARD PRACTICE technology as the BASE LINE.

My focus has been energy saving building construction. I assume the need for the benefit is perpetual. I also assume the building, with normal maintenance, will last forever. Most of you will be ready to part company with me after that last statement, but hold on for a moment. When you calculate the REPLACEMENT COST MULTIPLIER for a long lasting item like a building, you find there is almost no difference between a lifetime of 100 years and an infinite number of years.

PERFORMANCE RATIO can take both LIFETIME and benefit PERIOD into account. For those who are interested, I present the general formula for PERFORMANCE RATIO at the end of this paper. For now I shall deal with the special case using the above assumptions for PERIOD and LIFETIME.

$$(1) \quad PR = \frac{(BASE\ LINE\ COST)}{(ALTERNATIVE\ COST)}$$

PR > 1    alternative is BETTER
PR = 1    no change
PR < 1    alternative is WORSE

PERFORMANCE RATIO applied to the evaluation of energy conservation measures for building construction would take the following form:

$$(2) \quad PR = \frac{(\text{HEAT COST})_b}{(\text{HEAT COST})_a + (\text{NET COST})_a}$$

b = Base Line
a = Alternative

HEAT COST (HC) is the PRESENT VALUE of the YEARLY HEAT COST (HCy). HC is equal to HCy times a COST MULTIPLIER (MC). HEAT COST is the amount of money you would have to invest such that yearly interest on the investment would equal HCy plus a reinvestment amount to offset inflation. HC is a first cost reflecting all future heating costs.

$$MC = \frac{100 + F}{(I - F)}$$

F = Average Fuel INFLATION Rate
I = Average INTEREST Rate

YEARLY HEAT COST (HCy) is equal to the sum of building ENVELOPE Conductance (U•A) and VENTILATION Heat Loss Rate (Qv), multiplied by the number of DEGREE DAYS per year (DD), and by the ENERGY COST (EC). The FIRST-COST equivalent of total FUTURE heat cost (HC) is equal to the yearly heat cost (HCy) times the multiplier (MC).

$$HCy = COST/YEAR = (Uo•Ao + Qv)•DD•EC$$

$$\text{and}... \quad HC = HCy • MC = (Uo•Ao + Qv)•DD•EC•MC$$

$$PR = \frac{HC_b}{HC_a + NC_a} \quad \text{same as equation (2)}$$

If the environmental factors (DD•EC•MC), represented by (K), are divided out, PR will appear as shown in equation (3). This is the PERFORMANCE RATIO for an entire building.

$$\text{if}... \quad K = DD•EC•MC \quad (K=\text{ENVIRONMENT CONSTANT})$$

$$(3) \quad PR = \frac{(U_b•A_o + Q_{vb})}{(U_a•A_o + Q_{va}) + NC/K} \quad (\text{building})$$

Notice, the value (K) represents the combined term for yearly degree days (DD), energy cost (EC), and the multiplier (MC). (K) represents all the factors over which the designer has no control, and which are site specific. A change in (K) can change the relative value of designs under consideration. Therefore, a design that is optimal in one location may not be the best design somewhere else. You should use PR for design comparison **only** when the PR values are calculated using the same value for (DD). (EC) and (MC) may vary **only** if the two designs require different fuel.

```
Uo = U-VALUE of Envelope     (BTU/SQ.FT./DEG.F./HOUR)
Ao = Surface AREA of Building Envelope   (SQ.FT.)
Vo = VOLUME of Building Envelope     (CU.FT.)
Qv = ACH•Vo•0.018 air change LOSS (BTU/DEG.F./HOUR)
Qv = CFM•60•0.018 (CFM•60=CU.FT./HOUR, 0.018=SHair)
DD = DEGREE DAYS   (FAHRENHEIT DEGREES at location)
EC = ENERGY COST/BTU/DAY = ECbtu•24  (24=HOURS/DAY)
```

## APPLICATION TO BUILDING ENVELOPE SYSTEMS

It is not necessary to include terms for **both** envelope **and** ventilation heat losses when you want to examine separate building sections and components. The following example confines PR to the problem of envelope heat losses (U•A).

### Graphic EXAMPLE   (numbers used have no units, and are for *example* only)

```
      HC base
PR = ─────────────────────────────         K•A = 4  (chosen for EXAMPLE)
      HC alternate + NC alternate           HC  = K•A/R   (HEATING COST)
                                            NC  = Ra-Rbase   (NET COST)

   BASE       ALTERNATIVES - - - - - - - - - - - - - - - - - - - - - - - - - - ->

   R  Rb=1    R  Ra=1.5   R  Ra=2    R  Ra=2.5   R  Ra=3     R  Ra=3.5   R  Ra=4
   R  NC=0....R .........  R .........  R .........  R .........  R .........  R .........
   HC         R  NC=0.5   R  NC       R  NC       R  NC       R  NC       R  NC
   HC         HC          R  NC=1     R  NC       R  NC       R  NC       R  NC
   HC         HC          HC          R  NC=1.5   R  NC       R  NC       R  NC
   HC         HC          HC          HC          R  NC=2     R  NC       R  NC
   HC         HC          HC          HC          HC          R  NC=2.5   R  NC
   HC         HC          HC HC=2     HC HC=1.6   HC          HC          R  NC=3
   HC         .. HC=2.67                          .. HC=1.33  HC HC=1.14  HC
   HC HC=4                                                                HC HC=1
                          PR=1.33
               PR=1.26                PR=1.29
                                                  PR=1.2
                                                              PR=1.1
   ...PR=1 ..................................................................PR=1 ...
```

In this demonstration of PR, NET COST is assumed to be proportional to R-VALUE. Adding attic insulation would be a good example. In the real world, the difference between competing designs does not often allow a simple relationship between PERFORMANCE and NET COST. This does not diminish the validity of PR, or its usefulness to the design process.

326

Moving on to real problems, lets look at how a building's heat losses add up. The envelope sections, such as roofs and walls, add together toward the total (UoAo). You may use PR to evaluate specific envelope sections (UsAs).

So, for a given Building SECTION

$$HCs = Us \cdot As \cdot DD \cdot EC \cdot MC \quad and.. \quad K=DD \cdot EC \cdot MC$$

so... $HCs = Us \cdot As \cdot K$ and.. U=1/R
$HCs = (1/Rs) \cdot (As \cdot K)$

$$(4) \quad PR = \frac{(1/R_b)}{(1/R_a) + (NC/(As \cdot K))}$$

Rb = R-VALUE of base line envelope SECTION
Ra = R-VALUE of alternative envelope SECTION
As = AREA of envelope SECTION (As = Ab = Aa)

## PERFORMANCE RATIO FOR SECTIONS OF UNIT AREA

UNIT AREA, like unit pricing, makes it easier to compare component costs. The SQUARE FOOT is the unit used in the USA. The SQUARE METER is used nearly everywhere else. By using the NET COST per UNIT AREA (COST/AREA), section AREA (As) can be removed, leaving PERFORMANCE RATIO unchanged.

NC = NET COST =(COST of B)-(COST of A)
NUIC = NET COST per UNIT AREA
(NET UNIT INCREMENTAL COST)
so... NUIC = NC/As (and... NC = NUIC·As)

$$(5) \quad PR = \frac{(1/R_b)}{(1/R_a) + (NUIC/K)}$$

## HEAT RECOVERY VENTILATION (HRV) SYSTEMS

PERFORMANCE RATIO also works with ventilation systems. The BASE LINE used here is very simple, a standard *(rather leaky)* house. Equation (6) assumes the leakage rate for BASE LINE is equal to the HRV rate. *(This is not really fair to our HRV system, but you can make your own extrapolation).* Therefore, the difference in CFM capacity between different HRV systems does not affect PERFORMANCE RATIO. This means, you can compare any two HRV systems no matter what their CFM.

You can get into trouble comparing HRV systems. One system may run at a steady rate, while another cycles on and off. Some use a defrost system that cuts in on demand, and some preheat incoming air, depending on outside temperature. Any attempt to correct for these differences will depend on installation site conditions. Affected terms are PWR, EFF, and CFM.

The assumption regarding LIFETIME, used for building construction, does not hold up for HRV systems. If you want a more accurate assessment, you may wish to replace the NET COST (NC) term with a series of incremental costs, multiplied by the appropriate REPLACEMENT COST MULTIPLIER (MR) for the respective equipment LIFETIMES. *(See the general formula for PR at the end of this article).*

HC = Qv·K and.. HRVs use ELECTRICITY

so... K = DD·(ECkwh·0.007032)·MC

NC = (HRV system COST)-(BASE LINE COST)

Qv = CFM·60·0.018 = CFM·1.08 (60=MINUTES/HOUR)
CFM = CFM of HRV (Choose HRV with adequate CFM)
EFF = HRV EFFICIENCY RATING as a PERCENT
PWR = Continuous POWER RATING in WATTS
P = PWR·103.8·MONTHS(of operation)/YEAR
Equation (6) accounts for HRV POWER usage.

$$(6) \quad PR = \frac{1}{(1-EFF/100)+(((NC/K)+(P/DD))/Qv)}$$

## PERFORMANCE RATIO OF AIR TIGHTNESS SYSTEMS

The following PR formulas may be used to evaluate different infiltration barrier systems. Compare nearly identical buildings, after standard depressurization testing to obtain CFM or ACH values.

$$PR = \frac{Qv_b}{Qv_a + (NC/K)}$$

also... Qv = CFM·1.08 (CFM=CUBIC FEET/MIN)
Qv = ACH·Vo·0.018 (ACH=AIR CHANGES/HR)
Vo = VOLUME of building (CUBIC FEET)

K = DD·EC·MC

$$(7a) \quad PR = \frac{CFM_b}{CFM_a + (NC/(1.08 \cdot K))}$$

$$(7b) \quad PR = \frac{ACH_b}{ACH_a + (NC/(Vo \cdot 0.018 \cdot K))}$$

## DIFFERENT ENERGY SOURCES

If different energy sources are used for the BASE LINE system and ALTERNATIVE system, then you must use different (K) values for each. The value of (EC) will surely be different, and (MC) may change if the inflation rate is different for the two energy sources.

Kb = DD·ECb·MCb (DD is CONSTANT)
Ka = DD·ECa·MCa

$$(8) \quad PR = \frac{(U_b \cdot Ao + Qv_b) \cdot K_b}{(U_a \cdot Ao + Qv_a) \cdot K_a + NC}$$

and..

$$PR = \frac{(K_b/R_b)}{(K_a/R_a) + NUIC}$$

$$PR = \frac{(Qv_b \cdot K_b)}{(Qv_a \cdot K_a) + NC}$$

327

## PRACTICAL APPLICATION OF PERFORMANCE RATIO

PERFORMANCE RATIO will be more useful if you establish a BASE LINE design, and compare all future designs to this base line. I use a STANDARD PRACTICE design for my base line. This way, I always know if a new design is better than standard practice. And, the PR value can be directly compared with PR values calculated for other designs, using the same (K).

Compare PR values, including those for the same design, under different site conditions *(different* (K) *values)*, ONLY to assess the effect of those different conditions.

The first step to using PR is determining a value for (K). Once you have chosen (K), it does not change over the course of optimizing PR for all components, in any number of buildings using the same energy source, in a given area.

$$K = DD \cdot EC \cdot MC$$

DD = DEGREE DAYS   (local FAHRENHEIT DEGREES)

EC = ECbtu•24 = ECkwh•0.000293•24 = ECkwh•0.007032

EC = ECkwh•0.007032 (ECkwh=COST/KWH    electricity)
EC = ECoil•0.017/CE (ECoil=COST/GAL       fuel oil)
EC = ECgas•0.024/CE (ECgas=COST/THERM natural gas)

Gas or electric COST equals UTILIZATION rate PLUS TAX.

CE = combustion CONVERSION EFFICIENCY (eg. 65-95%)

MC = (100+F)/(I-F)
I  = Projected AVERAGE INTEREST RATE
F  = Projected AVERAGE FUEL INFLATION RATE

Calculating (MC) requires a careful choice of interest and inflation rates. Small differences in (I) and (F) can make a big difference in the size of (K). Luckily, PERFORMANCE RATIO is fairly insensitive to small changes in the value of (K). Use a bit of care, and take the long view. I have calculated a few sample (K) values to give you an idea of the range.

for... MC=25  and...

DD=7500  EC=(0.06 ECkwh)•(0.007032)  K= 79.1
DD=7500  EC=(0.10 ECkwh)•(0.007032)  K=131.9
DD=8500  EC=(0.06 ECkwh)•(0.007032)  K= 89.7
DD=8500  EC=(0.10 ECkwh)•(0.007032)  K=149.4

A good BASE LINE for comparing alternate wall structures is the standard 2x4 stud wall (1/2 inch sheetrock, vapor barrier, studs 16 inches o.c., bottom plate, double top plate, 3.5 inch fiberglass batt insulation, 3/4 inch sheathing, and 3/4 inch siding) with a composite R-VALUE *(including air films)* of R=12.77. It is convenient to use the standard 2x4 stud wall quoted here because (Rb) has been established, and it should be easy to cost locally.

Rb    = R-VALUE of BASE LINE structure  (B)
Ra    = R-VALUE of ALTERNATE structure  (A)
NUIC = (COST(A)/SQ.FT.) - (COST(B)/SQ.FT.)

PR = (1/Rb)/((1/Ra)+(NUIC/K))

Vary your design. Calculate the resulting PR, and choose the variation with the maximum PERFORMANCE RATIO.

## REAL WORLD EXAMPLE

A study, sponsored by Energy, Mines, and Resources, CANADA, used CPI to examine the relative advantage of several advanced wood frame wall designs. They were compared to a standard 2x4 stud wall. I have selected a few of the wall descriptions, in the order listed in the study report. They are presented here with the CPI given in the report, and a PR calculated using K=95 (DD=9000, EC=0.06•(0.007), and M=25). Canadian dollars have been converted to US dollars for NUIC, but CPI values have been left as given because we only need to look at relative size, and note the order.

| WALL DESCRIPTION | R-VALUE | NUIC | (CPI) | (PR) |
|---|---|---|---|---|
| (1) (2x6) 24 inch o.c. 5/8 inch fiberboard sheathing | 20.0 | .31 | 47 | 1.47 |
| (2) (2X6) 16 inch o.c. 1 inch Glasclad insulated sheathing with Tyvek | 24.4 | .65 | 29 | 1.64 |
| (3) (2x6) 16 inch o.c. 2 inch Glasclad insulated sheathing with Tyvek | 28.8 | 1.07 | 20 | (1.70) |
| (4) Double Stud Wall | 40.0 | 2.97 | 9 | 1.39 |

Look at the CPI values. The wall design representing the least change has the highest CPI. As the designs move farther away, the CPI values become smaller. The study report goes on to observe that, the upgrade from a 2x4 to a 2x6 system *SHOULD BE NOTED* because it achieved a CPI approaching twice the CPI of the next highest wall system. This leads architects, builders, and home buyers to the wrong conclusion.

Now look at the PR values. The system of choice, in terms of money spent for value received, is wall (3). Wall (2) runs a close 2nd. You should note, any value of (K) between 75 and 195 will produce the same results. Above (K=195), even the very expensive double stud wall starts looking pretty good. The range of possible wall designs is far greater than shown here, but you will not find the winners without a tool like PERFORMANCE RATIO.

## PERFORMANCE RATIO - THE UNABRIDGED VERSION

The following is a more general, and technical discussion of PERFORMANCE RATIO.

I have introduced the subject in a form that may be easily, and immediately applied to energy conserving home construction. The PR relationships shown in equations (2)-(8) represent a special application of PERFORMANCE RATIO. The general form of PERFORMANCE RATIO can handle situations where BENEFITS continue without end, or for a PERIOD of limited duration. Equipment in one design may have a *very* long LIFETIME with no need for replacement. Another design may require regular replacement of fixed LIFETIME equipment. Any logical combination of these conditions may be compared. This includes designs with considerably different lifetimes.

```
C  = OPERATING COST (initial yearly COST)
R  = EQUIPMENT COST (initial REPLACEMENT cost)
MC = Operating COST MULTIPLIER
MR = Equipment COST MULTIPLIER
```

$$PR = \frac{C_b \cdot MC_b + R_b \cdot MR_b}{C_a \cdot MC_a + R_a \cdot MR_a}$$

C•MC and R•MR may be SUMS where COST elements have different lifetimes or inflation rates. Thus, PERFORMANCE RATIO can handle complex systems.

$$PR = \frac{\sum(c_{bi} \cdot mc_{bi}) + \sum(r_{bi} \cdot mr_{bi})}{\sum(c_{ai} \cdot mc_{ai}) + \sum(r_{ai} \cdot mr_{ai})}$$

```
where for i=1 to n...   c_1+c_2+...+c_n = C
              and...    r_1+r_2+...+r_n = R
```

```
I  = INTEREST  Rate (as a percentage)
F  = INFLATION Rate (as a percentage)
     (INFLATION may be DIFFERENT for EACH COST.)
L  = LIFETIME in years
P  = PERIOD in years
```

$$II = (1+I/100)^L$$
$$FF = (1+F/100)^L$$

When calculating OPERATING COST for an INFINITE PERIOD of TIME use:

$$MC = (100+F)/(I-F)$$

$$MR = 1+(FF/(II-FF))$$

$$MR = 1 \quad \text{(for L=200 years or more)}$$

When calculating OPERATING COST for a LIMITED PERIOD of TIME use:

$$MC = ((100+F)/(I-F)) \cdot (1-((100+F)/(100+I))^P)$$

$$MR = 1+(FF/(II-FF)) \cdot (1-(FF/II)^{[(P/L)-1]})$$

$$MR = 1 \quad \text{(for L=PERIOD)}$$

PERFORMANCE RATIO calculations for some long-lifetime designs may be simplified when only a portion of the COST accounts for the BENEFIT. In building thermal envelope design, only the FIRST COST difference contributes to any difference in the BENEFIT. With MR=1, substitute Rb=Rb-Rb=0, and Ra=Ra-Rb=NC in the general equation for PR above. If you also say HC=HCy•MC=C•MC, true for thermal envelope designs, the general equation turns into equation (2).

I developed PERFORMANCE RATIO with building design in mind. However, first and future cost problems of this type are common. For instance, try comparing standard incandescent lights with the new, high efficiency fluorescents. Even choosing a new car falls into this category.

\* \* \*

The author has developed an innovative building system, THERMAL EFFICIENCY CONSTRUCTION. R-40 wood frame walls, built using TEC, achieve PR values greater than 2.2 at K=95. He has also authored computer software making it easy to calculate building heatload, composite R-values, and of course, PERFORMANCE RATIO.

You may contact the author directly for further information by calling 518-359-9300, or writing to him at Thermal Efficiency Construction, Mount Arab, Box 786, Tupper Lake, NY 12986.

## APPENDIX A

COST-PERFORMANCE-INDEX (CPI) is defined by the following relationship:

$$CPI = \frac{Kcpi \cdot ((1/R_b)-(1/R_a))}{NUIC}$$

```
and..  Kcpi = DD•EC
```

(Kcpi) accounts for climate and energy cost. It is a multiplier of the entire relationship. Consequently, (Kcpi) has absolutely no affect on the relative order of competing designs - a red flag for anyone considering using CPI.

Compare this to YEARS-TO-PAYBACK (YP), commonly known as SIMPLE PAYBACK:

$$YP = \frac{NC}{(HCy_b - HCy_a)}$$

(HCyb - HCya) is the NET yearly HEATING COST savings for the alternate design.

For a building envelope SECTION...

$$HCy = (1/R) \cdot A \cdot DD \cdot EC = (1/R) \cdot A \cdot Kyp$$

```
where.. Kyp = DD•EC
```

(Kyp) is a common factor of both (HCyb) and (HCya). Therefore, (Kyp) is a multiplier like (Kcpi), and with the same consequences.

```
and... NC = NUIC • A          so...
```

$$YP = \frac{NUIC}{Kyp \cdot ((1/R_b)-(1/R_a))}$$

```
therefore...    CPI = 1/YP
```

A few minor manipulations show that YP is the inverse of CPI. This means both methods will produce identical results, on their inverse scales, when used to judge alternative designs. YP may be useful to someone who wants to know how quickly an investment will be recovered. This information will *not* determine the better option.

This appendix describes the method used to derive the multipliers, (MC) and (MR). The approach is straightforward, and the math is simple. I shall start by finding the COST MULTIPLIER (MC) for an infinite PERIOD.

```
IF      I=Interest  (as a percent)

for an INCREMENT of time (say 1 year), and

        F=Inflation (as a percent)

for the same INCREMENT of time,

THEN    i=(1+I/100) and f=(1+F/100)
```

are multipliers that may be used to calculate the new value of an AMOUNT, after the given INCREMENT, when the amount is subject to an increase resulting from interest, or inflation.

We want a multiplier (MC) that, when multiplied by a cost (C), will deliver an AMOUNT equal to the present value of all future costs. This AMOUNT (lets call it A), if invested at the prevalent interest rate, would produce sufficient interest to cover ALL future costs, even as those costs increase with inflation.

This means the AMOUNT (A), despite steady depletion by future costs, would not fall to ZERO until the entire PERIOD of time (infinity for this calculation) has expired.

Lets look at cumulative INCREMENTS of time. And, for the sake of argument, assume at each INCREMENT it is the final INCREMENT of the PERIOD.

$$Ai-Cf=0 \text{ so.. } A=C(f/i)$$
$$(Ai-Cf)i-Cf^2=0 \text{ so.. } A=C((f/i)+(f/i)^2)$$
$$((Ai-Cf)i-Cf^2)i-Cf^3=0 \text{ so.. } A=C((f/i)+(f/i)^2+(f/i)^3)$$

We note the series...    $A=C [z+z^2+z^3+...+z^n]$

And...  $A=C [MC]$    so..  $MC = [z+z^2+z^3+...+z^n]$

for...  $Z=(f/i)=(1+F/100)/(1+I/100)$  and.. n=PERIOD

This series converges:   $MC_{n=\infty} = Z/(1-Z)$  (for F<I)

$$MC = (100+F)/(I-F)$$

Sometimes we wish to compare alternatives where the BENEFIT PERIOD is finite. We shall now find (MC) for a finite PERIOD of time (P), a series of (P) terms.

$$MC = [Z+Z^2+Z^3+...+Z^P] \quad\quad And,..$$

the original infinite series may be expressed as:

$$MC_\infty= [Z+Z^2+Z^3+...+Z^P] + Z^P [Z+Z^2+Z^3+...+Z^n]$$

$$MC_\infty= MC + Z^P (MC_\infty) \quad so... \quad MC = MC_\infty (1-Z^P)$$

$$MC = ((100+F)/(I-F))(1-((100+F)/(100+I))^P)$$

I have derived (MC) for operating costs. These are costs (C), similar to an electric bill, where you receive a benefit, and pay the bill afterward. The charges come due in roughly the same regular manner as interest payments on a bank deposit.

We shall now consider replacement costs (R), and the multiplier (MR). Replacement costs begin with initial cost (first cost). You pay in advance, and then enjoy the benefits. This is a fundamental difference between (R) and (C). Each element of this first cost has an associated LIFETIME. Elements, like planning, may be considered to have an infinite life. Hard construction elements may have such long LIFETIMES we may consider them to last forever. Many elements will require replacement at regular intervals, and some elements may have valuable useful life at the conclusion of the BENEFIT PERIOD.

The replacement cost multiplier (MR) times the REPLACEMENT COST (R) is equal to the FIRST COST plus the PRESENT VALUE of any future replacement, based on first cost LIFETIME.

This is expressed as R·MR where R=(REPLACEMENT COST).

```
MR = 1 + future replacement PRESENT VALUE factor
```

If LIFETIME is equal to BENEFIT PERIOD, there will never be need for replacement, OR investment recovery, so for L=P :

```
MR = 1
```

For any case where LIFETIME is significantly longer or shorter than BENEFIT PERIOD, we must calculate (MR) differently.

Replacement occurs only at the end of LIFETIME. LIFETIME is measured in *multiple* INCREMENTS. (I) and (F) are based on *SINGLE* INCREMENTS. This requires definition of effective interest and inflation rates, similar to a calculation of compound interest.

```
II = i(effective)=(1+I/100)^L
FF = f(effective)=(1+F/100)^L
ZZ = Z(effective)=FF/II
```

We must also define an effective PERIOD ($P_{eff}$). LIFETIME becomes the effective INCREMENT. The number of replacements equals P/L less 1 because replacement is not required at the end of the BENEFIT PERIOD.

```
Peff = (P/L)-1
```

Using $MC = (Z /(1-Z)) (1-Z^P)$ as a guide, substitute ZZ for Z, and $P_{eff}$ for P, keeping in mind the addition of 1 to the whole thing to account for FIRST COST.

```
MR = 1 + (ZZ/(1-ZZ)) (1-ZZ^[(P/L)-1])

MR = 1 + (FF/(II-FF))(1-(FF/II)^[(P/L)-1])
```

In the case where the PERIOD (P) goes to infinity, the relationship condenses to:

```
MR = 1 + (FF/(II-FF))
```

* * *

RICHARD BENTLEY, Mount Arab, Tupper Lake, NY 12986 (518-359-9300)

# Chapter 56
# PCB Ballast Disposal
M. Dong, B. McGagg

## INTRODUCTION

When implementing a lighting retrofit project, removing and disposing of the old ballasts can be a problem. The installation of new electronic ballasts in fluorescent light fixtures causes the retirement of millions of pre-1979 ballasts which contain polychlorinated biphenyls, also known as PCBs.

It is estimated that there are 400 million to 1.6 billion ballasts currently in service in the U.S. Approximately half of these contain PCBs. Since each ballast has one ounce of virtually pure dielectric fluid, there are roughly 10 to 40 million pounds (nearly 1 to 4 million gallons) of PCBs in our country's buildings.

A typical 100,000 square-foot building contains 1250 fixtures and 2500 ballasts. If built prior to 1979, this translates into roughly 150 pounds of PCBs or 12 gallons of PCB dielectric fluid.

## HOW TO IDENTIFY
## PCB BALLASTS

Non-PCB ballasts are required to be marked "NO PCBs" as of July 1, 1978. This label is usually printed on the manufacturer's label. If you can't find the "NO PCBs" label, then assume that it is a PCB ballast.

For added security look for the date stamp on the back of the ballast, as ballasts made before 1979 generally contain PCBs. Universal and Advance ballasts have the last two digits of the year, e.g., "78" for 1978, while General Electric ballasts have a two-letter code. All General Electric codes ending with letters A-R and T-Y denote ballasts made in the 1960's and 1970's. Ballasts made in the 1980's do not contain PCBs.

We recommend sorting PCB and non-PCB ballasts because there is a dramatic difference in the disposal and recycling costs.

## LAX AND CONFLICTING
## DISPOSAL REGULATIONS

Under the Toxic Substances Control Act (TSCA) non-leaking small PCB capacitors, such as the type in fluorescent light ballasts, may be disposed of as municipal solid waste, e.g., in a sanitary landfill.

Under the Superfund laws, a release or threat of release of more than one pound (the Reportable Quantity) of PCBs into the environment triggers an immediate notification and cleanup requirement. Approximately 16 ballasts contain one pound of PCBs. Some regulators have interpreted this to mean that the disposal of 16 or more ballasts in a sanitary landfill is a release and, as such, would trigger a Superfund action.

Under state laws, there are some 15 states which classify PCB ballasts as hazardous waste and ban PCBs from their sanitary landfills (see Figure 1). In another 15 states there are special handling or approval requirements. We recommend that you check with your state's environmental agency for specifics.

## HOW TO IDENTIFY LEAKERS

Leaking ballasts are regulated for disposal and they cannot be put in the trash. "Leakers" (leaking ballasts or capacitors) are items in which PCB oil has flowed onto the exterior surface of the ballast or capacitor. PCBs are a clear or yellow oil, and most PCB leaks are visible. If you see oil on the surface of your ballast, consider it to be a leaker.

Many companies also classify ballasts with leaking asphalt as leakers. Unless the asphalt is contaminated with PCBs, it is not a leaker. Some generators err on the conservative side because much of the asphalt potting material in ballasts is PCB-contaminated.

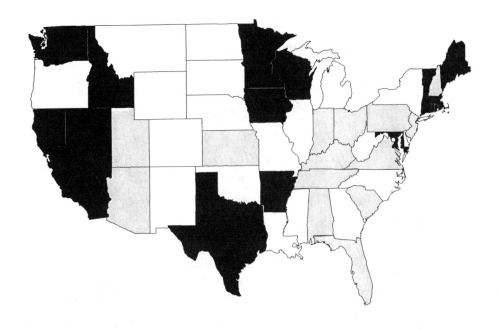

■ States which ban PCB ballasts from sanitary landfills

▨ States which may have special policies or requirements
regarding disposal of PCB ballasts

FIGURE 1.   STATE BALLAST DISPOSAL REGULATIONS

### TIPS ON BALLAST REMOVAL

Wear chemically resistant gloves when handling the ballast as the exterior surface may contain trace quantities of PCBs.  When handling leakers a chemically resistant suit, e.g., one made of Tyvek®, is also recommended to reduce human contact with PCBs. Dispose of protective equipment as contaminated PCB waste along with the ballasts.

All leaking ballasts should be placed in double plastic bags and separated from all other ballasts.  The bags should be placed in steel drums and labelled with the yellow "Caution Contains PCBs" sticker.

### TIPS ON PACKING

After the ballasts have been removed they should be taken to the shipping/receiving area, packed in steel drums, and labelled for shipment.

Most companies use 55-gallon steel drums for packing ballasts but other DOT  containers can be used. Occasionally, some use DOT-approved bins constructed of steel.

When purchasing drums, specify 17C 55-gallon open head steel drums approved for transporting hazardous liquids.  New drums need not be purchased; used or reconditioned drums are suitable if they have been properly cleaned, tested and labelled.  Reconditioned drums can usually be purchased for $20-$30 each in major metropolitan areas.  A typical empty steel drum weighs 55 pounds.

Pack the ballasts with care.  Don't overpack the drums or crush the ballasts because this could cause leaks and increase your disposal costs.  A typical drum will hold 150-250 F40 ballasts from 4-foot light fixtures or 60-100 F96 ballasts from 8-foot light fixtures.  We have seen as many as 300 F40 ballasts fit into one drum, but we don't recommend putting more than 250 ballasts into each drum for safety reasons.

A drum filled with ballasts will weigh 700-800 pounds on average. Drum weight should not exceed 1000 pounds for safety purposes.  Some companies only half-fill the barrel because they are difficult to move manually or require special equipment.

As an added precaution, put 1-3 inches of absorbent material in the bottom of the barrel to soak up any leaking PCB oil. Kitty litter or sawdust will do. If you plan to landfill the non-leaking ballasts, put extra absorbent material in the bottom, e.g., 6-12 inches, plus absorbent material in the interstitial areas between ballasts. This is required by Federal law (TSCA).

## LABELLING, MANIFESTING AND TRANSPORTING BALLASTS

All barrels of leaking ballasts should bear the yellow "Caution Contains PCBs" label. This is a standard label which can be purchased from most label companies.

FIGURE 2. FEDERAL UNIFORM HAZARDOUS WASTE MANIFEST

All barrels of non-leaking and leaking ballasts should contain a material profile with: the name, address and telephone number of the waste generator; the date on which the ballasts were first removed; a description of the material ("Discarded Light Ballasts"); and the new DOT Shipping Description ("RQ, Polychlorinated Biphenyls, 9, UN2315, PGII").

We recommend using the Federal Uniform Hazardous Waste Manifest (see Figure 2), except in those states which require use of the state Hazardous Waste Manifest.

Generally speaking, only the 15 states which classify PCB ballasts as hazardous waste require a licensed hazardous waste hauler to transport non-leaking PCB ballasts. Under TSCA only leakers must be transported by a registered PCB hauler.

DISPOSAL OPTIONS

After removal there are five common disposal options for PCB ballasts.

## Leaving Disconnected Ballasts In the Fixture

This is not recommended by fire inspectors or fire insurers because it greatly increases the toxicity of a fire and the clean-up costs after a fire. The PCBs could volatize during a fire and oxidize into dioxins or furans, deadly carcinogens.

Leaving the disconnected ballast in the fixture also makes it easy for the building owner to reconnect the old ballast when the new ballast fails, causing a "persistence" problem.

## Sanitary Landfills

This practice is not recommended and is illegal in 15 states. The option is cheap in the short term, but could result in future Superfund liabilities.

## Chemical Waste Landfills

These are legal and relatively inexpensive to use (25-50¢ per pound or $1-2 per ballast from a 4-foot fixture). However, most landfills are not designed to accept PCB liquids or materials with over 500 ppm PCBs. Ballasts have 500,000 to 1 million ppm of PCBs in liquid form. This option could also lead to Superfund liabilities.

## Whole Ballast Incineration

This ensures permanent destruction of the PCBs. However, PCB incineration capacity is limited and expensive ($1.50-3.00 per pound or $6-10 per ballast from a 4-foot fixture).

## Recycling/Incineration

This option destroys only the PCBs and recycles the remaining metals, which comprise 80% of the ballast by weight. This is 30-50% less expensive than whole ballast incineration.

See Figure 3 for relative costs of various disposal options.

## Short-Term Cost of Ballast Disposal
### (excludes environmental cost)

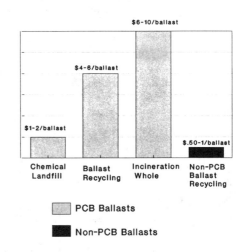

FIGURE 3.    SHORT-TERM COST OF BALLAST DISPOSAL

CONCLUSION

Group replacement of PCB ballasts presents a unique opportunity to rid a building of PCBs and dispose of them properly. Without group replacement, disposing of small quantities of pre-1979 ballasts as hazardous waste would be expensive or, alternatively, the ballasts would be discarded in the dumpster. This could result in the contamination of our local landfills and groundwater. However, with group replacement, proper disposal becomes much more economical.

What may seem like an impediment to upgrading a lighting system is actually an opportunity to decontaminate a building of PCBs and dispose of them in an environmentally sound manner.

# Chapter 57

# The Economics of Supplying the Supplementary Heat in a Closed Loop Water Source Heat Pump System

R.P. Johnson, V.E. Bartkus, J.B. Singh

The paper describes the details of a research and demonstration project that will be completed in August 1992 at a healthcare facility in northeastern Pennsylvania. The purpose of the project is to compare the economics of several methods of supplying the supplementary heating in a facility served by a closed loop water source heat pump system. The systems being tested include a storage hot water tank with electric resistance heaters and three air source heat pumps that have the ability to supply the same heat during on-peak hours as well as off-peak hours.

The paper compares the projected operating costs of the following:

1. Gas boiler supplying the supplementary heat.

2. Stored hot water supplying the supplementary heat which is generated and stored during off-peak hours using resistance heat on PP&L's off-peak rate.

3. Stored hot water supplying the supplementary heat generated during off-peak hours using the air source heat pumps on PP&L's off-peak rate.

4. Hot water generated by the air source heat pumps supplying the supplementary loop heating on PP&L's general service and time-of-day electric rates.

It is generally known in the HVAC industry that a closed loop water source heat pump system can provide one of the most efficient means of space conditioning to a building with high internal gains by transferring the excess heat available in one part of the building to another part of the building where it may be needed for heating.

The following flow diagram (Figure 1) depicts the relationship of the air source heat pumps with the storage tanks and the building closed water loop.

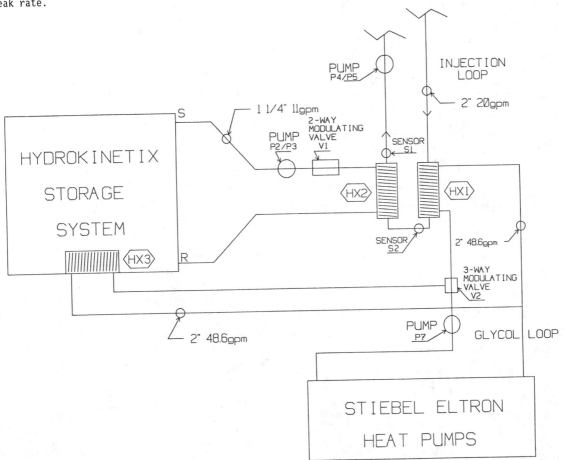

FIGURE 1. THE RELATIONSHIP OF STORAGE TANK, HEAT PUMPS, AND THE CLOSED LOOP HEAT PUMP LOOP

Another important feature of the system is that the loop piping brings the natural source and sink from outdoors to indoors enabling future connection of heat-adding devices as well as heat extracting devices to the same loop. The versatility and use of this loop as a heat source and heat sink is unlimited. The ever-present restraint of a limited dollar resource may be the only limitation. For example, if in a typical building using water source heat pumps, one-third of the heat pumps are in cooling mode, the building does not require supplementary heating. There are many buildings throughout the country which use the closed loop water source heat pump system for their HVAC system. Most of them use an electric boiler or a fossil-fuel boiler for supplementary heat. The question is, just how efficient are these systems and are the boilers the only economical way to supply the supplementary heating? To answer this question, Pennsylvania Power & Light Company has undertaken a research project in its service territory which is expected to be completed and in service by August 1992.

## PP&L RESEARCH OBJECTIVES

1. To monitor energy use of a resistance heater supplying the supplementary storage heat during the off-peak hours on the PP&L off-peak rate (resistance heater charging the storage tank).

2. To monitor energy use of air-to-water heat pumps supplying the supplementary storage heat during the off-peak hours on the PP&L off-peak rate with a C.O.P. of 3 (air-to-water heat pumps charging the storage tank).

3. To monitor energy use of air-to-water heat pumps supplying the supplementary heat on the PP&L time-of-day rate with a C.O.P. of 3 (air-to-water heat pumps supplying the heat directly to the loop and to the storage tank).

| Heat Pump Performance At Various Outside Temperatures (Information From The Manufacturer) | | | | |
|---|---|---|---|---|
| | 45°F | 36°F | 36°F* | 5°F* |
| Hot Water Supply | 95°F | 95°F | 131°F | 131°F |
| Output (Kw) | 28.6 | 25.2 | 22.5 | 11.8 |
| Compressor Input (Kw) | 9.5 | 9.2 | 10.7 | 7.9 |
| C.O.P. | 3.0 | 2.7 | 2.1 | 1.5 |
| *Dual Compressor | | | | |

## DESIGN CRITERIA

Type of Facility: Medical Office Building In Wilkes-Barre, Pennsylvania

Occupancy: 8:00 a.m. to 5:00 p.m., five days a week.

One floor at 12,000 square feet.

Additional floor to be added in future for a total of 24,000 square feet.

Design cooling load = 32 tons (12,000 square feet).

On-peak hours: 7:00 a.m. to 7:00 p.m.

Customer's instruction to design the off-peak electric storage system to accommodate the future expansion.

Heat loss = 124,000 Btuh.

Internal heat gain = 81,840 Btuh lighting.

Ventilation load = 214,000 Btuh.

Supplementary electric heat required = vent load - internal heat gain + heat loss = 256,160 Btuh.

Because a closed loop water source heat pump system is used, the credit must be taken for the heat of compression.

Since the heat pump C.O.P. is 3, reduce the supplementary heating requirement by one-third. The net supplementary heat = 170,770 Btuh.

Heat loss (winter unoccupied period) = 124,000 Btuh.

Net heat loss (unoccupied period) = 2/3 x 124,000 = 82,670 Btuh.

### CALCULATION OF HEATER SIZE

Supplementary heat required during the on-peak period = 82,670 x 3 hours + 170,770 x 9 hours = 1,784,970 Btu.

Heating required during the unoccupied 12 hours = 82,670 Btuh x 12 hours = 992,040 Btu.

Total heat required during the 24-hour period = 2,777,010 Btu.

$$\text{Heater size} = \frac{2,777,010 \text{ Btu}}{3,413 \text{ Btuh/kw} \times 12 \text{ hours} \times 0.9 \text{ (eff.)}}$$

$$= 75 \text{ kw.}$$

Incremental size increase to accommodate future expansion = 51 kw.

Total heater size = 126 kw.

### CALCULATION OF STORAGE CAPACITY

Loop water = 60°F to 90°F. Storage tank to store water at 130°F.

Temperature difference = 130°F - 60°F = 70°F (130°F needed to heat the loop water to 60°F).

$$\text{Storage volume} = \frac{1,784,970 \text{ Btu}}{8.33 \text{ lb./gal.} \times 1 \text{ Btu/lb.-°F} \times 70°F}$$

Volume = 3,061 gallons.

Use a 3,750 gallon tank for the first floor as well as to accommodate the future expansion.

### INSTALLATION COSTS

| Installation Costs For The 12,000 Square Foot Building (Excluding Future Expansion) Electric Off-Peak Storage System Versus Gas | | | |
|---|---|---|---|
| | Installed Cost | PP&L Grant | Net Cost |
| Gas Boiler | $8,000 | 0 | $8,000 |
| 3,000 Gallon Storage Tank with 126 Kw Heater at 480 Volt | $15,300 | $14,200 | $1,100 |
| PP&L grant is $100 per shifted kw for an electric heating type thermal storage system, $100 per shifted ton for cooling type thermal energy storage system, and $50 per ton for the water source heat pumps. | | | |

PROJECTED OPERATING COSTS

Loop temperature: 60°F to 90°F.

Heat loss as given before.

Gas fuel efficiency: 70%.

| Comparison Of The Gas Boiler With Off-Peak Electric Resistance Heater Charging The Tank | | | |
|---|---|---|---|
| System | Energy Usage | Rate | Annual Costs |
| Gas Boiler | 2,572 CCF | $0.61/CCF | $1,574 |
| Thermal Storage System | 52,771 Kwh | 4.4¢/Kwh | $2,305 |

| Comparison Of The Gas Boiler With Air-To-Water Heat Pump In Lieu Of The Resistance Heater Charging The Tanks During The Off-Peak Hours | |
|---|---|
| System | Annual Costs |
| Gas Boiler | $1,574 |
| Thermal Storage System | $870 (C.O.P. = 3) |

Chapter 58

# Improving Manufacturing Energy Efficiency: The Energy Analysis and Diagnostic Center at the University of Florida

B.L. Capehart, S. Ray, N. Altibi

## INTRODUCTION

The University of Florida Energy Analysis and Diagnostic Center (UFEADC) is part of an industrial service program funded by the U.S. Department of Energy and coordinated by the University Science Center in Philadelphia, PA. The main activity of the EADCs is to perform energy audits for small and medium size manufacturing facilities and to make recommendations that would increase their energy efficiency, reduce their energy costs, and help them become more profitable and competitive.

This paper describes the EADC program, discusses the operation of the UFEADC, and summarizes the results of the UFEADC program. The UFEADC has completed 40 industrial audits in just under two years, and has identified and analyzed more than fifty different Energy Conservation Opportunities (ECOs). An ECO is presented to the plant management as an efficiency measure which if implemented will provide an energy and dollar savings with an associated simple payback period typically under two years. In many cases these energy control programs will result in reduced air and water emissions as well as reduced energy consumption.

## THE EADC PROGRAM

The EADC program has been in operation for almost fifteen years, and has helped hundreds of small and medium sized manufacturing companies reduce their energy consumption and reduce their energy costs. EADCs are located on university campuses in eighteen states: Arizona, California, Colorado, Florida, Georgia, Indiana, Iowa, Kansas, Massachusetts, Missouri, New Jersey, New York, Ohio, Oklahoma, Oregon, Tennessee, Texas, and Wisconsin. The U.S. Department of Energy, Office of Industrial Technologies, funds the EADC program and contracts with the University City Science Center in Philadelphia, PA to manage the twenty centers, provide them technical support, and collect and analyze the data on industrial efficiency potentials that the EADC's develop.

The EADC program is one of the most cost-effective programs that the U.S. Department of Energy funds, and the program is being expanded by adding three new centers each year for the next few years. Each EADC has a faculty director and assistant director, and typically uses graduate and undergraduate student assistants to help perform the detailed industrial audits. The faculty director or assistant director go on every audit, and are usually accompanied by two or three student assistants. The audit team visits the industrial facility, performs an on-site audit, and returns to the university campus to complete the detailed energy audit report for the company.

The EADC program serves only manufacturing companies, and offers free energy audits to companies that have SIC codes in the 20xx - 39xx range (manufacturing), have fewer than 500 employees, have energy bills less than $1.75 million per year, and have gross sales of less than $75 million per year. The EADC audit is performed at no cost to the client company, and the audit report is held in confidence. Over 3100 manufacturing plants have been audited since the start of the program. The average energy cost savings found in an EADC audit is $44,000 per year, and can be obtained with equipment and operational changes that pay back in two years or less. Based on follow-up interviews with companies, over 50% of the energy cost savings recommended in the EADC audit reports has been achieved through implementation of the equipment changes or operational changes.

The EADC program accomplishes several goals toward improving the energy efficiency and manufacturing competitiveness of the United States. There is a direct benefit in helping individual companies improve the energy efficiency of their operation and reducing their energy costs. There is also an indirect benefit in providing a large pool of trained university graduates - mostly in engineering - in the complex area of industrial energy efficiency. Engineering graduates from EADC programs are often sought out by electric and gas utilities to staff their energy audit and energy conservation programs, by engineering consulting firms and government agencies working in the energy area, and by companies interested in improving their energy efficiency and reducing their energy costs.

The University of Florida EADC was established in November, 1990. It performed 15 audits in its first year of operation, and is now performing 30 audits per year. The director of the UFEADC is a professor in the Department of Industrial & Systems Engineering, and the assistant director is a professor in the Department of Chemical Engineering. The UFEADC employs two half-time graduate assistants, and around ten part-time undergraduate student assistants from several different engineering departments.

## THE ENERGY AUDIT

The energy audit is one of the first tasks to perform when initiating an effective energy cost control program. The UFEADC program provides cost-free audits for Florida industries to help them identify energy cost reduction opportunities. The UFEADC performs energy audits for manufacturing facilities within 150 miles of the university. Primary client companies are the industrial energy users whose energy bills are $100,000/year to $1,750,000/year, with gross sales of less than $75 million/year. As a first step in preparing for the audit, we request copies of the company's utility bills to evaluate energy usage patterns at the facility. A plant layout diagram and a list of equipment are also essential to understanding the types of processes which are major energy users at the facility and the types of equipment which may be tested for operating efficiency. An energy analysis consists of a detailed examination of how a facility uses energy, what the facility pays for that energy, and finally, a recommended program for changes in operating practices of energy consuming equipment that will be cost effective and save dollars on energy bills. The audit is usually one day in duration and focuses on how energy is being lost in the plant or the process. The energy audit primarily involves a physical inspection of the energy distribution system and energy using devices for identification of improved energy management opportunities.

## THE AUDIT REPORT

The audit report consists of an audit summary, energy consumption and cost bar charts, a general description of the facility including the manufacturing processes, and analysis of all energy conservation opportunities (ECOs). This report is based on the observations and technical data collected during the on-site energy audit. Each individual ECO is presented separately. The discussion includes the method of implementation, detailed calculations of energy and dollar savings, associated implementation costs, and calculation of the simple payback period.

The energy audit report presents a complete package of information on improving energy efficiency in the facility. Each ECO is independent of the other ECOs. A typical report takes about 100 person-hours, or approximately 6 to 8 weeks to finish. A preliminary report is sent to the facility within one week of the audit to give an idea of the energy savings possibilities that exist. This is a quick overview of the audit results and gives more obvious energy savings potentials which can be implemented immediately. Sometimes a preliminary report focuses on a particular machine or process which is out of control or not efficient at all; this allows the management to take some immediate action without waiting for the final audit report to arrive.

The first step in preparing the report is to calculate the average energy cost of the facility from its energy bills. These figures can reveal trends and irregularities in energy use and costs. They also allow the relative merits of energy conservation and load management opportunities to be assessed. We contact the utility company to find their rate structure, to determine if any incentive programs for energy efficiency improvements are available, to examine the availability of an interruptible rate for the customers, and to see if there is a rebate for the manufacturing company owning its own transformers. From this information, we recommend the best way to save money utilizing different programs offered by their utility company. Many of the facilities we audit are not aware of these utility incentives and have often made equipment changes that would have been eligible for a utility incentive.

The audit report recommends that each facility set up an energy accounting system. Figure 1 shows the table for calculation of the cost of electricity. Figure 2 shows the KWh consumption and figure 3 shows a line graph to keep track of energy consumption. This will help the company understand the utility rate structure, and how to use it effectively. It will also help keep track of energy consumption anomalies that indicate a potential energy use that should be examined in greater depth. The energy accounting system should also be designed to keep track of energy use per dollar of product sold. If anomalies are the result of increased production, this will show up in the accounting system. If the energy consumption is increasing faster than the product sales, the company may need to look for additional energy conservation opportunities. Keeping records in graphical form provides an easy visual reference and helps to highlight trends and potential problems.

The next step in constructing the audit report is to describe the facility and its major energy consuming equipment. We focus on the large energy consuming processes or equipment, and propose alternative technologies to perform the work in a more energy efficient way. This involves in-depth analyses of recent technological developments, determination of costs to implement the new technologies, evaluation of the energy cost savings expected, and finally, a calculation

| SUMMARY OF ELECTRIC ENERGY USAGE AND COSTS | | | | | |
|---|---|---|---|---|---|
| Month | Energy Consumed (KWh) | Energy Cost ($) | Total Demand (KW) | Demand Cost ($) | Total Cost Including Taxes ($) |
| December | 279,360 | 17,020.25 | 812 | 4,587.80 | 21,608.05 |
| January | 307,200 | 17,667.39 | 812 | 4,587.80 | 22,255.19 |
| February | 288,960 | 16,549.76 | 812 | 4,587.80 | 21,137.56 |
| March | 287,040 | 17,138.59 | 812 | 4,587.80 | 21,726.39 |
| April | 359,520 | 22,037.65 | 820 | 4,633.00 | 26,670.65 |
| May | 359,520 | 22,674.05 | 838 | 4,734.70 | 27,408.75 |
| June | 371,040 | 23,727.09 | 838 | 4,734.70 | 28,461.79 |
| July | 358,080 | 22,248.58 | 838 | 4,734.70 | 26,983.28 |
| August | 348,480 | 20,034.23 | 838 | 4,734.70 | 24,768.93 |
| September | 368,640 | 21,233.93 | 838 | 4,734.70 | 25,968.63 |
| October | 328,800 | 18,960.54 | 838 | 4,734.70 | 23,695.24 |
| November | 310,560 | 17,793.90 | 838 | 4,734.70 | 22,528.60 |
| Totals | 3,967,200 | 237,085.96 | 9,934 | 56,127.10 | 293,213.06 |
| Averages | 330,600 | 19,757.16 | 828 | 4,677.26 | 24,434.42 |

| | |
|---|---|
| Average Cost per KWh | = $0.074/KWh |
| Average Cost per KW per month | = $5.649/KW/month |
| Average Cost of Off-Peak Use | = $0.060/KWh |

FIGURE 1

ELECTRICAL CONSUMPTION (KWh)
December 1990 - November 1991

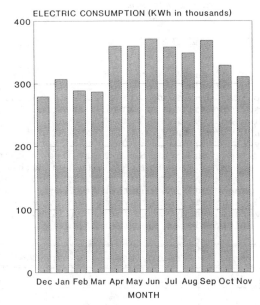

FIGURE 2

ELECTRICAL CONSUMPTION (KWh)
December 1990 - November 1991

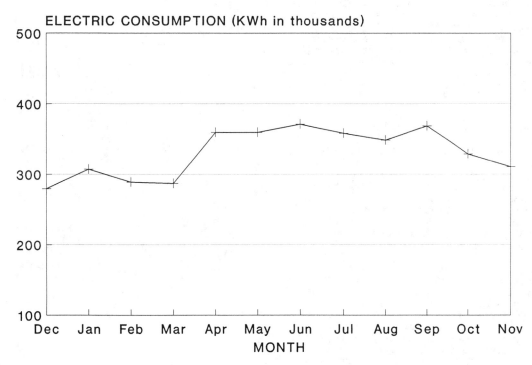

FIGURE 3

of the payback period. Typical technologies that we examine are high efficiency lighting, boiler and gas or oil heater operation, high efficiency motors, peak load reduction through equipment scheduling, high efficiency HVAC equipment, waste heat recovery devices, alternative industrial processes, and energy management control systems.

Energy Conservation Opportunities:

The amount of energy used in a facility varies depending on the type of business and the geographical location, along with many other factors. The amount of money that a facility pays for energy depends on how much energy they use, when they use it, and the local utility rate structure. Often the items that use the most energy are not the items that cost the most. For example, although heating is the biggest energy use, you may find that more is spent on lighting than heating. As an example, a comparison of average annual energy usage versus energy costs for a small business in the United States is shown below.

| Items | Energy Use | Energy Cost |
|---------|------------|-------------|
| Heating | 54% | 22% |
| Cooling | 4% | 9% |
| Lights | 22% | 37% |
| Fan | 12% | 21% |
| Other | 8% | 11% |

Regardless of the energy used in a facility and the cost associated with it, reducing overall energy costs means greater profit for the business. Once it is decided to implement energy savings programs, employees should know about the plans and goals. Getting them involved will not only help in achieving energy goals, but it will also generate bright new ideas for energy savings as well.

**RESULTS**

The UFEADC has performed 40 audits in just under two years. The remainder of this paper discusses some of the data and results from those audits. As additional audits are performed, our data files will be expanded and updated to incorporate the new information. This data base on industrial audits should provide useful information to a number of utilities and government organizations interested in the energy efficiency of small to medium sized manufacturing companies.

We have calculated and recorded the average cost of electricity that utility companies charge to the facilities in our region of the country. Depending on the rate structure, usage pattern, and the location, cost of electricity varies considerably. Graph 1 shows the cost per KWh for eleven different utility companies around Gainesville, Florida. In Graphs 1 & 2, utility # H, has a very high KWh cost, but does not have a separate demand charge. Their rate structure is such that the

demand charge is included in the KWh cost. The average cost per KWh for these manufacturing companies in our area is around $0.08. Some facilities pay substantially less than this cost which most likely indicates that they are on an interruptible rate structure. Similarly Graph 2 shows the cost per KW for different utility companies.

Graph 3 shows the energy usage per year of the different facilities we have audited. Facilities designated R4 and R13 have a very high energy consumption. This indicates that those facilities are energy intense manufacturing operations and run 24 hours per day compared to other facilities. Graph 5 shows the potential percentage reduction of the total energy use after the energy audit performed by the UFEADC. The largest reduction is about 39% of the present usage. Graph 6 shows the energy cost reduction potential after the audit. It is interesting to observe that the percentage reduction in cost is not necessarily accompanied by the same percentage reduction in energy use. For example, shifting peak load to off peak time will reduce the demand and hence reduce the demand cost, but total energy use will be same as before.

Graph 8 shows that the average cost of energy is about 1.5% of the total sales. That means 1.5% of the total cost goes toward the energy to produce that item. Chemical process based manufacturing facilities generally spend 9-11% of the total cost toward energy.

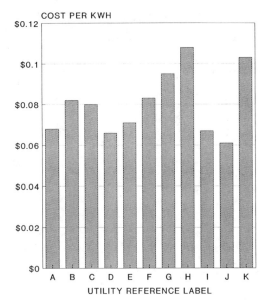

## UTILITY COST OF ELECTRICITY
## COST PER KWH

GRAPH 1

## UTILITY COST OF ELECTRICITY
## DEMAND COST

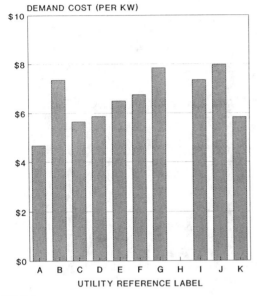

GRAPH 2

## TOTAL ENERGY USAGE/YEAR
## BEFORE AND AFTER THE AUDIT
## MMBTU/YR

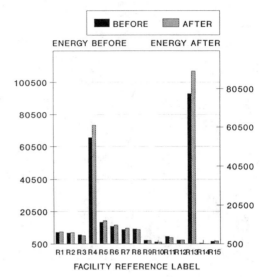

GRAPH 4

## AVERAGE ELECTRICITY USAGE
## KWh & KW USAGE PER MONTH

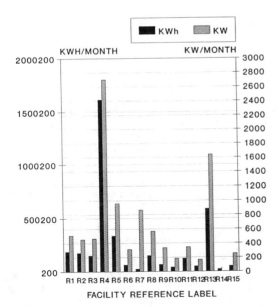

GRAPH 3

## ENERGY USE REDUCTION
## % REDUCTION AFTER AUDIT

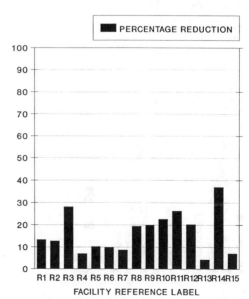

GRAPH 5

343

## TOTAL ENERGY COST PER YEAR
## BEFORE AND AFTER THE AUDIT

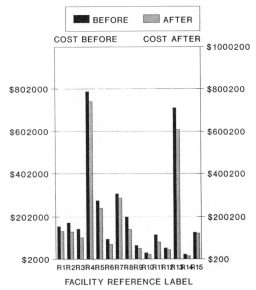

GRAPH 6

## ENERGY USAGE
## % OF THE ANNUAL SALES

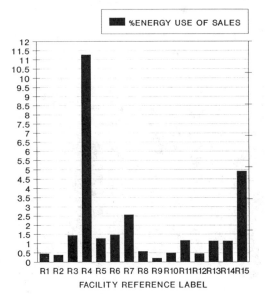

GRAPH 8

## ENERGY COST REDUCTION
## % REDUCTION AFTER AUDIT

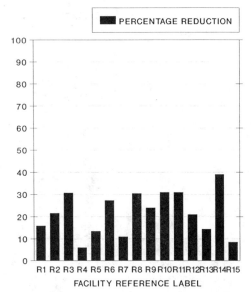

GRAPH 7

### CONCLUSIONS

Energy audits are an important first step in the overall process of reducing energy costs for any industry. A thorough audit identifies and analyzes the changes in equipment and operations that will result in cost-effective energy cost reduction. The energy auditor plays a key role in the successful conduct of an audit, and also in the implementation of the audit recommendations.

The EADC program provides a valuable service to the small and medium sized manufacturing companies in the United States. Reducing energy costs is a key ingredient in an overall plan to improve the competitiveness of our industries. The EADC centers offer highly skilled help to manufacturing companies who might not otherwise seek out help from their utilities or from consultants to find cost-effective ways to control their energy costs.

# REFERENCES

1.  U.S.Department of Energy, "Energy Conservation Trends" September 1989.

2.  U.S.Department of Energy, "Tips for Saving Energy in Small Business"

3.  National Energy Strategy, First Edition 1991/1992, Washington, DC, 1991.

4.  Albert Thumann, P.E, "Handbook of Energy Audits", Second Edition, 1983.

5.  Energy Analysis and Diagnostic Center, University of Florida, "Energy Audits Reports" 1991/1992.

# Chapter 59
# Process Energy Reduction
W.E. Lowthian

## ABSTRACT

Process Energy Reduction (PER) is a demand-side energy reduction approach which complements and often supplants other traditional energy reduction methods such as conservation and heat recovery. Because the application of PER is less obvious than the traditional methods, it takes some time to learn the steps as well as practise to become proficient in its use. However, the benefit is significant, often far outweighing the traditional energy reduction approaches. Furthermore, the method usually results in a better process having less waste and pollution along with improved yields, increased capacity, and lower operating costs.

## INTRODUCTION

This paper presents an effective method for reducing energy use, called Process Energy Reduction (PER). It is effective even where traditional supply side conservation measures and heat recovery have been fully implemented. However, the most effective time to apply PER is prior to any other energy reduction measures.

The paper discusses the method, how it differs from other energy reduction approaches, and how it was applied in three cases. Since space is limited, details of the method are not presented. Additional information can be obtained from the references or the author.

## PER

Process energy reduction (PER) is a relatively new approach to reducing energy cost. It is a *demand-side* approach that focuses on the process loads at the end of the energy conduit, whereas traditional cost reduction methods focus on the supply-side. PER applies specific analysis and innovation techniques which result in a modified or new process for producing a product or service which uses less energy or lower cost energy. This method questions current or --- in the case of a new design --- proposed operating conditions, practices and procedures.

Another way to understand PER is to realize that you haven't done Process Energy Reduction unless you have *modified the process*.

The potential from PER can be an energy cost reduction of as much as 80 percent. Collateral benefits include reduced pollution, less waste and better quality --- consequences with positive economic benefits that often surpass energy savings.

### How process energy reduction is different.

Traditional commercial and industrial energy audits often start at the "wrong" end of the energy conduit. Audits that start at the boiler house or in the equipment room are useful, but may miss the greatest opportunities --- in the end-use areas. We must recognize that simply

tuning boilers and refrigeration units creates a false sense of satisfaction about reducing energy costs. You unusually can achieve much larger savings at the demand end where the steam, chilled water, and other energy are used.

The four traditional approaches to reducing the cost of energy include:
1) *Reduce the unit cost (price) of purchased energy.* For example, buy well-head gas or sign-up for alternate electric rates involving peak-shaving and the like.
2) *Improve energy conversion efficiencies.* For example, improve the efficiency of converting fuel to steam or hot water, electricity to chilled water, compressed air or lighted lamps.
3) *Conserve.* This can be done passively (eg. via insulation to reduce heat loss) or actively (eg. via installing automatic switches to shut off unneeded use.)
4) *Recover or recycle* from discharge streams. For example, use exhaust heat, pressure recovery or vapor recompression.

These four approaches - energy purchase, conservation, delivery, and recovery for secondary use - involve the supply side, that is, systems supplying energy to a point of use. These are *supply-side* strategies.

PER, by contrast, focuses on *demand* by the energy user --- the user being a process, system, or piece of equipment which uses the energy. It aims to reduce the demand and to change the demand to a less expensive energy form. Because PER reduces demand and introduces alternative technologies, it also can significantly affect the supply-side energy, sometimes eliminating the need to take any traditional supply-side action to reduce cost.

In summary, first you try to improve the process efficiency (ie. reduce demand.) Then, you investigate other energy cost reduction steps. (ie. work on the supply side.)

### PER demand

For an electric utility, demand is the instantaneous amount of power required at any moment; it is the amount of power the utility must supply. Because utilities have built little supply capacity in the last decade, they are using demand management and reduction as major elements of their strategy to provide reliable supply to customers. While the utility looks at shifting or reducing electrical loads, PER requires you to look at demand in a more basic sense. For example, a PER investigation of electrical energy, requires you to advance down the power supply conduit to the motor, then to the motor shaft, on to the pump impeller, pausing to check the volume and pressure of the liquid being moved, and finally to the process itself. During this whole exercise, you should ask yourself questions such as: "Why is the flow rate what it is?" "Why is the pressure as high as it is?" "What is the energy achieving?" "What is the function of the energy being used?"

In the case of thermal energy, say steam, the PER analysis follows the steam line to the heat exchanger, then to the fluid being heated, then to the particular unit operation (eg. distillation) or reaction. The questions include "Why were these particular process conditions selected?" "Are the observed conditions the design conditions?" "What is the function of the heat?" "Of the unit operation (eg. separation of chemical components in the case of distillation.)" "Is there another way (eg. crystallization) to achieve to the chemical separation?" "Why is the separation required?" "What purity is required?" (Higher purity takes more energy, but may not be necessary.)

Establishing the purpose or function of the energy, that is, *Why* the energy is being used, is critical for the PER. Only after you have defined the purpose, function or task of each part of the system can you suggest fundamentally different alternatives. Once alternatives are developed and selected the more traditional approaches can be pursued. You can then examine the energy supply for improvements in price, conversion efficiency and conservation. Finally, after you have chosen a new or modified process, you can investigate energy recovery --- if you still need it.

### Process Vs. System

The PER methodology sometimes appears to be contrary to the more established approaches For example, PER considers heat recovery as a "failure" to fully develop a process. The ideal process would use all the heat, not exhaust some which is then recovered for secondary use. PER also may seem to concentrate on points that, initially, appear inconsequential. This is the case when you draw a distinction between *process* and *system*. However, distinguishing between the two is helpful --- if not crucial --- to understanding and applying PER effectively.

PER concentrates on process, the ultimate demand, while other energy strategies tend to work on the system (ie. equipment, piping, etc.) While work on the system is necessary to develop a comprehensive solution to a problem, the first area to attack is the process. PER goes *inside* the system to work on the process being carried out by and inside the system.

What is meant by process? For PER, it is any operation or function in a facility that uses energy. The process is carried out by and usually contained by a system. For example, bread baking (process) is carried out be any oven (system) using energy (heat). Alcohol is distilled (process) by an evaporator (system) using energy (heat). Cooling (process) a room is achieved by an air conditioner (system) using energy (electricity). Illuminating (process) a shopping mall is carried out by electric lighting (system) using energy (electricity).

In each case the system is the collection of equipment that performs the process. The process produces the end product or result: bread, alcohol, comfort, and illumination. Because of the physical reality of the system, it is easy to think only in terms of a system revision. A system change can save energy and often will change the process somewhat. But, PER requires a deeper examination of the process pressing further to examine the purpose or function of the process, why it operates as it does and how the ultimate goal might be accomplished better through a change that modifies the process.

In each case, when you focus on the process, or more particularly the *function* of the process, you usually can imagine additional ways (often radically different ways) to reduce the energy required to meet the system's purpose. PER looks for a better method (process) to achieve the same end. That better method results in a better, more efficient system.

The example presented in this paper, "A Case of Changing the Process," provides an illustration of process and system changes."

### Setting up a PER program

A Process Energy Reduction program has four major phases:
1) Program Development (PD)
2) Process Energy Analysis (PEA)
3) Process Energy Innovation (PEI)
4) Program Implementation. (PI)

*Phase 1 - Program Development* has two goals: 1) to establish if sufficient potential value exists to set up a PER program; and 2) to set up the structure for the program, including crucial backing by management.

*Phase 2 - Process Energy Analysis* documents and analyzes quantitatively how an operation uses energy. It is an in-depth energy audit that looks not only at *how much* energy is used, but at *how* and *why* the energy is used and how it achieves the desired results.

*Phase 3 - Process Energy Innovation* develops better ways to achieve a process modification --- that is, to achieve the effect or end purpose of the process while using less energy or lower cost energy. PEI may produce one of two results: a process improvement --- a modest improvement which slightly alters the process --- or a process change, one involving completely different technology.

*Phase 4 - Program Implementation* implements the ideas developed in Step 3, PEI. If the ideas are straightforward engineering projects, then program implementation is similar to any other design project implementation. If the ideas must go through further development, PI can be more like a R&D project. Often, many potential projects of varying size and complexity are generated, requiring an involved program, stretching over several years.

### EXAMPLE 1
### A CASE OF CHANGING THE PROCESS

An example involving salt crystallization will help clarify how a Process Energy Reduction program deals with the difference between "system" and "process." The example involves removal of a salt form an agueous chemical solution, but could apply to sugar production or similar operations.

An existing batch process, designed in the 1950's, performed the following steps:
o Drain the hot salt solution from the main process to a tank
o Pull a vacuum on the tank to boil off water and cool the solution (a natural consequence of vacuum toiling)
o Allow the chemical salt crystals to form in the concentrated, cooler "mother liquor"
o Pump the tank contents through a filter to remove the salt crystals and return the low-salt solution to the main production process.

This operation was a high energy user because steam jets were used to create the vacuum by consuming 25,000 lb/hr of 150 lb steam for each of the seven batch tanks. Steam cost was about $300,000/yr even though steam was unusually cheap ($2.16/1,000 lb).

Initially, system improvements to save energy costs were discussed. More efficient steam - vacuum jets, better sizing and sequencing of jets, cooler condensing water, use of vacuum pumps instead of jets, etc. were discussed. Little benefit would have been derived, certainly not enough to justify and capital expenditure.

A PER program was initiated to look deeper. In Phase 1, Program Development (PD), an expanded problem definition was developed so that the Potential Value of improvement could be judged. Other problems (ie. potential value if a solution were found) included: high crystal contamination, marginal capacity, high operating labor and high maintenance. The potential value was high, so the PER program was continued.

The second Phase, Process Energy Analysis (PEA) established all the particulars of the existing process, including:
   o  Energy use and cost
   o  Product salt quality and market price
   o  Actual, design and required capacity
   o  Cost and pollution impact as a result of insufficient capacity
   o  Effect of batch sequencing on capacity and quality
   o  Crystal growth rate, size, quality
   o  Filtration parameters
   o  Required operator attention and cost
   o  Historical maintenance attention and cost

It was obvious that the system was being pushed past the original design parameters; what had once been a profitable side operation was losing money as a result of low quality and high operating costs. The only justification for operation was avoidance of still higher costs for disposal of the salt cake.

PEA also established the fundamental requirements of an upgraded process and cataloged available plant site resources. A key resource was excess low-cost steam-driven brine chiller capacity. These steam-turbine-driven units operated on 400 psig steam exhausting 150 psig or 25 psig steam, which the plant could use elsewhere, replacing steam that was produced by pressure let-down.

With PEA finished, the third Phase, Process Energy Innovation (PEI) was initiated. The ultimate purpose of the steam was established: it turned out that cooling was very important while the concentration effect from evaporating had very little effect on crystallization. Knowing that, allowed the investigators to turn to other methods (processes) for cooling. Also, other separation methods (processes) were discussed and evaluated. PEI developed many improvement ideas, some speculative, some straightforward. The final process choice included two major changes:

1)  Converting the process from batch to continuous operation
2)  Using the idled power house refrigerated brine system for cooling, eliminating the steam vacuum system.

These two process changes required the system (ie. equipment) to be modified. However, as is often true, the basic equipment was retained (avoiding large capital costs) and changes were in additional or different ancillary equipment and in design details.

The energy cost savings was the original steam cost of $300,000/yr. Also eliminated was the large condenser cooling water load. In addition, as a result of steady-state continuous operation, crystal contamination was no longer a problem, capacity was doubled, operation was

far more automated and maintenance costs were expected to drop. Since the modified process employed co-generation (chilled water production with process steam used elsewhere), the plant also reduced coal consumption and $CO_2$ emissions.

In summary, by changing the process significant energy savings and other benefits were obtained. Without a process change few if any of the benefits could have been achieved.

Was it easy to change the process? Yes and no. The original equipment manufacture at first was negative, but then endorsed the idea and did the redesign work. There were some operational and crystal quality problems initially, as there often is with any new installation, but these were worked out. Other parts of the change, the heat transfer equipment, etc. were straight forward. The project produced was an attractive payout.

## EXAMPLE 2
## INDUSTRIAL VENTILATION AS A PROCESS

"Process" covers a much larger range than merely reactions or operations in chemical plants and the like. Industrial ventilation, for example, is a process for producing a comfortable and clean work environment. The following example illustrates the wide application of PER.

A production area for making plated steel wire was excessively hot and humid in the summer because several hundred wire drawing machines operated simultaneously in the area. Each machine had a 25-40 hp motor and an open warm water bath for cooling the drawn wire and dies. Temperature could reach 120°F in some locations during the summer. Productivity would fall off and absenteeism rise. Both indicated worker distress and the potential for serious health consequences. The owner wanted a solution.

The plant engineer looked at supplying the room with cool air. To cool this area, conventional air conditioning would have required 600 tons of refrigeration and an electrical demand of 475 kW. The cost of system, site power expansion, and operating and demand charges were felt to be prohibitive by the owner.

Because of this, the owner agreed to begin a PER program approach to determine if some approach could be developed which provided the required comfort while meeting tight financial criteria. PER was started with the conviction that an as yet unidentified solution could be found.

After performing the initial Program Development, Process Energy Analysis established the conditions in key locations in the building, sources of heat and humidity, air flow, daily temperature patterns, and other factors that affected the existing conditions.

After analysis, it became clear that the main problem was neither with the heat and humidity per se' nor with insufficient air ventilation. Instead, the problem was with allowing the machine exhaust to mix with make-up ventilation air in the room before it was exhausted. This caused room temperatures to rise 10-20°F higher than outdoor temperatures.

Process Energy Analysis prepared the way for Process Energy Innovation, the phase in which alternatives are developed. The main problem was to prevent the hot, humid air from the wire drawing machines from mixing with the total room air. Also, since ventilation air was taken from above the roof, air was heated by the solar load several degrees on still, sunny days. Finally, delivering moving air to worker locations was determined

349

to be an important method to increase the effective comfort produced by the ventilation.

Many ideas were developed along these and other lines. Key ideas which were part of the final project included:
1) Reducing roof temperature via a white coating
2) Using a system of curtains and supply and exhaust points to control air flow. The air flow was configured so that it entered the room, passed over the workers, passed on to the machines where it picked up moisture and heat, and then exhausted up through ceiling openings without mixing with the general room air. In this way, ventilation alone would be able to nearly match the conditions anticipated for the original air conditioning.
3) Using spot cooling at selected workplace locations.

The capital cost for the PER program project was about half that of the conventional air conditioning based system. The project also reduced electrical demand to 75 kW, thereby avoiding new site power, and decreased operating costs to about 40 percent of the original approach. In addition, there were collateral benefits. By controlling the pattern of air flow, workers no longer were exposed to operations contaminants. The solution also improved motor life by removing the motors from operating in hot, humid, contaminated air.

In this example, the key to developing improvement ideas was to understand the "process" of room cooling (ventilation) and heating (machine exhaust.) Once understood, the process could be changed so that much less cooling was required. In the simplest form, the original approach allowed cooling air and exhaust to mix, whereas the new approach kept them separate --- and placed people in the cool air for most tasks.

### EXAMPLE 3
### PAINT DRYING

The industrial facility in this example had conducted a site-wide energy audit. The audit team identified several energy conservation project opportunities in the boiler/utility area and utility distribution systems. An analysis of the steam system indicated the paint department was a major user of steam. The paint process was conventional; production parts were painted in a batch spray room, followed by a drying operation. Sufficient potential value was identified in the painting department to embark on a PER program.

The facility completed Phase 1, Program Development, in which they identified a target process in the paint department: paint drying. The next PER effort obtained management support, selected a PER team and wrote a PER program plan. The PER team then took charge of the next three phases of the program: Phase 2, the Process Energy Analysis; Phase 3, Process Energy Innovation; and Phase 4, Program Implementation.

In the Process Energy Analysis phase, the PER team developed an one-line energy balance confirmed that the paint drying operation used half of the site-generated steam. The annual cost of the paint drying step was about $355,000 for steam and $119,000 for electricity.

Additional facts gathered in this phase showed paint drying was a production bottleneck. Also, it often resulted in poor product quality due to surface imperfections.

The third phase, Process Energy Innovation, challenged the existing process with the facility's initial goal: reducing energy cost. The PER team focused on steam and tried to produce a list of possible improvements. But ideas did not really start appearing until the goal was defined differently. Instead of *improving paint drying*, the team determined that the *function* of the operation was to *produce a product with a nice surface*. Redefining the goal encourages the generation of many more ideas as well as more fundamental ideas for improvements. Some of the ideas generated included:
- Improve steam heating efficiency.
- Use less-or a different-solvent.
- Raise drying room temperature.
- Add a chemical to speed drying.
- Substitute plastic coating for paint.
- Switch to a nonheat cure coating.
- Heat parts surface, not room and air.
- Convert to a plastic part.

However, this list did not address other, nonenergy goals. As discussion proceeded, it became clear that capacity and quality were the big department concerns, while energy cost was relatively minor. The PER team then worked with these department concerns and arrived at a list of possible process changes and alternatives.

In the Program Implementation phase, the team selected three process modifications 1) use a polymer dispersion water-based paint, 2) add a chemical to speed curing and 3) heat parts with infrared heaters instead of steam. They also added other improvements to the program.

The results of PER in paint drying at the facility were dramatic. By adopting the process modifications, the firm reduced paint-drying energy cost by more than 50 percent. Furthermore, the facility converted the multi-step batch spray/dry room process to an integrated continuous process. Together, these changes resulted in increased production, productivity and product quality.

### ACKNOWLEDGEMENT

The author wishes to thank Walter P. Smith for his contributions to the development of the Process Energy Reduction approaches and methodology.

### REFERENCES

1) Lowthian, Walter E., "Process Energy Cost Reduction," Strategies for Reducing Natural Gas, Electric, and Oil Costs; Proceedings of the Twelfth World Energy Engineering Conference, October 24-27, 1989.
2) Lowthian, Walter E., and Smith, Walter P., "Process Energy Reduction,", Engineer's Digest, July, September, and December 1991.

Chapter 60

# Wastewater Treatment Technologies to Satisfy 1990's Energy Conservation/ Pollution Prevention Goals

L.W. Keith, A.R. Beers

## BACKGROUND

Anheuser-Busch, like most other companies, relied through the mid-1970's on end-of-pipe, energy-intensive aerobic treatment systems for its wastewater. Little if any attention was placed on source reduction. There are several factors that help explain why industry had adopted this approach. Energy was relatively cheap, sludge disposal was not a major problem and many municipalities provided wastewater treatment capacity to industry as an inducement for industry to locate there. The saying for A-B was "We know how to make beer — municipalities know how to treat our wastewater — let's not mix the two."

The 1973 oil embargo and the resulting mid-1970's energy crisis changed Anheuser-Busch's wastewater treatment philosophy. The days of cheap energy and wastewater treatment were gone. This was only exaggerated by the more stringent treatment requirements resulting from the passage of PL92-500 (Clean Water Act). Increasing sludge disposal problems with associated increased disposal costs also occurred.

From the mid-1970's to the mid-1980's Anheuser-Busch performed significant developmental work on land application of wastewater. This technology, which requires only about 10% of the energy of aerobic activated sludge treatment systems and produces no sludge for disposal, was installed at six Anheuser-Busch locations. During this time period considerable improvement was made in the area of waste load reduction. However, the main driving force was economics; that is, it was done if cheaper than wastewater treatment. Anheuser-Busch still had a basic end-of-pipe treatment philosophy.

It was realized that land application could not be utilized everywhere, and aerobic treatment costs and sludge disposal costs were continuing to rise. For these reasons, in the early 1980's A-B began developmental work on anaerobic treatment, a technology not widely used at that time for treatment of food industry wastewater. This biological process, which operates in the absence of oxygen, requires only about 20% of the energy and produces 60% less sludge than conventional activated sludge systems. This process is actually a net producer of energy since the methane that is produced in this process is recovered and used as a fuel.

Anheuser-Busch installed its first full-scale anaerobic treatment system in 1985. Additional anaerobic systems were started up in 1991 at A-B's Jacksonville, Florida, and Baldwinsville, New York, breweries, with a third brewery anaerobic treatment system scheduled for start-up in 1993 when production begins at the Cartersville, Georgia, brewery.

A significant change is taking place today that will guide industry from the 1990's into the twenty-first century. In the past, pollution prevention and waste minimization were merely buzzwords. Today, and increasingly in the future, they will become ingrained philosophies for all successful industries. Life cycle analysis and demonstrating sustainable development (meeting the needs of the present without compromising the ability of future generations to meet their own needs) will likely be as important to the Board of Directors and stakeholders as a project's Return On Investment.

There will continue to be increased emphasis on pollution prevention and waste minimization. However, most industry, including A-B, will for the foreseeable future continue to require some degree of end-of-pipe treatment for its wastewater. Anheuser-Busch, through planning, has a portfolio of wastewater treatment alternatives that fit well into satisfying the 1990's pollution prevention and waste minimization requirements.

## TECHNOLOGY REVIEW

### Residuals Handling

Systems that fit into this category are installed for source reduction, but for the purposes of this presentation are included in the overall costs associated with the processing of wastewater. There are several high-strength streams that are segregated at the brewery and therefore can be processed separately from the remaining end-of-pipe wastewater flow. The streams are classified as either alcoholic or non-alcoholic, the former being treated in a distillation system, the latter in an evaporator. The still is used for production of 190 proof ethanol, and the evaporator is used for production of syrup as a supplement to animal feed.

While these systems, being essentially heat treatments, are large steam and electricity users, their economic justification is tied to a marketable product and the fact that concentrated carbohydrate streams are usually handled more efficiently this way than in conventional aerobic biological treatment systems. However, evaporator condensate and still bottoms are sidestreams that require further treatment.

## Aerobic Treatment

As previously noted, aerobic treatment has been the standard for removal of organic matter in both municipal and industrial wastewater for decades. The so-called activated sludge process delivers a clean effluent suitable for direct discharge to a receiving stream. However, it does so for a price. The process generates large volumes of sludge for disposal and can consume large amounts of chemical nutrients, but attention here will be to system energetics.

The majority of energy required in aerobic treatment results from maintaining a dissolved oxygen residual in the treatment basin to support the essential organisms and for supplying enough oxygen to complete the conversion of the organic substrate to carbon dioxide. A secondary energy requirement is agitation of the basin so that wastewater and biomass maintain intimate contact. Modern designs attempt to satisfy both process needs using the same equipment, but the power requirements to support aerobic treatment of wastewater from a large brewery can easily be 3000 – 6000 hP. There are numerous aerobic system configurations but the oxygen and mixing demands are satisfied by large blowers, mixers or a combination thereof.

## Anaerobic Treatment

Taking advantage of bacteria that thrive in the absence of oxygen, anaerobic technology has a major energy advantage over aerobic treatment. The key to this process is the alternate metabolic pathway utilized by these organisms. Instead of converting all organic

carbon to carbon dioxide, the majority is converted to methane. This characteristic in turn leads to the secondary energy advantage of the anaerobic process — production of usable fuel. Finally, because of the ability for the anaerobic organisms to sustain high waste volumetric loadings compared to their aerobic counterparts, vigorous mixing is accomplished naturally by the methane production.

The result is a dramatic reduction in energy requirements. However, there are two major shortcomings in widespread application of this technology. First, the effluent is not suitable for direct discharge to a receiving stream, because the metabolic pathway leaves refractory organic matter. Therefore, an additional aerobic "polishing" step is needed. Second, there is a temperature minimum (about 85°F) for viability of the anaerobic organisms. As a result, cool, dilute wastewaters are not treated cost-effectively by this process. However, the utilization of anaerobic treatment on warm, concentrated wastewater can create substantial energy savings, as will be demonstrated in the Case Study.

## Land Application

Land application, or spray irrigation of wastewater as a treatment means is nearly self-explanatory. The liquid is stored in tanks and surface-applied to large fields to support turf or other crop growth. The application rate is dictated by various loading parameters and climatic conditions.

Of all the technologies herein considered, land application is the least mechanical and as such, has the lowest unit energy cost to operate. The only electrical demands are: pumps to convey the wastewater to the application site, pumps and blowers to mix and aerate the waste, and pumps to convey the wastewater to the distribution pivots. The energy efficiency of this treatment method draws upon the utilization of naturally occuring soil organisms for breakdown of organic matter.

Although this technology offers a low energy option, it has limited utility because the land requirements are great and specific soil and climate types are needed. Anheuser-Busch presently has two breweries using this environmentally friendly technology.

### CASE HISTORY — ENERGY CONSERVATION

In cases where land application of wastewater is neither applicable nor economical, Anheuser-Busch breweries have discharged directly into municipal treatment systems. The one exception is the Baldwinsville, New York, brewery, which has an on-site treatment facility. When the brewery was built in the mid-1970's, an activated sludge, or aerobic treatment process was installed. As already mentioned, this practice was typical during the days of cheap energy and abundant landfills.

By the mid-1980's, the cost of operating this treatment plant had increased considerably. When the brewery was expanded in 1989, and additional treatment capacity was needed, the treatment plant was modified using the anaerobic process. The benefits of anaerobic versus aerobic treatment are threefold: energy conservation, sludge reduction and process enhancement (stability). This paper will focus on the first of these benefits.

This case study will compare the overall energy costs of treating brewery wastewater before and after the addition of the anaerobic process. This energy balance addresses both the treatment facility itself and residuals handling systems at the brewery. The analysis accounts for electrical and fuel requirements.

The pre-anaerobic treatment scenario included an evaporator and distillation column at the brewery for processing concentrated waste streams. The remaining, "dilute" wastewater was routed to the treatment plant, at which the soluble organic matter was consumed in the aerobic process. A simplified process flow diagram is shown in Figure A. After installation of anaerobic treatment, the evaporator and still were shut down. As will be shown, anaerobic treatment is more energy-efficient than these residuals systems. Thus, all brewery wastewater is now discharged directly to the treatment plant. This enriched waste stream is ideal for the anaerobic process. However, because the treatment in this step is not sufficient for stream discharge, an aerobic polishing step is still required. As will be shown, the aerobic energy consumption is greatly reduced as a result of anaerobic pretreatment. Figure B shows the modified flow schematic. Biogas, or methane is produced, some of which is needed to heat the wastewater. The majority is conveyed to the brewery powerhouse to offset fuel purchases.

Table 1 shows the wastewater treatment energy balance before and after anaerobic treatment.

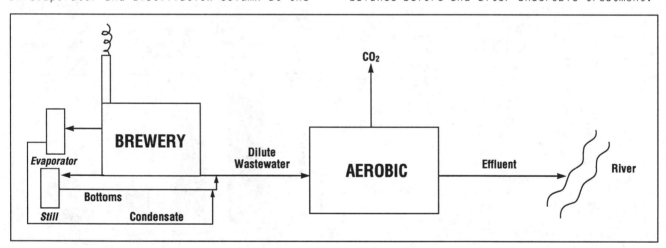

FIGURE A.   Pre-Anaerobic Treatment Scheme

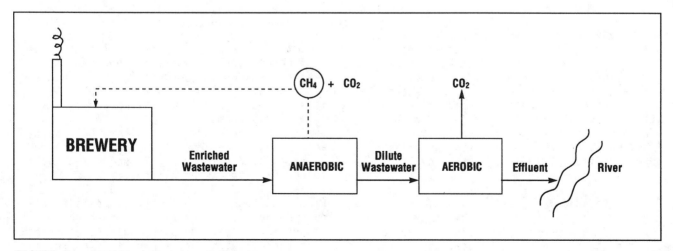

FIGURE B.   Modified Treatment Scheme

The bottom line indicates a net energy cost savings of 75%. These savings are realized in several areas. First, the shutdown of the residuals handling systems saves about 6.2 ¢/lb BOD. Even though this nearly doubles the wastewater organic loading to the treatment plant, the aerobic system electrical costs are still cut considerably. Note that the incremental increase in electrical requirements for the anaerobic system are relatively small. The reason for this was previously explained.

| | BEFORE ANAEROBIC | AFTER ANAEROBIC |
|---|---|---|
| Residuals Handling | 6.2 | 0 |
| Aerobic Treatment | 8.5 | 2.7 |
| Anaerobic Treatment | 0 | 1.1 |
| Biogas Credit | 0 | (1.9) |
| TOTAL | 7.6* | 1.9 |

Note: Units of ¢/lb BOD treated
*Weighted average

TABLE 1.    Wastewater Energy Balance Baldwinsville Case

The other major area of energy savings is the biogas generation, which is shown as a credit. This gas volume presently offsets approximately 15% of the brewery fuel purchases. Corporate utility rate projections call for an escalation in fuel rates during the 90's, which bodes well for application of the anaerobic technology. Being a net producer of energy rather than a consumer, the anaerobic system economics become more favorable as rates rise.

The foregoing analysis demonstrates the substantial economic advantage that can result from selection of an alternate treatment technology. Of further interest in this case is the fact that, when all fixed treatment costs are considered (primarily labor), the marginal cost for treating additional wastewater actually becomes negative. This becomes an important factor when expansion plans are evaluated.

This study covered a unique case for the Company, one with an existing treatment facility. However, there will be cases where anaerobic pretreatment only, with effluent discharged to the municipality, will be mutually beneficial to both the Company and the City, especially in a situation where the latter's excess treatment capacity is limited. Anheuser-Busch is continuing to investigate opportunities for application of this technology to other locations.

LIFE CYCLE COST ANALYSIS

In the 15-year period from 1975 to 1990, as depicted on Figure C, water/wastewater treatment costs went from being the lowest cost

to the highest cost utility for Anheuser-Busch. During this period, unit wastewater treatment costs increased tenfold. Even though this exponential jump is in part related to increasing energy costs, unit electric costs, only increased 130% during this same 15-year period. Other factors, including more restrictive discharge limits requiring a higher level of treatment, and significant increases in sludge disposal costs are two reasons for this difference.

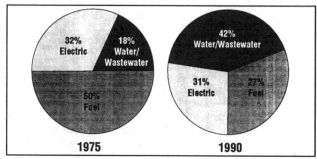

FIGURE C.    Brewery Utility Costs — % of Total

As has been previously discussed and as shown on Figure D, from an overall energy standpoint the ranking of wastewater treatment alternatives from lowest to highest energy user is land application, followed by anaerobic/aerobic, followed by residuals treatment, with aerobic treatment being the most energy intensive.

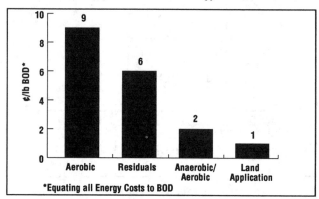

FIGURE D.    Energy Costs for Treatment Alternatives

Selecting a treatment system that is the lowest energy user is important; however, from a business standpoint, selecting the treatment system with the lowest overall life cycle cost is essential. When all is said and done, a company must remain competitive to stay in business. Therefore, initial capital costs, as well as annual operation and maintenance costs, are both important in selecting the appropriate treatment alternative.

Figure E shows the unit capital costs based on Anheuser-Busch experience for aerobic, anaerobic/aerobic and land application treatment technologies. As shown, from an initial capital standpoint, an anaerobic/aerobic system costs approximately one-half that of the aerobic system. Land application treatment costs approximately one-third of the capital of an equivalent aerobic system. From an annual operation and maintenance standpoint, as shown on Figure F, anaerobic/ aerobic and land application costs are approximately one-half and one-third the costs, respectively, of aerobic treatment costs.

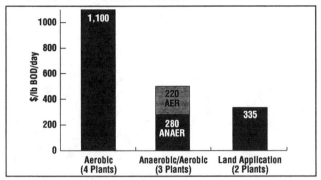

FIGURE E. Capital Costs for Treatment Alternatives

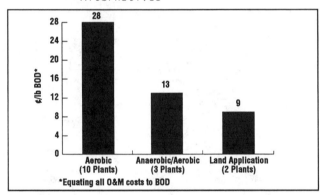

FIGURE F. O & M Costs For Treatment Alternative — A-B Experience (1990$)

Figure G depicts the life cycle cost analysis for the three treatment alternatives. Based on a typical Anheuser-Busch brewery, unit wastewater treatment costs per pound of BOD treated are 59¢/lb, 27¢/lb, and 18¢/lb for aerobic, anaerobic/aerobic and land application technologies, respectively.

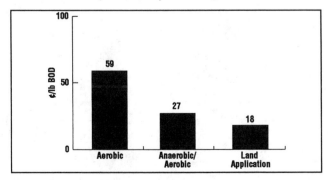

FIGURE G. Total Treatment Costs for Various Alternatives (Capital amortized 20 years @ 8%, 1990$)

From an energy and life cycle cost analysis, we have a win/win. The ranking of treatment systems from an overall cost and energy standpoint is identical. That is, the system with the lowest life cycle cost also uses the least energy.

## CORPORATE VISION

Discussions so far have centered around energy and life cycle costs for various end-of-pipe treatment technologies. A major change is taking place in industry today. Industry is starting to realize that raw materials and the ability of the earth to assimilate pollution are finite. The successful industries in the twenty-first century will be those that adapt their thinking to assure that their operations not only comply with all regulations but support life cycle analysis and sustainable development goals.

Even though pollution prevention and waste minimization are and will continue to play an important role in day-to-day operational decisions, end-of-pipe treatment will continue to be essential, at least for the foreseeable future. In fact, it will be imperative in the future that end-of-pipe treatment decisions also pass the rigors of life cycle and sustainable development analysis.

For Anheuser-Busch, it is felt that the anaerobic/aerobic and land application treatment technologies that we helped develop and employ today place us in a good position for the future. First, the majority of the raw materials utilized in our products are renewable and sustainable crops. If anaerobic treatment is utilized, this system is actually a net producer of energy. When this technology is followed by land application, which is done at the Jacksonville, Florida, brewery, all remaining nutrients and water are recycled back to the soil, therefore completing the cycle much as would happen in nature.

In summary, much work needs to be done to support future environmental goals. Every aspect of an industry's operation will need to be examined closely, and dramatic changes will be required to assure long-term future success. This re-evaluation must include other methods of end-of-pipe treatment. Much additional development work needs to be done in this area. However, it is felt that with the technologies discussed here, Anheuser-Busch is in an excellent starting position heading into the twenty-first century.

*Larry W. Keith is director of environmental engineering and development and Allen R. Beers is senior environmental engineer, Anheuser-Busch Companies, Inc.*

# Chapter 61
# CAD Active Flowsheets for Process Energy Analysis

P. Wilson

Process Energy Reduction, discussed elsewhere, is a methodology for reducing the energy demand by processes. The second phase (or step) of this method is Process Energy Analysis (PEA). This phase establishes the type and amount of energy consumption in each process step or system and develops one-line balances for each energy system (e.g. the steam system). For large facilities, establishing individual equipment energy usage and the one-line balances can be a very time consuming effort. This paper describes how process simulation coupled with a graphics front end allows one to rapidly create flowsheets with mass and energy balances. These "Electronic Flowsheets" can be constrained by process criteria into a complete simulation model. All this is done in a graphics mode.

## MILL DESCRIPTION

### Process

The process considered in this paper is a paper mill which produces bleached food board. The mill is currently increasing its tonnage from 1570 oven dried tons per day (ODTPD)to 1880 ODTPD. Pulp and paper making operations use large quantities of water and energy. The major sources of energy at this mill site are wood (in tree lengths), wood waste, electric power and natural gas.

In general terms, the processing of wood into paper is outlined in the accompanying block diagram and is as follows:

Tree length wood is debarked in rotating drums with the bark being used as fuel. The debarked wood is then chipped into chips approximately one inch square by 1/4 inch thick. The chips are stored in piles along with purchased chips. Hardwood and softwood chips are handled and stored separately.

The digesters require about 3500 ODTPD of screened chips, about half of which are hardwood. Fines from the chip screens are added to the fuel pile. Hardwood and softwood is processed separately right up to the paper machine blending systems.

In the digesters, wood chips are cooked with recycled chemicals at temperatures of up to 350 deg. F. Some fresh chemical makeup in the form of caustic and sulfur is required also. The wood chips are converted into pulp in the digesters by the dissolution of the lignin that binds the wood fiber together. In the washing and screening stage, the dissolved lignin is removed from the pulp at about 15% solids. This dissolved lignin is known as black liquor.

The black liquor also contains spent cooking chemicals. To recover the chemicals in an economic fashion, the black liquor is concentrated to 55 to 70% solids in multiple effect evaporators. At these levels, the concentrated black liquor has sufficient organic content (principally lignin) to burn. At solids in excess of about 60%, no auxiliary fuel is required. The black liquor is fired in a specially designed recovery boiler to produce steam and recover the digesting

KRAFT PAPER MILL
PROCESS FLOW DIAGRAM

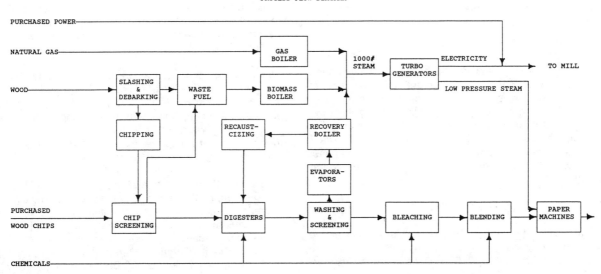

chemicals. The spent chemicals are recovered as molten salts at the bottom of the furnace and then dissolved in water. The predominant sodium salt is sodium carbonate and this is converted to sodium hydroxide in a recausticizing operation after leaving the recovery boiler. The recovered chemicals, in the form of "white liquor", are recycled back to the digesters.

Screened and washed pulp is then bleached. This occurs at between 3.5 and 12% solids levels. Typically, four or five stages of bleaching are required with washing occurring between all the intermediate stages. Unfortunately, true countercurrent washing cannot be used and considerable quantities of fresh water are used in the bleaching process. All the make-up water has to be heated to about 165 deg. F.

The bleached pulp is then blended into the desired portions of hardwood and softwood and chemicals. At this time, mechanical energy is applied to the pulp to defibrillate it. This is called refining and uses about 5 horsepower days per ton, on average.

As the blended pulp approaches the paper machine, it is diluted to about 0.5% solids with recycled paper machine water. It is then dewatered on a series of gravity and suction dewatering devices to about 20% solids to begin forming the paper sheet. It is then further dewatered to 45% solids in a pressing operation and is dried to its final solids content of 94% on rotating steam heated cylinders. The dried paper is then cut into shipping rolls or sheeted and is wrapped and shipped.

## Energy

Wood waste is used to fire a biomass boiler. In this mill, the biomass boiler is base loaded. Since the recovery boilers do not swing much, a fossil fuel boiler is used as a swing boiler to compensate for surges in the steam demands. The swing boiler is fired on natural gas.

All boilers produce 1000 psig steam. This steam is reduced to 300 psig, 150 psig and 50 psig steam through turbine prime movers and turbogenerator sets. Very little steam is blown down through pressure reducing stations (PRV's) during normal operations. The power produced by the turbogenerators is used to augment purchased power used to drive the process motors. The steam is all consumed internally to heat the processes and to dry paper.

## Water

For simplicity, water flows are not shown on the flowsheet. However, as mentioned above, large quantities of water are used throughout the process of converting wood to paper. Plant discharge is in the order of 50,000,000 gallons per day while total pumping is several times that amount. In addition, electrical power is required to pump this water and steam is required to heat it. Thus, in a pulp and paper complex, energy management must also encompass water management.

## THE PROBLEM

In May 1990, the pulp and paper mill described above contracted to purchase a new pulping line. This line consists of a single, 1000 ODTPD continuous digester,

washing, screening and a dedicated bleach plant. This was purchased to allow one existing, obsolete fiber line to be shut down, and two others to be operated at lower capacity than current operation. The objective was to reduce the production of dioxin to non-measurable levels and to effect a modest plant tonnage increase.

To operate the new pulp line, 110,000 pounds per hour (lb/hr) of steam (split between 50 psig and 150 psig), 6500 GPM of 160 deg. F water and 5000 horsepower was required. Furthermore, if fresh water was to be used, and additional 225,000 lb/hr of 50 psig steam was required to heat this water to 160 deg. F.

This facility was blessed with an ample water supply and a matching waste water treatment system. Both systems are capable of handling 50,000,000 gallons per day (34,700 GPM). As there was no apparent penalty for freely using water, over a period of years, more and more water was used. Consequently, in May, 1990, there was no more fresh water available and the waste water treatment plant was also at capacity.

In addition to not having enough water to meet the requirements of the new pulping line, it also was realized that there was not enough steam capacity in the existing boilers to meet the new steam requirements. Finally, to meet the increased power requirements, a new electrical feeder line and a substation were found to be necessary.

In brief, the mill found that it had contracted for a new pulping line for which it did not have sufficient water, steam or power using the existing utilities under the existing operating conditions. It was at this point that they requested a mass and energy study to investigate if they could change their operations to allow the new pulping line to be started up without having to provide new water handling or steam generating facilities.

## THE SOLUTION

Using CADSIM/MASSBAL, an electronic flow sheet software package, a computer model of the mill and the new pulping line was constructed to determine the optimum configuration for energy economy. At the same time, a block flow diagram of the total mill was constructed and a mass and energy balance was run to describe the existing conditions. The mass and energy balance numbers were then checked against actual mill operating data to reconcile the model and the model was adjusted where it did not.

Using mass and energy balance information for the optimum configuration of the new pulping line, a number of changes were made to the design of the new pulping line before detailed engineering of the new line began. Then, a number of "what if" scenarios were investigated to determine what water streams could be diverted to the new pulping line, reused or otherwise conserved.

The overall thrust was to attempt to cascade cold water to hot by using fresh water on devices that required clean cold water, then collecting this water and reusing it on devices that required warmer water and so on. In conjunction, a secondary cascade of clean to dirty was perused. As a result of this investigation, the potential for reducing the total water flow by 10,000,000 gallons per day was identified. Also steam savings of 250,000 lb/hr were identified.

A plan to realize the most economic water and steam savings was then implemented with the following results:

|  | Tons Paper ODTPD | Water Saved MMGPD | Steam Saved LB/HR |
|---|---|---|---|
| May 1990 | 1570 | 0 | 0 |
| July 1992 | 1880 | 6,400 | 111,000 |

As the investigation to save steam and water progressed, it became apparent that the mill also would benefit from a steam and power balance. This was because a number of steam users were switched from 150 psig steam to 50 psig steam and the total steam pull was being decreased. As the steam pulls were being determined in July 1990, it was observed that steam was being reduced across PRV's rather than being let down through turbines.

Consequently, a steam and power balance was prepared and added to the overall electronic flow sheet analysis. A number of scenarios were prepared that explored eliminating steam flows across PRV's and maximizing steam flows through turbines to the 50 psig header. The result of this line of investigation resulted in one of two gas fired boilers being shut down due to some immediate steam savings and the realization that some additional steam could be generated from the biomass boiler. Furthermore, by changing steam users from 150 psig steam to 50 psig steam and reconfiguring to minimize blowdown across PRVs, an additional 4.2 MW of power could be generated under existing conditions.

## CONCLUSIONS

Within a month of starting with incomplete flowsheets and incomplete information, comprehensive electronic flow sheets and balances for fiber, water, steam and electricity were available for the existing mill and the new line. The instantaneous nature of the flowsheet allowed various "what if" questions to be answered in a matter of minutes --- a task which would take weeks otherwise.

Just as important, the flowsheet approach allowed energy usage by various equipment and systems to be closely estimated even when complete information was absent. Having these values is critical to Process Energy Analysis in order to establish existing conditions as a starting point for developing ideas for improvements.

Process simulation is a computer model that emulates actual real-life situations. The power of this tool enables the process engineer to create "Electronic Flowsheets" in a CAD environment and then rapidly execute mass and energy balances in the same graphics mode. The balance results are presented instantly on the flowsheet (or P&ID's if these have been developed), thereby making a highly readable document. The advantages of this to operations and engineering personnel are:

Many process conditions can be evaluated in a short span of time. Each scenario can be presented on a separate flowsheet (or set of P&ID's) within minutes of completing each balance.

CADSIM flowsheets can be expanded into P&ID's without duplication of effort.

MASSBAL is a linear program, therefore, all solutions are optimal for the given process conditions.

Mill operating data can be reconciled with the simulation of the process. In this way, the accuracy of individual measurements can be determined.

# Chapter 62
# Exergy Analysis and Thermoeconomics in Search of Cost Effective Solutions Part 1: Exergy Analysis

R.J. Krane, G. Tsatsaronis

## ABSTRACT

Many decisions to be made during design, operation, retrofitting and repowering of energy systems refer to thermodynamic variables (temperatures, pressures, mass flow rates, etc.) and to equipment costs that depend on these variables. One of the most important final selection criteria, however, is the cost of the product(s) generated by the energy system. It is apparent that an appropriate combination of energy balances and economic evaluations must be advantageous to the cost optimization process. It is also apparent that we can reduce inefficiencies and costs more effectively if we understand their sources and mechanisms of formation.

An exergy analysis identifies the real "energy waste" (inefficiencies) in each component of an energy system. A thermoeconomic analysis combines an exergy analysis with cost balances conducted at the component level. A thermoeconomic analysis reveals the real cost sources, calculates the costs of different products generated by the same energy system, simplifies and, in cases of very complex systems, enables the cost optimization process, and facilitates decision-making procedures in energy systems.

The first part of the paper presents the most important aspects of exergy analysis. The second part of the paper focuses on applications of thermoeconomic analyses. Examples from cogeneration systems and integrated gasification-combined cycle power plants are discussed.

## NOMENCLATURE

| Symbol | Meaning [units] |
|---|---|
| c | cost per exergy unit [$/MMBtu] |
| $\dot{D}$ | cost flow rate [$/hr] |
| e | specific exergy [Btu/lbm] |
| $\dot{E}$ | exergy flow rate [MW or MMBtu/hr] |
| g | gravitational acceleration |
| h | specific enthalpy [Btu/lbm] |
| I | investment cost [$] |
| KE | kinetic energy |
| $\dot{m}$ | mass flow rate [lbm/hr] |
| P | pressure [psia] |
| PE | potential energy |
| $\dot{Q}$ | heat transfer rate [MW or MMBtu/hr] |

| Symbol | Meaning [units] |
|---|---|
| r | relative cost difference between average cost per exergy unit of product and average cost per exergy unit of fuel [%] |
| t | time |
| T | temperature [K] |
| U | internal energy [Btu] |
| V | velocity [ft/s] |
| $\dot{W}$ | power [MW] |
| z | elevation relative to the earth surface [ft] |
| Z | annual capital costs associated with a plant component [$] |

### Greek letters

| | |
|---|---|
| $\beta$ | capital-recovery factor [%] |
| $\gamma$ | coefficient expressing the part of the annual fixed operating and maintenance costs that depends on the net investment cost for a plant component [%] |
| $\epsilon$ | exergetic efficiency [%] |
| $\eta$ | thermal efficiency of the total system or isentropic efficiency of a compressor or turbine [%] |
| $\tau$ | annual number of hours of plant operation at the nominal capacity [hr] |

### Subscripts

| | |
|---|---|
| CV | control volume |
| D | exergy destruction |
| e | exiting stream |
| F | fuel |
| i | entering stream |
| k | plant component |
| L | loss |
| OM | operation and maintenance |
| P | product |
| 0 | environment |

### Superscripts

| | |
|---|---|
| OPT | optimum |
| Q | heat transfer |
| W | power |
| • | time rate of the corresponding variable |

## INTRODUCTION

Engineers engaged in the operation, analysis, comparison, and optimization of energy systems are usually interested in the answers to the following five questions:

(1)  What are the **real** thermodynamic losses ("energy wastes")?,

(2)  What are the **true** causes of the inefficiencies?,

(3)  How do we correctly evaluate the inefficiencies?,

(4)  What are the **real** cost sources?, and

(5)  How does each thermodynamic inefficiency affect the cost of the final products?

This paper provides answers for these important questions. The answers to the first three questions fall within the realm of **exergy analysis**, which is the subject of Part 1 of the paper. The answers to the last two questions may be found in the field of **thermoeconomics**, which is discussed in Part 2.

## EXERGY ANALYSIS

### Some Concepts from Elementary Thermodynamics

Constraints on the length of this paper prevent a detailed discussion of exergy analysis or a complete explanation of it's practical importance in the field of energy engineering. Within the limitations imposed by these constraints, however, we shall attempt to present the basic notions of exergy analysis and explain its usefulness to the energy engineer. This task begins by recalling some well-known concepts from classical thermodynamics.

The law of conservation of mass may be stated as "mass is neither created nor destroyed; that is, mass is conserved". For a control volume this law may be written as

$$\frac{d\,m_{cv}}{dt} + \sum \dot{m}_e - \sum \dot{m}_i = 0 \qquad (1)$$

where the first term represents the rate of change of mass stored in the control volume and the last two terms give the net rate at which mass flows across the control surface.

The first law of thermodynamics may be stated as "energy is neither created nor destroyed; that is, energy is conserved." The first law is written for a control volume as

$$\dot{Q}_{cv} + \sum \dot{m}_i \left[ h_i + \frac{V_i^2}{2} + gz_i \right]$$

$$= \frac{d(U + KE + PE)}{dt} + \sum \dot{m}_e \left[ h_e + \frac{V_e^2}{2} + gz_e \right] + \dot{W}_{cv} \qquad (2)$$

where the first term on the left-hand side is the net rate of heat transfer across the control surface, and the second term on this

side is the rate at which energy is carried into the control volume by entering mass flowrates. The first term on the right-hand side is the rate of change of energy stored in the control volume, the second term is rate at which energy is carried out of the control volume by exiting mass flowrates, and the third term is the net rate of work done on or by the control volume. The present motive for reviewing the laws of conservation of mass and energy is to emphasize that both are **conserved** quantities.

### The Failure of the First Law to Adequately Characterize the True Worth of an Energy Resource

Next, we will show that the law of conservation of mass and the first law alone fail to depict some of the most important aspects of energy resource utilization. We will then show that this failure stems directly from the fact that mass and energy are conserved quantities. This, in turn, will provide the motivation for introducing the concept of exergy.

We will make initially some interesting observations and then address the answers to questions that follow from these observations. First, note that a large utility company in the eastern United States sells energy in two forms: electricity and steam. Their relative pricing for these two forms of energy is given by

$$\begin{bmatrix} \text{Price of} \\ \text{1000 Btu of Steam} \\ \text{(0.87 lbm} \\ \text{at 250 lbf/in}^2) \end{bmatrix} \approx \frac{1}{2} \begin{bmatrix} \text{Price of} \\ \text{1000 Btu of} \\ \text{Electricity} \\ \text{(0.29 kWh)} \end{bmatrix} \qquad (3)$$

This leads us to ask "how does a closely regulated utility get away with such **disparate prices for the same amount of energy?** We should also note that despite the price differential the utility's customers purchase much more electricity than steam and do not complain about the differential! Why? Is a BTU not a BTU? The answer to this latter question is of course, "yes, all BTU's are equal, but, **some are worth more than others because energy has a quality associated with it as well as a quantity**". It is this attribute of quality that is responsible for the price differential for the same amount (quantity) of energy.

Now consider the very large isolated system (a system that exchanges no heat, mass, or work with its surroundings) shown in Figure 1. The system consists of a quantity of fuel, a burner, and air in abundance [1]. All parts of the system are initially at the same temperature, $T_i$. At some instant, fuel is introduced into the burner and ignited. As time progresses, combustion of the fuel proceeds until the supply is exhausted. Upon completion of the combustion process, the system contains a mixture of air and combustion products at a temperature, $T_i + dt$, which is only slightly greater than the initial temperature, $T_i$. Several observations may now be made regarding this process. First, since the system is isolated, the law of conservation of mass and the first law assure us that the mass and energy of the system are conserved; that is

$$\begin{bmatrix} \dfrac{\text{final system mass}}{\text{initial system mass}} \end{bmatrix} = 1 \qquad (4)$$

and,

$$\left[\frac{\text{final system energy}}{\text{initial system energy}}\right] = 1. \qquad (5)$$

Next, we recognize that the original combination of fuel and air is intrinsically more valuable than the final mixture of slightly warm air and combustion products because the original combination has a greater potential to "do something useful", such as generate electricity or produce superheated steam. Thus, we see that the "potential for use", or **quality**, of the original system has been largely **destroyed** and that this destruction has taken place without getting any of the possible benefits.

We have now shown that the first law: (1) focuses on the quantity of energy, (2) fails to account for the quality of energy, and (3) does not provide us with sufficient information to establish the true thermodynamic value of an energy resource. We also know from experience that the first law permits the design of energy systems that work, but usually not in an optimum manner. Therefore, we may conclude that we should identify and employ some measure of the quality of energy. The "quality of energy" is synonymous with its capacity, or potential, to cause change [2]; that is, "to do something useful", such as heat a room, compress a gas, or promote an endothermic chemical reaction. In thermodynamics, we characterize the quality of a given quantity of energy by its exergy.

### The Definition of Exergy

The exergy of an energy carrier is defined as the **maximum useful work that can be done by the carrier under the conditions imposed by the environment**. Exergy is also known in the literature by a number of other names such availability, available energy, maximum useful work, etc. In most cases the exergy represents the useful part of energy, the part of the given form of energy that can be transformed into any other energy form.

The example of the combustion of a fuel in an isolated system discussed above shows that the quality of energy can be degraded; that is, its potential for use can be destroyed. Thus, we conclude that exergy may be destroyed, or exergy is not conserved.

It is easily shown that an exergy balance on a control volume gives

$$\frac{dE_{CV}}{dt} = \sum_{j=1}^{n}\left[1 - \frac{T_0}{T_j}\right]\dot{Q}_j - \dot{W}_{CV} + P_0\frac{dV_{CV}}{dt} \\ + \sum_i \dot{m}_i e_i - \sum_e \dot{m}_e e_e - \dot{E}_D. \qquad (6)$$

The left-hand side of the equation gives the rate of change of exergy stored in the control volume. The first term on the right-hand side is the rate at which exergy is carried across the control surface by heat transfers to and from the control volume, the second term is the rate at which exergy is carried

across the control surface by work transfers, and the third term is the rate of exergy transfer across the control surface by PdV-type work done on the environment by an expanding control volume. The fourth and fifth terms on the right-hand side give the net rate at which exergy is carried across the control surface by entering and leaving mass flowrates. The last term on the right-hand side represents the rate of exergy **destruction** within the control volume by irreversibilities.

The exergy of shaft work, a flow of electricity, kinetic energy, or potential energy is exactly equal to the amount of each of these quantities. (Each BTU of energy in one of these forms can, theoretically, be converted to 1 BTU of useful work.) The exergy of a heat transfer, $\dot{Q}$, at a specific temperature "T" is given by

$$\dot{E}^Q = \dot{Q}\left[1 - \frac{T_0}{T}\right]. \qquad (7)$$

Some of the common irreversibilities that destroy exergy include fluid friction, flow throttling, heat transfer across a finite temperature difference, mixing of dissimilar fluids, Joulean ($I^2R$) heating in an electrical conductor, and chemical reactions.

We will now show that efficiencies based on exergy, rather than on energy, give the **true** measure of thermodynamic performance.

### Exergetic Efficiency

The first law may be written for a control volume in a steady state, steady flow situation as

$$\left[\begin{array}{c}\text{Energy}\\\text{In}\end{array}\right] = \left[\begin{array}{c}\text{Desired}\\\text{Energy}\\\text{Out}\end{array}\right] + \left[\begin{array}{c}\text{Energy}\\\text{"Loss"}\end{array}\right] \qquad (8)$$

or

$$= \left[\begin{array}{c}\text{The "Energy}\\\text{Sought"}\end{array}\right] + \left[\begin{array}{c}\text{Energy Carried Out Of}\\\text{The Control Volume By}\\\text{Leaks And Extraneous}\\\text{Heat Transfers}\end{array}\right]. \qquad (9)$$

Based on these equations, we define

$$\left[\begin{array}{c}\text{1st Law,}\\\text{or Thermal,}\\\text{Efficiency}\end{array}\right] = \eta = \left[\dfrac{\begin{array}{c}\text{Desired}\\\text{Energy}\\\text{Out}\end{array}}{\text{Energy In}}\right] \qquad (10)$$

$$= \left[1 - \frac{\text{Energy Loss}}{\text{Energy In}}\right].$$

This definition immediately shows us that the thermal, or first law efficiency: (1) deals only with the **quantity** of energy and does not take the **quality** of energy into account, (2) focuses attention on "reducing losses"; that is, it promotes "good housekeeping", or "BTU-chasing", type activities, (3) does not emphasize the possible efficiency of energy use (as we shall see is done by second law efficiencies), (4) cannot be generalized in a meaningful way for complex systems in which the desired output is some combination of heat and work (as in a cogeneration plant). For such reasons we find it desirable to employ **exergetic efficiencies** (second-law efficiencies).

An exergy balance on a control volume in steady state, steady flow may be written as

$$\begin{bmatrix} \text{Exergy} \\ \text{In} \end{bmatrix} = \begin{bmatrix} \text{Desired} \\ \text{Exergy} \\ \text{Out} \end{bmatrix} + \begin{bmatrix} \text{Exergy} \\ \text{"Losses"} \end{bmatrix} + \begin{bmatrix} \text{Exergy} \\ \text{Destroyed} \end{bmatrix}. \quad (10)$$

Based on this equation, we define the exergetic efficiency. To understand the term exergetic efficiency, it is helpful to think of each component as having a **"product"**, which represents the desired result from the component, and a **"fuel"**, which represents the driving force for the process, or the resources used to obtain the "product". Definition of the "product" must be consistent with the **purpose** of using the component being considered (References [3] through [6]). In the following, the terms "fuel" and "product" for a plant component are used without quotation marks. Using this terminology, the exergetic efficiency ($\epsilon$) of a component is defined as the ratio of the exergy in the product ($E_P$) to the exergy in the fuel ($E_F$):

$$\epsilon = \begin{bmatrix} \dfrac{\text{Exergy of the Product}}{\text{Total Exergy Used to Generate}} \\ \text{the Desired Product} \end{bmatrix} = \frac{E_P}{E_F} \quad (12)$$

or

$$\epsilon = \begin{bmatrix} 1 - \dfrac{\text{Exergy Losses}}{\text{Total Exergy Used}} - \dfrac{\text{Exergy Destroyed}}{\text{Total Exergy Used}} \end{bmatrix}. \quad (13)$$

From these equations it is readily seen that: (1) the importance of a given quantity of energy in the overall exergetic efficiency is weighted by its exergy, or quality, and (2) the overall exergetic efficiency emphasizes the need to reduce both losses and irreversibilities in order to improve system performance.

Values of the energetic (first-law) and exergetic (second-law) efficiencies for five different systems, or devices, are presented in Table 1. The exceptionally low exergetic efficiencies for the home gas furnace, the electrical resistance heater and the electric clothes dryer are the result of using very high quality energy to perform relatively low quality heating tasks. The discrepancies between the values of the first and second law efficiencies for these devices clearly illustrate the fact that a first-law efficiency does not correctly account for the high quality of the energy used in these devices. The inability of the first-law (thermal) efficiency to adequately portray the true performance of many devices and processes will now be examined in detail for the well-known throttling process.

## TABLE 1
**Comparison of Average Energetic (First-Law) and Exergetic (Second-Law) Efficiencies of Energy-Conversion Systems/Devices. All Values are Given in Percent**

| System/Device | $\eta$ | $\epsilon$ |
|---|---|---|
| Large Electric Motor | 98 | 98 |
| Large Steam Boiler | 92 | 49 |
| Home Gas Furnace | 85 | 13 |
| Electric Resistance Heater | 100 | 17 |
| Electric Clothes Dryer | 50 | 9.5 |

## Comparison of the First and Second Law Approaches for a Simple Throttling Process

"Throttling" is defined as the steady-state, steady-flow process in which the pressure of a flowing stream of fluid is reduced across a restriction in the flow passage. Throttling is a ubiquitous process which occurs in many devices and systems of practical engineering interest.

Consider the uninsulated throttle with a leak shown in Figure 2. Applying the law of conservation of mass to the control volume for the steady state, steady flow process shown in Figure 2 yields

$$\begin{bmatrix} \text{Mass Flowrate} \\ \text{Into The Throttle} \end{bmatrix} = \begin{bmatrix} \text{Mass Flowrate} \\ \text{Leaving The Throttle} \end{bmatrix} + \begin{bmatrix} \text{Mass Flowrate} \\ \text{"Lost" In The Leak} \end{bmatrix} \quad (14)$$

or

$$\dot{m}_i = \dot{m}_e + \dot{m}_L . \quad (15)$$

Similarly, applying the first law to this control volume gives

$$\begin{bmatrix} \text{Rate At Which} \\ \text{Energy Is} \\ \text{"Lost" By Heat} \\ \text{Transfer} \end{bmatrix} + \begin{bmatrix} \text{Rate At Which Energy} \\ \text{Is Carried Into} \\ \text{The Throttle By} \\ \text{The Entering Mass} \\ \text{Flowrate} \end{bmatrix}$$
$$= \begin{bmatrix} \text{Rate At Which Energy} \\ \text{Is Carried Out Of} \\ \text{The Throttle By} \\ \text{The Exiting Mass} \\ \text{Flowrate} \end{bmatrix} + \begin{bmatrix} \text{Rate At Which} \\ \text{Energy} \\ \text{Is Lost} \\ \text{Through} \\ \text{The Leak} \end{bmatrix} \quad (16)$$

or

$$\dot{Q} + \dot{m}_i h_i = \dot{m}_e h_e + \dot{m}_L h_e. \quad (17)$$

Equations (10) and (19) may now be used to construct the following first-law efficiency for the throttling process:

$$(\eta)_{th} = \begin{bmatrix} \dfrac{\text{Desired} \\ \text{Energy} \\ \text{Out}}{\text{Energy In}} \end{bmatrix} = \begin{bmatrix} 1 - \dfrac{\text{Energy} \\ \text{"Losses"}}{\text{Energy In}} \end{bmatrix} \quad (18)$$

or

$$(\eta)_{th} = \left[\frac{\dot{m}_e h_e}{\dot{m}_i h_i}\right] = \left[1 - \frac{\dot{m}_L h_e}{\dot{m}_i h_i} + \frac{\dot{Q}}{\dot{m}_i h_i}\right] \qquad (19)$$

The second term on the right-hand side represents the energy "lost" due to the leak, while the third term gives the energy "lost" due to heat transfer. Thus, a "first law", or **"energy audit"**, type approach would suggest plugging the leak and insulating the throttle to improve the performance of the process. These actions would yield a first-law efficiency of 1; that is, the first law result would state that the throttling process is 100 percent efficient and that no further improvements are possible.

In a similar fashion, if an exergy balance is now performed on the control volume containing the throttle, we obtain the following result

$$\left[\begin{array}{c}\text{Rate At Which}\\\text{Exergy Is Carried}\\\text{In By The Entering}\\\text{Mass Flowrate}\end{array}\right] - \left[\begin{array}{c}\text{Rate At Which}\\\text{Exergy Is "Lost"}\\\text{Due To}\\\text{Heat Transfer}\end{array}\right]$$

$$- \left[\begin{array}{c}\text{Rate At Which}\\\text{Desired Exergy}\\\text{Is Carried Out}\\\text{By The Exiting}\\\text{Mass Flowrate}\end{array}\right]$$

$$- \left[\begin{array}{c}\text{Rate At Which}\\\text{Exergy Is "Lost"}\\\text{Through The}\\\text{Leak}\end{array}\right] - \left[\begin{array}{c}\text{Rate At Which}\\\text{Exergy Is}\\\text{Destroyed By}\\\text{Irreversibilities}\end{array}\right] = 0. \qquad (20)$$

Equations (13) and (20) are now used to obtain the following second-law efficiency for the throttling process:

$$\epsilon = \frac{\left[\begin{array}{c}\text{Rate At Which}\\\text{Desired Exergy}\\\text{Is Carried Out}\\\text{By Exiting Mass}\\\text{Flowrate}\end{array}\right]}{\left[\begin{array}{c}\text{Rate At Which}\\\text{Exergy Is Carried}\\\text{In By Entering}\\\text{Mass Flowrate}\end{array}\right]} = \left[\frac{\dot{m}_e e_e}{\dot{m}_i e_i}\right]$$

$$= \left[1 - \frac{\left[1 - \frac{T_0}{T_e}\right]}{\dot{m}_i e_i} - \frac{\dot{m}_L e_e}{\dot{m}_i e_i} - \frac{\dot{E}_D}{\dot{m}_i e_i}\right]. \qquad (21)$$

The second term on the right-hand side of Equation (21) represents the exergy "lost" due to heat transfer, while the third term gives the exergy "lost" due to the leak. Finally, the last term represents the exergy destroyed by irreversibilities. Thus, a "second law", or **exergy audit**, approach would also suggest plugging the leak and insulating the throttle to improve the performance of the process. If, however, these actions were

taken and were completely effective, the exergetic efficiency, $\epsilon$, would still be less than 1 due to the presence of the irreversibility term. Therefore, the exergetic efficiency, unlike the energetic efficiency, informs us that throttling is an inherently inefficient process and leads us to consider a possible alternative process to accomplish the desired reduction in pressure of the flowing stream of fluid.

## A Candidate Replacement for a Throttling Process

When it is technically and economically viable, an exergy analysis suggests replacement of a throttle by a power recovery turbine (in gases), or a hydraulic turbine (in liquids) and the subsequent recovery of some useful work while reducing the pressure of the flowing stream of fluid as shown in Figure 3. The corresponding energy analysis not only fails to suggest a more efficient alternative for an insulated throttle with no leaks, but deceptively evaluates the throttling process as being perfect, such that there is not even a perceived need for improvement.

## CONCLUSIONS

In summary, we may conclude that an exergy analysis calculates the useful energy associated with an energy carrier and identifies:

(1)     the **real "energy wastes"**; that is, the exergy destructions and the exergy losses, and

(2)     the **real performance** of each plant component as characterized from the thermodynamic viewpoint by an exergetic efficiency.

Finally, we may also conclude that an exergy analysis does not show how much a particular inefficiency costs a plant operator. To determine such costs, **thermoeconomics**, which is the topic of Part 2 of this paper, must be employed.

## REFERENCES

1.     Moran, M. J. and Shapiro, H. N., <u>Fundamentals of Engineering Thermodynamics</u>, John Wiley & Sons, Inc., 1992.

2.     Gaggioli, R. A., "Second Law Analysis for Process and Energy Engineering," in <u>Efficiency and Costing</u>, American Chemical Society, Washington, D.C., ACS Symposium Series 235, 1983, pp. 3-50.

3.     Tsatsaronis, G. and Winhold, M., "Thermoeconomic Analysis of Power Plants," EPRI Final Report, AP-3651, August 1984.

4.     Tsatsaronis, G. and Winhold M., "Exergoeconomic Analysis and Evaluation of Energy Conversion Plants. Part I – A New General Methodology," <u>Energy – The International Journal</u> <u>10</u> (1985) No. 1, pp. 69-80.

5.     Tsatsaronis, G. and Winhold, M., "Exergoeconomic Analysis and Evaluation of Energy Conversion Plants. Part II – Analysis of a Coal-Fired Steam Power Plant,"

Energy – The International Journal <u>10</u> (1985) No. 1, pp. 81-94.

6.      Tsatsaronis, G., Winhold, M., and Stojanoff, C. G., "Thermoeconomic Analysis of a Gasification-Combined-Cycle Power Plant," EPRI Final Report AP 4734, August 1986.

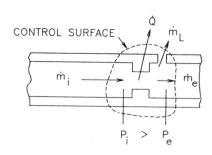

**Figure 2.  Uninsulated Throttle with a Leak**

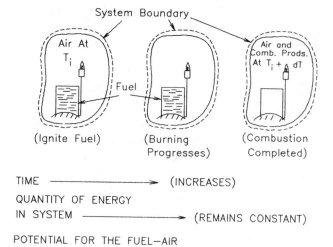

**Figure 1.  Combustion Process in an Isolated System**

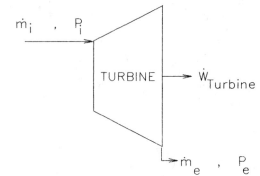

**Figure 3.  Possible Replacement for a Throttling Process**

# Chapter 63
# Exergy Analysis and Thermoeconomics in Search of Cost Effective Solutions Part 2; Thermoeconomics

G. Tsatsaronis, R.J. Krane

## NOMENCLATURE

See Part 1.

## INTRODUCTION

This paper briefly discusses the thermoeconomic evaluation and optimization of energy systems. The techniques involved are somewhat specialized and will not be described in detail here but will be summarized to the level necessary to discuss some applications and conclusions. More details on thermoeconomics are given in References [1] through [6].

Exergy is not only a measure of the true thermodynamic value of an energy carrier but is also closely related to the economic value of the carrier since users pay only for the useful part of energy. **A thermoeconomic analysis combines an exergy analysis with an economic analysis at the component level.** The objectives of a detailed thermoeconomic analysis include all the objectives of an exergy analysis (see Part 1 of this paper) in addition to the following:

- To shed light on the cost formation process, and, thus, facilitate studies to effectively reduce the product costs in an energy system.

- To estimate economically optimal operating conditions for a given design configuration.

- To understand the interactions between the thermodynamic performance of each plant component and the cost of the final plant product(s).

- To calculate the production costs of various products generated in the **same** process.

- To enable cost minimization studies in very complex energy systems.

In the following, thermoeconomics and some applications to energy systems are briefly discussed.

## THERMOECONOMIC EVALUATION

In addition to mass, energy, and exergy balances, **cost balances** are formulated for each system component by assigning a cost value to the exergy (not the energy) of each stream entering or exiting the component. This procedure, **exergy costing**, is based on the finding that exergy is the only rational basis for assigning costs to streams as well as to "energy waste" (exergy destruction and exergy losses) in an energy-conversion process. For a steady state process the cost balance on a control volume gives

$$\dot{Z} + \sum_i \dot{D}_i = \sum_e \dot{D}_e \qquad (1)$$

The second term on the left-hand side and the term on the right-hand side of the equation represent the cost rate associated with the entering and exiting streams. Since exergy is used as the basis for costing, the cost rate $\dot{D}$ is the product of exergy flow rate, $\dot{E}$, and cost per exergy unit, c, for the stream being considered.

$$\dot{D} = \dot{E}c \qquad (2)$$

The first term on the left-hand side of Equation (1) represents the cost rate associated with owning and operating the devices and/or systems within the control volume. This cost rate can be calculated from the initial capital investment expenditure, I according to the following equation.

$$\dot{Z} = \frac{(\beta + \gamma)I}{\tau} \qquad (3)$$

Here, $\beta$ is the capital recovery factor and $\tau$ represents the annual number of hours of plant operation at the nominal capacity. The coefficient $\gamma$ expresses that part of the annual operating and maintenance costs that depends on the net investment cost.

After calculating the cost per exergy unit, c, for all streams in a plant, the cost per exergy unit of fuel ($c_F$) and the cost per exergy unit of product ($c_P$) are calculated for each component. The cost of exergy destruction, $\dot{D}_D$, which expresses the cost of fuel used just to cover the irreversibilities in the component being considered, is given by

$$\dot{D}_D = c_F \dot{E}_D \qquad (4)$$

The real cost sources in a system component are (1) the cost of exergy destruction, $\dot{D}_D$, (2) the cost of exergy loss, $\dot{D}_L$, and (3) the capital cost $\dot{Z}$. A comparison of $\dot{Z}$ with $\dot{D}_D$ and $\dot{D}_L$ for a plant component indicates whether the cost of the final product(s) can be reduced by increasing the capital investment and, consequently, the efficiency* of the component being analyzed, or whether a reduction in the component capital investment would be more cost effective. Traditionally, these decisions are made for the entire plant; thermoeconomics allows the comparison between "fuel costs" (cost of exergy destruction) and investment cost to be made at the plant component level. This represents a significant advantage of thermoeconomics.

Several thermoeconomic variables ([1] through [6]) are used to evaluate the performance of plant components from the cost viewpoint and to identify the most cost effective design changes. A very useful variable for the thermoeconomic evaluation at a plant component is the relative cost difference, r, between cost of fuel and cost of product in the component

$$r = \frac{c_P - c_F}{c_F} = \frac{\dot{D}_D + \dot{Z}}{c_F \dot{E}_P} = \frac{1 - \epsilon}{\epsilon} + \frac{\dot{Z}}{c_F \dot{E}_P} \qquad (5)$$

This equation shows that the exergy unit of product costs more than the exergy unit of fuel because of the exergy destruction and the capital costs associated with the component.

## THERMOECONOMIC OPTIMIZATION

Cost optimization for a complex energy-conversion plant is usually expensive and requires knowledge of engineering, science, and business. The goal of optimization is to find the design configuration and the values of the system variables (the temperature, pressure, and chemical composition of flow streams, equipment size, materials, etc.) that minimize the cost of the total plant product(s). As discussed above, this involves a trade-off between capital and fuel costs for the entire system. Typical problems in the design and operation of energy systems have many workable solutions – sometimes an infinite number. Selecting the best solution requires engineering judgment, intuition, and critical analysis.

In many cases a rigorous cost optimization for a complex energy system is not possible because some of the cost functions that are needed to express the capital cost of a component as a function of thermodynamic variables (temperatures, pressures, etc.) are either unavailable or inaccurate. But even in cases in which all the information is available and acceptably accurate, it is expensive and time-consuming to formulate and solve an optimization problem with an extremely large number of equations, constraints, and highly interdependent variables.

Traditionally, design optimization includes the following steps. First, a detailed system configuration is developed; material and energy balances are conducted for this configuration. Then, product costs are estimated through an economic analysis. The third step includes development of a modified/new configuration that accounts for the corresponding material and energy balances. Subsequently the product costs

for the new configuration are calculated. Since this is a trial and error process, the last two steps are repeated several times.

Development of new process configurations is based, among other factors, on the experience and intuition of design engineers. Several decisions must be made with respect to thermodynamic variables. The final selection criterion, however, is economic. It is apparent that judiciously combining the thermodynamic and economic analyses, as in the thermoeconomic analysis, is advantageous to the optimization process.

When sufficient cost information is available, thermoeconomics allows calculation of the cost optimal exergetic efficiency and the cost optimal relative cost difference r for each plant component. A comparison between the actual and the cost optimal values of exergetic efficiency and relative cost difference r considerably simplifies the cost optimization process.

## BENEFITS OF THERMOECONOMICS

Today the field of thermoeconomics has matured to the point where it is a valuable analytical tool for the design, operation, and maintenance of energy systems; it is not yet, however, a fully developed discipline. Thus, studies involving further development of some aspects of thermoeconomics are currently being carried out in parallel with applications of this field to practical problems.

The effectiveness of reducing costs in the design or operation of an energy system increases when we understand the **real** causes and sources of costs. A thermoeconomic analysis identifies these sources and indicates the changes required to reduce product costs. This information, complemented by the engineer's intuition and judgment, assists in the effective reduction of the product costs in energy systems on a relatively short time scale compared with traditional approaches. Decisions about the design, operation, and repair or replacement of equipment are facilitated.

In addition, thermoeconomics provides an objective cost allocation to more than one product of the same process. For instance, a thermoeconomic analysis of a cogeneration plant (which produces electricity and process steam) will provide the cost of steam and the cost of electricity separately. The cost ratio of steam to electricity calculated by the analysis does not necessarily have to be reflected in their selling prices, but the plant operators should know the real cost of generating each form of energy. In an IGCC power plant, thermoeconomics calculates separately the cost at which electric power is generated in the gas turbine and the steam turbine.

The thermoeconomic analysis also shows how much raw fuel is required to produce each stream in the system. Finally, thermoeconomics helps managers decide how to allocate research and development funds to improve plant components that contribute most significantly to the product costs.

It is true that many conclusions obtained by a thermo-economic optimization could also be obtained through a large number of conventional energy and economic analyses. The

---

*An increase in the component efficiency results in a decrease in the cost of exergy destruction.

368

advantage of thermoeconomics, however, is that it replaces an expensive and subjective search for cost reduction with an objective, well-informed, systematic, and, therefore, shorter search in which all of the cost sources are properly identified and evaluated. The savings in both engineering and computer time are significant.

In the following, two applications of thermoeconomic optimization are presented.

## APPLICATION OF THERMOECONOMICS TO A COGENERATION SYSTEM [6]

In Reference [6] the thermoeconomic optimization techniques were applied to the cogeneration plant shown in Figure 1. This plant generates a net electric power of 30 MW and provides 14 kg/s saturated steam at 20 bar. The purpose of this study was to demonstrate the application of optimization techniques to a plant with two products, electricity and steam. Therefore, no commercially available gas turbine was assumed and the decision variables in the optimization were the pressure ratio $P_2/P_1$, the isentropic efficiencies of the air compressor $\eta_{AC}$ and the gas turbine $\eta_{GT}$ as well as the temperatures of the air at the air-preheater exit ($T_3$) and of the combustion gas at the gas-turbine inlet ($T_4$). All other thermodynamic variables were calculated as a function of the decision variables. The investment costs for the five plant components were calculated as a function of the thermodynamic properties.

Table 1 compares the values of the decision variables and the objective function used in the optimization. The initial design represents a good plant design developed using first-law principles. Application of the thermoeconomic optimization techniques as discussed in Reference [6] resulted after four fast iterations in the optimized design with the values shown in Table 1. Compared with the initial design, the total costs of the optimized design were reduced by more than 7 percent.

## TABLE 1

### Comparison of the Values of the Decision Variables and the Objective Function for the Initial and Optimized Design of the Cogeneration System, Figure 1.

| Variable | Initial Design | Optimized Design |
|---|---|---|
| Pressure Ratio, $P_2/P_1$ | 10.0 | 10.0 |
| Compressor Isentropic Efficiency $\eta_{AC}$ [%] | 86.0 | 85.0 |
| Gas Turbine Isentropic Efficiency $\eta_{GT}$ [%] | 86.0 | 87.5 |
| Temperature $T_3$ [K] | 850 | 900 |
| Temperature $T_4$ [K] | 1,520 | 1,485 |
| Objective Function (Total Cost Rate) [$/hr] | 1,410 | 1,309 |

## APPLICATION OF THERMOECONOMICS TO AN IGCC POWER PLANT [5]

Several integrated gasification-combined-cycle (IGCC) power plants are currently under development to provide a clean, efficient, and cost effective option for generating electric power from coal. Through a joint site-specific project with the U.S. Department of Energy (DOE), Morgantown Energy Technology Center (METC), Southern Company Services, Inc. (SCS) conducted a comprehensive study to determine the characteristics of IGCC power plants with respect to thermal and environmental performance, capital costs, and electricity costs. This evaluation was conducted to be as specific as possible to the Southern Company. The results of that study are summarized in Reference [7].

Among the power plant configurations developed and compared in that study, the so-called Case 1 design configuration was found to be an attractive IGCC power plant configuration. This plant uses four air-blown KRW coal gasifiers, a hot-gas cleanup system, and two GE MS7001F gas turbines. However, no attempt was made to minimize the cost of electricity (COE) in the results presented in Reference [7]. Indeed, final conclusions from the comparison of different IGCC design configurations should only be drawn after these configurations have been optimized from the economic viewpoint or at least after the potential for further cost and efficiency improvements has been estimated.

To optimize the design of Case 1 using advanced thermoeconomic optimization techniques, SCS entered into a supplementary project with DOE/METC. The simulation and optimization studies reported here were conducted by the Tennessee Technological University (TTU) Center for Electric Power under a subcontract to SCS. SCS was responsible for overall project management and cost estimates in the power island. The M. W. Kellogg Company provided TTU with material and energy balances in addition to cost estimates for the gasification island. Some other companies (General Electric, Industrial Filter and Pump Manufacturing, and the Henry Vogt Machine Company) provided performance and cost data for specific equipment items.

### Description of the IGCC Power Plant

The IGCC power plant configuration for Case 1, as reported in Reference [7], is the base case for the studies discussed here. In the following, we will refer to this case as original Case 1. This section briefly describes this case. Additional details may be found in Reference [7].

Figures 2 and 3 show simplified flow diagrams of the gasification island and the power island, respectively. The gasification island converts coal to a clean combustible gas that fuels a combustion turbine. The combustion turbine exhaust heat is used in a heat recovery steam generator (HRSG) to produce steam that drives a turbine generator. The integration between the gasification island and the steam cycle mainly involves (a) generation of saturated steam in the gasification island and use of this steam in the steam cycle and (b) supply of steam at various temperature and pressure levels by the steam cycle to cover the demands of the gasification island.

In the following, the numbers given in parenthesis refer to the material streams shown in Figures 2 and 3.

The air booster compression system (Area 250) supplies the air necessary for the gasifier operation (5) and for the regeneration of the zinc-ferrite desulfurizer (29). Air for this system is obtained by extraction from the compressor of the gas turbine (4).

Flue gas from the sulfator (48) provides the heat to dry the coal to a moisture content at 4.98 weight percent. The coal is gasified in a KRW pressurized, fluidized-bed gasifier. Hydrogen sulfide, produced from the sulfur in the coal, is removed from the gas phase by reacting with calcium oxide that is obtained through the decomposition of limestone. The limestone in the gasifier serves as the primary desulfurization step in the plant. The product gas from the gasifier (6) enters a cyclone that separates most of the fine particulates that escape the gasifier bed and returns them to the bed.

The gas exiting the cyclone (7) is partially cooled in the product gas cooler where HP steam is generated. Additional cooling is provided by quenching with steam (39). The amount of quench steam is determined by the desired moisture content of the gas (30 percent by volume) in order to achieve a satisfactory operation of the zinc ferrite unit.

The product gas (159), now around 1,015°F, then passes through a non-recycle cyclone and a ceramic candle gas filter where all of the remaining particulates are removed from the gas. The collected solids are transferred to a depressurization lockhopper from which the solids, now at atmospheric pressure, are sent through a water-cooled conveyor to the sulfation area.

Since chlorides can severely affect the structural integrity of the zinc ferrite sorbent, a chloride guard is used to remove chlorides from the fuel gas (35). Zinc ferrite was selected as the external bed sorbent for high-temperature coal gas desulfurization because of its effectiveness and capability for sulfur absorption combined with its regenerative characteristics. In the design of the original Case 1, 86.5 percent of the coal sulfur is removed in the gasifier. After the additional removal in the zinc ferrite reactors, the total sulfur removal in the gasification island is 99.4 percent.

The zinc ferrite is regenerated through oxidation of the zinc and iron sulfides with air. The regeneration gas (17) is recycled to the gasifier and the sulfur dioxide in the gas is captured by the limestone in the gasifier bed. The major part of the desulfurized product gas (84) enters the exit-gas cooler where it is cooled to a temperature of 1,000°F, which represents the maximum valve temperature for fuel-supply to the gas turbine. A small portion of the clean product gas (20) is cooled in the recycle gas cooler, compressed, and recycled back to the gasifier (42) and the gas filter (15).

The mixture of spent (sulfided) limestone, ash, and fines (22) is prepared for disposal in the fluidized-bed sulfator. This system is used to oxidize the calcium sulfide to calcium sulfate, a chemical compound similar to gypsum, which can be readily disposed of in a dry landfill. The calcium sulfide oxidation is highly exothermic. At temperatures below 1,600°F, little

sulfur dioxide is formed. During this process, any residual carbon remaining in the fines is combusted. The heat is recovered by in-bed heat exchanger tubes that keep the bed temperature less than 1,600°F without the need for high excess air. The gas from the combustor is cooled by an additional heat exchanger to approximately 1,400°F before being routed to the coal preparation section of the plant for coal drying.

Two General Electric MS7001F combustion gas turbines were assumed in the combined cycle. These advanced combustion turbines will have a firing temperature of about 2,300°F. Fuel gas (32) is introduced to the gas turbine combustor along with air (73) supplied by the compressor, which is driven by the gas turbine expander. The hot gas exiting the combustor (74) is supplied to the hot gas expander, which in turn drives the gas turbine generator.

The exhaust gas from each combustion turbine (75) enters a heat-recovery steam generator that provides steam generation and superheating of high-pressure (HP) and intermediate-pressure (IP) steam, reheating of IP steam, and feedwater preheating. The combined-cycle steam turbine consists of a high-pressure, intermediate-pressure, and low-pressure sections. The HP section accepts the 1,500 psia/1,000°F steam (101) from the two HRSGs. The exhaust steam (104) from the HP turbine is reheated to 1,000°F by the HRSGs and returns to the IP turbine (105). The IP exhaust steam (141) is then routed to the LP turbine from which it is condensed at a design backpressure of 3.5" Hg.

Condensate from the condenser (118) enters two vertical motor driven condensate pumps and subsequently passes through the gland seal condenser. Steam for this heating is provided by the steam seal regulator (SSR). Subsequently, the condensate (121) is heated in the low-pressure feedwater heater (FWH2) before it enters (122) the two deaerators, which are an integral part of each HRSG. Finally, the electric motor driven HRSG feed pumps supply the feedwater (124) to its HRSG feedwater inlets (125, 129) and to the gasification process (36, 46, 49).

## Cost Optimization

Application of the thermoeconomic optimization techniques resulted in the cost optimal design of Case 1CO1, which is characterized by the following design changes. The corresponding design options and values used in the original Case 1 are given in parenthesis.

1. The coal moisture at the gasifier inlet is 11.12 weight percent (4.98 weight percent).

2. The gasification temperature is 1,920°F (1,900°F).

3. The raw gas is cooled in the product gas cooler to $T_{12} = 1,168°F$ ($T_{12} = 1,252°F$).

4. The pressure of the HP steam generated in the gasification island is $P_{16} = 2,055$ psia ($P_{16} = 1,600$ psia).

5. The temperature and mass flow rate of the quench steam, which is mixed with the gas at the exit of the product gas

cooler, are $T_{39}$ = 663°F ($T_{39}$ = 500°F) and $\dot{m}_{39}$ = 401,759 lbm/hr ($\dot{m}_{39}$ = 389,707 lbm/hr). The ratio $\dot{m}_{39}/\dot{m}_1$ is smaller in Case 1CO1 than in the original Case 1. Note that the temperature and moisture content of the gas after quenching, stream 159, remained constant during the optimization studies.

6. The combustion gas exiting the sulfator at $T_{48}$ = 1,098°F is filtered, mixed with the gas turbine exhaust, and supplied to the HRSG. (In the original Case 1, the combustion gas exited the sulfator at $T_{48}$ = 1,400°F and was used for coal drying.) As a result of this change, more HP saturated steam is generated in the sulfation area in Case 1CO1 than in the original Case 1.

7. The boiler feedwater (BFW) preheater in the air booster compression area preheats low-pressure (high-pressure) feedwater. The heat rejection in the subsequent trim cooler is 0.86 MW (10.62 MW).

8. The recycle gas, stream 20, is extracted from the main gas stream at the outlet of the exit gas cooler (at the outlet of the zinc ferrite system).

9. The recycle gas cooler is used to preheat low-temperature (high-temperature) feedwater.

10. The steam cycle of Case 1CO1 does not generate or use any IP steam.

11. The HRSG of Case 1CO1 contains no steam drums. The heat supplied to the HRSG is used for superheating and reheating steam and for feedwater preheating but not for steam generation. HP steam generation in Case 1CO1 occurs exclusively in the gasification island.

12. The main steam pressure at the HP turbine inlet is about $P_{101}$ = 1,850psia ($P_{101}$ = 1,450 psia) and at the HP turbine outlet $P_{139}$ = 500 psia ($P_{139}$ = 350 psia). Thus, no extraction from the HP turbine is required in Case 1CO1. The blast steam and quench steam are taken at the HP turbine exhaust.

13. The steam required for the deaerator operation is extracted from the LP turbine in Case 1CO1, whereas it is generated in the FWH1 of the HRSG in the original Case 1. The deaerator operating pressure is 20 psia (24.5 psia).

14. No desuperheating of the quench steam is required in Case 1CO1. The design mass flow rate of stream 149 in Case 1CO1 is zero.

The following is an example of the usefulness of thermoeconomic evaluation techniques. The adiabatic mixing of streams 39 (steam) and 12 (gas exiting the product gas cooler) results in an extremely high exergy destruction rate of 17.6 MW (to be compared with the net power generation in the total plant of 458 MW) and a cost rate associated with the exergy destruction in the mixing of about 168 dollars per hour of plant operation at the nominal capacity. The design changes 1, 3, 5 and 12 have their origin in the realization of the consequences of the mixing of streams 39 and 12 on the overall plant efficiency and cost effectiveness. The exergy destruction in the adiabatic mixing process represents an "energy waste" that is easily detected in an exergy analysis but cannot be identified through an energy balance. Thus, if only first-law principles would have been used in the mixing process, a 100 percent efficiency and no associated costs would have been calculated. This means that no improvements related to this process would have been suggested.

The net heat rate of Case 1CO1 is 8,351 Btu/kWh (8,595 Btu/kWh in the original Case 1). The total capital requirement of the cost optimal Case 1CO1 is 649 (615 in the original Case 1) million 1990 dollars, or \$1,346/kW (\$1,342/kW). The thirty-year levelized cost of electricity at 85 percent capacity factor is 38.3 mills/kWh in Case 1CO1 and 39.0 mills/kWh in the original Case 1.

The difference in cost of electricity between Case 1CO1 and the original Case 1 results in savings of over 2.4 million constant (mid-1990) dollars per year of plant operation. Compared with the original Case 1, the thirty-year pre-tax present value of the cost savings in Case 1CO1 is 30.0 million constant mid-1990 dollars.

## CONCLUSIONS

Thermoeconomics provides extremely useful tools in the efforts to reduce the cost of the products of energy-conversion plants. It identifies the cost sources and the mechanisms of cost formation in these plants and suggests technical solutions for cost reduction. When first-law principles are used, some of these solutions cannot be developed or cannot be suggested with the same confidence (with respect to their cost effectiveness) as when thermoeconomic evaluation techniques are employed.

An exergy audit, when only fuel costs are considered, or a thermoeconomic audit, when fuel and capital investment costs must be taken into account simultaneously, significantly improves our understanding of the true performance of energy systems. There is little doubt that in the future these audits will replace the traditional energy audit. Appropriate computer software developed for this purpose will facilitate and simplify the required calculations.

## REFERENCES

1. Tsatsaronis, G. and Winhold, M., "Thermoeconomic Analysis of Power Plants," EPRI AP-3651, RP2029-8, Final Report, Electric Power Research Institute, Palo Alto, CA, August 1984.

2. Tsatsaronis, G. and Winhold, M., "Exergoeconomic Analysis and Evaluation of Energy Conversion Plants. Part II – Analysis of a Coal-Fired Steam Plant," Energy – The International Journal 10 (1985) No. 1, pp. 81-94.

3. Tsatsaronis, G., Winhold, M. and Stojanoff, C. G., "Thermoeconomic Analysis of Gasification-Combined-Cycle Power Plants," EPRI AP-4734, RP2029-8, Final Report, Electric Power Research Institute, Palo Alto, CA, August 1986, 172 pp.

4.  Tsatsaronis, G. and Valero, A., "Thermodynamics Meets Economics," Mechanical Engineering, August 1989, pp. 84-86.

5.  Tsatsaronis, G., Lin, L., Pisa, J. and Tawfik, T., "Thermoeconomic Design Optimization of a KRW-Based IGCC Power Plant," Final Report prepared for the U.S. Department of Energy, DOE Contract No. DE-FC21-89MC26019, November 1991.

6.  Tsatsaronis, G. and Pisa, J., "Exergoeconomic Evaluation of Energy Systems – The CGAM Problem," in Thermoeconomic Analysis of Energy Systems (A. Valero, G. Tsatsaronis and M. A. Lozano, editors), ASME, New York, 1992.

7.  Southern Company Services, "Assessment of Coal Gasification/Hot-gas cleanup Based Advanced Gas Turbine Systems," Final Report prepared for the U.S. Department of Energy, Morgantown Energy Technology Center, Contract No. DE-FC21-89MC26019, December 1990.

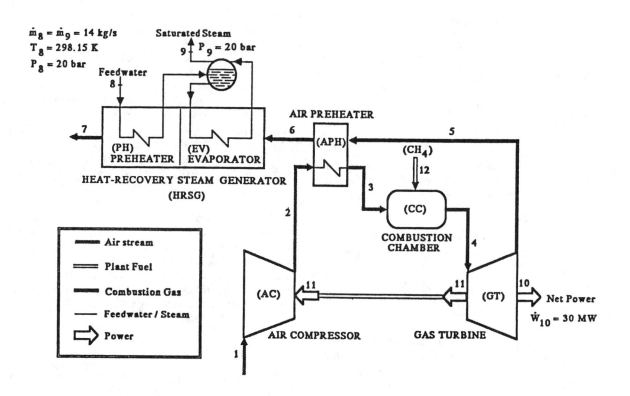

Figure 1.  Flow Diagram of the Cogeneration System

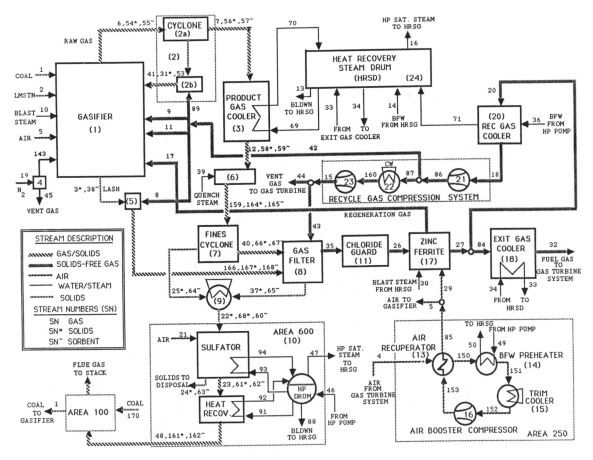

Figure 2. Flow Diagram of the Gasification Island in the Original Case 1

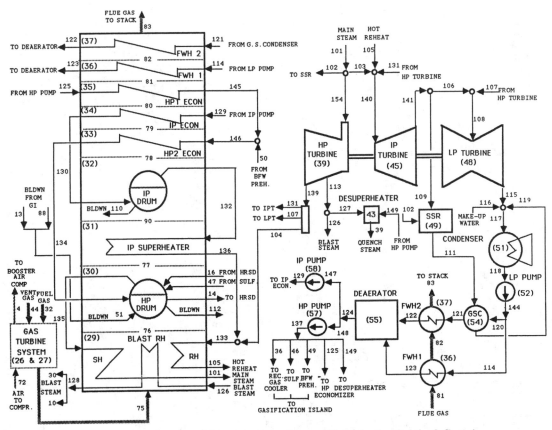

Figure 3. Flow Diagram of the Power Island in the Original Case 1

# Chapter 64

# Control of Energy Use via Computerized Facility Energy Management Systems in a Heavy Industrial Plant

S.S. Bagstad

This presentation describes an effort to implement a modern energy data collection, analysis, and control system into ALCOA's Cleveland Works, a forging operation with much equipment originally dating from the World War II era.

## BACKGROUND

### The facility/operation

The complexity of energy control by any method is enormous at Cleveland Works due to the job shop nature of the operation. Very little equipment operates in a continuous production-line mode. Large numbers of individual operations are spread throughout the Works. Operations performed change on a daily and sometimes hourly basis. Production items flow from one production center to another with constantly varying schedules.

Although many of the physical facilities date back to the 1940's, there is often little resemblance inside to original facility layout. Over the years, equipment has been added, removed, and extensively modified and updated. One major change that effected Works energy use was the closure of the Permanent Mold Casting Division in 1988. This Division accounted for roughly ten percent of overall energy use at Cleveland Works. Operations are now subdivided into three (3) major plant areas, although there are regular overlaps of operations.

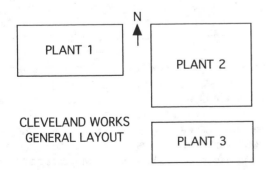

CLEVELAND WORKS
GENERAL LAYOUT

Most utilities enter the plant from the North along Harvard Avenue. Generally Plants 2 & 3 utilities are combined. Electric service has one main meter, with internal subdivision to three submeters for

Plant 1 and two submeters for Plants 2 & 3. Gas has one meter for Plant 1 and one for Plants 2 & 3, although a separate Plant 3 meter is being pursued. Water has two submeters each for Plant 1 and Plants 2 & 3. Steam(coal) has one meter for Plant 1 and one meter for Plants 2 & 3. Some individual pieces of equipment have energy-monitoring meters.

## ENERGY USE

Major energy uses at Cleveland Works include electricity, natural gas, water, and coal. Minor or secondary uses include compressed air, steam, fuel oil, diesel, propane, and gasoline. Over the years, there have been several occasions of increased emphasis on reducing energy use, most recently in 1986-87. The following chart shows major utility use for the last ten (10) years.

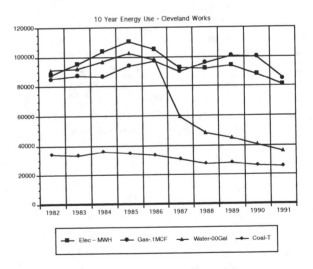

Note that some unusual units have been used to allow scaling of all major utilities to fit on the same chart. The 1986-87 reduction efforts do show clearly. Despite efforts to establish one, there has been no solid link shown between production levels and energy use.

## 1992 ENERGY DIRECTIONS

### Comparison to TQC, Safety

Cleveland Works uses specialized people to assist with plantwide efforts areas such as Total Quality Control and Safety. The intent is not that these groups are responsible for performance in these areas, but rather that they are resources to help and guide the operating groups within the Works to improvement. The Energy group formed at the start of 1992 has the same sort of focus.

Energy Vision

The Energy Vision adopted for Cleveland Works has four (4) points:

1. All use will be controlled. No energy consuming equipment will be allowed to run continuously.

2. All use will be needed. At its simplest, this means equipment will be turned on, used, then turned off.

3. The best energy form will be used. This means, for example, that steam will not be used for heating where gas is more appropriate.

4. Useful energy information will be readily available. Everyone with the need will have ready access to "user friendly" energy information.

Continuous Improvement

Developments beginning in 1991 led into increased emphasis on energy use reductions for 1992 and beyond. A broad-based attack on a large number of identified opportunities is now underway toward an ambitious reduction of ten (10) percent in 1992 use. In some areas, major changes will occur. One of the major changes identified for implementation is a Facility Energy Management System (FEMS).

FEMS

History-EMS

Early efforts at energy control led to installation in 1985 of a demand monitoring system (EMS) that has seen limited success in reducing electrical peak demands. Since initial installation, it was tried and rejected on a variety of production equipment; eventually it was installed on roughly 80 loads that had insufficient power use to significantly affect demand. Since that time, it has had sporadic success through eventual connection of four (4) significant process loads.

Some of the problems related to the existing system

are not its own. There has been a natural reluctance to "cause pain" in production areas, particularly given the difficulty of verifying the correctness of a given choice of operating method. Other difficulties that have proven uncorrectable with the existing system include lack of data storage/analysis ability, limited information sharing, and insufficient monitoring scope.

The Answer?

Earlier in 1992, a conclusion was reached that we were unable to make accurate operating decisions concerning energy use without a better system. We realized that we use enormous amounts of energy in the forms of electricity, natural gas, water, and coal; yet our knowledge of where and how this energy is being used is very limited.

Most energy control efforts to this point have focused on general practices and specific studies of particular equipment of interest at a given time. While this can be effective in answering specific questions, it does not lend itself well to the need for information to readily evaluate continuous improvement possibilities. Manual efforts to collect energy information are necessarily limited, and often data collection may require enough trouble to make it seem not worth the struggle.

In a number of cases, we have been confused during high electric use periods, hearing the production departments comments that "we're running the same equipment as we did yesterday, so it can't be our fault."

The lack of energy information/control, it should be noted, is not necessarily due to lack of equipment and/or instrumentation. As is surely the case with many heavy industrial plants, we have process controls everywhere; the "energy" problem is that they concern themselves only with the specific equipment controlled. Their orientation is normally toward control of a process variable such as temperature or pressure, rather than to efficient use of gas or electricity needed to achieve a given setpoint of that variable.

Although initially the new FEMS will have a conservative monitoring/advising role rather than automatically reducing use by itself; this is expected to change as we gain experience with its use. The system will include all major plantwide utility meters including electric, gas, water, steam, and compressed air. Selected high energy use equipment will also be included, with data acquisition and control both by the individual item as well as summed by production complex and plant area.

The Benefits

There are four (4) major benefits identified in this initial phase of the FEMS installation.

1. Automatically track power use in production complexes to identify high energy jobs/equipment to allow energy to become part of planning. This is expected to help avoid high electrical peak demands.

2. Automatically initiate "smart" peak demand alerting in areas contributing to high demands. Trend use information immediately available to allow quick decision. Provide feedback both for shutdown/setback and restart. This is expected to help react intelligently when in high electrical use periods.

3. Selectively alert for operating conditions on gas-burning equipment that may suggest possible energy use reduction such as temperature setback.

4. Generally at all monitored uses, alert to unusual conditions such as abnormally high energy use that will help reduce waste.

PROGRESS/PLANS

As this paper is written, we are nearing award of a system contract. As specifications and our needs were developed, we were helped by a variety of means. Engineer's Digest had a recent summary of energy management software[1]. Plant Engineering had a reference article more related to electrical control[2]. Finally, a general energy management system feature article appeared in Heating/Piping/Air Conditioning[3]. Contacts within our own company were helpful, as were contacts made both through vendors and independently, through groups such as our Ohio Manufacturer's Association. All of these are essential to best fit any new system into what you are trying to accomplish.

Some of the factors identified as essential to our success are speed, ease of use, expandability, flexibility, and ability to work with existing plant systems. One of the more unusual requirements is ability to interface with our voice paging system as one method of alerting plant people to unusual energy use conditions requiring prompt attention.

By the time of the WEEC, we will have the FEMS in at least limited use, and have examples of what it is doing and will do for us. We already have envisioned two added expansion phases for each of the following years to help reach our goals. These will include addition of remaining large individual energy users, additional submetering, and more "traditional" energy

management items such as HVAC and an expanded role in our boiler house. Assumption of the role of our existing EMS will also be needed. Finally, other areas such as lighting, fire, security, and other general plant functions will be considered.

Our basic bottom line is that you can only control what you can measure, and that you must have useful data to make informed decisions. Our new FEMS will give us these capabilities.

References

[1]Engineer's Digest, March 1992, p. 38.

[2]Ed Palko, Interactive Electric Power Management Systems, Plant Engineering, April 9, 1992, p. 61-64.

[3]Ron Anderson, Gems To Look For In EMCS, Heating/Piping/Air Conditioning, November 1991, p. 47-52.

# Chapter 65
# Energy Education - A Multidisciplinary Approach

H.G. Nezhad

## INTRODUCTION

One of the major global issues of the 1990s will be how to best use our scarce energy resources while maintaining a high economic growth rate and improving environmental quality. In fact, the survival of our civilization depends very much on the wise use of conventional energy sources and the development of renewable resources.

Although securing our future energy needs requires joint efforts by governments, the public, and industry, the most crucial role is that of energy educators who are needed to train manpower and educate the public. In the past, education has played mainly a reactive role in crisis situations. We must become proactive now. I strongly believe that through appropriate energy education at all levels of our society, we can prevent future energy and environmental crisis and at the same time provide our people with a safe environment and an adequate supply of energy.

## ENERGY EDUCATION

### Existing Energy Programs

Existing programs in educational institutions can be divided into three main categories:

1. Research centers involved in multidisciplinary energy research;

2. Informal programs consisting of energy-related courses at the undergraduate and graduate levels offered through different departments; also, workshops, seminars, conferences, etc.;

3. Formal degree programs.

Formal degree programs can be divided into four categories:

1. Two-year programs offered by community colleges and technical schools which are training energy technicians;

2. Engineering-oriented programs;

3. Policy-oriented programs; and

4. Business/management-oriented programs.

### Energy Management Education

Management of energy resources requires a new breed of professionals who have a clear understanding of the technological, economic, environmental, and sociopolitical aspects of energy. This exciting field also calls for technically competent marketers who can promote advanced technologies for energy efficiency improvements and utilization of renewable energy resources.

According to the *AMA Management Handbook*, "A successful energy management program involves much more than simply turning off lights and adding insulation. Ideally, it should be a total program that involves every area of the business-research, process development, manufacturing, marketing, and financial and strategic planning. It must also reach outside the company, to include suppliers, customers, various government and legislative agencies and the general public."

A program as complicated as this demands an unusual mix of skills from its managers, ranging from purely technical expertise to a flair for marketing and salesmanship.

### The Energy Management Program at Moorhead State University

The Energy Management Program at Moorhead State University (MSU) is an interdisciplinary program. In addition to studying the liberal arts and improving their communication skills, the energy management majors learn about the scientific, technological and managerial aspects of energy management.

MSU's Energy Management Program offers a B.S. degree in Energy Management with a concentration in an area of student's choice. The program consists of three major components as shown in figure 1.

FIGURE 1

A MACRO VIEW OF THE ENERGY MANAGEMENT
CURRICULUM AT MSU

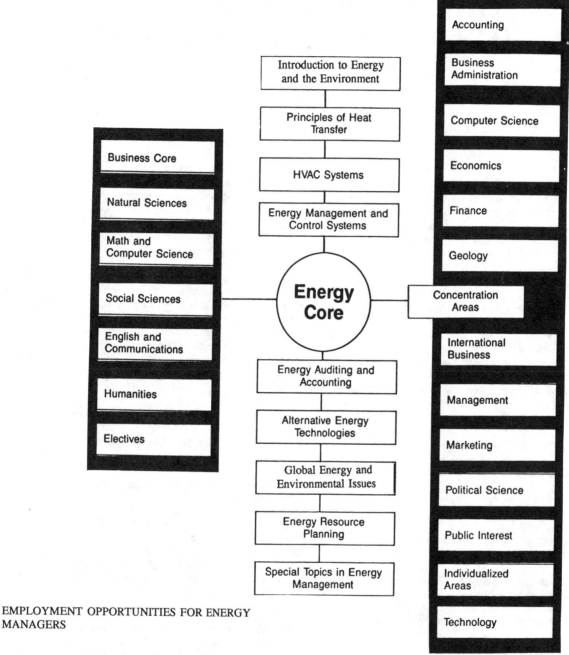

EMPLOYMENT OPPORTUNITIES FOR ENERGY
MANAGERS

MSU's Energy Management Program is such an
interdisciplinary program needed for the 1990s and beyond.
The graduates of this program, who are among the pioneers
in this field, are in demand by:

    o.    Electric utility companies;
    o.    Manufacturing and distributing companies
        involved
        in the production and marketing of energy
        products;
    o.    Energy consulting firms;
    o.    Government agencies dealing with energy and
        environmental programs.

A survey conducted by Accountemps, a personnel service in
California, claims that:

"U.S. businesses will be looking for more well-rounded
college graduates in the next decade.  This survey indicates
that while liberal arts was big in the 1960s, business
administration was big in the 1970s, and computer science
was big in the 1980s, all three will be equally important to
success in the 1990s and beyond.  Having an awareness of a
broad range of disciplines will help workers relate better to
sweeping changes in technology, politics, and global
economics."

Some of the positions held by professionals with similar training include:

- o. Energy Services Specialist;
- o. Sales Engineer;
- o. Energy Auditor;
- o. Financial Analyst;
- o. Fuel Accountant;
- o. Rate Analyst;
- o. Customer Representative;
- o. Marketing Analyst;
- o. Energy Conservation Specialist;

I conducted an employment-needs survey in 1990 (Table 1). According to this survey, most of the positions available were in marketing (about 26%) followed by energy management system design/installation/operation (13%)

## TABLE 1
## EMPLOYMENT - NEEDS SURVEY

| AREAS OF EMPLOYMENT | TOTAL EMPLOYMENT OF RESPONDANTS | PERCENT OF TOTAL |
|---|---|---|
| Energy Auditing | 605 | 7 |
| Marketing | 2250 | 25.9 |
| Socioeconomic Impact Analysis | 179 | 2.1 |
| Alternative Source Analysis | 285 | 3.3 |
| Energy Management Systems Design/Installation/ Operation | 1169 | 13.5 |
| Energy Use, Procurement and/or Supply Analysis | 784 | 9 |
| Energy Accounting | 599 | 6.9 |
| Utility Rate Analysis | 299 | 3.4 |
| Environmental Impact Analysis | 148 | 1.7 |
| Energy Policy Analysis | 252 | 2.9 |
| Energy Resource Planning | 347 | 4 |
| Other Areas | 1290 | 14.8 |
| TOTAL ENERGY-RELATED POSITIONS | 8,688 | 100% |
| TOTAL EMPLOYMENT IN ALL AREAS | 220,287 | |

Number Surveyed: 200
Number Reponded: 55

# Chapter 66

# The Economics of Window Selection: An Incremental Approach

W.T. Dixon

The options available to Energy Service Companies when improving the energy performance of an existing building are often driven by short-term payback cycles. The value of a measure is based on how quickly it pays for itself. The more quickly the energy savings created by the measure exceed the cost of purchasing and installing the measure, the more comfortable the engineer feels recommending that improvement. This is not to say that this is always the logic applied, but it seems to be the conventional wisdom in many design circles.

In the best cases, the short-term approach will quickly retire the debts associated with a particular retrofit and provide a dependable, albeit limited net savings stream for the property owner. The engineer has thus successfully "cream-skimmed" the most easily obtained energy savings for his client. The problem with this short-term approach is that it automatically eliminates other conservation measures which, over longer time horizons, could add far more value for the customer. The installation of new, extremely energy efficient replacement windows is a case in point.

During preliminary discussions with our clients, (typically Public Housing Authorities or owners of subsidized, multi-family housing), the conversation eventually turns to the issue of replacement windows. The perception by many of the people we talk to is that new windows are a luxury. The decision to install new windows is driven by maintenance costs and, in some cases, resident complaints over operability or draftiness associated with the existing windows. Typically the windows are not handled as part of the mainstream energy conservation program. If the client has already installed new windows, he probably based his selection on the low bidder of a unit that has marginal thermal performance. Every property has a budget and compromises must often be made to meet budgets. The purchaser may have not gotten the Cadillac of windows, but at least he got a good deal on the window that he did buy. His maintenance problems have been solved for the near term and resident complaints have gone down, for now.

The client who has not yet installed new windows wants to go a similar route. He wants new windows, but wants to place greater emphasis on "real" energy conservation measures, such as insulation and control systems. Again, the basis of the client's perception is the faster payback schedule of these types of measures. Table 1 gives an actual example of a group of conservation measures that might be typical for a multifamily building.

This simple example shows the individual payback period for each improvement is listed. The overall payback period is 7 years. Notice that window replacement is not part of this solution to improve the building's thermal performance. Intuition tells us that the costs of putting in new windows cannot be justified on the basis of energy savings alone. But what type of windows would one purchase if there was a need for replacement windows as part of an overall design solution?

Table 2 shows a listing of some of the most common window types with their U values and an estimate of a range of their total installed costs [1]. The table includes wood and aluminum windows. It could be expanded to included other frame materials, but these two are what we prefer to specify. The basic window type assumed in this table is a 48" x 48" double hung window. Our firm often specifies double hung replacement windows because they give the resident more flexibility in controlling the air movement in their living space. The actual U values have been generated using Lawrence Berkeley Labs' WINDOW 4.0 program [1]. In all cases, the windows with low-e coatings are configured for a climate with a large number of degree days, such as Boston's.C.

Table 2 also shows costs per installed square foot. These cost ranges demonstrate a basic economic fact: in general, one must pay more for a window if one wants greater thermal performance.

Given the spectrum of windows to chose from, what can the energy engineer expect in terms of "real world" energy savings from a particular unit? More importantly, does it make sense for the specifier to consider one of the high tech, higher priced models? How about an intermediately priced model? An example of an actual project where above average (in terms of thermal performance) windows were installed will help to answer these questions.

Table 3 lists the basic "before" and "after" features of a high-rise building in Cambridge, Massachusetts that received an energy retrofit. The windows specified for this building were wood windows with double glazed, low-e glass. The bulk of the dollar cost savings (approximately 60%) were due to the conversion of the building from electric heat and domestic hot water to a central, gas-fired, heating and domestic hot water system. However, I have concluded that the Btu energy savings of some 20% are due primarily to the new windows. (The energy savings for this building were determined from actual utility bills from before and after the thermostat settings within the apartments without compromising resident comfort.

Figure 1 portrays balance point values that occur in a typical apartment at the Cambridge site. One set of points shows how the balance point goes down without any change to the apartment thermostat setting. The second set of points demonstrates the more dramatic reduction of the balance point if the apartment thermostat is turned down. As the graph demonstrates, the lower the u value, the more the balance point can be lowered.

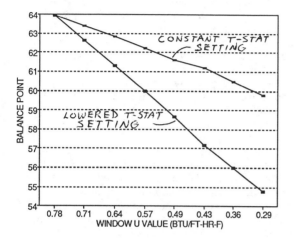

FIGURE 1. BALANCE POINT AS A FUNCTION OF U VALUE

The main consequence of the reduced balance point can be seen in Figure 2. The graph demonstrates that the number of degree days for the building also are reduced more quickly if the apartment thermostats are set lower. Once again, by using windows with lower u values, this effect is magnified. The main point is that if degree days are treated as a direct measure of energy consumption, this "comfort effect" of the reduced apartment thermostats is significant. At Inman Square Apartments, the radiators are equipped with new, non-electric zone valves that have an upper limit of 75 degrees Fahrenheit. The average apartment temperature prior to the retrofit was 79 degrees Fahrenheit. Of the 20% savings attributed to the windows (u value of .43 Btu/ft-hr-F), four fifths of this results from the lower thermostat settings. The tighter, more efficient windows makes this possible. Residents have adjusted to the new system and many speak highly of its consistent performance.

In addition to the long term savings achievable with energy efficient windows, there are other one-time cost savings that can be captured if widows are part of the retrofit package. The more energy efficient the windows installed in a building, the lower will be the building's hourly heat loss. This in turn means that heating distribution system can be downsized from the start if coupled with high performance windows. If a new hydronic heating system is to be installed, radiator lengths can be shortened and many of the pipe diameters can be reduced. This translates into substantial savings in construction costs. Table 4 shows how the Inman

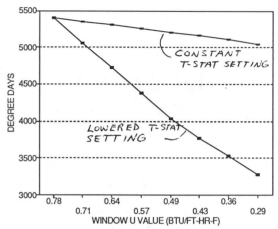

FIGURE 2. DEGREE DAYS AS A FUNCTION OF U VALUE

Square budget was adjusted through the specification of high performance wood windows.

The table demonstrates how one might further improve on the performance of "Case 1" by purchasing higher performance windows, the greater cost of which will be partially off-set by the downsizing of the new heating distribution system. "Case 2" is the actual budget for the project. "Case 3" was our original budget which included wood windows with an u value of .29. Unfortunately, the supplier had difficulty meeting the financial requirements of the project, and we were forced to go with a wood window with a u value of .43.

Based upon the experience of Inman Square, what basic guidelines do we use to select a new window given the wide spectrum of product performance? Here are some suggestions:

Wood, Aluminum, or Vinyl

The material a window is made from is, in a rough sense, a fair determinate of its thermal. However referring to Table 2, one can see that there is actually an overlap of u values between aluminum and wood. One should not always assume that a wood window will outperform an aluminum window. Vinyl windows (not covered herein) should also be compared with wood and aluminum. If the client wants wood windows, as in the case of Inman Square, then the choice is simplified. Given the narrow range of marginal paybacks on high performance wood windows (Table 2), it makes sense to get the highest performing window that the project can afford.

Package Solutions

Consider the thermally efficient window upgrade as part of a group of improvements. Table 2 reminds us that a wood window with a u value of .41 or less has a 50 year plus marginal payback. However, when combined with other measures that have much shorter simple payback periods, the net result can be an overall payback period of 20 years or less. Table 5 shows an example of this.

| MEASURES | ESTIMATED TOTAL COST | FUEL | ANNUAL PROJECTED SAVINGS | SIMPLE PAYBACK |
|---|---|---|---|---|
| BOILER ROOM | $60,948 | GAS | $12,060 | 5.1 |
| THERMOSTATS | $37,710 | GAS | $2,345 | 16.1 |
| VENTILATION | $16,287 | GAS | $2,010 | 8.1 |
| TOTAL | $114,945 | | $16,415 | 7.0 |

TABLE 1. SAMPLE CONSERVATION MEASURES

| DEGREE DAYS: | 5,400 | PER YEAR[2] |
|---|---|---|
| EXIST. U: | 0.79 | BTU/(SQFT-HR-F) |
| AVG GAS $: | 0.77 | PER THERM |
| HT. SYS. EFFICIENCY: | 100% | |

| FOR 4' X 4' DOUBLE HUNG WINDOW | U VALUE BTU/SQFT /HR/F [1] | AVG COST [2] $/SQ-FT | NET ENERGY SAVINGS PER YEAR THERMS/SQF | NET COST SAVINGS PER YEAR $/SQFT | AVG SIMPLE PAY-BACK YEARS | AVG PAY-BACK ON MARGIN OF ADD COST YEARS |
|---|---|---|---|---|---|---|
| AL,DG (NO THERMAL BREAK) | 0.78 | 8.50 | 0.013 | 0.01 | ——— | ——— |
| AL,DG | 0.63 | 17.50 | 0.207 | 0.16 | 110 | ——— |
| AL,DG,LOWE | 0.56 | 18.50 | 0.298 | 0.23 | 81 | 4 |
| WD,DG | 0.49 | 31.50 | 0.389 | 0.30 | 105 | 47 |
| AL,DG,HTMIRR | 0.46 | 23.00 | 0.428 | 0.33 | 70 | 17 |
| WD,DG,LOWE | 0.43 | 36.50 | 0.467 | 0.36 | 102 | 53 |
| WD,DG,LOWE,ARG | 0.41 | 37.00 | 0.492 | 0.38 | 98 | 51 |
| WD,DG,HTMIRR,ARG | 0.31 | 41.00 | 0.622 | 0.48 | 86 | 49 |
| WD,DG,SUPER8 | 0.29 | 49.00 | 0.648 | 0.50 | 98 | 63 |

AL= ALUMINUM

DG= DOUBLE GLAZED

LOWE= LOW-E COAT ON ONE SURFACE

WD= WOOD

ARG= ARGON-FILLED GLAZ. SPACE

HTMIRR= ONE LAYER OF MYLAR W/ LOW-E COATING

SUPER8= TWO LAYERS OF MYLAR W/ LOW-E COATING

TABLE 2. LIST OF VARIOUS WINDOW TYPES

| ITEM | BEFORE | AFTER |
|---|---|---|
| HEATING | * BASEBOARD * ELECTRIC | * CENTRAL * GAS, HYDRO |
| DHW | * INDIVIDUAL * ELECTRIC | * CENTRAL * GAS FIRED |
| VENTILATION | * ROOF FANS * 24 HRS/DAY | * ONLY WHEN * T> 30 DEG |
| WINDOWS | * ALUMINUM, * NO THERMAL * BREAK | * WOOD, * LOW-E * ARGON |

TABLE 3. INMAN SQUARE APARTMENTS BEFORE AND AFTER RETROFIT

renovation.) At this point, several key assumptions need to be spelled out. They are as follows:

1. The electric heat with an efficiency of 100% was replaced by a pair of gas-fired boilers with an estimated efficiency of 85%.

2. The original individual electric hot water heaters in the apartments were a significant source of internal gains due to stand-by losses.

3. The energy savings resulting from the switch to the new central DHW system are not significant.

4. The maximum annual energy savings that are produced as a result of the controls on the eleven roof exhaust fans is 5%. However, because of the very drafty nature of this building, these savings are somewhat negated. To isolate and maximize the possible energy savings of the windows, the savings due to these controls are considered negligible. The author recognizes that the precise determination of the air flow patterns in a building such as this one both before and after a retrofit is a very complex problem, and will not be attempted herein.

Based upon the window types listed in Table 2, the window used on this project, at $37.00 per square foot, was almost twice as expensive to purchase and install as the basic aluminum window with a thermally broken frame. The simple payback on the unit is over ninety years. However, this simple payback is actually less than the 110 years of the basic aluminum window with simple double glazing and no low-e coating.

The installation of windows at this building helps to reduce energy consumption in three ways. The first is through their greater resistance to conductive heat loss. The combination of wood frames and low-e glass are important design features. The other two ways are less obvious. The window's thermal efficiency means higher interior glass surface temperatures. Persons sitting near the window experience reduced body heat loss via radiation. Based on independent laboratory tests of a typical window model [3], the new windows are also tighter i.e. more resistant to air infiltration than windows similar in make to the old, less efficient windows. The combination of these subtle effects increases resident comfort. Based upon my experience, this increased comfort makes it possible to reduce

| BUDGET ITEM | CASE 1 | CASE 2 | CASE 3 |
|---|---|---|---|
| CARPENTRY | $33,556 | $33,556 | $33,556 |
| WINDOWS | $236,500 | $358,728 | $451,000 |
| DRYWALL | $67,719 | $67,719 | $67,719 |
| SPRINKLERS | $216,741 | $216,741 | $216,741 |
| BOILERS | $123,744 | $123,744 | $123,744 |
| RADIATORS/PIPING | $194,629 | $181,005 | $168,334 |
| ELECTRICAL | $55,450 | $55,450 | $55,450 |
| TOTAL | $928,339 | $1,036,943 | $1,116,544 |
| PERCENTAGE OF BASE COST | 100.0% | 111.7% | 120.3% |

TABLE 4. CONSTRUCTION BUDGET COMPARISONS FOR DIFFERENT WINDOWS

| MEASURES | ESTIMATED TOTAL COST | FUEL | ANNUAL PROJECTED SAVINGS | SIMPLE PAYBACK |
|---|---|---|---|---|
| WINDOWS | $300,000 | ELECTRIC | $6,000 | 50.0 |
| BOILER ROOM | $60,948 | GAS | $12,060 | 5.1 |
| THERMOSTATS | $37,710 | GAS | $2,345 | 16.1 |
| VENTILATION | $16,287 | GAS | $2,010 | 8.1 |
| TOTAL | $414,945 | | $22,415 | 18.5 |

TABLE 5. SIMPLE PAYBACK SCHEDULE FOR RETROFIT INCLUDING WINDOWS

## Keep Abreast of Window Technology

New developments in window technology are happening all the time. As these technologies become more commonplace, their prices come down. This means that conservation measures involving energy efficient windows will make even more economic sense in the months and years ahead. This shift in the economics of windows will help to further enforce the perception that highly efficient windows can be a key part of a complete energy retrofit.

REFERENCES

1.  "Window 4.0," March 1992, Windows and Daylighting Group, Lawrence Berkeley Laboratory.

2.  Bids solicited by Citizens Conservation Corporation between July 1990 and July 1991.

3.  Laboratory tests conducted by laboratories recognized by the American Architectural Manufacturer's Association.

4.  Solar Architecture: The Direct Gain Approach, Timothy E. Johnson, 1981, McGraw-Hill Book Company.

Special thanks to John Snell and Bill Bartovics for their guidance on this paper.

Chapter 67

# Optimization of a Dual-Fuel Heating System Utilizing an EMS to Maintain Persistence of Measures

J.S. Wolpert, S.B. Wolpert, G. Martin

## ABSTRACT

An older small office building was subjected to a program substituting gas for electric heat to reduce energy cost and improve comfort. This program was carried out on a trial basis for approximately one year and was permanently instituted, with the installation of an energy management system (EMS) the following year.

This paper will present a description of the facility, its usage patterns, and the measures taken to introduce the fuel-switching program. The impacts on energy usage and cost as well as comfort will also be reported.

This program was initiated by a preliminary audit of the facility conducted by the service contractor in conjunction with the area gas wholesaler. This combination of familiarity with the specific building (the service organization) and broad experience into heating strategies (the utility) resulted in postulating an innovative plan of action.

During the audit it was observed that the heating set points for the gas-fired equipment was kept fairly low. This was the result of the desire to keep the cooling set point low and the use of auto-changeover thermostats. The result of this was that the system utilized the gas heat to come up to 68-70° with the majority of the zones then relying on their electric heat to bring temperatures into the 73-75° range. In addition to impacting energy costs, this approach generated numerous comfort complaints. As a further electric penalty, the low cooling set point resulted in a heavy reliance on electric heat (reheat) all summer.

The basis of the proposed strategy was to reduce the heavy usage of electric heat by making the building comfortable through reliance more heavily on gas heat. This was tested by raising the heating set points for the RTUs. The success of this approach, along with the comfort considerations and the desire for further savings, led to the installation of an EMS. This allowed further refinements of the control strategy, which are briefly described.

When completed, the fuel-switching led to an increase in annual gas costs of 125% with a corresponding decrease in electric cost of nearly 30% for an annual utility cost savings of over 19%.

## INTRODUCTION

While there are numerous reports of energy savings resulting from projects where existing equipment was replaced or significant amounts of new equipment was added, generally at significant capital cost. In contrast to this are potential energy savings available from operation and maintenance (O&M) measures which, if obtainable, would occur at fairly low capital cost. While documentation of these O&M savings has been much harder to find, there are good indications that this can be a significant resource (1-6).

This paper describes a fuel-switching project where simple operational changes lead to a re-distribution in energy usage patterns accompanied by a marked reduction in peak electrical demand and by a reduction in annual costs. While the specifics of this site may not occur that frequently, the approach of combining various field-experienced personnel can be broadly applied.

## BUILDING DESCRIPTION

The facility described in this project is a 12,750 square foot, three story municipal office building of brick and glass construction, and was 15 years old at the time of this work commenced (1986-88). The building has some insulation but is hampered in both comfort and energy use by large areas of single-pane glass. This glazing does have a mirrored film to help reduce solar gains.

This office building is located in Boulder, Colorado, a climate with an average of 5,460 heating (base 65°) and 745 cooling (base 65°) degree days. The ASHRAE 1% design conditions are 2°db, (winter) and 93°db, 64°wb(summer), and extreme weather conditions of -15° db/99° db are not uncommon. Note that the typically low humidity levels and cool nights makes for ideal economizer operation. In addition, located at 5,445 ft. above sea level in a climatic zone with low cloud cover, the solar gains can be quite significant.

This building is used exclusively for offices with the majority of occupancy from 8AM through 6PM, Monday through Friday. As discussed, there is some limited weekend use and, subsequent to this work, some extension of operating hours.

## MECHANICAL SYSTEM DESCRIPTION

The building's HVAC needs are served by a combination of constant volume packaged roof-top units (RTUs) with gas heat and additionally with electric resistance heat in the terminal boxes of each zone. The building is zoned such that the East RTU serves all three floors on the east side while the West RTU serves the west side. Each zone, controlled by a single thermostat, typically consists of a few offices and is served by branch ducting with an electric re-heat box.

The two constant volume, single fan, RTUs are each equipped with gas heat with high/low firing capability, dual R-22 hermetic compressors, and air-side economizers. As designed, these units were each controlled by a 24 vac thermostat with 2-stage heating/cooling capability and automatic changeover, located respectively in 3rd floor offices on the east and west sides. In addition, a building time clock was provided to cycle the units and the accompanying electric heat off during the unoccupied periods with an override timer (6-hour twist timer) for each half of the facility as well as a low-temperature thermostat to cycle the heating (both gas and electric) during colder weather.

In the area of miscellaneous loads, the domestic hot water is provided by one electric water heater, there is a single elevator in an external structure (discussed later), typical office equipment, fluorescent lighting estimated at about 2.5 watts/sq.ft., and a population density of 250-300 sq.ft./person.

## AUDIT RESULTS

During an audit of the facility in Aug. of '86 by the authors, the occupants of the building reported frequent discomfort. A large portion of these complaints appeared to arise from the use of a single thermostat to control each RTU. This problem appeared to be compounded by the tendency of the occupants of those two zones to set the cooling set point fairly low (72-73° F, undeterred by the locking cover) and thus force the heating low as well (as these were auto-changeover thermostats). While the electric reheat could partially compensate for this, the overall satisfaction level was low and a significant energy cost penalty was suspected. In addition, during the winter months this approach resulted in slow morning recovery and left the entire building too cold on days when the outdoor temperature was fairly low.

Additionally, it was observed that the HVAC time clocks were no longer in-service (having been bypassed to eliminate problems with the accompanying air-flow switches keeping the electric re-heat from operating) and that the AC condenser coils, while clean on the surface, were restricting air-flow and in need of high-pressure washing. The remaining system components were in fairly good condition having been subjected to a moderate planned maintenance program.

## PERFORMANCE MODIFICATIONS

Following the audit, it was decided to test a new control strategy that was expected to both improve comfort and reduce energy costs. The approach taken was to raise the heating/cooling set points on the thermostats controlling the two RTUs. Initially it was decided to demonstrate this strategy without any major capital investments and an appropriate plan was developed. In brief, this included setting the thermostats at approximately 75-76° cooling/73-74° heating, locking the thermostat covers once again, and having the service contractor check the settings on at least a weekly basis (of critical importance as reviewed in the Discussion section ).

The time clocks were also returned to service and the coils (condenser and evaporator) in both RTUs were cleaned in early spring. In addition, the facility was put on an aggressive preventative maintenance program to assist and maintain these improvements and to gain other benefits including extending equipment life.

## RESULTS

Monthly electric use for 1986-87, shown in Figure 1, illustrates the impact of the performance modifications described above. As shown, the monthly kWh drop significantly after Aug. '86 and remains low through much of '87. Note that the monthly patterns also show more seasonal variation (with the winter, non-AC months being lowered) and that Sep.-Dec. of '87 show some return to earlier, higher usage patterns.

Monthly electric demand for the same period is portrayed in Figure 2. Like the pattern for kWh (Fig. 1), there is a marked drop beginning in Aug. '86 and lasting for an equivalent period (approximately one year until Aug. '87), followed by a partial return to earlier patterns.

Monthly natural gas consumption (845 Btu/cf), shown in Figure 3, exhibit a similar but inverse relationship. As illustrated, gas consumption rises significantly starting in Sep. '86 and remains relatively high through Jul. '87. Like both electric energy and demand, this pattern returns to earlier (pre-Aug. '86) behavior in the last few months of '87.

The resulting annual energy performance for the two years, as shown Table 1, indicates a significant drop in total site consumption from 106 to 99 MBtu/sf-yr (10%). As expected from the monthly data, electric energy has dropped 25%, electric demand (12 month total) 1%, and natural gas has risen 28%.

| Energy | --- Annual Use --- | | Comparison | |
|--------|------|------|------|---|
| Type | 1986 | 1987 | % 87/86 | |
| | | | | |
| kWh | 252080 | 187840 | 75 | |
| kW | 907.2 | 898 | 99 | |
| CCF | 5789 | 7401 | 128 | |
| MBtu/sf-yr | 105.8 | 99.3 | 90 | |
| | | | | |
| TABLE 1. | 1986 vs. 1987 Annual Energy Performance | | | |

The economics of this are portrayed in Figure 4 with an overall savings in the range of $1,900 or 10%. As seen with the energy performance data, the cost of both electric energy and demand has dropped (25% and 1% respectively) while that of gas has risen (17%).

## DISCUSSION

The overall reduction in utility cost of 10% between the two years was certainly of value. Given the low first-cost of the measures used to achieve it, it is certainly cost-effective. As expected with fuel switching strategies, the drop in electric use was accompanied by an increase in gas consumption. Also as anticipated, the $453 increased gas cost was more than offset by the corresponding drop in electric cost of $1673.

An added, less anticipated benefit was the overall energy savings (27%) that resulted from this undertaking. We suspect this arose from the combined benefits of running the AC compressors less at higher set points, from the reduced power needs and run times resulting from clean condenser/evaporator coils, and certainly from the reduction in electric re-heat during AC season when the building was not being overcooled. Of interest is the observation that when demand rose again in Sep. and Dec. of '87 (Fig. 2), electric energy rose also (Fig. 1), suggesting that this was a month long effect (probably from re-setting the thermostats) as opposed to a short-term event that would have only impacted demand. Corroborating this is the low gas consumption (Fig. 3) during this period.

Of interest is the degradation of savings during the last months of '87. As noted in the Results section electric energy, demand, and gas consumption all returned towards their pre-project levels after Jul.-Aug. '87. In reviewing the service records, it became clear that this had arisen out of less attention being paid to the two RTU thermostats. This appears to have occurred due to two main reasons. First, after approximately one year of successfully "baby

sitting" the thermostats, and having demonstrated the value of the strategy, the service personnel were less than totally motivated in this area. Second, having demonstrated the value of this approach the decision had been made to install an energy management system (EMS) and from October on the service personnel were occupied with this task. Both of these occurrences serve to underscore the difficulty of maintaining savings that are based on operational procedures, (a problem that is beginning to draw more attention), of the value of having some form of energy accounting system to monitor these changes, and some procedure in place to take corrective action (7).

Since the implementation of this procedure spanned both years (approximately Aug. '86 - Jul. '87), the use of annual energy reductions is somewhat misleading, resulting in understating of the benefits of this approach. This of course can be somewhat corrected for by using more appropriate periods of comparison. When one uses Aug. '86 through Jul. '87 as the test period and compares this to the periods of Jan. - Jul. '86 plus Aug. - Dec. '87, the results are much more dramatic, as shown in Table 2.

| Energy | - Twelve Month Use - | | Comparison | |
|--------|------|------|------|---|
| Type | base | test | % test/base | |
| | | | | |
| kWh | 255600 | 184320 | 72 | |
| kW | 1057.8 | 747.4 | 71 | |
| CCF | 4056 | 9134 | 225 | |
| MBtu/sf-yr | 95.3 | 109.9 | 115 | |
| | | | | |
| TABLE 2. | Reference vs. Test Period | | | |

Using this more representative comparison period, the twelve month impact of this control strategy is significantly greater with kWh reduced 28%, annual kW reduced 29%, and natural gas increased 125%. Likewise, overall twelve month savings are increased to $3,811 (a cost reduction of 19%). Also of interest is the observed increase in site (as opposed to source) energy use of 15%.

As mentioned above, this project resulted in the installation of an EMS in late '87. This system allowed the above strategy to be adopted on a continuous basis and added a number of control logic improvements. A wide range of these improvements were added, with a few of the more significant listed as follows:

    o reliable performance of the time
    clock functions
    o using input from a number of zones
    (as opposed to two previously) to
    control the RTUs
    o duty-cycling the electric heat when
    it was enabled
    o preventing AC compressors (two per
    RTU) from operating when economizer was
    sufficient
    o locking out the electric heat when
    the 2nd-stage AC compressor was enabled

o using a winter AM warm-up routine that prevented electric heat operation and raised the gas heating set point 1° above normal to further minimize the need for re-heat when the system went to occupied mode.

The installation of these measures, problems encountered, and their impacts/persistence over the past four years, will be discussed in a later publication.

In conclusion, we feel this project successfully demonstrated the value of careful utilization of a dual-fuel system to both improve comfort and reduce operating costs. Like numerous other facilities, this site offered significant savings from operation and maintenance measures (at low capital cost). This work also underscores the challenge of maintaining savings from efficiency measures. While this particular case received an EMS to deal with some of these issues, a less expensive approach (such as programmable, locking thermostats) could have been effectively employed. Finally, although not discussed here, this approach is also well suited to providing improved indoor air quality (IAQ) through the use of increased outside air while improving operating costs. This lends support to the argument that increased ventilation does not have to lead to increased costs (5).

## ACKNOWLEDGEMENTS

We would like to thank the support and cooperation of the following city employees. Stan Zemler, Environmental Affairs Manager, for his recognition of the value of documenting performance and his support of the work. Dan Buckner, Maintenance Dept. Manager for his support on all phases of this work over the years. Mark Brunner, Maintenance Mechanic, for his cooperation and attention to the day-to-day building details.

## REFERENCES

1. Smilie, J., Louisiana Cooperative Extension Service 1984 Commercial AC Maintenance Study, reported in Contracting Business, 71-91, (1985).

2. Washington State Energy Office, Institutional Operations and Maintenance Energy Savings Demonstration Program, by Francis Sheridan, Linda Dethman, and Perter Spinney; WAOENG-86-07 (Olympia, 1986).

3. Haberl, J. and Vajda, J., 1988. "Use of Metered Data Analysis to Improve Building Operation and Maintenance: Early Results From Two Federal Complexes," Proc. of the ACEEE 1988 Summer Study, Volume 3, Washington, D.C.

4. Wolpert, J. and Robbins, C., "Improving An Older Building Through Field Audits And Operational Changes," Proc. of the Fifth Forum on Practical Applications of Building Energy Efficiency, Dallas, TX, May 13-14, 1991, pp. 88-100.

5. Ventresca, J. and Schrack, J., "Measured Indoor Air Quality and Energy Demand with Increased Fresh Air Ventilation," Proc. of the 14th World Energy Engineering Congress, Atlanta, GA, Oct. 23-25, 1991, pp. 549-558.

6. Wolpert, J. and Rozek, L., "Short Term Monitoring As A Design Evaluation Tool," Proc. of the HVAC Controls & Energy Conservation '92 Conference," Boston, MA, June 10-11, 1992.

7. Claridge, D., et. al., "Analysis of Texas Loanstar Data," Proc. of the Seventh Symposium on Improving Building Systems in Hot and Humid Climates , Fort Worth, TX, Oct. 9-10, 1990, pp. 53-60.

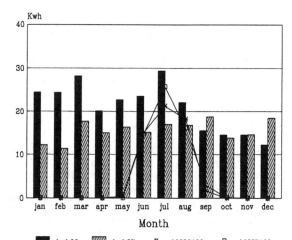

FIGURE 1: ELECTRIC USAGE

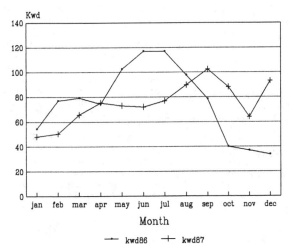

FIGURE 2: ELECTRIC DEMAND

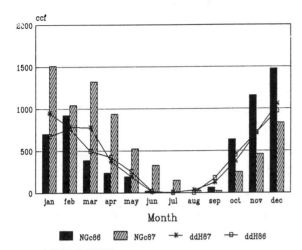

FIGURE 3: NATURAL GAS USAGE

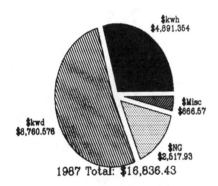

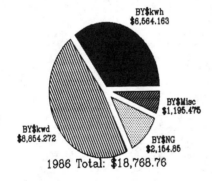

FIGURE 4: ANNUAL UTILITY COST PROFILE

# Chapter 68
# Load Factor Optimization of Fire Tube Boilers

V. Bortone

## ABSTRACT

This study was performed as a result of experiences acquired through participation in the Energy Analysis and Diagnostic Center at The University of Kansas(KU-EADC). The EADC program is sponsored by the U.S. Department of Energy and is managed by the University City Science Center in Philadelphia, Pennsylvania. The program funds 18 University-based centers across the country for the purpose of providing energy audits for small-and medium-sized industrial facilities at no cost to the client firm.

During industrial energy audits carried out by KU-EADC, a complete energy balance on boilers is performed. The data collected show that a significant percentage of boilers are oversized for the actual load. The dynamic efficiency of boilers is low when operating at low load factors.[1] Usually EADC recommends installing a smaller boiler as an energy conservation opportunity. Installing a smaller boiler is feasible only when the current load factor is below 20% with long annual operating times. Implementation of this recommendation is rare because of the high initial cost, long payback and low confidence in results.[2] A better approach is to consider the following recommendations according to each case, including those cases in which load factors of boilers are higher than 20%:

a.- Upgrading the burner control system to consider switching between on/off and high/low/off or modulating control.[3]

b.- Installing flue damper on/off control systems.

c.- Reducing the fireside heating surface by installing tube plugs. This will require to fine tuning the boiler burner to suit the new conditions.

d.- Reducing the size of the burner in combination with "c" can be justified when the load factor is low.

The objective of this study is to simulate retrofitting the boiler with the recommendations given above in accordance with the estimated load factor. The data for the simulation were obtained from KU-EADC files. Sixty audits were evaluated. Table 1 gives the data for the 19 boilers found in the 60 industrial plants during years 1988-1989.

The results of simulation give the expected energy and cost saving if retrofitting

Table 1. Historical Data

| BOILERS DATA YEARS 1988-1989[a] | | | | |
|---|---|---|---|---|
| CASE # | "HP"[b] | "HY"[c] | "LF"[d] | "GP"[e] |
| 1 | 100 | 1,760 | 0.78 | 3.57 |
| 2 | 63 | 6,000 | 0.04 | 3.42 |
| 3 | 188 | 6,000 | 0.34 | 3.31 |
| 4 | 630 | 8,760 | 0.42 | 3.42 |
| 5 | 15 | 6,000 | 0.33 | 4.02 |
| 6 | 60 | 2,976 | 0.90 | 3.50 |
| 7 | 325 | 7,200 | 0.46 | 2.71 |
| 8 | 60 | 2,460 | 0.96 | 3.65 |
| 9 | 400 | 6,000 | 0.66 | 3.44 |
| 10 | 150 | 6,048 | 0.94 | 2.95 |
| 11 | 1050 | 5,200 | 0.82 | 4.10 |
| 12 | 200 | 4,464 | 0.71 | 3.95 |
| 13 | 140 | 4,200 | 0.16 | 3.86 |
| 14 | 1,750 | 6,840 | 0.82 | 5.70 |
| 15 | 185 | 6,048 | 0.16 | 3.08 |
| 16 | 300 | 6,000 | 0.59 | 4.00 |
| 17 | 40 | 2,240 | 0.63 | 4.49 |
| 18 | 300 | 3,840 | 0.39 | 4.31 |
| 19 | 600 | 4,860 | 0.45 | 2.74 |

[a] Collected from 60 Energy Audits.
[b] "HP" Boiler Horse Power
[c] "HY" Yearly Hours of Operation
[d] "LF" Boiler Load Factor
[e] "GP" Natural Gas Price($/MMBtu)

had been implemented. The simulation results give better understanding to justify further research and development in this area of energy conservation opportunity.

## PROBLEM FORMULATION

The dynamic operating efficiency of fire tube boilers decreases as the load on the boiler is reduced below the rated load (dynamic efficiency represents the actual operating efficiency of a boiler as it cycles through the varying loads placed on it throughout the operating period). This decrease is due to the standby losses from the boiler (radiation and convection losses from the boiler surface and stack), purging losses, and cycling losses. Approximate reductions in boiler efficiency (dynamic) due to operation at less than rated load are given in Table 2. For simulation purposes, dynamic efficiency values are based on steady state efficiency of 80%.

A simulation model was developed utilizing a Lotus 1-2-3[4] spreadsheet with the @RISK add-in program.[5]

The annual energy savings, ES, to be realized from increasing the boiler efficiency to a fixed value of 80%, which is the maximum at rated loads between 80-90% (Table 2), can be estimated as follows:

$$ES = HP \times CC \times LF \times HY \times (1-CEF/0.80)$$

Where:

HP= rated boiler horse power, hp
CC= conversion constant, 33,480 Btu/hp
LF= current rated load factor, no units
HY= yearly hours of operation, no units
CEF= current boiler dynamic efficiency, no units

The historical data for boiler horse power "HP" were divided into five groups. This division is convenient to simplify the final analysis. The probability for each class was determined using historical frequencies from Table 1 with the following results:

Class A1 probability = 0.22

Class A2 probability = 0.28

Class A3 probability = 0.22

Class A4 probability = 0.17

Class A5 probability = 0.11

The distribution for each class is simulated by truncated normal or truncated lognormal distribution. The values in parentheses denote mean, std. deviation, minimum, and maximum, respectively. Therefore, the representation of the variables A1, A2, A3, A4 and A5 is given by the following distribution functions:

Class A1: HP= @TNORMAL(56,9,40,63)

Class A2: HP= @TNORMAL(153,32,100,188)

Class A3: HP= @TNORMAL(281,48,200,325)

Class A4: HP= @TNORMAL(543,102,400,630)

Class A5: HP= @TLOGNORM(1400,350,1050,1750)

As an example, Figure 1 shows the truncated normal distribution of class A1 boilers, and Figure 2 shows the truncated lognormal distribution of class A5 boilers.

The probability to find a boiler in a given plant was determined using the fact that 19 boilers were found in 60 audits for two years of KU-EADC operations. Thus, this probability is 19/60 or 0.32.

The current dynamic efficiency of the boiler "CEF" is determined by using the function @HLOOKUP as a function of the rated load factor. The look up values for CEF are given in Table 2.

The cost saving, CS, is determined by:

$$CS = ES \times GP$$

Where:

GP= natural gas price, $/MMBTU

The distribution of natural gas price "GP" can be approximated by:

$$GP = @TNORMAL(3.7,0.68,2.71,5.7)$$

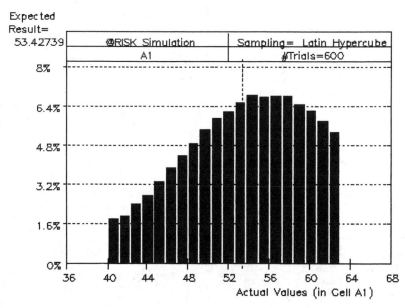

Figure 1. Truncated Normal Distribution For A1 Class Boilers.

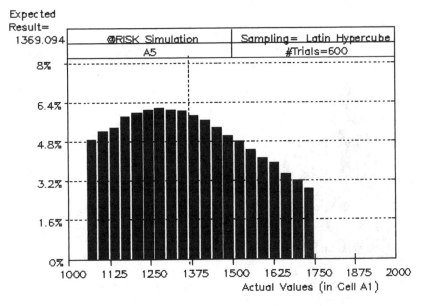

Figure 2. Truncated Lognormal Distribution for A5 Class Boilers.

The distributions for load factor "LF" and yearly operating time "HY" are simulated by:

LF= @TNORMAL(0.56,0.27,0.04,0.96)

HY= @TNORMAL(5100,1782,1760,8760)

Table 2[a]. Boiler Efficiency Vs. Fraction of Rated load

| Fraction of Rated Load | EFFICIENCY | |
| --- | --- | --- |
| | Dynamic/ Steady State | Dynamic Efficiency[b] |
| 0.05 | 0.60 | 0.48 |
| 0.10 | 0.79 | 0.63 |
| 0.15 | 0.86 | 0.69 |
| 0.20 | 0.90 | 0.72 |
| 0.25 | 0.92 | 0.74 |
| 0.30 | 0.94 | 0.75 |
| 0.35 | 0.95 | 0.76 |
| 0.40 | 0.96 | 0.77 |
| 0.50 | 0.97 | 0.78 |
| 0.60 | 0.98 | 0.79 |
| 0.70 | 0.98 | 0.79 |
| 0.80 | 0.99 | 0.80 |
| 0.90 | 1.00 | 0.80 |

---

[a] Weil-McLain Engineering Data, derived from studies by the National Bureau of Standars and Brookhaven National Laboratory.

[b] Based on 80% steady state efficiency

## RESULTS AND DISCUSSION

Three hundred interactions were run to simulate one year of KU-EADC operation, which is equivalent to 9,000 energy audits. The distribution of annual energy savings and annual cost saving were found. Figure 3 shows the distribution of energy savings in millions of BTUs if the recommendation is implemented. Figure 4 illustrates the costs savings in dollars per year. Table 3 gives the statistical results for each variable. The expected energy savings and cost savings for one year EADC operation (30 industrial energy audits) are 4,957 MMBtu/yr and $18,900/yr. For the expected 10 boilers found in one year means that at least $1,890/yr are available to pay for the equipment for each boiler working at low load factor.

The results confirm that this will be an important opportunity to conserve energy and natural gas, which is a nonrenewable natural resource. The result obtained for 30 energy audits can be extrapolated using the distribution of medium and small industries served by KU-EADC.[6] There are 906 small and medium size facilities that are eligible for KU-EADC energy audits (i.e. within 150 miles of Lawrence, Kansas). Thus, the total energy savings and cost savings in this region could be 149,701MMBtu/yr and $570,780/yr respectively.

Table 4 shows the contribution per boiler class in percentage of total energy savings. Special attention should be given to boilers of classes A5 and A6 since the greatest potential (63%) belongs to these groups.

Therefore, we can conclude that boiler manufacturers and specialized firms should conduct more research to improve the efficiency of existing fire tube boilers when their rated load factor is low. New technologies should provide practical solutions to retrofit existing boilers.

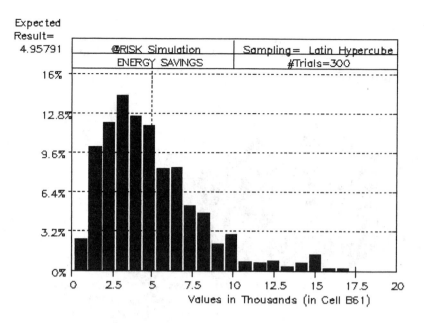

Figure 3. Distribution of Energy Savings "ES"

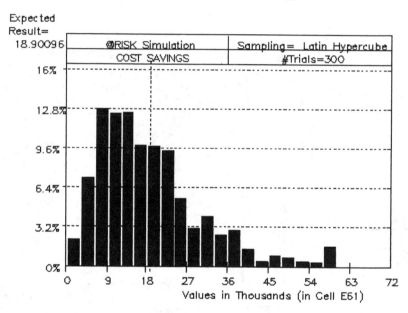

Figure 4. Distribution of Cost Savings "CS"

Table 3. Statisticals Results for Energy
Savings and Cost Savings

|  | MEAN | STANDAR DEVIATION | MINIMUM | MAXIMUM |
|---|---|---|---|---|
| ES[a] | 4,957 | 3,097 | 113 | 17,144 |
| CS[b] | 18,900 | 11,902 | 348 | 59,981 |

[a] "ES" Energy Savings (MMBtu/yr)

[b] "CS" Cost Savings ($/yr)

Table 4. Contribution in % Energy Savings per
Boiler Class

| BOILER CLASS | % CONTRIBUTION |
|---|---|
| A1 | 4.47 |
| A2 | 13.78 |
| A3 | 19.02 |
| A4 | 29.06 |
| A5 | 33.64 |

**REFERENCES**

1. F. William Payne, "Efficient Boiler Operations Sourcebook," Fairmont Press, 1991.

2. University City Science Center, "Frequency of DIECO Occurrences, Data Base 1981-1989," Philadelphia.

3. S.G. Dukelow, "Improving Boiler Efficiency," Kansas State University and Kansas Energy Office, 1981.

4. Lotus 1-2-3 is a registered trademark of Lotus Development Corporation.

5. Risk Analysis and Simulation Add-in for Lotus 1-2-3. @RISK is a registered trademark of Palidase Corporation.

6. Peter Tenpas, "Distribution of Industries by SIC Code for KU-EADC Region," The University of Kansas.

# Chapter 69

# Rate Intervention - An Alternative Energy Pricing Strategy

S.M. MacNish

Rate intervention is a good deal. It has provided IBM's three Mid-Hudson Valley sites the opportunity to reduce our electric expense by over twenty percent between 1987 and 1991.

## WHAT IS RATE INTERVENTION?

Rate intervention is the only legal process prescribed by a state utility regulator or state legislature which allows the comments of an interested party to be heard and entered in the record of a rate proceeding.

Think of intervention as participation. It is your way to participate in the utility's rate-making process.

Using New York State as an example, let's look at the intervention ("participation") process in more detail.

## WHY INTERVENE?

As I have said, intervention can be very rewarding. For example, one utility serves IBM's three major production plants in New York's Mid-Hudson Valley. Six years ago, the three plants participated in an electric rate case. It was a very successful intervention. We avoided a $6 million plus increase in electricity costs for that rate year.

Our approach to intervention and the rate-making process, while driven by economics, is to establish and maintain "cost-of-service" based rates. Cost-of-service based rates reflect the true costs incurred by the utility to provide the requires service to each specific class of customer - residential, commercial or industrial.

Perhaps the best example of a cost of service is the fuel adjustment charge that most utilities have. Every kilowatt-hour of electricity requires a specific amount of fuel to generate. The fuel adjustment mechanism in the electric rate allows the utility to bill a customer for the fuel used to meet that customer's electrical requirements.

Where that fuel adjustment charge is restricted by the regulators to only contain actual fuel costs, it reflects a "passthrough" of the fuel cost directly to the customer. It is a true "cost of service" in this case.

What we have seen evolve in recent years

is that regulators have added other non-fuel expenses to the fuel adjustment cost. The cost of Demand Side Management programs, things like energy efficient light bulbs that are given to residential and commercial customers, are being placed in the fuel adjustment charge. Where those programs are not open to the industrial customer, clearly charging the industrial customer for those programs through the fuel adjustment charge is not in keeping with "cost-of-service" principles.

While the dollar savings are attractive, it may soon become a necessity for companies to intervene, regardless of the savings potential, just to keep the rate-making process fair and equitable.

What is "fair and equitable"? Rates are fair and equitable when you pay only what it costs to serve you. When rates are based on the true "cost of service" - the real cost of generating electricity and distributing it to your facility - you don't pay anyone else's share of the costs and no one else pays yours.

Simply put, if you are paying more than what it actually costs to serve you, someone is paying less.

Traditionally, the commercial and industrial consumers of energy have paid more than their share of the costs of generation, transmission and distribution. This has been the result of a regulatory assumption that commercial and industrial consumers could pass this overcharge on to their customers without any adverse effects on their businesses.

In today's world, this assumption is not valid - if, indeed, it ever was. Most industrial energy users also have a large network of local suppliers who purchase their electricity at the commercial rate. If those suppliers' expenses are inflated by incorrectly priced energy costs, their price to their industrial customer may not be competitive - making that industrial customer non-competitive or forcing the industrial to find a more competitive supplier elsewhere.

In New York's Mid-Hudson Valley, industry pays $1.26 for $1.00 worth of non-fuel related electric costs. Based on the amount of electricity used by the industrial class in that region, the excess cost paid by industry that flows as a subsidy to the residential classes primarily amounted to over $12 million in 1991.

Since 1982, charges in excess of cost of service similar to the demand side management charges and inappropriate allocation of production plant have cost the Mid-Hudson Valley industrial customers over $70 million.

While the overcharges have occurred, intervention has enabled industry to avoid an additional $100 million in excess charges over the last ten years. In 1991 alone, as much as $15 million in charges above cost of service was eliminated.

It is unfortunate that the term INTERVENTION sounds confrontational or adversarial, because it usually is not.

We have all operated under what I will call the "reasonable person" theory. This is the idea that, somewhere in any organization, there is a reasonable person. If I can get to that person, we can resolve our differences. It is a great theory, but it does not work in a regulated monopoly because, in most cases, there is no individual serving on the regulating body who has had any "hands-on" experience in an open, unregulated, competitive marketplace.

There is one major point to remember in intervention. If you do not intervene, your position may not get into the record. And since the decision is based solely on what appears in the record, if you do not intervene, you may have no influence on the final decision.

New York State's lotto game had a slogan - You can't win if you don't play. What we have found is that you can't even maintain a semblance of rate stability or consistency unless you play the intervention game, and keep playing.

HOW TO INTERVENE

In order to participate, you must be recognized.

In New York, rate intervenors are controlled in a manner similar to lobbyists. Intervenors register with the Public Service Commission. While individuals may intervene on their own, corporations are expected to be represented by legal counsel.

In addition, while a company can participate on its own, doing so raises questions in the minds of the regulatory body with regard to the credibility and staying power of a corporate intervenor.

More success is possible as a member of a recognized industrial energy user group.

WHO PARTICIPATES?

A rate case can assemble quite a cast of characters, so let's look at each party, keeping the New York experience in mind.

The Public Service Commission or Public Utility Board is either elected by the general public or appointed by the Governor.

The Commissioners are advised by their senior staff - one senior staff department for each major regulated utility type - Power or Electricity, Gas, Telephone and Water.

In order to hear testimony in a rate case and to assemble a record of evidence, each rate filing is assigned to an Administrative Law Judge as a case. The ALJ accepts testimony, moderates the cross examination, decides on the admissability of testimony when it is contested and writes a recommended decision on the disposition of the rate request, which is then passed on to the senior staff.

The PSC's position in the case is presented and defended by the PSC trial staff.

The utility which filed the rate request presents and defends its position with expert witnesses.

The Consumer Protection Board is the state's consumer advocate. In New York, the CPB may soon share this responsibility with the Governor's newly created Citizens Utility Board.

The Attorney General oversees the process to insure that it meets all legal requirements.

The Economic Development people are there to advocate a position that will encourage job growth in the state.

The Senators and Assemblymen participate as consumer advocates in most cases.

The industrial groups are there to counter some of the adverse bias toward industry.

The residential advocates are usually there to emphasize the adverse impacts of any rate increase on the average consumer.

With all the parties involved, the process is long and complex. In New York it takes eleven months from the day the utility files a rate request for the commissioners to hand down a decision.

WHAT IS THE PROCESS?

Let's step through a case now, from its beginning with a utility filing a rate request. A utility files for a rate increase in order to maintain the rate of return on its investment in capital assets. The rate of return is affected by a number of factors, including increased labor and maintenance expense and sales figures below forecast.

This filing is the proverbial five pounds of paperwork. In the last filing by our local utility, the proposed rates were put forth in a three quarter inch book, backed up with about six inches of expert witness testimony and exhibits. Some of the topics covered in a typical case includes a sales forecast, operating budget, capital asset structure, expectations of rate of return on investment, the cost of serving the various classes of customers, allocation of the revenue requirement between the customer classes and design of the rates to be used to insure that the revenue requirement is met.

The intervenors then begin the complex process of structuring their participation. The issues that each wishes to address are decided, the intervenor position is mapped out, the intervenor selects his expert witnesses and develops his position. The cross examination of the utility witnesses is planned.

Once the utility's witnesses have been cross examined, the intervenors file their testimony and whatever rebuttal to the utility's testimony that they may feel is necessary to demonstrate the value of the intervenor's position.

All of the intervenors make their witnesses available for cross examination by both the utility and other intervening parties and the rebuttal cycle is repeated.

At this point, receiving of testimony and the ability to respond to that testimony is ended. The record of evidence is closed.

Summaries of position and replies to those summaries are then filed with the ALJ, who retires to his chambers with the complete body of documentation and comes up with his recommendation on the disposition of the case.

The intervening parties are then allowed one brief to respond to the ALJ's recommendation and one brief to respond to other parties' comments on the ALJ recommendation.

Now the senior staff meets to review this expanded body of documentation - the testimony, the cross examination, all of the rebuttal, the briefs, the reply briefs, the ALJ recommendation and its attendant briefs and replies - to advise the commissioners and assist them in generating the "Opinion" that closes the rate request filed by the utility eleven months previous.

The documents in an average case will stand four feet high by the end of the case.

## WHAT REACTIONS SURFACE?

Local media tend to report the facts in an unbiased manner, once they understand the issues. A well prepared, well presented press conference can put your position forth in the best light.

Local utilities will, for the most part, encourage intervention. Our utility told us that the only way we would be heard was to intervene. They realize that on some points, there will be opposing positions. However, they also recognize that there will be other issues where the industrial customer and the utility are looking for the same result.

Area residents usually hail the industrial participant, at least the first time out, because we are seen as taking up the fight against the utility who wants to raise resident's rates.

Area politicians think like area residents.

Most industrial employees tend to understand that in order to be competitive in the world market, their company must have the lowest cost, highest quality suppliers. If the industrial customer is subsidizing other customers, it is not getting the lowest rates and it may not be competitive.

Many times, industrial management tends to be uneasy about intervention the first time out. There is the question of the perception of a company as a good corporate citizen and how something that appears to be adversarial to the local community will impact that good corporate citizen view.

## ARE THE REWARDS WORTH THE EFFORT?

We certainly think so. When industry participated in a case for the first time in the Mid-Hudson Valley, they were hailed by the consumer advocates for finally getting involved. There was no adverse press then. And in the six years that industry has been an active participant in the intervention process, that has remained the situation with one or two minor exceptions.

Before intervention, industry had a very good operating relationship with our local utility. They still have it.

In that first intervention, the local utility filed for a $27 million rate increase. The final opinion awarded them an $8.7 million rate reduction - a $36 million reduction over their initial request. Industry had expected a $14 million increase - so their intervention was at least partly responsible for an additional $23 million reduction. The industrial share of the savings was over $6 million. They avoided this $6 million plus rate increase at a cost of $440 thousand.

In the industrials' second intervention, the local utility proposed a $2.7 million reduction to be equally divided in thirds for the residential, commercial and industrial customer classes. The Commission's decision gave no reduction to the residential class, one quarter to the commercial class and the industrial class received the remaining three quarters. The industrials received a reduction of $800 thousand more than originally announced. The intervention cost to the industrials was under $250 thousand. And even here, where the residential customers were not given the $900 thousand reduction they thought they were going to get, there was no adverse public reaction.

Late in 1990, the local utility petitioned the Public Service Commission to change the method of allocating fuel adjustment charges. The proposal would have eliminated all incentive for the utility to manage and contain fuel cost increases. The industrials submitted comments detailing how this worked against PSC policy. The PSC denied the petition and the industrials avoided a possible fuel adjustment charge increase of as much as $750 thousand annually. This was a "sleeper" intervention. The total cost for developing and filing comments was about $2,500. With the cost avoidance potential of $750 thousand, the payback on the cost of commenting was just over one day.

In the latest case, the local utility proposed an increase of over $30 million. The final decision allowed an increase of $18 million, some $3.5 million more than expected. However, the utility filing proposed that the industrial customers have an increase equal to the systems average increase. Based on the PSC decision, the system average increase was 4.6% or almost double the 2.4% that the industrial rates were actually increased. The difference translated into a $2.4 million saving for the industrials. For those industrials who participated in the intervention, the payback is in the range of three months.

One of the rewards of intervention that does not flow directly to the industrial customer is the savings that go to the other customers on the utility system. In the Mid-Hudson Valley, the residential and commercial customers served by the same utility that serves IBM have saved an estimated $105 million in the six years that IBM has been participating in the rate-making process. This is based on the value of the actual rate increases allowed compared to the historic value of rate increases prior to IBM intervention.

So what rewards have the industrials in the Mid-Hudson Valley seen?
- No adverse reaction from their employees.
- No adverse publicity or reaction from the community.
- No change in the operating relationship with the local utility.
- Paybacks on the cost ranging from one day to six months.
- An accumulated savings over the last six years to industry of over $45 million at an intervention cost of under $3.0 million.
- A utility financially healthier than it was six years ago.

I think you would agree that the rewards are worth the effort.

Thank you.

I would be happy to answer any questions you may have.

Stephen M. Mac Nish
Site Energy Coordinator
IBM Corporation
P.O. Box 950, D/772, B/414
Poughkeepsie, NY 12602
914-433-9380

# Chapter 70

# Vibration Diagnostic Analysis As Part of Energy Audit and Energy Management Application

C.C. Chen, H.M Rideau, S.D. Davis

## INTRODUCTION

As awareness about total energy concepts continues to grow, the design as well as the operation and maintenance of HVAC energy systems has become increasingly important. In many facilities, HVAC systems have been one of the major energy elements within their overall energy management plan. Significant amounts of energy and money can be saved by proper maintenance of an HVAC system. In many facilities however, maintenance is an afterthought, and the personnel who perform maintenance are not appropriately trained. Many lack the fundamental background to employ new concepts and technology which are now available through state-of-the-art advances.

In the traditional approach to HVAC machinery maintenance, scheduling repairs is difficult because the need for repair usually cannot be assessed without disassembling the machine (such as pump, fan, blower, motor, and compressor). If a problem is serious enough to be readily apparent, damage has probably already occurred without a means of externally determine machine conditions, scheduling is inaccurate.

Modern technology provides a number of methods for externally determining the condition of machinery. The most effective of these is vibration analysis. When a defect occurs in a machine, the results is an increase in vibration level. By regularly measuring this vibration level, defects can be detected before they have a chance to cause extensive damage or failure. More importantly, by analyzing the vibration signal, the nature of the defect can often be determined. As part of Louisiana's Industrial/Commercial Energy Reduction Program, we implemented the Vibration Diagnostic Analysis as part of our energy audit for the overall energy management plan. This paper discusses our experience in implementing vibration diagnostic tests in HVAC Systems and the testing results.

## ICERP DESCRIPTION

Significant amounts of energy and money can be saved in both industrial and commercial sectors by proper operations and maintenance of energy systems. Since 1986, the Louisiana Energy Division within the Department of Natural Resources (DNR) has utilized Petroleum Violation Escrow (PVE) funds for a wide range of energy conservation programs and projects. The Center for Energy and Environmental Studies and Southern University (CEES-SU) has been contracted by the Energy Division of the Department of Natural Resources, in the conduction of a three year Industrial/Commercial Energy Reduction Program through providing energy audits to commercials and industrial entities in the State. Additionally, recommending on energy consumption strategies, assistance in establishing ongoing training programs, and other post-audits assistance will be provided to increase the potential for realizing opportunities to increase actual energy savings. Such audits and follow-up activities are termed Level II Energy Audits. A total of two-hundred eighty (280) energy audits will be performed throughout the state during the three years of the project.

## TRAINING FOR VIBRATION DIAGNOSTIC ANALYSIS

As awareness about total energy concepts continue to grow, the design as well as the operation and maintenance of energy systems has become increasingly important. As a result of the cooperation and technology transfer between Exxon Company and the Department of Mechanical Engineering Technology (MET) at Southern University, MET laboratory courses have greatly enhanced not only the performance testing but also the operation and maintenance of HVAC systems.

During the Fall Semester 1989, we had the opportunity to develop one HVAC related vibration analysis lab. This lab is designed to analyze HVAC machinery's vibration with Modern Dynamic Signal Analyzers. University systems are used as a hands-on project.

ICERP student auditor has been required to take this vibration Analysis lab. The content of this Vibration Analysis Lab is listed below:

A. Machinery Maintenance Based on Vibration Analysis

B. Vibrating Monitoring Program

C. Converting Monitoring to an Electrical Signal

D. Reducing Vibration to its Components

E. Vibration Characteristic of Common Machinery Faults

F. Advanced Analysis and Documentation

G. Dynamic Signal Analysis

H. Case Histories

Equipment Used for Project

Computer      Transducer

Software      Monitor

## VIBRATION DIAGNOSTIC ANALYSIS
## EXAMPLE AND RESULTS

Woman's Hospital is a 270,000 square foot facility supplied by a Central Heating and Cooling system which utilizes hot water for heating and chilled water for air conditioning. Heat dissipation for the cooling system is accomplished by for Marley cooling towers with constant overflow. The heating system is supplied by three (3) 150 horsepower fire-tube boilers. Each boiler with a capacity of 5,021,000 BTUs/hr, has an internal blower which is externally driven by a 5 horsepower motor. By this method, fresh air is supplied to the boiler for combustion. Our vibration test did not cover the blowers; however, the four Reheat pumps (boiler pumps), Chillers No. 1 and No. 3, System pump No. 4 and the Primary Loop pumps were included in the analysis. The air conditioning system uses a Primary and Secondary Loop system. Chilled water is recirculated through the chillers and is pumped through the air handling on demand.

In our Vibration Analysis Report, we included seventy-two (72) points for measurement. Of these points, only forty of which were active. In our finding, three points were found ton be above the preset alarm limits. These points will be included in the Exception Report.

The breakdown of the Exception Report is as follows:

| Point # | Train | Amplitude | | Alarm |
|---|---|---|---|---|
| 27 | Primary Loop Pump #2 | 0.235467 | Inches/sec | 0,200 |
| 31 | Primary Loop Pump #2 | 0.219681 | Inches/sec | 0.200 |
| 66 | Reheat Pump #4 | 0.3868 | Inches/sec | 0.200 |

A spectrum was taken on points 27, 31, and 66 which is also included at the end of the Upload Statistics Report (see figure A, B, C). Points 27 and 31 are slightly above the present alarm of 0.200 Inches/sec. Since these points have high velocity readings at multiples of run speed, a low High Frequency Detection reading, mild pump cavitation is suspected. However, point No. 66 (Motor Outboard Velocity) has a velocity reading well above the second alarm limit.

Our recommendation is a continual observation for increased level of vibration on these points of exception. Overall, the readings on the other 69 points are below the lower alarm limits which is indicative of excellent running equipment.

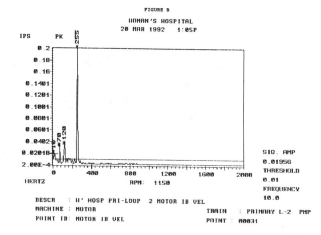

FIGURE B

WOMAN'S HOSPITAL
20 MAR 1992   1:05P

DESCR   : W' HOSP PRI-LOOP 2 MOTOR IB VEL
MACHINE : MOTOR                          TRAIN   : PRIMARY L-2 PMP
POINT ID: MOTOR IB VEL                   POINT   : 00031

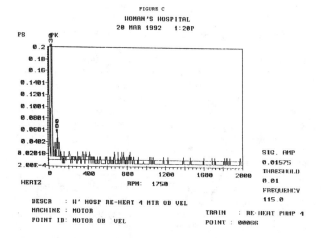

FIGURE C

WOMAN'S HOSPITAL
20 MAR 1992   1:20P

DESCR   : W' HOSP RE-HEAT 4 MTR OB VEL
MACHINE : MOTOR                          TRAIN   : RE-HEAT PUMP 4
POINT ID: MOTOR OB  VEL                  POINT   : 00066

Page No.   1
03/19/92
WOMAN'S HOSPITAL                    Route: WOMANS    (Std. Measurements)

LAST MEASUREMENT REPORT

| POINT ID | POINT | UNIT | LAST VALU | CUR. VALU | ALARM NO1 | % | DATE | MEASUR |
|---|---|---|---|---|---|---|---|---|
| ** TRAIN : CHILLER 1 | | | | | | | | |
| * MACHINE : MOTOR | | | | | | | | |
| MOTOR OB AX VEL | 00001 | IPS | .0 | 0.05985 | 0.20000 | 0 | 03/20/92 | OVERAL |
| MOTOR OB SE | 00002 | G/HFD | .0 | 0.01325 | 0.50000 | 0 | 03/20/92 | OVERAL |
| MOTOR OB VEL | 00003 | IPS | .0 | 0.07620 | 0.20000 | 0 | 03/20/92 | OVERAL |
| MOTOR IB SE | 00004 | G/HFD | .0 | 0.02122 | 0.50000 | 0 | 03/20/92 | OVERAL |
| MOTOR IB VEL | 00005 | IPS | .0 | 0.04267 | 0.20000 | 0 | 03/20/92 | OVERAL |
| ** TRAIN : CHILLER 2 | | | | | | | | |
| * MACHINE : COMPRESSOR | | | | | | | | |
| COMP IB VEL | 00014 | IPS | .0 | 0.03615 | 0.20000 | 0 | 03/20/92 | OVERAL |
| COMP OB VEL | 00015 | IPS | .0 | 0.03659 | 0.20000 | 0 | 03/20/92 | OVERAL |
| COMP OB AX VEL | 00016 | IPS | .0 | 0.07282 | 0.20000 | 0 | 03/20/92 | OVERAL |
| * MACHINE : MOTOR | | | | | | | | |
| MOTOR OB AX VEL | 00009 | IPS | .0 | 0.04652 | 0.20000 | 0 | 03/20/92 | OVERAL |
| MOTOR OB SE | 00010 | G/HFD | .0 | 0.01323 | 0.50000 | 0 | 03/20/92 | OVERAL |
| MOTOR OB VEL | 00011 | IPS | .0 | 0.03628 | 0.20000 | 0 | 03/20/92 | OVERAL |
| MOTOR IB SE | 00012 | G/HFD | .0 | 0.01315 | 0.50000 | 0 | 03/20/92 | OVERAL |
| MOTOR IB VEL | 00013 | IPS | .0 | 0.03569 | 0.20000 | 0 | 03/20/92 | OVERAL |
| ** TRAIN : PRIMARY L-2  PMP | | | | | | | | |
| * MACHINE : MOTOR | | | | | | | | |
| MOTOR OB VEL | 00029 | IPS | .0 | 0.13756 | 0.20000 | 0 | 03/20/92 | OVERAL |
| MOTOR IB SE | 00030 | G/HFD | .0 | 0.00974 | 0.20000 | 0 | 03/20/92 | OVERAL |
| MOTOR IB VEL | 00031 | IPS | .0 | 0.23546 | 0.20000 | 0 | 03/20/92 | SPEC+0 |
| ** TRAIN : PRIMARY L-2  PMP | | | | | | | | |
| * MACHINE : MOTOR | | | | | | | | |
| MOTOR OB AX VEL | 00027 | IPS | .0 | 0.21968 | 0.20000 | 0 | 03/20/92 | SPEC+0 |
| MOTOR OB SE | 00028 | G/HFD | .0 | 0.01084 | 0.20000 | 0 | 03/20/92 | OVERAL |
| ** TRAIN : PRIMARY LOOP PMP | | | | | | | | |
| * MACHINE : MOTOR | | | | | | | | |
| MOTOR OB AX VEL | 00017 | IPS | .0 | 0.12012 | 0.20000 | 0 | 03/20/92 | OVERAL. |
| MOTOR OB SE | 00018 | G/HFD | .0 | 0.00733 | 0.20000 | 0 | 03/20/92 | OVERAL |
| MOTOR OB VEL | 00019 | IPS | .0 | 0.05985 | 0.20000 | 0 | 03/20/92 | OVERAL |
| MOTOR IB SE | 00020 | G/HFD | .0 | 0.00737 | 0.20000 | 0 | 03/20/92 | OVERAL |
| MOTOR IB VEL | 00021 | IPS | .0 | 0.04925 | 0.20000 | 0 | 03/20/92 | OVERAL |
| ** TRAIN : RE-HEAT PUMP 1 | | | | | | | | |
| * MACHINE : MOTOR | | | | | | | | |
| MOTOR OB AX VEL | 00037 | IPS | .0 | 0.04951 | 0.20000 | 0 | 03/20/92 | OVERAL |
| MOTOR OB SE | 00038 | G/HFD | .0 | 0.02319 | 0.50000 | 0 | 03/20/92 | OVERAL |
| MOTOR OB  VEL | 00039 | IPS | .0 | 0.04131 | 0.20000 | 0 | 03/20/92 | OVERAL |
| MOTOR IB SE | 00040 | G/HFD | .0 | 0.05239 | 0.50000 | 0 | 03/20/92 | OVERAL |
| MOTOR IB  VEL | 00041 | IPS | .0 | 0.03481 | 0.20000 | 0 | 03/20/92 | OVERAL |
| * MACHINE : PUMP | | | | | | | | |
| PUMP IB SE | 00042 | G/HFD | .0 | 0.06209 | 0.50000 | 0 | 03/20/92 | OVERALL |

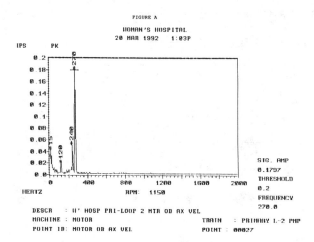

FIGURE A

WOMAN'S HOSPITAL
20 MAR 1992   1:03P

DESCR   : W' HOSP PRI-LOOP 2 MTR OB AX VEL
MACHINE : MOTOR                          TRAIN   : PRIMARY L-2 PMP
POINT ID: MOTOR OB AX VEL                POINT   : 00027

L A S T   M E A S U R E M E N T   R E P O R T
-------------------------------------------------

| POINT ID | POINT | UNIT | LAST VALU | CUR. VALU | ALARM NO1 | % | DATE | MEASUR |
|----------|-------|------|-----------|-----------|-----------|---|------|--------|
| ** TRAIN : RE-HEAT PUMP 1 | | | | | | | | |
| * MACHINE : PUMP | | | | | | | | |
| PUMP IB VEL | 00043 | IPS | .0 | 0.04078 | 0.20000 | 0 | 03/20/92 | OVERAL |
| | | | | | | | | |
| ** TRAIN : RE-HEAT PUMP 2 | | | | | | | | |
| * MACHINE : MOTOR | | | | | | | | |
| MOTOR OB AX VEL | 00046 | IPS | .0 | 0.06884 | 0.20000 | 0 | 03/20/92 | OVERAL |
| | | | | | | | | |
| ** TRAIN : RE-HEAT PUMP 4 | | | | | | | | |
| * MACHINE : MOTOR | | | | | | | | |
| MOTOR OB AX VEL | 00064 | IPS | .0 | 0.17425 | 0.20000 | 0 | 03/20/92 | OVERAL |
| MOTOR OB SE | 00065 | G/HFD | .0 | 0.07328 | 0.50000 | 0 | 03/20/92 | OVERAL |
| MOTOR OB VEL | 00066 | IPS | .0 | 0.33868 | 0.20000 | 0 | 03/20/92 | SPEC+O |
| MOTOR IB SE | 00067 | G/HFD | .0 | 0.06002 | 0.50000 | 0 | 03/20/92 | OVERAL |
| MOTOR IB VEL | 00068 | IPS | .0 | 0.18281 | 0.20000 | 0 | 03/20/92 | OVERAL |
| | | | | | | | | |
| * MACHINE : PUMP | | | | | | | | |
| PUMP IB SE | 00069 | G/HFD | .0 | 0.01143 | 0.50000 | 0 | 03/20/92 | OVERAL |
| PUMP IB VEL | 00070 | IPS | .0 | 0.13834 | 0.20000 | 0 | 03/20/92 | OVERAL |
| PUMP OB SE | 00071 | G/HFD | .0 | 0.00851 | 0.50000 | 0 | 03/20/92 | OVERAL |
| PUMP OB VEL | 00072 | IPS | .0 | 0.08782 | 0.20000 | 0 | 03/20/92 | OVERAL |

MAXIMUM AMPLITUDE IN SPECTRUM REPORT
-------------------------------------

| POINT | POINT ID | UNTS | PEAK AMP | LINE | FREQ HZ | DATE | MACHINE |
|-------|----------|------|----------|------|---------|------|---------|
| **PLANT   : WOMAN'S HOSPITAL | | | | | | | |
| 00027 | MOTOR OB AX VEL | IPS | 0.179687 | 54 | 270.00 | 20 MAR 1992 | MOTOR |
| 00031 | MOTOR IB VEL | IPS | 0.207031 | 51 | 255.00 | 20 MAR 1992 | MOTOR |
| 00066 | MOTOR OB   VEL | IPS | 0.351562 | 1 | 5.00 | 20 MAR 1992 | MOTOR |

## CONCLUSION

Vibration monitoring analysis already has produced substantial cost savings in large systems in industry. However only relatively recently has vibration analysis or monitoring been applied to large central HVAC systems. We would like to use our experience as an example how vibration analysis and monitoring may be incorporated in the energy audit and energy management application.

# SECTION 5
# ADVANCES IN LIGHTING
# EFFICIENCY AND APPLICATIONS

# Chapter 71
# Structuring Lighting Retrofit Projects for Success

J.L Fetters

## Abstract

Several trends are converging to create a substantial market for lighting retrofits in these uncertain economic times . Low interest rates are making investments in buildings more attractive than alternative financial investnments such as CD's. With activity in the new construction market at an all time low, savvy contractors are turning to the retrofit market - restoring, renovating and upgrading existing buildings. Heightened environmental concerns are fueling lighting incentive programs from the electric utilities and the EPA. Improvements in lighting technology are arriving in the marketplace at an accelerated rate. Building occupants are demanding higher quality workplaces and managers are seeking higher levels of productivity.

Replacing older lighting equipment can substantially improve lighting efficiency, decrease energy and maintenance costs and, at the same time, improve the workplace by increasing lighting quality Lighting retrofit projects have a demonstrated track record, reducing lighting costs on the order of 50%. This experience can be applied to help structure retrofit projects. But, in order to reap all the benefits available from a rretrofit project, it must be structured for success.

The retrofit option introduces a unique series of issues for building owners, managers and engineers. The best way to prevent these issues from undermining the success of retrofit projects is to anticipate and completely plan for them.

Successful retrofit projects run smoothly and stay within budgetary constraints. Three important considerations will guide the successful project:

1) Start comprehensive planning early,
2) Investigate existing conditions, and
3) Be sensitive to owner/occupants needs keep building operational.

## Comprehensive Planning

There are several benefits of comprehensive planning. All of these benefits contribute to a more successful retrofit project with fewer delays and disruptions. Detailed planning will include 1) thoroughly investigating the scope of the project, 2) clearly communicating the scope of the project, and 3) developing a reasonable schedule for the project.

## Investigate Scope of Project

If planning is started early, disruptive surprises can be eliminated, and equipment with long lead times can be ordered in time to meet the retrofit schedule. Identifying the long lead time material and contacting manufacturers well ahead of the project start date helps avoid costly delays. It also helps ensure that you get higher efficiency equipment that may have longer lead times. At the Columbus Works of AT&T, the lighting retrofit equipment is ordered by the lighting engineer. Removing this routine from the installer's responsibility provides the quality control that may be missing when the installer provides substitutions because of lower cost or because other equipment was more readily available. It also ensures that the equipment is available before the project start date.

Environmental considerations should also be included in the specifications of the project, outlining the installer's obligations for lamp and ballast disposal. It may be necessary to subcontract disposal or recycling services. If there is asbestos present in the demolition process, asbestos abatement planning must also be included.

## Communicate Scope of Project

Communicating the scope of the project to those concerned. both installer and occupants, is extremely important to the success of retrofit projects. Any changes to the schedule should also be communicated as soon as they are recognized. When people are kept informed, they are more cooperative and the retrofit project is completed in a timely and smooth manner.

### Develop a Reasonable Schedule

Once the scope of the project is developed, delivery lead times will be known and the time to complete each step estimated, completion dates can be assigned. Disruptions to the schedule are less likely to occur and costly overtime can be eliminated if time is allowed for the inevitable slippage that occurs on many projects. Assigning completion times that require superhuman efforts or obtaining materials shipped by air freight are sometimes necessary on extremely fast-track projects, but they should not become the norm because of lack of planning.

### Investigate Existing Conditions

Unlike new construction projects, retrofit projects often face many unknowns. This is the reason that a detailed and thorough investigation of the existing conditions is made; to reveal unknowns and confirm existing conditions. For example: the voltage of the various building lighting systems may not be the same throughout a building, particularly if parts of the building were originally lighted with incandescent fixtures and parts with fluorescent luminaires. In addition, present wiring may not meet current electrical codes.

As-built drawings are often not available. So, for older buildings, learning to recognize the potential for hidden conditions is a valuable asset. If these conditions are not determined early, discovering them after the project is underway will cause delays, overrunning the project budget with increased costs for additional materials and labor hours.

### Keep the Building Operational

Most retrofit projects involve work in buildings that are occupied. Planning should take into consideration how different phases of the project will affect the occupants. Disruption of office routines or factory processes is a major concern for results oriented managers. An important part of the planning for lighting retrofits requires sensitivity to the needs of the owners and occupants by keeping the building operational. This may involve phasing the work in order to minimize disruptions to occupants. Work may need to be accomplished when an area is not occupied, such as at night or during weekends. Planning may also involve completing one section of a facility at a time so that occupants can be moved from one completely operational area to another. Any additional costs for these moving strategies are usually recovered by maintaining worker productivity.

### A Prescription for the Successful Retrofit Project

Successful retrofit projects will follow a process in a specific sequence with five major phases:
1) Evaluation
2) Exploring Options
3) Planning
4) Installation
5) Post-occupancy Evaluation

### Evaluation

#### Lighting Survey
The objectives of the lighting survey are to obtain enough meaningful information to evaluate the lighting systems for potential retrofit opportunities. This step also identifies all the existing conditions of the areas being considered for retrofit. The survey should include a count of the fixtures, lamps and controls for each space. Each area should be measured for physical dimensions and the illuminance measured for each visual task identified. Interviewing the occupants and owners may be desirable to uncover problems with the existing lighting system and to help discover the objectives of the work group. Cost data must be collected to determine the operating costs for the existing systems.

#### Assessing Existing Systems
Assessment is a "pause-and-reflect" step that helps to concentrate on the condition of the lighting systems, the physical condition of the space and to help determine if the existing lighting is appropriate for the visual tasks that are being performed in the space now. Many times it is found that the tasks have changed but the lighting systems did not,

creating a mis-match of improper lighting for the task. This is why it is <u>not</u> advisable to simply replicate existing lighting levels.

Part of the assessment step should be devoted to calculating the unit power density (UPD) to determine if the watts per square foot calculation reveals an unusually high energy use for the lighting system.

Another function of this step is to consider what effect this change will have on the occupants. Many people do not like change and may oppose your retrofit plans only because it represents another disruption in their lives. These people can undermine the best retrofit project. They can become project allies by a good communications PR effort.

## Exploring Options

### <u>Preparing Options List</u>

Some of the available retrofit options will be screened out during the assessment phase because they are not appropriate for the application. The remaining options will be explored during this phase by preparing a list of appropriate options for the retrofit project under consideration. The list should include lamp options (CFL, T8, T10, T12, MH, HPS, etc), ballast options (energy saving, electronic, etc.), fixture options (remove, clean, reflectors, etc.), controls options (switching, occupancy sensors, etc.), ceiling options (replace tile, paint, etc.), wiring options (hard-wired, flexible wiring system, etc.), and emergency/night lighting options.

### <u>Compare Equivalent Packages</u>

A few equivalent packages or systems based on the options explored in the previous step are developed at this step. The number of fixtures and the illuminance level in foot-candles is calculated for each system to be considered. First costs and annual operating costs are calculated for each system. If a life-cycle cost method is used, it is calculated for each package at this time. Each system unit power density (UPD) is calculated for comparison. All the benefits of each system are identified in this step.

### <u>Select Package</u>

In preparation for selecting the final package or system, a criteria is prepared based on the most important attributes to the end-user. Some attributes to consider in the criteria preparation are;

efficiency, lighting quality, cost, and appearance. Next, the candidates under consideration are rank ordered according to the criteria. The last stage of this step is to select the final package from the rank ordering of candidates. This logical process will take out some of the bias and subjectivity from the selection process and will result in a more objective choice.

## Planning

### <u>Prepare Final Design</u>

In this step, the final design is prepared and then calculations of illuminance (FC), costs, and UPD are performed. Specifications and plans are drawn, fully describing the what, when and how of the project. Construction conditions and any special conditions are written into the specification.

### <u>Meet With the "Customer"</u>

The "customer" may be the owner or the occupants or both. Meeting will help to achieve a successful project by describing the design and how the retrofit will be different from the existing lighting system. This meeting can be used to help prepare the customer for change and to outline the way in which the project will be accomplished by the installer. The schedule and costs are discussed as appropriate. It is not advised that occupants be kept "in the dark" about the changes to their work space if success is desired. In fact, by informing the occupants of this change, you can help them understand the benefits to them and they can help you improve the space for them. Solicit their feedback to the project and listen to their comments. While you will need to sort out non-lighting issues, it is worth doing.

### <u>Incorporate Feedback</u>

If the comments indicate that changes need to be made in the structuring of the project it is done at this time. Incorporate the feedback into the design and modify the project documents. Communicate that you have listened to comments and have made the listed changes.

## Installation

There may need to be a trial installation phase that precedes the final installation. Whether a trial is included or not, the following steps apply to both the trial installation and final installation.

### Meet With Installer

Developing a good rapport with the installer will contribute to the success of the retrofit project, because at this point the ultimate success lies with the installer. The installer must know what the project entails in exacting detail and your expectations of his performance must be painstakingly reviewed. The costs of the project need to be reviewed and an accounting method for field changes be outlined.

### Visit Job Site

At the beginning and the retrofit project, visiting the job site is the only way to adequately monitor job progress and quality of workmanship. You can assist in solving the inevitable field situations that develop on all projects and help the installer adapt for these conditions.

### Inspect Completion

At the end of the retrofit installation, a close inspection will reveal any missing or improper work. A visual inspection for the quality of the installation will allow any items to be posted to a punch list with the installer's representative present. Agreement on a time to complete the punch list will save arguments later. Metering to verify savings may be desired when the punch list is accomplished.

### Post-Occupancy Evaluation

A follow-up step after occupancy contributes to success by obtaining written comments from the installer which can be incorporated in the next project of this type. Written comments may also be solicited from the occupants of their evaluation of their new lighting system. An evaluation form may be the best way to accomplish this task. Review the forms and tabulate the results.

### A Key Tool for Lighting Retrofits

Participants in the EPA Green Lights Program have an effective lighting retrofit tool in the first edition of the *Lighting Upgrade Manual*. Although the manual does not detail everything the end user might need to know in executing a comprehensive lighting retrofit, it does contain a detailed set of "first steps" for almost any lighting retrofit project planning process. This manual represents the first installment in what is to be a regularly updated reference manual for lighting retrofit planners.

### Conclusion

Someone once said that nothing succeeds like success. As more successful retrofit projects are accomplished, the elements of that successful project can be applied to the next project. Building on success by this self bench- marking process will result in a constantly improving retrofit process.

Chapter 72
# Providing a Lighting Retrofit Program for Multiple Locations

S. Boresow

ABSTRACT

A very common and effective approach for determining the costs and benefits of a lighting retrofit project at any facility is to complete a detailed survey of the facility's current lighting system and obtain proposals for completing the work required. Gathering this information can be tedious and expensive, but is still quite manageable. However, applying this same approach to several (or several hundred) facilities, can be extremely costly and equally difficult to manage. The analysis that is described, utilizes an effective software simulation program that provides accurate estimates for solutions, and also determines the degree of risk associated with the solution(s) generated. Suggestions for appropriate application for simulation (rather than calculation) and risk analysis are provided as a tool for project analysis.

INTRODUCTION

There is no doubt about it; when thoroughly investigated and properly applied, Energy Managers, Lighting Managers and Facility Managers will confirm that LIGHTING TECHNOLOGY IS AVAILABLE TODAY that will reduce lighting energy costs, reduce the cooling requirements of some buildings, and enhance their working environments with better lighting conditions.

Every lamp, reflector, occupancy sensor, or fixture salesperson could show you how to save from 30% to 70% of your current lighting energy costs at any one building. To insure that the "wrong solution" for lighting upgrades is not applied, a facility manager must completely understand the requirements of the building tenants, and apply the current technologies to existing systems, without adding costs to the clients, or compromising necessary light levels.

However, when trying to develop an effective lighting efficiency program for many facilities, one cannot apply the traditional roles and responsibilities of a Lighting Manager that should be used at a single facility. It becomes an unmanageable situation for someone to determine the tasks being performed, the various hours of operations of the facility, the utility charges, or the number or types of fixtures at each facility.

The Contract Services Organization (CSO) of AT&T has responsibility for building operations at over 1000 facilities across the country. One of the goals for the Energy Product Management Group was to develop a program and a strategy for implementing lighting system upgrades and efficiency improvements at targeted facilities. This plan would need to be approved and supported by upper management before implementing it at our many field locations across the country.

The successful approval of any project or program will be based on an accurate and well documented economic analysis. The basis of this paper is to show how an economic analysis was developed for a large scale lighting retrofit program using simulation techniques with basic spreadsheet application. After approval of the economic analysis, the success of the program will depend on the implementation plan developed.

SOFTWARE BACKGROUND

While enrolled in an Engineering Systems Simulation class and working toward a Masters in Engineering Management at the University of Kansas, I learned about a software add-in manager to Lotus 1-2-3 called @RISK, pronounced "at risk".

Most often, spread sheet applications are used to "calculate" a solution based on previously supplied "average" information. For example, one can calculate the energy savings in a facility if the following are known:

- exact number of fixtures
- fixture wattages
- average annual hours of operation
- utility rebates per fixture

One of the errors in applying averages to a calculation, is that the average being used assumes a normal distribution, when, in fact, the distribution may not be normal. To get around that subject, engineers often find themselves having to run countless of calculations, changing variables for each iteration.

One of the advantages of an iterative simulation model, is that a distribution of answers is achieved, not just one 'calculated' answer. Simulation allows one to combine all the uncertainties of the project (or model) into one spreadsheet. Also, the number of iterations per simulation can be specified, providing statistically verified results and continuous risk analysis for any variable.

For this study, a simulation model was built using Lotus 1-2-3 version 2.3 in conjunction with @RISK, an ADD-IN manager to Lotus 1-2-3 with sophisticated capabilities of risk analysis and simulation. @RISK provides over thirty different probability distributions to spreadsheet capabilities. The ones used in this analysis are:

**THE TRUNCATED NORMAL DISTRIBUTION**

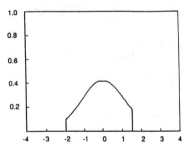

The @RISK function is @tnormal (mean, standard dev., minimum, maximum)

**THE TRIANGULAR DISTRIBUTION**

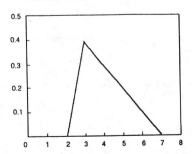

The @RISK function is @triang (most likely, minimum, maximum)

413

Shown below is a comparison between a spreadsheet that provides calculations and a spreadsheet that provides distribution ranges for simulation techniques.

## COMPARISON BETWEEN TYPICAL SPREADSHEETS USING

| CALCULATION TECHNIQUES | SIMULATION TECHNIQUES |
|---|---|
| • Provide an average number of fixtures per 100 square feet of office space (uses an average based on normal distribution) | • Provide an average number of fixtures per 100 square feet and include the maximum, the minimum, and the standard deviation allowed (uses a truncated normal distribution) |
| • Provide average costs for projects (uses an average based on normal distribution) | • Provide most likely costs with the minimum and maximum expected (uses a triangular distribution) |
| • Provide average hours of operation (uses an average based on normal distribution) | • Provide average hours of operation, maximum, minimum and the standard deviation (uses the truncated normal distribution) |

## APPROACH

This study identifies twenty areas around the country where CSO manages significant amounts of office space. Data on square footages of facilities, utility company energy charges, utility sponsored rebates (if available), and project pricing were collected or estimated. The simulation study is based upon retrofitting two, three and four lamp fixtures with T8 lamps and electronic ballasts.

## ASSUMPTIONS

Even with simulation techniques, one can still make assumptions that can be used in spreadsheet functions. The following assumptions very easily could have been represented in the spreadsheet with a distribution function. However, these are just examples of fixture types. Any percentages totaling less than 100% could be used here.

Fixture types:
• 40% of the fixtures contain four lamp systems

• 20% of the fixtures contain three lamp systems

• 15% of the fixtures contain two lamp systems but will be tandem wired to act as a four lamp system Lamp type:

• 50% of the lamps are standard lamps, or 40 watts

• 50% of the lamps are energy efficient lamps, or 34 watts

Other assumptions made for this analysis are that utility company rebates are applied where currently being offered, and that a reduction in lighting load can reduce the cooling requirements for HVAC systems. For every reduction of 5 watts of light, an equivalent 1 watt can be reduced from the cooling requirement of the facility. This national average of 20% was used to account for HVAC Energy Savings.[5]

## RESULTS

Several graphical reports were developed with the software used, showing the results of the simulation model. Graphs #1A shows the distribution of savings, and that the expected savings for the entire retrofit program are $3.54 million. Graph 1B shows the corresponding probability risk analysis. For example, if one wanted to know the probability, or "risk", that savings will be $3.3 million (not quite the expected amount), the software program will respond with the level of risk. In this example, the probability that savings will be $3.3 million is about 17%.

Graph #1A

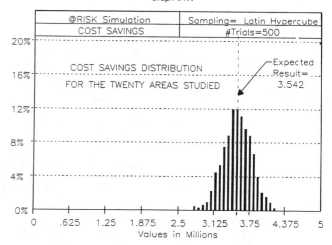

Graph #1B

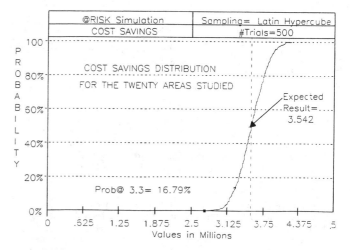

| Expected Savings | $3,542,898 |
|---|---|
| Minimum Savings | 2,747,158 |
| Maximum Savings | 4,243,469 |
| Standard Deviation | 253,518 |

Graphs #2A shows the distribution of program costs with a very narrow, almost normal curve. The expected costs for this project are $7.2 million. On graph #2B, the example provided shows that the probability that costs will be less than or equal to $7.3 million, is about 80%.

Graph #3A shows the distribution of project payback with an expected payback of about 1.4 years. Graph #3B allows one to determine the overall program risk. For example, the probability that the program could have a 1.5 year payback is shown to be almost 88%.

Graph #2A

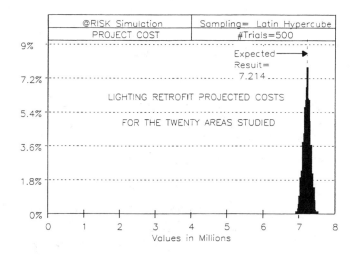

Graph #3A

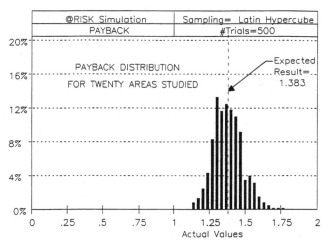

Graph #2B

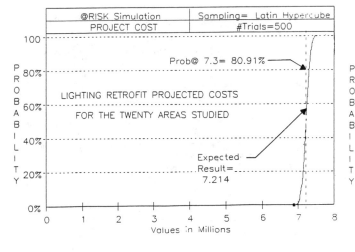

Graph #3B

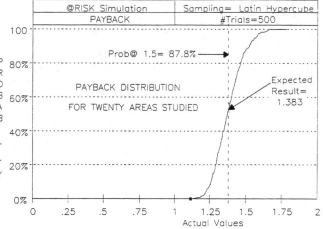

| Expected Costs | $7,214,889 |
|---|---|
| Minimum Costs | 6,921,059 |
| Maximum Costs | 7,523,203 |
| Standard Deviation | 99,289 |

Graph #3C provides a representation of paybacks for each project area. On this graph the expected payback and the minimum and maximum paybacks are identified for each project area. This would be very useful if trying to allocate money for projects with the quickest payback, and the lowest risk factor.

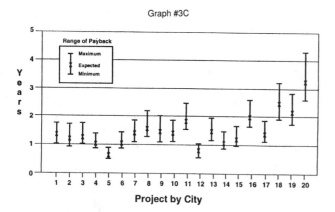

Graph #3C

| Expected Payback | 1.38 years |
| Minimum Payback | 1.12 years |
| Maximum Payback | 1.78 years |
| Standard Deviation | .10 years |

## APPLICATIONS

This simulation technique can be very helpful for energy managers, project engineers, technical sales representatives, and others responsible for making decisions. Here, it was used to prove the economics of a large scale, multi-location lighting retrofit project to upper management. Simulation and risk analysis can be applied to the following areas, to name a few:

- corporate planning
- environmental impacts and planning
- engineering reliability
- operational analysis
- cost analysis

Specifically, lighting salespeople would benefit from this by providing much more accurate cost/savings proposals, and energy managers would be better able to analyze the level of risk they are willing to take with any project, regardless of its size.

In order to obtain more accurate results, a recommendation would be to try to fit the data to a specific distribution curve (perform a chi square analysis), and use that distribution curve with the proper arguments, in this simulation package.

## THE REST OF THE PLAN

Now that we have seen that the economics of a properly constructed and targeted lighting retrofit program, the rest of a successful, implementation plan follows like this:

- Obtain management commitment for energy saving projects.
- Establish technical training seminars for the facility managers.
- Prepare budget for targeted projects.
- Prioritize where budgeted expenses will provide the greatest ROI.
- Obtain project proposals and schedule projects.
- Implement retrofit projects.
- Track energy consumption, light levels and savings for projects.
- Recognize and reward individuals for their energy efficiency improvements and cost reductions obtained.
- Reinvest savings in other energy efficiency improvements.

## CONCLUSION

As new products and technology become available to improve the efficiency of current lighting systems, it is important to consider new approaches for establishing and analyzing a projects' economics. Software is available that will improve the accuracy of any analysis. Also, statistical verification and probability distribution analysis are available and can play a major role in project analysis and acceptance.

## REFERENCES AND ACKNOWLEDGMENTS

1. Occhino, C.C., "Today's Lighting Management", *Proceedings of the 14th World Energy Engineering Congress*, Atlanta, GA, October 23-25, 1991.

2. @RISK Version 1.55, *Risk Analysis and Simulation Add-In for Lotus 1-2-3*, New York, Palisade Corporation, January 1990.

3. Lotus and 1-2-3 are registered trademarks of Lotus Development Corporation.

4. RISK is a trademark of Parker Brothers, Division of Tonka Corporation.

5. Mendelsohn, C., "The Lighting-Air Conditioning Environmental Domino Effect", *Proceedings of the 14th World Energy Engineering Congress*, Atlanta, GA, October 23-25, 1991.

Chapter 73

# Performance Comparison of Direct and Indirect Lighting Systems

F. Rubinstein, O. Morse, T. Clark

**Abstract --** The performance of a retrofitted indirect lighting system was compared to the performance of a typical de-lamped direct lighting system in a partitioned office space. Power, illuminance and luminance measurements were made for the de-lamped direct lighting system and after installation of the indirect lighting system with various lamp and ballast combinations. Using the same lamps and ballasts, average workplane illuminance was slightly higher with indirect lighting than with direct lighting. With indirect lighting, workplane lumen efficacy was 4.5% lower due to the higher power draw of the lamps in the more open and cooler indirect fixtures. Indirect lighting with 36 watt T-8 lamps and electronic ballasts achieved an initial average workplane illuminance of 45 foot-candles in the partitioned office space at only 1.1 w/ft$^2$.

## I. INTRODUCTION

Indirect lighting is not a new concept. But despite a number of potential advantages, the vast majority of commercial and industrial building space is lit with direct lighting systems. Indirect lighting offers many benefits in office spaces. First, by illuminating the ceiling, the ceiling brightness is much more uniform than with a direct lighting system. Secondly, with indirect lighting, the wall brightness as well as the brightness of any vertical partitions may be higher than with direct lighting. Third, indirect lighting systems may cause less distracting glare from the computer screens. Finally, indirect lighting systems are potentially less susceptible to the shadowing effects of partitions and storage cabinets built into typical furniture systems.

However, conventional wisdom has it that indirect lighting provides approximately 20% less illumination at the workplace than equivalent direct lighting systems and is too expensive to install in existing offices. Recently, a relatively inexpensive retrofit indirect fixture has been introduced to the marketplace, requiring a re-examination of this conventional wisdom. The installed cost of this new retrofit indirect system is substantially less than that of many other indirect systems installed in existing offices. (Depending upon on the location, size, and nature of the job, the installed cost of the retrofit indirect lighting system will range from $2.00/ft$^2$ to $4.00/ft$^2$). Due to this low installed cost, indirect lighting becomes an economically attractive option for a number of areas within the office environment. However, to determine its overall attractiveness, one needs to determine the impact of the retrofit indirect light fixture on energy consumption and on the quality of the light in the office.

This paper compares the energy and luminous performance of a standard direct lighting system and an indirect lighting system in a typical partitioned office area and a conference room. Changes in other luminous quantities such as ceiling and wall luminances and the reflected glare off a computer screen are also examined.

## II. METHODS

The test site is a suite of offices in Sunnyvale, CA. Approximately 915 ft$^2$ are partitioned offices and circulation path. The remaining area, 176 ft$^2$, is a small conference room. In the open office area, 5'-6" partitions are used to create 7 ft by 8 ft work stations. Each work station has two work surfaces mounted 30" above the floor. One of the work stations has storage units (binder bins) mounted on the partition above one of the work surfaces; the other work stations have no obstructions on the partitions. Overhead lighting was provided throughout the open-office

area by 13 2x4 recessed fluorescent luminaires on 8 ft by 8 ft centers (Fig. 1). The ceiling system in which the luminaires are mounted is standard NEMA G type dropped ceiling. The original fixtures contained standard energy-efficient magnetic ballasts. The conference room contained two 2x4 recessed fixtures. To avoid any confounding effects of lumen maintenance, all luminaires were initially cleaned and all the lamps used in the tests were aged for approximately 100 hours.

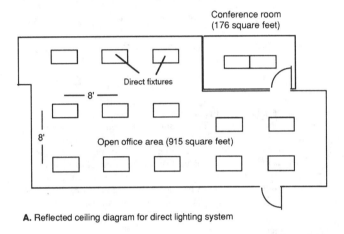

**A.** Reflected ceiling diagram for direct lighting system

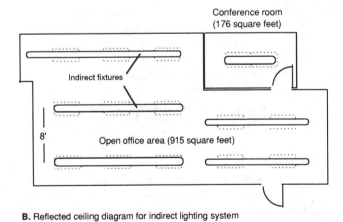

**B.** Reflected ceiling diagram for indirect lighting system

Fig. 1.   Reflected ceiling diagrams showing locations of direct fixtures before retrofitting (A) and location of indirect lighting fixtures (B). In (B), the 24 ft and 20 ft uplights contain 6 lamps each. The two 16 ft uplights in the open office area and the single 8 ft uplight in the conference room contain 4 lamps each. The number of lamps and ballasts remained the same for both indirect and direct lighting systems.

The lighting system was configured in four different manners. The original lighting system consisted of four-lamp 2'x4' direct fluorescent fixtures. On move-in, the tenant had removed two lamps from each fixture because the original system provided nearly 100 fc at a power density of over 2.2 watt/ft² -- far more than required to meet IES recommended levels for the tasks being performed. Therefore, we selected the 2-lamp fixtures to be our basecase. To obtain a baseline light level of 50 foot-candles initially, the reflectors and diffusers were cleaned and the fixtures re-lamped with two "extended output" (EO) lamps to create the basecase direct lighting system. The EO lamps are standard fluorescent lamps except that they contain a slightly more efficient phosphor giving a rated output of 3400 lumens as opposed to 3050 lumens for a lamp with cool white phosphor. (The original fixtures had four standard F40T12 cool white lamps). The remaining three systems used the retrofitted indirect lighting system with different combinations of lamp and ballast as indicated in Table 1.

Table 1. Lighting System Configurations Examined

| Name | Fixture | Lamp Type and Manufacturer | Rated Lamp Lumens | Ballast and Manufacturer |
|---|---|---|---|---|
| Direct T-12 (Baseline) | Direct 2x4 recessed troffer | 2-40W T12 GE F40SXL/SP35 | 3400 | Advance Kool Coil RQM-2S40-3-TP |
| Indirect T-12 | Indirect | 2-40W T12 GE F40SXL/SP35 | 3400 | Advance Kool Coil RQM-2S40-3-TP |
| Indirect T-10 | Indirect | 2-42W T10 Philips F40AX35 | 3700 | Advance Kool Coil RQM-2S40-3-TP |
| Indirect T-8 | Indirect | 2-36W T8 Osram F36T8/35K | 3450 | Osram Quicktronic QT-2x36/120IS |

The retrofit indirect lighting system was installed after completing the baseline measurements on the baseline (de-lamped) direct lighting system. The indirect lighting system (manufactured by Finelite) is mechanically connected to the existing T-bar with aircraft cables to hang 18" below the ceiling plane. The lamps in the indirect fixtures receive electric power from special lamp connectors that make electric contact with the lamp holders installed in the original down lights. The lens for the downlight is replaced with an opaque ceiling tile of similar appearance.

Lighting Measurements

Lighting quality and quantity were assessed by measuring:
1.  Illuminances at representative locations at task surfaces
2.  Luminance distribution on representative portion of one wall
3.  Luminance distribution on representative section of ceiling
4.  Luminances at computer screen and nearby surround

**Illuminances**

Illuminances at workplane height were measured using a recently calibrated Minolta T1 photometer. Illuminances were measured at locations both immediately underneath luminances as well as under storage cabinets and at other locations shielded from direct light from nearest ceiling luminaires.

**Luminance distribution on wall**

To measure the luminance distribution on the wall, a representative wall area in the open office space was selected. Luminances were measured horizontally along the wall every 6 inches along lines 1 ft and 2 ft below the ceiling. Measurements were made starting from the fixture centerline to the next adjacent fixture. The wall along which we made the measurements was 3 ft from the nearest ceiling fixture centerline. Luminance was measured using a Minolta LS100 luminance meter (field of view of 1 degree) aimed normal to the measurement points. The points at which luminance was measured were marked with a grid to allow good reproducibility.

**Luminance distribution on ceiling**

The ceiling luminance distribution was measured on a 9 by 9 grid of points on 6 inch centers. The entire grid was a 4 ft by 4 ft square with the corner of the grid at the center of one of the original fixture locations. The grid location was marked with white tacks in the ceiling

to assure that we were measuring the luminances at the same locations for all lighting system configurations. We used symmetry to extrapolate the grid to obtain the entire luminance distribution between four adjacent fixtures.

**Luminances on computer screen and surround**

A typical workstation with computer was selected for detailed luminance measurement. The purpose of these measurements was to compare the luminance distribution on the computer screen with the direct and indirect lighting systems to compare their performance relative to the recommendations in IES RP-24 [1]. A color VDT screen was adjusted to normal viewing intensity and filled mostly with white characters on a blue background. Some areas of the screen were left without characters and were measured to obtain the background luminance. The screen was left at the same intensity setting and the same screen display was used for all lighting measurements. In addition, a vertical transcription stand with a piece of paper was mounted immediately next to the screen similar to what would be found on a document holder for a word processing application. The areas visible around and behind the VDT screen including portions of partition walls were measured to obtain the surround luminance. Note that no outside windows were visible from the workstation.

**Electrical measurements**

Separate dedicated branch circuits fed the lighting in the office area and the conference room. Thus we measured power by attaching a power meter (Valhalla 2101A) to the branch circuits in the electrical closet. Before any measurements, the lighting system in each configuration was allowed to run for at least a half hour to reach equilibrium. Throughout all the measurements, input voltage varied less than ±1%.

**III. RESULTS**

Electrical Measurements

The results of the electrical measurements are given in Table 2. The input power is somewhat higher with the T-12 indirect system than with the T-12 direct system. Only the T-8 indirect case has lower power than the basecase. Note that the input power to the indirect T-12 system is about 9% higher than the direct T-12 case even though the lamps and ballasts are identical. This is due to the fact that the lamps in the indirect fixtures run cooler and therefore draw more power than the same lamps in the direct recessed fixtures.

Table 2. Electrical Measurements

| Location | Input Voltage (V) | Current (amps) | Power (watts) | Change in Power (%) |
|---|---|---|---|---|
| Direct T-12 (baseline) Office | 119.1 | 9.39 | 1098 | 0.00% |
| Direct T-12 (baseline) Conf. Room | 119.4 | 1.5 | 175 | 0.00% |
| Indirect T-12 Office | 120.1 | 10.12 | 1194 | 8.74% |
| Indirect T-12 Conf. Room | 119.9 | 1.53 | 180 | 2.86% |
| Indirect T-10 Office | 119.4 | 10.66 | 1240 | 12.93% |
| Indirect T-10 Conf. Room | 120 | 1.62 | 189 | 8.00% |
| Indirect T-8 Office | 119.9 | 8.62 | 1014 | -7.65% |
| Indirect T-8 Conf. Room | 120.2 | 1.32 | 156 | -10.86% |

Illuminance Measurements

Illuminance measurements for the four lighting configurations are given in Table 3. Eight measurement locations in the open-office area, which we term the primary locations, are representative of horizontal illuminance at 30" above the floor at typical task locations. Four of these points are roughly between luminaires, the remainder more immediately underneath the luminaires. The primary locations in the conference room were at desk height primarily underneath the ceiling fixtures.

Table 3. Illuminance Measurements in Foot-candles

| Location | Direct T12 | Indirect T12 | Indirect T10 | Indirect T8 |
|---|---|---|---|---|
| *Primary locations, office* | | | | |
| A | 38 | 39 | 44 | 46 |
| B | 35 | 38 | 42 | 45 |
| C | 42.5 | 43 | 49 | 54 |
| D | 33 | 43 | 48 | 53 |
| 2 | 44 | 37 | 42 | 47 |
| 3 | 46 | 32 | 34 | 41 |
| 5 | 20 | 32 | 36 | 41 |
| 11 | 21 | 25 | 27 | 29 |
| **Ave  &lt;A-D,2,3,5,11&gt;** | **35** | **36** | **40** | **45** |
| Stdev &lt;A-D,2,3,5,11&gt; | 10 | 6 | 7 | 8 |
| | | | | |
| *Secondary locations, office* | | | | |
| 1 | 14 | 31 | 36 | 38 |
| 6 | 7 | 10 | 11 | 12 |
| 7 | 13 | 13 | 14 | 16 |
| 9 | 12 | 24 | 26 | 28 |
| 10 | 19 | 30 | 33 | 35 |
| Ave &lt;1,6,7,9,10&gt; | 13 | 22 | 24 | 26 |
| | | | | |
| *Primary locations, conference room* | | | | |
| E | 53 | 43 | 49 | 52 |
| F | 58 | 45 | 51 | 56 |
| G | 61 | 46 | 53 | 58 |
| H | 62 | 47 | 54 | 59 |
| corner | 18 | 23 | 25 | 29 |
| Ave &lt;E-H,corner&gt; | 50 | 41 | 46 | 51 |
| | | | | |
| **Grand Ave** | **33** | **33** | **37** | **41** |
| Grand Stdev | 18 | 11 | 13 | 14 |
| | | | | |
| *Vertical illumination, office* | | | | |
| 8 | 27 | 33 | 34 | 41 |
| 12 | 10 | 18 | 19 | 22 |

## Wall Luminance Measurements

The measured wall luminance distribution for the direct T-12 system and indirect T-12 system are plotted in Fig. 2A and 2B, respectively. At 1 ft below the ceiling plane, the luminance from the indirect lighting system is uniform and 2 to 4 times as bright as the luminance with the direct fixtures. At 2 ft below the ceiling plane, the luminance of the indirect and direct systems are roughly the same between fixtures, but the wall luminance is much lower with direct lighting along the fixture centerline.

**A.** 1 ft below ceiling

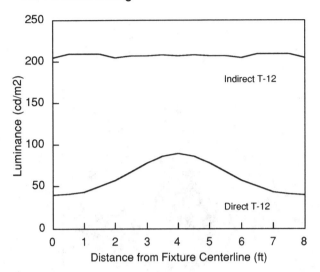

**B.** 2 ft below ceiling

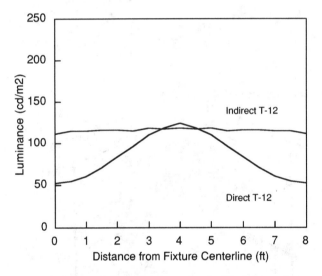

Fig. 2. Luminances of representative section of wall for indirect and direct T-12 lighting systems.

## Ceiling Luminance Measurements

The ceiling luminance distribution for the indirect and direct T-12 lighting systems are plotted as 3-D surfaces in Fig. 3. Note that the vertical axis plots log luminance. This quantity is more closely related to perceived brightness and is also easier to compare the large differences between these types of lighting systems.

419

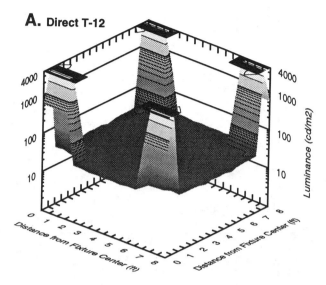

## A. Direct T-12

## B. Indirect T-12

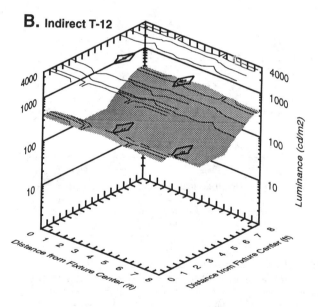

Fig. 3. Luminance distribution on 8 ft by 8 ft portion of ceiling. The corners of the plots correspond to the centerpoints of four adjacent fixtures. The ceiling luminance distribution is shown in (A) for the direct T-12 system and in (B) for the indirect T-12 system. The contour lines shown are on 100 cd/m$^2$ increments.

The ceiling luminance data was analyzed and averaged over 0.6 m by 0.6 m areas as specified by RP-24 [1]. Since we measured the luminance every 6 inches, we averaged over a square 5 x 5 grid of points to obtain average minimum and maximum luminances. These averages and max to min ratios are presented in Table 4.

Table 4. Summary of ceiling luminance measurements
Luminances in candela/meter$^2$

|  | Ave | Standard Deviation | Min[a] | Max[a] | Max/Min |
|---|---|---|---|---|---|
| T-12 Direct | 254 | 821 | 26.2 | 2081 | 79.2 |
| T-12 Indirect | 237 | 119 | 105 | 387 | 3.67 |
| T-10 Indirect | 272 | 139 | 119 | 439 | 3.7 |
| T-8 Indirect | 282 | 146 | 129 | 465 | 3.62 |

[a] Averaged over 0.6 m by 0.6 m per [1]

### Computer Screen Measurements

The results of the luminance measurements at the computer screen are given in Table 5.

Table 5. Luminance measurements on computer screen
Luminances in candela/meter$^2$

|  | T-12 Direct | T-12 Indirect | T-10 Indirect | T-8 Indirect |
|---|---|---|---|---|
| Screen, No text | 8 | 10 | 10 | 11 |
| Screen, Text | 13 | 14 | 18 | 15 |
| Screen, Glare, No text | 22 | 22 | 24 | 28 |
| Vertical Paper | 49 | 59 | 65 | 69 |
| Horizontal Paper | 77 | 87 | 97 | 105 |
| Pt A @ Horiz. Desk | 15 | 15 | 20 | 17 |
| Pt B @ Horiz. Desk | 13 | 17 | 18 | 20 |
| Partition surround | 28-33 | 38-48 | 41-50 | 43-53 |

Note that the luminance of the screen with text and the screen without text increases slightly with the indirect lighting but the luminance of the highlight reflected in the screen remains about the same. It is also seen that the luminances of all vertical surfaces, including the surround luminance behind the screen and luminance of the vertically oriented paper immediately adjacent to the screen, are higher in the case of indirect lighting.

### Workplane Lumen Efficacy

A key parameter for assessing the ability of a lighting system to efficiently provide light at the workplane is the workplane lumen efficacy. This parameter is computed by dividing the average workplane illuminance by the lighting power density. Workplane lumen efficacy has units of lumens/watt and is therefore analogous to the lamp/ballast system efficacy except that it accounts for effect of the luminaire and the application conditions. Workplane lumen efficacy for the various examined lighting system configurations are given in Table 6. The average of the primary illuminance points in the open-office space (Table 3) were used for the estimate of workplane illuminance. Note that the T-10 and T-12 indirect cases have higher lighting power densities than the basecase while the T-8 case is lower. Compared to direct lighting with the same lamps and ballasts, indirect lighting only slightly decreases workplane lumen efficacy. In the case of the T-8 system, workplane lumen efficacy is increased nearly 38%. This improvement is due to the highly efficient lamp/ballast combination for this system.

Table 6. Workplane lumen efficacy for various tested systems

| Location | Power (watts) | Lighting Power Density (W/ft$^2$) | Ave. Light (fc) | Workplane Lumen Efficacy (l/w) | % Change in Workplane Lumen Efficacy |
|---|---|---|---|---|---|
| Direct T-12 (baseline) Office | 1098 | 1.20 | 35 | 29.1 | 0.0% |
| Indirect T-12 Office | 1194 | 1.30 | 36 | 27.8 | -4.5% |
| Indirect T-10 Office | 1240 | 1.36 | 40 | 29.6 | 1.7% |
| Indirect T-8 Office | 1014 | 1.11 | 45 | 40.1 | 37.8% |

## Installation Costs

Table 7 summarizes the installed costs for the indirect lighting system equipped with the 36 watt T-8 lamps and electronic ballasts.

Table 7
Installed cost for T-8 indirect system

|  | Office Area | Conference Room |
| --- | --- | --- |
| Fixture Cost | $2,280 | $190 |
| Electronic Ballast and Lamp Costs | $425 | $66 |
| Installation | $570 | $45 |
| Total Installed Cost | $3,275 | $301 |
| Installed Cost per Square Foot | $3.58 | $1.71 |

The installed cost for the indirect T-8 system was therefore approximately $3.28/ft$^2$ for both the open-office area and the conference room.

## IV. DISCUSSION

Comparing the light measurements between the direct T-12 and the indirect T-12 case reveals several interesting differences between the two types of systems. For locations directly underneath the fixtures (points A-D in the conference room) the illuminance is about 22% lower in the indirect case than in the direct. But at other locations, such as points E-H, which are located at desk height in the partitioned office area roughly between luminaires, the illuminance is actually 11% higher with indirect lighting. It is also clear that for locations near partition walls or underneath storage cabinets, (points 1-11) that the light levels are generally somewhat higher with indirect lighting. This is especially true of vertical illuminance measurements. This is significant since it indicates that the presence of partitions and storage cabinets, which are so common in many open-office spaces, more negatively affects the delivered illuminance from direct lighting systems than indirect lighting.

Examination of the ceiling luminance distribution indicates that, with direct lighting, the luminance varies nearly 80 to 1 when luminances are averaged over 0.6 m by 0.6 m patches as specified by [1]. The average luminance of the direct ceiling fixture is well over 2000 cd/m$^2$, which is considerably higher than the 850 cd/m$^2$ luminance limit required by RP-24 for direct lighting fixtures for computer tasks. With indirect lighting, ceiling luminance varies only about 3.6 to 1, which surpasses the RP-24 preferred ceiling luminance uniformity of 4:1 for indirect lighting for computer tasks.. Note also that the highest ceiling luminance for all indirect lighting configurations examined never exceeded 850 cd/m$^2$, which is RP-24's limit for ceiling luminance with indirect lighting.

The luminance patterns on the wall immediately below the ceiling are quite different between indirect and direct lighting. With direct lighting, the wall luminance is non-uniform and generally relatively low. With indirect lighting, the luminance is overall higher, and is highest at the ceiling and decreases down from the ceiling. Also the luminance pattern horizontally is very uniform for indirect lighting. This is important for providing a uniform luminance background that is not distracting when reflectively viewed in a computer screen.

Indirect lighting did not reduce the measured veiling reflections off the computer screen thus it did not improve the visibility of the screen relative to the direct lighting system. Also the glare highlight was not reduced with indirect lighting. Qualitatively, however, with the direct lighting system, sharply defined images of five down light lenses can be clearly seen reflected in the VDT screen. The reflection of the ceiling in the screen, in the case of indirect lighting, is less distracting than the sharply defined reflection of the direct luminaires. The relatively uniform luminance of the wall and ceiling that can be observed with indirect lighting has no sharp discernible borders, unlike the situation with direct lighting. Thus, with indirect lighting, the computer operator is less tempted to continually adjust eye focus because the glare, though present, is more diffuse and less specific. This should tend to reduce operator fatigue, even though quantitatively, there is little difference between the two lighting systems.

The T-8 indirect lighting system provided at average initial workplane illuminance of 45 foot-candles at 1.1 w/ft$^2$. These T-8 lamps draw 36 watts rather than the 32 watts drawn by most T-8 lamps. The electronic ballast used for these lamps is also very efficient and drives the 36 watt lamps with a ballast factor of 1.05. Had we used standard T-8 lamps and electronic ballasts, the supplied illuminance would have been approximately 36 foot-candles initial but the system would draw only 0.87 w/ft$^2$.

## V. CONCLUSIONS

When using the same lamps and ballasts, an indirect lighting system provided about the same amount of lumens at the workplane in a partitioned open-office space as a direct lighting system with the same type of lamp and ballast. Using very efficient T-8 lamps and electronic ballasts indirect lighting provided approximately 45 foot-candles at a power density of only 1.1 w/ft$^2$. The luminances on the walls and ceilings were significantly higher and more uniform with the indirect lighting. The workplane illuminance uniformity was also significantly improved. The indirect lighting system met all the requirements for indirect lighting as specified in RP-24 but did not significantly improve the visibility of the screen relative to the direct lighting case.

## References

[1] Illuminating Engineering Society of North America, "IES Recommended Practice for Lighting Offices Containing Computer Visual Display Terminals," RP-24, 1989.

# Chapter 74
# New Efficient Lighting Products and Security Lighting - Are They Compatible?

R.A. Tucker

## SECURITY LIGHTING

Properly applied, light sources and lighting systems not only enhance a building's attractiveness and usability, they also create a secure environment. An effectively lighted area can minimize pedestrian hazards and auto accidents. Good security lighting also eliminates the darkness that vandals, thieves, and felons thrive on. Unfortunately, lighting quality has sometimes been sacrificed for the sake of energy efficiency, and resulting savings offset by poor aesthetics and user dissatisfaction. Trade-offs in quality and efficiency are not necessary, however, thanks to recent developments in light source technology.

## LIGHTING CHOICES

Progress in light source technology has given designers more options for security lighting systems. Each family of light sources has its own characteristics. Matching those characteristics to the requirements of a particular security lighting project is the goal of the lighting designer. The designer's primary objective should be to optimize energy use, not to minimize it.

In order to make the best decisions, the designer should first consider security objectives. Are would be intruders to be deterred or apprehended? Is greater visible light antagonistic to security requirements? Will visible light creat a nuisance for personnel or neighbors? Is there advantages to covert surveillance with invisible lighting?

In the design of an exterior CCTV (closed circuit TV) security system, light can make the difference between good and bad results. The illuminated scenes visible to the eye generally are less acceptable to a CCTV camera. Two to three footcandles is enough light to prevent accidents, for instance, but 20 to 30 footcandles may be necessary for a surveillance camera. Infrared light, on the other hand, can provide a site profile and security lighting benefits without the problems associated with visible lighting systems. (Note: A CCTV expert should be consulted for best results.)

## SECURITY LIGHT SOURCE TECHNOLOGY

Once security objectives have been established, the designer can begin weighing the pros and cons of different light source families and the possibilities for energy management. One question in particular is worth considering: Can existing fixtures be upgraded with more efficient light sources?

As noted, light sources fall into two broad categories - visible and invisible. Visible light sources are categorized here as filament and arc discharge. Infrared (and near-infrared) is the invisible illumination available to designers and specifiers.

### Filament

While the incandescent lamp family is the least efficient of the light sources, it offers the advantages of compactness, flexibility, and excellent color rendition. Halogen capsule technology, pioneered for automobile headlamps, has led to the development of many new general lighting sources in this family. Forty-five -watt and 90-watt halogen capsule PAR lamps, for example, can replace 75-watt and 150-watt PAR incandescent lamps respectively. The halogen capsule lamps deliver the same usable light output and beam spread and maintain the same lamp life as conventional incandescent PAR sources, but they use 40 percent less energy.

Newly designed 75-watt halogen and 60-watt halogen-IR PAR lamps allow the user to reduce the energy use even more without sacrificing light or life.

### Arc Discharge

Fluorescent: These fluorescent light sources have long been used for safety and security lighting in stairwells, hallways, elevator lobbies, passageways, and corridors. Recent innovations with cathode designs, different fill gas, and dual-coat phosphor technology have led to four-foot, 32-watt, T-12 fluorescent lamps that operate on existing rapid-start, standard, and low wattage energy saving ballasts. These new lamps can reduce power usage by up to 20% with a 7 to 12 percent reduction in light output.

The most energy efficient fluorescent light source is the reduced diameter T-8 lamp. In addition to using rare earth phosphors efficiently, this lamp employs solid-state, electronic ballasts to provide an exceptionally high lumen per watt efficacy. Retrofitting a 40-watt T-12 system with the four-foot T-8 system yields the same amount of light but costs 40 percent less to operate.

The T-8 lamps come in 2-,3-,4-,5- and a new 8-foot straight lamp version, as well as three U-shaped lamps of 16-, 24-, and 31-watts. All T-8 lamps are compatible with luminaire sockets designed for T-12 lamps. The rapid start lamps, straight or bent, use medium bi-pin bases and the 8-foot lamp has a single pin base. A new ballast is required for this lighting system, however, because the T-8 lamps operate at 265 milliamps (ma), while T-12 lamps operate at 430ma. These T-8 lamps have a rated life of 20,000 hours and excellent lumen maintenance characteristics. They are available in 3100K, 3500K and 4100K color temperatures.

Compact fluorescent lamps are available for security lighting applications that have traditionally used low-wattage incandescent lamps. Available in a range of from 5 to 26 watts, the compact fluorescents offer both life and efficiency advantages combined with compatible color temperature and high color rendering. They have an integral starter, operate on simple choke ballasts, are single-ended, and have plug-in, two-pin bases. These preheat lamps have a life rating of 10,000 hours - four to ten times the life of standard incandescents.

Most building exit signs are lighted with incandescents. The incandescent sources used are less efficient and have short life ratings. This results in an on-going battle to keep these inefficient signs lighted. Compact fluorescent lamps provide a unique solution. Conversion kits are available to retrofit existing full size exit signs so they use less energy and last longer without sacrificing any light.

With the use of compact fluorescent adapters, a 25-, 40-, or 60-watt existing incandescent fixture can be retrofitted with 5-, 7-, 9-, 13-, or 18-watt compact fluorescent lighting, yielding energy savings of up to 70 percent. The adapters simply screw into standard, medium-base incandescent sockets, and the lamps plug into the adapters.

Even more compact double twin-tube or quad lamps are available for situations in which single, twin-tube compact fluorescents are too long. Quad lamps come in 9-, 13-, 18-, and 26-watt sizes and in colors of 2700K, 3500K, and 4100K. Dimming equipment is also available for the 18- and 26-watt quad lamps.

High Intensity Discharge: The high intensity discharge (HID) group of lamps is comprised of three basic types: High pressure sodium, metal halide, and mercury vapor. This family of lamps and lighting equipment has been most popular where high light efficiency and long life are desired. Until recently, 175 watts was the lowest wattage metal halide lamp available. Now there is a family of low wattage metal halide lamps ranging from 32- to 150-watts, available in a tubular, double-ended configuration, a single-ended with a medium base, or a PAR 38 reflector lamp with various beam spreads and a medium base.

Other refinements in metal halide technology have increased the light output of horizontally operated lamps by as much as 15 percent. These lamps have special position oriented mogul (POM) bases that properly position the arc tube for optimum performance. Vertically operated lamps have made up to 11 percent efficiency gains, also because of arc tube geometry modifications.

Standard metal halide equipment requires approximately 5 to 15 minutes to restart after a power interruption. Relatively new instant restart metal halide equipment has the capability to relight instantaneously with the use of a high voltage ignitor. Light output is restored at various levels dependent on the length of the power outage.

High pressure sodium lamps are extremely efficient and have a long life - 24,000 hours for most types. Medium base lamps offer the same life and lumen packages as their mogul based counterparts but are more compact. These smaller lamps have led to more compact, more efficient luminaries. Medium base high pressure sodium lamps are available in 35-, 50-, 70-,100-, and 150-

watt sizes.

When extinguished, even by a momentary power interruption, HID lamps generally require a period of time to cool before restarting. The length of restart times, which varies from one to ten minutes depending on lamp type, has required many designers of HID systems to provide standby lighting in the form of (1) separate systems or (2) tungsten halogen lamps installed in a select number of fixtures for low level lighting until the HID lamps restart. To compensate for restart time, high pressure sodium lamps with two arc tubes have been introduced. These are available in 70-, 100-, 150-, 200-, 250-, 400-, and 1000-watt sizes and operate on existing ballasts. One arc tube in these lamps operates normally while the other remains off. If power is interrupted, the lamp extinguishes; then when power is restored, the second arc tube strikes, providing immediate, low level illumination. When this arc tube warms up, it becomes the primary source while the other acts as a standby in the event of another power interruption. In some installations, these lamps eliminate the need for auxiliary standby lighting systems.

INVISIBLE LIGHT

Infrared Light

Infrared light is often overlooked by lighting designers because it is not fully understood. Although not necessarily an energy-efficient source, infrared light is excellent for security lighting, especially when visible light may be a nuisance.

To varying degrees, a spectral distribution of visible light includes some infrared, but it is possible to design a light source that produces only invisible light in the near-infrared spectral range of 800 to 1,000 nanometers (nm-unit used to measure light wavelengths). The human eye stops seeing light at about 800nm; hence, the near-infrared portion (800 to 1100nm) is invisible. Most standard silicon diode target (SDT) and CCD cameras can "see" infrared light very well.

Available in line voltage in 300-watt and 500-watt sizes, and in low voltage, 24 volt and 6.3-watts, a near-infrared floodlight illuminates an area for a black-and-white SDT and CCD camera about as well as a visible light source of the same wattage illuminates the area for the human eye. This type of lighting system is ideal for situations where security lighting is required but where visible light may disturb neighbors, encourage loitering, call attention to a secured site, alert intruders to the presence of security monitoring, or counteract a lower or covert site profile.

The keys to infrared fixture performance are thin-film dichroic lamp coatings and absorbing filters. Dichroic coatings can reflect or transmit certain light wavelengths. In a fixture that generates invisible light, a dichroic cold coating is applied to the front of the lamp to reflect unwanted visible light wavelengths to the back of the fixture while allowing the infrared wavelengths to pass through it. A dichroic hot coating is applied to the rear lamp surface to reflect useful infrared light forward while transmitting the visible and long infrared wavelengths out the back of the lamp.

Near-infrared light is not measurable with a standard light meter. The best way to lay out a system is with a field demonstration with the cameras and monitor set up. An infrared light meter (radiometer) is available, but it is best to field test the system to ensure the best results.

## THE FUTURE

The selection of light sources has, without a doubt, become more complex. As demands to decrease energy use and to increase safety and security grow, more new light sources will be developed. The filament source family, for example, will see expanded use of halogen technology. The use of double-coat phosphor technology and smaller lamp geometry will expand the application of fluorescent lamps. High frequency, solid-state ballasts will increase the efficiency of both fluorescent and HID lighting systems; and HID light sources will become more compact.

Various utilities offer incentives or rebates to off-set some of the first cost for an energy efficient lighting system by paying cash directly to the end user. Government regulations and standards are being developed that will set requirements and limits for lighting systems for the design community. The interest in more efficient lighting exhibited by the EPA in their Green Lights program certainly appeals to voluntary efforts based on the general good of the country.

As designers continue to operate in this arena of heightened energy awareness, lighting will remain a prime candidate for cost-saving ideas. However, there is a delicate balance that lies between lighting a space efficiently and lighting it properly. Considering two factors will help designers achieve this balance. The first involves determining light quality and quantity by safety and security task analysis. The second involves keeping abreast of new technology.

## CONCLUSION

To be compatible, energy efficient lighting must provide the same quantity and quality of illumination as needed for effective security lighting. There are a number of energy saving lamps available now that can do just that. Lighting retrofits, however, should be implemented with a security objective in mind. Various codes, new technology and good judgement are the key ingredients for an effective security lighting system. With so much at stake, it is best to rely on a lighting professional.

## REFERENCES

1. Bachner, John P., "Effective Security Lighting", Journal of Security Administration, 1985.

2. Tucker, R. Arnold, "New Light Sources for Security Lighting", The Construction Specifier, September 1989.

3. Gregerson, John, "Designing for Security", Building Design & Construction, March 1991.

## Chapter 75
# T-8 Profits for Improved Lighting and Energy Efficiency

M. Heis

## Introduction

Fifth Third Center is a 32 story office tower located in Cincinnati, Ohio. The building was completed in 1968 and during 1987, the owners became very interested in modernizing the building systems. Two of the systems targeted were the HVAC and lighting systems. The goal was to improve tenant comfort while reducing operating costs. During the period of 01/88 to 06/92, the building has been able to reduce its utility bills by $400,000 per year while improving tenant comfort. The average payback for a project has been 2 years or less. A major part of the lighting modernization program is the application of T-8 technology. This article discusses the application and performance characteristics of T-8 lamps, electronic ballasts and three lamp, 2 x 4 fixtures.

## Lamps

The goal of the lighting retrofit was to improve lighting quality while reducing energy consumption. We found that T-8 lamps provided substantial reductions in power input while providing full light output. With four lamp fixtures, T-8 lamps and electronic ballasts reduced input watts by more than 40% (compared to the existing four lamp fixtures using magnetic ballasts).

The T-8 designation refers to the lamp diameter expressed in one-eights of an inch. The T-8 lamp is one inch in diameter. The standard T-12 lamp is 1.5 inches in diameter.

The smaller T-8 lamp diameter allows for the use of expensive rare earth phosphors more economically, making a higher performance lamp affordable for general office lighting use. Also, the T-8 diameter allows improved fixture photometry, increasing fixture efficiency. Because of the rare earth phosphors, T-8 lamps have a coloring rendering index (CRI) of 80. Cool white T-12 lamps have a CRI of 62 and warm white T-12 lamps a rating of only 52. In general, the higher the CRI number, the better the color rendering properties of the light source. T-8 lamps are also available in three correlated color temperatures - 3100K, 3500K and 4100K.

Lumen maintenance is also higher for the T-8 lamp. After 8000 hours of operation, the light output of a F40CW lamp will drop by 15% or more from its initial light level, while the F032 T-8 lamp light output will only drop by 10%.

## Ballasts

The amount of light that a lamp produces is determined by the Ballast Factor. The Ballast Factor is an indication of the amount of light produced by the ballast/lamp combination. The ballast efficacy factor is an expression of lumens per watt, for a given system. By the proper selection of ballasts, light output from a fixture can be the rated light output (according to lamp specifications), increased light output or reduced light output. The ballasts that we tested with the T-8 lamps ranged from 51 watts to 72 watts for a two lamp T-8 system. The 51 watts was achieved using the Triad Low Power electronic ballast while the 72 watts was from an Advance Mark V VIC-2540-TP. As you can see, input watts can vary significantly depending on the ballast selected. Although the Mark V had a higher light output, we chose to use the more efficient Triad Low Power electronic ballast. Electronic ballasts were used because we preferred the advantages of the electronic ballasts over magnetic ballasts. These benefits include higher energy efficiency, quiet operation (no hum), cooler operation, longer life, lighter weight and no flicker.

To further reduce our energy consumption and initial cost, we used 4-lamp ballasts wherever possible. The 4-lamp Triad Low Power ballast uses only 95 watts to power four T-8 lamps. This compares with 102 watts if two 2-lamp ballasts are used (and 2 ballasts cost more than 1 ballast). In order to use 4 lamp ballasts in 3 lamp fixtures, the fixtures were tandem wired. A 4-lamp and a 2 lamp ballast were located in the master fixture with tandem wiring to a slave fixture. The 4 lamp ballast is wired to the outer two lamps in each fixture and the 2 lamp ballast is wired to the center lamp in each fixture.

## Luminaires

A software program was used to select the most efficient luminaires for general office illumination. Three lamp, 2 x 4 fixtures were selected by the program. Two lamp, 2 x 2 fixtures were selected for corridors and the elevator lobbies. About 80% of the fixtures were 2 x 4, static troffers with .125 thick acrylic prismatic lenses. The remaining 20% were 2 x 2 static troffers and 2 x 4, 3 lamp parabolic, 18 cell, 3" deep parabolic luminaires. The three lamp, 2 x 4 system was found to be much more efficient than a four lamp, 2 x 4 system. The least efficient system would have been a four lamp, 2 x 4, parabolic system.

## Switching

Because three lamp fixtures were used, a three light level system was designed. The center lamp in each fixture is controlled independently of the outer two lamps. This allows reduced light levels after hours for housekeeping or other special activities. The single lamp operation provides approximately 30 FC. Three lamp operation is used for normal office work. Two switches are provided for each zone, one for the center lamps, and one for the outer two lamps.

## Air Conditioning Reduction

Using energy efficient lighting greatly reduces air conditioning load in office spaces. On an annual basis, per KWH of lighting energy reduction, from 12 to 32% reduction in KWHs used for A/C can be expected. The percentage depends on the building characteristics and climate. Generally, a higher cost savings can be expected because most areas have ratchet charges based on the summer electrical demand. In addition, A/C equipment can often be down-sized because of the lower heat generation of the lighting system. Air conditioning requirements are reduced by one ton for each 3.5 KW reduction in lighting load.

## System Description

The new lighting system is a 3 light level system. Each 2 x 4 fixture contains 3 lamps. The center lamp is controlled independently of the outer two lamps. The three-lamp fixtures have two switches. The left hand switch (red dot) controls the center (or inside) lamp and the right hand switch (blue dot) controls the outer two lamps.

The common area light fixtures are on a lighting control system. The center lamp is turned on automatically at 6 am on work days. If light is needed before 6 am or "after hours", the switch can be turned on and the lights will come on. If the switch is already in the "on" position and the lights are off, turn the switch off and back on. This will override the control system and bring the lights on. The lights can be turned off by operating the switch anytime. The lighting control system will turn the lights off at 2 am if they are left on. The outer two lamps are turned on by the employees as the arrive in the morning. The outer two lamps will be turned off at approximately 6:30 pm unless the department has extended hours. If the lights should go out while employees are still working in the area, the light switch can override the system. The switch should be turned off and then back on. The center lamp provides 30 footcandles of light which is a good level for general work and moving around. However, the full 90 footcandles is recommended for office work. Two lamps will provide approximately 60 footcandles of light. This is the minimum level of light recommended for office work. The system provides all three levels.

Individual offices and rooms generally are not controlled by the lighting control system. They must be turned on and off by the employees working in these areas.

A great deal of electricity, money and pollution can be saved by employees turning their lights off when they leave their offices. On hot days, turning the lights office in an office during lunch will allow the A/C to better cool the offices.

An office with four 3 lamp fixtures will use 300 watt hours of electricity in one hour. It will also contribute 300 watts of load to the air conditioning system and cause .48 pounds of pollution to be produced by C G & E (plus possibly another .48 pounds of pollution from the A/C system). By turning lights off when they are not needed you will:
1. Save energy dollars.
2. Reduce air pollution.
3. Reduce the air conditioning load.
4. Extend the life of the lamps & ballasts.

## New Lighting System Data (Typical Floor)

Total Lighting Wattage - 16,000 watts (new system)
Total Lighting Wattage - 33,000 watts (old system)

Watts per fixture (2x4) - 75 watts (new system)

Watts per fixture (2x4) - 160 watts (old system)

Color Rendition Index (CRI) - 80 high color quality (new system)
Color Rendition Index (CRI) - 62 average color quality (old system)

Lumen output efficiency - 120 lumens/watt (new system)
Lumen output efficiency - 75 lumens/watt (old system)

Lumen output efficiency - 15 lumens/watt (old incandescent)

Cost to operate lights with the new system for one year - $2,745.00
Cost to operate lights with the old system for one year - $5,662.00

A/C needed to offset lights on new floor - 4.5 tons
A/C needed to offset lights on old floor - 9.3 tons

Coal burnt by CG&E to light new floor for one year - 43,034 pounds
Coal burnt by CG&E to light old floor for one year - 88,758 pounds

Estimated pollution caused by new lighting per floor - 74,880 pounds $CO_2$; 499 pounds $SO_2$ and 299 pounds NO.
Estimated pollution caused by old lighting per floor - 154,440 pounds $CO_2$; 1,030 pounds $SO_2$ and 618 pounds NO.

New technology T-8 lamps provide fully light output while using substantially less energy. T-8 lamps use high efficiency rare earth phosphors and a dual coat phosphor process to achieve high light output with excellent color balance. The higher CRI of the T-8 lamp means that colors will be less distorted and more like their "true" colors as seen in sunlight. The annual pollution caused by the production of electricity to power the new lamps is estimated to be 80,000 pounds less than the pollution caused by the production of electricity to power the old lamps.

# Chapter 76

# New Lighting Options: What Users Will Find - And What They Still Need

L. Audin

## INTRODUCTION

The last five years have seen an explosion of new lighting products, and the acceptance of technologies that, only a decade before, had been confined to the laboratory. But while it is true that the variety of high efficiency lighting options has never been greater, there are still gaps in the product line, and unfulfilled needs in the lighting efficiency community. Following is an overview of some of the latest products, followed by conjecture and suggestions for the next wave of lighting miracles.

## THE LEADING EDGE

### Ballasts

The electronic ballast for fluorescent lamps is becoming generally accepted as the appropriate replacement for most core-and-coil ballasts. Supported by generous utility rebates, these solid state devices are now available from over a dozen manufacturers, and the supply bottlenecks of the last three years appear to have diminished.

In response to users, several ballast makers are now also providing specialized versions that allow greater energy savings at little or no increase in cost. While the early versions of electronic ballasts served only two T-12 or T-8 lamps at normal output, one can now purchase electronic ballasts with ballast factors significantly above or below 1.0, with proportional changes in wattage. Driven by retrofit installers that often combine lamp and ballast changeouts with reflectors that may also increase fixture efficiency, these ballasts offer major new flexibility in altering light levels without changing the number or layout of existing fixtures.

For those desiring greater light output in the T-8 package, another lamp ballast option (presently available from only one lamp vendor), uses a proprietary lamp that offers a boost in light from existing fixtures. Additional flexibility and economy results from use of new low harmonic single, three and four lamp ballasts that offer easy installation of multiple level switching, tandemed ballasts and reballasting of built-in task lighting (which typically uses a single lamp).

Most exciting is the recent unveiling of "wireless" dimmable ballasts and controls that install as easily as standard ballasts and require no additional wiring. Shown earlier this year, the controllers use power

line carrier technology and infrared sensing to allow communication between the controllers and the ballast, and the user and the controller, respectively. One manufacturer has built into his controller an infrared occupancy sensor that shuts off (or dims) the lights when a room is unoccupied, and provides a hand-held remote that allows the user to dim lighting from any location in the room - an excellent option for those making visual presentations in a large lecture hall.

But solid state electronics has not stopped with standard fluorescents. Instead, it has now entered the realm of compact fluorescent (CF) and high intensity discharge (HID) lamps. While previously confined to one-piece screw-in CF lamps, miniature electronic ballasts became available in this country as separate units about two years ago and are now also available in models designed for new fixtures. Unlike some of their predecessors, these newer CF ballasts have low harmonics, are transient protected, and offer high ballast factors. For metal halide and "white" high pressure sodium lamps in the 50 to 150 watt range, electronic ballasts designed for new fixtures offer significantly reduced size, noise and ballast losses, making them easily worth the premium cost.

### Lamps

Several new lamps have created additional options for lighting designers. The first eight foot T-8 "Octron" lamp was unveiled at Lightfair last May, along with an electronic ballast designed to fire two of these lamps. Retrofitters can now easily upgrade existing eight foot fixtures, and costs for using the efficient and high quality T-8 system will drop since wiring and socket costs will be cut nearly in half for such fixtures.

New "compact" HID lamps (under 175 watts) offer a wider range of choices for replacement of high wattage incandescent lamps. A new line of metal halide PAR lamps, for example, should provide an opportunity for retrofit (or replacement) of existing incandescent fixtures while cutting power consumption by at least two-thirds, and greatly increasing lamp life. Some of these new lamps are designed for use in open fixtures, further increasing their light output while reducing maintenance. Several additions to the "white" (i.e., high CRI) high pressure sodium family likewise allow for low cost retrofitting. When combined with the new electronic ballasts becoming available for them, many new designs become possible due to reduced size, noise and heat output.

Even the realm of the compact fluorescent has not remained still. Previously available only as an import, "flat", or 2-D, CF lamps are now being marketed domestically, along with several new fixture designs. Looking a little like a square Circline lamp, these 2-D sources could foster luminous surfaces, small drum-shaped fixtures, and unique indirect lighting.

Two lamp manufacturers have produced screw-in CF lamps that use three U-shaped structures where previously only dual-U "quad" lamps existed. Doing so increases light output while not increasing lamp length. One model is also the first multiple light level CF lamp. Operating in a standard 3-way socket (it's actually three 9 watt lamps in one housing), it provides 3 levels of lighting, just like a standard 3-way incandescent lamp.

Another addition to the fluorescent family is the double-ended subminiature lamp. Looking more like lab thermometers or overgrown swizzle sticks, these thin tubes are less than a quarter inch in diameter but are otherwise identical to their larger brothers. Designed for use where only a small amount of light is needed, the subminiatures will likely supplant miniature incandescent lamps in decorative applications and internal equipment lighting. They may also create whole new ways of lighting tasks, signage, and high-end merchandising.

The final new offspring of the lamp industry is a distant cousin from the others. Long on the test benches of several laboratories, the electrodeless fluorescent lamp has arrived. In standard fluorescent lamps, the electrodes emit electrons by heating coatings that break down slightly each time the lamp is started. The electrons stimulate gaseous mercury into producing ultraviolet light that is converted to visible light by lamp phosphors. As these coatings are "boiled off", lamp lifetime is reduced. The electrodeless system uses microwaves (in the radio frequency part of the spectrum) to excite the mercury's own electrons into a plasma. As they shift back and forth between being independent or rejoining their nuclei, these electrons also emit ultraviolet light that excites phosphors. The electrodeless system thus promises longer lamp life, since there are no coatings to boil off.

Originally introduced in Europe in 1991, the first incarnations of this system appeared as screw-in bulbs designed to compete with incandescent and screw-in CF lamps. There may be some controversy, however, because two companies are laying claim to the technology in the U.S. When a major European lamp maker unveiled its version in early May of this year at the Lightfair lighting show in New York, it claimed a potential 60,000 hour lifetime, but no general media coverage was sought. Less than a month later, a small west coast technology firm, in a major media blitz, showed off its 20,000 hour version, pitching it to the general consumer market as the sole supplier of lamps that will "last 14 years." While nearly all standard fluorescent lamps are already rated for 20,000 hour lifetimes, most CF lamps last only 7 to 10,000 hours, so either system would be an improvement. As far as energy efficiency is concerned, neither does better than CF lamps.

On the other hand, this new technology raises the usual questions concerning radio interference (both makers say there will be none), safety in case of bulb breakage (the answers were less clear here), cost (comparable to CF lamps), and availability (not until 1993, assuming there are no suits over patent infringement).

Fixtures

Just as new lamps and ballasts have expanded the lighting designer's choices, so has the development of new fixtures, especially in spaces containing video display terminals (VDT). Avoiding screen glare has stimulated interest in indirect lighting fixtures, but most require pendant-mounting at least 12 to 18 inches below a ceiling, which may be unattractive or impossible in spaces with low ceilings or raised floors. Similarly, offices equipped with temporary partitions may have problems with a static arrangement of ceiling fixtures, if the partitions are high enough to block some of the light.

Enter the high efficiency mobile indirect light fixture. Using HID or high wattage Biax lamps, these fixtures can be mounted on top of partitions or cabinets, or stand alone as floor lamps. The pattern can be adjusted to accomodate the room layout as it changes and, when combined with task lighting, yields a low wattage per square foot to meet energy codes.

Speaking of task lighting, new fixtures are now available to replace incandescent desk lamps. Using electronic ballasts that provide instand and flicker-free illumination, they allow easy replacement of fixtures using up to 100 watt incandescent lamps. Purchase prices are presently high, however, and payback would be long if the fixtures are used only a few hours a day.

When replacing high wattage incandescent fixtures, designers now have a variety of new options, msot of them using multiple Biax lamps, or "compact" HID sources. While few are inexpensive, most are attractive; some even duplicate the historic appearance of "old style" globes. Surprisingly, most of them are being produced by small, relatively unknown, manufacturers staffed by people apparently more imaginative and market-oriented than the better known (and often less innovative) brand names. To accomodate, for example, a chain of restaurants seeking to replace its pendant-mounted globe fixtures (each holding a "long-life" 200 watt incandescent lamp), one small outfit created a prism shaped structure holding a reduced-wattage electronic ballast, surrounded by three vertically-mounted 18 watt Biax lamps (one on each side of the prism). The whole structure slips into a globe, yielding the same light output as the original globe fixture, but using only 30% of the wattage.

Other excellent examples of innovation are coming out of companies that began solely as reflector fabricators. Several of them now make and market entire fixtures, focussed on the retrofit/upgrade market. When a building owner seeking to replace his ceiling-recessed fixtures was handicapped by loose asbestos above the hung ceiling, one such manufacturer fabricated an attractive, semi-recessed fixture that slipped into the existing fixture's housing (after all old parts had been removed). Extending slightly below the ceiling line, it improved beam spread and reduced the number of lamps needed to maintain an acceptable light level. At no time was it necessary to enter the hung ceiling. No such fixtures existed prior to meeting this challenge, nor were several major manufacturers even interested in discussing the problem. Now the reflector maker is the sole supplier of fixtures ideally suited for a niche market that encompasses thousands of buildings in older urban areas.

## Exit Signs

With the advent of lower cost exit signs using light emitting diodes (LED), CF retrofit kits for exit signs may soon become obsolete. Now approved even in cities with tough safety codes, LED exit signs use less wattage than the best CF retrofit kit, have "cleaner" electrical characteristics, and never require relamping: lifetime on LED's in continuous operation may exceed 50 years. Initially quite expensive, the signs are now available in quantity for less than $70. If a utility rebate is available for new fixtures, this price is reduced even further, and the 24 hour operation of such signs usually yields paybacks under 3 years. In older buildings that have seen several upgrades, it may also be easier to completely replace a variety of exit signs instead of trying to find and adapt different retrofit kits to accomodate the existing signs.

## Retrofit Kits

Somewhere between new CF downlights and existing incandescent downlights is the CF retrofit kit. In the past, most kits used a screw-in CF ballast and lamp, possibly including a new reflector. Such devices are easy to install, but leave open the option for a user or relamper to replace them later with yet another incandescent, thereby discontinuing energy savings. New kits are now available that replace the downlight's cap (in which the socket is located) with a new cap holding one or two CF lamp sockets. This allows the CF lamps to be used with the existing fixture's reflector. The new cap comes attached to a remote ballast that, in turn, connects to the old cap. This assembly resides in the hung ceiling, so future CF relamping and energy savings are assured.

There is a downside, however: fixture efficiency will likely drop significantly since that reflector was not designed to focus the light emanating from a CF lamp's surface, but rather from a smaller, and more symmetrical, incandescent filament and globe. Photometric comparisons of this type of kit with the same fixture holding an incandescent lamp show reductions in efficiency

sometimes exceeding 40%. The result is lower wattage, but much lower light output, especially when two CF's are installed side-by-side in one fixture. Even replacing the reflector may not help much: properly focussing the output of a CF lamp usually involves a reflector opening and depth greater than that needed for an incandescent lamp of the same light output.

The best retrofit kits appear to be those that use a new larger reflector housing a single vertical "quad" style CF, recessed deeper into the fixture to reduce glare and maintain symmetry. Retrofitters should set up side-by-side tests of the existing and altered fixtures to be sure the desired results are obtained. It should also be noted that most retrofit kits still use magnetic ballasts which are noisier and use more power than electronic ballasts that are available with the better kits.

One other way to maintain savings due to retrofitting is to use screw-in kits that have now been theft-proofed. Utilizing a special tool for their insertion into a standard socket, these kits cannot be removed without again using the special tool.

## THE CUTTING EDGE

Several welcome ideas have recently emerged from the lighting labs and may soon see application in high efficiency lighting. First among them is the quantification of the benefits of "scotopically-rich" light. Put simply, the human eye responds at two light levels, one dominated by light common during the day (i.e., brighter and at "warmer" color temperatures), the other during the evening (i.e., darker and at "cooler" temperatures). By increasing the light output of high CRI bluer "cooler" light (color temperatures above $4000^\circ$ K), the pupil shrinks, sharpening focus and improving seeing.

Such light can have the effect of significantly enhancing vision, potentially allowing a reduction in foot-candles (as measured by a standard light meter) without impeding task performance. While ideally this may mean use of lamps providing $5500^\circ$ K light, some compromises may be necessary to gain acceptance by those accustomed to $3000^\circ$ K incandescents, or warm white fluorescents. There is a psychological component to the perceived comfort of color temperature, and further research is needed to derive an optimal color temperature for various tasks. What this research does show, however, is that lighting efficiency is more than just watts and foot-candles. It also shows that "warm" sources, such as incandescent and high pressure sodium, do not (at the same foot-candle level) provide as much useful light as cooler sources, such as high CRI fluorescent or metal halide.

Another useful discovery relates to a fluorescent lamp's physical temperature. Especially noticeable with compact fluorescents, high lamp wall temperatures result in lower lumen output. As a lamp warms up, it may reach maximum output in a minute or two, but then gradually lose over 10% of its output as it reaches equilibrium temperature with its fixture housing. Two immediately obvious methods to keep lamps cooler have been tried with success: better fixture venting, and a thermal "bridge" that conducts heat from the lamp, dissipating it through the fixture chassis. While both measures will slow the rate at which fixtures reach full output, the difference is not significant unless the fixture is on only momentarily (such as in a closet or bathroom). At least two fixture manufacturers have already designed new products with improved venting, and a retrofit kit manufacturer is considering adding a thermal bridge to his products.

Further consideration is needed, however, by safety and code enforcement bodies since fixture venting into a hung ceiling may violate some fire codes, and UL listing of some fixtures may be lost when a thermal bridge is added. Neither concern should be difficult to address, and we look forward to further applications of these simple - and often elegant - ways to squeeze more lumens out of the same wattage.

## OVER THE EDGE

So far we have only covered recently introduced products and techniques. Now we shall consider what may come soon - and what remains to be developed.

## The Integrated Lighting Source

Several trends are leading to combination of the lamp and its ballast. Imagine, for a moment, that the 60,000 hour electrodeless lamp has come into being in a four foot T-8 version. Why not seek a self-ballasted version, since the lifetime of the lamp now approaches that of the ballast, which will shrunk by being miniaturized? The fixture's old ballast would be disconnected and power brought directly to the sockets. Routine relamping would be eliminated by the extended lifetime. But lamps still routinely lose some output due to wear on the phosphors, so imagine a built-in photocell that monitors light output and raises it as a lamp depreciates, maintaining brightness over the entire lifetime of the lamp.

By why stop there? Let's seal the fixture, and fill it with an inert gas like nitrogen, so its reflector cannot oxidize and its lens remains clean. We now have a replaceable unit that fits into a shell, either that of an old fixture or a housing (preferably equipped with modular wiring) designed to hold the replaceable fixture. When the unit burns out, it is exchanged for a new unit and the burned out casing goes to a recycling plant where the steel, plastic, glass, aluminum and mercury are all re-used, thereby minimizing solid waste and avoiding improper disposal of lamp mercury.

While it is doubtful that such an "integrated" light source would ever have universal application, it would be a cost-effective replacement for the millions of standard size recessed and surface-mounted fixtures presently installed in typical offices, factories, stores, labs and institutions. And if the task or layout were to change, the replaceable units need only be un-

plugged, the lightweight shells rearranged, and the units reinstalled.

## Zero Glare - Without the "Cave"

The continued proliferation of VDT's creates both a need and an opportunity for ceiling fixtures that provide glare-free light, but do not create the cave-like ambience typical of the parabolic "eggcrate"-style louver. In general, avoidance of direct glare means distribution of light below 30° or above 60° from nadir (i.e., 0° is directly below a fixture). While properly designed indirect lighting does this quite well, it usually requires task lighting for both psychological and technical reasons. Indirect lighting may also be severely limited by low ceiling height. Enter the semi-recessed downlight. It doesn't exist yet, but prototypes seen recently at lighting shows may yet evolve into it.

The concept is relatively simple, and may even lend itself to creation of retrofit kits. All recessed downlights have difficulty spreading their light much beyond 30° from nadir without creating glare. The net result is severe scalloping on walls (unless wall sconces or recessed wall washers are added, increasing cost and potentially creating localized glare sources). Why not consider fixtures that recess into the ceiling (to hold sockets, ballasts and fixture structure), but emerge from the ceiling as louvered cylinders that shine down inside the 30° zone, but also up beyond the 60° zone limit? In effect, such fixtures would provide both direct downlight and indirect uplight, bouncing light off the ceiling and nearby walls.

Coated with specular silver on the inside of the cylindrical louvers, they would be highly efficient since very little light would be trapped or subjected to multiple reflections. Lamps would remain cooler from the directed updraft of warm air through the louvers. Such fixtures would take great advantage of vertically oriented Biax lamps that would be partially recessed (surrounded by a parabolic reflector for downlighting) and protrude partially below the ceiling line, surrounded by the cylindrical louvers. Provided with an appropriate screw-in ballast, a 39 watt Biax lamp could replace a 150 watt incandescent lamp in the typical inefficient downlight, providing better, more evenly distributed light due to the greatly increased fixture efficiency.

The same tactic could be used with linear fluorescent fixtures. Horizontal louvers (attached to the fixture below the ceiling line) divert light - normally emitted into the glare zone - up to the ceiling and upper walls, reducing the ratio of luminance from the darkest to the brightest surfaces, and eliminating the dark ceilings often associated with low brightness designs. A rectangular orifice at the botton of the louver assembly provides glare-free downlight.

## The "Ideal" Track Light

High efficacy light sources have become common in downlights, wall sconces and task lights, providing numerous viable options for economical energy efficiency. The same cannot be said, however, for track and spot lighting. While at least a dozen CF and HID track light fixtures are presently sold by several major manufacturers, only one or two provide close equivalency to their incandescent rivals. In a few cases, manufacturers have simply used housings previously designed for linear halogen lamps and altered them to hold CF or HID lamps. The net result is a high efficacy source in a low efficiency fixture, yielding insufficient light output and lacking the concentrated punch of an incandescent PAR lamp.

The problem appears to lie in a misunderstanding of the way light is (and needs to be) focussed. We have become accustomed to the relatively small size of most spot light fixtures, which do their job easily because of the very small size of the incandescent lamp's luminous source; i.e., its filament. CF lamps, on the other hand, are really a set of cylindrical luminous surfaces, making concentration of their light much more difficult. To treat a typical CF lamp like a point source requires a reflector many times the size of the lamp, making the fixture cumbersome and aesthetically unappealing. One of the most efficient CF track lights seen so far utilizes a vertically-mounted 22 watt "quad" style lamp in a 9 inch reflector - yet it barely replaces a 75 watt incandescent reflector flood lamp (which is not a tightly focussed source).

In numerous attempts to eradicate incandescent lamps from his facility, this user has gained new respect for the 90 watt halogen PAR lamp, and especially the 60 watt halogen infrared PAR lamp. At this time, there is no track or spot fixture that can equal these sources and still achieve an acceptable payback, to say nothing of acceptable aesthetics. To some degree, one and two lamp horizontal 39 watt Biax lamps in a single housing can replace two incandescent floods, and several HID fixtures can replace incandescent spots on a one-for-one basis, but the wattage reduction is nowhere near that obtained by replacing an incandescent downlight or sconce.

To yield the same photometric performance as a 90 watt PAR Capsylite, for example, requires use of a 50 watt white HPS lamp, typically using a bulky magnetic ballast that draws an additional 8 watts. The net reduction of only 32 watts comes at a cost of more than $200, which yields a payback exceeding 20 years, at typical electric rates. The HPS fixture is also bulky, heavy and unappealing. A more acceptable look can be obtained with fixtures using double-ended HQI metal halide lamps, but either the photometrics are wrong, or the wattage reduction is once again small compared to the fixture cost.

There is a need for a small, electronically ballasted (preferably "instant on") metal halide fixture using the 35 or 70 watt single ended HQI lamp, enclosed in an attractive reflector that can be pointed in any direction. There are thousands of galleries, clothing stores, institutions and museums that would buy such a product. It would require no new wiring, could be installed by

a custodian, and would yield major savings both in energy and relamping, due to the much greater lifetime of HID lamps. It is difficult to understand why this source has been so little used in this country, since it approximates the point sources in halogen lamps sold so successfully in the last 20 years. Perhaps it is due to a failure of imagination, or a misguided notion that energy codes are a passing fad.

Improving Retrofit Sophistication

The typical designer of retrofit installations lacks any formal lighting training and instead relies on the ability of a few off-the-shelf devices to replace existing obsolete equipment, on a one-for-one basis. While this may work acceptably more often than not, it allows new lighting problems to be created or old problems maintained. Experience with several retrofit firms shows that it is not unusual to find the following flaws in a typical large installation:

1. Uneven task light levels due to failure to account for existing fixture spacing and/or the photometrics of the replacement device.

2. Excessively high (or low) levels, leading to wasted watts or the eventual loss of savings by the gradual influx of incandescent task lighting to meet occupants' needs.

3. Lost savings opportunities due to failure to fully address existing incandescent lighting.

4. Lack of new lighting controls, incorrect analysis of their real payback, and/or improper choice of type and location (especially for sensors).

While not a panacea, the creation of a certification framework for lighting professionals is essential in order to place a "floor" on the incompetence seen in so many installations. Doing so will reduce the number of "horror stories" that impede acceptance of high efficiency lighting, and probably increase the net savings of future installations. It should also reduce the re-installation of inefficient lighting, added to a poorly lit space to correct the problems.

Several professional groups, including AEE and IES, are promoting and/or providing training, testing and certification of lighting professionals. If utilities and state-sponsored energy programs required that such a professional "sign off" on efficient designs, it is likely that the quality of the work would increase, some fly-by-night operations would close up shop, and efficient design would become the norm rather than remain an aberration.

To aid such professionals, some new lighting analysis tools are needed, one being luminance analysis, and a low cost metering device to help perform it. At present, the concept of luminance (i.e., light reflected or transmitted from a surface) is not well understood or utilized by the lighting retrofitters, some of whom believe that the foot-candle meter is the sole judge of an acceptable installation. Since we rarely look at direct light, and the eye notices relative brightness of surfaces more than absolute levels, the acceptability of an installation may actually be determined to a greater degree by the ratio of the luminances of surfaces in the normal field of vision than by the illumination at any given spot. When those ratios exceed certain levels, we may experience indirect glare, veiling reflections (especially on VDT screens), or the "cave effect" when walls ar darkened by louvered lenses with sharp cutoff angles.

Unfortunately, such meters are presently used more in lighting labs than by lighting installers, and are relatively expensive. Coupled with the lack of any code requirement or training in the use of such equipment, it may be a long time before such valuable analysis is applied to evaluating an existing or proposed design. In the meantime, occupants and building administrators will continue to be bothered by poor lighting distribution, and fooled by ignorant installers wielding a standard foot-candle meter.

These deficiencies provide the established lighting design industry - never happy with the upstart lighting efficiency trade - with valid criticism of many energy conservation efforts. We would all do well to heed such criticism when it focusses on this glaring (no pun intended) deficiency in our work.

CONCLUSION

This paper attempted to outline the state-of-the-art in high efficiency lighting, and to guide that industry toward recognizing and fulfilling unmet needs, in order to improve its quality and impact on energy use. Comments by readers are appreciated, and may be directed to the author at his Columbia University office.

# Chapter 77

# Gearing Lighting Retrofit Projects to the End User

M.S. Gould

## ABSTRACT

Products designed to reduce lighting energy consumption are of particular interest to facility engineers, lighting designers, and energy management professionals. Data supplied by manufacturers can be helpful in explaining features of these products, but it is difficult to judge their performance with this (often optimistic) information alone. Products such as electronic ballasts, occupancy sensors, and dimming systems are continually developed and refined, yet insufficient field data are made available to the end user. Sparse data exist on the effect that these products have on the building occupants and on building systems.

This paper briefly reviews lighting technologies, and then defines lighting product impact parameters such as system operation, maintenance, aesthetics, safety, occupant comfort, and potential for energy savings. Savings calculation methods are presented, including significant variables and non-economic factors. Recommended (or tolerable) values for these parameters are given, followed by an illustrative evaluation of lighting products available in 1992 in view of these characteristics and recommended values.

## Background

In the United States, energy costs consume 30 percent of the operating budget of commercial buildings (Bevington and Rosenfeld 1990, p. 77). These same buildings also have the largest potential for reducing energy consumption. This is not a coincidence. First of all, much of the existing building stock was built when energy costs were not as significant. Second, in many buildings the initial construction costs are considered ahead of long-term operating costs. Finally, because maintenance budgets are generally cut to meet tight budgets, buildings are often not operated as designed.

The EPA claims that if energy-efficient lighting were used wherever profitable, annual savings would amount to $18.6 billion, annual carbon dioxide emissions would fall by 232 million tons, and sulfur dioxide emissions would be reduced by 1.7 million tons per year (Geberer 1991, p. 49). As with many statistics, the hugeness of the numbers makes them difficult to comprehend. The important point, however, is that by installing cost-effective, currently available energy-efficient lighting technologies, the United States can go a long way toward reducing its dependence on oil imports and slow the release of harmful gases into the atmosphere.

In describing the huge potential for energy-efficient lighting, it should not be forgotten that many businesses and institutions have already implemented aggressive energy management programs. In order to accrue additional energy savings, energy management projects will require more complete engineering, coordination, and preparation to ensure success, and no longer be able to depend solely on the easy "quick fixes."

It is important to observe at the outset that reducing energy consumption is not the same as reducing comfort. Technologies and implementation techniques now exist for using electricity more efficiently while actually improving services (Fickett 1990, p. 65). In fact, many of the new lighting systems offer less glare, less audible noise, more pleasant color, and reduced flicker. These aesthetic improvements can mean increased visual performance and worker productivity.

Since energy costs are significant and the potential for savings high, many companies view energy management as a worthwhile investment. Lighting accounts for the direct consumption of 40 percent of the electrical power load of commercial buildings. In specialized applications such as retail and display lighting, that percentage is often higher.

Since these products can require a large capital investment--and therefore must compete with investment or growth funds--project risk must be minimized. But a gap exists in the information available to lighting professionals. Although energy efficiency lighting products are tested, the results are often presented in a format to stimulate sales rather than to be useful to the end user.

The format of this paper is organized to be the most useful to those planning and implementing energy efficiency projects. For this reason, each section ends with a one page summary that identifies the major decisions to be made before a project is considered.

## FULL-SIZED FLUORESCENT LAMPS

This section begins with a discussion of the different types of lamps available followed by important selection criteria.

### Energy-Saving Lamps

Installing 34-watt F40T12 lamps to replace 40-watt F40T12 lamps is a very popular energy-saving strategy. By changing the composition of gases in fluorescent lamps, the lamp voltage, and therefore wattage, can be reduced. The energy consumption of a lamp is reduced by 14 percent at the expense of some light output. This is an easy conversion, since the 34-watt lamps are designed to use the same ballast as the 40-watt lamp.

In some cases, however, this simple conversion is inappropriate. Since energy-saver lamps reduce light output, they should never be installed in an area that is already at or below recommended light levels. Also, 34-watt energy-saving lamps should not be used in new construction applications. With less light output per luminaire, more luminaires may be required to obtain the desired light levels. Although this point seems obvious, energy-saver lamps can be found in many recently completed buildings. Some energy-saving lamps have trouble starting at ambient temperatures below 60°F (Kaufman ed. 1984, p. 8-24). In addition, some energy-saving lamps have compatibility problems with older standard fluorescent ballasts, leading in some cases to local overheating and explosive destruction of the older ballasts.

## T-10 Fluorescent Lamps

These lamps are designed to be an interchangeable alternative to the T-12 lamp. The principle advantage of the T-10 is increased lumens-per-watt ratio and a small increase in optical efficiency when compared with T-12 lamps (Eley, Benya, and Verderber 1990, p. 8). Two disadvantages are that the lamp cost is higher and that they are currently produced by only a few of the lamp manufacturers. Since T-10 lamps are rated to consume 42 watts-per-lamp they do not reduce energy consumption if they are replaced one-for-one with T-12 lamps. (The use of T-10 lamps is also discussed in the optical reflector section.)

## T-8 Fluorescent Lamps

The T-8 lamp uses a tri-stimulus rare earth phosphor coating which provides higher efficiency, improved lamp lumen depreciation, and good color rendering when compared to the T-12 lamp (Verderber 1989, p. 9). By comparison, the total light output of the 32-watt T-8 lamps is less than the typical 40-watt T-12 lamp. The efficacy, however, is higher--at ninety lumens-per-watt--than the 40-watt T-12, which is around eighty lumens-per-watt. T-8 lamps can be used in the same fixtures as T-12 lamps, but because of their 265 milliampere current requirement, they require a ballast that is incompatible with T-12 or T-10 lamps (standard fluorescent lamps are designed for 430 milliampere operation). The cost of a T-8 lamp and ballast is comparable to that of a T-12 lamp and ballast.

It should be mentioned that before tri-phosphor lamps were introduced, designers had to decide between lamps with high light output or lamps with good color rendering. For example, a standard cool white lamp has a CRI of around sixty-two and a lumen-per-watt ratio of seventy-nine, while a deluxe cool white lamp has a higher CRI of eighty nine but a lower lumen-to-watt ratio of fifty-five. By comparison a typical T-8 lamp in the cool white color temperature range (4,100K) has a CRI of seventy-five and a lumen-per-watt ratio of ninety, combining excellent efficiency with very good color rendering properties.

## Impact Analysis

Maintenance: Institutions or businesses with a large and diverse building stock are often reluctant to specify more than one type of lamp to be used in their facilities. Many of these groups attempt to settle on a standard lamp in order to simplify ordering and stocking. In addition, there is no guarantee that a special lamp will be replaced with a comparable lamp after it burns out. Training must be provided to maintenance crews so that they understand why different lamps are specified for different areas. These potential problems should be considered and special arrangements should perhaps be made when evaluating different lamp options.

## Summary of Important Criteria for Fluorescent Lamp Selection

The first step in selecting a fluorescent lamp is not to consider the lamps but rather the space where the lamps will be used. Whether these priorities are based on first cost, aesthetics or energy cost, once the needs of occupants have been decided the following lamp selection criteria can be used:

o    Color Rendering Index: Generally, the more important the aesthetics of a lighting design the higher the CRI should be. A lamp with a CRI of seventy-five or higher is considered adequate for most office and school situations.

o    Color Temperature: "Warm" or "Cool" colors can be selected depending on preference. Warm White lamps are typically rated at 2,700K and Cool White lamps are 4,100K.

Mixing lamps of different color temperature is not recommended.

o    Lumen Output: Each brand of fluorescent lamp has a rated light output that can be obtained from lamp manufacturers. Most engineers and designers involved with fixture selection and layout use this number. A better guide to lamp performance is the lumen-per-watt ratio.

o    Lumen-Per-Watt Ratio (Efficacy): This is the best direct measurement of performance. This value is a function of many factors including the type of ballast used and the lamp operating temperature. Manufacturer's literature can be helpful in making rough comparisons.

o    Compatibility: The proper size and shape lamp must be selected to fit the proposed fixture. Selecting standard shape and length lamps can reduce ordering and stocking costs. It is important to note that T-12 and T-10 lamps can operate on the same ballast while T-8 lamps require a ballast with a different input rating. Multi-lamp ballasts are now available that can operate all kinds, but apparently not with the greatest efficiency for any one type.

Once these factors have been weighed, the decision-maker can balance the benefits of improving color quality and aesthetics with potentially higher first costs. While these factors are important when weighed independently, they cannot be thought of separately from the associated ballast, fixture, and lens that make up the complete luminaire.

## COMPACT FLUORESCENT LAMPS

Compact fluorescent lamps are available as energy-saving alternatives to standard incandescent lamps. Although these lamp-ballast combinations can initially cost as much as ten times more than incandescent lamps, compact fluorescents are often cost effective. While specifications vary from manufacturer to manufacturer, an eighteen watt compact fluorescent usually replaces a sixty to seventy watt incandescent, in view of equivalent light output. In addition, compact fluorescents have an operating life of 10,000 hours, compared with 750 hours for a standard incandescent.

Compact fluorescent lamps generally can be used as replacements for incandescent "A" or "T" lamps. But because most compact fluorescents are larger, heavier, and shaped slightly differently than incandescents, they cannot be used to replace incandescents in all situations.

Two different types of compact fluorescents are available, an integral type and a modular type. Integral compact fluorescents are sold as an inseparable single lamp and ballast unit. Most integral lamps look like a slightly oversized incandescent bulbs. Modular compact fluorescents, often referred to by the trade name "PL" lamps, have a separate plug-in lamp and ballast. The advantage of the modular approach is that the ballast can be reused when the lamps burn out. Typical modular compact fluorescent can be found with lamp wattages ranging from five to thirteen watts. Most integral models are between fifteen and twenty watts.

## Savings Calculation Methods

Calculating the energy savings for installing compact fluorescents is straightforward and without the pitfalls that make some energy calculations difficult. The only variables needed are the hours of operation, the wattage of the existing lamps, and the wattage of the proposed lamps. A more rigorous estimate of the total savings resulting from compact fluorescent lamping or relamping project would have to include other economic factors such as maintenance and relamping savings, which are project specific.

Impact Analysis

System Operation: Compact fluorescent projects generally require less planning and have a quicker payback than most other types of lighting projects. Potential mistakes can be avoided by considering the following factors:

    o    Compatibility: When compact fluorescents first became available, there was an incentive for manufacturers to design and produce lamps quickly. Because of this, there are many different sizes and shapes of lamps and bases on the market. Stocking replacement lamps for a variety of models and manufacturers is cumbersome. Versatility should be considered when selecting lamp models. Standardization of lamp sizes and bases will alleviate this problem.

    o    Power Factor: Power factor is the ratio of watts input divided by the line volts multiplied by the line amps.

*Power Factor= (Watts input)/(line volts x line amps)*

Non inductive or capacitive loads such as an incandescent light bulb have a 100 percent or "unity" power factor. If high power factor equipment is specified in new construction, more luminaires can be placed on a given circuit than with lower power factor equipment. Also, most utilities charge a penalty to customers with a total power factor under 85 percent. According to the IES, a high power factor is above 90 percent (Kaufman ed. 1984, p. 8-35).

Currently, not all compact fluorescent lamps have built-in power factor correction. Most of the lamps listed have a power factor of around 50 percent. (It is important to remember that although a high power factor is usually preferred, a fifteen-watt low power factor compact fluorescent is still half the amperage load of a sixty-watt incandescent.)

o    Flicker: Some compact fluorescent lamps have electronic ballasts that reduce or eliminate flicker. Flicker may be noticeable in some task lighting applications, but is generally not a problem in most compact fluorescent installations. (There is a more detailed discussion of flicker in the electronic ballast section.)

o    Heat Buildup: There is strong evidence that the light output of compact fluorescents decreases as the temperature of the lamps increases. A 1990 Advance Lighting Technologies report prepared for the California Energy Commission points out that rated lumens are measured at 77°F, a condition that is likely to occur only in an open fixture. At 95°F the light output of compact fluorescents decreases by 7 percent, at 113°F the light output decreases by 17 percent, and so on. Since a common application of compact fluorescents includes recessed-can luminaires and other reduced air circulation luminaires, some light loss should be expected. Both lighting researchers and manufacturers are developing products with built-in heat sinks to address this problem (Siminovich, Rubenstein, and Verderber 1990, p. 1).

Maintenance: Relamping costs can be significantly reduced with compact fluorescent lamps when compared to incandescent lamps. Most compact fluorescents have an operating life from between 9,000 and 10,000 hours. In many cases, the reduced replacement costs are greater than the energy savings! For example, a compact fluorescent rated at 10,000 hours life will last for just over three years in a typical

nine-hour-per-day 360 days-per-year environment. Under these same conditions, a 750 hour incandescent will need to be changed over four times per year (or thirteen times for every time a compact fluorescent is changed). Using costs at Stanford University in this example, with energy at $.06/kWh and labor rates at $30 per hour, the energy savings would be $8.16 per year, whereas the maintenance savings would be $21.60. Even with long-life incandescent lamps (2,500 hours rated life) there still is a $6.50 annual maintenance savings with the compact fluorescent. This simple example points out an important side benefit of compact fluorescents.

Aesthetics, Safety, and Comfort Issues

Aesthetics: The color "quality" of compact fluorescent lamps is generally very high because of the use of high color rendering rare earth phosphors. Most of these lamps have a good to excellent color rendering index (CRI) rating over 80 and up to 85. There is also a wide range of color temperatures available, from 2,700K to 5,000K. The 2,700K color temperature is most often selected because it most closely resembles the color of the standard incandescent lamp (Eley, Benya, and Verderber 1990, p. 2). Caution should be taken to avoid mixing lamps of different color temperatures in the same area.

Summary of Important Criteria For Compact Fluorescent Lamp Selection

Compact fluorescent lamps have proven to be a cost effective alternative to incandescent bulbs. Since most compact fluorescents fit into the same socket as incandescent bulbs they can be used in many commercial and residential applications.

o    Color Rendering Index: As with standard fluorescent lamps, the selection of a specific compact fluorescent depends on the space intended for use. If a compact fluorescent lamp is replacing an incandescent bulb in an area where aesthetics are important, then a high CRI should be selected. On the other hand, if the compact fluorescent lamps are installed in a non-critical area, the higher CRI may not warrant the extra cost.

o    Lumen Output: Early compact fluorescent lamps could only supply the equivalent lumen output of a sixty-watt incandescent. Today there are compact fluorescents with much higher lumen output. Caution should be taken to purchase the model of compact fluorescent with the proper desired light output.

o    Lumen-Per-Watt Ratio (Efficacy): As with standard fluorescent lamps, this is the best direct measure of performance. Manufacturer's literature can be helpful in making rough comparisons. Compact fluorescent lamps with electronic ballasts can be expected to have a higher lumen-per-watt ratio than compact fluorescent lamps with a core and coil ballast.

o    Color Temperature: "Warm" or "Cool" colors can be selected depending on preference. Warm White lamps are typically 2700K and Cool White lamps are 4100K. Mixing lamps of different color temperature is not recommended.

o    Compatibility. The proper size and shape lamp must be selected to fit the proposed fixture. When buying compact fluorescents with a modular lamp and ballast, the price and availability of obtaining separate replacements should be considered. Selecting standard shaped and length lamps can reduce the number of lamps and ballasts needed to be stocked as replacements.

o    Power Factor: Many compact fluorescent lamps are considered to have a low power factor. A small premium price can be paid to purchase compact florescent lamps with built-in power factor correction. In extreme cases, low power factor may lead to electrical circuit overloading and potential penalties from the electric utility.

o    Heat Buildup: Compact fluorescent lamps produce peak light output at about 77° F. Higher temperatures found in many enclosed fixtures cause a decrease in light output. Compact fluorescent lamps are available with heat sinks to help alleviate this problem.

## OPTICAL REFLECTORS

### Introduction

A common method of increasing the efficiency of fluorescent luminaires is to install optical reflectors. If a reflective material is installed on the inside of a fluorescent luminaire, more of the lumens produced by the fluorescent lamps will be emitted from the luminaire. When the efficiency increase is sufficient to enable lamp removal, energy savings result.

The standard four-lamp, two-foot by four-foot fluorescent luminaire is the product most often targeted by reflector manufacturers and represents about 90 percent of sales. Optical reflectors are also available for two-foot by two-foot and eight-foot luminaires.

When optical reflectors were first introduced, performance claims were often exaggerated. Advertisements implied that after an optical reflector was installed, two lamps could be removed from a four-lamp luminaire without any loss in light output. This type of oversimplification, combined with the large numbers of inexperienced manufacturers/distributors marketing reflectors, caused the reputation of the reflector industry to suffer. The reputation of the industry has, however, improved, now that performance claims are more consistent with actual performance. At the same time, the industry has a better understanding of the best applications and limitations of optical reflectors.

Two steps should be taken before considering the installation of optical reflectors. The first step is to obtain light level readings with a high quality light meter. The second step is to compare those readings with the light levels recommended by the Illuminating Engineering Society (Kaufman ed. 1987) for the particular tasks performed in that space. Only if the light levels are above the IES recommended levels should optical reflectors accompanied by lamp removal be considered.

### Materials Used to Construct Optical Reflectors

Optical reflectors are either rigid or filmlike. Rigid reflectors must be cut and bent to fit in a particular luminaire. The three most common materials used to make optical reflectors are:

o    Anodized Aluminum: Aluminium reflectors are cut from a specular polished aluminum sheet. (In the reflector industry, the word "specular" describes a mirror-like quality where the reflection is predominantly regular.) The range of total reflectivity is 85 to 90 percent.

o    Anodized Aluminum with Dielectric Coating: A dielectric coating is added to an anodized aluminum sheet to increase reflectivity. The range of total reflectivity is 88 to 94 percent.

o    Specular Silver Laminate: Silver reflectors are made by coating or impregnating a polyester film with elemental silver. The film is typically bonded to an aluminum substrate. The range of total reflectivity is 91 to 95 percent.

By comparison, the white enamel paint found in most older luminaires and some new luminaires has a reflectance of 80 to 85 percent. Modern white powder paints generally exhibit a reflectance of about 90 percent (Lindsey 1989, p. 110).

Choosing among these three types of reflectors depends on priorities defined by the user. These priorities include cost, reflectivity, and additional maintenance required, if any. The anodized aluminum reflectors tend to be the least expensive (thirty dollars), and the dielectrically coated reflectors the most expensive (forty-five dollars). The price of specular silver reflectors falls between the two. Installation of the reflectors is commonly quoted at between ten dollars and twelve dollars. This usually includes installation of the reflector, cleaning the fixture, and replacing the lamps. Labor costs will, of course, increase for nonstandard fixtures and high ceilings. These are 1991 estimated costs and vary among manufacturers, but they give an idea of the cost of this technology.

According to a February 1991 survey of reflector manufacturers conducted by the Energy User News, there are currently twenty-four manufacturers of optical reflectors. Many of these make more than one type. Eighteen manufacture specular silver reflectors, eighteen make anodized aluminum, and two make the dielectric coated mirror reflectors. All the manufacturers offer warranties of at least five years and up to twenty-five years.

To reduce some of the costs associated with optical reflectors, self-adhesive reflective film has been marketed. Unlike reflective material bonded to a rigid substrate, the film consists of a reflective material with an adhesive backing, and is placed on the inside of fluorescent luminaires. Although material costs are cheaper, these savings may be absorbed by the additional labor required to line the luminaires with this adhesive film. There is also a fundamental design restriction. According to Lindsey (1989 p. 111), "Reflectors which are applied directly to the interior surfaces of the fixture are generally less efficient than semi-rigid reflectors since they conform to the fixture contours and cannot be formed to direct light in any specific manner." DiLaura and Kambich (1987, p. S-2) found that luminaires with sloped sides exhibit an increase in efficiency when lined with film, whereas luminaires with straight sides did not. In a fixture with straight sides, the light output is reduced by the multiple reflections that occur before the light is emitted.

Although manufacturers and vendors consider reflectivity an important part of sales promotions, from a building occupant's perspective the difference between materials may not be significant. Depending on the reflector design, the material used may have little effect on light output (Paumgartten 1989, p. 104). For example, specular silver is more reflective than polished aluminum, yet even the most attentive user is unlikely to be able to tell the difference between the two once an installation is complete. When a reflector is installed, it must be remembered that lamps and ballasts are often replaced and the luminaire lens is also cleaned. These changes are often more significant than differences in reflectivity between reflector materials.

## Reflector Design

Many authors agree that the design of the reflector is critical to performance (Lindsey 1989, p. 111) and (Brekken 1987, p. 72). In this case the word design refers to bending the reflector to maximize the light output of the luminaire. Not only can light output be increased, but an optical reflector can be designed to fit different lighting tasks. In an office environment, for example, the reflectors are designed to focus the maximum amount of light at desk level. In a hallway, however, the amount of light concentrated on the floor is usually not important. So, instead of focusing the light downward creating a tunnel like appearance, the reflector can be designed to focus the light outward onto the hallway walls.

## Savings Calculation Methods

Once it has been determined that adequate light levels will be maintained after the optical reflector installation, performing the energy savings calculation is simple. Of the three possible variables, both hours of operation and number of luminaires remain constant. The third, watts per fixture, is the unknown. If two lamps are removed from a four-lamp fixture, the luminaire wattage will be reduced by half. Therefore, if one lamp is removed from a three-lamp luminaire the energy consumption will be reduced by one-third. (In fact, the saving could be slightly higher.)

There are two common ways to wire a three-lamp luminaire. The first is to connect two outside lamps to one ballast and have the middle lamp operated by a one-lamp ballast. The second method also has the two outside lamps connected to one ballast but instead of a single-lamp ballast, two adjoining luminaires share a ballast to operate the center lamps. In other words, for every two adjoining luminaires, there are three two-lamp ballasts. Since a single-lamp ballast and lamp is less efficient per lamp than a two-lamp ballast, the energy savings are slightly higher in the first case.

Since all lighting sources emit heat as well as light, removing lamps will reduce the building heat load and possibly reduce air-conditioning costs. This kind of energy savings is very building specific and therefore difficult to calculate accurately. Complicating the matter further, during the heating season heat from the lights, although not a very efficient heat source, is still a part of the heat supply in some buildings. A rough figure that seems to have some industry acceptance is that for every kilowatt of lighting power reduction, .25 kilowatts of cooling power are saved. It is the opinion of the author, however, that project economics should be acceptable without adding this additional factor.

## Impact Analysis

Considering Optical Reflector Alternatives: A cost-conscious energy manager will consider other luminaire modifications before considering optical reflectors. As stated earlier, a light meter is required to determine the potential for installing optical reflectors. It is also important to consider that the lamp output will be reduced as the lamps age (lumen depreciation) and the fixture will get dirty over time. These factors combine to reduce total luminaire output.

Once light level measurements are taken, the energy engineer can use this simple key to decide if optical reflectors are appropriate. (Although the costs will vary, cheaper options are listed first.)

If an area is overlit:
o    Delamp without an optical reflector.

o    Install more efficacious lamps with lower wattage and light output.
o    Delamp without a reflector and replace remaining lamps with higher output lamps/ballasts.
o    Replace the old luminaire with a new fixture consisting of fewer lamps.
o    Delamp and install an inexpensive reflector.
o    Delamp and install a carefully designed high-quality reflector.

If an area is properly lit:
o    Install a more efficacious lamp/ballast system with the same light output.
o    Delamp without a reflector and replace remaining lamps with higher output lamps/ballasts.
o    Delamp and install a carefully designed high qualityreflector; replace remaining lamps with higher output lamps/ballasts.

If an area is underlit:
o    Install lamps/ballasts with increased light output.
o    Optical reflectors could be installed instead of adding additional lamps and ballasts to boost light output. This does not reduce energy consumption, but rather avoids additional energy consumption (Brekken 1987, p. 68).

System operation: When retrofitting with optical reflectors, the possibility of two-level or "dual" switching is often lost when lamps are removed from a fixture. In mixed use areas, having two lighting levels adds versatility. For example, when viewing a computer screen, glare and eye strain can be reduced with lower light levels. If higher light levels are required for reading or writing that is easily accomplished. Fixtures could be rewired to retain this capability, but only at a large extra expense.

Maintenance: More attention to maintenance is required in areas with optical reflectors. Since the luminaires have fewer lamps, burnouts are more noticeable. The reflector should also be cleaned periodically so light levels are maintained. In most office areas dusting the lamps and cleaning the lens and reflector may only be necessary every two or three years. In more dusty environments, one or more cleanings per year may be required. The specular silver reflector scratches easier than either the dielectric coated reflector or the anodized aluminum reflector. Because of this, repeated cleaning could diminish the specular ability of the specular silver reflector.

## Aesthetics, Safety, and Comfort Issues

Once installed, optical reflectors change the characteristic of a luminaire. In the best installations, light output is at or near original levels and energy consumption is reduced. In poor installations, energy savings may still be realized but dark spots and uneven light distribution may result. Unless the building occupant is directly underneath a luminaire, he or she may have substantially less light. A study performed at the University of California, Berkeley found a 16 to 19 percent decrease in uniformity of light levels over a test room (Kessel 1990, p. 25). A small test installation is a prudent method of verifying claims made by the manufacturer and ensuring acceptable uniformity. In doing so, there is the added advantage that the building occupants can see how the reflectors will look before they are installed in their area. In this way the building occupants become a part of the energy management team and help to ensure the project's success.

Unlike electronic ballasts or compact fluorescent lamps, optical reflectors are not in themselves energy savers. Optical reflectors increase the light output of fluorescent fixtures, often allowing lamps to be removed. Although optical reflectors are a proven lighting technology, other, often cheaper, techniques can also be used. Simple delamping or lower output lamp/ballast combinations can also save energy and at the same time provide the desired light levels. After other options are considered, the following factors should be included in the selection of optical reflectors:

o    Materials: Optical reflectors are constructed from either anodized aluminum, anodized aluminum with a coating, or a specular silver laminate. The aluminum class of reflectors may perform better in dirty or dusty environments.

o    Design: From a performance perspective, optical reflector design is more critical than material selection. Since there are too many fixture designs to standardize reflector shape, reflectors must be custom designed for each project. Poor optical reflector design can focus too much light downward leaving the space with uneven levels of light.

o    Combining Technologies: Since labor is an important component of reflector projects, it may be cost effective to also consider installing electronic ballasts, T8 lamps, and a new fixture lens at the same time.

## ELECTRONIC BALLASTS

Electronic ballasts have shown great promise as energy-saving devices. Manufacturers claim a 10 to 20 percent energy reduction when compared with core-and-coil ballasts. Electronic ballasts perform the same function as standard core-and-coil ballasts (i.e., to regulate current flow and voltage to the fluorescent lamps), but use solid state technology to rectify the incoming 60 Hz power and convert it to a much higher frequency (typically 25,000 Hz.). This high frequency operation has the double benefit of allowing the ballasts to operate with lower losses, making them more efficient than core-and-coil ballasts, and at the same time improving the operating efficiency of the fluorescent lamps.

Aside from energy savings, electronic ballasts offer several other advantages over core-and-coil ballasts. One advantage is the potential for reduced flicker, a problem for those who work around video display terminals (VDT's), as well as a suspected cause of adverse physiological reactions to fluorescent lights. In addition, some electronic ballasts offer a dimming control feature that can increase energy savings and flexibility.

Three factors have made energy managers cautious about purchasing electronic ballasts: a high premature failure rate with early electronic ballasts; a potential for excessive harmonics and conducted electro-magnetic interference (EMI); and a higher cost per unit. Many manufacturers have improved internal ballast circuitry and quality testing techniques to diminish these problems.

### Savings Calculation Methods

Accurately calculating the energy savings for electronic ballasts is difficult. Ballast manufacturers claim 14 to 20 percent energy savings, but several factors influence the actual energy savings: the existing ballast/lamp combined energy consumption; the proposed ballast/lamp combined energy consumption; and the hours of operation. To complicate the evaluation further, there are no universally accepted standards against which to compare electronic ballasts. To remedy this problem, the American National Standards Institute (ANSI) is working (1991) on an update of Standard C82 to include electronic ballasts.

Electronic ballasts are priced from twenty-two to seventy-five dollars per ballast. (By comparison, an energy-saver magnetic ballast costs from twelve to sixteen dollars.) The more expensive electronic ballasts generally have special features such as dimming capabilities or supply power to three or four lamps instead of two lamps. Among the electronic ballasts with common features there is no evidence that there is a correlation between cost and quality. Before paying a higher cost for dimmable ballasts, users should be certain they need to be able to vary the light levels over such a large range. (Often only two light levels are necessary. This can usually be accomplished with dual switching at a lower cost.)

### Impact Analyses

Since most ballasts are hidden inside luminaires, building occupants are unaware of ballast changes or retrofits. Unless there is an unusually high number of early ballast failures, the ballast project should be transparent to the building occupants. The following factors should be studied before a ballast installation is considered:

### System Operation

o    Ballast Factor: Ballast factor is a comparison of the lumen output from a laboratory reference ballast with that of the commercial ballast and is commonly expressed as a percentage. Ballast factor can also be described as the lumen output of actual lamp-ballast divided by the lumen output of a reference lamp-ballast. Typical values range from 80 to 95 percent, although some newer ballasts have a ballast factor of greater than one. A single ballast will have a different ballast factor for different lamps. (For example, the ballast factor will typically be lower for F40T12 energy-saving 34 watt lamp when compared to the standard 40 watt F40T12 lamps). In a retrofit situation, the new ballast factor should be at least equal to the ballast factor of the ballast being replaced (unless the light level is too high). In new construction, the ballast factor should be considered as a part of the lighting design. A higher ballast factor means more light output, possibly reducing the number of luminaires required. As an example, the Certified Ballast Manufacturers (CBM) require a ballast to have a minimum ballast factor of .925 with a 40 watt F40T12 lamp (Verderber and Morse 1985, p.3-3).

o    Voltage Regulation: Because small voltage changes occur from time to time, the ballast should be able to accommodate these with a minimum of change in light output. A large change in light output may disturb building occupants. An electronic ballast should be expected to handle a 10 percent voltage fluctuation without affecting user comfort. Voltage regulation is commonly expressed as a percentage output variation compared to a percentage input. For example, an acceptable light variation for a standard 120 volt ballast might be minus 8 percent at 108 volts and plus 8 percent at 132 volts.

o    System Efficacy: Efficacy--efficiency expressed in lumens per watt--is the best cost performance measure of the lamp and ballast system performance. Electronic ballasts have been shown to be more efficacious than core-and-coil ballasts. Sometimes this efficacy improvement is at the expense of light output. This is a problem when light levels are already close to or below minimum recommended levels. The total amount of light output, along with system efficacy, should be considered in every electronic ballast installation.

o        Harmonics and Conducted Electro-Magnetic Interference (EMI): In simple terms, harmonics are high frequency variations of the fundamental sixty Hz sinusoidal wave form. In three phase balanced distribution systems, the load can become unbalanced from harmonics, causing the neutrals to carry additional current and in some cases to become over loaded. The electronic switching in the ballast can introduce harmonics that are transmitted back into the power supply. A small percentage of harmonics will go unnoticed, but larger amounts can disturb sensitive electronic equipment. Many electronic ballasts now manufactured have levels of harmonics and EMI that meet or are below the levels proposed by ANSI and IEEE (Eley, Benya, and Verderber 1990, p. 6).

o        Power Factor: The section on compact fluorescent lamps has a discussion of power factor. Many of the electronic ballasts produced in 1991 have a power factor above 90 percent.

o        Crest Factor: Crest factor is the ratio of the peak lamp voltage to the root mean square (RMS) voltage. This value should be between 1.4 and 1.8. Values out of this range will shorten lamp life.

Aesthetics, Safety, and Comfort Issues

o        Percent Flicker: One of the important advantages of electronic ballasts is the potential to reduce or eliminate flicker. The IES Reference Manual describes flicker as a cyclic variation in instantaneous light output (Kaufman ed. 1984, p. 8-30). Since this variation is twice the input frequency (120 Hz modulation when 60 Hz power is supplied), flicker can be virtually eliminated at the frequency range that electronic ballasts operate in (between 20 and 30 kHz). Magnetic ballasts operate at 33 percent flicker. A reduction in percentage flicker can improve lighting conditions, especially for those who work around VDT's (Helms and Belcher 1991, p. 144). It should also be noted that when designing particular circuits, some manufacturers may choose between improving power factor and increasing the percentage of flicker (Verderber and Morse 1985, p. 3-3). Not all electronic ballasts reduce flicker. Electronic ballasts without rectifier output filters can have flicker as high as standard magnetic ballasts.

o        Audible Noise: Ballast noise or hum is the result of vibrations caused by the magnetic elements in a core-and-coil ballast. The vibration is from the expanding and collapsing magnetic field in the laminated core of the ballast. This magnetic vibration may be amplified if the ballast is improperly seated into a metal fixture. A properly manufactured solid state ballast should reduce or eliminate the buzzing noise associated with conventional core and coil ballasts (Alling 1990, p. 5). Each company publishes sound ratings that indicates a relative sound output. The highest sound rating "A" is used for most indoor applications.

o        PCB Ballasts: Until the middle 1970s polychlorinated biphenyls were used in the capacitors of core and coil ballasts. Federal law no longer allows the use of this chemical. Ballasts without the "Contains No PCB's" label may need to be treated as hazardous waste. (Ballasts containing PCB's are generally not considered a health risk unless they are leaking.)

Maintenance Considerations

o        Lamp Life: Some manufacturers claim that electronic ballasts extend the life of fluorescent lamps. In most cases this claim is based on accelerated life bench testing. Most of the electronic ballasts available today have not been on the market long enough for longevity field test data to be complete. Since lamp life is a function of many factors, it may be difficult to extrapolate test data to other sites. In addition, the many possible combinations of lamps and ballasts further complicates the issue. Although some buyers have experienced reduced lamp life when electronic ballasts were first introduced, installations at Stanford University have been free of this problem.

o        Lamp Burnouts: There are two strategies for controlling fluorescent lamp burnouts. Sometimes the electronic ballasts will only operate if the circuit is complete (e.g., if one lamp burns out the ballast will shut itself off along with any other lamps powered by that ballast). This "series" strategy is intended to protect the ballast circuitry. The second "parallel" strategy is to let the good lamps operate even with a burnt out lamp. There are several advantages to this parallel strategy. When new ballasts are installed, new lamps are usually also installed. If one of the new lamps happens to be defective, it will be unclear to the installer if it is the lamp or ballast that is not working. This can waste time, especially if the ballast supplies three or more lamps. In areas where few luminaires are present, if the whole luminaire goes out there may not be enough light available for safe egress. This can be a problem particularly in areas with dispersed luminaires.

o        Warranty and Service: Not all of the companies that have marketed electronic ballasts are still in business. High failure rates and the associated bad publicity is the main reason those companies were not able to stay in business. Warranty and service should therefore be part of the product evaluation. Most companies offer at least a two-year warranty. Some warranties include a labor allowance of up to ten dollars per ballast. Service is managed either factory-direct or through the distributor. For further protection, ballast buyers should consider the financial strength of the company offering the warranty.

Summary of Important Criteria for Electronic Ballast Selection

When planning an electronic ballast project, ballast performance, manufacturer warranty, and ballast cost are the key considerations. Since no universally accepted standards exist for electronic ballast comparison, it is difficult to rate different makes and models. At a minimum, each manufacturer should have the following criteria available:

o        Lumen-Per-Watt Ratio (Efficacy): Although this is the best direct measure of ballast performance, the fluorescent lamp used to obtain this measurement strongly contributes to the end result. Efficacy figures are available from manufacturers, but care should be taken to verify that the same types of lamps or class of lamps are used in each comparison.

o        Percentage Flicker: The potential to reduce flicker is an important benefit of the electronic ballast. This value should be published in the manufacturer's sales literature.

o        Harmonics: The amount of harmonics and electromagnetic interference generated by each model of electronic ballast should be low. Although most electronic ballasts emit acceptable amounts of harmonics, high values of harmonics can disturb sensitive electronic equipment.

o       Crest Factor: Crest factor values should be between 1.4 and 1.8 since values outside this range can reduce lamp life.

Other important ballast performance selection criteria should also be presented in the manufacturer's sales literature, such as voltage regulation, power factor, and ballast factor.

In addition to ballast performance, the warranty offered by the manufacturer should be an important part of the ballast selection criteria. A two year warranty is an acceptable minimum. It is also prudent to estimate the ability of the manufacturer to honor the warranty.

Although cost is an important part of every energy efficiency analysis, the wide difference in the per-ballast-cost of different electronic ballasts warrants special mention. This higher cost may be due to extra energy saving features built-in to the electronic ballast. If this is the case, the additional benefit of these features must be made a part of the economic analysis.

## OCCUPANCY SENSORS

Manual Control v. Occupancy Sensors
One of the most frustrating tasks for the energy manager is convincing building occupants to turn off the lights. Light switches are simple to operate, yet even a short stroll through any school or office building reveals lights left on. People either forget to turn off lights or, in larger areas, are reluctant to turn lights off in large areas where others might be affected. But manual control, where possible, is still the preferred method of on/off lighting control and should be considered before any discussion of occupancy sensors. The advantages of manual control are obvious: no additional installation or engineering costs, no nuisance shutoff or "ghost" detection, and very little training. Users may also get in the habit of thinking about energy and may turn off computers, printers and other office equipment.

Despite these advantages, experience shows us that manual lighting control can only be used effectively in controlled areas. These might include laboratories or libraries where a single person is responsible for watching a large area. Public areas such as classrooms, conference rooms, hallways, and open offices are places where manual switching is often wasteful. They are the only devices that can automatically respond to unpredictable occupancy of a space (Verderber 1988, p. 25).

Types of Occupancy Sensors
Occupancy sensor operation is simple. When no movement is detected in a controlled space for a given period of time the sensor will operate a relay to shut the lights off. The two most popular methods of doing this are with either ultrasonic or infrared sensing. Although limited, microwave and audio sensors are also available. In a 1991 directory of lighting products, fourteen manufacturers are listed (EUN). About two-thirds of the companies make infrared units, and the remaining third specialize in ultrasonic. At least two companies manufacture both types, and a single unit utilizing both technologies simultaneously has recently been introduced.

Although the specific method of operation varies, ultrasonic sensors detect movement by responding to frequency changes produced by interference with a moving object (Doppler shift). Infrared sensors, on the other hand, are passive and respond to movement of heat sources within the unit's range. They are called passive because they detect, rather than transmit, energy (Khosla 1986, p. 8-14).

Most sensors have two adjustable controls. The first is a time delay that allows the operator to set the interval between the last time the sensor detects motion and the time the lights switch off. The second adjustment allows the user to set the unit's sensitivity, or, more specifically, how much movement is required to activate the sensor. Even though different models of sensors are available for use in specific room shapes and sizes, the sensitivity adjustment allows for more precise coverage. For example, cubicle walls, carpeting, movement outside windows or doors, and air movement from HVAC ducts, can all affect the sensor's operation. In addition, rooms are occupied differently. Active areas such as cafeterias require a different sensitivity level than a quiet office with someone working on a personal computer. Potential problems can be moderated by the sensitivity adjustment.

Neither type of sensor is intrinsically better than the other. Because they are not directional, ultrasonic sensors work well in areas with obstacles such as cubicle walls or partitions. This, however, can also be a disadvantage when the coverage area spills into areas such as corridors or adjacent rooms. Infrared sensors, on the other hand, are cheaper to manufacture and somewhat simpler in design, so they are generally less expensive.

Savings Calculation Methods
Although the equation for determining energy savings from occupancy sensors is straightforward, obtaining accurate assumptions for the calculation can be difficult. The most accurate method is to set up a simple field test. All that is required are two inexpensive hour-meters and an occupancy sensor. The first hour-meter is used to determine how much time the lights are on during a given period of time. The second hour-meter records only the amount of time the sensor would operate if it was controlling the lights instead of just the hour-meter (actually, this is sensing the hours the space is occupied). The difference in these two readings gives an accurate idea of potential energy savings. Of course, the longer the test the more accurate the results. Take caution to select a site that represents the potential project.

At Stanford University, such a test was performed on seven classrooms. The number of hours saved on an annualized basis ranged from 600 hours to 2,730 hours. The average number of hours saved was 1,300. Because the amount of "off" time used in the equation really drives the savings calculation, care should be taken to determine this number accurately.

A detailed study performed at TRW Inc. identified nearly 3,000 hours of annual off-time from using occupancy sensors (Andis 1988, p. 42).

Installation Cost Elements: Several things affect the cost of installing occupancy sensors:

o       Room size, shape and obstructions (large and/or odd sized rooms require more sensors for complete coverage).

o       Ceiling Height (ceilings higher than twelve feet may require the construction of temporary scaffolding during installation. This can be further complicated by sloping floors, or permanent furniture).

o       Type of Ceiling (T-Bar or "drop" ceilings allow easy access for the low voltage wiring from the switch to the relay/transformer and the sensor.) Without an access space, some sort of wire mold or conduit will be needed to protect the wiring. The disadvantage of using wire molding is that it takes more time to install and, because it is visible, may need to be painted.

o    As an extra precaution in areas with special safety requirements, such as laboratories or hospitals, it may be advisable to remove one or two luminaires from the circuit switched by the sensors. Then, in the unlikely event that a sensor fails or is falsely tripped, there will be enough light for occupants to leave the room safely. (Laboratories or rooms with safety hazards may require extra sensors or extra wiring for a night light.)

Cost Effective Installations: As discussed in the Savings Calculation Methods Section, not all rooms are good candidates for sensor installations. Labor and material costs may be the same for a room with two luminaires or twenty luminaires. The energy savings, however, are a direct function of the number of luminaires (and the hours they can be turned off). Therefore, a room must have a certain number of luminaires to be cost effective (depending on the watts per fixture).

Impact Analyses

The following issues should be considered as part of any occupancy sensor installation. Each particular item should be weighted according to the pattern of occupancy, type of space, and economic priorities of the company or institution.

System Operation: Aside from the time and sensitivity adjustments, most occupancy sensors include an LED to indicate sensor operation and range, a bypass to remove the sensor from the lighting circuit, and an override used to switch off the lights for showing slides or movies. Several manufacturers offer "slave sensors" to work in combination with a "master sensor" to extend coverage range. Since adding features to a sensor usually only requires additional circuitry, lack of a particular feature may reflect the manufacturer's design philosophy. For example, not all sensors include a bypass switch. Some claim that the occupant will use the bypass to defeat the sensor, and thus impede energy savings. Others claim that making a bypass available is preferable to having someone not familiar with sensor operation or lighting circuits attempt to adjust or repair it. Ideally, the bypass can be used to reduce the inconvenience to the building occupant. Sensor adjustments or repairs can be made by competent personnel after the sensor has been disabled.

System Design and Maintenance: The success of any sensor installation is largely dependent on proper design and maintenance to insure proper operation. Several things must be done early in the engineering and installation parts of the project to avoid problems.

o    Enough sensors must be used to cover the space properly. Although this seems obvious, competitive bidders often reduce the number of sensors used to gain the low bid. This can result in nuisance shutoff.

o    Sensors should not be used to the limits of their coverage capabilities. If a room is one-thousand square feet, a sensor should be selected that can cover a larger area, or two six-hundred square foot sensors should be used.

o    In-house personnel must be trained in sensor operation. Unfortunately, the newest or most unfamiliar item will be the first suspected in any lighting problem. If the electricians know how the sensors operate and how they were installed, the chances increase that they will be adjusted correctly.

o    If a large project is completed with many different types of rooms and wiring schemes, a single line sketch of the room should be required of the installer to show the location of new relays or transformers. This is especially critical in areas that have complicated switching layouts. Trouble shooting time can be reduced with simple, organized installation details.

o    Two features make testing and trouble shooting easy: the first is the LED indicator and the second is the short time test mode. The LED is illuminated when the sensor detects motion. This is necessary to check the sensor's range. The short-time test-mode bypass sets the sensor timer to shut off the lights after only 15 seconds. Both of these features decrease the amount of time needed to trouble shoot the sensors.

o    Although the cost of energy is much greater than the cost of lamps, the time delay and sensitivity should be set to avoid excessive lamp cycling. This will help prevent early lamp burnout.

o    It is useful to mount and wire a sensor to something portable so it can be used for demonstration or training purposes. This is especially easy to do with the wall switch units.

Aesthetics, Safety, and Comfort Issues: Unlike electronic ballasts or optical reflectors, occupancy sensors are a high visibility product. Building occupants are quickly aware of sensor malfunctions. For this reason, proper installation is critical. Although many people will put up with early tuning adjustments, few will put up with repeated problems.

In 1983, the health impact of ultrasonic occupancy sensors was considered by the California Energy Commission. Ultrasonic sensors are "active" by nature: that is, they emit high frequency sound. This tone is above the levels audible to the human ear (25 kHz). Two groups, (the American National Standards Institute and the Department of Health Services) have concluded that the sound pressure levels (dB) emitted by ultrasonic sensors do not adversely affect the health of workers. A high quality sensor will also be free of any subharmonics and emit only a "pure" tone. Infrared sensors, by virtue of their passive operation nature, have no potential adverse effects.

Wall Switch Sensors

In an effort to expand the cost effective use of occupancy sensors manufactures have recently developed the wall switch sensor. These units replace normal single-pole electrical switches. Wall switch sensors use the same infrared or ultrasonic technology as large room sensors. By only replacing the existing wall switch, labor and material costs are significantly reduced over the large room units.

Wall switch sensors are not cost effective in many small office settings. (A small office, for the purpose of this discussion, is a completely enclosed space less than 300 square feet in size and with local lighting controls.) It is important to mention that a typical office is occupied nine hours a day, two hundred sixty days per year (2,340 hours per year). If the building occupants already turn the lights off manually at night, there are few hours to reap energy savings. An office with six 40-watt lamps (two three-lamp luminaires) must have the annual on time reduced by over two-thousand hours to gain a two year payback, assuming a sensor cost of fifty-five dollars and an energy cost of six cents per kWh. On the other hand, in office settings where the lights are continually left on at night the simple payback is usually quick. Although this sort of time reduction is possible, it is certainly not a conservative estimate. (Even the most remiss building occupant is likely to turn out the lights when locking up for the night.) With the lights already off at night, the sensor must be able to turn off the lights for over eight hours per day 260 days per year to reach the 2,000 hours needed for a two year payback. Rooms with more lamps, higher energy costs and cheaper sensors will, of course, pay back quicker.

Although some wall sensors will cover areas as large as eight-hundred square feet, perhaps their best application is in single offices or conference rooms with few obstructions.

Several manufacturers have introduced a wall switch sensor with a built-in photocell control. Not only will the sensor turn off the lights when no one is in the room, but it will also turn off the lights when a preset amount of daylight available, making the fluorescent lights unnecessary. Since traditional indoor photocell control is rarely cost effective in small areas, this sensor will be particularly useful in perimeter offices and other daylit rooms.

Summary of Important Criteria for Occupancy Sensor Selection

Occupancy sensors can be used to provide local on/off lighting control for unoccupied areas. Occupancy sensors can be installed in most areas, but areas with high ceilings, non-rectangular shapes, and with obstructions tend to require more sensors and therefore are often less cost effective. Because there are so many different types of occupancy sensors most manufacturers provide both engineering and product selection assistance.

There are two major types of occupancy sensors, passive infrared and active ultrasonic. The selection to use one type over the other will depend on the project specifics.

The following additional factors should be considered:

o    Enough sensors should be used in each area to assure full coverage.

o    Sensors should not be used to limits of their coverage capabilities.

o    In-house personnel should be trained in occupancy sensor installation and repair.

o    Single line drawings should be made for areas with complicated switching schemes.

o    Each sensor should have both sensitivity and time delay adjustments.

o    A bypass to remove the sensor from the lighting circuit is an important feature.

o    For testing the sensors range, a built-in LED indicator light is vital.

## CONCLUSION

With a bright future ahead, what is the next logical step for the lighting efficiency industry? Quantum leaps have already been made with the introduction of new technologies such as the electronic ballast and the compact fluorescent lamp. Continued progress will be made as researchers refine existing technologies and introduce still newer technologies. These technologies, however, will not realize their full environmental and economic potential unless manufacturers, researchers, utilities, and government agencies work to help end-users properly implement lighting efficiency projects.

## BIBLIOGRAPHY

Alling, W.R. 1990. Performance of Electronic Ballasts. Danville, California: LMP Corporation, 1990. Photocopied.

Andis, Jerry D. 1988. Selecting Motion Sensor Technology for a Large-Scale Lighting Project. Energy Engineering 85 (January): 39-46.

Arthur, A.A., R.R. Verderber, F. Rubinstein, and O. Morse. 1982. Electromagnetic Interference Measurements of Fluorescent Lamps Operated With Electronic Ballasts. IEEE Transactions on Industry Applications, November-December, 647-652.

Bevington, Rick and Arthur Rosenfeld. 1990. Energy for Buildings and Homes Scientific American, September, 76.

Black, Paul. 1989. Energy Management By Lighting Retrofits. Facilities Manager, Fall, 42.

Brekken, R.A. 1987. Specular Fluorescent Reflectors-Some Considerations. Journal of the Illuminating Engineering Society. 16 (Summer): 67-75.

DiLaura, D.L. and D.G. Kambich. 1987. Luminaire Retrofit Performance. Palo Alto, California: Electric Power Research Institute. EM-5094

Eley, Charles, Jim Benya, and Rudy Verderber. 1990. Advanced Lighting Technologies Application Guidelines. Sacramento, California: Building and Appliance Efficiency Office, Division of the California Energy Commission. PB400-90-014.

Fetters, John L. 1990. Design Criteria for Lighting: Balancing Quality, Cost, and Flexibility. Energy Engineering 87: 13-28.

Fickett, Arnold P., Clark Gellings and Amory Lovins. 1990. Efficient Use of Electricity. Scientific American 263 (September): 64-75.

Ford, Laura Bird, and David Ranieri. 1990. Glare Evaluation Calculations Applied to Visual Display Terminals. Journal of the Illuminating Engineering Society 19 (Summer): 3-21.

Geberer, Raanan. 1991. EPA Formulates Program to Promote Efficient Lighting Technologies. Energy Users News, January, 16.

Gould, Scott. 1989. Cautious Application of Electronic Ballasts. Edited by Albert Thumann. Lighting Efficiency Applications. Lilburn, Ga: Fairmont Press.

Harms, H. P., L.P. Leung, and R.R. Verderber. 1984. Electromagnetic Interference From Fluorescent Lighting Operated With Solid State Ballasts in Various Sites. Berkeley: Lawrence Berkeley Laboratory, LBL Report 17998.

Heerwagen, Judith H. and Heerwagen Dean R. 1986. Lighting and Psychological Comfort. Lighting Design and Application, April, 47.

Helms, Ronald N. and Belcher, M. Clay. 1991. Lighting For Energy-Efficient Luminous Environments. New Jersey: Prentice Hall

Howard, Theresa. 1990. Vendors, Users Cite Increased Use of Sensor Controls. Energy User News, November, 11.

Isaksen, L. 1987. Survey of Utility Lighting Programs. Palo Alto, California: Electric Power Research Institute, EM-5093.

_____. 1987. Personal Computer Software for Lighting Design and Analysis. Palo Alto, California: Electric Power Research Institute, EM-5463.

Jewel, J. E., S. Selkowitz, and R. R. Verderber. 1980. Solid State Ballasts Prove to be Energy Savers. Lighting Design and Application, January, 36.

Johnston, C. 1985. Lighting Energy Management-With Reflectors. <u>Facilities Manager</u>, Winter, 24.

Kaufman, John, ed. 1984. <u>Illuminating Engineering Society Lighting Handbook, Reference Volume</u>. New York, New York: Illuminating Engineering Society of North America.

_____. <u>Illuminating Engineering Society Lighting Handbook, Application Volume</u>. New York, New York: Illuminating Engineering Society of North America.

Kessel, Jeff. 1990. Performance of Retrofit Optical Reflectors. <u>Strategic Planning for Energy and the Environment</u> 10 (Fall): 25-34.

Khosla, N. K., and J. P. Bachner. 1986. <u>Lighting Handbook for Utilities</u>. Palo Alto, California: Electric Power Research Institute, EM-4423.

Landis, Karl E. 1988. The VDT Office: Consider the Worker's Needs First. <u>Electrical Systems Design</u>, April, 30.

Lindsey, J.L. 1988. Specular Retrofit Reflectors For Fluorescent Troffers. In <u>Integration of Efficient Design Technologies: Proceedings of the 10th World Energy Engineering Congress, in Atlanta Georgia, September 29-October 3, 1987</u>, edited by Albert Thumann. 41-52.

McCully, R.A. 1990. Development History of More Efficient Lamp Designs. <u>Energy Engineering</u> 87: 29-45.

Mehta, D. Paul, and Albert Thumann. 1989. <u>Handbook of Energy Engineering</u>. Lilburn, GA: Fairmont Press.

Neils, M.F. 1986. Retrofitting Optical Reflectors IntoExisting Fluorescent Fixtures, Application Note 76. San Francisco, California. Pacific Gas and Electric Co.

_____. 1986. Energy Efficiency Retrofits on Existing Fluorescent Fixtures, Application Note 80. San Francisco, California: Pacific Gas and Electric Co.

"Occupancy Sensor Product Guide." <u>Energy User News</u>, March 1989, pp. 10-12.

Paumgartten, Paul. 1989. <u>Fluorescent Reflectors: The Main Consideration.</u> Edited by Albert Thumann. <u>Lighting Efficiency Applications</u>. Lilburn, Ga: Fairmont Press.

Rosenfeld, Arthur H. 1988. Energy Conservation, Competition and National Security. <u>Strategic Planning and Energy Management</u> 8: 5-30.

Siminovitch, Micheal, Francis Rubenstein, Rudy Verderber, and Douglas Crawford. 1990. Energy Conservation from Thermally Efficient Fluorescent Fixtures. <u>Strategic Planning and Energy Management</u> 9 3: 45-65.

_____. 1990. Thermal Performance Characteristics of Compact Fluorescent Fixtures. In <u>Proceedings Lighting Efficiency Congress, Santa Clara, California, March 27-30, 1990</u>, edited by Richard Sequest. 1-14.

Verderber, R. R. 1980. Electronic Ballast Improves Efficiency. <u>Electrical Consultant</u>, November-December, 22.

Verderber, R. R. and O. Morse. 1985. <u>Performance ofElectronic Ballast and Other New Lighting Equipment</u>. Berkeley: Lawrence Berkeley Laboratory, LBL Report 20119.

_____. 1988. Review of Lighting Control Equipment and Applications. <u>Energy Engineering</u> 85 (January): 19-28.

_____. 1989. Advanced Lighting Technologies and Products. <u>Strategic Planning and Energy Management</u> 9: 6-15.

# SECTION 6
# ELECTRICAL SYSTEM
# OPTIMIZATION

# Chapter 78
# Harmonics and Energy Management

M. Andresen

It's hard to believe that during the 1980's several electricity-related milestones occurred. 1982 marked the 100th anniversary of Edison's first commercial generating station (DC) and 1989 was the 100th anniversary for the first HVAC generating station on a large scale. For many, the thought that commercial electricity is only 100 years old is akin to thinking the wheel has only been around for a similar period of time. Hasn't AC power been used forever? Obviously, no, not forever. And although much has changed in the last 100 years, many aspects of our electrical system have remained somewhat constant. AC power is still generated as a sine wave; common low voltage utilization is still around 110-120 Vrms; three-phase transmission is still the most common form of getting power from here to there. Much is the same - even with all the technical advances in design and technology. And, until recently, there wasn't much happening that seriously rocked the boat.

Then, along came computers and the age of power electronics was born. More specifically, the age of power conversion. It seems that after all the work Tesla, Westinghouse, and a host of others have done to make AC power work effectively, we now have to get back to Edison's idea of using DC power, albeit within the computer and not necessarily to the computer. The focus on conversion technology has increased dramatically over recent years, resulting in all manner of power supplies, converters, controllers, etc., being placed into our neat, pretty picture of AC power.

The result has been a bonanza for manufacturers, but our power system may be paying a price for it. Today, there are numerous energy conservation incentives to use more of these types of technologies in place of the old "standard" loads our power system is used to.

The difference, and thus the price to pay, revolves around waveshape. Sine waves dominated the scene, as both voltage and current, until power converters showed up. Power converters do not draw current, typically, as a sine wave. Since the whole power system has developed with a sine wave mentality, what happens if current and/or voltage is non-sinusoidal? The answer lies is the distortion-analysis realm commonly called harmonics.

Harmonics affect the distribution of power. Harmonics shake the foundation of power measurement. Harmonics disrupt the very equipment which is usually generating them. The more harmonic-generating equipment the power system must support, the greater the potential for harmonic related problems.

To complicate matters, those who seek to implement energy management techniques quite often do not understand the issues of harmonics, and thus are at their mercy. The very piece of equipment designed to reduce costs, for example, may cost more.

This interaction between harmonics and energy management is the focus of this paper. An overview of what harmonics are and how they are created will be presented first. Then, discussions on how harmonics impact several energy management issues will be given.

## HARMONICS OVERVIEW

When we talk about harmonics we are first of all talking about steady-state signals. The study of power system harmonics does not generally include looking at transient waveshapes or high frequency noise bursts. Since the steady-state power ideally is sinusoidal, harmonic analysis involves deviation, or distortion, from a sine wave. Thus, a pure sine wave of voltage has no distortion and no harmonics, and a non-sinusoidal waveshape (also called "non-linear") has distortion and harmonics. Several examples of current and voltage waveshapes from harmonic-generating devices are shown below.

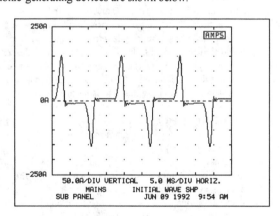

FIGURE 1.   CURRENT FROM A PC

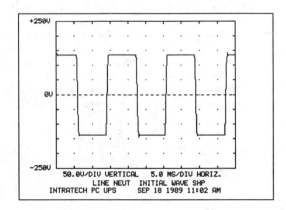

FIGURE 2.   OUTPUT VOLTAGE FROM AN
OFF-LINE UPS (SPS)

If, as these graphs indicate, non-sinusoidal waveshapes exist in the power system, then where do they come from? Have utilities decided to give us poor power? Are they no longer creating sinusoidal power? The answer is quite simple. The utilities are still providing voltage as a sine wave. In fact, the utilities are doing a better job of providing electrical power than ever before. The problem is not the voltage from the utility, but rather the loads being used by customers. Harmonic generating loads are being installed all over the country at an increasing rate. These loads fall into one of three categories:

- Arcing Devices such as high intensity discharge lighting and arc furnaces
- Saturable Reactors such as lightly loaded transformers and ferroresonant devices
- Power Conversion Devices such as power supplies and variable speed drives

An Electric Power Research Institute (EPRI) study suggests that by the year 2000 as much as 50%-60% of the total U.S. electricity production will be consumed by non-linear loads. Imagine if all the HVAC units in a typical building (maybe 50% of the total load) were replaced by variable speed drives which generate harmonics. Then, the fluorescent lights (30% of the load) were "upgraded" to electronic ballasts. Now, instead of only 10% of the building using harmonic loads, 90% of the loads generate harmonics. If this were to become a trend, it could cause utilities great concern. The irony is that many utilities are offering financial incentives to customers who install the VSDs and electronic ballasts.

### Fourier Analysis

Clearly, some method of systematically analyzing harmonics is needed in order to determine how they impact the power system. In the late 1700's a mathematician named Fourier developed such a method. Today it is called Fourier Analysis. Fourier found a way to describe distorted, periodic waveforms in terms of sine waves. In essence, he could decompose a distorted waveform into a set of pure sine waves with certain characteristics. These characteristics are:

- The repetition rate of the wave - that is, how often it repeats itself - is called the fundamental frequency (typically 60 Hz in power systems).
- The fundamental waveshape is a pure sine wave.
- All additional sine waves are integer multiples of the fundamental frequency.
- These additional sine waves - called harmonics - may vary from the fundamental in magnitude and phase shift.
- The variation in magnitude is called the Distortion Factor (DF) and equals the ratio of the harmonic amps (or volts) to the fundamental amps (or volts).
- If the positive half cycle of the distorted waveshape looks like a mirror image of the negative half cycle, the wave is said to be symmetrical and will have no even order harmonics (2nd, 4th, 6th, etc.).
- The summation of the fundamental and all harmonics will equal the original distorted waveform.

At first the idea that a bunch of sine waves can equal a really bad waveshape sounds ludicrous. To demonstrate this, let's look at the harmonic spectrum of Figure 1. This spectrum was obtained from a BMI 3030A PowerProfiler.

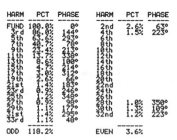

| HARM | PCT | PHASE | HARM | PCT | PHASE |
|------|-----|-------|------|-----|-------|
| FUND | 100.0% | 0° | 2nd | 2.6% | 63° |
| 3rd | 86.0% | 144° | 4th | 1.5% | 223° |
| 5th | 63.6% | 293° | 6th | | |
| 7th | 40.7% | 78° | 8th | | |
| 9th | 19.4% | 213° | 10th | | |
| 11th | 13.7% | 338° | 12th | | |
| 13th | 8.6% | 100° | 14th | | |
| 15th | 4.7% | 414° | 16th | | |
| 17th | 3.0% | 312° | 18th | | |
| 19th | 3.6% | 66° | 20th | | |
| 21st | 1.4% | 183° | 22nd | | |
| 23rd | 0.9% | 246° | 24th | | |
| 25th | 1.2% | 348° | 26th | | |
| 27th | 0.9% | 98° | 28th | 1.0% | 350° |
| 29th | 1.1% | 177° | 30th | 1.3% | 109° |
| 31st | 1.4% | 295° | 32nd | 1.2% | 223° |
| 33rd | 1.1% | 48° | | | |
| ODD | 118.2% | | EVEN | 3.6% | |

FIGURE 3. HARMONIC SPECTRUM OF FIGURE 1.

Given that the fundamental current is about 35 Arms, we can see from this spectrum that:
- The fundamental is, by definition, 100%.
- The magnitude of each harmonic is the distortion factor (DF) times the fundamental, so the 3rd harmonic is 86% of 35 Arms = 30.1 Arms
- The frequency of each harmonic is the harmonic number times the fundamental, so the 3rd is 180 Hz, the 5th is 300 Hz, etc..
- Since reference is made to the fundamental, the Total Harmonic Distortion (THD) can be over 100%.

To determine how the 118.2% number was figured out, Fourier found that the total distortion is not the sum of the individual distortion factors, but rather the geometric sum. The formula below works for all harmonics (THD), or for only even or odd harmonics (as shown in Figure 3).

$$ THD = (DF_2^2 + DF_3^2 + DF_4^2 + \ldots + DF_n^2 )^{1/2} $$

If the listed distortion factors are put into a spreadsheet designed to generate sine waves of varying magnitude and phase shift, a similar waveshape to Figure 1 will be seen. This was done (through the 19th harmonic) with the results shown in Figure 4.

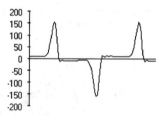

FIGURE 4. SPREADSHEET RESULT FROM FIGURE 3.

So, as hard as it may be to believe in Fourier analysis, it does work, and it has become the standard approach to most harmonic analysis issues.

### Voltage Distortion

Our discussion so far has focused on current distortion. This is not to say that the voltage is never distorted. Voltage is constantly being distorted as it travels from the generator to the branch circuit outlet. Voltage distortion usually occurs in two ways.

First, we must recognize that Ohm's Law not only applies to RMS levels, but also to actual waveshapes. If Ohm's Law says that there should be a 5 volt drop, the resultant waveshape will show this drop. If the drop is sinusoidal, then the resultant voltage will not be any more distorted than it was. However, if the voltage drop is not sinusoidal, then the resultant voltage wave may very well become more distorted than it was. As an example, consider Figure 5 below.

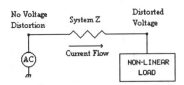

FIGURE 5.    TYPICAL BRANCH CIRCUIT

As the current is conducted along the path from source to load, it interacts with the impedance of the wires. During the times when there is no current flowing (the time between the current pulses from Figure 1) there will be no voltage drop. When current is flowing the high peak currents cause a large voltage drop near the voltage peak. The subsequent drop appears to "cut off" the top of the voltage in what is commonly called "flat-topping" (see Figure 6.).

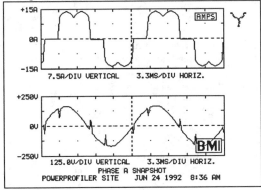

Non-distorted V          Distorted V drop          Resultant

FIGURE 6.    VOLTAGE DISTORTION DUE TO OHM'S LAW

Second, voltage distortion can be a direct result from certain types of power conversion devices - specifically, three phase rectifiers. The phenomenon involved is called "line notching" and is a by-product of many of the power electronics used in these rectifiers. As the rectifier operates, the power electronic devices are turning on and off quite rapidly. Where problems come up is that as one is turning on, another is turning off and the two overlap slightly. This overlap creates a very brief short circuit (called commutation) which, in turn, causes a fast voltage drop. This drop is seen on the voltage waveform as a notch. Figure 7 shows an example of both the current and voltage from a 6-pulse rectifier. Notice how the notching on the voltage directly lines up with the change in current.

```
+15A                                    AMPS    Y

0A

-15A
     7.5A/DIV VERTICAL      3.3MS/DIV HORIZ.

+250V

0V

-250V                                           BMI
     125.0V/DIV VERTICAL      3.3MS/DIV HORIZ.
              PHASE A SNAPSHOT
     POWERPROFILER SITE    JUN 24 1992  8:36 AM
```

FIGURE 7.    LINE NOTCHING FROM A 6-PULSE
RECTIFIER

So, our power system must not only be able to handle current distortion, but also voltage distortion.

### IMPACT ON ENERGY MANAGEMENT

But after everything is said and done, what's the big deal? So what if distortion exists? How does if affect the power system, and how does it impact energy management issues? Why is it said to be the source of *problems*? This is discussed next.

### Measurement Accuracy

When considering the fact that we can't (or shouldn't) detect electricity by our senses, we must provide equipment to measure and characterize it for us. The good news is that this equipment exists and works well. The bad news is that all too often we whole-heartedly believe the equipment without understanding its limitations - thus leading to wrong results. This is the case when using one of the most common electrical measurement devices, the multimeter.

To understand why our common multimeters can be inaccurate we must start with the question - how does one measure an AC signal? There are two basic methods of doing this. The first method is to take the average value of a half cycle. For a sine wave, this works out to be the peak times 0.636. The second method is to determine the effective, or usually called the RMS, value. For a sine wave, this is the peak times 0.707. The $64,000 question is which one is the right one? In order to equate AC to DC we must use the RMS value.

When meters began to be commercially developed it was far easier and cheaper to find the average value of a signal. Then, in order to provide an RMS reading, the average value was multiplied (in the meter) by a constant called the form factor. The form factor is the ratio of a signal's RMS value to its average value, and for a sine wave, the form factor equals 1.11. Due to our "sine wave mentality", this form factor was (and still is) used in the multimeter design as the constant multiplier.

This process worked excellently through the years and multimeters were specified as "average detecting, RMS calibrated" meters. Now comes the monkey wrench. When harmonics began emerging the form factors of many power signals were no longer 1.11. The form factor for the pulsed current wave of Figure 1 is about 2.0. Its RMS value is 50 Arms and its average/RMS calibrated value is 27 Arms. Quite a difference. When harmonics are present, only a true RMS measuring device can provide an accurate reading. If your multimeter is an average/RMS calibrated one, it will not give correct readings when harmonics are present - and who knows if the voltage or current you want to measure is distorted?

To make matters worse, the error introduced by the averaging meter can be unsafe. Imagine plugging in this load from Figure 1 on your 30 amp circuit and trying to find out why the breaker keeps tripping. The average/RMS calibrated multimeter says 27 Arms, when the load is really consuming 50 Arms. Measurement accuracy can only be ensured by using true RMS devices.

### Neutral Current

Another area where harmonics have altered our basic concept of power regards the neutral conductor in a three-phase, wye system. It has long been held that if a wye subpanel is perfectly balanced there will be little to no current in the neutral. Many electricians still check their panel installation by measuring the neutral. If the current is small, they think they have done a good job. This process works only if the currents are sinusoidal. Three currents, phase-shifted by 120°, all flowing through the same neutral will cancel each other out. This is shown in Figure 8.

Given the same panel, if the currents were equal in magnitude, but were distorted, potentially high levels of neutral current could occur. Figure 9 shows an example using typical currents from computers. Notice that the waveshapes do not cancel out even though they are balanced.

451

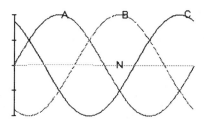

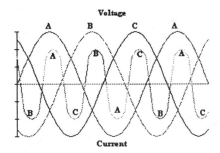

FIGURE 8. PHASE CURRENTS AND RESULTANT
NEUTRAL CURRENT IN A BALANCE
WYE SYSTEM

FIGURE 9. 3rd HARMONIC NEUTRAL CURRENT AS
SUM OF DISTORTED PHASE CURRENTS

The unique feature of this phenomenon is the 180 Hz frequency - the 3rd harmonic in a 60 Hz system.

Although neutral current is nothing new, high levels of neutral current is. The National Electrical Code (NEC), in the majority of cases, allows for two particular items regarding the neutral conductor. First, a neutral can be derated, or sized smaller than the phase conductor. Second, when determining the maximum number of wires within a conduit (needed for controlling the conduit heating effect), the neutral can be ignored. In both of these circumstances, high neutral currents can pose serious safety and fire hazards. This can be especially true with modular office partitions where large computer loads, shared neutrals, and poor inter-module connections can cause numerous problems.

Another concern over high neutral currents surrounds the levels of neutral-to-ground voltages at outlets. Many electronic devices have specific requirements for N-G voltage magnitudes. The dominant cause of this voltage is the neutral current interacting with the neutral conductor impedance. High currents, especially with long branch circuit runs, can create significant N-G voltages which may disrupt computers and the like. Neutral currents and N-G voltages can no longer be ignored or assumed to be at acceptable levels.

Transformer Overheating

One of the main components in the power system is the transformer. A large number of transformers are involved in the transmission and distribution of power from the utility to the receptacle. All transformers are designed to some capacity level, usually rated in kVA. Ultimately, however, the power limitation of the transformer is not determined by its capacity, but by the internal level of heat.

The majority of heat is generated in a transformer by two areas of losses - the winding loss ($I^2R$) and the eddy current loss. Since RMS current has the same heating effect regardless of harmonic content, the presence of harmonics does not alter the winding losses. On the other hand, the eddy current loss is "proportional to the square of the load

current and the square of frequency" (ANSI C57.110-1986, 4.1.2). Thus, for a given RMS current value, the more harmonics the higher the losses and the higher the internal temperature.

At some point, if the distorted load current increases, the internal temperature reaches a maximum level. To go beyond this jeopardizes the integrity of the winding insulation and may lead to failure. The corresponding kVA at this maximum temperature level is *less* than the normal rating, and the transformer should be *derated*. A 100 kVA transformer, for example, might have to be derated to 80 kVA maximum load to stay within its temperature requirements.

Please note that transformer derating does not eliminate or reduce harmonic content. It merely indicates the transformer capability given the current harmonic content. The new K-Factor transformers are specially designed to supply these harmonic currents without the need to be derated. They do not eliminate harmonics either.

Power Factor Correction

Correcting the power factor has long been a technique to improve the transmission of power. Since our power system is largely inductive, the current tends to lag, or come after, the voltage. The sine wave mentality led to the development of what is referred to as "the power triangle", Figure 10, shown with a lagging power factor.

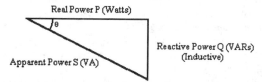

FIGURE 10. POWER TRIANGLE SHOWING WATTS,
VOLT-AMPS, AND VARS

From this triangle we see that real power, what we are most interested in, can be calculated as:

$$P = S \times \text{Power Factor} \qquad \text{where Power Factor} = \cos\theta$$

The smaller the angle (and the smaller the VARs), the larger the power factor and the closer the Watts are to the kVA. The easiest way to reduce the angle and the VARs is to offset the inductive VARs with capacitive VARs as shown in Figure 11.

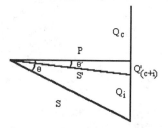

FIGURE 11. POWER FACTOR CORRECTION
USING A CAPACITOR

When the reactive VARs of the capacitor are added to those of the inductance, the total VARs (Q') are significantly reduced, the angle is smaller, and the resultant apparent power (S') is less. Since the voltage has not changed, the lower S' means less current is needed to get the same real power P as before. This is the beauty of PF correction with capacitors - lower current for the same real power. Thus, capacities are increased, utility costs are reduced, and system burden is reduced.

As stated earlier, though, when harmonics are present the power triangle is no longer applicable as it is. The triangle works for only one frequency. Harmonics introduce many frequencies into the system. Recall the pulsed current waveshape of Figure 1. Where is the zero crossing to determine θ? Even if there was some kind of zero crossing, the power factor would not be the cosine of the displacement angle. Standard power factor measurements and PF correction calculations no longer work with harmonics. So, what do we do?

To accurately measure power factor, we need simply remember the definition:

Power Factor = Watts / Volt-Amps

If we accurately measure the true RMS values of the voltage and current, and the total power (say, with digital sampling), then PF falls out easily. This is the *true* power factor and will follow how the utility looks at power.

So, can we use the true power factor to determine capacitor sizing to correct for low PF? No. If a capacitor is placed into a power system where the voltage is still sinusoidal, it will draw sinusoidal current. Sinusoidal capacitor current will only offset sinusoidal inductive current. Any harmonic frequencies will not be corrected. If this procedure is attempted, problems can occur as discussed in the following example.

Example: A customer has a computer system on a panel. The panel is rated for 100 Arms per phase, and the system has these characteristics:
- All single phase loads.
- Current draw of about 75 Arms per phase.
- Measured watts of 4.66 kW
- True PF of 0.52 lag
- VARs are calculated as $\sqrt{(VA^2 - W^2)}$ = 7.7 kVAR

It is desired to correct the low PF to about 0.98 in order to reduce the current draw and open up capacity for more loads. After installing the properly sized capacitor, based on the calculated VARs, the following was measured:
- Total current draw of 100 Arms per phase
- True PF of 0.39 lead

Why wasn't the current reduced? Why did the power factor get worse? What happened?

The answer, again involves harmonics. What the customer did not take into account was the level of harmonic distortion. Since, as stated above, a capacitor can only correct for the sinusoidal component of the current (which is the current's fundamental sine wave), the customer miscalculated the VAR requirement. The capacitor will only offset the VARs at the fundamental - it will not correct for harmonics. After installing the capacitor, the waveshapes in Figure 12 were recorded.

Notice that the current waveshape shows leading power factor because the leading capacitor current dominates as the fundamental. The current pulse from the computer system is very evident and is not significantly changed. No canceling occurs to reduce the current level, rather the current is increased. None of the desired objectives were achieved because the wrong application was attempted. What should have been determined was either the fundamental VARs, or the displacement power factor. The dPF is the cosine of the angle between the fundamental voltage (a sine wave) and the fundamental current (also a sine wave). In the example above, the dPF is about 0.94, indicating that any capacitance could easily overcorrect to a leading power factor, which is exactly what happened.

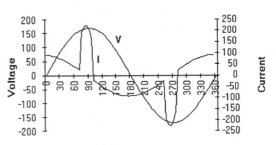

FIGURE 12. CURRENT WAVESHAPE OF PULSED CURRENT AND CAPACITOR

CONCLUSION

To summarize what this paper has presented:

- Voltage and current non-sinusoidal waveshapes exist in our power system.
- These harmonics result from the prolific use of non-linear loads.
- The use of these types of loads is increasing dramatically, partly due to the push to implement energy management techniques involving harmonic generating equipment.
- Harmonic analysis can identify specific harmonics, their frequency, magnitude, and phase shift referenced to the fundamental.
- Harmonic distortion forces the use of true RMS multimeters for measurement accuracy.
- High levels of neutral current and N-G voltages are now possible.
- Transformers may overheat and fail even though they are below rated capacity.
- Low power factors due to harmonics cannot be corrected by the installation of capacitors.
- Knowledge of the fundamental VARs or the displacement power factor is needed to use capacitors alone for power factor correction.

The harmonic related problems presented are by no means an exhaustive list. Many other concerns arise when harmonics are involved in the power system. The critical issue behind these problems is that many of the devices being recommended from an energy management point of view are contributing to the harmonic levels, and thus to the potential for harmonic problems. We can no longer live in the sinusoidal mentality if we are to be effective in saving energy and reducing costs.

# Chapter 79

# Two-Speed Step Drives - A Variable Speed Drive Is a Terrible Thing to Waste When All You Want to Do Is Save Some Kilowatt Hours

D.K. Tillson

IN HEATING, VENTILATING and AIR CONDITIONING (HVAC) SYSTEMS, significant quantities of Electrical Energy can be saved by providing equipment to enable the drives for Air Handling Units, Chilled Water Circulating Pumps, and Condenser Water (Cooling Tower Water) circulating pumps to operate at reduced speed when maximum conditions do not exist.

BUT, there is little need for a completely variable speed capability.

AND, the cost, complexity and reliability of the equipment and associated controls for variable speed inverter type drives is several times what is needed for some simple stepped speed drives.

WE HAVE FOUND THAT IN MANY SYSTEMS, 80% OF ALL THE ENERGY THAT COULD BE SAVED WITH A COMPLETELY VARIABLE SPEED DRIVE WITH SOPHISTICATED CONTROLS TO ALLOW THE SPEED TO VARY WITH THE LOAD, CAN BE SAVED WITH A SIMPLE TWO SPEED DRIVE OPERATING AT 100% AND 70% SPEEDS AND CONTROLLED BY A SINGLE 24 VOLT CONTACT CLOSURE!

The cost can be recovered in one to one and a quarter years in situations where the equipment is running on a 24 Hour basis and with electric rates at 4.5 cents per Kwhr or higher.

(So that we may understand the type of equipment that can be used, the second page of this paper is devoted to diagrams and photographs of some 2 speed step drives as manufactured by one company. The page should be used as a reference as various points are made.)

## WHAT MAKES THESE SAVINGS POSSIBLE?

There are four major factors that make this energy saving possible.

- The Designers Dilemma
- The Nature of Nature (Weather Facts)
- The Cube Function
- The Wonder Machine (Induction Motor)

A short discussion of each of these factors will remind the reader of what he most likely already knows.

## The Designer's Dilemma

The designer's problem comes from the fact, and his inherent knowledge, that a system that is inadequate (too small) will cause him a great deal of trouble and anguish and even legal liability. A system that is too large will not normally be noticed by the people who pay for the design because the consequences are primarily increased first cost and increased energy use over the years.

Add to this situation the fact that calculations for Heating and Cooling Loads are by nature only estimates;

the use of the building spaces is not always known for certain, the construction may vary in response to yet-to-be-designed or accepted alternatives, new materials may be used that affect the loads, even other buildings may be built that influence the present peak load vs the design peak load. Equipment may be put into the spaces now or in the future that adds to or deducts from the design load.

Further, complicating the matter is the fact that pipe and equipment only comes in standard sizes. The designer who needs a 4.2 inch pipe is going for a 6 inch etc. etc.

Further, there is need to consider the recovery time for the system if it is down for a long power outage. If a hotel is down because of a power outage for long enough that the spaces are badly out of limits, what is it worth to be able to get the system back quickly?

Further, it may be necessary to size for the smoke evacuation requirements to keep the building from serious freezing damage. (A situation which is likely to never occur!)

Further, it is necessary to consider a fouling factor for some types of equipment so that it can be expected to perform within the needs of the facilities without constant maintenance (or more realist·cally with the normal lack of maintenance).

And to top it all, the designer must by necessity design for the peak design conditions for the area concerned, conditions which seldom occur, but nevertheless, do occur and remain for hours or days.

SO IS IT ANY WONDER THAT YOU OFTEN FIND SITUATIONS WHERE THE SYSTEM IS MUCH, MUCH TOO LARGE FOR THE NEEDS MOST OF THE TIME.

## Now Let Us Look At The Nature of Nature

First remember that there are 8,760 Hours in a year.

In our area (Greensboro, NC) the design conditions for summer are 91 deg F dry bulb. (Many still use the old figure of 95 deg F.)

How many hours a year is the temp at or above design condition. Would you believe only 90 Hours? (The US Weather Data from our weather station says that is the case.) BUT WHAT IS STARTLING TO ME IS THAT THIS IS ONLY ONE POINT ZERO THREE PER CENT OF THE TIME! 1.03% ! ALL THE REST OF THE TIME THAT THE SYSTEM IS ON, IT IS TOO BIG.

98.97% OF THE TIME ITS TOO BIG, EVEN IF IT WAS DESIGNED WITH NONE OF THE FACTORS MENTIONED ABOVE BEING CONSIDERED! WITH SOME OF THE SAFETY FACTORS IN;

# Typical Diagrams and Photographs of 2-Speed Step Drives by One Manufacturer

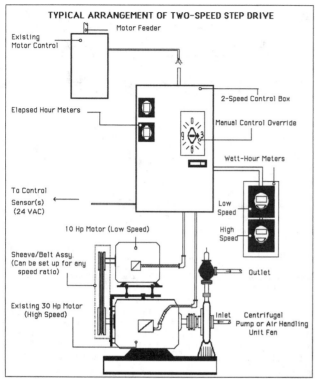

TYPICAL ARRANGEMENT OF TWO-SPEED STEP DRIVE

- Existing Motor Control
- Motor Feeder
- Elapsed Hour Meters
- 2-Speed Control Box
- Manual Control Override
- Watt-Hour Meters
- To Control Sensor(s) (24 VAC)
- Low Speed
- High Speed
- 10 Hp Motor (Low Speed)
- Sheave/Belt Assy. (Can be set up for any speed ratio)
- Outlet
- Existing 30 Hp Motor (High Speed)
- Inlet
- Centrifugal Pump or Air Handling Unit Fan

**100 Hp Chilled Water Pump**

**100 Hp Chilled Water Pump (partially assembled)**

**30 Hp Air Handling Unit**

**Two 25 Hp Condenser Water Pumps**

**60 Hp Air Handling Unit**

**15 Hp Hot Water Pump**

**50 Hp Condenser Water Pump**

Courtesy of Tillson Engineering Laboratory, Box 996, Jamestown, NC

456

We have taken the dry bulb temperature information and
made two charts which are shown below.   The first one
shows how many hours each batch of 5 deg temperature
ranges occurred.

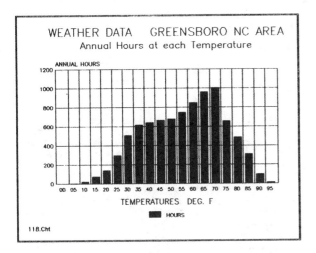

It is interesting to note that the most hours are in
the 70 deg F. bin.  But more important, THE GREAT
MAJORITY OF THE HOURS ARE BETWEEN 30 DEG AND 80 DEG.
(actually 27.5 to 82.5)  Since design conditions are
often taken at 95 deg and 10 deg; a first approximation
of when the system could reduce to 70% capacity,
(speed) is to take the inside temperature less the
outside temp at design and use 30% of that difference
to deduct from the design temp to guess at where the
system might be able to shift to 70%.  The answer is 90
deg.  So in a situation that has a large part of its
cooling load dependent on outside conditions, We can
guess that somewhere around 90 deg outside air temp. we
will need to go to Maximum from the 70% Normal Speed.
All the rest of the time we can run at the lower speed.

I know this is over simplified, but the point is that
even with sizeable internal loads the load profile has
a shape dictated by the outside conditions, and there
will be some temperature at which the system can run at
70%.  Will it be 90 or 85 or 80?  We don't really know;
and it won't be the same every day because of other
variables.  Does it matter?  Yes, but not much.

        THE HOURS ABOVE 90 DEG ARE 112; 1.25%
        THE HOURS ABOVE 85 DEG ARE 421; 4.80%
        THE HOURS ABOVE 80 DEG ARE 910; 10.38%

        IT IS ALMOST A CERTAINTY THAT THE SYSTEM CAN
        OPERATE AT REDUCED SPEED AT LEAST 90% OF THE TIME!

The Second Chart:  This graph shows how many hours each
year are above any given temperature.

Since many cooling systems do not need to operate in
the colder months, this chart gives a basis for
estimating how many hours the systems will operate if
you know at what temperature you have to start the
chillers.  In our area the systems usually have to
start at about 55 deg.  Obviously this depends on what
is going on in the building, the use of outside air for
cooling, etc. etc.  But as an example, if you start
your equipment at 55 degrees outside temp, then the
graph indicates there will be about 5500 hours each
year at or above that temp. and  that will be the hours
your chiller, chilled water pumps and condenser water
pumps operate.  In some systems here and particularly a
little farther north, use of heat exchangers may get

some "free cooling" for meeting much of the load.   The
chilled water pumps and the condenser water pumps are
still running "Flat Out" regardless of whether the
water is being cooled by a chiller or by the heat
exchanger.  The Air Handling Units on the other hand
will be running continuously all year long in many
applications.

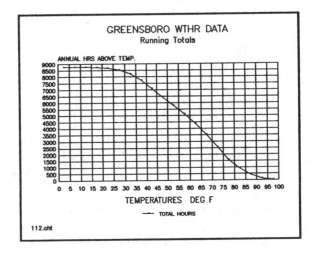

You may say, but this is weather data for your area
only.  But the shape of the curve is going to remain
much the same.  It simply moves laterally along the
temperature axis.  And, the design temperatures move
with it.  This can be shown by the next chart which
shows the Charlotte, Greensboro, and Asheville
(mountains) N.C.  charts all on one common graph.
Observe the similar shape.  Note that Charlotte which
is south of Greensboro moves toward the higher
temperature end of the chart while Asheville which has
much cooler summer conditions moves toward the cooler
end of the chart.

THE POINT IS THAT REGARDLESS OF WHERE THE SYSTEM IS,
THE NUMBER OF HOURS AT DESIGN CONDITIONS WILL BE VERY
SMALL.

(The 2 speed drive system with which we are most
familiar reduces the speed to 70% of the existing speed
and the flow (CFM) is reduced similarly.  So the
question becomes how many hours can the system operate
with air flow of 70% of maximum?  We will discuss this
point later.)

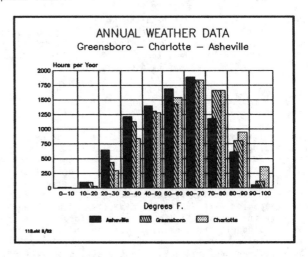

But remember, THE MAIN POINT IS THAT there are 8760 hrs
in a year and less than 1.3% of them are at or above
the design condition!

## What About This Cube Function?

The natural laws of physics apply to air and other fluids such as water. The energy required to force these fluids through a pipe or duct is related to the quantity being moved. But the relationship is not a simple one to one where twice as much fluid moved would take twice as much energy. The relationship is a cube function which means that if you double the quantity of fluid flowing in an enclosed system, it will take 2cubed or 8 times as much energy to move it! This also applies to objects moving through fluids such as boats and airplanes. Their propellers are basically pumps, blowers, or fans the same as the fans in air handling units and the impellers in centrifugal pumps.

Please note that we are not talking about pumping systems where water is actually moved to some other location, such as from one lake to a higher lake, but only circulation systems where you still have the same water when you quit as when you started. The water is being used as a CONVEYOR of heat and the need for the pump is the same as the motor on a belt conveyor. But the belt itself is not going anywhere.

> When the only resistance to the flow of the fluid is the friction of the fluid in the containing system, then the energy required to move the fluid through the system varies as the cube of the quantity of fluid moved.

> This is the case in chilled water pumps, condenser water pumps (except for the distance between pans in the Cooling Tower), hot water circulating pumps and Air Handling Units.

> Another physical fact is that the quantity of fluid moved varies directly with the speed of the pump (or fan).

So, if you double the speed of the pump (or fan) you will double the quantity of fluid flowing,(gpm, or cfm) and if you double the quantity of fluid flowing it will require 8 times as much energy to do it!

So why is this so important? Because it also works in reverse.

IF YOU REDUCE THE SPEED OF A PUMP OR BLOWER BY HALF YOU WILL REDUCE THE QUANTITY OF FLUID MOVED BY HALF; AND

> YOU WILL NEED ONLY ONE EIGHTH OF THE
> ENERGY TO MOVE IT. (0.5 X 0.5 X 0.5 = 0.125 )

So if you reduce the air handling unit's fan speed to 70% of what it was, you will reduce the air quantity to 70% of what it was and you will reduce the electric energy required for the motor to (0.70 x 0.70 x 0.70 = 0.343 ) 34.3% of what was needed before.

YOU CAN MOVE 70% OF THE AIR FOR 35% OF THE ENERGY! What a bargain, particularly when the system is inherently too big more than 95% of the time.

Duty Cycling vs Speed Reduction: This brings us to an interesting comparison. Many installations have recognized the fact that they do not need full capacity most of the time, and have initiated a program of duty cycling to save that energy. For instance if we have 10 Air Handling Units of 10 HP each; and if we think that we can do with 70% of the capacity, then we can run each unit only 70% of the time on a rotating basis and still handle the cooling or heating load. A 15 min. cycle with 10.5 min. on and 4.5 off will be 70%. The effect on the occupants is not always good, and the notable difference in full flow down to zero flow are drawbacks as well as the need for a computer for the timing function. The motors are started and stopped

many times a day contributing to their wear and tear and particularly to belt drive wear. In peak load times the spaces may go out of control and not recover in the following on cycle. The energy saved is significant and as expected is 30% or 30 HP in this example. The system is still using 70 HP.

Now compare this with slowing all of the 10 units down to 70% speed. No on-off conditions. No loss of control of space. No serious air distribution problems. Continuous operation at a lower general noise level without the notice of occupants.

AND; IT WILL ONLY REQUIRE 34 HP TO DO IT, NOT 70 HP!
66 HP WILL BE SAVED INSTEAD OF 30 HP!

## THE WONDER MACHINE: The Induction Motor

When you think about it, there is almost no machine as simple and as near to perfection as the 3 phase squirrel cage rotor induction motor. It has only one moving part and two bearings, and nothing touches anything or passes any electric current to the rotor. It is mass produced in standard designs and you can get a 20HP for $550 and it can and will run for years and never stop.

THE ONLY PROBLEM WITH THIS MACHINE IS THAT ITS SPEED IS CONTROLLED BY THE FREQUENCY OF THE AC POWER SOURCE AND THE PHYSICAL WINDING WITHIN THE MOTOR AND IT CANNOT BE RUN AT ANY OTHER SPEED. FURTHER, THE ONLY SPEEDS AVAILABLE ARE SUBMULTIPLES OF THE POWER LINE FREQUENCY. THE HIGHEST IS 60 CYCLES PER SECOND TIMES 60 SECONDS PER MINUTE WHICH IS 3600 REVOLUTIONS PER MINUTE AND THE NEXT IS 1800 RPM; THEN 1200 RPM; THEN 900 RPM; THEN 600 RPM ETC. (all reduced slightly by the slip of the induction motor; i.e. 3500 RPM; 1750 RPM; 1140 RPM; etc.)

> THE POINT IS THAT THIS MOTOR CAN ONLY GO ONE SPEED WITH A GIVEN LOAD AND A GIVEN PHYSICAL WINDING AND A POWER SOURCE FREQUENCY THAT CANNOT BE VARIED. (because it serves many other customers.)

Now enters the hand of economics and practicality. This wonderful motor has been standardized and mass produced by many manufacturers and competition has set the price. But the minute you want to get something even slightly different than this standardized motor you find that:

1. It isn't readily available in local stocks.

2. It costs a whole lot more.

3. You may have to buy more than one to even get a price quote.

4. Delivery is not too swift. ( An intolerable situation for Air Handling Units which hardly ever have any standby equipment.)

The result is a general use of the simple mass produced motor even in situations where it single speed characteristic makes it unsuitable.

Of course, it is possible to make two speed induction motors by putting two windings with a different arrangement of magnetic poles in the same frame. For instance a motor can be made that will run at either 1800 (1750) RPM or at 1200 (1150) RPM. It is actually two motors in one and normally requires a larger frame size. Its efficiency is not too good. This is not exactly the ratio of speeds that we want, but it is close, 65.7%, and the energy saved could and can be significant.

458

SO WHY DON'T WE SEE A LOT OF THESE ON
PUMPS AND AIR HANDLERS?

I don't know.  We should.  It must be because:

1. They are expensive and the equipment to start and
protect them is expensive.

   (The 20 HP motor that can be bought for 550
   dollars costs 1450 in a 2 speed version and the
   equipment to start, protect, and control which
   speed is used costs 900 instead of 325 for the
   standard one speed.  Total 875 for one speed 2350
   for two speed.  2.7 times as much plus increased
   installation costs.)

   (Is it worth difference?  Absolutely, Yes!)

2. If a winding burns out you lose both windings, the
motor is out of service, so you need some spares and
you will need an expensive rewind.

3. They are not available for immediate replacement
from local sources.

4. Motor Control equipment is much more expensive.

5. Nobody has put together a package and made a good
marketing effort.

6. In retrofitting situations, the installed costs by
the usual method of contracting get way out of hand
since the contractor has many unknown and one-time
costs as well as his overhead and profit. Deciding
exactly what equipment to purchase from the thousands
of sizes and makes of motors and starting equipment
needed to do the job and meet code requirements is a
time-consuming undertaking, and is not cost effective
on a one time basis.

Now however, packaged equipment is available to be used
on a retrofit basis, which will provide two speeds for
air handling units or pumps with a choice of speed
ratios from 50% to 95% and with separate standard 1750
RPM motors for a guaranteed price of 160 dollars per HP
for a 20 HP unit. (and if the smaller motor which runs
most of the time burns out or loses a bearing, you have
an immediate alternate already in place.  Remove the
belt and the unit can run again giving you time to
replace or repair the damaged motor as a non-emergency
routine repair; and at a Standard Motor off the shelf
price.)

The chart below shows the relationship of other sizes.
As usual, on a cost per HP basis, the larger units cost
less.  The energy savings are directly related to HP
expended, so the payoffs get better and better as the
sizes increase.

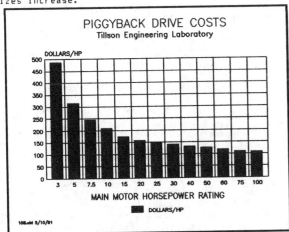

Chart 4 shows the cost relationship between the use of
this concept of two standard off the shelf motors
mounted on top of each other with a simple belt drive,
and the conventional two winding two speed motors.

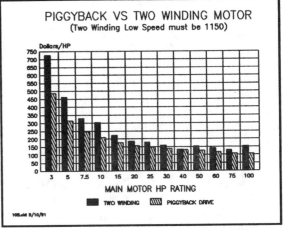

As you can see the costs are comparable.  Either one is
an acceptable method of saving a significant number of
kilowatt hours.

EVERY AIR HANDLING UNIT AND CIRCULATING PUMP IN THE
COUNTRY SHOULD HAVE A MEANS OF RUNNING AT A REDUCED
SPEED AND ENERGY REQUIREMENT DURING THE THOUSANDS OF
HOURS EACH YEAR WHEN HEATING AND/OR COOLING LOADS ARE
LESS THAN MAXIMUM.

CERTAINLY THOSE OVER 5HP THAT ARE RUNNING AS MUCH AS
4000 HRS PER YR. OUGHT TO HAVE THIS CAPABILITY.

YOU DO NOT NEED A VARIABLE SPEED DRIVE TO REAP THESE
ENERGY SAVINGS.  IN FACT SOMETIMES IT IS BETTER NOT TO
HAVE COMPLETE VARIABILITY BECAUSE THEN SOMEONE OR
SOMETHING HAS TO DECIDE ON A CONTINUOUS BASIS WHAT
SPEED TO RUN THE SYSTEM.  THIS GETS INTO COMPLICATED
(READ EXPENSIVE) CONTROLS AND SENSORS TO FEED
INFORMATION TO THE CONTROLS.

THE TWO SPEED DRIVES CAN OPERATE ON SOMETHING AS SIMPLE
AS AN OUTDOOR AIR THERMOSTAT.

   For Instance:  Consider this Control Strategy.  When
   outside air is over 90 run on High Speed. All other
   times run at reduced speed' say 70%.

HOW SIMPLE CAN YOU GET?!

   Or use two outside air thermostats.

(Control Strategy:  When outside air is over 90 or
under 25 run on High Speed.  All other times run at
reduced speed.)

In our area there are only 234 hours under 25 degF and
100 hours over 90 degF; 334 hours total time on High
Speed for the simple controls above.  That leaves 8426
Hours on the reduced speed and using 34% of the energy.

THAT'S RIGHT MORE THAN 96% OF THE TIME THE SYSTEM WOULD
BE ON REDUCED SPEED.

If that is a little to simple for you, add a return air
temp override, or a mechanical time switch override, or
put it on the building computer, or whatever.

THE KEY IS TO CONSIDER THE SYSTEMS NORMAL CONDITION TO
BE OPERATION ON THE LOWER SPEED AND THEN TO LET SOME
PARAMETER OR CONDITION OF YOUR CHOICE FORCE IT TO HIGH.

RUN IT ON CRUISE -- WITH SPURTS OF HIGH AS REQUIRED TO
DO THE JOB.

459

## So What About Controlling Pumps?

Well, again the bottom line of all the design work and all the factors in the building operation, the cooling load calculations, ad infinitum are there for you to see if you will only look.

If your system is designed for a delta T of 10 degF and it is going out at 48 and coming back at 53, a delta T of 5 degF, then what is happening?

Obviously the load is only half of design. But what is more significant, you are sending **twice** as much water through the system as is needed.

ALWAYS REMEMBER, WE ARE TRYING TO MOVE HEAT, NOT WATER! WATER IS SIMPLY THE VEHICLE THAT IS CARRYING THE HEAT. EACH POUND OF WATER IS CAPABLE OF CARRYING 10 BTU, BUT IT IS COMING BACK WITH ONLY FIVE.

The amount of Heat to be moved out of a space is equal to what the space in question is gaining from all sources.

    IT IS NOT CHANGED ONE IOTA BY HOW MUCH WATER YOU SEND THRU THE SYSTEM!

AN ANALOGY IF YOU WILL: Suppose you were operating a concrete plant and at maximum capacity you need 10 trucks full of sand per day. The trucks can make one trip per day so you have purchased 10 trucks. Operating cost is $100 per trip.

On this particular day you are operating at 50% of your maximum; so you have two choices about your sand trucks

        1. Send all 10 trucks and fill each one half full.

        2. Send only 5 trucks and fill them as usual saving the $500 cost of the other trips.

Which will you do?

There is only one sensible answer.

    BUT WHEN WE HAVE THE SAME PROBLEM IN OUR WATER CIRCULATING SYSTEM, WE CONTINUE TO SEND ALL THE TRUCKS AND BRING THEM BACK HALF FULL!

                WHY?

BECAUSE THE WONDERFUL INDUCTION MOTORS WHICH DRIVE OUR PUMPS WILL ONLY GO ONE SPEED.

Now, back to the control for a 2 Speed pump drive; what could be better than return water temperature? Set it for 10 deg delta T, or better yet set if for 12 deg delta T with a differential of say 2.5 degrees. This will kick the pumps up to Hi only when the spaces are producing enough heat to need the full flow.

What about flow through the evaporator of the Chiller?

This is not really a problem since we are only reducing the flow with pumps to 63% of the maximum. One of the major manufacturers of Centrifugal Chillers indicates that the water flow thru the evaporator can vary from 0.80 to 2.80 GPM per ton. (you will remember that a delta T of 10 degF gives a flow of 2.4 GPM per ton. 63% of that is 1.5 GPM per ton, well above the minimum. It is necessary to avoid getting into a laminar flow condition which could happen at flows lower than the minimum recommended.) Condensers have a similar range of acceptable flows.

(Actually the evaporator average temperature is lower than design and the power used by the chiller is somewhat larger when the design delta T is not being achieved. If design temp out is 48 with 10 deg delta T, then average Temp is 53, but with only 5 deg delta T, Avg temp is 50.5! This is 2.5 degrees colder. If the total lift is from say 53 to 83 = 30 degF then this 2.5 extra degrees is an 8.33% increase in the Chiller power required. The answer to this is to raise the leaving water temp. or send less water.)

SO, THE BOTTOM LINE IS WHY SEND 10 TRUCKS TO HAUL 5 LOADS OF SAND?

There is another point too which I guess needs to come into the picture about here. All the energy put into the chilled water pumps ends up where? You guessed it. In the form of heat in the chilled water. So a 20HP Chilled water pump is putting 20 x 0.746 Kw/HP = 14.92 Kw of electric energy into the chilled water as heat. (That is the equivalent of more than 3 residential electric water heaters!) So whatever we save in HP pumping the water will have an additional saving in less chiller compressor energy needed. Calculations indicate that the chiller has to use 0.18 HP to remove the heat put into the system by 1 HP driving the pumps.

ACTUALLY THIS IS TRUE OF THE AIR HANDLING UNIT FANS TOO. ALL THE ENERGY USED IN MOVING THE AIR THRU THE SYSTEM ENDS UP AS HEAT IN THE AIR AND MUST BE REMOVED BY THE REFRIGERATION EQUIPMENT WHEN IT IS RUNNING.

OBVIOUSLY, REDUCING THE HP TO PUMP WATER AND MOVE AIR HAS THE ADDED EFFECT OF ELIMINATING THE NEED TO REMOVE THE HEAT THAT IT WOULD HAVE PRODUCED.

We can measure the energy saved at the pumps, but it is a little hard to see the savings in the chillers, but they are there none the less.

          SO, WHERE ARE WE?

PERHAPS WE HAVE BY NOW CONVINCED THE READER THAT IT IS A GOOD THING NOT TO RUN PUMPS AND AIR HANDLING UNITS FLAT OUT AT MAXIMUM SPEED ALL THE TIME.

    (and we haven't even talked about the lower noise, better filtration, longer equipment life, and better operating control valves.)

    An Aside: We sometimes run into someone who says "you can't vary the fan speed because ....... etc."

    CONSIDER:

    Your car has a four speed fan.

    Residential air conditioning has a 2 or 3 speed fan capability.

    Even Window Air Conditioning Units have 2 or 3 speed fans. (which often drive both the condenser and the room air fans.)

    Your overhead paddle fan has 3 speeds.

    Even your kitchen hood has two or more speeds.

    It is interesting that noe of these are doing this to save energy. They are doing it for convenience, better control, noise, comfort, longer life, and because it is possible.

    Direct Current motors like you have in the car can easily run at different speeds by simpley changing the voltage supplied. Small peanut power AC motors can afford to have multiple windings and high slip (low efficiency operation) to get the benefits of the speed changes. The efficiency is often very low and power factor worse. Even room size fan coil units for commercial operation have 2 or 3 speed blower (fan) motors.

BUT YOUR BUILDING CAN ONLY RUN AT ONE SPEED; AND WITH ONLY ONE CHOICE IT HAS TO BE <u>FLAT OUT.</u>

The same thing happens with pumps. Some people say the pumps can only run at one speed. Baloney! It is the motors that can only run at one speed! The pump doesn't care at what speed it runs. It has different capabilities at different speeds of course. One of them is that it uses a great deal less energy if it runs slower. Consider the automobile cooling water pump. How many speeds does it run? Consider your heart, how many speeds does it run? (HOW WOULD YOU LIKE TO HAVE A HEART THAT COULD ONLY RUN AT ONE SPEED? WHAT SPEED WOULD YOU CHOSE? MAXIMUM? YOU WOULD ALMOST HAVE TO IN ORDER TO RUN AWAY FROM TROUBLE OR PLAY ANY SPORT OR FOR THAT MATTER TO REPRODUCE THE RACE. BUT IT SURE WOULD BE HARD TO SLEEP.)

(WONDER HOW LONG YOUR HEART WOULD LAST UNDER THOSE CONDITIONS.)

<u>BUT THIS IS THE CONDITION UNDER WHICH WE OPERATE OUR BUILDINGS.</u>

And then there is always someone who says that because the building is 12 stories high, the pump has to run fast and use lots of energy to get the chilled water to upper floors, or the condenser water to the cooling towers on the roof. THINK ABOUT IT. This is baloney too! In a closed system the pump input energy goes into circulating the water only. The change in pressure across the pump is what is important, not the height of the column of water. For every gallon that goes up, one comes down.

LET US TAKE A LOOK NOW AT HOW MUCH ENERGY CAN BE SAVED BY THE SEVERAL METHODS OF FLOW CONTROL AND THEN COMPARE THAT TO WHAT CAN BE SAVED WITH A TWO SPEED DRIVE.

(The only reason that a two-speed step drive is being advocated is because it is simpler, cheaper, easier to control, more dependable, easier to maintain, uses common widely available parts and most important, is more likely to get installed because of all the above. Variable Speed Drives have many, many applications where there complete variability is indispensable; a takeup reel for a paper machine for instance, or a formula mixing application where the ingredient conveyors are variable speed, and on and on; but that variability is not essential in this application.)

ON THE OTHER HAND THERE IS NO QUESTION THAT YOU COULD SAVE MORE WITH THE VARIABLE SPEED DRIVE THAN WITH A TWO STEP DRIVE, AND FOR THAT MATTER WITH A 3 STEP DRIVE THAN WITH A 2 STEP DRIVE, ETC.

THE REAL QUESTION IS WHY AREN'T WE DOING IT?

WHICH BRINGS US TO THE OTHER REAL QUESTION WHICH IS:

HOW MUCH OF THE TOTAL POSSIBLE ENERGY SAVINGS CAN WE GET USING A SIMPLE, EASILY CONTROLLED TWO SPEED DRIVE INSTEAD OF THE FULLY VARIABLE SPEED.

(After all a variable speed drive is just a stepped drive with an infinite number of steps.) SO, HOW MANY STEPS IS ENOUGH? REMEMBERING THAT FOR EACH STEP WE ADD, WE WILL NEED SOME DECISION POINT AND CONTROL TO DECIDE WHEN THE DRIVE WILL RUN ON EACH STEP.

There are a number of published graphs showing the energy used by variable speed drives. The one below shows the cube curve and it also shows the curves for the brute force technique of outlet dampers (or valves) and for the inlet venes used with fans. (Incidentally, the use of two speed drive with inlet vanes looks to be a winning combination for VAV (variable air volume) systems. A suggested control strategy would be to run the system at reduced speed say 70% until the vanes go wide open and then if return air or outside air indicates a further need for more air, speed the system up to maximum, returning to the 70% speed when the conditions are satisfied.)

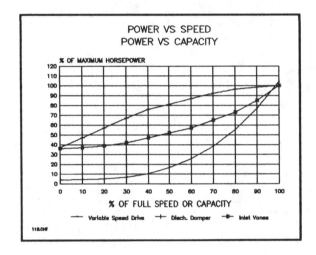

THE SAME CHART WITH THE A TWO SPEED SYSTEM OPERATING AT 70% IS SHOWN NEXT TO GIVE A COMPARISON.

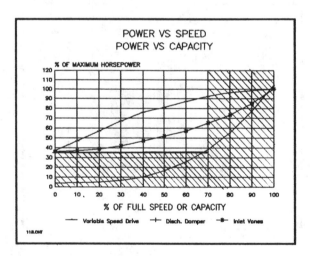

THE AREA UNDER THE CURVES ON THE CHART IS AN INDICATION OF THE POWER REQUIRED WITH EACH SYSTEM. BUT THERE IS ANOTHER FACTOR TO CONSIDER:

<u>THE LOAD PROFILE</u>

If the system operated an equal amount of time at each point on the curves, then the area under the curves would truly represent the amount of energy that would be required to operate the system. Such a system would look like this.

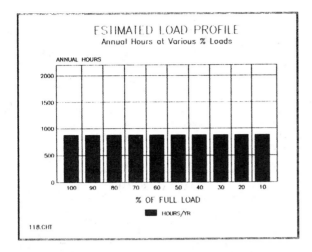

But this is not what happens.

First, the system hardly ever runs at 100% as we have discussed.

Second, the system almost never runs at 10% or 20% load either.

According to some Annual Load Profile information which has been developed in working with VAV systems, the system actually runs most of its time at 60% with 50% next, then 70% and 40% with 80%, 30% and 90% bringing up the rear.

The graph for that information looks like this:

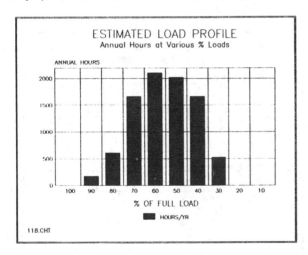

The load profile for each different installation is going to vary, but there is no doubt that it is going to look very much like the second graph and not much like the first. In other words most of the hours that a system runs are going to be in the 40 to 70% of load range.

This gets us to a very important question. If we are going to have a two speed drive,

WHAT SHOULD THE SECOND SPEED BE?

This becomes a tradeoff, because we want to get as many hours as we can on the lower speed to use less energy; but we also want to use the lowest possible speed for the low speed so that the energy requirement per Hour is as low as possible. (We would also like to be able to switch back and forth from Lo to Hi without

disturbing the occupants.)

From an examination of the Load Profile Graph it seems that we would want to go to low speed at somewhere around 70% Load. It is interesting to note at this point that a two winding induction motor can only run at either 1150 RPM or 850 RPM if the fan is now being driven by a 1750 RPM motor, which is the usual case. It is obvious that the lower speed, 48.6%, is much too low. Yet we have seen some two speed motors used where the lower speed was half the higher one. Actually the only speed available electrically with two windings in the same motor is 1150 or 65.7%. This is really a bit too low too, but well worth doing as I indicated before as far as cost goes. The problems of rewinding, and/or quick replacement of damaged motors is another matter. Both windings are always ruined when either burns out with this type motor.

There is another factor and that is at what lower speed will the outside air requirements still be met and the room air distribution still be acceptable. As far as outside air for ventilation goes, we need to understand that just because we slow the fan down to 70% of its maximum volume, doesn't mean that we are cutting down the quantity of outside air. If a 20,000 CFM fan is running with 10% outside air then the space is receiving 2000 CFM. If we slow the fan down to deliver only 14,000 CFM we can still have the same 2000 CFM of outside air by setting the controls and dampers properly. We are now using 2000/14000 = 14.3% outside air. The cooling or heating load caused by this outside air has not changed either.

Room Air Distribution patterns will change and some rebalancing at the lower speed may be needed.

SO, LETS LOOK AT A TABLE THAT SHOWS WHAT HAPPENS IF WE COMBINE THE TWO IDEAS INTO AN APPROXIMATION OF HOW THE REAL WORLD WORKS.

THE TABLE WILL DEVELOP SOME FIGURES SHOWING WHAT QUANTITY OF ELECTRIC ENERGY WILL BE USED ANNUALLY WITH:

  A. THE SITUATION AS IT IS WITH THE USUAL SINGLE
     SPEED INDUCTION MOTOR.

  B. THE SITUATION AS IT WILL BE USING A TWO SPEED
     MOTOR DRIVE WITH THE LOWER SPEED BEING 70% OF
     THE HIGHER.

  C. THE SITUATION AS IT WILL BE USING AN INVERTER
     DRIVE TO PROVIDE COMPLETE VARIABLE SPEED
     CAPABILITIES.

| 20 HP AHU LOAD PROFILE 118.CHT | OPERATING TIME IN HOURS/YR | Accum. HOURS | KW | Add for 96% Eff at Max | KW-HRS | Two Speed KW | KW-HRS | Single Speed KW | KW-HRS |
|---|---|---|---|---|---|---|---|---|---|
| 100 | 10 | 10 | 18.20 | 0.76 | 190 | 18.20 | 182 | 18.20 | 182 |
| 90 | 170 | 180 | 13.27 | 0.76 | 2,385 | 18.20 | 3,094 | 18.20 | 3,094 |
| 80 | 608 | 788 | 9.32 | 0.76 | 6,128 | 18.20 | 11,066 | 18.20 | 11,066 |
| 70 | 1,664 | 2,452 | 6.24 | 0.76 | 11,652 | 6.24 | 10,383 | 18.20 | 30,285 |
| 60 | 2,102 | 4,554 | 3.93 | 0.76 | 9,861 | 6.24 | 13,116 | 18.20 | 38,256 |
| 50 | 2,016 | 6,570 | 2.28 | 0.76 | 6,119 | 6.24 | 12,580 | 18.20 | 36,691 |
| 40 | 1,664 | 8,234 | 1.16 | 0.76 | 3,203 | 6.24 | 10,383 | 18.20 | 30,285 |
| 30 | 526 | 8,760 | 0.49 | 0.76 | 658 | 6.24 | 3,282 | 18.20 | 9,573 |
| 20 | | 8,760 | 0.15 | 0.76 | 0 | 6.24 | 0 | 18.20 | 0 |
| 10 | | 8,760 | 0.02 | 0.76 | 0 | 6.24 | 0 | 18.20 | 0 |
| 0 | | 8,760 | 0.00 | 0.76 | 0 | 6.24 | 0 | 18.20 | 0 |
| | | | | | | | | | |
| VARIABLE SPEED | 40,195 | | | | 40,195 | | 64,087 | | 159,432 |
| TWO SPEED | 64,087 | | | | | | | | |
| ONE SPEED | 159,432 | | | | | | | | |

* Courtesy of Tillson Engineering Laboratory

With the systems running as they are now with a single speed capability, a 20 HP motor will use 160,000 Kwhrs. The use of an Inverter type variable speed drive will result in the use of 40,200 Kwhrs for a savings of 119,800 Kwhrs annually. The use of a two speed drive

462

will require 64,100 Kwhrs for a savings of 95,900 Kwhrs.

THE SAVINGS ACHIEVED WITH THE SIMPLE TWO SPEED DRIVE ARE EQUAL TO 80% OF THE SAVINGS AVAILABLE WITH FULL VARIABLE SPEED CAPABILITY! (95,900/119,800 x 100 = 80%)

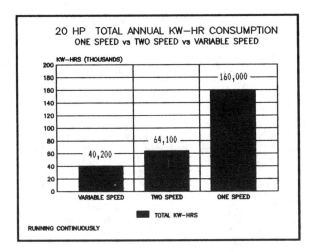

* we also studied 3 step drives, and if the speeds are carefully chosen to match the load profile of the facility, then they can save another 5 to 8 per cent. But it is not worth the difference in cost, complexity and control to get the other step.

At 5 cents per Kwhr, the two speed will save 95,900 x .05 = $4,795; and such equipment is available for $3,600 installed. (Payback in 9 Months!)

The Variable Speed Drive would save $ 1,295 dollars more, but it and its control equipment will cost a great deal more, and the reliability factor must be carefully considered, as well as who can maintain it, troubleshoot it, and replace it quickly when needed.

Another way to look at it is to decide how long it will take to payback the difference in cost of the Variable Speed System over the Cost of the Two Speed System with the difference in savings of say $1300.

### SOAP BOX TIME

SURELY WE CAN FIND THE FUNDS TO MAKE THESE SAVINGS IN ENERGY HAPPEN.

USING PRECIOUS ENERGY RESOURCES MERELY TO SWISH WATER AND AIR AROUND THROUGH PIPES AND DUCTWORK AT SPEEDS AND QUANTITIES THAT ARE SELDOM IF EVER NEEDED JUST BECAUSE WE HAPPEN TO HAVE USED A LESS EXPENSIVE MOTOR HAS GOT TO BE DUMB, SINFUL, STUPID, UNPROFESSIONAL, UNAMERICAN AND @#%*&$! WE NEED TO STOP IT NOW!

AND YOU REMEMBER WHAT IS JUST AS BAD OR WORSE; ALL THAT EXTRA ELECTRICITY THAT WE USED HAS BEEN CONVERTED TO HEAT; IT IS IN THE AIR THAT WE ARE TRYING TO COOL OR IN THE WATER THAT WE ARE TRYING TO COOL AND WE ARE GOING TO HAVE TO USE SOME MORE ELECTRICITY IN THE REFRIGERATION EQUIPMENT TO GET IT OUT. (Turns out to be about another 18% ! )

I SAY AGAIN, LETS STOP THIS WASTE NOW.

WHAT IS THE MATTER WITH OUR MANAGERS? IS BETTER THAN

### 100% RETURN ON MONEY NOT GOOD ENOUGH?

WELL, IF IT'S NOT, THEN THE FUNDS CAN BE FOUND TO USE ON A SHARED SAVINGS BASIS. THESE SAVINGS ARE BASED ON THE LAWS OF NATURE (PHYSICS) NOT THE LAWS OF CONGRESS; THESE KWHR SAVINGS ARE REAL NOT JUST DOLLAR SAVINGS THAT PLAY TO THE RATE STRUCTURE OF THE ELECTRIC UTILITY COMPANIES.

I SAY AGAIN, AS ENERGY ENGINEERS WORTH OUR SALT, WE MUST STOP THIS WASTE NOW!

When you really get down and think about it, every businessman and corporation in America ought to be willing to do anything he can to help conserve our energy resource and help solve the environmental pollution as long as it doesn't cost his company anything. If money can be borrowed at 10% and equipment life is as much as 10 years, then 100,000 worth of equipment costs a company only $16,275 per year. If they can save that much in electricity costs then

THEY SHOULD DO IT! AND IF THEY DON'T SOMEBODY IS GOING TO MAKE THEM BEFORE LONG.

That is basically a 5 year payback! But here we are talking about less than a year!!!

Can you imagine owning a $100,000 house and collecting rent of $ 8,300 per month! That is how good this is in many instances.

I SAY AGAIN, THIS WASTE OF ENERGY HAS GOT TO BE STOPPED.

THINK OF THE POSSIBILITIES IN LOAD LIMITING TO REDUCE DEMAND AT CRITICAL TIMES. FOR INSTANCE A SLIGHT PRECOOLING OF THE BUILDING MIGHT LET YOU SLIP THROUGH THE PEAK HOUR OR TWO WITH ALL FANS AND ALL PUMPS ON LOW WITH A DEMAND OF 35% OF WHAT IT IS NOW.

### SUMMATION

A great advance in technology was the introduction and refinement of the inverter type variable speed drive, sophisticated solid state equipment that allows machinery to be speed controlled by varying the frequency of the power to the drive motor.

However, many HVAC applications will never have such equipment installed, because of the cost, and the complexity of both the inverters themselves and the sensors and controls needed to decide at what speed to run.

Consequently many Kwhrs are being wasted that could be saved.

TWO STEP DRIVES can capture 80% of the total possible savings that variable speed drives capture;

- At less cost

- With simpler controls

- With greater reliability

- Using "off the shelf" components.

- Using technology already known and understood by electricians.

Secondly; The nature of weather conditions require designers of HVAC systems to provide for maximum conditions that occur less than 8% of the time. (Summer Cooling maximums occur less than 2% of the time.)

The nature of centrifugal pumps and blowers (HP is a function of the cube of the speed) creates large potential kwhr savings when fans and pumps can be operated at lower speeds.

TWO SPEED DRIVES are herein advocated as an immediate, cost effective way to achieve the lion's share of the possible savings.

Some of the points in favor are:

Control: Control is simplified with an either/or decision compared to infinite possibilities of variable speed. No problem with going too low and creating flow problems through chillers or lack of sufficient ventilation air in spaces.

Costs: Initial cost, installation cost, maintenance cost and life cost are all going to be better with the two speed drive. What are the costs of system failure and downtime? How can it be avoided?

Efficiency: Inverter drives range from 94 to 96% efficient at their maximum output, but they have nearly the same actual kilowatt losses at the reduced outputs as well. This makes their efficiency much lower at the speeds they will be running.

Retrofit: Much of the work we have done in this field is in retrofitting existing systems. Variable Air Volume (VAV) systems is not what we are usually talking about. All systems can benefit from the idea of running the system on CRUISE at 70% air and 64% water flow; and then making something require it to go to MAXIMUM; and not let it stay there any longer than needed. VAV systems which now use inlet vanes to control the air flow in the system can benefit by two speed also. Running the system at 70% of maximum until the vanes are wide open and then, if outside air or return air temperatures indicate the need, speed the drive up to maximum. This system can very nearly meet the savings of a completely variable speed drive.

Dependability: Electronic Drives have improved, but they will never be as ruggedly dependable nor as simple as a two speed step drive. Safety trip-outs are often as bad as equipment breakdowns. Rotating electro-mechanical equipment and big old contactors can easily weather most transient problems.

Demand Limiting: Opportunities for limiting total demand at critical times are inherent in the utilization of this equipment. Airflow changes are often unnoticeable. Even duty cycling from 100% to 70% can be used.

Power Factor: With both motors running near there nameplate HP; power factor is good.

Interface with Existing Controls: Pneumatic and normal electric controls as well as digital controls are no problem. One simple 24 VAC contact is all it takes. Contact open --Drive runs on Normal (Low); Contact closed --Drive runs on Maximum (High). Easily controlled by Computer Energy Management Systems; Time clocks, Thermostats, Electro-Pneumatic Switches etc. Controls in parallel will switch to High if any one of them calls for it; controls in series will switch to high only if all of them call for it.

Softstart: The equipment with which we are most familiar includes circuitry to force the system to start on the smaller motor even if the controls are calling for high speed. This cuts the starting torque by two thirds, and the starting amps by two thirds. (Important considerations when the system needs to come back up after a power outage, or when running on standby generators.) With simple tie-in controls standby generators can be sized to only run the smaller motors during the emergency.

Noise Reduction: The primary focus here has been energy savings, but in many instances the reduction in air flow noise can be a great extra benefit.

Longer Life for Driven Equipment Too: Bearing and belt life are functions of the speed of the equipment. This means the main motor bearings and the blower unit bearings will last longer at 70% speed.

BOTTOM LINE

Many energy conservation projects will not be done because the only way to do them is either too complex or too costly. The use of simple two-speed step-drive may allow more projects to be initiated, and therefore more kilowatt hours saved, less fuel burned, less environmental damage overall. WITH PAYBACKS OF ABOUT 1 YR IN AREAS WITH ELECTRIC COST OF 5 CENTS PER KWHR, THESE DRIVES CAN PROVIDE AN INCENTIVE FOR ENERGY SAVINGS WHERE OTHER EQUIPMENT HAS BEEN CONSIDERED TOO COSTLY OR UNMANAGEABLE.

WHAT GETS DONE ARE PROJECTS WITH FAST PAYBACKS FROM THE CASH STREAM OF ELECTRIC ENERGY SAVINGS.

IT NEEDS TO BE DONE NOW BY YOU

GOOD ENGINEERS MAKE SIMPLE THINGS THAT WORK!

REFERENCES:

Acknowledgement is made of the general use of the following manuals, handbooks and catalogs:

[1]  Handbook of Air Conditioning System Design; Carrier Air Conditioning Company; McGraw Hill Book Company.

[2]  Catalogs on Centrifugal Chillers and Air Handling Units, including selection; var., Trane Corp.

[3]  Catalogs, Pump Curves, and Design Manuals for Hydronic Systems, var.; Bell & Gossett Div. of ITT

[4]  Mark's Standard Handbook for Mechanical Engineers; E.A. Avallone, T. Baumeister III, eds.; Ninth Ed.; McGraw-Hill Book Company.

[5]  Standard Handbook for Electrical Engineers; A.E. Knowlton, Editor-in-Chief; McGraw-Hill Book Co.

[6]  General Catalog No. 380; W. W. Grainger, Inc, Skokie, IL, 1992, for prices and availability of needed motors and equipment.

[7]  Catalogs of the Lewellen Manufacturing Co., Columbus, Ind.; for suggested design and information in relation to variable-speed belt drives.

[8]  Manual for Technical Assistance Program; N.C. Energy Division, North Carolina Department of Commerce; Prepd. by Advanced Energy Concepts, Inc.

[9]  U.S. Weather Service; for annual temperature hourly temperature records.

[10] Direct and Alternating Currents; E. A. Loew; McGraw-Hill Book Company.

Chapter 80

# Alternatives to Electrical Cogeneration: The Direct Application of Steam Engines

W.C. Phillips

## ABSTRACT

Although small to medium sized industrial facilities are aware of electrical cogeneration, often they are too small for it to be economically justifiable. The direct application of steam turbine power to equipment formerly powered by electric motors, such as air compressors, chillers and pumps, can allow them to use steam capacity to reduce electrical demand and consumption, bypassing cogeneration. For many of these industrial facilities, this direct application of a steam turbine would be easy to undertake since boilers, air compressors and chillers are often located close to each other.

There are substantial reasons why the direct application of steam turbines can actually be preferable to small scale cogeneration. Cogeneration converts the heat energy of steam into circular mechanical motion and then converts the circular mechanical motion into electricity. Each conversion entails a loss of energy due to friction and other conversion losses. A substantial amount of the generated electricity is then converted back into circular motion with electric motors, again incurring energy losses due to the less than 100 percent efficiency of the motors. Directly applying the mechanical motion of turbines eliminates both the motion-to-electricity (generator) and the electricity-to-motion (motor) conversion losses.

Excess steam capacity during the summer is not unusual for facilities that use steam to provide winter heating. Similarly, most of these facilities experience a large electrical demand peak during the cooling season due to the electricity needed to operate centrifugal chillers. Using the excess steam capacity via a turbine to power the chillers can allow the boilers to operate at a higher loading (often increasing boiler efficiency) while reducing electrical consumption and demand during precisely those periods when demand reduction is most needed. Steam absorption chillers can also provide these advantages, but there is a large existing installed base of centrifugal chillers where retrofitting with turbines may be more economical than replacing them
with absorption units. In facilities where the steam generating capacity is sufficient, air compressors provide an appropriate year-round application for turbine power.

This paper is the result of an on-going project being conducted by the Energy Division, State of North Carolina, Department of Economic and Community Development, in conjunction with the University of North Carolina at Charlotte. The author is Project Manager for the Energy Division, and the information contained in this paper was developed with Professors William Shelnutt and John Patton of UNC-Charlotte.

The objective of this project is to educate the operating engineers and managers of industrial facilities, specifically small to medium sized manufacturing facilities, on the technical application and economic justification of steam turbine power. It is believed that these facilities are under-utilizing this technology due to a general lack of information, intimidation with the technology and lack of assurance as to the savings available.

## BACKGROUND - USE OF STEAM TURBINES IN INDUSTRY

Steam turbines have been used for many years in industrial applications. They have been shown to be effective prime movers for industrial process machines as well as for direct drivers of plant equipment such as chillers, compressors, pumps, and fans (Neerkin, 1980, pp 63). Steam turbines have proved their long term reliability and relatively low maintenance requirements. The characteristics of steam as a working fluid are very well known, making possible steam turbine designs matching virtually any practical range of steam pressures and temperatures needed for process steam use and available from the steam generator (e.g.,boiler). Steam turbines can be made to operate at variable speed by properly controlling steam flow, offering substantial energy savings for many applications.

## Steam Turbine Mechanical Drives -- an Alternative to Electrical Cogeneration

A popular use of industrial steam turbines in the last ten or twenty years has been to drive electrical generators to produce electrical power. Generally the electrical power has been used internally in the industrial plant, to offset power costs for purchased electricity. In some cases excess electrical power is sold to the utility serving the plant, at some designated rate. In other cases a cogenerating plant is placed near an end user of steam, i.e., an industrial site, where the host (cogenerating plant) sells electricity to the electrical utility and process steam to the industrial site. The term "co-generation" has been used to refer both to generating electrical power (perhaps for sale to a utility) and to generation of mechanical power directly applied to industrial process machines and plant equipment. One accepted definition of **cogeneration is "... the sequential use of a primary energy source to produce both shaft power and useful thermal energy"** (McConnell, 1985). The inference is that the power is generated as a complementary process to the steam needs of the industrial plant. For example, an industrial power plant may need to produce steam for an industrial process, but the steam boiler is capable of producing steam at pressures and temperatures suitable to drive a steam turbine which would exhaust steam at conditions adequate to the process. A cogeneration system would consist of the steam turbine exhausting to the process. The shaft power developed by the steam turbine could be used to drive an electrical generator. This would be what many refer to as (electrical) "cogeneration". The electrical power could be used internally within the plant, or, if it exceeds the needs of the facility, it could be sold to the local utility. Alternatively, the shaft power could be used to drive plant equipment or process machines directly. Good candidates for such applications would include air compressors, chillers, pumps, and fans. Whether such application is suitable depends largely on the match of load and duty cycles between the process steam needs, the shaft power requirements of the machines, and on the economics of the system.

## ENERGY SOURCE CONSIDERATIONS

### Primary Fuel Sources

In addition to high grade fuels such as oil, natural gas, and coal, there have been considerable efforts to develop technology for combustion of low-grade fuels such as municipal wastes, high sulphur coals, and low grade coals. However, much of the work has been directed toward large municipal facilities producing 20 MW or more of electrical power. Industrial waste disposal systems can typically support generation of less than 2 MW. When the savings in costs of disposal in landfills is added to savings in process heat, and cogenerated power, the balance may tip in favor of small industrial waste disposal/ cogeneration systems. The advent of small fluidized bed waste incinerators

could produce, for example, 2 MW of electrical power or a combination of 500 kW of electrical power and 28,000 lb/hr of process steam (Colosimo, pp 21-24).

The possibility of using biomass fuels may be interesting to some industries. These fuels consist of wood, wood waste, and a variety of agribusiness residues, including bagasse (sugar cane refuse), cotton gin trash, vineyard prunings, nut shells, and animal manures. A 1982 study (Tillman, 1982) compared four systems using wood fuel: (1) a 100,000 lb/hr, 50 psig process steam boiler, (2) a 110,500 lb/hr 850 psig, 850 F topping cycle boiler feeding a topping cycle turbine-generator which exhausts 100,000 lb/hr of 50 psig steam to the process, (3) a combined Brayton cycle (compressed air) gas turbine fed indirectly by a wood combustor and heat exchanger and exhausting to a heat recovery steam generator which produces 300 psig steam driving a steam turbine-generator, which in turn exhausts 100,000 lb/hr of 50 psig steam to the process, and (4) a wood gasifier Brayton cycle gas turbine-generator exhausting into a heat recovery steam generator which produces 100,000 lb/hr of 50 psig steam to the process. Results showed that the Rankine cycle topping cycle cogeneration system (system 2) supplemented by power generated in condensing power plants as needed was the most efficient approach to biomass-fired cogeneration. This system could, of course, generate electrical power or shaft power to plant machinery.

### Fuel Availability and Cost Considerations

As has been mentioned previously, a primary factor in choosing between AC motors and steam turbine mechanical drives is the common connection of heat to process needs. If the fuel supply is also dictated by the process demand level, additional care must be taken to insure that there will be a balance among the three, fuel supply, turbine driven shaft power, and process heat. In evaluating these alternatives, the costs of fuel should take into account the costs of handling, transportation, and disposal of combustible wastes for the case of not using them as fuel. When such costs are considered, the lower fuel costs may permit justification of cogenerated shaft power and increased capital investment in boiler equipment (McConnell, 1985).

### Distributed Energy Sources

Three basic alternatives have been identified for satisfying the shaft power and thermal energy requirements of a process industry (McConnell, 1985): (1) low pressure boilers and electric drives, (2) high pressure boilers with superheaters plus mechanical-drive turbines for drive systems, and (3) high pressure boilers with superheaters plus steam turbine generators and electric drives. Of course, there may be hybrid variations on each of these basic types, such as a mechanical drive turbine supplied with extraction steam from a turbine generator. As has been state earlier, **in any system, there must be a demand for thermal energy for a process or for space heating in order to justify mechanical drive turbines.** In other words, there must be an opportunity for cogeneration. This will generally mean that there must be an opportunity for a topping cycle. Bottoming cycle systems are generally not justifiable economically except for unusual situations such as using condensing turbines for driving boiler feed pumps in large utility power plants (McConnell, 1985, pp 375).

**Low Pressure Boilers and Electric Drives:** In this type of system, the cogeneration option is not taken. It has the advantages of lowest investment. The thermal energy needs of the process dictate the steam pressures and temperatures, which are kept as low as will satisfy the process needs (usually without a superheater) in order to maximize boiler efficiency. Boilers are usually gas or oil fire. Electrical power demands are satisfied by purchased power from the utility.

**High Pressure Boilers with Superheaters Plus Mechanical Drive Turbines:** In this type of system, there is a greater capital investment due to more expensive boilers and piping. The higher pressures and temperatures in the boiler create a cogeneration opportunity with various topping cycles. Solid fuel and perhaps combustible wastes can be considered because of the cogeneration payback potential.

**High Pressure Boilers with Superheaters plus Steam Turbine Generators and Electric Drives:** These systems can be full electrical cogeneration systems capable of supplying electrical power back to the utility. They have the highest capital costs, and may be justified when the cost of electricity is relatively high. Sometimes condensers are added to extraction turbine generators to eliminate load swings on the utility tie-line.

### Direct Drive System Applications

**General Considerations – Matching Application with Energy Source**

Although each case must be judged on the existing process heat needs, shaft power needs, and electrical power needs of the facility, we attempt here to generalize the types of considerations which must be taken into account.

Some knowledgeable writers suggest that energy utilization is significantly enhanced by the application of large, efficient turbine-generators rather than a group of smaller, less efficient mechanical drive steam turbines for small plant loads. A hypothetical example (Kovacik, 1983) showed a 70% increase in power output, per 100 million BTU/hr net heat to the process, for a 5000 kW turbine-generator compared to smaller 500 HP single stage steam turbine mechanical drive units producing the same net heat to processes. Even when the losses associated with the transformation and distribution of energy from the turbine-generator system are taken into account, the net increase in shaft power available was reported as approximately 57% (an additional 2000 HP). (The assumptions were

for initial steam at 600 psig, 750 F; process steam at 50 psig; process returns at 180 F; and no feedwater heating.) The dominant factor here is the very significant difference in efficiencies of the smaller mechanical drive turbines (45%) versus the larger turbine-generators (72%).

Of course, in an existing installation, the question is a different one: would the application of a smaller steam turbine to take advantage of existing steam capacity be more efficient than the use of an electric motor to power plant machinery? Also, we must ask specifically whether there is a need for the quantities of turbine exhaust steam energy which will be produced as the turbine satisfies its shaft power output requirements. **A careful consideration of the load profile of the process system heat needs and the driven machine's shaft power load profile is therefore essential to evaluate any given system.**

### Facilities Drives Case Studies

Mechanical drive steam turbines may be applied to a number of different types of machines. These turbines must be designed with the application in mind, which may have quite different conditions than those for driving electrical generators. The design requires consideration of the varying speed of operation which may be required while producing full load torque or a substantial portion of this torque, a consideration of vibratory resonance at various speeds, and consideration of the start-up sequence.

**Fans:** Steam turbines are frequently used to drive forced or induced draft fans for fossil fueled boilers. For start-up or low load operation they normally have either a tandem electric motor drive or a connection to an independent steam supply such as a main steam supply line.

**Pumps:** Steam turbines have been used extensively to drive boiler feedwater pumps, where the pump and turbine can be speed matched. The most common practice in larger systems is to use condensing, non-extracting turbines with inlet steam in the range of 200 psig which is extracted from intermediate stages of higher pressure turbines. (Baumeister, 1978, pp 9-47).
Although the advantages of increased power plant efficiency by using turbines for feedwater pumps have been widely recognized, it was not until the 1970's energy crises that intensive attention was paid to maximizing this advantage through increased turbine efficiency. For large, high pressure utility systems, this is particularly important. One author notes that for a 2400 psig fossil fueled system, a 1% increase in turbine efficiency translates to a two or three BTU/kWh improvement in system heat rate. For these large pumps, turbine efficiency levels of 80 to 84 percent are commonplace, and improved methods of measuring efficiency accurately are increasingly important (Finck, 1980).

**Refrigeration Machines:** Back pressure turbines are most often used in water chilling plants for driving a centrifugal compressor which shares the cooling load with one or more absorption units (ASHRAE, 1983, pp 33.8). The exhaust steam from the turbine, usually at about 15 psig, is used to heat the absorption unit's concentrator. The use of both the available energy in the steam by the turbine and the thermal energy in the exhaust by the absorption unit results in lower energy input per unit of refrigeration output than is obtainable by either system operating alone. Again, the system design must resolve the problem of balancing the turbine exhaust flow (as dictated by the centrifugal compressor's demand) with the absorption unit's demand for steam flow.

**Gas Compressors:** Gas compressors are good candidates for turbine drive applications if process load conditions make good use of the exhaust energy.

An example of an air compressor system in the U.K. driven by a back pressure turbine reported in the literature (Reay, 1984) showed attractive economics. The air compressor required input shaft power of 285 kW (382 HP) to produce 56.5 $M^3$/min compressed air at 7 bar (103 psia). A single stage turbine drives the compressor with 9860 kg/hr (21,700 lb/hr) of steam at 17 bar (250 psia) and 20 C (36 F) superheat. The turbine exhausts steam at 3.5 bar (51 psia) for process use. Hourly savings compared to an electric motor drive for the compressor showed a payback of about 7000 hours.
Case histories of two gas compressors (Finnerman, 1983) discussed solution of torsional vibrational problems of the steam turbine driven systems. One of the compressors was a single stage bicycle crank compressor driven by a 2-stage steam turbine through a 7.486 to 1 speed reducer producing 850 BHP at 3600/480 RPM. The other was a two-stage, two-cylinder opposed, reciprocating compressor driven by a two-stage steam turbine through a 12.987 to 1 double speed reducer producing 540 BHP at 5000/385 RPM. The vibrational problems were resolved by flywheel, coupling, and governor changes.

In Japan, Mitsubishi Heavy Industries has reported using mechanical drive steam turbines for variable speed drives for liquid natural gas compressors as an energy saving measure (Takanaga, 1982). A major effort was expended in undertaking efficiency improvements in the turbines themselves.

## District Heating and Cooling Applications

It is frequently stated that much of the heat supplied by the fuel in a conventional steam turbine application is lost in the condenser, on the order of 40 to 50 percent. Even though this rejected heat has low available energy, it may be used profitably to displace higher level energy which may be currently used for district heating and cooling. In cogeneration applications, the steam may be extracted between the low and high pressure stages of the turbine and routed to a district water heater using what can be referred to as a condensing tail turbine or a back pressure turbine exhausting with sufficient steam energy to handle the heating and/or cooling loads (Denesdi, 1980).

Some caution has been recommended (Viar, 1981) against creating an excessive supply of exhaust steam through numbers of small, inefficient steam turbines, which is in turn used in steam driven absorption refrigeration machines to satisfy cooling loads. It was suggested that sometimes it is better to reduce operation of the more inefficient turbines (where electric motors would be more efficient) than to try to find uses for the steam. Each application should be evaluated on the basis of the economic return before a decision is made.

--------**Case Study: Ingersoll Milling Machine Co., Rockford, Ill.; Gas fired Reciprocating Engine Cogeneration System with Cooling System Alternatives.**

In July 1988, Ingersoll Milling Machine Company in their Rockford, Illinois plant installed a 3250 Kw cogeneration system consisting of five 915-HP natural gas fired, ebullient cooled, reciprocating engines with heat recovery steam generators (at 12 psig). The system reduced the annual total energy costs by 30.3%, reduced electrical energy costs by 28%, and reduced steam costs by 43% in the first year of operation. Due to the high cost of peak-hour electricity (about 70% of electricity expenses), the system operates the 13 peak hours per day Monday through Friday. The cost of the system, including major rerouting of the steam lines, was $2.4 million, with payback calculated at 3 years. The system has exceeded the first year avoided cost by 9% and was expected to do even better in the next year.

As the system was being installed, Ingersoll evaluated using the low-pressure steam from the cogeneration units in the summer months through absorption coolers to air condition the plant. The cooling load was estimated to be 1400 tons, but only 600 tons of cogeneration steam output was available. Three alternates were considered: (1) installation of 1400 tons of steam fired absorption units and a chilled water loop throughout the plant, with the additional steam under maximum load conditions being supplied by the boiler plant; (2) installation of a 600 ton absorption chiller, two 400-ton centrifugal chillers, and a chilled water loop throughout the plant; and (3) install packaged rooftop air conditioning units with a total capacity of 1400 tons and two 800-kW natural gas fired engine-generator sets to drive the rooftop units. Ingersoll decided to install alternate 3, the rooftop units. The advantages cited were lower initial costs than alternatives (1) and (2), reasonable operating costs through inexpensive power produced by the engine generators, and no demand charges. Disadvantages were lower energy efficiency, higher maintenance costs than the other two alternatives. No performance data on the air conditioning systems were yet available.

## Multiple Steam Header Pressures for Process, Hot Water, Space Heating and Cooling and Similar Systems

Many plants have a multi-level steam header

distribution system. In this case the maximum steam pressure may be used directly for certain process applications (e.g., drying processes). Medium and low pressure steam may also be required for process, hot water, heating, and cooling applications. With such a diverse system there are numerous opportunities for utilizing backpressure steam turbines to provide the low pressure steam while driving a mechanical system with the turbine. A careful analysis is usually required to determine the load profile and load matching of the various subsystems. Even after a suitable application is identified, it is often the run-time experience or the control system which determines the efficiency or effectiveness of the overall system.

## ANALYSIS OF THREE FACILITIES

As a part of this project, evaluations of steam turbine power were made at three facilities where management had volunteered to have the analysis done.

Despite the possibilities of electrical demand reduction using a turbine to power a centrifugal chiller, with the electrical rates currently in effect in North Carolina the best return on investment occurs when the turbine can be used year-round, as with an air compressor. Hence, all three facilities were evaluated on turbine powered air compressors. At all three facilities, the replacement of electric motors with steam turbines was technically feasible.

At Facility A, a textile plant in western North Carolina, the marginal cost of electricity is $0.03665 per KWh and the demand cost is $3.28 per KW. The cost of steam was calculated to be $5.23 per 1000 lbs. The cost of replacing a 400 HP motor on an air compressor with a steam turbine was estimated at $253,845. Based on a load analysis of the compressor's operation, it was determined that $71,659 would be saved per year in electrical costs. The estimated steam turbine maintenance cost was $2,528 per year with the energy cost of operating the turbine estimated at $8,890. This yields a net annual savings of $60,151 for a simple payback of 4.2 years.

Facility B, a furniture plant, has the advantage of "free" fuel from waste wood, but the disadvantage of using a small (100 HP) air compressor. The marginal cost of electricity here is $0.03981 per KWh and the demand cost is $3.45 per KW. The cost of replacing the motor with a steam turbine was estimated at $110,400. The electrical savings resulting from this replacement was estimated at $13,327 per year, with turbine maintenance estimated at $633 per year. Given the "free" fuel source, the steam energy cost was listed at zero (an incremental increase in wear on the steam generating system was not considered). Despite this, the simple payback is 8.7 years. Using a rebuilt turbine instead of a new turbine would reduce the capital investment by about $12,000, and the simple payback would drop to approximately 7.7 years.

Facility C, a pharmaceutical plant in eastern North Carolina, is on a "time-of-use" electrical rate with an on peak rate of $0.03125 per KWh and $19.56 per KW and an off peak rate of $0.02625 per KWh and $14.25 per KW. The cost of steam was calculated to be $3.00 per 1000 lbs. The cost of replacing their 400 HP air compressor motor with a steam turbine was estimated at $253,169. The electrical savings were estimated at $126,249 per year, with turbine maintenance costing $2,532 and a steam consumption cost of $50,592 per year. This yields a net savings of $73,126 per year for a simple payback of 3.4 years.

At the time of this paper, Facility C has definitely committed to installing the turbine, and Facility A is continuing to consider it. Because of the long payback, the turbine installation is no longer under consideration at Facility B.

## CONCLUSION

Based on the research and site surveys conducted for this project, we conclude that the application of steam turbines to loads in the 100-400 HP range is technically feasible at a variety of locations, and replacing a 400 HP motor can yield a calculated simple payback in the range of 3-4 years. As a part of this project, the installation at Facility C will be closely monitored, with the actual installation costs, maintenance costs, energy costs and savings fully documented. This data will be presented in another paper at a later date.

## References

American Society of Heating, Refrigerating and Air-Conditioning Engineers, Inc., ASHRAE Handbook - 1983 Equipment, ASHRAE and Air-Conditioning Engineers, Inc., Atlanta, (1983).

Baumeister, T., ed., Mark's Standard Handbook for Mechanical Engineers, McGraw-Hill Book Co., New York, (1985).

Denesdi, L., "Fuel Savings with Turbines Modified for District Heating", Power Engineering, 84-2, (Feb. 1980), 62-63.

Finck, E. J., "Performance Testing of Feedwater Pump Turbines", Electric Forum, 6-2, (1980), 28-30.

Finnerman, T. J., "Case Histories on Steam Turbine Driven Low Speed Reciprocation Compressors", Proceedings - Machinery Vibrations Monitoring and Analysis Seminar and Meeting, (1983), 181-186.

Kovacik, J.M., "Industrial Cogeneration System Application Considerations", Proceedings of the 12th Turbomachinery Symposium, (1983), 129-137.

McConnell, J.E., "Economics for Selection of Drives: ac Motors or Steam Turbine Mechanical Drives", IEEE Transactions on Industry Applications, IA-21, (Mar-Apr 1985), 375-381.

Neerkin, R., "Use Steam Turbines as Process Drivers", Chemical Engineering, 87-17, Aug. 25, (1980).

Reay, D.A., "Engineering Systems Approach to Small Scale Combined Heat and Power", Journal of Heat Recovery Systems, 4-1, (1984), 37-42.

Takanaga, H., Katayama, K., and Iida, K., "Performance Improvement of Mechanical Drive Steam Turbines", Proceedings of the 11th Annual Turbomachinery Symposium, (1982), 51-59.

Tillman, D. A., Schnorr, R. D., and Sale, J. W., "Alternative Cogeneration Systems Using Biomass Fuels", Proceedings of the American Power Conference, 44, (1982), 371-377.

Viar, W. L., "Economics of Steam Turbine Use in Industry", AIIE (Cat n p-254), (1981), 67-72.

# SECTION 7
# FEDERAL ENERGY MANAGEMENT

# Chapter 81
# New Directions in Federal Energy Management

M. Ginsberg

The fuel embargo of 1973, followed by the oil disruption of 1979 heightened national security concerns over the availability and price of foreign oil to sustain all sectors of the U.S. economy. As a result of our growing dependence on foreign oil and diminishing resources at home, the Federal government has worked since 1974 to identify and implement a variety of measures to reduce energy consumption in Federal buildings and operations. Federal energy expenditures peaked at almost $14 billion in 1982 but has now been reduced to approximately $10 billion a year. However, much needs to be done to further reduce Federal energy expenditures.

Since the 1973 oil embargo, successive Presidents and sessions of Congress have proposed a variety of initiatives to reduce Federal energy consumption and expenditures. Through a series of legislative initiatives and Presidential authorities, the Federal Energy Management Program (FEMP) was established and then expanded to address a broad range of energy-related issues affecting the Federal sector. Administered by the U.S. Department of Energy, FEMP coordinates the design and implementation of energy-saving programs for Federal buildings and operations. This includes working with other Federal agencies through interagency committees to interpret and implement Federal policy, to provide technical assistance to other Federal agencies, and to collect and report Federal energy consumption data to Congress. Our activities are based on Presidential authorities and Congressionally-mandated directives. In addition, with the passage of the Clean Air Act Amendments of 1990, concerns over global climate change and a range of man-made and natural pollutants, environmental issues now play a critical role in our nation's energy policy. As a major consumer of energy, the Federal sector can serve as an important model for other sectors of the economy as a result of some of the innovative and cost-effective measures planned or currently underway. My talk today will focus on the Federal government's plans to ensure the energy efficient design and operation of Federal facilities, with an emphasis on life-cycle cost analyses.

## NEW DIRECTIONS

Building on the foundation of existing Federal authorities, the legislation addressing the National Energy Strategy (NES) offers an aggressive program to reduce energy consumption in Federal facilities. Based on Senate bill S. 2166 and House bill H.R. 776, the legislation increases Federal energy goals and provides new incentives and analytical and design tools to meet these goals. As this article goes to press, a separate, specific title is devoted specifically to Federal Energy Management.

It is my challenge along with other Federal agency energy coordinators to implement the Federal energy management provisions and bring years of discussion into reality. There are complicated and diverse new tactics that expand the ability of Federal energy managers to meet the goal shared by the President and Congress to reduce energy consumption in Federal buildings by 20 percent by the year 2000, over a 1985 energy consumption baseline. This year's legislation also expands our responsibility to include water conservation and renewable energy measures in Federal facilities.

Achieving the NES goal will result in a reduction of Federal energy expenditures by an estimated $10 billion and eliminate the need for 2000 megawatts, which would cost $4 billion in new generating plants. The impact on new product development and growth in the marketplace is enormous. The parallel benefit to the environment will be equally significant.

The new directions reflected in these Federal initiatives can be categorized in four areas:

- Identification of energy savings opportunities;
- Establishment of Federal energy incentive programs;
- Financing and procurement procedures; and
- Deployment of energy-efficient and renewable energy technologies.

## IDENTIFYING ENERGY SAVINGS OPPORTUNITIES

Analyzing energy use in Federal buildings is as much an art as it is a science. Much like a doctor who has sophisticated diagnostic tools but still needs keen instinct to interpret the technical findings, an energy diagnostician needs both tools and training to be effective.

The comprehensive energy bill expands FEMP's responsibilities with greatly enhanced training requirements and audit teams to perform on-site evaluations. Building on existing FEMP training programs that focus on lighting, shared energy savings, and life-cycle costing procedures, the 1992 law requires that DOE offer regular, biennial conference workshops in each of the 10 standard Federal regions. The training workshops will cover such topics as energy management, conservation, efficiency, and planning strategies. To ensure that Federal energy managers are thoroughly equipped to meet their goals, there is a requirement that they be trained in the fundamentals of building energy systems, energy codes and applicable professional standards, energy accounting and analysis, life-cycle cost methodology, fuel supply and pricing, and instrumentation for energy surveys and audits. This training could be offered by public or private educational institutions, Federal agencies or professional associations such as the Association of Energy Engineers.

Technology-based tools have been developed by the Federal Energy Management Program to provide Federal facility managers with simple-to-use, fuel-neutral expert systems and software packages. Life-cycle cost analysis, required by law, is embedded in the software. The Federal Energy Decision Screening, or FEDS, Level 1 offers a 2-4 hour process to rank energy opportunities at Federal sites. Using a Minuet graphic display interface, FEDS is a sophisticated software package that addresses the unique needs of large, Federal building complexes. In a similar way, the Federal Lighting Expert System, called FLEX, is a decision-screening program for lighting opportunities. Matched with a Lighting Technology Screening Matrix, FLEX offers facility managers the tools for determining optimal, cost-effective lighting options for existing buildings. These tools have been developed by FEMP's partners at Pacific Northwest Laboratory and the National Renewable Energy Laboratory. Options for more efficient lighting have also been prepared with the active involvement of the Illuminating Engineering Society.

When I mention relighting programs in Federal facilities, I am proud of our efforts to develop a strong partnership with the Environmental Protection Agency and its Green Lights program. To aggressively pursue relighting in Federal agencies, we have developed the Federal Relighting Initiative/Green Lights, a DOE-EPA Partnership. This partnership combines the goals and expertise of each agency to significantly increase the pace of relamping Federal facilities in combination with utility-based demand-side management programs currently in existence (or planned) throughout the U.S.

The legislation also requires that Federal buildings be screened by January 1, 1994, to identify all viable energy-saving measures that offer 10-year paybacks. That's challenging, but the FEDS system and audit teams can help meet this goal. The required audit teams would be given instrumentation and other advanced equipment needed to perform energy audits of Federal facilities.

## Agency Incentives

To provide incentives to agencies, Congress authorized energy savings to be dispersed according to the following formula:

- one-third of savings to support energy-saving projects;
- one-third of savings for building improvement programs; and
- one-third of savings to be returned to the general fund of the Treasury.

With this provision, each agency can retain two-thirds of all savings for energy and building improvements, a significant incentive for Federal agencies to implement energy-saving measures in their facilities.

To acknowledge the important role played by Federal energy managers, individual cash awards up to $2500 are authorized. One hundred or more successful managers could be recognized each year with funds authorized by this legislation.

## Financing and Purchasing

Perhaps the greatest opportunity to affect Federal energy consumption is in the areas of the financing and procurement of energy conservation and renewable energy measures. Initial capital costs pose the same problems for Federal agencies as they do for the private sector. To help overcome that problem, Congress established a dedicated fund and an approach to expand the use of private sector investment resources.

A Federal Energy Efficiency Fund is established to provide needed capital to implement energy and water conservation and renewable energy projects. With priority given to projects leveraged with demand-side management and individual agency resources, the fund offers a significant incentive to accelerate implementation of these energy-saving measures. Once established, the Department would issue quarterly solicitations for agency projects.

Recognizing problems with existing Federal shared energy savings laws that produced eleven Federal projects and $47 million of private sector investment since 1986, the bill requires the use of performance contracting, which has been used widely by schools and local governments throughout the country. By adding performance contracting to the Federal procurement process, agencies will have a streamlined approach to select pre-qualified energy service contractors and a procurement process adapted to the unique requirement of the energy services. Even as we speak, rules and procedures are being promulgated to put this provision into effect.

There are those who believe this process could revolutionize the way Federal agencies finance their energy-saving projects. Performance contracting encourages capital formation and offers a proven approach to attract needed initial investment capital to supplement Federal appropriations and utility-based demand-side management programs.

With the Federal Energy Efficiency Fund and performance contracting added to utility rebates and agency appropriations, there should be adequate capital to meet the President's goal of 20 percent savings by the year 2000, and to implement the most cost-effective measures with 10-year paybacks.

## Deploying Energy Technologies

One of the most exciting aspects of this program and one that provides Federal leadership in the development and market impact of new technologies, is a greatly expanded deployment program.

DOE is authorized to spend up to $5 million for energy technologies that are commercially available but not in widespread use in the public and private sectors. Such technologies shall be selected on the basis of: cost-effective, system reliability; level of Federal market penetration; potential agency needs of and market for the technology; and agency commitment to use the technology to supply at least 10 percent of the agency's potential needs.

Although FEMP's main mission is the deployment of proven, cost-effective technologies, this test-bed demonstration process provides the government the opportunity to demonstrate to other sectors of the economy, the benefits of cutting-edge technologies realized in Federal facilities.

## New Initiatives

Supported by the 1992 comprehensive bill and other Federal legislation, energy management in Federal facilities will continue to move in new directions. I intend to build on the goals of existing Federal legislation by advocating increased use of solar energy; partnerships with national laboratories, other Federal agencies, and experts from the private sector; accelerated implementation of energy-saving measures; and increased procurement clout to meet Federal energy goals. Briefly, I would like to describe my ideas to you.

Solar Energy: As Arizona's Energy Director during most of the 1980's, I acquired an appreciation for the values of solar energy, not only in sun-rich states like Arizona, but throughout the country. Passive solar buildings are valuable in Minnesota, and solar cars are proliferating from New England to Washington state. Of course, the economics vary, but there are plenty of cost-effective solar applications available in Federal facilities. They range from remote photovoltaic electric production at Tonto National Forest, to hot water systems at national parks and large- scale systems being developed at military bases. To focus on this important energy source, a new award for outstanding solar projects will be presented at this year's Federal Energy Award Program ceremony on October 30, 1992.

Partnerships: With a challenge this size, we cannot meet the goals alone. Continued and expanded partnerships with industry, support offices, states, and DOE's national laboratories will provide us important new resources to call upon.

Accelerated Implementation: The FEMP model approach has offered a broad-based performance-based system to evaluate opportunities. In addition, I propose a proven prescriptive approach that provides the Federal energy manager with a checklist to combine several energy savings measures like lights and motors that he or she can take to a utility or energy services company for implementation on an accelerated schedule to achieve savings in a shorter timeframe.

Procurement Clout: The Federal government buys $8 billion in office equipment. Much of this technology is inefficient, resulting in a steep increase in energy costs as the equipment gains widespread use. An estimated $150 million is used to power computers, copiers and faxes making this the fastest growing energy-consuming segment in the Federal sector. We are currently working with industry to capture the genius used to produce energy-efficient laptops (low energy users because they depend on batteries) to produce a new generation of energy-saving office equipment. This effort can be applied to other technologies and products to provide market leadership that should not only increase availability but reduce cost resulting from increased volume. Using the procurement clout of the Federal government can significantly expand markets and lead to widespread availability of new energy efficient products at lower prices due to increased volume.

SUMMARY

With the implementation of these legislative requirements, Federal energy management should reach the 20 percent goal by the year 2000, and result in billions of dollars of energy cost savings and a reduction in pollution emissions by tons.

With the professional and technical expertise of the engineering community and our partners in other agencies, the states, and industry, I am proud to be part of the new directions in Federal energy management.

# Chapter 82

# The Role of the Government Energy Efficiency Act in the National Energy Act of 1992

L. Good, D.R. Williams

## Abstract

Last year Senator John Glenn's **Government Energy Efficiency Act** to reform energy management in the Federal Government was adopted entirely into the Senate's comprehensive energy bill. This year key portions of an equivalent bill were incorporated into the House of Representatives' comprehensive energy bill after intensive lobbying by AEE's National Capital Chapter. According to a House staffer who played a key role in the bill, the section on energy manager training was included as a direct result of the Chapter's persuasion.

Each bill passed in its respective house. At the time of this writing, in the spring of 1992, the two houses are scheduled to go into conference and attempt to merge their separate bills into one **National Energy Act of 1992.**

The 102nd Congress seems determined to establish a national energy policy before election time, but the two houses take very different approaches to the problem. The bill could be voted into law during or just before the 15th World Energy Engineering Congress (WEEC). This paper will discuss some of the strengths and loopholes that apply to the Federal sector. The presentation of this paper at WEEC in October will bring AEE members up to the minute on these developments.

## Introduction

On February 19, 1992, by a vote of 94 to 4, the United States Senate passed an omnibus energy bill entitled **S.2166, the National Energy Security Act of 1992,** which contains the following titles:

Title I - Findings and Purposes
Title II - Definitions
Title IV - Fleets and Alternative Fuels
Title V- Renewable Energy
Title VI - Energy Efficiency
Title VIII - Advanced Nuclear Reactor
         Commercialization
Title IX - Nuclear Reactor Licensing
Title X - Uranium
Title XI - Natural Gas
Title XII - Outer Continental Shelf
Title XIII - Research, Development,
         Demonstration and
         Commercialization Activities
Title XIV - Coal, Coal Technology, and
         Electricity
Title XV - Public Utility Holding Company Act
         Reform

On May 27, 1992, by a vote of 381 to 37, the United States House of Representatives passed an omnibus energy bill entitled **H.R. 776, The Comprehensive National Energy Policy Act,** which contains the following titles:

Title I - Energy Efficiency
Title II - Natural Gas Pipelines
Title III - Alternative Fuels - General
Title IV - Alternative Fuels - Non-Federal
         Programs
Title V - Availability and Use of Replacement
         Fuels, Alternative Fuels, and
         Alternative Fueled Private Vehicles
Title VI - Electric Motor Vehicles
Title VII - Electricity
Title VIII - High-Level Radioactive Waste
Title IX - Uranium Enrichment Corporation
Title X - Remedial Action at Active Processing
         Sites
Title XI - Uranium Enrichment Health, Safety,
         and Environmental Issues
Title XII - Renewable Energy
Title XIII - Coal
Title XIV - Strategic Petroleum Reserve
Title XV - Octane Display and Disclosure
Title XVI - Green House Warming - Energy
         Implications
Title XVII - Additional Federal Power Act
         Amendments
Title XVIII - Oil Pipeline Regulatory Reform
Title XIX - Miscellaneous

These two bills amend the **National Energy Policy Act of 1988** as well as PUCHA and PURPA, and are to be merged to form one comprehensive national energy policy. Included in each of these two major bills are the major parts of the **Government Energy Efficiency Act**, originally a separate bill, which contained two titles:

Title I - Federal Agency Energy Efficiency and Management
Title II - Federal Alternative Fuel Vehicle Procurement and Management

It was designated **S.1040** in the Senate and **H.R.2916** in the House. It was added to the Senate omnibus bill virtually in its entirety, and appears in **Title VI, Energy Efficiency,** and in **Title IV, Fleets and Alternative Fuels.** It was added to the House omnibus bill in a more fragmented form, and appears in **Title I, Energy Efficiency,** and in **Title III - Alternative Fuels - General.**

## To Put its Own House in Order

By the conservative estimate of the Congressional Office of Technology Assessment (OTA), the Federal Government is wasting about $1 billion/yr in energy. Other witnesses at congressional hearings place the waste near $4 billion. Senator John Glenn recognizes the scope of the problem better than most legislators. In his opening remarks at a Governmental Affairs Committee hearing on energy earlier this year, he stated, "Americans are sick and tired of seeing the Government fritter away taxpayer dollars on wasteful spending..... Government should cut out the waste and accomplish more with what it has...... Energy efficiency is a prime example of where the Federal Government could do more with less."

Until now our country has been operating with no serious energy philosophy. Written policies of the past, such as President Bush's executive order to reduce Federal energy consumption, have been unenforced. The de facto policy has been largely laissez faire. Lack of strong direction caught the country by surprise during the oil shortage of 1973-74 and Iraq's conquest of Kuwait, an oil supplier, in 1991.

If the new energy bill is passed and enforced, the Federal Government will accomplish several positive things to put its own house in order:

1. Make agencies more accountable for their energy consumption.
2. Train energy managers.
3. Set clear targets for improvement of energy efficiency.
4. Eliminate barriers to procurement of energy efficient products.
5. Convert a portion of its vehicle fleets to cleaner, more efficient fuels.

These are some of the strengths of the two energy bills.

### Cons

On the negative side, the energy bills, like any others, have soft spots. Regarding the Federal Government sector:

Subtitle B of Section 121 of the House bill exempts a federal agency from the requirements of the bill if "compliance....would be impractical," or "if the requirements will pose an unacceptable burden open the agency." One report per building complex, describing the burden, exempts the agency unless contested within 90 days by the Secretary of Energy.

The same subtitle states that an agency shall "designate facility energy supervisors." But Section 123 says that agencies "shall....ensure that facility energy managers are trained energy managers " There is no schedule for accomplishing the training. Neither house's bill contains testing standards by which to measure an energy manager's qualifications. A determined agency may have nothing to stop it from simply changing facility managers' titles to "energy manager" to satisfy the law.

Also, "The Secretary may waive the requirements.... if the agency is taking all practical steps to meet the requirements..." This is a matter of opinion and interpretation. In a recent House hearing, GSA claimed that it was already exceeding the requirements of the energy bill, and that it should not be subject to further regulation. An agency that will not be told what to do may be able to opt out of the requirements.

Loopholes like these could expose the law to gross abuse.

The most serious shortcoming may be the lack of funding. Without more adequate funding, it will be difficult to reverse the backward slide of energy efficiency in the Federal Government. The amounts appropriated in the two bills are a few million here, a few hundred thousand there. This will not begin to accomplish the worthy goals set forth, and they may go the way of so much other legislation that suffered early starvation.

A solution to this problem may be the Energy Efficiency Bank, a self sustaining financing mechanism that lends money to agencies for energy efficiency projects. The money comes from a combination of $200 million seed money plus a tax on each agency based on its energy use. If this concept is incorporated into the final bill, it may offer a revolutionary means of sustaining energy improvements in the Federal Government well into the future. The Bank's payback obligation, as opposed to a typical three year appropriation, also offers the hope of changing users' long term habits in favor of efficiency and good management.

### Market Proving Ground

The Government Energy Efficiency Act, which started life in the Senate as S.1040, was not intended to create a technological proving ground for new products. H.R. 3397, The Federal Facility Energy Efficiency and Environmental Improvement Act does that. S.1040 takes off-the-shelf technology and installs it in government buildings and vehicle fleets. It creates a market proving ground, which accomplishes several things:

1. It drives the prices of newer products down quickly. Due to the mass buying power of the Federal Government, it can get better deals on expensive new products through volume discounts. That, in turn, leads to cost reductions in mass production which are passed on to the public in a competitive marketplace. This accomplishes more to make new products affordable than decades of public purchasing. Thus, new technology leapfrogs into American homes and businesses.

2. It familiarizes users with new products. Federal employees are the users of federal equipment. As these federal employees become accustomed to spending eight hours/day with occupancy sensors, energy efficient desk lamps, or driving natural gas vehicles, they will lose their reluctance to purchase these same products at home. This will plant the seeds. There are millions of federal employees and on site contractors. They will spread the word and expand new markets.

Familiarization on a larger scale requires different methods. Individual government employees will not notice the effect of most big ticket items like economizers or energy efficient chillers. The larger items are of more interest to industry. To familiarize industry with large scale equipment, the Federal Government should have technical demonstrations. This paper proposes that the Federal Government invite his big constituents, the manufacturers and their representatives, developers, contractors and other major purchasers of energy and energy equipment, into open houses for the purpose of publicizing how companies can benefit. The information needs to be shared and shared often.

Demonstration requirements are written into the bills, but they are not specific. They do not suggest that government invite industry in for plant tours of successful installations, financial seminars, technical seminars or any concrete action that would educate and convince industry that the investments are profitable. The Federal Government needs to take such initiate to spur technology transfer. The government cannot lead by example if the examples are a secret.

## Leading by Example

Dr. Robin Roy implied convincingly and emphatically in his OTA publication, **Energy Efficiency in the Federal Government: Government by Good Example?** that the Federal Government has set a poor example for the rest of the nation. James Schlesinger, the first Secretary of Energy, noted in his address to the Johnson Control's 1991 Energy Forum that the public would be inclined to follow a good example by the Federal Government. Both of these experts insist that the government should try.

**S.1040, The Government Energy Efficiency Act** (Titles IV and VI in the Senate version and Titles I and III in the House version of the comprehensive energy bill) does just that. These titles take a leadership role among other titles in that they tell the nation to "Do as I do," not just "Do as I say." The other titles regulate the public sector. In the titles of **S.1040** the Federal Government is regulating itself.

The need for the government to regulate itself is serious. Federal management of its own energy use has been dismal compared to

    a) what private industry has been doing, and
    b) the potential for what could be done.

The Federal Government lags at least 10 years behind the private sector in developing its energy management. Mark Hopkins, of the Alliance to Save Energy, testified at a House hearing that a 3M corporate building complex spends $1 for every $7 in energy costs, a rate 600 times higher than DOD's. Many government buildings are not even metered, yet America has shown that it is willing to go to war to secure petroleum supplies.

Energy issues do not get the constant, sensational press coverage given to other scandals like the House banking abuses or the illicit affairs of some politicians. These spectacles, however, serve as a general indicator of public opinion on government accountability. The American public expects its government to set a good example and to be good stewards. On energy matters, the public expects the government to lead the country by example to a more efficient economy. If taxpayers feel that the government has been a good steward of its resources, they are much more likely to follow their elected leaders through tough decisions.

## Conclusion

James Schlesinger, the first Secretary of Energy, said, "Americans believe they have a right to cheap energy." As long as the Federal Government treats energy as a virtually free resource, the rest of the country lacks a role model. The citizen's only guide for energy management is the marketplace, and the United States has some of the cheapest energy prices in the world. This does not encourage good management.

If the Federal Government takes the moral high ground and recognizes that fossil fuel is a precious natural resource and pollution of the planet must be halted, then the **National Energy Act** will lead the nation by example. Such an example will inspire individuals to be better national citizens, and America will, in turn, become a better world citizen. This is the most valuable role that the **Government Energy Efficiency Act** can play in the **National Energy Act of 1992.**

# Chapter 83
# Energy Conservation in the Federal Sector

M. Ginsberg

As a representative of the Nation's largest energy consumer, spending $10 billion annually, it is an honor to participate in the World Energy Congress. I have the responsibility along with other members of this panel to reduce energy costs in the Federal sector. Obviously, with a challenge of that size, we cannot do it alone. So, I appreciate the Association of Energy Engineers convening this and other panels to discuss energy conservation in Federal facilities. I hope our discussion can lead to accelerated energy savings in the public and private sectors.

I am the Director of the U.S. Department of Energy's Office of Federal Energy Management Programs (FEMP). First established by Congress in 1974, FEMP coordinates the design and implementation of a variety of energy-saving programs for Federal buildings and operations. This includes working closely with other Federal agencies through interagency committees to interpret and implement Federal policy, to develop and provide technical assistance to other Federal agencies, and to collect and report data on Federal energy consumption to Congress. Our activities are based on Presidential authorities and Congressionally-mandated directives.

Let me put the challenge of my Office in the context of Federal energy consumption, since few energy managers deal with energy costs of this size. Of the $10 billion spent annually, about 40 percent or $4 billion is expended annually for electricity, natural gas, and other energy sources to operate Federal buildings. The other sixty percent goes to gasoline and transportation fuels as well as industrial process energy. Almost half a quad is needed to keep about 500,000 Federal buildings operating annually. That would be about 200 average-sized electric power plants.

Twenty-nine Federal agencies report their energy consumption to us on a quarterly basis. The current Federal building stock has a considerable number of buildings over twenty years old. The inventory consists of typical office buildings, residences, hangers and hospitals, warehouses and space launch buildings.

Federal facilities are located in deserts and remote Alaskan tundra as well as the largest urban centers throughout the U.S. The buildings range from small post offices to national treasures such as the Statue of Liberty. On the face of it, this is a daunting and diverse challenge. And, let me assure you, as one goes deeper, it only becomes more complex and difficult to address.

My task is to assist agencies in implementing Congressional and Presidential direction that should result in a $2 billion reduction in energy expenditures in the year 2000. Cumulative savings from 1985-2000 would exceed $10 billion. Existing technology markets will be expanded, new energy-saving products will be developed, and the environment will benefit from a significant decrease in pollution emissions. If we reduce the need for 2000 megawatts, our nation could save $4 billion in avoided power-generation construction costs.

## THE MANDATE

It is with this significant potential in mind that led Congress to address Federal energy management as early as 1977 with the Energy Conservation and Production Act. That set a goal of 10 percent savings from a base of 1975 to 1985. The Federal Energy Management Improvement Act of 1988 strengthened existing legislation by setting a new goal - to achieve 10 percent savings from 1985 to 1995. This Act established the requirement for life cycle-cost analysis for selecting energy-saving measures for Federal facilities and established the Interagency Energy Management Task Force, which assists FEMP in the implementation of Federal policy and new energy-saving initiatives for the Federal sector.

In April 1991, President Bush signed Executive Order 12759, which expanded the existing Federal goal to 20 percent by the year 2000 over the base year of 1985, and 10 percent fuel-savings by 1995. The Executive Order also included provisions that addressed energy efficient procurement practices, the use of alterative fuels in Federal fleets, and encouraged Federal participation in utility-based demand side management. Passage of legislation addressing the National Energy Strategy (NES) provides the most comprehensive course of action thus far to address energy and water conservation and renewable energy measures for the Federal sector. Passed by both houses of Congress, the legislation awaits a conference committee as this articles goes to press. In another paper,

I address in more detail, the new directions required by this year's historic legislation.

Keep in mind that, even with this arsenal of legislation and Presidential direction, my office has limited authority over the actions of other agencies to achieve Federally-mandated goals or energy savings. My office provides encouragement, technical assistance, and data collection and reporting support. The good news is there are now a number of innovative incentives to encourage individual agencies to implement energy saving measures in their facilities and operations. For example, the new legislation includes a provision that allows agencies to retain energy savings for additional building improvements and provides cash awards for employees who successfully implement energy saving measures.

Federal Energy Management Programs

Congress and the Department of Energy have devoted six professional staff members and a $4 million budget to support this program. For fiscal year 1993, which began October 1, 1992, the President's budget request includes $5.7 million for FEMP. With these funds, FEMP will address Federal energy consumption issues in three areas: planning and guidance; technical assistance; and technology deployment.

Planning Coordination, Reporting, and Analysis: At the heart of planning and guidance is energy consumption data. Twenty-nine agencies report their energy consumption in a format that goes into Congressionally-mandated annual reports. Data is reported in aggregated, agency-wide totals with buildings reported in Btus per gross square feet. FEMP receives the total square footage of buildings along with electricity, natural gas, steam and fuel oil data used to operate these facilities. The data is reported in both units of measure and dollar costs and documented in an Annual Report to Congress.

This activity also supports FEMP's energy awareness and annual awards program for the Federal sector. We participate in the Federal government's annual Energy Awareness Month program, which is conducted each October; FEMP distributes an energy efficiency poster to all Federal agencies for display in their facilities throughout the U.S. We also provide agencies with guidance on how to set up and conduct their own energy awareness programs. Each year, the Federal Energy Award program recognizes the outstanding achievements of Federal energy managers for their energy savings projects in Federal facilities and operations. Awards are presented to fifteen individuals, five groups of four and under, and fifteen large working groups. An awards ceremony is held in late October, in which plaques are presented to award recipients.

Finally, an evaluation methodology has been developed and implemented to assist in tracking Federal energy savings. The methodology includes before and after studies, metering, and related analysis. Until recently, four Mobile Energy Laboratories traveled around the country, providing valuable evaluation experience while performing on-site analysis at Federal facilities. An advisory group provides oversight of the technical elements of the evaluation process.

Federal Guidance and Assistance: Technical guidance and assistance includes development of analytical tools, innovative financing techniques, and technical training.

Based on our considerable experience in Federal energy management, FEMP has determined that facility managers require technology-based support to identify the most optimal energy measures for Federal facilities. A Federal Energy Decision Screening software package is being developed for FEMP by Pacific Northwest Laboratories for use in Federal facilities. The purpose of this software program is to provide facility managers in a few hours with a simple way of determining what energy opportunities make the most sense in terms of energy savings and cost-effectiveness. Imbedded in this program is life-cycle cost analysis. A related tool has been developed specifically for lighting.

As a result of existing legislation, which authorizes shared energy savings contracting, FEMP has also begun to address the need for capital to support energy efficiency improvements in Federal facilities. To date, eleven contracts have been completed, representing an investment of $47 million. Current procurement procedures have slowed the shared energy saving process in the Federal sector with just eleven projects since 1986. However, more attention has been directed to procurement issues and Federal energy managers are now better informed about the shared energy savings methodology. For example, we have trained 413 workshop attendees in 21 sessions during the last two years.

FEMP also conducts training sessions on life-cycle cost analysis and lighting. With the requirements of 10 CFR 436, a Federal regulation that specifies the procedure to be used, we have conducted 16 Workshops for over 300 participants in a computer setting that combines life-cycle costing with A Simple Energy Analysis System (ASEAM), a whole building analytical software program. The lighting training program will be offered in concert with the Illuminating Engineering Society. We will "train the trainers" and the Society's local chapters will conduct the actual training workshops. Another new training program - the Federal Energy Decision Screening program, will be conducted and will focus on building energy opportunity analysis. In addition, the design of workshops on demand-side management and passive solar design techniques are now being considered by FEMP.

Technology Deployment: One of the most important elements of the Federal Energy Management Program is the deployment of existing and cutting-edge technologies. This is accomplished through the "Federal Relighting Initiative" and a technology test-bed demonstration program.

On January 26, 1990, the Department of Energy announced a major new initiative to relight Federal facilities to enhance energy efficiency and productivity. The initiative is tied directly to utility-based demand-side management and several demonstrations are currently underway in Federal facilities. The most advanced demonstration is at Fort Lewis in Takoma, Washington. Takoma Public Utilities, Bonneville Power Administration, the Department of Energy and the Army's Forces Command have joined in this effort to reduce the base's energy consumption by 5 average megawatts, enough to power 2700 Takoma homes for one year. About $12 million will be invested; 85 percent of the funding will be contributed by Takoma Public Utilities and 15 percent will be provided by the Army. Bonneville will "buy conservation" to help meet its resource acquisition goals. This project will result in a case study for DOE to use to encourage other Federal agencies to conduct similar programs in their facilities. Together, we have a Win-Win-Win-Win program.

DOE's Forrestal Headquarters building in Washington, DC, will be relamped with the installation of 41,000 new energy-efficient ballasts and tubes. As this presentation goes to press, three firms are providing their best and final offers to DOE's procurement office for this relighting project.

Commercially available technologies that have not yet achieved widespread use will be demonstrated in a test-bed program. A Cooperative Research and Development Agreement (CRADA) has been signed with Thermo-King and the Willow Grove Naval Air Station in the service territory of Philadelphia Electric Company. Two 15-ton gas cooling units will provide heating and cooling for the Post Exchange. A successful demonstration of this technology will result in the expanded use of such energy-efficient, gas cooling approaches.

## FEDERAL ENERGY MANAGEMENT

The three program areas described form the basis of our organization. Within this structure, there are several other specific approaches I would like to describe. In addition, recently enacted and pending Federal legislation will significantly alter Federal energy activities.

Implementation of the Executive Order I mentioned earlier, requires the procurement of energy efficient products and services. Work is underway with Federal procurement officials to address this requirement in an orderly way. The best example is the procurement of office equipment. The Federal government spends approximately $8 billion annually for office equipment and requires an estimated $150 million in power to support this equipment. This is the fastest growing energy-consuming segment of the Federal government due to the explosion of LANs, copiers, and faxes - we do not expect this growth area to slow down any time soon.

To address the energy used by office equipment, FEMP has initiated a cooperative effort with the General Services Administration, the Environmental Protection Agency, and industry.

The purpose of this agreement is to identify technical solutions to reduce the amount of energy consumed by office equipment and to develop and conduct facility manager and employee awareness campaigns to implement these energy-saving measures. GSA intends to notify industry of its intent to obtain for the Federal sector, office equipment that is energy-efficient. This effort may result in the incorporation of energy-efficient office equipment standards into the Federal Acquisition Regulations - thus further confirming energy-efficiency as a high priority for the procurement of products and services for the Federal government.

The second approach is a conscientious effort at partnership-building. I am a strong believer that we must reach out to allies who can help make Federal facilities more energy efficient. Internally at DOE, we are expanding the use of resources in the Department's Offices of Building Technologies, Utility Technologies, and Technical and Financial Assistance. We intend to make our ten regional Support Offices our "eyes and ears" to identify new opportunities and deliver technical assistance services at a more local level. In a similar way, DOE field offices and national laboratories can also play a major role in this effort. Outside the Department, I am putting together industry roundtables, specific task workshops, and working groups. Composed of industry representatives, public and private sector experts, and appropriate resources, these initiatives will expand our knowledge base, refine our approaches, and provide us with the practical experience that should lead to greater success in reaching our energy goals for the Federal sector.

## CONCLUSION

By providing guidance and technical assistance, training and assistance with financing mechanisms, and developing strong new partnerships, I am confident that we can meet the goals established by existing legislation to increase energy efficiency and reduce energy costs in Federal facilities.

# Chapter 84
# Implementing Energy Conservation Strategies or How to Plan Your Program to Be a Winner

T.H. Walker

**BACKGROUND**: The General Services Administration (GSA) is an agency of the Federal Government's Executive Branch organized in 1949. The U.S General Services Administration is the business manager for the Federal Government. GSA's business activities are undertaken through four major services with a nationwide staff of approximately 20,000 employees. These four services are:

o Public Building Service
o Information Resource Management Service
o Federal Property Resources Service
o Federal Supply Service

GSA's Energy Management Program encompasses many responsibilities in diverse areas of these Services. These areas include:

o Federal Facilities
o Recycling Programs
o Product Procurement
o Alternative Fuel Vehicles

GSA is the second largest real property management civilian agency with 176 million GSF in approximately 1600 Federally owned buildings. Also, GSA manages Federal leases in an additional 6000 buildings. The utility costs for these facilities exceeded $200 million in fiscal year 1991.

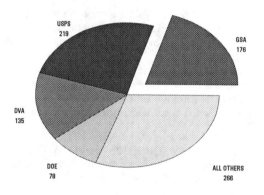

**FEDERAL BUILDINGS AND FACILITIES\***
**MILLION SQUARE FEET**

USPS 219
GSA 176
DVA 135
DOE 78
ALL OTHERS 266

\*Excluding Department of Defense

FIGURE 1: Federal Buildings and Facilities

GSA is responsible for purchasing most items required for the day-to-day operation of all government agencies, as well as, responsible for managing the general purpose office space occupied by these agencies. It wasn't always that way. Until GSA was formed, each agency and department took care of their own needs.

As one of the largest providers of goods and services, GSA's Federal Supply Service (FSS) contracts for items, such as, pens, pencils, office equipment, light fixtures, air conditioners, household appliances, fleet vehicles and numerous other items.

For all Federal agencies major objectives and directives are implemented through a complex system of Executive Orders and Laws. These EO's and Laws can be issued in the form of major documents such as the National Energy Strategy (Issued by President Bush in 1991). Some individuals, not familiar with Congressional procedures may not be aware of the energy issues contained in various (seemingly unrelated) Bills. This year more than 40 Bills were introduced before Congress with energy related sections which impact real property management. These Bills require analysis and comments to assure the proper result from what may have been a well-intended requirement.

A very brief history of legislative activities directed at energy conservation include the following milestones:

**LEGISLATIVE MILESTONES:**

o  In 1975 the Energy Policy and Conservation Act (EPCA), passed by Congress, addressed energy conservation issues in the Federal Government. It included energy management goals for operation and procurement of buildings, and also required the Federal automotive fleet meet or exceed the corporate average fuel economy (CAFE) standards.

o  In 1977, Executive Order 12003 (EO) issued by the President, established a goal to reduce energy consumption in Federal buildings by 20 percent (on a per square foot basis) by the year 1985 as compared to 1975. This EO also established life-cycle costing standards for Government decision makers.

o  In 1978 the National Energy Conservation Policy Act (NECPA) further extended the management goals first promoted by EPCA and the EO12003.

o  In 1982, Executive Order 12375 amended EO's 11912 and 12003 and reduced the requirements for the Federal fleet to meet the CAFE standards.

o  In 1988, The Federal Energy Management Improvement Act (FEMIA) established a goal to reduce energy consumption in buildings by ten percent by 1995 as compared to 1985.

o  In 1991, Executive Order 12759 further mandated energy reduction goals for buildings and industrial facilities by 20 percent by the year 2000 as compared to 1985.

During this same time period covered by these legislative activities, GSA engaged in  energy conservation efforts, including the following:

**ENERGY CONSERVATION EFFORTS IN GSA:**

**PAST ACCOMPLISHMENTS:**

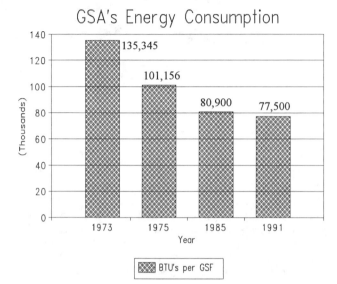

FIGURE 2:  GSA's Energy Consumption

o  Between 1973 and 1975, GSA reduced energy consumption by approximately 25% by implementing low cost/no cost operation and maintenance improvements

o  Between 1975 and 1985, GSA further reduced its energy consumption by more than 20% by continuing the management practices started in 1973 and implementing energy conservation improvements to its buildings

o  Petroleum conversion programs resulted in reducing GSA petroleum use by 75% between 1973 and 1985

New goals established in PL 100-615 and EO 12759, set the course for Federal agencies into the next century. The job of implementing these goals fell to each individual agency with the understanding that each agency knows the problems of its missions and can incorporate this knowledge into its plans.

## GSA MISSION:

In GSA, our mission is:

o  provide quality services required by our tenants and clients
o  ensure the best value to the Government and the public
o  enhance our clients ability to accomplish their mission.

To effectively incorporate energy conservation goals into our strategy, reasonably defined goals that could be achieved without compromising essential mission requirements were established. In the military program, you may have heard, "If it doesn't Fly, Fight Or Shoot, it doesn't matter." This may be a catchy phrase, that emphasizes the importance of organization "Missions," but officials in DoD have placed energy programs on par with other important goals.

GSA has a Central Office which is responsible for policy development, program monitoring and oversight. GSA has 10 regional offices and carry out those policies. Each region has a full-time Energy Coordinator in addition to energy conservation staff as necessary. These Coordinators were brought together shortly after the passage of the Federal Energy Management Improvement Act of 1988 to develop GSA's energy program. These programs include a comprehensive strategy (Energy Reduction Plan) to achieve goals outlined in Public Law without affecting the comfort, health and safety of building tenants. Important points in this plan include:

## FIVE POINT ENERGY REDUCTION PLAN:

> Point #1. Increased conservation planning and monitoring;
>
> Point #2. Identification and implementation of energy conservation opportunities (ECO's);
>
> Point #3. Improve building operations;
>
> Point #4. Enhance tenant and employee energy awareness; and
>
> Point #5. Develop incentives for energy conservation in leased buildings

**Point #1** - You may be familiar with Mr. Wayne Stebbins, Staff Electrical Engineer, for Hoechst-Celanese Company and a regular speaker at Assocoation Of Energy Engineers Conferences. He has shared with us his "Two 'M' Rule" which states, "If you can't measure it, you can't manage it!" To this end, the establishment of our Energy Usage and Analysis Center (EUAS) in Fort Worth, Texas has met with complete success. This Center analyzes energy consumption for more than 5,000 utility bills each month. Energy costs average approximately $1.00 per square foot (and usually range from $0.50 to $2.00 per square foot) to operate Federal Buildings. The EUAS data assists GSA in targeting high energy using facilities for energy conservation opportunities, and enables GSA to monitor the success of conserving energy.

**Point #2** - GSA's has set-aside more than $30 million funding each year in fiscal years 1991 and 1992 for special energy conservation projects. These projects include:

o  Retrofitting Existing Light Systems
o  Installation of Motion Sensors to Control Lights
o  Installing Energy Efficient Exit Signs
o  Converting to Energy Efficient Motors
o  Installing Energy Management Control Systems
o  Replacing HVAC and Damper Control Systems
o  Improving Storm/Insulating Windows
o  Retrofitting Existing Chiller and Boiler Systems
o  Replacing or Repairing Steam Traps

In Fiscal Year 1992, more than 200 projects were funded nationwide for this "Energy Conservation Set-Aside" Program. In addition, GSA is incorporating energy conservation and life-cycle costs into normal repairs, alterations and procurement of energy efficient products and services as reflected in newly revised building standards. If you would like aditional information on these or other energy conservation retrofit projects, contact the Real Property Management and Safety Office, Energy Branch, on 501-1563, and we will put you in contact with the appropriate Regional Energy Coordinator.

**Point #3** - The efficient operation of Federal buildings has been the cornerstone of early conservation efforts. An excellent guideline for identifying low cost/no cost energy conservation opportunities is the Architect's and Engineer's Guide to Energy Conservation in Existing Buildings (Publication DOE/RL/01830P-H4). This guide was prepared by the Federal Energy Management Program to provide energy managers, Federal Energy Coordinators, contractors, and other decision makers with current information for improving energy efficiency and analysis methods. This guide is supported by ASEAM (A Simplified Energy Analysis Method) public domain computer program for simulating energy use in buildings.

**Point #4** - Tenant and employee awareness programs are managed by individual GSA building managers to promote energy conservation goals in unison with enhancing the efficiency, effectiveness and productivity of the workplace. Many opportunities exist for idividuals to participate in energy conservation. Some simple tasks as turning out lights in unoccupied rooms and shutting off unnecessary equipment not only contributes to energy savings but also promotes the overall goal of a quality work environment. Additional tasks to reduce unnecessary overtime and optimize building system schedules is accomplished with the full participation and cooperation of tenants and employees.

**Point #5** - GSA has sought and obtained appropriations language which allows GSA to retain rebates from utility companies, and to assign those rebates to lessors who make energy conservation improvements in their buildings. In leased buildings where GSA pays the utility costs, the provision of this financial incentive will create a win-win situation for both the lessor and GSA. These rebates will reduce the cost of building modernization to the lessor and GSA will pay lower utility bills.

These activities integrate the need to protect our environment and conserve energy resources with our essential mission. As stated by Mr Richard Austin, Administrator, GSA, "Environmental protection and energy conservation are vital to all Americans." It is our goal to protect our environment, conserve our natural resources by expanding our efforts in recycling, waste reduction, and the purchase of energy efficient products and services.

**IMPEDIMENTS TO ENERGY CONSERVATION:**

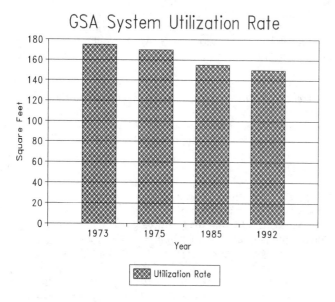

**FIGURE 3: GSA System Utilization Rate**

o The past success to reduce energy consumption makes it difficult to continue to achieve reduction that use new benchmarks to base percentage goals. GSA energy usage has reduced since 1973 according to the following data:

-- 1973 - Exceeded 130,000 BTU/GSA
-- 1975 - Exceeded 100,000 BTU/GSF
-- 1985 - Approximately 78,000 BTU/GSF
-- 1991 - Approximately 76,800 BTU/GSF

(Note: The 1991 performance can be compared to the Governmentwide average last year of approximately 132,000 BTU/GSF, as well as, private commercial buildings at 110,000 BTU/GSF)

o GSA has been reducing space utilization rates systematically throughout Government office buildings

- 1973, 175 SF/Person
- 1975, 170 SF/Person
- 1985, 155 SF/Person
- 1990, 150 SF/Person (including common/shared work areas)

(Note: This practice can be appreciated by understanding that under the 1990 guidelines described above, the average size for systems furniture workstation is now 49 SF.)

o Energy Projects have lower paybacks and lower savings-to-investment ratios

o Government-wide initiatives which have adversely impacted building energy usage include:

-- Flexible work hours:
   Increasing building operations from 8 to 11 hours per day
-- Increased use of office equipment:
   Desk top computers, individual printers
-- Conversion to energy intensive workplace:
   Systems furniture and individual work stations
-- Indoor air quality issues:
   Increased outdoor air ventilation

**OTHER GSA ENERGY CONSERVATION INITIATIVES:**

o **RECYCLING:**

-- Initial effort to establish a recycling program in GSA started in 1976. In 1990, GSA focused efforts on high-grade white paper (50-80 percent of the commercial office waste paper) which is proving successful.

-- Federal Agency Recycling Conferences provide increased public and media awareness.

-- Additional programs to include newspapers, aluminum containers, and glass are environmentally sound practices although program costs exceed revenue generated

These buildings (which may be government-owned or -leased) serve a wide variety of tenant demands, such as, office buildings, hospitals, warehouses, courtrooms, and others.

o **FEDERAL SUPPLY SERVICE:**

-- The purchase of energy consuming items in the FSS schedule includes information on life-cycle costs (LCC) for products such as electric motors, refrigerators, air conditioners and others

-- Initiatives have begun to expand LCC information for all energy consuming products in the FSS schedule including lightbulbs, computers, typewriters, and other products

-- Identify energy conservation products on the FSS New Item Introductory Schedule (NIIS) to supply building managers and tenants, including:

- Lighting controls (motion detectors) to turn off lights
- "Window Quilt" to reduce infiltration
- Solar type film and window shades which absorb heat
- Fuel economizers for gas furnaces
- Reflective film for retrofitting light fixtures

**SUMMARY:**

As the largest single consumer of energy in the United States, the Federal Government has a responsibility to be energy efficient. GSA is developing long-range plans and implementing actions that will achieve the goals outlined in Law and Executive Order. These actions impact all aspects of the Government and the results will benefit the entire Nation. As President Bush stated when signing Executive Order 12759, "This Order is a component, an important component, of the National Energy Strategy. And it demonstrates our commitment to a balanced approach for achieving an energy future that is secure, that is efficient, and that is environmentally sound." The General Accounting Office report, GSA - A Status Report on Energy Conservation Efforts, stated GSA developed a comprehensive building energy conservation plan which is a "... well-designed strategy for achieving energy savings." Please join in the GSA commitment to protect our environment and conserve our natural resources.

**Acknowledgements:** I would like to thank James Woods, Linda Garner, George Banko, and Eric Dunham for the support and assistance they provided during the preparation and review of this document.

References:

1.  Annual Report to Congress on Federal Government Energy Management and Conservation Programs Fiscal Year 1991; U.S. Department of Energy.

2.  Summary Report of the Real Property Owned by the United States Throughout the World as of September 30, 1990; U.S. General Services Administration.

3.  Energy Efficiency in the Federal Government (Government by Good Example?), Congress of the United States, Office of Technology Assessment.

4.  1992 Annual Energy Outlook; Energy Information Administration.

5.  Architect's and Engineer's Guide to Energy Conservation in Existing Buildings; U.S. Department of Energy.

6.  Life-Cycle Costing Manual for Federal Energy Management Program, NBS Handbook 135, National Institute of Standards and Technology.

7.  1992 Strategic Plan of the Public Building Service, U.S. General Services Administration.

8.  Code of Federal Regulations, General Services Administration, 41 CFR Part 101-20, Management of Buildings and Grounds.

9.  General Services Administration - A Status Report on Energy Conservation Efforts, GAO Report to the Chairman, Subcommittee on Public Buildings and Grounds, January 1992.

10. Energy Eficient Design of New Buildings Except Low-Rise Resdidential Buildings, ASHRAE/IES 90.1-1989.

11. Facilities Standards for the Public Buildings Service, PBS-PQ100, General Services Administration.

12. National Energy Conservation Policy Act (NECPA) of 1978.

13. Federal Energy Management Improvement Act (FEMIA) of 1988.

14. Executive Order 12759, Federal Energy Management.

# Chapter 85

# Lighting Technology Specifications for Relighting Federal Buildings

L. Harris, C.W. Purcell, H. Gordon, H. McKay

## INTRODUCTION

The Federal Energy Management Program (FEMP) of the U.S. Department of Energy has established the Federal Relighting Initiative (FRI) -- a broad-based, multiyear effort to help agencies modernize lighting systems in all Federal buildings and facilities. The theme for this Federal initiative is <u>Relighting for Energy Efficiency and Productivity</u>. Its goal is to encourage the retrofit of high-quality, life-cycle cost effective lighting systems in all Federal buildings. Through the initiative, DOE will provide agencies with technical and management assistance in a number of areas, including project screening and identification, staff training, technology demonstration, utility negotiation support, and direct modernization assistance. In addition, DOE is developing an integrated package of easy-to-use tools to help agency managers with the relighting process:

* A standard Federal process for identifying, characterizing, and prioritizing agency relighting opportunities

* An approach for characterizing the existing lighting in a facility to assist with project design

* A lighting technology screening matrix to quickly focus upon a limited number of appropriate lighting technology options

* Simplified approaches to calculating minimum life-cycle costs for lighting retrofit configurations

* Technology data sheets to assist with technology evaluation

* Equipment and systems specifications that can be employed by these agencies to ensure relighting bids that feature quality lighting systems.

A key element of this initiative is the development of a set of Master Lighting Technology Specifications that permit the designer, specifier, and/or Government Contracting Official to accomplish the following:

1. Identify and understand performance criteria for new, energy-efficient technologies that have been developed for lamps, fixtures, and ballasts, as well as lighting controls and control strategies

2. Understand the influence of the specifications on lighting quality and other related performance characteristics

3. Identify manufacturers that make products that can meet the requirements

4. Establish installation procedures to achieve lighting quality and energy savings objectives.

---

[1] Pacific Northwest Laboratory is operated for the U.S. Department of Energy by Battelle Memorial Institute under contract DE-AC06-76RLO 1830

## DISCUSSION

Under an FRI project, a set of Master Lighting Technology Specifications was developed for use by the Federal sector in relighting buildings. The specifications will cover all major lighting technologies. The initial set was developed and issued for comprehensive peer review in December 1991. Extensive comments were received from industry, Federal sector participants (DOD, GSA, NASA, DOE, etc.), national laboratories, professional lighting organizations, private lighting professionals, and recognized experts in the lighting community. The document underwent extensive revision and was reissued in June 1992 for a second round of peer review.

The current FRI Lighting Technology Specifications are organized into two sections: (1) Technical Notes and (2) Master Specifications. The Technical Notes contain explanations that enable the users to understand the background and reasons for specification requirements. The Master Specifications are organized in the Construction Specifications Institute (CSI) format and are intended to form the basis for competitive bidding and contracting to undertake relighting initiatives.

### 1. Technical Notes

The Technical Notes have been developed to assist the designer, specifier, or government representative in specifying cost-effective energy efficient lighting technologies contained in the Master Specification. The Notes include background information, recommended requirements for bidders, a glossary, a discussion of products, and a section covering commissioning and maintenance and operations. They deal with common applications of technologies and are not intended to be used as design guidelines or replace professional design expertise. They are not part of the actual Master Specifications.

The Technical Notes portion of the tool first provides background and perspective to the users. Federal energy managers have widely varied backgrounds experience and training. The Technical Notes are designed to present a broad overview of lighting issues to provide a "leveling" effect for the agency team and users thus ensuring at least a minimum level of understanding for the team members. This understanding of terms and technical issues will allow the managers to make more informed decisions when dealing with bidders and suppliers. The notes provide a background that will be useful to managers at all levels and provide guidance for preparing the project specifications as well as detail and justification for specific elements and sections of the specification.

The Notes also provide some guidance and recommendations about what should be required in a contractor submittal. The recommended requirements include documentation on computer generated plots of illuminance, for example, to determine that maintained light levels are being considered rather than just initial light levels. This will help ensure that maintained levels do not fall below the minimum requirements in critical areas.

The Technical Notes include a glossary of terms to provide explanations and references for using and editing the Master Specifications. The glossary includes such terms as Ballast Efficacy Factor, Ballast Factor, Color Rendering Index, and total harmonic distortion. While the list is not totally comprehensive, it does provide the basics and additional references are given to provide sources for additional terms or more detailed definitions.

In the "Products" section are discussions of fluorescent luminaries, reflectors, ballasts, and lamps. These cover broad areas of what to evaluate and expect in using and specifying each of the various products required for a project. The discussion on reflectors is particularly detailed and includes a recommended procedure for measuring their performance when installed.

Also in the "Products" section is a "Manufacturers Product Certification" form. This will enable manufacturers to be included on the List of Acceptable Manufacturers by certifying that a specific product meets the performance requirements of the Master Specifications in all aspects. This List of Acceptable Manufacturers will be maintained by the Department of Energy, and the updated list can be obtained by the specification writer on request. DOE will keep the list updated as new certifications are received from the manufacturers.

The final discussion in the Technical Notes briefly covers the basic aspects of commissioning, and operations and maintenance requirements. Since the commissioning area for lighting often receives less emphasis then the equipment installation, it needs to be discussed and implemented as part of the project. A strong, comprehensive operations and maintenance manual is vital if the system is to continue to operate as designed (and commissioned) and achieve the long-lasting energy efficiency desired.

The notes are intended to be used by the Federal manager to provide background; in conjunction with other FRI material, the notes will enhance their understanding of the entire project as well as the requirements for specifications development.

## 2. Master Specifications

The Master Specifications are intended to be used in preparing project specifications at the conclusion of the design process, which is the eleventh step in the FRI process (see fig 1), preceded by economic studies and existing condition surveys which verify the building as a suitable candidate for relighting. If the agency does not have sufficient lighting design expertise in-house, the project managers are expected to add such expertise to the project team to assist at several stages in the process; one of these stages is preparing project specifications.

The master lighting specifications are intended to provide default values and a common qualitative and economic benchmark for all Federal projects. If detailed analysis and specific project requirements favor different technologies or strategies, an appropriately qualified lighting professional may modify the specifications. While the specifier can modify the specifications to include products or technologies not currently contained, this should only be done following a thorough evaluation of energy conservation goals, lighting quality, and life cycle cost analysis. Lighting technologies which reduce energy further, or cost less than those included in these specifications may do so at the expense of lighting quality. In the absence of such technical justifications, however, the nature of the FRI process discourages capricious changes.

The characteristics of the technologies and strategies included in the specifications are intended to set a high standard for both product quality and lighting quality.

The development and use of these specifications is intended to spur product development by providing a large market for high quality, energy efficient technologies acceptable to users.

The current version of the specifications section contains state-of-the-art, energy efficient, interior fluorescent lighting technologies that are intended to fulfill the general relighting requirements for existing Federal facilities as part of the FRI. Currently, the specifications include a range of components and product performance characteristics for typical 4' fluorescent luminaries, reflectors, lamps, and ballasts. The subsequent updates to these specifications will incorporate the energy efficient lighting technologies of compact fluorescent, exit signs, occupant sensors, daylight sensors, time controls, and HID sources.

The specifications section has been developed as a combination of descriptive, performance, and reference standard specifications in order to accommodate the varying levels of technological development and testing. Reference standards have been utilized when applicable to establish acceptable performance characteristics. The specified product requirements are intentionally stringent in order to achieve maximum value for Federal expenditure and to encourage research and development in energy efficient products.

To be included in the Master Specifications, a product needs to meet several criteria, including the following:

* wide application potential

* maintenance of minimum standards of lighting quality

* energy efficiency

* cost-effectiveness

* production by at least three (3) U.S. manufacturers.

Many manufacturers of conventional products, even those who had previously supplied products for government facilities, will not be able to meet these specifications without improvement in the performance of their products. These specifications will also be updated on a regular basis in order to capture the benefits of technology and market advancements.

To further enhance the utility of the specifications, editing comments providing instruction to the specifier are inserted as capitalized statements or italicized comments; these are to be removed by the specifier during preparation of the specification. Additionally, the Master Specifications reference the List of Acceptable Manufacturers. This list will contain the manufacturers' names and product designations of those products that are certified by their manufacturer as being in compliance with specific portions of the Master Specifications.

FIGURE 1.

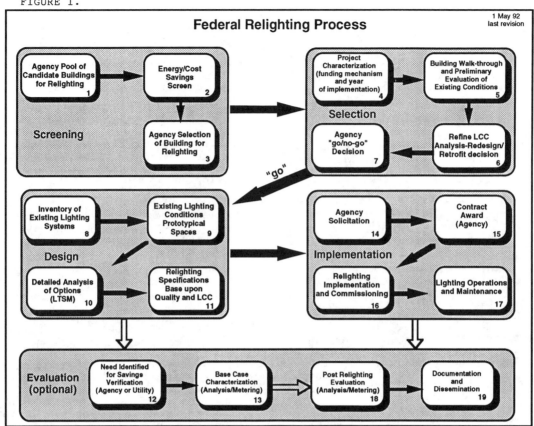

**Federal Relighting Process**

1 May 92
last revision

**Screening**

1. Agency Pool of Candidate Buildings for Relighting
2. Energy/Cost Savings Screen
3. Agency Selection of Building for Relighting

**Selection**

4. Project Characterization (funding mechanism and year of implementation)
5. Building Walk-through and Preliminary Evaluation of Existing Conditions
6. Refine LCC Analysis-Redesign/Retrofit decision
7. Agency "go/no-go" Decision

"go"

**Design**

8. Inventory of Existing Lighting Systems
9. Existing Lighting Conditions Prototypical Spaces
10. Detailed Analysis of Options (LTSM)
11. Relighting Specifications Base upon Quality and LCC

**Implementation**

14. Agency Solicitation
15. Contract Award (Agency)
16. Relighting Implementation and Commissioning
17. Lighting Operations and Maintenance

**Evaluation (optional)**

12. Need Identified for Savings Verification (Agency or Utility)
13. Base Case Characterization (Analysis/Metering)
18. Post Relighting Evaluation (Analysis/Metering)
19. Documentation and Dissemination

## SUMMARY

The Department of Energy's Federal Relighting Initiative, under the Federal Energy Management Program (FEMP), now offers a comprehensive process to assist agencies in meeting the DOE energy mandate that states that Federal facilities shall use 20% less energy by the year 2000, based on 1985 consumption, and shall improve lighting to increase productivity with relighting projects. The process provides a systematic approach in the screening, selection, design, implementation and evaluation of relighting projects. The Master Specifications help assure the acquisition of high-quality, life-cycle cost-effective lighting systems.

The process begins with the screening of the agency's building stock to identify the most promising relighting candidates and concludes with implementation support and system performance assessment. The tools developed by FRI are designed to assist agencies during each phase of the relighting process. The tools are based upon the Federal life-cycle cost approach, thereby complying with 10 CFR, part 436, and the Federal life-cycle cost requirement.

The Master Specifications package is one of the main tools in the FRI process and is intended to promote technologies which exhibit the highest level of performance and quality which is typically cost justified. To ensure adequate cost competition, that level of performance is set at the highest level that will still allow three U.S. manufacturers to compete. As products improve, the performance standards will be set at increasingly higher levels.

The specifications contain very stringent criteria and will require manufacturers to certify that their products meet the specifications when they submit bids on projects. The specifications are designed to assist the Federal manager or specifier in quickly developing solicitation packages that will result in Federal buildings being relighted in the most life-cycle cost effective manner with the highest quality energy efficient lighting available on the market. The ultimate goal of the FRI is to improve energy efficiency and productivity.

## ACKNOWLEDGMENTS

This paper was prepared with the support of the U.S. Department of Energy. The opinions, findings, conclusions and recommendations expressed herein are solely those of the authors and do not necessarily reflect an official policy or position of the Department of Energy.

# Chapter 86

# Selecting Energy Conservation Projects at the General Services Administration

J.E. Woods

**BACKGROUND:** The General Services Administration is the agency responsible for general purpose office space property management in the Federal Government. GSA is the second largest civilian property management agency with 176 million square feet in approximately 1600 Federally owned buildings. Also, GSA manages Federal leases in an additional 6000 buildings for a combined total of more than 240 million occupiable square feet.

The Public Building Service in GSA provides operating services to Agencies occupying space and charges rent comparable to commercial rates. Revenues from rent are approximately $4 billion annually.

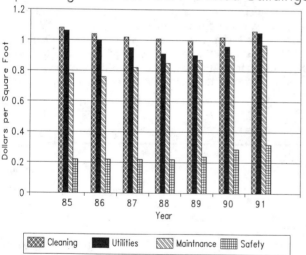

FIGURE 1: Operating Costs for GSA-Owned Buildings

Offsetting these revenues are operating expenses for utilities, cleaning, maintenance services, and other items. Utility costs are tracked by the Energy Usage and Analysis System Center (EUAS) in Fort Worth, Texas. This Center receives information from approximately 5,000 utility bills each month and analyzes these bills for accuracy and proper rate structures. Where GSA pays the utilities, costs for these facilities exceeded $200 million in fiscal year 1991.

**ENERGY GOALS:** In recognition of the Federal Government's opportunities to conserve energy, Congress passed the Federal Energy Management Improvement Act of 1988 which mandated that each Federal Agency reduce its energy consumption by ten percent by 1995 as compared to 1985 (measured in Btu per gross square foot). Further, in 1991, Executive Order 12759, Federal Energy Management, increased this goal and required a reduction of 20 percent BTU per gross square foot by fiscal year 2000.

GSA responded to these legislative mandates by developing a "5 Point Energy Reduction Plan." This plan encompasses many initiatives which will incorporate energy conservation actions in the full spectrum of GSA operations, maintenance, repair and alterations, and capital investment program. A cornerstone of GSA's energy reduction plan" is the Energy Conservation Retrofit Projects.

**ENERGY PROJECTS:** GSA has 10 regional offices. These regional offices develop energy conservation projects from a variety of sources, such as tenant requests, building managers, energy audits, A&E studies, or other sources. These regions submit requests for project funding to GSA's Central Office for review and approval. Project approvals are based on factors outlined in "Life Cycle Costing Manual for the Federal Energy Management Program." These factors include:

o Initial Cost
o Savings-to-Investment Ratio
o Energy Savings
o Payback

GSA has set-aside more than $100 million for retrofit projects in the last four years from 1990 through 1993. Typically these projects include:

o Retrofitting Existing Light Systems
o Installation of Motion Sensors for Lights
o Installing Energy Efficient Exit Signs
o Converting to Energy Efficient Motors
o Installing Energy Management Systems
o Replacing HVAC and Damper Control Systems
o Improving Storm/Insulating Windows
o Retrofitting Chiller and Boiler Systems
o Replacing or Repairing Steam Traps

Numerous utility companies supply electricity and other utilities to GSA with a wide variety of rate structures. Those companies with "Demand-Side Management" programs offer an incentive to install energy conservation technologies, such as, T-8 fluorescent lighting, or high efficiency electric motors. These rebate programs present an opportunity to provide energy conservation projects by offsetting a portion of the installation cost.

Demand-Side Management programs offered by utility companies can provide the margin of savings which can "make or break" some of these projects. Similar projects in different utility service territories have very different cost/benefit calculations.

When the offices at the General Services Administration were being renovated and the wooden desks were being replaced with new systems furniture, GSA examined the overhead lighting and found an opportunity to reduce energy consumption, save utility costs and improve lighting for the workers. The existing lighting was 2' x 4' recessed ceiling troffers that used four 40-watt lamps and two standard ballasts. Most fixtures had two lamps removed and one ballast disconnected for energy conservation. This "delamping" resulted in a mixed appearance, with light and dark areas in the ceiling.

The new lighting used 2' x 4' fixtures with parabolic reflectors, prismatic lenses and tandem wired two fixtures to operate from one electronic ballast using T-8 lamps with high color rendition qualities. General lighting was achieved using less than one watt per square foot (below ASHRAE/IES goals). Task lighting is added at individual workstations where needed. This project not only saved energy and improved the quality of the workplace, but it also qualified for a rebate from the local utility company which helped defer some of the initial costs.

**PROJECT ANALYSIS:** An example of Life Cycle Costing is presented in Table 1 (retrofitting existing 2' x 4' recessed fluorescent troffer with 40 watt lamps, typical in many older office buildings, with 2' x 4' recessed fluorescent troffer, parabolic reflectors, prismatic lenses and two T-8 lamps, high color rendition qualities. Two fixtures are tandem wired and operated from one electronic ballast).

To achieve a comparison of costs and savings, the Federal Building Life-Cycle Costing (BLCC) program requires information on:

1. Installations cost
2. Energy consumption
3. Maintenance and repair costs
4. Replacement and salvage value

To avoid the cliche that "Figures Lie and Liars Figure," we will make assumptions that do not favor the new project.

1. No additional costs to maintain the old vs. the new system.
2. No additional costs for maintaining additional ballasts of the old system.
3. No future replacement project required within the 15 year study period.
4. No intangible benefits from the new system, such as, increased worker productivity, improved safety, better quality of light.

Even in the worse case LCC analysis the new lighting project results in a net savings of more than $28,000 as compared to a "Do Nothing" scenario. This analysis clearly shows that a "Do Nothing" approach to existing systems actually costs more than investing now in improved technologies and energy conservation projects.

| Present-Value Life-Cycle Cost | | | |
|---|---|---|---|
| | Existing System | New System | Savings |
| Fixtures: | 160 | 125 | |
| Ballasts | 160 | 64 | |
| Total Watts: | 16,320 | 7,000 | |
| Total KW/Yr | 65,280 | 28,000 | |
| Initial Investment | $978 | $11,736 | -$10,758 |
| Future Costs: | | | |
| Annual O&M Costs | $1,942 | $1,942 | $0 |
| Energy Costs | $69,037 | $29,621 | $39,415 |
| Subtotal | $70,979 | $31,563 | $39,415 |
| TOTAL P.V. LCC | $71,957 | $43,299 | $28,657 |
| Savings-to-Investment Ratio (SIR) = 3.66 | | | |
| Adjusted Internal Rate Of Return (AIRR) = 14.06% | | | |

Table 1 - Comparison of Present-Value Costs

This analysis can be repeated with different assumptions (just to reassure those building owners and managers that "A dollar invested today, will save money later").

The convenience and ease of the BLCC program allows existing data files to be recalled and modified and saved under new names. With this convenience in mind, a second "Base Case" was examined in which the number of existing fixtures was equal to the number of new fixtures. This second "Base Case" is considered because it could be argued that all of the savings in the first example was due to the reduced number of fixtures, when it would be very possible to remove the excess number of existing fixtures to equal the exact number required for the workstations in the new floor plan.

In spite of these unfavorable factors, the new lighting project still results in a net savings of more than $11,000 as compared to a "Worst Case" scenario. In addition, with the participation in "Demand Side Management" programs the initial first cost is reduced and the benefits improved.

GSA developed a national policy and strategy to participate with Demand-Side Management programs. Originally, Federal agencies had little incentive to participate in these programs because all refunds and other proceeds were returned to the Treasury. Thus, any agency that went to the trouble to design a project, apply for the rebate, fund the additional costs for the energy conservation technology, schedule the construction, and "walk" the project through, at the end of all these efforts, the agency did not get any financial gain (except for reduced utility costs in future, which probably resulted in reduced appropriations).

This counterproductive cycle was broken when GSA developed Appropriations language which allowed for rebates to be retained by the agency. This language has been adopted by legislation and should continue to apply for future budgets.

Not all energy conservation opportunities (ECO's) are as clearly life-cycle cost effective as the lighting project examined in the above examples. More than 100 ECO's are discussed in the Architect's and Engineer's Guide to Energy Conservation in Existing Buildings, National Institute of Standards and Technology. ECO's include:

o Building Equipment Operation
o Building Envelope
o HVAC Systems
o Water Heating Systems
o Lighting Systems
o Power Systems

GSA has an established "Building Evaluation Report" (BER) program. This program insures that GSA facilities will be reviewed periodically (usually within 5 years) and recommendations are made for improving the facility to current standards. In this way, we protect the Government interests and insure that Federal facilities do not become obsolete.

The newly implemented "Statement of Work" for these BER's include requirements for life-cycle cost analysis for energy consuming systems, as well as building envelope systems. A building modeling program is available for evaluating Federal facilities. This public domain program, A Simplified Energy Analysis Method (ASEAM) is developed and supported by the Federal Energy Management Program (FEMP).

**SUMMARY:** To achieve energy reduction goals, GSA plans to use the tools mentioned above:

o Improved Operations and Maintenance
o Energy Conservation Retrofit Projects
o Capital Investment Programs
o Federal Building Life-Cycle Costing
o Building Evaluation Reports

Energy reduction goals, mandated by Law, established a 1985 baseline at which time GSA used approximately 84 MBtu/GSF in Government-owned and -leased buildings. (At the time of publication, GSA's energy performance for fiscal year 1992 was approximately 79 MBtu/GSF.)

The "bottom-line" to meet these goals, means GSA must reduce energy consumption to:
o 75 MBtu/GSF by fiscal year 1995
o 67 MBtu/GSF by fiscal year 2000

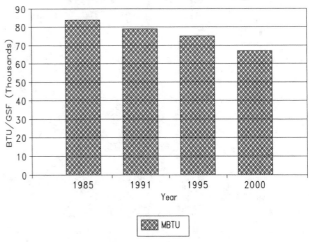

FIGURE 2: Energy Performance

Testimony in Congress by the Office of Technology Assessment and the General Accounting Office indicated that GSA's "5 Point Energy Reduction Plan" is being implemented to achieve these goals. If this plan is successful in GSA it will mean substantial savings ($40 million annually) to the Federal Government and ultimately a savings to the taxpayer.

**Acknowledgements: I would like to thank the following individuals for the support and assistance they provided during the preparation and review of this document: George Banko, Eric Dunham, Sieglinde Fuller, and Linda Garner.**

References:

1. Annual Report to Congress on Federal Government Energy Management and Conservation Programs Fiscal Year 1991; U.S. Department of Energy.

2. Summary Report of the Real Property Owned by the United States Throughout the World as of September 30, 1990; U.S. General Services Administration.

3. Energy Efficiency in the Federal Government (Government by Good Example?), Congress of the United States, Office of Technology Assessment.

4. Architect's and Engineer's Guide to Energy Conservation in Existing Buildings; U.S. Department of Energy.

5. Life-Cycle Costing Manual for Federal Energy Management Program, NBS Handbook 135, National Institute of Standards and Technology.

6. 1992 Strategic Plan of the Public Building Service, U.S. General Services Administration.

7. General Services Administration - A Status Report on Energy Conservation Efforts, GAO Report to the Chairman, Subcommittee on Public Buildings and Grounds, January 1992.

8. Energy Eficient Design of New Buildings Except Low-Rise Resdidential Buildings, ASHRAE/IES 90.1-1989.

9. Facilities Standards for the Public Buildings Service, PBS-PQ100, General Services Administration.

10. National Energy Conservation Policy Act (NECPA) of 1978.

11. Federal Energy Management Improvement Act (FEMIA) of 1988.

12. Executive Order 12759, Federal Energy Management.

# Chapter 87

# Measured Energy Savings from Using Night Temperature Setback

R.F. Szydlowski, L.E. Wrench, P.J. O'Neill

The measured energy savings resulting from using night temperature setback in typical light-construction wooden office buildings was determined. Researchers installed monitoring equipment in a six-building sample of two-story wooden buildings at Fort Devens, Massachusetts. Data obtained during both single-setting and night-setback operating modes were used to develop models of each building's heat consumption as a function of the difference between inside and outside temperature. These models were used to estimate seasonal savings that could be obtained from the use of night-setback thermostat control.

The measured savings in heating energy from using night temperature setback for the six Fort Devens buildings ranged from 14% to 25%; the mean savings was 19.2%. Based on an energy cost of $0.65/therm of natural gas, the estimated average cost savings of using automatic setback thermostats in these buildings is $780 per year per building.

## INTRODUCTION

During March 1990, the Fort Devens Directorate of Logistics (DOL) conducted a test to counter the popular misconception about nighttime temperature setback during the heating season--that the energy saved by lowering the temperature at night is lost when the building temperature is brought back up to comfortable levels during the day. To disprove this, two similar World War II-style two-story wooden administrative buildings, 4,720 ft$^2$ each, were selected for a short-term test. Recorders that measured run-time were wired into the forced-air heating system fan circuits at each building. The fan run-time measurements were used to estimate gas combustor on-time. The control building (Building 2203) was maintained at 70°F, regardless of occupancy (single-setting). In the test building (Building 2204), the occupants manually controlled the thermostat to 70°F during occupied hours and to 55°F while unoccupied (night-setback). Both buildings were occupied 10 hours daily during a 24-hour test period. The recorded fan run-times for the control and the test buildings were 9 hours and 3.5 hours, respectively, indicating a potential 60% energy savings from use of nighttime temperature setback.

However, this result was questioned because of 1) uncertainties about similarities of building envelope and heating systems of the two apparently identical buildings; 2) possible differences between the fan and the combustor operating times; 3) relatively mild outside air temperatures during the 24-hour test period; 4) problems associated with extrapolation of the single 24-hour test results to seasonal performance; and 5) application of the night temperature setback. Fort Devens personnel requested an independent, detailed energy analysis to verify the annual energy savings and provide the incentive necessary to continue installation of night-setback thermostats in all similar buildings throughout Fort Devens. In response, Pacific Northwest Laboratory (PNL) conducted a field test at the Fort during the 1991-1992 winter to measure the energy savings resulting from the installation of automatic night-setback thermostats.

An overview of that field test is presented in this paper. The buildings selected for the test are described first, followed by documentation of the test procedure. Next, the various analyses performed on the collected data are discussed, along with the results. Observations and conclusions drawn from the results are offered in the final sections.

## BUILDING DESCRIPTION

Six "identical" two-story wooden structures, all currently used for administrative functions, were selected for this test. Each building has approximately 4,800 ft$^2$, and all were built circa 1941. This type of construction is typical of approximately 200 buildings at Fort Devens and of many more throughout U.S. military installations.

Based on the condition of their envelopes, the six buildings were grouped into three classes as follows:

- Class I: Buildings 1628 and 1629 are the most recently renovated and are believed to be the most energy-efficient.

- Class II: Buildings 1620 and 1622 were apparently renovated 10 or more years ago, and appear to be moderately energy-efficient.

[1] The U.S. Army Forces Command (FORSCOM) has tasked Pacific Northwest Laboratory (PNL), as the lead laboratory supporting the U.S. Department of Energy Federal Energy Management Program (DOE-FEMP) mission, to provide technical assistance to characterize and modernize energy systems at FORSCOM installations. The Pacific Northwest Laboratory is operated by Battelle Memorial Institute for the U.S. Department of Energy under Contract DE-AC06-76RLO 1830.

The goal of the DOE-FEMP is to facilitate energy efficiency improvements at federal facilities. This is accomplished by a balanced program of technology development, energy efficiency resource and energy supply assessment, and facility modernization. For efficiency resource and energy supply assessment, FEMP provides metering equipment and trained analysts to federal agencies exhibiting a commitment to understand and improve energy use efficiency and reduce energy costs.

Class III: Buildings 2285 and 2286 appear to be in much the same condition as when they were built--basically uninsulated wooden shells. They were expected to have the worst energy performance.

The mean occupancy in each varies widely, from 5 to 25 people, depending on the specific building and ongoing activities.

All six buildings are heated with gas-fired, forced-air furnaces. The furnace combustors are of similar types and heat ratings. The building temperatures are controlled by two thermostats. The main thermostat, which controls the furnace and was replaced with an automatic setback thermostat for this study, is located on the first floor. A second thermostat, located on the second floor, controls a damper that regulates the airflow rate into the second story. Without this two-zone control, the second story often becomes overheated on relatively warm, sunny days.

Identical automatic night-setback thermostats were installed in five of the buildings. The thermostat selected was designed to directly replace a conventional thermostat wired in a 24-volt control system. The electro-mechanical thermostat's features included a battery-powered solid-state clock, capability for multiple setback/setup time setpoints, two temperature setpoints (occupied/day and unoccupied/night periods), a temporary setback override for unexpected occupancy, and a very simple programming process. This thermostat does not have the capability of separate weekday/weekend setback settings.

More sophisticated microprocessor-controlled thermostats are commercially available. Additional features that should increase energy savings include more time and temperature setpoints, separate weekday/weekend schedules, and optimized start capability for automatic adjustment of setup time. The Fort Devens Directorate of Engineering and Housing (DEH) staff's informal evaluation of such thermostats indicated that their programming was too complicated and they were therefore not appropriate for general installations.

The 120-volt control system in the sixth building, Building 1628, was not compatible with the 24-volt design limit of the thermostats. The occupants in this building were asked to manually adjust the thermostat temperature settings during the field test.

### TEST PROCEDURE

The six buildings were monitored during the period extending from 28 November 1991 to 31 March 1992. Field Data Acquisition System (FDAS) data loggers were then installed in each building. The FDAS is a stand-alone microprocessor-controlled data logger, developed at PNL, that is capable of processing electric power and analog and digital signals. The FDAS recorded a time series record (TSR) every integration period, which was selected as 1 hour for this test. Electric power and analog channel TSRs were based on a 2-second scan rate that is averaged for the integration period. The digital channel TSRs were an accumulated count of all pulses during the integration period. The TSRs recorded by the FDAS loggers were automatically downloaded to a computer at PNL via telephone modem on a daily basis.

The FDAS loggers recorded the following data channels for each building:

· gas valve (furnace) on-time, fraction of hour

· gas valve (furnace) on-cycles (number of times on), count per hour

· first floor inside air temperature, °F

· second floor inside air temperature, °F

· total (A + B phase) electric power, watts.

In addition, a pulse initiator was installed on an existing positive displacement gas meter on Building 1629 (originally installed for a previous test) to allow direct measurement of that building's gas consumption. The gas meter measurement resolution was 5 ft$^3$ of gas per pulse. No gas meters were available on the other five test buildings. These gas consumption measurements were used in the analysis to estimate the firing rate of the combustors in the furnaces of all six buildings.

Meteorological data were collected at Buildings 1629 and 2285. The data channels consisted of outside air temperature (°F) and direct horizontal solar insolation (W/m$^2$).

The number of times the gas valve turned on (on-cycles) and the amount of valve on-time were monitored to track gas consumption in the buildings without gas meters. Electric power data served as a proxy for building occupancy and as a measure of internal gains.

Although guidance was given to the building occupants regarding setback/setup time and temperature setpoints, specific setpoints were not mandated. Many occupants had expressed concern that a large night setback would leave the building uncomfortably cold for an extended period in the morning because the furnace would not have enough capacity to recover. And previous projects have shown that occupant comfort is critical to acceptance and continued long-term use of night setback. Therefore, each building's occupants were asked to use setback/setup setpoints with which they were comfortable, instead of the traditional 68°F occupied and 50°F unoccupied recommendations. All features, including both setback/setup times and temperature setpoints, were readily accessible to the building occupants at all times.

The thermostats were modified with electrical relays and telephone modem-based controllers that allowed the researchers to remotely select the single-setting or night-setback mode. The test design called for switching between single-setting or night-setback modes on a weekly basis throughout the heating season, without building occupant knowledge or participation. However, problems with the remote controllers required the occupants to actively participate in selecting or disabling night-setback operation during most of the test.

Temperature sensors were placed within 6 inches of each thermostat. Plots of inside temperatures were checked weekly to help ensure that building occupants were complying with the thermostat control mode. Figure 1 illustrates typical 24-hour temperature profiles for Building 1629 during both single-setting and night-setback modes.

### ANALYSIS RESULTS

Four analyses were conducted on the data collected during the field test.

#### Gas Combustor Heat Rate Estimate

The first task in the analysis was to estimate the rate of gas consumption for the furnace combustors.

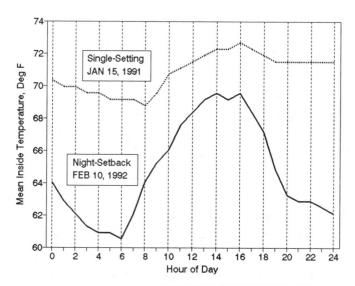

FIGURE 1. TYPICAL HOURLY INSIDE TEMPERATURES FOR BUILDING 1629 IN SINGLE-SETTING AND NIGHT-SETBACK MODES

Gas consumption, based on the gas flow meter readings, was plotted against the furnace gas valve on-time for Building 1629, as shown in Figure 2. The resulting highly correlated linear relationship implies that the combustion rate for Building 1629 was constant over the monitoring period.

Given the measured gas consumption ($V_{gas}$, ft$^3$) and gas valve on-time ($t_{on}$, hour), which were recorded as hourly integration period TSRs, and the average heat content of the gas ($H_{gas}$, 1030 Btu/ft$^3$), a fixed valued based on utility bills, the combustor heat rate ($Q_{comb}$, Btu/hr) was calculated using

$$Q_{comb} = \frac{V_{gas} \times H_{gas}}{t_{on}} \qquad (1)$$

A total of 2,944 TSRs were used to calculate hourly combustor heat rates. TSRs with no gas combustion were excluded from this calculation. All the hourly gas combustor heat rates were then averaged for the

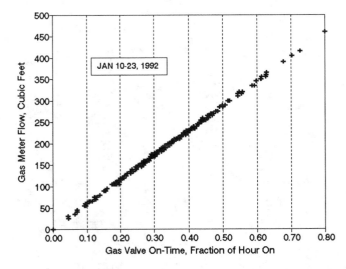

FIGURE 2. CORRELATION OF GAS VALVE ON-TIME AND GAS CONSUMPTION

complete test period. The mean gas combustor heat rate and associated standard deviation are listed in Table 1.

TABLE 1. GAS COMBUSTOR HEAT RATE ESTIMATE STATISTICS

| Mean | 619,398 Btu/hr |
|---|---|
| Standard Deviation | 14,128 Btu/hr |

## Heat Consumption Calculation

The heat consumption calculation for Building 1629 was based on the gas volume measured by the installed gas flow meter. The hourly heat consumption for the building ($Q_{bldg}$, Btu/hr) is simply

$$Q_{bldg} = V_{gas} \times H_{gas} \qquad (2)$$

For the remaining five buildings, which had no gas flow meters, the heat consumption was calculated using the mean combustion rate for Building 1629, as shown in Table 1, and the furnace on-time for each specific building:

$$Q_{bldg} = 619,398 \; Btu/hr \times t_{on} \qquad (3)$$

This is a reasonable assumption because the combustors in all six buildings were rated at similar heat rates and operated under similar conditions. Errors in absolute heat consumption do not affect each building's percent energy savings calculation, which are based on monitoring of each building during both single-setting and night-setback modes. Each building was used as its own control.

## Regression Analysis

The hourly values for heat consumption, electric power, direct solar horizontal insolation, inside temperature, and outside temperature were aggregated to create daily means for each measured variable. Scatter plots were then made of the daily mean heat consumption against each of the other measured quantities, as well as against the difference between the mean inside and mean outside temperatures (inside-outside ΔT). There was a significant difference between weekday and weekend heat consumption, and the inside-outside ΔT variable was the one most highly correlated to heat consumption. These scatter plots were indicative of "typical" small- to medium-size, light- to medium-construction office buildings.

The daily mean data were then grouped according to day type (weekday and weekend/holiday). A least-squares linear regression against inside-outside ΔT was then calculated for each group. The regression model used was

$$Q_{bldg} = a \; + \; b \times \Delta T_{inside-outside} \qquad (4)$$

where **a**, the intercept, is the heat consumption for equal inside and outside temperatures (inside-outside ΔT equals zero), and **b**, the slope, is the change in heat consumption for a 1-degree change in the inside-outside ΔT. The regression results for each building, including the R-squared statistic and the number of days available for each regression, are summarized in Table 2.

501

TABLE 2. REGRESSION ANALYSIS RESULTS

| Bldg | Day Type | a Btu/hr | b (Btu/hr)/°F | R-squared | Number of Days |
|------|----------|----------|---------------|-----------|----------------|
| 1620 | Weekday | -44826 | 4645 | 0.852 | 77 |
| | Weekend | -9550 | 4024 | 0.831 | 36 |
| 1622 | Weekday | -34804 | 3516 | 0.659 | 58 |
| | Weekend | -11520 | 3258 | 0.617 | 30 |
| 1628 | Weekday | -19569 | 2100 | 0.729 | 80 |
| | Weekend | -27826 | 2804 | 0.878 | 32 |
| 1629 | Weekday | -61508 | 5696 | 0.892 | 86 |
| | Weekend | -30668 | 5388 | 0.914 | 35 |
| 2285 | Weekday | -22368 | 7030 | 0.646 | 74 |
| | Weekend | -50183 | 8264 | 0.800 | 34 |
| 2286 | Weekday | -74892 | 7694 | 0.862 | 77 |
| | Weekend | -66799 | 7648 | 0.913 | 34 |

Because the slope (b) is a function of the energy efficiency of the building envelope and heating system, the slope should be similar for both weekday and weekend day types. The mean difference was 11%. Most of the difference can be explained by building envelope variations resulting from the frequency of door and window openings and application of window coverings.

The intercept (a) divided by the slope (b) represents the reduction in outside air temperature, as compared to the inside air temperature, before heating system operation is required. This outside air temperature is commonly called the balance point. Increased internal heat generation from equipment and people ("free" heat) during occupancy will result in a decreased balance point. As expected, the mean balance points measured were 8.8°F and 6.0°F below the inside air temperature for weekday and weekend periods, respectively.

Energy Savings Calculations

The daily mean data, already divided into weekday and weekend groups, were further subdivided by thermostat operation mode (i.e., single-setting or night-setback). The mean inside-outside ΔT, over the monitoring period, was calculated for each of the four groups. These inside-outside ΔTs were then used in regression Equation 4 to estimate mean hourly weekday and weekend heat consumption for single-setting and night-setback thermostat operation.

Heating energy savings are a direct result of a lower mean inside operating temperature due to nighttime temperature setback. The difference between the mean single-setting inside-outside ΔT and the mean night-setback inside-outside ΔT (setback ΔT) is used to calculate the heating energy consumption savings, based on the Equation 4 regression. Figure 3 illustrates this process for Building 1629.

The heating season weather conditions experienced during this test were representative of a typical winter at Fort Devens. The mean outside air temperature measured during the heating season (November 1991 through March 1992) at Fort Devens was 31.8°F, compared to 35.4°F for Typical Meteorological Year (TMY) data for Boston, Massachusetts (the nearest city with available data). However, Fort Devens is

located inland from Boston and has slightly cooler heating season temperatures.

Estimates of the seasonal consumption for single-setting and night-setback thermostat operation were then calculated. For each operational mode, the mean hourly consumption for the weekdays was multiplied by the number of weekdays in the season and 24 hours in the day. Similar calculations were performed for weekend conditions. The weekday and weekend consumptions were summed to obtain the estimate of seasonal consumption. Those estimates are summarized on the bar chart in Figure 4.

Also shown in Figure 4 are the percent savings associated with setback operation, and the mean, occupied and unoccupied inside air temperatures for each building. Most of the high inside temperatures were measured in the least energy-efficient buildings (Buildings 2285 and 2286). These temperatures probably reflect occupants' efforts to compensate for uncomfortable draft and cold wall conditions.

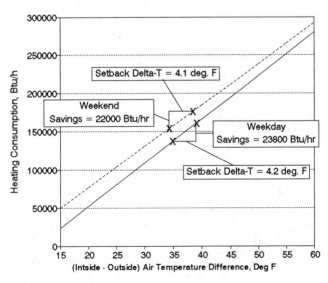

FIGURE 3. USE OF THE REGRESSION MODEL TO CALCULATE MEAN HOURLY SAVINGS FOR WEEKDAYS AND WEEKEND/HOLIDAYS

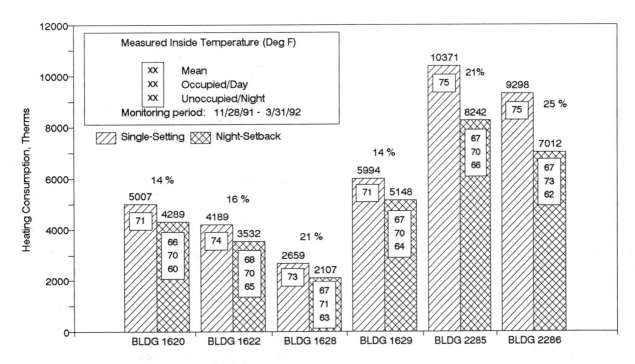

FIGURE 4. SEASONAL HEATING CONSUMPTION ESTIMATES IN BOTH SINGLE-SETTING AND NIGHT-SETBACK MODES

Finally, the seasonal consumption estimates were normalized to the same mean inside temperatures for each building (72°F for the single-setting mode, 66°F for the setback mode). The results of those calculations are shown in Figure 5. This calculation removes the occupant effect with regard to variations in temperature setpoints.

DISCUSSION

The measured energy savings resulting from using night temperature setback thermostats for the six Fort

Devens buildings ranged from 14% to 25%; the mean savings was 19.2%. The mean seasonal energy consumption was 6,255 therm/year for single-setting and 5,055 therm/year for night-setback. However, there is a 3.9-to-1 range of seasonal energy consumption, from 2,659 therm/year for the best building to 10,371 therm/year for the worst building. Even considering the mean of Class I and II, which included those recently renovated and those renovated 10 or more years ago, and Class III, those with virtually no insulation, there is a 2.2-to-1 range of seasonal energy consumption, from 4,462 therm/year for

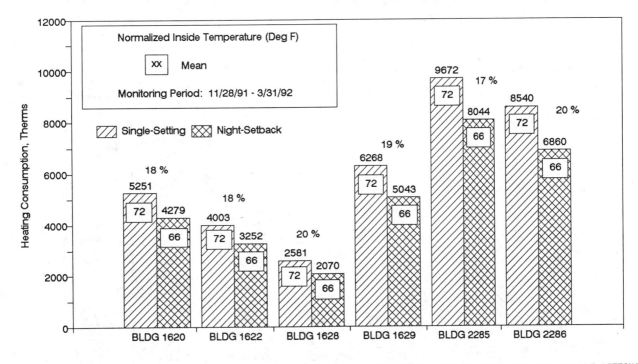

FIGURE 5. SEASONAL HEATING CONSUMPTION ESTIMATES, NORMALIZED TO 72°F MEAN INSIDE TEMPERATURE (FOR SINGLE-SETTING MODE) AND 66°F MEAN INSIDE TEMPERATURE (FOR NIGHT-SETBACK MODE)

the better buildings to 9,835 therm/year for the worst buildings.

The difference between the two buildings within each building envelope class was 20% for Class I, 125% for Class II, and 11% for Class III. This means that for a night-setback test that selected two "identical" buildings--one as a control and the second as a test-- the potential energy savings associated with the test building ranges from 11% to 125%, even if night setback were not implemented. That was probably the main reason for the high 60% energy savings measured by DOL in the March 1990 Fort Devens nighttime-setback test. This problem was avoided in the PNL test by using the same building for both control (single-setting) and test (night-setback) modes.

The inside air temperature data indicated that the temperature setpoints of the thermostats were frequently changed by the occupants during the test period. Because the purpose of this test was to measure "realistic" energy savings, the occupants were not discouraged from setpoint modifications, as long as there was some temperature setback during the night-setback cycles of the test.

During the single-setting periods, the mean inside air temperature was 73°F. During periods with night-setback, the mean inside air temperatures were 71°F during daytime and 64°F during nighttime--a mean setback of 7.3°F. The daytime temperature decreased during night-setback periods, from 73°F to 71°F, even with identical daytime thermostat temperature settings. This is a result of an early morning warmup period, which included most of the day in some buildings during cold days because the furnace did not have the capacity to quickly recover from night setback.

Building 1628 was one of the best in terms of energy efficiency, which typically results in a lower energy savings percentage. But its energy savings percentage was as high as that of Building 2285, one of the worst. Unlike the remaining buildings, the manually

operated temperature setback in Building 1628 (an automatic setback thermostat could not be installed) remained set back all weekend. In the buildings with automatic setback thermostats, the setpoint was automatically set up during the day on weekends, even though the buildings were unoccupied. This finding suggests that additional savings (7% in this case) could be realized by installing thermostats "smarter" than those used in this test.

Based on a cost of $0.65/therm of natural gas, the estimated average savings in energy costs is $780 per year per building. The annual energy costs for single-setting and night-setback modes and the annual energy cost savings for each of the six buildings are shown in Figure 6. The mean energy cost savings from use of heating season night setback ranged from a high of $1485/year for the worst building to $359/year for the best building. The mean of the Class III buildings was $1435/year, compared to the four better buildings, Class I and II, at $450/year--a 2.2-to-1 range.

## CONCLUSIONS

The energy savings measured in this study are "real," repeatable in other similar buildings, and will have long-term persistence. The reason is that the setback/setup time and temperature setpoints were selected by the building occupants based on their respective building's heating system characteristics and their personal comfort range. Many other projects have demonstrated that mandated time and temperature setpoints, which do not allow for individual variations in occupancy patterns, heating system recovery rates, local temperature variations, and variations in peoples' comfort range, will eventually be disregarded--resulting in less-than-predicted energy savings.

The measured energy savings resulting from use of heating season nighttime temperature setback in six two-story wooden office buildings at Fort Devens was 19.2%. The associated average energy cost savings is

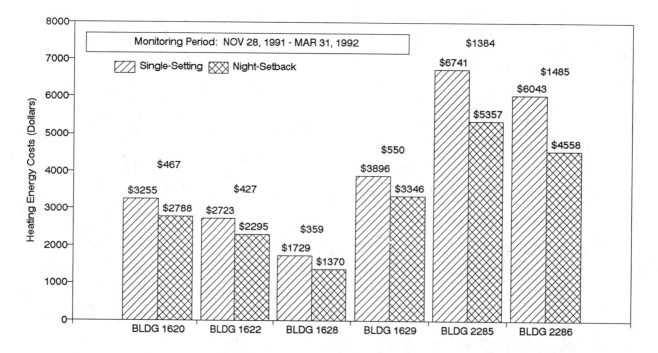

FIGURE 6. SEASONAL HEATING COST ESTIMATES IN BOTH SINGLE-SETTING AND NIGHT-SETBACK MODES

$780 per year per building. The simple payback time is less than one month of the heating season, based on a $100 cost for purchase and installation of a simple automatic setback thermostat.

Although the $450/year energy cost savings associated with the four better buildings is economically attractive, the $1435/year energy cost savings associated with the worst buildings indicates that a priority should be set for installation of automatic setback thermostats in the worst buildings first.

Purchase and installation of night-setback thermostats is cost-effective for all similar office buildings that are going to be occupied for more than one month of the next heating season. For a $20,000 investment, application of night setback to the 200 similar buildings at Fort Devens will yield cost savings of approximately $150,000 per year for natural gas. Because the heat loss mechanisms are common to most small-to-medium office buildings, similar energy savings can also be expected for a much wider range of buildings.

ACKNOWLEDGMENTS

The authors would like to thank Bobby Orr and his staff at the Fort Devens Directorate of Engineering and Housing for their support in installing the automatic setback thermostats. Appreciation is extended to PNL staff whose efforts supported the study: John Schmelzer for monitoring equipment preparation and installation, Su Thelen for remote data collection, and Andrea Wood for data analysis. Thanks go also to Shannon McDaniel, Shannon Electric, for installation of monitoring equipment.

# Chapter 88
# Energy Service Contracting in DOD

D.E. Dahle

## INTRODUCTION

The U.S. Department of Defense (DOD) annually consumes about $3 Billion in energy to operate facilities at military installations worldwide, representing about 80% of utility operating expense for all Federal facilities. Recent legislation and a Presidential Executive Order have directed DOD by Fiscal Year 2000 to reduce facility energy consumption by 20%, from the level of energy used in Fiscal Year 1985. To achieve this goal it is estimated that energy efficiency improvement investments between $2-3 billion would be required. Considering the competition for resources within DOD as it experiences downsizing and restructuring, DOD will need to seek opportunities to tap alternative investment strategies through energy service contracting to leverage Federal resources. Shared Energy Savings and Operations and Maintenance Energy Services contracting activities in the Department of the Navy will be used to address how such acquisition methods can contribute to achieving DOD energy efficiency goals.

The Navy (including Marine Corps) operates and maintains a worldwide inventory of energy-consuming buildings in excess of 550 million square feet. In Fiscal Year 1991, the Navy spent over $850 million for purchased utilities and fuels, 70% of which was for electricity. The Navy's shore establishment is an infrastructure, where the average age of buildings is over 40 years. Like most public works functions in times of budget austerity, facility energy efficiency improvements compete with other operational and maintenance requirements for capital investment resources. Additionally, building systems preventative maintenance is commonly deferred which further degrades building energy efficiency.

## TRADITIONAL ENERGY PROJECT IMPLEMENTATION

To set the stage for discussing innovative energy service contracts the Navy and DOD are pursuing, let's look at the traditional methods DOD uses to implement facility energy efficiency improvements. DOD energy projects are implemented by three basic methods, dependent on the level of Government funding used.

Each military installation can use available operating and maintenance (O&M) funds to install energy conserving equipment, generally not exceeding $75,000. Energy projects costing $75-200,000 require "special project" O&M funding from higher echelon commands, where project documentation is prepared and submitted up the chain of command for prioritization (i.e. payback period) and approval based on available funding. For projects exceeding $200,000, Military Construction (MILCON) funds must be appropriated by Congress. MILCON project documents are prepared and submitted through higher commands for prioritization and forwarding to Congress in DOD annual budget requests, usually a 3-5 year process.

Once funded, all these projects are typically implemented by contracting for Architect or Engineer services to prepare design specifications. Then the construction portion of the project is acquired through construction bidding based on least cost. Maintenance of installed energy efficiency improvements and associated energy savings potential is provided by the military installation's staff or by maintenance service contract.

## SHARED ENERGY SAVINGS CONTRACTING AUTHORITY

In April 1986, Congress passed a law which provided Federal agencies the authority to enter into long term (up to 25 year) contracts for Shared Energy Savings (SES) services. The SES law, codified as 42 USC 8287, allows Federal acquisition of facility energy efficiency improvements financed by private capital, where contractor return on investment is recouped through a share of savings directly resulting from contractor's energy savings measures. This authority requires that the resulting contract include a method for establishing the baseline energy use and cost, from which to measure the energy savings achieved. Payments for energy services are paid out of annually appropriated utility budget cost avoidance.

SES contracts can be viewed as "privatization of building energy management" offering the advantages of performance-based, turnkey energy project implementation. SES contracts utilize the energy service company's (ESCO) innovation, financing and profit motivation to sustain reduced energy consumption and cost throughout the contract term. A key benefit is the long-term commitment of preventative and corrective maintenance and Government personnel operations training which is integral to SES contracts.

## DEVELOPING NAVY SES CONTRACTING POLICY

Acquisition of SES services by Navy, like all Federal procurements is governed by the Federal Acquisition Regulations (FAR) and related DOD and Navy specific requirements. Despite the fact that there is latitude in FAR interpretation, it is clear that the FAR was not designed to easily accommodate SES, since it is a hybrid containing elements of design, construction, service and multi-year contracts. Development of SES contracting policy, required a team of engineering, contracts, and legal counsel personnel. This team was challenged to create and implement procurement guidelines that recognize the risk sharing and partnership needs of privately financed energy projects, while complying with existing FAR policy and procurement related statutes.

SES contracts are unique, innovative and personnel resource intensive, as each acquisition presents unforseen (real and perceived) risks to be addressed and establishes program precedents for its successors. As in any organization, new programs that demand a high learning curve to fully understand the technical, financial and contracting issues are met with resistance. Only experience and SES contract successes will remove the barriers to full scale implementation. A key and continuing role for SES policy development personnel will be to seek out legislative relief of statutory and procurement policy requirements which continue to burden the ESCO industry with unacceptable financial risk.

## ESTABLISHING ENERGY BASELINES

SES contracts must include a method to measure the savings achieved from contractor installed energy measures. Establishing an energy baseline represent the most critical and technically challenging requirement for SES contracts, as it becomes the basis for contractor payment throughout the multi-year term. Few Navy or DOD installations, which often comprise hundreds of buildings, have metering beyond the "fence" (utility service point) to establish historical energy consumption for facility energy baselines.

Initial pilot project sites were selected where building electric and gas meters existed, but such sites are small in number. Thus the ability to establish energy baselines for large scale projects is at best difficult. There are two basic approaches to establishing energy baselines for SES projects. The Government can develop a baseline which is a contract requirement and used to determine payments for all prospective contractors. Or, the contract solicitation can seek a contractor-proposed baseline and savings measurement method, tailored to the proposed technologies to be installed, for government review and approval prior to contract award.

### Government Established Baseline

For the Navy's first two pilot projects, which had metered facilities, Government engineers collected years of data on energy consumption, weather, building occupancy, and any other factor considered to significantly impact building energy use. From this data, statistical multiple linear regression models were developed to predict future energy consumption, as if contractor measures had not been installed. Payments would be based on comparing actual monthly metered consumption with monthly model predictions. Models proved to be reasonably accurate on an annual basis ($\pm$ 2%), however on a monthly basis wide variations of $\pm$ 20% or more were common, when model predictions were compared to actual consumption prior to implementing SES project. Government established baselines were expensive to develop and increased financial risk to the contractor, however they offered the advantage of simplifying Government proposal evaluation due to a common baseline approach.

### Contractor Proposed Baseline Method

By allowing the contractor to propose the method by which the baseline and significant adjustment factors will be developed, the approach can be linked to the energy savings measures being proposed. For example, if the project scope is limited to lighting systems, engineering estimates may be considered adequate, if operating hours can be mutually agreed to. However, for energy savings measures involving HVAC modifications or use of energy management and control systems, building and large system submetering before equipment installation is more appropriate. Based on the availability of low cost instrumentation devices on the market today, the submetering requirements envisioned to establish building and system load profiles, energy baselines, and dominant variables which affect consumption is achievable. The Government will have to evaluate the reasonableness, reliability, and accuracy of the contractor's proposed baseline and energy savings measurement methods. Government proposal evaluation is more difficult, however it is a risk sharing approach which reduces the contractor's financial risk and increases interest in large scale (installation-wide) SES contracts.

## THE PERFORMANCE-BASED SES SOLICITATION

Team building is the key element in this phase of the SES project. Participants must include representatives from project site (facility management/maintenance staff, management, budget/accounting, contracts, counsel), servicing utility company, contracting activity acquisition team, and agency SES program managers. A successful project is dependent upon the Government's ability to reach a consensus on acquisition approach and objectives, contract requirements, and commitment of resources (mostly personnel) to proceed with the SES procurement.

The Navy has developed a generic SES solicitation, which can be modified using site specific data and requirements. The following provides a summary of key elements in the Navy's standardized approach to acquiring performance-based SES services.

- Contract Scope
  - Types of Energy (electric, gas, oil, steam)
  - Facilities to be Included
    Selected Buildings
    Utility Systems
    Basewide
  - Types of Energy Measures
    Lighting Only
    Any Measure
    O&M Improvements

- General Requirements
  - Government Mission Definition
  - Minimum Annual Energy Savings
  - Standards of Service
    Space Temperature/Humidity Ranges
      Occupied
      Unoccupied
    Ventilation Minimums
    Light Level Minimums
    Hours of Operation (typical)
    Special/Mission Critical Operations
  - Restrictions on Allowable Measures
    Mission Critical Functions
    Significant Environmental Impacts
    Cogeneration Output > Federal Use

- Audits & Baseline Requirements (After Contract Award)
  - Approval of Audit Report Documenting Existing Conditions before Construction
  - Approval of Final Baseline and Measurement Methods

- Design Requirements
  - Meet State and Local Codes
  - Meet Manufacturer or Engineering Standards
  - Review of Design and Plans for:
    Life Safety Compliance
    Fire Regulations Compliance
    Interfaces to Government Equipment

- Construction Requirements
  - Minimize Mission Impacts
  - Approval of Construction Schedules
  - Siting Approval for New Facilities
  - Allowable Utility Outages
  - Safety & Quality Control

- Service Requirements
  - Govt Acceptance of Installed Measures
  - Maintenance of Installed Measures
  - Government Personnel Training
  - Service Response Capability

- Other Compliances
  - Environmental Regulations (Fed, State, Local)
  - OSHA Regulations
  - Base Regulations
  - Labor Laws (DOL Wages)

- Deliverables
  - Insurance/Bonding/Financing Commitment
  - Detailed Facility Audit & Baseline After Award
  - Design/Construction Plans
  - Installed/Tested Energy Measures
  - Training/O&M Manuals/As-Builts
  - Annual Energy Savings for each Contract Year

- Proposal Requirements
  Technical
    Proposed Energy Measures
    Baseline & Measurement Approach
    Management Approach/Subcontracting
    O&M/Training Approach
    Financial Plan & Experience
  Price
    Proposed Contract Term
    Annual Energy Savings per Year
    Share of Cost Savings per Year

The Navy slects the contractor offering the "most advantageous proposal" to th Government, considering technical and price factors with equal weight.

SES PILOT PROGRAM RESULTS/LESSONS LEARNED

Naval Hospital, Long Beach, CA

Procurement Type: Two-step Sealed Bid

Solicited: 8/87

Awarded: 9/1/89

Scope: Open, 10 Year Term, 420,000 SF complex

Annual Purchased Utilities: $1.5M (80% electric, 20% gas)

Baseline Method: Government Established Statistical Model

Contractor Proposed Energy Projects:
(1) Lighting Retrofits in general use areas
(2) 2 MW Cogeneration system - gas fired IC engines
(3) 600 ton absorption chiller using cogen waste heat
(4) Energy Management System (EMS) controlling cogen/chiller system, existing boilers, electric chillers and emergency generator sets.

Annual Energy Savings Proposed: $ 1.1M/yr

Contract Requirements:
- 60% reduction in purchased utilities (mostly electric)
- Contractor payments to be 88% (avg.) share of cost savings
- Savings measured using statistical baseline model

Contractor Investment: $3M

10 Year Govt Share of Savings: - est. $1M

Contract Status: Contract terminated for default - 8/90

Lessons Learned:
· Compliance with National Environmental
  Policy Act
    - 1 Proposal with a environmentally
    controversial approach
    - Required Environmental Assessment
    before final offers
    - 1 year delay in project

· Selected contractor was joint venture
    - Created new company upon contract award
    - Required negotiation of novation
    agreement

· Financing commitment not secured by prime
  contractor immediately after award
    - Interest rates increased sharply during
    post award negotiations
    - Contractor unable to secure financing
    within term
    - Bonding requirements increased
    financing cost/risk

· Continuity of field acquisition personnel
  essential
    - Government personnel turnover produced
    post-award negotiation delays

Building 3400, Naval Training Center, Great
Lakes, IL

Procurement Type: Negotiated Request for
Proposal (RFP)

1st Solicitation: 9/86

Canceled: 9/87

2nd Solicitation: 5/88

Awarded: 12/20/89

Scope: Open, 10 Year Term, 240,000 SF Building

Annual Purchased Utilities: $900K (50%
electric, 50% gas)

Baseline Method: Contractor Proposed,
Government Approved

Contractor Proposed Energy Projects:
(1) Lighting Retrofits throughout building
(2) Building wide EMS controlling forced air
    HVAC system, which includes 2 10 MBTU/hr
    boilers, a 700 ton absorption chiller, 7
    supply and 3 return air handling systems.

Annual Energy Savings Proposed: $ 180K/yr

Contract Requirements:
    - 15% and 25% reduction in electric and
    natural gas respectively
    - Contractor payments (savings share) - 95%
    during first 7 years, 60% (avg.) in last 3
    years
    - Savings measured using baseline based on
    engineering estimates and fixed rate of
    energy intensity growth

Contractor Investment: $500K

10 Year Govt Share of Savings: - est. $500K

Contract Status:
    - Installation complete installation
    - Actual annual cost savings ~ $200K/yr

Lessons Learned:
· 1st Solicitation used Government baseline
  model
    - Unacceptable to proposers
    - Solicit canceled as baseline change
    deemed "out of scope"

· Natural Gas Procurement Awarded at Project
  Site
    - Awarded during negotiations
    - Reduced economic potential for
    boiler/chiller retrofits
    - Reduced potential Government share
    during contract term

· Use of non-domestic lighting products
    - Delays installation acceptance awaiting
    Buy American Act waiver

· Post award meeting on site establishes
  partnership early
    - Information exchange, coordination,
    agreements

Naval Air Station, Patuxent River, MD

Procurement Type: Negotiated RFP

Solicited: 5/89

Awarded: 4/13/90

Scope: Interior Lighting Systems, 10 Year
term, 52 buildings

Annual Purchased Utilities: Est. $300-350K
Electric (10% of base utility cost)

Baseline Method: Contractor Proposed,
Government Approved

Contractor Proposed Energy Projects:
(1) Lighting Retrofits in 50 Buildings
    17 different lighting measures - mostly
    fluorescent fixture retrofits

Annual Energy Savings: $ 72K/yr

Contract Requirements:
    - Electric consumption reduction of 1500
    MWH/yr
    - Electric peak demand reduction of .4
    MW/month
    - Contractor payments to be 95% share of
    cost savings
    - Savings measured using engineering
    estimates

Contractor Investment: $350K

10 Year Govt Share of Savings: - est. $35K

Contract Status:
    - Installation complete
    - Actual investment $550K
    - Actual annual energy savings > $150K

Lessons Learned:
· Marginal Project Economics for 10 year
  term ($.025/KWh, $7.50/KW peak)
    - Result is low Government share over
    term

· Requirement for lamp replacement during
  term unreasonable

510

- Negotiated lamp inventory maintained at site

· No provision to renegotiate share when audit revealed greater savings potential
    - Future contracts to allow renegotiation of share if audit reveals savings 10-15% greater than proposed

## DOD DIRECTED TO STREAMLINE SES CONTRACTING

In the late 1980's several trends emerged, resulting in legislation to stimulate improved SES procurement practices, which were:
    · Congressional dissatisfaction with the low utilization of Federal SES contracting authority
    · Development and growth of unique Demand Side Management (DSM) programs within Electric Utility Industry
    · Maturing of ESCO industry and greater use of lease financing for performance based SES contracts after '86 Tax Reform

In November 1990, energy legislation (10 USC 2865) was enacted directing DOD to streamline SES contracting procedures. Authority cited 2 specific procurement approaches to be developed: (1) Use A Request for Qualifications (RFQ) procedure to establish a pre-qualified list of ESCOs on annual basis, from which 3 firms could be selected to submit proposals for SES contract negotiation and award; and (2) directly negotiate (limit competition) with ESCOs competitively selected and approved for gas or electric utility Demand Side Management (DSM) contracts. Additionally, Executive Order 12759, signed by the President in April 1991, reiterated the need for removal of procurement impediments to increase SES contracting and participation in Utility DSM programs.

### RFQ for SES Qualified Contractor List

The Navy developed proposed contracting procedures for establishing pre-qualified list of ESCOS and recommended all DOD services participate to develop a DOD-wide list. This procedure has not been implemented as of June 92, but execution is planned for late 1992.

### SES With Utility DSM Contractors

The Navy has solicited proposals for a SES contract at the Naval Surface Warfare Center, Indian Head, MD, from four ESCOs competitively selected for DSM services by Potomac Electric Power. SES services are being sought for all facilities at Indian Head, except high security weapons production facilities. Recognizing the high proposal preparation cost for a basewide project, the Navy has developed a new procurement approach. 18 buildings were selected as representative of the nearly 100 buildings within the project scope. ESCOs are requested to prepare preliminary proposals to save a minimum of 600 MWH/yr, based only on the 18 selected buildings.

From these proposals, the ESCO whose technical approach and proposed price is most advantageous to the Government will be selected. Then, only the selected ESCO will be requested to prepare more detailed technical and price proposals, with a minimum annual energy savings requirement of 3000 MWH/yr (total base consumption is 35000 MWH/yr). The Government will negotiate with selected contractor to reach a "fair and reasonable" price for contract award. If an agreement cannot be reached, the Government will request the second best ESCO, based on preliminary proposals, to submit a detailed proposal for negotiation.

So far, this approach has demonstrated potential to reduce the time and financial risk of Federal SES contract proposal preparation and evaluation for large scale Navy projects. The Request for Proposal was issued in February 92 and contract award to the first selected firm by late Fall '92 is realistic. The Navy plans to seek approval to try this procurement approach at other proposed SES sites.

### Sole Source SES With Serving Utility

Another contracting approach being tried at Marine Corps Base Camp Pendleton, CA, is modeled after an Army procurement in Washington State at Fort Lewis, where basewide energy services were negotiated on a sole source basis with the local utility. In this case, the local utility offers complete project financing and applies Public Utility Commission approved DSM financial incentives to the reduce the capital cost (50-85%), which is recouped through Government payments from energy savings after measures are installed. As part of such a contract, the utility is required to competitively select ESCOs to perform the installation, monitoring and maintenance of energy savings measures.

### Potential of Streamlining SES Contracts

The new SES procurement approaches described above are expected to demonstrate improvements in the timeliness and cost effectiveness (higher Government savings share) of utilizing the ESCO and Utility industries. Additionally large scale (basewide) projects allow SES contracts to tap the vast energy savings potential at Navy and Marine installations.

## OPERATION AND MAINTENANCE ENERGY SERVICES (OMES) CONTRACTING

OMES contracts were conceived and developed to fulfill a need to improve the flexibility and cost effectiveness of implementing low cost retrofits and repairs to "tune up" energy and utility systems at Navy and Marine Corps installations. OMES combines, in one contract, the traditionally separate procurement of services to: (1) survey buildings for low cost energy conservation measures (ECMs); and (2) install Government selected ECMs to achieve energy and cost savings identified in surveys.

OMES are Indefinite Quantity, Deliver Order service contracts, where the Government specifies quantities and types of: (1) DOD buildings to be audited; (2) low-cost ECMs typically found and proven to reduce utilities expenses (i.e. steam traps, programmable thermostats, etc.);  and (3) negotiated labor and material required to implement ECMs not easily pre-specified and identified during audits (i.e repair or adjustment of HVAC system actuators and dampers).  OMES contracts provide a single, flexible contracting vehicle, for facility energy managers, to order and purchase building audits and ECM installations, as local or higher command energy project funding becomes available.

Contractor work is ordered in increments. The first delivery order will direct the contractor to perform $10-20,000 worth of building or steam trap surveys to be completed within a specified time period.  The results of audits and surveys are provided to the Government, identifying a prioritized list of repairs or retrofits with 2 year paybacks or less.  The Government then elects to place an order(s) for all, some or none of the pre-priced or negotiated projects generated by contractor.  The Government may also order additional audits/surveys after initial order to continuously generate potential ECMs. Should the contractor not perform in a fully satisfactory manner, the Government has the option to pay the contractor for work performed and terminate the remaining quantity of potential work, at no additional cost.

Although OMES is not a pure performance based contract like SES, a strong contractor motivation exists to satisfy the Government, in order to be eligible to receive additional delivery orders.  OMES contracting also provides the continuity and quick turnaround advantages of having a single contractor identify and implement potential ECMs.  The 2 year payback or less criteria for ECMs, pre-priced ECMs and incremental ordering of work, reduces the chance of overdesigning or "goldplating" survey results to maximize profits on the installation work.

The Navy has generated a generic OMES contract solicitation and a supplement for Federal users, providing guidance to adapt and modify the OMES for site specific requirements. Since no specific contracting authority (like SES) is applicable, an OMES contract can be acquired for one year plus four option years, as allowed by FAR for any service contract.

### OMES CONTRACTING RESULTS

#### Pilot OMES Projects

The Navy awarded 2 pilot, one year, OMES contracts in 1989 at Naval Construction Battalion Center, Port Hueneme, CA and at the Charleston, SC Naval complex.

·Audit/Survey Work Ordered:          $ 25K
·Energy Project Work Ordered:        $186K
·Estimated Annual Savings:           $218K
·Payback on Project Work Ordered:    0.85 Years
·Payback on Total Investment:        0.97 Years

#### 1990 OMES Projects

Based on the successful OMES pilot projects, 4 more OMES contracts were acquired in 1990:

(1) Naval Air Station, North Island, CA (small purchase < $25K)
(2) Regional Contract covering Navy bases in 11 Southeast states
(3) Regional Contract in Northwest covering Naval Air Station Whidbey Island, WA and Naval Supply Center, Puget Sound, WA
(4) Regional Contract covering Naval bases at Pearl Harbor, HI, Guam and Midway Islands

·Audit/Survey Work Ordered:          $214K
·Energy Project Work Ordered:        $225K
·Estimated Annual Savings:           $421K
·Payback on Project Work Ordered:    0.54 Years
·Payback on Total Investment:        1.04 Years

#### 1991/92 OMES Projects

In late 1991 and early 1992, 3 more OMES contracts were awarded:

(1) Regional Contract for Navy bases in Los Angeles County
(2) Regional Contract for Navy bases in Washington, DC and surrounding counties in Maryland
(3) Naval Air Engineering Center, Lakehurst, NJ

To date, each of the above three contracts have ordered initial audit/survey work at an average cost of $14K.  No project work has been ordered to identify payback on project work or total investment.  The Lakehurst, NJ contract has the potential for high payback on Navy investment, since the selected contractor is one of New Jersey Central Power & Light's (CP&L) utility DSM service contractors.  As a result, pre-priced project work at the Lakehurst site was provided at substantially lower price than competing contractors, due to the application of CP&L's financial incentive for contractor delivered energy savings from a CP&L customer.

### SUMMARY

SES and OMES energy service contracting programs have demonstrated that the Navy and DOD have acquisition tools available to reduce utility operating costs at DOD facilities.  As DOD budget cuts decrease installation operating and maintenance accounts, SES and OMES contracting programs offer a viable alternative to absorb budget and personnel reductions, sustain mission capability, and achieve energy efficiency goals.

# Chapter 89
# DOD Low Energy Model Installation Program

D.F. Fournier, Jr.

## INTRODUCTION

The Model Low Energy Installation Program is a demonstration of an installation-wide, comprehensive energy conservation program that meets the Department of Defense (DoD) energy management goals of reducing energy usage and costs by at least 20%. It employs the required strategies for meeting these goals, quantifies the environmental compliance benefits resulting from energy conservation and serves as a prototype for DoD wide application. This project will develop both analysis tools and implementation procedures as well as demonstrate the effectiveness of a comprehensive, coordinated energy conservation program based on state-of-the-art technologies.

A military installation is in reality a small to medium sized city. It generally has a complete utilities infrastructure including water supply and distribution, sewage collection and treatment, electrical supply and distribution, central heating and cooling plants with thermal distribution, and a natural gas distribution system. These utilities are quite extensive and actually consume about 10-15% of the energy on the facility not counting the energy going into the central plants.

This small city has many types of buildings. There are family housing units, both single and multi-family; lodging facilities; office complexes; medical facilities; community buildings such as theaters, restaurants, chapels, and physical fitness centers; and many light industrial operations.

Like any other city, the military installation has both permanent residents and a large commuting population. Since neither population pays for any energy used in the city, they are not necessary motivated to or interested in saving energy.

Analyzing the energy flow in this city can be a daunting task. Unlike the civilian sector, there are very few meters installed and the energy flow in the city is not well defined. This program will develop the tools and techniques that will enable the energy managers to determine where the energy is going and how it is being used. This will show what buildings need to be made more efficient and where to make the capital investments necessary to stop waste and increase efficiency. Additionally, these efficiency improvements should not adversely impact the residents of the city.

The model installation will showcase the technologies required to reduce energy consumption, provide a test-bed for new techniques and equipment, and serve as a base case for developing the analytical tools and methods. Collateral to this energy improvement would be an environmental benefit.

## BACKGROUND

These are changing times for the US military. While undergoing downsizing, base closures, and force restructuring, the DoD must also continue to develop new ways of doing business that are friendlier the environment. Providing a better place for our service men and women and their families to live and work is also an imperative. Historically, the military mission of an installation was the preeminent endeavor, and all resources were dedicated to support that mission. As shown in Figure 1, this tended to be a one-way street. In today's more environmentally aware atmosphere, a new way of doing business on military bases must continue to evolve. More emphasis must be placed on the social and environmental structures that support the military mission. Quality of life issues along with energy and environmental issues must have equal standing with mission issues. Two-way streets must link this triad since they are certainly inter-related and impact one another in both positive or negative ways. Our program seeks to develop ways to beef up the "green" corner of the triangle and make the linkage positive.

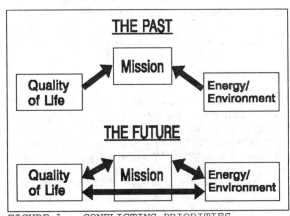

FIGURE 1.   CONFLICTING PRIORITIES

513

In the early 80's, the DoD vigorously pursued an energy management program designed to reduce its energy consumption and costs. Through this effort, overall facility energy consumption in 1985 was decreased by 20% compared to 1975, resulting in a cost savings of several billion dollars. Unfortunately, these savings were achieved through the application of "quick and easy" energy initiatives such as control settings and building envelope renovations. Currently, the Army pays about one billion dollars a year for its facility energy. From fiscal year 1985 to 1991, the Army's facility consumption dropped about 14%. This is good progress considering that facility square footage increased 6% during the same time-frame. Taking a closer look reveals that heating energy decreased 21%, but that electrical energy usage increased 11%. This electrical growth caused the total reduction to be less and has actually led to an increase in costs over the time period. While electrical consumption represents only 29% of the energy usage, it amounts to 53% of Army energy costs.

The estimated emissions from heating plants on Army facilities in the continental US and the estimated emissions from utility plants which provide electricity to our Army posts are shown in Figure 2. These estimates were generated using standard emission factors and national averages for utility plants. The overall trend is fairly constant. The emissions from Army plants are decreasing, but the emissions from utility-owned electrical generating plants are significant and growing, thus keeping the total about the same. In each case, the emissions from utility-owned plants due to Army electrical consumption were greater than those from Army-owned heating plants.

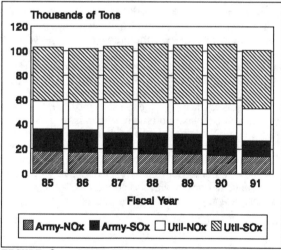

FIGURE 2. ARMY FACILITY $NO_x$ AND $SO_x$ EMISSIONS

The estimated carbon dioxide emissions from both Army plants and utility plants are shown in Figure 3. Note again that the $CO_2$ emissions from the utility plants are about the same as from Army-owned heating plants. The overall trend here is also fairly constant due to the electrical consumption growth. The utility portion is growing and compensates for the army plant reductions. Also note that $CO_2$ emissions are millions of tons versus thousands of tons for the other emissions shown in Figure 2.

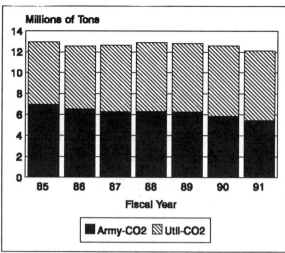

FIGURE 3. ARMY FACILITY $CO_2$ EMISSIONS

## ENERGY POLICY

In response to Presidential Executive Order 12579 on Federal Energy Management, Defense Energy Program Policy Memorandum (DEPPM) 91-2 was issued. This document incorporates new goals, indicates the recommended approaches to energy reduction, and provides an incentive to installations. The new goals require a 20% reduction in Btu/Sq Ft by the year 2000 based on 1985 usage. The implementation strategy is fairly comprehensive and requires a multi-faceted approach.

The DoD will strive to improve operation and maintenance activities that have an impact on energy consumption. There is also a new Energy Conservation Investment Program to implement a $50 million/year capital investment strategy. In reality, $50 million per year will not be sufficient. The typical investment required to achieve energy efficiency is between one and two years' energy bill, and for the Army alone this is an investment of $1 to $2 billion. Since the requisite investment capital is not available within the DoD, it is apparent that we must seek external sources of capital investment. Thus, we intend to take advantage of Demand Side Management (DSM) Programs from public utilities, shared energy savings

opportunities, and third party energy supply initiatives. Naturally, as part of any plan to improve energy efficiency, fuel switching to cleaner and lower cost sources, along with renewables, will be occurring.

The last element of the program is rewarding the installations that make the effort to save energy. Title 10 US Code, Section 2865, allows retention of two thirds of the energy cost savings through the next fiscal year. One half is to be used for moral, welfare, and recreation, or other quality of life improvements. The other half is to be used for additional energy saving investments.

Finally, emphasis must be placed on actions which achieve environmental compliance through conservation as a least cost approach.

There are significant, positive environmental benefits from meeting energy saving goals. Although the Army has already achieved significant emission reductions from its own facilities, this has been somewhat offset by the increase in emissions due to increased electrical consumption. Therefore, one goal is to stop and actually reverse the growth in electrical consumption. This has been the toughest area to achieve reductions. Also, there will continue to be fuel switching over the next decade which would result in even greater emission reductions from Army sources. The potential emission reductions that would result from a 10% drop in Army electrical consumption and a 15% drop in heating fuel usage using 1991 as the base year are as follows:

| | |
|---|---|
| Oxides of Nitrogen - | 5,000 tons |
| Oxides of Sulfur - | 6,000 tons |
| Particulates - | 2,000 tons |
| Carbon Dioxide - | 1,300,000 tons |

As the numbers indicate, there are significant positive environmental benefits from an effective energy management program.

## MODEL ENERGY INSTALLATION

The DoD has a comprehensive overall strategy package, but currently lacks the analysis tools and methodology to effectively implement it.

The objective of the Model Energy Installation Program is to demonstrate the actual implementation of the DoD energy policy. The program will take a representative installation and use all of the defined strategies to reduce energy usage and costs by 20%. Methods and tools to quantify the environmental benefits and to enable this process to be repeated at other installations throughout the Department of Defense will be developed.

The installation's energy production facilities will be evaluated and how best to meet the combined thermal and electrical loads will be determined. This may involve fuel switching and cogeneration schemes. Proven, "off the shelf" technologies that are available today that will not only save energy but will also reduce the operation and maintenance workload for the installation will be used. Implementation of these technologies should be either invisible to the building occupant or actually improve the physical comfort in the building.

It is also imperative to accomplish the demonstration using resources that are presently available to the engineering staff at the installation. An integrated team made up of agencies and organizations to which the engineer family already has access will demonstrate the effectiveness of using the appropriate talent to solve a problem. The installation engineering staff also needs capital for investment. The program will take advantage of existing investment programs, regional utility DSM programs, and other alternative financing schemes such as shared savings and third party initiatives.

The plan of attack for this research project is to take a methodical and deliberate path through the process of evaluating the energy flow on a military installation, determining the cost effective approaches to reducing it, and implementing those approaches.

The initial step is to determine where the energy is going by developing usage patterns and analysis tools that can be applied to the model installation and similar facilities. Generally, very little metering exists on these installations and basic analysis tools need to be developed that characterize energy usage in different types of typical military buildings. Surveys, audits and system evaluations will provide the necessary information from which to build models. These models will allow the user to assess the potential for savings, target the appropriate buildings and utility systems, and determine what modifications to make.

Integral to improving the physical operations on an installation is enhancement of energy awareness and educating the engineer work force. A survey of building occupants to determine general attitudes and how they perceive their work environment as it relates to its energy aspects will be taken. As much as possible occupant desires will be incorporated into any building modification projects.

Since capital resources are not readily available to implement energy projects, a methodology to insure that existing repair and maintenance projects along with any military construction projects incorporate appropriate energy efficient technology will be developed and implemented. We must instill the concept of "negawatts" into the design process and eliminate inefficient technology.

Assessing energy reduction progress on a large installation can be very difficult, especially if there is significant new construction, old building demolition, and troop restationing actions underway. Therefore, a method of predicting future energy consumption incorporating such factors as changes in square footage and population will be developed. This will allow an evaluation of the real progress in energy reduction.

Identification of energy conservation opportunities is the logical next step in the process. This will be accomplished by the standard approach of building and system audits and evaluations. This work will be broken into several thrust areas, such as central energy plants, building systems, and exterior utilities. Based on the results of these studies, a computerized method of coding and prioritizing the available energy conserving opportunities will be developed. In order to enable this to be one of the decision factors in determining implementation priority the environmental impact of each opportunity will also be part of the data package. Since military bases tend to have many similar buildings, retrofit templates for these standard types which would be applicable on most installations will also be developed. The key data required for decision factors will be identified and made easy to input for different installations.

Once the opportunities are identified, phased implementation plans which will define the capital resources required and provide recommendations on which funding source is appropriate and feasible. These implementation plans will show priorities and options which will enable the installation management to decide on how best to proceed.

Throughout the development process, the appropriate technical transfer documentation for the tools and methodologies will be created. This will include such things as metering strategies, energy pattern models, energy conservation opportunity templates, and the planning data base. An overall guidance document and an expert system are also planned.

Some of the typical technologies that will be implemented during the program are efficient lighting, super efficient motors, variable speed drives, high efficiency boilers and furnaces, ground coupled heat pumps, variable speed air conditioning, direct digital control of HVAC, load management, and microclimate techniques. As highlighted earlier, electrical energy reduction is to be a prime target area. Many of these technologies are specifically directed at reducing electrical consumption and demand. The other aspect to note is that these are all proven technologies that are currently available and will generate energy reductions that will persist.

## MILESTONES AND FUNDING

This to be a five year program. The first year's effort will be dedicated to developing the tools and strategy necessary to carry out the program. All the data for the selected installation will also be gathered in the first year. The remaining years involve the actual implementation of the program. This includes designing and constructing the projects, implementing DSM with utility, monitoring our progress, and analyzing the results. Some technical transfer will be accomplished in the first year, but most will be in the succeeding years as we develop knowledge based on implementation of the program.

The initial program funding is from the Strategic Environmental Research and Development Program. This amounts to $2.7 million and will cover the first year costs and the development of the tools and methodologies. For the implementation phases, the program will require about $22 million and will rely on the same funding types available to the local installation engineer staff. Maximum advantage will be taken of demand side management resources from the local utility and third party funding for energy plant renovation. A reinvestment funding stream based on the savings as they accrue will also be implemented. Other project funds will come from the Energy Conservation Investment Program and the Operations and Maintenance Accounts.

## SELECTED INSTALLATION

Since this program has so much potential, the US Army Forces Command Headquarters has agreed to fund our initial efforts and will help as much as possible with the funding in the out-years. Fort Hood, Texas, one of their largest installations, has agreed to be the prototype.

Fort Hood is the home of two army divisions and a corps headquarters. It is indeed a city, having an effective population of 63,000 and a resident population of 35,000. The population is currently lower than typical but will trend upwards over the next year or so as a new division phases in. There are over 5,100 buildings comprising about 26 million square feet. The two primary energy sources used at Fort Hood are electricity and natural gas. Their energy bill is $22 million per year, with about $16 million going for electricity and $6 million for natural gas. Family Housing uses about 24% of the energy and Operation & Maintenance Army funded facilities the rest.

## EXPECTED BENEFITS AND RESULTS

A prime benefit of the program is the demonstration of a cost-effective way to implement the new energy policy. This program will illustrate the impact of comprehensive planning and management that exploits the savings inherent in an integrated approach that views thermal and electrical loads together as a system. The program will also determine which technologies will survive on a military installation so we can be assured of long term savings.

Another benefit of the program is the demonstration of energy conservation as a least cost approach to environmental compliance. After all, this approach will not only reduce environmental impact, but also have a significant return on investment. The tools to identify and quantify the environmental affects will be in hand, along with a process for employing these tools to develop a least-cost compliance strategy.

A team will be built that has the expertise to get the job done and is readily accessible to the local engineer staff. The partners will come from both the private and public sectors and encompass the research community, the local installation, and the local utilities.

The program will have several specific results. It will showcase the latest energy technologies in an atmosphere which does not necessarily embrace new technology. The program will reduce energy usage and costs while simultaneously improving the environment and demonstrating that the comfort and productivity of a building's occupants need not be compromised in the process. Last but not least, The DoD will have the tools and methodology to cost effectively repeat the process at other installations or at other places that fit the process. This is a solid program with an executable plan that will result in great benefit to the overall energy and environmental programs. It will foster the holistic approach to energy and environmental problems at DoD facilities.

# SECTION 8
# HVAC SYSTEM OPTIMIZATION

Chapter 90

# Applications of Heat Pipes for HVAC Dehumidification at Walt Disney World

P.J. Allen, K. Dinh

## ABSTRACT

This paper presents the theory and application of heat pipes for HVAC dehumidification purposes. In HVAC applications, a heat pipe is used as a heat exchanger that transfers heat from the return air directly to the supply air. The air is pre-cooled entering the cooling coil and reheated using the same heat removed from the return air. While consuming no energy, the heat pipe lets the evaporator coil operate at a lower temp-erature, increasing the moisture removal capabilities of the HVAC system by 50% to 100%.

WALT DISNEY WORLD is currently testing several heat pipe applications ranging from 1 to 240 tons. The applications include (1) water attractions (2) museums/artifacts areas (3) resort guest rooms and (4) locker rooms. Actual energy usage and relative humidity reductions are shown to determine the effect-iveness of the heat pipe as an energy efficient method of humidity control.

## HISTORY OF HEAT PIPES

Having first been developed near the turn of the century, the heat pipe is not in itself a new invention. They were know in France under the name "caloduc". In the United States, the heat pipe was first suggested by Mr. Gaugler in 1942. In 1963, a U.S. Patent was granted to Mr. Grover, and there after several other scientists rapidly developed the underlying theories. Major development works were conducted in the 60's at the Los Alamos Scientific Laboratory, bringing the heat pipe device to the attention of the world scientific community.

Early heat pipes were constructed out of hollow metal tubes which were sealed at both ends, vacuumed and charged with a small amount of evaporative fluid. They contained a "wick" to transport the fluid from one end of the heat pipe to the other.

Heat pipes were not applied to HVAC systems until recently primarily because of their high cost. Over the past decade, two factors have also contributed to make heat pipes a choice consideration for modern HVAC designers: (1) the improvement in the techniques and materials of construction which create very tight and well insulated structures and (2) the new realization of an urgent need for better Indoor Air Quality.

Khanh Dinh improved the construction of heat pipes in the early 1980's. He was granted the first of several heat pipe U.S. Patents in 1986. The heat pipe construction methods which he developed brought the heat pipe cost down to a level that was commercially afforable. The new heat pipe systems offer the same extra-ordinary heat transfer performance associated with traditional heat pipes but at less cost. They also offer many desirable characteristics, such as low air drag, and material compati-bility with present HVAC equipment.

## HOW DO HEAT PIPES WORK?

The evaporation and condensation of a liquid such as water absorbs and releases a very large amount of energy. For example, the evaporation of one single pound of water takes more than 1,000 BTU's of energy while heating and cooling the same pound of water by one degree takes only 1 BTU. The heat pipe uses this phase-change principle to give it extremely fast heat transfer characteristics. As heat is added to one end of the heat pipe, the liquid vaporizes and in doing so absorbs a large amount of heat. This gas then moves to the other, "colder" end of the pipe where it quickly condensed back into a liquid, releasing the heat absorbed during the vaporization process.

In the case of a heat pipe which has been totally vacuumed, the working fluid will adopt the vapor pressure of the fluid at the mean temperature of the pipe. Such a system is very reactive to any change in temperature of the pipe: a small temperature rise at any point will vaporized the liquid, a small temperature drop will cause the vapors to condense. Thus, for heat transfer applications with a small delta T, the heat pipe is an ideal choice.

## HVAC DEHUMIDIFICATION WITH HEAT PIPES

In an air conditioning system, the lower the evaporator operating temperature, the more moisture is condensed out. The heat pipes "wrap around" the evaporator coil, with one half of the heat pipe in the incoming air stream and the other half in the outgoing stream.

The cool air leaving the evaporator chills one end of the heat pipe, and results in a heat transfer to the heat pipe located in the warmer return air stream. This transfer of heat from the warm incoming air to the cooled outgoing

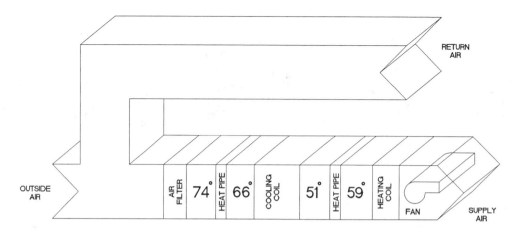

Figure 1. Heat Pipe HVAC Process

air creates the effect of pre-cooling the air going into the evaporator coil and then reheating the air immediately afterward. Figure 1 shows a graphic summary of this process.

While consuming no energy, the heat pipe lets the evaporator coil operate at a lower temperature, increasing the moisture removal capabilities of the HVAC system by 50% to 100%. With lower humidity, the indoor air feels more comfortable at higher thermostat settings, which result in net energy savings.

HEAT PIPE APPLICATIONS AT WALT DISNEY WORLD

WALT DISNEY WORLD, located in Orlando, Florida, is world renowned for Theme Parks and Resort Hotels. The hot and humid climate of Central Florida make the need for dehumidification especially important for the comfort of our guests. The use of heat pipe systems provide an energy efficient method for dehumidification. The following applications are a few examples of how heat pipes have been successfully applied at WALT DISNEY WORLD.

Small World Attraction

The Small World attraction is located in the MAGIC KINGDOM and features a boat ride through an animated scenes from around the world. The

Figure 2. Small World Attraction

facility is approximately 52,000 sq. ft. and the floor area is filled with water for the boat ride. Humidity levels average 75% in the facility without dehumidification. If left un-checked, these high humidity levels promote mold and mildew growth on the show sets and animated figures. Dehumidification is required to maintain a 60% relative humidity level.

The Small World Attraction is air conditioned with one large HVAC system. Dehumidification is achieved by sub-cooling the air to remove the moisture, then reheating the air to maintain comfortable space temperatures. Additionally, a "ride water heat exchanger" is used to chill the ride water to further decrease the humidity levels in the attraction.

A heat pipe was installed on the HVAC system at Small World in December, 1991 to minimize the chilled and hot water used in the dehumification process. The results shown below were based on sample BTU measurements taken throughout the year before and after the heat pipe was installed.

| UTILITY | BEFORE HEAT PIPE (MMBTU'S/DAY) | AFTER HEAT PIPE (MMBTU'S/DAY) | PCT |
|---|---|---|---|
| Spring/Fall Period: | | | |
| Hot Water | 6.68 | 2.14 | -68% |
| Chilled Water | 11.83 | 9.61 | -19% |
| Summer Period: | | | |
| Hot Water | 10.07 | 1.20 | -88% |
| Chilled Water | 20.61 | 17.15 | -17% |

As shown above, both chilled and hot water were reduced. During the summer period, reheat was almost completely eliminated with the heat pipe system.

Animation Pavilion

The Animation Pavilion is located in the Disney/MGM Studio Tour and features a behind-the-scenes tour of the art of animation. Animators prepare drawings and animation cells which are used in filmed animation features. Tight control of humidity and temperature levels are required in this area. Guest enter a pre-show area which display original animation cells from past Disney Classics. Severe damage to the cells can occur if high humidity levels occur. As a result, the animation cells are displayed in a tightly-sealed case which uses a special desiccant material to maintain a 50% relative humidity level.

Figure 3. Animation Cell Art Work

The HVAC which serves the pre-show area uses a dehumidification cycle which subcools the air to remove the moisture, then reheats the air to maintain comfortable space temperatures. In December, 1991, a heat pipe was installed on this unit to further enhance the dehumification capability of the HVAC system. Test results have indicated that the natural gas consumption used to make heating hot water for the Animation Pavilion has been reduced approximately 62% as the result of the heat pipe addition.

## Norway Stave Church Art Museum

The Stave Church is located at the Norway Pavilion at EPCOT Center. The Stave Church is used to display Norwegian artifacts to guests visiting the attraction. Since the opening of the Norway Pavilion, high humidity levels were experienced in the Stave Church during the hot and humid summer months.

Figure 4. Norway Stave Church

The Stave Church is conditioned by a single zone, face and by-pass HVAC unit. Because of the HVAC configuration, it was impossible to retrofit a heat pipe around the existing chilled water coil on the HVAC system. Instead, a new design was developed that involved the installation of a dedicated DX heat pipe dehumidifier system in parallel to the existing chilled water unit. With this design the dehumidifier unit could be turned on whenever the humidity setpoint was exceeded to provide maximum latent heat removal. The following results were obtained:

| PHASE OF PROJECT | RELATIVE HUMIDITY |
| --- | --- |
| Before Installation | 66% |
| After HVAC System Mods | 57% |
| After Heat Pipe Addition | 52% |

As part the of heat pipe installation, the chilled water HVAC system was cleaned and adjusted to original specifications. As shown below, a marked improvement over the original relative humidity levels was experienced after these modifications were made. However, the chilled water unit alone was not able to maintain the 52% relative humidity setpoint. Typical runtimes for the DX heat pipe dehumidifier unit vary from 3 to 4 hours daily and occur when EPCOT Center is open.

## Caribbean Beach Resort Guest Room

Caribbean Beach is a Resort Hotel located at WALT DISNEY WORLD. The guest rooms are conditioned by a one-ton PTAC through-the-wall unit. Shortly after opening, the guest rooms were retrofited with dedicated dehumidifier units to correct problems associated with high guest room humidity levels. A prototype PTAC heat pipe unit was developed and tested at Caribbean Beach. This unit installed directly in front of the PTAC unit and a new enclosure was made to cover the entire assembly.

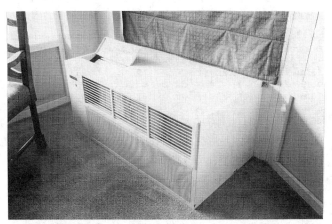

Figure 5. Guest Room Heat Pipe

A test was conducted to determine the effectiveness of the PTAC heat pipe unit in reducing guest room relative humidity levels. Two guest rooms at the Caribbean Beach were instrumented to record the data in the test. One room had a heat pipe modified PTAC unit.

The other room was used as a control for comparison purposes. The results from the test are shown below:

| TEST PHASE | ROOM W/ HEAT PIPE | CONTROL ROOM | PCT |
|---|---|---|---|
| 1. Before Heat Pipe Enabled (Dehumidifiers disabled) | 53% | 55% | -3% |
| 2. Heat Pipe Enabled (Dehumidifiers disabled) | 47% | 57% | -18% |
| 3. Heat Pipe Enabled (Dehumidifiers enabled) rooms) | 52% | 57% | -8% |

As shown above, before the heat pipe system was installed, there was virtually no difference between the two rooms. After the heat pipe was installed, the heat pipe room shown a significant reduction in relative humidity compared to the control room. During the final phase of testing, after the stand-alone dehumidifiers were enabled in both rooms, the heat pipe equipped room still showed lower relative humidity levels. It should be noted that the heat pipe is activated only when the PTAC is operating. Thus, the heat pipe equipped room relative humidity is effected when guests turn the PTAC on/off and raise/lower the temperature setpoints.

A modification has been developed to install the heat pipe directly inside existing PTAC enclosure. Aesthetically, this is preferred and helps reduce the retrofit cost even further. Testing is underway to determine the effectiveness of this unit. Preliminary test results indicate that the modified PTAC unit removes the same amount of moisture as the stand-alone dehumidifier unit.

Locker Room HVAC systems

In January, 1991, the Florida Model Energy Efficiency Code prohibited the use of electric strip heat for reheat purposes in a dehumidification process. Thus, new facilities constructed in Florida must use natural gas generated hot water or other methods to provide reheat.

Two new facilities at WALT DISNEY WORLD use heat pipes in 100% outside air HVAC systems which served locker rooms. Without dehumidification, these spaces would be very humid and result in extensive mold and mildew growth. Heat pipes were installed on these systems to reduce the reheat energy consumption and also meet the Florida Model Energy Code requirements. At the time of this paper, no specific tests had been performed to measure the effectiveness of these heat pipe applications.

CONCLUSION

The results of the first heat pipe applications used at WALT DISNEY WORLD has shown that heat pipes are an energy efficient method for dehumidification. Further heat pipe applications are planned for the future in areas which require extensive dehumidification and use large amounts of reheat energy.

# Chapter 91
# Desiccant Wheel and Heat Pipes Dehumidification Technologies

Y.A.M. Elgendy

ABSTRACT

In many heat pump and air conditioning applications, the cooling and dehumidification coil is unable to meet the dehumidification requirements of the load. High thermal performance heat pipe heat exchanger with large heat transfer surface area and desiccant wheel augmentations promise to improve the dehumidification performance and raise the efficiency of cooling equipment via increase the apparatus dew point of the cooling coil.

This study is designed to investigate the potential of utilizing a high performance heat pipe heat exchanger and a solid rotary desiccant wheel to maintain comfort levels with energy saving. Design improvement for the heat pipe and desiccant wheel would result in a HVAC system with low operating costs on account of the improved cooling COP.

## INTRODUCTION

Use of heat pipes and desiccants in HVAC systems for dehumidification purposes has been investigated. In any air conditioning process, the enthalpy change of moist air can be consider to have two components, the latent component at constant temperature, and the sensible component at constant moisture. The latent heat ratio of a conventional cooling and dehumidification coil is often smaller than the latent heat ratio of the load. This mismatch is often ignored, which degrades the comfort conditions, or is compensated with reheat, which decreases energy efficiency. The most efficient means of increasing the latent heat ratio is a heat pipe or a desiccant wheel to exchange heat from the return air (upstream of the coil) to the downstream, supply air as shown in Figures 1 and 2. The heat pipe augmentation or the rotary desiccant wheel unit will provide a better match between the latent load of the space and the latent load capabilities of the equipment. Figure 1 shows the heat pipe augmentation schematic as well as the process illustration on a psychrometric chart. The warm and humid return air is passed through the heat pipe heat exchanger unit which removes the reheat energy to the supply air. The air exits the cooling coil at point 3 closer to the apparatus dew-point. However, The cooling coil needs to perform less sensible cooling load and more latent cooling is accomplished. Then the cold and wet air exits the condenser section of the heat pipe unit to provide free reheat to the supply air. Supply air leaving the heat pipe heat exchanger unit is dry and moderately cool to meet the indoor comfort conditions.

The heat pipe is a device of very high thermal conductance, in order of several hundreds time the thermal conductance of copper.

Solid rotary desiccant wheels is similar in effect to heat pipe technology in that dehumidification process. Solid rotary desiccant wheels could provide air at correct conditions but without depressing the coil temperature, an undesirable but unavoidable result when air is precooled with heat pipes. The warm and humid air is passed through the solid rotary desiccant wheels, as shown in Figure 2, and removes moisture from the moist desiccant wheel. The air exits the wheel cooler and wetter and therefore closer to the dew-point of the moist air. The coil, therefore needs to perform less sensible cooling as in the case of the heat pipe, and more latent cooling is accomplished. After the cold and wet air exits the cooling coil, it is passed the solid rotary desiccant wheels. The solid rotary desiccant wheel provides free reheat and removes the excess moisture from the air. Supply air leaving the solid rotary desiccant wheel is dry and moderately cool.

Desiccants are porous materials with large surface area which upon contact with moist air exhibit a great affinity for water vapor molecules which condenses and adheres to surface of the pores. This surface effect is called physical adsorption. The most common desiccant dehumidification configuration is the rotary desiccant wheel as shown in Figure 2. The parallel passage rotary desiccant wheel has achieved the highest heat transfer to pressure drop ratio compared with other tested geometries [2]. The desiccant wheel performs the dehumidification portion of the load without the use of CFC's.

The solid rotary desiccant wheel concept promises to raise the efficiency of cooling equipment via increase the apparatus dew point of the cooling coil.

## CONCEPT

Heat pipe augmentation may utilize with a conventional cooling coils by reheating the supply air with energy obtained from the precooling the return air in HVAC systems.

This process will reduce the apparatus dew-point of the coil, as shown in Figure 1, improving its dehumidification without adversely affecting efficiency. Also, it will decrease the excessive sensible heat ratio of a typical coil and bring the coil dehumidification capacity nearer into balance with the characteristics of the load. The improved match will minimize the requirement for reheat to maintain specified indoor comfort conditions. A high thermal performance heat pipe with large heat transfer surface area is designed [3, 4, and 5] to provide a high effectiveness heat pipe heat exchanger unit.

The concept of moisture exchange through the desiccant wheel is shown in Figure 2 the system schematic as well as the process illustrated on a psychrometric. The warm and humid return air is passed through the desiccant wheel and removes moisture from the moist desiccant wheel. The air exits the wheel cooler and wetter and therefore closer to the dew-point of the moist air. The cooling coil, therefore, needs to perform less sensible cooling as in the case of the heat pipe, see Figure 1, and more latent cooling is accomplished. After the cold and wet air exits the cooling coil, it is passed through the desiccant wheel. The desiccant wheel removes the excess moisture from the air as well as providing free reheat. Supply air leaving the desiccant wheel is dry and moderately cool which is the correct conditions to maintain comfortable indoor conditions in many applications.

The desiccant wheel cooling concept also promises to raise the efficiency of traditional vapor compressor cooling equipment via increase of apparatus dew-point of the cooling coil.

## ADVANTAGES OF HEAT PIPES

The benefits of heat pipe augmentation are attractive. Utilizing heat pipe heat exchanger unit between the return air and the supply air, as shown in Figure 1, provides the following advantages:
1. The precooling of the air before it reaches the cooling coil reduces the apparatus dew-point of the coil improving its dehumidification without adversely affecting efficiency.

2. Decreasing the excessive sensible heat ratio of a typical coil.

3. The reheat energy does not add to the energy requirement for the system.

4. Providing a better match between the latent load of the space and the latent load capabilities of the equipment.

## ADVANTAGES OF DESICCANT WHEEL

The potential advantages of desiccant assisted cooling cycles are:

1. Control of both wet bulb and dry bulb temperature without the use of reheat.

2. Increasing the load ratios between the latent and sensible heat due to trends in architecture.

3. The desiccant wheel has achieved the highest heat transfer to pressure drop ratio compared with other geometries.

4. Dehumidification becomes increasingly inefficient as the latent load increases.

5. Regeneration energy can be partially supplied by compression heat or waste condenser.

6. Regeneration temperature are also compatible with flat solar collectors.

In addition, the desiccant wheel has the following effects on the environment:

1. The desiccant wheel performs the dehumidification portion of the load without the use of CFC's.

2. Desiccant dehumidifiers adsorb both particulate and vapor pollutants such as CO, NO2, SiO2 which as been reported by Gas Research Institute in 1986.

3. As air tightness increases, the ability of HVAC systems to remove trapped contaminants will become an important feature.

4. Pollutants are purged during regeneration.

## SIMULATION MODEL

The desiccant wheel model or the heat pipe augmentation model is integrated with the cooling coil model to simulate the system. The simulation model for the moisture exchange process analogous to heat pipe heat exchanger and the desiccant well are studied. Figure 3 shows the modeling of desiccant beds and the thermal resistance for the moisture particle with the temperatures and the relative humidities. Several simulation

models for the moisture particle inside the desiccant wheel could be applied to study the thermal performance of the desiccant such as Gas and Solid Side Rate Controlled Model (GSSRCM), Gas Side Rate Controlled Model (GSRCM), and Transport Idealized Wheel Model (TIWM). The GSSRCM is a detailed model appropriate for thicker beds and study of various desiccants. The GSRCM is a realistic behavior of thin desiccant beds for desiccants whose artificially degraded mass transfer coefficient is well established. The TIWM is operating charts and optimization studies for commonly used desiccants. The computational among these model is very costly.

The GSSRCM model is proposed to simulate the desiccant wheel in this research which incorporates the diffusivity of the adsorbent. The other models require empirical data. The system of equations which have been applied in the GSSECM model are: the conservation of mass and energy, the mass transfer rate, the heat transfer rate, the enthalpy of moist air, the enthalpy of desiccant, the adsorption isothermal, the pressure drop, the inlet moist air states, and the initial bed state or periodic steady state boundary conditions. The GSSECM model using a parabolic moisture concentration profile, as shown in Figure 4, has been adapted from Chain [2] in modeling the diffusion process inside the desiccant particle.

## RESULTS AND CONCLUSIONS

Use of heat pipes and desiccant wheels for dehumidification purposes have been investigated. Heat pipe augmentation and desiccant wheel promise to improve the dehumidification performance of conventional cooling coil by reheating the supply air with energy obtained from precooling the return air. This process will reduce the excessive sensible heat ratio of a typical coil and bring the coil dehumidification capacity nearer into balance with the characteristics of the load. The improved match will minimize the requirement for reheat to maintain specified indoor comfort conditions. Therefore, expensive resistance or combustion reheat can be eliminated.

Potential exists for moisture exchange to occur return air is warmer, lower relative humidity air exiting coil is cold and nearly saturated. Also, the cooling coil performs increased dehumidification. Also, the evaporator temperature of the vapor compression unit can be raised, therefore, increasing the unit's COP.

Various approaches to modeling the heat pipe augmentation and the solid rotary desiccant wheels have been studied. The models have concentrated on the computational efficiency, which is important in HVAC simulations.

REFERENCES

1. Dunn, P. and Reay, D. A. "Heat Pipes" Thired Edition, Pergaman Press, Oxford, 1982.

2. Chant, Eileen " Transient and Steady State Simulations of an Advanced Desiccant Enhanced Cooling and Dehumidification Cycle", Ph. D. Thesis, Georgia Institute of Technology, 1991.

3. Elgendy, Youssef " Heat Pipes For Residential Heat Pump" Unpublished Report Submitted to Georgia Power Company, Atlanta, Georgia, 1990.

4. Elgendy, Youssef " Variable Speed Ericsson Engine Heat Pump System", The 13th World Energy Engineering Congress (WEEC), The Association of Energy Engineers, Atlanta Georgia, USA, October 10-12, 1990.

5. Elgendy, Youssef "Simulation of a Modular Variable Speed Gas Fired Heat Pump", The 14th World Energy Engineering Congress (WEEC), The Association of Energy Engineers, Atlanta, Georgia, USA, October 1991.

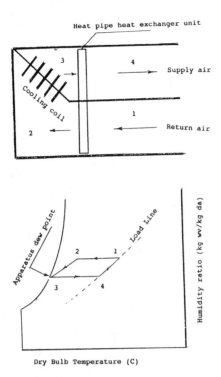

Heat pipe heat exchanger unit

3

4 → Supply air

Cooling coil

1 ← Return air

2

Apparatus dew point

Load Line

2   1

3   4

Humidity ratio (kg wv/kg da)

Dry Bulb Temperature (C)

Figure 1 Cooling and dehumidification with
heat pipe heat exchanger unit

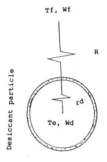

Tf, Wf

R

Desiccant particle

rd

Te, Wd

Figure 3 Modeling of desiccant bed

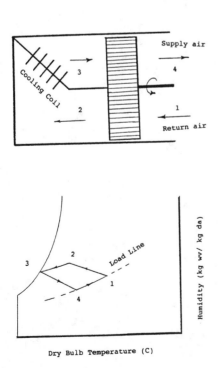

Cooling Coil

3

4   Supply air

2

1   Return air

3

2

Load Line

1

4

Humidity (kg wv/ kg da)

Dry Bulb Temperature (C)

Figure 2 Cooling and dehumidification with
desiccant wheel unit

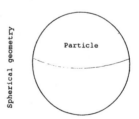

Spherical geometry

Particle

Planar geometry of a particle

Moisture content on particle

r = 0   r = R   r

Parabolic moisture concentration profile

Figure 4 Modeling the diffusion process inside
the desiccant particle

Chapter 92

# Comparative Study of a Conventional Electric Chiller System Versus Cool Storage with Conventional Air Distribution or Cool Storage with Cool Air Distribution

P.R. Bramble, J.B. Singh

## ABSTRACT

This paper describes a conceptual study analyzing conventional electric cooling versus electric cooling with ice storage and either conventional or cold air distribution. The facility under consideration was a medical outpatient complex. The analysis reported here is a preliminary study to select the most economical cooling option for the facility based on the first-installed costs, maintenance costs and energy costs. Our analysis indicates that an ice storage system with cool air distribution results in the most economical of the three systems studied, due to the economies resulting from reduced chiller sizes, as well as smaller pipe, duct, fan and pump sizes. These equipment size reductions result in lower operating and maintenance costs, as well as lower first-installed costs, when compared to the conventional electric cooling system alone.

## INTRODUCTION

Conventional electric cooling with a centrifugal chiller is a time-tested way to air-condition a facility. However, as electric utilities become short on capacity and demand penalties rise, state-of-the-art technologies must now be analyzed to reduce total cooling costs as well as first-installed equipment costs.

This paper is an attempt to study all relevant factors of ice storage systems and compare them to centrifugal chillers. This analysis addresses first-costs, operating costs and maintenance costs, compliance with design requirements and conformance to codes.

The results achieved and the conclusions reached here may be applicable in electric utility service areas where the rate structure is similar to that of the Pennsylvania Power & Light Company (PP&L). Even greater operating savings may result with ice storage in areas where the utility rate structure has higher demand penalties than PP&L.

## WHY ICE STORAGE?

### Reduced Energy Costs

Thermal Electric Storage (TES) systems are an HVAC technology used to shift on-peak electric usage to off-peak periods when energy costs are lower. Installation of these systems may result in lower costs for both the customer and the utility, now and in the future.

With ice storage systems, energy cost savings result due to reduced on-peak utility demands. This is done by creating ice during the off-peak period. Load shifting allows utilities to defer construction of capital intensive power plants, while better utilizing existing

facilities. Since PP&L has no demand charge during off-peak periods, energy cost savings result.

With conventional operation, a chiller will operate during the occupied period ONLY, and will be subject to the utility's maximum demand which traditionally occurs during the "on-peak" period.

Under PP&L rate structure, this on-peak period is a customer-selected 8-hour block of time (7A-3P; 8A-4P; or 9A-5P) when maximum demand is billed. Any **demand occurring BEFORE OR AFTER this "on-peak" period**, or on weekends and holidays, **will not be billed**. Therefore, it is in the customer's best interest to limit demand during the on-peak period to lower total energy costs.

### Reduced Equipment Costs

With the aid of higher-temperature rise for water and air, TES systems permit reduced chiller sizes (and reduced sizing of ducts, pipes, pumps and fans when cold air distribution is also used). This results in lower equipment costs than those of a conventional chiller system.

The PP&L grant of $100 per avoided ton offered at the time of this analysis makes the TES system even more attractive when compared to the conventional chiller system.

### Reduced Maintenance Costs

Since the thermal storage mass contains no moving parts, ice TES systems are considered simple and reliable and are designed to last for 20 to 25 years with only minor maintenance.

The tanks used by leading manufacturers are inert, being made of a seamless plastic, and are generally filled with plastic coils which are not likely to rupture or leak. Additional maintenance of most ice systems is limited to maintaining the water/glycol levels and adding a small amount of algicide each year.

Chiller maintenance costs are normally estimated based on system tonnage, so down-sizing the chiller can result in lower nominal maintenance costs. Since the compressor runs continuously with the partial ice-storage system, rather than in frequent on/off cycles that increase wear and tear of conventional chillers, actual maintenance with partial ice TES is typically competitive with or less than that of a conventional chiller.

## WHY PARTIAL AND NOT TOTAL-ICE STORAGE?

A TES system can provide either **full** or **partial ice storage** capacity. A "full storage" system is designed to produce and *"store" all cooling requirements* during the "off-peak" period and draw from these reserves during the "on-peak" period. This is done without running the chiller "on-peak" or increasing the on-peak billing demand.

**Partial storage systems** are designed to **run continuously** throughout the day. This *levelizes the cooling load* by spreading usage throughout a 24-hour period. Although a down-sized chiller will run during the on-peak period, the resulting on-peak billing demand will still be significantly lower than that resulting from a conventional chiller system. Both operating and equipment costs can result by decreasing chiller sizing.

The decision to choose between a partial and a full-storage system normally depends on the balance between first-costs and operating costs.

PP&L rate structure dictated that a partial ice storage system would be more cost-effective than a full storage system. For this application, higher capital costs of larger chillers and tanks could not be justified by only marginally greater avoided demand costs with the full storage system.

## CONVENTIONAL VS. COLD AIR DISTRIBUTION

### The Pros

With partial ice storage, it is possible to use either conventional air distribution or cold air distribution. Cold air distribution is possible if the thermal storage mass is maintained between 34°F and 38°F. Cold supply air can then be distributed at temperatures between 45°F and 50°F.

The cold air distribution system studied required 20% less cold air than the conventional system. (This was based on a 20° ΔT for conventional air distribution and 1 CFM per sq. ft. required, vs. a 25° ΔT for cold air distribution and .8 CFM per sq. ft. required.) This reduction in required supply air allowed mechanical equipment such as ducts, piping, pumps and fans to be down-sized for significant cost savings compared to the conventional air distribution system.

As estimated here, the low-temperature air distribution approach reduced first-installed costs by $168,100 over the 55°F supply air design.

### The Cons

Two additional factors must be addressed when comparing conventional and cold air distribution:

(1) Increased duct work and terminal unit insulation with cold air distribution.

(2) Increased maintenance with fan-powered boxes required for cold air distribution vs. maintenance of regular VAV boxes for conventional air distribution.

More attention must be given to duct and terminal insulation with a cold air distribution system. However, it is a "once-and-done" job that can be handled by proper supervision and inspection during construction without significant added costs. However, failure to do so could result in unnecessary condensation in the ceiling space and spoiled ceiling tiles.

Fan-powered boxes required for cold air distribution have a marginally higher maintenance cost than the VAV boxes used with conventional air distribution. However, this slight added maintenance cost is more than made up by avoided energy costs with the cold air distribution system.

Also, several manufacturers use induction boxes rather than fan-powered boxes for cold air distribution. In either case, fan maintenance costs are not considered very significant in terms of overall system operation.

## BASIS FOR ANALYSIS

The following design parameters were used, based on the Health Code Standards prevalent in the construction industry. It is our recommendation that these guidelines should not be used for a hospital, but for a diagnostic center with requirements approaching those of a hospital.

The space analyzed was a 200,000 square foot building to be used as an up-scale, outpatient treatment facility.

Walls are of medium color brick with R-20 insulation. Windows and skylights are of "Low-E" glass and have an R-3 insulation value. The roof is light-colored and insulated to R-40.

| | |
|---|---|
| Inside Space Temperature: | 75°F Summer |
| Outside Design Temperature: | 90°F DB/74°F WB |
| Hours of Operation: | Monday thru Saturday 7:00 a.m.-12:00 Midnight. Closed Sunday. All systems "off" during unoccupied period. |
| Occupant Load: | 100 sq. ft./person = 2,000 people 250 BTUH sensible/person = 500 MBH 250 BTUH latent/person = 500 MBH |
| Lighting Load: | 2.5 watts/sq. ft. = 500 KW |
| Misc. Equipment Load: | 3.0 watts/sq. ft. = 600 KW |
| Conventional Air Distribution: | 1 CFM per sq. ft. |
| Cold Air Distribution: | .8 CFM per sq. ft. |
| Minimum Outside Air: | 50,000 CFM |
| Operating Rooms: | 50% R.H. (maintained by local electric steam humidifiers) |
| Air Handling Units: | 9 AHU's |
| Mixing Boxes: | 400 boxes with 500 CFM capacity each and hot water reheat |

## DESCRIPTION OF SYSTEMS ANALYZED

For analytical work, only rooftop-type air handling equipment was considered.

Fans had adjustable speed drives. The estimate included primary pumping and secondary pumping. Each cooling coil had its own secondary pump.

A HEPA (high efficiency particulate air) type filtration system was included for the outpatient operating rooms. Humidification equipment was also included in this area to maintain humidity around 50 percent.

Parallel boxes were estimated for the exterior zones and upper floor. Series-type boxes were estimated for the interior zones. The conventional option included variable air volume (VAV) boxes in lieu of fan-powered boxes.

## SYSTEMS ANALYZED

The systems that we analyzed are as follows:

(1) **Conventional Centrifugal Chiller Using R-123 Refrigerant**

The system distributes 42°F chilled water and air at 50°F conventional distribution temperatures. A cooling tower is required. Regular VAV boxes have hot water reheat.

(2) **Partial Ice Storage System with Conventional Air Distribution**

The system distributes 38°F to 42°F chilled water and air at 50°F conventional distribution temperatures. The chiller is a rotary screw or a reciprocating chiller using R-22 refrigerant. A cooling tower is required. Regular VAV boxes have hot water reheat.

(3) **Partial Ice Storage System with Cold Air Distribution**

The system distributes 38°F water with glycol and cold air distribution at 45°F. The chiller is a rotary screw or reciprocating chiller using R-22 refrigerant. A cooling tower is required. Fan-powered boxes have hot water reheat.

## SIZING EQUIPMENT

### Conventional Chiller

Given: Conventional Chiller Capacity = 765 tons

To calculate total 24-hour cooling requirement, add on-peak cooling requirements and "off-peak" cooling requirements:

```
  765 tons x .75 (Diversity) x 9 hrs (peak occupied load 7A-4P)
+ 765 tons x .30 (Diversity) x 8 hrs (evening load 4P-12A)
= 6,999 ton-hours required in a 24-hour period
```

### Down-Sized Chiller

To size for a smaller chiller using ice storage, assume that the machine will run 24 hours a day to meet total cooling requirements, unlike the conventional chiller, which runs only during the occupied mode to meet cooling needs.

$$\frac{6,999 \text{ ton-hours}}{24 \text{ hour run time}} = 300 \text{ tons (down-sized chiller)}$$

Assume that the down-sized chiller will continue to run during the utility's 8-hour "on-peak" period while being supplemented by the ice storage system. Ice storage requirements will then be calculated as the difference between total cooling requirements and on-peak chiller capacity:

```
     Total ton-hour requirement
(-) On-peak ton-hours produced by the down-sized chiller

  =    Net Latent Cooling Capacity Requirement
```

```
Total Ton-hour Requirement = 765 tons x .75 Div. x 8 hrs = 5,400 ton-hours
                                    .85 efficiency*

(-) On-peak Cooling Output = 300 tons x 8 hrs =      (-) 2,400 ton-hours

  = Net Latent Cooling Capacity Requirement    =        3,000 ton-hours
                                                            ice storage
```

\* Note: Assume that a 15% (1 - .85 = .15) reduction efficiency allows for standby losses and equipment and system efficiencies.

### Sizing Check

After the preliminary sizing, it is necessary to verify that the 300-ton machine is capable of the required output, since the output of the down-sized chiller actually decreases by 15% to 30% in the ice-building mode.

$$\text{Actual chiller output in ice-building mode} = \frac{300 \text{ tons}}{1.15} = 260 \text{ tons}$$

These 260 tons of available refrigeration capacity must be able to produce enough ice in the 12-hour available off-peak time period to store at least 3,000 ton-hours latent cooling.

```
CHECK: 3,000 Ton-hours = 11.5 Hours off-peak time required to produce
         260 tons         3,000 ton-hours latent cooling

11.5 Hours Off-peak + 8.0 Hours On-Peak = 19.5 Hours

→ 4.5 Hours Remain in 24-hour period

24-hour total ton-hour production:

  8.0 hours x (300 tons) = 2,400 ton-hours on-peak chiller output
 11.5 hours x (260 tons) = 2,990 ton-hours off-peak ice building capacity
  4.5 hours x (300 tons) = 1,350 ton-hours off-peak chiller output
                           6,740 ton-hours total
```

Since 6,740 ton-hours approximately equals the 6,999 ton-hour total cooling requirement, we assumed that the 300-ton chiller was adequate for estimating purposes. A computer model of a one-week design period will be required for final sizing. This model must be capable of adjusting chiller efficiency, which varies with loading, based on outside dry and wet-bulb temperatures.

### Avoided Tons

Avoided tons are significant when calculating cooling costs, since PP&L billing is based on the maximum 15-minute on-peak demand in the month.

```
  765 = Tons Conventional Chiller Requirement
- 300 = Tons Partial Storage Chiller Requirement
  465 = Avoided Tons x .76 KW/ton = 353 KW avoided
                                        on-peak demand
```

This avoided demand was reflected in projected annual cooling costs.

### Grants

At the time of this analysis, PP&L offered a grant of $100 per avoided ton to promote TES systems. For both the conventional chiller and the partial ice storage option, a spare chiller was required for back-up in case of failure of a primary unit. Calculation of avoided tons and available grant money were done as follows:

**Conventional:** Two 400-ton units are to be in service, with one 400-ton unit as a spare

2 x 400 tons = 800 tons installed capacity

**Ice Storage:** One 300-ton unit is to be in service, with one 300-ton unit as a spare

1 x 300 tons = 300 tons installed capacity

Avoided Tons: 800 tons - 300 tons = 500 tons

PP&L Grant: 500 tons x $100/ton = $50,000


## RESULTS

### A. Equipment Costs -- Installed (1)

| | Conventional Chiller ($) | Partial Ice Storage with Conventional Distribution ($) | Partial Ice Storage with Cold Air Distribution ($) |
|---|---|---|---|
| Chillers | 421,000 (2) | 210,000 (3) | 210,000 (3) |
| Cooling Tower | 45,600 | 27,600 | 27,600 |
| Tower Pump | 6,900 | 5,200 | 5,200 |
| Chilled Water Pumps | 5,200 | 4,200 | 4,200 |
| Tank | --- | 174,000 | 174,000 |
| AHU's | 479,000 | 479,000 | 379,000 |
| Secondary CW Pumps | 12,600 | 8,870 | 8,870 |
| Exhaust Fans | 10,900 | 10,900 | 10,900 |
| Return Fans | 21,400 | 21,400 | 18,800 |
| Htg./Vent. Units | 20,600 | 20,600 | 20,600 |
| O.R. Filtration & Humidification | 50,000 | 50,000 | 50,000 |
| Hot Water Pumps | 4,600 | 4,600 | 4,600 |
| Hot Water Boiler (gas-fired) | 86,200 | 86,200 | 86,200 |
| Piping (4) | 289,400 | 289,400 | 289,400 (5) |
| Air Distribution (6)(ductwork) | 671,500 | 671,500 | 480,000 |
| Mixing Boxes | 202,800 | 202,800 | 322,400 |
| Variable Speed Drives (Fans) | 32,300 | 32,300 | 29,300 |
| H&V Unit for non-A/C areas | 20,600 | 20,600 | 20,600 |
| Subtotal | $2,380,600 | $2,319,170 | $2,141,670 |
| PP&L Grant | --- | (-)50,000 | (-)50,000 |
| Final Cost | $2,380,600 | $2,269,170 | $2,091,670 |
| | $11.90/sq.ft. | $11.35/sq.ft. | $10.46/sq.ft. |

(1) These costs do not include controls.

(2) Three 400-ton chillers (two operating plus one back-up).

(3) Includes two 300-ton chillers (one back-up).

(4) Includes installed costs for piping, accessories, valves, and insulation.

(5) For estimating purposes, additional savings from reduced pipe sizes were not considered.

(6) Includes installed costs for all the ductwork, diffusers and insulation.


### B. Energy/Operating Costs

The following is the tabulated summary of the KWH usage for the three HVAC systems studied. Calculations were based on PP&L's LP-4 rate for "Time-of-Day" billing for primary service at 12,470 volts. The effects of base usage and demand costs are reflected in total operating costs. ‡

| | Conventional Chiller (KWH/Year) | Partial Ice Storage with Conventional Distribution (KWH/Year) | Partial Ice Storage with Cold Air Distribution (KWH/Year) |
|---|---|---|---|
| Chiller | 752,512 | 752,512 | 752,512 |
| Chiller/Ice Efficiency Loss | --- | 57,600 | 57,600 |
| Ice Storage Standby Loss | --- | 161,568 | 161,568 |
| Secondary Pumps, Supply, Return & Exhaust Fans | 2,116,864 | 2,116,864 | 1,944,033 |
| Free-Cooling Loss | --- | --- | 109,440 |
| Hot Water Pumps | 83,830 | 83,830 | 83,830 |
| Total HVAC KWH/Year | 2,953,206 KWH/YR | 3,172,374 KWH/YR | 3,108,983 KWH/YR |
| Total HVAC Cost/Year | $ 190,114 | $193,216 | $ 186,030 |

‡ The PP&L Rate Structure is as follows:

$6.39 per kilowatt for the first 200 kilowatts of the Billing KW.
$4.33 per kilowatt for all additional kilowatts of the Billing KW.

5.32 cents per KWH for the first 150 KWH per kilowatt of the Billing KW.
4.46 cents per KWH for the next 100 KWH per kilowatt of the Billing KW.
4.03 cents per KWH for the next 150 KWH per kilowatt of the Billing KW.
3.60 cents per KWH for all additional KWH.


### C. Maintenance Costs

The total building requirement of 765 tons cooling was used to estimate maintenance costs. Choice of boxes was based on total building cooling requirements.

These estimated maintenance costs appear to be very conservative for the partial ice storage systems, since down-sized chillers will run continuously, unlike conventional chillers, which run on demand. This will tend to minimize wear and tear during start/stop of equipment, therefore lowering total maintenance costs of partial ice storage systems.

**(1) Conventional Chiller:**

765 tons x $50/ton = $38,250/year

Maintenance costs provided by the chiller manufacturer for VAV boxes with reheat in hospital applications typically run between $40 and $50 per ton.

**(2) Partial Ice Storage with Conventional Air Distribution & VAV with Reheat:**

765 tons x $50/ton + 3% ($210,000) = $44,550/year

Maintenance costs provided by the manufacturer for this application are typically $44 to $54 per ton plus 3 percent of chiller machine costs for additional maintenance on the ice storage portion of the system.

(3) Partial Ice Storage with Cold Air Distribution &
    Fan-powered VAV Boxes:

765 tons x $54/ton x 3% ($210,000) = $47,610/year

Maintenance costs provided by the chiller
manufacturer for this application are typically
$44 to $54 per ton plus 3 percent of chiller
machine costs for additional maintenance on the
ice storage portion of the system.

## SUMMARY AND RECOMMENDATIONS

| | HVAC Equipment Costs ($/Year) | HVAC Energy Costs ($/Year) | HVAC Maintenance Costs ($/Year) |
|---|---|---|---|
| Conventional Chiller | $ 2,380,600 | $228,364 | $38,250 |
| Partial Ice Storage with Conventional Air Distribution | $ 2,240,070 | $237,766 | $44,550 |
| Partial Ice Storage with Cold Air Distribution | $ 2,061,970 | $233,640 | $47,610 |

A TES system should be considered in utility service
territories which have demand charges similar to or
higher than those of PP&L. Most large commercial
buildings with adequate space to accommodate TES tanks
are good candidates for this technology. As this study
indicates, **first-installed costs of partial ice-storage
systems can be lower than those of a conventional
chiller system.** Since estimated maintenance costs and
energy costs are competitive with those of the
conventional, there can be an "immediate" or very short-
term payback associated with this system.

General guidelines for choosing between full and partial
storage systems are not addressed here. However,
additional equipment costs for a full storage system
should be weighed against the (avoided) cost of utility
demand charges. Grants offered by utilities to promote
this system concept should also factor into this
decision.

Cold air distribution becomes much more attractive than
the conventional air distribution system with partial
ice storage when a building has significant cooling load
and long hours of use. In such cases, significant
energy savings result from the reduced pump and fan
sizes, which must run 24-hours a day, adding to total
energy usage.

Energy costs calculated here are considered very
conservative when estimating for the TES systems. As an
example, actual standby losses and system efficiency
losses of installed systems should be somewhat less than
those shown here. **Credit for thermal storage in the
piping system was not taken into account here; and
greater savings from reduced sizing of secondary pumps
and fans was also not adequately accounted for in the
estimate.** The penalty for "free-cooling losses" for the
cold air distribution system is also considered very
conservatative. Also, maintenance costs for the ice
storage systems are considered very conservative.

Although results of this paper favor cold air
distribution with partial ice storage, savings would be
even greater and more strongly point to selecting this
system design if the facility operated 24 hours a day.
Likewise, if PP&L had higher demand charges or a
"rachet", the results would once again have shown
convincingly that partial ice storage with cold air
distribution was the ideal HVAC system for this project.

# Chapter 93
# Comparison of Electric Versus Gas-Fired Cooling Options

T.P. Szlenski, J.B. Singh

### INTRODUCTION

Much interest has been focused on gas cooling recently. Phase-out of CFCs, demand-side management programs, relative cost of natural gas, and aggressive marketing by gas utilities have all brought gas cooling to the forefront of cooling options available today. This paper compares electric cooling with available gas-cooling options. It discusses the advantages and disadvantages of each option, including operating, maintenance, and installed costs. The analysis indicates that, in areas of the country with high electric charges, gas cooling may be a viable option; but in most cases, it still does not present an economical choice. The higher efficiency and the lower maintenance costs of the electric options outweigh the operating cost savings from decreased electric use of the gas options.

### HISTORY

In the 1950s and 1960s, gas-fired absorption cooling was widely used. In buildings and facilities where steam was used as a winter heating source, the use of absorption cooling in summer made good economic sense. The gas and oil used as fuel sources were comparatively economical and were widely available. Single-effect absorption units were easy to maintain due to few moving parts. The energy efficiency was low (C.O.P. = 0.7) and the cost of water and sewer was not of much concern. Proper emphasis on condenser water treatment was critical. The crystallization of lithium bromide was to be guarded against. It required several days to decrystallize resulting in a shut down of the absorber.

During the 1950s and 1960s, there was little concern about the energy costs. After the energy crisis of the early 1970s, the manufacture and sale of these inefficient single-effect machines started declining. Maintenance also became a major problem with the older units. During the increase in oil and gas prices of the 1970s, most of the single-stage absorption units were retrofitted with energy-efficient electric chillers in areas with favorable electric rates. While the use of the absorption technology took a nose dive in the United States, it caught on in Japan. Electric machines today constitute the vast majority of cooling equipment purchased in the United States.

### MODERN GAS COOLING EQUIPMENT

#### Double Effect Absorption

Due to the inefficiency of the single-effect absorption process, double-effect direct-fired, and indirect-fired absorption machines were developed. The Coefficient of Performance (C.O.P.) of these machines is 1.0 to 1.3. The earlier United States-made machines required high head room and developed tube problems which have been corrected in recent models. Almost all the premier chiller manufactur-ers today have a collaboration with a Japanese manufacturer of these refrigeration machines. The Japanese models require less head room than United States makes. Absorption units weigh much more than their electric counterparts. The weight is a significant factor if the chiller is to be installed on upper floors due to the increase in the structural cost of the building. The handling and rigging costs of these heavy machines become very significant if installation is required in an upper story of a high-rise building.

Double-effect absorption machines have low energy use and should be applied in areas of the country where the electric rates are high and the utility provides grants to offset the significant first-cost price differential of absorption chillers.

All the absorption equipment uses significant electrical energy in the form of power required to drive the concentrator pump, absorber pump, refrigerant pump, and evaporator pumps. The condenser water pump and the cooling tower fans are larger than those required by an electric chiller. Since the water use in a modern absorption chiller is higher than in an electric chiller, this cost can also be significant. Depending upon the manufacturer, availability of parts may also be a problem.

Where there is economical waste heat available, such as exhaust gas from a steam turbine or incinerator-generated heat, single-effect machines may still be economical despite their higher first cost.

#### Indirect-Fired Chillers

Some indirect-fired machines use high temperature hot water as an energy source. Most indirect-fired machines, however, use medium to high pressure steam. This requires a licensed boiler operator around the clock, significantly impacting the operating cost of a facility.

#### Direct-Fired Chiller/Heaters

During the heating season, almost all the capacity of the direct-fired chiller can be used for heating. In summer, the rejected heat can be used to supply domestic hot water. The direct-fired, double-effect machines do not require a licensed boiler operator. It is often possible to eliminate or do away with the need for installing a heating boiler, thus saving the cost of constructing a boiler room.

#### Gas Engine-Driven Chillers

Gas engine-driven chillers have components similar to an electric chiller and use CFCs and HCFCs. The low-cost electric hermetic or semi-hermetic motor compressor is replaced by a comparatively more expensive natural gas or diesel engine and an open drive compressor.

## MODERN ELECTRIC COOLING EQUIPMENT

Electric vapor compression machines still have higher efficiencies than absorption units. Most manufacturers make refrigeration machines for alternate refrigerant R-123 and one manufacturer makes a machine which uses R-134A, which has no ozone depletion potential. The rotary screw and scroll type compressors have improved efficiencies, quieter operation, and greater reliability. The emphasis on efficiency improvement for part load operation and increased use of air-cooled condensing, especially for smaller-sized equipment, yields economical first costs and attractive operating and maintenance costs for electric rotary chillers. An additional strategy increasingly being evaluated for use in air-conditioning and process applications is the use of thermal storage for heating as well as for cooling purposes. Especially in the south, cool storage with cold air distribution has been found to be more economical as compared to conventional cooling and conventional air distribution. Another important strategy increasingly being looked into is the use of ammonia in comfort air-conditioning systems. Ammonia systems have been in use in the food processing and warehousing facilities for a long time. They are ozone safe. There is no reason why ammonia systems could not be used for supplying cooling through an indirect heat transfer so that it does not impact the occupied environment.

## PRESENT STATE OF GAS COOLING

After limited use in almost the last 20 years in the United States, absorption units have generated significant appeal and acceptance recently. Concern for the CFCs, ability to assist electric utilities in their demand-side management, and deferring the cost of electric generation and distribution have all made gas cooling more attractive. One great drawback of most modern gas-cooling equipment is the lack of operating data because the more energy-efficient, double-effect absorption gas-cooling systems have only short history. Another important consideration is their high purchase costs. These could not be justified for use even in areas with high electric rates if it were not for heavy subsidization by utilities. Therefore, an analysis of all the relevant costs -- first cost, installation cost, energy cost, maintenance and operating costs, water cost, amortization, depreciation, taxes, and insurance -- must be factored in to arrive at the most economical life-cycle cost of the proposed installation.

## COST COMPARISON

Cost comparisons of cooling systems usually only include energy and first costs. A complete analysis must include other costs, such as maintenance, water and sewer charges, and auxiliary energy use. We will neglect depreciation, taxes, and insurance as too variable to be included in a general estimate.

## Assumptions

Equipment Operating Hours: Some typical equipment operating hours for an office facility are as follows:

| Location | Total Equipment Operating Hours/Year |
|---|---|
| Miami | 3,450 |
| Atlanta | 2,700 |
| Newark | 2,300 |
| Chicago | 2,000 |

For this analysis, we will assume 2,000 hours as total equipment operating hours per year and 1,000 hours as equivalent full-load cooling hours.

A typical electrical chiller demand schedule (used in this cost comparison) is as follows:

| Month | Percent Of Full Load Kw |
|---|---|
| April | 40 |
| May | 60 |
| June | 80 |
| July | 100 |
| August | 100 |
| September | 80 |
| October | 60 |

Water costs: Typical cost for water is $2.00 per 1,000 gallons in the authors' area. This includes the cost for water, chemical treatment, and sewer charges to dispose of cooling tower blow down. Typical use for the various cooling options is estimated to be the annual operating hours times the following[1]:

| System | Gallons/Ton-Hour |
|---|---|
| Single-Stage Absorption | 8.0 |
| Double-Stage Absorption | 6.2 |
| Gas Engine-Driven Chiller | 4.3 |
| Direct Gas-Fired | 6.2 |
| Electric Centrifugal | 4.0 |

Maintenance Costs: Annual package chiller system maintenance costs are detailed in Table 1.

| Annual Maintenance Costs* | | | | | |
|---|---|---|---|---|---|
| System | 100 Tons | 200 Tons | 400 Tons | 500 Tons | 600 Tons |
| Electric Centrifugal | $3,700 | $ 6,000 | $ 8,000 | $ 9,000 | $10,800 |
| Single-Stage Absorption | 4,600 | 7,000 | 9,600 | 11,000 | 13,200 |
| Double-Stage Absorption | 4,800 | 7,600 | 10,000 | 11,500 | 13,800 |
| Direct Gas-Fired | 5,000 | 8,000 | 10,400 | 12,000 | 14,400 |
| Gas Engine-Driven Chiller** | 6,000 | 10,600 | 17,200 | 20,500 | 24,600 |

*From reference 1.
**The maintenance on the engines should average $0.0115 per ton per operating hour. This is added to the electric chiller maintenance cost to arrive at the total cost.

TABLE 1. PACKAGE CHILLER MAINTENANCE COSTS

Operating Energy Use: Energy use for electric chillers, including auxiliaries, is 0.65 kw/ton-hour for an HCFC-123 machine. It will be lower for a high-efficiency electric machine at a slight incremental cost. For gas-cooling equipment, the gas usage is as follows[1]:

| System | High Heat Value Input In Btu/Ton-Hour* |
|---|---|
| Single-Stage Absorption | 22,000 |
| Double-Stage Absorption | 12,200 |
| Direct Gas-Fired | 13,000 |
| Gas Engine-Driven Chiller | 9,300 |
| *Assuming 82% boiler efficiency. | |

Unit auxiliary use includes lube oil pumps, controls, solution pump, and evaporator pumps, etc. Primary and secondary chilled water pumps and supply and return fans, being common, have not been included in the analysis. For electric centrifugal machines, auxiliary usage is already included in kw/ton as previously mentioned[1]:

| System | Kw/Ton |
|---|---|
| Single-Stage Absorption | 0.010 |
| Double-Stage Absorption | 0.021 |
| Direct Gas-Fired | 0.024 |
| Gas Engine-Driven Chiller | 0.040 |

Condenser water pump electrical usage was estimated as follows[1]:

| System | Kw/Ton |
|---|---|
| Single-Stage Absorption | 0.110 |
| Double-Stage Absorption | 0.094 |
| Direct Gas-Fired | 0.096 |
| Gas Engine-Driven Chiller | 0.054 |
| Electric Centrifugal | 0.048 |

Cooling tower fan usage is as follows[1]:

| System | Kw/Ton |
|---|---|
| Single-Stage Absorption | 0.138 |
| Double-Stage Absorption | 0.113 |
| Direct Gas-Fired | 0.143 |
| Gas Engine-Driven Chiller | 0.087 |
| Electric Centrifugal | 0.079 |

Cost Summary

The total annual costs for the various systems at five tonnages were calculated. Table 2 details the installed costs of the various systems. A gas cost of $3.00/mcf and electric costs of $0.05/kwh (average cost scenario) and $0.10/kwh (high cost scenario) were used. The final annual costs, which include electric, gas, maintenance, and water costs, are detailed in Tables 3 and 4. These clearly show that electric cooling is the most economical choice except in high electric cost areas. Even with high electric cost detailed in Table 4, some of the gas-cooling options have only a slight annual cost advantage, with poor paybacks on the added costs. Tables 5 and 6 show amortized life-cycle costs of the 100 ton and 500 ton chillers, respectively. Where rebates are available and electric costs are higher, gas cooling may offer a better payback.

## Chiller Installed Cost
### includes chiller, tower, pumps & piping

| Tons | Single-Stage Absorption | Double-Stage Absorption | Gas Engine Driven | Direct Gas Fired | Electric Chiller |
|---|---|---|---|---|---|
| 100 | $117,000 | $183,000 | $107,000 | $139,000 | $67,300 |
| 200 | 178,600 | 222,700 | 160,650 | 189,600 | 112,500 |
| 400 | 291,000 | 357,200 | 287,000 | 335,200 | 185,200 |
| 500 | 330,750 | 424,500 | 342,000 | 408,000 | 232,600 |
| 600 | 397,000 | 483,000 | 397,000 | 483,000 | 251,400 |

TABLE 2. INSTALLED COSTS[2,3]

## Total Annual Cost
### includes electric, gas, maintenance & water costs
### Average Electric Cost Scenario

| Tons | Single-Stage Absorption | Double-Stage Absorption | Gas Engine Driven | Direct Gas Fired | Electric Chiller |
|---|---|---|---|---|---|
| 100 | $15,710 | $12,080 | $11,415 | $12,695 | $9,185 |
| 200 | 29,220 | 22,160 | 21,430 | 23,390 | 16,970 |
| 400 | 54,040 | 39,120 | 38,860 | 41,180 | 29,940 |
| 500 | 66,550 | 47,900 | 47,575 | 50,475 | 36,425 |
| 600 | 79,860 | 57,480 | 57,090 | 60,570 | 43,710 |

TABLE 3.  ANNUAL COST, AVERAGE ELECTRIC COST

## Total Annual Cost
### includes electric, gas, maintenance & water costs
### High Electric Cost Scenario

| Tons | Single-Stage Absorption | Double-Stage Absorption | Gas Engine Driven | Direct Gas Fired | Electric Chiller |
|---|---|---|---|---|---|
| 100 | $17,020 | $13,220 | $12,320 | $14,010 | $13,070 |
| 200 | 31,840 | 24,440 | 23,240 | 26,020 | 24,740 |
| 400 | 59,280 | 43,680 | 42,480 | 46,440 | 45,480 |
| 500 | 73,100 | 53,600 | 52,100 | 57,050 | 55,850 |
| 600 | 87,720 | 64,320 | 62,520 | 68,460 | 67,020 |

TABLE 4.  ANNUAL COST, HIGH ELECTRIC RATE

### 100 Ton Chiller

| System | Net Present Worth | Simple Payback (Years) |
|---|---|---|
| Single Stage Absorption | ($329,728) | Never |
| Double Stage Absorption | ($340,118) | Never |
| Gas Engine Driven | ($258,330) | 53 |
| Direct Fired Gas | ($309,207) | Never |
| Electric Chiller | ($219,090) | Base |
| Assuming: 8% cost of money, 4% escalation of water & maintenance, 2.25% escalation of electric, 4.5% escalation of gas and 23 year life of all equipment. | | |

TABLE 5.  AMORTIZED LIFE CYCLE COST -- 100 TON CHILLER

### 500 Ton Chiller

| System | Net Present Worth | Simple Payback (Years) |
|---|---|---|
| Single Stage Absorption | ($1,256,537) | Never |
| Double Stage Absorption | ($1,083,208) | 85 |
| Gas Engine Driven | ($988,900) | 29 |
| Direct Fired Gas | ($1,110,549) | Never |
| Electric Chiller | ($875,203) | Base |
| Assuming: 8% cost of money, 4% escalation of water & maintenance, 2.25% escalation of electric, 4.5% escalation of gas and 23 year life of all equipment. | | |

TABLE 6.  AMORTIZED LIFE CYCLE COST -- 500 TON CHILLER

# REFERENCES

[1]CFCs and Electric Chillers, EPRI Document No. TR-100537, prepared by Gilbert & Associates, Gloucester Point, Virginia. Majority of the data for this article is derived from this document with permission from Electric Power Research Institute (EPRI), 1992.

[2]HVAC Systems Evaluation, Harold R. Colen, P.E., R. S. Means Company, Inc., Kingston, Massachusetts, 1990.

[3]Means Mechanical Cost Data, 15th Edition, R. S. Means Company, Inc., Kingston, Massachusetts, 1992.

# Chapter 94
# EMCS Upgrade to 3rd Generation Not an Easy Task

C.E. Neal

## ABSTRACT

The Energy Management Control System (EMCS) for
Sheppard AFB was started in 1976 with contract
completion in 1981.  With other additions the system
grew to over 8,000 points with 350 Field Panels.
Over 35 miles of coax for data transmission were
installed.  In 1987 an effort was started to move to
the "new" generation for the central system.  At the
same time coax replacement with fiber optics was
started.  This paper discusses the problems
encountered which caused a change in plans and a
move to 3rd generation system.  There are many
things to consider when attempting an upgrade.
Conflicting information will make the task that much
harder.  This paper will attempt to show some of the
problems encountered and lessons learned to help
others avoid such difficulties.

## INTRODUCTION

In the May 92 issue of Engineer's Digest, an article
by Mark Serridge, Machine Health Monitoring
Specialist, Bruel & Kjaer, talks about condition
monitoring systems being better-than-ever
maintenance tools.  He said "imagine... You are a
maintenance engineer for an oil company in Dhahran
(Saudi Arabia), in the desert.  It is hot, but with
air conditioning your office is silent save the fan
on your PC and the hum of the office a/c.  Your
screen displays a map of 11 oil installations, all
your responsibility.

Microwave links and satellites connect the oil
fields to your screen.  Yellow lights glow next to
each site on the map.  It's been like this for
weeks.  You relax.

Smiling in anticipation, you think about disks that
should arrive Thursday.  After you load them into
your computer, they will send reconfigurations and
software instructions to all condition monitoring
systems at you 11 sites.  You then, for the first
time, will be able to monitor the condition of your
reciprocating pumps.  This prospect pleases you.
While you've grown accustomed to total
predictability from rotary and turbo machinery, the
reciprocating machines still can present surprises
that sometimes ruin a longed-for weekend.  It
pleases you more that adding this extra power
involves no more than plugging a disk into your
computer (the extra transducers and cabling will be
installed by Wednesday, and the monitors themselves
are totally reprogrammable).

An orange, flashing alert light in Al Mubarraz drags
you from your complacency.  You guide the pointer on
your screen to Al Mubarraz and click the mouse

once.  Immediately, you see a plan of the critical
machines there.  The orange light flashes next to
the power train of the electricity generator.  You
click onto that and see the same light flashing next
to the gearbox between the generator and turbine.
One more click reveals the warning comes from the
accelerometer on the bearing on the generator side
of the driven shaft.  All other transducers read
yellow.  One more click initiates  10 analysis of
the accelerometer signal; it's the envelope spectrum
measurement generating the alarm.  You immediately
suspect the bearing.

You call up the expert system resident on your hard
disk.  It confirms your suspicions.  It advises you
the cage on the bearing is failing but reveals you
have no reason to panic.  According to automatic
trend information, you should have three weeks-the
time the bearing will last-in which to get required
parts to the site.  You send this news through the
system to the slave terminal at Al Mubarraz and
relax again."

You may say this is a dream system that may be
developed sometime in the future.  The technology is
there for this to be a reality on your system.  The
days of just using your EMCS to turn equipment on
and off and adjust temperatures are over.  Now is
the time to use the system for what it was once
envisioned, and that is maintenance management.
With the reductions in manpower and multiskilling of
our military technicians, the ability to quickly and
accurately determine a problem will become a
critical part of our EMCS operations.  Getting there
may not be easy and there may be some "wrong turns"
that you make.  The Sheppard experience may help you
make the right turns.

## FIRST GENERATION SYSTEM

The first generation EMCS for Sheppard Air Force Bas
was started in 1976.  When the original contract was
completed, the system comprised of over 100
facilities with over 8,000 hardware points using 35
miles of coax cable for the data transmission link.
The system was classed a "C", which means it
provided energy management through special
application programs and operator intervention as
well as providing the capability to troubleshoot
mechanical and utility systems.

A vast amount of information could be made
available.  The computer was to be the cure-all of
our HVAC problems.  As a result, "everything" was
connected.  As time went on it was realized that
itwas not necessary to "see" everything.  It was
also realized that the computer could not work
wonders if the mechanical equipment was not in good
working order along with the controls.  With so many

things connected it was very expensive to maintain. The system needed cleaning up.

Points were eliminated that would not "make us money". We found which application programs worked and which didn't. After considerable effort to make the programs work, several were discontinued. Through all of this the customer suffered to some extent. Considerable operator involvement was necessary to make the remaining programs work. This became very labor intensive and little time was left for diagnostics.

FIGURE 1.   FIRST GENERATION CENTRAL

FIGURE 2.   FIRST GENERATION DISK DRIVES

FIGURE 3.   FIRST GENERATION FIELD PANELS

The data transmission medium (DTM) began to deteriorate. The North Texas area has many spring electrical storms which cause havoc with the system. The errors induced in the system from the DTM plus other field sensor problems gave the operators fits. However, in spite of all the problems, EMCS made great strides in reducing energy consumption. Sheppard Air Force Base was able to make the target reduction for FY 1985 which was 20% less than FY 75 consumption. The system had proven its worth. As more applications were being considered and the desire to take advantage of new advances were considered, coupled with an increased effort at energy reduction, it was very clear that the EMCS needed to be upgraded.

## SECOND GENERATION SYSTEM

The DTM was one of the first things to look at. After considerable discussion with our headquarters it was decided to go with fiber optics. We were to install an 8 fiber cable. All parties believed that it would be possible to multiplex up to 512 channel on a single fiber. This would more than take care of our needs. The base would be configured into a ring concept and the work would be done in stages. We were to use two fibers for EMCS, two for fire reporting, two for security systems, and two for intercom or other applications. This would satisfy all requirements. For the same size cable the fiber count could have easily been doubled with a nominal increase in cost. This is something to consider, especially if any type of area wide networking is planned with other data medium. The first phase was funded and installed. It was not until the second phase was under contract that we were informed by the contractor it could not be constructed as designed. It can not be emphasized enough to ask all the questions you can when you contemplate any EMCS upgrade. The problem here was that the EMCS vendor did not have all the answers and the vendor thought we were going in the right direction.

FIGURE 4.  INSTALLING FIBER OPTICS

FIGURE 5.  FIBER OPTIC SPLICE DEVICE

The first thing that we found out was that our EMCS signal was not standard  and therefore could not be multiplexed without having special boards built. The cost were out of the question.  The signal was not one of the standard RS type signals.  It also began to look like more than two fibers would be required for fire reporting to maintain a dual loop capability.

All along the plans were to connect phase II to the end of phase I and use the same two fibers used in phase I.  After the project was under contract, we were notified this would not be possible.  There was a maximum number of fiber optic transmitter/receiver cards allowed on a channel.  (Each building where

there was an EMCS drop required a board.)  The designer said that 16 drops was maximum though it may be possible to get a few more on.  As a result two other fibers were required from phase I to get phase II back to the central.  Looking back it is hard to see where things could have been done differently.  We thought the right questions were being asked.  Add that to the fact that salesman didn't know there was a problem made a bad situation worse.  We had to keep changing plans to make things work.  One lesson is to not react before you are ready.  It may be best to lose funding than to jump when not ready.  Ask all the questions you can and be sure before you start on that upgrade project. The problem is that even if you think you asked the right questions there may be some surprises along the way.  Be prepared to be flexible.

FIGURE 6.  NEW WAY TO HANG CABLE

Due to the age of the central computer a move to the next generation computer was started.  This computer would have better graphics capability and better applications programs.  Efforts were started in 1987 to get the system.  Due to funding problems (not able to get a project funded) the system was purchased through the supply system in "pieces". Once all came in, a contract was let to assemble and bring on line.  This took several years to complete.  Two channels were connected to this computer.  The application programs were much better and the graphics capabilities showed promise.  One major problem was that another computer was necessary to bridge the gapor interface with the field.  At first, this was not thought to be a very expensive proposition.  This proved false.  By the time the computer was up and running with two channels connected, it was decided that another way had to be found.

One thing that you will find is that the state of the art is moving so fast it is hard to stay up with it all.  Some decisions that you think are solid may prove not to be.  While trying to figure out how to get around the expense problem, a new technology came on the scene.  This was a PC based system taking EMCS from a hardware dependent system to a software dependent system.

## THIRD GENERATION SYSTEM

During the completion and first year operation of the second generation system (the first system was still on line) efforts were underway to install Multiloop Direct Digital Control (DDC). This was done by getting pilot project approval. The DDC controllers would not "talk" to either the first or the second generation computer without having to install field gateway devices. After several controllers were installed, a project was funded to connect the DDC controllers to the second generation computer. The contractor came back with a value engineering proposal to install a new generation system that was PC based for the DDC controllers to interface with. This was to become the backbone of the EMCS system and one on which all other decisions were based.

Our new third generation system has all the capabilities you can think about. The graphics package is very good with all sorts of "bells and whistles". Text can be created that is dynamic (temperatures and status show changes while you are reading text). There is also the familiar text mode of operation that is used extensively for troubleshooting. The system works under the familiar PC Windows operating system. A very good spread sheet program is included. With it, points can be selected for dynamic trending. You can see, graphically, the relationships of up to six different inputs. The applications primarily side in the DDC controllers and the central becomes a data gathering and analysis center. The Systems Engineer can modify DDC programs and upload them to the controller or all controllers at the same time. The operators can override the DDC operation if needed.

FIGURE 7. DDC CONTROLLERS

FIGURE 8. THIRD GENERATION CENTRAL COMPUTER.

As luck would have it, all DDC controllers were along the existing fiber optic system. Therefore, the controllers used two unused fibers for the DTM link with the new computer. By the time the computer was on line there were 18 DDC controllers to be connected with others scheduled. Sheppard Air Force Base had received blanket approval for DDC on all O&M and MILCON projects. Negotiations between the EMCS vendor and mechanical contractors were getting us DDC.

By now all the right people were involved in the planning including top management of the EMCS vendor. We all knew where we wanted to go and how we were going to get there. The key was to go to gateways around the base that would take inputs from all the varied EMCS field panels and convert their signals to a standard RS signal for transmission back to the central. When this project is completed the first two generation systems will be retired. Learning from past experiences has dictated that any future contract action will be by request for proposal. Things move so quickly in the computer area that a system is obsolete before you can get the specification on the street. An RFP is the only way to go.

Even with the new system surprises come along. We are limited to 29 controllers on a single peer bus. One project coming on line will have 24 plus controllers. This will require its own fiber optic path back to the central. Sheppard Air Force Base has a very large construction program underway to take care of courses from bases that are closing. All so far will have DDC. There is no reason to think that anything other than DDC will be installed.

## CONCLUSION

Sheppard is making progress in developing a system for the 1990's that will also function well into the future by being able to upgrade quickly at a reasonable cost. When you look at the technology that is available, the need to connect your generating plants and water plants, base irrigation systems and other functions not yet thought about, it is clear that the Al Mubarraz story can take place at your installation. We can all agree that this must be the wave of the future and all actions must be to that end. Hopefully our story will guide your thinking so mistakes are not made.

# Chapter 95

# Documenting Success of Energy Management Cost Reduction Initiatives

A. Stewart

The scope of this paper is to offer methods to document energy saving projects. The examples used are based on actual industrial facilities. I will define concepts to be used in the analysis of the industrial work place energy consumption. With the concepts defined we can begin to apply the documentation strategy for some specific examples. Why should we be interested in auditing the results of energy projects?

Nearly every industrial facility has embarked on the road to energy efficiency. As one of my plant engineer associates relates "If all our energy saving programs were working as stated the power company would be paying us." The underlying principles in this statement are true. Does it mean we as technicians, engineers and managers of energy projects have failed? No, we have however failed to finish the job and document the results. My experience has shown there is good support and enthusiasm for those energy projects we begin. It is also my experience that a well documented successful project provides many levels of satisfaction. Large energy management projects involve a major financial commitment. Documenting the results provides all those who supported the project from finance, management and the technical staff the positive reinforcement to support your future projects. We should begin by defining what an energy audit is and what is the expected result of an audit.

## The Energy Audit

The energy audit is a document which tabulates the results of energy related savings associated with a specified course of action. The most important aspect of the energy audit is to measure the actual consumption and account for deviations in the expected energy consumption. Audits should be produced on a timely basis which may be daily, weekly, monthly or quarterly as necessary to achieve your goals. Energy audits will vary in complexity depending on the utility rate cost structure, utility billing cycles, weather, production volumes, and frequency of equipment changes.

Energy audits can be used for a wide variety of projects. In the most simple case we eliminate some energy consuming activity. For example we eliminate the operation of some equipment on weekend hours. In the more complicated case we modify the method of consuming energy. For example we replace an air-conditioning system with a more efficient unit. In our home environment we could expect to see reduced utility bills to document the latter example. However, in the industrial environment many changes in energy consumption are occurring simultaneously. We must identify change in our energy consumption pattern quickly because of the potential for waste and the ability for the workers to describe the events leading up to the change. Some change may be due to new equipment operation but we should be able to record the reasons for change.

## Historical Utility Information

Two years worth of billing data are required, three years are better. You should also have two years production data again three are better. I look for change in consumption or production data over the years and seek out those within the plant who can explain why the changes occurred. Based on the energy data and production data I begin to model the performance of the facility. The first pass at my model will be by hand calculation. A recent audit showed the most recent year to have reduced energy demand and energy. After conducting several interviews I learned one of the larger machines was out of service for the previous summer period. Additionally, the plant had moved to just in time production and had drawn down all of the products stockpiled the previous year. A rail strike also had caused abnormal production as raw materials were not available. All of these conditions yielded an energy usage and cost below the trend of previous years. This reconciling historical data to facility use and production levels is a critical component of the audit. Fine tuning will occur throughout the audit but your ability to compensate for change in the facility use or production levels will be only as accurate as your original calculations for the first few audits. Major changes in your baseline data well into the audit process can lead management to lose confidence in you audit.

A first pass at developing the major energy cost centers can be accomplished as shown in the table. A cost center can be energy use for a specific piece of equipment or a larger department level. Cost centers should be established to make resource management more effective. This particular table is based on the total annual consumption with demand values at a maximum. This process can be repeated for summer and winter months .

The plant is approximately 260K square feet.
**Assume 50% office/productuion and 50% warehouse.**
Office/production at 2Watt per SF.
Warehouse at 1 Watt per SF.

| | | KW | Annual hrs | MKWH |
|---|---|---|---|---|
| Lighting | | | | |
| Office/production | 260KSF*.50*2W/SF = | 260 | 8760 | 2.28 |
| Warehouse | 260KSF*.50* 1W/SF= | 130 | 8760 | 1.14 |
| | | | | |
| Air compressors | | | | |
| 3 at 200HP | 3*200HP*.8KW/HP= | 450 | 4300 | 1.94 |
| | | | | |
| Battery chargers | | | | |
| 16 at 10KW | 16*.4*10= | 64 | 1900 | 0.12 |
| | 40% usage factor | | | |
| HVAC | | | | |
| 350 Tons at 1.1KW/Ton= | | 440 | 5000 | 2.20 |
| Roof Top HVAC units | | 100 | 4500 | 0.45 |
| Process cooling requirements | | | | |
| at 150 Tons *1.1KW/Ton | | 165 | 6500 | 1.07 |
| | | | | |
| Process loads | | 900 | 6500 | 5.85 |
| Process chilled water 150 Tons | | 165 | 6500 | 1.07 |
| | | | | |
| Miscellaneous power | | 100 | 1000 | 0.10 |
| | | ======== | | ======== |
| | TOTAL | 2674 | | 16.12 |

Calendar year 1990 showed 2765KW and 15.9MKWH energy use

## Utility Rate Structure

Many different rate structures are in place across our country. The most common similarities are the treatment of energy consumption (KWH) and energy demand (KW) as two separate entities for billing purposes. Most rate structures (or tariffs) provide the maximum benefit to those facilities were the load can be maintained at a constant level all year long. For most of us this type of load profile is unattainable. We must recognize how to use the rate structure to our advantage. Energy demand costs can comprise over 50 percent of your bill. Further with 12 month ratchet clauses a high consumption level in one metering period (usually 15 to 30 minutes) can cause a new peak demand which must be paid for over the next 12 months. A thorough audit will begin with a complete understanding of your rate structure as KWH saved must be computed at the marginal purchase rate. That is the rate the utility will charge for one additional KWH. Which is a very different number from the average cost of a KWH (Total utility bill divided by the Total utility cost). Energy demand must also be computed at the marginal rate. The required rate information will be explained on the tariff filed with your Public Service Commission.

## Utility Billing Cycles

Most utilities still read the meter by hand. The exact time and date cause the monthly bill from year to year to have different periods. For example the January 1991 bill may have 33 days and the January 1992 may have 29 days. If the bill is not factored for the proper number of days the data from January 1992 could look overly opti-

mistic. It is important to make sure that the proper number of week days and weekend days are accounted for as these days have very different energy usage in most facilities.

## Weather Adjustment

Manual methods for developing energy audits have long relied on the concept of degree-days. This method of accounting for the impact of weather is rooted in the residential energy auditing process. The premise of this system is that there is a temperature at which the building envelop and contents are in thermal equilibrium with the outside conditions. It was reasoned that a typical home is in equilibrium at approximately 65 degrees Fahrenheit. Measurements support the reliability of the 65 degree Fahrenheit outside air temperature figure as the balance point where internal home heat loads cancel external heat loss in modern home structures. After determining the balance point at 65 degrees Fahrenheit some method of quantifying the effects of higher and lower outside air temperatures was required. The mean temperature for each day was chosen as the representative temperature for each particular day. The effect of higher (or lower) temperatures could now be quantified as the difference between 65 degrees Fahrenheit and the mean temperature for the day. Mean temperatures above the 65 degrees Fahrenheit would be referred to as cooling degree days and mean temperatures below 65 degrees Fahrenheit would be heating degree days. For example, if the mean temperature was 55 degrees Fahrenheit then that day would be counted as having 10 heating degree days. As the resistance to heat flow is linear with the thermal gradient between two surfaces, so it was decided to aggregate the sum of the hours above (or below) the 65 degree Fahrenheit.

Having established the beginnings of the degree day method for quantifying weather impact on facilities we now need to examine the suitability for industrial facilities. We desire to establish the balance point for thermal equilibrium. In industrial plants it is common to require cooling as low as 55 degrees Fahrenheit outside temperatures. Generally, air side economizers allow outside air to be used for cooling with outside air temperatures below 55 degrees Fahrenheit. Some unique applications will require cooling to 45 degrees Fahrenheit outside air temperature. (Large internal heat loads without the benefit of air side economizers can require the use of mechanical refrigeration.) Standard degree-day data will be presented for use based on the 65 degree Fahrenheit balance point. For use with your facility the data will require adjustment for your balance point temperature.

To establish a new balance point we must remember that the degree-day is based on the mean temperature. For example let's assume the balance point is 55 degrees Fahrenheit and the data we are adjusting shows a particular month has 600 heating degree-days. For a thirty day month we calculate the following:

Deg-days=(deg-day data) - ((65-55)*30 days)

Deg-days=600 -(10*30)

Deg-days=300 degree-days

We are able to take advantage of the fact that the degree-day data is based on the mean temperature so to reduce the balance point by 10 degrees we subtract 10 degree-days for each day of the month.

Heating systems tend to respond in a linear fashion to the colder temperatures. So the adjustments we made above should help the correlation between heating fuels consumption and weather data.

Cooling systems tend to respond in nonlinear fashion to weather data. Two main reasons exist for the nonlinear response:

1. When large cooling plants are started the loads are low and cooling plant efficiency is low. The result is much higher energy consumption than would be expected for the connected loads. The cost to produce a unit of cooling can approach twice the cost per unit when the cooling system is well loaded. (The cooling system consists of the chiller, pumps, fans, and air handlers,)

2. Most chillers in use require the entering water temperature to the condenser to be 85 degrees F. With lower outside air (below say 85 degrees F, main concern here is wet bulb temperature) the wet bulb temperature can be expected to be in the low to mid 70 degrees (for Atlanta, GA). The result of 95+ degree Fahrenheit out side air temperatures and mean coincident wet bulb (75+ degrees Fahrenheit) can drive the condenser water above the 85 degree Fahrenheit design levels resulting in increased energy consumption per cooling unit produced. Residential air conditioning on the other hand responds more uniformly to the increase in outside air temperatures as the unit adjusts run time to meet the cooling loads.

My goal with the above discussion for degree-day calculations is as follows:

1. Demonstrate the validity of the heating energy usage correlation with degree-day data and the appropriate balance point for heating.

2. Demonstrate the nonlinear response for most industrial facilities of cooling energy load and cooling degree-days.

3. Based on the discussion for chiller energy use it should be evident that an unusually hot day can set a new demand peak for your facility without appreciably affecting the overall weather data for the month.

4. A computer model of your facility with hourly chiller load data will provide the most useful data to manage energy consumption and energy demand for the annual cycle. The portion of energy consumption subject to weather impact will be easily established. The error in extrapolating from the weather data of the thirty year average will be much smaller than the error from degree-day data.

This is one of the most difficult areas for the auditor. The goal in this area is to establish a correlation between the number of products produced and the energy consumed. A very true statement is "You cannot manage that which you cannot measure". Now is the time you desire those separately metered histories, but in most plants the data does not exist. Almost immediately you realize that production will have fixed cost and variable cost. Many machines used in industry consume energy whether producing product or sitting idle but ready to produce. The operation of this machine is a fixed cost, independent of throughput. An example of such a situation would be a large heated tank for cleaning machine parts. Often the energy use between production and idle is insignificant. In large plants there may be several machines producing the very same end product however each machine may have a different energy consumption. This can be the case for injection molding machines where the mold used is based on the current requirement for containers. A machine with variable cost for energy is, for example, a metal stamping press. We should remember that almost all machines have some fixed cost. If your facility is served by a utility with an energy demand ratchet operation of your equipment for one measuring period of 15 or 30 minutes will incur demand charges for the next 12 months, whether you use the machine again or not.

One area to examine is the amount of processed material. If historical data can show a correlation to processed material you may use the volumes for energy correlation. In my studies I have found areas where for example certain types of resins may be worked two or three times if the product is not acceptable on the first pass. The amount of energy can vary widely per unit of processed material. There will be some waste associated with most processing, the waste may or may not be quantified.

Additional utilities in use are compressed air, vacuum air, water, chilled water, steam, and hot water. Many more utilities are in use in plants. Some of these utilities are shared between production and personnel comfort heating and cooling systems. Part of your task will be to prorate the utility usage. It may be determined that a particular utility should be metered, however in most applications you will have to estimate utility consumption based on knowledge of the load served. It helps me to estimate the individual loads and then develop the expected total consumption. Total consumption can be reconciled with the total available quantity for each utility. For example chiller logs will be helpful to determine maximum consumption for chilled water, however process and non-process usage will have to be determined.

**Measuring Results**

A metering plan should be developed as the result of your work. The analysis performed above will show where each utility is most exposed to waste. Additionally, you may wish to meter to establish cost centers. Cost centers help us develop budgets that can be achieved. Many utilities can be wasted without visible warning signs, metering will quickly pinpoint such losses. Leaking steam traps can significantly increase energy consumption, without meters and a baseline for appropriate consumption in may be several months before major leaks are detected.

The results of your energy program should be proudly displayed for all. I can think of no better way to get support for your program than to put up some nice color charts that demonstrate your success. Charts should show comparisons to historical billing data for the following areas: energy cost, total Btu values, KWH, KW, and other sources of energy. All to often we believe the results of various energy saving projects are inherently obvious. With all the change going on in most plants savings get lost or offset by new consumption. This level of accounting can best be handled by a computerized energy management system. One of the most important events to occur is a physical inventory of all plant energy consumers.

## Physical Audit

We have already talked about the need for good utility consumption history. Now we need to know how the plant equipment has changed over the last few years. We could go to each department and take inventory, however, that process could take months. A better approach would be to visit your purchasing department and ask for a list of all equipment purchased for the last two years. By tracking down each piece of equipment you will develop the energy consumption profile from your interviews with the end user of the new equipment. Also the end user can tell you if some equipment was replaced or removed. Some plants regulated by federal agencies may go through extensive testing of machines and produce no product. If in doubt ask the equipment user. The result of your work will be a table in the energy audit which adds new loads and subtracts removed loads. New loads will be added to your baseline data so you can project where the current energy consumption would have been without the energy initiatives.

## Summary

This paper discusses the building blocks for a successful energy audit in the post-energy project phase. This comprehensive approach is warranted to fully disclose results of energy initiatives. Many of the tasks discussed can and should be automated. Analysis of deviation for energy consumption is most effective if completed a short period after the event. Weeks after a major change in energy consumption patterns no one may remember what caused the event.

# Chapter 96
# The Art of Performing a "Walk-Through" Energy Audit

R.R. Vaillencourt

A dictionary definition of the word "engineering" is: "1. the science of making practical application of pure sciences." Similarly, the word "art" has, as two of its meanings: "1. the principles governing any craft or skill. 2. skilled workmanship or execution." We, as energy engineers, must strive to emphasize the practical application of whatever knowledge we have acquired, and we must do so skillfully.

Why? Because in the world of building managers and production managers energy conservation has been a synonym for suffering. As energy engineers we really haven't done much to dispel these fears. In many cases we have earned the reputation for going off half-cocked. A reputation for squeezing off the flow of BTUs with little regard for anything else.

To counter this we must continuously learn the "principles governing our craft". And since many of these principles affect non-engineering facts of life, we must apply them skillfully. We must know when they are important enough to push for and when to back off. This is art. The elements of style, finesse, subtlety, etc., must be constantly balanced with facts and reality. Engineering realities, financial realities, cultural realities, and the most frustrating of all: human nature.

A walk through energy audit consists of two distinct operations. The first is to determine with as much accuracy as is possible exactly what the existing conditions are. This is accomplished during the walk-through stage. The second stage is defining and evaluating Energy Conservation Measures.

The limitations of a walk-through audit should be clearly understood. You cannot completely understand any complicated processes and even most simple ones as they apply in any specific application. However, the process auxiliaries will, in most cases, be standard applications of pumps, fans, cooling (air and water), lighting, etc. The goal is to suggest ways to provide these functions in such a way that the process is "unaware" of a change, yet the operating expense is reduced and reliability is unchanged, or improved.

This approach will not produce detailed plans and specifications. The goal is to point out the possibilities with enough detail and cost/savings estimates to indicate which ideas deserve an in depth study.

This paper will assume that the reader already has the necessary basic energy engineering training and skills. The main goal will be to: 1) leave them with an attitude that will foster cooperation from plant personnel, and 2) to attempt to list specific areas in commercial/industrial applications that they can quickly identify, quantify the potential for savings, and outline key information to gather during the audit.

**"Tilting at windmills hurts you more than the windmills."** [1]

Have you ever wondered why a production supervisor is <u>not</u> pleased to see you? And if not openly hostile, he is at best uncooperative.

That's because Energy Management means changing his procedures, retraining his men, and giving him more paperwork. He is a successful production supervisor because he <u>produces</u>. Why should he go out of his way to do something that will only make <u>you</u> look good? And give him more headaches. What's in it for him?

It's alright to tell him about making the company more competitive or profitable, and I'm sure he agrees with those goals. But my experience has shown me that in reality <u>his</u> next raise or promotion depends **entirely** upon whether he gets the product out on time without mistakes. What does that have to do with energy management? Nothing. That's <u>your</u> problem, not his. <u>Your</u> next raise or promotion depends on how much you reduce the company's energy bills. Nobody comes to you and asks you why orders are not being filled on time.

Believe me, this is a **big** windmill.

**"You live and learn. Or you don't live long."**

"We should not expect to utilize in practice all the motive power of combustibles. The attempts made to attain this result would be far more hurtful than useful if they caused other important considerations to be neglected. The economy of the combustible is only one of the conditions to be fulfilled in heat engines. In many cases it is only secondary. It should often give precedence to safety, to strength, to the durability of the engine, to the small space which it must occupy, to small cost of installation. etc."

Sadi Carnot; 1824

What does this have to do with a walk through audit? Or windmills? Everything. To get this person on your side you must state clearly, and more importantly, you must <u>believe</u> that efficiency is not the only parameter that merits your attention. You only have a few hours to spend with the plant engineer. You <u>need</u> him to keep you out of trouble. You need him on your side. You need to convince him that you are not blind to his needs and are not going to make a name for yourself without any care for his problems.

**"In handling a stinging insect, move very slowly."**

By far, the hardest thing to overcome when dealing with a client plant engineer is that he is, in many cases, defensive. This is <u>completely</u> understandable.

First: He lives, breathes, eats and sleeps with his facility. Whether he wants to, or not, the plant will find him when they need him.

Second: He is always looking for a better way to get something done. Not just energy, but: storage, material handling, purchasing supplies, water, sewage, pollution control, hazardous waste management, maintenance, installations, demolitions, etc., etc., etc. Most of the time some "bean counter" is pushing an idea that he read about in Popular Science. Having been there, I know how you can start with a chip on your shoulder. All it takes is for someone to come in off the street, make a proposal to some production manager (that is the same thing you have been talking about for two years) that gets approved in two weeks, and you can get bitter.

Third: There is no way that anyone off the street can know his plant and processes better than him.

Fourth: He has the attitude: If there was a better way to do it, I would have done it already.

These attitudes are very difficult to avoid developing if you are the plant engineer, and very difficult to overcome if you are the one coming in "off the street".

As a conservation engineer, remember that it is his plant and he has dealt with a lot of "snake oil salesmen". They waste his time and annoy the daylights out of him. Admit immediately that you know he knows more than you about his plant. But try and point out that he isn't expected to know everything about the latest technology. Maybe you do have something to offer. Together, you might be able to sort out what will, or will not, work for him.

The hardest thing for an energy auditor to deal with is the wrong information. There is no way (see #3, above) that he can tell that it's wrong. If he's smart, he will take a long time to describe what will happen, or needs to happen. Hopefully, in this discussion enough information will be passed between you so that both the auditor and the plant engineer know enough to keep each other out of trouble.

That is the essence of this last discussion. KEEP EACH OTHER OUT OF TROUBLE.

If this attitude is made clear to the customer you will be seen as an asset. Your goals are the same as his. You are there to present options. To improve the profitability and the productivity. You are really there to help him.

"What are the facts? Again and again and again - what are the facts? Shun wishful thinking, ignore divine revelation, forget what 'the stars foretell', avoid opinion, care not what the neighbors think, never mind the unguessable 'verdict of history' - what are the facts, and to how many decimal places? You pilot always into an unknown future, facts are your single clue. Get the facts!"

It is my recommendation that you purchase, develop, copy, or steal an audit checklist form. You only have a short time to perform the audit and usually no access for a second visit to get what you missed. Trust me. You will not get everything. But with a good form to prompt you, you won't forget the obvious things.

Find a form and always be ready to modify it. It doesn't matter how many pages you carry. Obviously many of the pages will not apply to the plant that you are doing. But the fact that you note "N/A" where appropriate will give you the confidence that you did not forget it entirely.

The last page should be a list of questions left unanswered when you left, but promised to be answered by plant personnel. A copy of this page with a delivery date should be left with the person at the plant responsible for getting the answers to you.

Keep this list short! Usually this consists of energy consumption records and costs, specific equipment operating times and strategies, horsepower of inaccessible motors, etc. Try very hard to keep it to information that you would like to have. If there is a piece of information that you feel that you need to do your work, try very hard to get it while you are there.

Many times the best intentions of the plant personnel are forgotten when they are faced with putting out daily fires. If the information is necessary for a complete and accurate report, you may be "on hold" for a long time.

"Expertise in one field does not carry over into other fields. But experts often think so. The narrower their field of knowledge the more likely they are to think so."

I recommend that you avoid making recommendations for production processes unless you are asked. It doesn't matter that you were the Corporate Energy Manager for a textile company for over five years. All that means is that you can easily recognize textile machinery and its basic function.

What you should look at is all the auxiliary equipment and functions that support the process. Specifically, cooling water, heating method, exhaust, fume/dust collection, etc. The goal is to provide all these services for the least cost such that the process never experiences a change in their ability to function.

"Never appeal to a man's 'better nature'. He may not have one. Invoking his self-interest gives you more leverage."

I used the term "least cost" on purpose. In order to be useful to the plant, your goal must be to save money. Certainly you are concentrating on the energy consumption. But the reason you are looking at the energy consumption is to reduce its expense aspect to the profitability of the operation as a whole.

"Climate is what we expect, weather is what we get."

Give the plant engineer full power of veto! You may think that you know the climate. The plant engineer knows what the ice and snow feels like! If he indicates that a certain measure is not worth it to him, by all means try to find out why and even try to change his mind. But if he still insists - drop it!

I can't say this strong enough! You don't have to know or accept his reasons. You don't have to agree with him. You do have to give him that power.

"It may be better to be a live jackal than a dead lion, but it is better still to be a live lion. And usually easier."

My own experiences with failed conservation measures taught me an important lesson: Most of the failures occurred when I went for every last BTU. That's when performance fell into the "marginal" or "unsatisfactory" category. The surprise was that the entire project was considered a failure and discarded! If you push the plant engineer unnecessarily I guarantee the project is doomed to failure.

If you prove to him that you are on his side and he has veto power, you will get the first projects implemented.

Now you can build from this success to push for the ones you held back before, if you still want to.

The goal of the previous discussion is to help you develop a style and attitude that will encourage cooperation and support from inside the plant. Such support will improve the accuracy and the volume of information that you can acquire in the short time provided.

## "If it can't be expressed in figures, it is not science; it is opinion."

As you perform your calculations, you start to walk a fine line between engineering and opinion. The final numbers are only as good as your assumptions. The best approach is to take the attitude: "This is what I thought I saw and heard. If these assumptions are reasonably correct then the report is reasonably correct."

The walk through audit report is meant to be a <u>first cut</u> report only. The idea is to identify measures that appear to be worth a detailed evaluation. **Many** of these measures will not pass a second cut. Quite often due to feasibility or product quality conflicts, not economics. Your job is to point out the opportunity, ballpark the potential, **and make them tell you "why not".**

You have accomplished your goal. The measure has not been overlooked. It has been evaluated and discarded for logical reasons.

## "The truth of a proposition has nothing to do with its credibility. And vice versa."

So what do you look for?

<u>Lighting:</u> Find out if they are happy with the light levels. Make your initial recommendations based upon a lumen for lumen retrofit. Don't change the color without making sure all interested parties agree.

No pun intended: lighting is the most visible change you can make. If you make a change that is too noticeable, a lot of people will complain. Don't bother them with meters, or color swatches, etc. Don't confuse the issue with facts. They will complain.

When I say "lumen for lumen", try not to cheat. At least start with comparing initial lumens to initial lumens. If you think that they are grossly over lit, then try to compare depreciated lumens to initial lumens. **But tell the plant engineer!** Make him part of the decision.

Exterior lighting should be retrofit to HPS.

I, personally, do not recommend low pressure sodium lights for anything but the most basic security applications. It is my belief that it takes more than just lumens to allow effective "seeing". The monochromatic light grossly distorts all colors such that <u>contrast</u> and <u>perception</u> are greatly impaired. While objects become visible, they are difficult to identify without concentrating on them. This may be fine when the goal is to illuminate objects for safety and security. But if the tasks require identification and recognition, even if it's not too critical, the task becomes very difficult.

<u>Pumps:</u> Centrifugal pumps used to circulate cooling (or heating) water to hvac or process applications offer major savings potential. Look for throttling valves. Not just at the outlet from the pump, but at the various end use equipment. Many process cooling water loops are supplied by a pump that runs constantly, pressurizing a plantwide header with various machine taps ending in a valve (solenoid or manual) at each machine.

Each of those machine valves varies the flow requirement from the pump. I usually recommend a variable speed drive (VSD) controlled by a pressure sensor in the header. As a valve opens, the flow increases and the pressure drops. This will speed up the pump to maintain the pressure setpoint. As a valve closes, the flow will decrease and the pressure will rise, slowing the pump down.

This measure should also be evaluated for HVAC chilled water loops with two-way, modulating valves at each coil.

Cooling towers transfer the heat from the condenser side of refrigeration machines to the outside air. Installing a VSD controlled by condenser inlet temperature will ensure that the gpm (mass flow rate) is matched to the btu rejection requirements. (This measure should be coordinated with the VSD recommendation for the cooling tower fan.)

**Caution!** Check with the equipment manufacturer to determine the <u>minimum flow rate</u> required to maintain turbulent flow through the condenser and evaporator tubes.

Another common application is a boiler feedwater pump that runs continuously while the actual inlet flow to the boiler is controlled by a modulating float valve. The calculations must take into account the fact that the pump must provide a minimum pressure higher than the boiler pressure. This means that there is a minimum horsepower requirement even if the flow is negligible.

The key things to look for are: Circulating fluids, throttled flow, stepped flow variations, pumps in continuous operation against a control valve.

Things to look out for are: constant high flow requirements, non-variable fluid transfer systems, positive displacement pumps.

<u>Fans:</u> Many building exhaust fan systems are grossly oversized and over-operated. They are designed for the worst occupancy conditions and run that way continuously for 24 hours a day. A VSD will allow plant personnel to match the exhaust quantities to the requirements without making major modifications. The best part of this is that you can reduce the exhaust by duty cycling without completely stopping it. This will not add any excess strain or wear on the equipment and, more importantly, it will avoid complaints.

Cooling tower fans provide additional air circulation through cascading water to increase the cooling effect of conduction and convection. As the air temperature drops (specifically the wet bulb) less air flow will be required to provide the same cooling effect. A VSD controlled by discharge water temperature will allow the fan speed and energy to automatically match the cooling requirements. (If the cooling tower pump VSD application is also implemented, the controls should be designed such that the pump is brought up to full speed before the fan is enabled to start at slow speed.)

Many variable air volume (VAV) systems were originally designed without cfm control devices. Second generation VAV systems utilized pressure relief dampers, or fan outlet and inlet dampers to control fan output. All these systems can benefit from the installation of a VSD and removal of the other control methods.

Things to look out for: dust collection system fans require a minimum cfm to maintain carrying velocity throughout the duct system, high static pressure fans quite often are not centrifugal fans, certain fan speeds may result in resonant frequency vibration amplification (this can be avoided with VSD options).

<u>Building Envelope Options:</u>    Most  of  the  time,
modifications to the building envelope are too expensive
to provide an acceptable payback period **unless it saves
electric heat.**

<u>Heat Recovery:</u>    High  temperature  exhaust  streams  can
produce hot water.  Process cooling is often accomplished
by running city water through a heat exchanger, cooling
the process fluid and heating the city water.  The more
audits you do, the more you'll be surprised to see this
clean,  hot  water  dumped  down  the  drain.    The  first
question is whether the plant can use that much hot
water.

If not, look into a cooling tower and water recirculation
system.  This will use more energy, but will save major
amounts of money in water and sewer charges.  (Remember,
you are there to <u>help save money</u>, not just energy.)

Things to look for are: stacks above the roof, drainage
pits in the floor, and water vapor in the air.  Listen
for water splashing or air moving through a duct.  Touch
(carefully) the pipes and the ducts.

Things to look out for: no place to use the recovered
heat,  contaminated  fluid  streams  that  can  destroy
recovery equipment, cooling contaminated exhaust air to
the point that the contaminates are condensed out of the
stream.

In conclusion, bear in mind that a walk through audit has
many limitations.   But it is a necessary first step.
Plant Engineers are doing it all the time that they are
in their plant.  You may be inside for the first time,
but you can accomplish much if you use all your senses,
your experiences, and your wits.  It is often a question
of balance.  Don't get greedy and don't be lazy.

And remember:

    **"Never underestimate the power of human stupidity."**

Especially your own.

    **"One man's 'magic' is another man's engineering."**

And, finally;

        **"A motion to adjourn is always in order."**


[1] All  quotes  are  from  Robert  Heinlein's  "Notebooks  of
Lazarus Long" as found in his book "Time Enough For Love"

# Chapter 97

# Monitoring & Controlling Large Computers & Support Systems

J.P. Cilia

## ABSTRACT

Distributed Direct Digital Control (DDDC) for building and facility automation systems has been implemented and operational at IBM for many years. This DDDC system monitors and controls chillers, boilers, lighting, heating, ventilating and air-conditioning. Finding new ways to monitor and control untapped high potential users of energy and support unmanned areas for optimum operation and support is a major concern for IBM Corporation. The desire to remotely monitor and control unmanned computer raised floor areas resulted in the development of the System View Site Manager Services (SSMS) offering.

Besides powering on-off computers and peripherals, SSMS can communicate environmental information such as room temperature, relative humidity, fire, smoke and security system status, and alarms through the same network.

This paper describes the steps required to design and implement a system for a computer raised floor area. This unique installation will remotely monitor and control large frame computers, peripherals, and environmental systems simultaneously. Expansion of SSMS using NetView Automation throughout the plant and the enterprise is also covered.

## UNDERSTANDING YOUR SYSTEMS AND OPERATIONS

The same requirements to understand your mechanical and electrical systems apply to Data Process (DP) equipment. These basic requirements are necessary for the monitoring and controlling of DP equipment residing inside large buildings, hospitals, college campuses, or plants.

In order to reduce operating costs, there has been a trend in the 90's to reduce staff personnel within all fields of a business. The DP field is no exception. Reducing staff personnel implies that the existing operation has too many bodies to perform certain tasks or, in most cases today, cost reductions are imposed in every area of the business in order to be competitive in the world market. This plan of action requires some kind of automated systems to replace most of the tasks performed by your DP personnel.

This section is intended to provide the reader with a basic picture of the major DP equipment and operation required to operate, manage, and support any large buildings, hospitals, college campuses, or plants.

## Hardware

Today, most companies use a large number of computers and peripherals to operate, manage and support their business. Typical examples are office automation and telecommunication.

To show the varieties of hardware in the DP environment, a partial list of potential hardware located in your site are identified.

- Workstations
  - Personal computers (PC's)
  - Printers, plotters and displays
- Mid-Range and Large Systems
  - Processors
    - ▲ Control units
    - ▲ Printers, plotters, terminals
    - ▲ Magnetic Media
      - △ Direct access storage devices (DASD's) and tapes
- Telecommunications Systems
  - Modems
  - Communication controllers

## Operation

Today, integration of office automation, computers, manufacturing automation and peripherals is accomplished by one or more networks which transfer data from one system to another.

This connectivity provides the door to the host computer using expert system software and artificial intelligence to achieve the highest productivity at the minimum cost. Existing automation packages are available from many manufacturers and software companies to provide such support. The operation, management, and support of a site is done through the host computer. The host computer determines which systems, nodes and control units should be operational at different times of the days.

You can see the major part of understanding how your DP equipment operates is absolutely required if you want to control any of your DP equipment. This task usually requires a team of people working in different areas of your DP environment. Many meetings will be necessary to gather all relevant data in order to gain a true understanding of the operation of your DP equipment.

REQUIREMENT GATHERING

Now that you understand how your DP equipment operates, the next step is to specify necessary requirements to decide what you can turn on or off and when. A major problem not yet covered should be coming to your mind. How can you make sure that a computer is not working, i.e., idling, before you shut it down? This question will be discussed and answered later under the Process Data Monitoring section of this paper.

Equipment Survey

This task requires that one or more experts on your DP equipment checks whether the hardware you chose to monitor and control has existing connections for the power-control interface (PCI). Many computer manufacturers like IBM, have provided PCI for some of their hardware since 1966. One of the most common interfaces is the "standard 6-wire interface". In the event that some of the DP equipment you select do not have a PCI, you can go back to the unit manufacturer and request such a connection to be installed. This PCI provides the necessary connection to remotely power up and down (control function) a device and to confirm whether the unit is up or down (monitor function).

Environment monitoring and control is also required to facilitate the operation of your DP room and to reduce operating costs by shutting down air-conditioning units (ACU's) as well as monitoring the room temperature and humidity. Other information such as security and fire/smoke alarm can be used to provide a local and/or remote alert to enhance the operation of your DP area and reduce the chance of plant shut-down due to a system malfunction. Additional energy management strategies can be used to control peripheral equipment such as terminals and printers to reduce energy consumption during scheduled operation shutdown.

Process Data Monitoring

The final and most challenging task is, in my opinion, the monitoring of your application programs. I will use a simple scenario to explain this process. Let's assume for a moment that you can power off an office automation system configured as follows: one computer, one control unit, and several attached DASD's and terminals. Your site is unoccupied after 8:00pm every Friday until 6:00am Monday. You plan to shutdown your office automation system by Friday, 10:00pm, for the weekend. Before turning off the equipment and its support systems, such as ACU's, you want to make sure that nobody is "LOGGED ON" the network. This requires a software package capable of reading all the attached devices on the network, i.e., nodes, and determines if each node is activated or de-activated. The application program will read the actual time of day (TOD) and day of week (DOW), determine it is Friday, 10:00pm, and initiate a pre-defined strategy. This strategy will start a program and simulate key strokes on the screen, as if a person were typing on the keyboard. The program reads the status of the nodes on the screen and, if all identified nodes are logged off, the program proceeds to shutdown the DP equipment and its support systems in a pre-defined

sequence. If one or more nodes are logged on, the program will hold the shutdown process for another hour or two and try again. This strategy is just one of many possible ways that can be utilized to schedule a weekend shutdown of your DP equipment. Let's assume that the system tried again two hours later and one node is still logged on. It is midnight and usually the building is empty. There are at least two reasons that can be derived by this monitoring process. First, the person forgot to log off his terminal before leaving his office. The second one is potentially a serious problem; the person is still in the office, unable to move for help. You automation system can display an alert on a terminal and simultaneously send a message on the pager of your security guard at the front entrance of the plant. The message on the pager will identify the building and room number where the node is installed. If the guard does not acknowledge such alert within a pre-defined time by dialing back the computer with a specific code to clear the alert, the system can escalate and call one or more predefined pages until confirmation is acknowledged by the system.

The process requires a software program to allow the user to interface and communicate with the office automation system as well as providing the necessary functions to monitor and control the equipment. One approach used in IBM has been to utilize a Personal System/2 (PS/2) to act at the gateway between DP equipment, application software, and the host computer. The host computer will have an automated expert program package which will provide the necessary interfaces with all major application programs running your enterprise. This automated expert program will monitor computer systems, networks and software. In the event of a problem, an alert and possible corrective action can be handled. Automated operations products such as IBM NetView and Automated Operations Control (AOC) are available to predict system outages and re-route workload to improve system availability. Figure 1 describes how an IBM Enterprise Systems Architecture/390 (ESA/390) host computer is connected to remote sites using Enterprise Systems Connection (ESCON) products with SSMS.

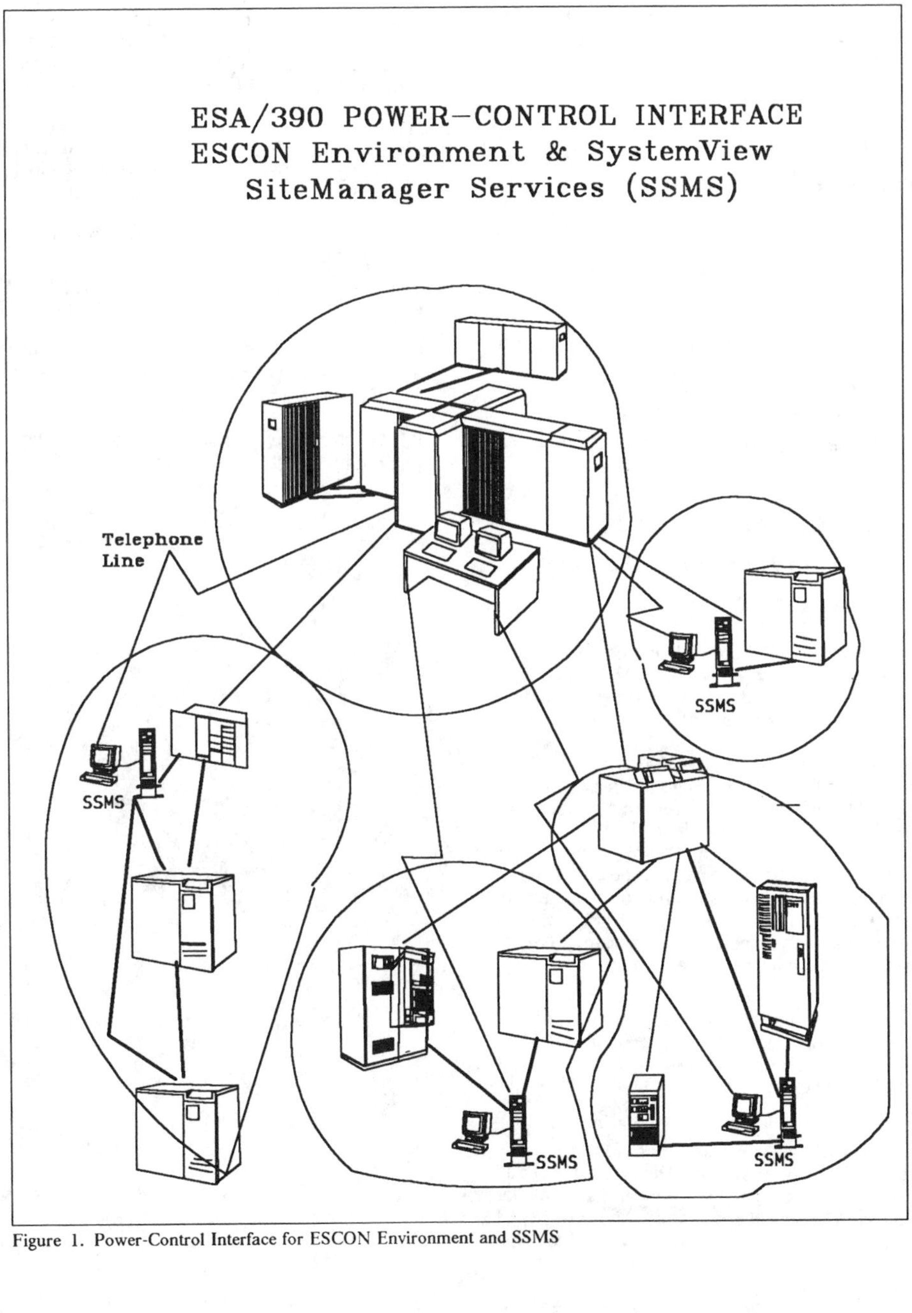
ESA/390 POWER-CONTROL INTERFACE
ESCON Environment & SystemView
SiteManager Services (SSMS)
Telephone
Line
SSMS
SSMS
SSMS
SSMS

Figure 1. Power-Control Interface for ESCON Environment and SSMS

## HARDWARE AND SOFTWARE COMPONENTS

### PS/2

- PS/2 Model 8580, 20 Mhz, 110 MB hard disk, 8 MB

- Color Display Model 85XX

- Mouse Model 8770

- Proprinter Model 42XX

Communication cards are used to communicate to the host computer, to other computers and terminals for monitoring application programs.

### Communications

- Dual Async Adapter/A (RS232)

- Synchronous Data Link Control (SDLC) Adapter

- 3270 Emulation

- 5250 Emulation

- X.25 Adapter

- IBM PS/2 300/1200/2400 bits/second Internal Modem

### Local Area Network (LAN)

- IBM Token-Ring Network 16/4 Mbit/second Adapter/A

- Ethernet Adapter

- IBM PC Network Broadband Adapter II/A

- IBM PC Network Baseband Adapter/A

### Environmental Monitoring and Control

Different components are used to interface with the computers, peripherals and environment. The same approach used for standard Building Automation System (BAS) is applied for the DP equipment.

The PS/2 is connected to an Environmental Master Controller (EMC) which acts as a policeman between the PS/2 and attached DP equipment and sensors. EMC is linked to the PS/2 through a standard RS-232 port. The EMC has two RS-485 communication trunk lines running at 51.2 KBaud to a maximum of 4000 feet for each trunk line. Each trunk line can support up to 31 Environmental Local Controllers (ELC's). EMC has a 3-cell rechargeable battery to backup memory for a minimum of 72 hours in case of a power failure.

ELC has an input/output capacity to handle 11 analog and/or digital inputs for monitoring and 8 digital and/or analog outputs for controlling devices. The communication between the ELC on the trunk line is done via a two-wire.

Connection between field sensors and the ELC are direct plug-in with a DB-9 connector. Input and output connectors are color coded to facilitate installation. Normally open (NO) and normally closed (NC) contacts as well as 2000 Ohms RTD, 4-20 mA and 1-5Vdc are supported.

Connection from the ELC to the computers and peripherals is done through the PCI 6-wire, PCI 2-wire and PCI-RPC (Remote power control). Each PCI provides connection for power control and monitoring. Different PCI's voltage and current load are available to handle most common DP equipment.

### Software Base Components

The software used to run the PS/2 and to monitor and control DP equipment is integrated in two packages: PS/2 operating system (OS/2 version 2.0), and SSMS. OS/2 provides the different interfaces necessary to handle the hand checking between the PS/2 components and the communication to the outside world. The extended services (ES) of OS/2 includes the communication manager providing the necessary drivers to interface with the host computer, LAN's and other computers. SSMS interacts directly with external systems by using the existing protocols supported under the ES communication manager capabilities of OS/2. SSMS provides the sensors and controllable configuration lists of all sensors and devices attached to the system as well as the drivers to communicate with EMC and the pagers. Other screens to select which alert and messages to be forwarded to different pager numbers and devices that can be powered on or off are also available.

## IMPLEMENTATION

Figure 2 shows a typical application between DP equipment, host computers, devices, and sensors.

Connectivity and application monitoring software (dialog) are integrated under the communication manager of OS/2 extended services.

PCI's and environmental monitoring and control are provided by the ELC's and the PCI's devices.

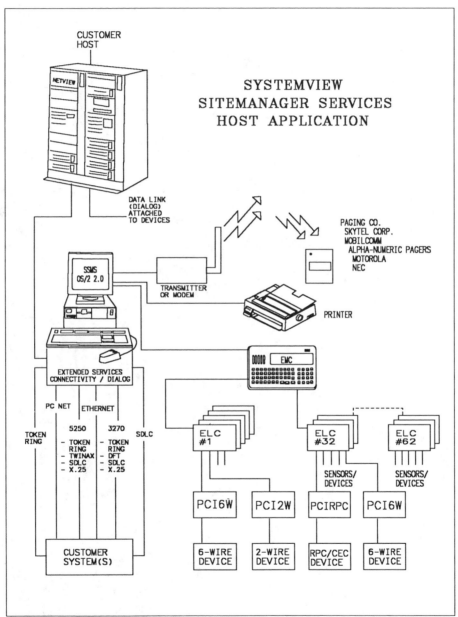

Figure 2. Typical application utilizing SSMS

# Chapter 98

# The New EMCS Generation: Smarter, Faster, More Flexible, and More Options

K.B. Silveria

A leading conversation topic when building owners get together is most likely to be the search for effective, reliable, and flexible methods of controlling HVAC equipment. More than ever, today's competitive economic climate continues to pressure building owners to reduce operating expenses–fuels, electricity, maintenance, and equipment repair and replacement–without sacrificing occupant comfort and safety. HVAC building control system manufacturers have introduced new products to improve Energy Management and Control Systems (EMCS) that incorporate electronic direct digital control (DDC).

EMCS first costs have dropped, and as a result their use has increased. Over the long term, building owners can look forward to energy savings and lower building operating costs because of more sophisticated, user-responsive Energy Management and Control Systems. In the following pages, I will present technical information relative to both pneumatic control systems and EMCS utilizing DDC, outline applications for both types of systems, identify a typical EMCS architecture, evaluate integration of specialty building systems (fire alarm, security, lighting) to an EMCS and identify future EMCS technological advancements.

## Pneumatic Control Systems

An automatic control system is identified by the method of transmitting input and output signals(i.e. compressed air, electric, electronic, digital) and by the type of signal (analog or digital). By definition, pneumatic systems utilize varying air pressure signals, typically analog, to transmit sensor inputs and controller outputs.

A typical pneumatic controller will receive an analog pneumatic signal from a sensor which is proportional to the value of the control variable being measured. The controller subsequently compares this input pressure signal to the desired air pressure input (setpoint), and in turn transmits an analog output signal to a terminal control device, based upon the comparison of the input pressure to the setpoint pressure (refer to Figure 1).

Pneumatic control systems can apply different control modes (proportional control, two-position control, and step control). The majority of installed pneumatic control systems utilize proportional type control.

Proportional control by definition actually proportions the output capacity of the terminal control device to correspond to the load requirements of the specific process (refer to Figure 2). Proportional control requires the terminal control device to modulate to a position proportional to the deviation (offset) of the value of the controlled variable from the setpoint. Thereby, the terminal control device responds and modulates linearly with a change in the value of the controlled variable. As a result of this linear function (terminal control device vs. control point) an offset is inevitable. (See Figure 2.) The fundamental characteristic of incurring an offset due to proportional control systems should be clearly understood when applying a pneumatic control system.

Pneumatic control systems have generally been applied to buildings where economy is important and control accuracy is not critical to the operation of the building. Figure 4 identifies the characteristics, advantages/disadvantages, and applications for pneumatic control systems which should be understood and prioritized when evaluating implementation of this type of system.

## Direct Digital Control (DDC)

Computer-based EMCS have been available as an alternative to pneumatic control systems since the mid 1960s. They were typically applied to large buildings or campuses and required large mainframe computers for processing all the control strategies. As a result, these systems were complex, expensive, and unreliable and placed unreasonable demands on operating personnel. Loss of the mainframe computer meant loss of the entire control system. The 1970s resulted in advancement in the central computer technology. General purpose mini-computers where now being utilized as the central processing unit. Minicomputers provided more processing power for monitoring, control and report generation in addition to the ability to incorporate multiple operator interface terminals. Added memory capacity allowed processing of data into more meaningful reports as well as allowing for significant improvements in operator interface software (ex. color graphics). Introduction of microprocessors with relatively inexpensive and high density memories, opened

up a whole new world of control system technology. These microprocessors were developed with the idea of placing them in local distributed controllers which in turn handled all the computer processing required for a specific control application. Microprocessor programs could implement control functions previously performed by minicomputers and provide local control at a cost and performance level suitable for individual HVAC mechanical equipment. With the advent of microprocessor controllers came the ability to incorporate DDC. DDC became defined as a digital computer having the ability to measure particular variables, process this information via control algorithms and control a terminal device to maintain a given setpoint. The term "digital" refers only to the fact that input/output information is processed digitally, and not that input (sensors) or outputs (transducers) devices were digital. Typically all inputs and outputs relative to a DDC system are analog signals and then are converted to digital signals by the microprocessor for control purposes.

DDC systems offer advantages over pneumatic control systems as noted in Figure 5. Microprocessor memory costs continue to decrease while their capabilities continue to increase. The compact physical size of microprocessors means smaller controller housing and shipping cartons which further reduce overall costs. DDC systems utilize software to program microprocessors and therefore provide tremendous flexibility for controlling and modifying sophisticated control applications. Changing control sequences by modifying software, allows users the ability to continually improve the performance of control systems throughout a building.

DDC control systems can be programmed for building HVAC system control as well as perform facility-wide energy management routines such as electrical peak demand limiting, start-stop time optimization programming, site-wide chilled water reset, lighting control, time-of-day scheduling, and outdoor air free cooling control,

to name a few. An EMCS utilizing DDC can integrate HVAC control functions with energy management functions in order to ensure they operate in accordance with one another resulting in higher energy savings. DDC systems have become much more reliable over earlier DDC systems due to the continual development in microprocessor technology in addition to improved software design technology provided by the EMCS manufacturers. As a result, DDC systems today are reliable and easier to use. DDC (Accurate Control)

The most significant benefits that DDC systems offer are the additional control modes (integral and derivative), which result in quicker and more accurate control. Pneumatic systems, as a result of their design, inherently offer proportional control which results in an offset. The wider a particular throttling range, the more offset incurred by a proportional controller. The development of the microprocessor and DDC has improved and simplified the use of two control modes (integral and derivative). These modes provide improved accuracy due to the elimination of offset. They respond to the rate of change to the control point which achieves the setpoint much faster whenever the load varies. DDC (Proportional - Integral - Derivative Control)

The majority of DDC systems available today incorporate proportional-integral-derivative control. These control systems offer more accurate, precise and efficient control of building HVAC systems. The important question is: What does integral and derivative control offer that traditional proportional control does not? Proportional plus integral (PI) control provides automatic reset of the control point. PI control eliminates offset by automatically changing the proportional band or throttling range until the control point approaches the setpoint. A typical proportional control mode has a defined position for the terminal control device for each offset from setpoint whereas integral control adjusts the terminal control device while shifting the

proportional band. The constant shifting of the proportional band maintains the controlled variable at setpoint by correcting the control signal to the terminal control device.

Whenever the load changes, the controlled variable will change and an offset will occur. The proportional (P) control immediately responds to this change resulting in an offset which is then measured by the PI control which adjusts the control output signal. The rate of response for the PI control is adjustable through software to provide the response required for the specific control application.

Proportional-integral-derivative (PID) control adds the derivative control function to the control process. The derivative function applies corrective action to the output signal based upon the rate at which the controlled variable deviates from setpoint. Derivative control enhances PI control by increasing the rate at which the controlled variable is brought to the setpoint following an offset. As the controlled variable approaches the setpoint, derivative control reduces the corrective actions to the output signal in order to prevent the controlled variable from passing the setpoint on the other side (overshoot). As is with PI control, PID control is typically adjustable for most DDC systems and allows the user the ability to change the rate time setting which determines the effect of derivative control on a specific control system application.

## EMCS Architecture

The primary objective of an EMCS utilizing DDC is to centralize the monitoring and supervisory control of a building or group of buildings to reduce maintenance labor and operating costs while maintaining a safe and comfortable working environment.

The first automation systems were fully hardwired systems with all of the data input and control output points wired directly back to the EMCS data center in a central location. These

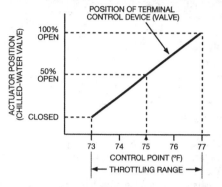

FIGURE 2 – PROPORTIONAL CONTROL, LINEAR RELATIONSHIP

VALVE POSITION VERSUS CONTROL POINT
NOTE: THE PROPORTIONAL OR LINEAR FUNCTION DEPICTED ABOVE ILLUSTRATES THAT OFFSET IS INEVITABLE WHEN THE CONTROL POINT CHANGES DUE TO A CHANGE IN COOLING LOAD.

automation systems allowed an operator to remotely start/stop equipment, monitor and alarm temperatures and reset specific controller setpoints. As expected, these systems were expensive due to the extensive wiring.
In the early 1960s, multiplexed wiring became the technology for an EMCS. Multiplexing permitted more data to be transmitted with fewer wires. Multiplexing used relays to selectively connect a set of centrally located selection switches and control wires which were connected to remote mechanical systems. A communication trunk included the wiring required for remote start/stop, status, control point adjustment, and temperature indication for specific mechanical equipment.

EMCS today have benefitted from the personal computer technology. Powerful PC's provide the processing capability equivalent to previous minicomputer based systems offered in the 1970s for a lot less money. PCs provide large quantities of random access memory (RAM) and hard disk storage which can operate with any of the largest EMCS. As a result of PC technology, present EMCS systems may now take advantage of sophisticated third-party software packages which can be utilized for custom report generation, spread sheets, word processing programs and various other management functions. Previous EMCS systems had this software developed by the EMCS manufacturers but these proved to be cumbersome to use and difficult to customize.

The PC offers the use of sophisticated operator interface color graphics software. Most EMCS manufacturers have made significant developments in color graphic software programs which have greatly simplified their EMCS uses. Graphic generation with previous systems was very complex and often required the EMCS technician to generate them, adding to the overall cost of the system. PCs made a computer-based EMCS economically justifiable to not only sophisticated owners but also to less sophisticated facilities or buildings.

## FIGURE 1
## PNEUMATIC AND DDC CONTROL DETAILS

**PNEUMATIC CONTROL DETAIL**

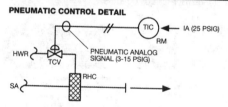

**DIRECT DIGITAL CONTROL DETAIL**

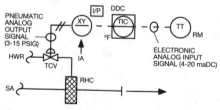

| | |
|---|---|
| TIC_RM PNEUMATIC ROOM THERMOSTAT | HWR = HOT WATER RETURN |
| TT_RM ELECTRONIC ROOM TRANSMITTER | IA = INSTRUMENT AIR |
| DDC DDC TEMPERATURE CONTROL ALGORITHM | RHC = REHEAT COIL |
| XY CURRENT TO PNEUMATIC TRANSDUCER | SA = SUPPLY AIR |
| | TCV = TEMPERATURE CONTROL VALVE |

EMCS available now have a specific hierarchical configuration of the microprocessor-based digital controllers as well as the front-end personal computer (refer to Figure 6). The specific configuration levels associated with a system depend on the actual needs and requirements of a particular building or campus of buildings. Configurations vary from manufacturer to manufacturer but the configuration shown in Figure 6 is the most common.

The lowest level of microprocessor-based controllers shown in Figure 6 provide direct digital control of terminal equipment such as variable air volume boxes, induction boxes, fan powered boxes, terminal reheat, heat pumps, fin tube radiation, etc. Proportional-integral-derivative (PID) control software in addition to energy management software functions are directly resident in these terminal equipment controllers. At this terminal equipment level, sensor inputs (VAV box airflow, room temperature) and actuator outputs (VAV box damper actuator, reheat coil) interface directly with the controllers and mechanical equipment being controlled. A communication trunk provides communication networking to allow information to be shared between other terminal equipment controllers and all other level controllers. Many manufacturers offer communication ports to these controllers for directly connecting a portable operator interface device used to assist in field set-up and trouble-shooting of terminal equipment. This level of technology has provided the end user a tremendous ability to implement Energy Management techniques such as occupied/unoccupied scheduling of any area of a building, resulting in reduced airflow volumes and night setback temperatures which greatly reduce operating energy costs. Monitoring and controlling terminal equipment centrally reduces maintenance costs by allowing maintenance personnel to respond quickly and accurately to building HVAC equipment failures.

The system level controllers are larger in both memory and input/output point capacity than terminal equipment controllers. The system level controllers offer more flexibility in custom programming of direct digital control algorithms and are typically applied to major pieces of mechanical equipment such as large built-up air handling units, variable air volume systems with return fan tracking, central utility plants, etc. Larger mechanical equipment is often more critical and complex and therefore requires customized software for the specific sequence of operation to be effective. A significant feature which the system level controller offers, is the ability to handle multiple control loops and functions such as PID control, Energy Management routines, alarm monitoring, smoke control and many others. Terminal equipment controllers by comparison are typically single control loop controllers with very specific pre-written software routines which only allow the user to modify setpoints. System controllers are the most significant aspect of an EMCS because they monitor and control the majority of mechanical equipment. System level controller technology varies from manufacturer to manufacturer. Therefore, when evaluating an EMCS, the specifying engineer must thoroughly evaluate the different manufacturers' system level controllers for memory capacity, input/output point capacity, ease of programming and for quantity of terminal level controllers which can be connected to it. Evaluating system level controllers will provide the best insight to the specific capabilities and performance of the overall EMCS.

The operator interface level is the level in which an operator accesses the EMCS communication network for specific data. The operator interface hardware in today's systems will be a personal computer or multiple computers with integral color graphics, alarm/log printer(s), application software, communication trunk interface devices, and possibly a telephone modem for remote accessibility. The operator level PC incorporates software to implement; 1) system password level security; 2) formatting of data into logical and organized groups; 3) engineering software which allows for customizing DDC programs for downloading to specific system controllers; 4) report generation; 5) maintenance scheduling and inventory reports; 6) time of day/holiday scheduling of equipment and buildings; and 7) verification of occupant complaints.

### TABLE 1—PNEUMATIC CONTROL SYSTEM

| | | |
|---|---|---|
| Inherently proportional control | Good for simple control applications. Results in offset from control set point | 1) Basic commercial office buildings |
| Uses low cost, reliable actuators for dampers and valves | First cost and operating cost are lower. | 2) Elementary and secondary schools |
| Controllers and thermostats require frequent recalibration | Higher operating and maintenance costs | 3) Small hospitals |
| Explosionproof | May be used in explosionproof areas for terminal equipment controls | 4) University buildings |
| Requires air compressor, drier and filtration equipment | Increased operating and maintenance costs. May result in higher first cost when very low dewpoint, compressed-air temperatures are required | |
| Additional pneumatic hardware required when modifying equipment sequence of operation | Requires adding pneumatic equipment and field labor to modify sequence of operations | |

### EMCS Data Communications Protocol

The specific method of communication within an EMCS is significant because of the amount of data being processed simultaneously. The specific methods of data transfer between DDC controllers and the operator interface PC varies from manufacturer to manufacturer. However, communication protocols can be simplified into two distinct categories, poll/response communication versus peer-to-peer communications.

## Peer-To-Peer Communication Protocol

The most prevalent communication protocol for state of the art systems offered today is peer-to-peer communication. With peer-to-peer communications (sometimes referred to as token ring passing network), a pre-established time slot is automatically passed from one communication trunk device (i.e. PC or system level DDC controller) to another. This time slot designates when a trunk device has sole access to the communication trunk for data transferring. This software time slot is passed in an order sequence and does not require the trunk devices to be in proximity of one another.

A peer-to-peer network does not have a communication master or center point, due to the fact that every trunk device at some point has a time slot allowing it to operate as the master. Peer-to-peer communication offers distinct advantages: 1) direct communication between controllers does not require communication through operator interface PC, 2) communication is not dependent on one device, and 3) global information can be communicated to all controllers quickly and easily.

## Poll/Response Communications Protocol

Most of the earlier systems utilized poll/response communications which required a central communication master. The master was responsible for periodically polling all the system level controllers for data such as equipment status, alarms, and input/output point value information. Each controller was assigned a binary address which it responded to when it appeared on the communication trunk. Although poll/response communications is relatively simple and straightforward, it is very slow when applied to large systems. The communication procedure requires the master to; 1) poll a specified address; 2) wait for a controller response; 3) identify the data requested for transfer; 4) wait for the acknowledgement of the request; 5) receive the data to be transferred; and 6) acknowledge it was properly received.

Although this method of communication is not widely utilized at the system controller level today, it does continue to be utilized for the terminal equipment level controllers by many manufacturers. Where control and monitoring point densities are low and alarm response times are not critical, poll/response proves to be both effective and economical for interconnection between system level controllers and terminal equipment level controllers.

Current development of EMCS has not resulted in a standard communications protocol. Many discussions are taking place about a standard protocol which would allow for direct integration of one manufacturers EMCS to a completely different manufacturer's EMCS. This technology has been incorporated with many of the industrial control systems but has not been accomplished by commercial manufacturers. A standard communications protocol is significant because it would permit a user to competitively bid all EMCS projects for a facility rather than having to extend an existing system because integration is not available.

## TABLE 2—DIRECT DIGITAL CONTROL

| | | |
|---|---|---|
| Inherently precise control using proportional-integral-derivative control modes | Good for applications incorporating accurate environmental control criteria (temperature, humidity, airflow, etc.) | 1) Large corporate office buildings |
| Performs complex sequence of operations for large mechanical equipment | DDC software allows users to customize sequences easily | 2) Research and development facilities |
| Incorporates energy management routes as a standard offering | Allows users to easily implement energy saving routines without adding additional hardware | 3) Academic research and development facilities |
| System can be expanded easily | Permits users to extend DDC throughout building or campus by simply extending communication trunk and adding DDC controllers | 4) University campuses 5) Computer facilities |
| Centralizes and integrates control and monitoring for HVAC and any subsystems | Reduces maintenance labor and allows for faster response to equipment failures to ensure a safe, comfortable work environment | 6) Medium and large hospitals |
| Continuous technological developments with microprocessor memory size and processing capability | User will have leading technology available. The disadvantage is that it can be expensive to incorporate into older generation systems | |

## FIGURE 3 PROPORTIONAL-INTEGRAL-DERIVATIVE CONTROL

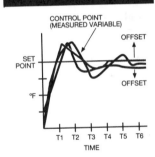

— PROPORTIONAL CONTROL
— PROPORTIONAL-INTEGRAL CONTROL
— PROPORTIONAL-INTEGRAL-DERIVATIVE CONTROL

## Integration of Subsystems

Often in large facilities there is a desire to integrate subsystems (see Figure 6) such as fire, security, access control and lighting to the site EMCS. Integration can consist of primarily two types; 1) hardwired integration; and 2) network integration as detailed in Figure 6. Either method allows important information to be communicated on the EMCS communication trunk for remote monitoring and reporting purposes.

Hardwired Integration allows for the specific subsystem (i.e. fire, security, etc.) to operate in a stand-alone (separate) fashion with only specific point information provided to the EMCS. The subsystem transmits alarms, status, and value information to the EMCS via directly hardwired point connections which are outputs from the subsystem and inputs to the EMCS. The EMCS is then programmed to process this information for operator's use. This type of integration is useful when dealing with an existing stand-alone subsystem which would otherwise be difficult to integrate. Hardwired integration, however, can be expensive for large systems due to the duplication of wiring required between systems. This interconnected wiring is typically not electrically supervised. Because it is not monitored for continuity, in the event of a wiring failure it will not notify the system operator.

## Network Integration

Network integration allows system level DDC controllers for the EMCS and building subsystems to all communicate with a common operator interface PC, allowing an operator the ability to access information for any subsystem. The building systems are integrated by software as opposed to the hardwired method. Manufacturers differ in the hardware configuration of integrating these systems. Some manufacturers have dedicated communication trunks linking system level controllers for particular a subsystem which are then brought back and integrated at the operator interface level as shown in Figure 6. Other manufacturers interconnect all subsystem system level controllers on a common communication trunk where subsystem data is carried across one common communication trunk. Either variation of network integration is effective. Network integration often results in a lower first cost when dealing with large new systems, and accommodates complex sequence of operations for interrelated systems such as fire and security, lighting and smoke control. Caution is advised when implementing this type of integration with regards to configuring the software. Data must be addressed and prioritized to ensure communication transmission speeds are adequate for each specific subsystem.

## EMCS Future Technology

The last couple of decades have established several technological milestones for Energy Management and Control Systems. In fact, the last one to two years for several manufacturers has resulted in significant changes to their existing product lines.

## BACnet

In January, 1987 an ASHRAE Standards Committee formed a Standards Project Committee (SPC-135P) committed to establishing the criteria for an EMCS industry standard communications protocol. The name for this standard communication protocol is BACnet, which stands for Building Automation and Control Networks. BACnet will establish standardized methods for communicating data across an EMCS communication trunk. Information will consist of physical output and input points, software points, alarm information, event programming, control logic and any other informa-

tion required to be shared on a trunk.

All EMCS manufacturers provide a communication protocol, however, it is very specific to their system hardware and software. The ability to provide network integration of different manufacturer's systems on a commercial level is not presently available. BACnet is trying to standardize communications to allow different EMCS systems to exchange information (Network Integration) on the same dedicated communication trunk. The ability to integrate systems will relieve end users from being committed to a single source manufacturer for all additional EMCS projects.

Many of the major manufacturers are represented on this ASHRAE committee and are demonstrating interest in configuring their future systems with this concept in mind. Only time will tell if new developments in EMCS will conform to the concept of BACnet.

## ARCNET-ETHERNET

Some manufacturers have just introduced the ability to network personal computers on industry standard communication networks (ARCNET and ETHERNET). This differs from the BACnet concept in that the integration takes place only at the computer (operator interface) level and does not integrate different EMCS systems. This exchange of information can take place at much higher communication rates which allows large facilities with multiple operator PC stations, the ability to access information from several stations quickly and without affecting the communication rate at the system controller level.

## Adaptive Control

HVAC mechanical equipment sequence of operations are becoming increasingly complex. This complexity is a result of stricter criteria established by national codes (ASHRAE Minimum Outdoor Air Requirements, for example) and by end users within institutions which require highly accurate control systems. Therefore, control systems have to account for the requirements of greater accuracies. A response to this requirement has been adaptive control. However, with these modes of

control, parameters were established for the most common load conditions. A controller set-up to control accurately under one set of conditions may not always respond well when the conditions or load significantly changes. EMCS manufacturers are beginning to provide their DDC systems with the ability to perform adaptive control. Adaptive control (sometimes referred to as self-tuning control) automatically monitors the control performance of a particular control loop and automatically adjusts its proportional-integral-derivative parameters to improve this performance. This additional feature improves the control loop response to more complicated and dynamic processes.

FIGURE 4 – EMCS ARCHITECTURE

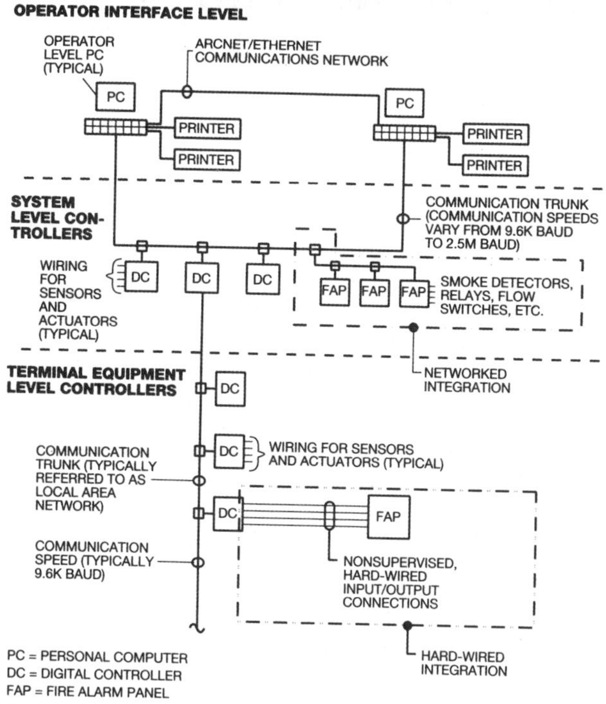

**OPERATOR INTERFACE LEVEL**

PC = PERSONAL COMPUTER
DC = DIGITAL CONTROLLER
FAP = FIRE ALARM PANEL

## Advances Continue

Manufacturers will continue to make strides in the area of terminal equipment DDC controllers. They will continue to become more cost effective resulting in more buildings implementing DDC for variable air volume boxes, heat pumps, etc. These controllers will be developed with more computer memory capacity, and the ability to implement more complex customized control logic. Many manufacturers are introducing terminal equipment controllers for fume hood face velocity control in research applications allowing building operators to monitor and ensure safety for all research personnel. System level DDC controllers will continue to be improved by expanding memory capacity up to 1.5 MB and incorporating 32K bit processors that larger groups of data can be exchanged at a faster rate.

The 1980s resulted in many innovative developments in the EMCSs. The continued development of the microprocessor in the 1990s will only prove to enhance the capabilities of Energy Management and Control Systems utilizing direct digital control.

## GLOSSARY OF TERMS

Adaptive or Self-Tuning Control:
This control adjusts the controller output to optimize the performance of the system under all load conditions. This control allows the controller the ability to evaluate its performance and adjust parameters in order to improve its accuracy and response.

Algorithm:
A software calculation method which results in a controller output signal based upon input information.

Analog Signal:
A control signal which is continuously variable (ex. temperature in a room).

Baud Rate:
Digital information communication rate measured in bits per second. 9.6K baud rate refers to 9600 bits/second while 2.5M baud refers to 2,500 bits/second.

Communication Network:
Provides microprocessor controllers and personal computers the ability to share information over a transmission medium (pair of wires, coax cable or fiber optic cable).

Communications Protocol:
A set of conventions or rules which determine the format and content of data messages between microprocessor controllers.

Control Point
The actual value of the controlled variable (setpoint plus or minus offset).

Control Variable:
The condition or quantity which is measured and controlled (ex: temperature, flow, humidity, etc.)

Cycling:
A periodic change in the controlled variable from one value to another. Cycling which occurs continuously is referred to as "hunting".
Proportional - Integral - Derivative (PID) Control:
This control mode enhances PI control by adding a feature which accounts for the rate of change (derivative) of the offset incurred by the controlled variable. This feature allows setpoint to be achieved much quicker and more accurately.

Sensor:
A control device which monitors a particular control variable (ex. temperature, humidity).

Sequence of Operation:
The specific sequence of events or instructions which must occur in order for a mechanical system to operate as designed. Instructions are programmed via DDC software within a microprocessor controller.

Setpoint:
The value at which a controlled variable is to be maintained.

Step Control:
This is a control mode which sequences a switch assembly (ex: electric resistant heat) based upon the value of the controlled variable.

Terminal Control Device:
A device utilized to change the value of the controlled variable (ex: control valve or damper)

Throttling Range:
In a proportional controller, the range through which the controlled variable must vary to modulate the terminal control device from its fully open position to fully closed. This is also referred to as the proportional band.

Two Position Control:
A simple system in which the terminal control device is either fully open or closed and there is no intermediate position.

Direct Digital Control (DDC):
Control which is performed by electronic microprocessor based controllers which utilize computer digital processing for monitoring analog sensor inputs and controlling analog actuator outputs.

Digital Signal:
A control signal which is either on or off (ex. fan start/stop).

Energy Management and Control System (EMCS):
A system which centralizes the monitoring, control, and management of a building or group of buildings.

Hierarchical Configuration:
A system architecture in which the personal computers and microprocessor controllers are arranged in terms of levels. The levels determine the significance of data transmitted and received as well as the communication rates of speed.

Offset:
The difference between the setpoint and the control point. Also referred to as deviation.

Operator Interface Device:
The device permitting the user to access data and software within the EMCS (ex: personal computer, portable PC or simplified CRT monitor.)

Pneumatic Control System:
A system which utilizes compressed air signals to monitor and control mechanical equipment.

Proportional (P) Control:
Control mode in which the terminal control device is moved to a position proportional to the deviation of the control point from the setpoint.

Proportional - Integral (PI) Control:
In addition to proportional control this mode provides reset of the control point automatically. As a result control offset is virtually eliminated. This is accomplished by the controller continually shifting the throttling range.

About The Author

Kent B. Silveria is an Energy Management and Control Systems Engineer with CUH2A Inc., Princeton, New Jersey-based interdisciplinary design firm. He has a B.S. in Mechanical Engineering from Bucknell University, and is active in ASHRAE, the Instrumentation Society of America, and the International Society of Pharmaceutical Engineers. His involvement with large building EMCS for CUH2A projects includes: Eli Lilly and Company, Indianapolis; Pfizer Inc., Groton, Conn.; Lederle Laboratories Division, American Cyanamid Company, Pearl River, N.Y.; and Rhône-Poulenc Rorer Pharmaceuticals, Inc., Collegeville, Pa.

Chapter 99
# Cost Justification of Chiller Replacement

T.J. Baker, R.A. Baumer

## Introduction

We often hear of products with paybacks that are too good to be true. Just a few weeks ago, a client received a recommendation from a national service company's local office. In the letter the company recommended that "due to the age and condition of the boiler ...that the school consider replacing the boiler... The cost for the new boiler can usually be recovered by lower fuel bills in 2 to 3 years." This was for an installation in Southeast Texas where the boiler is only used 4 to 5 months per year.

Analysis shows the above claims to be nonsense. A new boiler would cost about $47,000 installed. Current total gas bills for the facility are $15,630 per year. They would have to shutoff the gas to the facility to have a three year payback. In fact, only two-thirds of the gas is used to heat the facility so we have only $10,000 to write off against the new boiler. How much will the greater efficiency save? A 30% savings due to greater efficiency produces $3,000 per year in gas savings to offset the $47,000 cost, a 16 year payback. And much of the efficiency savings can be realized by adjusting the existing boiler.

In another case a client wanted to investigate replacement of a twenty year old chiller plant with more efficient equipment. We investigated the project and determined that the payback would be greater than ten years. They did not operate the equipment during the summer and at less than 50% of capacity the balance of the year.

About a year later, the same client repeated the request but with the information that another engineer had come up with piece of equipment that will generate a two year payback. ECF requested that the client have the other engineer submit his calculations so that we could prepare a DOE Grant Application.

When we received the other engineers calculations, we found a major flaw in them. He had assumed, probably to satisfy the client, that the buildings operated 365 days per year, 24 hour per day. In reality this was a school building operating 180 days per year, 8 hours per day, and not operating in the peak cooling load period.

The claims about savings can often be substantiated. If they meet your payback criteria you should proceed as fast as possible. However, the claims have to be examined on the basis of the assumptions made to produce the savings.

## Existing Conditions

If you suspect that you have equipment that needs to be replaced you have to analyze your existing conditions. The case of lighting retrofits will be used as a simple example because we eliminate the weather variable. This example demonstrates the necessity to determine existing conditions.

The first thing to do is to determine the energy usage of the existing fixtures. Find several groups of fixtures, that have all lamps lit and measure the wattage of the circuits. This can be done simply at the wall switch or the breaker where the circuit is switched. Divide the measured wattage by the number of lamps to determine the watts per lamp.

On an old lighting system we are likely to calculate over 40 watts per lamps. On a recent well specified system we may find numbers closer to 36 watts per lamp using high efficiency 34 watt lamps. Most manufactures claim 30 watts per lamp for new high efficiency ballasts and lamps. Thus, the claims for a 25% or greater savings.

However, in order to calculate payback you have to observe the operating conditions of the fixtures under consideration. If lamps operate ten hour per day, five days a week, 52 weeks per year, that calculates to 2600 hours per year. For a business open 24 hours a day, 365 days per year, the hours are 8760 hours per year. The different is better than three to one. Continous operation will always have a" good" payback.

At $0.08/KWH (including demand) with a 10 watt savings we save $2.08 per year for the one installation vs $7.00 per year for the continuous operation. At an installation cost for new ballast of $35, we have a 5 vs 17 year payback.

Accurate knowledge of existing conditions cannot be over-emphasized. Measure what you can and observe the rest at several times to a have a fair estimate of actual usage.

Lighting is an easy evaluation once the operating hours are determined. There is little reason to consider weather conditions and how they impact our calculations. The purpose of this paper is to demonstrate chiller BIN type analysis. As you look at this example you will see how the engineer mentioned above went wrong. The example also implies how we go wrong adjusting cooling loads using cooling degree days.

## Chiller Replacement

We have the following conditions:

The facility, a jail, uses 10,000 gallons per day of 140 degree hot water. The water is heated with electricity. The demand charge is $7.44 per KW and the energy charge is $0.0294. Energy cost per year would be $18,000 and demand charges on 504 KW are $45,000 per year. A decision has been made that we cannot use gas to heat the water due to safety considerations. City water is river water and the temperature varies from 55 degrees in the winter to 80 degrees in the summer. Air conditioning is needed in the jail on all but the coldest days. At about 30 degrees there is no further need for AC. Operating data, indicates that internal load is 50% of the chiller load and that 185 tons will satisfy design conditions. (This was the actual conditions is a specification prepared by one of the authors and replied to by the other in an award winning bid.)

## Building Cooling Load Profile

First, we will simulate the manner in which the building cooling load varies in the form of a cooling load profile. The profile will be used in conjunction with average weather data to simulate machine operation on an annual basis.

Based on the above condition, the maximum cooling load that the jail experiences in 185 tons. This data is translated into a profile point of 185 tons at 95 deg F, dry bulb.

It has also been described that about 50% of the jail's cooling requirement is an internal load. This information is translated into a load point of 93 tons at 55 deg F.

The indication of no cooling load at 30 degrees is translated into a load point of 0 tons at 30 deg F.

Due to the high percentage of internal load and cooling need below 55 deg F use of a straight line to connect the load points would not provide as accurate data. Therefore, a hyperbole was utilized. In high humidity areas, such as Southeast Texas, this practice has provided more realistic studies. Figure 1 displays the building cooling load profile which will be used in this analysis.

In addition to the building cooling load, varying at different weather conditions, the domestic hot water needs also change. In mid winter, entering cold water temperature drops to 55 F. To simulate this effect, entering hot water temperature has also been selected for each temperature bin.

## Weather Data

The operation of the facility is continuous, 24 hours/day. The chiller operates all year, whenever cooling is needed.

Using this data, a specific set of area weather data was selected. The data in Figure 2 is for Houston, Texas and was obtained from local utility.

## Chiller Energy Consumption Calculations

With the building load profile and weather data, we have clearly identified 9 load points at which we can estimate energy consumption. To determine chiller energy consumption, there are two items which need to be taken into consideration: compressor and condenser fan KW.

In this analysis we will consider a machine with three rotary screw compressors providing infinitely variable slide valve capacity control, and thus, excellent part load efficiency. Accurate part load compressor KW profile for the machine being considered is in the manufacturer's brochures. Such a curve was used to determine the compressor KW for the BIN of 65 deg and higher. Below 65 deg the curve data was increased about 50% to allow for keeping head pressure high for improved equipment performance.

Condenser fan energy is determined by both cooling load and entering air temperature. The fans are controlled to maintain minimum discharge pressure for each compressor refrigeration circuit independently. For each load point, required condenser fan energy is calculated from the manufacturer's data. Table 1 shows the compressor KW, condenser KW from manufacturer's part load operating data.

### TABLE 1
### ESTIMATED ANNUAL ENERGY CONSUMPTION
### DUNHAM-BUSH ACWC-200-SD

| TEMP BIN | HOURS | TONS | COMPR KW | COND KW | TOTAL KW | ANNUAL KWH |
|---|---|---|---|---|---|---|
| 10-19 | 18 | - | - | - | - | - |
| 20-29 | 130 | - | - | - | - | - |
| 30-39 | 422 | 45 | 30 | 1.8 | 31.8 | 13,419 |
| 40-49 | 667 | 75 | 51 | 3.6 | 54.6 | 36,418 |
| 50-59 | 958 | 93 | 63 | 7.2 | 70.2 | 67,251 |
| 60-69 | 1638 | 108 | 73 | 10.8 | 83.8 | 137,264 |
| 70-79 | 2237 | 125 | 98 | 14.4 | 112.4 | 251,438 |
| 80-89 | 2171 | 147 | 121 | 21.6 | 142.6 | 309,584 |
| 90-99 | 519 | 181 | 205 | 21.6 | 226.6 | 117,605 |
| | | | | | | 932,979 |

## Heat Recovery Savings.

The machine selected has two lead circuits equipped with desuperheating domestic hot water heat exchangers. The heat exchangers are designed to heat 7 GPM from 50F to 140F and 20 GPM from 110 to 140F when the screw compressors are fully loaded. Consequently, when the chiller is fully loaded, there is more than adequate heat available to meet the hot water demands of the building. In the following calculations heating simulation is based on a constant 7 GPM hot water demand. However, on colder days, heating demands will exceed heat recovery capacity available from the partially loaded refrigeration system.

The bin analysis detailed below in Table 2 will take these various factors into consideration. Heating requirements and heat recovery capacity will be expressed in terms of KW for simplicity. This table shows that whenever the temperature exceeds 65 deg F we have adequate waste heat to satisfy all of the requirements. Based upon $0.0294/KWH energy charge, we will save $15,800 per year or about 88% of the energy charge.

TABLE 2
ESTIMATE ANNUAL HEAT RECOVERY SAVINGS
DUNHAM-BUSH ACWC-200-SD

| TEMP BIN | HOURS | EWT | COMPR KW | REQD KW | SAVED KW | ANNUAL KWH |
|---|---|---|---|---|---|---|
| 10-19 | 18 | 55 | - | 87.1 | - | - |
| 20-29 | 130 | 55 | - | 87.1 | - | - |
| 30-39 | 422 | 60 | 30 | 82.0 | 30.0 | 12,660 |
| 40-49 | 667 | 65 | 51 | 76.9 | 51.0 | 34,017 |
| 50-59 | 958 | 68 | 63 | 73.8 | 63.0 | 60,354 |
| 60-69 | 1638 | 72 | 73 | 70.0 | 70.0 | 114,660 |
| 70-79 | 2237 | 75 | 98 | 66.6 | 66.6 | 148,984 |
| 80-89 | 2171 | 80 | 81 | 61.5 | 61.5 | 133,516 |
| 90-99 | 519 | 80 | 135 | 61.5 | 61.5 | 31,918 |
| | | | | | | 536,109 |

EWT -Entering hot water temperature
COMP KW - Avail. compressor heat for reclaim
REQD KW - Hot water heating required
SAVED KW - Actual reclaimed KW

Demand Cost

Table 2 shows that 75% of the time the chiller can supply the required heating capacity. However, during the remainder of the time electric heating will be required to supplement the shortfall. To determine the exact requirements for supplemental electric heat would require a daily analysis for the cold months. In Table 3 we have estimated the months when supplemental heat is required and the percentage of full load demand.

Conservatively, demand charges are expected to be reduced from $45,000 to $13,600 per year or a net savings of $31,400.

TABLE 3
ESTIMATE ANNUAL DEMAND COST
DUNHAM-BUSH ACWC-200-SD

| MONTH | EXPECTED HIGH | EXPECTED LOW | KW TO HEAT WATER | COST |
|---|---|---|---|---|
| JAN | 65 | 31 | 504 | $3,750 |
| FEB | 65 | 31 | 504 | 3,750 |
| MAR | 75 | 45 | 252 | 1,875 |
| APR | 85 | 50 | 126 | 937 |
| MAY | 95 | 55 | 63 | 469 |
| JUN | 95 | 65 | 0 | 0 |
| JUL | 95 | 65 | 0 | 0 |
| AUG | 95 | 65 | 0 | 0 |
| SEP | 95 | 65 | 0 | 0 |
| OCT | 85 | 60 | 63 | 469 |
| NOV | 75 | 50 | 126 | 937 |
| DEC | 65 | 40 | 252 | 1,875 |
| | | | | $13,593 |

Analysis

Project cost is estimated at $230,000. The energy savings is $15,800 and the demand savings is $31,600 for a total of $47,700. The payback is just under five years. This would be considered high for most corporate customers; however, this is in line with the DOE ICP program and State funding was obtained.

Although, the above analysis is acceptable, several questions should be reviewed before a go decision is made.

How was the 185 ton chiller size derived? If the machine is too big the payback may be different. If too small it will have to be supplemented by the existing system, which may not be a bad choice since during the summer, the machine is much too big for hot water heating.

Is the water use data accurate and what affect will changes have on variances in the volume? In fact, the jail population is expected to decrease 25% in the next year. Will this reduce the hot water load and if it does will the payback be affected? How is the credit for the reduced load to be handled?

Is 88% saving in energy cost realistic? Since the 99% design point for heating is 30 deg F, it is very likely the chiller will run year round.

Is the 70% reduction in demand realistic? The analysis is conservative. Since an Energy Management System exist to manage the heating of water it is probable the demand saving will be greater that stated. However, there are some major assumptions on winter electric water heating demand.

This unit is expected to operate 365 days per year. However, if the unit were not to operate during the summer the high end of the energy savings would not be realized. Definitely the 95 deg F bin would be lost and a good portion of the 85 deg F bin.

Although, we addressed these questions they are often ignored. However, it is , in our opinion, poor practice to request funds when the payback may be in question. Especially, if the payback could be longer that we are estimating. Our project may not be the best to receive the limited capital funds of the company. We feel it is always better to have better payback than projected on a project. Then the decision to fund the project was definitely a wise one.

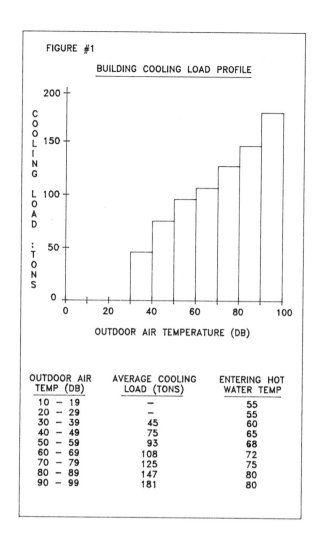

FIGURE #1

BUILDING COOLING LOAD PROFILE

| OUTDOOR AIR TEMP (DB) | AVERAGE COOLING LOAD (TONS) | ENTERING HOT WATER TEMP |
|---|---|---|
| 10 — 19 | — | 55 |
| 20 — 29 | — | 55 |
| 30 — 39 | 45 | 60 |
| 40 — 49 | 75 | 65 |
| 50 — 59 | 93 | 68 |
| 60 — 69 | 108 | 72 |
| 70 — 79 | 125 | 75 |
| 80 — 89 | 147 | 80 |
| 90 — 99 | 181 | 80 |

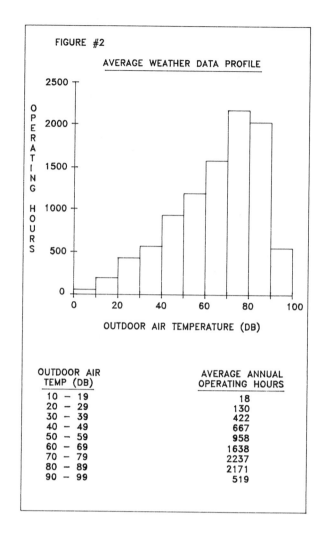

FIGURE #2

AVERAGE WEATHER DATA PROFILE

| OUTDOOR AIR TEMP (DB) | AVERAGE ANNUAL OPERATING HOURS |
|---|---|
| 10 — 19 | 18 |
| 20 — 29 | 130 |
| 30 — 39 | 422 |
| 40 — 49 | 667 |
| 50 — 59 | 958 |
| 60 — 69 | 1638 |
| 70 — 79 | 2237 |
| 80 — 89 | 2171 |
| 90 — 99 | 519 |

# Chapter 100

# Optimizing Cooling Tower Performance Refrigeration Systems, Chemical Plants, and Power Plants All Have a Resource Quietly Awaiting Exploitation - Cold Water!

R. Burger

Cooling towers, because of their seeming simplicity, are usually orphans of the facilities operation. We are all aware that cooling towers are the step-children of the chemical process plant, electric power generating station, and refrigeration system.

While engineers are pretty well convinced of the importance of their sophisticated equipment, and rightly so, they take the cooling towers and the cold water returning from them for granted.

Design Conditions are specified for the particular requirements before a cooling tower is purchased. This relates to the volume of circulating water, hot water temperature on the tower, cold water temperature discharge, and wet bulb temperature (consisting of ambient temperature and relative humidity). After the tower is put on the line and the cold water temperature or volume becomes inadequate, engineers look to solutions other than the obvious. While all cooling towers are purchased to function at 100% of capability in accordance with the required Design Conditions, in actual on-stream employment, the level of operation many times is lower, downwards to as much as 50% due to a variety of reasons:-

1. The present service needed is now greater than the original requirements which the tower was purchased for.

2. "Slippage" due to usage and perhaps deficient maintenance has reduced the performance of the tower over years of operation.

3. The installation could have been originally undersized due to the low bidder syndrome (1).

4. New plant expansion needs additional water volume and possibly colder temperatures off the tower.

## State-of-the-Art Upgrading

Users of cooling towers are not particularly concerned with the thermal analysis involving calculus, or delving into the complicated hydraulics and aerodynamic principles of selection for their equipment. Rather, it appears that their immediate requirements are for an intelligent investigation and answers to the question, "We have this piece of equipment which is part of our facility. What can we do to remedy the situation?" This paper will address that question in the hopes that it well better serve the hands-on-operator.

In order to upgrade a cooling tower to produce higher levels of colder water which will conserve energy with it's utilization, let us briefly review the elements involved and

compare the conventional construction with modern day technology.

There are three major elements of the cooling tower we will investigate, whether it be counterflow or crossflow, which consists of:-
1. Air handling
2. Water distribution
3. Heat transfer surfaces

The upgrading of these elements will be investigated in order of ascending costs and then case histories will be presented to document the rapid return of investment (ROI), by optimizing the performance of the cooling tower.

1. Air Handling.
a. The least expensive fix to improve air handling and increase the volume is by pitching blades to a maximum angle consistent with the motor plate

Figure 1. State-Of-The-Art high efficiency drift eliminators and cellular fill can upgrade NOMINAL cooling towers upwards to 50%.

571

amperage requirements.

b. Installation of velocity regain (VR) fan cylinders will generate approximately 7% more air due to relieving the exit pressure which the fan works against. This brings into effect Bernoulli's principle which states that increasing the velocity of a fluid will reduce its pressure or conversely: reducing the pressure of a fluid will increase it's velocity (and effective volume).

c. In conjunction with the VR stack, air flow can be enchanced if a right angle fan deck and fan cylinder are removed and an eased inlet is provided for.

d. Installing a larger motor and/or fan should be considered to increase the air flow to obtain higher levels of performance.

2. Water Distribution.

a. Crossflow water distribution patterns are set by the flow requirements and orifices (holes) located in the hot water distribution basin which are fixed in position. The conventional orifice drops the solid column of water on a lattice work of wood which splashes the water about the top of the fill. A higher level of performance can be obtained by removing the redistribution splash deck and replacing it with efficient cellular redistribution decks or target orifice nozzles. Both of these procedures will provide a more uniform distribution at the top of the tower thereby utilizing the entire height for cooling rather than a portion of it for water breakup and splash resulting in a net lower temperature.

b. Water troughs or enclosed flumes in counterflow towers should be changed to a low-pressure spray piping system.

c. Existing spray systems can be greatly improved by installing noncorroding PVC piping in conjunction with nonclogging, noncorroding square spray ABS plastic nozzles.

3. Heat Transfer Surfaces.

a. The most dramatic improvement in the performance of the tower can be obtained by installing, on a retrofit basis, cellular fill, available from a number of manufacturers.

b. Whether it be counterflow or crossflow configurations, change out to high-efficiency, dense-film fill also known as cellular fill, can result in improvements as much as 10 to 15°F (5.5 to 8.4°C), colder water which could equal upwards to a 50% or more increase in capacity of the existing tower.

c. The main factor in this extraordinary improvement is that in utilizing

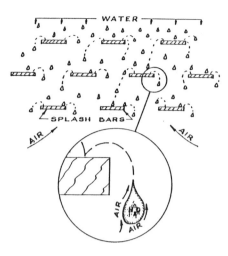

Figure 1a.    75 yearold splash bar technique is still being installed in cooling towers. while adequate, it is outmoded.

conventional splash bars, the water must bounce from slat to slat on it's way from top to bottom of the crossflow or counterflow tower and the exterior of the droplet is cooled, Figure 1a. If a high enough vertical travel is engineered, the water will be cooled to Design Conditions. Bear in mind, however, the more wood that is put into the tower, the higher the static pressure loss and larger horsepower motor and fan diameters are required.

Cellular Fill Principle. Cellular fill works on the principle that the droplet of water is stretched into a thin film as the water proceeds vertically downward through the cells, thereby permitting the available crossflow or counterflow air to cool the entire droplet more rapidly, Figure 2.

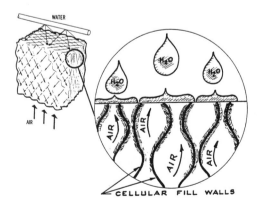

Figure 2.   Cellular fill changes droplet to thin film which is cooled faster and colder in  much shorted vertical distance

Even though the static pressure per cubic ft of cellular fill is much higher than the static pressure per cubic ft of wood fill, considerably less depth of cellular fill is required to produce the same or greater cooling results, thereby generating less total pressure drop which will provide a greater available volume of usable cooling air.

d. While the fill upgrading change out from wood splash bars to cellular could be the most expensive first cost retrofit procedure, it produces the highest level of improvement in performance which will provide for a more rapid ROI.

## Function of Lower Temperatures

The role of the cooling tower is to remove waste heat in the chemical or petrochemical reaction. In a condensation process, it is obvious that colder condensing water temperatures will increase unit production at a lower unit cost. The degree of elevation of the process temperature above ambient conditions is the sum of the tower's approach of the cold water to the wet bulb temperature, the cooling range (which equals the temperature rise in the heat exchanger), and the terminal difference in the exchanger. A reduction in operating temperature, always desirable for economic

results (4). Thus, a cooling system consuming $450,000 of electric or steam energy to power the turbines can reduce this utility cost by approximately $45,000.00 per year for a 4°F (2.2°C) colder water from the cooling tower. This can amount to over $500,000.00 or more in ten years, depending upon the ever rising utility costs.

## Case History I

Blow Through Squirrel Cage Tower. The subject three cell metal tower had a water distribution system of 960 small orifice nozzles on 1½" pipe, Figure 3, and the air conditioning machinery it had to cool was operating at high head temperatures and pressures as a result of not providing a sufficient level of cold water. The clogged and corroded water distribution system was removed from the tower and the rusted clogged steel plate corrugated wet decking fill was also disposed of. After sandblasting and coating with two part catalized coal tar epoxy, the new spray system consisting of 36 nozzles on 3" diameter PVC pipes was installed together with new PVC cellular fill.

Figure 3. Forced draft cooling tower complex, retrofitted with cellular film fill, square spray pattern, and cellular eliminators, produced 4 Degrees F. colder water at Design.

reasons, may be obtained by increasing the capability of the cooling tower's performance (2).

The importance of colder water for the compression of gases is evident in that all compressors have one thing in common: a major portion (80%) of the energy is converted to heat. This rejected heat must be continuously removed at the same rate it is generated or the compressor will overheat and shut down. Reducing the operating temperature of the compressor will proportionately reduce the energy input requirements. In other words, the colder the water returns to the equipment, the less energy is required to produce the same degree of work at lower costs (3).

In a refrigeration system, whether it be for process cooling or room temperature reduction (comfort cooling), colder water requires less energy to operate this system. Enthalpy charts indicate that for every degree F (.5°C) of colder water returning from the cooling tower within the operating range of the compressors, 2⅛% less energy will be required by the compressor to produce the same cooling

## Case History II

Petrochemical Plant, Gasoline. This case history clearly indicates the importance in value of the utilization of colder water from a well-engineered and rebuilt cooling tower functioning at optimum levels of performance.

Design Conditions of the two cell counterflow tower, Figure 4, were to originally cool 6500 GPM (1476 m³/hr) from entering the tower at 108°F (42.2°C) leaving at 90°F (32.2°C) during an ambient wet bulb temperature of 78°F (25.6°C). The manufacturer's data and associated fan curves indicated that the two 18 ft (5.5 m) diameter air foil aluminum fans utilizing 40 HP (30 kw) drivers will produce 300,000 ACFM of air (8500 m³/min per fan). This was designed to provide a delta T of 18°F (10°C) with a 12°F (6.6°C) approach to the wet bulb.

During the field inspection of this unit, the cooling tower engineers interviewed operating personnel who indicated at best, the tower was producing 70 to 75% capability at full heat load.

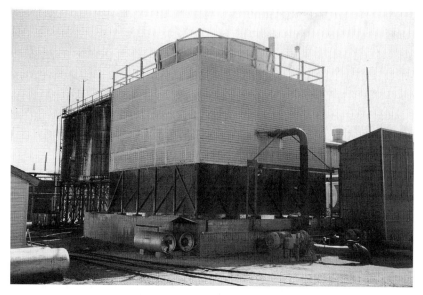

Figure 4. Petrochemical two cell counterflow tower doubled capacity from cooling 6,500 gpm originally, to 10,500 after new spray system and cellular fill installed.

Pullman-Kellogg was awarded a contract to double the capacity of the Alkylation Unit and determined quite early in the engineering phase of the program that the cooling tower was indeed a weak link in the process. To yield the projected quantity of increased product, 10,500 GPM (2385 m³/hr) of water approximately 60% greater capability of the existing 6500 GPM (1476 m³/hr) rate must be circulated through the system, which initially indicated erection of a new tower.

However, new tower delivery scheduling, plot plan constraint problems and budgetary requirements dictated that if the existing tower could be rebuilt to accommodate the newer capacity, considerable savings in time, real estate, and dollars would accrue over the alternative installation of new OEM equipment.

In order to provide sufficient cooling water for the doubled output of the new projected requirements, the old 6500 GPM (1476 m³/hr) tower would have to be upgraded to cool 10,500 GPM (2385 m³/hr) of water from entering at 108°F (42.2°C) at 78°F (25.6°C) wet bulb.

It was also evident that if the additional gallonage was not added to the tower after retrofit, the rebuilt facility would have the capability of cooling the 6500 GPM (1476 m³/hr) from 108° (42.2°C) to 84°F (28.9°C) at 78°F (25.6°C) wet bulb indicating a new capacity of providing a 24°F (13.3°C) delta T with a 6°F (3.3°C) approach to the wet bulb.

A further discussion at management level indicated that a new requirement of doubling the plant's output again is being considered which would now require cooling 15,500 GPM (3520 m³/hr) of cooling water. Engineering calculations (5) indicate that with additional rebuilding, the existing tower will have the capability of cooling this increased requirement.

While spending considerably more money, it would be cost-effective when the new cooling water rate could be used to produce approximately 1000 additional bbl (159 m³)/day of lead-free, high-octane gasoline. The savings in plot area and new construction would more than offset the labor and materials involved in

excavating the underground piping to change from 12 to 14 inch (3.7 to 4.3 m) diameter together with installing new 60 HP (45 kw) motors and 20 ft (6.1 m) diameter fan blades required to generate sufficient cooling air.

This clearly illustrates the viability of modern retrofit techniques which can upgrade this original design from cooling 6500 GPM (1476 m³/hr) to a new level of 15,500 GPM (3520 m³/hr).

The upgrading and modern retrofit consisted of changing the water distribution from old-fashioned water troughs and inefficient wood splash bar decking fill, to energy-absorbing, high-efficiency heat transfer PVC cellular fill, Figure 5, and PVC non-corroding water distribution system utilizing large orifice (1¼ inch (3.175 cm) diameter) ABS nonclogging square spray pattern nozzles.

The installation of the high thermal transfer, cellular fill surfaces provided over a 50% increase in capability, new water distribution patterns were extremely uniform, and the new cellular drift eliminators functioned at lower static pressure levels.

Case History III

The Power Generating Plant. The question of rebuilding large capacity exiting cooling towers for industrial power plants to modernize them to provide necessary additional capacity for plant expansion or to augment the performance with a new O.E.M. erected cell requires a professional inspection and evaluation of the situation.

Many generating power plants require expansion necessitating additional water volume through the cooling tower and/or colder water discharge to maximize production and meet new requirements.

The original operating conditions and new design requirements for the field erected doubleflow crossflow cooling tower, Figure 6, in this example are:

Figure 5. Large orifice square spray pattern nozzles permit uniform water distribution over the highly efficient heat transfer surfaces of cellular fill.

Old Operating Conditions

| | |
|---|---|
| Six 24' diameter fans | (7.3 m) |
| Six 75 HP motors | (60 kw) |
| 35,000 Gallons per minute | (7950 m³/hr) |
| 114°F Entering water | (45.5°C) |
| 91°F Discharge water | (32.7°C) |
| 80°F Wet bulb temperature | (26.6°C) |

New Design Requirements

| | |
|---|---|
| 42,000 Gallons per minute | (9540 m³/hr) |
| 114°F Entering temperature | (45.5°C) |
| 88°F Discharge water | (31.1°C) |
| 80°F Wet bulb temperature | (26.6°C) |

The existing conventional wood slat wet decking splash bar fill was in moderately sound condition but the heat transfer rate was considerably sub-standard compared to Design Requirements. The drift eliminators were inefficient, broken up, and permitting excessive solid water droplets to be drawn out of the tower. New PVC high performance drift eliminators that were retrofitted.

Thermal calculations indicated that if the highly efficient "V" bar fill shown on Figure 7 was installed on 8 inch (20 cm) vertical centers and 4 inch (10 cm) horizontal centers, the splash and film surface provided by this configuration would adequately meet the new Design Requirements.

The mechanical equipment rails were deteriorated and required a change out necessitating the use of a crane to remove entire units, rebuild them and later put them back into position, Figure 8.

To handle additional water volume, the distribution holes in the hot water basin were enlarged and metered orifice Polyvinyl Chloride target nozzles were installed.

Figure 6. "V" Bar combination splash and film bars can effectively upgrade large cross-flow towers to produce more cooling and circulate more water.

## Cost Comparison

To engineer, fabricate and erect an additional cell would have required a new concrete basin extention, plumbing, electrical, and erection and would require four months to accomplish from date of order. The turn-key construction cost would be $310,000.00. To be added to this price, the new tower would require an additional 75 HP (60 kw) motor operating approximately 48 to 50 weeks of the year, 24 hours a day would require approximately $30,000.00 electrical input energy costs at an average 5¢ per Kwh, Figure 9. This electrical penalty would be added and escalated yearly.

Rebuilding was selected, because in addition to the considerable savings, the new facility had to be put on line after a 14 day plant turnaround. This required two crews of cooling tower specialists working ten hour shifts to accomplish the tight schedule. The new self-extinguishing PVC fill, drift eliminators, and mechanical equipment rails were all retrofitted within the tight time frame. The work was performed at a cost of $181,740.00, or a savings of $128,260.00 for the P & L Utility (6) plus the add-on cost of $30,000.00 per year.

In this thirty-five year old tower the 48 ft (14.6 m) high unit was in good structural condition, the ancillary equipment such as the mechanicals, piping, and electrical were reuseable and with normal inplant maintenance procedures, a minimum of ten to fifteen years, and savings of $130,000.00, four months time, with no additional charge burdens, made it eminently feasible to rehabilitate this existing equipment.

## Conclusion

The cooling towers are hidden bonanzas for energy conservation and dollar savings when properly engineered and maintained. In many cases, the limiting factor of production is the quality and quantity of cold water coming off the cooling tower. The savings accrued in energy conservation and additional product manufactured can be an important factor on the operator's company's profit and loss sheet (7).

Energy management analysis is a very important consideration in today's escalating climate of costs of energy. It is advisable to consider a thorough engineering inspection and evaluation of the entire plant to leave no stone unturned in the search to reduce energy consumption (8). The cooling tower plays the major role on waste heat removal and should be given a thorough engineering inspection and evaluation by a specialist in this field. This can be performed at nominal cost and a formal report submitted with recommendations, budget costs, and evaluation of the thermal, structural, and mechanical condition of the equipment. This feasibility study will assist in determining the extent of efficiency improvement available with costs and projected savings.

It can be stated that practically all cooling towers can be upgraded to perform at higher levels of efficiency which can provide a rapid, cost-effective payback. However, while all cooling tower systems might not provide such a dramatic cost payback as these case histories, the return of a customer's investment in upgrading his cooling tower can be a surprising factor of operation and should not be neglected.

## References

1. The Marley Cooling Tower Co., "Energy Consideration in Cooling Tower Application", April 22, 1976.

2. "ASHRAE Equipment Handbook", Chapter 21, 1975, p. 11.

3. Stoven, K., "Energy Evaluation in Compressed Air Systems", Plant Engineering, June 1979.

4. Allied Chemical Corp., "The Pressure Enthalpy Diagram: It's Construction, Use, and Value".

5. Burger, Robert, "Cooling Tower Technology", Chapter 8, 1979, Revised 1989.

6. Southwest Public Utility, location upon request.

7. Willa, J., "Proper Cooling Tower Operations Makes Money", Cooling Tower Annual Institute Meeting Paper, 1975.

8. Mathur, S., "Energy Today", Hydrocarbon Processing, July 1980.

Chapter 101

# Back to the Future - Reinventing Centralized HVAC

S.J. Clark, K. Bass, S. Brown

## THE TREND TOWARD DECENTRALIZED IIVAC SYSTEMS

Modern commercial heating systems began when engineers started designing buildings with central boilers and one-pipe, and then two-pipe, steam distribution systems. In this century, that system was supplemented with a second set of pipes which could then be used to distribute cooling throughout a building. In the 1950's, steam heat was replaced with hydronic heat and numerous buildings were built using four-pipe systems.

The major drawback of four-pipe heating/cooling was relatively high initial cost. The cost of materials and labor for running four individual pipes to each zone of a building were prohibitive. Two-pipe and three-pipe systems were used to save on initial costs, but with significant performance penalties. The demand for systems that provide individual zone temperature controls led to the development and use of distributed HVAC systems which produce the heating or cooling effect in the zone where it is to be used. In the last thirty years, we have seen a dramatic increase in the use of systems like water source heat pumps, package terminal air conditioners and heat pumps, and packaged unitary equipment. This trend towards decentralized systems came when energy costs were cheap and electrical supplies seemed endless. In today's reality of limited and ever more expensive electrical power resources, it is time to reevaluate the costs of decentralized HVAC systems.

## HVAC: CENTRALIZED VERSUS DECENTRALIZED

Two major factors have driven the HVAC industry towards decentralized systems. Both are the initial cost. First, a decentralized system can often be installed without the cost of having an engineering firm design it. While a centralized system is almost always engineered, most building owners can order their own PTACs. Even small unitary systems are often installed without engineering services. Secondly, the initial cost of the systems are almost always less than a centralized systems with four pipes distributing the heating and cooling throughout a facility.

An additional negative aspect often associated with central systems is the picture of oversized equipment running inefficiently, running at low loads, and large horsepower pumps continuously circulating heating and cooling energy even when no loads are present. These negative aspects of the centralized HVAC systems can be eliminated or minimized through intelligent engineering design.

The disadvantages of decentralized HVAC systems are inherent with the nature of those systems and cannot be engineered away. Here are some of the inherent advantages centralized systems have over decentralized HVAC systems:

1) <u>Decreased Maintenance</u>: Simply counting the number of parts that can, and eventually will, fail when you have a hundred small air conditioning units is enough to give most repairmen nightmares.

2) <u>Improved Maintenance</u>: Not only do central systems have significantly fewer components to maintain and repair, but typically all components are located within a mechanical room, making them visible and accessible to the engineering staff. For this reason, central equipment is almost always far better maintained than numerous small pieces of equipment.

3) <u>Energy Efficiency</u>: Chillers are readily available which can provide an hour of air conditioning at nearly half the electrical use associated with packaged DX air conditioning equipment. Likewise, boiler plants can be optimized to be 20 to 30 percent more efficient than a packaged furnace.

4) <u>Flexibility</u>: We don't know what the optimum energy sources for heating and cooling will be in ten or twenty years but, with a central system, changing heating/cooling energy sources is relatively simple. Its also easy to incorporate features such as thermal storage, co-generation, chiller heat recovery, demand limiting, gas fired cooling etc. On the other hand, distributed systems offer no flexibilty in incorporating many of these features. Just try to incorporate thermal storage in a building cooled by a hundred, through-the-wall air conditioning units.

5) <u>CFC Loss Control</u>: Switching to ozone-safe refrigerants and controlling loss of ozone depleting refrigerants will be a major concern for building owners very soon. This problem is simplified when there is one central chiller plant versus numerous, through-the-wall air conditioners or unitary pieces of equipment.

6) <u>Aesthetics and Accoustics</u>: A good HVAC system should not be seen or heard. While this is an achievable goal with central systems it is nearly impossible with distributed systems, particularly systems where the compressor is located within occupied space.

So, from the viewpoint of owning, operating, or upgrading, central systems can be far superior. Intelligent engineering also allows us to minimize the additional first cost associated with centralized systems.

A major reason central heating and cooling systems are considerably more expensive than packaged unitary equipment is the cost of running heating and cooling fluids back and forth in piping throughout a building. Fortunately, how we construct our buildings has changed to allow us the advantages of four-pipe central systems with minimal extra piping costs.

The system is the Integrated Piping System. In this system the HVAC distribution lines are integrated with the domestic hot water and sprinkler lines. By serving two different functions with a single pipe, costs are reduced and considerable efficiencies are gained. The domestic hot water supply line now doubles as the heating water supply line. The low temperature of domestic hot water is quite well suited to heating our modern, well insulated buildings. The domestic hot water recirculation line size has to be increased to handle its second function of returning the heating hot water. The size of the domestic hot water heater is also considerably increased so that it now can also serve its purpose of being the heating plant for the building.

The fire suppression sprinkler piping layout must also be conducive to serving as the chilled water supply and return lines. The lines must now be insulated and sized to serve both functions of chilled water distribution and fire sprinkler uses. Because most modern commercial buildings have fire sprinkler systems and because the uniform fire code allows and directs the integration of the sprinkler lines with HVAC purposes, this dual purpose is easy to achieve.

The first cost savings of integrating hot water, sprinkler, and HVAC piping system into one system is obvious and very significant. The savings on piping costs allows central systems to compete better with the less expensive packaged unitary systems. When owning and operating costs are all looked at together, central HVAC systems actually are less expensive.

## DESIGNING INTEGRATED PIPING SYSTEMS

Combining the HVAC system with the fire sprinkler system is not a new concept. It has been heavily promoted by American Air Filter utilizing water-source heat pumps and called the Tri-Water System. In this system, condensor water for the water source heat pumps flows through the sprinkler lines. The drawback of this system is that it requires each room to have an independent compressor along with its associated noise controls and energy costs. The Tri-Water System was introduced in the mid 1970's, and a number of buildings were built integrating the fire sprinkler lines with water source heat pumps. Technology is basically the same for fire sprinkler lines used to distribute chilled water with the addition of insulation on the sprinkler lines.

Also introduced in the mid 1970's by Raypak was a system called Radronics. This system used the water heater as a boiler and the hot water piping for distribution to fan coils throughout the building. Since that time, a number of other manufacturers have introduced fan coils that connect into the domestic hot water heater, particularly for residential use.

So, while neither idea of using the domestic hot water lines or the sprinkler lines for HVAC systems is new, the concept of utilizing both simultaneously is new and has significant benefits. Using both sets of lines greatly reduces the cost of centralized systems, which will allow many buildings to enjoy the benefits of central heating and cooling on an economic basis. The synergistic benefits of combining these three piping systems to accomplish the three different functions could radically alter the way we design and construct buildings. The swing back to centralized heating/cooling plants will push manufacturers to develop more products to serve this area, causing the benefits to be increased further.

Environmental factors pushing us toward more efficient buildings could also drive energy codes to the point of requiring the use of centralized systems. One of the strongest proponents for change in how we build our buildings is coming from a new source, the electric Utility Company.

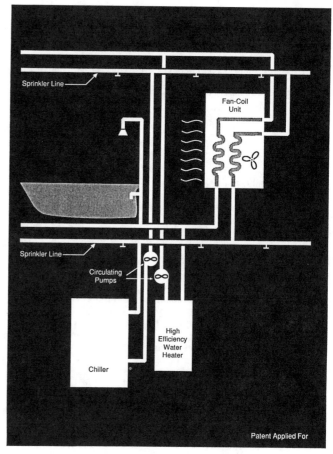

Integrated Fan-Coil System

## UTILITY PERSPECTIVE

I am a Commercial Key Account Executive with The Montana Power Company. It's my job to interface with our largest commercial customers. That includes the retail, the hotel/motel, and the banking industries. Of those groups, nothing currently compares with the activity in the Montana hotel/motel industry.

Those of you who are familiar with Montana, doubtless have discovered what I discovered when I moved to Montana from my home state of Texas three years ago. Not unlike Georgia, Montana's sheer beauty and tremendous recreation opportunities make it a great place to vacation and have fun. In fact, tourism and recreation are one of our leading industries. In 1991, $828 million was spent on tourism and recreation within our state. $141 million of that was spent with the lodging industry. Small peanuts some places, but real substance in a state that is big on space, but short on people.

Montana is more than a summer destination. The fall, winter and spring seasons are growth industries, which has led to expansion of lodging facilities throughout the state. Over the past year-and-a-half, we have seen the completion or the beginning of construction of 15 motel properties within our service territory. It is hard to complain about such aggressive economic development, but it has thrown out some real challenges for our utility. In general, we are seeing budget-class motels springing up. This means that comfort conditioning systems are specified in the plans to be all electric package terminal air-conditioning and heating units. This type of air-conditioning and heating is popular with budget class properties. Upfront cost, ease of installation are outstanding advantages when your budget is tight and your deadline is, too. But when it comes to day-to-day operating costs and customer comfort, there probably is no worse way to go.

How are we affected by this type of system? We are a winter-peaking utility. These types of systems are a tremendous adder to our peak. Even though there is some need for air-conditioning during certain times of our summer, this demand does not closely rival the amount of heating demand that we see in the winter. In pure and simple terms, we find ourselves spending $2,100 to provide capacity in order to generate $200 in revenue. It does not take a brain surgeon to determine that this is about as welcome as polecat roadkill for breakfast.

In early 1991, Montana Power commissioned design studies to be conducted on two motels that were going to be built. One in Great Falls, the other in Missoula. The one in Missoula was the 4B's Motel. The design study was an effort to explore alternatives to the package terminal air-conditioning and heating units. In all, four alternatives were examined. The initial results were disappointing. It was concluded that the package terminal air-conditioning and heating units were by far the most attractive way to go on the basis of first cost. The payback for the other systems ranged from 8 to 20 years. It has been our experience that most commercial customers require somewhere in the neighborhood of a 3 to 4-1/2 year payback for efficiency upgrades in order to justify the additional upfront cost on projects. The 4B's was geared up to begin construction of its 65-unit motel in Missoula when Steve Clark approached me and said that he might have a plan to compete with the PTAC units. Steve said his plan involved utilizing fan coil units similar to what is used with a four-pipe system. But we would not have to use dedicated supply and return lines; we would just use the piping that is already in place. Hence, the beginning of what we have come to refer to as the amazing integrated fan coil system.

We approached the 4B's with the idea and asked for a delay in construction in order to take a chance on saving energy dollars with a system that had never been used before. The owners reluctantly gave us two weeks to provide them with some economic analysis in order to help them make a decision. Steve reopened the design study and added this additional alternative to the study that already had been completed.

This time we had found a system that could compete with the package terminal air-conditioning units. The upfront economics showed that they would see about a $12,000 a year energy cost savings, plus $1,600 a year maintenance savings. Because going with this system would require a substantial amount of change orders, the incremental cost was not an actual reflection of what future projects would realize. In order to offset those punitive costs, Montana Power agreed to provide an incentive if the 4B's would go with the newly designed system.

Our agenda was two-fold. First, we wanted to eliminate the addition of another 100 kilowatts of demand coming onto our system for only winter use, with very little summer use. Second, we wanted a case study that might serve as a catalyst to change the way motels were built in our service territory. This incentive, along with Steve's confidence that the system would work, was enough to convince the owners of the 4B's.

Our experience to date shows that the 4B's made the right decision. The 4B's has a sister motel of similar size with the package terminal air-conditioning units for heating and cooling. Comparing the two facilities over the last seven months, the 4B's---with the integrated fan coil system---is running about half the energy cost of the older 4B's with the electric package terminal air-conditioning units.

Figure 1 is the comparison of kWh usage between the Reserve Street facility, the one with the integrated fan coil system, and the Brooks Street facility, the one with the package terminal air-conditioning and heating units.

Figure 2 is the kilowatt demand comparison.

Figure 3 is the gas usage comparison.

Figure 4 is the total energy cost comparison.

The experience we gained from this project has allowed us to effectively promote the "integrated fan coil system." The Great Falls motel where we conducted the other design study has opted to go with the "integrated fan coil system." Also, we were able to convince a motel owner in Bozeman to implement the

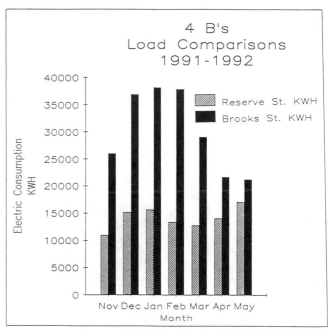

Figure 1

"integrated fan coil system" in his new facility. All three facilities are very similar in size and design. Through our work with these three facilities, we have developed a rebate level based on a standard room basis that can be offered to perspective motel builders. We hope that as mechanical contractors and general contractors gain experience in constructing facilities with the "integrated fan coil system," the system will become standard practice. In the long-term, no incentives should be necessary to entice people to utilize this type of system. It will speak clearly for itself and will say "use me and save money." And it will only have to whisper. Because the unit is so quiet, that alone is a strong incentive to motels in competitive markets.

The key to bring about these changes will come from an engineering community comfortable with, and capable of, designing buildings which integrate the piping systems.

## INTEGRATED SYSTEMS DESIGN

The design process for integrated system is essentially the same process for designing a conventional four-pipe system; however, the extra effort in optimizing the design of the integrated system will be apparent in its installed cost and operating performance. Here are the steps we recommend for designing an HVAC system using integrated piping system.

Step #1: Optimize Building Loads Utilizing energy efficient building materials and lighting systems allows a designer to minimize the cooling and heating requirements for a space. This, in turn, can result in smaller equipment for heating or cooling the space, and reducing flow rates required for the heating and cooling water. Taking advantage of technologies like tinted low-E glass and compact fluourescent light bulbs often can reduce the required mechanical equipment size by one full size. This savings can offset the increased envelope and lighting costs, as well as produce savings on piping and pumps.

Step #2: Minimize Flow Rate The use of low flow, high delta-T heating and cooling coils allows buildings to be heated or cooled with minimal flow rates. Again, this allows the use of smaller pipes and pumps to distribute the heating and cooling water. Having a high delta-T also means that return water temperatures are near the space temperature, thus minimizing pipe heat loss.

Step #3: Design Variable Flow Systems By using two-way valves on most of the coils throughout the system the flow can be allowed to vary, providing that the chiller plant and pumping system are designed to accomplish the variable flow.

Step #4: Optimize Location of Fan Coil Units and Air Handlers Locate the fan coil units as near as possible to hot water risers serving sinks or showers. Route sprinkler piping so it also passes near fan coil units.

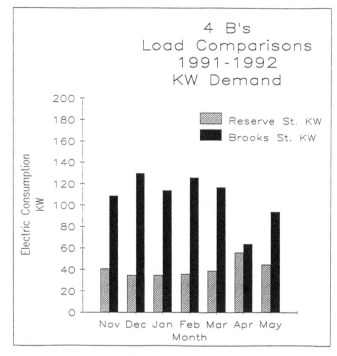

Figure 2

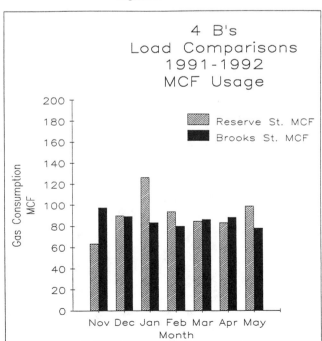

Figure 3

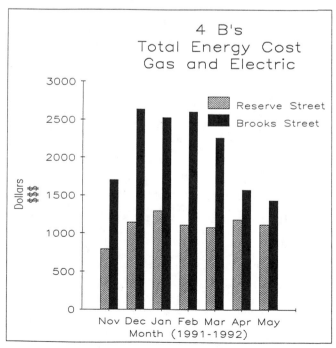

Figure 4

Step #5: Optimize Piping Distribution Systems  There will be trade-offs in determining the optimum piping system that can serve both chilled water supply and return as well as for sprinkler water supply. This may require engineers skilled in these two disciplines to work closely together, or for one engineer to expand his knowledge into a new area.

Step #6: Central Plant Design  The central heating plant now serves both the domestic hot water load and the building heating load. Obviously, engineering judgement is required in sizing the heating plant for the simultaneous peak of all loads or in allowing for reasonable diversity. Obviously, at a ski resort lodge, no diversity would be the best policy, while at a summer resort, it may be safe to assume that the peak heating load does not occur at the same time as the peak domestic hot water load. With a single heating plant now serving two different loads, it is easier to economically justify a higher efficiency boiler.

It also is important to satisfy the varying loads by using a modulating burner or staging of boilers. Keep in mind that the boiler plant will have numerous hours at very light loads. Obviously the heating plant, all pumps, fan coils, cylanoid, valves and other components in contact with the domestic hot water must be designed and rated for such use. The hot water is typically supplied in the 120 degree Fahrenheit to 140 degree Fahrenheit range. It is important to insure that the boiler can operate at those levels with no adverse effects. We recommend copper tube boilers with integral recirculating pumps to prevent boiler hot spots during operation at low loads. A pressure release valve is, of course, recommended with any domestic hot water system, but expansion tanks are not necessary.

Step #7: Central Chiller Plant Design  For ease in piping, we recommend that the chiller be located as near as possible to the fire sprinkler service entrance. At this point, the fire sprinkler line should spread into two main supply lines, one which will double as chill water supply and the other as chill water return. Locate a check valve in the line that will become supply just upstream of where the chilled water supply pipe ties in. This will prevent short circuiting of the chilled water. From the point of connection of the chilled water to the system all sprinkler piping, which will have chilled water flowing through it, must be insulated. In climates with freezing temperatures, we recommend that the chiller be placed indoors and connected to either a remote air-cooled condenser or a cooling tower. All components, including the chiller and fan coil coils that are connected to the fire sprinkler system, that must be rated in accordance with the fire code, usually to 175 psig. In many buildings, the use of plastic sprinkler piping is allowed and we encourage that use to reduce the initial cost of the system, as well as reducing the problem of corrosion within the metal fire sprinkler piping.

Step #8: Optimizing The System  Central systems offer a wide variety of options to allow an engineer to optimize the design in terms of economy and performance. Obviously, it is important to select efficient equipment, especially the boilers, chillers, and pumps. Secondly, optimize control strategies to minimize energy use at part-load conditions. Additional possible features in the integrated building design include digital controls, automatic setback of unoccupied rooms, thermal storage, gas-fired cooling, geothermal cooling, solar heating, heat recovery from the chiller, and even co-generation. Creatively applying these and other state-of-the-art technologies can result in buildings that operate at a fraction of the cost of the buildings using decentralized systems.

We can design buildings that are better for our customers, their customers, the utilities and the environment by using integrated piping systems.

# Chapter 102
# Hot Gas Defrosting Analysis of a Flat Plate Cooler

R.A. Sherif, S.A. Sherif

## ABSTRACT

The objective of this paper is to compute the defrosting time of a flat plate cooler originally maintained at a sub-freezing temperature. The cooler is assumed to have a specified frost layer at the time the defrosting process is activated, and the defrost time is predicted for different frost surface temperatures, heat flux, frost thickness, and frost properties.

## INTRODUCTION

The build up of frost on coolers maintained at sub-freezing temperatures has been shown to have a detrimental effect on their performance. Previous studies indicate, however, that a small build up may be desirable since the rough frost surface acts as a finned one, thus temporarily improving the heat transfer rate. Additional frost build up increases its insulating effect and causes a deterioration in the heat transfer performance of the cooler. Periodic frost removal becomes necessary and may be achieved employing several known methods such as electric resistance heating, hot gas reverse cycle, or hot water spray heating.

Previous defrosting studies are few, and most of them lack the kind of quantitative contribution that is needed if the process is to be optimized. Important defrosting studies include those of Kerschbaumer [1], Sanders [2], Stoecker et al. [3], Abdel-Wahed et al. [4], and Zakrzewski [5]. The work by Zakrzewski is indeed very significant since he presented an exhaustive model describing an optimum defrost cycle for an air cooler.

The purpose of this paper is to present a model for defrosting a horizontal flat plate cooler employing the hot gas reverse cycle defrosting method. The analysis is transient in nature and assumes a constant heat flux during the defrosting cycle. Frost properties such as thermal conductivity and density are assumed constant for purposes of the analysis, but are assigned values based on empirical correlations and the initial frost surface temperature. The model predicts the defrost time as a function of the applicable heat flux, hot gas and frost temperatures, frost thickness, and frost properties.

## ANALYSIS

Figure 1 describes the physical model and the coordinate system. An initial frost layer of thickness $S_i$ and surface temperature $t_{pi}$ is defrosted by the application of a constant heat flux q at the inside (bottom) surface. This can be achieved by reversing the flow of refrigerant so that heat is released in the evaporator. During the process, both the refrigerant temperature $t_H$ and the refrigerant side film coefficient of heat transfer, h, are assumed constant. The constant heat flux assumption requires that the plate surface temperature, $t_s$, also remain constant throughout the process. The energy balance equation in the frost layer during the defrosting process can be expressed as follows:

$$q = -\rho_f L \frac{dS}{d\tau} + \frac{K_f(t_s - t_p)}{S} \qquad (1)$$

where

$\rho_f$ = frost density, kg/m³
$K_f$ = frost thermal conductivity, kW/m.K
$S$ = frost thickness at time $\tau$, m
$t_p$ = frost surface temperature at time $\tau$, °C
$t_s$ = plate surface temperature, °C
$\tau$ = time, seconds
$L$ = latent heat of fusion of the frost = 79 kJ/kg

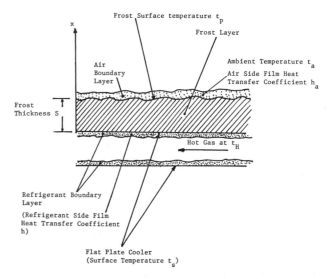

FIGURE 1 PHYSICAL MODEL OF A FLAT PLATE COOLER

In a previous investigation, Abdel-Wahed et al. [4] assumed a constant frost surface temperature during a hot water defrosting process and obtained an expression for the frost thickness as a function of time. In this paper, the frost surface temperature will be assumed to change linearly with the frost thickness with a convective boundary condition on the frost upper surface. This can be expressed by:

$$h_a (t_p - t_a) = \frac{K_f}{S} (t_s - t_p) \qquad (2)$$

where $h_a$ is the air side film heat transfer coefficient and $t_a$ is the ambient temperature in the vicinity of the frost surface.

The heat flux term q may also be expressed in terms of the film coefficient of heat transfer on the hot gas side, h, and the temperature difference between the hot gas and the plate surface. This gives:

$$q = h (t_H - t_s) \qquad (3)$$

Solving Equation (2) in the frost surface temperature, $t_p$, the following equation is obtained:

$$t_p = \frac{h_a t_a S + K_f t_s}{h_a S + K_f} \qquad (4)$$

which when substituted in Equation (1) yields the following energy balance equation:

$$\frac{dS}{d\tau} = \frac{K_f h_a (t_s - t_a) - h(t_H - t_s)(h_a S + K_f)}{\rho_f L (h_a S + K_f)} \qquad (5)$$

Equation (5) can be integrated by separating the variables as follows:

$$\int_{S_i}^{S} \frac{-\rho_f L (h_a S + K_f) dS}{h_a h(t_H - t_s)S + K_f[h(t_H - t_s) - h_a(t_s - t_a)]} = \int_0^\tau d\tau \qquad (6)$$

The left hand side of Equation (6) may be integrated by using integration tables. This yields the following (after manipulation):

$$\tau = \frac{\rho_f L}{h^2(t_H - t_s)^2} \{h(t_H - t_s)(S_i - S) + K_f(t_s - t_a) \cdot$$
$$\log_e[\frac{h h_a(t_H - t_s)S_i + \{h(t_H - t_s) - h_a(t_s - t_a)\}K_f}{h h_a(t_H - t_s)S + \{h(t_H - t_s) - h_a(t_s - t_a)\}K_f}]\} \qquad (7)$$

Equation (7) provides a formula for computing the time as a function of the frost thickness and other relevant parameters. For a complete frost removal, S=o and Equation (7) gives $\tau_{def}$ as follows:

$$\tau_{def} = \frac{\rho_f L}{h^2(t_H - t_s)^2} \{h(t_H - t_s)S_i + K_f(t_s - t_a)$$
$$\log_e [ 1 + \frac{h h_a(t_H - t_s)S_i}{\{h(t_H - t_s) - h_a(t_s - t_a)\}K_f}]\} \qquad (8)$$

It is to be noted that the defrost time is always a positive non zero quantity for $S_i > o$. For $S_i = o$ (i.e. no initial frost layer), the defrost time is zero (since there is no defrosting needed).

It should be borne in mind when applying this model that the melt is assumed not to accumulate in the frost layer during the defrosting cycle. Also, the values of the frost density and thermal conductivity will be altered once defrosting is activated. Both the frost density and conductivity will increase as the frost surface temperature increases. This was documented in the literature by Hayashi et al. [6] and Sanders [2]. Hayashi's formula for the frost density is

$$\rho_f = 650 \exp[ 0.227 \, t_p] \qquad (9)$$

where $-25°C < t_p < 0°C$, and $\rho_f$ is in kg/m$^3$. One interesting aspect about Equation (9) is that the frost density is a sole function of its surface temperature. Sanders' formula for the frost thermal conductivity, on the other hand, is expressed as follows:

$$K_f = 0.001202 \, \rho_f^{0.963} \qquad (10)$$

where $K_f$ is in W/m.K and $\rho_f$ is in kg/m$^3$. Also, the plate temperature has to lie between $-22°C$ and $+11°C$.

If conduction effects through the frost layer are neglected, $K_f$ is set to zero and the thickness would vary linearly with time. This may be expressed as follows:

$$\tau = \frac{\rho_f L (S_i - S)}{h(t_H - t_s)} \qquad (11)$$

and when S=o, the defrosting time is obtained according to:

$$\tau_{def} = \frac{\rho_f L S_i}{h(t_H - t_s)} \qquad (12)$$

## RESULTS AND DISCUSSION

As seen in the previous section, the model is primarily useful for predicting two different quantities; (1) the defrosting time for a given initial frost thickness as a function of the hot gas temperature; and (2) the frost thickness-time history of a given frost layer undergoing a defrosting cycle. These predictions are illustrated in Figures 2 through 4.

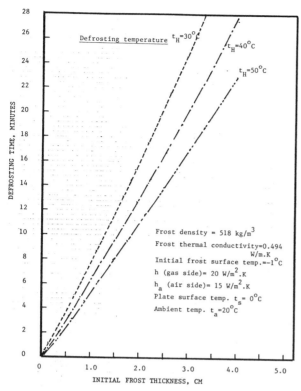

FIGURE 2 EFFECT OF HOT GAS TEMPERATURE ON DEFROST TIME

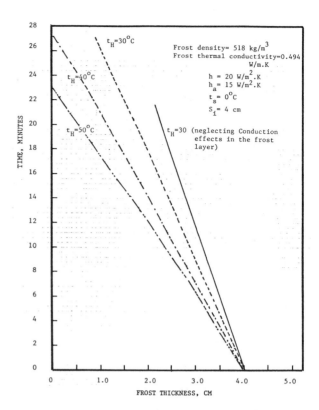

FIGURE 4 FROST THICKNESS-TIME PROFILES DURING THE DEFROST CYCLE

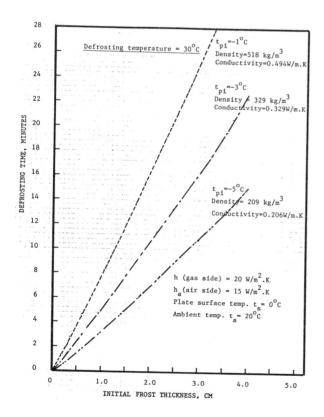

FIGURE 3 EFFECT OF FROST NATURE ON DEFROST TIME

Figure 2 displays the defrost time as a function of the original thickness of the frost layer for three hot gas temperatures of 30°C, 40°C, and 50°C. These are typical condensing temperatures in refrigeration applications. The initial frost layer surface temperature is assumed to be -1°C. This temperature determines the frost-density and thermal conductivity according to Equations (9) and (10), respectively. It is important to note that, in an actual defrosting process, the frost surface temperature, and, consequently, the frost density and conductivity will not remain constant throughout the process. While this continuous variation was not accounted for in this model, a quasi-static variation was accounted for by computing the correct values of the density and conductivity based on the initial frost surface temperature. This can be seen in Figure 3, where the defrosting time as a function of the initial frost thickness is plotted for a number of initial frost surface temperatures.

An examination of Figures 2 and 3 reveals that the defrosting time increases almost linearly as the frost thickness increases. As can be seen from Equation (7), there are two main terms in the frost thickness-time profile, a linear term and a logarithmic term. The relative significance of both terms changes depending on the values assumed by the different parameters. Generally, the linear term becomes more dominant for larger defrosting heat fluxes (as evidenced by larger defrosting temperatures, $t_H$, and/or larger refrigerant side heat transfer coefficients). However, even in cases involving a smaller defrosting heat flux, the effect of the logarithmic term is significantly less than the linear one.

Another observation can be made by examining Figure 2. Despite the obvious result that an increase in the defrosting temperature decreases the defrosting time, the rate of decrease of the latter is non-linearly related to the rate of increase of the former. This non-linear relationship becomes more significant for thicker frost layers. For example, an increase in the hot gas temperature from 30°C to 40°C results in a larger defrost time reduction than an equal increase in temperature from 40°C and 50°C (see Fig. 2). Also, for a larger initial frost thickness, the reduction in defrost time is significantly less between 40°C and 50°C than between 30°C and 40°C. This means that the energy consumed at larger defrosting temperatures is not proportional to the savings in the time of defrost, and optimum decision rules regarding which defrosting temperature to apply should be obtained based on the type of application and the system economics.

Figure 3 reveals a similar trend between the defrosting time and the frost layer thickness but in connection with changing the nature of the frost layer. As the frost surface temperature increases, the frost becomes denser and more thermally conductive. Naturally, a denser frost layer is harder to defrost than a lighter one. However, a more thermally conductive layer is easier to defrost than a less thermally conductive one. In other words, there are two opposing effects when the frost becomes denser. Examination of Figure 3 indicates that the density effect is significantly more dominant than the thermal conductivity effect as evidenced by a lower curve at -3°C than -1°C, for example. However, again there is a similar phenomenon associated with defrosting denser frost layers vis-a-vis the change in the frost surface temperature. This observation can be understood by noticing that the decrease in defrosting time between the -1°C-frost and the -3°C-frost is significantly larger than the corresponding decrease between the -3°C-frost and the -5°C-frost. Again, this effect is more pronounced for thicker frost layers.

A general frost thickness-time profile can be obtained employing Equation (7). This results in the profiles shown in Figure 4 for a 4-cm frost layer. These profiles are useful in predicting the instantaneous frost layer thickness at any time during the defrost cycle. Again, the underlying assumption is that the melt is continuously removed away from the frost layer. Figure 4 also shows what the profile would have looked like had conduction effects through the frost layer been neglected. This is shown for the case where the defrosting temperature is 30°C. As mentioned earlier, the thickness-time profile neglecting conduction effects is a straight line. Examination of Equation (11) indicates that the slope and ordinate intercept are $-\rho_f L/[h(t_H-t_s)]$ and $\rho_f L S_i/[h(t_H-t_s)]$, respectively.

Finally, a note is in order regarding the film coefficients of heat transfer on the gas and air sides. The coefficients were given the values 20 and 15 $W/m^2 \cdot K$, respectively, based on typical applications. Larger values for either $h$ or $h_a$ would result in smaller defrosting times.

CONCLUSIONS

A simple model for predicting the defrost time and the frost thickness-time history in hot gas reverse cycle defrosting of a flat plate cooler was presented. The model revealed a number of interesting observations regarding the effectiveness of this defrosting method for thicker frost layers. In such cases, it might be advisable to employ more frequent defrosting cycles, or use a defrosting method with more direct heat transfer mechanisms (such as hot water spray methods). It should be borne in mind when applying this model that it is limited to a linear temperature profile in the frost layer, a quasi-static variation of the frost properties, and a constant defrosting heat flux. This last assumption resulted in a constant cooler surface temperature throughout the defrosting process.

ACKNOWLEDGEMENTS

The first author is grateful to the invaluable help received from Mrs. Alice Jempson in typing and preparation of the manuscript. Support from the Department of Mechanical Engineering at the University of Florida is also gratefully acknowledged.

REFERENCES

1. Kerschbaumer, H.G., "Analysis of the Influence of Frost Formation on Evaporators and of the Defrost Cycles on Performance and Power Consumption of Refrigeration Systems," Proceedings of the XIII International Congress of Refrigeration, Paper No. 3.11, Washington, D.C., 1971.

2. Sanders, C. Th., "The Influence of Frost Formation and Defrosting on the Performance of Air Coolers," Ph.D. Dissertation, Technische Hogeschool, Delft, The Netherlands, 1974.

3. Stoecker, W.F., Lux, J.J., and Kooy, R.J., "Conserving Energy in Industrial Refrigeration Systems by Reducing Condensing Temperatures-Effect on Hot Gas Defrost," ASHRAE RP-193 Final Report, 1983.

4. Abdel-Wahed, R.M., Hifni, M.A., and Sherif, S.A., "Hot Water Defrosting of a Horizontal Flat Plate Cooling Surface," International Journal of Refrigeration, Vol. 6, No. 3, May 1983, pp. 152-154.

5. Zakrzewski, B., "Optimal Defrost Cycle for the Air Cooler," International Journal of Refrigeration, Vol. 7, No. 1, January 1984, pp. 41-45.

6. Hayashi, Y., Aoki, A., and Yuhara, H., "Study of Frost Formation Based on a Theoretical Model of the Frost Layer," Heat Transfer - Japanese Research, Vol. 6, No. 3, 1977, pp. 79-94.

# SECTION 9
# ALTERNATIVE ENERGY DEVELOPMENT

# Chapter 103

# Solar Water Heating: The Making of a Simple, Standard Appliance

D.L. Block

## Abstract

Within the solar community we have carried on never-ending discussions about the performance of solar water heaters. As a long-time solar advocate and researcher, I am continually asked, "When will solar usage become widespread?" We who are in the solar business all face this question, and we must respond. Our answers usually take the form of some discussion on efficiency improvements, life-cycle costs, level playing field or environmental factors. But the only real way to answer this question is: "Use of solar will be widespread when a solar water heater is considered to be just another standard appliance." Increased installations is the key, and the solar technology with the greatest near-term potential for increased installation is solar water heating (SWH). Simply put, solar water heating has to be successful for solar in general to be successful.

Since the demise of the federal tax credits in 1985, the annual number of new solar water heating installations has decreased dramatically. By 1991, the industry stabilized, and installations have increased moderately. However, the present number of annual installations will not make solar usage widespread. There is a crying need for a dramatic increase. For there to be a dramatic increase, there must be a dramatic change in the way both we and the public think about SWH. We, as the solar community and the industry, must be the leaders in this change. What must we do?

There are three issues that we are directly responsible for and which have a direct impact on increasing SWH installations. The issues are: public perception, system performance requirements and system simplification. To positively affect these issues, we must take steps to ensure that:

- SWH is considered a standard appliance by the public
- The performance of SWH can be presented as simply as the performance of gas and electric systems.
- The complexity of SWH systems and components is minimized to allow for improved installation and reliability.

The following discusses each of these issues in some detail.

## I. Solar as a Standard Appliance

Every time a system is installed, the first words out of a new owner's mouth are, "I will be happy to monitor the performance of my system for you."

We must change the attitude and thinking that solar is "experimental" and in need of monitoring. We need to express the attitude that we <u>know</u> the performance of solar water heating and that SWH systems are conventional appliances -- no more in need of monitoring than a refrigerator.

Table 1 illustrates why we know the performance of SWH and why it is important for us to make this case. The table was constructed based on a literature search for references on the performance of three types of water heaters -- solar, electric and gas. The critical data are the number of citations with the word "performance" in the title and in English. There are 2580 for solar, 2 for electric, and 8 for gas water heaters.

I believe it is safe to state that when we see 2580 references on solar water heater performance, we can rest assured that we have studied their performance in enough detail to know the answers. With 10 total citations for electric and gas water heaters, it is also clearly obvious that no one is interested in their performance; it is simply assumed that they perform up to standards.

The point is: <u>solar water heaters are standard appliances and must be thought of and presented as standard appliances</u>. We know their performance and are ready to install them. This positive attitude requires no more than a change in our thinking and a direct transfer of this change to the consuming public.

One final comment needs to be made on performance. Although we have 2500 citations on SWH performance, we only have three citations on the time-of-day usage of SWHs. Time-of-day performance of SWH is the most significant data to utility companies and their demand-side management programs.

## II. Simplified Presentation of Solar Water Heating Performance

While we know and are confident of the performance of SWH systems, we still must have a means by which to present their performance to both the solar community and the consuming public. It is also critical that both groups have a simple, clear means of comparing SWH systems with other water heating systems. The only performance parameter that meets these goals is an energy factor (to be defined later).

I note that it is highly probable that the 2580 evaluations of SWH performance cited in Table 1 have probably led to 2580 different methods of presenting that performance. In fact, the presentation of performance has become more complex in time, involving mazes of tables and multiple multiplication factors. Let me cite a specific example -- the Florida Energy-Efficiency Code for Building Construction (Reference 1), which I believe clearly presents the need for performance simplification.

For every new home constructed in Florida, the builder must file an energy-efficiency code evaluation. The Code requires that water heating be given consideration by the builder. Table 2 shows that five types of water heating systems are considered in the Code. It also shows the rating method and code steps considered for selection of a system type by a builder.

With regard to solar and its consideration by the builder, the critical characteristic in Table 2 is the number of code steps: solar requires 8 steps for selection compared to only 1 or 2

TABLE 1. LITERATURE CITATIONS ON PERFORMANCE OF SOLAR WATER HEATERS*

| Item Description | Number of Citations | Number of Citations with Performance as Major Topic and in English |
|---|---|---|
| Solar water heaters, solar water heating and performance | 3232 | 2580 |
| Electric water heaters, electric water heating and performance | 104 | 2 |
| Gas water heaters, gas water heating and performance | 90 | 8 |

*Information obtained from U.S. DOE publications data base (Energy Science & Technology).

TABLE 2. WATER HEATING CHARACTERISTICS OF THE FLORIDA ENERGY EFFICIENCY CODE

| System | Rating | Rating Method | Rating Range | Code Steps |
|---|---|---|---|---|
| Gas | Energy Factor [1] | DOE | .54 - .75 | 1 |
| Electric | Energy Factor [1] | DOE | .80 - 1.0 | 1 |
| Heat Pump | Energy Factor [1] | GAMA [3] | 2.0 - 3.5 | 2 |
| Solar | Solar Fraction [2] | FSEC | 0.1 - 1.0 | 8 |
| Desuperheater | (Test only) | N/A | AC/HP | 2 |

[1] Energy Factor - A measure of water heater overall efficiency in terms of energy output compared to energy consumption over a 24-hour usage cycle (Range: 0 to infinity)

[2] Solar Fraction - The percentage of annual water heating load that can be supplied by a solar water heating system (Range: 0 to 1.0)

[3] GAMA - Gas Appliance Manufacturers Association

steps for all other systems. Is it any wonder that Florida builders select options other than solar? At present, efforts are being made to change the Florida Code in a manner that would apply an energy factor to solar and, thus, would require that the builder follow only 2 code steps. This change will be considered by Code officials this year and may well serve as a national model.

Referring again to Table 2, I propose that SWH systems adopt the same rating factor that applies to other water heating systems -- an energy factor. An energy factor is defined as follows:

$$EF = \frac{Q}{E + E_a}$$

Where:

EF = energy factor
Q = heat delivered to the household by the water heating system
E = electricity (gas) energy used by the storage tank (burner)
$E_a$ = electrical energy to operate circulating pump and controls for solar

The above energy factor definition is the same for all water heating systems and can be thought of as the amount of energy supplied, divided by the amount of conventional energy used. The energy factor for electric and gas systems is always less than one, since they cannot supply more energy than they consume. For solar systems, energy factors generally range from 3 to 10, which implies that solar supplies 3 to 10 times the conventional energy it uses. Note that the energy factor can be calculated from an SWH solar fraction ($f_s$) by the relation of $1/(1 - f_s)$.

The primary argument against using an energy factor lies in the premise that solar performance is different at each location or city within the U.S. While this statement is valid, it erroneously implies that a rating procedure is to be used as a design tool. The energy factor is to be used for rating solar systems and for comparing solar with other system types, and not as a design tool. Design and sizing are functions to be carried out by the solar manufacturer and company representatives -- not builders or consumers. It is also important to note in Table 2 that solar is the only water heating system that is considered to be climate sensitive. We all know that desuperheaters and heat pumps are also climate sensitive.

To calculate energy factors, we must make some assumptions as a baseline. I have studied this question and propose the following values:

o Water usage of 64.3 gallons per day
o Inlet water temperature of 58°F
o Outlet water temperature of 135°F
o Solar insolation of 1500 Btu/ft2 · day, and ambient temperature of 67.5°F
o Collector facing south at a tilt of 45°
o Solar systems evaluated using TRNSYS.

The water usage and inlet and outlet water temperature values presented above are the same as those used by rating organizations and the U.S. Department of Energy to calculate the energy factors for electric and gas water heaters. The solar-specific values selected are the values used for the system tests specified by SRCC Standard OG-200 (Reference 2). To ensure accuracy, TRNSYS is used for modelling purposes. The TRNSYS use should be relatively easy, since it is being developed and used for SRCC Standard OG-300.

590

Table 3 presents a sample listing and the energy factors for some solar water heating systems that are certified by the Florida Solar Energy Center. The sample listing includes the system model number, collector area, rated storage volume and energy factor. Each system has one energy factor, and that value is directly comparable to the energy factors of other system types, such as a gas or electric. If this rating system is to be applied, the final result would be a listing of solar systems, such as shown in Table 3, in a book similar to the GAMA Consumer Directory of Certified Efficiency Ratings for gas water heaters.

A final, important note on energy factors: they have the potential for providing the impetus and mechanism for including solar water heaters as a part of the National Appliance Energy Conservation Act. Inclusion of solar in the NAECA would imply that SWH is a simple, standard appliance -- the goal that needs to be achieved.

good system performance. Second, our national research efforts have concentrated on performance instead of materials and manufacturing improvements. Very simply stated, our most important problem is to simplify solar systems and components in ways that will improve installations and increase reliability. Our efforts need to focus on these two issues.

As an industry, we still do not have a reliable mechanical check valve. We still use copper absorber plates and glass cover plates -- materials that were developed for solar in the 1940s. We still install by soldering.

That's the solar industry. Now look at the plumbing industry. Today, plumbing has become so simple that the average homeowner can easily replace a sink, fix a toilet, or put in new plumbing fixtures. This can be done without ever using solder or a torch, much less calling a plumber. And in the plumbing industry itself, slip couplings and plastic or stainless steel flexible lines are now commonplace.

TABLE 3. SAMPLE LISTING OF SOLAR WATER HEATING SYSTEMS

| SYSTEM NUMBER | COLLECTOR MODEL | GROSS COLLECTOR AREA (ft²) | RATED STORAGE VOLUME (GALLONS) | ENERGY FACTOR |
|---|---|---|---|---|
| **AA, INC.** | | | | |
| S8010A | SD6A | 40.6 | 80 | 6.8 |
| S8010B | SD7CRW | 40.4 | 80 | 7.3 |
| S8010C | SD7CRW | 31.3 | 80 | 4.1 |
| S8011A | SD7CRW | 49.7 | 120 | 20.4 |
| S8011B | SD6A | 40.6 | 120 | 7.8 |
| | | | | |
| **BB COMPANY** | | | | |
| S5059A | MSC-26 | 52.0 | 80 | 10.2 |
| S5059B | MSC-40 | 40.7 | 80 | 6.0 |
| S5065A | MSC-26 | 26.0 | 66 | 2.8 |
| S5065B | MSC-32 | 32.7 | 66 | 3.9 |
| | | | | |
| **XXX, INC.** | | | | |
| S7001A | ESC 6520 | 58.0 | 80 | 7.3 |
| S7001B | ESC 6520 | 77.3 | 80 | 11.3 |
| S7002A | ESC 6520 | 77.3 | 120 | 11.3 |
| S7002B | ESC 6520 | 96.7 | 120 | 25.5 |
| S7007 | ESC 6520 | 38.7 | 80 | 3.5 |
| | | | | |
| **XYZ CORP.** | | | | |
| S4099 | A.S.K. SS-12 | 63.0 | 100 | 7.8 |
| S5100 | A.S.K. SS-12 | 31.5 | 80 | 2.9 |
| S5101 | A.S.K. SS-12 | 31.5 | 66 | 2.8 |
| | | | | |
| **ABC COMPANY** | | | | |
| S4110A | MSC-32 | 65.5 | 120 | 11.3 |
| S4110B | MSC-40 | 81.3 | 120 | 12.8 |
| S4111A | MSC-32 | 32.7 | 66 | 3.3 |
| S4111B | MSC-40 | 40.7 | 66 | 4.4 |
| S4112A | MSC-40 | 40.7 | 80 | 4.6 |
| S4112B | MSC-32 | 32.7 | 80 | 3.4 |
| S4113 | MSC-32 | 65.5 | 80 | 11.3 |
| S4115A | MSC-26 | 26.0 | 40 | 2.3 |
| S4115B | MSC-32 | 32.7 | 40 | 3.1 |
| S4116A | MSC-26 | 26.0 | 52 | 2.4 |
| S4116B | MSC-32 | 32.7 | 52 | 3.1 |

III. System and Component Simplification

This final issue is extremely important, but its resolution is far from simple. Resolving this issue must be pursued, because how it is dealt with may well determine the success of solar technologies for the future.

Two points are important here. First, experience over the past 15 years has shown us that proper installation is the key to

The solar industry must begin to move into the modern era and toward simplification. Imagine the consequences if a solar system could be manufactured in a process that would allow its purchase price to be less than $1,000 from the local building supply store; imagine the number of sales if solar installation were so simple it could be done by the average homeowner. System installations would increase by many magnitudes.

I cannot resolve these issues here, but let me list what I believe to be important goals for the SWH industry and R&D community:

- Development of new absorber plate and glazing materials
- Manufacturing cost reductions by such techniques as extrusion processes
- System and component simplifications
- Installation simplifications.

In summary, solar DWH must reduce system costs for large-scale usage. The easiest way to reduce these costs is through improvements in the manufacturing process and installation, and development of new materials. Imagine the public's perception of solar technologies if solar water heaters were no more "special" than a refrigerator.

IV. References

1. "Energy-Efficiency Code for Building Construction," Florida Department of Community Affairs, Tallahassee, FL, 1990.

2. "Test Methods and Minimum Standards for Certifying Solar Water Heating Systems," Standard 200-82, Solar Rating and Certification Corporation, Washington, DC, February 1985.111

Chapter 104

# Photovoltaics As a Demand-Side Management Option: Benefits of a Utility Customer Partnership

H. Wenger, T. Hoff, R. Perez

## INTRODUCTION

Pacific Gas and Electric Company (PG&E) has been involved in photovoltaic (PV) research for more than a decade. PG&E's efforts have ranged from basic cell research to the development of PV for utility-scale applications (PVUSA).[1] These projects have covered a range of research designed to enhance technical understanding and speed commercialization of PV for utility use. Throughout, PG&E has found PV to be a reliable, low maintenance, non-polluting energy producer that matches PG&E's loads.

Many in the PV community believe utility networks will eventually provide a large enough market to drive PV system costs down and thus establish PV as a significant power producing technology. Utilities have not found currently-available PV technology cost-effective, however, except for niche applications utilizing small off-grid power supplies.[2]

The most promising utility-owned applications appear to be strategically sited PV systems within the transmission and distribution network. These applications maximize local and system benefits to the utility.[3] Current PV system costs, however, still exceed value, making PV uncompetitive. The same is true for customer-owned systems located on the demand side of the meter.[4]

This paper combines previous efforts by proposing a utility-customer partnership. Such a partnership improves the economic feasibility of deploying grid-connected PV by maximizing the net benefit for parties on both sides of the meter. PV within this utility-customer partnership is called PV DSM, a utility-sponsored photovoltaic demand-side management program. This paper draws largely on a recent PG&E report[5] and presents the PV DSM concept, sample calculations for a test case, and compares PV DSM with more conventional utility-customer energy efficiency measures.

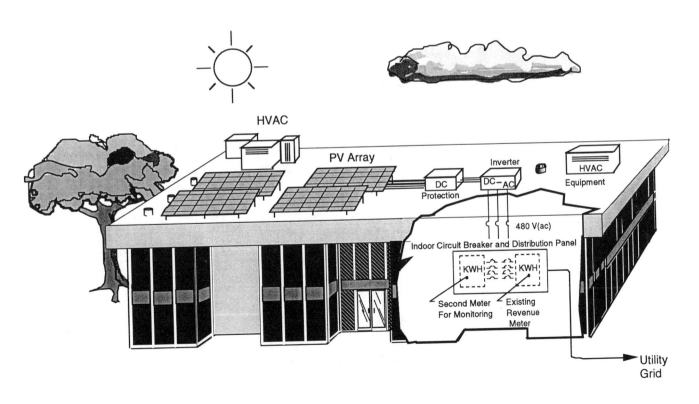

Figure 1. Customer-sited PV system illustration.

## TECHNICAL OVERVIEW: WHAT IS PV DSM?

Figure 1 is an illustration of the major components of a customer-sited PV system. The PV array converts sunlight directly into DC. A power conditioning system electronically inverts the DC power into AC power, which is fed directly into the building distribution panel for consumption.[*] A kilowatt-hour meter is used to monitor PV energy production.

There are many ways to structure a PV DSM program. For the purposes of this paper, the utility's role is to use financial incentives, such as rebates, to encourage customers in areas of high utility value to purchase and install PV systems. This arrangement is similar to traditional utility-sponsored DSM programs.

The definition of PV DSM presented in this paper stipulates that the PV power system delivers electricity solely to the customer's load and does not back-feed power to the utility grid. This can be achieved either by sizing the PV system so that power output never exceeds customer load, or by installing a device to prevent back-feeding excess power to the grid. This stipulation renders the PV system "transparent" to the utility and makes it comparable to the installation of energy efficient appliances.

To illustrate, consider a high efficiency air conditioner replacement program. Both air conditioning loads and PV system output are highly correlated with sunlight availability. Thus, both high efficiency air conditioners and PV systems have similar impacts on a building's peak load and electricity consumption. As long as PV power is used to serve the

building's loads only, the utility does not know whether the customer has a PV system or a high efficiency air conditioner.

Figure 2 demonstrates this concept by showing the effect of PV on a typical day's load of a representative commercial office building with daytime occupancy, using actual load data from PG&E's Research and Development building. The building load is dominated by the air cooling (HVAC) system. The power output from a 15 kW PV system located on the roof of the building is subtracted from the HVAC load.[**]

The peak load occurs at 2:30 PM and is about 102 kW without the PV system. A PV DSM system reduces peak load to 88 kW, and effectively acts like a high efficiency HVAC system: it reduces the HVAC load by 23 percent at peak and provides consistent load shaving throughout the day.

Figure 3 demonstrates this concept further by using a year's worth of HVAC load data from PG&E's Research and Development building. Three load duration curves[***] are plotted. The top curve is the load duration curve (LDC) for the original HVAC system; the HVAC load peaks at about 70 kW. The second curve is the LDC for a *hypothetical* HVAC system. This "efficient" HVAC system has 21.5 percent less demand during all operating conditions than the original HVAC system. The third LDC is for the original HVAC system coupled with a 30 degree tilted fixed flat-plate PV system. The PV system is rated at 15 kW (21.5 percent of the HVAC peak load).

These curves show that the two demand-side management options provide similar peak load reductions and annual energy savings. That is, from the utility's perspective, the

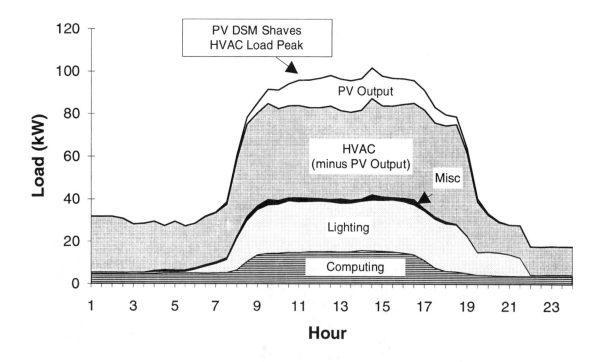

Figure 2. PV output matches PG&E R&D building daily load and shaves peak, June 21, 1990.

---

[*]PV system output could alternatively be directed to a specific piece of equipment, such as an air cooling unit.

[**] PV output is simulated using actual on-site weather data.[6]

[***] Load data in a load duration curve are re-sorted from chronological order to descending load order. The highest load of the year is at the far left of the plot and the lowest load is at the far right of the plot.

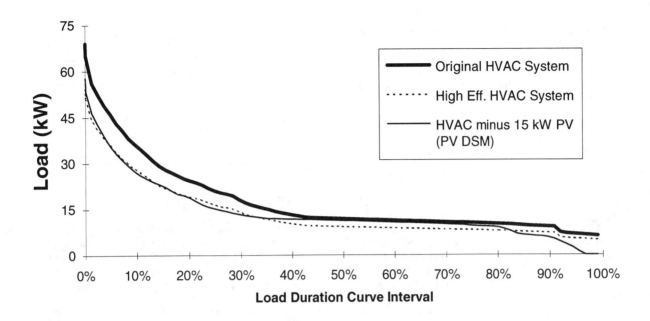

Figure 3. HVAC Load Duration Curves for PG&E's R&D Building (7/90 to 6/91).

original HVAC system coupled with the PV system (PV DSM) behaves like a high efficiency HVAC system. In particular, the top third of the load duration curves are essentially identical. (The top of the LDC curve is of critical importance to utility planners, since capital expenditure decisions are based on peak loads.) Thus, PV output correlates extremely well with specific building equipment loads. This finding is consistent with past studies, which indicate that PV output matches the load profile of many PG&E distribution feeders, and the PG&E system as a whole.[3,7]

An effective PV DSM program would initially use customer-sited PV systems to relieve peak loads in areas constrained by transmission and distribution capacity. Distribution circuits with a high saturation of commercial customers appear to be favorable targets for PV DSM, since commercial loads closely match PV output. Other reasons favoring commercial over residential applications for early market entry include tax advantages, easier control, fewer interconnects, and lower maintenance and administration costs. This paper, therefore, focuses on commercial applications of PV DSM. (The residential market, however, is potentially substantial, and changes in economic assumptions, cost-effectiveness tests, and tax treatments could make PV DSM attractive to residential customers in the future).[5]

## COST-EFFECTIVENESS TESTS

Utilities use several cost-effectiveness tests when performing a DSM program evaluation. These tests include: ratepayer impact measure (RIM), total resource cost (TRC), participant cost, utility cost, and societal cost tests.[8] RIM directly measures the impact on rates and thus is of greatest interest to ratepayers and capacity planners. TRC is often used by DSM planners at PG&E as the bottom line evaluation tool because it considers a program's overall impacts. The participant cost test directly measures the economic impact on the particular

customer participating in the DSM program; it is of greatest interest to that customer.

In the authors' view, the most appropriate tests for the evaluation of PV DSM are the RIM and participant cost tests, and a TRC test that includes participant tax impacts. The RIM test is necessary because it describes the impact of a program on ratepayers. The participant cost test is necessary because it describes the impact on a customer's financial resources and gives insight to the number of customers likely to participate.

DSM evaluations at PG&E have traditionally used a TRC test that treats participant tax impacts as transfer payments: taxes are excluded. Treating taxes as transfer payments is appropriate for traditional DSM because the impact of such action is usually small. However, such treatment of taxes for PV DSM may not be appropriate. Due to the high capital cost of PV systems, the utility will give rebates that cover only a small portion of the total system cost and the customer will likely finance most of the system. Thus, there are significant tax benefits available to the PV DSM participant that are not available to traditional DSM program participants. As shown in the following section, these tax related benefits account for about half of the total value to the participant. Excluding them from TRC calculations may give a distorted picture of the feasibility of PV DSM.

In order to satisfy the demands of traditional DSM evaluations while not unnecessarily penalizing PV DSM, TRC is presented in two ways. First, it is presented as traditionally calculated (referred to as "Traditional TRC"); that is, participant tax impacts are excluded. Second, it is presented as suggested above (referred to as "Suggested TRC"); that is, participant tax impacts are included.

## PV OWNERSHIP SCENARIOS

Various efforts have been made to economically integrate PV into the utility network. Three financial approaches are presented here to illustrate how the PV DSM partnership concept evolved:

1. **Utility ownership** of the PV system, installed on the supply-side of the meter;

2. **Customer ownership** of the PV system installed on the demand-side of the meter without incentives from the utility; and

3. **A utility-customer partnership**, where the utility provides customer incentives to purchase and install the PV system on the demand-side of the meter.

Financial results are presented in 1992 dollars per kW of PV.[*]

## Utility Ownership

First, consider the case of a strategically sited utility-owned PV system on the supply-side of the meter. The value of this type of "grid-support" system has previously been evaluated for a specific test case in PG&E's distribution network.[3] Figure 4 presents the results of this analysis by its two components: (1) "Bulk System Benefits", which account for the avoidance of energy and capacity costs from bulk generating stations; and (2) "Distributed Benefits", which account for the benefits to the local substation and distribution system, such as hardware life extension, electrical loss reduction, and voltage support. Cost exceeds value even when distributed benefits are included, rendering the installation uneconomic.

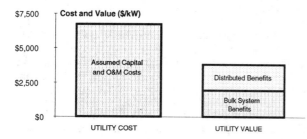

Figure 4. Utility Ownership: Cost exceeds value to the utility.

## Customer Ownership Without Utility Incentives

Figure 5 shows the cost/value results for the case of a customer-owned system, installed without the direct involvement of the utility. Such installations have been labeled demand-side management (DSM) systems because of their ability to meet the peak electrical load of, for example, commercial buildings.[4,9] This approach places costs, responsibility, and benefits of PV directly with the customer. The value to the customer is gained through savings on the utility bill, federal and state solar tax credits, and other tax benefits. Although the economics are better than the utility ownership scenario, this approach is also not cost-effective.

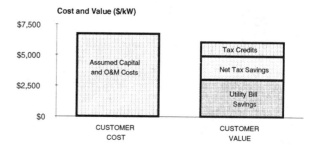

Figure 5. Customer ownership without utility incentives: cost exceeds value.

## Utility-Customer Partnership

Figure 6 depicts a utility-customer partnership where the utility encourages customers to install PV systems through the use of rebates. The result is that both the utility and the participating customer benefit, since value exceeds cost from both perspectives.

Table 1 shows the details of these results from several perspectives: RIM test, participant cost test, and total resource cost tests. As described earlier, the TRC test is presented in two ways: Traditional TRC and Suggested TRC. The results are presented in terms of net present value (NPV), where NPV equals value minus cost. A DSM measure is viable when the NPV is greater than or equal to zero, and when the benefit-cost ratio is greater than or equal to one.

Table 1. Cost-Effectiveness Tests ($/kW).

| Cost Category | Test Perspective | | | |
| | RIM | Partici-pant Cost | Tradi-tional TRC | Suggested TRC |
| --- | --- | --- | --- | --- |
| Avoided Marginal Costs | $3,800 | | $3,800 | $3,800 |
| Rebates to Participants | -$ 750 | $ 750 | | |
| Reduced Utility Bills | -$3,000 | $3,000 | | |
| Net Tax Impact[**] | | $1,896 | $ 0 | $1,896 |
| Tax Credits | | $1,161 | $ 0 | $1,161 |
| Installed Cost | | -$6,500 | -$6,500 | -$6,500 |
| Maintenance Cost | | -$ 240 | -$ 240 | -$ 240 |
| NPV | $ 50 | $ 67 | -$2,940 | $ 117 |
| Benefit/Cost Ratio | 1.01 | 1.01 | .56 | 1.02 |

Table 1 shows that the utility-customer partnership is financially viable from all three perspectives: rates decrease for ratepayers (RIM test); the participating customer earns the desired rate of return (participant cost test); and the combined result decreases costs from the Suggested TRC perspective.

---

[*] Table A-1, at the end of this paper, contains the customer and PV economic assumptions used in the evaluation.

---

[**] The Net Tax Impact on the participant has positive and negative components. Positive benefits include decreased taxes due to system depreciation ($1,733), loan interest deductions ($1,738), and O&M expense deduductions ($96). Costs include increased taxes from reduced utility bills which can be deducted as a business expense (-$1,204), rebate tax (-$269), and tax credit taxes (-$198). Adding these figures together yields a net tax benefit of $1,896.

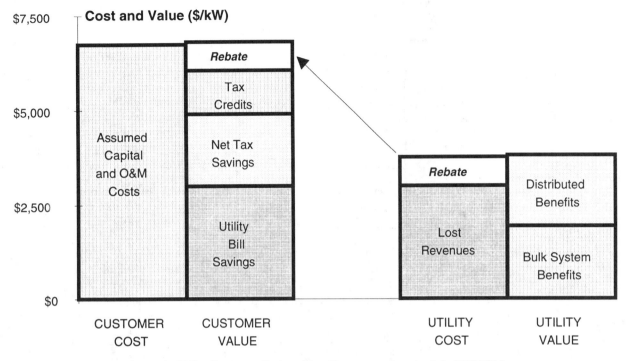

Figure 6. Utility-Customer Partnership: The economic potential of PV DSM.

## SENSITIVITY OF RESULTS

The results are highly dependent on the economic assumptions. The intent of this paper is to present the concept and not to provide a comprehensive analysis. There are literally hundreds of thousands of different scenarios which would change the results in either direction.

Figure 7 puts the magnitude of variation of the results into perspective. This figure illustrates the sensitivity to assumption changes by providing three scenarios. The middle line in the figure is the test case used in this paper. The upper line ("favorable tax benefits") assumes that the Federal government offers a 20 percent rather than a 10 percent tax credit, and that the utility rebate is not taxed. The lower line ("no tax benefits") is a worst case scenario in which there are no tax credits and

the customer is in a tax bracket that eliminates the value of all tax write-offs. Even with these few changes, the break-even capital cost (the cost at which the Suggested TRC benefit/cost ratio is 1) ranges from $3,600/kW to $9,600/kW. In other words, a few assumption changes have a large impact on the viability of a PV DSM partnership.

As shown in Figure 7, capital cost plays a major role in driving the economic viability of PV DSM. Unfortunately, due to the size of the grid-connected PV market, projecting the capital cost under a mature PV DSM program is difficult. In 1990, only 3 percent, or 500 kW, of the 15 MW of PV manufactured in the U.S. were used in grid-connected applications. The total number of U.S. grid connected PV systems installed to date is probably less than 300, the majority of which employ one-of-a-kind designs.

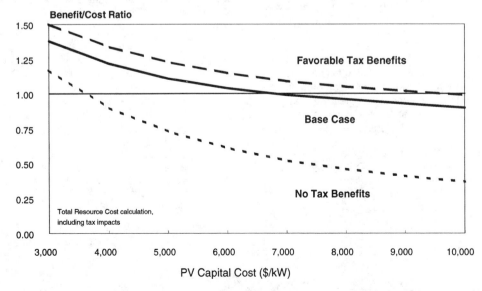

Figure 7. Impact of the customer's financial assumptions and costs on PV DSM viability.

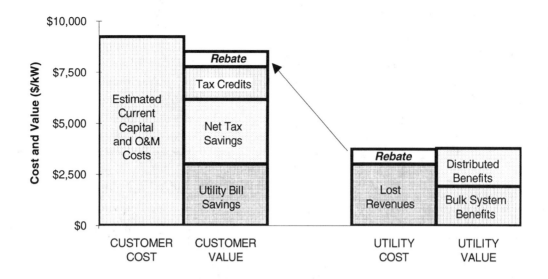

Figure 8. The economics of a PV DSM partnership at a capital cost of $9000/kW.

A one-of-a-kind customer-sited PV system presently costs around $9,000/kW. Figure 8 shows the cost/value relationship at this capital cost. Although the value to the customer increases with an increase in capital cost, PV is not cost-effective under these conditions.

This section demonstrates that PV DSM's viability is highly dependent on the customer's financial profile as well as PV system cost. It is therefore difficult to draw definitive conclusions regarding market size and the target capital cost which will open the doors to economic viability. In-depth sensitivity and market analyses will be completed in future research at PG&E in an attempt to better characterize the potential of a PV DSM program. Other drivers of PV DSM cost-effectiveness include customer rate schedule, loan debt/equity ratio, loan life, interest, discount, and tax rates, and rebate level.

### COMPARISON OF PV DSM TO OTHER DSM PROGRAMS

This section compares PV DSM to other conventional DSM measures using data from PG&E's only locally targeted DSM program.[10] The program, located in the Delta District, targets a high growth area near San Francisco.

DSM programs were evaluated in the Delta District using RIM and TRC tests. The TRC test used excluded tax impacts by treating them as transfer payments. Rather than presenting all of the programs, only those programs with the lowest and highest RIM and TRC benefit-cost ratios in each category (residential and commercial) are included.

Figure 9 shows that PV DSM is in the range of the Delta programs from a RIM perspective. A PV DSM program would have similar rate impacts as other conventional programs.

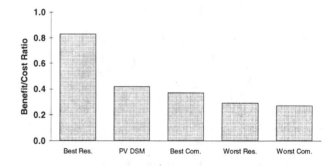

Figure 9. RIM benefit-cost ratios for DSM programs in the Delta District vs. PV DSM.

Figure 10 shows TRC benefit-cost ratios. The PV DSM TRC is presented in two ways: including tax impacts (Suggested TRC) and excluding tax impacts (Traditional TRC). Treating taxes as transfer payments (Traditional TRC) significantly reduces PV DSM's viability. PV DSM may be competitive with other DSM programs on a TRC basis, however, when tax impacts are included.

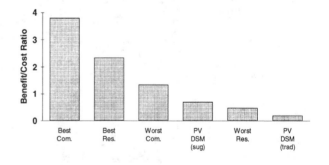

Figure 10. TRC benefit-cost ratios for DSM programs in the Delta District vs. PV DSM.*

---

* PV DSM is evaluted at a capital cost of $9,000/kW.

598

## SUMMARY

PG&E is actively pursuing demand-side management programs.[11] Most of these DSM programs are designed to reduce customer loads through the use of devices that are of higher efficiency than those currently owned by customers (e.g., high efficiency HVAC, appliances, and lighting). The utility is able to encourage the use of such devices through rebates and other incentive programs. If the DSM programs reduce peak capacity and annual energy demands, the utility defers capital expenditures for new generation and for transmission, substation, and distribution system upgrades.

This suggests another option for the utility planner. PV DSM has the potential to offer the same, if not more, benefits to the utility as other DSM programs. With rebates or other utility incentives, the customer may be allowed to make a financially prudent decision by installing a PV system on his side of the meter. Both the utility and the customer may benefit economically when PV is deployed as a utility-sponsored DSM program. This partnership pushes grid-connected PV closer to cost-effectiveness.

Due to current capital costs and regulatory treatment of taxes, however, PV will probably not play a major role in PG&E's comprehensive plan to reduce system load in the next several years. Nevertheless, a near-term market goal of even a few megawatts of PV DSM per year would be a major breakthrough for the PV industry, and would serve as a catalyst for speeding cost reductions.

## ACKNOWLEDGMENTS

A number of individuals deserve special recognition for their valuable contributions and willingness and ability to stretch beyond convention: Gerry Braun, Jim Eyer, Bill Fairchild, Bill Follette, Grayson Heffner, Steve Hester, Joe Iannucci, Christina Jennings, Dennis Keane, Ken Lau, Dick Maclay, Ren Orans, Dan Shugar, Bruce Smith, Amy Tessler, Carl Weinberg, and Chuck Whitaker. Thank you for your support!

## REFERENCES

1. PG&E PV Conference Papers 1984-1990 and 1991 PG&E PV Conference Papers, Pacific Gas and Electric Company, Report 007.3-91.2 and 007.5-92.3, March 1991 and March 1992.

2. Jennings, C., *Cost-Effective Photovoltaics at PG&E*, Pacific Gas and Electric Company, Report 007.3-89.4, June 1989.

3. Shugar, D., Orans, R., Suchard, A., El-Gassier, M. and A. Jones, *Benefits of Distributed Generation in PG&E's T&D System: A Case Study of Photovoltaics Serving Kerman Substation, Pacific Gas and Electric Company*, Report Forthcoming.

4. Perez, R. and R. Stewart, *An Opportunity for Photovoltaic Development in the Northeast: Non-Remote, Non-Grid-Interactive Systems*, Atmospheric Sciences Research Center, SUNY at Albany, Publication no. 1322, June 1988.

5. Hoff, T. and H. Wenger, *Photovoltaics as a Demand-Side Management Option, Phase I: Concept Development*, Pacific Gas and Electric Company, Report 007.5-92.4, June 1992.

6. Wenger, H, *PVGRID: A Micro-Computer Based Software Package for Central Station Photovoltaic System Analysis*, University of Colorado, Department of Engineering, Boulder, CO, June 1987.

7. Hoff, T. and J. Iannucci, *Maximizing the Benefits Derived from PV Plants: Selecting the Best Plant Type and Location*, Pacific Gas and Electric Company, Report 007.3-89.8, November 1989.

8. California Public Utilities Commission and California Energy Commission, *Standard Practice Manual: Economic Analysis of Demand-Side Management Programs*, December 1987.

9. Bailey, B., Doty, J., Perez, R. and R. Stewart, *Performance of a Photovoltaic Demand-Side Management System*, Proc. of 1991 ISES Solar World Congress, Denver, CO, August 1991.

10. Wiersma, B. and R. Orans, *The Delta Project: Reducing T&D Costs with CEE*, Pacific Gas and Electric Company, June 1991.

11. *Annual Summary Report on Demand Side Management Programs in 1990 and 1991*, Pacific Gas and Electric Company, March 1991.

# APPENDIX

Table A-1. Commercial Customer Economic and PV System Assumptions.

| | Customer |
|---|---|
| Incremental federal tax rate | 34.0% |
| Incremental state tax rate | 9.3% |
| Equipment depreciation[1] | 5 years |
| Federal tax credit[2] | 10.0% |
| State tax credit[3] | 10.0% |
| Customer's invested equity[4] | 20.0% |
| Loan interest rate | 12.0% |
| Loan term (years) | 25 years |
| Energy escalation rate | 5.5% |
| General inflation rate | 5.0% |
| Customer's discount rate | 12.0% |
| Property Taxes[5] | none |
| First year energy rate[6] | $0.082/kWh |
| First year demand charge rate[7] | $79/kW |
| Rebate from utility | $750/kW |

| | PV System |
|---|---|
| Installed capital cost | $6,500/kW |
| First year maintenance cost | $0.01/kWh |
| Annual capacity factor | 24% |
| System life | 25 years |

[1] Federal and state depreciation schedules use five-year, 200 percent declining balance.

[2] Federal tax credit expires 6/30/92 but is currently under review for extension.

[3] California state tax credit, available for non-residential customers, expires on 12/31/93.

[4] In its July 1990 Energy Technology Status Report, the California Energy Commission used a 70/30 debt/equity ratio for qualifying facilities (QFs).

[5] Solar equipment is exempt from property taxes in California through 12/31/93.

[6] PG&E's Schedule E-19S average rate, weighted by PV output, effective 8/1/91.

[7] Demand charge savings is a weighted value based on an 80 percent PV capacity factor during summer peak loads ($73) and 25 percent capacity factor during winter peak loads ($6).

*The views, opinions, and evalutions presented herein do not necessarily reflect those of the Pacific Gas and Electric Company. The authors alone are responsible for the contents of this paper.*

*This paper is taken in part from a PG&E report "Photovoltaics as a Demand-Side Management Option, Phase I: Concept Development." If you would like to order the report, please contact Gretchen Bedard, Pacific Gas & Electric Company, Department of Research and Development, San Ramon, California, 94583 (telephone: 510-866-5577).*

Chapter 105

# Environmental Externalities and Alternative Energy Choices

L.J. Williams

## INTRODUCTION

This paper will introduce and explain the economic concept of an "externality" and how it applies to environmental issues. The theory was developed by economists more than a half century ago. Much of the current interest in the idea is aimed at its application to environmental issues in the regulated electric and gas utility industries. A good deal of this current interest began with the publication of the Pace University report on the <u>Environmental Costs of Electricity</u> [1]. The report is widely cited but, unfortunately, seriously flawed. Two important examples of this will be shown later in this paper.

The widespread interest in the application of the environmental externality concept apparently arose out of the desire of regulators and others to "level the playing field" for Demand Side Management (DSM) activities and renewables. The rapid growth of DSM over the past 10 to 15 years has occurred without any boost from externalities. By including the complete private and social costs of traditional electric generating technologies, it is thought that DSM and renewables will get an additional boost. Although current activity aims at the application of the environmental externality concept to the regulated utilities sector, it clearly has potential for much wider application. This issue will also be examined. The current status of various regulatory actions at the state level will be reviewed.

When making alternative energy choices the ideal goal is to achieve the best mix of technologies through the inclusion of environmental externalities in a least cost integrated framework. An Integrated Resource Planning (IRP) framework must be used to compare the costs and benefits of traditional generation technologies with, DSM, and renewables. In this setting all alternatives compete on an equal basis to arrive at the best combination of technologies. In practice, an important part of the externalities calculation has not yet been developed. This missing part is the demonstration of a practical method to quantify environmental impacts and to value the damages of resulting environmental burdens resulting from alternative energy choices on a site specific basis.

Along with the capital, fuel, and O&M, the costs of generation technology must include the costs of abating pollution. The benefits to society are a cleaner environment. A socially efficient amount of pollution control is obtained by equating the costs of abatement with the benefits of reduced pollution. Uncertainty is an intrinsic part of the benefit side of the problem. The abatement cost for various technologies is easier to quantify. To the extent that pollution damage costs are not included in the resource decision, the damages are considered "environmental externalities". Both abatement costs and the damage costs must be considered. Unfortunately, early efforts to include environmental externalities in the resource choice tried to avoid the hard issue of quantifying benefits of reduced environmental damages and simply used the highest control costs as a proxy for benefits. This is completely wrong and can lead to inefficient and socially harmful decisions.

Fortunately, the control cost idea has been rejected by most policy makers and prominent researchers in the field. Furthermore this method is not being considered in either of two important research efforts on environmental externalities that are currently underway. This paper will conclude with a discussion of these research efforts.

## OVERVIEW OF THE EXTERNALITY ISSUE

The theory and practice of externalities was introduced by the British economist A.C. Pigou in the 1930's [2]. Ronald Coase won the Nobel Prize in economics in part for his paper on "The Problem of Social Cost" [3]. The theory and practice of externalities has played a large role in a variety of areas that do not include environmental effects. These include law and economics, transportation economics, urban economics, research and development, and economic development. The application of this concept to

---

* This paper represents the views of the author and not of EPRI or the electric utility industry.

environmental issues is an important one. See Baumol and Oates [4] for a comprehensive discussion.

## What is an Externality?

The U.S. market economy is increasingly viewed by the world as a model for efficiently producing and allocating goods and services. A key assumption of a market economy is that the prices of goods and services generally reflects both the costs to produce them and the value that consumers place on obtaining them. This equating of costs (to producers) and benefits (value to consumers) happens at "the margin". For example, computer manufacturers will increase the number of computers they produce as long as their incremental cost of producing (including capital, labor and materials) the next computer is less than the price (value to the next buyer) for which it can be sold.

The implicit assumption is that all the costs of producing the computers are reflected in the price paid by the consumers who buy them. Externalities arise when some of the costs are not taken into account by the producer of the goods or services. For example, suppose that potentially harmful solvents used in the manufacture of the integrated circuits are simply sent down the drain, rather than disposed of properly (at greater expense). The burden of the solvents will place greater expense on taxpayers when sewage treatment plants must use more expensive methods to treat these harmful substances. If not handled properly at the treatment plant, the general public will face increased health risks. These social costs become external to the market for computers. Computer owners benefit and others in society pay the price for the "externality".

Clean air, clean water, and a clean environment are scarce resources that society values. Emissions of industrial wastes use up or damage some of these valued resources. Environmental externalities arise when the value of these damages are not internalized into the cost structure of the industry responsible for producing the damages. The cost of these damages are borne by society and not by the customers who pay less than the total cost of producing the goods.

## Internalizing the Costs of Emissions

Ideal World: If we had free and perfect information about all the relevant costs and benefits related to emissions, there are a series of simple principles that could be used to internalize the costs of emissions. These principles follow from the economics of externalities. They are:

- Any specific emissions target should be achieved at the lowest cost.

- Optimal emissions are achieved by balancing benefits and costs.

- Final goods prices should reflect the emissions control cost as well as the residual emissions damage cost.

- Emissions taxes or marketable permits can internalize costs.

The first principle is illustrated by the simple two source emission example shown in Figure 1. Source 1 has a relatively fast rising marginal cost of pollution abatement. Source 2's control costs rise more slowly. To achieve the lowest control cost, at a specific level of emissions reduction, the high control cost source would reduce its emissions less than the low control cost emitter. The lowest cost of emitting a specific amount of pollution is always found by equating the marginal costs of control across the relevant pollution emitters. This efficient method is in sharp contrast to the existing command and control regulations that specify standards, either on a technology or a performance basis. The Clean Air Act specifies New Source Performance Standards (NSPS) which are technology standards. In areas meeting the National Ambient Air Quality Standards (NAAQS), they require the use of Best Available Control Technology (BACT) for $SO_2$ and other criteria pollutants. Performance based standards leave the choice of control strategy to the emitter. In both cases the four simple principles outlined above are violated. The result has been to raise the cost of a specified level of environmental protection to much higher levels than is necessary.

The recent Clean Air Act Amendments move toward market based regulation by creating Emission Allowances for $SO_2$. Each $SO_2$ emitter must have sufficient emission allowances (EA's) to cover all the $SO_2$ emitted during the year. The Act permits trading these EA's on a nationwide basis. This results in incentives for the low cost $SO_2$ controller to reduce emissions by a larger amount than the high cost controller. In this way there should be movement toward equalizing the marginal costs of control across different sources of $SO_2$.

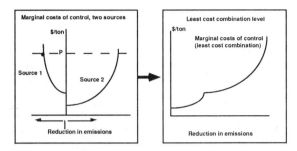

FIGURE 1. ANY SPECIFIC EMISSIONS TARGET SHOULD BE ACHIEVED AT MINIMUM COST.

Balancing benefits and costs to achieve optimal emissions levels is shown in Figure 2. The benefit in this case is the reduction in environmental damages from a specific pollutant. The efficient level of pollution is shown where the marginal cost of control curve crosses the marginal cost of damage curve. Notice that the optimal level of pollution is not zero. Social welfare is decreased when the costs of control exceed the benefits.

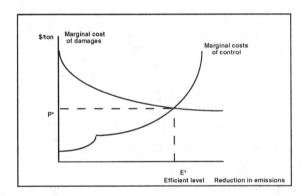

FIGURE 2. OPTIMAL EMISSIONS ARE ACHIEVED BY BALANCING BENEFITS AND COSTS.

The discussion so far has focused on the pollution market. That is, the release of emissions, their transport and conversion, and the environmental damages caused by these pollution products. Internalizing the costs of pollution by balancing benefits and costs to arrive at the best control levels and having these costs internalized in the decision making of polluting industries does not finish the job of internalizing the social costs of pollution.

The final step requires an examination of the market for the goods produced by the polluting industry. The principles apply to any industry, but for this final step let us consider the electric utility industry. Figure 3 shows an idealized version of the market for electricity. The customer demand for electricity is downward sloping, reflecting

the increasing demand for electricity as prices decline. The lowest supply cost of electricity characterizes the case that would prevail if there were no pollution controls and the costs of abatement did not enter into electric utility decision making. This cost is called the marginal private cost of electricity. Based on the discussion above this marginal private cost would be increased once the costs of controlling emissions at an optimal level are internalized. Finally the costs of residual emissions damages must be added to arrive at the fully internalized marginal social cost of electricity. By internalizing the residual damages the markets for final goods will shift slightly away from the products that have these residual damages and toward those which do not.

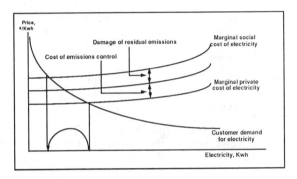

FIGURE 3. TO MAXIMIZE ECONOMIC EFFICIENCY, FINAL GOODS PRICES SHOULD REFLECT THE EMISSIONS CONTROL COST AND THE RESIDUAL EMISSIONS DAMAGE COST.

Non-Ideal World: Implementing the above principles in the real world faces a number of serious problems. Among them are the following:

- The prices of all goods should reflect control and damage costs, not just goods reulated by Public Utility Commissions.

- Estimates of damage costs are expensive to obtain and have large uncertainties. Therefore it is hard to balance benefits and costs.

- Current emissions target levels are not achieved at lowest cost due to the extensive use of command and control environmental regulations.

Piecemeal Regulation Problem

The fact that only some PUC regulated utilities are now using or considering environmental externality "adders" leads to several potentially serious problems. Additionally, not all power producers in a state are subject to PUC regulation. This leads to the "bypass" problem. If residual emissions from only some PUC regulated utilities or power producers are internalized, there are adverse price consequences for their customers that are not experienced by the customers of other power producers and other industrial and commercial emitters. As a result these non-regulated sectors will tend to grow faster with adverse environmental consequences. For example there will tend to be more self-generation, direct service by independent power producers to retail and commercial customers, and the conversion of areas to the municipal utility operating structure. These producers of electricity are generally not subject to PUC externality regulation.

Other piecemeal problems would arise if some states adopt regulations that increase customer costs and other nearby states do not. Utilities may attempt to purchase power from across the borders in an attempt to meet customer demands for lower cost power, or economic activity may tend to migrate toward the states with lower cost power. These difficulties can lead to higher costs and higher emissions.

Partial quantification could also produce unintended environmental degradation. For example, if externalities adders were only aimed at air emissions, utilities would have incentives to improve air quality, perhaps by increasing water pollution. Also, if adders were used to affect the choice of new generation, the result could bias decisions toward older generation capacity not covered by the adders. The overall result could be environmental degradation at higher cost.

Another problem arises from the failure to account for the consequences of using externality adders in the context of existing and future national environmental policies. For example, under the recent Clean Air Act Amendments, every $SO_2$ emitter must have emission allowances (EA's) to cover its emissions. These allowances are to be traded in a national market. If a state in New England uses adders to deter $SO_2$ emissions, there will be no effect on national $SO_2$ total discharge. This will be capped at 8.9 million tons per year beginning in 2000. The New England adders will not reduce national emissions of $SO_2$. However, New England could reduce the demand for $SO_2$ emission allowances. This could have the perverse effect of making it cheaper for utilities in Ohio to emit $SO_2$, thereby increasing acidic deposition in New England.

A final point: using the externality concept only on PUC regulated utilities is a "second best" policy. It violates the first principle, above, of achieving specific emission targets at the lowest possible cost. For example, it

is almost certain that mobile emitters in the transportation sector are not being controlled at the same marginal costs as are stationary sources. Additional environmental benefits would come at lower cost if all stationary sources of pollution in non-PUC regulated industries were subject to the externality concept that is applied to some PUC regulated utilities. Further benefits would come if the mobile emitters also were subject to the externality concept that is applied to some PUC regulated utilities.

For further discussion of these and related issues see Schmalensee[5], Lave[6], Joskow[7], Butraw and Krupnick[8], and Freeman et. al.[9].

## UNCERTAINTY IN ESTIMATING BENEFITS

The appropriate use of the environmental externalities concept becomes problematic due to the practical problems associated with estimating the marginal cost of reducing damages (marginal benefits). To avoid adverse consequences of the type discussed above, the proper approach must look at the complete fuel cycle and account for all of the externalities, both environmental and non-environmental. This evaluation must be done for each specific site at which externalities can play a role in the outcome. The value of damages from a pound of lead may vary enormously depending on whether it is dispersed in drinking water, in peeling paint in aging homes, or dispersed over some unpopulated area. The actual damage valuations cannot be simply estimated in California and transferred to Massachusetts or Wisconsin.

Attempting to implement a damage function approach at a specific site is an appropriate but difficult task. For any specific externality (and there may be hundreds of effects associated with a single fuel cycle), there will be uncertainty associated with the amount of source emission at a given time, uncertainty about the transport and conversion effects, uncertainty about the dose-response functions of the many receptors, and the valuations of the physical impacts that finally result. Morgan et. al. stressed the importance of the proper treatment of uncertainties in their paper "Technical Uncertainty in Quantitative Policy analysis: A Sulfur Air Pollution Example" [10]. They

"conclude[d that] one can set a fairly high upper bound on the health impacts (from sulfate particulates from a 1000 Mwe coal fired power plant) of a few thousand excess deaths per year. Between this bound and the lower bound of no effects there is no agreement across the set of air pollution health effects experts about the likely health impacts of sulfate. Within this group you can get almost any answer, including the answer that with 100 percent probability there are no adverse health impacts, depending on which expert one talks to."

## Wide Range in Damage Estimates

Given the uncertainties and the non-transferability of results it is not surprising that a very large range of damage estimates are cited in various places. Table 1 shows just a few of these numbers.

| | Cost in $/ton | | | |
|---|---|---|---|---|
| | Pace | NYPSC | Mass./Tellus | Mass./La ve |
| $CO_2$ | 14 | 1 | 22 | 2-10 |
| $NO_x$ | 1,640 | 1,832 | 6,500 | 70-450 |
| $SO_2$ | 4,060 | 832 | 1,500 | 60-990 |
| TSP | 2,380 | 333 | 4,000 | 100-1,500 |

* First number is best estimate.
Second is high estimate.

TABLE 1. ALTERNATIVE DAMAGE ESTIMATES

Notice that the $NO_x$ damage estimates vary by a factor of 100. A further demonstration of the problems inherent in these numbers can be seen by a closer look at the Pace Report adders for central station coal and nuclear power.

## Coal Case From Pace Report

Table 1 on page 351 of the Pace Report [1] shows a total externality adder of 6.8 cents per delivered kWh of electricity from an existing coal fired central station power plant. It is instructive to examine the basis on which Pace calculated this number. With some arithmetic one can calculate that 65 percent of this adder derives from $SO_2$ and 25 percent from $CO_2$. The remaining 10 percent derives from $NO_x$ and particulates. Table 1 above shows that $CO_2$ damage estimates range from $1 to $22 per ton. This is problematic since the damages from $CO_2$ are highly uncertain and the ranges may not represent bounds to the problem. A further problem is that climate change is a global externality and the actions taken on a local level may have no effect. The policies to deal with it must be global. If regulated utilities turned off all their boilers, 97 percent of global anthropogenic greenhouse gas emission would continue.

Next, examine the $SO_2$ adder. To arrive at the $4,060/ton of $SO_2$ damages, Pace estimates that 87 percent of the damage is due to human health effects and 13 percent due to visibility and corrosion damage. The health effects number relies on a single paper published in 1979. Although the

paper was in the peer reviewed scientific literature, the Pace study ignores all the research that has occured since then. A vast existing research base needs to be reviewed. Two ongoing research projects on this issue will be reviewed later in this paper.

## Nuclear Case from Pace Report

The Pace Report estimates an externality adder for nuclear power plants of 2.91 cents/kWh. With some arithmetic one can show that Pace obtains 79 percent of this adder from the possibility of a catastrophic nuclear accident. They further estimate that 17 percent follows from decommissioning a plant and 4 percent from the routine operation of a plant. These numbers are seriously limited. The Pace numbers are based on the Chernobyl accident using flawed methods. The estimates for decommissioning a plant are also limited. No plant has been decommissioned. Estimates from other sources remain speculative.

Professor Marvin Goldman (Professor Emeritus in the Department of Radiological Sciences at UC Davis) was commissioned by the Department of Energy to examine the Pace analysis of nuclear externalities. He provided the following main criticisms:

1. Pace used gray publications rather than the extensive peer-reviewed scientific literature.
2. Confused meltdown with massive radioactive release.
3. Used outdated estimates of Chernobyl-related doses and possible consequences.
4. Failed to address current fatal radiation cancer risk coefficients with regard to effects of dose rate in reducing risk.
5. Calculated cost bases on questionable assumptions regarding the accidents impact on health.

A peer-reviewed article from Science [11] offers a different view of Chernobyl:

"Outside the 30-km zone surrounding Chernobyl, the incremental increase in fatal cancer risk is a fraction of a percent and is not likely to ever be detected epidemiologically...in Europe..., an increment of 0.01%...these risk estimates do not rule out zero as a possibility."

## CURRENT REGULATORY STATUS

Regulatory interest in the externality issue is widespread. See Figure 4 for a broad overview of how the issue looks on a state by state basis. By the second quarter of 1992 34 states have either included externalities in their decision making, are considering to do so, or have considered them but have stopped short of requiring their use. The main target is utility resource planning decisions; alternative energy choices. The situation changes fast and by the time this paper is presented and published, Figure 4 will most likely be out of date. EPRI member utilities can stay up to date on this issue through the <u>Environmental Externalities Information Clearinghouse on EPRINET</u>. This is an interactive electronic information service that includes:

- State-by-State Regulatory Treatment of Externalities

- Bibliography of Externalities Literature

- Summary of Key Externalities Literature

- News Shorts

- Calendar of Related Activities

- Background and Analysis

- Interactive Bulletin Board on Selected Topics and Issues

The externality adder approach has been the most common way of "internalizing" the environmental impacts of residual emissions in the resource selection decision. However, other methods are also in use. These include rate of return and avoided cost incentives. Some states have used non-monetized methods: environmental impacts used as a "tie breaker", and various non monetary weighting and points systems.

Although the externality numbers that have been used are very uncertain, they are large and can make a significant impact on resource selection. See Figure 5 for a hypothetical comparison of three generation technologies and the changes that occur after including externality adders for $CO_2$, $NO_x$, and $SO_2$.

The status of regulatory information in California and Wisconsin will be described next. Although California is not necessarily representative, it's size and impact on other states make it an important case to understand. Wisconsin activity provides an interesting contrast. This information was taken from EPRI's Environmental Externalities Clearinghouse in June of 1992 and may have changed since then.

<u>Regulatory Status in California</u>

This summary is based on secondary sources by EPRI's contractor for the Clearinghouse, Barakat & Chamberlin, Inc. There are requirements in California for utilities to consider the environmental externalities associated with electricity production in resource planning, bidding decisions, and in rates paid for long-term QF

contracts. Environmental externalities are not incorporated into utility operating decisions, or utility ratemaking decisions.

The California Energy Commission (CEC) and the California Public Utilities Commission (CPUC) both play a role in the regulatory treatment of environmental externalities. The CEC addresses externalities in its biennial "Electricity Reports" (ER). Through ER 90, the CEC recommended monetized externalities values for air emissions to be used in resource planning. Based in part on the CEC's recommendations, the CPUC requires the consideration of environmental externalities in resource planning and in bidding.

Externalities were also addressed in the 1989 California collaborative process. While the collaborative resulted in utility incentives for conservation, aggressive DSM goals, proposals for a pilot DSM bidding program, and many other steps designed to promote energy efficiency in California, the group was unable to reach a consensus on environmental externalities. Adders of 10% to 25% were proposed, but some participants felt that the stringent environmental controls already imposed on utilities in California sufficiently internalized environmental externalities.

<u>CEC Valuation of Environmental Externalities:</u> The CEC has estimated values for emissions offsets and residual emissions for use in energy planning. Emissions offsets for non attainment pollutants are required under the California Clean Air Act. Offsets are required at a 1.1:1 ratio in the San Francisco area, and a 1.2:1 ratio in the Los Angeles and San Diego basins. Offsets can be obtained from both utility and non utility sources. However, the CEC uses marginal control costs for retrofitting utility boilers to estimate the market value of $NO_x$ reductions. Costs vary by air districts based on the level of $NO_x$ emissions reductions required and range from $13/kW to $45/kW (1987$). The CEC has developed residual emission values for use in resource planning. The CEC anticipates that values assigned to residual emissions levels will make low-emitting, natural gas resources cost-effective a year or two sooner than they would otherwise be. However, the CEC indicates that residual emissions values will not shift energy production toward renewables because of their higher capital costs - residual emissions values would have to be increased by 4-10 times current values to cause such a shift.

To estimate values for residual air emissions in-state, the CEC uses marginal costs of control measures imposed by air quality regulators. Residual emission values vary by APCD. Out-of-state residual emissions

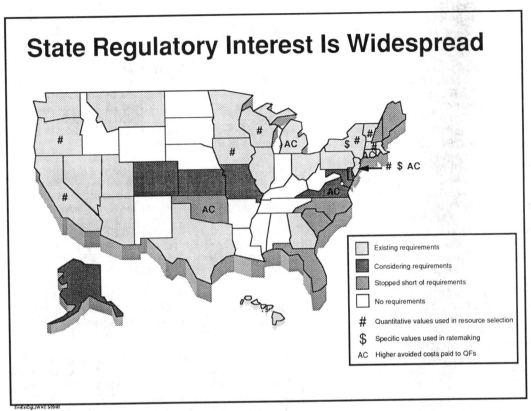

# State Regulatory Interest Is Widespread

Existing requirements

Considering requirements

Stopped short of requirements

No requirements

\#    Quantitative values used in resource selection

\$    Specific values used in ratemaking

AC    Higher avoided costs paid to QFs

FIGURE 4. STATE REGULATORY STATUS

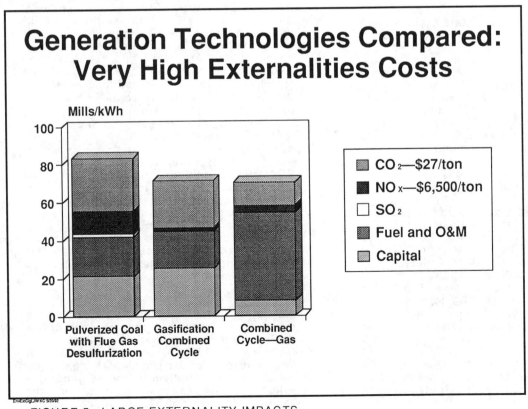

# Generation Technologies Compared: Very High Externalities Costs

Mills/kWh

$CO_2$—\$27/ton

$NO_x$—\$6,500/ton

$SO_2$

Fuel and O&M

Capital

Pulverized Coal with Flue Gas Desulfurization

Gasification Combined Cycle

Combined Cycle—Gas

FIGURE 5. LARGE EXTERNALITY IMPACTS

values are based on existing air quality in national parks. The Commission's value for carbon is simply a "placeholder" until the CEC's "Global Climate Change" study is completed.

In-state residual emissions values for the SCAQMD reflect best available control technology (BACT). BACT is required because of the non attainment status of the basin. Both the in-state and out-of-state residual emission values for the SCAQMD are shown in Table 2. The CEC has applied these values in societal cost-effectiveness analyses for Southern California Edison. These values should not be extended to other parts of the state because the costs are specific to the control measures mandated by the South Coast Air Quality Management District. Other air quality management districts have not fully analyzed the costs of measures required for attainment of standards in their areas.

TABLE 2. AIR POLLUTION EXTERNALITY VALUES FOR THE SCAQMD FROM THE 1990 "ELECTRICITY REPORT" (1987$/TON)

| Pollutant | SCAQMD | Out-of-State |
|-----------|--------|--------------|
| NO$_x$ | $11,600 | $2,700 |
| SO$_2$ | $11,500 | $1,000 |
| ROG | $ 3,300 | $3,000 |
| PM10 | $ 7,800 | $ 800 |
| CO$_2$ | $ 7.1 | $ 7.1 |

Preparation of ER 92 has started and values for residual emissions are being updated. The CEC proposes to again use control costs as proxies for emissions values. Control measures costing more than $100,000/ton are excluded because the CEC does not expect that these measures would be adopted in the foreseeable future. These values would change as air quality districts revise their implementation plans and emissions control requirements. In future planning cycles, the CEC is interested in using environmental damage estimates in place of control costs.

CPUC Requirements Regarding Externalities (QF Bidding): The CPUC requires consideration of environmental externalities in QF bidding. In its latest "Biennial Resource Plan Update" (BRPU), dated June 1991, the CPUC ordered utilities to include "non price" adders in QF bidding. The CPUC identified nonprice adders for: regional environmental impacts; employment and economic development impacts; impacts on the use of renewable resources; enhanced energy efficiency and conservation of natural resources; system reliability and dispatchability; resource, fuel or technology diversity; and reduced vulnerability to future rate increases.

In the bidding process, QFs compete against a utility's identified deferrable resource (IDR). The only bidding criteria is price, although threshold conditions screen QF applicants for other factors, such as front-loading. Utility resources can be selected if they pass cost-effectiveness screening and are "needed" (as determined by the CEC), and if the capacity is not bid by QFs. The non price adders are added to the prices of competing resources. This affects both resource selection and the size of the payment to winning QFs.

The CPUC has ordered utilities to use the difference in residual emissions between QFs and the utility's IDR to determine the appropriate adder (or subtractor) payments for long-run QF contracts. The CPUC has directed Southern California Edison (SCE) to use the SCAQMD residual emission values (the values recommended in ER 90) for calculating adders. Pending final action by the San Diego APCD, the CPUC has directed San Diego Gas and Electric (SDG&E) to also use the SCAQMD values since control measures for the San Diego area will be at least as strict as those in the SCAQMD.

Pacific Gas & Electric (PG&E), which is in the Bay Area Air Quality Management District (BAAQMD), is treated differently because air quality problems are less severe in northern California and thus the SCAQMD values are too high to be applicable. Until the BAAQMD produces a compliance plan from which control costs can be extracted, the CPUC directs PG&E to use the SCAQMD values, multiplied by a factor of 29% (29% is the ratio of ER 90's estimates of NOx control costs in northern California [$13/kW] and NO$_x$ control costs in southern California [$45/kW]). CO$_2$ is an exception - PG&E is directed to use the unadjusted value of $7 per ton. PG&E is also directed to convert the $/kW NO$_x$ control costs into $/ton figures for the next BRPU.

For emissions other than those valued by SCAQMD, utilities are to use the externalities values from the 1990 study conducted by the Pace University Center for Environmental Legal Studies, "Environmental Costs of Electricity." However, the CPUC said that future versions of the ER and BRPU should derive their own values for land and water impacts from new electric resources.

Resource Planning: In its June 1991 BRPU, the CPUC also directed utilities to file resource plans that incorporate environmental externalities. The CPUC requires the filing of two cost scenarios - one where the environmental costs are calculated as if all electricity were generated within the utility's service area, and the second where the externalities values adopted by the Nevada Public Service

Commissions are to be used as a proxy for the environmental costs of electricity generated in air quality attainment areas outside of the utilities service area.

Regulatory Status in Wisconsin

The Wisconsin Public Service Commission (PSC) previously required the consideration of environmental externalities in resource planning through two means (Docket 05-E-5, April 6, 1989). First, utilities were required to assign a 15% credit to the cost of non combustion technologies to account for air emissions externalities in new resource decisions. Second, utilities were required to make a qualitative consideration of other externalities. The order did not specify the type of externalities to which the utilities were required to give qualitative consideration. Nor did it require the utilities to use specific methods or criteria.

However, several utilities challenged the 15% credit in court and won their case. The court indicated that the authority of the PSC to impose more stringent environmental requirements than those of the state legislature and the Department of Natural Resources is constrained. The PSC cannot deny a certificate of public necessity and convenience for a new generating facility on the basis of air pollution if the plan meets all state and federal environmental standards. The Court said that the potential elimination of proposed generating options in the planning process through use of the 15% adder would in effect constitute the same prohibited denial.

The Wisconsin utilities and the PSC are currently working together to develop a way to consider residual environmental effects in integrated resource planning. Participants are leaning toward a monetization approach. The utilities favor a damage-based willingness-to-pay approach. PSC staff witnesses favor a cost-of-control method. The Commission is expected to rule on this issue July 1992. The author has heard that more than 16,000 pages of information were compiled for this effort. This is an example of how the "free and perfect information" assumption of the "Ideal World" breaks down for the actual world we live in.

The Commission has discussed (but has not formally considered) requiring utilities to incorporate environmental externalities into dispatch and power purchase decisions. This summary is based on phone conversation with PSC staff in April 1992.

RESEARCH CURRENTLY UNDERWAY

Two major research efforts that will make a large impact on the environmental externalities issue are presently underway. No preliminary results are available, so a brief summary of the goals, timetables, and sponsors will be provided here.

New York State Environmental Externalities Cost Study

The objective of this study is to develop a methodology that would permit New York State regulatory agencies and utilities to estimate the environmental externalities for electric supply and Demand Side Management options. This methodology may be used in other states undertaking the same task. The research will help utilities and regulators:

• To understand the limitations and complexities of existing approaches to estimating environmental externalities for electric resource options.

• To develop improved methodologies for estimating environmental externalities.

• To apply the methodologies to estimate environmental externalities from future generation or DSM options in New York and other states.

It is being conducted under an order issued by the New York State Public Service Commission. The major contractor for the project is RCG/Hagler, Bailly, Inc (RCG).

A five member Management Board is directing the program. The Board is composed of representatives from the New York Department of Public Service, the New York State Energy Research and Development Authority, the Empire State Electric Energy Research Corporation, EPRI, and Resources for the Future, an independent expert selected by the other four members. The coordinating contractor, Industrial Economics, Inc. is overseeing the work as a consultant to the Management Board under contract to the Energy Authority. Dr. A. Myrick Freeman III, Professor of Economics at Bowdoin College, serves as the Project Coordinator for Industrial Economics.

EPRI's participation is currently limited to aspects of the program which clarify the limitations and complexities of existing approaches to estimating environmental externalities for electric resource options.

The 30-month study began in December 1991. The study will produce information workshops, task reports, a final report, and a personal computer software model for estimating environmental externalities

External Costs of Fuels Cycles Study

This research effort is jointly sponsored by the U.S. Department of Energy and the Commission of the European Communities.

609

The U.S. research team includes workers at the Oak Ridge National Laboratories and Resources for the Future. They will study the following fuel cycles:

- Biomass
- Oil
- Natural Gas
- Hydro

The European team will examine:

- Nuclear
- Wind
- Photovoltaic

Both teams will work on:

- Coal
- Conservation

The initial phase of the study formally began in February 1991 and concludes in early 1993. Unlike the Pace University Report, this research will assume there are no generic damage values. Human population densities and characteristics, topography, flora, fauna, wind patterns, weather and climate all differ from place to place, so that different damage estimates can result from the same emissions.

CONCLUDING REMARKS

The environmental externalities issue offers great promise to policy makers and the public to improve environmental quality at the same time that the costs for obtaining that quality are reduced. That is the motivating force behind all the activity that is observed in so many states. However, whether that promise can be realized is not yet clear. This is true due to the complexity of the issue and the many practical difficulties that enter once the simplicity of the textbook case is qualified by the costly and complex measurements required by the real world application of the simple underlying principles.

References

1. Ottinger, Richard L., et al. 1990. Environmental Costs of Electricity (New York, Oceana Publications).

2. Pigou, A.C. 1938. The Economics of Welfare (London, Macmillan and Co.).

3. Coase, R.H. (October, 1963) "The Problem of Social Cost", Journal of Law and Economics III.

4. Baumol, W.J. and Oates, W.E. 1988. The Theory of Environmental Policy, (Cambridge and New York, Cambridge University Press).

5. Schmalensee, R.L. 1991. Testimony before the Massachusetts Departmement of Public Utilities, D.P.U. 91-131.

6. Lave, L. 1991. Testimony before the Massachusetts Departmement of Public Utilities, D.P.U. 91-131.

7. Joskow, P. L., 1992. "Dealing With Environmental Externalities: Let's Do It Right!", Edison Electric Institute Issues and Trends Briefing Paper No. 61.

8. Burtraw, D. and Krupnick, A.J. February 1992. "The Social Costs of Electricity: How Much of the Camel to Let into the Tent?" Discussion Paper, Resources for the Future.

9. Freeman III, A.M., Burtraw, D., Harrington, H., and Krupnick, A.J. 1992. "Accounting for Environmental Costs in Electric Utility Resource Supply Planning", Discussion Paper QE92-14, Resources for the Future.

10. Morgan, G.M., Morris, S.C. Henrion, M., Amaral, D.A.L., and Rish, W.R. September 1985, "Technical Uncetainty in Quantitative Policy Analysis: A Sulfur Air Pollution Example", Risk Analysis .

11. Anspaugh, L.R., Catlin, R.J., Goldman, M. December 16, 1988. "The Global Impact of the Chernobyl Reactor Accident", Science.

# SECTION 10
# THERMAL ENERGY STORAGE

## Chapter 106
# Centralized Rooftops with TES: Saves Retrofit Money and Energy

C.D. MacCracken

### ABSTRACT

Sixty percent of commercial air conditioning tonnage is in unitary equipment, mainly rooftops. Only 22% is in central chiller systems. And yet, combining cool storage with rooftops has been totally neglected until recently.

Now, centralized rooftop retrofit systems are taking hold in which cold glycol is pumped across the roof to the rooftop coils from a convenient centralized chiller ice storage package. The rooftop compressor and condenser are abandoned. Easy conversion of the coils from refrigerant to glycol is described.

Savings of 20% to 30% in first cost, energy usage and demand charges are all documented. Many other advantages such as ease of service, roof insurance bonding, redundancy, no roof penetration nor indoor work, and zone temperature control are detailed.

Comparative costs, paybacks, and energy savings in new construction central chiller/ice storage systems also are given. The rapidly growing worldwide market for off-peak air conditioning is identified.

### GREEN ROOFS

The greatest potential energy savings in the air conditioning field can be achieved by converting rooftop units to central systems with ice storage.

The total energy use in commercial buildings is about 20 quads (quadrillion Btu's)[1] of which about 10 quads are associated with peak period air conditioning. Of this 60% are rooftops. This means that about 6 quads are used for this purpose.

Since the existing rooftops average 10 years old and are operating at as high as 2.0 kw/ton compared to central systems at 1.0 kw/ton, 1 kw/ton can be saved at peak periods in very large quantity.

$$\frac{6 \text{ quads} \times 10^{12} \text{Btu/hr} \cdot \text{quad} \times 1 \text{ kw/ton}}{12 \times 10^{3} \text{Btu/ton-hr}} = 500 \text{ MM kw}$$

(500,000 megawatts)

On a seasonal basis, however, the savings will be much lower. Actual operating tests so far have ranged between 13 and 30% kwh savings and data will soon be in from other installations. Demand side savings have been in the 30 to 39% range.[2]

### SAVINGS

#### The Partial Storage System

Ice storage is used in a partial storage mode for many reasons:

- The 40% size chillers are less expensive, easier to handle, and can never incur full demand charges as full storage chillers can.

- Air cooled chillers are used which because of the 18 to 20F lower night dry bulb temperature use less energy making ice than non-storage systems do in the day. See Figure 1.[3]

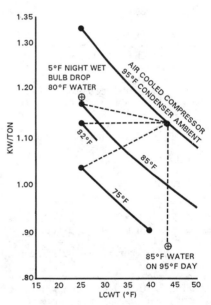

FIGURE 1. RECIPROCATING AIR COOLED COMPRESSOR PERFORMANCE CURVE.

- Ice storage provides redundancy in case of chiller outage, gives infinite modulation in cooling potential, eliminates top/start compressor operation, allows compressor operation at maximum efficiency point, services unanticipated overloads, and provides low temperature for highly efficient cold air systems which lead to improved comfort.

#### First Cost Savings

Rooftops have been sold in large quantity largely due to lower cost than central systems. How can we now believe that retrofitting with a central system can cost less than replacing with new rooftops? Here are the reasons:

- The cost of a central system benefits from combining multiple units in one, from working on the ground instead of a roof, from piping being conveniently accessible, from centralized controls, and from much less refrigerant.

613

- Replacement of rooftop units means use of a crane or helicopter at two different times because most old curbs do not fit new equipment, it usually means not only a new curb and roofing changes, but also duct alterations requiring inside work above ceiling level.

- Alteration of roof penetrations often means termination of the insurance roof bond.

- The downsizing of the chiller with the lost capacity made up by lower cost ice storage is a major factor in cost savings, plus the centralization which provides economy of scale.

- First cost is also affected by rebates which are offered by many utilities varying from $50 to $500/avoided kw or ton which can be a strong accelerator but is not a self-starter.

- Rooftop centralization in Cherry Hill Middle School under Public Service Electric & Gas and in Gloucester College, Deptford, NJ under Atlantic Electric Co. both came in well under the cost of replacing rooftops.

## Operating Cost Savings

Operational cost is primarily controlled by the utility electric rate and involves the number of hours on-peak, the demand charge, the on-peak/off-peak differential, the window rate (a combination of partial and full storage), seasonal or shoulder rate changes, and in some cases a year-long ratchet where every month is charged as a peak month or near to it. It works like this:

- The number of utilities are divided into:
  - 203 private investor owned
  - 1807 municipals
  - 928 co-ops
  - 206 governmental
  - 3144

Almost every one has different rate schedules, different load curves, climates, populations, urban/rural ratios, state regulatory policies, etc., so it is difficult for a manufacturer to meet all the needs.

- The most economically effective rate for off-peak air conditioning (OPAC) is a combination of high demand, short peak and perhaps a ratchet, but the most successful OPAC utility is T.U. (Texas Utilities) and it uses a window rate and no ratchet.

- Often the partial storage design is partial only during very warm weather and is run as full storage much of the year; this can provide large demand savings provided there is no ratchet.

- Compared to average demand (kw) savings, the off-peak energy (kwh) savings in dollars are small; however if the off-peak energy rate is half or less than the on-peak rate, some owners will use as much ice as possible (ice priority strategy) because it is cheaper even though it is less efficient; chiller priority, which uses as little ice as possible, is the usual partial storage strategy.

- Operating cost savings have averaged about 30% by EPRI's instrumentation due primarily to the strategy but also because of higher efficiency of new larger equipment compared to old rooftops.

## Energy Savings

It is commonly thought that making ice at lower temperature is less efficient, but this is not so when the ice is made at night 15 or 20°F cooler than peak time and air cooled chillers are used.[3] Rooftops all use air cooling. In fact, night ice making is often 9% more efficient than daytime operation. Many other matters add to this:

- Some of the improvement is due to the old rooftop condensers and compressors which are often dirty and corroded with age.

  The new larger centralized equipment has higher efficiency because the smaller reciprocating compressors are no match for new scrolls, screws, and particularly centrifugals for jobs totalling 200 or 300 tons or more.

- The location on hot flat roofs compared to ground areas shielded from the sun is considerable.

- The compressors have less on/off operation because the ice cooling can be infinitely modulated as stated before; the rooftop coil and fan are fed the precise amount of cooling desired by modulating by-pass valves in the circulating brine (ethylene glycol 25%) system.

- For maximum efficiency and low operating cost a service contract with the local equipment supplier is recommended; efficiencies 30% better than non-storage rooftops have been observed in the second year's performance, while 12% savings was typical the first year.

## REFITTING COILS

The immediate reaction to the rooftop centralization concept (Roofberg™ System) is to look for a new liquid coil for each rooftop unit. A much better plan is to reheader the evaporator inlet as described below:

- Based upon personal experience a skilled torch craftsman can convert two coils per day.

- The procedure is shown in Figures 2 to 7 and in the handout manual.

- Replacement coils to fit an old design unit are expensive specials and require sourcing, transportation, adapting, piping, disposal, and waste material.

- The ice provides a large delta T, such as 38°F compared to 44°F for the typical coil, and thus can adapt to non-counterflow and less coil rows than usual liquid coils require.

- A great deal can be saved in this way which aids in overall lower cost.

- The biggest job is installing insulated supply and return piping across the roof to service all the old rooftop coils and fans.

## A MONEY MAKER FOR CONTRACTORS

Contrary to installation of central systems in commercial buildings a Roofberg project can be done without aid of an outside engineer. As a contractor you will appreciate installing a system that uses existing rooftop blowers, cooling coil and ductwork. Load requirements can be taken from the old rooftop sizes.

There is only one centralized location for compressors and controls, and service is extremely convenient at outdoor ground level.

You'll win the job, though, because of the benefits you can offer the building owner.

First, tell him the Roofberg system will cost less than replacing his old rooftops, and since there's no need to alter insured roof openings, revise ducts, or hoist heavy equipment, you won't interrupt his business.

Next, tell him that with half the tonnage plus off-peak ice, he'll save a lot of money on demand and energy.

To close the sale, inform him that one-piece polyethylene tanks won't corrode, and have no moving parts to wear out.

REFERENCES

1. Davis,S.C. & Morris,M.D.1992. Transportation Energy Data Book: Edition 12. Oak Ridge National Laboratory,Oak Ridge,TN March p.EN-2

2. Pandya,D.1990. Central Cool Storage Receives "A" at School. Heating/Piping/Air Conditioning, March.

3. MacCracken,C.D.1991. Off-peak Air Conditioning: A Major Energy Saver. Ashrae Journal,Dec.pp.12-23.

FIGURE 2.   OLD ROOFTOP UNITS AT A NEW JERSEY MIDDLE SCHOOL PRIOR TO CONVERSION TO ICE STORAGE.

FIGURE 3.   OLD DIRECT EXPANSION REFRIGERANT COIL PRIOR TO CONVERSION TO GLYCOL BRINE.

FIGURE 4.   USING A PIPE NIPPLE TO HAMMER BACK THE END PLATE, EXPOSING TUBE ENDS FOR BRAZING.

FIGURE 5.   OLD DX COIL AFTER CONVERSION TO BRINE HEADER.

FIGURE 6.   INSULATED LINES CONNECT CONVERTED COILS TO AN AIR COOLED BRINE CHILLER ON THE GROUND.

FIGURE 7.   AIR COOLED CHILLER AND ICE STORAGE TANKS.

# Chapter 107
# The Design Aspects of Ice Storage
R.L. Liechty

## INTRODUCTION

Thermal storage has been recognized as a valuable advantage in HVAC mechanical design for a long time. Ice storage has the reduced volume advantage over chilled water storage by utilizing the benefit of the latent heat associated with a change in state.

Ice storage is often promoted as a technology which can potentially provide significant operating cost savings due to lower demand and, to a lesser degree, energy savings. Because of this, electric utilities (summer peaking in particular) often provide incentive programs to encourage customers to use electricity off-peak. Although this provides a mutual economic benefit to both utility and user, the benefits extend beyond the monetary. The use of low temperature chilled water can produce better indoor comfort by reducing humidity levels and improve both real and perceived indoor air quality.

## ASSESSMENT OF THE OPPORTUNITY, NEW AND EXISTING

Although there is an obvious penalty of higher KW use at the chiller associated with generating ice, when compared with generating warmer chilled water, the overall picture needs to analyzed.

## NEW SYSTEMS

In planning the installation of new equipment the opportunity to utilize smaller equipment is apparent. When applied to meet loads of relatively short duration as exemplified by a church or theater, the economics can be very favorable.

Cold primary air distribution (40-51 deg.F) as a design parameter makes ice storage the system of choice. By utilizing greater delta T design temperatures smaller fans and smaller two-speed pumps can be utilized. By distributing low temperature air, ducts can be reduced in size. Although additional insulation is required on low temperature duct systems, this is typically not a significant cost factor due to the fact that there is less of it.

Since chillers are designed to operate at full capacity during the ice making mode, these too are generally significantly smaller than would be the case by conventional design. Ice building typically reduces compressor cycling which in effect helps to decrease mechanical maintenance costs due to fewer start/stop cycles.

## RETROFITTING EXISTING SYSTEMS

One must evaluate the capability of the existing equipment to produce low temperature chilled water. If replacement of the present chiller equipment is required, what physical constraints exist which influence replacement. Replacement often presents opportunities, but is not a requirement.

If an existing system is being expanded or if cooling loads have increased, an increase in the design delta T and reduction in supply temperature may permit the existing equipment to be modified and piping to remain and be reused. Ice storage can offer increased total capacity without having to install additional equipment if adequate unoccupied hours are available. This is particularly helpful in addressing additional lighting and/or increased ventilation loads in existing buildings. The new ASHRAE STANDARD 62 recommends ventilation air rates of 35 CFM per person.

## DETAILED ANALYSIS OF COOLING LOADS

The most important aspect of any HVAC design is the proper estimating and evaluation of the building load profile. This profoundly impacts both the selection of equipment and the determination of storage capacity required. The building load profile represents energy over time, and is the basis for evaluating storage capacity. This not only involves an analysis of the daily load cycle, but also the weekly cycle. Following is a typical graphical daily cooling load profile.

# COOLING LOAD PROFILE

## HOURLY (TONS OF COOLING)

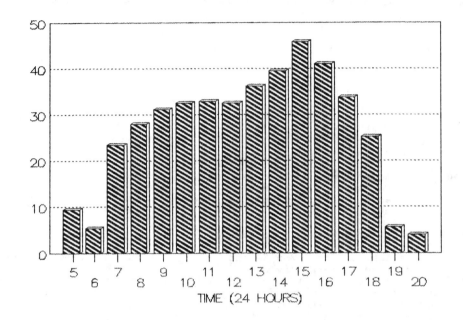

Note that although the ventilation load may be non-existent during the initial cooling of the building prior to occupancy, thermal lag and/or after hours solar gains may need to be addressed. The cumulative ton-hours of cooling will dictate the storage capacity required. Once an accurate picture of the load is generated, the evaluation of full versus partial storage options can be weighed. Humidity migration due to poor construction techniques should also be considered when evaluating loads.

Often the strategy employed will be highly utility dependent; nonetheless, the following points are offered for consideration.

### STRATEGY

Many utilities encourage off-peak use by reducing the cost of power purchased during off-peak hours. Often times this rate is half to two-thirds the on-peak rate. The reduced cost per KW often compensates for the reduction in efficiency associated with generating colder temperatures.

The shift of electrical demand to off-peak hours is another significant driver in the economic picture. In the case of a full storage system, on-peak demand for the cooling medium can be reduced to the operation of a chilled water pump. Since ice is generated at night, there is usually an advantage in utilizing the cooler temperatures to reject heat at the cooling tower or air cooled condensing unit.

Direct financial incentives and rebates offered by utilities are also an important factor to consider in the evaluation process.

### FULL STORAGE VERSUS PARTIAL STORAGE

Several factors impact the decision to pursue full or partial capacity storage. The following "General Rule of Thumb" guidelines are offered to help direct the initial course.

### RULE OF THUMB GUIDELINES

Relatively uniform cooling loads of 9 hours or longer per day are often best served by a partial storage design concept. This allows a significant base load to be generated during no-load or low-load conditions off-peak. The chiller is then allowed to run on-peak with a higher chilled water setpoint and better KW/TON efficiency to supplement the cooling system. A typical chilled water setpoint for ice building would be 28 deg.F with a 1.1 KW/TON rating. With an on-peak setpoint of 50 deg.F the same machine would have an associated operating efficiency of 0.8 KW/TON.

Short duration cooling loads of 6-8 hours, or relatively non-uniform loads can typically take advantage of a full storage strategy which keeps the chiller off-line during the peak hours of the day. Two speed chilled water pumping, or variable speed pumping may also be beneficial to minimize on-peak demand and electric energy use.

Allocating space for ice storage within the building will typically require a volume of 3.5 to 4.0 C.F. per TON-HR. This is highly dependent upon storage configuration and access to the space allocated. External direct buried storage tanks can reduce space allocation volume to as little as 1.8 C.F. per TON-HR.

## APPLICATION OF COMMERCIALLY AVAILABLE EQUIPMENT

The commercial market has responded to the need for standardized equipment in the industry. There are several options open to the designer which allows both flexibility and ease in application. Charging and discharge rates will vary with each manufacturer. Following is a summary of systems I am aware of with a very brief synopsis of operating characteristics.

## SYSTEM TYPES

### STATIC ICE STORAGE

Ice on pipe with external melt out. Ice is built and stored directly on the evaporator surface. Chilled water is circulated around the ice during melt out.

Ice on pipe with internal melt out. Ice is built and stored on the surface of coiled tubing. Brine or glycol/water solution is circulated through the conventional chilled water loop.

Encapsulated water modules, lenses or ice balls are frozen in a tank by circulating brine solution around them, and melted in like manner.

### DYNAMIC ICE STORAGE

Ice harvesters or shuckers build ice on evaporator plates and utilize hot refrigerant gas periodically to warm the plates causing the ice to drop into ice water tanks creating a slurry of ice and water.

# Chapter 108

# Case Study of a Combined Thermal Energy Storage (TES) and Gas Engine Drive Chiller System to Replace 500-Ton Chiller

K. Scheiss

## SUMMARY

This paper describes how creative energy engineering can successfully replace an existing 490 tons centrifugal chiller with a combined TES (120 tons ice/1,300 ton-hour) - Gas Engine Driven Chiller (200 tons) to reduce electrical demand charges and use heat recovery to reduce the burden of very inefficient multizone units for the Mount Carmel High School in the Poway Unified School District (PUSD) in California. An innovative method is applied to transport the recovered heat to the swimming pool. Rebates from San Diego Gas & Electric Company (SDG&E) and grants from the California Energy Commission (CEC) made this project a very economical proposition.

## FEASIBILITY STUDIES

A feasibility study initiated by SDG&E was conducted in two phases. The initial study determined the potential energy engineering projects that presented themselves when an existing centrifugal chiller needs to be replaced. The basic most economical project was chosen and then further refined during the second phase which would form the project which PUSD presented to obtain the grant from the CEC.

## SYSTEM DESCRIPTION

### Description of Existing System

A 490 ton Airtemp centrifugal chiller is supplying chilled water to various multizone units. The peak summer cooling load is in the 400 ton region. The chiller is oversized and is often required to operate at low loads. In winter the chiller is subjected to cycling as it cuts out at approximately 25% load. Low load conditions also occur during the summer vacations, when only the administration building requires cooling. This method of operation increases wear and tear and reduces the life expectancy of the chiller.

The air handling units served by the 4-pipe system from the central plant are of the multizone type. Multizone units waste energy by controlling space temperature by mixing heated and cooled air. Eight of the multizone units are worse than the conventional double deck multizone units. The cooling coils are situated on the suction side of the supply fan and cool all air to the coil-leaving design temperature before the air is heated by face and by-pass dampers across the heating coil.

Even though the multizone units waste considerable energy, it is not economically feasible at present to replace these units under the umbrella of an energy conservation project. If the units would be in such a condition that they need to be replaced, it is possible to propose an energy improvement project using improved energy savings systems.

As funds are scarce under the present economic climate it is necessary to address the energy wasted by the multizone units. A direct driven gas engine chiller allows the recovery of considerable heat. The more cooling is produced, the larger the recoverable heat. If recovered heat can be utilized to heat the hot decks of the multizone units, the energy wastage can be reduced until the time when the multizone units can be replaced.

The initial study yielded the following results:

| PROJECT | EXTRA COST* | ANNUAL SAVINGS | STORAGE CAPACITY | LOAD REDUCT. | PAYBACK YEARS |
|---|---|---|---|---|---|
| Full Storage | $243,000 | $38,207 | 2,750 T-H | 400 TNS | 6.0 |
| TES+100 Ton Gas | $354,000 | $54,497 | 1,960 T-H | 400 TNS | 6.5 |
| TES+150 Ton Gas | $343,000 | $59,878 | 1,600 T-H | 400 TNS | 5.7 |
| TES+200 Ton Gas | $334,000 | $61,436 | 1,226 T-H | 400 TNS | 5.4 |

* COST = The cost of replacing the existing chiller with a new one of 400 tons is subtracted. The feasibility of the special project using TES and a gas-fired chiller with heat recovery is determined.    T-H = Ton-Hours

## Potential for TES

Mount Carmel High School purchases power from San Diego Gas & Electric under the AL-TOU (time-of-use) rate schedule applicable to metered demand. The present demand charges (Jan 1992) are $17.54/KW for the summer and $4.08/KW for the winter period with a non-time related (non-coincident) demand charge of $3.71/KW all year round. There is also a 4 cent per KWH cost difference between on-peak and off-peak during summer and 3.8 cents during winter. The on-peak windows are from 11:00 to 18:00 hours in summer and 17:00 to 20:00 hours in winter.

Usually, two cost saving methods are possible with TES. The on-peak demand charge can be reduced if the air conditioning compressors can be kept off during the on-peak periods. The demand charge will be reduced by the total (KW) load shifted. The different rate charges per KWH allow for less expensive cool production during the night. Therefore, the energy cost of the cooling required during the on-peak hours can be reduced by producing it at the less expensive off-peak rate.

The problems associated with low cooling load conditions can also be solved with TES by using the storage capacity of the system to cool all day long. The heat exchanger has no problem providing a low delta temperature to a relatively large circulating chilled water quantity.

## Potential for Heat Recovery

Two gas-fired boilers are located in the main mechanical equipment room and smaller local units supply the gymnasium and the two swimming pools. The boilers in the main MER provide hot water for the heating water distribution system, feeding the multizone units.

With the relatively constant need for heat of the multizone units and for the pool all year round, the use of a natural gas engine-driven water chiller with heat recovery may be economically feasible. There are various packaged commercial water chillers on the market using screw compressors or reciprocating compressors. The packages are designed and assembled for fast, easy installation and efficient servicing. The variable speed capability of the gas engine provides efficient and easy adjustment to low cooling load requirements.

Using gas for cooling purposes increases gas consumption during the traditional low gas consumption periods and in addition relieves the electrical consumption during the electrical peak periods to achieve summer peak cooling.

## THERMAL ENERGY STORAGE - FULL STORAGE

A full storage system using ice as storage medium requires a chiller with a cooling capacity of 250 "ice" tons and a storage capacity of 2,750 ton-hours. An ice storage system is used for cost comparison.

Figure 1 shows the full storage TES system. During low load requirements only one pump is required to operate. It is estimated that the additional savings are 50% of 45,834 KWH for reduced pumping energy. The operational sequence for peak cooling is shown on Figure 2.

## TES COMBINED WITH DIRECT DRIVEN GAS ENGINE CHILLER AT POOL

### General

The storage capacity of a TES system can be reduced and its payback improved if gas-engine driven chillers supplement the TES system to provide cooling during the electrical peak periods during summer. Gas driven chillers equipped with heat recovery from the engine jackets and exhaust gases can be used to cool whenever it is beneficial to recover heat and cool at the same time.

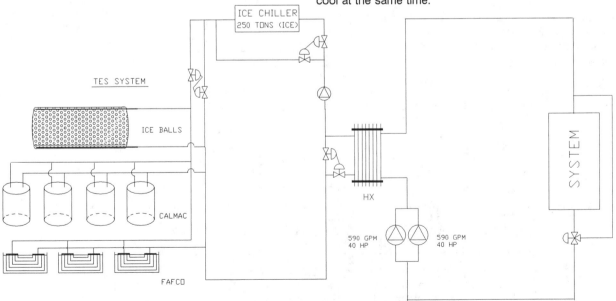

FIG. 1

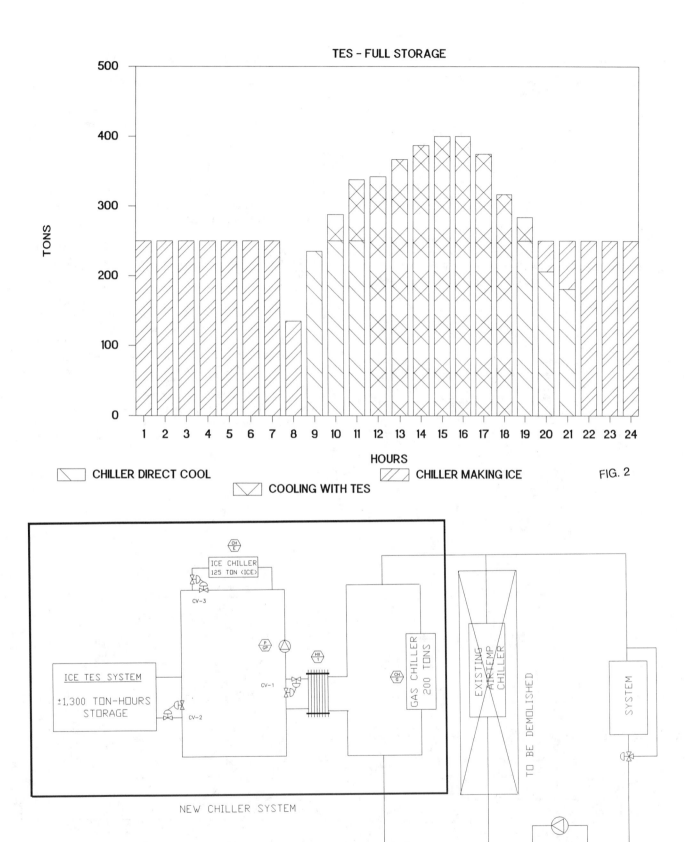

TES - FULL STORAGE

CHILLER DIRECT COOL          CHILLER MAKING ICE          FIG. 2

COOLING WITH TES

SCHEMATIC DIAGRAM OF CHILLED WATER SYSTEM

FIG. 3

623

### Heat Recovery Potential

The recovered heat of a direct gas driven engine can be utilized to relieve the load on the main boilers or the boiler of the swimming pools.

The largest part of the gas consumption of the two main boilers is used to heat the hot decks of the multizone units. It is possible to recover heat and dump it into the pools. Due to the location of the swimming pool boiler, long pipe runs are required to bring the hot water from the point of recovery to the pools. An alternate method is to place the gas-fired chiller near the swimming pool and connect the chiller to the central chilled water distribution system at the nearest point in or near the gymnasium. The pipe size at the point of connection is 4"dia. Placing the gas-fired chiller near the pool reduces the cost caused by the long distance from the MER to the pool, but it also limits the chiller size to the maximum acceptable water flow quantity through the 4" pipe connection.

### System Hydronics for Chilled Water

With the gas fired chiller being located at one of the remote ends of the central distribution systems it is essential that the chilled water distribution system be changed to a variable water volume system. Not only will this enable the system to work and allow the operation of the gas-fired chiller during low cooling requirements, but it will also save considerable energy by reducing the circulated water quantity to the load.

### Direct Driven Gas Engine Chiller with TES System

A gas-engine driven chiller and an ice making chiller are connected in parallel through a flat plate heat exchanger. The direct gas-driven chiller is located near the swimming pool equipment room to allow for heat recovery. The storage capacity and ice chiller size is calculated for three different direct driven gas engine chillers (100, 150 and 200 tons). The gas-driven chillers would support the full storage TES system during the electrical on-peak period for the five summer months. For the remainder of the year the gas-fired chiller should be used as the primary chiller in order to recover as much heat as possible to heat the pools.

### Study Phase II: 200 Ton Direct Driven Gas Engine Chiller with TES System

During the period leading up to the second study the proposals were re-evaluated. Install the gas-fired chiller near the pool was obviously a compromise. It would be better engineering to have the chillers together in the central plant room without having to feed chilled water "backwards" to the system when using the gas-fired chiller.

Why not use the hot water distribution system to transport the recovered heat to the pool? This can be easily achieved by placing the gas chiller in the main plant room and by pumping the recovered heat into the heating water circuit before the

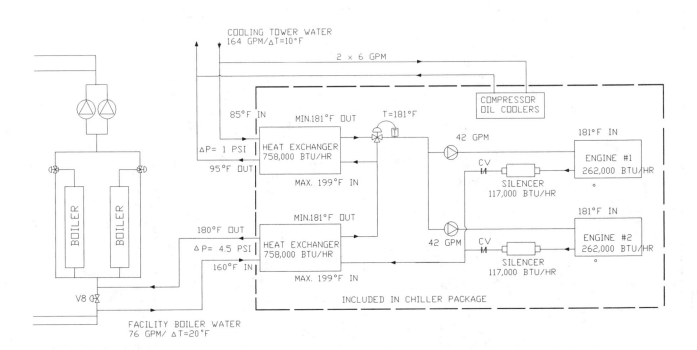

FIG. 4

624

return enters the boilers. Any heat recovered will reduce the load on the boiler, whether it replaces heat wasted by the multizone units or heats the pool.

Phase II of the study then focused on this idea and the following project was developed for application of a California Energy Commission grant:

A 200 ton gas-engine driven chiller and an ice-making chiller of 120 ice tons capacity through a flat plate heat exchanger are connected in parallel. The storage capacity is 1,226 Ton-hours. The direct gas-driven chiller will be located in the main mechanical equipment room. The heat recovered will be pumped into the central heating distribution system. To facilitate full usage of all recoverable heat, it is proposed to expand the heating circuit at the gymnasium and provide a heat exchanger to pump the heat into the swimming pool.

At this stage of investigation, the ice-making chiller could be any ice storage system application. The storage capacity required is 1,226 ton-hours for a full storage TES system with the gas-driven chillers operating and supporting the ice storage system during the electrical on-peak period for the summer months when the school is open. During the July and August vacation months when most classrooms are not used, it is possible to use the TES system to bridge the seven hours peak period without using the gas-fired chiller. During these two months the heating requirements for the pool are so small that heat recovery is not required. For the remainder of the year the gas fired chiller should be used as the primary chiller in order to recover as much heat as possible to heat the heating circuit for the air handling units and the pools.

With the main heat recovery occurring at the proposed heat exchanger located in the swimming pool equipment room, it is essential that some 3-way valves in the heating water distribution system are changed to 2-way valves. The extension to the heat exchanger will act as a by-pass at the extreme point of the circuit.

Figure 3 shows the chilled water system with the gas-fired chiller and the TES system. Figure 4 shows the schematic diagram of the heat recovery heat exchanger integrated with the central heating water system. The operational sequence during peak cooling load conditions is shown on Figure 5.

The project cost at feasibility study stage were estimated as follows:

| | |
|---|---|
| Total project cost | $574,000 |
| Projected cost annual savings | $98,000 |
| SDG&E Rebate | $92,300 |
| CEC grant (50%) | $287,000 |

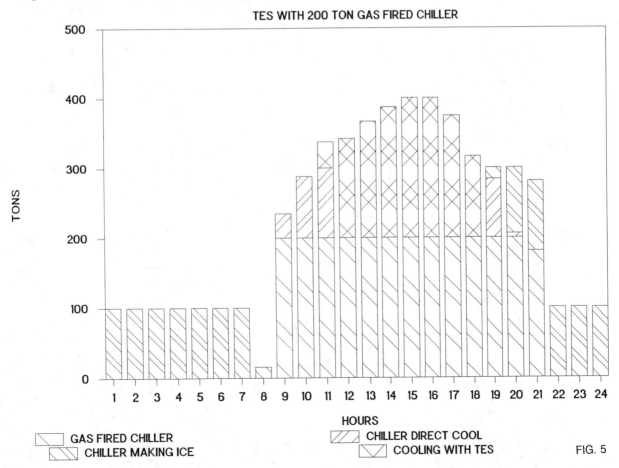

TES WITH 200 TON GAS FIRED CHILLER

GAS FIRED CHILLER
CHILLER MAKING ICE
CHILLER DIRECT COOL
COOLING WITH TES

FIG. 5